CONSTITUTIONAL LAW

CONSTITUTIONAL LAW: CASES IN CONTEXT

VOLUME I
FEDERAL GOVERNMENTAL POWERS AND FEDERALISM

James C. Foster
Oregon State University

Susan M. Leeson
Oregon Court of Appeals

PRENTICE HALL, UPPER SADDLE RIVER, NEW JERSEY 07458

Library of Congress Cataloging-in-Publication Data

FOSTER, JAMES C. (JAMES CARL)
    Constitutional law: cases in context/James C. Foster, Susan M.
Leeson
      p.   cm.
      Leeson's name appears first on the earlier edition.
      Includes bibliographical references and index.
      Contents: v. 1. Federal governmental powers and federalism.
      ISBN 0-13-568775-6 (v. 1)
      1. Constitutional law—United States—Cases.   I. Leeson, Susan M.
II. Title.
KF4549.F675   1998
342.73'00264—dc21   97-27675
                                                         CIP

Editorial director: Charlyce Jones Owen
Editor-in-chief: Nancy Roberts
Acquisitions editor: Michael Bickerstaff
Assistant editor: Nicole Signoretti
Marketing manager: Christopher DeJohn
Editorial/production supervision
    and electronic page makeup: Kari Callaghan Mazzola
Interior design and electronic art creation: John P. Mazzola
Cover design: Bruce Kenselaar
Buyer: Bob Anderson

This book was set in 10/12 Cheltenham Book by Big Sky Composition
and was printed and bound by Courier Companies, Inc.
The cover was printed by Phoenix Color Corp.

© 1998, 1992 by Prentice-Hall, Inc.
Simon & Schuster/A Viacom Company
Upper Saddle River, New Jersey 07458

Printed in the United States of America
10   9   8   7   6   5   4   3   2   1

ISBN 0-13-568775-6

PRENTICE-HALL INTERNATIONAL (UK) LIMITED, *London*
PRENTICE-HALL OF AUSTRALIA PTY. LIMITED, *Sydney*
PRENTICE-HALL CANADA INC., *Toronto*
PRENTICE-HALL HISPANOAMERICANA, S.A., *Mexico*
PRENTICE-HALL OF INDIA PRIVATE LIMITED, *New Delhi*
PRENTICE-HALL OF JAPAN, INC., *Tokyo*
SIMON & SCHUSTER ASIA PTE. LTD., *Singapore*
EDITORA PRENTICE-HALL DO BRASIL, LTDA., *Rio de Janeiro*

In memory of Alpheus Thomas Mason

CONTENTS

CHAPTER 6   PROPERTY RIGHTS VERSUS GOVERNMENTAL POWERS   724

HISTORICAL ERA CONTENTS

The Third Era (1941–1971)—Civil Rights and Civil Liberties

PREFACE

We undertook writing this text knowing well that the field of constitutional law is crowded with texts—casebooks and noncasebooks alike. Our starting premise is that the study of doctrine—divorced from history, politics, and the workings of the legal system—leaves students with an abstract, incomplete understanding of the Supreme Court as one of the three coordinate branches of the national government. Shorn of the social and institutional contexts within which it operates, the Court and the constitutional decisions it hands down cannot be understood adequately. We also know from experience that students quickly forget abstract doctrine and often recall little about their study of constitutional law except the discipline of reading and briefing cases. Notwithstanding those concerns, we believe that Supreme Court opinions are an invaluable primary source of information about the third branch and its role in the American political system. Because we are committed to the study of constitutional law in a liberal arts setting, we have sought to give greater depth and dimension to Supreme Court opinions by placing them in their historical, political, and legal contexts.

In *Constitutional Law: Cases in Context*, we present landmark decisions of the Supreme Court of the United States in subject matter categories that reflect doctrinal evolution. Nevertheless, our approach to each of these doctrinally organized cases remains contextual: Every case excerpted in this text is presented in terms of the circumstances giving rise to the controversy, the constitutional arguments of the parties to that controversy, the doctrines, rules, and policy choices the Court announces in resolving that controversy, and the salient consequences resulting from the judicial outcome of that controversy. Thus, while this book arranges Supreme Court decisions doctrinally, it treats them historically. We also offer an Alternative Table of Contents by Historical Era for those who prefer to study and teach constitutional law chronologically. As is characteristic of two-volume constitutional law texts, the first volume focuses on federal government powers and federalism, while the second focuses on protections against governmental powers.

Several features distinguish this text from others, including the *Setting* and *Highlights of Supreme Court Arguments* sections, extensive excerpts of opinions, and *Questions* and *Comments* following each case that are designed not only to promote greater understanding of the opinions, but to stimulate reflection and thoughtful class discussion. Because our goal in preparing these materials is to encourage further study, we also offer *Suggestions for Further Reading* at the end of each section.

The *Setting* that precedes each case provides a richer factual statement and insight into the parties and their controversy than typically appears in the opinions themselves. The *Setting* also explains the primary social and political forces that gave rise to the litigation. In addition, the *Setting* traces the evolution of a case from the time it was filed to its appearance on the Supreme Court's docket, explaining the reasoning of lower court judges along the way and demonstrating the legal climate of opinion in which the case arrived at the Supreme Court. It is our hope that the *Setting* will facilitate better understanding of cases and constitutional issues and that it will provoke students to learn more about the historical and political contexts in which the cases arose and were decided.

Supreme Court doctrine does not simply emerge from the minds of the justices. Rules are shaped by the adversary contest between the parties at every stage of the litigation process. In the section entitled *Highlights of Supreme Court Arguments*, we summarize the legal theories offered to the justices by each of the parties. Contained in those theories is the rule of law that each side hopes the Court will adopt. Sometimes the Court endorses one or more of those theories in fashioning a rule. On other occasions, the opinion suggests that the parties' arguments, while essential, were not determinative. As additional backdrop for each case, we identify the organizations (and, occasionally, the individuals) that submitted *amicus curiae* briefs in support of each side. We hope that students will want to know more about what motivates the organizations that join in the adversary competition to shape the Constitution, and will undertake research into how at least some of those organizations came into being, how they are funded, and how they work.

Excerpts of the Supreme Court's opinions tend to be more lengthy in this text than in other casebooks. This reflects our commitment to having students grapple with original sources rather than merely being told what the Court decided. In reading the excerpts, students are exposed to the ideas, thought processes, language, and debates among the justices that contribute to the development of constitutional doctrine. They also learn firsthand that there are few if any doctrines in constitutional law that are so well-established as to be beyond debate.

The *Questions* and *Comments* that follow each opinion serve a variety of functions. *Comments* provide additional information about a case or the parties to it, immediate political or legal consequences, and related and subsequent Supreme Court decisions. *Questions* are designed to facilitate better understanding of the case, its relationship to other cases and issues, and the dynamics of the interaction among the justices. *Questions* also are devised to stimulate thought about the extent to which the Court's opinion resolved or exacerbated the controversy presented to it. Often the *Questions* reflect the differences in perspective of the authors, both of whom have taught constitutional law for many years and one of whom is now a state appellate court judge. We hope that the *Comments* and *Questions* will provide additional incentive to students to inquire into the political and social reactions to the Court's decisions, for rarely, if ever, is the Supreme Court's opinion the last word on an issue.

ANNUAL SUPPLEMENTS AND WEB SITE

Beginning with the 1997–98 Term, we will provide annual, free supplements to faculty who adopt *Constitutional Law: Cases in Context*. The supplements will follow the same format as the text. Links to supplementary Supreme Court decisions will be available on Prentice Hall's web site, http://www.prenhall.com. We anticipate revising the text every four years. Questions should be referred to your local Prentice Hall sales representative.

ACKNOWLEDGMENTS

We have accumulated many debts in writing *Constitutional Law: Cases in Context*, which we gratefully acknowledge here.

Richard Breen, Willamette College of Law librarian, and his reference staff have continued to go to extraordinary lengths to provide us with access to microfiche records and briefs of cases as well as to make available the other resources in the law library. The library staff at the Supreme Court of the United States has graciously welcomed back a former judicial fellow to use original sources and found her a place to work, even when the library was closed for recarpeting. Supreme Court Deputy Clerk Frank Lorson provided statistics for the Court's 1995 Term, which appear in chart form in Chapter 1.

Oregon State University graduate Donna Shaw worked closely with Professor Foster on this book, providing research assistance and intelligent, thoughtful, and enthusiastic feedback. Willamette College of Law students Kara Daley, Wendy Johnson, Kevin Swartz, and Teuta Veizaj provided helpful research and comments.

Various professional colleagues provided numerous forms of support, encouragement, and suggestions during the period this book was being prepared: Henry Abraham, Audrey Bach, Donald Balmer, John Brigham, Vicki Collins, Donald Crowley, Steve DeLancey, Susan Dwyer-Schick, James Elkins, Donna Erickson, Leo Flynn, Howard Gillman, Edward Goldberg, Sheldon Goldman, Joel Grossman, Sandra Guy, William Haltom, Barbara Hayler, William Husband, Sam Jacobson, Patricia Lindsey, Carolyn Long, Michael McCann, Bob Noll, Don Reisman, Robert Sahr, Stuart Scheingold, Brent Steel, and Kenneth Wagner. We remain grateful for their ongoing efforts. Judge Leeson's colleagues at the Oregon Court of Appeals have provided insight and suggestions for approaches to particular cases.

The text has also had the benefit of critical reading by these reviewers selected by Prentice Hall: Carolyn Nestor Long, *Washington State University*; Bette Novit Evans, *Creighton University*; Ronald Kahn, *Oberlin College*; Jerome O'Callaghan, *SUNY Cortland*; Donald G. Balmer, *Lewis and Clark College*; William Haltom, *University of Puget Sound*; and Mary Thornberry, *Davidson College*. Although anonymous to us at the time, we appreciate the interest they took in this project and the efforts they put into refining it. This book is better for their suggestions.

Similarly, this book has benefited significantly from the various editorial and production assistance rendered by Prentice Hall personnel. At the outset, we want to thank Michael Bickerstaff, Political Science Acquisitions Editor at Prentice Hall, for his interest in this text and his support for it. Assistant Editors, Jennie Katsaros, and later, Nicole Signoretti, professionally shepherded the book through the drafting, reviewing, and revising process. A special, heartfelt thanks goes to Kari Callaghan Mazzola of Big Sky Composition for her expertise, creative suggestions, and cheerful cooperation.

Support staff at Oregon State University—Karen Thayer, Political Science Office Coordinator, and Shannona Miller, Political Science Office Specialist—teamed to provide essential support. Their imaginative composition, tireless revision, and quick turnaround time facilitated this project.

Finally, we both thank our long-suffering spouses. From Professor Foster, as always, to Laurel Lynn Ramsey for your love, your perseverance, and for schooling me in practical romance. From Judge Leeson, as always, to Richard Samuel Hall Jr., whose love of mathematics and logic spills over into the study of history and constitutional law at the most convenient times.

J. C. F.
Corvallis, Oregon

S. M. L.
Salem, Oregon

CHAPTER 1

UNDERSTANDING THE SUPREME COURT

In the 1830s, Frenchman Alexis de Tocqueville observed that "Scarcely any political question arises in the United States that is not resolved, sooner or later, into a judicial question."[1] This book expands on that theme. It examines landmark controversies in American politics that were resolved, sooner or later, into questions of constitutional law argued before the Supreme Court of the United States. Each case arose out of discrete social and political circumstances. Most were litigated in state or federal courts and worked their way to the Supreme Court, where advocates urged that Court to adopt their particular theory or theories of the Constitution. Resolution of each of the cases by the Supreme Court required the justices to interpret one or more provisions of the Constitution of the United States. The Court's decisions have furthered the development of constitutional doctrine and have had significant social and political consequences as well. The Court's decisions continue to give life and meaning to the Constitution, a relatively short document that was adopted in 1789 and amended only twenty-seven times since then.[2]

THE SUPREME COURT'S DEFINING POWER: JUDICIAL REVIEW

In interpreting the Constitution since 1803, the Supreme Court has exercised the power of judicial review, a power it claimed for itself in the famous case of *Marbury v. Madison*, 1 Cranch 137 (1803). Judicial review is the power of the Supreme Court to determine the constitutionality of acts of Congress, the executive, a state, or even a provision of a state constitution under the Constitution of the United States. In short, it is the power to declare what the Constitution means.[3]

---

[1] Alexis de Tocqueville, *Democracy in America*, Phillips Bradley, ed., 2 vols. (New York, NY: Vintage, 1945), I: 290.

[2] Refer to the Constitution of the United States reproduced at the end of this book as Appendix A. Also see Sanford Levinson, ed., *Responding to Imperfection: The Theory and Practice of Constitutional Amendment* (Princeton, NJ: Princeton University Press, 1995); and David E. Kyvig, *Explicit and Authentic Acts: Amending the U.S. Constitution, 1776–1995* (Lawrence, KS: University of Kansas Press, 1996).

[3] See Henry J. Abraham, *The Judicial Process*, 6th ed. (New York, NY: Oxford University Press, 1993), pp. 270–288. *The Constitution of the United States: Analysis and Interpretation*, Johnny H. Killian, ed. (Washington, D.C.: U.S. Government Printing Office, 1987), pp. 1883–2113 lists the congressional and state statutes the Supreme Court has reviewed and held unconstitutional through 1982.

Although the Supreme Court has exercised the power of judicial review at least since 1803 and its authority to do so is almost universally accepted, there has always been controversy over the propriety of the Court's exercise of judicial review in particular cases and circumstances.[4] This book examines cases that demonstrate dramatically the constitutional and political consequences of the exercise of judicial review. Those cases have involved controversies that range from early disagreements over whether Congress has the authority to charter a national bank, to issues such as the legality of slavery, school segregation, abortion, and the rights of the criminally accused.

Alexander Hamilton described the paradox of judicial review in *Federalist No. 78*: it is *essential* and it is *fragile*. Judicial review is essential, Hamilton reasoned, because some "department of the proposed government" must enforce constitutional limitations:

> Limitations ... can be preserved in practice no other way than through the medium of courts of justice, whose duty it must be to declare all acts contrary to the manifest tenor of the Constitution void. Without this, all the reservations of particular rights or privileges would amount to nothing.

Judicial review is fragile because:

> Whoever attentively considers the different departments of power must perceive that, in a government in which they are separated from each other, the judiciary, from the nature of its functions, will always be the least dangerous to the political rights of the Constitution; because it will be least in a capacity to annoy or injure them. The executive not only dispenses the honors but holds the sword of the community. The legislature not only commands the purse but prescribes the rules by which the duties and rights of every citizen are to be regulated. The judiciary, on the contrary, has no influence over either the sword or the purse; no direction either of the strength or of the wealth of the society, and can take no active resolution whatever.

Hamilton concluded that courts "may truly be said to have neither force nor will but merely judgment; and must ultimately depend upon the aid of the executive arm even for the efficacy of its judgments."[5]

In the process of examining the cases that follow, readers are invited to debate with Hamilton whether judicial review is essential to the American form of government. Even if judicial review is not essential, Hamilton was correct that it is fragile. Readers also are invited to understand that the legiti-

---

[4] The first time the Supreme Court actually reviewed a statute it did so without explicitly claiming the power of judicial review. In *Hylton v. United States*, 3 Dallas 171 (1796), the Court upheld the constitutionality of the 1794 federal Carriage Tax Act. Because it upheld this act of Congress, the Court did not have to call attention to the fact that it had tacitly exercised the power of judicial review.

[5] *The Federalist Papers*, Clinton Rossiter, ed. (New York, NY: Mentor, 1961), pp. 466, 465.

macy of the power of judicial review is contingent on the justices' ability to write persuasively, on the willingness of other branches of government to enforce the Court's decisions, and on the perception of the American public that the Court's decisions are authoritative.[6]

One question that arises repeatedly throughout this book is whether judicial review has been exercised wisely, consistently, or legitimately in a particular case or series of cases dealing with the same subject. A recurring theme is that, to be authoritative, the Court's opinions not only must resolve the legal controversies posed by the parties, but its interpretation of the Constitution must respond persuasively to ongoing tensions involving the relationship of the Court to Congress and the executive branch (separation of powers), to the relationship between the states and the national government (federalism), and to the political realities of the times in which the decisions are written. An important lesson from this book is that many, if not all, of the fundamental constitutional questions that were left unresolved by the Constitutional Convention remain unresolved, notwithstanding a civil war and more than two centuries of the Supreme Court's exercise of judicial review.

PERSPECTIVES ON CONSTITUTIONAL INTERPRETATION

Reduced to its simplest terms, a lawsuit involves application of the law to facts.[7] At trial, parties to a lawsuit seek to persuade the trier of fact (judge or jury) that their version of the facts is correct. The judge then applies the law to the facts and enters judgment accordingly. Appellate litigation before the Supreme Court involves debates only about the correct rule of law to apply to the facts that have been found at trial.[8] In each of the cases in this book, the Supreme Court's determination of the rule of law applicable to the facts has required an interpretation of one or more provisions of the Constitution.

Constitutional interpretation is an intricate, difficult task. That is so, in part, because there is significant disagreement in this country about what constitutional interpretation entails.[9] This book views constitutional interpreta-

---

[6] The extent and limits of the Supreme Court's power of judicial review has been much debated. See, for example, Robert A. Dahl, "Decision Making in a Democracy: The Supreme Court as a National Policy Maker," 6 *Journal of Politics* (1957): 279; David Adamany, "Legitimacy, Realigning Elections, and the Supreme Court," 73 *Wisconsin Law Review* (1973): 790; Richard Funston, "The Supreme Court and Critical Elections," 69 *American Political Science Review* (1975): 793; Jonathan D. Casper, "The Supreme Court and National Policy Making," 70 *American Political Science Review* (1976): 50; and Roger Handberg and Harold F. Hill Jr., "Court Curbing, Court Reversals, and Judicial Review: The Supreme Court versus Congress," 14 *Law and Society Review* (1980): 309.

[7] See the Appendix to this chapter for a brief overview of the litigation process.

[8] One small exception to this rule is that the Supreme Court sits as a fact-finding body in the rare cases when it exercises original jurisdiction, spelled out in Article III of the Constitution.

[9] John H. Garvey and T. Alexander Aleinikoff, eds., *Modern Constitutional Theory: A Reader*, 3rd ed. (St. Paul, MN: West, 1994), pt. II.

tion as a creative act, constrained by rules of law. Supreme Court Justice Oliver Wendell Holmes, for example, contended that

> [W]hen we are dealing with words that also are a constituent act, like the Constitution of the United States, we must realize that they have called into life a being the development of which could not have been foreseen completely by the most gifted of its begetters....[10]

In Justice Holmes's view, the men who drafted the Constitution in Philadelphia in the summer of 1787 were "begetters" of words that are also "constituent acts"; that is, those who interpret constitutional words actively make the Constitution meaningful. Consequently, the meaning of the Constitution is not fixed. It is not a collection of axiomatic formulas that dictate the results in particular cases. From this perspective, the Constitution provides an adaptable framework for analyzing legal issues and relationships between and among the branches of government and levels of government.

Chief Justice John Marshall provided additional insight into the complexities of constitutional interpretation when he wrote that

> A constitution['s] ... nature ... requires, that only its great outlines should be marked, its important objects designated, and the minor ingredients which compose those objects be deduced from the nature of the objects themselves....[11]

From Marshall's perspective, constitutional interpretation involves a process of deducing from general principles answers to specific questions. Those answers are never self-evident from the words of the document.

Justice Thurgood Marshall provided yet another perspective on the difficulties of constitutional interpretation. In a speech commemorating the bicentennial of the Constitution in 1987, Justice Marshall observed that

> The men who gathered in Philadelphia in 1787 could not have ... imagined, nor would they have accepted, that the document they were drafting would one day be construed by a Supreme Court to which had been appointed a woman and the descendent of an African slave. "We the People" no longer enslave, but the credit does not belong to the framers. It belongs to those who refused to acquiesce in outdated notions of "liberty," "justice," and "equality," and who strived to better them.[12]

---

[10] *Missouri v. Holland*, 25 U.S. 416 (1920). Compare William Rehnquist's view, distinguishing Holmes's understanding "with which scarcely anyone would disagree," from the view taken by many lawyers that "nonelected members of the federal judiciary may address themselves to a social problem simply because other branches of government have failed or refused to do so" (*Views from the Bench*, Mark W. Cannon and David M. O'Brien, eds. [Chatham, NJ: Chatham House, 1985], pp. 127, 128). Chief Justice Rehnquist quotes favorably Holmes's *Missouri v. Holland* view of the Constitution in his *The Supreme Court: How It Was, How It Is* (New York, NY: Morrow, 1987), p. 315.

[11] *McCulloch v. Maryland*, 4 Wheaton 316 (1819).

[12] Speech delivered at the Annual Seminar of the San Francisco Patent and Trademark Law Association, May 6, 1987. Reprinted in 101 *Harvard Law Review* (1987): 1, 5.

From Justice Marshall's perspective, the Constitution of 1787 was an incomplete document. Consequently, one aspect of constitutional interpretation entails construing the document in a way that fosters the justice, general welfare, and liberty to which the Constitution aspires.[13]

Despite the differences among these three justices' perspectives, they have in common the understanding that the Constitution is essentially adjustable and that judicial interpretation is a creative act.[14]

THE CONSTITUTION AS A RESPONSIVE DOCUMENT

The history of the Constitutional Convention reveals that the drafters anticipated and even intended that the Constitution be a responsive document. One reason is that on virtually every issue they faced between May and September 1787, the drafters resolved their disagreements through compromise. Embedded in the Constitution, those compromises have been the source of continuous debate and litigation.

The Great Compromise, for example, provided a solution to the disagreement over how the states should be represented in Congress: as geographic entities or by population. Under the compromise, population was accepted as the basis for representation in the House of Representatives, while each state was seen as a single geographic entity and was guaranteed equal representation in the Senate. Whether people or places should be represented in legislatures has remained a controversial subject, although the focus of the debate has shifted from Congress to state legislatures and units of local government. The Supreme Court's so-called Reapportionment Revolution of the 1960s is an example of the ongoing debate over principles of representation that was never finally resolved at the Constitutional Convention. (See Volume II, Chapter 6.)

Another compromise at the Constitutional Convention allowed the delegates to move past impasse over the question of whether Congress or the states would have responsibility for regulating of commerce. At its core, that debate raised the question of whether sovereignty—ultimate governing authority—would reside with the U.S. government or remain with the states. That impasse was resolved by including among Congress's enumerated powers in Article I, section 8, the power to regulate commerce "among the several states," while leaving regulation of commerce off the list of powers prohibited to the states in Article I, section 10. The compromise regarding the regulation

---

[13] See the Preamble to the Constitution in Appendix A to this volume.

[14] The first dictionary definition of *constitution* is the act or process of setting up, of establishing, of beginning. Chief Justice Marshall and Justices Holmes and Marshall agree that the Supreme Court's interpretation of the Constitution involves acts of creating meaning. As the late political philosopher Hannah Arendt observed, "Political institutions, no matter how well or how badly designed, depend for their continued existence upon acting [human beings]; their conservation is achieved by the same means that brought them into being" (Hannah Arendt, *Between Past and Future: Eight Exercises in Political Thought* [New York, NY: Viking Press], p. 153).

of commerce left unresolved the specific relationship between Congress's commerce power and the states' inherent powers to regulate, commonly known as the police powers, reserved to the states in the Tenth Amendment. It also left to another day the task of drawing lines between *inter*state and *intra*state commerce. Debate over the limits on Congress's power to regulate commerce—to say nothing of defining commerce—has occupied the Supreme Court's attention ever since, arising out of cases involving a wide range of facts. As it did at the Constitutional Convention, the debate over regulating commerce inevitably rekindles the debate over sovereignty. (See especially Chapter 3 of this volume.)

Yet another important compromise at the Constitutional Convention that allowed the delegates to move past impasse concerned slavery. The Three-Fifths Compromise involved counting "other Persons" (a euphemism for slaves) as three-fifths of "free persons" for purposes of apportioning representatives in the House of Representatives, thereby assuring the South substantial representation in the House. Other slavery compromises included giving Congress the power to prohibit the migration or importation of slaves but postponing its authority to exercise that power until at least the year 1808.[15]

The Constitution contains other significant compromises. Coupled with the ambiguous terms in which many Constitutional provisions were written, and the inherent ambiguities of language itself, those compromises have ensured that the Supreme Court always has had before it cases and controversies capable of transforming the constitutional landscape. As the late constitutional historian and scholar Alpheus Mason put it, the Supreme Court is America's "ongoing Constitutional Convention."[16]

Understanding the Supreme Court Historically

Although the cases in this text are organized by subject matter, the material introducing each case provides a glimpse into the historical contexts out of which the cases emerged. This approach blends an historical perspective on

---

[15] William M. Wiecek counts "no less [sic] than ten clauses in the Constitution that directly or indirectly accommodated the peculiar institution" (*The Sources of Antislavery Constitutionalism in America* [Ithaca, NY: Cornell University Press, 1977], pp. 62–63).

[16] This was the theme of Professor Mason's 1979 National Endowment for the Humanities Summer Seminar at Princeton University.

The late Robert G. McCloskey observed in his history of the Supreme Court: "If the framers had tried to settle all 'constitutional' questions that confronted them; if they had even assumed the more modest task of specifically circumscribing the judicial power; if the doctrine of legislative supremacy had been a little more firmly intrenched in 1789; if judges like Marshall had been a little more inclined toward abnegation and a little less inclined toward politics, the uncertainties would be very different, the tale would be of another order. But then the country it was told about would not be the historical United States" (*The American Supreme Court* [Chicago, IL: University of Chicago Press, 1960], pp. 24–25). See also Robert G. McCloskey, *The American Supreme Court*, 2nd ed., revised by Sanford Levinson (Chicago, IL: University of Chicago Press, 1994). Compare Laurence H. Tribe and Michael C. Dorf, *On Reading the Constitution* (Cambridge, MA: Harvard University Press, 1991).

the cases with the contemporary academic preference for analy
work of the Supreme Court in terms of the development of constitutional
doctrine. However, the Court may also be understood as an institution
whose work reflects three distinct eras and an emerging fourth era. Each era
is marked by particular constitutional concerns and distinctive patterns of
interpretation. An understanding of those eras provides helpful perspective
when examining the Court's responses to particular categories of constitutional controversies.[17]

THE FIRST ERA (1793–1876)—DEFINING AMERICAN GOVERNMENT

In the first era, the Court was concerned primarily with issues of federalism.
Federalism is the term that describes a form of government in which the
states and the central government share governing powers and responsibilities. The term also describes the ongoing debate over the balance of power
between the two levels of government.

The Supreme Court's assertion of the power of judicial review in 1803
ensured that it would play an important role in defining the powers delegated
to the national government by the Constitution and those reserved to the
states under the Tenth Amendment. Early decisions, frequently written by
Chief Justice John Marshall, held that a strong national government is consistent with the constitutional principle of limited government. Those decisions
declared that the national government has extensive powers to regulate and
promote interstate commerce and that the judiciary is responsible for protecting the rights of private property owners against incursions by both national
and state legislatures.

Contrary to the fears of states' rights advocates, the Court during this
era, particularly under the leadership of Chief Justice Roger Brooke Taney, left
undisturbed many of the important prerogatives that the states had enjoyed
since the Revolution. Significantly, the Court declared that the Bill of Rights
imposes limits only on the national government, not on the states.

Near the end of this era, the Civil War and the Thirteenth, Fourteenth,
and Fifteenth Amendments purged the Constitution of the scourge of slavery,
but they did not resolve the question of whether sovereignty lies with the
national government or with the states. In 1869, the Supreme Court merely
restated the ambiguity that has been present in the constitutional system
since its beginning, when the Court declared that "The Constitution, in all its
provisions, looks to an indestructible Union, composed of indestructible
States."[18] The Court's early interpretations of the Civil War Amendments, however, severely crippled the national government's attempts to address the
deep social and political problems left in the wake of slavery.

---

[17] A Table of Contents that reflects the historical eras described below is provided at the beginning of this book for those who prefer to study constitutional law historically.

[18] *Texas v. White*, 7 Wallace 700 (1896).

THE SECOND ERA (1877–1940)—GOVERNMENT AND ECONOMY

The Supreme Court's second era was concerned primarily with interpreting the Constitution in the light of the nation's rapidly changing economy. The Court played a major role in determining the social as well as economic consequences of the industrial revolution by scrutinizing many state and federal regulatory statutes and by striking down important pieces of regulatory legislation. The Court defined the Due Process Clause of the Fourteenth Amendment in substantive, economic terms, declaring that due process guarantees "liberty of contract" and that the government may not intervene on behalf of labor to equalize the bargaining power between owners and workers.

The Court's opinions regarding economic regulation during this era clung tenaciously to James Madison's notion that government must remain a "neutral" umpire between competing economic interests, above and outside the competition between economic interests like capitalists and laborers. The Court's economic doctrine—commonly called economic substantive due process—and its view that government is constitutionally prohibited from ordering private market relationships, had the consequence of advancing the interests of private property owners and business enterprises during this era.

By contrast, the Court during this period construed the Civil War Amendments as giving Congress virtually no remedial powers to ameliorate the racial, social and political legacies of slavery. Racial unrest and the nation's first Communist "Red Scare" after World War I failed to jar the fundamentally conservative Supreme Court. Near the end of this era, the nation sank into a deep, worldwide economic depression that called into question the viability of both capitalism and America's constitutional government.

In 1937, the Court's approach to economic regulation took a dramatic turn. In the face of threats by President Franklin Roosevelt to "pack" the Court with justices willing to declare constitutional his far-reaching social and economic reform programs designed to pull the country out of the Great Depression, the Court abruptly abandoned its constitutional opposition to government regulation of market relations. It declared: "Liberty under the Constitution is ... necessarily subject to the restraints of due process, and regulation which is reasonable in relation to its subject and is adopted in the interests of the community is due process."[19] The Court began validating economic regulatory legislation at both the national and state levels.

THE THIRD ERA (1941–1971)—CIVIL RIGHTS AND CIVIL LIBERTIES

In the third era, the justices shifted their focus from scrutinizing government regulation of the economy to protecting civil rights and civil liberties. The Due Process Clause of the Fourteenth Amendment, once a vehicle for voiding economic regulation, became a vehicle for extending many of the provisions of the

---

[19] *West Coast Hotel v. Parrish*, 300 U.S. 379 (1937).

Bill of Rights against state governments. Racial and ethnic minorities and other disenfranchised groups, such as criminal defendants, increasingly turned to the courts to achieve results denied to them in the partisan political sphere. During Chief Justice Earl Warren's leadership of the Court, these groups were frequently rewarded for their efforts. The Fourteenth Amendment's Equal Protection Clause, along with the Due Process Clause, became the engine of a judicial revolution in rights that ranged from school desegregation and reapportionment to privacy rights and the protection of the criminally accused. Hallmarks of this era were the Court's views that "at the very least," the Equal Protection Clause "demands that racial classifications ... be subjected to the 'most rigid scrutiny,'" and that "[n]othing can destroy a government more quickly than its failure to observe its own laws...."[20]

To advocates of states' rights, this third era in the Court's history appeared to sound the death knell of federalism as a balance between state and federal prerogatives. Following the Supreme Court's lead, Americans increasingly looked to the national government for solutions to social problems and frequently preferred litigation over legislative lobbying to establish rights and prerogatives.

A FOURTH ERA? (1972–PRESENT)—PRAGMATIC CONSERVATISM

Although proximity makes problematic an assessment of the Court's most recent history, there are indications that the past quarter century has been transitional. Republican Presidents Nixon, Reagan, and Bush appointed ten justices to the Court between 1969 and 1991, and President Clinton has appointed two justices since 1993. Although the Republican appointees have derailed the activist civil liberties and civil rights agenda of the Warren Court, they have not destroyed it.

In general terms, the Court's present conservatism is not of the activist variety advocated by the presidents who appointed most of today's justices. Instead, it is a pragmatic conservatism that is at once a reaction to the previous Warren Court policy agenda and a hybrid of it. While the heady days of skirmishes at the judicial frontiers over expanding equal protection and criminal due process are gone, the justices exhibit a quasi-libertarian concern to protect civil and, recently, property rights. The contemporary Court also has revitalized its traditional role of policing separation of powers and has resurrected a concern for states' rights in the federal system. This is not a revolutionary court of either the political left or right. One observer contends that the Court reflects the deep fissures dividing the society of which it is a part: "These are finger-to-the-wind days for the Justices."[21]

---

[20] The quotations are from *Loving v. Virginia*, 388 U.S. 1 (1967), and *Mapp v. Ohio*, 367 U.S. 643 (1961), respectively.

[21] Jeffrey Toobin, "Chicken Supreme: The Rehnquist Court Is Political in Every Way" (reviewing James F. Simon, *The Center Holds: The Power Struggle inside the Rehnquist Court* [New York, NY: Simon & Schuster, 1995]), *The New Yorker*, August 14, 1995, p. 82.

UNDERSTANDING THE SUPREME COURT POLITICALLY

The Supreme Court has always operated at the intersection of law and politics.[22] It is at once a court of law that resolves disputes on a case-by-case basis by applying rules and precedents to specific facts, and a branch of the U.S. government that makes public policy. The consequence is that when the Supreme Court exercises its power of judicial review to resolve a constitutional question, it shapes American politics by using legal rules, rights, principles, and precedents to fashion policy.

An example from the 1996 Term is *Romer v. Evans*, 513 U.S. 1146 (1996). (See Volume II, Chapter 7.) The Court held, by a 6–3 vote, that a Colorado statewide initiative—a provision of the Colorado Constitution known as "Amendment 2" that precluded all legislative, executive, or judicial action at any level of state or local government to protect persons based on their "homosexual, lesbian or bisexual orientation, conduct, practices or relationships"—violates the Equal Protection Clause of the Fourteenth Amendment. As a legal matter, the Court ruled that Amendment 2 classified persons based on their status, a form of classification the Equal Protection Clause does not permit. "We must conclude," wrote Justice Anthony Kennedy, "that Amendment 2 classifies homosexuals not to further a proper legislative end but to make them unequal to everyone else. This Colorado cannot do. A State cannot so deem a class of persons a stranger to its laws." The Court's holding in *Romer v. Evans* unquestionably has affected public policy in the area of gay and lesbian rights.

The importance of the Supreme Court as a coordinate branch of government cannot be overstated, because it means that rarely, if ever, are the Court's decisions on a controversial topic final. As constitutional scholars Louis Fisher and Neal Devins put it,

> The process is not linear, with the courts issuing the final word. The process is circular, turning back on itself again and again until society is satisfied with the outcome.[23]

The cases in this text demonstrate that point time and again.

Early in its history, for example, the Court was asked to declare the extent of Congress's power to regulate interstate commerce under Article I,

---

[22] See the essays collected in Martin Shapiro, *Law and Politics in the Supreme Court: New Approaches to Political Jurisprudence* (New York, NY: Free Press, 1964), esp. Chapter 1. Political scientist Mark A. Graber makes a similar point about the Court and politics: "[T]he Supreme Court is the one place in American politics where there is still some space between electorates and governing officials[.]... The issue is ... not whether [the Justices] are ... disinterested Platonic philosophers ... but what their place actually is in the web of American politics, and whether that place is desirable." Graber, Mark A. [mgraber@bss2.umd.edu]. "REPLY: The Supreme Court's New Term." In *LAWCOURTS*. [lawcourts-l@usc.edu]. 4 November 1996.

[23] Louis Fisher and Neal Devins, *Political Dynamics of Constitutional Law*, 2nd ed. (St. Paul, MN: West, 1996), p. 9.

section 8, clause 3. Its decisions declared that Congress has broad, though not exclusive, regulatory powers. Those decisions generated intense political reactions in the states, including threats of secession. During the Great Depression of the 1930s, the Court's Commerce Clause jurisprudence again fomented a political firestorm, leading President Franklin Roosevelt to attempt to "pack" the Court with justices who would read the Commerce Clause and other constitutional provisions to legitimate his far-reaching social and economic legislation. Even in the 1990s, the Court's Commerce Clause decisions are marked by sharp divisions among the justices and are the source of intense political debate about whether the national government or the states should have the power to make particular governing decisions.[24] Despite the power of judicial review, the Court's Commerce Clause decisions have never been the final word on the meaning of that constitutional provision and the balance of power between the national government and the states. (See especially Chapter 3 of this volume.)

Abortion politics in the wake of *Roe v. Wade*, 410 U.S. 113 (1973), provides another illustration of the circular, coordinate policymaking process to which Fisher and Devins refer.[25] (See Volume II, Chapter 7.) When *Roe* came to the Court, most state statutes prohibited nontherapeutic abortions. Those laws dated back to the late nineteenth and early twentieth centuries and reflected the lobbying efforts of organizations like the American Medical Association. More than forty interest groups and some 350 individuals signed sixteen joint *amicus curiae* briefs supporting one side or the other in the legal controversy in *Roe*, in which the Court was asked to declare unconstitutional a Texas statute that banned abortions.

The Supreme Court's 7–2 decision in *Roe* invalidated the Texas statute but it did nothing to end the abortion controversy. Instead, the decision mobilized abortion opponents. By 1989, changes in the Supreme Court's personnel fueled speculation that *Roe* might be overruled. Two of the majority votes in *Roe*—Justices Powell and Stewart—had been replaced by Justices Kennedy and O'Connor, both appointed by antiabortion President Ronald Reagan. Reagan elevated Justice Rehnquist, who had dissented in *Roe*, to chief justice following Chief Justice Burger's retirement, and appointed Justice Scalia to the vacant seat. In *Webster v. Reproductive Health Services*, 492 U.S. 490 (1989), the Court by a 5–4 vote dashed the hopes of antiabortion forces that *Roe* would be overruled, but the *Webster* decision did send a signal that the Court would approve more restrictive regulation of the abortion practice than it had previously. (See Volume II, Chapter 7.)

---

[24] See *United States v. Lopez*, 514 U.S. 549 (1995), excerpted in Chapter 3 of this volume.

[25] Compare the case study on *Roe v. Wade* in Charles A. Johnson and Bradley C. Canon, *Judicial Policies: Implementation and Impact* (Washington, D.C.: Congressional Quarterly, 1984), pp. 4–14. Also see Neal Devins, *Shaping Constitutional Values: Elected Government, the Supreme Court, and the Abortion Debate* (Baltimore, MD: The Johns Hopkins University Press, 1996); and Gerald N. Rosenberg, *The Hollow Hope: Can Courts Bring about Social Change?* (Chicago, IL: University of Chicago Press, 1991).

Clearly, the Supreme Court's exercise of its power of judicial review in *Roe v. Wade* did not resolve the abortion controversy.[26] Rather, *Roe* helped to make abortion a national issue, while before *Roe* abortion politics and law had played out primarily in the states. Like the Court's decisions regarding Congress's power to regulate interstate commerce, *Roe* illustrates the way in which Supreme Court justices engage in a "continuing colloquy with the political institutions and with society at large."[27] "Judges," observed Ruth Bader Ginsburg in 1992, the year before she was appointed to the Supreme Court, "play an interdependent part in our democracy. They do not alone shape legal doctrine but ... they participate in a dialogue with other organs of government, and with the people as well."[28]

Stories illustrating the circular, coordinate nature of Supreme Court policymaking can be told about every case in this book.[29] Each of the Court's landmark constitutional decisions has emerged out of a hotly contested political environment and has involved constitutional issues about which lower courts have been in disagreement. Although each decision has yielded a rule of constitutional law that has contributed to the evolution of legal doctrine, none has put an end to the political controversy that spawned the litigation. Consequently, it is fair to ask—do Supreme Court decisions matter?[30]

The realistic answer to that question is—it depends. Compliance with a particular judicial decision depends on how the decision is perceived by various groups in American society.[31] According to political scientists Charles A. Johnson and Bradley C. Canon, perception is shaped along four dimensions: (1) a person's attitude toward the specific policy announced in the Supreme Court's decision; (2) a person's attitude toward the Court; (3) a person's perception of the practical consequences of the decision; and (4) a person's per-

---

[26] See Robert Blank and Janna C. Merrick, *Human Reproduction, Emerging Technologies, and Conflicting Rights* (Washington, D.C.: Congressional Quarterly, 1995).

[27] Alexander Bickel, *The Least Dangerous Branch: The Supreme Court at the Bar of Politics* (Indianapolis, IN: Bobbs-Merrill, 1962), p. 240.

[28] Ruth Bader Ginsburg, "Speaking in a Judicial Voice," 67 *New York University Law Review* (1992): 1198. See Richard Funston, *A Vital National Seminar: The Supreme Court in American Political Life* (Palo Alto, CA: Mayfield, 1978).

[29] Many outstanding case studies of Supreme Court decisions already have been published. Among them are Gordon E. Baker, *The Reapportionment Revolution: Representation, Political Power, and the Supreme Court* (New York, NY: Random House, 1966); Fred W. Friendly, *Minnesota Rag: The Dramatic Story of the Landmark Supreme Court Case That Gave Meaning to Freedom of the Press* (New York, NY: Vintage, 1982); Richard Kluger, *Simple Justice* (New York, NY: Vintage, 1977); Anthony Lewis, *Gideon's Trumpet* (New York, NY: Vintage, 1964); C. Peter Magrath, *Yazoo: The Case of Fletcher v. Peck* (New York, NY: Norton, 1967); John T. Noonan, *The Antelope* (Berkeley, CA: University of California Press, 1977). Tracing the political and social consequences of any of the cases in this book is an excellent source of topics for student research papers.

[30] See Lauren Bowen, "Do Court Decisions Matter?" in *Contemplating Courts*, ed. Lee Epstein (Washington, D.C.: Congressional Quarterly, 1995), pp. 376–389.

[31] Stuart A. Scheingold refers to this process of perception as the "compliance calculation," in his *The Politics of Rights: Lawyers, Public Policy, and Political Change* (New Haven, CT: Yale University Press, 1974), pp. 123–130. Compare Michael W. McCann, *Rights at Work: Pay Equity Reform and the Politics of Legal Mobilization* (Chicago, IL: University of Chicago Press, 1994); and John Brigham, *The Constitution of Interest: Beyond the Politics of Rights* (New York, NY: New York University Press, 1996).

ception of how the decision will affect their role in society. Johnson and Canon write: "Behavioral responses … are often linked to acceptance decisions. Persons who do not accept a judicial policy are likely to engage in behavior designed to defeat the policy or minimize its impact…. Those who accept a policy are likely to be more faithful or even enthusiastic in interpreting, implementing, and consuming it."[32] In most landmark Supreme Court decisions, the relevant population extends well beyond the immediate parties to the case. At the federal level, lower courts, Congress, the president, and one or more administrative agencies all make compliance calculations. Fifty state executives and state legislatures, and multiple state courts also must decide how to respond to the Court's decisions. Local law enforcement officials, school board members, bar associations and legal academics, and interest groups also are among salient populations whose responses can affect whether Supreme Court decisions meet with compliance.

As a policymaking body, observes political scientist Lawrence Baum, the Supreme Court "is neither all-powerful nor insignificant." He concludes:

> [T]he Court is perhaps most important in creating conditions for action by others. Its decisions put issues on the national agenda so that other policy makers and the general public consider them. The Court is not highly effective at enforcing rights, but it often legitimates efforts to achieve them and thus provides the impetus for people to take legal and political action. Its decisions affect the positions of interest groups and social movements, strengthening some and weakening others.[33]

THE SUPREME COURT IN THE AMERICAN JUDICIAL SYSTEM

As noted previously, the Supreme Court is not merely a coordinate branch of the national government. It also operates within a federal system. However, this was not always the case. The Articles of Confederation did not provide for a judicial branch as such, only for a mechanism to hear disputes between and among states. Each of the state governments had a judicial branch, however, so the proposal at the Constitutional Convention for a national judiciary to

---

[32] Johnson and Canon, *Judicial Policies*, pp. 23–24. Johnson and Canon identify four particularly important "populations" (groups): the interpreting population, the implementing population, the consumer population, and the secondary population. Ibid., pp. 15–22, 24.

See also Rosenberg, *The Hollow Hope*; Bradley C. Canon, "Courts and Policy: Compliance, Implementation, and Impact," in *The American Courts: A Critical Assessment*, ed. John B. Gates (Washington, D.C.: Congressional Quarterly, 1991); Sheldon Ekland-Olson and Steve J. Martin, "Organizational Compliance with Court-Ordered Reform," in *The Law & Society Reader*, ed. Richard L. Abel (New York, NY: New York University Press, 1995); Robert A. Carp and Ronald Stidham, *Judicial Process in America*, 3rd ed. (Washington, D.C.: Congressional Quarterly, 1996), Chapter 11; Stewart Macaulay, Lawrence M. Friedman, and John Stookey, eds., *Law & Society: Readings on the Social Study of Law* (New York, NY: Norton, 1995), Chapter 4; Sheldon Goldman and Austin Sarat, eds., *American Court Systems: Readings in Judicial Process and Behavior*, 2nd ed. (New York, NY: Longman, 1989), Chapters 13 and 14; and Stephen L. Wasby, *The Impact of the United States Supreme Court* (Homewood, IL: Dorsey, 1970).

[33] Lawrence Baum, *The Supreme Court*, 5th ed. (Washington, D.C.: Congressional Quarterly, 1995), p. 272. Also see Lawrence Baum, "Courts and Policy Innovation," in Gates, *The American Courts*. Political scientist Stuart A. Scheingold termed the process Baum describes as the "politics of rights." See Scheingold, *The Politics of Rights*.

consist of at least one "supreme tribunal" created little stir. The delegates also agreed easily to the proposition that judges should hold their offices during good behavior. With no debate at all, the delegates voted to extend the national judicial power to cases in equity as well as law.[34] Giving the national judiciary power to dispense both legal and equitable remedies significantly consolidated the judicial function at the national level.[35]

Debate at the Convention was more divisive over the method for appointing federal judges, however. By a split vote, the delegates finally agreed to nomination by the president and confirmation by the Senate. Following extensive debate, the delegates rejected a proposal for a Council of Revision consisting of the president and a "convenient number of the national judiciary" that would have examined all acts of Congress before those acts went into effect. The delegates also debated, but rejected, a proposal for a joint judicial-executive veto of congressional legislation. Instead, the delegates gave Congress power to establish "inferior courts" and to determine the size and internal organization of the Supreme Court.

In the Judiciary Act of 1789, Congress created thirteen federal district courts that were to meet in four sessions annually, and three circuit courts, to hold court twice a year in each district within the circuit. The jurisdiction of the district courts was quite narrow; most of their work consisted of admiralty cases. The circuit courts had some appellate jurisdiction over the district courts, but primarily they were trial courts for cases involving suits between citizens of different states (known as diversity of citizenship cases). Few routes of appeal existed for litigants who were dissatisfied with circuit court judgments. The Supreme Court's appellate caseload during its formative years consisted primarily of cases appealed from decisions of state courts.

Circuit courts initially were staffed by two Supreme Court justices and one district court judge. In 1793, Congress reduced the circuit-riding burden on Supreme Court justices somewhat by requiring only one justice to sit each year as a circuit judge in each district.

The federal judicial structure created by the Judiciary Act of 1789 remained essentially intact until 1891, when Congress established a set of intermediate federal courts of appeal, now known as the U.S. Courts of Appeals. Figure 1.1 gives an overview of the U.S. judicial system as it looks today.

The Supreme Court sits at the top of a complex system of federal and state courts over which it exercises appellate jurisdiction. It also sits as a trial

---

[34] In England, and in the states, separate tribunals administered legal and equitable remedies. Courts of law resolved cases involving statutes or the common law, granting monetary damages to parties who prevailed in civil litigation and imposing fines and prison terms on defendants convicted of crimes. Courts of equity administered "remedial justice." They determined the appropriate relief in situations where rules of law were incomplete or inadequate. Equitable remedies included ordering specific conduct on the part of the litigants after the suit, and issuing temporary and permanent injunctions to compel or prohibit certain actions.

[35] Peter Charles Hoffer provides an historical account of equity in Anglo-American jurisprudence and shows the Supreme Court's use of equitable principles in twentieth century civil rights and affirmative action cases in *The Law's Conscience* (Chapel Hill, NC: University of North Carolina Press, 1990).

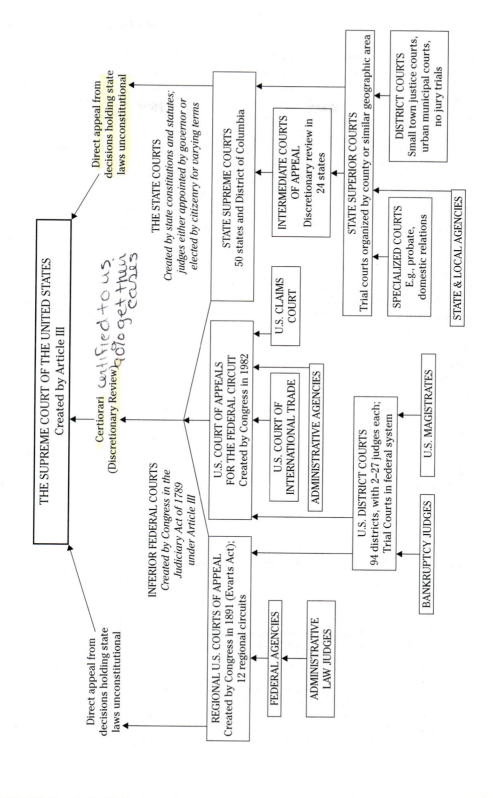

FIGURE 1.1 THE AMERICAN DUAL COURT SYSTEM

court in an extremely small number of cases, outlined in Article III, which comprise its original jurisdiction. The Supreme Court becomes involved in only a tiny fraction of the cases filed in American courts each year. Not many cases filed raise constitutional questions; not many cases that do raise constitutional questions work their way to the Supreme Court.

As Figure 1.1 also shows, the judicial system comprises both federal and state courts. State court systems have existed since the Revolution. Their organization originally reflected their English heritage. Congress's power to create "inferior" federal courts stirred political controversy among the states because of the fear that federal courts would rob state courts of their jurisdiction. Subject to the limitations in the Constitution of the United States, their own state constitutions and state law, state courts have general authority to try and decide a vast range of cases, including criminal prosecutions, personal injury cases, marital disputes, probate of estates, and land and commercial transactions. Federal courts, by comparison, are courts of limited jurisdiction. They are authorized to decide only those cases and controversies over which the Constitution of the United States or acts of Congress made pursuant to the Constitution give them jurisdiction.[36] Figure 1.2 shows boundaries of the twelve regional federal circuit courts of appeal. Those courts hear appeals from the U.S. district courts located within their boundaries.[37]

AUTHORITY OF THE SUPREME COURT

JURISDICTION

The authority of a court to try and decide a case is called jurisdiction.[38] It is of two kinds, personal and subject matter. A court does not have jurisdiction to hear a case unless it has the authority to compel the participation of the

---

[36] The distinctions between the jurisdiction of state and federal courts are set out by Fannie Klein in *Federal and State Court Systems—A Guide* (Cambridge, MA: Ballinger Publishing Co., 1977), p. 1.

[37] The Court of Appeals for the Federal Circuit is the exception to the rule of regional courts of appeal. It is a jurisdictional instead of a geographical appeals court. Created in 1982 through a merger of the U.S. Court of Claims and the U.S. Court of Customs and Patents, it hears appeals in cases from the U.S. Court of Federal Claims, the U.S. Court of International Trade, the U.S. Court of Veterans Appeals, the International Trade Commission, the Board of Contract Appeals, the Patent and Trademark Office, and the Merit Systems Protection Board. The Court of Appeals for the Federal Circuit also hears appeals from certain decisions of the secretaries of the Department of Agriculture and the Department of Commerce, cases arising from district courts involving patents, and minor claims against the federal government.

The regional courts of appeal frequently interpret federal law differently, creating what are known as "intercircuit conflicts." Often the Supreme Court will await intercircuit conflicts on an issue before accepting a case for review. That way, the justices have the benefit of the reasoning of federal appellate judges in various parts of the country on an issue.

[38] Students interested in exploring details of the Court's jurisdiction, issues of justiciability, and aspects of practices and procedures before the Supreme Court are referred to Robert L. Stern, Eugene Gressman, Stephen M. Shapiro, and Kenneth S. Geller, *Supreme Court Practice*, 7th ed. (Washington, D.C.: Bureau of National Affairs, 1993). The authors note in their preface that the goal of the book is to "set forth in a single volume to the extent possible everything that a lawyer would want to know as to how to prosecute or defend a case in the Supreme Court." Also see Susan Low Bloch and Thomas G. Krattenmaker, eds., *Supreme Court Politics: The Institution and Its Procedures* (St. Paul, MN: West, 1994).

FIGURE 1.2   TWELVE REGIONAL FEDERAL CIRCUIT COURTS OF APPEAL (*Source: Map courtesy of Edward Bennett Williams Law Library, Georgetown University Law Center.*)

parties (personal jurisdiction) and the authority to render a binding decision on the issues (subject matter jurisdiction). As noted previously, state courts traditionally have been recognized as courts of general jurisdiction. They are assumed to have the authority to resolve all cases and controversies submitted to them by their own residents. Federal courts, by contrast, are courts of limited jurisdiction. They may exercise judicial power only if authority has been conferred by the Constitution or by federal statute. A party who files a case in federal court must prove that the court has jurisdiction through reference to the constitutional or federal statutory provision conferring the right to litigate in a federal court. Failure to prove federal jurisdiction results in automatic dismissal of the case, no matter how compelling the issues.

The Supreme Court exercises jurisdiction over two categories of cases. Article III of the Constitution gives it original jurisdiction over "cases affecting Ambassadors, other public Ministers and Consuls, and those in which a State shall be a Party." The Court's jurisdiction over these cases may be exclusive or concurrent with other federal or state courts. Only a few cases have ever been brought involving foreign diplomats. Disputes between states over land, boundaries, and water and mineral rights have provided the bulk of the Court's work in this realm, although these cases are rare and have comprised only a small fraction of the Court's overall caseload. When the justices hear cases in the exercise of their original jurisdiction they sit as a trial court, making findings of fact as well as conclusions of law.

The Supreme Court has appellate, or review, jurisdiction in all other cases, subject to regulations and exceptions made by Congress. Congress has considered limiting the Court's appellate jurisdiction many times over the years. During the past two decades, legislation has been introduced to curb the Court's appellate jurisdiction in four controversial areas in particular: abortion, prayer in public schools, school busing, and the rights of criminal defendants.[39] Until recently, however, the typical pattern of congressional action has been to provide litigants with more rather than fewer opportunities to request appellate review, while at the same time giving the Supreme Court more discretion over the appellate cases it will hear. The Judiciary Act of 1925, for example, replaced review as a matter of right from state and circuit courts of appeal with discretionary review by writ of certiorari.[40] The 1925 legislation did not eliminate a range of direct appeals provided by Congress, such as in cases where a federal court had invalidated a state statute or when a state court declared federal legislation unconstitutional. Beginning in 1948, however, Congress began to eliminate opportunities for nondiscretionary appeals. Following passage of the 1988 Act to Improve the Administration of

---

[39] According to attorney Ronald L. Goldfarb, as of November 1996, there were 194 resolutions for constitutional amendments pending in the House of Representatives and 55 pending in the Senate. Among these resolutions were proposed amendments designed to reverse several Supreme Court opinions, including decisions on abortion and term limits. "The 11,000th Amendment: What's Wrong with the Rush to Revise the Constitution," *Washington Post*, Sunday, November 17, 1996, C4.

The legitimacy of congressional curbs on the Court's jurisdiction is discussed by Henry M. Hart Jr., "The Power of Congress to Limit the Jurisdiction of the Federal Courts: An Exercise in Dialectic," 66 *Harvard Law Review* (1953): 1362; Leonard Ratner, "Congressional Power over the Appellate Jurisdiction of the Supreme Court," 109 *University of Pennsylvania Law Review* (1960): 157; Leonard Ratner, "Majoritarian Constraints on Judicial Review: Congressional Control of Supreme Court Jurisdiction," 27 *Villanova Law Review* (1982): 929; and Charles E. Rice, "The Constitutional Basis for the Proposals in Congress Today," 65 *Judicature* (1981): 190.

See also C. Herman Pritchett, *Congress versus the Supreme Court* (Minneapolis, MN: University of Minnesota Press, 1961); Walter F. Murphy, *Congress and the Court: A Case Study in the American Political Process* (Chicago, IL: University of Chicago Press, 1962); Stuart S. Nagel, "Court-Curbing Periods in American History," 18 *Vanderbilt Law Review* (1965): 925; Raoul Berger, *Congress v. The Supreme Court* (Cambridge, MA: Harvard University Press, 1969); John R. Schmidhauser and Larry L. Berg, *The Supreme Court and Congress: Conflict and Interaction, 1945–1968* (New York, NY: Free Press, 1972); Handberg and Hill, "Court Curbing, Court Reversals, and Judicial Review: The Supreme Court versus Congress"; Louis Fisher, *Constitutional Dialogues: Interpretation as Political Process* (Princeton, NJ: Princeton University Press, 1988); William N. Eskridge Jr., "Overriding Supreme Court Statutory Interpretation Decisions," 101 *Yale Law Journal* (1991): 331; Abner Mikva and Jeff Bleich, "When Congress Overrides the Court," 79 *California Law Review* (1991): 729; and Linda Greenhouse, "How Congress Curtailed the Courts' Jurisdiction," *New York Times*, October 27, 1996, E5.

[40] The certiorari process is explained on pp. 23–24.

Justice, almost all rights of direct appeal were eliminated.[41] Today, the certiorari process gives the Court almost complete discretion over the cases it will hear in the exercise of its appellate jurisdiction. Figure 1.3 shows the sources of Supreme Court cases docketed during the 1995 October Term.

In recent years, the Court has denied review (or the parties have withdrawn requests for review) in over 90 percent of the cases for which review has been sought. As a result, the Supreme Court hears and decides only a very small proportion of the total number of cases filed each year. The number of cases the Court hears and decides has been declining in recent years. During its 1980 Term, for example, the Court granted review in 232 (10.4 percent) of 2,256 cases on the Appellate Docket, and 27 (1.3 percent) of 2,017 cases on the Miscellaneous Docket.[42] In the 1989 Term, the numbers diminished to 171 (8.4 percent) of the 2,028 cases on its Appellate Docket and in 32 (1.1 percent) of the 2,878 cases on its Miscellaneous Docket. By its 1994 Term, the Court granted review in merely 83 (3.9 percent) of the 2,151 cases on its Appellate Docket, and only 10 (.02 percent) of the 4,979 cases on its Miscellaneous Docket. For the Supreme Court's 1995 Term, the figures are 92 (4.4 percent) of the 2,099 cases on its Appellate Docket, and 13 (.03 percent) of the 4,507 cases on its Miscellaneous Docket.[43]

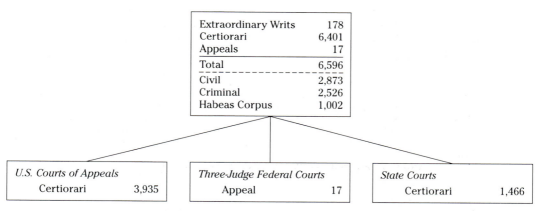

FIGURE 1.3   CASES DOCKETED OCTOBER TERM 1995 (*Source: Clerk's Office, Supreme Court of the United States.*)

---

[41] Exceptions to the elimination of the right to appeal include appeals in reapportionment cases, suits under the Civil Rights and Voting Rights Acts, antitrust laws, and the Presidential Election Campaign Fund Act.

[42] The Appellate Docket consists of all cases for which the parties pay counsel and relevant filing fees. The Miscellaneous Docket includes cases filed in *forma pauperis* ("as a pauper," that is, permission to sue without paying any court costs).

[43] 104 *Harvard Law Review* (1990): Table I, p. 367; 104 *Harvard Law Review* (1990): Table II, p. 363; 109 *Harvard Law Review* (1995): Table II, pp. 344–345; 110 *Harvard Law Review* (1996): Table II, p. 371. Annually, the first issue (November) of each volume of the *Harvard Law Review* contains a section called "The Statistics." This section contains tables reporting, for instance, the actions of individual justices, voting alignments, unanimity, 5–4 decisions, final disposition of cases, disposition of cases reviewed on writ of certiorari, and subject matter of dispositions with full opinions.

JUSTICIABILITY

In addition to defining the Supreme Court's jurisdiction, Article III of the Constitution specifies that the Court has power over "cases and controversies." Article III provides no definition of those terms, however. Over the past two hundred years, the "case" and "controversy" requirement has evolved into a broad threshold doctrine known as justiciability. Justiciability refers to the propriety of examining a dispute in a judicial forum. While the doctrine has many dimensions, the five most important for purposes of understanding Supreme Court litigation are summarized below.[44] They are among the factors that the justices consider when deciding whether to hear a case.

1. *No Advisory Opinions*   As a matter of policy, courts will not issue an advisory opinion in advance of an actual case or controversy between identifiable parties. This policy was established in 1793 when George Washington directed his secretary of state, Thomas Jefferson, to write a letter to the first chief justice of the United States, John Jay, asking the Supreme Court to advise the president on twenty-nine hypothetical questions of international law and neutrality. Jay declined, saying to do so would violate the separation of powers.

The Court's refusal to issue advisory opinions was reinforced in 1911, when it refused to hear a case brought by parties in order to obtain an opinion on the constitutionality of Congressional statutes enacted in 1902 and 1907 that affected Indian lands. The statutes altered the original distribution of Cherokee tribal property and had the practical effect of reducing the amount of lands and funds to which certain Indians are entitled. This redistribution of property raised constitutional questions, which one of the statutes authorized the parties to take to the Supreme Court of the United States. Justice Day wrote that this authorization required the Court "to give opinions in the nature of advice concerning legislative action—a function never conferred upon it by the Constitution...." *Muskrat v. United States*, 219 U.S. 346 (1911).

no case a contravcy

2. *No "Political Questions"*   In order to protect the judiciary from becoming embroiled in partisan politics and to protect their integrity as an independent, coequal branch of government, American courts declared early in their history that they would not hear cases that raise so-called "political questions."[45] If a court believes a case raises issues that are properly decided by the legislative and/or executive branches at the state or federal level, it will declare the case nonjusticiable, citing the doctrine against deciding political

---

[44] For a complete analysis of the justiciability doctrine, see the latest edition of Charles Alan Wright, et al, *Federal Practice and Procedure* (*Manual for Complex Litigation*) (St. Paul, MN: West Publishing, 1969–).

[45] The Court formally announced the "political question" doctrine in *Luther v. Borden*, 7 Howard 1 (1849). However, Chief Justice John Marshall wrote in *Marbury v. Madison*, 1 Cranch 137 (1803), that "The province of the court is, solely, to decide on the rights of individuals, not to inquire how the executive, or executive officers, perform duties in which they have a discretion. Questions, in their nature political ... can never be made in this court."

questions. A modern example of the Supreme Court's use of the doctrine is *Gilligan v. Morgan*, 413 U.S. 1 (1973). The Court held that questions involving the training and discipline of National Guard troops are nonjusticiable because the constitutional responsibility for organizing, arming, and disciplining the military is committed to Congress and the executive branch.

The line between a "political" and "legal" question usually is very hard to draw. Declaring that a case is nonjusticiable on the grounds that it raises a political question frequently is synonymous with deciding the issue: it effectively gives judicial sanction to a resolution by a nonjudicial body. The Supreme Court's use of the political question doctrine thus provides insight into the justices' views of the kinds of issues that they believe merit judicial resolution, which in turn is an insight into the justices' view of the proper role of the courts in our political system.

3. Parties Must Have Standing to Sue

In order to be involved in a lawsuit, parties must have definite and concrete interests in the litigation and must have adverse legal interests. With rare exceptions, third parties cannot assert the rights of others. Failure to satisfy any of the elements of the standing rule can result in dismissal of the action. An environmental dispute provides an example. In 1972, the Court rejected the Sierra Club's challenge to a proposed recreational development. The Sierra Club claimed to represent the interests of the scenery, natural and historical objects, and wildlife of the Mineral King Valley in California. The Court rejected the challenge, ruling that the Sierra Club alleged no facts showing itself or its members adversely affected by the development. The Court dismissed the case on the grounds that the Sierra Club lacked standing to sue.[46]

Like the political question doctrine, the justices exercise the standing rule with considerable flexibility. Their explanation of why a party does or does not have standing to sue provides additional perspective on their understanding of the proper exercise of judicial power. (See Chapter 2 of this volume.)

4. No Adjudication of Cases That Are Not "Ripe" or Are Moot

The concepts of ripeness and mootness refer to the time when it is appropriate for judicial resolution of an issue. If a case is dismissed for lack of ripeness, it means that the justices believe a decision would be premature for some reason. Most often, cases are dismissed for lack of ripeness because other avenues of redress, including legislative and administrative proceedings, are available, are in progress, or are pending. In cases invoking the Supreme Court's equitable jurisdiction, the justices will dismiss for lack of ripeness if they conclude that the threatened injury is too "speculative" to warrant their intervention.

An example of the Court's refusal to decide cases that it believes are not ripe for adjudication is *United Public Workers v. Mitchell*, 330 U.S. 75 (1946). In

---

[46] *Sierra Club v. Morton*, 405 U.S. 727 (1972).

that case, federal employees sought an injunction against enforcement of the federal Hatch Act, which prohibits certain federal employees from engaging in political activities. The employees sought the injunction on the ground that the First, Fifth, Ninth, and Tenth Amendments to the Constitution entitles them to engage in certain political activities. The Court refused to decide the case, claiming that the issues it posed were too speculative for judicial resolution. "A hypothetical threat is not enough," wrote Justice Reed. "It would not accord with judicial responsibility to adjudge ... between the freedom of the individual and the requirements of public order except when definite rights appear upon the one side and definite prejudicial interferences on the other."

Conversely, cases must be "live" throughout the adjudicatory process. If circumstances terminate the adverseness of the parties to a controversy before their case reaches the Supreme Court, the Court's jurisdiction ceases and the case is deemed "moot." A case can be moot if a party drops out of the litigation or if the parties decide to settle their dispute at any time during the process.

A lawsuit filed in 1971 by a white male, Marco DeFunis, that challenged the University of Washington Law School's affirmative action plan as reverse discrimination, demonstrates the mootness doctrine. By the time DeFunis's case reached the Supreme Court in 1974, he was enrolled as a student in the law school on order of a state superior court and was assured of graduation. The Supreme Court refused to rule on the constitutionality of the law school's affirmative action program because DeFunis no longer was an injured party.[47]

Like the other doctrines discussed in this section, the Court does not apply the mootness doctrine rigidly. In deciding the constitutionality of the Texas abortion statute in *Roe v. Wade*, 410 U.S. 113 (1973), for example, the Court rejected the threshold argument that the birth of the plaintiff's baby rendered the case moot. Justice Harry Blackmun noted that if mootness standards were applied strictly, it would never be possible for a woman to challenge such statutes because the normal course of litigation is much longer than the normal course of a pregnancy.

5. A Case Will Not Be Resolved on Constitutional Grounds If It Can Be Resolved on Other Grounds   A final example of judicial self-restraint is the self-imposed rule that courts will avoid construing the Constitution if there are other grounds on which to decide a case. Hence, where possible, courts will resolve cases under the terms of a state or federal statute or in accordance with common law precedents if they can do so. Constitutional resolution of a case is avoided if possible. The theory behind this rule is that courts should not prematurely foreclose debate on issues by resolving them

---

[47]*DeFunis v. Odegaard*, 416 U.S. 312 (1974). Similarly, the Court dismissed as moot two constitutional challenges to the congressional joint resolution extending the ratification period for the proposed Equal Rights Amendment. The cases arrived at the Court after the extended time period had elapsed without the requisite number of states ratifying. *National Organization for Women v. Idaho* and *Carmen v. Idaho*, 459 U.S. 809 (1982).

on constitutional grounds. In practice, however, as noted earlier, resolving an issue on constitutional grounds may actually expand and intensify debate.

These examples demonstrate that justiciability rules are not cast in concrete. Rather, they are gate-keeping norms that the Court uses in deciding whether to accept cases for resolution in order to manage its work load and to conserve its authority.[48] On occasion the Supreme Court has stretched the rules in order to hear a case. On other occasions it has strictly invoked the rules to avoid deciding a case that from the perspective of the parties or public policy would benefit from resolution. Exercising the gate-keeping function is never automatic. It always involves discretion.[49]

SUPREME COURT REVIEW

The procedures for having a case reviewed by the Supreme Court of the United States have varied over the years. Today, almost 99 percent of the Court's appellate docket is created by petitions for writs of certiorari. Under this process, a party seeking Supreme Court review requests the Court by petition (in the form of a legal brief) to issue a writ directing the lower court to send the record of the case to the Supreme Court for review. Usually the opposing party submits a petition explaining why the Court should not issue the writ. Occasionally, the parties will submit a joint petition requesting the Court to issue a writ of certiorari.

By custom, a writ of certiorari is issued when four of the nine justices vote to issue it. Under the pressure of increasing case loads, this custom, known as the "rule of four," has applied to an increasingly smaller number of

---

[48] In his concurring opinion to *Ashwander v. T.V.A.*, 297 U.S. 288 (1936), Justice Louis Brandeis thought it important to summarize the following seven rules developed by the Supreme Court "for its own governance" to avoid "passing upon a large part of all the constitutional questions pressed upon it for decision":

1. The Court will not pass upon the constitutionality of legislation in a friendly, nonadversary, proceeding.
2. The Court will not anticipate a question of constitutional law in advance of the necessity of deciding it.
3. The Court will not formulate a rule of constitutional law broader than is required by the precise facts to which it is to be applied.
4. The Court will not pass upon a constitutional question although properly presented by the record, if there is also present some other ground upon which the case may be disposed of.
5. The Court will not pass upon the validity of a statute upon the complaint of one who fails to show that he is injured by its operation.
6. The Court will not pass upon the constitutionality of a statute at the instance of one who has availed himself of its benefits.
7. When the validity of an act of the Congress is drawn in question, and even if a serious doubt of constitutionality is raised, it is a cardinal principle that this Court will first ascertain whether a construction of the statute is fairly possible by which the question may be avoided.

Compare Henry J. Abraham's discussion of "The Sixteen Great Maxims of Judicial Self Restraint," *The Judicial Process*, pp. 348–370.

[49] Some view the Court's justiciability rules as contributing to its institutional conservatism. See M. Glenn Abernathy and Barbara A. Perry, *Civil Liberties under the Constitution*, 6th ed. (Columbia, SC: University of South Carolina Press, 1993).

cases, currently around 2 percent. Most often review is granted by a majority vote and unanimity on case selection is remarkably high.[50]

On average, about one case per term reaches the Court through certification. Under this procedure, if a federal court of appeals is unclear about a question of law, and hence is unable to decide a case, it may certify the legal question to the Supreme Court. The Court has discretion over whether to accept a case on certification and in recent years has shown little inclination to do so. If the Supreme Court refuses to accept a case on certification, the lower court must decide the legal question and enter a judgment. A dissatisfied party may then seek Supreme Court review.

Parties may petition the Court to issue other writs that require review of a case before the writ is issued or denied. An example is the writ of mandamus, through which a party petitions the Court to order a judge or other government official to perform a legally mandated duty. The Court must determine the nature of the duty before issuing or declining to issue such a writ. The Supreme Court issues writs of mandamus infrequently. As noted earlier, the 1988 Act to Improve the Administration of Justice gave the Supreme Court virtually complete discretion over deciding which cases to accept for review.

SUPREME COURT REVIEW PROCESS

In recent years, the Court has been asked to review between four thousand and five thousand cases during its annual eight- or nine-month term (the first Monday in October through late June or early July). All requests for review are analyzed by the office of the Clerk of the Court. If the requests satisfy the procedural requirements spelled out in the Court's rules, they are assigned docket numbers. Filings are screened by the justices or, more often, by their law clerks.[51] Since 1972, the justices have combined resources in a "cert pool," where their clerks share responsibility for winnowing the few cases to be heard from the vast majority that are rejected. Currently, all the justices except John Paul Stevens participate in the "cert pool." The decision whether to accept or deny review of cases is made by the justices in closed conference. The Court recently has reduced the number of certiorari cases discussed at conference through a device called Special List I, or "the discuss list." Before conference, the chief justice circulates a list of certiorari cases that he deems worthy of discussion. Other justices add to the list if they choose. According to former Justice William Brennan, only about 30 percent of the docketed cases appear on the discuss list, and most of those eventually are denied review.[52]

If a case is accepted for Supreme Court review, it normally is processed

---

[50] David M. O'Brien, *Storm Center: The Supreme Court in American Politics*, 4th ed. (New York, NY: Norton, 1996), pp. 234–236.

[51] Law clerks typically are high-ranking recent graduates of the nation's prestigious law schools who have had previous experience as clerks for state or federal judges.

[52] William Brennan, "The National Court of Appeals: Another Dissent," 40 *University of Chicago Law Review* (1973): 473, 479.

through several distinct steps on the way to a decision. The process is as follows:[53]

1. Submission of Briefs   The first step is for legal counsel to submit written briefs. Today, the appellant (the losing party below) has forty-five days to file a brief on the merits after being notified by the Clerk of the Court that its case has been accepted. The respondent (the winning party below) then has thirty days to file a brief that responds to the appellant's brief and seeks to persuade the Supreme Court to affirm the decision of the most recent court to rule on the case. The briefs summarize the facts, describe the rulings of the lower court(s), and identify and argue the legal points and constitutional theories that each side wishes the Court to consider. In true adversary fashion, the appellant is permitted to submit a reply brief that refutes the points made in the respondent's brief.

In order to get a broader perspective on a case, the Court can approve requests from various groups to submit *amicus curiae* or "friend of the Court" briefs. Parties *amici* can include individuals, organizations, and governmental units that have an interest in the outcome of the case but that are not parties. In the past three decades, the *amicus* brief has become a vehicle by means of which diverse interest groups lobby the Court to adopt a particular rule of law.[54]

The briefing process is carefully governed by Court rules. If a brief is particularly well-written or organized, it might be used by a justice to structure an opinion in the case.

2. Oral Argument   Oral argument takes place several weeks after the justices have received the briefs and records of a case and have had an opportunity to read them and conduct preliminary legal research. The justices hear arguments four days a week during each Term. Under current Supreme Court

---

[53] On occasion, the Court has issued a decision in a case at the time it decides to review it, suggesting that the justices do not believe completion of all steps is essential in every case. See *Spain v. Rushen*, 464 U.S. 114 (1983), for an example of the majority deciding without benefit of argument that error committed at the trial level was "harmless."

[54] See Samuel Krislov, "The *Amicus Curiae* Brief: From Friendship to Advocacy," 72 *Yale Law Journal* (1963): 694; Nathan Hakman, "Lobbying the Supreme Court: An Appraisal of Political Science 'Folklore,'" 35 *Fordham Law Review* (1966): 15; Lucius Barker, "Third Parties in Litigation: A Systematic View of the Judicial Function," 29 *Journal of Politics* (1967): 41; Karen Orren, "Standing to Sue: Interest Group Conflict in Federal Courts," 70 *American Political Science Review* (1976): 723; Karen O'Connor and Lee Epstein, "Research Note: *Amicus Curiae* Participation in U.S. Supreme Court Litigation: An Appraisal of Hakman's 'Folklore,'" 16 *Law and Society Review* (1982): 701; Karen O'Connor and Lee Epstein, "The Rise of Conservative Interest Group Litigation, 45 *Journal of Politics* (1983): 479; Robert C. Bradley and Paul Gardiner, "Underdogs, Upperdogs, and the Use of the *Amicus* Brief: Trends and Explanations," 10 *Justice Systems Journal* (1985): 78; Stephen L. Wasby, "The Multi-faceted Elephant: Litigator Perspectives on Planned Litigation," 15 *Capital University Law Review* (1986): 143; Gregory A. Caldeira and Donald J. McCrone, "Of Time and Judicial Activism: A Study of the U.S. Supreme Court, 1800–1973," in *Supreme Court Activism and Restraint*, eds. Stephen C. Halpern and Charles M. Lamb (Lexington, MA: Lexington Books, 1988); Gregory A. Caldeira, "*Amici* before the Supreme Court: Who Participates, When, and How Much?" *Journal of Politics* (1990); Lee Epstein, "Courts and Interests Groups," in *The American Courts: A Critical Assessment*, eds. John B. Gates and Charles A. Johnson (Washington, D.C.: Congressional Quarterly, 1991); and Kevin T. McGuire, "*Amici Curiae* and Strategies for Gaining Access to the Supreme Court," 47 *Political Research Quarterly* (1994): 821.

rules, each side has thirty minutes for oral argument, unless the Court grants a written request for an extension of time. Occasionally the Court permits more than one attorney to argue a case, or allows counsel for parties *amicus* to argue.

Before the Court's docket became so crowded, much more time was allowed for oral argument. In the early days of the Court, for example, argument could go on for days. By the mid-1800s, the time had been shortened to two hours per side; later, to one hour per side. The current rule governing the length of oral argument has been in effect since 1970. Since 1993, the Clerk of the Court has been sending attorneys a booklet containing advice on how to prepare for and make oral arguments.

Oral arguments range from dull expositions by counsel of the points in their briefs to heated exchanges between counsel and the bench or even between justices. Justices can and do interrupt arguments at any time with questions and counter-arguments. Oral argument allows the justices, as well as legal counsel, to test and debate constitutional theories. Reporters who cover the Court and legal scholars who seek to predict how the justices will decide a case listen to oral arguments carefully for clues about the justices' views and probable votes. Predicting outcomes based on questions posed or comments made during oral argument is as problematic as it is fascinating.[55] Expression of an opinion or point of view during oral argument is not necessarily an indication of how a particular justice or group of justices will vote.

Students of the judicial process and justices themselves disagree about the importance of oral argument.[56] Primarily, oral argument provides the jus-

[55] Anyone interested in participating in this parlor game can study the verbatim transcripts of oral arguments in especially significant cases printed in the *New York Times*. Access to the *New York Times* on the Internet is available at [http://www.nytimes.com/].

[56] Elder Witt, *Congressional Quarterly Guide to the U.S. Supreme Court*, 2nd ed. (Washington, D.C.: Congressional Quarterly, 1990), p. 739.

Journalists Joan Biskupic and Linda Greenhouse fueled the debate over the importance of oral argument. Biskupic wrote an article about the highly competitive, often arrogant, elite "Supreme Court bar." In her article, Biskupic recounts an episode when Matt Coles, director of the American Civil Liberties Union's Lesbian and Gay Rights Project, unsuccessfully tried to persuade Jean Dubofsky, who had argued as plaintiff's attorney against Colorado Amendment 2 in state court—*Evans v. Romer*, 854 P2d 1270 (Colo. 1993); *Evans v. Romer*, 882 P2d 1335 (Colo. 1994)—to relinquish the case to a law professor "who had helped on the case and had more experience before the justices." Dubofsky's performance at oral argument met with "mixed reviews" from Supreme Court bar critics. However, "[i]n the end," noted Biskupic, "she won— showing that the quality of the oral argument, while scrutinized by the media, lawyers and justices themselves, does not determine the outcome of the case." "Legal Elite Vie for Court Time in Pursuit of Supreme Challenge," *Washington Post*, December 2, 1996, A19. Biskupic does not report that Jean Dubofsky served on the Colorado Supreme Court from 1979 until 1987.

Linda Greenhouse apparently takes a different view of the importance of oral argument in a recent article about *Glickman v. Wileman Bros.*, No. 95-1184, a First Amendment case in which a group of California fruit growers challenged a government-required advertising program. Greenhouse observed that the growers' attorney bungled his oral argument time: "Thomas Compagne ... failed to exploit the numerous openings the government's argument had made for him. Instead, he resisted the justices' numerous invitations to present a coherent First Amendment theory and kept returning to the details of the fruit business, ignoring warnings that he was turning his constitutional challenge into a mundane administrative-law case in which the court had little reason to be interested." "High Court Hears Case about Commercial Speech." [http://www.nytimes.com/]. 3 December 1996.

tices an opportunity to question counsel about legal theories contained in the briefs and to raise points that individual justices deem important and that may not have been addressed in the briefs.

Occasionally, the Court will order reargument in a case. Usually such an order requires the parties to submit new briefs and to appear at another oral argument. Reargument will be ordered if members of the Court conclude that important points of law were not argued adequately or that other issues need to be addressed by counsel before the Court issues an opinion. Reargument tends to be ordered when the Court considers the case to be of especially great magnitude from the perspective of public policy. School desegregation, reapportionment, and abortion are modern examples of cases raising issues for which the justices have required reargument.

3. Conference on the Merits   Following oral argument, a case is declared "submitted." This means that the case is ready for discussion among the justices at their conference, for a tentative vote on the outcome, and for the assignment of the case to a justice to draft an opinion.

Supreme Court conferences are one of the last vestiges of complete secrecy in American government. Since the mid-1950s, conferences have occurred on Friday. Although there are two large conference rooms in the Supreme Court building, the justices meet in a smaller, more private room adjacent to the chief justice's chambers. No one is allowed in the conference room except the justices, and no one knows exactly what occurs during the gatherings. Tradition has it that before taking their seats to discuss cases that have been submitted, the justices shake hands with one another to symbolize the collegial nature of their decision-making process. The chief justice presides at the conference.

Conventional wisdom among students of the Court was that discussion and voting at conference proceed in two stages. According to this account, the chief justice is the first to express an opinion about a case, with other justices speaking in order of seniority. Following discussion, the justices vote on the case in reverse order of seniority.[57] However, recent scholarship and remarks by Chief Justice William Rehnquist call this version into question.[58] It is now believed that the justices discuss and vote in a single process conducted in descending order of seniority after the chief justice. Conference discussions are more in the nature of "straw polls," revealing initial positions rather than final outcomes. These exchanges begin a process of bargaining, negotiating, and maneuvering that continues through the opinion-writing stage.

---

[57] Congressional Quarterly, *Guide to the U.S. Supreme Court* (Washington D.C.: Congressional Quarterly, 1979), p. 739.

[58] Robert C. Bradley, "What Is Actually Happening behind the Closed Doors?" 6 *Law, Courts, and Judicial Process Section Newsletter*, Washington, D.C.: American Political Science Association (Summer 1989): 1–2. Chief Justice Rehnquist made his remarks on "This Honorable Court," 2 pts., Public Broadcasting System, Washington, D.C., WETA, 1987, pt. 2. Compare Rehnquist, *The Supreme Court*, pp. 289–290.

A majority vote of the nine justices is required to decide a case. A tie vote, if only eight or six justices participate, has the effect of leaving the lower court's decision in force. A majority vote also is required in order for a case to have precedential value. On occasion, a majority of the justices will agree on the result in a case but will fail to agree on the reasoning leading to that outcome.[59] A plurality decision is one that commands a majority of votes on the result but lacks majority agreement on the particular reasoning supporting that result. Such opinions have been on the increase in recent years.[60] A justice who agrees with the outcome but who disagrees about the reasons supporting it, usually files a concurring opinion that explains the grounds on which he or she would decide the case. None of the opinions in a plurality decision has value as precedent. Lawyers and judges nonetheless cite plurality opinions in an attempt to build majority support for an opinion in a subsequent case. Plurality opinions can frustrate lower courts, which are required to apply Supreme Court doctrine, because they send ambiguous and sometimes conflicting signals. They also are signals to lawyers to relitigate an issue if they desire a clear rule of law and doctrinal development in an area.

4. Opinion Drafting and Circulating   Traditionally, a chief justice who votes with the majority determines which justice will write the opinion.[61] If the chief justice votes with the minority, the most senior associate justice voting with the majority makes the assignment. Opinion drafting can be a long, tedious process, particularly if the justices voting in the majority disagree with one another about the reasoning that supports their position. Because every justice's chambers is run like a private law firm, with highly controlled access, not much is known about the process of opinion writing or the role of law clerks.[62] Recent scholarship, however, appears to confirm what has long been suspected: the drafting process can be highly con-

---

[59] A famous example is *Youngstown Sheet and Tube Co. v. Sawyer*, 343 U.S. 579 (1952). While holding unconstitutional President Truman's seizure of steel mills during the Korean War, 6–3, all six justices voting to overrule Truman's action wrote opinions. Over time, the consensus among students of the Court is that Justice Jackson's concurring opinion in *Youngstown*, not Justice Black's opinion for the Court, is the most constitutionally influential.

[60] William Reynolds, *Judicial Process in a Nutshell* (St. Paul, MN: West Publishing Co., 1980), pp. 27–31. Cf. the letters from Chief Justice Rehnquist and Professor Henry J. Abraham published in 7 *Law, Courts, and Judicial Process Section Newsletter*, Washington D.C.: American Political Science Association (Fall 1989): 8–9.

[61] Bob Woodward and Scott Armstrong report that Chief Justice Warren Burger deviated from this practice on several occasions, most notably in the 1973 abortion cases *Doe v. Bolton*, 41 U.S. 179 (1973) and *Roe v. Wade*, 410 U.S. 113 (1973). See *The Brethren* (New York, NY: Simon & Schuster, 1979), pp. 170–189, 417–438.

[62] See Woodward and Armstrong, *The Brethren*; and Jennifer Conlin, "Decisions, Decisions: Supreme Court Clerks Share Heady Secrets, Midnight Oil, and a Year of Hidden Power," *The Washingtonian* (June 1990), p. 65. Compare John Bilyeu Oakley and Robert S. Thompson, *Law Clerks and the Judicial Process: Perceptions of the Qualities and Functions of Law Clerks in American Courts* (Berkeley, CA: University of California Press, 1980).

tentious, sometimes involving emotional exchanges among two or more of the justices.[63]

When the justice assigned to write the opinion has a draft ready for circulation, it is sent to other justices for discussion. Sometimes it is necessary to rewrite certain sections of an opinion or to change language in an opinion in order to retain votes for the proposed majority opinion. If a justice decides to switch sides after a draft opinion has been circulated, the entire writing process may have to begin again.

As much as members of the Court may strive for consensus, any justice has the prerogative to write a concurring or dissenting opinion. Concurring opinions explain the reasons for joining the majority but give other grounds for arriving at that conclusion. Dissenting opinions explain disagreement with the majority view and frequently state the minority view of what the law should be.

Before John Marshall became chief justice in 1801, the Supreme Court followed the English practice of issuing opinions *seriatim*; that is, each justice wrote an individual opinion about the case. Chief Justice Marshall thought that it was important for the Court to speak as an institution, with one voice. During his chief justiceship, very few of the Court's decisions contained dissenting or concurring opinions. Over the years, however, both dissenting and concurring have become Court traditions. Some justices, like Oliver Wendell Holmes Jr., have gone down in history as "great dissenters," whose minority views at the time eventually became the Court's majority position on an issue. Justice Stephen J. Field's dissents on the issue of property rights in *The Slaughter-House Cases*, 16 Wallace 36 (1873), and *Munn v. Illinois*, 94 U.S. 113

---

[63] For example, see Bernard Schwartz, *The Unpublished Opinions of the Warren Court* (New York, NY: Oxford University Press, 1985), esp. Chapter 8, pp. 240–303.

Justice Oliver Wendell Holmes, reflecting on the High Bench to which he had been appointed eleven years previously, mused in a 1913 speech: "We are very quiet there, but it is the quiet of a storm center, as we all know." Holmes's characterization of the Supreme Court's precincts as "quiet" is an idealization that runs counter to both the findings of scholars and to news reports about current hard feelings among the justices. Compare Chief Justice William Howard Taft's metaphor: "The Supreme Court, a stormy petrel in the politics of the country." Also compare Justice Anthony Kennedy's recent observation: "[A]fter one of these cases is decided, the five in the majority … don't have a lot of smiles and handshakes and high fives. There's a *quietness*. There's stillness, as you recognize, no matter which case, which position prevails, that there are long-term consequences that are the result of our verdict." Jeffrey Rosen, "Annals of Law: The Agonizer," *The New Yorker*, November 11, 1996, p. 89.

Also see C. Herman Pritchett, "Divisions of Opinion among Justices of the U.S. Supreme Court," 35 *American Political Science Review* (1941): 890; Walter F. Murphy, *Elements of Judicial Strategy* (Chicago, IL: University of Chicago Press, 1964); Thomas G. Walker, Lee Epstein, and William J. Dixon, "On the Mysterious Decline of Consensual Norms in the United States Supreme Court," 50 *Journal of Politics* (1988): 361; and Howard Ball, *Hugo L. Black: Cold Steel Warrior* (New York, NY: Oxford University Press, 1996). Compare Phillip J. Cooper, *Battles on the Bench: Conflict inside the Supreme Court* (Lawrence, KS: University Press of Kansas, 1995).

On the well-known contemporary hard feelings between Justice Antonin Scalia and Justice Sandra O'Connor, see Donald Baer, "Now the Court of Less Resort," *U.S. News and World Report*, July 17, 1989; David Garrow, "The Rehnquist Years," *New York Times Magazine*, October 6, 1996, pp. 68–69; and Joan Biskupic, "Nothing Subtle about Scalia, the Combative Conservative." [http://www.washingtonpost.com]. 27 February 1997.

(1877), became the majority position in *Chicago, Milwaukee and St. Paul Railroad Company v. Minnesota*, 134 U.S. 418 (1890), less than twenty years later. (See Chapter 6 of this volume.) A more contemporary example is Justice William Rehnquist's prediction in his dissent in *Garcia v. San Antonio Metropolitan Transit Authority*, 469 U.S. 528 (1985), that the Court's view of states' rights relative to the power of the national government would soon change. Only ten years later, a triumphant Chief Justice Rehnquist, in *United States v. Lopez*, 514 U.S. 549 (1995), declared unconstitutional a federal statute on the ground that it usurped the states' police powers. (See Chapter 5 of this volume.)

Whether the presence of dissenting and concurring opinions undermines public and legal respect for the Supreme Court as an institution continues to be debated. Dissenting and concurring opinions deserve to be studied as carefully as majority opinions, however, because often they signal shifting coalitions on the bench, suggest alternative litigation strategies, or indicate the need to litigate again narrow questions of law to undermine or solidify a particular doctrine.

Like all American appellate courts, the Supreme Court is a "multimember, multi-issue body."[64] This means that the justices' decision-making process is collegial, even if not always congenial.[65] Political scientists have formulated several different approaches to explain the group interactions that produce judicial opinions.[66]

Small-group analysis focuses on the way in which interpersonal give-and-take shapes judicial opinions. Adherents to this methodology posit that appellate decisions can be explained by the way that judges seek to maximize their influence over decisions by employing, consciously or unconsciously, three interrelated strategies: persuasion on the merits; bargaining; and threatening sanctions such as withdrawing a vote, willingness to dissent or, in extreme instances, going public. The chief justice can be a particularly important player in this small group decision-making process if that person has the intellectual skill, the appropriate personality, and the will to exert influence and become *primus inter pares* (first among equals).[67]

Other students of the Court argue that although small group process clearly plays a role in shaping judicial outcomes, other methodologies provide more instructive explanations of appellate judges' collegial behavior. One of these approaches is attitude theory. Attitude theorists posit that appellate

---

[64] This is Sanford Levinson's description. Levinson, Sanford. [slevinson@mail.law.utexas.edu]. "REPLY: Court Bashing." In *LAWCOURTS*. [lawcourts-l@usc.edu]. 5 November 1996.

[65] See O'Brien, *Storm Center*, Chapters 4 and 5.

[66] This discussion of approaches to studying collegial decision making is derived from Carp and Stidham, *Judicial Process in America*, pp. 342–364. Also see the exchange between professor Howard Gillman and professors Lee Epstein and Jack Knight on "The New Institutionalism" in 7, 8 *Law and Courts* (Winter 1996–97/Spring 1997): 6, 4.

[67] See David J. Danelski, "The Influence of the Chief Justice in the Decisional Process," in *Courts, Judges, and Politics: An Introduction to the Judicial Process*, 4th ed., eds. Walter F. Murphy and C. Herman Pritchett (New York, NY: Random House, 1986).

judges view cases in broadly socioeconomic terms and decide them according to their personal values and attitudes. From this perspective, judges with similar attitudes join together in voting coalitions, termed blocs. Attitude theorists study the content of appellate judges' opinions to learn the values that shape them. Based on these content analyses, attitude theorists identify the level of cohesiveness among bloc members and assign mean indices of "interagreement" among judges making up the bloc. Cohesiveness and interagreement can run along political, social, and economic lines. For instance, Glendon Schubert analyzed Supreme Court voting blocs in terms of political liberals who support civil rights and liberties and political conservatives who support law enforcement.[68]

Fact pattern analysis is another social science methodology for studying appellate judicial behavior. According to fact pattern analysts, the particular circumstances of each case are the best explanatory variables of any given judicial outcome. "Facts" include more than the details of the specific dispute. The gender and race of the parties, their social status, and whether their attorneys are appointed or privately retained all figure in the eventual result. Key factors are weighted employing sophisticated mathematical equations that are machine processed to determine how different facts combine to affect judicial opinions.[69]

None of these methodologies explains completely appellate court decisions or decision making, and none of their practitioners claim that they do. Scholars in recent years have conceded that models representing a *combination* of various approaches "provide much greater explanatory power than any of them taken alone."[70] Supreme Court decisions, it appears, are shaped by "multiple forces" and "the intertwining of these forces."[71]

5. Announcement of Decisions   The Court's announcement of opinions on Decision Day is one of its most dramatic and public functions. Decision Day can occur whenever a case has been decided, or it can await the end of the Court's Term, when many decisions are issued at once. When opinions in controversial cases are expected, Decision Day can take on a circus-like atmosphere as reporters, curious onlookers, and antagonistic groups jostle to learn what the Court has decided.

In the Court's early days, justices sometimes read their entire opinions to the waiting press and public on Decision Day. Today, members of the press receive printed copies of opinions contemporaneously with the justices' announcement. The justice who drafted the opinion is called on by the chief

---

[68] Glendon Schubert, *Judicial Policy Making* (Glenview, IL: Scott, Foresman, 1974).

[69] Fred Cort, "Quantitative Analysis of Fact-Patterns in Cases and Their Impact on Judicial Decisions," in *American Court Systems*, eds. Goldman and Austin Sarat, p. 351.

[70] Carp and Stidham, *Judicial Process in America*, p. 365. See, for example, Tracey E. George and Lee Epstein, "On the Nature of Supreme Court Decision Making," 86 *American Political Science Review* (1992): 323.

[71] Baum, *The Supreme Court*, p. 183.

justice to announce the result. Rarely does a justice read an entire majority opinion from the bench. Occasionally, however, in a controversial case, a dissenting justice will make a "bench speech" explaining why, in his or her view, the case has been decided incorrectly. Perhaps the most famous outburst from the bench was delivered by Justice James C. McReynolds as he read his dissent from one of the Gold Clause Cases in 1935.[72] Justice McReynolds opposed the Court's upholding of Congress's decision to end the gold standard as the measure of the value of the American currency. During his bench speech he exclaimed, "This is Nero at his worst. The Constitution is gone!" Thirty-six years later, Justice William Brennan dissented from a 1971 decision holding that some foreign-born American citizens could lose their citizenship if they violated a residency requirement enacted by Congress in 1952. In his bench speech, Justice Brennan read from his opinion: "Since the Court this Term has already downgraded citizens receiving public welfare, and citizens having the misfortune to be illegitimate, I suppose today's decision downgrading citizens born outside the United States should have been expected."[73]

CASELOAD OF THE SUPREME COURT

The work of the Supreme Court in the eighteenth century has been described as "leisurely," although the workload of the individual justices was heavier because of their responsibilities to serve on circuit courts as well as on the Supreme Court. Before 1801, only eighty-seven appellate cases appeared on the Court's docket.[74] When Chief Justice John Marshall took office that year, a mere fifty-six cases had been decided by the Court in its entire history.[75]

The Court's workload increased as the country changed, however. Factors including quickening commercial activity, mechanical innovations such as the steam engine, population growth, and the addition of new territories during the first half of the nineteenth century resulted in a steady increase in the number of cases coming to the Supreme Court. The Civil War and the rapid industrial expansion that followed caused sharp increases in the Court's docket later in the century. By the 1870s, the Court was encountering backlogs.[76] Congress sought to eliminate the congestion in 1891 by creating the intermediate circuit courts of appeal described earlier. The impact on the Supreme Court's caseload was dramatic but short-lived.[77] Conflicts between labor and management, governmental efforts to regulate the circumstances

---

[72] *Norman v. Baltimore & Ohio Railroad Company*, 294 U.S. 240 (1935).

[73] *Rogers v. Bellei*, 401 U.S. 815 (1971). For more examples, see Abraham, *The Judicial Process*, pp. 220–223.

[74] Julius Goebel Jr., *History of the Supreme Court of the United States, Vol. 1: Antecedents and Beginnings* (New York, NY: Macmillan, 1971), pp. 662–665.

[75] John P. Frank, *Cases and Materials on Constitutional Law* (Chicago, IL: Callaghan & Co., 1952), p. 29.

[76] O'Brien, *Storm Center*, pp. 179–184.

[77] William Howard Taft, "The Jurisdiction of the Supreme Court under the Act of February 13, 1925," 35 *Yale Law Journal* (1925): 1.

and conditions of industrial production, and World War I sent the Court's docket skyrocketing again, leaving the justices with such a backlog that cases not advanced out of their filing order could not be heard for more than a year after filing.[78] The Judiciary Act of 1925, which gave the Court discretion over whether to issue writs of certiorari, was one remedy. Virtual elimination of mandatory appeals was another.

In response to social movements organized since World War II on behalf of groups including blacks, women, welfare recipients, and the environment, Congress has enacted numerous laws that create rights and make them enforceable in federal courts.[79] The Supreme Court's docket has reflected the dramatic increase in federal litigation that followed. The Court has responded to its caseload increases in a variety of ways, including the "cert pool" discussed earlier, hiring more administrative staff, automating many procedures, and adopting rules that limit the length of briefs and the amount of time allocated to each side for oral arguments. Nonetheless, as noted previously in the chapter, the Court still must process between four thousand and five thousand applications for review each year. Currently, also as noted above, the Court grants full review in fewer than one hundred cases each year.[80]

SUGGESTIONS FOR STUDYING SUPREME COURT DECISIONS

The Supreme Court's opinions are the point of departure for understanding constitutional law. Of course, as suggested throughout this chapter, those decisions must be understood in their historical, political, and institutional contexts. There are three steps to understanding Supreme Court opinions: finding them, reading them, and analyzing them.

FINDING SUPREME COURT DECISIONS

Reports of Supreme Court Decisions   Alexander Dallas, a Philadelphia lawyer, began publishing the decisions of the Supreme Court of Pennsylvania in the 1790s and began including Supreme Court decisions in 1793.[81] He argued several cases before the Court and used his reports to advertise his availability as an advocate.[82] In 1800, William Cranch, a judge on the District of Columbia circuit court, began publishing a set of reports that contained only Supreme Court decisions. He found the venture unprofitable.[83] In 1817, Chief

---

[78] Ibid., p. 2.

[79] Cass R. Sunstein, *After the Rights Revolution: Reconceiving the Regulatory State* (Cambridge, MA: Harvard University Press, 1990).

[80] See the figures on review granted discussed on p. 19.

[81] G. Edward White, *The History of the Supreme Court of the United States, Vol. 3: The Marshall Court and Cultural Change* (New York, NY: Macmillan, 1988), p. 385.

[82] Carl Swisher, *History of the Supreme Court of the United States, Vol. 5: The Taney Period* (New York, NY: Macmillan, 1974), p. 293.

[83] White, *The Marshall Court and Cultural Change*, p. 387.

Justice John Marshall lent his support to a bill that had been introduced in Congress a year before to hire the reporters of decisions as government employees and to require that they publish each year's decisions promptly.[84] With Marshall's support, the bill passed.

Beginning in 1789, reports of Supreme Court decisions were cited according to the name of the reporter: Alexander *Dallas* (1789–1800); William *Cranch* (1801–1815); Henry *Wheaton* (1816–1827); Richard *Peters* Jr. (1828–1842); Benjamin *Howard* (1843–1860); Jeremiah *Black* (1861–1862); John *Wallace* (1863–1874); and William *Otto* (1875 and 1882). Since 1875, the official reports of Supreme Court decisions have been by volume number (counting Alexander Dallas's first report as number one). The volume number is followed by the designation, "U.S.," the page number on which the opinion appears, and the year of the decision. The official citation for *United States v. Carolene Products Co.,* for example, is 304 U.S. 144 (1938). That means that the report of the decision is found in volume 304 of the *United States Reports,* beginning at page 144, and was decided in 1938.

Supreme Court decisions also are published in two commercial reporters, the *Lawyers' Edition* of the United States Supreme Court Reports published by the Lawyers' Cooperative Publishing Company, and the *Supreme Court Reporter,* published by the West Publishing Company. The *Lawyers' Edition* includes notes and annotations that assist attorneys with legal research. Cases in the *Lawyers' Edition* are cited by volume, the designation "L.Ed.," the page number on which the opinion appears, and the year the decision was rendered. In the *Lawyers' Edition, United States v. Carolene Products Co.* is reported as 82 L.Ed. 1234 (1938). The *Supreme Court Reporter* follows a similar format. Cases in that system are reported by volume, the designation "S.Ct.," the page number on which the opinion appears, and the year of the decision. *United States v. Carolene Products Co.* appears in the *Supreme Court Reporter* as 58 S.Ct. 778 (1938). Both the *Lawyers' Edition* and the *Supreme Court Reporter* provide cross-references to the United States Reports.

Supreme Court Decisions on the Internet   Supreme Court decisions are also available on the Internet. Following are directions to some useful Internet sites:

1. Cornell University's Legal Information Institute (LII) search page: [http://fatty.law.cornell.edu/]

    This archive service provides decisions from May 1990 to the present. From the LII site, it is possible to link to:

    a. the LII archive of 325 Selected Historic Decisions

    b. the FedWorld/FLITE archive of decisions from 1937–75

---

[84] William Crosskey, *Politics and the Constitution,* vol. 2 (Chicago, IL: University of Chicago Press, 1952), Appendix G, pp. 1243–1245.

c. "Oyez, Oyez, Oyez," [http://oyez.at.nwu.edu/oyez.html], which provides access to audio files of Supreme Court oral arguments (Access to these arguments requires RealAudio software.)

2. The LII Supreme Court Justices page: [http://www.law.cornell.edu/supct/justices/fullcourt.html]

This service provides access to brief biographies of present Supreme Court justices, as well as the major opinions, concurrences, and dissents that each has written.

3. *USA Today* search vehicle: [http://167.8.29.8/plweb-cgi/ixacct.pl]

Select "News" category, type "Supreme Court" in the search field, click on "Search," then click on "Supreme Court Index." This service provides news articles about the Supreme Court and copies of its most recent decisions.

4. "CourtTV" Library page: [http://www.courttv.com/library/supreme/]

This service provides recent Supreme Court opinions and brief biographies of current justices. (The "CourtTV" home page is: [http://www.courttv.com])

Supreme Court opinions also are available on CD-ROM:

1. Law Office Information Systems (LOIS), currently contains *U.S. Reports* of eight to nine thousand (1949 to present) Supreme Court decisions.

2. HoweData contains all three hundred thousand of the Supreme Court's decisions on a single disk.

3. In addition to the *Supreme Court Reporter*, West Publishing offers all three hundred thousand Supreme Court decisions on multiple CD-ROM disks plus West and Lawyers' annotations and hard copies of advance sheets (opinions before they are bound and indexed in reporters).

Readers are encouraged to supplement their understanding of the Supreme Court by using any of the above sources to locate and read unedited decisions in addition to the cases in this text.

READING SUPREME COURT DECISIONS

At first glance, a Supreme Court opinion is an intimidating piece of writing. The prose often is dense, interspersed with obscure Latin phrases. Seemingly important statements frequently are interrupted by citations to other opinions. Older opinions pose a particular challenge. Writing styles in the nineteenth and early twentieth centuries were very different from today's straightforward approach, sometimes making it difficult to understand exactly what a justice meant. Although the going may be difficult at the outset, the effort of reading, dissecting, and understanding a Supreme Court opinion is richly rewarding. No one else's summary of an opinion can substitute for the understanding that comes from grappling with the original source.

An appellate opinion usually contains the following elements. First is a statement of the facts. Second is an explanation of the decisions of lower courts as the case worked its way to the Supreme Court. Third is a description of the legal issue or issues raised by the facts. Fourth is an explication of the law, which is an explanation of the constitutional provision or provisions at issue and why the Court construes that provision or provisions as it does. It is in this portion of an opinion that one usually finds the rule of law that contributes to the evolution of constitutional doctrine in a particular area. Fifth is an application of the law to the facts of the case, which explains the Court's holding. Finally, if necessary, the opinion responds to concurring or dissenting opinions in an effort to persuade the reader that the majority's approach is correct. It is common for these elements to appear in the order described. Sometimes, however, a justice will vary the order.

Concurring and dissenting opinions follow much the same format. However, it is not uncommon for concurrences and dissents to contain facts that the majority has ignored or discounted and that, in the author's view, are critical to the legal issues or should affect the outcome. Concurring and dissenting opinions invariably contain a statement of the rule of law that the justices adhering to that view believe the Court should have adopted. In addition, it is not uncommon for concurring and dissenting opinions to explain what those justices believe will be the mischievous consequences of the majority opinion.[85]

In this book, the facts and decisions by lower courts are provided in the *Setting*. The goal is to provide a more complete factual statement and more historical context than usually is provided in the opinion. The information in each *Setting* is derived from the briefs submitted by the parties to the Court and from contemporary and historical sources. Each *Setting* section also describes the history of the case from the time it was filed until it appeared before the Supreme Court.

The first step in reading a Supreme Court opinion is to thoroughly understand the facts and parties, why the parties were involved in the litigation, and what result and rule of law each hoped the Supreme Court would declare. The next step is to read and *reread* the Court's opinion. The purpose of the first reading is to get a general understanding of what the Court did and why, and whether there are concurring and dissenting opinions attacking the majority. The second reading requires a more detailed analysis of the elements of the opinion described above. It is useful during the second reading to consult the glossary of legal terms at the end of this text. The first two readings of an opinion are prelude to the third step, which is reducing the case to a short synopsis called a brief.

BRIEFING AND ANALYZING SUPREME COURT DECISIONS

A brief of an opinion is a decidedly different product than a legal brief submitted to the Supreme Court by the parties. The purpose of an opinion brief is to dissect a decision into its component parts. The process of preparing an opin-

---

[85] See Ruggero J. Aldisert, *Opinion Writing* (St. Paul, MN: West Publishing, 1990). Although meant to be a guide to judges about how to write opinions, it also provides insights to readers of judicial opinions.

ion brief helps to guarantee that the reader understands the Court's decision. Briefs subsequently provide a thumbnail sketch of doctrinal development in a particular subject field and should contain the following elements:

1. Name and case citation
2. Succinct summary of the facts
3. Statement of the constitutional question or questions before the Court
4. Legal holding or holdings; i.e., how the Court answered the legal question or questions
5. The rule of law announced in the majority opinion and which justice wrote it
6. A short summary of the reasoning that led to the holding and rule
7. A summary of the concurring and dissenting opinions, if any, and which justices wrote them
8. A short evaluation of the opinion:

    Does the opinion answer all the questions posed or does it leave some unanswered?

    Is the reasoning persuasive?

    Are there hidden assumptions in the opinion?

    Does the opinion encourage more litigation on the subject?

    What are the broader implications of the opinion in terms of political, social, or economic considerations?

The goal of a brief is to be just that—brief. With practice, briefs become relatively straightforward to prepare and are invaluable in helping to develop the critical reading and analytical skills required in the study of constitutional law.

APPENDIX: LITIGATION STAGES ON THE WAY TO THE SUPREME COURT

Unless a case falls into that very small category qualifying for the Supreme Court's original jurisdiction, it must pass through several stages at the state or federal level before reaching the Supreme Court. The vast majority of cases filed each year do not survive all the steps and hence do not reach the Supreme Court. If a case raises a constitutional question, in general terms the following steps would be involved on the way to Supreme Court review.[86] These steps reflect the fact that the American system of justice is adversary in nature, which has been described as a "fight theory" rather than a "truth theory" system of justice.[87]

---

[86] A more detailed description of this process is found in Susan M. Leeson and Bryan M. Johnston, *Ending It: Dispute Resolution in America* (Cincinnati, OH: Anderson Publishing Co., 1988), Chapter 2.

[87] Jerome Frank, *Courts on Trial* (New York, NY: Atheneum, 1969).

PRETRIAL ACTIVITY

This step involves a range of activities, including the filing of the case in the proper court, submission and resolution of any pretrial motions, determination of whether a judge or jury will serve as fact finder, and discovery, which is the process by which each side learns the factual basis of the opposing side's claims. The overwhelming number of cases filed in state and federal courts are resolved at the pretrial stage. Many are dismissed because of defects in the pleadings. Others are abandoned when parties discover they lack the proof required to prevail at trial. The vast majority of cases (both civil and criminal) are settled through negotiation. A settlement is binding and nonappealable. If the parties agree, even a case that raises constitutional issues can be settled through negotiation, but the resulting settlement establishes no precedent.

TRIAL

The function of a trial is to decide which side has presented legally sufficient evidence to allow it to prevail. A trial is the prototype of the adversary process. Each side presents its strongest evidence and witnesses to persuade the fact finder that it should prevail. Each also seeks to discredit the other side's evidence and its witnesses. The plaintiff in a civil case or the state in a criminal case always has the initial burden of coming forth with evidence to prove why the status quo should change.

A trial is a highly controlled process, governed by strict rules of evidence and procedure. Rarely do parties represent themselves at trial; the services of a legally trained advocate usually are sought because even minor, unintentional errors can be fatal to the case. Parties whose case involves constitutional questions must raise them at the trial level in order to preserve the right to litigate them on appeal and before the Supreme Court. It is rare that a trial judge will be willing to apply a new constitutional rule. Most trial judges understand their role as limited to applying existing constitutional rules.

Some cases enter the judicial system through administrative agency hearings. Typically, administrative hearings deal with statutory rather than constitutional issues, but questions of agency procedures can raise constitutional questions. Routes of appeal exist from agency judgments in both state and federal court systems. Section 702 of the federal Administrative Procedure Act specifically guarantees the right of judicial review of decisions of federal administrative agencies. Most state administrative procedure acts contain similar guarantees.

APPELLATE REVIEW

All court systems in the United States provide one level of appeal to parties who lose at trial, assuming they choose to pursue the appeal. On appeal, the loser at the trial level (known as the petitioner or appellant) seeks to have the

appellate court overturn the decision of the trial court. The wir
(known as the respondent or appellee) defends the judgment belov

The appellate process differs dramatically from the trial pro
are no witnesses, testimony, or juries. Federal appellate judges typically sit in
panels of three, where they review the written submissions, called briefs, prepared by each party's attorney. Briefs outline the factual or legal errors that
are alleged to have occurred at trial and argue the appropriate legal remedy.
After they have reviewed the briefs and the trial record, the judges hold oral
argument. Each side is given a specified amount of time to argue its case and
to respond to questions from the judges. After oral argument the case is
deemed submitted for decision and no additional information about the case
is permitted. Although they differ from trial proceedings, appellate proceedings remain adversary in nature. The parties continue to disagree about the
legal significance of the facts that were established at trial.

Appellate judges apply various standards of review when scrutinizing
cases. These standards of review determine the level of inspection the judges
give to the trial record. If a case raises factual questions, for example, appellate judges tend to defer to trial court determinations and require the appellant to show that the trial court committed clear error. If a case raises a question of law, on the other hand, as is always true in constitutional litigation,
appellate courts review for errors of law or in some instances apply a *de novo*
standard of review, which allows the appellate court to review the entire
record of the trial and the correctness of the legal determinations made during trial. Appellate judges typically issue written opinions explaining the standard of review they apply in a case, their judgment affirming or reversing the
trial court, and the reasons for their holding or holdings.

Most state court systems provide for a second appeal, but give the
state's highest appellate court (commonly, but not always, called the state
supreme court) substantial discretion over which cases they will hear. Only
the party that lost at the first level of appeal may pursue the second level of
appeal in state courts.

CHAPTER 2

JUDICIAL POWERS

JUDICIAL REVIEW

Marbury v. Madison
1 Cranch 137 (1803)

SETTING

The framers of the Constitution sketched the judiciary in only skeletal form, leaving it to Congress to provide details. One of the many tasks facing the first Congress, therefore, was fleshing out the structure and jurisdiction of the federal courts outlined in Article III. This was done in the Judiciary Act of 1789, enacted by a Congress dominated by members of the Federalist Party. The Federalists advocated a strong national government and a powerful federal judiciary.

The Judiciary Act provided for a Supreme Court consisting of a chief justice and five associate justices. The act also created thirteen federal district courts and district court judgeships, and three federal circuit courts. Circuit courts were staffed by two Supreme Court justices and a sitting district judge. One consequence of this circuit court staffing arrangement was that Supreme Court justices were required to travel thousands of miles each year to carry out their circuit court duties.

The Judiciary Act of 1789 also spelled out the jurisdiction of the lower federal courts and the appellate jurisdiction of the Supreme Court. Section 13, the part of the Judiciary Act at issue in *Marbury v. Madison*, gave the Supreme Court original jurisdiction over cases involving writs of mandamus, which are directives from courts of higher jurisdiction to lower tribunals or other government officers commanding them to perform particular acts.

The Federalist Party controlled the new American government until 1800. In elections held that year, Thomas Jefferson's Republican Party took control of both houses of Congress. The bitterly contested presidential election of 1800 resulted in an electoral college tie. In February 1801, after being deadlocked through thirty-six ballots, members of the House of Representatives elected Jefferson president of the United States by a single vote. Before Jefferson took office on March 4, 1801, outgoing President John Adams and the lame-duck Federalist Party in Congress took specific actions to make the federal judiciary into a Federalist stronghold.

First, John Adams nominated his outgoing secretary of state, John Marshall, as the nation's fourth chief justice, succeeding the aging and feeble Oliver Ellsworth, who had resigned the post in October 1800. Marshall was confirmed by the Senate in January 1801. Second, the Federalist Congress passed the Judiciary Act of 1801. It created six circuit courts of appeal and six-teen new judgeships, thereby relieving members of the Supreme Court from their hated circuit-riding duties. The new judgeships also gave President Adams the opportunity to appoint Federalists to the life-tenure positions. In addition, the Judiciary Act reduced the size of the Supreme Court from six to five, making it more difficult for incoming President Jefferson to nominate new justices. Third, Congress passed the Organic Act for the District of Columbia. The Organic Act authorized President Adams to appoint as many justices of the peace as he deemed necessary to serve five-year terms in the District of Columbia.

On March 2, Adams signed commissions for forty-two so-called "mid-night judges," including District of Columbia justice of the peace commissions for William Marbury, Dennis Ramsay, Robert Townshend Hooe, and William Harper. All forty-two appointments were confirmed by the Senate on March 3. The same day, Adams instructed Secretary of State John Marshall (whose appointment as chief justice of the United States had been confirmed the previous January 27) to deliver the commissions.

When President Thomas Jefferson took office on March 4, he learned that his predecessor had packed the judiciary with Jefferson's "most ardent political enemies," an act Jefferson considered an "outrage on decency." Jefferson also discovered that Marshall had failed to deliver all the commissions by midnight March 3, 1801, when the Adams administration ended. James Madison, Jefferson's designated secretary of state, was not yet in Washington, D.C., so Jefferson named his attorney general, Levi Lincoln, acting secretary of state and ordered Lincoln not to deliver seventeen of the remaining commissions. Among the commissions not delivered were those appointing Marbury, Ramsay, Hooe, and Harper. At the 1801 Term of the Supreme Court, Marbury and the others invoked the Supreme Court's original jurisdiction under Section 13 of the Judiciary Act of 1789, asking it to instruct James Madison, who became secretary of state on May 2, 1801, to show cause why a writ of mandamus should not issue, ordering him to deliver their commissions as justices of the peace.

Republican frustration at Federalist efforts to create a judicial preserve culminated in repeal of the Judiciary Act of 1801 and enactment of the Judiciary Act of 1802. It eliminated the sixteen circuit court judgeships created by the 1801 act (consequently reinstating Supreme Court justices' circuit riding duties), and restored the number of Supreme Court justices to six. Fearing the Supreme Court might hold abolition of the judgeships unconstitutional, the 1802 act also suspended the Supreme Court's term for fourteen months, guaranteeing that it would not meet again until 1803. *Marbury v. Madison* was pending at the time the repeal was adopted.

HIGHLIGHTS OF SUPREME COURT ARGUMENTS

TESTIMONY ON BEHALF OF MARBURY, ET AL.

◆ Department of State clerks Daniel Brent and Jacob Wagner refused to testify, claiming that they were not bound to disclose any facts relating to the business or transactions of the office. In response to an order by the Court to answer questions in writing or to state objections they had to testifying, Wagner testified that he did not know whether all the commissions had been recorded, including those of Marbury, Ramsay, Hooe, and Harper. Brent testified that he was almost certain Marbury's and Hooe's commissions had been made out, and that Ramsay's had not been. He believed none of the commissions had been sent out or delivered.

◆ Attorney General Levi Lincoln refused to answer questions, claiming he was not bound to answer about any facts that came officially to his knowledge while acting secretary of state. He subsequently responded in writing to questions about the existence of the commissions. He stated that he had seen commissions for justices of the peace, but did not believe any had been sent out.

◆ James Marshall testified that he had been instructed by the secretary of state to deliver as many as twelve commissions on March 4, 1801, but had been unable to deliver all of them. He returned the undelivered commissions to the secretary of state.

LEGAL ARGUMENTS FOR MARBURY, ET AL.

◆ The power to issue a writ of mandamus is an inherent part of the Supreme Court's appellate jurisdiction over lower courts. Power to issue the writ was granted explicitly in Section 13 of the Judiciary Act of 1789. English and American precedents support the Supreme Court's power to issue writs of mandamus in appropriate cases.

◆ The secretary of state operates in two distinct capacities. In one capacity he acts as a public minister, an officer of the United States. In the other he acts as an agent of the president. When the secretary of state acts as an agent of the president, he is accountable to the president alone. When he acts in his ministerial capacity, carrying out the official duties of the office, he is accountable to the public. The writ of mandamus is an appropriate method of holding the secretary of state accountable for ministerial duties.

◆ It is appropriate for the Supreme Court to issue a writ of mandamus to the secretary of state under the circumstances of this case because as keeper of public records the secretary of state is a public minister and is publicly accountable for his actions. Once the president signs a commission for an office not held at the president's will, and the commission is in the secretary of state's office, nothing remains but for the secretary to perform the ministerial act imposed by law of delivering the commission.

Note: Secretary of State James Madison was not represented by counsel and put on no case.

SUPREME COURT DECISION: 6–0

MARSHALL, C.J.

... In the order in which the court has viewed this subject, the following questions have been considered and decided.

1st. Has the applicant a right to the commission he demands?

2d. If he has a right, and that right has been violated, do the laws of his country afford him a remedy?

3d. If they do afford him a remedy, is it a mandamus issuing from this court?

The first object of inquiry is,...

Has the applicant a right to the commission he demands?...

It is ... decidedly the opinion of the court, that when a commission has been signed by the President, the appointment is made; and that the commission is complete when the seal of the United States has been affixed to it by the Secretary of State....

Mr. Marbury, then, since his commission was signed by the President, and sealed by the Secretary of State, was appointed; and as the law creating the office, gave the officer a right to hold for five years, independent of the executive, the appointment was not revocable, but vested in the officer legal rights, which are protected by the laws of his country.

To withhold his commission, therefore, is an act deemed by the court not warranted by law, but violative of a vested legal right.

This brings us to the second inquiry; which is, ... If he has a right, and that right has been violated, do the laws of this country afford him a remedy?

The very essence of civil liberty certainly consists in the right of every individual to claim the protection of the laws, whenever he receives an injury. One of the first duties of government is to afford that protection....

The government of the United States has been emphatically termed a government of laws, and not of men. It will certainly cease to deserve this high appellation, if the laws furnish no remedy for the violation of a vested legal right.

If this obloquy is to be cast on the jurisprudence of our country, it must arise from the peculiar character of the case....

[T]he question, whether the legality of an act of the head of a department be examinable in a court of justice or not[,] must always depend on the nature of that act.

If some acts be examinable, and others not, there must be some rule of law to guide the court in the exercise of its jurisdiction....

By the constitution of the United States, the President is invested with certain important political powers, in the exercise of which he is to use his own discretion, and is accountable only to his country in his political character and to his own conscience. To aid him in the performance of these duties, he is authorized to appoint certain officers, who act by his authority, and in conformity with his orders.

In such cases, their acts are his acts; and whatever opinion may be entertained of the manner in which executive discretion may be used, still there exists, and can exist, no power to control that discretion. The subjects are political. They respect the nation, not individual rights, and being intrusted to the executive, the decision of the executive is conclusive. The application of this remark will be perceived by adverting to the act of congress for establishing the department of foreign affairs. This officer, as his duties were prescribed by that act, is to conform precisely to the will of the President. He is the mere organ by whom that will is communicated. The acts of such an officer, as an officer, can never be examinable by the courts.

But when the legislature proceeds to impose on that officer other duties; when he is directed peremptorily to perform certain acts; when the rights of individuals are dependent on the performance of those acts; he is so far the officer of the law; is amenable to the laws for his conduct; and cannot at his discretion sport away the vested rights of others.

The conclusion of this reasoning is, that where the heads of the departments are the political or confidential agents of the executive, merely to execute the will of the President, or rather to act in cases in which the executive possesses a constitutional or legal dis-

cretion, nothing can be more perfectly clear than that their acts are only politically examinable. But where a specific duty is assigned by law, and individual rights depend upon the performance of that duty, it seems equally clear that the individual who considers himself injured, has a right to resort to the laws of his country for a remedy....

The question whether a right has vested or not, is, in its nature, judicial, and must be tried by the judicial authority. If, for example, Mr. Marbury had taken the oaths of a magistrate, and proceeded to act as one; in consequence of which a suit had been instituted against him, in which his defence had depended on his being a magistrate, the validity of his appointment must have been determined by judicial authority.

So, if he conceives that, by virtue of his appointment, he has a legal right either to the commission which has been made out for him, or to a copy of that commission, it is equally a question examinable in a court, and the decision of the court upon it must depend on the opinion entertained of his appointment....

It is, then, the opinion of the Court,

1st. That by signing the commission of Mr. Marbury, the President of the United States appointed him a justice of peace for the county of Washington, in the District of Columbia; and that the seal of the United States, affixed thereto by the Secretary of State, is conclusive testimony of the verity of the signature, and of the completion of the appointment, and that the appointment conferred on him a legal right to the office for the space of five years.

2d. That, having this legal title to the office, he has a consequent right to the commission; a refusal to deliver which is a plain violation of that right, for which the laws of his country afford him a remedy.

It remains to be inquired whether,

3d. He is entitled to the remedy for which he applies. This depends on,

1st. The nature of the writ applied for; and,

2d. The power of this court....

This writ, if awarded, would be directed to an officer of government, and its mandate to him would be, to use the words of Blackstone, "to do a particular thing therein specified, which appertains to his office and duty, and which the court has previously determined, or at least supposes, to be consonant to right and justice." Or, in the words of Lord Mansfield, the applicant, in this case, has a right to execute an office of public concern, and is kept out of possession of that right....

This ... is a plain case for a mandamus, either to deliver the commission, or a copy of it from the record; and it only remains to be inquired,

Whether it can issue from this court.

The act to establish the judicial courts of the United States [Judiciary Act of 1789] authorizes the Supreme Court "to issue writs of mandamus in cases warranted by the principles and usages of law, to any courts appointed, or persons holding office, under the authority of the United States" [Section 13].

The Secretary of State, being a person holding an office under the authority of the United States, is precisely within the letter of the description, and if this court is not authorized to issue a writ of mandamus to such an officer, it must be because the law is unconstitutional, and therefore absolutely incapable of conferring the authority, and assigning the duties which its words purport to confer and assign.

The constitution vests the whole judicial power of the United States in one Supreme Court, and such inferior courts as congress shall, from time to time, ordain and establish. This power is expressly extended to all cases arising under the laws of the United States; and, consequently, in some form, may be exercised over the present case; because the right claimed is given by a law of the United States.

In the distribution of this power it is declared that "the Supreme Court shall have original jurisdiction in all cases affecting ambassadors, other public ministers and consuls, and those in which a state shall be a party. In all other cases, the Supreme Court shall have appellate jurisdiction."...

If it had been intended to leave it in the discretion of the legislature to apportion the judicial power between the supreme and inferior courts according to the will of that body, it would certainly have been useless to have proceeded further than to have defined the judicial power, and the tribunals in which it should be vested. The subsequent part of the section is mere surplusage, is entirely without meaning, if such is to be the construction. If congress remains at liberty to give this court appellate jurisdiction, where the constitution has declared their jurisdiction shall be original; and original jurisdiction where the constitution has declared it shall be appellate; the distribution of jurisdiction, made in the constitution, is form without substance.

Affirmative words are often, in their operation, negative of other objects than those affirmed; and in this case, a negative or exclusive sense must be given to them, or they have no operation at all.

It cannot be presumed that any clause in the constitution is intended to be without effect; and, therefore, such a construction is inadmissible, unless the words require it....

When an instrument organizing fundamentally a judicial system, divides it into one supreme, and so many inferior courts as the legislature may ordain and establish; then enumerates its powers, and proceeds so far as to distribute them, as to define the jurisdiction of the Supreme Court by declaring the cases in which it shall take original jurisdiction, and that in others it shall take appellate jurisdiction; the plain import of the words seems to be, that in one class of cases its jurisdiction is original, and not appellate; in the other it is appellate, and not original. If any other construction would render the clause inoperative, that is an additional reason for rejecting such other construction, and for adhering to their obvious meaning.

To enable this court, then, to issue a mandamus, it must be shown to be an exercise of appellate jurisdiction, or to be necessary to enable them to exercise appellate jurisdiction....

It is the essential criterion of appellate jurisdiction, that it revises and corrects the proceedings in a cause already instituted, and does not create that cause. Although, therefore, a mandamus may be directed to courts, yet to issue such a writ to an officer for the delivery of a paper, is in effect the same as to sustain an original action for that paper, and, therefore, seems not to belong to appellate, but to original jurisdiction. Neither is it necessary in such a case as this, to enable the court to exercise its appellate jurisdiction.

The authority, therefore, given to the Supreme Court, by the act establishing the judicial courts of the United States, to issue writs of mandamus to public officers, appears not to be warranted by the constitution; and it becomes necessary to inquire whether a jurisdiction so conferred can be exercised.

The question, whether an act, repugnant to the constitution, can become the law of the land, is a question deeply interesting to the United States; but, happily, not of an intricacy proportioned to its interest. It seems only necessary to recognize certain principles, supposed to have been long and well established, to decide it.

That the people have an original right to establish, for their future government, such principles, as, in their opinion, shall most conduce to their own happiness is the basis on which the whole American fabric has been erected. The exercise of this original right is a very great exertion; nor can it, nor ought it, to be frequently repeated. The principles, therefore, so established, are deemed fundamental. And as the authority from which they proceed is supreme, and can seldom act, they are designated to be permanent.

This original and supreme will organizes the government, and assigns to different departments their respective powers. It may either stop here, or establish certain limits not to be transcended by those departments.

The government of the United States is of the latter description. The powers of the legislature are defined and limited; and that those limits may not be mistaken, or forgotten, the constitution is written. To what purpose are powers limited, and to what purpose is that limitation committed to writing, if these limits may, at any time, be passed by those intended to be restrained? The distinction between a government with limited and unlimited powers is abolished, if those limits do not confine the persons on whom they are imposed, and if acts prohibited and acts allowed, are of equal obligation. It is a proposition too plain to be contested, that the constitution controls any legislative act repugnant to it; or, that the legislature may alter the constitution by an ordinary act.

Between these alternatives there is no middle ground. The constitution is either a superior paramount law, unchangeable by ordinary means, or it is on a level with ordinary legislative acts, and, like other acts, is alterable when the legislature shall please to alter it.

If the former part of the alternative be true, then a legislative act contrary to the constitution is not law; if the latter part be true, then written constitutions are absurd attempts, on the part of the people, to limit a power in its own nature illimitable.

Certainly all those who have framed written constitutions contemplate them as forming the fundamental and paramount law of the nation, and, consequently, the theory of every such government must be, that an act of the legislature, repugnant to the constitution, is void.

This theory is essentially attached to a written constitution, and, is consequently, to be considered, by this court, as one of the fundamental principles of our society. It is not therefore to be lost sight of in the further consideration of this subject.

If an act of the legislature, repugnant to the constitution, is void, does it,

notwithstanding its invalidity, bind the courts, and oblige them to give it effect? Or, in other words, though it be not law, does it constitute a rule as operative as if it was a law? This would be to overthrow in fact what was established in theory; and would seem, at first view, an absurdity too gross to be insisted on. It shall, however, receive a more attentive consideration.

It is emphatically the province and duty of the judicial department to say what the law is. Those who apply the rule to particular cases, must of necessity expound and interpret that rule. If two laws conflict with each other, the courts must decide on the operation of each.

So if a law be in opposition to the constitution; if both the law and the constitution apply to a particular case, so that the court must either decide that case conformably to the law, disregarding the constitution; or conformably to the constitution, disregarding the law; the court must determine which of these conflicting rules govern the case. This is of the very essence of judicial duty.

If, then, the courts are to regard the constitution, and the constitution is superior to any ordinary act of the legislature, the constitution, and not such ordinary act, must govern the case to which they both apply.

Those, then, who controvert the principle that the constitution is to be considered, in court, as a paramount law, are reduced to the necessity of maintaining that courts must close their eyes on the constitution, and see only the law.

This doctrine would subvert the very foundation of all written constitutions. It would declare that an act which, according to the principles and theory of our government, is entirely void, is yet, in practice, completely obligatory. It would declare that if the legislature shall do what is expressly forbidden, such act, notwithstanding the express prohibition, is in reality effectual. It would be giving to the legislature a practical and real omnipotence, with the same breath which professes to restrict their powers within narrow limits, and declaring that those limits may be passed at pleasure.

That it reduces to nothing what we have deemed the greatest improvement on political institutions, a written constitution, would of itself be sufficient, in America, where written constitutions have been viewed with so much reverence, for rejecting the construction. But the peculiar expressions of the constitution of the United States furnish additional arguments in favour of its rejection.

The judicial power of the United States is extended to all cases arising under the constitution.

Could it be the intention of those who gave this power, to say that in using it the constitution should not be looked into? That a case arising under the constitution should be decided without examining the instrument under which it arises?

This is too extravagant to be maintained.

In some cases, then, the constitution must be looked into by the judges. And if they can open it at all, what part of it are they forbidden to read or to obey?

There are many other parts of the constitution which serve to illustrate this subject.

It is declared that "no tax or duty shall be laid on articles exported from any state." Suppose a duty on the export of cotton, of tobacco, or of flour; and a suit instituted to recover it. Ought judgment to be rendered in such a case? [O]ught the judges to close their eyes on the constitution, and only see the law?

The constitution declares "that no bill of attainder or ex post facto law shall be passed."

If, however, such a bill should be passed, and a person should be prosecuted under it; must the court condemn to death those victims whom the constitution endeavors to preserve?

"No person," says the constitution, "shall be convicted of treason unless on the testimony of two witnesses to the same overt act, or on confession in open court."

Here the language of the constitution is addressed especially to the courts. It prescribes, directly for them, a rule of evidence not to be departed from. If the legislature should change that rule, and declare one witness, or a confession out of court, sufficient for conviction, must the constitutional principle yield to the legislative act?

From these, and many other selections which might be made, it is apparent, that the framers of the constitution contemplated that instrument as a rule for the government of courts, as well as of the legislature.

Why otherwise does it direct the judges to take an oath to support it? This oath certainly applies in an especial manner, to their conduct in their official character. How immoral to impose it on them, if they were to be used as the instruments, and the knowing instruments, for violating what they swear to support!...

Why does a judge swear to discharge

his duties agreeably to the constitution of the United States, if that constitution forms no rule for his government? [I]f it is closed upon him, and cannot be inspected by him?

If such be the real state of things, this is worse than solemn mockery. To prescribe, or to take this oath, becomes equally a crime.

It is also not entirely unworthy of observation, that in declaring what shall be the supreme law of the land, the constitution itself is first mentioned; and not the laws of the United States generally, but those only which shall be made in pursuance of the constitution, have that rank.

Thus, the particular phraseology of the constitution of the United States confirms and strengthens the principle, supposed to be essential to all written constitutions, that a law repugnant to the constitution is void; and that courts, as well as other departments, are bound by that instrument.

The rule must be discharged.

QUESTIONS

1. In *Marbury v. Madison* Chief Justice John Marshall explicitly claimed the power of judicial review. Summarize the doctrine of judicial review as explained by Marshall. How does it enhance the powers of the judiciary?

2. In *Marbury*, did Chief Justice Marshall declare that the judicial department has the final say to pass on constitutional questions affecting its own authority, or did he make the broader claim that the Supreme Court has the sole authority to pass on the constitutionality of acts of the executive and legislative branches as well? Is one claim more defensible than the other?

   While some laud judicial review as necessary to make the Supreme Court coequal with the other two branches of the federal government, others are concerned that judicial review sets the judiciary above the elected legislative and executive branches. Should nine judges, appointed for life, exercise such influence over the fundamental rules and principles governing American society?

3. Can Chief Justice Marshall's defense of judicial review in *Marbury* be divorced from his general commitment to enhancing the powers of the national government, or from his desire to enhance the institutional position of the Supreme Court? Was Marshall making a principled argument, seizing power, or both?

4. Justice John B. Gibson of the Pennsylvania Supreme Court articulated several objections to judicial review in his dissent in *Eakin v. Raub*, 12 Sargeant & Rawle 330 (Pa. 1825). The *Eakin* majority held that the Pennsylvania Supreme Court was authorized to consider the constitutionality of acts passed by the state legislature. Among Gibson's reasons for rejecting judicial review:

a. At common law, the powers of the judiciary extended only to the administration of "distributive justice," without extending to anything of a political cast. The power of judicial review is preeminently political.

b. Legislatures are the repositories of the sovereignty that the people have thought fit to impart. Unless the power of judicial review is explicitly granted, the judiciary has no authority to exercise it. The exercise of judicial review is nothing more than an act of sovereignty, which resides with legislatures or with the people.

c. Political turmoil could result from the refusal of the legislature or executive to acquiesce in a decision resulting from the exercise of judicial review.

d. In a republican form of government the legislative branch of government necessarily is superior to every other. Judicial review makes the judiciary a coordinate and equal branch, if not superior to the legislature.

e. All officers of the government take an oath to support the Constitution. Legislators must consider the constitutionality of laws in the process of enacting them. *prove to much*

f. The judiciary is not infallible. An error committed by legislators can be corrected at the polls. An error committed by the judiciary, however, admits of no remedy short of constitutional amendment, a difficult political process which could contribute to political instability.

Is Marshall's defense of judicial review in *Marbury* or Gibson's rejection of it in *Eakin* more constitutionally defensible?

5. In 1936, Justice Owen Roberts wrote: "When an act of Congress is appropriately challenged in the courts as not conforming to the constitutional mandate, the judicial branch of government has only one duty: to lay the article of the Constitution which is invoked beside the statute which is challenged and to decide whether the latter squares with the former. All the court does, or can do, is to announce its considered judgment upon the question." *United States v. Butler*, 297 U.S. 1.

Does Chief Justice Marshall consider the exercise of judicial review as mechanically as Justice Roberts apparently does? If Supreme Court justices have more discretion than Justice Roberts's view seems to imply, what prevents them from exercising judicial review arbitrarily?

6. In the three cases from the modern era that follow in this section, identify the appropriate and inappropriate exercises of the power of judicial review.

COMMENT

It is instructive to compare Chief Justice Marshall's defense of judicial review in *Marbury v. Madison* with Alexander Hamilton's analysis in *Federalist* No. 78 (*The Federalist Papers*, Clinton Rossiter, ed. [New York, NY: Mentor, 1961]). The two arguments are strikingly similar.

JUDICIAL REVIEW

Cooper v. Aaron
358 U.S. 1 (1958)

SETTING

Although the Civil War and the Thirteenth Amendment, ratified in December, 1865, put an end to the institution of racial slavery in the United States, they did little to eliminate the racism that underlay that "peculiar institution." After the Civil War, America remained a deeply segregated society. Blacks were prevented from voting and found it virtually impossible to achieve economic independence. Segregation was practiced in most facets of American life, including the public schools throughout the country. In 1896, the Supreme Court put its imprimatur on racial segregation, declaring that laws requiring blacks to ride in separate railroad cars did not violate the Fourteenth Amendment's guarantee of equal protection of the laws. *Plessy v. Ferguson*, 163 U.S. 537 (1896).

Not until after World War II, a conflict during which black soldiers fought for, distinguished themselves for, and died for their country in segregated units, did the political and legal attack on separate but equal doctrine begin to gain significant ground. In 1954, in *Brown v. Board of Education* (*Brown I*), 347 U.S. 483, a unanimous Supreme Court declared the long-standing practice of racial segregation in public schools unconstitutional under the Equal Protection Clause of the Fourteenth Amendment. The Court also repudiated the doctrine of "separate but equal" that had enjoyed judicial approval since 1896. *Brown I* is regarded conventionally as one of the landmarks in U.S. constitutional law. However, it was met with hostile resistance, especially in the South. In *Brown v. Board of Education* (*Brown II*), 349 U.S. 294 (1955), the Court ordered that school desegregation be accomplished with "all deliberate speed." Defiance of lower court orders implementing the *Brown II* decision, as well as violence and threats of violence, were not uncommon.

In 1956, for example, Federal Bureau of Investigation (FBI) Director J. Edgar Hoover reported to President Dwight D. Eisenhower and the members of his cabinet that "racial tension has been mounting almost daily since the Supreme Court banned segregation in public schools ... [and] required that integration be established at the earliest practicable date." The Ku Klux Klan, originally founded in 1867 to maintain white supremacy, "was pretty much defunct ... in the early 1950s." The Klan had been resurrected in August 1955 by Eldon Edwards, an Atlanta automobile assembly plant worker. Edwards's organization, the U.S. Klans, Knights of the Ku Klux Klan, Inc., established active branches in Georgia, Alabama, South Carolina, and Florida. Between January 1955, and January 1959, in the eleven former Confederate states, there were 210 reported violent incidents that resulted from racial tensions following the *Brown* decision. Ranging from Klan rallies and cross burnings to death threats, the incidents included murders of six blacks, twenty-nine assaults with firearms, and forty-four beatings. Between 1955 and 1958, ninety southern homes were damaged by explosives, gun fire, arson, and stoning.

In 1957, the Little Rock, Arkansas, School Board moved to integrate its schools in conformity with its understanding of the mandate of *Brown II*. Arkansas Governor Orval Faubus responded by declaring Little Rock's schools off-limits to black children and sending in the National Guard to prevent nine black children from entering Little Rock's public schools. A federal judge enjoined Governor Faubus from resisting public school integration and ordered that the National Guard be removed. Nevertheless, the black children's attempts to return to school were thwarted by angry white mobs. Mob violence provoked President Eisenhower, who had been reluctant to intervene in state affairs, to act. Saying that the situation in Arkansas was damaging American prestige and weakening American influence abroad, causing our enemies to gloat "over this incident," President Eisenhower ordered the National Guard into federal service on September 24, 1957, and sent some one-thousand paratroopers into Little Rock to reopen the schools and enforce order.

William Cooper and the other members of the Little Rock Independent School District and Virgil Blossom, Superintendent of the Little Rock Schools, subsequently filed a petition in the U.S. District Court for the Eastern District of Arkansas seeking a two-and-one-half year delay in implementing the desegregation plan that had been adopted by the school district and approved by the relevant federal courts. The National Association for the Advancement of Colored People (NAACP), on behalf of black students such as John Aaron, opposed the petition.

The district court granted the school district's petition, after which the NAACP appealed to the U.S. Circuit Court of Appeals for the Eighth Circuit. That court reversed. The Supreme Court of the United States granted Cooper and Blossom's petition for writ of certiorari. It then convened a special session of the Court on August 28, 1958, and again on September 11, to hear arguments.

HIGHLIGHTS OF SUPREME COURT ARGUMENTS

BRIEF FOR COOPER

◆ Efforts to implement *Brown II*, 349 U.S. 294 (1955), in Little Rock schools have proved disastrous despite good faith efforts. Mobs have overtly interfered with school operations; bloodshed appears inevitable.

◆ It is doubtful that a court has the practical power to deal with the kind of opposition to school desegregation the school district is encountering. A school district neither can nor should be expected to pursue the forces of violence arrayed in the local community.

◆ School officials should be allowed to further the district's educational programs and adhere to law and order. Under the circumstances, the Little Rock School District should be allowed to postpone its desegregation efforts.

States power

AMICUS CURIAE BRIEFS SUPPORTING COOPER

The Defenders of State Sovereignty and Individual Liberties of Arlington, Virginia; attorney William Burrow on behalf of himself and the Negro and white people of the South.

BRIEF FOR AARON

◆ Neither overt public resistance, nor the possibility of it, are reasons to delay the Court's order from the *Brown* decisions.

◆ Even if tensions disturb the educational process, they are preferable to the complete breakdown of education that will result from teaching children that courts of law would bow to violence.

AMICUS CURIAE BRIEF SUPPORTING AARON

United States.

SUPREME COURT DECISION: 9–0 *all wrote*

THE CHIEF JUSTICE, MR. JUSTICE BLACK, MR. JUSTICE FRANKFURTER, MR. JUSTICE DOUGLAS, MR. JUSTICE BURTON, MR. JUSTICE CLARK, MR. JUSTICE HARLAN, MR. JUSTICE BRENNAN, AND MR. JUSTICE WHITTAKER.

As this case reaches us it raises questions of the highest importance to the maintenance of our federal system of government. It necessarily involves a claim by the Governor and Legislature of a State that there is no duty on state officials to obey federal court orders resting on this Court's considered interpretation of the United States Constitution. Specifically it involves actions by the Governor and Legislature of Arkansas upon the premise that they are not bound by our holding in *Brown v. Board of Education*, 347 U.S. 483 [(1954)].... We are urged to uphold a suspension of the Little Rock School Board's plan to do away with segregated public schools in Little Rock until state laws and efforts to upset and nullify our holding in *Brown v. Board of Education* have been further challenged and tested in the courts. We reject these contentions....

On May 20, 1954, three days after the first *Brown* opinion, the Little Rock District School Board adopted, and on May 23, 1954, made public, a statement of policy entitled "Supreme Court Decision—Segregation in Public Schools." In this statement the Board recognized that:

> It is our responsibility to comply with Federal Constitutional Requirements and we intend to do so when the Supreme Court of the United States outlines the method to be followed....

While the School Board was thus going forward with its preparation for desegregating the Little Rock school system, other state authorities, in contrast, were actively pursuing a program designed to perpetuate in Arkansas the system of racial segregation which this Court had held violated the Fourteenth Amendment....

On February 20, 1958, the School Board and the Superintendent of Schools filed a petition in the District Court seeking a postponement of their program for desegregation. Their position in essence was that because of extreme public hostility, which they stated had been engendered largely by the official attitudes and actions of the Governor and the Legislature, the maintenance of a sound educational program at Central High School, with the Negro students in attendance, would be impossible. The Board therefore proposed that the Negro students already admitted to the school be withdrawn and sent to segregated schools, and that all further steps to carry out the Board's desegregation program be postponed

for a period later suggested by the Board to be two and one-half years.

After a hearing the District Court granted the relief requested by the Board....

In affirming the judgment of the Court of Appeals which reversed the District Court we have accepted without reservation the position of the School Board, the Superintendent of Schools, and their counsel that they displayed entire good faith in the conduct of these proceedings and in dealing with the unfortunate and distressing sequence of events which has been outlined. We likewise have accepted the findings of the District Court as to the conditions at Central High School during the 1957–1958 school year, and also the findings that the educational progress of all the students, white and colored, of that school has suffered and will continue to suffer if the conditions which prevailed last year are permitted to continue.

The significance of these findings, however, is to be considered in light of the fact, indisputably revealed by the record before us, that the conditions they depict are directly traceable to the actions of legislators and executive officials of the State of Arkansas, taken in their official capacities, which reflect their own determination to resist this Court's decision in the *Brown* case and which have brought about violent resistance to that decision in Arkansas....

One may well sympathize with the position of the Board in the face of the frustrating conditions which have confronted it, but, regardless of the Board's good faith, the actions of the other state agencies responsible for those conditions compel us to reject the Board's legal position....

The controlling legal principles are

plain. The command of the Fourteenth Amendment is that no "state" shall deny to any person within its jurisdiction the equal protection of the laws. "A State acts by its legislative, its executive, or its judicial authorities. It can act in no other way. The constitutional provision, therefore, must mean that no agency of the State, or of the officers or agents by whom its powers are exerted, shall deny to any person within its jurisdiction the equal protection of the laws. Whoever, by virtue of public position under a State government ... denies or takes away the equal protection of the laws, violates the constitutional inhibition; and as he acts in the name and for the State, and is clothed with the State's power, his act is that of the State. This must be so, or the constitutional prohibition has no meaning." *Ex parte Virginia*, 100 U.S. 339 (1880)....

What has been said, in the light of the facts developed, is enough to dispose of the case. However, we should answer the premise of the actions of the Governor and Legislature that they are not bound by our holding in the *Brown* case. It is necessary only to recall some basic constitutional propositions which are settled doctrine.

Article VI of the Constitution makes the Constitution the "supreme Law of the Land." In 1803, Chief Justice Marshall, speaking for a unanimous Court, referring to the Constitution as "the fundamental and paramount law of the nation," declared in the notable case of *Marbury v. Madison*, that "It is emphatically the province and duty of the judicial department to say what the law is." This decision declared the basic principle that the federal judiciary is supreme in the exposition of the law of the Constitution, and that principle has ever since been respected by this Court and the Country as a permanent and indispensable feature of our constitutional system. It follows that the interpretation of the Fourteenth Amendment enunciated by this Court in the *Brown* case is the supreme law of the land, and Art. VI of the Constitution makes it of binding effect on the States "any Thing in the Constitution or Laws of any State to the Contrary notwithstanding." Every state legislator and executive and judicial officer is solemnly committed by oath taken pursuant to Art. VI, Section 3 "to support this Constitution." Chief Justice Taney, speaking for a unanimous Court in 1859, said that this requirement reflected the framers' "anxiety to preserve it [the Constitution] in full force, in all its powers, and to guard against resistance to or evasion of its authority, on the part of a State...." *Ableman v. Booth*, 21 Howard 506 (1859).

No state legislator or executive or judicial officer can war against the Constitution without violating his understanding to support it. Chief Justice Marshall spoke for a unanimous Court in saying that: "If the legislatures of the several states may, at will, annul the judgments of the courts of the United States, and destroy the rights acquired under those judgments, the constitution itself becomes a solemn mockery." A Governor who asserts a power to nullify a federal court order is similarly restrained. If he had such power, said Chief Justice Hughes, in 1932, also for a unanimous Court, "it is manifest that the fiat of a state Governor, and not the Constitution of the United States, would be the supreme law of the land; that the restrictions of the Federal Constitution upon the exercise of state power would be but impotent phrases."...

The right of a student not to be segregated on racial grounds in schools so maintained is indeed so fundamental and pervasive that it is embraced in the concept of due process of law. The basic decision in *Brown* was unanimously reached by this Court only after the case had been briefed and twice argued and the issues had been given the most serious consideration. Since the first *Brown* opinion three new Justices have come to the Court. They are at one with the Justices still on the Court who participated in that basic decision as to its correctness, and that decision is now unanimously reaffirmed. The principles announced in that decision and the obedience of the States to them, according to the command of the Constitution, are indispensable for the protection of the freedoms guaranteed by our fundamental charter for all of us. Our constitutional ideal of equal justice under law is thus made a living truth.

FRANKFURTER, J., CONCURRING

While unreservedly participating with my brethren in our joint opinion, I deem it appropriate also to deal individually with the great issue here at stake....

The duty to abstain from resistance to "the supreme Law of the Land," as declared by the organ of our Government for ascertaining it, does not require immediate approval of it nor does it deny the right of dissent. Criticism need not be stilled. Active obstruction or defiance is barred. Our kind of society cannot endure if the controlling authority of the Law as derived from the Constitution is not to be the tribunal specially charged with the duty of ascertaining and declaring what is "the supreme Law of the Land." Particularly is this so where the declaration of what "the supreme Law" commands on an underlying moral issue is not the dubious pronouncement of a gravely divided Court but is the unanimous conclusion of a long-matured deliberative process....

That the responsibility of those who exercise power in a democratic government is not to reflect inflamed public feeling but to help form its understanding, is especially true when they are confronted with a problem like a racially discriminating public school system. This is the lesson to be drawn from the heartening experience in ending enforced racial segregation in the public schools in cities with Negro populations of large proportions. Compliance with decisions of this Court, as the constitutional organ of the supreme Law of the Land, has often, throughout our history, depended on active support by state and local authorities. It presupposes such support. To withhold it, and indeed to use political power to try to paralyze the supreme Law, precludes the maintenance of our federal system as we have known and cherished it for one hundred and seventy years....

QUESTIONS

1. *Cooper* was decided over 150 years after *Marbury v. Madison*. Does *Cooper* merely restate the understanding of judicial review Chief Justice John Marshall asserted in *Marbury*, or does it considerably enlarge upon that understanding? Is the doctrine of judicial review

more, or less, defensible when it is exercised contrary to popular opinion?

2. Did the justices in *Cooper* ground their authority over Little Rock school officials in the claim that what they say is supreme because the Constitution is what the justices say it is, or in the assertion that the Court's decisions must be respected because the justices are acting under the Constitution, which is supreme? What is the difference?

3. Alexander Hamilton argued in *Federalist* No. 78 that the Supreme Court, having neither the power of the sword nor of the purse, but solely of its "judgment," that is, its reason, "will always be the least dangerous branch to the political rights of the Constitution." Hamilton added that the Supreme Court "must ultimately depend upon the aid of the executive arm even for the efficacy of its judgments" (*The Federalist Papers*, Clinton Rossiter, ed. [New York, NY: Mentor, 1961]). Do Hamilton's observations provide insight into the extraordinary step the justices took when all nine signed the *Cooper* opinion? Does Justice Frankfurter's concurrence detract from the authority of the Court and undermine the power of judicial review? Would a dissent?

4. Interposition—the doctrine underlying the "massive resistance" strategy that gave rise to *Cooper*—holds that sovereign states may nullify a federal government mandate they deem unconstitutional or beyond the powers delegated to the national government. The doctrine of interposition has a long history in the United States. As early as the 1798–99 Kentucky and Virginia Resolutions two states objected that the federal Alien and Sedition Acts, which criminalized criticism of the government, were unenforceable because they violated the Constitution. *one soutient*

Can the doctrine of interposition coexist with the doctrine of judicial review? What contemporary issues might pit the two doctrines against one another? Is one doctrine more consistent with the Constitution?

COMMENTS

1. *Cooper* was handed down in September 1958. In response to the Supreme Court's decision, Governor Orval Faubus closed the city's schools for the 1958–59 academic year. They opened a year later only after a federal court declared the school closing unconstitutional (*Aaron v. McKinley*, 173 F. Supp. 944 (E.D. Ark 1959)) and President Eisenhower reluctantly federalized the Arkansas National Guard to enforce the order. Faubus used his defiance of the Court's decision in *Cooper* in his successful campaigns for governor of Arkansas in 1958, 1960, 1962, and 1964.

2. Political scientist David O'Brien notes that only in "extraordinary cases" do all the justices sign an opinion "to emphasize their agreement." Such was the situation in *Cooper*. O'Brien reports that Justice Brennan prepared the original draft of the decision, but that

> then all nine justices gathered around a table and rewrote portions of the opinion. The justices' collective drafting of *Cooper v. Aaron* was exceptional, though reminiscent of the nineteenth-century opinion-writing practice. The justices also took the unusual step of noting in the opinion that three—Brennan, Stewart, and Whittaker— were not on the Court when the landmark ruling in *Brown* was handed down but that they would have joined that unanimous decision if they had been. All nine justices then signed the Court's opinion in order to emphasize their unanimity and because Frankfurter insisted on adding a concurring opinion. This departure from the usual practice of having one justice sign the opinion was strongly opposed by Douglas. But all agreed to depart in this way so that Frankfurter's concurring opinion "would not be accepted as any dilution or interpretation of the views in the Court's joint opinion." (David M. O'Brien, *Storm Center: The Supreme Court in American Politics*, 4th ed. [New York, NY: Norton, 1996], p. 266)

O'Brien provides this explanation for Justice Frankfurter's insistence on publishing a concurring opinion in *Cooper*:

> Because many southern lawyers and law professors had been his students at Harvard Law School, Frankfurter insisted that it was important for him to lecture them on the soundness of the Court's decision not to permit delays in school desegregation.

Frankfurter's obstinacy angered Chief Justice Warren, and Justices Black and Brennan, and was strongly opposed by Douglas (O'Brien, *Storm Center*, p. 327).

JUDICIAL REVIEW

United States v. Nixon
418 U.S. 683 (1974)

SETTING

On June 17, 1972, during the presidential campaign between President Richard Nixon and Senator George McGovern, five people in the employ of the Committee to Re-Elect the President (popularly labeled "CREEP") broke into the office of the Democratic National Committee headquarters located in the

Watergate complex in Washington, D.C. Bernard Barker, Virgilio Gonzalez, Eugenio Martinez, James McCord Jr., and Frank Sturgis were apprehended by a Watergate security guard. The five were charged with attempted burglary and attempted interception of telephone and other communications. On September 17, 1972, these five—along with former White House consultant E. Howard Hunt and G. Gordon Liddy, counsel to the CREEP Finance Committee—were indicted for conspiracy, burglary, and violation of federal wiretapping laws. At trial in January 1973, Hunt, Barker, Gonzalez, Martinez, and Sturgis pleaded guilty. Liddy and McCord were tried and convicted.

President Nixon attempted to dismiss the break-in as a "third-rate burglary," but investigations by the Federal Bureau of Investigation, the House Banking and Currency Committee, various individual members of Congress, and the press suggested that campaign wrongdoing was not limited to the Watergate break-in. The investigations uncovered evidence that numerous Nixon campaign officials had engaged in extensive political sabotage, including organizing the burglary of the office of Pentagon expert Daniel Ellsberg's psychiatrist and attempting to tamper with the judge presiding over the subsequent trial for the Ellsberg break-in. Ellsberg had embarrassed the administration earlier by leaking to the press the so-called Pentagon Papers, a detailed and damning examination of America's Vietnam policy. The investigations also uncovered such activities as illegal campaign contributions, administrative favors for corporate contributors, the sale of ambassadorships, intentional destruction of government records, secret bombings of Cambodia, disruption of various Democratic campaign activities (dubbed "dirty tricks" by the media) and payment of "hush money" to try to cover up the growing Watergate scandal.

In February 1973, the Senate created a Select Committee on Presidential Campaign Activities to look into "the extent … to which illegal, improper, or unethical activities" had occurred during the 1972 presidential campaign and election. The committee soon came to be known as the Watergate Committee. On April 30, 1973, in an effort designed to control the damage threatening his presidency, Richard Nixon announced during a nationally televised talk that he had accepted the resignations of his two closest aides, John Erlichman and H. R. Haldeman, and had fired John W. Dean III, his White House counsel, who had confessed to Watergate Committee investigators that he had taken part in a conspiracy to conceal the Watergate illegalities. During this talk, Nixon assured the public, "There can be no whitewash at the White House."

The Watergate Committee held its first public hearings the following May. In an attempt to avoid disclosing information damaging to his administration, President Nixon claimed that his aides were cloaked with executive privilege and could not be compelled to testify. Nonetheless, committee chair Sam Ervin pressured Nixon's former counsel, John Dean, into a public confession of his participation in the attempt to conceal Watergate illegalities. Dean's testimony implicated several others on the president's closest staff and the CREEP. Subsequently, several presidential and campaign staff members resigned. Some admitted attending meetings at which a plan was discussed to place electronic eavesdropping devices in the Democratic headquarters. On May 18, 1973, Attorney General-designate Elliot L. Richardson asked former Solicitor General and Harvard Law School professor Archibald Cox to serve as a special prosecutor to investigate charges arising from the collection of scandals collectively known as "Watergate." President Nixon pledged his full cooperation.

On July 16, 1973, Alexander Butterfield, former White House aide and head of the Federal Aviation Administration, disclosed during testimony before the Watergate Committee that the president had surreptitiously tape-recorded those discussions as well as telephone conversations with members of his cabinet and staff. Later that day, a statement from the White House confirmed that President Nixon's conversations since early 1971 had been tape-recorded. The revelation sparked efforts to obtain the tapes in the quest for a "smoking gun" that would verify President Nixon's involvement in the Watergate cover-up.

A week after Butterfield's revelations, President Nixon refused requests from both the Watergate Committee and Special Prosecutor Cox for access to the tapes. The president subsequently ordered Cox to cease his efforts to acquire the tapes through a court order. When Cox nonetheless went to court seeking a judicial order, the president ordered his attorney general to fire him. On October 20, 1973, Attorney General Elliot Richardson and his assistant, William Ruckelshouse, submitted their resignations rather than fire Cox. Solicitor General Robert Bork then carried out the order. October 20 came to be know as the "Saturday night massacre."

President Nixon's firing of Cox unleashed a firestorm of criticism and led to calls for his impeachment. Attempts to accelerate implementation of a damage-control strategy did little to stem proliferating calls for President Nixon's resignation. During a televised press conference on November 17, 1973, an exasperated Nixon seemed to confirm his critic's allegations of impropriety and illegality by protesting: "I made my mistakes, but in all my years of public life, I have never profited, never profited from public service. I have earned every cent. ...Well, I am not a crook." Soon thereafter the House of Representatives began to inquire whether grounds existed for impeachment. In an effort to stem the rising tide of criticism, President Nixon named a new special prosecutor, Texas trial lawyer Leon Jaworski. Grand jury investigations of various members of the president's staff and the CREEP proceeded.

On March 1, 1974, a grand jury of the U.S. District Court for the District of Columbia returned an indictment against former Attorney General John Mitchell and six other members of President Nixon's White House staff and the CREEP for various offenses, including conspiracy to defraud the United States and to obstruct justice. In the course of considering its indictment, the grand jury decided by a vote of 19–0 that President Nixon was part of the conspiracy and notified Jaworski to identify Nixon (among others) as an unindicted co-conspirator in connection with subsequent legal proceedings.

In order to obtain additional evidence that Jaworski believed was in Nixon's custody and that would be important to the government's proof in the trial against those named in the indictment, Jaworski asked the U.S. District

Court for the District of Columbia to issue a subpoena *duces tecum* to the president, pursuant to Rule 17(c) of the Federal Rules of Criminal Procedure, requiring him to bring evidence with him as a witness. The court issued the subpoena on April 18, 1974. It ordered the president to make available twenty tape-recorded conversations dealing with Watergate by May 2.

On April 30, the president released to the public and submitted to the House Judiciary Committee conducting the impeachment inquiry 1,216 pages of edited transcripts of forty-three conversations dealing with Watergate. Portions of the twenty subpoenaed conversations were included. On May 1, the president's counsel filed a formal claim of executive privilege in the district court and a motion to quash the subpoena. The president's counsel also moved to expunge the grand jury's finding and to enjoin all persons except the president and his counsel from ever disclosing the grand jury's action.

On May 20, following an *in camera* (in chambers, in private) hearing, the district court denied the motions to quash and expunge. It held that the courts, not the president, were the final arbiter of the applicability of a claim of executive privilege. Under the circumstances of this case, the court concluded, the presumption of executive privilege was overcome by the special prosecutor's *prima facie* (on the face of it) demonstration of need sufficiently compelling to warrant judicial examination in chambers. It ordered the president or any of his subordinates in control of the subpoenaed material to deliver original copies to the court and taped copies of those portions of the subpoenaed recordings for the transcripts that had been released to the public on April 30. The district court stayed its order pending timely appellate review and ordered that the matters filed remain under seal when transmitted as part of the record.

On May 24, President Nixon appealed the district court's order to the U.S. Court of Appeals for the D.C. Circuit. On the same day, Special Prosecutor Jaworski filed a petition for a writ of certiorari before judgment with the Supreme Court of the United States. The president cross-petitioned, raising the issue of a grand jury's authority to charge an incumbent president as an unindicted co-conspirator in a criminal proceeding. The petitions were granted on May 31 with an expedited briefing schedule. The case was set for argument on July 8, 1974.

HIGHLIGHTS OF SUPREME COURT ARGUMENTS

BRIEF FOR THE UNITED STATES

◆ The Court has jurisdiction over this case because the subpoena was issued pursuant to a criminal prosecution. The Court is not deprived of jurisdiction just because the dispute is between two members of the executive branch.

◆ The speculative possibility that the president might disregard a valid court order does not strip the Court of its jurisdiction.

◆ The case is justiciable because there is an actual, adversary controversy between the special prosecutor and the president that can only be resolved judicially. Nothing in the constitutional grant of power to the president deprives courts of their constitutional power to resolve a dispute involving the claim of executive privilege.

◆ The president's claim of executive privilege is tantamount to a denial of constitutional limitations. Since *Marbury v. Madison* it has been recognized that every other officer of the executive branch is subject to judicial process.

◆ Courts' powers to issue subpoenas to the president have been recognized for many years, both because of the principle that no man is above the law, and because of the need for evidence in the conduct of criminal prosecutions.

◆ The conversations described in the subpoena relating to Watergate are outside the executive privilege for confidential communication because they are not related to deliberations comprising part of a process by which governmental decisions and policies are formulated.

◆ Even if the conversations described in the subpoena to the president might have been covered by executive privilege on the grounds of need for confidentiality, the president waived that privilege when he released 1,216 pages of transcript from 43 presidential conversations to the public and the House Judiciary Committee.

AMICUS CURIAE BRIEFS SUPPORTING THE UNITED STATES   *want the access to tapes*

Gordon Strachan and John Ehrlichmann; The American Civil Liberties Union.

BRIEF FOR PRESIDENT NIXON

◆ This intra-branch conflict between the president and the special prosecutor is not justiciable because it involves a political question arising out of the president's exercise of a textually demonstrable grant of power from Article II. The only appropriate procedure for the alleged abuses is impeachment.

◆ Separation of powers precludes judicial review of the use of executive privilege by a president. Executive privilege is one of the inherent parts of executive power and has been asserted at least twenty-eight times since 1796.

◆ An incumbent president cannot lawfully be charged with a crime by a grand jury. The functioning of the executive branch depends ultimately on the president's personal capacity—legal, mental, and physical. If he cannot function freely, there would be a critical gap in the constitutional structure.

SUPREME COURT DECISION: 8–0

(Rehnquist, J., did not participate.)

BURGER, C.J.

… The threshold question presented is whether the May 20, 1974, order of the District Court was an appealable order and whether this case was properly "in" the Court of Appeals when the petition for certiorari was filed in this Court…. [The court answers yes.]…

In the District Court, the President's counsel argued that the court lacked jurisdiction to issue the subpoena because the matter was an intra-branch dispute between a subordinate and superior officer of the Executive Branch and hence not subject to judicial resolution....

Our starting point is the nature of the proceeding for which the evidence is sought—here a pending criminal prosecution. It is a judicial proceeding in a federal court alleging violation of federal laws and is brought in the name of the United States as sovereign.... Under the authority of Art. II, § 2, Congress has vested in the Attorney General the power to conduct the criminal litigation of the United States Government.... It has also vested in him the power to appoint subordinate officers to assist him in the discharge of his duties.... Acting pursuant to those statutes, the Attorney General has delegated the authority to represent the United States in these particular matters to a Special Prosecutor with unique authority and tenure. The regulation gives the Special Prosecutor explicit power to contest the invocation of executive privilege in the process of seeking evidence deemed relevant to the performance of these specially delegated duties....

So long as this regulation is extant it has the force of law....

Here ... it is theoretically possible for the Attorney General to amend or revoke the regulation defining the Special Prosecutor's authority. But he has not done so. So long as this regulation remains in force the Executive Branch is bound by it, and indeed the United States as the sovereign composed of the three branches is bound to respect and to enforce it. Moreover, the delegation of authority to the Special Prosecutor in this case is not an ordinary delegation by the Attorney General to a subordinate officer: with the authorization of the President, the Acting Attorney General provided in the regulation that the Special Prosecutor was not to be removed without the consensus of eight designated leaders of Congress....

In light of the uniqueness of the setting in which the conflict arises, the fact that both parties are officers of the Executive Branch cannot be viewed as a barrier to justiciability. It would be inconsistent with the applicable law and regulation, and the unique facts of this case to conclude other than that the Special Prosecutor has standing to bring this action and that a justiciable controversy is presented for decision....

In a case such as this, ... where a subpoena is directed to a President of the United States, appellate review, in deference to a coordinate branch of Government, should be particularly meticulous to ensure that the standards of Rule 17(c) have been correctly applied.... From our examination of the materials submitted by the Special Prosecutor to the District Court in support of his motion for the subpoena, we are persuaded that the District Court's denial of the President's motion to quash the subpoena was consistent with Rule 17(c). We also conclude that the Special Prosecutor has made a sufficient showing to justify a subpoena for production *before* trial. The subpoenaed materials are not available from any other source, and their examination and processing should not await trial in the circumstances shown....

Having determined that the requirements of Rule 17(c) were satisfied, we turn to the claim that the subpoena should be quashed because it demands "confidential conversations between a President and his close advisors that it would be inconsistent with the public interest to produce."... The first con-

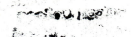

tention is a broad claim that the separation of powers doctrine precludes judicial review of a President's claim of privilege. The second contention is that if he does not prevail on the claim of absolute privilege, the court should hold as a matter of constitutional law that the privilege prevails over the subpoena duces tecum.

In the performance of assigned constitutional duties each branch of the Government must initially interpret the Constitution, and the interpretation of its powers by any branch is due great respect from the others. The President's counsel, as we have noted, reads the Constitution as providing an absolute privilege of confidentiality for all Presidential communications. Many decisions of this Court, however, have unequivocally reaffirmed the holding of *Marbury v. Madison* ... that "[i]t is emphatically the province and duty of the judicial department to say what the law is."...

No holding of the Court has defined the scope of judicial power specifically relating to the enforcement of a subpoena for confidential Presidential communications for use in a criminal prosecution, but other exercises of power by the Executive Branch and the Legislative Branch have been found invalid as in conflict with the Constitution.... Since this Court has consistently exercised the power to construe and delineate claims arising under express powers, it must follow that the Court has authority to interpret claims with respect to powers alleged to derive from enumerated powers....

We therefore reaffirm that it is the province and duty of this Court "to say what the law is" with respect to the claim of privilege presented in this case....

In support of his claim of absolute privilege, the President's counsel urges two grounds, one of which is common to all governments and one of which is peculiar to our system of separation of powers. The first ground is the valid need for protection of communications between high Government officials and those who advise and assist them in the performance of their manifold duties; the importance of this confidentiality is too plain to require further discussion. Human experience teaches that those who expect public dissemination of their remarks may well temper candor with a concern for appearances and for their own interests to the detriment of the decisionmaking process. Whatever the nature of the privilege of confidentiality of Presidential communications in the exercise of Art. II powers, the privilege can be said to derive from the supremacy of each branch within its own assigned area of constitutional duties. Certain powers and privileges flow from the nature of enumerated powers; the protection of the confidentiality of Presidential communications has similar constitutional underpinnings.

The second ground asserted by the President's counsel in support of the claim of absolute privilege rests on the doctrine of separation of powers. Here it is argued that the independence of the Executive Branch within its own sphere ... insulates a President from a judicial subpoena in an ongoing criminal prosecution, and thereby protects confidential Presidential communications.

However, neither the doctrine of separation of powers, nor the need for confidentiality of high-level communications, without more, can sustain an absolute, unqualified Presidential privilege of immunity from judicial process

under all circumstances. The President's need for complete candor and objectivity from advisers calls for great deference from the courts. However, when the privilege depends solely on the broad, undifferentiated claim of public interest in the confidentiality of such conversations, a confrontation with other values arises. Absent a claim of need to protect military, diplomatic, or sensitive national security secrets, we find it difficult to accept the argument that even the very important interest in confidentiality of Presidential communications is significantly diminished by production of such material for in camera inspection with all the protection that a district court will be obliged to provide.

The impediment that an absolute, unqualified privilege would place in the way of the primary constitutional duty of the Judicial Branch to do justice in criminal prosecutions would plainly conflict with the function of the courts under Art. III. In designing the structure of our Government and dividing and allocating the sovereign power among three co-equal branches, the Framers of the Constitution sought to provide a comprehensive system, but the separate powers were not intended to operate with absolute independence.... To read the Art. II powers of the President as providing an absolute privilege as against a subpoena essential to enforcement of criminal statutes on no more than a generalized claim of the public interest in confidentiality of non-military and nondiplomatic discussions would upset the constitutional balance of "a workable government" and gravely impair the role of the courts under Art. III.

In this case the President challenges a subpoena served on him as a third party requiring the production of materials for use in a criminal prosecution; he does so on the claim that he has a privilege against disclosure of confidential communications. He does not place his claim of privilege on the ground they are military or diplomatic secrets. As to these areas of Art. II duties the courts have traditionally shown the utmost deference to Presidential responsibilities.... No case of the Court, however, has extended this high degree of deference to a President's generalized interest in confidentiality. Nowhere in the Constitution, as we have noted earlier, is there any explicit reference to a privilege of confidentiality, yet to the extent this interest relates to the effective discharge of a President's powers, it is constitutionally based.

The right to the production of all evidence at a criminal trial similarly has constitutional dimensions. The Sixth Amendment explicitly confers upon every defendant in a criminal trial the right "to be confronted with the witnesses against him" and "to have compulsory process for obtaining witnesses in his favor." Moreover, the Fifth Amendment also guarantees that no person shall be deprived of liberty without due process of law. It is the manifest duty of the courts to vindicate those guarantees, and to accomplish that it is essential that all relevant and admissible evidence be produced.

In this case we must weigh the importance of the general privilege of confidentiality of Presidential communications in performance of the President's responsibilities against the inroads of such a privilege on the fair administration of criminal justice. The interest in preserving confidentiality is weighty indeed and entitled to great respect.

However, we cannot conclude that advisers will be moved to temper the candor of their remarks by the infrequent occasions of disclosure because of the possibility that such conversations will be called for in the context of a criminal prosecution.

On the other hand, the allowance of the privilege to withhold evidence that is demonstrably relevant in a criminal trial would cut deeply into the guarantee of due process of law and gravely impair the basic function of the courts. A President's acknowledged need for confidentiality in the communications of his office is general in nature, whereas the constitutional need for production of relevant evidence in a criminal proceeding is specific and central to the fair adjudication of a particular criminal case in the administration of justice. Without access to specific facts a criminal prosecution may be totally frustrated. The President's broad interest in confidentiality of communications will not be vitiated by disclosure of a limited number of conversations preliminarily shown to have some bearing on the pending criminal cases.

We conclude that when the ground for asserting privilege as to subpoenaed materials sought for use in a criminal trial is based only on the generalized interest in confidentiality, it cannot prevail over the fundamental demands of due process of law in the fair administration of criminal justice. The generalized assertion of privilege must yield to the demonstrated, specific need for evidence in a pending criminal trial....

Here the District Court treated the material as presumptively privileged, proceeded to find that the Special Prosecutor had made a sufficient showing to rebut the presumption, and ordered an in camera examination of the subpoenaed material. On the basis of our examination of the record we are unable to conclude that the District Court erred in ordering the inspection. Accordingly we affirm the order of the District Court that subpoenaed materials be transmitted to that court. We now turn to the important question of the District Court's responsibilities in conducting the in camera examination of Presidential materials or communications delivered under the compulsion of the subpoena duces tecum....

It is elementary that in camera inspection of evidence is always a procedure calling for scrupulous protection against any release or publication of material not found by the court, at that stage, probably admissible in evidence and relevant to the issues of the trial for which it is sought. That being true of an ordinary situation, it is obvious that the District Court has a very heavy responsibility to see to it that Presidential conversations, which are either not relevant or not admissible, are accorded that high degree of respect due the President of the United States.... We have no doubt that the District Judge will at all times accord to Presidential records that high degree of deference suggested in *United States v. Burr* [4 Cranch 470 (1807)] and will discharge his responsibility to see to it that until released to the Special Prosecutor no in camera material is revealed to anyone. This burden applies with even greater force to excised material; once the decision is made to excise, the material is restored to its privileged status and should be returned under seal to its lawful custodian.

Since this matter came before the Court during the pendency of a criminal prosecution, and on representations that time is of the essence, the mandate shall issue forthwith.

Affirmed.

QUESTIONS

1. Respond to the following question posed by attorney L. Michael Hager:

   > In *Nixon*, the Court discovered executive privilege where the Constitution itself was silent, and unabashedly weighed interests without a scale. Did not the Court thereby [exercise the power of judicial review to] usurp a policy-making function, infringing on the separation of powers? ("The Constitution, the Court, and the Cover-Up: Reflections on *United States v. Nixon*," 29 *Oklahoma Law Review* 591, 596, 1976)

2. There is no mention of "executive privilege" in either the text of the Constitution or in the debates of the Philadelphia Convention. Neither is judicial review mentioned in the Constitution. Does this mean that one branch of the federal government—the judiciary—was exercising extra-constitutional power to assess the extra-constitutional privilege of another branch—the presidency? If the Supreme Court had accepted President Nixon's argument of absolute executive privilege in *Nixon*, could not Congress plausibly contend that Congress alone may determine what legislation it is authorized to enact?

3. Law school professor Vincent Blasi wrote of *Nixon*: "At the time the Court decided to hear the tapes case on an expedited basis, the impeachment process was proceeding apace, and indeed the House Judiciary Committee was performing so impressively that many citizens were reexamining their previous low regard for Congress as an institution. Yet the Burger Court jumped in on its own initiative, and with a swift stroke essentially resolved the crisis.... *United States v. Nixon* represents nothing less than a bold and stunningly successful instance of judicial activism" ("The Rootless Activism of the Burger Court," in *The Burger Court: The Counter-Revolution That Wasn't*, ed. Vincent Blasi [New Haven, CT: Yale University Press, 1983], p. 201).

   Is *Nixon* an example of judicial activism? Is the decision in *Nixon* consistent with the doctrine of judicial review announced in *Marbury v. Madison*; with the exercise of judicial review in *Cooper v. Aaron*?

4. Suppose that President Nixon had chosen to defy the Court's ruling in *Nixon* and refused to hand the White House tapes over to federal prosecutors. What then? What does that possibility suggest about the fragile nature of the power of judicial review?

COMMENT

The Supreme Court handed down its decision in *Nixon* on July 24, 1974. The House Judiciary Committee voted articles of impeachment on July 27, 29, and 30. On Monday, August 5, President Nixon released the transcripts of three incriminating tapes as ordered by the Court, and admitted that he had attempted to stop investigations of the Watergate break-in for political as well as national security reasons. He also admitted that he had withheld evidence of his role in the cover-up from his lawyers and political supporters on the Watergate Committee. Nixon conceded that impeachment by the House of Representatives was "virtually a foregone conclusion" but stated that he hoped the Senate would vote to acquit him. Three days later, on August 8, 1974, realizing that his political support had disintegrated, Nixon announced his resignation, effective noon the next day. In addition to President Nixon's departure, the Watergate scandal resulted in the conviction of fifty-six government officials, including twenty members of the cabinet, the White House staff and the CREEP.

On September 8, 1974, Gerald R. Ford, Nixon's successor as president, surprised many by pardoning Nixon for all federal crimes "he committed or may have committed or taken part in" while president.

JUDICIAL REVIEW

Plaut v. Spendthrift Farm, Inc.
514 U.S. 211 (1995)

SETTING

In *Federalist* No. 9, Alexander Hamilton, writing as Publius, hailed the "distribution of power into distinct departments"—commonly known as the separation of governmental powers—as one of the "powerful means by which the excellencies of republican government may be retained and its imperfections lessened or avoided." However, the founders did not envision a constitutional system in which governmental branches are separated into airtight compartments. In *Federalist* No. 47, James Madison, also writing as Publius, began an exposition, completed in No. 51, in which he contended that effective separation requires some blending of powers. Referring to Montesquieu's famous caution against uniting legislative, executive, and judicial powers in the same person or body, Madison observed in *Federalist* No. 47 that Montesquieu "did not mean that these departments ought to have no *partial agency* in, or no *control* over, the acts of the other."

Separation of powers theory, while essential to our constitutional scheme, is not a doctrine with clear boundaries. Predictably, litigation began soon after ratification of the Constitution about the extent to which the activities of one branch impermissibly "encroach" on the exercise of power vested in another branch. A not uncommon theme has involved Congress's encroachment on judicial functions.

In *Hayburn's Case*, 2 Dallas 409 (1792), the Court ruled that the judgments of Article III courts adjudicating private rights cannot be reopened by the legislative branch. That case arose from a statute enacted by Congress in 1792 authorizing pensions for disabled Revolutionary War veterans. The statute provided for an applicant to file a claim with a federal circuit court, which was to certify and transmit the claim to the secretary of war stating an opinion about the amount to which the claimant was due. The justices determined that federal courts could not adjudicate claims under the act because "the business directed by this act is not of a judicial nature." *Hayburn's Case* stands for the proposition that an indispensable requirement for the exercise of Article III judicial power is the ultimate authority to adjudicate cases and controversies. However, *Hayburn's Case* was decided before *Marbury v. Madison* in 1803 and, despite its assertion about the power of federal courts to hold statutes enacted by Congress unconstitutional, *Hayburn's Case* lacked the authority it would have had if it had been announced after the Court had declared its power of judicial review. Since 1803, the Supreme Court has had the final say (except for constitutional amendments) about matters involving separation of powers. That the Court remains protectively on guard against what it perceives as legislative encroachment became clear during the 1995 Term in a case from Kentucky.

Spendthrift Farm, Inc., is a thoroughbred horse farm that specializes in breeding race horses and selling yearlings. It was founded in 1937 and named after a nineteenth-century winner of the Belmont Stakes. In 1983, Spendthrift was the first thoroughbred racing stable to sell its shares publicly on the stock market. Ed and Nancy Plaut purchased one thousand shares in January 1984 for $10,750; John Grady purchased one thousand shares that November for $12,000.

Spendthrift fell on hard financial times during the 1980s and its stock prices fell dramatically. The Plauts and Grady wished to file a securities fraud action against Spendthrift Farms but, like all other litigants, were required to do so within the limitations period established by law—commonly called the statute of limitations—for filing actions. In November 1987, the Plauts and Grady filed suit in the U.S. District Court for the Eastern District of Kentucky on behalf of themselves and similarly situated stock purchasers, charging that the prospectus under which they purchased their shares was fraudulent. Their suit was brought under Section 10(b) of the Securities Exchange Act of 1934 and Rule 10b-5 of the Securities and Exchange Commission, adopted pursuant to that act. When the suit was filed, the Exchange Act did not contain a statute of limitations specifically applicable to claims under Section 10(b) or

Rule 10b-5. In the absence of an express statute of limitations, most courts had held that private Rule 10b-5 actions were subject to state statutes of limitation. The Plauts' suit was filed within the statute of limitations recognized by Kentucky law.

While Plauts' action was pending before the district court, the Supreme Court in *Lampf, Pleva, Lipkind, Prupis & Petigrow v. Gilbertson*, 501 U.S. 350 (1991), ruled that private actions under Section 10(b) are subject to a uniform federal limitations period: suits may not be brought more than one year after the alleged fraud is discovered or more than three years after it occurs. In a companion case, *James B. Beam Distilling Co. v. Georgia*, 501 U.S. 529 (1991), the Court held that when a court applies a new holding to the parties before it, the same holding must be applied to similarly situated litigants in all pending cases. The Plauts' case was pending when *Lampf* and *Beam* were decided. Under those holdings, their suit had to have been filed by 1986. Because it was filed in 1987, the district court dismissed their suit and entered judgment for Spendthrift Farm. The Plauts did not appeal, and the judgment became final in September 1991.

Congress responded to *Lampf* and *Beam* four months later by amending the Securities Exchange Act of 1934. As one senator put it, *Lampf* "changed the rules in the middle of the game for thousands of fraud victims who already had suits pending." Section 27A(b) of the amended Securities Exchange Act blocked application of *Lampf*'s three-year filing period in cases pending when *Lampf* and *Beam* were decided and provided for reinstatement of any case that had been dismissed under *Lampf* as long as the plaintiff moved to reinstate the suit within sixty days of the statute's enactment. Section 27A(b) thus created a new statute of limitations and a new right to judicial review and adjudication for a defined class of securities plaintiffs. The Plauts filed a motion within the prescribed sixty days to reinstate their case.

The district court denied the Plauts' motion to reinstate the case on the ground that Section 27A(b) was unconstitutional. The U.S. Court of Appeals for the Sixth Circuit affirmed, relying on *Hayburn's Case* for the proposition that Section 27A(b) violates separation of powers doctrine. The appeals court concluded that Section 27A(b)'s reopening of final judgments of federal courts in cases involving private parties constitutes an exercise by Congress of judicial power.

The Plauts petitioned the Supreme Court for a writ of certiorari. While the petition was pending, the Court decided *First RepublicBank Corp. v. Pacific Mutual Life Insurance Co., sub nom., Morgan Stanley & Company, Inc. v. Pacific Mutual Life Insurance Company*, 511 U.S. 658 (1994). The *First RepublicBank* case also raised the issue of the constitutionality of Section 27A(b), but the Court split 4–4, thereby affirming the Court of Appeals without deciding the constitutional question. Justice O'Connor did not participate, perhaps because she owned stock in one of the several corporations involved in that litigation. Three weeks later, the Court granted the Plauts' petition for a writ of certiorari.

Highlights of Supreme Court Arguments

BRIEF FOR THE PLAUTS

♦ Section 27A(b) was a valid exercise of Congress's power to rectify the injustice visited on Plauts and others similarly situated by the retroactive application of *Lampf, Pleva, Lipkind, Prupis & Petigrow v. Gilbertson*, 501 U.S. 350 (1991). It survives separation of powers scrutiny because it does not authorize adjudication of individual cases by a nonjudicial branch.

♦ The absolute rule adopted by the Court of Appeals—that Congress may not retroactively disturb final judgments of the federal courts—does not comport with this Court's precedents or the flexible approach to the separation of powers doctrine contemplated by the framers.

♦ Separation of powers is not offended as long as the actions of one branch do not involve an attempt to increase the powers of that branch at the expense of the powers of another branch or usurp or impermissibly undermine the powers properly belonging to another branch. There is no constitutional significance, in a separation of powers analysis, to the expiration of a time period that is within the legislative power to establish.

♦ The test of Due Process under the Fifth Amendment for retroactive legislation is whether the legislation advances a legitimate legislative purpose furthered by rational means. Section 27A(b) meets that test.

♦ The doctrine of vested rights should be rejected in favor of a more lucid due process analysis provided by the rationality test.

AMICUS CURIAE BRIEFS SUPPORTING THE PLAUTS

United States; National Association of Securities and Commercial Law Attorneys; Pacific Mutual Life Insurance Company; Michael N. Dashjian.

BRIEF FOR SPENDTHRIFT FARM, INC.

♦ Although this case does raise substantial constitutional questions about the power of Congress to set aside final judgments of Article III courts and to substitute congressional rules of decision of judicial judgments in a closed case, those constitutional questions need not be addressed. For example, if Section 27A(b) is construed as not reaching completely closed cases, its constitutional implications need not be reached.

♦ If the Court does reach the constitutional issues, they are serious because the mechanism created by Section 27A(b) threatens separation of powers. Congress's broad power to enact rules of conduct for the judicial branch does not include the power to intrude on the judicial branch's exclusive power to render final decisions in cases and controversies between private litigants.

♦ Congress does not have the power to impose rules of decision on the courts in ways that interfere with the judiciary's ability to declare what the law is.

◆ Section 27A(b) is not an exercise of legislative power in any traditional or recognizable sense. It operates to mandate the application of a particular rule of decision in cases in which a contrary rule of decision has already been prescribed by the Supreme Court by requiring courts to reopen and then set aside judgments that have already been entered.

◆ If final judicial determinations in particular cases can be overturned by legislative or executive action, courts will become merely advisory bodies.

◆ The Due Process Clause of the Fourteenth Amendment, like separation-of-powers doctrine, prohibits Congress from selecting which final decisions of courts will be overturned and which unsuccessful litigants will be made into successful ones.

AMICUS CURIAE BRIEF SUPPORTING SPENDTHRIFT FARM, INC.

Washington Legal Foundation.

SUPREME COURT DECISION: *7–2*

SCALIA, J.

The question presented in this case is whether 27A(b) of the Securities Exchange Act of 1934, to the extent that it requires federal courts to reopen final judgments in private civil actions under 10(b) of the Act, contravenes the Constitution's separation of powers or the Due Process Clause of the Fifth Amendment....

We think ... that 27A(b) offends a postulate of Article III ... deeply rooted in our law.... Article III establishes a "judicial department" with the "province and duty ... to say what the law is" in particular cases and controversies. *Marbury v. Madison.* The record of history shows that the Framers crafted this charter of the judicial department with an expressed understanding that it gives the Federal Judiciary the power, not merely to rule on cases, but to decide them, subject to review only by superior courts in the Article III hierarchy—with an understanding, in short, that "a judg-ment conclusively resolves the case" because "a 'judicial Power' is one to render dispositive judgments."... By retroactively commanding the federal courts to reopen final judgments, Congress has violated this fundamental principle.

The Framers of our Constitution lived among the ruins of a system of intermingled legislative and judicial powers, which had been prevalent in the colonies long before the Revolution, and which after the Revolution had produced factional strife and partisan oppression. In the seventeenth and eighteenth centuries colonial assemblies and legislatures functioned as courts of equity of last resort, hearing original actions or providing appellate review of judicial judgments.... Often, however, they chose to correct the judicial process through special bills or other enacted legislation. It was common for such legislation not to prescribe a resolution of the dispute, but rather simply to set aside the judgment and order a new trial or appeal.... Thus, ... such legislation bears not on the problem of interbranch review but on the problem of finality of judicial judgments. The vigorous, indeed often radical, populism of the revolutionary legislatures and assemblies increased the frequency of legislative correction of judgments.... Voices from many quarters, official as well as private, decried the increasing legislative interference with the private-law judgments of the courts....

This sense of a sharp necessity to separate the legislative from the judicial power, prompted by the crescendo of legislative interference with private judgments of the courts, triumphed among the Framers of the new Federal Constitution.... The Convention made the critical decision to establish a judicial department independent of the Legislative Branch by providing that "the judicial Power of the United States shall be vested in one supreme Court, and in such inferior Courts as the Congress may from time to time ordain and establish." Before and during the debates on ratification, Madison, Jefferson, and Hamilton each wrote of the factional disorders and disarray that the system of legislative equity had produced in the years before the framing; and each thought that the separation of the legislative from the judicial power in the new Constitution would cure them. [In] Madison's *Federalist* No. 48, [there is] the famous description of the process by which "[t]he legislative department is every where extending the sphere of its activity, and drawing all power into its impetuous vortex.'"...

If the need for separation of legislative from judicial power was plain, the principal effect to be accomplished by that separation was even plainer. As Hamilton wrote in his exegesis of Article III, § 1, in *Federalist* No. 81: "It is not true ... that the parliament of Great Britain, or the legislatures of the particular states, can rectify the exceptionable decisions of their respective courts, in any other sense than might be done by a future legislature of the United States. The theory neither of the British, nor the state constitutions, authorizes the revisal of a judicial sentence, by a legislative act.... A legislature without exceeding its province cannot reverse a determination once made, in a particular case; though it may prescribe a new rule for future cases."

The essential balance created by this allocation of authority was a simple one. The Legislature would be possessed of power to "prescrib[e] the rules by which the duties and rights of every citizen are to be regulated," but the power of "[t]he interpretation of the laws" would be "the proper and peculiar province of the courts.".... The Judiciary would be, "from the nature of its functions, ... the [department] least dangerous to the political rights of the constitution," not because its acts were subject to legislative correction, but because the binding effect of its acts was limited to particular cases and controversies. Thus, "though individual oppression may now and then proceed from the courts of justice, the general liberty of the people can never be endangered from that quarter: ... so long as the judiciary remains truly distinct from both the legislative and executive." The *Federalist* No. 78.

Judicial decisions in the period immediately after ratification of the Constitution confirm the understanding that it forbade interference with the final judgments of courts. In *Calder v.*

Bull, 3 Dallas 386 (1798), the Legislature of Connecticut had enacted a statute that set aside the final judgment of a state court in a civil case. Although the issue before this Court was the construction of the Ex Post Facto Clause, Art. I, 10, Justice Iredell (a leading Federalist who had guided the Constitution to ratification in North Carolina) noted that

> the Legislature of [Connecticut] has been in the uniform, uninterrupted, habit of exercising a general superintending power over its courts of law, by granting new trials. It may, indeed, appear strange to some of us, that in any form, there should exist a power to grant, with respect to suits depending or adjudged, new rights of trial, new privileges of proceeding, not previously recognized and regulated by positive institutions.... The power ... is judicial in its nature; and whenever it is exercised, as in the present instance, it is an exercise of judicial, not of legislative, authority.

The state courts of the era showed a similar understanding of the separation of powers, in decisions that drew little distinction between the federal and state constitutions....

By the middle of the nineteenth century, the constitutional equilibrium created by the separation of the legislative power to make general law from the judicial power to apply that law in particular cases was so well understood and accepted that it could survive even *Dred Scott v. Sandford*, 19 [Howard] 393 (1857). In his First Inaugural Address, President Lincoln explained why the political branches could not, and need not, interfere with even that infamous judgment:

> I do not forget the position assumed by some, that constitutional questions are to be decided by the Supreme Court; nor do I deny that such decisions must be binding in any case, upon the parties to a suit, as to the object of that suit.... And while it is obviously possible that such decision may be erroneous in any given case, still the evil effect following it, being limited to that particular case, with the chance that it may be over-ruled, and never become a precedent for other cases, can better be borne than could the evils of a different practice....

Section 27A(b) effects a clear violation of the separation-of-powers principle we have just discussed. It is, of course, retroactive legislation, that is, legislation that prescribes what the law *was* at an earlier time, when the act whose effect is controlled by the legislation occurred—in this case, the filing of the initial Rule 10b-5 action in the District Court. When retroactive legislation requires its own application in a case already finally adjudicated, it does no more and no less than "reverse a determination once made, in a particular case." The *Federalist* No. 81. Our decisions stemming from *Hayburn's Case* [2 Dallas 409 (1792)]—although their precise holdings are not strictly applicable here—have uniformly provided fair warning that such an act exceeds the powers of Congress.... Today those clear statements must either be honored, or else proved false.

It is true, as petitioners contend, that Congress can always revise the judgments of Article III courts in one sense: When a new law makes clear that it is retroactive, an appellate court must apply that law in reviewing judgments still on appeal that were rendered before the law was enacted, and must alter the outcome accordingly.... Since that is so, petitioners argue, federal courts must apply the "new" law created by 27A(b) in finally adjudicated cases as well; for the line that separates lower court judgments that are pending on appeal (or may still be appealed), from lower-court judgments that are final, is determined by statute, ... and so cannot possibly be a constitutional line. But a distinction between judgments from which all appeals have been forgone or completed, and judgments that remain on appeal (or subject to being appealed), is implicit in what Article III creates: not a batch of unconnected courts, but a judicial department composed of "inferior Courts" and "one supreme Court." Within that hierarchy, the decision of an inferior court is not (unless the time for appeal has expired) the final word of the department as a whole. It is the obligation of the last court in the hierarchy that rules on the case to give effect to Congress's latest enactment, even when that has the effect of overturning the judgment of an inferior court, since each court, at every level, must "decide according to existing laws." *United States v. Schooner Peggy*, 1 Cranch 103 (1801). Having achieved finality, however, a judicial decision becomes the last word of the judicial department with regard to a particular case or controversy, and Congress may not declare by retroactive legislation that the law applicable to that very case was something other than what the courts said it was. Finality of a legal judgment is determined by statute, just as entitlement to a government benefit is a statutory creation; but that no more deprives the former of its constitutional significance for separation-of-powers analysis than it deprives the latter of its significance for due process purposes....

It is irrelevant ... that the final judgments reopened by 27A(b) rested on the bar of a statute of limitations. The rules of finality, both statutory and judge-made, treat a dismissal on statute-of-limitations grounds the same way they treat a dismissal for failure to state a claim, for failure to prove substantive liability, or for failure to prosecute: as a judgment on the merits.... Petitioners suggest, directly or by implication, two reasons why a merits judgment based on this particular ground may be uniquely subject to congressional nullification. First, there is the fact that the length and indeed even the very existence of a statute of limitations upon a federal cause of action is entirely subject to congressional control. But virtually all of the reasons why a final judgment on the merits is rendered on a federal claim are subject to congressional control. Congress can eliminate, for example, a particular element of a cause of action that plaintiffs have found it difficult to establish; or an evidentiary rule that has often excluded essential testimony; or a rule of offsetting wrong (such as contributory negligence) that has often prevented recovery. To distinguish statutes of limitations on the ground that they are mere creatures of Congress is to distinguish them not at all. The second supposedly distinguishing characteristic of a statute of limitations is that it can be extended, without violating the Due Process Clause, after the cause of the action arose and even after the statute itself has expired.... But that also does not set statutes of limitations apart. To mention only one other broad category of judgment-producing legal rule: rules of pleading and proof can similarly be altered after the cause of action arises ... and even, if the statute clearly so requires, after they have been applied in a case but before final judgment has been entered. Petitioners' principle would therefore lead to the conclusion that final judgments rendered on the basis of a stringent (or, alternatively, liberal) rule of pleading or proof may be set aside for retrial under a new liberal (or, alternatively, stringent) rule of pleading or proof. This alone provides massive scope for undoing final judgments and would substantially subvert the doctrine of separation of powers....

Apart from the statute we review today, we know of no instance in which Congress has attempted to set aside the final judgment of an Article III court by retroactive legislation. That prolonged reticence would be amazing if such interference were not understood to be constitutionally proscribed....

Finally, petitioners liken 27A(b) to Federal Rule of Civil Procedure 60(b), which authorizes courts to relieve parties from a final judgment for grounds such as excusable neglect, newly discovered evidence, fraud, or "any other reason justifying relief...." We see little resemblance. Rule 60(b), which authorizes discretionary judicial revision of judgments in the listed situations and in other "extraordinary circumstances," *Liljeberg v. Health Services Acquisition Corp.*, 486 U.S. 847 (1988), does not impose any legislative mandate-to-reopen upon the courts, but merely reflects and confirms the courts' own inherent and discretionary power, "firmly established in English practice long before the foundation of our Republic," to set aside a judgment whose enforcement would work inequity. *Hazel-Atlas Glass Co. v. Hartford-Empire Co.*, 322 U.S. 238 (1944)....

Separation of powers, a distinctively American political doctrine, profits from the advice authored by a distinctively American poet: Good fences make good neighbors....

It is so ordered.

BREYER, J., CONCURRING

I agree with the majority that 27A(b) of the Securities Exchange Act of 1934 is unconstitutional. In my view, the separation of powers inherent in our Constitution means that at least sometimes Congress lacks the power under Article I to reopen an otherwise closed court judgment.... But, it is far less clear, and unnecessary for the purposes of this case to decide, that separation of powers "is violated" *whenever* an "individual final judgment is legislatively rescinded" or that it is "violated 40 times over when 40 final judgments are legislatively dissolved." I therefore write separately....

Despite ... important "separation of powers" concerns, *sometimes* Congress can enact legislation that focuses upon a small group, or even a single individual.... Congress also sometimes passes private legislation.... And, *sometimes* Congress can enact legislation that, as a practical matter, radically changes the effect of an individual, previously entered court decree.... Statutes that apply prospectively and (in part because of that prospectivity) to an open-ended class of persons, however, are more than simply an effort to apply, person by person, a previously-enacted law, or to single out for oppressive treatment one, or a handful, of particular individuals. Thus, it seems to me, if Congress enacted legislation that reopened an otherwise closed judgment but in a way that mitigated some of the here relevant "separation of powers" concerns, by also providing some of the assurances against "singling out" that ordinary legislative activity normally provides—say, prospectivity and general applicability—we might have a different case.... Because such legislation, in light of those mitigating circumstances, might well present a different constitutional question, I do not subscribe to the Court's more absolute statement.

The statute before us, however, has no such mitigating features. It reopens previously closed judgments. It is entirely retroactive, applying only to those Rule 10b-5 actions actually filed, on or before (but on which final judgments were entered after) June 19, 1991.... It lacks generality, for it applies only to a few individual instances.... And, it is underinclusive, for it excludes from its coverage others who, relying upon pre-Lampf limitations law, may have failed to bring timely securities fraud actions against any other of the Nation's hundreds of thousands of businesses....

The upshot is that, viewed in light of the relevant, liberty-protecting objectives of the "separation of powers," this case falls directly within the scope of language in this Court's cases suggesting a restriction on Congress' power to reopen closed court judgments....

At the same time, because the law before us *both* reopens final judgments *and* lacks the liberty-protecting assurances that prospectivity and greater generality would have provided, we need not, and we should not, go further—to make of the reopening itself, an absolute, always determinative distinction, a "prophylactic device," or a foundation for the building of a new "high wal[l]" between the branches. Indeed, the unnecessary building of such walls is, in itself, dangerous, because the Constitution blends, as well as separates, powers in its effort to create a government that will work for, as well as protect the liberties of, its citizens.... That doctrine does not "divide the branches into watertight compartments," nor "establish and divide fields of black and white." *Springer v. Philippine Islands*, 277 U.S. 189 (1928). And, important separation of powers decisions of this Court have sometimes turned, not upon absolute distinctions, but upon degree. As the majority invokes the advice of an American poet, one might consider as well that poet's caution, for he not only notes that "Something there is that doesn't love a wall," but also writes, "Before I built a wall I'd ask to know/What I was walling in or walling out."...

STEVENS AND GINSBURG, J.J., DISSENTING

... In my opinion, if Congress had retroactively restored rights its own legislation had inadvertently or unfairly impaired, the remedial amendment's failure to exclude dismissed cases from the benefitted class would not make it invalid. The Court today faces a materially identical situation and, in my view, reaches the wrong result.

Throughout our history, Congress has passed laws that allow courts to reopen final judgments. Such laws characteristically apply to judgments entered before as well as after their enactment. When they apply retroactively, they may raise serious due process questions, but the Court has never invalidated such a law on separation-of-powers grounds until today....

The only remarkable feature of this enactment is the fact that it remedied a defect in a new judge-made rule rather than in a statute.

The familiar history the Court invokes, involving colonial legislatures' ad hoc decisions of individual cases, "'unfettered by rules,'" provides no support for its holding. On the contrary, history and precedent demonstrate that Congress may enact laws that establish both substantive rules and procedures for reopening final judgments....

Aside from 27A(b), the Court claims to "know of no instance in which Congress has attempted to set aside the final judgment of an Article III court by retroactive legislation." In fact, Congress has done so on several occasions. Section 27A(b) is part of a remedial statute. As early as 1833, we recognized that a remedial statute authorizing the reopening of a final judgment after the time for appeal has expired is "entirely unexceptionable" even though it operates retroactively. "It has been repeatedly decided in this court, that the retrospective operation of such a law forms no objection to it. Almost every law, providing a new remedy, affects and operates upon causes of action existing at the time the law is passed." *Sampeyreac v. United States*, 7 Peters 222 (1833). We have upheld remedial statutes that carried no greater cause for separation-of-powers concerns than does 27A(b); others have provoked no challenges. In contrast, the colonial directives on which the majority relies were nothing like remedial statutes....

The lack of precedent for the Court's holding is not, of course, a sufficient reason to reject it. Correct application of separation-of-powers principles, however, confirms that the Court has reached the wrong result. As our most recent major pronouncement on the separation of powers noted, "we have never held that the Constitution requires that the three branches of Government 'operate with absolute independence.'" *Morrison v. Olson*, 487 U.S. 654 (1988). Rather, our jurisprudence reflects "Madison's flexible approach to separation of powers." *Mistretta v. United States*, 488 U.S. 361 (1989). In accepting Madison's conception rather than any "hermetic division among the Branches," "we have upheld statutory provisions that to some degree commingle the functions of the Branches, but that pose no danger of either aggrandizement or encroachment." *Mistretta*. Today's holding does not comport with these ideals....

The majority's rigid holding unnecessarily hinders the Government from addressing difficult issues that inevitably arise in a complex society. This Court, for example, lacks power to enlarge the time for filing petitions for certiorari in a civil case after 90 days from the entry of final judgment, no matter how strong the equities.... If an Act of God, such as a flood or an earthquake, sufficiently disrupted communications in a particular area to preclude filing for several days, the majority's reasoning would appear to bar Congress from addressing the resulting inequity. If Congress passed remedial legislation that retroactively granted movants from the disaster area extra time to file petitions or motions for extensions of time to file, today's holding presumably would compel us to strike down the legislation as an attack on the finality of judgments. Such a ruling, like today's holding, would gravely undermine federal courts' traditional power "to set aside a judgment whose enforcement would work inequity.",...

"All we seek," affirmed a sponsor of 27A, "is to give the victims [of securities fraud] a fair day in court." A statute, such as 27A, that removes an unanticipated and unjust impediment to adjudication of a large class of claims on their merits poses no danger of "aggrandizement or encroachment." *Mistretta*. This is particularly true for 27A in light of Congress' historic primacy over statutes of limitations. The statute contains several checks against the danger of congressional overreaching. The Court in *Lampf* [*Pleva, Lipkind, Prupis & Petigrow v. Gilbertson*, 501 U.S. 350 (1991)] undertook a legislative function. Essentially, it supplied a statute of limitations for 10b-5 actions. The Court, however, failed to adopt the transition rules that ordinarily attend alterations shortening the time to

sue. Congress, in 27A, has supplied those rules. The statute reflects the ability of two coequal branches to cooperate in providing for the impartial application of legal rules to particular disputes. The Court's mistrust of such cooperation ill serves the separation of powers.

We have the authority to hold that Congress has usurped a judicial prerogative, but even if this case were doubtful I would heed Justice Iredell's admonition in *Calder v. Bull* [3 Dallas 386 (1798)], that "the Court will never resort to that authority, but in a clear and urgent case." An appropriate regard for the interdependence of Congress and the judiciary amply supports the conclusion that 27A(b) reflects constructive legislative cooperation rather than a usurpation of judicial prerogatives.

Accordingly, I respectfully dissent.

QUESTIONS

1. The effect of the Supreme Court's 1994 deadlock in *First RepublicBank v. Pacific Mutual Life Insurance Co.*, 511 U.S. 658, was to affirm the Fifth Circuit U.S. Court of Appeals' holding that Section 27A(b) of the Securities Exchange Act was constitutional. Because of that earlier decision, Pacific Mutual Life Insurance Company was allowed to reinstate its suit against First RepublicBank. In *Plaut*, by contrast, the Supreme Court's decision left the Plauts without a remedy. Is one inherent risk of the doctrine of judicial review that litigants who raise the same issues may be treated differently? Does the possibility of such a result undermine the legitimacy of the power of judicial review?

2. Justice O'Connor's recusal in *First RepublicBank* left the Supreme Court deadlocked 4–4. (When a lower court opinion is affirmed by an equally divided Court, the voting alignment is not reported.) Justice O'Connor did participate in *Plaut*, and this time the Court's consideration of the same constitutional issues as in *First RepublicBank* yielded a 7–2 vote. What factors might account for the 7–2 result, rather than the 5–4 outcome that seemed more likely after *First*

RepublicBank? Do those factors suggest that whenever the Supreme Court exercises the power of judicial review nonlegal influences will affect *how* the power is exercised?

3. The Supreme Court could have read Section 27A(b) as merely a codification of the Court's rulings in *Lampf, Pleva, Lipkind, Prupis & Petigrow v. Gilbertson*, 501 U.S. 350 (1991) and *James B. Beam Distilling Co. v. Georgia*, 501 U.S. 529 (1991), thereby avoiding the constitutional issues raised by the Plauts' civil action. Such an approach would have adhered to the principle of judicial self-restraint. What reasons might explain why the justices took an activist role in *Plaut* and addressed the constitutional issue? Is deciding a constitutional issue when the case could be resolved on subconstitutional grounds a proper exercise of judicial review?

4. Assuming the Court properly reached constitutional issues in *Plaut,* was separation of powers doctrine the correct basis for resolution of the constitutional question rather than the Fifth Amendment Due Process Clause? If one accepts the doctrine of judicial review on the terms articulated by Marshall in *Marbury*, must one accept as a corollary that judicial review gives the Court the discretion to resolve issues on whichever constitutional provision the Court prefers?

5. "Departmentalism" is the view that each branch of the federal government is authorized to interpret the constitutionality of its own actions. Thomas Jefferson, a staunch exponent of departmentalism, explained the view in a letter to his friend William Jarvis:

> The constitution has erected no such single tribunal, knowing that to whatever hands confided, with the corruptions of time and party, its members would become despots. It has more wisely made all the departments co-equal and co-sovereign within themselves. (Paul L. Ford, ed., *The Works of Thomas Jefferson* [New York, NY: Putnam's, 1905], XII:161)

What are the implications of departmentalism for the doctrine of judicial review? Is the doctrine of departmentalism any more or less acceptable as an alternative to judicial review today than it was in Jefferson's time?

SUGGESTIONS FOR FURTHER READING

Agresto, John, *The Supreme Court and Constitutional Democracy* (Ithaca, NY: Cornell University Press, 1984).

Barber, Sotirios A., *On What the Constitution Means* (Baltimore, MD: The Johns Hopkins University Press, 1984).

_____, *The Constitution of Judicial Power* (Baltimore, MD: The Johns Hopkins University Press, 1993).

Bickle, Alexander M., *The Least Dangerous Branch: The Supreme Court at the Bar of Politics* (Indianapolis, IN: Bobbs-Merrill, 1962).

_____, "The Decade of School Desegregation," 64 *Columbia Law Review* (1964): 193.

_____, *The Supreme Court and the Idea of Progress* (New Haven, CT: Yale University Press, 1978).

Bobbitt, Philip, *Constitutional Fate: Theory of the Constitution* (New York, NY: Oxford University Press, 1982).

_____, *Constitutional Interpretation* (Oxford, UK: Blackwell, 1991).

Brest, Paul, "A Conscientious Legislator's Guide to Constitutional Interpretation, 27 *Stanford Law Review* (1975): 585.

Brigham, John, *The Cult of the Court* (Philadelphia, PA: Temple University Press, 1987).

Clinton, Robert Lowry, Marbury v. Madison *and Judicial Review* (Lawrence, KS: University Press of Kansas, 1989).

Corwin, Edward S., "*Marbury v. Madison* and the Doctrine of Judicial Review," 12 *Michigan Law Review* (1914): 538.

_____, *The Doctrine of Judicial Review: Its Legal and Historical Basis, and Other Essays* (Princeton, NJ: Princeton University Press, 1914).

_____, *John Marshall and the Constitution: A Chronicle of the Supreme Court* (New Haven, CT: Yale University Press, 1919).

_____, *Court over Constitution: A Study of Judicial Review as an Instrument of Popular Government* (Princeton, NJ: Princeton University Press, 1938).

Duram, James C., *A Moderate among Extremists: Dwight D. Eisenhower and the School Desegregation Crisis* (Chicago, IL: Nelson-Hall, 1981).

Ely, John Hart, *Democracy and Distrust: A Theory of Judicial Review* (Cambridge, MA: Harvard University Press, 1980).

Farber, Daniel A., "The Supreme Court and the Rule of Law: *Cooper v. Aaron* Revisited," *University of Illinois Law Review* (1982): 387.

Faulkner, Robert K., *The Jurisprudence of John Marshall* (Princeton, NJ: Princeton University Press, 1968).

Federalist Society, "The Great Debate: Interpreting Our Constitution," Occasional Paper No. 2 (Washington, D.C.: The Federalist Society, 1986).

Fisher, Louis, "Constitutional Interpretation by Members of Congress," 63 *North Carolina Law Review* (1985): 701.

Garraty, John A., "The Case of the Missing Commissions," in *Quarrels that Have Shaped the Constitution*, rev. ed., John A. Garraty, ed. (New York, NY: Harper, 1987).

Garvey, John H., and T. Alexander Aleinikoff, eds., *Modern Constitutional Theory: A Reader*, 3rd ed. (St. Paul, MN: West, 1994).

Gunther, Gerald, "The Subtle Vices of the 'Passive Virtues'—A Comment on

Principle and Expediency in Judicial Review," 64 *Columbia Law Review* (1964): 1.

_____, "Judicial Hegemony & Legislative Autonomy: The *Nixon* Case and the Impeachment Process," 22 *UCLA Law Review* (1974): 30.

Hager, L. Michael, "The Constitution, the Court and the Cover-Up: Reflections on *United States v. Nixon*," 29 *Oklahoma Law Review* (1976): 591, 596.

Haines, Charles Grove, *The Role of the Supreme Court in American Government and Politics, 1789–1835* (Berkeley, CA: University of California Press, 1944).

_____, *The American Doctrine of Judicial Supremacy*, 2nd ed. (New York, NY: Russell and Russell, 1959).

Jacobsohn, Gary J., *The Supreme Court and the Decline of Constitutional Aspiration* (Totowa, NJ: Rowman & Littlefield, 1986).

Konefsky, Samuel J., *John Marshall and Alexander Hamilton* (New York, NY: Macmillan, 1964).

Lasser, William, *The Limits of Judicial Power: The Supreme Court in American Politics* (Chapel Hill, NC: University of North Carolina Press, 1988).

Levinson, Sanford, *Constitutional Faith* (Princeton, NJ: Princeton University Press, 1988).

Levy, Leonard W., ed., *Judicial Review and the Supreme Court: Selected Essays* (New York, NY: Harper and Row, 1967).

Maltz, Earl M., *Rethinking Constitutional Law: Originalism, Interventionism, and the Politics of Judicial Review* (Lawrence, KS: University Press of Kansas, 1994).

Meese, Edwin, III, "The Law of the Constitution," 61 *Tulane Law Review* (1987): 979.

Mikva, Abner J., "How Well Does Congress Support and Defend the Constitution?" 61 *North Carolina Law Review* (1983): 587.

Nagel, Robert F., *Judicial Power and American Character: Censoring Ourselves in an Anxious Age* (New York, NY: Oxford University Press, 1994).

National Legal Center for the Public Interest, *Politics and the Constitution: The Nature and Extent of Interpretation* (Washington, D.C.: The American Studies Center, 1990).

Peller, Gary, "Neutral Principles in the 1950s," 21 *Michigan Journal of Legal Reference* (1988): 561.

Perry, Michael J., *The Constitution, the Courts, and Human Rights: An Inquiry into the Legitimacy of Constitutional Policymaking by the Judiciary* (New Haven, CT: Yale University Press, 1982).

_____, *The Constitution in the Courts: Law or Politics* (New York, NY: Oxford University Press, 1994).

Slotnik, Elliot E., "The Place of Judicial Review in the American Tradition," *Judicature* (1987): 68.

Snowiss, Sylvia, *Judicial Review and the Law of the Constitution* (New Haven, CT: Yale University Press, 1990).

Sunstein, Cass R., *The Partial Constitution* (Cambridge, MA: Harvard University Press, 1993).

Van Alstyne, William, "A Critical Guide to *Marbury v. Madison*," *Duke Law Journal* (1969): 1.

Wechsler, Herbert, "Toward Neutral Principles of Constitutional Law," 73 *Harvard Law Review* (1959): 1

———, The Courts and the Constitution," 65 *Columbia Law Review* (1965): 1001.

Wellington, Harry H., *Interpreting the Constitution: The Supreme Court and the Process of Adjudication* (New Haven, CT: Yale University Press, 1990).

White, G. Edward, *Intervention and Detachment: Essays in Legal History and Jurisprudence* (New York, NY: Oxford University Press, 1994).

Wolfe, Christopher, *The Rise of Modern Judicial Review: From Constitutional Interpretation to Judge-Made Law* (New York, NY: Basic Books, 1986).

———, *Judicial Activism: Bulwark of Freedom or Precarious Security?* (Pacific Grove, CA: Brooks/Cole, 1991).

JUDICIAL REVIEW OF STATE ACTIONS

Chisholm v. Georgia
2 Dallas 419 (1793)

SETTING

Creation of a national judiciary in Article III of the Constitution proved to be a very controversial topic during the Philadelphia Constitutional Convention. One of the reasons opponents of the Constitution objected to it was that they feared that under Article III states would be subject to suit in federal court, which, it was argued, would destroy the states as sovereign political entities. During the Convention, Virginia delegate James Madison denied that states could be made defendants in federal suits, while fellow Virginian Edmond Randolph went on record stating that they could be. The question was not definitively resolved by the broad language of Article III, which refers merely to "The judicial Power of the United States."

Virginia delegate George Mason refused to sign the proposed

Constitution and lobbied against its ratification because of his fear that it would subject states to lawsuits in federal court. In *Federalist* No. 81, however, Alexander Hamilton declared such fears to be "without foundation." Hamilton wrote, "It is inherent in the nature of sovereignty not to be amenable to the suit of an individual *without its consent.* This is the general sense and the general practice of mankind; and the exemption, as one of the attributes of sovereignty, is now enjoyed by the government of every State in the Union" (emphasis in original).

Despite Hamilton's efforts to quell the fears of states' rights advocates, the question of whether states could be sued in federal court without their consent became the subject of litigation almost immediately after the Constitution was ratified. The first suit brought in the Supreme Court's 1791 Term, for example, was against the state of Maryland by a group of Dutch bankers as creditors. Other suits involving states as defendants also appeared on the Court's docket. Those suits caused great alarm among states' rights adherents, but it was a suit brought at the August 1792 Term that gave the Court its first opportunity to rule on whether states can be sued in federal court without their consent. The case arose out of a debt owed by the state of Georgia to the estate of a merchant.

On October 31, 1777, the state of Georgia, acting through agents Edward Davies and Thomas Stone, contracted with Robert Farquhar, a British merchant living in South Carolina, for the purchase of a large quantity of goods, to be delivered on or before December 1, 1777. Farquhar delivered the goods as promised, but Davies and Stone never paid for them, despite Farquhar's many demands. Farquhar still had not received payment in January 1784, when he accidentally drowned. The executor of his estate, Alexander Chisholm of Charleston, South Carolina, continued to attempt to collect the debt.

In 1789, Chisholm presented a petition to the Georgia legislature requesting payment of the debt. That body investigated the claim and found it to be valid, but concluded that the fault for failure to pay the debt lay with Davies and Stone, not with the state of Georgia. Chisholm then filed suit against Georgia in the U.S. Circuit Court for the District of Georgia. The court issued a summons to Governor Edward Telfair, requiring him or a representative of the state to appear. Legal proceedings were delayed while Telfair sought advice about how to respond to the suit. When the case was called for argument at the October 1791 Term, Telfair claimed that no federal court had jurisdiction over a suit against Georgia unless the state consented to it. Chisholm filed a demurrer, stating that the case should proceed, because Article III of the Constitution explicitly extends the judicial power of the United States to controversies between states and citizens of other states.

The circuit court agreed with Telfair and dismissed the case for want of jurisdiction. Chisholm then filed suit in the Supreme Court of the United States at its August 1792 Term.

Do not have 11'th Amend yet (handwritten)

HIGHLIGHTS OF SUPREME COURT ARGUMENTS

BRIEF FOR CHISHOLM

◆ The clear language of Article III gives the Supreme Court jurisdiction over a state as a defendant when it is sued by a private citizen of another state.

◆ There are many evils that could be enumerated that could not be corrected if a citizen could not sue the state.

◆ The present Constitution produced a new order of things. Whereas the Articles of Confederation derived its authority from the sovereign states, this Constitution derives its authority from the people. The Constitution diminishes the sovereignty of the states, at least to the point of making them defendants in some legal actions.

Note: The state of Georgia did not appear. However, on December 14, 1792, the Georgia House of Representatives adopted a resolution stating that Article III did not give the Supreme Court jurisdiction over suits against states by citizens of other states and declaring that the state would treat any judgment entered in the case as unconstitutional.

SUPREME COURT DECISION: 4–1

(delivered *seriatim*)

Supreme Court has no jurisdiction on this case (handwritten)

IREDELL, J.

... The question ... is will an action of *assumpsit* [a common law action for damages for the nonperformance of a contract] lie against a State? If it will, it must be in virtue of the Constitution of the United States, and of some law of Congress conformable thereto. The part of the Constitution concerning the Judicial Power is ... Art.3. sect. 2....

The Supreme Court hath ... First. Exclusive jurisdiction in every controversy of a civil nature: 1st. Between two or more States. 2nd. Between a State and a foreign State. 3rd. Where a suit or proceeding is depending against Ambassadors, other public ministers, or their domestics, or domestic servants. Second. Original, but not exclusive jurisdiction. 1st. Between a State and citizens of other States. 2nd. Between a State and foreign citizens or

No power to enforce (handwritten)

subjects. 3rd. Where a suit is brought by Ambassadors, or other public ministers. 4th. Where a consul or vice-consul, is a party. The suit now before the Court (if maintainable at all) comes within the latter description, it being a suit against a State by a citizen of another State.

The Constitution is particular in expressing the parties who may be the objects of the jurisdiction in any of these cases, but in respect to the subject-matter upon which such jurisdiction is to be exercised, uses the word "controversies" only. The [Judiciary Act] more particularly mentions civil controversies, a qualification of the general word in the Constitution, which I do not doubt every reasonable man will think well warranted, for it cannot be presumed that the general word, "controversies" intended to include any proceedings that relate to criminal cases, which in all instances that respect the same Government, only, are uniformly considered of a local nature, and to be decided by its particular laws....

A general question of great importance here occurs. What controversy of a civil nature can be maintained against a State by an individual? The framers of the Constitution, I presume, must have meant one of two things: Either 1. In the conveyance of that part of the judicial power which did not relate to the execution of the other authorities of the general Government (which it must be admitted are full and discretionary, within the restrictions of the Constitution itself), to refer to antecedent laws for the construction of the general words they use: Or, 2. To enable Congress in all such cases to pass all such laws, as they might deem necessary and proper to carry the purposes of this Constitution into full effect, either absolutely at their discretion, or at least in cases where prior laws were deficient for such purposes, if any such deficiency existed.... I conceive, that all the Courts of the United States must receive, not merely their organization as to the number of Judges of which they are to consist; but all their authority, as to the manner of their proceeding, from the Legislature only....

The Judicial power is of a peculiar kind. It is indeed commensurate with the ordinary Legislative and Executive powers of the general government, and the Power which concerns treaties. But it also goes further. Where certain parties are concerned, although the subject in controversy does not relate to any of the special objects of authority of the general government, wherein the separate sovereignties of the States are blended in one common mass of supremacy, yet the general Government has a Judicial Authority in regard to such subjects of controversy, and the Legislature of the United States may pass all laws necessary to give such Judicial Authority its proper effect. So far as States under the Constitution can be made legally liable to this authority, so far to be sure they are subordinate to the authority of the United States, and their individual sovereignty is in this respect limited. But it is limited no farther than the necessary execution of such authority requires. The authority extends only to the decision of controversies in which a State is a party, and providing laws necessary for that purpose. That surely can refer only to such controversies in which a State can be a party; in respect to which, if any question arises, it can be determined, according to the principles I have supported, in no other manner than by a reference either to pre-existent laws, or laws passed under the Constitution and in conformity to it....

If therefore, no new remedy be provided (as plainly is the case), and consequently we have no other rule to govern us but the principles of the pre-existent laws, which must remain in force till superceded by others, then it is incumbent upon us to enquire, whether previous to the adoption of the Constitution ... an action of the nature like this before the Court could have been maintained against one of the States in the Union upon the principles of the common law, which I have shown to be alone applicable. If it could, I think it is now maintainable here: If it could not, I think, as the law stands at present, it is not maintainable; whatever opinion may be entertained; upon the construction of the Constitution, as to the power of

Congress to authorize such a one. Now I presume it will not be denied, that in every State in the Union, previous to the adoption of the Constitution, the only common law principles in regard to suits that were in any manner admissible in respect to claims against the State, were those which in England apply to claims against the crown[.]...

I have now, I think, established the following particulars. 1st. That the Constitution, so far as it respects the judicial authority, can only be carried into effect by acts of the Legislature appointing Courts, and prescribing their methods of proceeding. 2nd. That Congress has provided no new law in regard to this case, but expressly referred us to the old. 3rd. That there are no principles of the old law, to which we must have recourse, that in any manner authorise the present suit, either by precedent or by analogy. The consequence of which, in my opinion, clearly is, that the suit in question cannot be maintained, nor, of course, the motion made upon it be complied with....

BLAIR, J.

... The Constitution of the United States ... is obligatory upon every member of the Union; for, no State could have become a member, but by an adoption of it by the people of that State. What then do we find there requiring the submission of individual States to the judicial authority of the United States? This is expressly extended, among other things, to controversies between a State and citizens of another State. Is then the case before us one of that description? Undoubtedly it is[.]... After describing, generally, the judicial powers of the

United States, the Constitution goes on to speak of it distributively, and gives to the Supreme Court original jurisdiction, among other instances, in the case where a State shall be a party; but is not a State a party as well in the condition of a Defendant as in that of a Plaintiff? And is the whole force of that expression satisfied by confining its meaning to the case of a Plaintiff-State? It seems to me, that if this Court should refuse to hold jurisdiction of a case where a State is Defendant, it would renounce part of the authority conferred, and, consequently, part of the duty imposed on it by the Constitution; because it would be a refusal to take cognizance of a case where a State is a party. Nor does the jurisdiction of this Court, in relation to a State, seem to me to be questionable, on the ground that Congress has not provided any form of execution, or pointed out any mode of making the judgment against a State effectual[.]...

WILSON, J.

... The question to be determined is, whether this State ... is amenable to the jurisdiction of the Supreme Court of the United States? This question, important in itself, will depend on others, more important still; and, may, perhaps, be ultimately resolved into one, no less radical than this "do the people of the United States form a Nation?"...

To the Constitution of the United States the term SOVEREIGN, is totally unknown. There is but one place where it could have been used with propriety. But, even in that place it would not, perhaps, have comported with the delicacy of those, who ordained and established that Constitution. They might have announced themselves "SOVEREIGN" people of the United States: But serenely conscious of the fact, they avoided the ostentatious declaration....

Let a State be considered as subordinate to the People: But let every thing else be subordinate to the State. The latter part of this position is equally necessary with the former. For in the practice, and even at length, in the science of politics there has very frequently been a strong current against the natural order of things, and an inconsiderate or an interested disposition to sacrifice the end to the means. As the State has claimed precedence of the people; so, in the same inverted course of things, the Government has often claimed precedence of the State; and to this perversion in the second degree, many of the volumes of confusion concerning sovereignty owe their existence....

Is the foregoing description of a State a true description? It will not be questioned but it is. Is there any part of this description, which intimates, in the remotest manner, that a State, any more than the men who compose it, ought not to do justice and fulfil engagements? It will not be pretended that there is. If justice is not done; if engagements are not fulfilled; is it upon general principles of right, less proper, in the case of a great number, than in the case of an individual, to secure, by compulsion, that, which will not be voluntarily performed? Less proper it surely cannot be.... A State, like a merchant, makes a contract. A dishonest State, like a dishonest merchant, wilfully refuses to discharge it: The latter is amenable to a Court of Justice: Upon general principles of right, shall the former when summoned to answer the fair demands of its creditor, be permitted, proteus-like, to assume a new appearance, and to insult

him and justice, by declaring I am a Sovereign State? Surely not....

I have now fixed, in the scale of things, the grade of a State; and have described its composure[.]... I find nothing, which tends to evince an exemption of the State of Georgia, from the jurisdiction of the Court. I find everything to have a contrary tendency....

[O]ur national scene opens with the most magnificent object, which the nation could present. "The PEOPLE of the United States" are the first personages introduced. Who were those people? They were the citizens of thirteen States, each of which had a separate Constitution and Government, and all of which were connected together by articles of confederation. To the purposes of public strength and felicity, that confederacy was totally inadequate. A requisition on the several States terminated its Legislative authority: Executive or Judicial authority it had none. In order, therefore, to form a more perfect union, to establish justice, to ensure domestic tranquillity, to provide for common defence, and to secure the blessings of liberty, those people, among whom were the people of Georgia, ordained and established the present Constitution. By that Constitution Legislative power is vested, Executive power is vested, Judicial power is vested....

Whoever considers, in a combined and comprehensive view, the general texture of the Constitution, will be satisfied, that the people of the United States intended to form themselves into a nation for national purposes. They instituted, for such purposes, a national Government, complete in all its parts, with powers Legislative, Executive and

Judiciary; and, in all those powers, extending over the whole nation. Is it congruous, that, with regard to such purposes, any man or body of men, any person natural or artificial, should be permitted to claim successfully an entire exemption from the jurisdiction of the national Government? Would not such claims, crowned with success, be repugnant to our very existence as a nation? When so many trains of deduction, coming from different quarters, converge and unite, at last, in the same point; we may safely conclude, as the legitimate result of this Constitution, that the State of Georgia is amenable to the jurisdiction of this Court....

CUSHING, J. *court has jurisiton*

The ... question in this case is, whether a State can, by the Federal Constitution, be sued by an individual citizen of another State?

The point turns ... upon the Constitution established by the people of the United States; and particularly upon the extent of powers given to the Federal Judicial in the second section of the third article of the Constitution.... The judicial power ... is expressly extended to "controversies between a State and citizens of another State." When a citizen makes a demand against a state, of which he is not a citizen, it is as really a controversy between a State and a citizen of another State, as if such State made a demand against such citizen. The case, then, seems clearly to fall within the letter of the Constitution. It may be suggested that it could not be intended to subject a State to be a Defendant, because it would effect the sovereignty of States. If that be the case, what shall we do with the immediate preceding clause; "controversies between two or more States, where a State must of necessity be Defendant." If it was not the intent, in the very next clause also, that a State might be made Defendant, why was it so expressed as naturally to lead to and comprehend that idea? Why was not an exception made if one was intended?

Again what are we to do with the last clause of the section of judicial powers, viz. "Controversies between a state, or the citizens thereof, and foreign states or citizens?" Here again, States must be suable or liable to be made Defendants by this clause, which has a similar mode of language with the two other clauses I have remarked upon. For if the judicial power extends to a controversy between one of the United States and a foreign State, as the clause expresses, one of them must be Defendant. And then, what becomes of the sovereignty of States as far as suing affects it? But although the words appear reciprocally to affect the State here and a foreign State, and put them on the same footing as far as may be, yet ingenuity may say, that the State here may sue, but cannot be sued; but that the foreign State may be sued but cannot sue. We may touch foreign sovereignties but not our own. But I conceive the reason of the thing, as well as the words of the Constitution, tend to show that the Federal Judicial power extends to a suit brought by a foreign State against any one of the United States.... States at home and their citizens, and foreign States and their citizens, are put together without distinction upon the same footing, as far as may be, as to controversies between them. So also, with respect to controversies between a State and citizens of another State (at home) comparing all the clauses together, the remedy is reciprocal; the claim to justice equal. As controversies between State and State, and between a State and citizens of another State, might tend gradually to involve States in war and bloodshed, a disinterested civil tribunal was intended to be instituted to decide such controversies, and preserve peace and friendship. Further; if a State is entitled to Justice in the Federal Court, against a citizen of another State, why not such citizen against the State, when the same language equally comprehends both? The rights of individuals and the justice due to them, are as dear and precious as those of States. Indeed the latter are founded upon the former; and the great end and object of them must be to secure and support the rights of individuals, or else vain is Government.

But still it may be insisted, that this will reduce States to mere corporations, and take away all sovereignty. As to corporations, all States whatever are corporations or bodies politic. The only question is, what are their powers? As to individual States and the United States, the Constitution arks the boundary of powers. Whatever power is deposited with the Union by the people for their own necessary security, is so far a curtailing of the power and prerogatives of States. This is, as it were, a self-evident proposition; at least it cannot be contested....

Upon the whole, I am of opinion, that the Constitution warrants a suit against a State, by an individual citizen of another State.

A second question made in the case was, whether the particular action of assumpsit could lie against a State? I think assumpsit will lie, if any suit; provided a State is capable of contracting.

JAY, C.J.

... The question now before us renders it necessary to pay particular attention to that part of the second section [of Article III of the Constitution], which extends the judicial power "to controversies between a state and citizens of another state." It is contended, that this ought to be construed to reach none of these controversies, excepting those in which a State may be Plaintiff. The ordinary rules for construction will easily decide whether those words are to be understood in that limited sense....

If we attend to the words, we find them to be express, positive, free from ambiguity, and without room for such implied expressions: "The judicial power of the United States shall extend to controversies between a state and citizens of another state." If the Constitution really meant to extend these powers only to those controversies in which a State might be Plaintiff, to the exclusion of those in which citizens had demands against a State, it is inconceivable that it should have attempted to convey that meaning in words, not only so incompetent, but also repugnant to it; if it meant to exclude a certain class of these controversies, why were they not expressly excepted; on the contrary, not even an intimation of such intention appears in any part of the Constitution....

I am clearly of opinion, that a State is suable by citizens of another State; but lest I should be understood in a latitude beyond my meaning, I think it necessary to subjoin this caution, viz, That such suability may nevertheless not extend to all the demands, and to every kind of action; there may be exceptions. For instance, I am far from being pre-

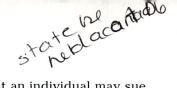

pared to say that an individual may sue a State on bills of credit issued before the Constitution was established, and which were issued and received on the faith of the State, and at a time when no ideas or expectations of judicial interposition were entertained or contemplated....

It is ordered, that the Plaintiff in this cause do file his declaration on or before the first day of March next.

Ordered, that certified copies of the said declaration be served on the Governor and Attorney General of the State of Georgia, on or before the first day of June next.

Ordered, that unless the said State shall either in due form appear, or show cause to the contrary in this Court, by the first day of next Term, judgment by default shall be entered against the said State....

QUESTIONS

1. Read Article III, section 2, of the Constitution. Does it clearly give the Supreme Court jurisdiction over the states? What language is dispositive? Compare the language of Article III with the language in the Preamble to the Constitution. Does the Preamble help to resolve the question? Political scientist C. Herman Pritchett wrote of the *Chisholm* decision:

   > [I]n *Chisholm*, the Supreme Court improperly and imprudently interpreted [the Constitution] as permitting a state to be made a defendant in a suit brought by citizens of another state. Georgia then refused to permit the decree to be enforced, and widespread protests against the Court's action resulted in its prompt reversal by adoption of the Eleventh Amendment. Later the Court [in *Hans v. Louisiana*, 134 U.S. 1 (1890)] itself admitted that the *Chisholm* decision was wrong. (*The American Constitution* [New York, NY: McGraw-Hill, 1959], p. 122)

   Does the language of Article III support Pritchett's view that *Chisholm* was "improperly and imprudently" decided? Do "improper and imprudent" decisions undermine the authority of judicial review?

2. Supreme Court historian Charles Warren reported that the *Chisholm* decision "fell upon the country with a profound shock. Both the Bar and the public in general appeared entirely unprepared for the doctrine upheld by the Court; and their surprise was warranted, when they recalled the fact that the vesting of any such jurisdiction over sovereign States had been expressly disclaimed and even resented by the great defenders of the Constitution, during the days of the contest over its adoption" (*The Supreme Court in United States History*, 2 vols. [Boston, MA: Little Brown, 1926], I: 96). Would the country find the *Chisholm* result shocking today? If not, what has changed regarding beliefs about state versus national sovereignty?

3. Counsel for Chisholm observed during oral argument that if a state resisted the exercise of the Supreme Court's jurisdiction over it, it

would fall to the executive to solve the problem that would result. Counsel observed,

> I will not believe that in the wide and gloomy theatre, over which his [the executive's] eye should roll, he might perchance catch a distant glimpse of the federal arm uplifted. Scenes like these are too full of horror, not to agitate, not to rack, the imagination. But at last we must settle on this result: There are many duties, precisely defined, which the states must perform. Let the remedy which is to be administered, if these should be disobeyed, be the remedy on the occasion, which we contemplate. The argument requires no more to be said; it surely does not require us to dwell on such painful possibilities.

In modern terms, what was Chisholm's counsel saying? Does his argument presuppose that the majority of states would be willing or unwilling to submit to the Court's jurisdiction?

COMMENTS

1. At the time *Chisholm* was decided, the Court followed the British tradition of issuing its opinions *seriatim*; that is, each justice stated his views in a series of separate opinions, with no single opinion representing the whole Court. Chief Justice John Marshall ended the practice of *seriatim* opinion writing. He strove to have the Court speak with one voice, merely one of his efforts to increase the authority and stature of the national judicial branch. Thomas Jefferson was a vehement opponent of ending the practice of *seriatim* opinion writing.

2. The negative political response to the Court's decision in *Chisholm* was intense. For example, the Georgia House of Representatives passed a bill in 1793 stating that "any Federal Marshall, or any other person," seeking to enforce *Chisholm v. Georgia* was "guilty of a felony, and shall suffer death, without benefit of clergy, by being hanged." At the next session of Congress after the *Chisholm* decision was announced a constitutional amendment was proposed to respond to it. The Eleventh Amendment was quickly approved by both the House and Senate. As ratified in February 1795, it provides that:

> The Judicial power of the United States shall not be construed to extend to any suit in law or equity, commenced or prosecuted against one of the United States by Citizens of another State, or by Citizens or Subjects of any Foreign State.

Chief Justice Marshall, the staunch advocate of both a strong national government and a powerful federal judiciary, was the first to construe the Eleventh Amendment. See *Cohens v. Virginia*, 6 Wheaton 264 (1821), excerpted on pp. 103–112.

3. Supreme Court historian Maeva Marcus reports that Alexander Chisholm did not actively pursue the case after 1794 because the Georgia legislature settled the Farquhar claim. As Marcus observes, the settlement was advisable because "even if the Supreme Court awarded damages in *Chisholm*, Georgia might never comply with the ruling, so it was better to take what he could get from the legislature" (*The Documentary History of the Supreme Court of the United States, 1789–1800*, vol. 5 [New York, NY: Columbia University Press, 1994], p. 135–136).

4. After delivering the *Chisholm* decision, the Court issued no further opinions for a year, because yellow fever was raging in Philadelphia, where the Court met at that time. *yellow fever*

JUDICIAL REVIEW OF STATE ACTIONS

Martin v. Hunter's Lessee
1 Wheaton 304 (1816)

SETTING

In *Marbury v. Madison*, John Marshall asserted the Supreme Court's power to nullify acts of Congress deemed to conflict with the Constitution. It was not clear from *Marbury*, however, whether the doctrine of judicial review included the power to rule on the constitutionality of state actions or to review the decisions of state courts. Section 25 of the Judiciary Act of 1789, which appeared to answer that question affirmatively and uphold the principle of federal supremacy, was not an issue in *Marbury*.

Section 25 authorized appeals to the Supreme Court of the United States from the highest state court under three circumstances: (1) when a state court had declared unconstitutional a federal law or treaty; (2) when a state court had upheld a state act that had been challenged as conflicting with the Constitution, treaties, or laws of the United States; or (3) when a state court had ruled against a right or privilege claimed under the federal Constitution or federal law. The character of jurisdiction conferred by Section 25 was at the center of the controversy in *Martin v. Hunter's Lessee*, a property case that also put the issue of states' rights versus federal judicial power high on the Court's agenda.

The case arose from the estate of Thomas Lord Fairfax, a British loyalist who fled to England during the Revolution. He owned some 300,000 acres of valuable timber and tobacco land on the Potomac River in Shenandoah County located in the Northern Neck of Virginia. Fairfax died in England in December 1781. By will, he bequeathed his prime American real estate to his nephew, Denny Martin, a British citizen. Martin was an enemy alien during the Revolutionary War. The State of Virginia contested Martin's inheritance, claiming that, under state law, aliens could not inherit property. Furthermore, Virginia had passed a series of laws confiscating the lands of British aliens during the Revolutionary War. It claimed that in 1777 Lord Fairfax's property had been confiscated by the state and that in 1789 it had sold a 788-acre tract of the property to David Hunter.

In 1791, David Hunter filed an action against Denny Martin in a district court of Virginia to eject Martin from the property. The trial court held for Martin in 1794. Further proceedings were postponed for sixteen years, while John Marshall, as a member of the Virginia legislature, negotiated a compromise between the state and the Fairfax heirs. That compromise failed to resolve the controversy between David Hunter and Denny Martin, however. In 1810, the Virginia Supreme Court of Appeals heard the case and reversed the trial court, giving judgment for Hunter. By the time the Virginia Supreme Court of Appeals ruled, Denny Martin had died. Philip Martin, his heir, removed the case to the Supreme Court of the United States.

In 1813, in *Fairfax's Devisee v. Hunter's Lessee*, 7 Cranch 603, the Supreme Court reversed the Virginia Supreme Court of Appeals. It ruled that the Treaty of Paris of 1783 and Jay's Treaty of 1795, affirming the rights of aliens to own land in the United States, overrode Virginia law. The Supreme Court remanded the case to the Virginia Supreme Court of Appeals with the instructions: "You are hereby commanded that such proceedings be had in said cause, as according to right and justice, and the laws of the United States, and agreeably to said judgment...."

On December 16, 1815, a unanimous Virginia Supreme Court of Appeals refused to recognize those instructions. It held that

> the appellate power of the Supreme Court of the United States does not extend to this Court, under a sound construction of the Constitution of the United States; that so much of the Twenty-fifth Section of the Act [Judiciary Act of 1789] ... to establish the Judicial Courts of the United States as extends the appellate jurisdiction of the Supreme Court to this Court, is not in pursuance of the Constitution of the United States ... and that obedience to [the Supreme Court's] mandate be declined by this court.

The Virginia court insisted that, when determining the validity of Virginia's laws, its interpretation could not be reviewed by the Supreme Court of the United States because the states were coequal sovereigns with the federal government.

The Virginia Court's refusal to comply with the Supreme Court's mandate resulted in a second writ of error, which brought the controversy back to the Supreme Court.

HIGHLIGHTS OF SUPREME COURT ARGUMENTS

BRIEF FOR MARTIN

◆ Ratification of the Constitution should have ended the debate about whether federal judicial authority extends to a review of state court decision.

◆ This government is no longer a confederacy. In its legislative, executive, and judicial authorities, it is a national government. The national government pervades their territory and acts upon all their citizens.

◆ Under the Constitution, the federal judiciary has exclusive authority to interpret treaties. Since state legislatures cannot make treaties, neither can state judiciaries expound upon them.

◆ The words "shall extend" in Article III, Section 2, describing the judicial power of the national government, express an imperative mandate. The power to review decisions of state courts on questions of federal law is inherent in the Supreme Court's appellate jurisdiction, because state courts are bound by the Constitution to adjudicate cases under the supreme law of the land.

BRIEF FOR HUNTER

◆ Section 2 of the Judiciary Act does not apply in this case because the original cause is not before the Supreme Court. The state court of appeals has done nothing, so there can be no error in its proceedings.

◆ Recognizing federal jurisdiction in this case would violate the genius, spirit, and tenor of the Constitution. The whole scheme of the Constitution aims at acting on citizens of the United States at large, not on state authorities.

◆ State courts are bound by treaties as a part of the supreme law of the land, and must construe them in order to obey them.

◆ The Constitution does not give the Supreme Court appellate jurisdiction. Such jurisdiction is neither expressed nor implied.

◆ Attempting to establish appellate jurisdiction over state court actions will begin a conflict between national and state authorities that may ultimately involve both in one common ruin. The taper of judicial discord may become the torch of civil war.

SUPREME COURT DECISION: 6–0

(Marshall, C.J., did not participate.)

STORY, J.

… The questions involved in this judgment are of great importance and delicacy. Perhaps it is not too much to affirm, that, upon their right decision, rest some of the most solid principles which have hitherto been supposed to sustain and protect the constitution itself.…

The constitution of the United States was ordained and established, not by the states in their sovereign capacities, but emphatically, as the preamble of the

*Question Georgia
section 25 should*

Art III

constitution declares, by "the people of the United States." There can be no doubt that it was competent to the people to invest the general government with all the powers which they might deem proper and necessary; to extend or restrain these powers according to their own good pleasure, and to give them a paramount and supreme authority. As little doubt can there be, that the people had a right to prohibit to the states the exercise of any powers which were, in their judgment, incompatible with the objects of the general compact; to make the powers of the state governments, in given cases, subordinate to those of the nation, or to reserve to themselves those sovereign authorities which they might not choose to delegate to either. The constitution was not, therefore, necessarily carved out of existing state sovereignties, nor a surrender of powers already existing in state institutions, for the powers of the states depend upon their own constitutions; and the people of every state had the right to modify and restrain them, according to their own views of the policy or principle. On the other hand, it is perfectly clear that the sovereign powers vested in the state governments, by their respective constitutions, remained unaltered and unimpaired, except so far as they were granted to the government of the United States.

These deductions do not rest upon general reasoning, plain and obvious as they seem to be. They have been positively recognised by one of the articles in amendment of the constitution, which declares, that "the powers not delegated to the United States by the constitution, nor prohibited by it to the states, are reserved to the states respectively, or to the people." The government, then, of the United States, can claim no powers which are not granted to it by the constitution, and the powers actually granted, must be such as are expressly given, or given by necessary implication. On the other hand, this instrument, like every other grant, is to have a reasonable construction, according to the import of its terms; and where a power is expressly given in general terms, it is not to be restrained to particular cases, unless that construction grow out of the context expressly, or by necessary implication. The words are to be taken in their natural and obvious sense, and not in a sense unreasonably restricted or enlarged.

The constitution unavoidably deals in general language. It did not suit the purposes of the people, in framing this great charter of our liberties, to provide for minute specifications of its powers, or to declare the means by which those powers should be carried into execution. It was foreseen that this would be a perilous and difficult, if not an impracticable, task. The instrument was not intended to provide merely for the exigencies of a few years, but was to endure through a long lapse of ages, the events of which were locked up in the inscrutable purposes of Providence. It could not be foreseen what new changes and modifications of power might be indispensable to effectuate the general objects of the charter; and restrictions and specifications, which, at the present, might seem salutary, might, in the end, prove the overthrow of the system itself. Hence its powers are expressed in general terms, leaving to the legislature, from time to time, to adopt its own means to effectuate legitimate objects, and to mould and model the exercise of its powers, as its own wisdom, and the public interests, should require.

With these principles in view, principles in respect to which no difference of opinion ought to be indulged, let us now proceed to the interpretation of the constitution, so far as regards the great points in controversy.

The third article of the constitution is that which must principally attract our attention. The 1st. section declares, "the judicial power of the United States shall be vested in one supreme court, and in such other inferior courts as the congress may, from time to time, ordain and establish." The 2d section declares, that "the judicial power shall extend to all cases in law or equity, arising under this constitution, the laws of the United States, and the treaties made, or which shall be made, under their authority; to all cases affecting ambassadors, other public ministers and consuls; to all cases of admiralty and maritime jurisdiction; to controversies to which the United States shall be a party; to controversies between two or more states; between a state and citizens of another state; between citizens of different states; between citizens of the same state, claiming lands under the grants of different states; and between a state or the citizens thereof, and foreign states, citizens, or subjects." It then proceeds to declare, that "in all cases affecting ambassadors, other public ministers and consuls, and those in which a state shall be a party, the supreme court shall have original jurisdiction. In all the other cases before mentioned the supreme court shall have appellate jurisdiction, both as to law and fact, with such exceptions, and under such regulations, as the Congress shall make."

Such is the language of the article creating and defining the judicial power of the United States. It is the voice of the whole American people solemnly declared, in establishing one great department of that government which was, in many respects, national, and in all, supreme. It is a part of the very same instrument which was to act not merely upon individuals, but upon states; and to deprive them altogether of the exercise of some powers of sovereignty, and to restrain and regulate them in the exercise of others.

Let this article be carefully weighed and considered. The language of the article throughout is manifestly designed to be mandatory upon the legislature. Its obligatory force is so imperative, that Congress could not, without a violation of its duty, have refused to carry it into operation. The judicial power of the United States shall be vested (not may be vested) in one supreme court, and in such inferior courts as congress may, from time to time, ordain and establish.... The judicial power must, therefore, be vested in some court, by Congress; and to suppose that it was not an obligation binding on them, but might, at their pleasure, be omitted or declined, is to suppose that, under the sanction of the constitution, they might defeat the constitution itself; a construction which would lead to such a result cannot be sound....

If, then, it is a duty of Congress to vest the judicial power of the United States, it is a duty to vest the whole judicial power. The language, if imperative as to one part, is imperative as to all. If it were otherwise, this anomaly would exist, that Congress might successively refuse to vest the jurisdiction in any one class of cases enumerated in the constitution, and thereby defeat the jurisdiction as to all; for the constitution has not singled out any class on which congress are bound to act in preference to others....

It being, then, established that the language of this clause is imperative, the next question is as to the cases to which it shall apply. The answer is found in the constitution itself. The judicial power shall extend to all the cases enumerated in the constitution. As the mode is not limited, it may extend to all such cases, in any form, in which judicial power may be exercised. It may, therefore, extend to them in the shape of original or appellate jurisdiction, or both; for there is nothing in the nature of the cases which binds to the exercise of the one in preference to the other....

[I]t is manifest that the judicial power of the United States is unavoidably, in some cases, exclusive of all state authority, and in all others, may be made so at the election of Congress.... Congress, throughout the judicial act [of 1789], and particularly in the 9th, 11th, and 13th sections, have legislated upon the supposition that in all the cases to which the judicial powers of the United States extended, they might rightfully vest exclusive jurisdiction in their own courts....

This leads us to the consideration of the great question as to the nature and extent of the appellate jurisdiction of the United States. We have already seen that appellate jurisdiction is given by the constitution to the supreme court in all cases where it has not original jurisdiction; subject, however, to such exceptions and regulations as Congress may prescribe. It is, therefore, capable of embracing every case enumerated in the constitution, which is not exclusively to be decided by way of original jurisdiction. But the exercise of appellate jurisdiction is far from being limited by the terms of the constitution to the supreme court. There can be no doubt that congress may create a succession of inferior tribunals, in each of which it may vest appellate as well as original jurisdiction. The judicial power is delegated by the constitution in the most general terms, and may, therefore, be exercised by Congress under every variety of form, of appellate or original jurisdiction. And as there is nothing in the constitution which restrains or limits this power, it must, therefore, in all other cases, subsist in the utmost latitude of which, in its own nature, it is susceptible.

As, then, by the terms of the constitution, the appellate jurisdiction is not limited as to the supreme court, and as to this court it may be exercised in all other cases than those of which it has original cognizance, what is there to restrain its exercise over state tribunals in the enumerated cases? The appellate power is not limited by the terms of the third article to any particular courts. The words are, "the judicial power (which includes appellate power) shall extend to all cases," &c., and "in all other cases before mentioned the supreme court shall have appellate jurisdiction." It is the case, then, and not the court, that gives the jurisdiction. If the judicial power extends to the case, it will be in vain to search in the letter of the constitution for any qualification as to the tribunal where it depends....

If the constitution meant to limit the appellate jurisdiction to cases pending in the courts of the United States, it would necessarily follow that the jurisdiction of these courts would, in all the cases enumerated in the constitution, be exclusive of state tribunals.... If some of these cases might be entertained by state tribunals, and no appellate jurisdiction as to them should exist, then the appellate power would not extend to all, but to some, cases. If state tribunals might exercise concurrent jurisdiction over all or some of the other classes of cases in the constitution without control, then the appellate jurisdiction of the United States might, as to such cases, have no real existence, contrary to the manifest intent of the constitution. Under such circumstances, to give effect to the judicial power, it must be construed to be exclusive; and this not only when the *casus foederis* [the case of a treaty] should arise directly, but when it should arise, incidentally, in cases pending in state courts. This construction would abridge the jurisdiction of such court far more than has been ever contemplated in any act of Congress.

On the other hand, if, as has been contended, a discretion be vested in congress to establish, or not to establish, inferior courts at their own pleasure, and congress should not establish such courts, the appellate jurisdiction of the Supreme Court would have nothing to act upon, unless it could act upon cases pending in the state courts. Under such circumstances it must be held that the appellate power would extend to state courts; for the constitution is peremptory that it shall extend to certain enumerated cases, which cases could exist in no other courts. Any other construction, upon this supposition, would involve this strange contradiction, that a discretionary power vested in congress, and which they might rightfully omit to exercise, would defeat the absolute injunctions of the constitution in relation to the whole appellate power.

But it is plain that the framers of the constitution did contemplate that cases within the judicial cognizance of the United States not only might but would arise in the state courts, in the exercise of their ordinary jurisdiction. With this view the sixth article declares, that "this constitution, and the laws of the United States which shall be made in pursuance thereof, and all treaties made, or which shall be made, under the authority of the United States, shall be the supreme law of the land, and the judges in every state shall be bound thereby, any thing in the constitution or laws of any state to the contrary notwithstanding." It is obvious that this obligation is imperative upon the state judges in their official, and not merely in their private, capacities. From the very nature of their judicial duties they would be called upon to pronounce the law applicable to the case in judgment. They were not to decide merely according to the laws or constitution of the state, but according to the constitution, laws and treaties of the United States—"the supreme law of the land."...

It must, therefore, be conceded that the constitution not only contemplated, but meant to provide for cases within the scope of the judicial power of the United States, which might yet depend before state tribunals. It was foreseen that in the exercise of their ordinary jurisdiction, state courts would incidentally take cognizance of cases arising under the constitution, the laws, and treaties of the United States. Yet to all these cases the judicial power, by the very terms of the constitution, is to extend. It cannot extend by original jurisdiction if that was already rightfully and exclusively attached in the state courts, which (as has been already shown) may occur; it must, therefore, extend by appellate jurisdiction, or not at all. It would seem to follow that the appellate power of the United States must, in such cases, extend to state tribunals; and if in such cases, there is no reason why it should not equally attach upon all others within the purview of the constitution.

It has been argued that such an appellate jurisdiction over state courts is inconsistent with the genius of our governments, and the spirit of the constitution. That the latter was never designed to act upon state sovereignties, but only upon the people, and that if the power exists, it will materially impair the sovereignty of the states, and the independence of their courts....

[T]he constitution ... is crowded with provisions which restrain or annul the sovereignty of the states in some of the highest branches of their prerogatives. The tenth section of the first article contains a long list of disabilities and prohibitions imposed upon the states. Surely, when such essential portions of state sovereignty are taken away, or prohibited to be exercised, it cannot be correctly asserted that the constitution does not act upon the states. The language of the constitution is also imperative upon the states as to the performance of many duties.... When, therefore, the states are stripped of some of the highest attributes of sovereignty, and the same are given to the United States; when the legislatures of the states are, in some respects, under the control of congress, and in every case are, under the constitution, bound by the paramount authority of the United States; it is certainly difficult to

support the argument that the appellate power over the decisions of state courts is contrary to the genius of our institutions. The courts of the United States can, without question, revise the proceedings of the executive and legislative authorities of the states, and if they are found to be contrary to the constitution, may declare them to be of no legal validity. Surely the exercise of the same right over judicial tribunals is not a higher or more dangerous act of sovereign power.

Nor can such a right be deemed to impair the independence of state judges. It is assuming the very ground in controversy to assert that they possess an absolute independence of the United States. In respect to the powers granted to the United States, they are not independent; they are expressly bound to obedience by the letter of the constitution; and if they should unintentionally transcend their authority, or misconstrue the constitution, there is no more reason for giving their judgments an absolute and irresistible force, than for giving it to the acts of the other co-ordinate departments of state sovereignty....

On the whole, the court are of opinion, that the appellate power of the United States does extend to cases pending in the state courts; and that the 25th section of the judiciary act, which authorizes the exercise of this jurisdiction in the specified cases, by a writ of error, is supported by the letter and spirit of the constitution....

The next question which has been argued, is, whether the case at bar be within the purview of the 25th section of the judiciary act [of 1789], so that this court may rightfully sustain the present writ of error....

That the present writ of error is

founded upon a judgment of the court below, which drew in question and denied the validity of a statute of the United States, is incontrovertible, for it is apparent upon the face of the record. That this judgment is final upon the rights of the parties is equally true; for if well founded, the former judgment of that court was of conclusive authority, and the former judgment of this court utterly void. The decision was, therefore, equivalent to a perpetual stay of proceedings upon the mandate, and a perpetual denial of all the rights acquired under it. The case, then, falls directly within the terms of the act....

But it is contended, that the former judgment of this court was rendered upon a case not within the purview of this section of the judicial act, and that as it was pronounced by an incompetent jurisdiction, it was utterly void, and cannot be a sufficient foundation to sustain any subsequent proceedings. To this argument several answers may be given. In the first place, it is not admitted that, upon this writ of error, the former record is before us. The error now assigned is not in the former proceedings, but in the judgment rendered upon the mandate issued after the former judgment. The question now litigated is not upon the construction of a treaty, but upon the constitutionality of a statute of the United States, which is clearly within our jurisdiction. In the next place, in ordinary cases a second writ of error has never been supposed to draw in question the propriety of the first judgment, and it is difficult to perceive how such a proceeding could be sustained upon principle. A final judgment of this court is supposed to be conclusive upon the rights which it decides, and no statute has provided

any process by which this court can revise its own judgments....

It is the opinion of the whole court, that the judgment of the court of appeals of Virginia, rendered on the mandate in this cause, be reversed, and the judgment of the district court, held at Winchester, be, and the same is hereby affirmed.

JOHNSON, J.

... [T]his question ... presents an instance of collision between the judicial powers of the union, and one of the greatest states in the union, on a point the most delicate and difficult to be adjusted....

I must claim the privilege of expressing my regret, that the opposition of the high and truly respected tribunal of that state had not been marked with a little more moderation. The only point necessary to be decided in the case then before them was, "whether they were bound to obey the mandate emanating from this court?" But in the judgment entered on their minutes, they have affirmed that the case was, in this court, *coram non judice* [in the presence of one not authorized to judge], or, in other words, that this court had not jurisdiction over it. This is assuming a truly alarming latitude of judicial power. Where is it to end?...

[This] collision has been, on our part, wholly unsolicited.... Had [the Virginia Supreme Court of Appeals] ... refused to grant the writ in the first instance, or had the question of jurisdiction, or on the mode of exercising jurisdiction, been made here originally, we should have been put on our guard, and might have so modelled the process of the court as to strip it of the offensive form of a mandate. In this case it might have been brought down to what probably the 25th section of the judiciary act meant it should be, to wit, an alternative judgment, either that the state court may finally proceed, at its option, to carry into effect the judgment of this court, or, if it declined doing so, that then this court would proceed itself to execute it. The language, sense, and operation of the 25th section on this subject, merit particular attention…. [I]n cases brought up from the state courts; the framers of that law plainly foresaw that the state courts might refuse; and not being willing to leave ground for the implication, that compulsory process must be resorted to, because no specific provision was made, they have provided the means, by authorizing this court, in case of reversal of the state decision, to execute its own judgment…. It is true, that the words of this section are, that this court may, in their discretion, proceed to execute its own judgment. But these words were very properly put in, that it might not be made imperative upon this court to proceed indiscriminately in this way; as it could only be necessary in case of the refusal of the state courts[.]…

QUESTIONS

1. The political significance of the *Martin* decision may be understood better by considering the consequences of an opposite conclusion: What if the Supreme Court could *not* review state court decisions that construed provisions of the Constitution of the United States? Justice Story contended that the exercise of this right of appellate review was not a "dangerous act of sovereign power." Clearly, Spencer Roane, Chief Judge of the Virginia Supreme Court of Appeals did not agree. What theories of state sovereignty and national-state relations informed Story's and Roane's positions?

2. Note that the Supreme Court sent its order directly to the Virginia trial court, the District Court of Shenandoah County, in Winchester, thereby avoiding further conflict with the Virginia Court of Appeals. It is believed that the trial court enforced the ruling favoring Martin that the Supreme Court had affirmed on appeal (Sheldon Goldman, *Constitutional Law: Cases and Essays*, 2nd ed. [New York, NY: Harper & Row, 1991], p. 166). If the trial court had refused to enforce the Supreme Court's ruling, what recourse would have been available to the Supreme Court?

3. Justice Oliver Wendell Holmes Jr. once observed: "I do not think the United States would come to an end if we lost our power to declare an Act of Congress void. I do think the Union would be imperiled if we could not make that declaration as to the laws of the several States" (*Collected Legal Papers* [New York, NY: Harcourt Brace, 1920], p. 295). Does this mean that the Supreme Court's decision in *Martin* is more

important than its decision in *Marbury*? Is not *Martin* more constitutionally defensible—textually, structurally, and logically—than *Marbury*? If
so, why was *Martin* so much more controversial than *Marbury*?

4. *Martin v. Hunter's Lessee* was written by a Republican justice, Joseph
   Story. John Marshall formally recused himself because he had been
   involved in both the abortive attempt to resolve this dispute out of
   court and because he and his brother, James, had contracted to pur-
   chase a large portion of the contested land from Fairfax's heirs.
   Nevertheless, Marshall worked actively behind the scenes to
   advance *Martin*'s appeal and to influence Justice Story's opinion.
   Justice Story spoke for a majority that included four other
   Jeffersonian Republican justices. Is it not curious that Jeffersonian
   Republicans would vote counter to states' rights?

5. Analyzing the doctrines, propositions, and arguments constituting
   the *Martin* decision, the late constitutional scholar Robert G.
   McClosky wrote: "This opinion contains, in more or less explicit
   statement, practically all the major items in the bag of tricks the
   Marshall Court was to use in future years against the minions of dis-
   union" (*The American Supreme Court*, 2nd rev. ed. [Chicago, IL:
   University of Chicago Press, 1994], p. 40). Identify the items in the
   Marshall Court's "bag of tricks."

JUDICIAL REVIEW OF STATE ACTIONS

Cohens v. Virginia
6 Wheaton 264 (1821)

SETTING

Between 1819 and 1823, Thomas Jefferson issued repeated warnings against
what he called the "consolidating tendency of the Court and Congress." In
1820 he wrote, "The Judiciary of the United States is the subtle corps of sappers and miners constantly working underground to undermine the foundations of our confederated fabric. They are construing our Constitution from
a coordination of a general and special government to a general and
supreme one alone." In 1821 he added, "The Legislative and Executive
branches may sometimes err, but elections and dependence will bring them
to rights. The Judiciary branch is the instrument which, working like gravity,
without intermission, is to press us at last into one consolidated mass."
Whether the Supreme Court would continue to "undermine" Jefferson's view

that the Constitution retained a confederate form of government became an issue in a case that reached the Supreme Court in 1821.

On May 3, 1802, Congress, pursuant to the authority granted to it in Article I, section 17, of the Constitution, enacted a law organizing the District of Columbia as a corporate body politic, and authorizing it to conduct lotteries for the purpose of raising money to finance civic improvements.

On January 1, 1820, the State of Virginia enacted a law making it a crime to buy or sell lottery tickets other than those authorized by the state. Six months later, on information provided by William H. Jennings, brothers and professional lottery agents P. J. and J. M. Cohen were indicted in the Norfolk Borough Court for selling District of Columbia lottery tickets to Jennings at their office in Maxwell's wharf, contrary to the Virginia law. The Cohens defended on the grounds that the federal law authorizing the D.C. lottery made their action legal and that the Virginia law did not apply to the sale of D.C. lottery tickets. Their defense was rejected by the Quarterly Session Court for the Borough of Norfolk, and the Cohens were convicted and fined $100. They petitioned for a writ of error to the Supreme Court of the United States under Section 25 of the Judiciary Act of 1789. The State of Virginia moved to dismiss the writ for want of jurisdiction.

HIGHLIGHTS OF SUPREME COURT ARGUMENTS

BRIEF FOR THE COHENS

◆ This Court has already determined in *Martin v. Hunter's Lessee* that it may exercise jurisdiction in any appellate form.

◆ The District of Columbia is a creature of the Constitution and acts of Congress relative to it must be determined by it and must be laws of the United States.

◆ Since the adoption of the Constitution there is no such thing as a sovereign state, independent of the union. The people are the sole sovereignty of this country.

◆ No one objects to a state enforcing its own penal laws; all that is claimed is that in executing them, the state should not violate the paramount laws of the United States.

BRIEF FOR VIRGINIA

◆ The Supreme Court lacks jurisdiction over this appeal because this is not a case arising under the Constitution, as witnessed by the plain language of Article III, section 2.

◆ The legislation authorizing the District of Columbia to conduct lotteries extends only to the boundaries of the District; it is not part of the laws of the United States and consequently is not a part of the supreme law of the land.

◆ Consistent with the rule in *Marbury v. Madison*, when a state is a party to litigation, the Supreme Court's jurisdiction must be original, not appellate.

◆ This is a criminal case, in which the laws of a sovereign and independent state have been violated. Because the state is one of the parties to a criminal prosecution, it is not amenable to any judicial power without its consent.

◆ Since enactment of the Eleventh Amendment, immediately after this Court's decision in *Chisholm v. Georgia*, it is clear that this Court cannot take jurisdiction over a case in favor of a citizen of another or a foreign state. It follows logically that this Court can never take jurisdiction in favor of a citizen against his own state.

SUPREME COURT DECISION: 5–0

MARSHALL, C.J.

... The defendant in error moves to dismiss this writ, for want of jurisdiction....

The first question to be considered is, whether the jurisdiction of this Court is excluded by the character of the parties, one of them being a State, and the other a citizen of that State?...

The counsel for the defendant in error have ... laid down the general proposition, that a sovereign independent State is not suable, except by its own consent.

This general proposition will not be controverted. But its consent is not requisite in each particular case. It may be given in a general law. And if a State has surrendered any portion of its sovereignty, the question whether a liability to suit be a part of this portion, depends on the instrument by which the surrender is made. If, upon a just construction of that instrument, it shall appear that the State has submitted to be sued, then it has parted with this sovereign right of judging in every case on the justice of its own pretensions, and has entrusted that power to a tribunal in whose impartiality it confides.

The American States, as well as the American people, have believed a close and firm Union to be essential to their liberty and to their happiness. They have been taught by experience, that this Union cannot exist without a government for the whole; and they have been taught by the same experience that this government would be a mere shadow, that must disappoint all their hopes, unless invested with large portions of that sovereignty which belongs to independent States. Under the influence of this opinion, and thus instructed by experience, the American people, in the conventions of their respective States, adopted the present constitution.

If it could be doubted, whether from its nature, it were not supreme in all cases where it is empowered to act, that doubt would be removed by the declaration, that "this constitution, and the laws of the United States, which shall be made in pursuance thereof, and all treaties made, or which shall be made, under the authority of the United States, shall be the supreme law of the land; and the judges in every State shall be bound thereby; any thing in the constitution or laws of any State to the contrary notwithstanding."...

With the ample powers confided to this supreme government, for these interesting purposes, are connected many express and important limitations on the sovereignty of the States, which are made for the same purposes. The powers of the Union, on the great subjects of war, peace, and commerce, and on many others, are in themselves limitations of the sovereignty of the States; but in addition to these, the sovereignty of the States is surrendered in many instances where the surrender can only operate to the benefit of the people, and where, perhaps, no other power is conferred on Congress than a conservative power to maintain the principles established in the constitution. The maintenance of these principles in their purity, is certainly among the great duties of the government. One of the instruments by which this duty may be peaceably performed, is the judicial department. It is authorized to decide all cases of every description, arising under the constitution or laws of the United States. From this general grant of jurisdiction, no exception is made of those cases in which a State may be a party. When we consider the situation of the government of the Union and of a State, in relation to each other; the nature of our constitution; the subordination of the State governments to that constitution; the great purpose for which jurisdiction over all cases arising under the constitution and laws of the United States, is confided to the judicial department; are we at liberty to insert in this general grant, an exception of those cases in which a State may be a party? Will the spirit of the constitution justify this attempt to control its words? We think it will not. We think a case arising under the constitution or laws of the United States, is cognizable in the Courts of the Union, whoever may be the parties to that case....

After bestowing on this subject the most attentive consideration, the Court can perceive no reason founded on the character of the parties for introducing an exception which the constitution has not made; and we think that the judicial power, as originally given, extends to all cases arising under the constitution or a law of the United States, whoever may be the parties.

It has been also contended, that this jurisdiction, if given, is original, and cannot be exercised in the appellate form.

The words of the constitution are, "in all cases affecting ambassadors, other public ministers, and consuls, and those in which a State shall be a party, the Supreme Court shall have original jurisdiction. In all the other cases before mentioned, the Supreme Court shall have appellate jurisdiction."

This distinction between original and appellate jurisdiction, excludes, we are told, in all cases, the exercise of the one where the other is given.

The constitution gives the Supreme Court original jurisdiction in certain enumerated cases, and gives it appellate jurisdiction in all others. Among those in which jurisdiction must be exercised in the appellate form, are cases arising under the constitution and laws of the United States. These provisions of the constitution are equally obligatory, and are to be equally respected. If a State be a party, the jurisdiction of this Court is original; if the case arise under a constitution or a law, the jurisdiction is appellate. But a case to which a State is a party may arise under the constitution or a law of the United States. What rule is applicable to such a case? What, then, becomes the duty of the Court? Certainly, we think, so to construe the constitution as to give effect to both provisions, as far as it is possible to reconcile them, and not to permit their seeming repugnancy to destroy each other. We must endeavor so to construe them as to preserve the true intent and meaning of the instrument.

In one description of cases, the jurisdiction of the Court is founded entirely on the character of the parties; and the nature of the controversy is not contemplated by the constitution. The character of the parties is every thing, the nature of the case nothing. In the other description of cases, the jurisdiction is founded entirely on the character of the case, and the parties are not contemplated by the constitution. In these, the nature of the case is every thing, the character of the parties nothing. When, then, the constitution declares the jurisdiction, in cases where a State shall be a party, to be original, and in all cases arising under the constitution or a law, to be appellate—the conclusion seems irresistible, that its framers designed to include in the first class those cases in which jurisdiction is given, because a State is a party; and to include in the second, those in which jurisdiction is given, because the case arises under the constitution or a law....

The constitution declares, that in cases where a State is a party, the Supreme Court shall have original jurisdiction; but does not say that its appellate jurisdiction shall not be exercised in cases where, from their nature, appellate jurisdiction is given, whether a State be or be not a party. It may be conceded, that where the case is of such a nature as to admit of its originating in the Supreme Court, it ought to originate there; but where, from its nature, it cannot originate in that Court, these words ought not to be so construed as to require it. There are many cases in which it would be found extremely difficult, and subversive of the spirit of the constitution, to maintain the construction, that appellate jurisdiction cannot be exercised where one of the parties might sue or be sued in this Court....

It is most true that this Court will not take jurisdiction if it should not: but it is equally true, that it must take jurisdiction if it should. The judiciary cannot, as the legislature may, avoid a measure because it approaches the confines of the constitution. We cannot pass it by because it is doubtful. With whatever doubts, with whatever difficulties, a case may be attended, we must decide it, if it be brought before us. We have no more right to decline the exercise of jurisdiction which is given, than to usurp that which is not given. The one or the other would be treason to the constitution. Questions may occur which we would gladly avoid; but we cannot avoid them. All we can do is, to exercise our best judgment, and conscientiously to perform our duty. In doing this, on the present occasion, we find this tribunal invested with appellate jurisdiction in all cases arising under the constitution and laws of the United States. We find no exception to this grant, and we cannot insert one....

We think, then, that, as the constitution originally stood, the appellate jurisdiction of this Court, in all cases arising under the constitution, laws, or treaties of the United States, was not arrested by the circumstance that a State was a party.

This leads to a consideration of the 11th amendment....

It is a part of our history, that, at the adoption of the constitution, all the States were greatly indebted; and the apprehension that these debts might be prosecuted in the federal Courts, formed a very serious objection to that instrument. Suits were instituted; and the Court maintained its jurisdiction. The alarm was general; and, to quiet the apprehensions that were so extensively entertained, this amendment was proposed in Congress, and adopted by the State legislatures. That its motive was not to maintain the sovereignty of a State from the degradation supposed to attend a compulsory appearance before the tribunal of the nation, may be inferred from the terms of the amendment. It does not comprehend controversies between two or more States, or between a State and a foreign State. The jurisdiction of the Court still extends to these cases: and in these a State may still be sued. We must ascribe the amendment, then, to some other cause than the dignity of a State. There is no difficulty in finding this cause. Those who were inhibited from commencing a suit against a State, or from prosecuting one which might be commenced before the adoption of the amendment, were persons who might probably be its creditors. There was not much reason to fear that foreign or sister States would be creditors to any considerable amount, and there was reason to retain the jurisdiction of the Court in those cases, because it might be essential to the preservation of peace. The amendment, therefore, extended to suits commenced or prosecuted by individuals, but not to those brought by States....

A writ of error is defined to be, a commission by which the judges of one Court are authorized to examine a record upon which a judgment was given in another Court, and, on such examination, to affirm or reverse the same according to law.... A writ of error, then, is in the nature of a suit or action when it is to restore the party who obtains it to the possession of any thing which is withheld from him, not when its operation is entirely defensive....

Under the judiciary act [of 1789], the effect of a writ of error is simply to bring the record into Court, and submit the judgment of the inferior tribunal to re-examination. It does not in any manner act upon the parties; it acts only on the record. It removes the record into the supervising tribunal. Where, then, a State obtains a judgment against an individual, and the Court, rendering such judgment, overrules a defence set up under the constitution or laws of the United States, the transfer of this record into the Supreme Court, for the sole purpose of inquiring whether the judgment violates the constitution or laws of the United States, can, with no propriety, we think, be denominated a suit commenced or prosecuted against the State whose judgment is so far re-examined....

It is, then, the opinion of the Court, that the defendant who removes a judgment rendered against him by a State Court into this Court, for the purpose of re-examining the question, whether that judgment be in violation of the constitution or laws of the United States, does not commence or prosecute a suit against the State, whatever may be its opinion where the effect of the writ may be to restore the party to the possession of a thing which he demands....

The second objection to the jurisdiction of the Court is, that its appellate power cannot be exercised, in any case, over the judgment of a State Court....

This hypothesis is not founded on any words in the constitution, which might seem to countenance it, but on the unreasonableness of giving a contrary construction to words which seem to require it; and on the incompatibility of the application of the appellate jurisdiction to the judgments of State Courts, with that constitutional relation which subsists between the government of the Union and the governments of those States which compose it.

Let this unreasonableness, this total incompatibility, be examined.

That the United States form, for many, and for most important purposes, a single nation, has not yet been denied. In war, we are one people. In making peace, we are one people. In all commercial regulations, we are one and the same people. In many other respects, the American people are one; and the government which is alone capable of controlling and managing their interests in all these respects, is the government of the Union. It is their government, and in that character they have no other. America has chosen to be, in many respects, and to many purposes, a nation; and for all these purposes, her government is complete; to all these objects, it is competent. The people have declared, that in the exercise of all powers given for these objects, it is supreme. It can, then, in effecting these objects, legitimately control all individuals or governments within the American territory. The constitution and laws of a State, so far as they are repugnant to the constitution and laws of the United States, are absolutely void. These States are constituent parts of the United States. They are members of one great empire—for some purposes sovereign, for some purposes subordinate.

In a government so constituted, is it unreasonable that the judicial power should be competent to give efficacy to the constitutional laws of the legislature? That department can decide on the validity of the constitution or law of a State, if it be repugnant to the constitution or to a law of the United States. Is it unreasonable that it should also be empowered to decide on the judgment of a State tribunal enforcing such unconstitutional law? Is it so very unreasonable as to furnish a justification for controlling the words of the constitution?

We think it is not. We think that in a government acknowledgedly supreme, with respect to objects of vital interest to the nation, there is nothing inconsistent with sound reason, nothing incompatible with the nature of government, in making all its departments supreme, so far as respects those objects, and so far as is necessary to their attainment. The exercise of the appellate power over those judgments of the State tribunals which may contravene the constitution or laws of the United States, is, we believe, essential to the attainment of those objects.

The propriety of entrusting the construction of the constitution, and laws made in pursuance thereof, to the judiciary of the Union, has not, we believe, as yet, been drawn into question. It seems to be a corollary from this political axiom, that the federal Courts should either possess exclusive jurisdiction in such cases, or a power to revise the judgment rendered in them, by the State tribunals....

Let the nature and objects of our Union be considered; let the great fundamental principles, on which the fabric stands, be examined; and we think the result must be, that there is nothing so extravagantly absurd in giving to the Court of the nation the power of revising the decisions of local tribunals on questions which affect the nation, as to require that words which import this power should be restricted by a forced construction. The question then must depend on the words themselves: and on their construction we shall be the more readily excused for not adding to the observations already made, because the subject was fully discussed and exhausted in the case of *Martin v. Hunter*....

We come now to the third objection ... that the judiciary act [of 1789] does not give jurisdiction in the case....

If the 25th section of the judiciary act be inspected, it will at once be perceived that it comprehends expressly the case under consideration....

In the enumeration of the powers of Congress, which is made in the 8th section of the first article [of the Constitution], we find that of exercising exclusive legislation over such District as shall become the seat of government. This power, like all others which are specified, is conferred on Congress as the legislature of the Union: for, strip them of that character, and they would not possess it. In no other character can it be exercised. In legislating for the District, they necessarily preserve the character of the legislature of the Union; for, it is in that character alone that the constitution confers on them this power of exclusive legislation. This proposition need not be enforced.

The 2d clause of the 6th article declares, that "This constitution, and the laws of the United States, which shall be made in pursuance thereof, shall be the supreme law of the land."

The clause which gives exclusive jurisdiction is, unquestionably, a part of the constitution, and, as such, binds all the United States. Those who contend that acts of Congress, made in pursuance of this power, do not, like acts made in pursuance of other powers, bind the nation, ought to show some safe and clear rule which shall support this construction, and prove that an act of Congress, clothed in all the forms which attend other legislative acts, and passed in virtue of a power conferred on, and exercised by Congress, as the legislature of the Union, is not a law of the United States, and does not bind them....

After having bestowed upon this question the most deliberate consideration of which we are capable, the Court is unanimously of opinion, that the objections to its jurisdiction are not sustained, and that the motion ought to be overruled.

Motion denied.

Comments

1. Two days after handing down the *Cohens* opinion, and after hearing arguments on the merits in the case, Chief Justice Marshall held that the May 3, 1802, act of Congress authorized the sale of lottery tickets only within the District of Columbia's boundaries. Consequently, the measure was local in nature and did not interfere with the penal laws of Virginia making it a crime to sell lottery tickets in that state.

2. Virginia officials perceived the state's stake in this case to be sub-

stantial. Counsel for Virginia argued, among other things, that if the Virginia law prohibiting the purchase of non-Virginia lottery tickets was stricken down, Congress would be able to devise all sorts of methods for impairing the revenue raising capacities of the states, as well as depriving the states of their authority to enact legislation protecting the morals of their people. Many Virginia officials and newspapers were outraged by Chief Justice Marshall's assertion in *Cohens* of federal judicial authority to review the decision of a state court. An anonymous doggerel that circulated in Virginia conveys the prevailing outrage against *Cohens*:

> Old Johnny Marshall what's got in ye
> To side with Cohens against Virginny.
> To call in Court his "Old Dominion."
> To insult her with your foul opinion!
> I'll tell you that it will not do
> To call old Spencer [Roane] in review.
> He knows the law as well as you.
> And Once for all, it will not do.
> Alas! Alas! that you should be
> So much against State Sovereignty!
> You've thrown the whole state in a terror,
> By this infernal "Writ of Error."

> (Cited in Leonard W. Levy, "*Cohens v. Virginia*," in *Encyclopedia of the American Constitution*, 4 vols., eds. Leonard W. Levy, Kenneth L. Karst and Dennis J. Mahoney [New York, NY: Macmillan], 1:307)

Despite the unpopularity of the *Cohens* decision, because Marshall had ruled that Congress had not intended that District of Columbia lottery tickets be sold outside of the District and the consequent affirmance of the Cohen brothers' convictions, Virginia was left with no Court order to disobey or to resist.

QUESTIONS

1. The Cohen brothers invoked Section 25 of the Judiciary Act of 1789 to appeal their state court convictions to the Supreme Court of the United States. Review the Court's decision in *Marbury v. Madison*. Why were the Cohens able to invoke the Judiciary Act after the Supreme Court's decision in *Marbury*?

2. In response to the outcry against the Court's decision in *Cohens*, Chief Justice Marshall wrote to Justice Story:

> For Mr. Jefferson's opinion as respects this department, it is not difficult to assign the cause. He is among the most ambitious, and I suspect among the most unforgiving of men. His great power is over

the mass of the people, and this power is chiefly acquired by professions of democracy. Every check on the wild impulse of the moment is a check on his own power, and he is unfriendly to the source from which it flows. He looks, of course, with ill will at an independent Judiciary. (Charles Warren, *The Supreme Court in United States History*, 2 vols. [Boston, MA: Little, Brown, 1935], 1: 562)

Marshall characterized the post-*Cohens* attack on the judiciary as an attack on the government itself:

> The whole attack, if not originating with Mr. Jefferson, is obviously approved and guided by him. It is therefore formidable in other States as well as in this, and it behooves the friends of the Union to be more on the alert than they have been. An effort will certainly be made to repeal the 25th Sec. of the Judiciary Act. (Ibid, 1: 562–563)

What insights into the nature of the union and the exercise of judicial power are contained in Jefferson's observations, quoted in the *Setting* to *Cohens*, and Marshall's reply, contained in his letters to Story?

4. *Martin* and *Cohens* are "companion cases" in the sense that *Martin* extends federal appellate jurisdiction to review state courts in civil cases raising federal questions, while *Cohens* does the same in criminal cases. A case that raises both federal and state questions muddies the legal waters. Under such circumstances, federal courts can invoke the "abstention doctrine," which allows the highest state court to interpret relevant state law and perhaps, in so doing, to eliminate the need for federal judicial review. The abstention doctrine is an example of the broader doctrine of judicial self-restraint. Is self-restraint any more advisable when the Supreme Court reviews state courts' decisions than when it reviews the decisions of lower federal courts? What constitutional factors are at issue?

JUDICIAL REVIEW OF STATE ACTIONS

Mapp v. Ohio
367 U.S. 643 (1961)

SETTING

One of the inherent powers of sovereignty that has always resided with the American states is administering criminal justice, which includes defining crimes, punishments, and defenses, and providing the processes through which criminals are investigated, arrested, tried, sentenced, and punished. American criminal laws have their origin in English common law (also known as judge-made law) and in statutes enacted by colonial legislatures. By 1600 in England, for example, judges had created and defined the felonies of murder, suicide, manslaughter, burglary, arson, robbery, larceny, rape, sodomy, and mayhem, as well as a long list of misdemeanors such as assault, battery, libel, perjury, and false imprisonment. At the same time that judges developed crimes, they developed defenses, such as insanity, coercion, and self-defense.

After the American War of Independence, states continued to recognize common law crimes, but state legislatures became increasingly active in defining statutory crimes, defenses, and punishments. The procedures followed by the states for investigating, arresting, "booking," indicting, arraigning, trying, and sentencing a person accused of committing a crime varied widely from state to state, as did definitions of crimes and available defenses.

The general warrant (also known as a writ of assistance) is a warrant issued by a magistrate commanding the arrest, search, or seizure of unspecified persons, places, or objects. It was a tool of criminal procedure used widely in Britain between the fourteenth and eighteenth centuries. In colonial America, general warrants were used to apprehend persons who smuggled commodities like tea in order to avoid paying what Americans perceived as tyrannical import taxes imposed by Parliament, and to produce evidence that was used against alleged smugglers in subsequent trials. General warrants also were used by the British authorities to seize private papers of American colonists who dared to protest colonial rule.

Although Americans generally detested general warrants when used by the British, officials in most colonies used them to collect taxes, discourage poaching, capture felons, or to discover stolen merchandise. In southern colonies, general warrants were useful to "slave patrols" in maintaining control over human chattel.

Following the Revolution, protections against general warrants were written into eight state constitutions. During the debate over ratification of the Constitution, several states proposed that a Bill of Rights be appended to the Constitution in order to restrain the national government. Submitted to the First Congress in April 1789, the Bill of Rights, as ratified, contains a guarantee of substantive rights such as speech, press, and religion. It also is a mini code of criminal procedure. The Fourth Amendment addresses warrants:

> The right of the people to be secure in their persons, houses, papers, and effects, against unreasonable searches and seizures, shall not be violated, and no Warrants shall issue, but upon probable cause, supported by Oath or affirmation, and particularly describing the place to be searched, and the persons or things to be seized.

For a century after ratification of the Fourth Amendment, American courts followed the common law rule that all evidence seized in a search was reliable, whether or not the evidence was obtained under the authority of a search warrant. Hence, all evidence was admissible at trial against an accused. (At common law, the remedy for an illegal search was a private tort action against the errant officer.)

In 1886, the Supreme Court implicitly discarded the common law rule of evidence when it excluded papers that federal agents had obtained in violation of the Fourth and Fifth Amendments. *Boyd v. United States*, 116 U.S. 616. Not until 1914, however, did the Supreme Court explicitly substitute the "exclusionary rule" for the common law rule. A unanimous Supreme Court held that evidence obtained in violation of constitutional rights could not be used against defendants at trial in federal court. The justices observed that if illegally seized evidence were admitted, the Fourth Amendment "might as well be stricken from the Constitution." *Weeks v. United States*, 232 U.S. 383.

Commentary on *Weeks* concluded that the decision did not specify whether the exclusionary rule was integral to the Fourth Amendment, or merely resulted from the Supreme Court's supervisory role over the federal judiciary. Even if the exclusionary rule were part of the Fourth Amendment, it was not clear from *Weeks* whether having evidence excluded was a personal right of a criminal defendant or just one of several possible deterrents against illegal searches by government officers.

Differences of opinion on these issues divided the justices when they had occasion to examine the implications of the Fourth Amendment for state law enforcement. In 1949, in *Wolf v. Colorado*, 338 U.S. 25, the Supreme Court held unanimously that "[t]he security of one's privacy against arbitrary intrusion by the police—which is at the core of the Fourth Amendment—is basic to a free society. It is therefore implicit in the 'concept of ordered liberty' and as such enforceable against the states through Due Process." Nevertheless, six justices refused to enforce the Fourth Amendment's core against the states by way of the exclusionary rule. Justice Frankfurter wrote for the majority that the *Weeks* rule "was not derived from the explicit requirements of the Fourth Amendment ... [but] was a matter of judicial implication." He noted that the United Kingdom and all nations of the British Commonwealth, as well as thirty American states, admitted illegally obtained evidence. Justice Rutledge complained in dissent that the exclusionary rule was indispensable in a democratic society. From 1914 until 1961 and the case of Dollree Mapp, the justices and legal commentators continued to debate whether the federal exclusionary rule announced in *Weeks* should also apply to the states.

On May 23, 1957, three Cleveland, Ohio, police officers went to Mapp's home in response to an anonymous phone tip suggesting that a bombing suspect named Vergil Ogiltree was hiding in her house. Three days before, a bomb had damaged the home of Don King. King was an alleged numbers racketeer who later became a championship boxing match promoter. Mapp had been married for a short time to Jimmy Bivins, briefly light heavyweight boxing champion during World War II. Subsequently, she was rumored to be the girlfriend of light heavyweight champion Archie Moore and was described as a confidante of numbers racketeers.

The officers knocked on the side door of Mapp's house. She stuck her head out an upstairs window and asked what they wanted. The police requested entry to make a search. Mapp refused to admit them until she called her attorney. She then refused to admit the police until they obtained a search warrant. A few hours later, another officer arrived along with a half-dozen back-ups. He brought with him a piece of paper that he claimed was a search warrant. Once again, Mapp was asked to consent to a search. When she refused for the second time, the police forcibly entered her house.

Mapp met the officers on the stair landing between floors. Suspicious about the document, she demanded to see it. Sergeant Carl Delau, the officer in charge, waved the paper in front of her. Mapp grabbed it and shoved it down the front of her turtleneck sweater. Delau demanded she return the paper. Mapp refused. Mapp's account and police accounts diverge at this point, but the officers eventually handcuffed her, retrieved the paper, and took Mapp to her bedroom where they told her to sit on her bed while they searched the rooms on the second floor.

In Mapp's bedroom police found four books, *Affairs of a Troubadour*, *Little Darlings*, *London Stage Affairs*, and *Memories of a Hotel Man*. They also discovered several hand-drawn penciled pictures of nude male and female models. The officers then searched Mapp's basement. They found a trunk containing numbers-racket paraphernalia. Mapp contended that the trunk and its contents belonged to Morris Jones, who once had rented a room in her house. The police also found their bombing suspect, Ogiltree, in the first-floor apartment of Mapp's house.

Mapp was prosecuted for possession of the numbers-racket paraphernalia, but she was acquitted. Subsequently, she was indicted for unlawfully and knowingly having in her possession lewd and lascivious books, pictures, and photographs in violation of the Ohio obscenity statute. Mapp's attorney moved to have the evidence suppressed on the ground that the officers were required to obtain a search warrant before conducting a search. The trial judge overruled her attorney's motion to suppress.

Mapp was convicted by a jury in the Court of Common Pleas of Cuyahoga County, Ohio. She was released on $2500 bail. Her conviction was affirmed by the Court of Appeals and the Supreme Court of Ohio. Four of the seven Ohio Supreme Court justices believed Mapp's conviction should be reversed because the Ohio obscenity statute was unconstitutional. The Ohio constitution, however, required all but one judge to concur in a decision declaring a law unconstitutional.

Mapp appealed to the Supreme Court of the United States.

HIGHLIGHTS OF SUPREME COURT ARGUMENTS

BRIEF FOR MAPP

◆ The statute under which Mapp was convicted is unconstitutional as applied to her. Mapp was neither in possession nor control of the lewd and lascivious documents left by a former roomer.

◆ The sentence imposed on Mapp was excessive, cruel, and unusual under the circumstances. The state court of appeals should have reviewed the sentence.

◆ Mapp's conviction was unconstitutional and void because the judge failed to correctly instruct the jury on the essential elements of the crime charged.

◆ The police conduct in procuring the books, pictures, and papers was oppressive and hence a violation of due process of law. In *Rochin v. California*, 342 U.S. 165 (1952), the Court declared that searches that "shocked the conscience" violate due process. In that case, a suspect in a drug case was taken to a hospital where he was forced to vomit two capsules of morphine swallowed when police entered his home and forced their way into his bedroom. The search of Mapp's home was equally shocking to the conscience.

AMICUS CURIAE BRIEF SUPPORTING MAPP

The American Civil Liberties Union.

BRIEF FOR OHIO

◆ The Ohio obscenity statute is constitutional in light of the Court's decision in *Roth v. United States*, 354 U.S. 476 (1957), which held that obscenity is not protected by the First Amendment.

◆ The sentence given Mapp was within the limit fixed by statute, and hence was not excessive.

◆ In a prosecution in a statute court for a state crime, state law is controlling on the admissibility of evidence obtained by an unreasonable search and seizure. The search in this case did not "shock the conscience" in the sense contemplated by *Rochin v. California*, 342 U.S. 165 (1952).

SUPREME COURT DECISION: 6–3

CLARK, J.

... While in 1949, prior to the *Wolf* [*v. Colorado*, 338 U.S. 25 (1949)] case, almost two-thirds of the States were opposed to the use of the exclusionary rule, now, despite the *Wolf* case, more than half of those since passing upon it, by their own legislative or judicial decision, have wholly or partly adopted or adhered to the *Weeks* [*v. United States*, 232 U.S. 383 (1914)] rule.... [W]e note that the second basis elaborated in *Wolf* in support of its failure to enforce the exclusionary doctrine against the States was that "other means of protection" have been afforded "the right to privacy.".... [T]hat such other remedies have been worthless and futile is buttressed by the experience of other States. The obvious futility of relegating the Fourth Amendment to the protection of other remedies has, moreover, been recognized by this Court since *Wolf*....

It, therefore, plainly appears that the factual considerations supporting the failure of the *Wolf* Court to include the *Weeks* exclusionary rule when it recognized the enforceability of the right to privacy against the States in 1949, while not basically relevant to the constitutional consideration, could not, in any analysis, now be deemed controlling....

Today we once again examine *Wolf*'s constitutional documentation of the right to privacy free from unreasonable state intrusion, and, after its dozen years on our books, are led by it to close the only courtroom door remaining open to evidence secured by official lawlessness in flagrant abuse of that basic right, reserved to all persons as a specific guarantee against that very same unlawful conduct. We hold that all evidence obtained by searches and seizures in violation of the Constitution is, by that same authority, inadmissible in a state court....

This Court has not hesitated to enforce as strictly against the States as it does against the Federal Government the rights of free speech and of a free press, the rights to notice and to a fair, public trial, including, as it does, the right not to be convicted by use of a coerced confession, however logically relevant it be, and without regard to its reliability. And nothing could be more certain that when a coerced confession is involved, "the relevant rules of evidence" are overridden without regard to "the incidence of such conduct by the police," slight or frequent. Why should not the same rule apply to what is tantamount to coerced testimony by way of unconstitutional seizure of goods, papers, effects, documents, etc.?...

[O]ur holding that the exclusionary rule is an essential part of both the Fourth and Fourteenth Amendments is not only the logical dictate of prior cases, but it also makes very good sense. There is no war between the Constitution and common sense. Presently, a federal prosecutor may make no use of evidence illegally seized, but a State's attorney across the street may, although he supposedly is operating under the enforceable prohibitions of the same Amendment. Thus the State, by admitting evidence unlawfully seized, serves to encourage disobedience to the Federal Constitution which it is bound to uphold....

Federal-state cooperation in the solution of crime under constitutional standards will be promoted, if only by recognition of their now mutual obligation to respect the same fundamental criteria in their approaches....

There are those who say, as did Justice (then Judge) Cardozo, that under our constitutional exclusionary doctrine "[t]he criminal is to go free because the constable has blundered." *People v. Defore*, 242 NY 21 (1926). In some cases this will undoubtedly be the result. But, as was said in *Elkins*, "there is another consideration—the imperative of judicial integrity." *Elkins v. United States*, 364 U.S. 206 (1960). The criminal goes free, if he must, but it is the law that sets him free. Nothing can destroy a government more quickly than its failure to observe its own laws, or worse, its disregard of the character of its own existence....

The ignoble shortcut to conviction left open to the State tends to destroy the entire system of constitutional restraints on which the liberties of the people rest. Having once recognized that the right to privacy embodied in the Fourth Amendment is enforceable against the States, and that the right to be secure against rude invasions of privacy by state officers is, therefore, constitutional in origin, we can no longer permit that right to remain an empty promise. Because it is enforceable in the same manner and to like effect as other basic rights secured by the Due Process Clause, we can no longer permit it to be revocable at the whim of any police officer who, in the name of law enforcement itself, chooses to suspend its enjoyment....

Reversed and remanded.

BLACK, J., CONCURRING

... I am still not persuaded that the Fourth Amendment, standing alone, would be enough to bar the introduction into evidence against an accused of papers and effects seized from him in violation of its commands. For the Fourth Amendment does not itself contain any provision expressly precluding the use of such evidence, and I am extremely doubtful that such a provision could properly be inferred from nothing more than the basic command against unreasonable searches and seizures. Reflection on the problem,

however, in the light of cases coming before the Court since *Wolf*, has led me to conclude that when the Fourth Amendment's ban against unreasonable searches and seizures is considered together with the Fifth Amendment's ban against compelled self-incrimination, a constitutional basis emerges which not only justifies but actually requires the exclusionary rule....

DOUGLAS, J., CONCURRING [OMITTED]

STEWART, J., DISSENTING [OMITTED]

HARLAN, FRANKFURTER, AND WHITTAKER, J.J., DISSENTING

In overruling the *Wolf* case the Court, in my opinion, has forgotten the sense of judicial restraint which, with due regard for *stare decisis*, is one element that should enter into deciding whether a past decision of this Court should be overruled. Apart from that I also believe that the *Wolf* rule represents sounder Constitutional doctrine than the new rule which now replaces it....

The occasion which the Court has taken here is in the context of a case where the question was briefed not at all and argued only extremely tangentially. The unwisdom of overruling *Wolf* without full-dress argument is aggravated by the circumstance that that decision is a comparatively recent one (1949) to which three members of the present majority have at one time or other expressly subscribed, one to be sure with explicit misgivings. I would think that our obligation to the States, on whom we impose this new rule, as well as the obligation of orderly adherence to our own processes would demand that we seek that aid which adequate briefing and argument lends to the determination of an important issue....

At the heart of the majority's opinion in this case is the following syllogism: (1) the rule excluding in federal criminal trials evidence which is the product of an illegal search and seizure is a "part and parcel" of the Fourth Amendment; (2) Wolf held that the "privacy" assured against federal action by the Fourth Amendment is also protected against state action by the Fourteenth Amendment; and (3) it is therefore "logically and constitutionally necessary" that the Weeks exclusionary rule should also be enforced against the States....

[W]hat the Court is now doing is to impose upon the States not only federal substantive standards of "search and seizure" but also the basic federal remedy for violation of those standards. For I think it entirely clear that the Weeks exclusionary rule is but a remedy which, by penalizing past official misconduct, is aimed at deterring such conduct in the future.

I would not impose upon the States this federal exclusionary remedy. The reasons given by the majority for now suddenly turning its back on Wolf seem to me notably unconvincing....

[T]he question remains, as it has always been, one of state power, not one of passing judgment on the wisdom of one state course or another. In my view this Court should continue to forbear from fettering the States with an adamant rule which may embarrass them in coping with their own peculiar problems in criminal law enforcement....

QUESTIONS

1. The criminal procedure aspects of *Mapp* and related cases are examined in greater detail in Volume II, Chapter 8 of *Constitutional Law: Cases in Context*. Here, the focus is on judicial review of states' actions. Administration of criminal justice has always been a primary responsibility of the states. To what extent does the Court's decision in *Mapp* strip the states of authority to determine the best way to administer their own criminal justice systems? Does the Fourth Amendment command such a result?

2. Identify the theories of judicial review that are implicit or explicit in the opinions of Justices Clark, Black, and Harlan. What constitutional values regarding national power, states' rights, and judicial protection of individual liberties underpin each theory?

3. Despite the fact that the parties had argued the constitutionality of the Ohio obscenity statute, focusing on the First Amendment, the Supreme Court framed the issues differently. The Court held against Ohio on Fourth Amendment grounds, extending the reach of the exclusionary rule. Was this an appropriate exercise of the power of judicial review? Does a decision so different from the emphasis of the parties presenting the issues make for good constitutional law?

Suggestions for Further Reading

Amar, Akhil, " A Neo-Federalist View of Article III: Separating the Two Tiers of Federal Jurisdiction," 65 *Boston University Law Review* (1985): 205.

_____, "Of Sovereignty and Federalism," 96 *Yale Law Journal* (1987): 1425.

Bator, Paul, ed., *Hart and Wechsler's The Federal Courts in the Federal System*, 3rd ed. (Westbury, NY: Foundation, 1988).

Black, Charles L., *Structure and Relationship in Constitutional Law* (Baton Rouge, LA: Louisiana State University Press, 1969).

Choper, Jesse, "The Scope of National Power vis-a-vis the States: The Dispensability of Judicial Review," 86 *Yale Law Journal* (1977): 1552.

Currie, David, "The Constitution in the Supreme Court: 1789–1801," 38 *University of Chicago Law Review* (1981): 819.

_____, "The Constitution in the Supreme Court, 1801–1835," 49 *University of Chicago Law Review* (1982): 646.

Fletcher, William, "A Historical Interpretation of the Eleventh Amendment: A Narrow Construction of an Affirmative Grant of Jurisdiction Rather Than a Prohibition against Jurisdiction," 35 *Stanford Law Review* (1983): 1033.

Friendly, Fred W., and Martha J. H. Elliott, *The Constitution: That Delicate Balance* (New York, NY: Random House, 1984), Chapter 8.

Gibbons, John, "The Eleventh Amendment and State Sovereign Immunity: A Reinterpretation," 83 *Columbia Law Review* (1983): 1889.

Jackson, Vicki, "The Supreme Court, the Eleventh Amendment, and State Sovereign Immunity," 98 *Yale Law Journal* (1988): 1.

Jackson, Robert H., *The Struggle for Judicial Supremacy: A Study in A Crisis in American Power Politics* (New York, NY: Knopf, 1941).

Jacobs, Clyde, *The Eleventh Amendment and Sovereign Immunity* (Westport, CT: Greenwood Press, 1972).

Mason, Alpheus Thomas, "Federalism: Historic Questions and Contemporary Meanings, the Role of the Court," in *Federalism: Infinite Variety in Theory and Practice*, ed. Earl Valerie (Itasca, IL: F. E. Peacock, 1968).

Mathis, Doyle, "*Chisholm v. Georgia*: Background and Settlement," 54 *Journal of American History* (1967): 19.

Monaghan, Henry P. "Foreword: Constitutional Common Law," 89 *Harvard Law Review* (1975): 1.

Neuborne, Burt, "The Myth of Parity," 90 *Harvard Law Review* (1977): 1105.

Note, "Judge Spencer Roane of Virginia: Champion of States' Rights—Foe of John Marshall," 66 *Harvard Law Review* (1953): 1242.

Orth, John V., *The Judicial Power of the United States: The Eleventh Amendment in American History* (New York, NY: Oxford University Press, 1987).

Schmidhauser, John R., *The Supreme Court as Final Arbiter of Federal-State Relations* (Chapel Hill, NC: University of North Carolina Press, 1958).

Warren, Charles, "Legislative and Judicial Attacks on the Supreme Court of the United States—A History of the Twenty-Fifth Section of the Judiciary Act," 47 *American Law Review* (1913): 1: 161.

STATE ACTION DOCTRINE

Civil Rights Cases
109 U.S. 3 (1883)

Setting

As previous cases in this chapter have illustrated, unresolved disagreements about states' rights and powers under the Constitution threatened to destroy the Union soon after its creation. The issue of states' rights in the context of slavery eventually reduced the nation to war. In December 1860, South Carolina repealed its ratification of the Constitution and seceded from the Union. Six other southern states soon followed South Carolina's lead. For the next four years, 1861 to 1865, the United States disintegrated into a great Civil War that left over six hundred thousand dead and the South in ruins.

The Civil War officially ended on April 9, 1865, when Robert E. Lee surrendered to Ulysses S. Grant at the Appomattox, Virginia, Court House. The Thirteenth Amendment, ratified at the end of 1865, abolished slavery and involuntary servitude. How to rebuild the Union and how to deal with former slaves, however, posed vexing problems. Abraham Lincoln, who had been president during the Civil War, proposed reconstruction of the Union "[w]ith malice toward none, with charity for all … to bind up the nation's wounds." That attitude extended to his proposals for the southern states, which he sought to rebuild economically and socially, if southerners would agree to take oaths to support the Constitution of the United States. Radical Republicans in Congress, however, opposed Lincoln's conciliatory approach. They advocated treating the former Confederacy like conquered provinces with no constitutional or political rights. Lincoln's assassination on April 14, 1865, left Reconstruction policy to be shaped by a tug-of-war between his successor, Andrew Johnson, a southerner from Tennessee, and a Congress dominated by Radical Republicans.

Six weeks before he died, President Lincoln had created a Freedmen's Bureau to help newly emancipated slaves to rebuild their lives. The Bureau provided former slaves with food, medical treatment, and assistance in finding jobs. It also sought to protect them from the Black Codes—state laws enacted to perpetuate the social relations of slavery by imposing invidious vocational, curfew, and other restrictions on blacks. When Congress attempted to extend authorization for the Freedman's Bureau in 1866, President Johnson vetoed the bill, arguing that it gave military courts too much power to resolve issues of discrimination or infringements of civil rights. Johnson's veto angered congressional Republicans, but they lacked the votes to override it. Instead, they enacted a Civil Rights Act in 1866. Johnson vetoed that legislation as well, claiming that Congress had no authority to interfere with the states on matters of civil rights. Johnson's veto so outraged moderate Republicans that they joined with the Radicals, overrode the veto, then passed a new Freedman's Bureau Act and proposed the Fourteenth Amendment.

The purpose of the Fourteenth Amendment was to respond to President Johnson's constitutional objections to the 1866 Civil Rights Act. The Fourteenth Amendment defines U.S. citizenship and reduces congressional representation of any state that does not allow adult male citizens to vote. It also contains clauses prohibiting state abridgment of U.S. citizens' privileges or immunities, and state deprivation of due process and equal protection of the laws. The Fourteenth Amendment was ratified in 1868.

In addition to adopting legislation and proposing a constitutional amendment to embarrass President Johnson, Radical Republicans sought to have him impeached and removed from office. Although that effort ultimately failed, the Republican Party nominated northern Civil War hero, Ulysses S. Grant, for president during Johnson's impeachment trial. Grant was elected in 1868, in part due to some 650,000 votes cast by blacks in the South. Eager to take advantage of and hold the black vote, Republicans proposed the Fifteenth Amendment, which forbids states and the national government from denying the right of citizens of the United States to vote "on account of race, color, or previous condition of servitude." The Fifteenth Amendment was ratified in 1870.

The former Confederacy did not passively accept these post-Civil War reforms. In the waning days of Reconstruction, white southerners, known as "Redeemers," overthrew hated northern "Carpetbaggers," reasserted control over their state governments and, in the name of white supremacy, enacted a variety of Black Codes restricting the recently freed slaves. Such laws required freedmen to hold steady jobs, imposed special penalties for violating labor contracts, and enforced harsh vagrancy and apprenticeship rules. Criminal codes extracted especially harsh and more arbitrary punishments for blacks than for whites. Newly freed slaves could not own weapons or appear in certain public places, and were often excluded from any occupation other than domestic and agricultural employment. Gradually, Black Codes evolved into statutes that came to be known as "Jim Crow" laws prohibiting blacks from using any white public facilities. Blacks were thereby confined to substandard schools and public accommodations, and consigned to social inferiority. Southern constitutions and state laws adopted after the War, which had been imposed by Radical Reconstructionists and their agents and enforced by federal military occupation, were slowly revised to prevent blacks from voting and to subject them to strict segregation. Secret organizations, such as the Ku Klux Klan, formed in 1867 as the "Invisible Empire of the South," arose to threaten, terrorize, and murder blacks who struggled against the prevailing social order. Congressional responses such as the Ku Klux Klan Acts that outlawed such activities were largely ineffectual and not enforced.

Ulysses S. Grant proved less effective as a president than as a Union general. His administration was rocked by scandals. By 1873 the nation was mired in a deep post-War economic depression known as a "panic." It was not until 1875 that Congress was able to complete action on another civil rights bill that had been proposed by Senator Charles Sumner in 1870. The 1875 Civil Rights Act guaranteed to all persons within the jurisdiction of the United States full and equal enjoyment of the accommodations of inns, public conveyances, theaters and other places of public amusement. The act imposed stiff civil and criminal penalties on violators. Like the 1866 Civil Rights Act which preceded it, questions about the constitutionality of the 1875 statute attended its adoption. It was seen by many as an incursion into states' rights and beyond the power of Congress.

As originally proposed by Senator Sumner, the Civil Rights Act also would have guaranteed equal access to blacks in public schools, churches, and cemeteries. These provisions were deleted after Sumner's death, as part of a compromise to rescue the bill from defeat by a coalition of northern and southern members of Congress opposed to school desegregation. The Civil Rights Act of 1875 became law on March 1, 1875, when signed by President Grant.

Challenges to the Civil Rights Act arose almost immediately. In October 1875, Murray Stanley, a Kansas innkeeper, was indicted in U.S. District Court for the District of Kansas for refusing to serve supper to Bird Gee because Gee was black. Stanley demurred to the indictment. The district court found itself unable to respond to Stanley's demurrer and certified two questions to the Supreme Court of the United States. First was whether the indictment stated an offense punishable by the laws of the United States or cognizable by the federal courts. Second was whether the Civil Rights Act of 1875 was constitutional.

HIGHLIGHTS OF SUPREME COURT ARGUMENTS

Note: Stanley's case was consolidated with three other criminal cases and one civil case, all brought under the Civil Rights Act for refusals to provide services to blacks. The criminal cases involved prosecutions against Samuel Nichols, an innkeeper in Missouri; Michael Ryan, owner of Maguire's theater in San Francisco, California; and Samuel D. Singleton, owner of the Grand Opera House in New York. The civil action was brought by Richard and Sallie Robinson against the Memphis & Charleston Railroad for refusing Mrs. Robinson a first-class railroad ticket in the ladies' car. The cases were known collectively as the *Civil Rights Cases*, and were argued at the 1879 and 1882 Terms of the Court.

BRIEF FOR THE UNITED STATES AT 1879 TERM

◆ The 1875 Civil Rights Act addresses public accommodations, guaranteeing equal access to facilities that are part of interstate commerce. Congress had power under the Commerce Clause to pass the Act.

◆ The Civil Rights Act is justified by the Fourteenth Amendment. Sponsors of the Fourteenth Amendment were clear that their intent was to give Congress power that had been of questionable constitutionality under the 1866 Act.

◆ The 1875 Civil Rights Act is a legitimate exercise of Congress's power under the Thirteenth Amendment. It is appropriate legislation to efface the residuum of slavery.

BRIEF FOR THE UNITED STATES AT 1882 TERM

◆ Inns are instrumentalities of interstate commerce and could be regulated by Congress even before passage of the Civil War Amendments.

◆ Innkeepers and theater operators carry on their businesses with licenses from the state. These businesses are quasi-public in nature, giving Congress the right to prohibit any discrimination based on race, color, or previous condition of servitude.

Note: No briefs were submitted on behalf of the defendants in the criminal cases.

BRIEF FOR MEMPHIS & CHARLESTON RAILROAD COMPANY

The conductor denied Mrs. Robinson access to the ladies' car because he thought she was a prostitute and Mr. Robinson was her paramour. Prostitutes are never allowed to sit in the ladies' car. Color was not a factor in the conductor's decision.

SUPREME COURT DECISION: 8–1

BRADLEY, J.

... Has Congress constitutional power to make [the 1875 Civil Rights Act]? Of course, no one will contend that the power to pass it was contained in the Constitution before the adoption of the last three [Thirteenth, Fourteenth, and Fifteenth] amendments....

The first section of the Fourteenth Amendment—which is the one relied on—after declaring who shall be citizens of the United States, and of the several States, is prohibitory in its character, and prohibitory upon the States. It declares that: "No State shall make or enforce any law which shall abridge the privileges or immunities of citizens of the United States; nor shall any State deprive any person of life, liberty, or property without due process of law; nor deny to any person within its jurisdiction the equal protection of the laws." It is State action of a particular character that is prohibited. Individual invasion of individual rights is not the subject-matter of the amendment. It has a deeper and broader scope. It nullifies and makes void all State legislation, and State action of every kind, which impairs the privileges and immunities of citizens of the United States, or which injures them in life, liberty or property without due process of law, or which denies to any of them the equal protection of the laws.... [The first section of the Fourteenth Amendment] does not authorize Congress to create a code of municipal law for the regulation of private rights; but to provide modes of redress against the operation of State laws, and the action of State officers, executive or judicial, when these are subversive of the fundamental rights specified in the amendment. Positive rights and privileges are undoubtedly secured by the Fourteenth Amendment; but they are secured by way of prohibition against State laws and State proceedings affecting those rights and privileges, and by power given to Congress to legislate for the purpose of carrying such prohibition into effect; and such legislation must necessarily be predicated upon such supposed State laws or State proceedings, and be directed to the correction of their operation and effect....

And so in the present case, until some state law has been passed, or some state action through its officers or agents has been taken, adverse to the rights of citizens sought to be protected by the Fourteenth Amendment, no legislation of the United States under said amendment, nor any proceeding under such legislation, can be called into activity, for the prohibitions of the amendment are against state laws and acts done under state authority....

An inspection of the [Civil Rights Act of 1875] shows that it makes no reference whatever to any supposed or apprehended violation of the Fourteenth Amendment on the part of the States. It is not predicated on any such view. It proceeds *ex directo* [immediately] to declare that certain acts committed by individuals shall be deemed offenses, and shall be prosecuted and punished by proceedings in the courts of the United States. It does not profess to be corrective of any constitutional wrong committed by the States; it does not make its operation to depend upon any such wrong committed....

If this legislation is appropriate for enforcing the prohibitions of the amendment, it is difficult to see where it is to stop. Why may not Congress with equal show of authority enact a code of laws for the enforcement and vindication of all rights of life, liberty, and property?... The truth is that the assumption that if the states are forbidden to legislate or act in a particular way on a particular subject, and power is conferred upon Congress to enforce the prohibition, this gives Congress power to legislate generally upon that subject, and not merely power to provide modes of redress against such state legislation or action. The assumption is certainly unsound. It is repugnant to the Tenth Amendment of the constitution....

The law in question, without any reference to adverse State legislation on the subject, declares that all persons shall be entitled to equal accommodations and privileges of inns, public conveyances, and places of public amusement, and imposes a penalty upon any individual who shall deny to any citizen such equal accommodations and privileges. This is not corrective legislation; it is primary and direct; it takes immediate and absolute possession of the subject of the right of admission to inns, public conveyances, and places of amusement. It supersedes and displaces State legislation on the same subject, or only allows it permissive force. It ignores such legislation, and assumes that the matter is one that belongs to the domain of national regulation. Whether it would not have been a more effective protection of the rights of citizens to have clothed Congress with plenary power over the whole subject, is not now the question. What we have to decide is, whether such plenary power has been conferred upon Congress by the Fourteenth Amendment, and, in our judgment, it has not....

But the power of Congress to adopt direct and primary, as distinguished from corrective, legislation on the subject in hand, is sought, in the second place, from the Thirteenth Amendment, which abolishes slavery....

The long existence of African slavery in this country gave us very distinct notions of what it was, and what were its necessary incidents. Compulsory service of the slave for the benefit of the master, restraint of his movements except by the master's will, disability to hold property, to make contracts, to have a standing in court, to be a witness against a white person, and such like burdens and incapacities, were the inseparable incidents of the institution....

The only question under the present head, therefore, is, whether the refusal to any persons of the accommodations of an inn, or a public conveyance, or a place of public amusement, by an individual, and without any sanction or support from any State law or regulation, does inflict upon such persons any manner of servitude, or form of slavery, as those terms are understood in this country?...

[W]e are forced to the conclusion that such an act of refusal has nothing to do with slavery or involuntary servitude, and that if it is violative of any right of the party, his redress is to be sought under the laws of the State; or, if those laws are adverse to his rights and do not protect him, his remedy will be found in the corrective legislation which Congress has adopted, or may adopt, for counteracting the effect of State laws, or State action, prohibited by the Fourteenth Amendment. It would be running the slavery argument into the ground to make it apply to every act of discrimination which a person may see fit to make as to the guests he will entertain, or as to the people he will take into his coach or cab or car, or admit to his concert or theater, or deal with in other matters of intercourse or business. Innkeepers and public carriers, by the laws of all the States, so far as we are aware, are bound, to the extent of their facilities, to furnish proper accommodation to all unobjectionable persons who in good faith apply for them. If the laws themselves make any unjust discrimination, amenable to the prohibitions of the

Fourteenth Amendment, Congress has full power to afford a remedy under that amendment and in accordance with it.

When a man has emerged from slavery, and by the aid of beneficent legislation has shaken off the inseparable concomitants of that state, there must be some stage in the process of his elevation when he takes the rank of a mere citizen, and ceases to be the special favorite of the laws, and when his rights as a citizen, or a man, are to be protected in the ordinary modes by which other men's rights are protected. There were thousands of free colored people in this country before the abolition of slavery, enjoying all the essential rights of life, liberty, and property the same as white citizens; yet no one, at that time, thought that it was any invasion of their personal *status* as freemen because they were not admitted to all the privileges enjoyed by white citizens, or because they were subjected to discriminations in the enjoyment of accommodations in inns, public conveyances, and places of amusement. Mere discriminations on account of race or color were not regarded as badges of slavery....

This conclusion disposes of the cases now under consideration....

HARLAN, J., DISSENTING

The opinion in these cases proceeds, it seems to me, upon grounds entirely too narrow and artificial. The substance and spirit of the recent amendments of the constitution have been sacrificed by a subtle and ingenious verbal criticism. Constitutional provisions, adopted in the interest of liberty, and for the purpose of securing, through national legislation, if need be, rights inhering in a state of freedom, and belonging to American citizenship, have been so construed as to defeat the ends the people desired to accomplish, which they attempted to accomplish, and which they supposed they had accomplished by changes in their fundamental law. By this I do not mean that the determination of these cases should have been materially controlled by considerations of mere expediency or policy. I mean only, in this form, to express an earnest conviction that the court has departed from the familiar rule requiring, in the interpretation of constitutional provisions, that full effect be given to the intent with which they were adopted.

The purpose of the first section of the act of congress of March 1, 1875, was to prevent *race* discrimination. It does not assume to define the general conditions and limitations under which inns, public conveyances, and places of public amusement may be conducted, but only declares that such conditions and limitations, whatever they may be, shall not be applied, by way of discrimination, *on account of race, color, or previous condition of servitude....*

The court adjudges that Congress is without power, under either the Thirteenth or Fourteenth Amendment, to establish [the Civil Rights Act of 1875], and that the first and second sections of the statute are, in all their parts, unconstitutional and void....

Before the adoption of the recent amendments it had become ... the established doctrine of this court that negroes, whose ancestors had been imported and sold as slaves, could not become citizens of a State, or even of the United States, with the rights and privileges guaranteed to citizens by the national Constitution; further, that one might have all the rights and privileges of a citizen of a State without being a citizen in the sense in which that word was used in the national Constitution, and without being entitled to the privileges and immunities of citizens of the several States. Still further, between the adoption of the Thirteenth Amendment and the proposal by Congress of the Fourteenth Amendment, on June 16, 1866, the statute books of several of the States ... had become loaded down with enactments which, under the guise of apprentice, vagrant, and contract regulations, sought to keep the colored race in a condition, practically, of servitude. It was openly announced that whatever might be the rights which persons of that race had as freemen, under the guarantees of the national Constitution, they could not become citizens of a State, with the rights belonging to citizens, except by the consent of such State; consequently, that their civil rights, as citizens of the State, depended entirely upon State legislation. To meet this new peril to the black race, that the purposes of the nation might not be doubted or defeated, and by way of further enlargement of the power of Congress, the Fourteenth Amendment was proposed for adoption....

The Fourteenth Amendment presents the first instance in our history of the investiture of Congress with affirmative power, by *legislation*, to *enforce* an express prohibition upon the states....

The assumption that this amendment consists wholly of prohibitions upon state laws and state proceedings in hostility to its provisions, is unauthorized by its language....

In view of the circumstances under which the recent amendments were incorporated into the constitution, and especially in view of the peculiar character of the new rights they created and secured, it ought not to be presumed that the general government has abdicated its authority, by national legislation, direct and primary in its character, to guard and protect privileges and immunities secured by that instrument. Such an interpretation of the constitution ought not to be accepted if it be possible to avoid it. Its acceptance would lead to this anomalous result: that whereas, prior to the amendments, Congress, with the sanction of this court, passed the most stringent laws—operating directly and primarily upon the States, and their officers and agents, as well as upon individuals—in vindication of slavery and the right of the master, it may not now, by legislation of a like primary and direct character, guard, protect, and secure the freedom established, and the most essential right of the citizenship granted, by the constitutional amendments. I venture, with all respect for the opinion of others, to insist that the national legislature may, without transcending the limits of the Constitution, do for human liberty and the fundamental rights of American citizenship, what it did, with the sanction of this court, for the protection of slavery and the rights of the masters of fugitive slaves....

It does not seem to me that the fact that, by the second clause of the first section of the Fourteenth Amendment, the states are expressly prohibited from making or enforcing laws abridging the privileges and immunities of citizens of the United States, furnishes any sufficient reason for holding or maintaining that the amendment was intended to deny Congress the power, by general, primary, and direct legislation, of protecting citizens of the United States, being also citizens of their respective States, against discrimination, in respect to their rights as citizens, founded on race, color, or previous condition of servitude. Such an interpretation of the amendment is plainly repugnant to its fifth section, conferring power upon Congress, by appropriate legislation, to enforce, not merely the provisions containing prohibitions upon the states, but all of the provisions of the amendment, including the provisions, express and implied, of the grant of citizenship in the first clause of the first section of the article. This alone is sufficient for holding that Congress is not restricted to the enactment of laws adapted to counteract and redress the operation of state legislation, or the action of state officers of the character prohibited by the amendment. It was perfectly well known that the great danger to the equal enjoyment by citizens of their rights, as citizens, was to be apprehended, not altogether from unfriendly state legislation, but from the hostile action of corporations and individuals in the States. And it is to be presumed that it was intended, by that section, to clothe Congress with power and authority to meet that danger....

[I]f it be ... adjudged that individuals and corporations exercising public functions may, without liability to direct primary legislation on the part of Congress, make the race of citizens the ground for denying them that equality of civil rights

which the constitution ordains as a principle of republican citizenship—then, not only the foundations upon which the national supremacy has always securely rested will be materially disturbed, but we shall enter upon an era of constitutional law when the rights of freedom and American citizenship cannot receive from the nation that efficient protection which heretofore was accorded to slavery and the rights of the master.

My brethren say that when a man has emerged from slavery, and by the aid of beneficent legislation has shaken off the inseparable concomitants of that state, there must be some stage in the process of his elevation when he takes the rank of a mere citizen, and ceases to be the special favorite of the laws.... It is, I submit, scarcely just to say that the colored race has been the special favorite of the laws.... Today it is the colored race which is denied, by corporations and individuals wielding public authority, rights fundamental in their freedom and citizenship. At some future time it may be some other race that will fall under the ban. If the constitutional amendments be enforced, according to the intent with which, as I conceive, they were adopted, there cannot be, in this republic, any class of human beings in practical subjection to another class, with power in the latter to dole out to the former just such privileges as they may choose to grant....

QUESTIONS

1. Summarize Justice Bradley's reasons for ruling that Congress exceeded its authority in passing the Civil Rights Act of 1875. Are those reasons constitutionally based?

2. What theories of judicial power underpin the majority and dissenting opinions in *The Civil Rights Cases*? Consider the thought that such

power, like many judicial formulations, is an accordion-like concept that can be expanded or contracted. To what extent is the Court's reluctance to expand its power over the states related to broader debates over states' rights?

3. How persuasive is the Solicitor General's argument that "Inns are instrumentalities of interstate commerce and could be regulated by Congress even before passage of the Civil War Amendments"?

4. Respond to the following question:

> Was it much of a solution ... for the Court to remit African-Americans, the country's newest citizens, to relief in the state legislative process when the common law or statutes of many states required those engaged in "public" callings—e.g., public utilities, common carriers, innkeepers—to serve all *white* persons who reasonably sought service? (Daniel A. Farber, William N. Eskridge Jr., Philip P. Frickey, *Constitutional Law: Themes for the Constitution's Third Century* [St. Paul, MN: West, 1993], p. 180)

COMMENT

Historian C. Vann Woodward wrote, "The court ... was engaged in a bit of reconciliation [in the *Civil Rights Cases*]—reconciliation between federal and state jurisdiction, as well as between North and South, reconciliation also achieved at the Negro's expense. ...The *Boston Evening Transcript* of 14 February 1899, admitted that Southern race policy was 'now the policy of the Administration of the very party which carried the country into and through a civil war to free the slave'" (*The Strange Career of Jim Crow*, 3rd rev. ed. [New York, NY: Oxford University Press, 1974], p. 71). (Justice Joseph Bradley, as a member of the special commission formed to resolve the contested 1876 Hayes-Tilden presidential election, cast his vote for Rutherford B. Hayes, the Republican candidate. Hayes had promised to remove federal troops occupying the former Confederate states.)

The *New York Times* editorialized approvingly about the decision in the *Civil Rights Cases* as follows:

> The fact is, that, so long as we have State governments, within their field of action we cannot by National authority prevent the consequences of misgovernment. The people of the State are dependent on their own civilized ideas and habits for the benefits of a civilized administration of laws. (Quoted in Charles Warren, *The Supreme Court in United States History*, 3 vols. [Boston, MA: Little, Brown and Company, 1923], III: 336–337)

The Civil Rights Act of 1875 was the last great Reconstruction statute. Congress did not pass another civil rights act until 1957, eighty-two years later.

STATE ACTION DOCTRINE

Shelley v. Kraemer
334 U.S. 1 (1948)

SETTING

A massive migration of blacks from the south, spawned by the northern industrial revolution and the southern poverty and racial oppression that followed the Civil War, continued into the Depression in the 1930s. That migration reached record numbers when the United States began mobilizing for World War II and blacks sought jobs in the defense establishment. In 1941, in response to the threat of a massive protest march on Washington, D.C., President Franklin Roosevelt issued an executive order barring racial discrimination in defense industries or government employment. The housing picture, however, was different. Property owners relied on devices like racially restrictive covenants, neighborhood association agreements, and agreements among real estate brokers to restrict the expansion of African-American residential communities in cities with increasing numbers of African-American workers.

Although racially restrictive municipal housing statutes had been invalidated in *Buchanan v. Warley*, 245 U.S. 60 (1917), racially restrictive covenants between private individuals—contractual agreements limiting the sale of real property to whites only—had been held beyond the reach of the Fifth Amendment (and, by implication, the Fourteenth Amendment) in a 1926 case arising from the District of Columbia. *Corrigan v. Buckley*, 271 U.S. 323. Constitutional, racially restrictive, private covenants maintained separation between the races, creating a rapid increase in social tensions and numerous legal battles.

St. Louis, Missouri, was one of many American cities where whites sought to contain African-Americans in clearly defined areas by use of racially restrictive covenants. In 1910, whites in a neighborhood in the northwestern part of the city formed the Marcus Avenue Improvement Association, which drew a "color line" along a number of blocks bordering a predominantly black neighborhood. The following year, the Association began putting racial restrictions in deeds to prevent persons of color from purchasing homes on that line or beyond.

In August 1945, J. D. and Ethel Lee Shelley, a black couple, told St. Louis realtor Robert Bishop (also the minister of their evangelical church) that they wished to buy a house. The following month, Bishop purchased a two-apartment house located at 4600 Labadie Avenue, one of the streets on the "color line" identified by the Marcus Avenue Improvement Association. Bishop bought the house in the name of Geraldine Fitzgerald, a white woman. Until

Fitzgerald's purchase, the property had been owned by a signatory to a restrictive covenant. Bishop then had Mrs. Fitzgerald sell the property to the Shelleys. When the Shelleys moved into the house in October, the Marcus Avenue Improvement Association filed suit on behalf of Louis and Fern Kraemer, who lived at 3542 Labadie Avenue, to enjoin the Shelleys from possessing the house on the ground that their possession violated the racially restrictive covenant covering the neighborhood. The Kraemers were selected as the plaintiffs because Mrs. Kraemer's parents had been signatories to the original restrictive covenants in the neighborhood in 1911.

The Circuit Court of the City of St. Louis dismissed the Kraemers' request for an injunction and overruled their motion for a new trial. It ruled that the restrictive covenant was not effective because it had not been signed by all the property owners in the area.

The Kraemers appealed to the St. Louis Court of Appeals, which transferred the case to the Supreme Court of Missouri. That court reversed the trial court on the strength of *Corrigan v. Buckley*, 271 U.S. 323 (1926). In its opinion the court stated that it deplored the living conditions of Negroes in St. Louis brought about by private segregation, but held that correcting the situation was "beyond the authority of the courts generally, and in particular in a case involving the contractual rights between parties to a law suit."

The Shelleys petitioned the Supreme Court for a writ of certiorari.

HIGHLIGHTS OF SUPREME COURT ARGUMENTS

Note: The case was consolidated with *McGhee v. Sipes*, raising the validity of restrictive covenants in the city of Detroit, Michigan.

BRIEF FOR THE SHELLEYS

◆ Restrictive covenants based exclusively on race or color violate the 1866 Civil Rights Act, which gives all citizens of the United States the same rights to inherit, purchase, lease, sell, hold, and convey real and personal property. Restrictive covenants, having goals opposite federal and state law, are as unenforceable as any other contract that violates public policy.

If restrictive covenants are legal, judicial enforcement of such covenants constitutes state action in violation of the Fourteenth Amendment. In St. Louis alone, judicial enforcement of restrictive covenants has created a housing crisis affecting over one hundred thousand Negro families, resulting in overcrowding, ill health, death, juvenile delinquency, and crime.

AMICUS CURIAE BRIEFS SUPPORTING THE SHELLEYS

United States; American Association for the United Nations; American Jewish Committee.

BRIEF FOR THE KRAEMERS

◆ This case raises no substantial federal question because no legislative enactment was involved to invoke any provisions of the Fourteenth Amendment. Courts, in adjudicating the contested rights of litigants, do not engage in the kind of state action prohibited by the Fourteenth Amendment.

◆ Private contracts between individuals are not touched by the Fourteenth Amendment or statutes enacted to enforce it.

◆ The Shelleys cannot complain of a due process violation. They had notice of the restrictive covenant when they purchased the home from Josephine Fitzgerald because it was recorded in the deed. No state action was involved in the restrictive covenant among the homeowners in the neighborhood in which the Shelleys sought to buy a house.

◆ Claims of equal protection and denial of privileges and immunities are also unavailing because there is no state action involved in restrictive covenants. This case is controlled by *Corrigan v. Buckley*, 271 U.S. 323 (1926).

◆ If the Shelleys are to prevail, the Court will have to promulgate a doctrine that would, through the Fourteenth Amendment, establish direct Federal control of the individual citizens of the United States and destroy State sovereignty.

AMICUS CURIAE BRIEF SUPPORTING THE KRAEMERS

National Association of Real Estate Boards.

SUPREME COURT DECISION: 6–0

(Reed, Jackson, and Rutledge, J.J., did not participate.)

VINSON, C.J.

... It cannot be doubted that among the civil rights intended to be protected from discriminatory state action by the Fourteenth Amendment are the rights to acquire, enjoy, own and dispose of property. Equality in the enjoyment of property rights was regarded by the framers of that Amendment as an essential pre-condition to the realization of other basic civil rights and liberties which the Amendment was intended to guarantee....

Since the decision of this Court in the *Civil Rights Cases* [of 1883], the principle has become firmly embedded in our constitutional law that the action inhibited by the first section of the Fourteenth Amendment is only such action as may fairly be said to be that of the States. That Amendment erects no shield against merely private conduct, however discriminatory or wrongful.

We conclude, therefore, that the restrictive agreements standing alone cannot be regarded as violative of any rights guaranteed to petitioners by the Fourteenth Amendment. So long as the purposes of those agreements are effectuated by voluntary adherence to their terms, it would appear clear that there has been no action by the State and the provisions of the Amendment have not been violated.

But here there was more. These are cases in which the purposes of the agreements were secured only by judicial enforcement by state courts of the restrictive terms of the agreements....

[F]rom the time of the adoption of the Fourteenth Amendment until the present, it has been the consistent ruling of this Court that the action of the States to which the Amendment has reference includes action of state courts and state judicial officials. Although, in construing the terms of the Fourteenth Amendment, differences have from time to time been expressed as to whether particular types of state action may be said to offend the Amendment's prohibitory provisions, it has never been suggested that state court action is immunized from the operation of those provisions simply because the act is that of the judicial branch of the state government....

We have no doubt that there has been state action in these cases in the full and complete sense of the phrase. The undisputed facts disclose that peti-tioners were willing purchasers of properties upon which they desired to establish homes. The owners of the properties were willing sellers; and contracts of sale were accordingly consummated. It is clear that but for the active intervention of the state courts, supported by the full panoply of state power, petitioners would have been free to occupy the properties in question without restraint....

We hold that in granting judicial enforcement of the restrictive agreements in these cases, the States have denied petitioners the equal protection of the laws and that, therefore, the action of the state courts cannot stand. We have noted that freedom from discrimination by the States in the enjoyment of property rights was among the basic objectives sought to be effectuated by the framers of the Fourteenth Amendment. That such discrimination has occurred in these cases is clear. Because of the race or color of these petitioners they have been denied rights of ownership or occupancy enjoyed as a matter of course by other citizens of different race or color....

Reversed.

COMMENTS

1. In 1938, the National Association for the Advancement of Colored People (NAACP) incorporated the Legal Defense and Educational Fund (Inc. Fund) to provide full-time staff to pursue civil rights litigation. The Inc. Fund became actively involved in litigating several issues, including residential segregation in cities, unequal education opportunities, and all-white primaries. Despite the Inc. Fund's interest in restrictive covenant cases, it did not become involved in *Shelley*. According to Richard Kluger, NAACP staff members Thurgood Marshall and Charles Houston thought the petition for certiorari in *Shelley* was premature because of the composition of the Supreme Court and because of attorney George Vaughn's lack of appellate experience. Nonetheless, they helped to file the appeal in *McGhee v. Sipes*,

(the case consolidated with *Shelley*) after Vaughn filed the petition in *Shelley*. Marshall was lead counsel on appeal in *McGhee*. (See Kluger, *Simple Justice* [New York, NY: Vintage Books, 1975], pp. 248–249.)

Counsel for the Shelleys relied primarily on legal arguments in attacking the restrictive covenants. Marshall and Houston relied more on the negative sociological effects of the covenants, submitting a brief patterned after Louis Brandeis's brief in *Muller v. Oregon*, 208 U.S. 412 (1908). (See Chapter 6, p. 826.) Their brief described the consequences of the ghettos created by restrictive covenants, including crowding, crime, delinquency, and racial tensions that affected the entire community.

2. In companion cases to *Shelley*, also argued by NAACP counsel—*Hurd v. Hodge* and *Urciola v. Hodge*, 334 U.S. 24 (1948)—the Court refused to enforce restrictive covenants in the District of Columbia. Counsel for Hurd and Urciola argued that the covenants violated the Due Process Clause of the Fifth Amendment. The unanimous Supreme Court (Reed, Jackson, and Rutledge not participating) avoided the constitutional question by holding that D.C. courts were prohibited by the Civil Rights Act of 1866 from enforcing the covenants. Justice Frankfurter, in a concurring opinion, argued that sound judicial discretion required denial of relief (i.e., refusal to enforce the covenants) in federal court where the granting of like relief in state courts would violate the Fourteenth Amendment.

3. Justices Reed, Jackson, and Rutledge did not participate in any of the restrictive covenant cases. Considerable speculation surrounded their absence, ranging from rumors that they themselves owned properties subject to restrictive covenants, to an "alternative rumor" that at least one had spoken out publicly against restrictive covenants.

Questions

1. What was the "state action" in *Shelley v. Kraemer* that in the Supreme Court's opinion subjected this controversy to judicial review? On what grounds is such an expansive definition constitutionally defensible?

2. Rather than devoting its attention primarily to whether there was state action, should the justices in *Shelley* have focused on whether that state action was unconstitutional? What is the difference between these two approaches?

3. Is failure by the state to bar discrimination a form of state action that denies people the equal protection of the laws?

4. The finding of "state action" in *Shelley* was essential for the plaintiffs

to prevail. The "state action" doctrine has continued to evolve, as the following cases illustrate. Read the following case summaries, then respond to the question posed after *Lebron v. National Railroad Passenger Corporation*, 513 U.S. 374 (1995), p. 139.

Case: *Williams v. United States*, 341 U.S. 97 (1951).

Vote: 5–4

Decision: A private detective holding a special police officer's card from the City of Miami, Florida, who was accompanied by a regular policeman and who beat robbery suspects to obtain confessions, acted under color of state law in violation of a federal statute. The statute made it an offense for any person, under color of law, to wilfully deprive others of any rights, privileges, or immunities secured or protected by the Constitution or laws of the United States.

Case: *Barrows v. Jackson*, 346 U.S. 249 (1953).

Vote: 6–1 (Reed and Jackson, J.J., did not participate.)

Decision: A racially restrictive covenant cannot be enforced in a suit for damages against a property owner who violated an agreement among neighbors in Los Angeles by selling her property to non-Caucasians without incorporating the racial restrictions. Action by the state court might result in a denial of constitutional rights to non-Caucasians.

Case: *Pennsylvania v. Board of Trustees*, 353 U.S. 230 (1957).

Vote: *Per curiam*

Decision: The board that operates a "college" created by a will probated in 1831 for "poor white male orphans, between the ages of six and ten years," is an agency of the state of Pennsylvania even though it acts as the trustee of the estate creating the institution. Refusal to admit Negro boys to the school therefore violates the Fourteenth Amendment.

Case: *Burton v. Wilmington Parking Authority*, 365 U.S. 715 (1961).

Vote: 6–3

Decision: A restaurant leased from the state of Delaware, located in a publicly owned and operated parking building, cannot refuse service to Negroes without violating the Equal Protection Clause of the Fourteenth Amendment. When a state leases public property under the circumstances presented in this case, the proscriptions of the Fourteenth Amendment must be complied with by the lessee as though they were binding covenants written into the lease agreement.

Case: *Peterson v. City of Greenville*, 373 U.S. 244 (1963).

Vote: 8–1

Decision: State action occurs when a city has an ordinance on its books that requires segregation in privately owned eating facilities. Enforcement of the state's trespass laws under such circumstances violates the Fourteenth Amendment.

Case: *Lombard v. Louisiana*, 373 U.S. 267 (1963).

Vote: 8–1

Decision: In the absence of a law requiring segregated eating places, the mayor, police chief, and other city officials of New Orleans made statements condemning sit-in demonstrations and urging lunch counter owners to resist protesters' demands. Such statements effectively required that public eating facilities be segregated. Consequently, following *Peterson*, "the State cannot achieve the same result by an official command which has at least as much coercive effect as an ordinance."

Case: *Griffin v. Maryland*, 378 U.S. 130 (1963).

Vote: 6–3

Decision: A Montgomery County deputy sheriff, employed as a special policemen by a privately owned amusement park, who enforced the park's policy of excluding Negroes engaged in state action in removing Negroes from the park. "If an individual is possessed of state authority and purports to act under that authority, his action is state action. It is irrelevant that he might have taken the same action had he acted in a purely private capacity...."

Case: *Reitman v. Mulkey*, 386 U.S. 369 (1967).

Vote: 5–4

Decision: A 1964 California ballot measure, Proposition 14, which amended the California constitution to prohibit that state from denying any person's right to decline to sell, lease, or rent real property as that person chooses, involves the state in racial discrimination in violation of the Fourteenth Amendment.

Case: *Jones v. Alfred H. Mayer Co.*, 392 U.S. 409 (1968).

Vote: 7–2

Decision: The 1866 Civil Rights Act bars private as well as state-supported racial discrimination in the sale and rental of housing. Congress's authority to enact the legislation stemmed from the Thirteenth Amendment rather than the Equal Protection Clause of the Fourteenth Amendment. The Thirteenth Amendment was adopted to remove the "badges of slavery" and gave Congress power to enforce that removal. The 1866 Civil Rights Act "plainly meant to secure [the right to buy and sell property] against interference from any source whatever, whether governmental or private."

Case: *Evans v. Abney*, 396 U.S. 435 (1970).

Vote: 5–3 (Marshall, J., did not participate.)

Decision: Management by a private trustee of a park bequeathed to the city of Macon, Georgia, on the condition that it serve whites only violates the Fourteenth Amendment because the park retains its public character. However, reversion of the land to the original heirs since it cannot be operated according to the terms of the will, and its subsequent closure as a park, does not violate the Fourteenth Amendment because the facility deprives blacks and whites equally of its use.

Case: *Moose Lodge No. 107 v. Irvis*, 407 U.S. 163 (1972).

Vote: 6–3

Decision: A private club operating under a Pennsylvania liquor license that refuses service at the club's dining room and bar solely on the basis of race does not violate the Fourteenth Amendment. Granting a liquor license does not sufficiently implicate the state in the club's discriminatory guest practices as to make those practices "state action" within the purview of the Equal Protection Clause.

Case: *Jackson v. Metropolitan Edison Co.*, 419 U.S. 345 (1974).

Vote: 6–3

Decision: A privately owned and operated utility corporation, holding a certificate of public convenience issued by the state of Pennsylvania, is not required to provide notice, a hearing, and an opportunity to pay any amounts found due before terminating electric service. Being a heavily regulated private utility with a partial monopoly does not sufficiently connect the state with the challenged termination to make the corporation's conduct "state action" for purposes of the Fourteenth Amendment.

Case: *Flagg Bros. v. Brooks*, 436 U.S. 149 (1978).

Vote: 6–3

Decision: A warehouseman's proposed private sale of goods entrusted to him for storage, as permitted by the self-help provisions of the New York Uniform Commercial Code, is not properly attributable to the state of New York and thus is not state action violative of the Fourteenth Amendment's Due Process and Equal Protection clauses.

Case: *Blum v. Yaretsky*, 457 U.S. 991 (1982).

Vote: 7–2

Decision: Privately owned nursing homes providing services that the state would not necessarily provide, even though they are state subsidized and extensively regulated, do not fall within the ambit of *Burton*. Periodically assessing whether Medicaid patients are receiving an appropriate level of care and, if less extensive care is required, transferring such recipients to a less costly facility, does not amount to state action.

Case: *San Francisco Arts & Athletics, Inc. v. United States Olympic Committee*, 483 U.S. 522 (1987).

Vote: 5–4

Decision: Federal sponsorship of the United States Olympic Committee (USOC) does not make it a governmental actor to whom the Fifth Amendment applies. Consequently, a USOC suit to enjoin use of the term "Olympics" to describe an athletic competition is not subject to challenge under the Fifth Amendment.

Case: *National Collegiate Athletic Association v. Tarkanian*, 488 U.S. 179 (1988).

Vote: 5–4

Decision: The National Collegiate Athletic Association's (NCAA) promulgation and enforcement of rules leading to the University of Nevada at Las Vegas's (UNLV) suspension of its head basketball coach, does not constitute state action. Neither UNLV's role in formulating NCAA rules and policies nor its adoption of those rules transformed NCAA into a state actor.

Case: *Edmonson v. Leesville Concrete Co.,* 500 U.S. 614 (1991).
Vote: 6–3

Decision: Exercise of peremptory challenges by Leesville Concrete Company in a district court to exclude jurors during *voir dire* on account of their race was pursuant to a course of state action. First, Leesville would not have been able to engage in alleged discriminatory acts without statutory authorization of the use of peremptory challenges in civil cases. Second, Leesville has made extensive use of government procedures administered solely by government officials, including the trial judge, himself a state actor. Moreover, the action in question involves the performance of a traditional governmental function since the peremptory challenge is used in selecting the jury, an entity that is a governmental body having no attributes of a private actor.

Case: *Lebron v. National Railroad Passenger Corporation,* 513 U.S. 374 (1995).
Vote: 8–1

Decision: The National Railroad Passenger Corporation, Amtrak, created by the Rail Passenger Service Act of 1970, is an entity of the U.S. government because it was created by Congress to serve specific federal objectives and is controlled by government appointees. Consequently, it is bound to respect the First Amendment guarantee of free speech. (The Court expressed no view about whether Amtrak's refusal to lease electronic billboard space to Lebron for an anti-Coors beer advertisement violated the First Amendment.)

Are there discernable doctrinal trends in the Supreme Court's approach to state action since *Shelley v. Kraemer*? If so, are they consistent? To what extent, if any, are judicial trends in defining the concept of "state action" related to broader trends in American politics?

Suggestions for Further Reading

Allen, Francis A., "Remembering *Shelley v. Kraemer*," 67 *Washington University Law Quarterly* (1989): 709.

Black, Charles, "Foreword: 'State Action,' Equal Protection, and California's Proposition 14," 81 *Harvard Law Review* (1967): 69.

Brest, Paul, "State Action and Liberal Theory," 130 *University of Pennsylvania Law Review* (1982): 1296.

Chemerinsky, Erwin, "Rethinking State Action," 80 *Northwestern University Law Review* (1985).

Choper, Jesse, "Thoughts on State Action," 57 *Washington University Law Quarterly* (1979): 757.

Frank, John P., and Robert F. Monro, "The Original Understanding of 'Equal Protection of the Laws,'" 50 *Washington University Law Quarterly* (1972): 421.

Glennon, Robert J. Jr., and John E. Nowak, "A Functional Analysis of the Fourteenth Amendment 'State Action' Requirement," *The Supreme Court Review* (Chicago, IL: University of Chicago Press, 1976).

Goldstein, Leslie F., "The Death and Transfiguration of the State Action Doctrine," 4 *Hastings Constitutional Law Quarterly* (1977): 1.

Goodman, Frank I., "Professor Brest on State Action and Liberal Theory, and a Postscript to Professor Stone," 130 *University of Pennsylvania Law Review* (1982): 1331.

Gressman, Eugene, "The Unhappy History of Civil Rights Legislation," 50 *Michigan Law Review* (1952): 1323.

Henkin, Louis, "*Shelley v. Kraemer*: Notes for a Revised Opinion," 110 *University of Pennsylvania Law Review* (1962): 473.

Horowitz, Harold W., "The Misleading Search for 'State Action,'" 30 *Southern California Law Review* (1957): 208.

Hyman, J. D., "Segregation and the Fourteenth Amendment," 4 *Vanderbilt Law Review* (1951): 555.

Lewis, Thomas P., "*Burton v. Wilmington Parking Authority*—A Case without Precedent," 61 *Columbia Law Review* (1961): 1458.

Note, "Federal Power to Regulate Private Discrimination: The Revival of the Enforcement Clauses of the Reconstruction Era Amendments," 74 *Columbia Law Review* (1974): 449.

Note, "State Court Approaches to the State Action Requirement: Private Rights, Public Values, and Constitutional Choices," 39 *Kansas Law Review* (1991): 495.

Peters, Roger Paul, "Civil Rights and State Non-Action," 34 *Notre Dame Lawyer* (1959): 303.

Schwarzchild, Maimon, "Value Pluralism and the Constitution: In Defense of the State Action Doctrine," *The Supreme Court Review* (Chicago, IL: University of Chicago Press, 1988).

Sunstein, Cass, "*Lochner's Legacy*," 87 *Columbia Law Review* (1987): 873.

Tushnet, Mark, "*Shelley v. Kraemer* and Theories of Equality," 33 *New York University Law School Law Review* (1988): 383.

Vose, Clement E., *Caucasians Only: The Supreme Court, the NAACP, and the Restrictive Covenant Cases* (Berkeley, CA: University of California Press, 1959).

Van Alstyne, William, and Kenneth Karst, "State Action," 14 *Stanford University Law Review* (1961): 3

Wechsler, Herbert, "Toward Neutral Principles in Constitutional Law," 73 *Harvard Law Review* (1959): 1.

Westin, Alan F., "The Case of the Prejudiced Doorkeeper," in *Quarrels That Have Shaped the Constitution*, rev. ed., ed. John A. Garraty (New York, NY: Harper and Row, 1987).

LIMITS ON FEDERAL JUDICIAL POWER: JURISDICTION

Cherokee Nation v. Georgia
5 Peters 1 (1831)

SETTING

The first European settlers in North America in the sixteenth century were Spaniards. After initial efforts to forcibly subdue indigenous peoples, the Spaniards created the "encomienda" system under which the King of Spain "entrusted" a particular group of Native American families to a specific Spanish settler in a relationship that was little better than slavery. By 1700, contact with Europeans had resulted in so many diseases ravaging the indigenous population that their numbers dwindled to some four million from approximately fifty million in the areas conquered by the Spaniards.

Arrival of British emigrants on the Atlantic Coast in the seventeenth century led to skirmishes and then outright wars with Native Americans. By the early nineteenth century, indigenous tribes had turned over hundreds of millions of acres of territory through various treaties and cessions to white settlers. As Americans moved inland to places like the Ohio River Valley, frontier squatters settled on other Indian lands. Native resistance precipitated fierce fighting such as the November 7, 1811, Battle of Tippecanoe, a precursor engagement of the War of 1812, which was motivated, in part, by Americans' hope to put an end to the "Indian menace." The War of 1812 ended in 1814 with the Treaty of Ghent that merely restored borders to what they had been before the war.

Beginning with the presidential administration of James Madison in 1809, the policy of the U.S. government was to remove Indians from lands that whites wished to occupy. *Cherokee Nation v. Georgia* arose out of the conflict between the policy of Indian removal and treaty rights previously negotiated between the United States and the Indian tribes.

Under a treaty signed between the United States and the Cherokee Indians in 1791, the Cherokees were guaranteed a tract of territory located within the boundaries of Georgia, North Carolina, South Carolina, Tennessee, and Alabama. In return, the Cherokees ceded other lands to the United States.

In 1802, the state of Georgia ceded lands now constituting the states of Alabama and Mississippi to the United States on the condition that the United States extinguish Indian titles to land within the remaining territory of Georgia. While Congress purchased millions of acres of Cherokee lands in Alabama and Mississippi beginning in 1805, it bought only about one-fifth of the Cherokee lands in Georgia.

Dissatisfied with the national government's progress in extinguishing Cherokee titles to land within its borders, the Georgia legislature passed a series of acts culminating in legislation in 1828 and 1829 that asserted complete sovereignty over the Cherokees and claimed that the national government lacked power to bind a state by a treaty made with Indians. The purpose of the Georgia legislation was to remove the Cherokees and to claim their lands. A series of events motivated the Georgia legislature to act when it did.

One event was an 1823 decision by the Supreme Court of the United States holding that Indians were entitled only to occupancy, not outright ownership, of the lands they inhabited, and hence could not convey clear title to private individuals who purchased from them. Speaking for a unanimous Court, Chief Justice Marshall acquiesced in the position argued by the United States:

> The United States ... have unequivocally acceded to that great and broad rule by which its civilized inhabitants now hold this country. They hold, and assert in themselves, the title by which it was acquired. They maintain, as all others have maintained, that discovery gave an exclusive right to extinguish the Indian title of occupancy, either by purchase or conquest; and gave also a right to such a degree of sovereignty as the circumstances of the people would allow them to exercise. *Johnson v. McIntosh*, 8 Wheaton 543, 587 (1823).

Another event that motivated the Georgia legislature was discovery of gold on Cherokee lands. A third was the Cherokees' declaration of their intent to remain on their lands in 1828, reflected in their adoption of a constitution for a permanent government.

Claiming that the Georgia legislation was unconstitutional under the Cherokees' treaty with the United States, the tribe sought the protection of federal troops against the efforts of the state to remove them. President Andrew Jackson responded that the president had no power to protect the Cherokees against the laws of Georgia. In May 1830, at President Jackson's recommendation, Congress passed new Indian removal legislation and appropriated $500,000 for Indian removal.

In 1831, at the recommendation of Daniel Webster, representatives of the Cherokee Nation hired former Attorney General William Wirt to file suit in the Supreme Court of the United States seeking an injunction to prevent the state of Georgia from enforcing its laws on Cherokee lands. The suit claimed that the Supreme Court had original jurisdiction over controversies between a state and a foreign nation, and that the Cherokees possessed the rights of self-government defined by treaty with the United States. Wirt asked that the Georgia legislation of 1828 and 1829 be declared unconstitutional because it conflicted with treaties that were the supreme law of the land.

On the day assigned for argument in the case, the Supreme Court received a supplemental claim on behalf of the Cherokee Nation. It asserted that in December 1830, Georgia had executed a Cherokee Indian, Corn Tassel, who had been arrested for murder in Cherokee territory. The supplemental claim asserted that Corn Tassel had been hanged in defiance of a writ of error allowed by Chief Justice Marshall upon review of Corn Tassel's conviction in a Georgia court. The governor of Georgia ordered Corn Tassel's execution in defiance of the authority of federal courts over the state. The Georgia legislature also denounced the Supreme Court's writ of error in the case and requested all officers of the state to disregard any judicial process served on them.

The supplemental claim recounted the passage of several additional laws by the state of Georgia after Corn Tassel's execution. One law authorized Cherokee lands to be surveyed and then distributed by lottery among the white people of Georgia. Another law voided all subsequent contracts made with the Cherokee Indians. A third law authorized the governor to take control of the gold, silver, and other mines in Cherokee country, and to protect the gold mines with armed forces. According to the supplemental claim, the governor of Georgia had stationed an armed force at the gold mines on Cherokee lands as part of his enforcement of these laws.

HIGHLIGHTS OF SUPREME COURT ARGUMENTS

BRIEF FOR CHEROKEE NATION

◆ The Supreme Court has original jurisdiction over this case because it involves a controversy between the Cherokees, a foreign nation, and a state of the United States.

◆ The controversy in this suit is of a judicial nature, warranting interposition of the Court's authority.

◆ An injunction prohibiting enforcement of the Georgia laws aimed at removing the Cherokees and taking their land is the only remedy under the circumstances.

Note: The State of Georgia refused to obey the Supreme Court's subpoena to appear.

SUPREME COURT DECISION: **6–2**

MARSHALL, C.J.

... If the courts were permitted to indulge their sympathies, a case better calculated to excite them can scarcely be imagined. A people once numerous, powerful, and truly independent, found by our ancestors in the quiet and uncontrolled possession of an ample domain, gradually sinking beneath our superior policy, our arts and our arms, have yielded their lands by successive treaties, each of which contains a solemn guarantee of the residue, until they retain no more of their formerly extensive territory than is deemed necessary to their comfortable subsistence. To preserve this remnant the present application is made.

Before we can look into the merits of the case, a preliminary inquiry presents itself. Has this court jurisdiction of the cause?

The third article of the Constitution describes the extent of the judicial power. The second section closes an enumeration of the cases to which it is extended, with "controversies" "between the State or the citizens thereof, and foreign states, citizens, or subjects." A subsequent clause of the same section gives the Supreme Court jurisdiction in all cases in which a state shall be a party. The party defendant may then unquestionably be sued in this court. May the plaintiff sue in it? Is the Cherokee Nation a foreign state in the sense in which that term is used in the Constitution?

The counsel for the plaintiffs have maintained the affirmative of this proposition with great earnestness and ability. So much of the argument as was intended to prove the character of the Cherokees as a State, as a distinct political society separated from others, capable of managing its own affairs and governing itself, has, in the opinion of a majority of the judges, been completely successful. They have been uniformly treated as a State from the settlement of our country. The numerous treaties made with them by the United States recognize them as a people capable of maintaining the relations of peace and war, of being responsible in their political character for any violation of their engagements, or for any aggression committed on the citizens of the United States by any individual of their community. Laws have been enacted in the spirit of these treaties. The acts of our government plainly recognize the Cherokee Nation as a State, and the courts are bound by those acts.

A question of much more difficulty remains. Do the Cherokees constitute a foreign state in the sense of the Constitution?...

The condition of the Indians in relation to the United States is perhaps unlike that of any other two people in existence. In the general, nations not owing a common allegiance are foreign to each other. The term "foreign nation" is, with strict propriety, applicable by either to the other. But the relation of the Indians to the United States is marked by peculiar and cardinal distinctions which exist nowhere else.

The Indian Territory is admitted to compose part of the United States. In all our maps, geographical treaties, histories and laws, it is so considered. In all our intercourse with foreign nations, in our commercial regulations, in any attempt at intercourse between Indians, and foreign nations, they are considered within the jurisdictional limits of the United States, subject to many of those restraints which are imposed upon our own citizens. They acknowledge themselves in their treaties to be under the protection of the United States; they admit that the United States shall have the sole and exclusive right of regulating the trade with them, and managing all their affairs as they think proper; and the Cherokees in particular were allowed by the treaty of Hopewell, which preceded the Constitution, "to send a deputy of their choice, whenever they think fit, to Congress." Treaties were made with some tribes by the State of New York under a then unsettled construction of the confederation, by which they ceded all their lands to that State, taking back a limited grant to themselves, in which they admit their dependence.

Though the Indians are acknowledged to have an unquestionable and, heretofore, unquestioned right to the lands they occupy until that right shall be extinguished by a voluntary cession to our government, yet it may well be doubted whether those tribes which reside within the acknowledged boundaries of the United States can, with strict accuracy, be denominated foreign nations. They occupy a territory to which we assert a title independent of their will, which must take effect in point of possession when their right of possession ceases. Meanwhile they are in a state of pupilage. Their relation to the United States resembles that of a ward to his guardians.

They look to our government for protection; rely upon its kindness and its power; appeal to it for relief to their wants; and address the President as their great father. They and their country are considered by foreign nations, as well as by ourselves, as being so completely under the sovereignty and dominion of the United States, that any attempt to acquire their lands, or to form a political connection with them, would be considered by all as an invasion of our territory, and an act of hostility.

These considerations go far to support the opinion that the framers of our Constitution had not the Indian tribes in view when they opened the courts of the Union to controversies between a State or the citizen thereof, and foreign states....

[T]he majority is of opinion that an Indian tribe or nation within the United States is not a foreign state in the sense of the Constitution, and cannot maintain an action in the courts of the United States....

The motion for an injunction is denied.

JOHNSON, J., CONCURRING

... I cannot but think that there are strong reasons for doubting the applicability of the epithet "State," to a people so low in the grade of organized society as our Indian tribes most generally are....

But it is said that we have extended to them the means and inducement to become agricultural and civilized. It is true: and the immediate object of that policy was so obvious as probably to have intercepted the view of ulterior consequences. Independently of the general influence of humanity, these people were restless, warlike, and signally cruel in their irruptions during the Revolution. The policy, therefore, of enticing them to the arts of peace, and to those improvements which war might lay desolate, was obvious, and it was wise to prepare them for what was probably then contemplated, to wit, to incorporate them in time into our respective governments: a policy which their inveterate habits and deep seated enmity has altogether baffled. But the project of ultimately organizing them into States within the limits of those States which had not ceded or should not cede to the United States the jurisdiction over the Indian territory within their bounds, could not possibly have entered into the contemplation of our government....

BALDWIN, J., CONCURRING

... In my opinion there is no plaintiff in this suit; and this opinion precludes any examination into the merits of the bill, or the weight of any minor objections. My judgement stops me at the threshold, and forbids me to examine into the acts complained of....

THOMPSON, AND STORY, J.J., DISSENTING

... In the opinion pronounced by the court, the merits of the controversy between the State of Georgia and the Cherokee Indians have not been taken into consideration. The denial of the application for an injunction has been placed solely on the ground of want of jurisdiction in this court to grant the relief prayed for. It became, therefore, unnecessary to inquire into the merits of the case. But thinking as I do that the court has jurisdiction of the case, and may grant relief, at least in part, it may become necessary for me, in the course of my opinion, to glance at the merits of the controversy....

Testing the character and condition of the Cherokee Indians ... it is not perceived how it is possible to escape the conclusion that they form a sovereign State. They have always been dealt with as such by the government of the United States, both before and since the adoption of the present Constitution. They have been admitted and treated as a people governed solely and exclusively by their own laws, usages and customs within their own territory, claiming and exercising exclusive dominion over the same; yielding up by treaty, from time to time, portions of their land, but still claiming absolute sovereignty and self-government over what remained unsold. And this has been the light in which they have, until recently, been considered from the earliest settlement of the country by the white people. And, indeed, I do not understand it is denied by a majority of the court that the Cherokee Indians form a sovereign State according to the doctrine of the law of nations; but that, although a sovereign State, they are not considered a foreign state within the meaning of the Constitution....

If we look to the whole course of treatment by this country of the Indians from the year 1775 to the present day, when dealing with them in their aggregate capacity as nations or tribes, and regarding the mode or manner in which all negotiations have been carried on and concluded with them, the conclusion appears to me irresistible that they have been regarded by the executive and legislative branches of the government not only as sovereign and independent, but as foreign nations or tribes, not within the jurisdiction nor under the government of the States within which they were located....

That the Cherokee Nation of Indians

have, by virtue of [treaties entered into with the United States beginning in 1775], an exclusive right of occupancy of the lands in question, and that the United States are bound under their guarantee to protect the nation in the enjoyment of such occupancy, cannot, in my judgment, admit of a doubt; and that some of the laws of Georgia set out in the bill are in violation of, and in conflict with those treaties and the Act of 1802 [under which Georgia ceded to the United States claims to western lands], is to my mind equally clear. But a majority of the court having refused the injunction, so that no relief whatever can be granted, it would be a fruitless inquiry for me to go at large into an examination of the extent to which relief might be granted by this court, according to my own view of the case....

The laws of Georgia set out in the bill, if carried fully into operation, go to the length of abrogating all of the laws of the Cherokees, abolishing their government, and entirely subverting their national character. Although the whole of these laws may be in violation of the treaties made with this nation, it is probable this court cannot grant relief to the full extent of the complaint. Some of them, however, are so directly at variance with these treaties and the laws of the United States touching the rights of property secured to them, that I can perceive no objection to the application of judicial relief. The State of Georgia certainly could not have intended these laws as declarations of hostility, or wish their execution of them to be viewed in any manner as acts of war; but merely as an assertion of what is claimed as a legal right; and in this light ought they to be considered by this court....

Upon the whole, I am of opinion:

1. That the Cherokees compose a foreign State within the sense and meaning of the Constitution, and constitute a competent party to maintain a suit against the State of Georgia.

2. That the bill presents a case for judicial consideration, arising under the laws of the United States, and treaties made under their authority with the Cherokee Nation, and which laws and treaties have been and are threatened to be still further violated by the laws of the State of Georgia referred to in this opinion.

3. That an injunction is a fit and proper writ to be issued to prevent the further execution of such laws, and ought therefore to be awarded.

And I am authorized by my brother Story to say that he concurs with me in this opinion.

QUESTIONS

1. Jurisdiction refers to the authority of a court to take cognizance of and decide a case. State courts are presumed to have jurisdiction over cases while federal tribunals are courts of limited jurisdiction. In order to be entitled to sue in federal court, a party must demonstrate that the Constitution or an act of Congress gives a federal court authority to decide the case. In Chief Justice Marshall's view, what elements in the Cherokee Nation's lawsuit are lacking with respect to the Supreme Court's jurisdiction? On what basis does

Justice Thompson disagree? What are the political implications of Marshall's and Thompson's approaches? Why might those implications have been different in 1831 than in our time?

2. In the American legal system, a party that is sued has an obligation to respond to the lawsuit and, if it fails to do so, the court enters a default judgment against it. In this case, the state of Georgia refused to defend the action brought against it, even though the Supreme Court issued a subpoena ordering it to do so. What factors might have entered into the Court's decision not to enter a default judgment against Georgia and to decide *Cherokee Nation* instead on jurisdictional grounds? What would have been the likely political consequences if the Court had entered a default judgment?

3. Historian G. Edward White reports that Justice Story wrote a letter to the Court's reporter, Richard Peters, about the dissent in *Cherokee Nation*. Story said that "neither Judge T. [Thompson] or myself contemplated delivering a dissenting opinion until the Chief Justice suggested to us the propriety of it, and his own desire that we should do it" (*History of the Supreme Court of the United States*, vols. 3 and 4, *The Marshall Court and Cultural Change, 1815–1835* [New York: Macmillan Publishing Co., 1988], p. 730).

   Chief Justice Marshall thought it important for the Supreme Court to speak with one voice and therefore eliminated the Court's practice of issuing *seriatim* opinions. Why might Marshall have invited a dissent in *Cherokee Nation*? Are there indications in his opinion that Chief Justice Marshall was uncomfortable with his own opinion?

4. When *Cherokee Nation* was decided, it was well known that President Andrew Jackson was not sympathetic to Indians. It was equally well known that Jackson was sympathetic to state policies calling for Indian removal. Congressional policy also supported Indian removal. If Chief Justice Marshall had ruled in *Cherokee Nation* that the Court had jurisdiction over the Cherokee's cause, and had ruled in their favor, it is likely that Jackson would have blinked at Georgia's defiance of the decision.

   What light does this prospect cast on Chief Justice Marshall's assertion in *Marbury v. Madison* that "it is emphatically the province and duty of the judicial department to say what the law is"? What light does this prospect cast on Alexander Hamilton's characterization in *Federalist* No. 78 of the Court as the "least dangerous branch"?

COMMENT

Just a year after the Court decided *Cherokee Nation*, it handed down its decision in *Worcester v. Georgia*, 6 Peters 515 (1832). That case involved a challenge to an 1828 Georgia statute that required all white persons living within Cherokee country after March 11, 1831, to take an oath of allegiance to the state and to obtain a residence license. Samuel A. Worcester and Elizur Butler, two missionaries living among the Cherokees, refused to apply for licenses. They were arrested, convicted by a Georgia Superior Court, and sentenced to four years of hard labor. Worcester appealed to the Supreme Court.

Chief Justice Marshall ruled that the Cherokee Nation was a "distinct community, occupying its own territory, with boundaries accurately described, in which the laws of Georgia can have no force, and which the citizens of Georgia have no right to enter but with the assent of the Cherokees themselves or in conformity with treaties and with the acts of Congress." Marshall also held that federal jurisdiction over Indian affairs was exclusive. The Georgia convictions of Worcester and Butler were therefore reversed.

The Georgia legislature responded to the Court's *Worcester* decision by adopting a resolution that stated: "Any attempt to reverse the decision of the Superior Court ... by the Supreme Court of the United States, will be held by this State as an unconstitutional and arbitrary interference in the administration of her criminal laws and will be treated as such...." Georgia refused to release Worcester and Butler. President Jackson made it clear he would not force Georgia to comply.

Ironically, the Cherokee crisis was defused when the South Carolina legislature passed a law in 1832 nullifying existing tariff laws of the United States. South Carolina saw the tariff as an infringement on states' rights. One section of the law attacked the Supreme Court's jurisdiction. President Jackson, a supporter of the tariff, responded to this state act of nullification by recommending that Congress enact legislation giving federal courts adequate powers to deal with nullification. The standoff quickly became a matter of compromise or dissolution of the Union.

Fearing an alliance would form between Georgia and South Carolina, resulting in armed rebellion, the Jackson administration sought to isolate Georgia's nullification actions from South Carolina's. It successfully pressured Georgia Governor Wilson Lumpkin to pardon Worcester and Butler without conceding the Supreme Court's jurisdiction over the case.

In 1835, some 13,000 Cherokees were removed forcibly to Oklahoma, consistent with U.S. policy of relocating Indians as far west as possible, to the "great American desert." Approximately 2,500 Cherokees died in the process of being herded into makeshift army stockades before their removal. Along the way west the Cherokees were subjected to humiliation by the soldiers assigned to protect them, theft by the civilians charged with resupplying them, and unremitting hostility from whites. Another 1,500 died during the forced march. *Worcester v. Georgia* thus culminated in the "Trail of Tears" for the Cherokee Nation.

LIMITS ON FEDERAL JUDICIAL POWER: JURISDICTION

Dred Scott v. Sandford
19 Howard 393 (1857)

SETTING

Two great sectional interests—the agrarian South with its slaveholding planta-
tion economy and the mercantile/shipping North with dreams of commercial
expansion—were pitted against one another early in America's history. Major
compromises over slavery, taxation, and representation were written into the
Constitution in an attempt to reconcile those interests. The Three-Fifths
Compromise in Article I, section 2, for example, provided that three-fifths "of
all other Persons" would be counted for purposes of apportioning congressional representation in the House of Representatives and for levying direct
taxes. Article I, section 9, prohibited Congress from prohibiting the
"Importation of such Persons as any of the States now existing shall think
proper to admit." Congress was given the power to regulate commerce in
Article I, section 8, but was prohibited by Article I, section 9, from imposing
taxes or duties on articles exported from any state, a power that might have
been used to tax slavery indirectly by imposing assessments on the products
of slave labor. As previous cases have demonstrated, the Union forged in 1787
threatened to come apart on several occasions over conflicts between states
and the national government. The slavery issue was deeply intertwined with
this controversy.

  During the 1830s, antislavery sentiment grew substantially, often
couched in terms of natural rights and Christian morality. William Lloyd
Garrison, for example, editor of the abolitionist newspaper *The Liberator,*
called the Constitution a covenant with death and an agreement with hell
because of its slavery provisions. The Missouri Compromise of 1820 sought to
resolve the question of the expansion of slavery by providing that for each
new free state admitted to the Union a slave state would be admitted as well.
The Missouri Compromise proved an unworkable truce in the face of burgeoning western migration and growing animosity between slavery proponents and
abolitionists. The Liberty Party, created in 1839, joined with antislavery
Democrats and "Conscience Whigs" in 1848 to form the Free-Soil Party. Free-
Soilers opposed the annexation of Texas by President John Tyler, a southerner who became president when William Henry Harrison died in office in
1841.

  In 1850 Congress attempted to settle the slavery controversy with
another compromise. The Compromise of 1850 consisted of five parts: (1)
California was admitted as a free state; (2) Texas gave up claims east of the

Rio Grande River for $10 million and would be admitted to the Union without prescription as to slavery; (3) Utah was organized as a territory with no slavery prescription; (4) slavery (but not the slave trade) was abolished in the District of Columbia; and (5) fugitive slave cases were placed under exclusive federal jurisdiction. During debate over the Compromise of 1850, several southerners expressed a desire to turn the problem over to the Supreme Court. The fifth provision of the Compromise created one legal channel for that possibility. Widespread nullification of the Fugitive Slave Act of 1850 in states like Ohio, Vermont, Michigan, Wisconsin, and Connecticut seemed certain to provide cases.

The Compromise of 1850 lasted only four years. The Kansas-Nebraska Act of 1854 eliminated both it and the earlier Missouri Compromise. The Kansas-Nebraska Act established a policy of Congressional noninterference with slavery in the territories, essentially inviting slave holders into them. The Act also provided for appeal to territorial courts and the Supreme Court of the United States in all cases involving slavery.

The Kansas-Nebraska Act prompted Free-Soilers, Whigs, and antislavery Democrats to form the Republican Party. As the Republican Party gathered strength in the North, radical southern leaders began to threaten secession from the Union. By the mid-1850s Supreme Court intervention seemed only a matter of time, because many cases had been filed to determine the status of slaves and their families who had resided for some time in free territories. Dred Scott was one.

Scott was a slave sold to John Emerson, an Army physician, in 1833, following the death of his original owner, Peter Blow. In 1834, Emerson took Scott from Missouri to the military post where he was assigned at Rock Island, Illinois, and held him as a slave until April 1836. Illinois was a free state. Then Emerson took Scott to the military post at Fort Snelling, on the west bank of the Mississippi River north of Missouri, and held him in slavery until 1838. Fort Snelling was in free territory under the Missouri Compromise of 1820.

In 1836, Emerson purchased a slave named Harriet Robinson, keeping her as a slave until 1838 while he was stationed at Fort Snelling. With Emerson's consent, Scott and Robinson were married. They had two children, Eliza and Lizzie. Eliza was born while the Scotts were at Fort Snelling.

In 1838, Emerson and the Scotts returned to Missouri, where Lizzie was born. Emerson died in 1843, leaving his slaves to his widow as part of his estate. In 1846, Scott, with the help of abolitionist lawyers, sued for his freedom. He claimed that his earlier residence in a free state and free territory had liberated him from slavery.

In 1852, in *Scott v. Emerson* (15 Missouri Rep. 682), the Missouri Supreme Court ruled against Scott. To do so, it had to overrule its 1836 decision, *Rachel v. Walker* (4 Missouri Rep. 350), which had held that the removal of a slave by his master to a free state made the slave forever free. Scott did not appeal the decision to the Supreme Court of the United States. Had he appealed, Scott would have confronted the Supreme Court's decision in *Strader v. Graham*, 10

Howard 82 (1851), which held that it lacked jurisdiction to declare whether slaves who had gone from Kentucky to Ohio were thereby made free. The Court held that the law of Kentucky, a slave state, governed the question.

In 1854, with the help of Peter Blow's children, Scott pursued a different legal route for his freedom. He filed an action in trespass in the U.S. Circuit Court for the District of Missouri against John F. A. Sandford (the correct spelling was Sanford), Mrs. Emerson's brother, to whom she had entrusted the administration of Dr. Emerson's estate when she moved to Massachusetts. The trespass alleged the illegal imprisonment of Scott, his wife, and his two children. Since Emerson lived in Missouri and Sanford was a citizen of New York, Scott claimed diversity of citizenship in his suit in order to have his case heard in federal rather than state court. Sanford defended solely on the grounds that the federal court lacked jurisdiction to hear the case (technically, a plea in abatement objecting to the place, mode, or time of the complaint). Sanford argued that Scott, because of his African descent, could not be a citizen of the United States and hence could not sue in federal court. The trial judge ruled that Scott was "enough of a citizen" to maintain the suit in federal court, but instructed the jury that, under the law of Missouri, Scott was a slave and that Sanford's acts therefore did not constitute false imprisonment or trespass. The jury found for Sanford. Scott petitioned the Supreme Court of the United States for a writ of error.

HIGHLIGHTS OF SUPREME COURT ARGUMENTS

Note: The case was first argued in February 1856. The Court ordered reargument in December 1856 because of a split of opinion among the justices on the jurisdictional question. Reargument focused on two questions: Whether the Supreme Court was to decide if the circuit court had jurisdiction to hear the case and whether Scott was a citizen of Missouri.

BRIEF FOR SCOTT

◆ Sanford waived the jurisdictional question by allowing the case to proceed on the merits before the circuit court. It is well-settled that a jurisdictional objection is not available at a later stage of a case if it is conceded at an earlier stage.

◆ If the Court believes the jurisdictional question was not waived, the law of Illinois, not the law of Missouri, should have been applied by the trial court in resolving this case. Under the Illinois constitution, Scott was emancipated by his residence there. If Scott was not emancipated by his residence in Illinois, he was emancipated by his residence in territory covered by the Missouri Compromise.

◆ Although certain temporary concessions to slavery were made by the Constitutional Convention, the fact that the slave trade could be prohibited in

1808 was an affirmative statement of the founders' policy against slavery's extension.

◆ Scott's capacity to sue in federal court should not be an issue in this case because social distinctions between whites and blacks are not recognized by courts. Persons of color have the capacity to sue and be sued, to own property, and the right to trial by jury. Free blacks are recognized as citizens in all the states, and Congress has extended citizenship to both Negroes and Indians through its power over naturalization. While it is true that Scott is not eligible to hold office or vote, he is a "quasi-citizen," entitled to be recognized by federal and state courts.

BRIEF FOR SANFORD

◆ Under the Constitution, children of foreign ambassadors, Indians, and persons of color may not be citizens. Because Scott is prohibited by the Constitution from being a citizen of the United States he cannot invoke the jurisdiction of the federal courts under the diversity of citizenship provision of the Constitution.

◆ The Illinois constitutional provision under which Scott claims his freedom prohibits only the introduction of slavery into the state; the rights of slave owners were restored when they and their property departed from Illinois. Emerson's temporary residence in the state, with no intent of establishing domicile there, did not entitle Scott to freedom.

◆ Slavery existed by law in all the territory ceded by France to the United States. Article IV, Section 3, relating to Congress's power to erect territorial governments, refers merely to the making of rules and regulations respecting the *lands* and other property of the United States. It does not give Congress power to pass laws regarding the permanent governance of territory belonging to the United States. The prohibition against slavery in the Missouri Compromise deprived slave-owning citizens of the right to move to land open to all others, with property recognized by the Constitution and protected by local laws.

SUPREME COURT DECISION: 7–2

TANEY, C.J.

... The question is simply this: Can a negro, whose ancestors were imported into this country, and sold as slaves, become a member of the political community formed and brought into existence by the Constitution of the United States, and as such become entitled to all the rights, and privileges, and immunities, guaranteed by that instrument to the citizen? One of which rights is the privilege of suing in a court of the United States in the cases specified in the Constitution....

The words "people of the United States" and "citizens" are synonymous terms, and mean the same thing. They both describe the political body who, according to our republican institutions, form the sovereignty, and who hold the power and conduct the Government through their representatives. They are what we familiarly call the "sovereign people," and every citizen is one of this people, and a constituent member of this sovereignty. The question before us is, whether the class of persons described in the plea in abatement compose a portion of this people, and are constituent members of this sovereignty? We think they are not, and that they are not included, and were not intended to be included, under the word "citizens" in the Constitution, and can therefore claim none of the rights and privileges which that instrument provides for and secures to citizens of the United States. On the contrary, they were at that time considered as a subordinate and inferior class of beings, who had been subjugated by the dominant race, and, whether emancipated or not, yet remained subject to their authority, and had no rights or privileges but such as those who held the power and the Government might choose to grant them....

Does the Constitution of the United States act upon [the negro] whenever he shall be made free under the laws of a State, and raised there to the rank of a citizen, and immediately clothe him with all the privileges of a citizen in every other State, and in its own courts?

The court think the affirmative of these propositions cannot be maintained. And if it cannot, the plaintiff in error could not be a citizen of the State of Missouri, within the meaning of the Constitution of the United States, and, consequently, was not entitled to sue in its courts....

In the opinion of the court, the legislation and histories of the times, and the language used in the Declaration of Independence, show, that neither the class of persons who had been imported as slaves, nor their descendants, whether they had become free or not, were then acknowledged as a part of the people, nor intended to be included in the general words used in that memorable instrument.

It is difficult at this day to realize the state of public opinion in relation to that unfortunate race, which prevailed in the civilized and enlightened portions of the world at the time of the Declaration of Independence, and when the Constitution of the United States was framed and adopted. But the public history of every European nation displays it in a manner too plain to be mistaken.

They had for more than a century before been regarded as beings of an inferior order, and altogether unfit to associate with the white race, either in social or political relations; and so far inferior, that they had no rights which the white man was bound to respect; and that the negro might justly and lawfully be reduced to slavery for his benefit. He was bought and sold, and treated as an ordinary article of merchandise and traffic, whenever a profit could be made by it. This opinion was at that time fixed and universal in the civilized portion of the white race. It was regarded as an axiom in morals as well as in politics, which no one thought of disputing, or supposed to be open to dispute; and men in every grade and position in society daily and habitually acted upon it in their private pursuits, as well as in matters of public concern, without doubting for a moment the correctness of this opinion....

No one of that race had ever migrated to the United States voluntarily; all of them had been brought here as articles of merchandise. The number that had been emancipated at that time were but few in comparison with those held in slavery; and they were identified in the public mind with the race to which they belonged, and regarded as a part of the slave population rather than the free. It is obvious that they were not even in the minds of the framers of the Constitution when they were conferring special rights and privileges upon the citizens of a State in every other part of the Union....

We proceed, therefore, to inquire whether the facts relied on by the plaintiff entitled him to his freedom....

In considering this part of the controversy, two questions arise: 1. Was he, together with his family, free in Missouri by reason of the stay in the territory of the United States herein before mentioned? And 2. If they were not, is Scott himself free by reason of his removal to Rock Island, in the State of Illinois, as stated in the above admissions?

We proceed to examine the first question.

The act of Congress, upon which the plaintiff relies, declares that slavery and involuntary servitude, except as a punishment for crime, shall be forever prohibited in all that part of the territory ceded by France, under the name of Louisiana, which lies north of thirty-six degrees thirty minutes north latitude, and not included within the limits of Missouri. And the difficulty which meets us at the threshold of this part of the inquiry is, whether Congress was authorized to pass this law under any of the powers granted to it by the Constitution; for if the authority is not given by that instrument, it is the duty of this court to declare it void and inoperative, and incapable of conferring freedom upon any one who is held as a slave under the laws of any one of the States.

The counsel for the plaintiff has laid much stress upon that article in the Constitution which confers on Congress the power "to dispose of and make all needful rules and regulations respecting the territory or other property belonging to the United States;" but, in the judgment of the court, that provision has no bearing on the present controversy, and the power there given, whatever it may be, is confined, and was intended to be confined, to the territory which at that time belonged to, or was claimed by, the United States, and was within their boundaries as settled by the treaty with Great Britain, and can have no influence upon a territory afterwards acquired from a foreign Government. It was a special provision for a known and particular territory, and to meet a present emergency, and nothing more....

This brings us to examine by what provision of the Constitution the present Federal Government, under its delegated and restricted powers, is authorized to acquire territory outside of the original limits of the United States, and what powers it may exercise therein over the person or property of a citizen of the United States, while it remains a Territory, and until it shall be admitted as one of the States of the Union.

There is certainly no power given by the Constitution to the Federal Government to establish or maintain colonies bordering on the United States or at a distance, to be ruled and governed at its own pleasure; nor to enlarge its territorial limits in any way, except by the admission of new States. That power is plainly given; and if a new State is admitted, it needs no further legislation by Congress, because the Constitution itself defines the relative rights and powers, and duties of the State, and the citizens of the State, and the Federal Government. But no power is given to acquire a Territory to be held and governed permanently in that character....

Upon these considerations, it is the opinion of the court that the act of Congress which prohibited a citizen from holding and owning property of this kind in the territory of the United States north of the line therein mentioned, is not warranted by the Constitution, and is therefore void; and that neither Dred Scott himself, nor any of his family, were made free by being carried into this territory; even if they had been carried there by the owner, with the intention of becoming a permanent resident....

On the whole, therefore, it is the judgment of this court, that it appears by the record before us that the plaintiff in error is not a citizen of Missouri, in the sense in which that word is used in the Constitution; and that the Circuit court of the United States, for that reason, had no jurisdiction in the case, and could give no judgment in it. Its judgment for the defendant must, consequently, be reversed, and a mandate issued directing the suit to be dismissed for want of jurisdiction.

NELSON, DANIEL, CAMPBELL, CATRON, WAYNE, AND GRIER, J.J., CONCURRING INDIVIDUALLY [OMITTED]

MCLEAN, J., DISSENTING

... On the 13th of July, the Ordinance of 1787 was passed, "for the government of the United States territory northwest of the river Ohio," with but one dissenting vote. This instrument provided there should be organized in the territory not less than three nor more than five States, designating their boundaries. It was passed while the Federal Convention was in session, about two months before the Constitution was adopted by the Convention. The members of the Convention must therefore have been well acquainted with the provisions of the Ordinance. It provided for a temporary Government, as initiatory to the formation of State Governments. Slavery was prohibited in the territory....

If Congress may establish a territorial government in the exercise of its discretion, it is a clear principle that a court cannot control that discretion. This being the case, I do not see on what ground the [Missouri Compromise] is held to be void. It did not purport to forfeit property, or take it for public purposes. It only prohibited slavery; in doing which, it followed the Ordinance of 1787....

CURTIS, J., DISSENTING

... To determine whether any free persons, descended from Africans held in slavery, were citizens of the United States under the Confederation, and consequently at the time of the adoption of the Constitution of the United States, it is only necessary to know whether any such persons were citizens of either of the States under the Confederation, at the time of the adoption of the Constitution.

Of this there can be no doubt. At the time of the ratification of the Articles of Confederation, all free native-born inhabitants of the States of New Hampshire,

Massachusetts, New York, New Jersey, and North Carolina, though descended from African slaves, were not only citizens of those States, but such of them as had the other necessary qualifications possessed the franchise of electors, on equal terms with other citizens....

Did the Constitution of the United States deprive them or their descendants of citizenship?...

I can find nothing in the Constitution which, *proprio vigore* [by its intrinsic meaning], deprives of their citizenship any class of persons who were citizens of the United States at the time of its adoption, or who should be native-born citizens of any State after its adoption; nor any power enabling Congress to disfranchise persons born on the soil of any State, and entitled to citizenship of such State by its Constitution and laws. And my opinion is, that under the Constitution of the United States, every free person born on the soil of a State, who is a citizen of that State by force of its Constitution or laws, is also a citizen of the United States....

It has been often asserted that the Constitution was made exclusively by and for the white race. It has already been shown that in five of the thirteen original States, colored persons then possessed the elective franchise, and were among those by whom the Constitution was ordained and established. If so, it is not true, in point of fact, that the Constitution was made exclusively for the white race. And that it was made exclusively for the white race is, in my opinion, not only an assumption not warranted by anything in the Constitution, but contradicted by its opening declaration, that it was ordained and established for the people of the United States, for themselves and their posterity. And as free colored persons were then citizens in at least five States, and so in every sense part of the people of the United States, they were among those for whom and whose posterity the Constitution was ordained and established....

I dissent, therefore, from that part of the opinion of the majority of the court, in which it is held that a person of African descent cannot be a citizen of the United States; and I regret I must go further, and dissent both from what I deem their assumption of authority to examine the constitutionality of the act of Congress commonly called the Missouri compromise act, and the grounds and conclusions announced in their opinion....

QUESTIONS

1. Chief Justice Taney dismissed the suit in *Dred Scott* on jurisdictional grounds. Having done so, was it necessary for him to reach the question of the constitutionality of the Missouri Compromise of 1820? Was it an error for him to do so? If so, was his error more political than legal?

2. Scott argued to the Court that Sanford had waived the jurisdictional issue by allowing the case to be argued on the merits in the circuit court. The general rule is that jurisdictional questions can never be waived and can be asserted at any stage of litigation. What would be

the consequences of allowing parties to create or destroy federal court jurisdiction?

3. Was it necessary for Chief Justice Taney to reach the issue of citizenship in order to resolve *Dred Scott*? In part, Taney's theory of citizenship reflected the view of South Carolina Senator John C. Calhoun that national citizenship derived from state citizenship and, consequently, that there could be no U.S. citizenship without state permission. Does the Constitution define "citizenship" as clearly or as exclusively as Taney's opinion contends?

4. Chief Justice Charles Evans Hughes referred to *Dred Scott* as one of the Supreme Court's worst "self-inflicted wounds." What was the most damaging aspect of the decision—the Court's holding on the jurisdiction issue; its holding on the question of blacks' citizenship; its holding on the 1820 Missouri Compromise; its view of the Constitution and constitutional interpretation; its fundamental rights analysis of property? Does the answer depend on whether one considers the short- or long-run consequences of *Dred Scott*?

5. Historian Carl Swisher claims the following:

> In the *Dred Scott* case the majority, although fully aware of the political implications of their work, persuaded themselves that they were resting their decision on the original meaning of the Constitution, and that in doing so they were merely performing their duty. (Carl B. Swisher, *History of the Supreme Court of the United States*, vol. 6, *The Taney Period, 1836–1864*, [New York, NY: Macmillan Co., 1974], pp. 631–632)

Assess the Court's understanding of "duty" in *Dred Scott*, both with respect to the relationship between law and politics and to declaring the original meaning of the Constitution.

COMMENTS

1. *Dred Scott* was only the second time in its history that the Supreme Court had invalidated an act of Congress as the result of the power of judicial review. The first was *Marbury v. Madison*. Ironically, Congress had repealed the Missouri Compromise by the time the Court declared it unconstitutional.

2. Justice Benjamin Curtis resigned shortly after the Court decided *Dred Scott*. His resignation followed an exchange of bitter letters with Chief Justice Taney over Curtis's claims that Taney had changed his written opinion in *Dred Scott* after hearing Curtis's dissent, and that Taney had refused to circulate his written opinion to the Court. Curtis's departure allowed Democratic President James Buchanan to appoint Nathan Clifford, a northerner with southern sympathies.

LIMITS ON FEDERAL JUDICIAL POWER: JURISDICTION

Ex parte McCardle
7 Wallace 506 (1869)

SETTING

The Supreme Court's decision in *Dred Scott v. Sandford* had the practical effect of declaring that Congress could do nothing about slavery in the territories. *Dred Scott* was among the precipitating causes of a bloody civil conflict that had threatened to break out between the northern and southern regions of the United States many times before April 1861. As explained in more detail in the *Setting* to the *Civil Rights Cases* (see p. 121), radical Republicans in Congress after the Civil War undertook to "reconstruct" the South. Their initial effort was creation of a Freedmen's Bureau in 1865 to educate and advance blacks. Southern states responded with Black Codes that bound blacks to the land through apprenticeship and vagrancy laws, segregated schools and public facilities, provided harsher punishments for blacks than whites convicted of the same crime, and made it hazardous for blacks to accuse whites of committing crimes against them. Congress's next major reconstruction effort was a Civil Rights Act in 1866 that set national standards for the protection of freed blacks. That act led to litigation about the extent of Congress's powers under the Fourteenth Amendment.

In February 1867, Congress passed legislation giving federal courts power to grant writs of habeas corpus "in all cases where any person may be restrained of his or her liberty in violation of the Constitution, or of any treaty or law of the United States." A writ of habeas corpus is a petition to a court alleging that a person is imprisoned illegally. The 1867 legislation gave the Supreme Court appellate jurisdiction over circuit court judgments in habeas corpus cases. The purpose of the act was to thwart southern state authorities who, as a form of harassment, were arresting blacks, federal government officials, and Republican politicians (derisively called "Carpetbaggers" by southerners) who went South to organize black voters. The following month, Congress passed a series of Reconstruction Acts over the veto of President Andrew Johnson. The acts divided the South into five military districts subject to martial law. In order to be readmitted to the union, southern states were required to call new constitutional conventions elected by universal manhood suffrage and to ratify the Fourteenth Amendment.

On November 8, 1867, William McCardle, a civilian citizen of Mississippi and the fourth military district created by the Reconstruction Acts, was arrested and brought before a military commission on order of General E. O. C. Ord, the district's commander. McCardle, editor of the *Vicksburg Times*, was charged with libel, inciting insurrection, disturbing the public peace, and impeding the reconstruction of the southern states because of a series of editorials he published between October 2 and November 6. One article, for example, expressed the view that General Ord, along with the commanding officers of the other military districts, were "satraps" who "should have their heads shaved, their ears cropped, their foreheads branded, and their precious persons lodged in a penitentiary."

McCardle filed a petition for a writ of habeas corpus with the Circuit Court for the Southern District of Mississippi, claiming unlawful restraint by military force. The circuit court issued the writ to General Ord. He returned it, admitting that he had McCardle in custody but denying that McCardle's incarceration was unlawful. Following a hearing, the circuit court remanded McCardle to military custody. McCardle appealed to the Supreme Court of the United States as allowed by the Act of February 1867. McCardle's case was argued in early March 1868 and was taken under advisement. McCardle meanwhile was freed on bail. He turned his attentions to organizing an all-white Democratic Party in Mississippi and continued to publish anti-Reconstruction editorials.

On March 27, 1868, while McCardle's case was under advisement, Congress repealed the Supreme Court's appellate jurisdiction over habeas corpus cases decided by circuit courts of the United States. The statute provided,

> That so much of the act approved February 5, 1867, entitled "An act to amend an act to establish the judicial courts of the United States, approved September 24, 1789," as authorized an appeal from the judgment of the Circuit Court to the Supreme Court of the United States, or exercise of any such jurisdiction by said Supreme Court, on appeals which have been, or may hereafter be taken, be, and the same is hereby repealed.

The Supreme Court scheduled arguments on the effect of the repealing act on McCardle's case at its December 1868 Term.

HIGHLIGHTS OF SUPREME COURT ARGUMENTS

BRIEF FOR MCCARDLE

♦ The Supreme Court acquired jurisdiction over this case from Article III of the Constitution, not from acts of Congress. The legality of McCardle's imprisonment presents a case arising under "the laws of the United States," to which the Court's jurisdiction extends. If the argument that the Court's jurisdiction is subject to Congressional legislation is accepted, the judicial power could be rendered null by Congressional inaction.

♦ It is universally known that the purpose of Congress's repealing act of March 27 was to prevent the Supreme Court from reversing the judgment of the circuit court in this case. The March 27 act amounted to an exercise by Congress of judicial power, which should not be permitted.

BRIEF FOR THE UNITED STATES

◆ The Supreme Court's appellate jurisdiction over this case derives exclusively from the act of February 1867.

◆ When the Supreme Court's jurisdiction depends on a statute, and the statute is repealed, jurisdiction ceases absolutely.

◆ It makes no difference at what point in a proceeding jurisdiction ceases. After it ceases, judicial power ceases.

SUPREME COURT DECISION: 9–0

CHASE, C.J.

... The first question necessarily is that of jurisdiction; for, if the act of March, 1868, takes away the jurisdiction defined by the act of February, 1867, it is useless, if not improper, to enter into any discussion of other questions.

It is quite true, as was argued by the counsel for the petitioner, that the appellate jurisdiction of this court is not derived from acts of Congress. It is, strictly speaking, conferred by the Constitution. But it is conferred "with such exceptions and under such regulations as Congress shall make."...

It is not necessary to consider whether, if Congress had made no exceptions and no regulations, this court might not have exercised general appellate jurisdiction under rules prescribed by itself....

The exception to the appellate jurisdiction in the case before us ... is not an inference from the affirmation of other appellate jurisdiction. It is made in terms. The provision of the act of 1867, affirming the appellate jurisdiction of this court in cases of habeas corpus is expressly repealed. It is hardly possible to imagine a plainer instance of positive exception....

We are not at liberty to inquire into the motives of the legislature. We can only examine into its power under the Constitution; and the power to make exceptions to the appellate jurisdiction of this court is given by express words.

What, then, is the effect of the repealing act upon the case before us? We cannot doubt as to this. Without jurisdiction the court cannot proceed at all in any cause. Jurisdiction is power to declare the law, and when it ceases to exist, the only function remaining to the court is that of announcing the fact and dismissing the cause. And this is not less clear upon authority than upon principle....

[T]he general rule, supported by the best elementary writers (Dwarris, Stat. 538), is, that "when an act of the legislature is repealed, it must be considered, except as to transactions past and closed, as if it never existed."...

It is quite clear, therefore, that this court cannot proceed to pronounce judgment in this case, for it has no longer jurisdiction of the appeal; and judicial duty is not less fitly performed by declining ungranted jurisdiction than in exercising firmly that which the Constitution and the laws confer....

Counsel seem to have supposed, if effect be given to the repealing Act in question, that the whole appellate power of the court, in cases of habeas corpus, is denied. But this [is] in error. The Act of 1868 does not except from that jurisdiction any cases but appeals from circuit courts under the Act of 1867. It does not affect the jurisdiction which was previously exercised.

The appeal of the petitioner in this case must be dismissed for want of jurisdiction.

COMMENTS

1. Congress's repeal of the Supreme Court's appellate jurisdiction over habeas corpus cases decided by federal circuit courts occurred in a highly charged political environment.

   On March 5, 1868, during the first argument of McCardle's case before the Supreme Court, the Senate began to organize to try the impeachment of President Andrew Johnson. The previous month the House of Representatives had voted eleven impeachment articles against Johnson for dismissing his secretary of war without Senate approval, contrary to the Tenure in Office Act of 1867, and for attempting to disgrace and ridicule the Congress by blatantly objecting to its Reconstruction policies. At the end of March, Chief Justice Chase presided over the impeachment trial. He insisted that the Senate sit as a court, not as a political party, in conducting the impeachment proceedings. Johnson was acquitted in late May 1868 when seven Republicans who supported Congressional Reconstruction voted for acquittal because they believed there was no legal ground for Johnson's conviction.

2. Justices Grier and Field dissented from the Court's delaying a decision in *McCardle* while awaiting congressional repeal of its jurisdiction. In an unpublished memorandum, Grier wrote: "By the postponement of the case we shall subject ourselves, whether justly or unjustly, to the imputation that we have evaded the performance of a duty imposed on us by the Constitution, and have waited for legislation to interpose to supersede our action and relieve us from our responsibility. I am not willing to be a partaker of the eulogy or opprobrium that may follow." McCardle's attorney, Jeremiah S. Black, was more blunt: "The court stood still to be ravished and did not even hallo while the thing was getting done" (quoted in Charles Fairman, *History of the Supreme Court of the United States*, vol. 6: *Reconstruction and Reunion, 1864–1888, Part One* [New York, NY: Macmillan Co., 1971], pp. 474, 478).

3. *McCardle* was the third in a series of legal challenges to Reconstruction. The Court avoided reaching the merits in the initial two cases that came before it by holding, in the first, that it lacked power to enjoin a president—*Mississippi v. Johnson*, 4 Wallace 475 (1867)—and, in the second, that a suit by a state raised a nonjusticiable "political" question. *Georgia v. Stanton*, 6 Wallace 50 (1868).

4. The status of the Court's habeas corpus jurisdiction was uncertain

following *Ex parte McCardle*. Later in the same Term in which it decided *McCardle*, the Court clarified matters somewhat in *Ex parte Yerger*, 8 Wallace 85 (1869). Edward Yerger, another Mississippi newspaper editor, was held by a military commission after conviction for murdering an army major. Yerger petitioned the Fifth Circuit Court of Appeals for a writ of habeas corpus. That court denied his petition. Yerger appealed to the Supreme Court, claiming that military commissions lacked jurisdiction to try civilians for civilian crimes. Limiting its opinion to the issue of jurisdiction, the Supreme Court held that, under the Judiciary Act of 1789, it had authority to review on certiorari a circuit court's denial of a petition for a writ of habeas corpus.

QUESTIONS

1. Law professor Charles Black Jr. maintains that the *McCardle* case "marks the extent of the vulnerability of the Judiciary to congressional control…" (*Perspectives in Constitutional Law* [Englewood Cliffs, NJ: Prentice Hall, 1963], p. 13). Does the Constitution support Black's view? Is there a difference between making a specific exception to the Court's appellate jurisdiction and totally abolishing its jurisdiction over a substantive area of law?

2. Congressional control over the Supreme Court's appellate jurisdiction is one method for checking the Court's power. What are other methods?

3. Less than a month after the *McCardle* decision was announced, Chief Justice Chase wrote to a district judge in Mississippi that "… had the merits of the *McCardle* case been decided the Court would doubtless have held that his imprisonment for trial before a military commission was illegal" (quoted in Charles Fairman, *History of the Supreme Court of the United States*, vol. 6: *Reconstruction and Reunion, 1864–1888, Part One* [New York, NY: Macmillan Co., 1971], p. 494).

   If Chief Justice Chase's conjecture had occurred, *McCardle* would have stymied Congressional Reconstruction. Was the Court wise to avoid claiming jurisdiction over McCardle's case? Even if the justices had asserted jurisdiction, would it have been appropriate to declare *McCardle* nonjusticiable as a "political" question?

4. Exercising jurisdiction over an issue often brings the Court into direct conflict with other branches of the federal government and/or the states. For instance, over the last thirty years, efforts have been undertaken in Congress to withdraw federal court jurisdiction over reapportionment of state legislatures, school busing, school prayer, and abortion. What do these conflicts suggest about the political character of federal appellate jurisdiction?

SUGGESTIONS FOR FURTHER READING

Anderson, William L., *Cherokee Removal: Before and After* (Athens, GA: University of Georgia Press, 1991).

Bestor, Arthur, "The American Civil War as a Constitutional Crisis," 69 *American Historical Review* (1964): 327.

Bickel, Alexander M., "Citizenship in the American Constitution," 15 *Arizona Law Review* (1973): 369.

Black, Charles L., "The Presidency and Congress," *Washington & Lee Law Review* (1975): 841.

Burke, Joseph C., "The Cherokee Cases: A Study in Law, Politics, and Morality," 21 *Stanford Law Review* (1969): 500.

Conference, " A Symposium on Judicial Activism: Problems and Responses," 7 *Harvard Journal of Law & Public Policy* (1984): 1.

Currie, David, "The Constitution in the Supreme Court: Civil War and Reconstruction," 51 *University of Chicago Law Review* (1984): 131.

Ehrlich, Walter, *They Have No Rights: Dred Scott's Struggle for Freedom* (Westport, CT: Greenwood Press, 1979).

Eisgruber, Christopher L., "*Dred* Again: Originalism's Forgotten Past," 10 *Constitutional Commentary* (1993): 37.

Fehrenbacher, Don E., *The Dred Scott Case* (New York, NY: Oxford University Press, 1978), pp. 316–319.

———, "The Dred Scott Case," in *Quarrels That Have Shaped the Constitution*, rev. ed., ed. John A. Garraty (New York, NY: Harper, 1987).

Finkelman, Paul, *An Imperfect Union: Slavery, Federalism, and Comity* (Chapel Hill, NC: University of North Carolina Press, 1981).

Foreman, Grant, *Indian Removal: The Emigration of the Five Civilized Tribes of Indians* (Norman, OK: University of Oklahoma Press, 1953).

Gunther, Gerald, "Congressional Power to Curtail Federal Court Jurisdiction: An Opinionated Guide to the Ongoing Debate," 36 *Stanford Law Review* (1984): 201.

Hart, Henry M. Jr., "The Power of Congress to Limit the Jurisdiction of Federal Courts: An Exercise in Dialectic," 66 *Harvard Law Review* (1953): 1362.

Hyman, Harold M., *A More Perfect Union* (New York, NY: Knopf, 1973).

Hyman, Harold M., and William M. Wiecek, *Equal Justice under Law: Constitutional Development, 1835–1875* (New York, NY: Harper and Row, 1982).

Kutler, Stanley L., *Judicial Power and Reconstruction Politics* (Chicago, IL: University of Chicago Press, 1968).

LaRue, Lewis, "The Continuing Presence of *Dred Scott*," 42 *Washington & Lee Law Review* (1985): 57.

Norgren, Jill, *The Cherokee Cases: The Confrontation of Law and Politics* (New York, NY: McGraw-Hill, 1996).

Perry, Michael J., *The Constitution, the Courts, and Human Rights* (New Haven, CT: Yale University Press, 1982).

Potter, David M., and Don E. Fehrenbacher, *The Impending Crisis, 1848–1861* (New York, NY: Harper and Row, 1976).

Prucha, Francis P., *Documents of United States Indian Policy*, 2nd ed. (Lincoln, NE: University of Nebraska, 1990).

Ratner, Leonard, "Congressional Power over the Appellate Jurisdiction of the Supreme Court," 109 *University of Pennsylvania Law Review* (1960): 157.

———, "Majoritarian Constraints on Judicial Review: Congressional Control of Supreme Court Jurisdiction," 27 *Villanova Law Review* (1982): 929.

Sager, Lawrence G., "Constitutional Limitations on Congress's Authority to Regulate the Appellate Jurisdiction of Federal Courts," 95 *Harvard Law Review* (1981): 17.

Stampp, Kenneth M., *The Peculiar Institution: Slavery in the Ante-Bellum South* (New York, NY: Vintage, 1956).

———, *America in 1857: A Nation on the Brink* (New York, NY: Oxford University Press, 1990).

Strickland, Rennard, *Felix Cohen's Handbook of Federal Indian Law* (Charlottesville, VA: Michie, 1982).

Tribe, Laurence M., "Jurisdictional Gerrymandering: Zoning Disfavored Rights out of the Federal Courts," 16 *Harvard Civil Rights-Civil Liberties Review* (1981): 129.

Van Alstyne, William, "A Critical Guide to *Ex parte McCardle*," 15 *Arizona Law Review* (1973): 229.

Wechsler, Herbert, "The Courts and the Constitution," 65 *Columbia Law Review* (1965): 1001.

Wiecek, William M., *The Sources of Antislavery Constitutionalism in America, 1760–1848* (Ithaca, NY: Cornell University Press, 1977).

Wilkinson, Charles F., *American Indians, Time and the Law: Native Societies in a Modern Constitutional Democracy* (New Haven, CT: Yale University Press, 1987).

Wilkinson, Charles F., and John M. Volkman, "Judicial Review of Indian Treaty Abrogation: 'As Long as Water Flows or Grass Grows upon the Earth'—How Long a Time is That?" 63 *California Law Review* (1975): 601.

Williams, Robert, *The American Indian in Western Legal Thought: The Discourse of Conquest* (New York, NY: Oxford University Press, 1990).

JUSTICIABILITY: POLITICAL QUESTIONS

Luther v. Borden
7 Howard 1 (1849)

SETTING

After the Revolution, the state of Rhode Island, unlike other states, did not adopt a new constitution. (Neither did it send delegates to the Constitutional Convention.) It continued instead under the form of government established by the charter of Charles the Second in 1663, with such alterations as the legislature found necessary to adapt the government to the needs of the newly independent state. The royal charter provided no means for amendment and authorized the legislature to prescribe the qualification of voters. The legislature limited suffrage to male property owners ("freeholders"). Rhode Island was a party to the Articles of Confederation and ratified the Constitution of the United States in 1790 under the charter government.

Groups dissatisfied with Rhode Island's limited suffrage under the charter government sought unsuccessfully to persuade the legislature to liberalize voting qualifications. In 1841, the Suffrage Association, led by Thomas Dorr, issued a declaration of principles claiming the right of the majority of citizens to draft a constitution for the governance of their state. The Suffrage Association called an unofficial constitutional convention at Providence. Delegates to the convention were elected at voluntary meetings. The convention drafted a constitution in October 1841 that extended the right of suffrage to every male citizen over twenty-one years of age who had resided for a year in the state and for six months in the town in which he planned to vote.

In November, after submitting the proposed constitution to the people, the unofficial convention declared that the document had been ratified by a large majority and declared it to be "the paramount law and constitution of the State of Rhode Island and Providence Plantations." The convention sent the new constitution to charter governor Samuel Ward King, directing him to communicate the results to the two houses of the state legislature.

In April 1842, the new government was organized through a series of town meetings. Thomas Dorr was elected governor and the new government went into operation in Providence on May 3, 1842. Dorr prepared to use force to assert the authority of what was known by then as the People's Constitution.

The charter legislature refused to recognize the new government, passed a resolution declaring it in violation of the rights of the existing government, and promised to defend the legal and constitutional rights of the people under the charter government. (The charter government also called a convention to draft a new constitution, which was ratified by the people in 1843.) On June 24, 1842, the charter government declared martial law and called out the militia to repel attacks threatened by Dorr and his followers. Governor King requested military aid from President John Tyler under Article 4, Section 4, of the Constitution of the United States. Tyler refused to send troops but promised that he would do so if violence erupted.

Luther v. Borden arose when Martin Luther, who had taken up arms in support of the Dorr government, brought an action in trespass against Luther Borden. Luther charged Borden and other state infantrymen with breaking and entering his house in Warren, Rhode Island, on June 29, 1842, armed with muskets and other dangerous weapons, and searching it without a warrant. He maintained that the People's Constitution superseded the charter government in 1842 and that Borden therefore was acting as a private citizen when he committed the trespass. Luther filed his suit in the U.S. Circuit Court for the District of Rhode Island, claiming to be a resident of Fall River, Massachusetts. His residency in Massachusetts entitled him to have his case heard in federal court because of diversity of citizenship between the parties. Borden's defense was that he entered Luther's house as an agent of the charter government, under authority of martial law, because at the time Luther was levying war on the state.

At trial Luther sought to introduce evidence of ratification of the People's Constitution. The Circuit Court refused to admit the evidence, ruling that the issues in the case were political rather than judicial. It instructed the jury that the charter government and the laws under which Borden acted were in full force at the time of Borden's alleged trespass and constituted a justification for his acts. Luther's attorney took exception to the jury instruction, then filed a writ of error with the Supreme Court of the United States.

HIGHLIGHTS OF SUPREME COURT ARGUMENTS

Note: *Luther v. Borden* was consolidated with a similar action against Borden filed by Rachel Luther, Martin Luther's mother, who was in Luther's house at the time of its search.

BRIEF FOR LUTHER

◆ The federal circuit court is the appropriate court to determine which government was in effect in Rhode Island at the time Borden entered Luther's home. The existence of two constitutions made the parties citizens of different states and hence subject to the jurisdiction of U.S. federal courts.

◆ A constitution, being the expression of the sovereign will of the people, takes effect from the time the people's will is unequivocally expressed. The Circuit Court should have allowed Luther's motion to submit evidence that the People's Constitution was adopted by the majority of the people of

Rhode Island. Denial of that opportunity, and the consequent failure to recognize the new constitution, amounted to a denial of the theory of free government in the states of the United States.

◆ The state's imposition of martial law in response to the Peoples' Constitution denied the people of Rhode Island the republican form of government guaranteed to every state under Article 4, Section 4, of the Constitution of the United States.

BRIEF FOR BORDEN

◆ The charter government of Rhode Island is a liberal, even radical, government of the people. By tradition in the state, all changes in suffrage must originate with the legislature. Rhode Island has taken several steps during the prior thirty years to satisfy the demands of those wishing to expand the suffrage. Even the People's Constitution requires constitutional change to occur through legislative channels.

◆ It is not for the Supreme Court to determine which is the rightful government of Rhode Island. Under our form of government, it devolves upon the president to determine which are and are not governments. The president recognized the authority of the charter government following the state's declaration of martial law.

◆ The right to vote, claimed by the rebellious forces as a natural right to justify their actions, is not one of the natural rights recognized by the Declaration of Independence. It is a political right. States are the sole judges of political rights.

◆ While no one doubts the sovereignty of the people, they have delegated a portion of their sovereign power to the government, which represents and speaks for them.

SUPREME COURT DECISION: 5–1

(Catron, McKinley, and Daniel, J.J., did not participate.)

TANEY, C.J.

... [T]he Constitution of the United States, as far as it has provided for an emergency of this kind, and authorized the general government to interfere in the domestic concerns of a State, has treated the subject as political in its nature, and placed the power in the hands of that department.

The fourth section of the fourth article of the Constitution of the United States provides that the United States shall guarantee to every State in the Union a republican form of government, and shall protect each of them against invasion; and on the application of the legislature or of the executive (when the legislature cannot be convened) against domestic violence.

Under this article of the Constitution it rests with Congress to decide what government is the established one in a State. For as the United States guarantee to each State a republican government, Congress must necessarily decide what government is established in the State before it can determine whether it is republican or not. And when the senators and representatives of a State are admitted into the councils of the Union, the authority of the government under which they are appointed, as well as its republican character, is recognized by the proper constitutional authority. And its decision is binding on every other department of the government, and could not be questioned in a judicial tribunal. It is true that the contest in this case did not last long enough to bring the matter to this issue; and as no senators or representatives were elected under the authority of the government of which Mr. Dorr was the head, Congress was not called upon to decide the controversy. Yet the right to decide is placed there, and not in the courts.

So, too, as relates to the clause in the above mentioned article of the Constitution, providing for cases of domestic violence. It rested with Congress, too, to determine upon the means proper to be adopted to fulfil this guarantee. They might, if they had deemed it most advisable to do so, have placed it in the power of a court to decide when the contingency had happened which required the federal government to interfere. But Congress thought otherwise, and no doubt wisely; and by the act of February 28, 1795, provided, that, "in case of an insurrection in any State against the government thereof, it shall be lawful for the President of the United States, on application of the legislature of such State or of the executive (when the legislature cannot be convened), to call forth such

number of the militia of any other State or States, as may be applied for, as he may judge sufficient to suppress such insurrection."...

The interference of the President, therefore, by announcing his determination, was as effectual as if the militia had been assembled under his orders. And it should be equally authoritative. For certainly no court of the United States, with a knowledge of this decision, would have been justified in recognizing the opposing party as the lawful government; or in treating as wrongdoers or insurgents the officers of the government which the President had recognized, and was prepared to support by an armed force. In the case of foreign nations, the government acknowledged by the President is always recognized in the courts of justice. And this principle has been applied by the act of Congress to the sovereign States of the Union....

Much of the argument on the part of the plaintiff turned upon political rights and political questions, upon which the court has been urged to express an opinion. We decline to do so. The high power has been conferred on this court of passing judgment upon the acts of the State sovereignties, and of the legislative and executive branches of the federal government, and of determining whether they are beyond the limits of power marked out for them respectively by the Constitution of the United States. This tribunal, therefore, should be the last to overstep its own jurisdiction. And while it should always be ready to meet any question confided to it by the Constitution, it is equally its duty not to pass beyond its appropriate sphere of action, and to take care not to involve itself in discussions which properly belong to other forums. No one, we believe, has ever doubted the proposition, that, according to the institutions of this country, the sovereignty in every State resides in the people of the State, and that they may alter and change their form of government at their own pleasure. But whether they have changed it or not by abolishing an old government, and establishing a new one in its place, is a question to be settled by the political power. And when that power has decided, the courts are bound to take notice of its decision and to follow it.

The judgment of the Circuit Court must therefore be affirmed.

WOODBURY, J., DISSENTING

... It looks, certainly, like pretty bold doctrine in a constitutional government, that, even in time of legitimate war, the legislature can properly suspend or abolish all constitutional restrictions, as martial law does, and lay the personal and political rights of the people at their feet....

The only point in connection with this matter which appears clearly to have been ruled at the trial was the legality or constitutionality of that act of Assembly [declaring martial law]. I think the ruling made was incorrect, and hence there has been a mistrial....

COMMENT

Thomas Dorr fled from Rhode Island in 1842 after an abortive attempt to seize a weapons arsenal in Providence. He was captured, convicted of treason, and sentenced to life imprisonment at hard labor. In *Ex parte Dorr*, 3 Howard 103 (1845), the Supreme Court of the United States unanimously denied a petition for a writ of *habeas corpus* brought by Dorr's friends. It ruled that a federal court could not issue a writ of *habeas corpus* to free a state prisoner unless it was for the purpose of making him a witness in a federal court proceeding. In response to indignation expressed throughout the country, the Rhode Island legislature granted amnesty to Dorr. He was released from prison on June 27, 1845.

In 1867, Congress gave federal courts power to "grant writs of *habeas corpus* in all cases where any person may be restrained of his or her liberty in violation of the constitution or of any treaty or law of the United States...."

QUESTIONS

1. *Luther v. Borden* stands for the proposition that some questions involving the Guaranty Clause of Article 4, Section 4, are nonjusticiable "political" questions. What are the implications of the "political question" doctrine for using federal courts to resolve social controversy? What cases, if any, presented in the text so far could have been resolved on "political question" grounds?

2. How does John Marshall's distinction in *Marbury v. Madison* between "ministerial duties" and "political functions" foreshadow the "political" question doctrine announced in *Luther*?

3. *Luther v. Borden* is often pointed to as both an example of judicial self-restraint and an exercise of judicial review to legitimize congressional power. What language in the opinion supports each view?

4. Compare *Luther* with *Cherokee Nation v. Georgia*. Did the justices have any practical alternative to refusing jurisdiction in either case? What consequences would have followed had the Court reversed the judgment of the circuit court in *Luther*? At the time *Luther* was handed down in 1849, sectional hostilities dividing North and South were escalating rapidly. Of what use might the "political question" doctrine be to the Court as it was called on to adjudicate disputes between increasingly polarized factions in the nation?

5. During the twentieth century, in the realm of foreign affairs, the Court has invoked the *Luther* doctrine so consistently to justify deferring to the partisan branches of government, particularly the executive, that the late constitutional scholar Robert G. McCloskey remarked: "[F]or better or worse the fact remains that these two great and increasingly important areas of public affairs [treaty powers and foreign affairs] are now subject to ... limits only ... by legislative and executive self-restraint and by the force of public opinion" (*The American Supreme Court*, 2nd rev. ed. [Chicago, IL: University of Chicago Press, 1994], p. 127).

   The "political question" doctrine is an example of judicial self-restraint. Is judicial self-restraint more, or less, justified in the realm of foreign affairs than in domestic affairs?

COMMENT

Not all cases asking the Court to accept jurisdiction under Article 4, Section 4, have involved facts as dramatic as those in *Luther*. For example, in *Pacific States Telephone and Telegraph Co. v. Oregon*, 223 U.S. 118 (1912), a unanimous Supreme Court held that it lacked jurisdiction to pass on the validity of a 1906 Oregon law that imposed taxes on telephone and telegraph companies. The law had been proposed and enacted under a 1902 state constitutional amendment reserving to the people the right of bypassing the legislature and initiating legislative proposals for direct popular vote. The Court declared that whether the initiative and referendum (also provided for in 1902) procedures destroyed Oregon's republican character is a "political" question.

JUSTICIABILITY: POLITICAL QUESTIONS

Baker v. Carr
369 U.S. 186 (1962)

SETTING

In *Federalist* No. 9, Alexander Hamilton praised the proposed Constitution on the grounds that it reflected a "new science of politics." A pivotal aspect of that science was "the representation of the people in the legislature by deputies of their own election." Like drafters of state constitutions before them, the drafters of the federal Constitution believed that representative (rather than direct) democracy would contribute to political stability and more intelligent laws.

Representative democracy requires establishment of geographical boundaries for election purposes (districting) and allocation of seats to those districts (apportionment). Who or what is represented in a legislative assembly frequently has a significant impact on the kinds of problems that assembly addresses and the laws it passes. Thus, districting and apportionment, while at first glance merely technical, have profound political consequences.

The Constitution reflects the "Great Compromise" of the Constitutional Convention that resulted in both people and states having representation in Congress. While population is the primary criterion for determining representation in the House of Representatives, each state has two U.S. Senators, regardless of population or geographical size. Many state constitutions followed a similar approach, guaranteeing representation of both people and geographical areas (usually counties) in their state legislatures.

The Industrial Revolution and the rapid urbanization that accompanied it led to considerable dissatisfaction with districting and apportionment schemes in many states. Legislatures dominated by rural, agrarian interests were perceived as unresponsive to modern problems and the needs of the growing numbers of city dwellers. Entrenched legislators were loathe to relinquish the power they would lose if they authorized redistricting.

Early in the twentieth century litigants turned to the Supreme Court, asking it to declare that failure to redistrict and reapportion denied them the right to a republican form of government guaranteed by Article IV, Section 4, of the Constitution. The Court consistently refused to grant relief, holding that questions raised under the Guaranty Clause were political questions and hence nonjusticiable.

In 1946, Northwestern University political science professor Kenneth

Colegrove took a new constitutional approach to the issue of districting and apportionment. He sought to have the division of the state of Illinois into Congressional districts declared invalid because of massive inequalities among the population of the respective districts. He maintained that unequal population districts violated his right to equal protection under the Fourteenth Amendment. A badly divided Supreme Court refused to hear an appeal in his case on the ground that he had not exhausted all the remedies available to him to change Illinois's districting plan before seeking judicial review. In the majority's view, Colegrove should have taken his complaints to the Illinois legislature and persuaded it to enact redistricting legislation. *Colegrove v. Green*, 328 U.S. 549 (1946). The professor's Fourteenth Amendment legal theory, however, gave new life to efforts to attack malapportionment, particularly at the state level. The theory was tested again in a reapportionment case filed in Tennessee in 1959.

The Tennessee constitution of 1870 created a two-house legislature with seats to be apportioned according to qualified voters in counties or districts. The constitution provided that elections would be "free and equal" and called for an enumeration of qualified voters and an apportionment of the legislature every ten years after 1871. The legislature reapportioned itself in 1901, but the apportionment was not based on an enumeration of qualified voters. The legislature defeated all bills proposing reapportionment after 1901.

In the late 1950s, Charles W. Baker and nine other qualified Tennessee voters from five counties claimed that as a result of population shifts since 1901, the legislative distribution was disproportionate to the population distribution in the state. By 1950, Baker calculated, twenty-three Tennessee counties had twenty-five direct representatives in the legislature when their total voting population entitled them to only two. Ten counties, including the one in which Baker resided, had twenty direct representatives but were entitled to forty-five under the state constitutional apportionment rule. Malapportionment of the state legislature gave Baker about one-tenth of a vote in choosing members of the state legislature.

In May 1959, Baker and his coplaintiffs filed suit against Tennessee Secretary of State Joe C. Carr, the state attorney general, the coordinator of elections, and members of the state board of elections. Their suit alleged denial of equal protection of the laws under the Fourteenth Amendment as a result of the Tennessee legislature's failure to reapportion its legislative districts based on the number of qualified voters. The suit sought a declaration that the 1901 Tennessee Act of Apportionment was unconstitutional, and an injunction restraining its enforcement. Baker asked the court to order an election at large or to direct Carr to hold an election in accordance with the formula provided by the state constitution.

A three-judge panel of the U.S. District Court for the Middle Division of Tennessee dismissed Baker's suit. The court said its action was controlled by *Colegrove v. Green*, 328 U.S. 549 (1946). In dismissing Baker's case, the district court observed that declaring Tennessee apportionment statutes unconstitutional would result in destruction of the state's government.

Baker appealed the dismissal to the Supreme Court, as allowed by federal statute from decisions of three-judge district court panels.

Highlights of Supreme Court Arguments

Note: The case was argued before the Supreme Court in April 1961 and reargued at the request of the Court the following October.

BRIEF FOR BAKER

◆ The practical effects of the inequality of voting rights in Tennessee is that the rural-dominated legislature discriminates against urban residents in the allocation of tax burdens and distribution of tax revenues. Repeated calls for a fair apportionment law have gone unheeded, making federal judicial assistance the only remedy.

◆ Dilution of voting rights denies equal protection of the laws guaranteed by the Fourteenth Amendment....

AMICUS CURIAE BRIEFS SUPPORTING BAKER

United States; Howard Edmondson (governor of Oklahoma, who ran for office on a reapportionment platform in 1958); residents of Nassau County, New York; four Kansas taxpayers; National Institute of Municipal Law.

BRIEF FOR CARR

◆ In order to have a case in controversy, Baker was required to sue parties with opposing interests. Neither Carr nor the other officials sued has any duties relating to legislative apportionment. Further, the plaintiffs have alleged no interests different from other Tennessee voters. This suit, in fact, is an action against the state of Tennessee and is forbidden by the Eleventh Amendment.

◆ Baker's complaint that Tennessee government is not republican in form because representation is not based on population was answered definitively by *Colegrove v. Green*, 328 U.S. 549 (1946). In cases since *Colegrove* this Court has properly refused to exercise its equity powers to resolve political issues arising from a state's geographical distribution of electoral strength.

◆ A different apportionment statute will be enacted if and when demanded of the legislature by the people. Healthy federalism requires that federal courts not exercise equitable powers in this delicate field.

SUPREME COURT DECISION: 6–2

(Whittaker, J., did not participate.)

BRENNAN, J.

... These appellants seek relief in order to protect or vindicate an interest of their own and those similarly situated. Their constitutional claim is, in substance, that the 1901 statute constitutes arbitrary and capricious state action offensive to the Fourteenth Amendment in its irrational disregard of the standard of apportionment prescribed by the State's Constitution or of any standard....

[T]he mere fact that the suit seeks protection of a political right does not mean it presents a political question....

We hold that the claim pleaded here neither rests upon nor implicates the Guaranty Clause [of Article 4, Section 4] and that its justiciability is therefore not foreclosed by our decisions of cases involving that clause. The District Court misinterpreted *Colegrove v. Green* [328 U.S. 549 (1946)] and other decisions of this Court on which it relied. Appellants' claim that they are being denied equal protection is justiciable, and if "discrimination is sufficiently shown, the right to relief under the equal protection clause is not diminished by the fact that the discrimination relates to political rights." *Snowdon v. Hughes*, 321 U.S. 1 (1944). To show why we reject the argument based on the Guaranty Clause, we must examine the authorities under it. But because there appears to be some uncertainty as to why [*Colegrove* and other earlier] cases did present political questions, and specifically as to whether this apportionment case is like those cases, we deem it necessary first to consider the contours of the "political question" doctrine....

The nonjusticiability of a political question is primarily a function of the separation of powers. Much confusion results from the capacity of the "political question" label to obscure the need for case-by-case inquiry. Deciding whether a matter has in any measure been committed by the Constitution to another branch of government, or whether the action of that branch exceeds whatever authority has been committed, is itself a delicate exercise in constitutional interpretation, and is a responsibility of this Court as ultimate interpreter of the Constitution. To demonstrate this requires no less than to analyze representative cases and to infer from them the analytical threads that make up the political question doctrine. We shall then show that none of those threads catches this case.

Foreign Relations: There are sweeping statements to the effect that all questions touching foreign relations are political questions.... Yet it is error to suppose that every case or controversy which touches foreign relations lies beyond judicial cognizance. Our cases in this field seem invariably to show a discriminating analysis of the particular question posed, in terms of the history of its management by the political branches, of its susceptibility to judicial handling in the light of its nature and posture in the specific case, and of the possible consequences of judicial action....

Dates of Duration of Hostilities: Though it has been stated broadly that "the power which declared the necessity is the power to declare its cessation, and what the cessation requires," here too analysis reveals isolable reasons for the presence of political questions, underlying this Court's refusal to review the political departments' determination of when or whether a war has ended....

Validity of Enactments: "The respect due to coequal and independent departments," and the need for finality and certainty about the status of a statute contribute to judicial reluctance to inquire whether, as passed, it complied with all requisite formalities. But it is not true that courts will never delve into a legislature's records upon such a quest.... The political question doctrine, a tool for maintenance of governmental order, will not be so applied as to promote only disorder.

The Status of Indian Tribes: This Court's deference to the political departments in determining whether Indians are recognized as a tribe, while it reflects familiar attributes of political questions, also has a unique element in that "the relation of the Indians to the United States is marked by peculiar and cardinal distinctions which exist no where else.... [The Indians are] domestic dependent nations ... in a state of pupilage. Their relation to the United States resembles that of a ward to his guardian." Yet, here too, there is no blanket rule....

Republican Form of Government: Luther v. Borden, though in form simply an action for damages for trespass was, as Daniel Webster said in opening the argument for the defense, "an unusual case." The defendants, admitting an otherwise tortious breaking and entering, sought to justify their action on the ground that they were agents of the established lawful government of Rhode Island, which State was then under martial law to defend itself from active insurrection; that the plaintiff was engaged in that insurrection; and that they entered under orders to arrest the plaintiff. The case arose "out of the unfortunate political differences which agitated the people of Rhode Island in 1841 and 1842," and which had resulted in a situation wherein two groups laid competing claims to recognition as the lawful government. The plaintiff's right to recover depended upon which of the two groups was entitled to such recognition; but the lower court's refusal to receive evidence or hear argument on that issue, its charge to the jury that the earlier established or "charter" government was lawful, and the verdict for the defendants, were affirmed upon appeal to this Court.

Chief Justice Taney's opinion for the Court reasoned as follows: (1) If a court were to hold the defendants' acts unjustified because the charter government had no legal existence during the period in question, it would follow that all of that government's actions—laws enacted, taxes collected, salaries paid, accounts settled, sentences passed—were of no effect; and that "the officers who carried their decisions into operation (were) answerable as trespassers, if not in some cases as criminals." There was, of course, no room for application of any doctrine of de facto status to uphold prior acts of an officer not authorized de jure, for such would have defeated the plaintiff's very action. A decision for the plaintiff would inevitably have produced some significant measure of chaos, a consequence to be avoided if it could be done without abnegation of the judicial duty to uphold the Constitution.

(2) No state court had recognized as a judicial responsibility settlement of the issue of the locus of state governmental authority. Indeed, the courts of

Rhode Island had in several cases held that "it rested with the political power to decide whether the charter government had been displaced or not," and that that department had acknowledged no change.

(3) Since "(t)he question relates, altogether, to the constitution and laws of (the) ... State," the courts of the United States had to follow the state courts' decisions unless there was a federal constitutional ground for overturning them.

(4) No provision of the Constitution could be or had been invoked for this purpose except Art. IV, [§] 4, the Guaranty Clause. Having already noted the absence of standards whereby the choice between governments could be made by a court acting independently, Chief Justice Taney now found further textual and practical reasons for concluding that, if any department of the United States was empowered by the Guaranty Clause to resolve the issue, it was not the judiciary:

Under this article of the Constitution it rests with Congress to decide what government is the established one in a State. For as the United States guarantee to each State a republican government, Congress must necessarily decide what government is established in the State before it can determine whether it is republican or not. And when the senators and representatives of a State are admitted into the councils of the Union, the authority of the government under which they are appointed, as well as its republican character, is recognized by the proper constitutional authority. And its decision is binding on every other department of the government, and could not be questioned in a judicial tribunal. It is true that the contest in this case did not last long enough to bring the matter to this issue; and ... Congress was

not called upon to decide the controversy. Yet the right to decide is placed there, and not in the courts.

So, too, as relates to the clause in the above-mentioned article of the Constitution, providing for cases of domestic violence. It rested with Congress, too, to determine upon the means proper to be adopted to fulfill this guarantee.... (B)y the act of February 28, 1795, (Congress) provided, that, "in case of an insurrection in any State against the government thereof, it shall be lawful for the President of the United States, on application of the legislature of such State or of the executive (when the legislature cannot be convened) to call forth such number of the militia of any other State or States, as may be applied for, as he may judge sufficient to suppress such insurrection."

By this act, the power of deciding whether the exigency had arisen upon which the government of the United States is bound to interfere, is given to the President....

After the President has acted and called out the militia, is a Circuit Court of the United States authorized to inquire whether his decision was right?.... If the judicial power extends so far, the guarantee contained in the Constitution of the United States is a guarantee of anarchy, and not of order....

It is true that in this case the militia were not called out by the President. But upon the application of the governor under the charter government, the President recognized him as the executive power of the State, and took measures to call out the militia to support his authority if it should be found necessary for the general government to interfere.... (C)ertainly no court of the United States, with a knowledge of this decision, would have been justified in recognizing the opposing party as the lawful government.... In the case of foreign nations, the government acknowledged by the President is always recognized in the courts of justice....

Clearly, several factors were thought by the Court in *Luther* to make the question there "political": the commitment to the other branches of the decision as to which is the lawful state government; the unambiguous action by the President, in recognizing the charter government as the lawful authority; the need for finality in the executive's decision; and the lack of criteria by which a court could determine which form of government was republican.

But the only significance that *Luther* could have for our immediate purposes is in its holding that the Guaranty Clause is not a repository of judicially manageable standards which a court could utilize independently in order to identify a State's lawful government. The Court has since refused to resort to the Guaranty Clause—which alone had been invoked for the purpose—as the source of a constitutional standard for invalidating state action....

We come, finally, to the ultimate inquiry whether our precedents as to what constitutes a nonjusticiable "political question" bring the case before us under the umbrella of that doctrine. A natural beginning is to note whether any of the common characteristics which we have been able to identify and label descriptively are present. We find none: The question here is the consistency of state action with the Federal Constitution. We have no question decided, or to be decided, by a political branch of government coequal with this Court. Nor do we risk embarrassment of our government abroad, or grave disturbance at home if we take issue with Tennessee as to the constitutionality of her action here challenged. Nor need the appellants, in order to succeed in this action, ask the Court to enter upon

policy determinations for which judicially manageable standards are lacking. Judicial standards under the Equal Protection Clause are well-developed and familiar, and it has been open to courts since the enactment of the Fourteenth Amendment to determine, if on the particular facts they must, that a discrimination reflects *no* policy, but simply arbitrary and capricious action.

This case does, in one sense, involve the allocation of political power within a State, and the appellants might conceivably have added a claim under the Guaranty Clause. Of course, as we have seen, any reliance on that clause would have been futile. But because any reliance on the Guaranty Clause could not have succeeded it does not follow that appellants may not be heard on the equal protection claim which they tender. True, it must be clear that the Fourteenth Amendment claim is not so enmeshed with those political question elements which render the Guaranty Clause claims nonjusticiable as actually to present a political question itself. But we have found that not to be the case....

We conclude that the complaint's allegations of a denial of equal protection present a justiciable constitutional cause of action upon which appellants are entitled to a trial and a decision. The right asserted is within the reach of judicial protection under the Fourteenth Amendment....

Reversed and remanded.

DOUGLAS, CLARK, AND STEWART, J.J., CONCURRING [OMITTED]

FRANKFURTER AND HARLAN, J.J., DISSENTING

The Court today reverses a uniform course of decision established by a dozen cases, including one by which the very claim now sustained was unanimously rejected only five years ago. The impressive body of rulings thus cast aside reflected the equally uniform course of our political history regarding the relationship between population and legislative representation—a wholly different matter from denial of the franchise to individuals because of race, color, religion, or sex. Such a massive repudiation of the experience of our whole past in asserting destructively novel judicial power demands a detailed analysis of the role of this Court in our constitutional scheme. Disregard of inherent limits in the effective exercise of the Court's "judicial Power" not only presages the futility of judicial intervention in the essentially political conflict of forces by which the relation between population and representation has time out of mind been and now is determined. It may well impair the Court's position as the ultimate organ of "the supreme Law of the Land" in that vast range of legal problems, often strongly entangled in popular feeling, on which this Court must pronounce. The Court's authority—possessed of neither the purse nor the sword—ultimately rests on sustained public confidence in its moral sanction. Such feeling must be nourished by the Court's complete detachment, in fact and in appearance, from political entanglements and by abstention from injecting itself into the clash of political forces in political settlements.

A hypothetical claim resting on abstract assumptions is now for the first time made the basis for affording illusory relief for a particular evil even though it foreshadows deeper and more pervasive difficulties in consequence. The claim is hypothetical and the assumptions are abstract because the Court does not vouchsafe the lower courts—state and federal—guidelines for formulating specific, definite, wholly unprecedented remedies for the inevitable litigations that today's umbrageous disposition is bound to stimulate in connection with politically motivated reapportionments in so many States. In such a setting, to promulgate jurisdiction in the abstract is meaningless.... For this Court to direct the District Court to enforce a claim to which the Court has over the years consistently found itself required to deny legal enforcement and at the same time to find it necessary to withhold any guidance to the lower court how to enforce this turnabout, new legal claim, manifests an odd—indeed an esoteric—conception of judicial propriety.... To charge courts with the task of accommodating the incommensurable factors of policy that underlie these mathematical puzzles is to attribute, however flatteringly, omnicompetence to judges. The Framers of the Constitution persistently rejected a proposal that embodied this assumption and Thomas Jefferson never entertained it....

In effect, today's decision empowers the courts of the country to devise what should constitute the proper composition of the legislatures of the fifty States. If state courts should for one reason or another find themselves unable to discharge this task, the duty of doing so is put on the federal courts or on this Court, if State views do not satisfy this Court's notion of what is proper districting....

The Framers carefully and with deliberate forethought refused so to enthrone the judiciary. In this situation, as in others of like nature, appeal for relief does not belong here. Appeal must be an informed, civically militant electorate. In a democratic society like ours, relief must come through an aroused popular conscience that sears the conscience of the people's representatives....

HARLAN AND FRANKFURTER, J.J., DISSENTING [OMITTED]

QUESTIONS

1. Explain why, according to Justice Brennan, *Luther v. Borden* raised nonjusticiable political questions while *Baker v. Carr* did not. After *Baker*, what criteria does the Court use to determine whether a case should be declared nonjusticiable because it involves political questions?

2. In an interview shortly after he left the Court, Chief Justice Earl Warren maintained that *Baker v. Carr* was the most important decision during his tenure on the Court. His selection of *Baker* rather than *Brown v. Board of Education*, 347 U.S 483 (1954), surprised many. Warren explained his choice this way:

   > If everybody in this country has an opportunity to participate on equal terms with everyone else and can share in electing representatives who will be truly representative of the entire community and not some special interest, then most of these problems we are now confronted with would be solved through the political process rather than through the courts. ("Warren Calls Vote Rulings Most Vital," *New York Times*, June 27, 1969, p. 17)

   What insights does this quotation provide into Warren's understanding of the function of the Supreme Court and judicially created tenets such as the political question doctrine?

3. Justice Frankfurter, a dissenter in *Baker*, wrote the majority opinion in *Colegrove v. Green*, 328 U.S. 549 (1946). He warned that entertaining reapportionment suits "cut[s] to the very being" of the political branches, and that "Courts ought not to enter this political thicket." In what ways does hearing reapportionment cases march the Court into the political thicket?

4. Law professor Gerald Gunther analyzes the political question doctrine as containing three discrete "strands": (1) the Constitution commits the final determination of some constitutional questions to agencies other than courts; (2) some constitutional questions cannot be resolved by judicially manageable standards or on the basis of data available to courts; and (3) some constitutional questions ought not be resolved by courts because they are too controversial or could present courts with enforcement problems (*Constitutional Law*, 12th ed. [Westbury, NY: Foundation, 1991], pp. 388, 1651). Are any of these "strands" a factor in *Baker*? In *Luther*?

5. After *Baker*, the political question doctrine has been raised in contexts other than reapportionment. Examples include the following:

After the May 1970 National Guard shooting at Kent State University, resulting in the death of four students, several Kent State students sued for injunctive relief. They sought to restrain the Governor of Ohio in the future from prematurely ordering Guard troops to a civil disorder and to restrain Guard leaders from future violations of student rights. In *Gilligan v. Morgan*, 413 U.S. 1 (1973) the Court divided 5–4 on the issue of justiciability. Writing for the majority, Chief Justice Burger wrote: "It would be difficult to think of a clearer example of the type of governmental action that was intended by the Constitution to be left to the political branches, directly responsible—as the Judicial Branch is not—to the elective process." The four dissenters thought the case should be dismissed as moot.

In 1979, Arizona Senator Barry Goldwater, joined by several senatorial colleagues, challenged the constitutionality of President Jimmy Carter's termination of a defense treaty with Taiwan without consulting the Senate. In *Goldwater v. Carter*, 444 U.S. 100 (1979) a fragmented Court voted 8–1 to direct a federal district court to dismiss the complaint. Writing for himself and three colleagues, Justice Rehnquist held that the case was political, hence nonjusticiable. Justice Powell disagreed, and would have dismissed the case as not ripe for judicial review. Justices Blackmun and White would have allowed oral arguments on the issues. Justice Brennan would have affirmed the district court's ruling that President Carter had the authority to abrogate the Taiwan treaty.

In *Walter L. Nixon v. United States*, 506 U.S. 224 (1993), the Court held unanimously that a challenge to the procedures adopted by the Senate to try the impeachment of a federal judge was a nonjusticiable political question. Following his 1986 conviction on two counts of lying to a grand jury, U.S. district court judge Walter L. Nixon refused to resign from the bench. He was subsequently impeached by the U.S. House of Representatives, 417–0, for "high crimes and misdemeanors." In trying Judge Nixon on two articles of impeachment, the Senate invoked its Rule XI, which authorizes a committee instead of the full Senate to hear the case. Upon recommendation of this committee, the full Senate voted to convict Judge Nixon on the two articles of impeachment. Nixon sued, claiming that Senate Rule XI violates Article I, Section 3, clause 6, of the Constitution that reads, the "Senate shall have the sole power to try all impeachments." Chief Justice Rehnquist wrote: "The parties do not offer evidence of a single word in the history of the Constitutional Convention or in contemporary commentary that even alludes to the possibility of judicial review in the context of the impeachment powers."

Do these cases raise issues any less needful of judicial resolution than *Baker v. Carr*? What insights into the political question doctrine and the doctrine of judicial self-restraint do the cases in this section provide in terms of being able to predict whether the Supreme Court will consider the merits of a case?

SUGGESTIONS FOR FURTHER READING

Bonfield, Arthur Earl, "*Baker v. Carr*: New Light on the Constitutional Guarantee of Republican Government," 50 *California Law Review* (1962): 245.

———, "The Guarantee Clause of Article IV, Section 4: A Study in Constitutional Desuetude," 46 *Minnesota Law Review* (1962): 513.

Cox, Archibald, *The Warren Court: Constitutional Decision as an Instrument of Reform* (Cambridge, MA: Harvard University Press, 1967).

Dellinger, Walter, "The Legitimacy of Constitutional Change: Rethinking the Amendment Process," 97 *Harvard Law Review* (1983): 386.

Dennison, George M., *The Dorr War: Republicanism on Trial, 1831–1861* (Lexington, KY: University of Kentucky Press, 1976).

Dixon, Robert G. Jr., *Democratic Representation: Reapportionment in Law and Politics* (New York, NY: Oxford University Press, 1968).

Elliott, Ward E. Y., *The Rise of Guardian Democracy: The Supreme Court's Role in Voting Rights Disputes, 1845–1969* (Cambridge, MA: Harvard University Press, 1975).

Gettleman, Marvin E., *The Dorr Rebellion: A Study in American Radicalism, 1833–1849* (Huntington, NY: R. E. Krieger, 1973).

Henkin, Louis, "Is There a 'Political Question' Doctrine?" 85 *Yale Law Journal* (1976): 597.

McCloskey, Robert G., "Foreword: The Reapportionment Case," 76 *Harvard Law Review* (1962): 54.

McKay, Robert B., "Political Thickets and Crazy Quilts: Reapportionment and Equal Protection," 61 *Michigan Law Review* (1963): 645.

Merritt, Deborah Jones, "The Guarantee Clause and State Autonomy: Federalism for a Third Century," 88 *Columbia Law Review* (1988): 1.

Mulhern, J. Peter, "In Defense of the Political Questions Doctrine," 137 *University of Pennsylvania Law Review* (1988): 97.

Neal, Phil C., "*Baker v. Carr*: Politics in Search of Law," in *The Supreme Court Review* (Chicago, IL: University of Chicago Press, 1962).

Note, "A Niche for the Guarantee Clause," 94 *Harvard Law Review* (1981): 681.

Redish, Martin, "Judicial Review and the Political Questions," 79 *Northwestern University Law Review* (1985): 1031.

Scharpf, Fritz W., "Judicial Review and the Political Question: A Functional Analysis," 75 *Yale Law Journal* (1966): 517.

Schuck, Peter H., "The Thickest Thicket: Partisan Gerrymandering and Judicial Regulation of Politics," 87 *Columbia Law Review* (1987): 1325.

Strum, Philippa, *The Supreme Court and "Political Questions": A Study in Judicial Evasion* (Tuscaloosa, AL: University of Alabama Press, 1974).

Tigar, Michael, "The 'Political Question' Doctrine and Foreign Relations," 17 *U.C.L.A. Law Review* (1970): 1135.

Tribe, Laurence H., "A *Constitution* We Are Amending: In Defense of a Restrained Judicial Role," 97 *Harvard Law Review* (1983): 433.

Wiecek, William M., *The Guarantee Clause of the U.S. Constitution* (Ithaca, NY: Cornell University Press, 1972).

JUSTICIABILITY: STANDING

Frothingham v. Mellon
262 U.S. 447 (1923)

SETTING

As explained in Chapter 1, litigants have no automatic right of access to federal courts. Among the "gatekeeping" rules governing access to federal courts is the requirement that the lawsuit raise a federal question. In addition, courts must have either subject matter or personal jurisdiction over the questions raised. A litigant also must have standing to sue. In *Ex parte Lévitt*, 302 U.S. 633 (1937), the Supreme Court summarized the standing-to-sue doctrine in these terms:

> It is an established principle that to entitle a private individual to invoke the judicial power to determine the validity of executive or legislative action he must show that he has sustained, or is immediately in danger of sustaining, a direct injury as the result of that action and it is not sufficient that he has merely a general interest common to all members of the public.

Frothingham v. Mellon is an early landmark in the Court's development of this doctrine.

Frothingham grew out of a controversy involving federal grants-in-aid to the states. Beginning in 1911 with the Weeks Act (designed to aid states with forest fire protection), Congress has used the grant-in-aid device to stimulate and assist states in achieving goals that the federal government deems desirable. Education, agriculture, military training, and highway construction were early subjects of grant-in-aid programs initiated by Congress and aimed at the states. Grants frequently are conditioned on the requirement that the state "match" the federal grant with state money. The political genius of the grant-in-aid is that no state is under direct compulsion to accept federal funds, but it is not easy for a state to reject offers of large sums of money from the federal government. Between 1911 and 1925, the total amount of federal grants-in-aid mushroomed from $200,000 to $93 million.

Those opposed generally to programs sponsored by the federal government or opposed to a particular program have sought various means to prevent grant-in-aid expenditures. An attempt to test the constitutionality of one grant-in-aid program arose in connection with the "Act for the promotion of the welfare and hygiene of maternity and infancy, and other purposes," commonly known as the Sheppard-Towner Act or the Maternity Act. It was passed by Congress in 1921 to reduce maternal and infant mortality and to protect the health of mothers and infants. The act appropriated monies to be expended for five years in cooperation with the states to improve the health of mothers and infants. In order for states to receive money from the Children's Bureau, they were required to submit plans for carrying out the act's provisions and to match federal funds with state funds each year. If the national Children's Bureau determined that a state had not expended funds properly, it was authorized to withhold payment to that state. In an era of social reaction and business dominance, many viewed the act as an unnecessary "frill" imposed on unwilling states by an aggressive national government.

One opponent of the Act was Harriet A. Frothingham, a citizen of Massachusetts and a U.S. taxpayer. She filed a suit in equity in the Supreme Court of the District of Columbia to enjoin Secretary of the Treasury Andrew Mellon and other federal officials from paying any money out of the federal treasury to support the Maternity Act. She claimed that promoting the welfare and hygiene of maternity and infancy was within the exclusive power of the states and that Congress was without power or authority to legislate or appropriate money for such a purpose.

The court dismissed Frothingham's complaint on the ground that it lacked jurisdiction. The Court of Appeals of the District of Columbia affirmed. Frothingham appealed to the Supreme Court of the United States. The case was consolidated with an original suit by the Commonwealth of Massachusetts raising related issues.

HIGHLIGHTS OF SUPREME COURT ARGUMENTS

BRIEF FOR FROTHINGHAM

◆ Taxpayers have a sufficient interest to entitle them to maintain a suit against a public officer for the purpose of enjoining an unauthorized payment of public funds or disposition of public property.

◆ It is the responsibility of the judiciary to restrain government agencies or officers when they attempt to act in excess of their authority.

◆ The Sheppard-Towner Act goes beyond the authority conferred on the government of the United States by the Constitution.

◆ If the appropriation of money for the "general welfare" is valid in this instance, the door is open for the subjection of the states of the union to the will of the United States.

AMICUS CURIAE BRIEF SUPPORTING FROTHINGHAM

Joint brief of Everett Wheeler and Waldo Morse.

BRIEF FOR MASSACHUSETTS

◆ Massachusetts has a sufficient interest in the case to allow it to sue as a party plaintiff because it is being asked by the Act to yield a part of its powers reserved by the Tenth Amendment or to give up its share of appropriations under the Act.

◆ This case is within the Supreme Court's original jurisdiction, is justiciable, and does not call for the decision of a political question.

AMICUS CURIAE BRIEF SUPPORTING MASSACHUSETTS

Former Massachusetts attorney general J. Weston Allen.

BRIEF FOR MELLON

◆ These actions in actuality are against the U.S. government, which cannot be sued without its consent.

◆ This Court lacks jurisdiction because this case does not involve a controversy between a state and citizens of other states.

◆ Even if money raised by federal taxes is being misspent, a state may not bring a suit on behalf of its citizens. There is no justiciable controversy in this case.

AMICUS CURIAE BRIEFS SUPPORTING MELLON

Attorneys general of Kentucky, Pennsylvania, Virginia, Minnesota, Colorado, Delaware, Indiana, Arkansas, Arizona, and Ohio.

SUPREME COURT DECISION: 9–0

SUTHERLAND, J.

... We have reached the conclusion that [this case] must be disposed of for want of jurisdiction, without considering the merits of the constitutional questions....

The appellant ... has no ... interest in the subject-matter, nor is any ... injury inflicted or threatened, as will enable her to sue....

The ... plaintiff alleges ... that she is a taxpayer of the United States; and her contention, though not clear, seems to be that the effect of the appropriations complained of will be to increase the burden of future taxation and thereby take her property without due process of law. The right of a taxpayer to enjoin the execution of a federal appropriation act, on the ground that it is invalid and will result in taxation for illegal purposes, has never been passed upon by this court.... The interest of a taxpayer of a municipality in the application of its moneys is direct and immediate and the remedy by injunction to prevent their misuse is not inappropriate. It is upheld by a large number of state cases and is the rule of this court.... The reasons which support the extension of the equitable remedy to a single taxpayer in such cases are based upon the peculiar relation of the corporate taxpayer to the corporation, which is not without some resemblance to that subsisting between stockholder and private corporation. But the relation of a taxpayer of the United States to the federal government is very different. His interest in the moneys of the treasury—partly realized from taxation and partly from other sources—is shared with millions of others, is comparatively minute and indeterminable, and the effect upon future taxation, of any payment out of the funds, so remote, fluctuating and uncertain, that no basis is afforded for an appeal to the preventive powers of a court of equity.

The administration of any statute, likely to produce additional taxation to be imposed upon a vast number of taxpayers, the extent of whose several liability is indefinite and constantly changing, is essentially a matter of public and not of individual concern. If one taxpayer may champion and litigate such a cause, then every other taxpayer may do the same, not only in respect of the statute here under review, but also in respect of every other appropriation act and statute whose administration requires the outlay of public money, and whose validity may be questioned. The bare suggestion of such a result, with its attendant inconveniences, goes far to sustain the conclusion which we have reached, that a suit of this character cannot be maintained....

The functions of government under our system are apportioned.... The general rule is that neither department may invade the province of the other and neither may control, direct, or restrain the action of the other.... We have no power *per se* to review and annul acts of Congress on the ground that they are unconstitutional. That question may be considered only when the justification for some direct injury suffered or threatened, presenting a justiciable issue, is made to rest upon such an act. Then the power exercised is that of ascertaining and declaring the law applicable to the controversy. It amounts to little more than the negative power to disregard an unconstitutional enactment, which otherwise would stand in the way of the enforcement of a legal right. The party who invokes the power must be able to show, not only that the statute is invalid, but that he has sustained or is immediately in danger of sustaining some direct injury as the result of its enforcement, and not merely that he suffers in some indefinite way in common with people generally. If a case for preventive relief be presented, the court enjoins, in effect, not the execution of the statute, but the acts of the official, the statute notwithstanding.... [T]he ... plaintiff [has] no such case. Looking through forms of words to the substance of their complaint, it is merely that officials of the executive department of the government are executing and will execute an act of Congress asserted to be unconstitutional; and this we are asked to prevent. To do so would be, not to decide a judicial controversy, but to assume a position of authority over the governmental acts of another and coequal department, an authority which plainly we do not possess.

[A]ffirmed.

Questions

1. State the rule of *Frothingham*. Is the standing rule constitutionally required or is it a rule fashioned by the judiciary to serve its own interests? If the latter, what are those interests?

2. Was Frothingham's case flawed because she failed to show injury, because she failed to demonstrate any connection between her injury and the Sheppard-Towner Act, or both? On what set of facts would Frothingham have had standing to sue? Lacking standing, what options were available to her to end a government program of which she disapproved? Are these options realistic? Adequate?

3. Might the Court have disposed of *Frothingham* by invoking the political question doctrine formulated in *Luther v. Borden*? Should it have done so? What are the practical differences between the doctrine of standing and the political question doctrine?

4. Writing for the majority in *Bi-Metallic Investment Co. v. State Board of Equalization of Colorado*, 239 U.S. 44 (1915), Justice Oliver Wendell Holmes Jr. observed:

   > Where a rule of conduct applies to more than a few people it is impracticable that every one should have a direct voice in its adoption. The Constitution does not require that all public acts be done in town meeting or an assembly of the whole. General statutes within the state power are passed that affect the person or property of individuals, sometimes to the point of ruin, without giving them a chance to be heard. Their rights are protected in the only way that they can be in a complex society, by their power, immediate or remote, over those who make the rule.... There must be a limit to individual argument in such matters if government is to go on.

   Is Holmes's argument consistent with the Court's view of standing in *Frothingham*?

Comment

In 1937, the Supreme Court held that, under Article I, § 6, cl. 2, a citizen has no standing to challenge the appointment of a Supreme Court Justice. *Ex parte Lévitt*, 302 U.S. 633. Albert Levitt challenged Hugo Black's appointment to the

Supreme Court because he was a sitting senator when Congress voted to increase the pension of federal justices retiring at seventy. Levitt argued that Black was being appointed unconstitutionally to an office, the "emoluments"of which had been "increased" during his term in the senate. In a *per curiam* opinion, the Court stated that

> A private individual may not invoke judicial power to determine validity of executive or legislative action without showing that he has sustained, or is immediately in danger of sustaining, a direct injury as result of action, and it is not sufficient that individual has merely a general interest common to all members of the public.

Curiously, although Levitt asked the Court to assume original jurisdiction, the opinion makes no reference to *Marbury v. Madison*.

JUSTICIABILITY: STANDING

Flast v. Cohen
392 U.S. 83 (1968)

SETTING

Lyndon Baines Johnson became president of the United States on November 22, 1963, following the assassination of President John F. Kennedy. Johnson brought to the office a commanding mastery of congressional politics based on lengthy careers in the U.S. House of Representatives (1939–1948) and the Senate (1948–1961). From 1955 until he became vice president in 1961, Johnson was the majority leader of the Senate. His reputation for getting legislation through Congress was legendary. In the spring of 1964, Johnson put a name on a group of social programs that he envisioned would transform America—the Great Society. After winning the November 1964 presidential election overwhelmingly, and with Democratic majorities in both the House and Senate, Johnson pushed his Great Society legislation through Congress. Two proposals were particularly important to Johnson—medical care for the elderly and federal aid to elementary and high school education to equalize educational funding disparities among the states.

Johnson called his $1.5 billion education bill "the key which can unlock the door to the Great Society." Previous federal aid to education bills had died in Congress because they contained provisions that channeled funds to parochial as well as to public schools, thereby raising concerns that such aid constituted an unconstitutional "establishment" of religion prohibited by the First Amendment. Johnson adroitly sidestepped that potential constitutional flaw by proposing aid to both public and parochial schools based on a "child benefit" theory: children, not schools, would receive the benefits of the monies appropriated for education. Johnson's well-known arm-twisting legislative skills resulted in his proposal being enacted as the Elementary and Secondary Education Act of 1965. It authorized Wilbur Cohen, secretary of the Department of Health, Education and Welfare (HEW) to provide federal funds to states and localities to help meet the special educational needs of educationally deprived children in school attendance areas that had high concentrations of children from low-income families.

The Elementary and Secondary Education Act was immediately challenged by opponents who believed that it violated the Establishment and Free Exercise Clauses of the First Amendment. Seven taxpayers from New York, headed by Florence Flast, sought to enjoin the use of federal funds to pay for guidance services and instruction in reading, writing, and other subjects in religiously operated schools and the purchase of textbooks and other instructional materials for use in such schools. They also sought a declaration that the expenditures were an unconstitutional violation of the First Amendment's prohibition against the establishment of religion in the United States.

A three-judge panel of the U.S. District Court for the Southern District of New York dismissed the complaint by a 2–1 vote. It ruled that under the doctrine of *Frothingham v. Mellon* taxpayers lacked standing to bring their action, that as a result no justiciable controversy existed, and that the court therefore lacked jurisdiction over the subject matter. The court observed that although *Frothingham* had been criticized, it had never been overruled and, accordingly, controlled this case.

Flast and her coplaintiffs appealed the dismissal directly to the Supreme Court of the United States, as allowed by statute from decisions of three-judge federal district court panels.

HIGHLIGHTS OF SUPREME COURT ARGUMENTS

BRIEF FOR FLAST

♦ The determination in *Frothingham* that the plaintiff lacked standing to sue was not a holding that the federal courts are without jurisdiction under Article III of the Constitution.

♦ *Frothingham* expressed a policy of judicial restraint based on factors that may have been valid in 1923 but have no equivalent validity today. All policy considerations dictate acceptance of jurisdiction in this case.

♦ This Court has never relied on *Frothingham* to dismiss a citizen's or taxpayer's suit under the First Amendment, or any other suit asserting a constitutional claim other than the narrow property right asserted in *Frothingham*.

AMICUS CURIAE BRIEFS SUPPORTING FLAST

Joint brief of Council of Chief State School Officers, American Association of School Administrators, National School Boards Association, National Association of State Boards of Education, and the Horace Mann League of the United States; Americans United for the Separation of Church and State; National Council of Churches; joint brief of the American Jewish Committee, American Jewish Congress, B'Nai B'rith Anti-Defamation League, Central Conference of American Rabbis, Jewish War Veterans of the U.S.A., National Council of Jewish Women, Rabbinical Assembly, Rabbinical Council of America, Union of American Hebrew Congregations, United Synagogue of America, and numerous local Jewish Community Councils; joint brief of Americans for Public Schools and Baptist General Association of Virginia.

BRIEF FOR COHEN

◆ A direct appeal to this Court is not authorized, because this case should not have been heard by a three-judge panel.
◆ If this Court rules that a federal taxpayer, as taxpayer, has standing to challenge specific expenditures of federal revenues without any case or controversy, federal courts will become councils of revision, empowered to review virtually any act of Congress or the Executive upon the request of hundreds of millions of "plaintiffs."
◆ If *Frothingham* is viewed as rule of restraint rather than a jurisdictional limitation, the circumstances here do not warrant exceptional treatment. There are ways for individuals with more immediate personal interests in the outcome of litigation to get their claims before state and federal courts.

AMICUS CURIAE BRIEFS SUPPORTING COHEN

Joint brief of fifteen parents and guardians of children who receive educational help under the Act; National Jewish Commission on Law and Public Affairs.

SUPREME COURT DECISION: 8–1

WARREN, C.J.

In this case, we must decide whether the *Frothingham* barrier should be lowered when a taxpayer attacks a federal statute on the ground that it violates the Establishment and Free Exercise Clauses of the First Amendment....

Although the barrier *Frothingham* erected against federal taxpayer suits has never been breached, the decision has been the source of some confusion and the object of considerable criticism. The confusion has developed as commentators have tried to determine whether *Frothingham* establishes a constitutional bar to taxpayer suits or whether the Court was simply imposing a rule of self-restraint which was not constitutionally compelled. The conflicting viewpoints are reflected in the arguments made to this Court by the parties in this case....

Whatever the merits of the current debate over *Frothingham*, its very existence suggests that we should undertake a fresh examination of the limitations upon standing to sue in a federal court and the application of those limitations to taxpayer suits.

The jurisdiction of federal courts is defined and limited by Article III of the Constitution. In terms relevant to the question for decision in this case, the judicial power of federal courts is constitutionally restricted to "cases" and "controversies." As is so often the situation in constitutional adjudication, those two words have an iceberg quality, containing beneath their surface simplicity submerged complexities which go to the very heart of our constitutional form of government. Embodied in the words "cases" and "controversies" are two complementary but somewhat different limitations. In part those words limit the business of federal courts to questions presented in an adversary context and in a form historically viewed as capable of resolution through the judicial process. And in part those words define the role assigned to the judiciary in a tripartite allocation of power to assure that the federal courts will not intrude into areas committed to the other branches of government. Justiciability is the term

of art employed to give expression to this dual limitation placed upon federal courts by the case-and-controversy doctrine.

Justiciability is itself a concept of uncertain meaning and scope. Its reach is illustrated by the various grounds upon which questions sought to be adjudicated in federal courts have been held not to be justiciable. Thus, no justiciable controversy is presented when the parties seek adjudication of only a political question, when the parties are asking for an advisory opinion, when the question sought to be adjudicated has been mooted by subsequent developments, and when there is no standing to maintain the action. Yet it remains true that "(j)usticiability is ... not a legal concept with a fixed content or susceptible of scientific verification. Its utilization is the result of many subtle pressures..." *Poe v. Ullman*, 367 U.S. 497 (1961).

Part of the difficulty in giving precise meaning and form to the concept of justiciability stems from the uncertain historical antecedents of the case-and-controversy doctrine....

Additional uncertainty exists in the doctrine of justiciability because that doctrine has become a blend of constitutional requirements and policy considerations. And a policy limitation is "not always clearly distinguished from the constitutional limitation." *Barrows v. Jackson*, 346 U.S. 249 (1953).... The "many subtle pressures" which cause policy considerations to blend into the constitutional limitations of Article III make the justiciability doctrine one of uncertain and shifting contours.

It is in this context that the standing question presented by this case must be viewed and that the Government's argument on that question must be evaluated. As we understand it, the Government's position is that the constitutional scheme of separation of powers, and the deference owed by the federal judiciary to the other two branches of government within that scheme, present an absolute bar to taxpayer suits challenging the validity of federal spending programs....

Standing is an aspect of justiciability and, as such, the problem of standing is surrounded by the same complexities and vagaries that inhere in justiciability. Standing has been called one of "the most amorphous (concepts) in the entire domain of public law." Some of the complexities peculiar to standing problems result because standing "serves, on occasion, as a shorthand expression for all the various elements of justiciability." In addition, there are at work in the standing doctrine the many subtle pressures which tend to cause policy considerations to blend into constitutional limitations.

Despite the complexities and uncertainties, some meaningful form can be given to the jurisdictional limitations placed on federal court power by the concept of standing. The fundamental aspect of standing is that it focuses on the party seeking to get his complaint before a federal court and not on the issues he wishes to have adjudicated. The "gist of the question of standing" is whether the party seeking relief has "alleged such a personal stake in the outcome of the controversy as to assure that concrete adverseness which sharpens the presentation of issues upon which the court so largely depends for illumination of difficult constitutional questions." *Baker v. Carr....*

When the emphasis in the standing problem is placed on whether the person invoking a federal court's jurisdiction is a proper party to maintain the action, the weakness of the Government's argument in this case becomes apparent. The question whether a particular person is a proper party to maintain the action does not, by its own force, raise separation of powers problems related to improper judicial interference in areas committed to other branches of the Federal Government. Such problems arise, if at all, only from the substantive issues the individual seeks to have adjudicated. Thus, in terms of Article III limitations on federal court jurisdiction, the question of standing is related only to whether the dispute sought to be adjudicated will be presented in an adversary context and in a form historically viewed as capable of judicial resolution. It is for that reason that the emphasis in standing problems is on whether the party invoking federal court jurisdiction has "a personal stake in the outcome of the controversy," and whether the dispute touches upon "the legal relations of parties having adverse legal interests." *Aetna Life Insurance Co. v. Haworth* [300 U.S. 27 (1937)]. A taxpayer may or may not have the requisite personal stake in the outcome, depending upon the circumstances of the particular case. Therefore, we find no absolute bar in Article III to suits by federal taxpayers challenging allegedly unconstitutional federal taxing and spending programs. There remains, however, the problem of determining the circumstances under which a federal taxpayer will be deemed to have the personal stake and interest that impart the necessary concrete adverseness to such litigation so that standing can be conferred on the taxpayer qua taxpayer consistent with the constitutional limitations of Article III.

The various rules of standing applied by federal courts have not been developed in the abstract. Rather, they have been fashioned with specific reference to the status asserted by the party whose standing is challenged and to the type of question he wishes to have adjudicated. We have noted that, in deciding the question of standing, it is not relevant that the substantive issues in the litigation might be nonjusticiable. However, our decisions establish that, in ruling on standing, it is both appropriate and necessary to look to the substantive issues for another purpose, namely, to determine whether there is a logical nexus between the status asserted and the claim sought to be adjudicated.... Such inquiries into the nexus between the status asserted by the litigant and the claim he presents are essential to assure that he is a proper and appropriate party to invoke federal judicial power. Thus, our point of reference in this case is the standing of individuals who assert only the status of federal taxpayers and who challenge the constitutionality of a federal spending program. Whether such individuals have standing to maintain that form of action turns on whether they can demonstrate the necessary stake as taxpayers in the outcome of the litigation to satisfy Article III requirements.

The nexus demanded of federal taxpayers has two aspects to it. First, the taxpayer must establish a logical link between that status and the type of legislative enactment attacked. Thus, a taxpayer will be a proper party to allege the unconstitutionality only of exercises of congressional power under the taxing

and spending clause of Art. I, [§] 8, of the Constitution. It will not be sufficient to allege an incidental expenditure of tax funds in the administration of an essentially regulatory statute.... Secondly, the taxpayer must establish a nexus between that status and the precise nature of the constitutional infringement alleged. Under this requirement, the taxpayer must show that the challenged enactment exceeds specific constitutional limitations imposed upon the exercise of the congressional taxing and spending power and not simply that the enactment is generally beyond the powers delegated to Congress by Art. I, [§] 8. When both nexuses are established, the litigant will have shown a taxpayer's stake in the outcome of the controversy and will be a proper and appropriate party to invoke a federal court's jurisdiction.

The taxpayer-appellants in this case have satisfied both nexuses to support their claim of standing under the test we announce today. Their constitutional challenge is made to an exercise by Congress of its power under Art. I, [§] 8, to spend for the general welfare, and the challenged program involves a substantial expenditure of federal tax funds. In addition, appellants have alleged that the challenged expenditures violate the Establishment and Free Exercise Clauses of the First Amendment. Our history vividly illustrates that one of the specific evils feared by those who drafted the Establishment Clause and fought for its adoption was that the taxing and spending power would be used to favor one religion over another or to support religion in general....

The allegations of the taxpayer in *Frothingham v. Mellon* were quite different from those made in this case, and the result in *Frothingham* is consistent with the test of taxpayer standing announced today. The taxpayer in *Frothingham* attacked a federal spending program and she, therefore, established the first nexus required. However, she lacked standing because her constitutional attack was not based on an allegation that Congress, in enacting the Maternity Act of 1921, had breached a specific limitation upon its taxing and spending power....

We have noted that the Establishment Clause of the First Amendment does specifically limit the taxing and spending power conferred by Art. I, [§] 8. Whether the Constitution contains other specific limitations can be determined only in the context of future cases. However, whenever such specific limitations are found, we believe a taxpayer will have a clear stake as a taxpayer in assuring that they are not breached by Congress. Consequently, we hold that a taxpayer will have standing consistent with Article III to invoke federal judicial power when he alleges that congressional action under the taxing and spending clause is in derogation of those constitutional provisions which operate to restrict the exercise of the taxing and spending power. The taxpayer's allegation in such cases would be that his tax money is being extracted and spent in violation of specific constitutional protections against such abuses of legislative power. Such an injury is appropriate for judicial redress, and the taxpayer has established the necessary nexus between his status and the nature of the allegedly unconstitutional action to support his claim of standing to secure judicial review....

Reversed.

DOUGLAS, J., CONCURRING

... I think ... it would ... be the part of wisdom, as I see the problem, to be rid of *Frothingham* here and now....

Taxpayers can be vigilant private attorneys general. Their stake in the outcome of litigation may be de minimis by financial standards, yet very great when measured by a particular constitutional mandate....

There has long been a school of thought here that the less the judiciary does, the better....

The judiciary is an indispensable part of the operation of our federal system. With the growing complexities of government it is often the one and only place where effective relief can be obtained. If the judiciary were to become a super-legislative group sitting in judgment on the affairs of people, the situation would be intolerable. But where wrongs to individuals are done by violation of specific guarantees, it is abdication for courts to close their doors....

We have a Constitution designed to keep government out of private domains. But the fences have often been broken down; and *Frothingham* denied effective machinery to restore them. The Constitution even with the judicial gloss it has acquired plainly is not adequate to protect the individual against the growing bureaucracy in the Legislative and Executive Branches. He faces a formidable opponent in government, even when he is endowed with funds and with courage. The individual is almost certain to be plowed under, unless he has a well-organized active political group to speak for him. The church is one. The press is another. The union is a third. But if a powerful sponsor is lacking, individual liberty withers—in spite of glowing opinions and resounding constitutional phrases.

I would not be niggardly therefore in giving private attorneys general standing to sue....

STEWART, J., CONCURRING

I join the judgment and opinion of the Court, which I understand to hold only that a federal taxpayer has standing to assert that a specific expenditure of federal funds violates the Establishment Clause of the First Amendment....

In concluding that the appellants therefore have standing to sue, we do not undermine the salutary principle, established by *Frothingham* and reaffirmed today, that a taxpayer may not "employ a federal court as a forum in which to air his generalized grievances about the conduct of government or the allocation of power in the Federal System."

FORTAS, J., CONCURRING

I would confine the ruling in this case to the proposition that a taxpayer may maintain a suit to challenge the validity of a federal expenditure on the ground that the expenditure violates the Establishment Clause....

HARLAN, J., DISSENTING

The problems presented by this case are narrow and relatively abstract, but the principles by which they must be resolved involve nothing less than the proper functioning of the federal courts, and so run to the roots of our constitutional system. The nub of my view is that the end result of *Frothingham v. Mellon* was correct....

The Court's analysis consists principally of the observation that the requirements of standing are met if a taxpayer has the "requisite personal stake in the outcome" of this suit. This does not, of course, resolve the standing problem; it merely restates it. The Court implements this standard with the declaration that taxpayers will be "deemed" to have the necessary personal interest if their suits satisfy two criteria: first, the challenged expenditure must form part of a federal spending program, and not merely be "incidental" to a regulatory program; and second, the constitutional provision under which the plaintiff claims must be a "specific limitation" upon Congress' spending powers.

The difficulties with these criteria are many and severe, but it is enough for the moment to emphasize that they are not in any sense a measurement of any plaintiff's interest in the outcome of any suit. As even a cursory examination of the criteria will show, the Court's standard for the determination of standing and its criteria for the satisfaction of that standard are entirely unrelated.

It is surely clear that a plaintiff's interest in the outcome of a suit in which he challenges the constitutionality of a federal expenditure is not made greater or smaller by the unconnected fact that the expenditure is, or is not, "incidental" to an "essentially regulatory" program....

Presumably the Court does not believe that regulatory programs are necessarily less destructive of First Amendment rights, or that regulatory programs are necessarily less prodigal of public funds than are grants-in-aid, for both these general propositions are demonstrably false. The Court's disregard of regulatory expenditures is not even a logical consequence of its apparent assumption that taxpayer-plaintiffs assert essentially monetary interests, for it surely cannot matter to a taxpayer *qua* taxpayer whether an unconstitutional expenditure is used to hire the services of regulatory personnel or is distributed among private and local governmental agencies as grants-in-aid. His interest as taxpayer arises, if at all, from the fact of an unlawful expenditure, and not as a consequence of the expenditure's form.

Apparently the Court has repudiated the emphasis in *Frothingham* upon the amount of the plaintiff's tax bill, only to substitute an equally irrelevant emphasis upon the form of the challenged expenditure.

The Court's second criterion is similarly unrelated to its standard for the determination of standing. The intensity of a plaintiff's interest in a suit is not measured, even obliquely, by the fact that the constitutional provision under which he claims is, or is not, a "specific limitation" upon Congress' spending powers. Thus, among the claims in *Frothingham* was the assertion that the Maternity Act deprived the petitioner of property without due process of law. The Court has evidently concluded that this claim did not confer standing because the Due Process Clause of the Fifth Amendment is not a specific limitation upon the spending powers. Disregarding for the moment the formidable obscurity of the Court's categories, how can it be said that Mrs. Frothingham's interests in her suit were, as a consequence of her choice of a constitutional claim, necessarily less intense than those, for example, of the

present appellants? I am quite unable to understand how, if a taxpayer believes that a given public expenditure is unconstitutional, and if he seeks to vindicate that belief in a federal court, his interest in the suit can be said necessarily to vary according to the constitutional provision under which he states his claim....

Although the Court does not altogether explain its position, the essence of its reasoning is evidently that a taxpayer's claim under the Establishment Clause is "not merely one of ultra vires," but one which instead asserts "an abridgment of individual religious liberty" and a "governmental infringement of individual rights protected by the Constitution." It must first be emphasized that this is apparently not founded upon any "preferred" position for the First Amendment, or upon any asserted unavailability of other plaintiffs. The Court's position is instead that, because of the Establishment Clause's historical purposes, taxpayers retain rights under it quite different from those held by them under other constitutional provisions.

The difficulties with this position are several. First, ... I say simply that, given the ultimate obscurity of the Establishment Clause's historical purposes, it is inappropriate for this Court to draw fundamental distinctions among the several constitutional commands upon the supposed authority of isolated dicta extracted from the clause's complex history....

The Court's position is equally precarious if it is assumed that its premise is that the Establishment Clause is in some uncertain fashion a more "specific" limitation upon Congress' powers than are the various other constitutional commands. It is obvious, first, that only in some Pickwickian sense are any of the provisions with which the Court is concerned "specific(ally)" limitations upon spending, for they contain nothing that is expressly directed at the expenditure of public funds....

It seems to me clear that public actions, whatever the constitutional provisions on which they are premised, may involve important hazards for the continued effectiveness of the federal judiciary. Although I believe such actions to be within the jurisdiction conferred upon the federal courts by Article III of the Constitution, there surely can be little doubt that they strain the judicial function and press to the limit judicial authority. There is every reason to fear that unrestricted public actions might well alter the allocation of author-

ity among the three branches of the Federal Government. It is not, I submit, enough to say that the present members of the Court would not seize these opportunities for abuse, for such actions would, even without conscious abuse, go far toward the final transformation of this Court into the Council of Revision which, despite Madison's support, was rejected by the Constitutional Convention....

[T]here is available a resolution of this problem that entirely satisfies the demands of the principle of separation of powers. This Court has previously held that individual litigants have standing to represent the public interest, despite their lack of economic or other personal interests, if Congress has appropriately authorized such suits.... I would adhere to that principle....

QUESTIONS

1. What is the rule in *Flast*? How does it differ from the rule in *Frothingham*? On what basis did three justices write separate concurrences in *Flast*?

2. *Amici* on behalf of Flast argued that her case differed from *Frothingham* in at least three critical respects. First, the ruling in *Frothingham* was intended to protect the federal government and the courts from a flood of litigation by taxpayers and that threat was eliminated by changes to the Federal Rules of Civil Procedure. Second, the claims in *Flast* involved personal, preferred First Amendment rights, not merely an economic interest. Third, *Frothingham* at core involved issues of federalism while *Flast* did not. Are these distinctions with a constitutional difference?

3. The *amicus* brief submitted by the National Jewish Commission on Law and Public Affairs argued that taxpayer suits against federal appropriations are not the appropriate way to protect First Amendment rights. It contended that, "Were the Court to narrow the standing rule, as appellants urge, taxpayers who opposed federal programs would simply couch their lawsuits in First Amendment terms," and that, "as a practical matter, a rule excluding First Amendment cases from the standing requirement would be the equivalent of overruling *Frothingham v. Mellon*."

To the extent that standing-to-sue rules reflect the doctrine of judicial self-restraint, does it make a difference that *Flast* involved a First Amendment issue while *Frothingham* was about taxes? Should the Supreme Court be more willing to entertain cases that implicate civil liberties?

COMMENT

The threshold question, whether a party has standing to sue, is dispositive in deciding whether particular issues can be litigated. The following selected case summaries exemplify how the Court approached questions of standing for about fifteen years after *Flast*:

Case: *Sierra Club v. Morton*, 405 U.S. 727 (1972)
Vote: 4–3 (Justices Powell and Rehnquist did not participate.)
Decision: A litigant has standing to seek judicial review under the Administrative Procedures Act only by showing that he or she has suffered, or will suffer, injury. The Sierra Club can show no individualized harm if federal officials allow an extensive ski development in the Mineral King Valley in the Sequoia National Forest.

Case: *United States v. Students Challenging Regulatory Agency Procedures (SCRAP)*, 412 U.S. 669 (1973)
Vote: 5–3 (Justice Powell did not participate.)
Decision: SCRAP's allegations that it is "adversely affected" or "aggrieved" are sufficient to withstand a motion to dismiss on grounds of lack of standing. *Sierra Club v. Morton* distinguished. Standing is not confined to those who show economic harm. A claim that specific and alleged illegal action by an administrative agency would directly harm SCRAP in its use of natural resources is adequate. Standing is not lost merely because many people suffer the same injury.

Case: *Schlesinger v. Reservists Committee to Stop the War*, 418 U.S. 208 (1974)
Vote: 6–3
Decision: Article I, section 6, clause 2, the "Incompatibility Clause," bars members of Congress from simultaneously holding any other office under the authority of the United States. An association of present and past members of the Armed Forces Reserves lacks standing to challange the Reserve status of members of Congress. They also lack standing to sue as taxpayers because they have failed to establish the nexus required under *Flast*.

Case: *United States v. Richardson*, 418 U.S. 166 (1974)
Vote: 5–4
Decision: A federal taxpayer lacks standing to challenge the statutes regulating the Central Intelligence Agency. To satisfy the requirements of *Flast*, a taxpayer must challenge the taxing and spending power of the government. Parties may not use federal courts as a forum to air generalized grievances about the conduct of government.

Case: *Warth v. Seldin*, 422 U.S. 490 (1975)

Vote: 5–4

Decision: Property owners, taxpayers, low-and-moderate income residents, and a nonprofit corporation lack standing to challenge a city's zoning regulations on the ground that they prevent low-and-moderate income persons from living in the city. Whether viewed as constitutionally-based on Article III's requirement of a "case in controversy," or as a prudential limit on the role of courts in resolving disputes involving "generalized grievances" or third-party rights or interests, standing requires a plaintiff to allege facts showing he or she is a proper party to invoke the court's powers.

Case: *Village of Arlington Heights v. Metropolitan Housing Development Corp.*, 429 U.S. 252 (1977)

Vote: 8–1

Decision: Metro Housing (MHDC) met constitutional standing requirements by showing injury fairly traceable to petitioners' acts. A single-family zoning requirement stood as an absolute barrier to construction of the multiple-family residences the MHDC contracted to build. Despite the contingency provisions in its contract, MHDC suffered economic injury resulting from pursuing its rezoning petition and noneconomic injury resulting from the defeat of its petition and the consequent failure of its objective to make low-cost housing available.

JUSTICIABILITY: STANDING

Valley Forge Christian College v. Americans United for Separation of Church and State, Inc. 454 U.S. 462 (1982)

SETTING

As the decisions handed down in the fourteen years after *Flast v. Cohen* demonstrate, the Court's standing-to-sue rules sent mixed messages and clouded the status of *Flast*. Was *Flast* a lasting modification of *Frothingham*, or a merely temporary departure from it? A Defense Department decision to dispose of a parcel of surplus federal property provided the Burger Court an opportunity to address again the question of whether taxpayers have standing to sue.

Article IV, section 3, clause 2, of the Constitution empowers Congress "to dispose of and make all needful rules and regulations respecting ... the property belonging to the United States." Acting under authority of this language, Congress adopted the Federal Property and Administrative Services Act of 1949, shortly after the end of World War II. The law directs each federal agency to maintain inventories of property it controls and to identify and transfer excess property to other agencies that could make use of it. The Federal Property and Administrative Services Act authorizes the secretary of health, education, and welfare—now the secretary of education—to take responsibility for disposing of surplus federal property "for school, classroom, or other educational use."

The surplus property at issue in *Valley Forge* was acquired by the U.S. government in 1942. It consists of approximately 181 acres of land near Phoenixville, Pennsylvania, about 30 miles northwest of Philadelphia. The property cost $41,500. Over the years, the property was improved with hospital buildings, warehouses, administration buildings, and barracks at a cost of over $13,000,000. For the next thirty years, the Army used the facility, known as the Valley Forge General Hospital, to provide medical care for members of the armed services.

In 1973, the secretary of defense announced the closing of 274 military installations, including the Valley Forge General Hospital. The facilities were considered "excess" to the requirements of all military branches of the Department of Defense. The property was reported as "excess" to the General Services Administration, which offered the facility to all other federal government agencies pursuant to the Federal Property and Administrative Services Act. No other agency indicated a need for the facility, so the property was declared "surplus." Pursuant to the 1949 Act, which had previously gone unchallenged, the hospital property at the facility was assigned to the then Department of Health, Education, and Welfare (HEW) for disposal to a health or educational facility. Various institutions—public and private—applied to receive a portion of the hospital land.

HEW selected Valley Forge Christian College (then known as Northeast Bible College), which is affiliated with the Assemblies of God Church, to receive approximately 77 acres of real property, buildings, and personal property that had been part of the Army's medical facility. HEW followed the recommendation of a local use committee in deciding to transfer the property to the college. The property had a market value of approximately $1,303,000 at the time of the transfer. The college was granted a "public benefit allowance," which required the college to earn its right to use and own the property by bestowing educational benefits for thirty years.

In August 1976, the college changed its name to Valley Forge Christian College, relocated its campus to the property and rehabilitated the property at a substantial cost.

In July 1977, after learning of the transfer by reading a news release, Americans United for Separation of Church and State, Inc., and four of its citizen-taxpayer individual directors, filed a complaint in the U.S. District Court for the District of Columbia. The case was transferred to the U.S. District Court for the Eastern District of Pennsylvania. Americans United claims to be one of the primary organizations in the United States that defends and promotes religious liberty. At the time it filed suit, its membership was approximately ninety thousand nationwide. The complaint alleged that the federal government had conveyed seventy-seven acres of land and buildings to a college that was basically a religious institution, that religion pervades its instruction, and that the grant therefore violated the Establishment Clause of the First Amendment. Americans United sought a judgment declaring the grant to be void and ordering return of the property to the United States.

The district court dismissed the complaint in reliance on *Flast v. Cohen*, stating that Americans United lacked standing to challenge the transfer of property. The U.S. Court of Appeals for the Third Circuit, by a 2–1 vote, reversed. It ruled that although the plaintiffs lacked standing under *Flast*, the interest of a citizen in a government that is obedient to the Constitution warrants standing to sue. The Supreme Court of the United States granted Valley Forge's petition for a writ of certiorari.

HIGHLIGHTS OF SUPREME COURT ARGUMENTS

BRIEF FOR VALLEY FORGE CHRISTIAN COLLEGE

◆ The transfer of property to the college was not an exercise of the taxing and spending power. It was an exercise of Congress's power under the Property Clause of Article IV, section 3, clause 2. Therefore, Americans United lacks standing to challenge the action.

◆ Three types of personal stake have been recognized in Establishment Clause challenges: traditional injury, taxpayer injury, and direct offense. Never has a plaintiff been granted standing solely on the basis of holding separationist views.

◆ The novel and unprecedented grant of standing to these plaintiffs violates the doctrine of separation of powers. It tilts the apportionment of power to the judiciary, offering the potential for intrusion into the powers of the other two branches of government.

BRIEF FOR AMERICANS UNITED FOR SEPARATION OF CHURCH AND STATE

◆ Valley Forge Christian College is a self-professed theological or divinity school that states as its primary purpose "to train leaders for church related ministries." The government apparently believes it has discovered a method by which it may funnel millions of dollars worth of valuable property to pervasively sectarian institutions with no one having standing to object.

◆ The college and the government seek to apply formalistic standing rules, no longer rigidly adhered to by this Court, to prevent Americans United from litigating their rights as guaranteed by the Establishment Clause of the First Amendment. Americans United and its directors have suffered an actual injury as a result of the government's unconstitutional conduct.

AMICUS CURIAE BRIEFS SUPPORTING AMERICANS UNITED

Joint brief of the American Jewish Congress, The Synagogue Council of America, and The National Jewish Community Relations Council; joint brief of the National Coalition for Public Education and Religious Liberty, New York Committee for Public Education and Religious Liberty, and Florence Flast.

BRIEF FOR THE UNITED STATES

◆ Although *Flast v. Cohen* slightly lowered the barrier to taxpayer suits, it prescribed definite limitations to prevent an inundation of taxpayer litigation. It expressly limited taxpayer challenges to those challenging an exercise of Congressional power under Article I, section 8's taxing and spending clause. Plaintiffs ask this Court to extend *Flast*, and that request should be rejected.

◆ Prudential considerations militate against recognition of general citizen standing. If this Court were to accept the notion that any citizen may bring suit to vindicate "important" constitutional guarantees without alleging personal injury, there would be an outpouring of citizen complaints. In this case, plaintiffs have failed to allege an injury to themselves as a result of the claimed unconstitutional conduct.

◆ There is no logical distinction between a plaintiff contesting the donation of money and a plaintiff contesting the grant of surplus—but valuable—property. The effect of the college's litigation strategy would be to remove from judicial scrutiny a substantial portion of constitutional abuses and to divide the Establishment Clause in enforceable and nonenforceable rights.

SUPREME COURT DECISION: 5–4

REHNQUIST, J.

... Article III of the Constitution limits the "judicial power" of the United States to the resolution of "cases" and "controversies." The constitutional power of federal courts cannot be defined, and indeed has no substance, without reference to the necessity "to adjudge the legal rights of litigants in actual controversies." *Liverpool S.S. Co. v. Commissioners of Emigration*, 113 U.S. 33 (1885)....

As an incident to the elaboration of this bedrock requirement, this Court has always required that a litigant have "standing" to challenge the action sought to be adjudicated in the lawsuit. The term "standing" subsumes a blend of constitutional requirements and prudential considerations ... and it has not always been clear in the opinions of this Court whether particular features of the "standing" requirement have been required by Art. III *ex proprio vigore*, or whether they are requirements that the Court itself has erected and which were not compelled by the language of the Constitution....

A recent line of decisions, however, has resolved that ambiguity, at least to the following extent: at an irreducible minimum, Art. III requires the party who invokes the court's authority to "show that he personally has suffered some actual or threatened injury as a result of the putatively illegal conduct of the defendant," *Gladstone, Realtors v. Village of Bellwood*, 441 U.S. 91 (1979), and that the injury "fairly can be traced to the challenged action" and "is likely to be redressed by a favorable decision," *Simon v. Eastern Kentucky Welfare Rights Org.*, 426 U.S. 26 (1976). In this manner does Art. III limit the federal judicial power "to those disputes which confine federal courts to a role consistent with a system of separated powers and which are traditionally thought to be capable of resolution through the judicial process." *Flast v. Cohen*....

Proper regard for the complex nature of our constitutional structure requires neither that the Judicial Branch shrink from a confrontation with the other two coequal branches of the Federal Government, nor that it hospitably accept for adjudication claims of constitutional violation by other branches of government where the claimant has not suffered cognizable injury....

Beyond the constitutional requirements, the federal judiciary has also adhered to a set of prudential principles that bear on the question of standing. Thus, this Court has held that "the plaintiff generally must assert his own legal rights and interests, and cannot rest his claim to relief on the legal rights or interests of third parties." *Warth v. Seldin*, 422 U.S. [490 (1975)]. In addition, even when the plaintiff has alleged redressable injury sufficient to meet the requirements of Art. III, the Court has refrained from adjudicating "abstract questions of wide public significance" which amount to "generalized grievances," pervasively shared and most appropriately addressed in the repre-

sentative branches. *Warth*. Finally, the Court has required that the plaintiff's complaint fall within "the zone of interests to be protected or regulated by the statute or constitutional guarantee in question." *Association of Data Processing Service Orgs. v. Camp*, 397 U.S. 150 (1970).

Merely to articulate these principles is to demonstrate their close relationship to the policies reflected in the Art. III requirement of actual or threatened injury amenable to judicial remedy. But neither the counsels of prudence nor the policies implicit in the "case or controversy" requirement should be mistaken for the rigorous Art. III requirements themselves. Satisfaction of the former cannot substitute for a demonstration of "'distinct and palpable injury' ... that is likely to be redressed if the requested relief is granted." *Gladstone Realtors v. Village of Bellwood*. That requirement states a limitation on judicial power, not merely a factor to be balanced in the weighing of so-called "prudential" considerations.

We need not mince words when we say that the concept of "Art. III standing" has not been defined with complete consistency in all of the various cases decided by this Court which have discussed it, nor when we say that this very fact is probably proof that the concept cannot be reduced to a one-sentence or one-paragraph definition. But of one thing we may be sure: Those who do not possess Art. III standing may not litigate as suitors in the courts of the United States....

The injury alleged by respondents in their amended complaint is the "depriv[ation] of the fair and constitutional use of [their] tax dollar." As a result, our discussion must begin with

Frothingham v. Mellon.... In rejecting [taxpayer status] as a cognizable injury sufficient to establish standing, the [*Frothingham*] Court admonished:

> The party who invokes the power [of judicial review] must be able to show not only that the statute is invalid but that he has sustained or is immediately in danger of sustaining some direct injury as the result of its enforcement, and not merely that he suffers in some indefinite way in common with people generally.... Here the parties plaintiff have no such case....

The Court again visited the problem of taxpayer standing in *Flast v. Cohen....*

Unlike the plaintiffs in *Flast*, respondents fail the first prong of the test for taxpayer standing. Their claim is deficient in two respects. First, the source of their complaint is not a congressional action, but a decision by HEW to transfer a parcel of federal property. *Flast* limited taxpayer standing to challenges directed "only [at] exercises of congressional power."...

Second, and perhaps redundantly, the property transfer about which respondents complain was not an exercise of authority conferred by the Taxing and Spending Clause of Art. I, Sec. 8[,] ... and [this] is decisive of any claim of taxpayer standing under the *Flast* precedent....

It remains to be seen whether respondents have alleged any other basis for standing to bring this suit....

We simply cannot see that respondents have alleged an injury of any kind, economic or otherwise, sufficient to confer standing. Respondents complain of a transfer of property located in Chester County, Pa. The named plaintiffs reside in Maryland and Virginia; their organizational headquarters are located in Washington, D.C. They learned of the transfer through a news release. Their claim that the Government has violated the Establishment Clause does not provide a special license to roam the country in search of governmental wrongdoing and to reveal their discoveries in federal court. The federal courts were simply not constituted as ombudsmen of the general welfare....

Were we to accept respondents' claim of standing in this case, there would be no principled basis for confining our exception to litigants relying on the Establishment Clause. Ultimately, that exception derives from the idea that the judicial power requires nothing more for its invocation than important issues and able litigants. The existence of injured parties who might not wish to bring suit becomes irrelevant. Because we are unwilling to countenance such a departure from the limits on judicial power contained in Art. III, the judgment of the Court of Appeals is reversed.

It is so ordered.

BRENNAN, MARSHALL, AND BLACKMUN, J.J., DISSENTING

... The Court makes a fundamental mistake when it determines that a plaintiff has failed to satisfy the two-pronged "injury-in-fact" test, or indeed any other test of "standing," without first determining whether the Constitution or a statute defines injury, and creates a cause of action for redress of that injury, in precisely the circumstance presented to the Court....

In 1947, nine Justices of this Court recognized that the Establishment Clause does impose a very definite restriction on the power to tax. The Court held in *Everson v. Board of Education*, 330 U.S. 1, that the "'establishment of religion' clause of the First Amendment means at least this:

> No tax in any amount, large or small, can be levied to support any religious activities or institutions, whatever they may be called, or whatever form they may adopt, to teach or practice religion.

The Members of the Court could not have been more explicit....

This basic understanding of the meaning of the Establishment Clause explains why the Court in *Everson*, while rejecting appellant's claim on the merits, perceived the issue presented there as it did. The appellant sued "in his capacity as a district taxpayer," challenging the actions of the Board of Education in passing a resolution providing reimbursement to parents for the cost of transporting their children to parochial schools, and seeking to have that resolution "set aside." Appellant's Establishment Clause claim was precisely that the "statute ... forced inhabitants to pay taxes to help support and maintain" church schools....

The Justices who participated in *Flast* were not unaware of the Court's continued recognition of a federally cognizable "case or controversy" when a local taxpayer seeks to challenge as unconstitutional the use of a municipality's funds—propriety of which had, of course, gone unquestioned in *Everson*....

It is at once apparent that the test of standing formulated by the Court in *Flast* sought to reconcile the developing doctrine of taxpayer "standing" with the Court's historical understanding that the Establishment Clause was intended to prohibit the Federal Government from using tax funds for the advancement of religion, and thus the constitutional imperative of taxpayer standing in certain cases brought pursuant to the Establishment Clause. The two-pronged "nexus" test offered by the Court, despite its general language, is best understood as "a determinant of standing of plaintiffs alleging only injury as taxpayers who challenge alleged violations of the Establishment and Free Exercise Clauses of the First Amendment," and not as a general statement of standing principles. *Schlesinger [v. Reservists Committee to Stop the War*, 418 U.S. 208 (1974)] (Brennan, J., dissenting). The test explains what forms of governmental action may be attacked by someone alleging only taxpayer status, and, without ruling out the possibility that history might reveal another similarly founded provision, explains why an Establishment Clause claim is treated differently from any other assertion that the Federal Government has exceeded the bounds of the law in allocating its largesse....

The two-part *Flast* test did not supply the rationale for the Court's decision, but rather its exposition: That rationale was supplied by an understanding of the nature of the restrictions on government power imposed by the Constitution and the intended beneficiaries of those restrictions.

It may be that Congress can tax for almost any reason, or for no reason at all. There is, so far as I have been able to discern, but one constitutionally imposed limit on that authority. Congress cannot use tax money to support a church, or to encourage religion....

Blind to history, the Court attempts to distinguish this case from *Flast* by wrenching snippets of language from our opinions, and by perfunctorily applying that language under color of the first prong of *Flast*'s two-part nexus test. The tortuous distinctions thus produced are specious, at best: at worst, they are pernicious to our constitutional heritage.

First, the Court finds this case different from *Flast* because here the "source of [plaintiffs'] complaint is not a congressional action, but a decision by HEW to transfer a parcel of federal property." This attempt at distinction cannot withstand scrutiny.... It may be that the Court is concerned with the adequacy of respondents' pleading; respondents have not, in so many words, asked for a declaration that the "Federal Property and Administrative Services Act is unconstitutional and void to the extent that it authorizes HEW's actions." I would not construe their complaint so narrowly.

More fundamentally, no clear division can be drawn in this context between actions of the Legislative Branch and those of the Executive Branch. To be sure, the First Amendment is phrased as a restriction on Congress' legislative authority; this is only natural since the Constitution assigns the authority to legislate and appropriate only to the Congress. But it is difficult to conceive of an expenditure for which the last governmental actor, either implementing directly the legislative will, or acting within the scope of legislatively delegated authority, is not an Executive Branch official. The First Amendment binds the Government as a whole, regardless of which branch is at work in a particular instance.

The Court's second purported distinction between this case and *Flast* is equally unavailing. The majority finds it "decisive" that the Federal Property and Administrative Services Act of 1949 "was an evident exercise of Congress' power under the Property Clause, Art. IV, Sec. 3, cl. 2," while the Government action in *Flast* was taken under Art. I, Sec. 8....

It can make no constitutional difference in the case before us whether the donation to the petitioner here was in the form of a cash grant to build a facility ... or in the nature of a gift of property including a facility already built.... Whether undertaken pursuant to the Property Clause or the Spending Clause, the breach of the Establishment Clause, and the relationship of the taxpayer to that breach, is precisely the same....

STEVENS, J., DISSENTING

... Today the Court holds, in effect, that the Judiciary has no greater role in enforcing the Establishment Clause than in enforcing other "norm[s] of conduct which the Federal Government is bound to honor.... Ironically, however, its decision rests on the premise that the difference between a disposition of funds pursuant to the Spending Clause and a disposition of realty pursuant to the Property Clause is of fundamental jurisprudential significance. With all due respect, I am persuaded that the essential holding of *Flast v. Cohen* attaches special importance to the Establishment Clause and does not permit the drawing of a tenuous distinction between the Spending Clause and the Property Clause....

QUESTIONS

1. As the cases in this section demonstrate, the mere occurrence of an illegal act does not by itself confer standing to sue. In order to have standing, the plaintiff must be able to show injury from the defendant. What injury did Americans United assert in *Valley Forge*? How does the injury it claimed differ from the injury that Flast suffered? If the injury in both cases stemmed from the First Amendment, what accounts for the outcome in *Valley Forge*?

2. The brief filed by the American Jewish Council, urging the Court to acknowledge that Americans United had standing to sue, argued that the standing issue in *Valley Forge* was "of critical importance to the ability of religious minorities to adequately protect their rights to religious freedom under the religion clause of the First Amendment." If you were a justice, how would you balance the need of individuals—and particularly minorities—to vindicate constitutional rights against the need to protect the federal courts from a flood of lawsuits and the possibility that courts would intrude on the other branches of government?

3. The Court's fluctuating views regarding standing-to-sue reflects a more fundamental debate over its social role. Restrictive standing rules may derive from a view that courts are charged with resolving concrete disputes between discrete individuals. Liberal standing rules may derive from a view that emphasizes the Supreme Court's role as supreme interpreter of constitutional norms. Which view is more constitutionally compelling? Is one more consistent with Chief Justice Marshall's doctrine of judicial review?

4. Throughout its history, the Supreme Court has formulated a variety of doctrinal rules, such as standing, as means of judging whether or not to exercise judicial review. The existence of these "gatekeeping" threshold questions acknowledges the contingent nature of the Court's power, and enables it to exercise discretion. The late Alexander Bickel referred to them as "passive virtues" ("The Supreme Court, 1960 Term—Foreword: The Passive Virtues," 75 *Harvard Law Review* [1961]: 40; *The Least Dangerous Branch: The Supreme Court at the Bar of Politics* [Indianapolis, IN: Bobbs-Merrill, 1962], Chapter 4). Professor Henry J. Abraham categorizes them as "the sixteen great maxims of judicial self-restraint" (*The Judicial Process*, 6th ed. [New York, NY: Oxford University Press, 1993], Chapter 9).

   Justice Louis Brandeis, in an influential concurring opinion in *Ashwander v. Tennessee Valley Authority*, 297 U.S. 288 (1936), identified seven "rules under which [the Court] has avoided passing upon the large part of all the constitutional questions pressed upon it for decision":

1. The Court will not pass upon the constitutionality of legislation in a friendly, nonadversary, proceeding, declining because to decide such questions is legitimate only in the last resort, and as a necessity in the determination of real, earnest, and vital controversy between individuals[.]... 2. The Court will not anticipate a question of constitutional law in advance of the necessity of deciding it.... 3. The Court will not formulate a rule of constitutional law broader than is required by the precise facts to which it is to be applied.... 4. The Court will not pass upon a constitutional question although properly presented on the record, if there is also present some other ground upon which the case may be disposed of.... 5. The Court will not pass upon the validity of a statute upon complaint of one who fails to show that he is injured by its operation.... 6. The Court will not pass upon the constitutionality of a statute at the instance of one who has availed himself of its benefits.... 7. When the validity of an act of the Congress is drawn in question, and even if a serious doubt of constitutionality is raised, it is a cardinal principle that this Court will first ascertain whether a construction of the statute is fairly possible by which the question may be avoided. [Internal quotation marks omitted.]

In light of the opinions excerpted in this chapter about judicial power, how would you characterize these so-called *Ashwander* rules? Are they binding strictures dictating access to the Court, or tools of convenience deployed strategically? Why should the Supreme Court ever avoid passing judgment on constitutional questions?

COMMENT

Valley Forge and the decisions summarized below illustrate what some commentators call the "New Standing," or the injury-in-fact doctrine. Supporters hail the doctrine as a judicious gatekeeping tool protecting courts from overflowing dockets and from intruding on the executive and legislative branches. However, the doctrine has been criticized both as a species of judicial activism that has the effect of limiting access to judicial forums, and as having only tenuous textual support in the Constitution.

Case: *City of Los Angeles v. Lyons*, 461 U.S. 95 (1983)
Vote: 5–4
Decision: When requesting injunctive relief, past exposure to illegal conduct does not in itself show a present case or controversy. That Lyons may have been illegally choked by police in 1976 does not establish a real and immediate threat that, were he again stopped for a traffic or other offense, the officer would again illegally choke him into unconsciousness. Standing requires that the injury or threat of injury be real and immediate, not conjectural or hypothetical.

Case: *Allen v. Wright*, 468 U.S. 737 (1984)

Vote: 6–3

Decision: Wright's claim that she is harmed by the fact of government financial aid to schools that discriminate does not constitute a judicially cognizable injury. Wright's claim that her children are injured by diminished ability to receive an education in racially integrated schools because of federal tax exemptions granted to some private schools that are racially discriminatory is judicially cognizable, but fails because the alleged injury is not fairly traceable to the government conduct challenged as unlawful. The constitutional core of the standing doctrine is that a plaintiff must allege personal injury fairly traceable to the defendant's allegedly unlawful conduct and likely to be redressed by the requested relief.

Case: *Bowen v. Kendrick*, 487 U.S. 589 (1988)

Vote: 9–0 (on standing), 5–4 (on merits)

Decision: Kendrick has standing to raise the claim that the Adolescent Family Life Act, as applied, is a violation of the Establishment Clause. The act authorizes federal grants to private organizations for research in the area of premarital adolescent sexual relations and pregnancy. Federal taxpayers have standing to raise Establishment Clause claims against exercises of congressional power under the taxing and spending power of Article I, § 8, of the Constitution.

Case: *Lujan v. Defenders of Wildlife*, 540 U.S. 555 (1992)

Vote: 7–2

Decision: In order to survive a summary judgment motion in an action challenging government policy affecting third parties—here, federally funded projects outside the United States potentially threatening to endangered species—Defenders of Wildlife must provide evidence showing that they have suffered an injury in fact. Assuming that Defenders of Wildlife established that funded activities abroad threaten certain species, they failed to show that one or more of their members would thereby directly be affected apart from the members' special interest in endangered species.

Case: *Northeastern Florida Chapter of the Associated General Contractors of America v. City of Jacksonville, Florida*, 508 U.S. 656 (1993)

Vote: 7–2

Decision: In an equal protection case, the "injury in fact" requirement of standing is satisfied by the denial of equal treatment resulting from the imposition of a barrier—here, majority contractors' inability to compete on an equal footing in the bidding process due to a minority set aside requirement—not by the ultimate inability to obtain a benefit. *Warth v. Seldin's* holding that a plaintiff must allege facts showing that practices harm *him* or *her* and that he personally would benefit from a court's intervention distinguished. Construction association in *Warth* argued that its members could not obtain zoning variances and permits, not that they could not apply for such variances and permits on an equal basis.

Suggestions for Further Reading

Brilmayer, Lea, "The Jurisprudence of Article III: Perspectives on the 'Case or Controversy' Requirement," 93 *Harvard Law Review* (1979): 297

———, "A Reply," 93 *Harvard Law Review* (1980): 1727.

Chayes, Abram, "The Supreme Court, 1980 Term—Forward: Public Law Litigation & The Burger Court," 96 *Harvard Law Review* (1982): 4.

Currie, David, "Misunderstanding Standing," in *The Supreme Court Review* (Chicago, IL: University of Chicago Press, 1981).

Fletcher, William A., "The Structure of Standing," 98 *Yale Law Journal* (1988): 221.

Jaffe, Louis, "Standing to Secure Judicial Review: Private Actions," 75 *Harvard Law Review* (1961): 255.

———, "The Citizen as Litigant in Public Actions: The Non-Hohfeldian or Ideological Plaintiff," 116 *University of Pennsylvania Law Review* (1968): 1033.

Monaghan, Henry P., "Constitutional Adjudication: The Who and When," 82 *Yale Law Journal* (1973): 1836.

Nichol, Gene R. Jr., "Causation as a Standing Requirement: The Unprincipled Use of Judicial Restraint," 69 *Kentucky Law Journal* (1980–81): 185.

———, "Rethinking Standing," 72 *California Law Review* (1984): 68.

———, "Injury and the Disintegration of Article III," 74 *California Law Review* (1986): 1915.

Scalia, Antonin, "The Doctrine of Standing as an Essential Element of the Separation of Powers," 17 *Suffolk Law Review* (1983): 881.

Scott, Kenneth E., "Standing in the Supreme Court: A Functional Analysis," 86 *Harvard Law Review* (1973): 645.

Sunstein, Cass, "Standing and the Privitization of Public Law," 88 *Columbia Law Review* (1988): 1432.

Tushnet, Mark, "The New Law of Standing: A Plea for Abandonment," 62 *Cornell Law Review* (1977); 663.

———, "The Sociology of Article III: A Response to Professor Brilmayer," 93 *Harvard Law Review* (1980): 1699.

CHAPTER 3

CONGRESSIONAL POWERS

CONGRESS'S EXPRESS POWERS: MARSHALL COURT

McCulloch v. Maryland
4 Wheaton 316 (1819)

SETTING

The "Necessary and Proper" clause of Article I, section 8, clause 18, was never actively debated during the Constitutional Convention but became a major topic of controversy during the ratification debates that followed. Opponents of the Constitution saw the clause as a potential source of unlimited expansion of the specific enumerated congressional powers in Article I. In particular, they were worried that the clause would become a vehicle for aggrandizing national taxing power while hobbling state taxing power. Defenders, like Alexander Hamilton, declared the clause "only declaratory of truth" and "perfectly harmless" (*Federalist* No. 33). James Madison echoed Hamilton, claiming that, without the Necessary and Proper Clause in the Constitution, "there can be no doubt that all the particular powers requisite as means of executing the general powers would have resulted to the government, by unavoidable implication" (*Federalist* No. 44). Ultimately, it was left to the judiciary to determine the meaning of the clause and, concomitantly, the implied extent of enumerated federal taxing and spending powers. The litigation that provided the occasion for doing so involved the constitutionality of a national bank.

In December 1790, in his second *Report on Public Credit*, Alexander Hamilton recommended chartering a national bank. He modeled his proposed financial institution on the Bank of England. Over the objections of Thomas Jefferson, who thought that creating a national bank exceeded the power of the federal government, Congress chartered the First Bank of the United States in 1791. The charter ran for twenty years. Although called a national bank, it was largely privately owned and privately managed. Only two of the bank's original ten million dollars in capitalization came from public funds; private investors furnished the rest. One-fifth of the bank's directors were named by the government. Its notes circulated as the nation's currency. The bank was authorized to lend money to the government and to act as a collecting and disbursing agency for the U.S. Treasury.

The bank was the object of political controversy from the start. Federalists saw a national bank as an essential means of promoting commerce. The bank's opponents perceived it as encroaching on state sovereignty and as a bastion of Federalist privilege. The Supreme Court never had the opportunity to rule on the constitutionality of the first bank. The 1791 charter lapsed in 1811 when Congress failed to renew it.

Five years later, responding to financial disruption resulting from America's war with England in 1812, Congress incorporated the Second Bank of the United States. It went into operation in January 1817. The directors of the bank located one branch in Baltimore, Maryland.

Management of the Second National Bank, like that of the First, was inefficient and frequently corrupt. It overextended credit, then overcontracted it, leading to serious financial depressions. In 1818, for example, when cotton prices fell precipitously, the bank called in many of its loans, causing many banks located in the West and South to fail. The downturn also caused depositors to try to redeem U.S. Bank notes in coined money. When the bank had difficulty backing its deposits, an economic panic ensued. The panic transformed lingering state opposition to the bank into open hostility.

At least seven states passed special taxes with the goal of driving the bank out of existence. The general assembly of Maryland passed a bill in February 1818 entitled, "an act to impose a tax on all banks, or branches thereof, in the State of Maryland, not chartered by the legislature." The tax took the form of a stamp, ranging from ten cents to twenty dollars, imposed on all U.S. Bank notes, depending upon their face value. Payment of the stamp tax could be avoided by an annual payment of $15,000. The penalty for each bank note issued on unstamped paper was $100.

The Maryland statute was enforced partly by state agents who were allowed to keep half of the fines they collected from banks that did not comply with the state law. In May 1818, agent John James visited the Baltimore branch of the bank. James McCulloch, the Baltimore branch cashier, made little secret of the fact that he issued bank notes on which he had refused to pay the tax. McCulloch summarily refused to pay the penalty that James demanded. The state of Maryland then sued McCulloch in the county court of Baltimore to recover the penalty.

The county court entered judgment for Maryland; the state court of appeals affirmed. McCulloch petitioned the Supreme Court of the United States for a writ of error.

HIGHLIGHTS OF SUPREME COURT ARGUMENTS

BRIEF FOR MCCULLOCH

◆ The first Congress created and incorporated a bank. Members of the Constitutional Convention passed into the first Congress. They must have understood their own work, and they determined that Congress had the power of incorporating a banking company even though the power was not explicitly stated in Article I. Nearly all succeeding Congresses have assumed the legal existence of such a power in the government. Many of those who doubted or denied the existence of the power when it was first exercised have acquiesced in it as a settled question.

◆ It was not the intention of the drafters of the Constitution to enumerate all the particular powers of Congress.

◆ The words "necessary and proper" are synonymous. Necessary powers are those that are suitable and fitted to an object. A bank is a proper and suitable instrument to assist the operations of the government in the collection and disbursement of revenue and for other purposes.

◆ If states are permitted to tax the bank, they have no limit but their discretion and the bank, therefore, must depend on the discretion of the state governments for its existence. An unlimited power to tax necessarily involves a power to destroy.

◆ The law of Maryland taxing this branch of the national bank cannot be sustained except on principles and reasoning which would subject every important measure of the national government to the revision and control of the state legislatures.

◆ Article 6 of the Constitution declares that laws made in pursuance of the Constitution are the supreme law of the land. This provision prohibits states from passing any acts that are repugnant to a law of the United States. The asserted power to tax any of the institutions of the United States presents directly the question of the supremacy of national laws over state laws.

BRIEF FOR MARYLAND

◆ The conditions that justified creation of a nationally chartered bank in 1791 do not exist today. Facilities for money transactions abound. Some of the powers of the Constitution, like the power to create a national bank, are of a fluctuating nature, depending on the circumstances at a particular time.

◆ The Constitution was formed and adopted by the people of the states. It did not convert the American people into one aggregate mass. States retain all powers which are not expressly relinquished to the national government. The existence of the Tenth Amendment is proof that the Constitutional Convention intended to define the powers of the national government with precision and accuracy.

◆ It is clear from the ratification debates in the Virginia and New York conventions, and from the *Federalist*, that the national power contended for in this case is repugnant even to those who supported the adoption of the Constitution.

◆ States need no reservation or acknowledgement of their right to tax the branches of the national bank. States retain all powers that are not expressly prohibited or necessarily excluded by the Constitution. The only express prohibition is found in Article I, section 10, which requires states to have congressional approval in some situations before levying imposts or duties on imports or exports. Advocates of the Constitution, including Publius in the *Federalist*, conceded that with this one exception, states would enjoy coequal authority with the national government on matters of revenue.

◆ Nothing in the nature of the property of bank stock exonerates it from taxation. The real and personal property of the bank does not belong to the United States. It is a purely private institution which disclaims any public character. It should not be clothed with the power and rights of the national government and demand subordination from state governments.

SUPREME COURT DECISION: 7–0

MARSHALL, C.J.

The first question made in the cause is, has Congress power to incorporate a bank?...

The power now contested was exercised by the first Congress elected under the present constitution. The bill for incorporating the Bank of the United States did not steal upon an unsuspecting legislature, and pass unobserved. Its principle was completely understood, and was opposed with equal zeal and ability.... The original act was permitted to expire; but a short experience of the embarrassments to which the refusal to revive it exposed the government, convinced those who were most prejudiced against the measure of its necessity, and induced the passage of the present law....

[T]he counsel for the state of Maryland have deemed it of some importance, in the construction of the constitution, to consider that instrument, not as emanating from the people, but as the act of sovereign and independent states....

It would be difficult to sustain this proposition. The convention which framed the constitution was indeed elected by the state legislatures. But the instrument, when it came from their hands, was a mere proposal, without obligation, or pretensions to it. It was reported to the then existing congress of the United States, with a request that it might "be submitted to a convention of delegates, chosen in each state by the people thereof, under the recommendation of its legislature, for their assent and ratification." This mode of proceeding was adopted, and by the convention, by congress, and by the state legislatures, the instrument was submitted to the people. They acted upon it in the only manner in which they can act safely, effectively and wisely, on such a subject, by assembling in conventions. It is true, they assembled in their several states—and where else should they have assembled? No political dreamer was ever wild enough to think of breaking down the lines which separate the states, and of compounding the American people into one common mass. Of consequence, when they act, they act in their states. But the measures they adopt do not, on that account, cease to be the measures of the people themselves, or become the measures of the state governments.

From these conventions, the constitution derives its whole authority. The government proceeds directly from the people....

It has been said, that the people had already surrendered all their powers to the state sovereignties, and had nothing more to give. But, surely, the question whether they may resume and modify the powers granted to government, does not remain to be settled in this country....

The government of the Union, then (whatever may be the influence of this fact on the case), is, emphatically and truly, a government of the people. In form, and in substance, it emanates from them. Its powers are granted by them, and are to be exercised directly on them, and for their benefit.

This government is acknowledged by all, to be one of enumerated powers. The principle, that it can exercise only the powers granted to it, would seem too apparent, to have required to be enforced by all those arguments, which its enlightened friends, while it was depending before the people, found it necessary to urge; that principle is now universally admitted. But the question respecting the extent of the powers actually granted, is perpetually arising, and will probably continue to arise, so long as our system shall exist....

If any one proposition could command the universal assent of mankind, we might expect it would be this—that the government of the Union, though limited in its powers, is supreme within its sphere of action. This would seem to result, necessarily, from its nature. It is the government of all; its powers are delegated by all; it represents all, and acts for all. Though any one state may be willing to control its operations, no state is willing to allow others to control them. The nation, on those subjects on which it can act, must necessarily bind its component parts. But this question is not left to mere reason; the people have, in express terms, decided it by saying, "this constitution, and the laws which shall be made in pursuance thereof," "shall be the supreme law of the land," and by requiring that the members of the state legislatures, and the officers of the executive and judicial departments of the states shall take the oath of fidelity to it.

The government of the United States, then, though limited in its powers, is supreme; and its laws, when made in pursuance of the constitution, form the supreme law of the land, "anything in the constitution or laws of any state to the contrary notwithstanding."

Among the enumerated powers, we do not find that of establishing a bank or creating a corporation. But there is no phrase in the instrument which, like the articles of confederation, excludes incidental or implied powers; and which requires that everything granted shall be expressly and minutely described. Even the 10th amendment, which was framed for the purpose of quieting the excessive jealousies which had been excited, omits the word "expressly," and declares only that the powers "not delegated to the United States, nor prohibited to the states, are reserved to the states or to the people;" thus leaving the question, whether the particular power which may become the subject of contest has been delegated to the one government, or prohibited to the other, to depend on a fair construction of the whole instrument.... A constitution, to contain an accurate detail of all the subdivisions of which its great powers will admit, and of all the means by which they may be carried into execution, would partake of a prolixity of a legal code, and could scarcely be embraced by the human mind. It would probably never be understood by the public. Its nature, therefore, requires, that only its great outlines should be marked, its important objects designated, and the minor ingredients which compose those objects be deduced from the nature of the objects themselves. That this idea was entertained by the framers of the American constitution, is not only to be inferred from the nature of the instrument, but from the language. Why else were some of the limitations, found in the ninth section of the 1st article, introduced? It is also, in some degree, warranted by their having omitted to use any restrictive term which might prevent its receiving a fair and just interpretation. In considering this question, then, we must never forget that it is a constitution we are expounding.

Although, among the enumerated powers of government, we do not find the word "bank" or "incorporation," we find the great powers to lay and collect taxes; to borrow money; to regulate commerce; to declare and conduct a war; and to raise and support armies and navies. The sword and the purse, all the external relations, and no inconsiderable portion of the industry of the nation, are entrusted to its government. It can never be pretended that these vast powers draw after them others of inferior importance, merely because they are inferior. Such an idea can never be advanced. But it may with great reason be contended, that a government, entrusted with such ample powers, on the due execution of which

the happiness and prosperity of the nation so vitally depends, must also be entrusted with ample means for their execution....

[T]he constitution of the United States has not left the right of congress to employ the necessary means for the execution of the powers conferred on the government to general reasoning. To its enumeration of powers is added, that of making "all laws which shall be necessary and proper, for carrying into execution the foregoing powers, and all other powers vested by this constitution, in the government of the United States, or in any department thereof."...

[T]he argument on which most reliance is placed [by the state of Maryland], is drawn from that peculiar language of this clause. Congress is not empowered by it to make all laws, which may have relation to the powers conferred on the government, but such only as may be "necessary and proper" for carrying them into execution. The word "necessary" is considered as controlling the whole sentence, and as limiting the right to pass laws for the execution of the granted powers, to such as are indispensable, and without which the power would be nugatory. That it excludes the choice of means, and leaves to congress, in each case, that only which is most direct and simple.

Is it true, that this is the sense in which the word "necessary" is always used? Does it always import an absolute physical necessity, so strong, that one thing to which another may be termed necessary, cannot exist without that other? We think it does not. If reference be had to its use, in the common affairs of the world, or in approved authors, we find that it frequently imports no more than that one thing is convenient, or useful, or essential to another. To employ the means necessary to an end, is generally understood as employing any means calculated to produce the end, and not as being confined to those single means, without which the end would be entirely unattainable. Such is the character of human language, that no word conveys to the mind, in all situations, one single definite idea; and nothing is more common than to use words in a figurative sense. Almost all compositions contain words, which, taken in their rigorous sense, would convey a meaning different from that which is obviously intended. It is essential to just construction, that many words which import something excessive, should be understood in a more mitigated sense—in that sense which common usage justifies. The word "necessary" is of this description. It has not a fixed character, peculiar to itself. It admits of all degrees of comparison; and is often connected with other words, which increase or diminish the impression the mind receives of the urgency it imports. A thing may be necessary, very necessary, absolutely or indispensably necessary. To no mind would the same idea be conveyed by these several phrases. The comment on the word is well illustrated by the passage cited at the bar, from the 10th section of the 1st article of the constitution. It is, we think, impossible to compare the sentence which prohibits a state from laying "imposts, or duties on imports or exports, except what may be absolutely necessary for executing its inspection laws," with that which authorizes congress "to make all laws which shall be necessary and proper for carrying into execution" the powers of the general government, without feel-

ing a conviction, that the convention understood itself to change materially the meaning of the word "necessary," by prefixing the word "absolutely." This word, then, like others, is used in various senses; and, in its construction, the subject, the context, the intention of the person using them, are all to be taken into view.

Let this be done in the case under consideration. The subject is the execution of those great powers on which the welfare of a nation essentially depends. It must have been the intention of those who gave these powers, to insure, so far as human prudence could insure, their beneficial execution. This could not be done, by confiding the choice of means to such narrow limits as not to leave it in the power of Congress to adopt any which might be appropriate, and which were conducive to the end. This provision is made in a constitution, intended to endure for ages to come, and consequently, to be adapted to the various crises of human affairs. To have prescribed the means by which government should, in all future time, execute its powers, would have been to change, entirely, the character of the instrument, and give it the properties of a legal code. It would have been an unwise attempt to provide, by immutable rules, for exigencies which, if foreseen at all, must have been seen dimly, and which can be best provided for as they occur. To have declared, that the best means shall not be used, but those alone, without which the power given would be nugatory, would have been to deprive the legislature of the capacity to avail itself of experience, to exercise its reason, and to accommodate its legislation to circumstances....

In ascertaining the sense in which the word "necessary" is used in this clause of the constitution, we may derive some aid from that with which it is associated. Congress shall have power "to make all laws which shall be necessary and proper to carry into execution" the powers of the government. If the word "necessary" is used in that strict and rigorous sense for which the counsel of the state of Maryland contend, it would be an extraordinary departure from the usual course of the human mind, as exhibited in composition, to add a word, the only possible effect of which is, to qualify that strict and rigorous meaning; to present to the mind the idea of some choice of means of legislation, not straightened and compressed within the narrow limits for which gentlemen contend.

But the argument which most conclusively demonstrates the error of the construction contended for by the counsel for the state of Maryland, is founded on the intention of the convention, as manifested in the whole clause. To waste time and argument in proving that without it Congress might carry its powers into execution, would be not much less idle than to hold a lighted taper to the sun. As little can it be required to prove, that in the absence of this clause, Congress would have some choice of means. That it might employ those which, in its judgment, would most advantageously effect the object to be accomplished. That any means adapted to the end, any means which tended directly to the execution of the constitutional powers of the government, were in themselves constitutional. This clause, as construed by the state of Maryland, would abridge, and almost annihilate this useful and necessary

right of the legislature to select its means. That this could not be intended, is, we should think, had it not already been controverted, too apparent for controversy....

The result of the most careful and attentive consideration bestowed upon this clause, is that if it does not enlarge, it cannot be construed to restrain the powers of Congress, or to impair the right of the legislature to exercise its best judgment in the selection of measures to carry into execution the constitutional powers of government....

We admit, as all must admit, that the powers of the government are limited, and that its limits are not to be transcended. But we think the sound construction of the constitution must allow to the national legislature that discretion, with respect to the means by which the powers it confers are to be carried into execution, which will enable that body to perform the high duties assigned to it, in the manner most beneficial to the people. Let the end be legitimate, let it be within the scope of the constitution, and all means which are appropriate, which are plainly adapted to that end, which are not prohibited, but consist with the letter and spirit of the constitution, are constitutional....

But were its necessity less apparent, none can deny its being an appropriate measure; and if it is, the decree of its necessity, as has been very justly observed, is to be discussed in another place. Should Congress, in the execution of its powers, adopt measures which are prohibited by the constitution; or should congress, under the pretext of executing its powers, pass laws for the accomplishment of objects not intrusted to the government; it would become the painful duty of this tribunal, should a case requiring such a decision come before it, to say, that such an act was not the law of the land. But where the law is not prohibited, and is really calculated to effect any of the objects intrusted to the government, to undertake here to inquire into the decree of its necessity, would be to pass the line which circumscribes the judicial department, and to tread on legislative ground. This court disclaims all pretensions to such a power....

It being the opinion of the court, that the act incorporating the bank is constitutional; and that the power of establishing a branch in the state of Maryland might be properly exercised by the bank itself, we proceed to inquire:...

Whether the state of Maryland may, without violating the constitution, tax that branch?

That the power of taxation is one of vital importance; that it is retained by the states; that it is not abridged by the grant of a similar power to the government of the Union; that it is to be concurrently exercised by the two governments are truths which have never been denied. But such is the paramount character of the constitution, that its capacity to withdraw any subject from the action of even this power, is admitted. The states are expressly forbidden to lay any duties on imports or exports, except what may be absolutely necessary for executing their inspection laws. If the obligation of this prohibition must be conceded—if it may restrain a state from the exercise of its taxing power on imports and exports—the same paramount character would seem to restrain, as it certainly may restrain, a state from such other exercise of this power, as is in its nature incompatible

with, and repugnant to, the constitutional laws of the Union....

We find, then, on just theory, a total failure of this original right to tax the means employed by the government of the Union, for the execution of its powers. The right never existed, and the question whether it has been surrendered, cannot arise....

That the power to tax involves the power to destroy; that the power to destroy may defeat and render useless the power to create; that there is a plain repugnance in conferring on one government a power to control the constitutional measures of another, which other, with respect to those very measures, is declared to be supreme over that which exerts the control, are propositions not to be denied. But all inconsistencies are to be reconciled by the magic of the word confidence. Taxation, it is said, does not necessarily and unavoidably destroy. To carry it to the excess of destruction, would be an abuse, to presume which, would banish that confidence which is essential to all government.

But is this a case of confidence? Would the people of any one state trust those of another with a power to control the most insignificant operations of their state government? We know they would not. Why, then, should we suppose, that the people of any one state should be willing to trust those of another with a power to control the operations of a government to which they have confided their most important and most valuable interests? In the legislature of the Union alone, are all represented. The legislature of the Union alone, therefore, can be trusted by the people with the power of controlling measures which concern all, in the confidence that it will not be abused. This, then, is not a case of confidence, and we must consider it as it really is.

If we apply the principle for which the state of Maryland contends, to the constitution, generally, we shall find it capable of changing totally the character of that instrument. We shall find it capable of arresting all the measures of the government, and of prostrating it at the foot of the states. The American people have declared their constitution and the laws made in pursuance thereof, to be supreme; but this principle would transfer the supremacy, in fact, to the states.

If the states may tax one instrument, employed by the government in the execution of its powers, they may tax any and every other instrument.... This was not intended by the American people. They did not design to make their government dependent on the states....

The court has bestowed on this subject its most deliberate consideration. The result is a conviction that the states have no power, by taxation or otherwise, to retard, impede, burden, or in any manner control, the operations of the constitutional laws enacted by congress to carry into execution the powers vested in the general government. This is, we think, the unavoidable consequence of that supremacy which the constitution has declared.

We are unanimously of the opinion, that the law passed by the legislature of Maryland, imposing a tax on the Bank of the United States, is unconstitutional and void.

QUESTIONS

1. Sort out the constitutional elements in *McCulloch*. Did Chief Justice Marshall rely primarily on his view of the federal union, his interpretation of enumerated congressional taxing and spending powers, or his reading of the Necessary and Proper Clause in upholding congressional authority to incorporate a bank?

2. How "elastic" does Chief Justice Marshall's opinion in *McCulloch* render the Necessary and Proper Clause? For instance, does *McCulloch* authorize Congress to exercise any implied taxing and spending power it believes it possesses, or does *McCulloch* require a relationship between ends and means? Of what pertinence to the issue of elasticity is Marshall's observation: "This provision is made in a constitution, intended to endure for ages to come, and consequently, to be adapted to the various crises of human affairs"?

3. By the time the Supreme Court heard *McCulloch*, debate over the constitutionality of a national bank was almost two decades old, dating to the 1791 exchange between Alexander Hamilton and Thomas Jefferson over Hamilton's proposal to incorporate a national bank. John Marshall himself had weighed into the debate over the extent of congressional powers in *United States v. Fisher*, 2 Cranch 358 (1805), holding that "[i]n construing [the Necessary and Proper Clause] it would be incorrect and would produce endless difficulties, if the

opinion should be maintained that no law was authorised which was not indispensably necessary to give effect to a specified power." During oral arguments in *McCulloch*, counsel for the United States observed that the constitutionality of a national bank essentially was taken for granted.

At the very time *McCulloch* was being argued, Congress was debating the Missouri Compromise and the fate of slavery in newly admitted states. Might Marshall's decision in *McCulloch* have less to do with the Second National Bank of the United States than with laying out his view about which level of government had constitutional authority to resolve the issue of slavery?

4. When *McCulloch* was decided there was but one national bank, with several branches. Under the present system of multiple national banks, Congress has authorized states to tax national banks at a rate no greater than the rate assessed against institutions that compete with national banks. The Court has approved. *Iowa-Des Moines National Bank v. Bennett*, 284 U.S. 239 (1931). What does this subsequent history suggest about the relationship between congressional and judicial power in the United States?

5. *Osborn v. Bank of the United States*, 9 Wheaton 738 (1824), replayed the constitutional issues raised in *McCulloch*. Ohio, openly flaunting its opposition to the *McCulloch* decision, continued to impose a $50,000 tax on branches of the Bank of the United States located in its boundaries. When the branches refused to pay, relying on *McCulloch*, the state sent agents to physically seize assets from Bank of the United States vaults in Chilicothe. The bank brought an action of trespass against state auditor Ralph Osborn to recover the money. Osborn defended on the ground that federal courts did not have jurisdiction because the bank's suit was in substance an action against a state in violation of the Eleventh Amendment.

Chief Justice Marshall held that federal courts had jurisdiction because the Eleventh Amendment applied only in cases in which a state was named as the defendant. His opinion defined in sweeping terms Congress's power to confer jurisdiction on federal courts under Article III, stating that the language "arising under" in that provision was broad enough to authorize federal courts to hear cases and controversies even in cases such as *Osborn*, where the trespass question was only indirectly related to a federal question.

As *Osborn v. Bank of the United States* demonstrates, Chief Justice Marshall's ruling in *McCulloch* upholding Congress's power to charter a national bank aroused tremendous opposition in the states. Virginia's Spencer Roane, for example, a noted anti-Federalist jurist, wrote under the pen name "Amphictyon" that the principles announced in *McCulloch* "tend directly to consolidation of the States and to strip them of some of the most important attributes of their sovereignty" (quoted in Charles Warren, *The Supreme Court in United States History*, 3 vols. [Boston, MA: Little, Brown and Company, 1923], I: 515). (Compare James Madison's *Federalist* No. 39.)

What "attributes" of state sovereignty, arguably, were stripped by the decision in *McCulloch*? Is a national taxing power inherently antithetical to states' rights?

COMMENT

One passage from *McCulloch* that is frequently quoted in subsequent Supreme Court decisions is: "In considering this question, then, we must never forget that it is a constitution we are expounding." Felix Frankfurter called this "the single most important utterance in the literature of constitutional law—most important because most comprehensive and most comprehending" (Felix Frankfurter, "John Marshall and the Judicial Function," 69 *Harvard Law Review* [1955]: 217).

Law professor Philip Kurland maintains that whenever a judge cites this passage "you can be sure that the court will be throwing the constitutional text, its history, and its structure to the winds in reaching its conclusion" (Philip Kurland, "*Curia Regis*: Some Comments on the Divine Right of Kings and Courts 'to Say What the Law Is,'" 23 *Arizona Law Review* [1981]: 582).

CONGRESS'S EXPRESS POWERS: MARSHALL COURT

Gibbons v. Ogden
9 Wheaton 1 (1824)

Substantive due process = 1. strict enforcement of 14 amendment and liberty of contract
2. when court looks to why action was passed and uses its own meaning

SETTING

Among the several failings of the Articles of Confederation was the lack of national power to govern and regulate commerce among the states, with foreign nations, and with the Indian tribes. States adopted and enforced their own commercial regulations, favoring their own residents. The Annapolis Convention was convened in September 1786 because of disagreements between Virginia and Maryland over safe commercial use of the Potomac River and Chesapeake Bay. The six states that gathered in Annapolis couched the need for constitutional revision in terms of economic crisis. Drafted by

Alexander Hamilton, their resolution read: "The power of regulating trade is of such comprehensive extent, and will enter so far into the general System of the federal government, that to give it efficacy, and to obviate questions and doubts concerning its precise nature and limits, may require a correspondent adjustment of the other parts of the Federal System."

At the Constitutional Convention in Philadelphia, the delegates debated the extent of national power to regulate commerce. Their discussion revealed the sectional tensions between southern and northern states that were to play an increasingly divisive role in the new nation. On August 29, 1787, Charles Pinckney of South Carolina introduced a motion supporting the proposition "That no act of the legislature for the purpose of regulating the commerce of the United States with foreign powers, among the several states, shall be passed without the assent of two-thirds of the members of each house." General Charles Cotesworth Pinckney, Charles Pinckney's cousin, disagreed. He said that "it was the true interest of the southern states to have no regulation of commerce, but considering ... the interest the weak southern states had in being united with the strong eastern states, he thought it proper that no fetters should be imposed on the power of making commercial regulations." Many southerners feared that Congress would exercise the commerce power to pass a navigation act that would disadvantage southern commercial interests. After discussing the interests dividing and uniting the several states, particularly involving the regulation of navigation, the Convention voted to strike the requirement of a two-thirds vote.

As finalized in Article I, section 8, clause 3, of the Constitution of the United States, the Commerce Clause reads: "The Congress shall have Power ... To regulate Commerce with foreign Nations, and among the several States, and with the Indian Tribes[.]" The first opportunity for the Supreme Court to interpret the Commerce Clause came in *Gibbons v. Ogden*. The case involved the development of a new mode of transportation: the steamboat.

Robert Fulton installed a steam engine on his vessel, the *Clermont*, in 1807. Dubbed "Fulton's Folly" by skeptics, Fulton's steam-powered ship revolutionized water transportation. The *Clermont* could travel one hundred fifty miles of the Hudson River, from New York City to Albany, in thirty-two hours. The first steamboat churned down the Mississippi River in 1811, and regular steamboat ferry service soon began on the Hudson River. Such new technology created lucrative business possibilities. By a series of acts passed by the New York legislature between 1787 and 1811, Robert Livingston and Robert Fulton acquired a monopoly over the use of steam navigation on all New York waters until 1838. The purpose of that monopoly, and similar monopolies granted by Massachusetts, New Hampshire, Pennsylvania, Georgia, and Tennessee, was to provide incentives for the development of steamboat technology. In 1815, Aaron Ogden, a former governor of New Jersey, acquired the monopoly given to Livingston and Fulton to navigate the waters between New York City and Elizabethtown, New Jersey.

Thomas Gibbons had been a business partner of Ogden. Their partnership broke up acrimoniously because of personal and business quarrels. Gibbons wanted to compete with Ogden's steamboat service to Elizabethtown but was unable to obtain a license to navigate in New York waters because of Ogden's monopoly. Gibbons subsequently purchased a federal license under the federal Coastal Licensing Act of 1793 and went into competition with Ogden under the authority of that license. Ogden sought an injunction from the New York Court of Chancery to prevent Gibbons from competing with him.

James Kent, Chancellor of New York (presiding judge of New York's court of equity), issued a permanent injunction against Gibbons to prevent him from competing with Ogden. The New York Court of Errors affirmed. Gibbons petitioned the Supreme Court of the United States for a writ of error.

HIGHLIGHTS OF SUPREME COURT ARGUMENTS

BRIEF FOR GIBBONS

◆ New York had no right to grant the monopoly over New York waters because that legislation regulates commerce, a power granted exclusively to Congress by Article I, section 8, clause 3, of the Constitution. The New York law also conflicts with Congress's power to promote the progress of science and useful arts.

◆ The Constitution never intended to leave the states with the power of granting monopolies of either trade or navigation.

◆ In adopting the Constitution, the American people transformed the several states into a general government, whose delegated powers by their nature must be exclusive. The general words of the document should be construed broadly in order to accomplish the ends intended by the people in that instrument.

◆ Defining commerce in a way that leaves a concurrent power with the states would be insidious and dangerous because no one would be able to say where it would stop. Conflicting and retaliatory state legislation might lead to civil war and the ultimate loss not only of the Constitution but of republican institutions.

BRIEF FOR OGDEN

◆ Every state law carries with it the general presumption in favor of its constitutionality.

◆ Before adoption of the Constitution the states were sovereign nations with respect to one another. They did not give up that sovereignty when they ratified the Constitution. The Constitution of the United States is one of limited and expressly delegated powers.

◆ An early draft of the Constitution read, "Congress shall have *the* power…." Elimination of the definite article in the final draft showed the intent of making the power to regulate commerce concurrent with the states rather than exclusive in the national government.

◆ The powers given to Congress by the Constitution should be interpreted according to commonly accepted meanings of its term. The word commerce means the exchange of one thing for another, the interchange of commodities, trade or traffic. Thus defined, New York retains a concurrent or shared power to regulate commerce and has authority under the Constitution to enact legislation such as the monopoly over steam navigation on its waters.

◆ The Constitution did not affect the state's power to regulate navigation in the waters within its borders. The New York legislation can be construed as a regulation of navigation rather than as a regulation of commerce.

SUPREME COURT DECISION: 6–0

(Thompson, J., did not become a member of the Court until after argument of the case.)

MARSHALL, C.J.

... The words [of the Constitution] are: "Congress shall have power to regulate commerce with foreign nations, and among the several states, and with the Indian tribes."

The subject to be regulated is commerce; and our constitution being, as was aptly said at the bar, one of enumeration, and not of definition, to ascertain the extent of the power it becomes necessary to settle the meaning of the word. The counsel for the appellee would limit it to traffic, to buying and selling, or the interchange of commodities, and does not admit that it comprehends navigation. This would restrict a general term, applicable to many objects, to one of its significations. Commerce, undoubtedly, is traffic, but it is something more; it is intercourse. It describes the commercial intercourse between nations, and parts of nations, in all its branches, and is regulated by prescribing rules for carrying on that intercourse. The mind can scarcely conceive a system for regulating commerce between nations, which shall exclude all laws concerning navigation, which shall be silent on the admission of vessels of the one nation into the ports of the other, and be confined to prescribing rules for the conduct of individuals, in the actual employment of buying and selling, or of barter.

If commerce does not include navigation, the government of the Union has no direct power over that subject, and can make no law prescribing what shall constitute American vessels, or requiring that they shall be navigated by American seamen. Yet this power has been exercised from the commencement of the government, has been exercised with the consent of all, and has been understood by all to be a commercial regulation. All America understands, and has uniformly understood the word "commerce" to comprehend navigation. It was so understood, and must have been so understood, when the constitution was framed. The power over commerce, including navigation, was one of the primary objects for which the people of America adopted their government, and must have been contemplated in forming it. The convention must have used the word in that sense; because all have understood it in that sense, and the attempt to restrict it comes too late....

To what commerce does this power extend? The constitution informs us, to commerce "with foreign nations, and among the several states, and with the Indian tribes."

It has, we believe, been universally admitted that these words comprehend every species of commercial intercourse between the United States and foreign nations. No sort of trade can be carried on between this country and any other, to which this power does not extend. It has been truly said, that commerce, as the word is used in the constitution, is a unit, every part of which is indicated by the term....

The subject to which the power is next applied, is to commerce "among the several states." The word "among" means intermingled with. A thing which is among others, is intermingled with them. Commerce among the states cannot stop at the external boundary line of each state, but may be introduced into the interior.

It is not intended to say that these words comprehend that commerce which is completely internal, which is carried on between man and man in a state, or between different parts of the same state, and which does not extend to or affect other states. Such a power would be inconvenient, and is certainly unnecessary.

Comprehensive as the word "among" is, it may very properly be restricted to that commerce which concerns more states than one.... The genius and character of the whole government seems to be, that its action is to be applied to all the external concerns of the nation, and to those internal concerns which affect the states generally; but not to those which are completely within a particular state, which do not affect other states, and with which it is not necessary to interfere, for the purpose of executing some of the general powers of the government. The completely internal commerce of a state, then, may be considered as reserved for the state itself....

We are now arrived at the inquiry, What is this power?

It is the power to regulate; that is to prescribe the rule by which commerce is to be governed. This power, like all others vested in Congress, is complete in itself, may be exercised to its utmost extent, and acknowledges no limitations, other than are prescribed in the constitution....

The power of Congress, then, comprehends navigation within the limits of every state in the Union; so far as that navigation may be, in any manner, connected with "commerce with foreign nations, or among the several states, or with the Indian tribes." It may, of consequence, pass the jurisdictional line of New York, and act upon the very waters to which the prohibition now under consideration applies.

But it has been urged with great earnestness, that although the power of Congress to regulate commerce with foreign nations, and among the several states, be co-extensive with the subject itself, and have no other limits than are prescribed in the constitution, yet the states may severally exercise the same power within their respective jurisdictions. In support of this argument, it is said that they possessed it as an inseparable attribute of sovereignty, before the formation of the constitution, and still retain it, except so far as they have surrendered it by that instrument; that this principle results from the nature of the government, and is secured by the tenth amendment; that an affirmative grant of power is not exclusive, unless in its own nature it be such that the continued exercise of it by the former possessor is inconsistent with the grant, and that this is not of that description....

The grant of the power to lay and collect taxes is, like the power to regulate commerce, made in general terms, and has never been understood to interfere with the exercise of the same power by the states; and hence has been drawn an argument which has been applied to the question under consideration. But the two grants are not, it is conceived, similar in their terms or their nature. Although many of the powers formerly exercised by the states, are transferred to the government of the Union, yet the state governments remain, and constitute a most important part of our system. The power of taxation is indispensable to their existence, and is a power which, in its own nature, is capable of residing in, and being exercised by, different authorities at the same time. We are accustomed to see it placed, for different purposes, in different hands.... In imposing taxes for state purposes, they are not doing what Congress is empowered to do. Congress is not empowered to tax for those purposes which are within the exclusive province of the states. When, then, each government exercises the power of taxation, neither is exercising the power of the other. But, when a state proceeds to regulate commerce with foreign nations, or among the several states, it is exercising the very power that is granted to Congress, and is doing the

very thing which Congress is authorized to do. There is no analogy, then, between the power of taxation and the power of regulating commerce....

The sole question is, can a state regulate commerce with foreign nations and among the state[s], while Congress is regulating it?...

[T]he framers of our constitution foresaw [the situation where a state law comes into conflict with an act of Congress], and provided for it, by declaring the supremacy not only of itself, but of the laws made in pursuance of it. The nullity of any act, inconsistent with the constitution, is produced by the declaration that the constitution is the supreme law.... [T]he act of Congress, or the treaty, is supreme; and the law of the state, though enacted in the exercise of powers not controverted, must yield to it....

It has been denied that [the words of the congressional coasting act] authorize a voyage from New Jersey to New York. It is true that no ports are specified; but it is equally true that the words used are perfectly intelligible, and do confer such authority as unquestionably as if the ports had been mentioned. The coasting trade is a term well understood. The law has defined it, and all know its meaning perfectly. The act describes, with great minuteness, the various operations of vessels engaged in it; and it cannot, we think, be doubted, that a voyage from New Jersey to New York is one of those operations....

The questions, then, whether the conveyance of passengers be part of the coasting trade, and whether a vessel can be protected in that occupation by a coasting license, are not, and cannot be, raised in this case. The real and sole question seems to be, whether a steam machine, in actual use, deprives a vessel of the privileges conferred by a license....

[A]ll inquiry into this subject seems to the court to be put completely at rest by the act already mentioned, entitled, "An act for the enrolling and licensing of steamboats."

This act authorizes a steamboat employed, or intended to be employed, only in a river or bay of the United States, owned wholly or in part by an alien, to be enrolled and licensed as if the same belonged to a citizen of the United States.

This act demonstrates the opinion of Congress, that steamboats may be enrolled and licensed, in common with vessels using sails. They are, of course, entitled to the same privileges, and can no more be restrained from navigating waters, and entering ports which are free to such vessels, than if they were wafted on their voyage by the winds, instead of being propelled by the agency of fire. The one element may be as legitimately used as the other, for every commercial purpose authorized by the laws of the Union; and the act of a state inhibiting the use of either to any vessel having a license under the act of Congress, comes, we think, in direct collision with that act....

[Reversed.]

JOHNSON, J., CONCURRING

... It is impossible, with the views which I entertain of the principle on which the commercial privileges of the people of the United States, among themselves, rests, to concur in the view which this Court takes of the effect of the coasting license in this cause. I do not regard it as the foundation of the right set up in behalf of the appellant. If there was any one object riding over every other in the adoption of the constitution, it was to keep the commercial intercourse among the States free from all invidious and partial restraints. And I cannot overcome the conviction, that if the licensing act was repealed to-morrow, the rights of the appellant to a reversal of the decision complained of, would be as strong as it is under this license....

The inferences, to be correctly drawn, from [Article I], appear to me to be altogether in favor of the exclusive grants to Congress of power over commerce, and the reverse of that which the appellee contends for....

QUESTIONS

1. Restate Chief Justice Marshall's definitions of "commerce," "among the several states," and "regulate." Does the Constitution compel such definitions?

2. The doctrinal roots of *Gibbons v. Ogden* trace back to the debates during the Constitutional Convention of 1787 over congressional commerce power, as well as to debates at the Annapolis Convention. The debate resurfaced subsequently in the argument between Alexander Hamilton and Thomas Jefferson over the language "among the several states" in the Commerce Clause. Hamilton interpreted the words in plenary terms, encompassing all commercial activity in the United States regardless of state lines (*Federalist* No. 22). (James

Madison articulated a similar position in *Federalist* No. 41.) Jefferson maintained that this language referred narrowly to commerce between two or more states; that is, *inter*state commerce.

If the definition of commerce was the subject of debate during the Constitutional Convention and after, and was not clear in the Constitution, to what standards should Chief Justice Marshall have looked in writing the opinion in *Gibbons*?

3. Did Chief Justice Marshall's decision in *Gibbons* adopt either position advocated by counsel in their arguments to the Court—namely, that states have a concurrent power to regulate commerce, or that Article I, section 8, clause 3, prevents the states from regulating all aspects of commerce? If Marshall adopted neither position, what was his view of congressional commerce power? What is the difference between Marshall's and Justice Johnson's views of Congress's commerce power?

4. *Gibbons* is sometimes referred to as the "Magna Carta of interstate commerce." Did Chief Justice Marshall's opinion free congressional regulation of commerce from all limitations? Is the federal judiciary the primary—or sole—protection against Congress exceeding its power under Article I, or is the political process a more effective bulwark? Consult *Federalist* Nos. 45 and 46 in formulating a response.

5. On February 13, 1829, James Madison wrote to J. C. Cabell that, in his opinion, the Commerce Clause was intended to be "a negative and preventive provision against injustice among the States themselves, rather than as a power to be used for the positive purpose of the General Government" (quoted in Daniel A. Farber, William N. Eskridge Jr., and Philip P. Frickey, *Cases and Materials on Constitutional Law: Themes for the Constitution's Third Century* [St. Paul, MN: West, 1993], pp. 863–864). What does Madison's opinion add to the constitutional meaning of the Commerce Clause?

6. How might narrow or expansive definitions of "commerce" in Article I, section 8, clause 3, affect regulation of slavery, an increasingly volatile political issue even in the 1820s?

7. In another case involving New York, closer to contemporary times, Justice Robert H. Jackson wrote, "The Commerce Clause is ... [a] prolific source of conflict with legislation of the States." *H. P. Hood & Sons v. DuMond*, 336 U.S. 525 (1949). The states are not mentioned in the Commerce Clause. How might state legislation cause conflicts with the Commerce Clause?

SUGGESTIONS FOR FURTHER READING

Baxter, Maurice G., *The Steamboat Monopoly:* Gibbons v. Ogden, *1824* (New York, NY: Knopf, 1972).

Catterall, Ralph C. H., *The Second Bank of the United States* (Chicago, IL: University of Chicago Press, 1903).

Choper, Jesse H., *Judicial Review and the National Political Process* (Chicago, IL: University of Chicago Press, 1980).

Dangerfield, George, "The Steamboat Case," in *Quarrels That Have Shaped the Constitution*, ed. John A. Garraty (New York, NY: Harper and Row, 1987).

Gunther, Gerald, ed., *John Marshall's Defense of* McCulloch v. Maryland (Stanford, CA: Stanford University Press, 1969).

_____, "Toward 'A More Perfect Union': Framing and Implementing the Distinctive Nation-Building Elements of the Constitution," in *Aspects of American Liberty—Philosophical, Historical, and Political: Addresses Presented at the Observance of the Bicentennial Year of American Independence by The American Philosophical Society* (Philadelphia, PA: The Society, 1977).

Hammond, Bray, *Banks and Politics in America from the Revolution to the Civil War* (Princeton, NJ: Princeton University Press, 1957).

_____, "The Bank Case," in *Quarrels That Have Shaped the Constitution*, rev. ed., ed. John A. Garraty (New York, NY: Harper and Row, 1987).

Pious, Harold J., and Gordon E. Baker, "*McCulloch v. Maryland*: Right Principle, Wrong Case," 9 *Stanford Law Review* (1957): 710.

Ribble, Frederick D. G., *State and National Power over Commerce* (New York, NY: Columbia University Press, 1937).

Sholley, John B., "The Negative Implications of the Commerce Clause," 3 *University of Chicago Law Review* (1936): 556.

Stern, Robert L., "That Commerce which Concerns More States than One," 47 *Harvard Law Review* (1934): 1335.

Wechsler, Herbert, "The Political Safeguards of the National Government," 54 *Columbia Law Review* (1954): 543.

CONGRESS'S EXPRESS POWERS: TANEY COURT

Mayor of the City of New York v. Miln
11 Peters 102 (1837)

SETTING

Although Chief Justice John Marshall defined commerce broadly in *Gibbons v. Ogden*, and gave the national government sweeping powers of regulation, he stopped short of ruling that Congress's regulatory power was exclusive.

However, the Court reiterated its broad interpretation of Article I, section 8, clause 3, in *Brown v. Maryland*, 12 Wheaton 419 (1827), the second Commerce Clause decision handed down by the Marshall Court. *Brown* held that a state could not impose a tax on imported goods in foreign commerce that remained in the possession of the importer and in their original package, and had not become "mixed up with the mass of property in the country." (Roger B. Taney, appointed Chief Justice in 1835, had represented Maryland in that litigation.)

Just two years later the Marshall Court held that states could exercise their "police powers" (the inherent power to legislate to protect public health, safety, welfare, and morals) to regulate commerce as long as Congress had not enacted legislation governing the same commerce. *Willson v. Black-Bird Creek Marsh Co.*, 2 Peters 245 (1829). *New York v. Miln*, another in this line of cases, arose out of the uncertainties about the relationship between Congress's power over commerce and the states' police powers under the Tenth Amendment.

In March 1788, almost a year before the Constitution went into effect, the New York legislature adopted "An act concerning passengers in vessels arriving in the Port of New York." The statute required that "[e]very city and town shall support and maintain their own poor." Other states passed similar laws at the suggestion of the final session of the Congress of the Confederation, which adopted a resolution in September 1788 calling for states to pass laws to prevent the transportation of "convicted malefactors" from foreign countries into the United States. Some of those laws were motivated by political opposition to Irish immigration. For example, the Report adopted by the Hartford Convention, a gathering of discontented New England Federalists between December 15, 1814, and January 5, 1815, complained of the "easy admission of naturalized foreigners, to places of trust, honor or profit, operating as an inducement to the malcontent subjects of the old world to come to these States, in quest of executive patronage...." The Hartford delegates resolved to ban naturalized citizens from holding national political office.

Responding to the growing flow of immigrants through its ports, New York regularly modified its passenger laws. The 1824 Passenger Act required the masters of all incoming ships to report the name, birth place, age, last legal settlement, and occupation of all passengers landing in New York from any foreign country or other state of the United States. The law also required masters of vessels bringing passengers into New York who had no legal settlement in the state to post bonds with the city to indemnify it for three years from all charges for the passengers' maintenance. The purpose of the act was to prevent an influx of foreigners into the state who might become paupers dependent on the state, exhausting its resources and causing crime and vagrancy. Failure to comply with the law resulted in a fine for each person not reported or reported falsely.

William Thompson was master of a ship named *Emily*. George Miln was the ship's New York receiver of goods. In August 1829, Thompson and approximately one hundred passengers arrived in the Port of New York on the *Emily*.

Thompson did not make the report required under the 1824 passenger statute. New York sued Miln in the Superior Court of the City of New York seeking $15,000, the amount of the penalties for violation of the statute. Miln entered a demurrer (disputing the legal sufficiency of New York's suit), thereby admitting the facts, but claimed that the New York statute was an unconstitutional regulation of interstate commerce. As an alien, he had the case removed from state court into the U.S. Circuit Court for the Southern District of New York.

The Circuit Court divided on whether to sustain Miln's demurrer. The judges then certified the case to the Supreme Court of the United States.

The case was first argued in 1834, with Chief Justice Marshall presiding. The Court divided on the outcome and the case was scheduled for reargument. John Marshall died in 1835. His replacement, Chief Justice Roger B. Taney, presided at the second argument, which occurred in 1837.

HIGHLIGHTS OF SUPREME COURT ARGUMENTS

BRIEF FOR NEW YORK

◆ The New York passenger law is a valid exercise of the state's police power because some sixty-five thousand migrants come into the Port of New York each year. The passenger law is justified by the right of New York to prevent the influx of strangers who have no claims on the community into which they come. Other Atlantic states face the same problem and have responded with similar legislation.

◆ Even if the New York statute is a regulation of commerce, such regulation is not prohibited because, under the Constitution, states retain concurrent power to regulate unless the power was given expressly to Congress by Article I, section 8, clause 3, or prohibited to the states by Article I, section 10.

◆ Article I, section 9, clause 1, assures states that they have the power to pass laws regarding the migration or importation of persons until the year 1808. After 1808, states assumed they would have concurrent power until Congress acted. Congress has not acted.

◆ *Gibbons v. Ogden* does not control this case because the question decided there was whether a state could regulate commerce while Congress was regulating it. Congress has passed no laws that conflict with the New York law; until Congress acts, which probably would be politically unwise, the state law is valid.

◆ The Court in *Gibbons* stated expressly that the Constitution never intended to deny to the states all legislation that might affect commerce. *Brown v. Maryland*, 12 Wheaton 419 (1827) also acknowledged the validity of state exercises of the police power in cases involving commerce, despite its narrow holding on the facts.

BRIEF FOR MILN

◆ The New York law violates the rule of *Gibbons v. Ogden* because it interferes with important commercial operations of the country, over which Congress has the sole power of regulation.

◆ New York's regulation of passengers is invalid because Congress already has occupied the field of passenger regulation. The New York law amounts to a prohibition on immigration and an infringement on Congress's power to set immigration standards. The field does not admit of concurrent regulation.

◆ The New York statute conflicts with U.S. treaties by imposing restrictions not spelled out in the treaties on subjects of countries united by treaty. American relations with foreign countries thus could be adversely affected by the New York law.

◆ The New York law is not a valid exercise of the state's police powers. The New York passenger statute goes beyond mere police power regulation to interfere with Congress's exclusive control over interstate commerce and commerce with foreign nations.

SUPREME COURT DECISION: 6–1

BARBOUR, J.

... If, as we think, [the New York law] be a regulation, not of commerce, but police; then it is not taken from the states. To decide this, let us examine its purpose, the end to be attained, and the means of its attainment. It is apparent, from the whole scope of the law, that the object of the legislature was, to prevent New York from being burdened by an influx of persons brought thither in ships, either from foreign countries, or from any other of the states; and for that purpose, a report was required of the names, places of birth, etc., of all passengers, that the necessary steps might be taken by the city authorities, to prevent them from becoming chargeable as paupers....

In *Gibbons v. Ogden*, the law of the state assumed to exercise authority over the navigable waters of the state; to do so, by granting a privilege to certain individuals, and by excluding all

others from navigating them by vessels propelled by steam; and in the particular case, this law was brought to bear in its operation directly upon a vessel sailing under a coasting license from the United States.... Now, there is not, in this case, one of the circumstances which existed in that of *Gibbons v. Ogden*, which, in the opinion of the court, rendered it obnoxious to the charge of unconstitutionality....

But we do not place our opinion on this ground. We choose rather to plant ourselves on what we consider impregnable positions. They are these: That a state has the same undeniable and unlimited jurisdiction over all persons and things, within its territorial limits, as any foreign nation; where that jurisdiction is not surrendered or restrained by the Constitution of the United States. That, by virtue of this, it is not only the right, but the bounded and solemn duty of a state, to advance the safety, happiness and prosperity of its people, and to provide for its general welfare, by any and every act of legislation, which it may deem to be conducive to these ends; where the power over the particular subject, or the manner of its exercise is not surrendered or restrained, in the manner just stated. That all those powers which relate to merely municipal legislation, or what may, perhaps, more properly be called internal police, are not thus surrendered or restrained; and that, consequently, in relation to these, the authority of a state is complete, unqualified and exclusive....

The right to punish, or to prevent crime, does in no degree depend upon the citizenship of the party who is obnoxious to the law. The alien who shall just have set his foot upon the soil of the state, is just as subject to the operation of the law, as one who is a native citizen. In this very case, if either the master, or one of the crew of the *Emily*, or one of the passengers who were landed, had, the next hour after they came on shore, committed an offence, or indicated a disposition to do so, he would have been subject to the criminal law of New York, either by punishment for the offence committed, or by prevention from its commission, where good ground for apprehension was shown, by being required to enter into a recognizance, with surety, either to keep the peace or be of good behavior, as the case might be; and if he failed to give it, by liability to be imprisoned in the discretion of the competent authority....

Let us compare this power with a mass of power, said by this court, in *Gibbons v. Ogden*, not to be surrendered to the general government. They are inspection laws, quarantine laws, health laws of every description, as well as

laws for regulating the internal commerce of a state, etc. To which it may be added, that this court, in *Brown v. State of Maryland* [12 Wheaton 419 (1827)], admits the power of a state to direct the removal of gunpowder, as a branch of the police power, which unquestionably remains, and ought to remain, with the states. It is easy to show, that if these powers, as is admitted, remain with the states, they are stronger examples than the one now in question. The power to pass inspection laws, involves the right to examine articles which are imported, and are, therefore, directly the subject of commerce; and if any of them are found to be unsound or infectious, to cause them to be removed, or even destroyed. But the power to pass these inspection laws, is itself a branch of the general power to regulate internal police. Again, the power to pass quarantine laws, operates on the ship which arrives, the goods which it brings, and all persons in it, whether the officers and crew, or the passengers; now the officers and crew are the agents of navigation; the ship is an instrument of it, and the cargo on board is the subject of commerce; and yet it is not only admitted, that this power remains with the states, but the laws of the United States expressly sanction the quarantines, and other restraints which shall be required and established by the health laws of any state; and declare that they shall be duly observed by the collectors and all other revenue officers of the United States.

We consider it unnecessary to pursue this comparison further; because we think, that if the stronger powers, under the necessity of the case, by inspection laws and quarantine laws, to delay the landing of a ship and cargo, which are the subjects of commerce and navigation, and to remove or even to destroy unsound and infectious articles, also the subject of commerce, can be rightfully exercised, then, that it must follow, as a consequence, that powers less strong, such as the one in question, which operates upon no subject either of commerce or navigation, but which operates alone within the limits and jurisdiction of New York, upon a person, at the time, not even engaged in navigation, is still more clearly embraced within the general power of the states to regulate their own internal police, and to take care that no detriment come to the commonwealth. We think it as competent and as necessary for a state to provide precautionary measures against the moral pestilence of paupers, vagabonds, and possibly convicts; as it is to guard against the physical pestilence, which may arise from unsound and infectious articles imported, or from a ship, the crew of which may be laboring under an infectious disease....

We are, therefore, of opinion, and do direct it to be certified to the circuit court ... that so much of the section of the act of the legislature of New York, as applies to the breaches assigned in the declaration, does not assume to regulate commerce between the port of New York and foreign ports....

THOMPSON AND BALDWIN, J.J., CONCURRING [OMITTED]

STORY, J., DISSENTING

... I admit, in the most unhesitating manner, that the states have a right to pass health laws and quarantine laws, and other police laws, not contravening the laws of Congress rightfully passed under their constitutional authority. I admit, that they have a right to pass poor-laws, and laws to prevent the introduction of paupers into the state, under the like qualifications. I go further, and admit, that in the exercise of their legitimate authority over any particular subject, the states may generally use the same means which are used by Congress, if these means are suitable to the end. But I cannot admit, that the states have authority to enact laws, which act upon subjects beyond their territorial limits, or within those limits and which trench upon the authority of Congress in its power to regulate commerce....

It has been argued, that the act of New York is not a regulation of commerce, but is a mere police law upon the subject of paupers; and it has been likened to the cases of health laws, quarantine laws, ballast laws, gunpowder laws, and others of a similar nature. The nature and character of these laws were fully considered, and the true answer given to them, in the case of *Gibbons v. Ogden*; and though the reasoning there given might be expanded, it cannot, in its grounds and distinctions, be more pointedly illustrated, or better expounded. I have already said, that I admit the power of the states to pass such laws, and to use the proper means to effectuate the objects of them; but it is with this reserve, that these means are not exclusively vested in congress. A state cannot make a regulation of commerce, to enforce its health laws, because it is a means withdrawn from its authority. It may be admitted, that it is a means adapted to the end; but it is quite a different question, whether it be a means within the competency of the state jurisdiction. The states have a right to borrow money; and borrowing by the issue of bills of credit, would certainly be an appropriate means; but we all know, that the emission of bills of credit by a state is expressly prohibited by the constitution. If the power to regulate commerce be exclusive in congress, then there is no difference between an express and an implied prohibition upon the states....

But how can it be truly said, that the act of New York is not a regulation of commerce? No one can well doubt, that if the same act had been passed by Congress, it would have been a regulation of commerce; and in that way, and in that only, would it be a constitutional act of Congress....

There is another consideration, which ought not to be overlooked in discussing this subject. It is, that Congress, by its legislation, has, in fact, authorized not only the transportation but the introduction of passengers into the country. The act of New York imposes restraints and burdens upon this right of transportation and introduction....

Such is a brief view of the grounds upon which my judgment is, that the act of New York is unconstitutional and void. In this opinion, I have the consolation to know, that I had the entire concurrence, upon the same grounds, of that great constitutional jurist, the late Mr. Chief Justice Marshall. Having heard the former arguments, his deliberate opinion was, that the act of New York was unconstitutional; and that the present case fell directly within the principles established in the case of *Gibbons v. Ogden* and *Brown v. State of Maryland.*

[handwritten: comes to commerce belong to Congress]

QUESTIONS

1. Summerize the majority's reasoning in upholding the 1824 New York Passenger Act. How did the Court distinguish between federal commerce power and state police power?

2. Justice Story indicated in his dissent that the late Chief Justice Marshall would not have approved of the result in this case. What language in *Gibbons* supports Story's assertion? What language in *Gibbons* would Marshall have had to change in order to secure a defeat for New York in *Miln*?

3. Article I, section 9, clause 1, was placed in the Constitution as part of the compromise over slavery at the Philadelphia Convention. Was New York's reliance on that provision as part of its defense of the 1824 Passenger Act appropriate?

COMMENT

Historian Carl Swisher observed that issues of commerce and slavery were locked in a "titanic struggle" during this period of American history (Carl B. Swisher, *History of the Supreme Court of the United States, Vol. 5: The Taney Period, 1836–1864* [New York, NY: Macmillan, 1974], p. 365). The case of *Groves v. Slaughter*, 15 Peters 449 (1841), illustrates how the Court dodged this struggle.

In 1832, the state of Mississippi amended its constitution to prohibit the importation of slaves for sale. However, it did not enact any legislation to enforce that prohibition. In 1836, Moses Groves purchased several slaves from Robert Slaughter for $7,875. Slaughter had imported the slaves a year earlier for sale as merchandise. Groves signed a personal note to Slaughter for the purchase. In 1837, the Mississippi legislature adopted legislation implementing the 1832 ban on the importation of slaves. The year 1837 also was a year of economic panic and Groves defaulted on the note. Slaughter sued for breach of contract. Groves defended by invoking the 1832 constitutional amendment. He declared that under that amendment, the transaction with Slaughter was void. Slaughter responded that the Mississippi constitutional amendment interfered with Congress's power to regulate interstate commerce. The case thus involved the explosive issues of slavery and the slave trade, Congress's commerce power, and the states' police powers.

When the case reached the Supreme Court, the justices decided it on the narrow ground that the 1832 constitutional amendment was not self-enforcing and hence had no effect without the 1837 implementing legislation. Justice Thompson's 5–2 majority opinion thus avoided the issues of the constitutional status of slaves and whether a state could prohibit the slave trade. In separate concurring opinions, Justice McLean asserted that slaves were persons, not property, while Chief Justice Taney argued that state power over blacks, regardless of their status, was exclusive and was not superseded by any federal power. Justice Baldwin dissented, concluding that the Commerce Clause denied states the ability to exclude the slave trade.

CONGRESS'S EXPRESS POWERS: TANEY COURT

Cooley v. Board of Wardens
12 Howard 299 (1851)

SETTING

Early Americans traveled only relatively short distances by horseback, stagecoach, and canoe. The nineteenth century, however, witnessed transportation innovations that transformed American life. By the 1830s, privately constructed and operated toll roads crisscrossed the country from the east coast to the Mississippi River, and a national road, authorized by Congress in 1822, stretched westward to Illinois by the early 1850s. Canal travel also developed quickly, providing farmers with markets for their goods and making western lands more valuable. As noted in the *Setting* to *Gibbons v. Ogden*, Robert

Fulton's introduction of the steam engine in America in 1807 further revolutionized transportation and the movement of goods and people. By the 1830s, travel by steamboat was popular, inexpensive, and fast. Transportation and commerce were revolutionized yet again with the first successful railroad, built in Pennsylvania in 1830. Within a decade, there were as many miles of rail track in the United States as there were canals.

Into the bustle of commerce made possible by only a few decades of transportation innovations, came a young Frenchman named Alexis de Tocqueville. In 1831, he spent seven months traveling throughout the country. He was so fascinated with the country and its people that he abandoned his original goal of writing about American prisons and instead wrote *Democracy in America*, one of the most insightful looks into American life and character ever written. Tocqueville was struck by what he called "two opposite tendencies" in America—nationalism and sectionalism—existing "like two distinct currents flowing in contrary directions in the same channel." How to promote and regulate the commerce made possible by transportation breakthroughs—and which level of government should do so—remained an issue following the Supreme Court's decisions in *Gibbons* and *Miln*. State governments took an active role in commercial and transportation developments during the important years between 1820 and 1850, deriving their authority from their inherent (or police) powers reserved in the Tenth Amendment. Given the constitutional grey areas separating the police power and the federal commerce power, state involvement in transportation and commerce assured that, just as Tocqueville predicted, legal conflicts pitting the states against the national government would continue.

The distinction between Congress's power under the Commerce Clause and state police powers grew increasingly confused in the early era of the Taney Court, whose chief justice was an unapologetic defender of states' rights. *Miln* was one victory for the states. A decade later, in *The License Cases*, 5 Howard 504 (1847), the Taney Court unanimously upheld the right of three New England states to license the sale of imported liquor within their borders. The justices, however, could not agree on a line of reasoning to support that result. Six of them wrote opinions, confirming Chief Justice Taney's observation that "[i]t is well known that upon this subject a difference of opinion [exists] among the members of this court."

In 1849, in *The Passenger Cases*, 7 Howard U.S. 283, the Court struck down a New York law that taxed passengers brought into a port of the United States. The purpose of the tax was to defray the costs of medical examinations of the passengers, to ensure that they did not have contagious diseases, and to hospitalize those who were found to be ill. The Court also invalidated a Massachusetts law that required ship masters to post a $1,000 bond for each passenger likely to become a public charge. Significantly, the Court could not agree on a majority opinion. Five justices concurred in holding that the state regulations were invalid, but for different reasons. Four justices, including Chief Justice Taney, dissented.

Cooley v. Board of Wardens arose in this muddled doctrinal context, again demonstrating the tension between states' rights and national commerce power that complicated America's burgeoning commercial growth. The controversy that led to the litigation in Cooley dated back to 1789, when Congress adopted an act declaring that states should continue to regulate the activities of river pilots until such time as Congress adopted a uniform system of regulation. The Pennsylvania legislature responded with a law in March 1803 that stated in part:

> ... [E]very ship or vessel arriving from or bound to any foreign port or place, and every ship or vessel of the burden of seventy-five tons or more, sailing from or bound to any port not within the river Delaware, shall be obliged to receive a pilot.... And if the master of any such ship or vessel shall refuse or neglect to take a pilot, the master, owner or consignee of such vessel shall forfeit and pay to the warden ... a sum equal to the half-pilotage of such ship or vessel, to the use of the Society for the Relief of Distressed and Decayed Pilots, their Widows and Children.

In 1832, the legislature exempted from the 1803 law vessels carrying coal mined in Pennsylvania.

Aaron B. Cooley was the receiver of goods for two ships, the *Undine* and the *Consul*. At different times he sailed both ships from Philadelphia without a pilot. The Board of Wardens of the Port of Philadelphia sued Cooley to recover the pilotage fees due under the statute. The case was heard by a Pennsylvania magistrate.

The magistrate ruled for the Board of Wardens and ordered Cooley to pay the fees. Cooley appealed to the Pennsylvania Court of Common Pleas. With respect to the *Consul*, Cooley argued that he was not required to pay the penalty because he was engaged in the coasting trade under a coasting license from the United States and that the schooner was traveling entirely within U.S. waters. With respect to the *Undine*, Cooley demurred to the charge, thereby admitting that he refused to pay the penalty and hire a pilot but denying that he was legally required to do so. The Court of Common Pleas also ruled in favor of the Port of Wardens. Cooley appealed both cases to the Supreme Court of Pennsylvania, which affirmed the Court of Common Pleas. Cooley then petitioned the Supreme Court for a writ of error. The Supreme Court consolidated the two cases.

HIGHLIGHTS OF SUPREME COURT ARGUMENTS

BRIEF FOR COOLEY

◆ The Pennsylvania statute requiring a pilot violates four constitutional provisions. First is Article I, section 8, clause 1, that requires duties, imposts, and excises to be uniform throughout the United States. That clause is self-enforcing; it does not require any act of Congress to implement it. Second is Article I, section 8, clause 3, delegating to Congress the power to regulate interstate commerce. The Pennsylvania statute regulates navigation. The Supreme Court in *Gibbons v. Ogden* held that navigation is commerce. Consequently, there can be no dispute that Pennsylvania's law is a state regulation of commerce. The power to regulate commerce is exclusive in Congress, preventing states from imposing their own regulations on it. Third, the law violates Article I, section 10, clause 2, prohibiting states from imposing imposts or duties on imports or exports without the consent of Congress, or from laying duties on tonnage without the consent of Congress. Congress did not authorize Pennsylvania to impose this tax for the support of "decayed pilots." In 1837 Congress even passed a law that repealed part of the Pennsylvania legislation in question. If the Pennsylvania law is upheld, states will have the power to impose taxes for any purpose and could make them so high as to exclude commerce altogether. Fourth, the Pennsylvania law violates Article I, section 9, clause 5 [correctly, clause 6], prohibiting states from giving preference to commerce in the ports of one state over those of another. The 1832 legislation exempting vessels in the Pennsylvania coal trade marks an invidious distinction in favor of one kind of commerce in one state.

◆ The Pennsylvania legislation is not a valid exercise of the state's police power under the Tenth Amendment. The purpose of the penalty for failure to take a pilot is to support a welfare institution that might or might not be useful. The police power does not reach so far.

BRIEF FOR PENNSYLVANIA

◆ Under the Constitution the states did not surrender to Congress the power to control the ports and harbors through which their commerce enters. Neither did the states surrender their power to protect the lives and property of people engaged in local commerce.

◆ The constitutional provisions cited by opposing counsel admit of a different interpretation. The requirement that duties, imposts, and excises be uniform throughout the United States refers only to impositions by Congress. The subject of pilotage is incapable of uniformity throughout the states and could not have been intended to be included by this clause.

◆ The prohibition on states to lay imposts or duties on imports or exports without the consent of Congress is inapplicable here because the Pennsylvania legislation is neither a duty nor impost on imports or exports. Penalties, if any, are levied against ships or vessels. If the tax is found to be a duty or impost within this clause of the Constitution, Congress consented to its imposition in 1789 and again in 1837 in legislation declaring that all pilots and ports of the United States should continue to be regulated in conformity with the existing laws of the states. Twelve other states have pilot laws similar to Pennsylvania's.

◆ The Pennsylvania law reflects an exercise of the state's police power, not a regulation of commerce. Even if it is a commercial regulation it is valid because the Commerce Clause did not eliminate the inherent or the coexisting power of the states to regulate local commerce. The pilot law is so local in effect as not to compete with Congress's power.

SUPREME COURT DECISION: 7–2

CURTIS, J.

... [W]e are brought directly and unavoidably to the consideration of the question, whether the grant of the commercial power to Congress, did per se deprive the States of all power to regulate pilots.... The grant of commercial power to Congress does not contain any terms which expressly exclude the States from exercising an authority over its subject matter. If they are excluded it must be because the nature of the power, thus granted to Congress, requires that a similar authority should not exist in the States....

Now the power to regulate commerce embraces a vast field, containing not only many, but exceedingly various subjects, quite unlike in their nature; some imperatively demanding a single uniform rule, operating equally on the commerce of the United States in every port; and some, like the subject now in question, as imperatively demanding that diversity which alone can meet the local necessities of navigation.

Either absolutely to affirm, or deny that the nature of this power requires exclusive legislation by Congress, is to lose sight of the nature of the subjects of this power, and to assert concerning all of them, what is really applicable to but a part. Whatever subjects of this power are in their nature national, or admit only of one uniform system, or plan of regulation, may justly be said to be of such a nature as to require exclusive legislation by Congress. That this cannot be affirmed of laws for the regulation of pilots and pilotage is plain. The act of 1789 contains a clear and authoritative declaration by the first Congress, that the nature of this subject is such, that until Congress should find it necessary to exert its power, it should be left to the legislation of the States; that it is local and not national; that it is likely to be the best provided for, not by one system, or plan of regulations, but by as many as the legislative discretion of the several States should deem applicable to the local peculiarities of the ports within their limits....

It is the opinion of a majority of the court that the mere grant to Congress of the power to regulate commerce, did not deprive the States of power to regulate pilots, and that although Congress has legislated on this subject, its legislation manifests an intention, with a single exception, not to regulate this subject, but to leave its regulation to the several States. To these precise questions, which we are called on to decide, this opinion must be understood to be confined. It does not extend to the question what other subjects, under the commercial power, are within the exclusive control of Congress, or may be regulated by the States in the absence of all congressional legislation; nor to the general question how far any regulation of a subject by Congress, may be deemed to operate as an exclusion of all legislation by the States upon the same subject. We decide the precise questions before us, upon what we deem sound principles, applicable to this particular subject in the state in which the legislation of Congress has left it. We go no further....

Affirmed.

DANIEL, J., CONCURRING [OMITTED]

MCLEAN, J., DISSENTING

... That a state may regulate foreign commerce, or commerce among the States, is a doctrine which has been advanced by individual judges of this court; but never before, I believe, has such a power been sanctioned by the decision of this court. In this case, the power to regulate pilots is admitted to belong to the commercial power of Congress; and yet it is held, that a State,

by virtue of its inherent power, may regulate the subject, until such regulation shall be annulled by Congress. This is the principle established by this decision. Its language is guarded, in order to apply the decision only to the case before the court. But such restrictions can never operate, so as to render the principle inapplicable to other cases. And it is in this light that the decision is chiefly to be regretted. The power is recognized in the State, because the subject is more appropriate for State than Federal actions; and consequently, it must be presumed the Constitution cannot have intended to inhibit State action. This is not a rule by which the Constitution is to be construed. It can receive but little support from the discussions which took place on the adoption of the Constitution, and none at all from the earlier decisions of this court....

WAYNE, J., DISSENTING [OMITTED]

QUESTIONS

1. Did Justice Curtis's opinion in *Cooley* clarify or further muddle the doctrinal confusion that existed in the wake of *Gibbons v. Ogden* and *New York v. Miln* over whether Congress's commerce power is exclusive of, or concurrent with, the states' police power?

2. *Cooley* stands for the proposition that *if* the subject of regulation is local, and *if* Congress has not occupied the field by enacting regulatory legislation, then states may regulate commerce. (An alternative view, known as the "negative" or "dormant" Commerce Clause doctrine, holds that the Commerce Clause empowers Congress to regulate commerce exclusively, whether or not it has acted to do so, a view that harkens back to Justice Johnson's concurring opinion in *Gibbons v. Ogden*.) Is the *Cooley* doctrine viable in an economy that transcends state lines? If not, was the doctrine doomed from the outset?

3. To a large extent, the Court's opinion in *Cooley* reflects a shift of perspective away from scrutinizing the nature and purpose of commerce power and toward examining the particular subject to be regu-

lated. For example, the purpose of the 1803 Pennsylvania statute was of less importance to the *Cooley* outcome than the subject it regulated. Which portions of the opinion illustrate this shift? Is the court's shift in perspective helpful in sorting out congressional or state powers to regulate commerce? Is the *Cooley* distinction between local and national subjects of regulation any more useful than the dichotomy between commerce and police powers?

4. Constitutional historian Charles Warren remarked that the decision in *Cooley* "was evidently in the nature of a compromise between the previously conflicting views of the Judges" (*The Supreme Court in United States History*, 3 vols. [Boston, MA: Little, Brown and Company, 1923], 2: 511). Is the *Cooley* compromise workable?

5. The same session that it decided *Cooley*, the Court handed down *Pennsylvania v. Wheeling and Belmont Bridge Company*, 13 Howard 518 (1852). A railroad bridge built over the Ohio River at Wheeling (in what was at the time part of Virginia) linked the Virginia segment of the Columbia Road with the segment in Ohio. Pennsylvania contended that the bridge was so low that it restricted steamboat traffic. The justices held that the bridge interfered with federal commerce power, as exercised by Congress under the coasting license acts, and that the bridge must either be raised or removed. In response, Congress passed a statute declaring that the bridge was not a navigational obstruction. The Court upheld that statute in the second *Wheeling Bridge* case, 18 Howard 421 (1856).

What does the first *Wheeling Bridge* case reveal about the relationship between economic developments, exemplified here by transportation rivals steamboats and trains, and constitutional developments? What does the second *Wheeling Bridge* case reveal about the relationship between the Court and Congress?

SUGGESTIONS FOR FURTHER READING

Cohen, William, "Congressional Power to Validate Unconstitutional State Laws: A Forgotten Solution to an Old Enigma," 35 *Stanford Law Review* (1985): 387.

Corwin, Edward S., *The Commerce Power versus States Rights: "Back to the Constitution"* (Princeton, NJ: Princeton University Press, 1936).

Frankfurter, Felix, *The Commerce Clause under Marshall, Taney, and Waite* (Chicago, IL: Quadrangle Books, 1964, originally published 1937).

Goodrich, Carter, *Government Promotion of American Canals and Railroads, 1800–1890* (New York, NY: Columbia University Press, 1960).

Higham, John, *Strangers in the Land: Patterns of American Nativism* (New Brunswick, NJ: Rutgers University Press, 1955).

Karst, Kenneth L., *Belonging to America: Equal Citizenship and the Constitution* (New Haven, CT: Yale University Press, 1989).

Konvitz, Milton R., *The Alien and the Asiatic in American Law* (Ithaca, NY: Cornell University Press, 1946).

Neuman, Gerald L., *Strangers to The Constitution: Immigrants, Borders, and Fundamental Law* (Princeton, NJ: Princeton University Press, 1966).

Reynolds, George G., *The Distribution of Power to Regulate Carriers between the Nation and the States* (New York, NY: AMS Press, 1968).

Roettinger, Ruth, *The Supreme Court and the State Police Power: A Study in Federalism* (Washington, D.C.: Public Affairs Press, 1957).

Ross, William G., *Forging New Freedoms: Nativism, Education, and the Constitution, 1917–1927* (Lincoln, NB: University of Nebraska Press, 1994).

Stern, Robert L., "The Problems of Yesteryear—Commerce and Due Process," 4 *Vanderbilt Law Review* (1951): 446.

Swisher, Carl B., *History of the Supreme Court of the United States, vol. 5: The Taney Period, 1836–1864* (New York, NY: Macmillan, 1974).

THE AGE OF ENTERPRISE

United States v. E. C. Knight Co.
156 U.S. 1 (1895)

SETTING

As seen in *Gibbons v. Ogden*, according to American law of the early nineteenth century, the term "monopoly" meant the privilege given by government to one person or company to exercise exclusive control over a certain area of commerce. Corporations frequently were formed to receive exclusive franchises—or monopolies—from state legislatures for the purpose of making public improvements such as roads, canals, or bridges. Such monopolies operated under the strict control of the state.

The rapid industrialization, scientific innovation, and economic expansion that occurred after the Civil War saw the development of a different form of monopoly. General incorporation statutes insulated business from governmental control. Corporations found other devices to limit competition in order to enjoy increased profits. One was the pool, a method by which competitors agreed to divide markets and share profits. A cooperative agreement among nominally competitive firms, a pool was an informal "gentlemen's agreement" to set prices. By the time the Interstate Commerce Act outlawed pools in 1887, they were already fading. Pools were replaced by trusts, an existing form of economic organization adapted by Samuel C. T. Dodd, John D. Rockefeller's lawyer. Trusts were created through shareholder transfers of stock from several companies to a common trust officer or officers who directed all operations. Within a very short span of time, huge trusts in oil, steel, rubber, copper, whiskey, tobacco, salt, and sugar managed to control entire industries. Between 1889 and 1903, nearly three hundred trusts were formed. Attorney Dodd observed, "[y]ou might as well endeavor to stay the formation of the clouds, the formation of the rains, or the flowing of the streams as to attempt by any means or in any manner to prevent organization of industry...."

A serious economic depression in 1873, and vast economic power concentrated in the hands of a few business corporations, combined to arouse public opinion against trusts and commercial monopolies by the late 1880s. Several states passed laws aimed at regulating business activities within their borders. By 1888, the national campaign platforms of both the Democratic and Republican parties contained planks opposing trusts and other oppressive business combinations. In August 1888, Republican Senator John Sherman of Ohio introduced an antitrust bill, which he termed "a bill of rights, a charter of liberty." The Sherman Anti-Trust Act became law in July 1890. Among other things, the act provided that "every contract, combination in the form of a trust, or otherwise, or conspiracy in restraint of trade and commerce among the several States is illegal, and ... persons who shall monopolize or shall attempt to monopolize, or combine or conspire with other persons to monopolize trade and commerce among the several States, shall be guilty of a misdemeanor." Section 4 gave circuit courts of the United States jurisdiction to prevent and restrain violations of the act.

In March 1892, the American Sugar Refining Company of New Jersey, incorporated under New Jersey laws, purchased controlling stock of the E. C. Knight Company, the Franklin Sugar Refining Company, the Spreckles Sugar Refining Company, and the Delaware Sugar House, all incorporated under Pennsylvania laws. These four companies, engaged separately in the manufacture and sale of sugar until their purchase by American Sugar, were responsible for approximately one-third of the refined sugar production in the United States. Following the purchase, American Sugar controlled all the sugar refineries in the United States, with the exception of Revere of Boston, whose annual production was about two percent of the nation's total.

In May 1892, the United States filed suit in the Circuit Court for the Eastern District of Pennsylvania against E. C. Knight and the other companies, charging that the purchases of the four sugar companies constituted combinations in restraint of trade and that in entering into the agreements the companies violated the Sherman Anti-Trust Act. The suit asked that the agreements be cancelled, that stock in the companies be redelivered to the respective companies, and that the companies be enjoined from further violations of the act.

The Circuit Court dismissed the suit, holding that no federal question had been raised because the facts presented failed to show a contract, combination, or conspiracy to restrain or monopolize trade. The Third Circuit Court of Appeals affirmed. The United States appealed to the Supreme Court of the United States.

HIGHLIGHTS OF SUPREME COURT ARGUMENTS

BRIEF FOR THE UNITED STATES

◆ As used in the Sherman Anti-Trust Act, the term monopoly should be applied in all cases in which one person sells alone the whole of any kind of marketable thing, so that only he can continue to sell it, fixing the price at his own pleasure. Monopoly includes controlling the market by contracts securing the advantage of selling alone or exclusively all, or some considerable portion, of a particular kind of merchandise or commodity to the detriment of the public.

◆ Because vast aggregations of commercial power have made their appearance so recently, the law has not had the advantage of the wisdom of a Marshall, Taney, Chase, Waite, or their peers in vindicating the power of the United States to suppress them.

BRIEF FOR E. C. KNIGHT

◆ The purchase and sale of stock in a corporation is a wholly local transaction, permitted by the laws of all the states in the provisions they make for the organization of incorporation statutes. Since the transaction in this case was local, it cannot be reached by federal legislation enacted on the strength of Congress's power to regulate interstate commerce.

◆ The Anti-Trust Act can do nothing but restrain the operation of the refineries of the several companies whose stock was purchased by American Sugar.

◆ The Anti-Trust Act does not define what constitutes a contract in restraint of trade or a monopoly. Because the statute seeks to put limitations on the general right to carry on business, it should be strictly construed.

◆ The agreement among the sugar companies is nothing more than an agreement to purchase and sell stock. It says nothing about fixing prices, limiting production, or preventing any of the companies from continuing to do business. The agreement reflects nothing more than the efficient carrying on of business in the corporate mode.

SUPREME COURT DECISION: 8–1

FULLER, C.J.

... Counsel [for the United States] contend ... that the monopolization referred to in the act of Congress is not confined to the common-law sense of the term as implying an exclusive control, by authority, of one branch of industry without legal right of any other person to interfere therewith by competition or otherwise.... But the monopoly and restraint denounced by the act are the monopoly and restraint of interstate commerce, while the conclusion to be assumed on this record is that the result of the transaction complained of was the creation of a monopoly in the manufacture of a necessary of life....

The fundamental question is whether, conceding that the existence of a monopoly in manufacture is established by the evidence, that monopoly can be directly suppressed under the act of congress in the mode attempted by this bill.

It cannot be denied that the power of a state to protect the lives, health, and property of its citizens, and to preserve good order and the public morals, "the power to govern men and things within the limits of its dominion," is a power originally and always belonging to the states, not surrendered by them to the general government, nor directly restrained by the Constitution of the United States, and essentially exclusive. The relief of the citizens of each state from the burden of monopoly and the evils resulting from the restraint of trade among such citizens was left with the states to deal with, and this court has recognized their possession of that power even to the extent of holding that an employment or business carried on by private individuals, when it becomes a matter of such public interest and importance as to create a common charge or burden upon the citizen; in other words, when it becomes a practical monopoly, to which the citizen is compelled to resort, and by means of which a tribute can be exacted from the community, is subject to regulation by state legislative power. On the other hand, the power of congress to regulate commerce among the several states is also exclusive. The constitution does not provide that interstate commerce shall be free, but, by the grant of this exclusive power to regulate it, it was left free, except as congress might impose restraints. Therefore it has been determined that the failure of Congress to exercise this exclusive power in any case is an expression of its will that the subject shall be free from restrictions or impositions upon it by the several states, and if a law passed by a state in the exercise of its acknowledged powers comes into conflict with that will, the Congress and the state cannot occupy the position of equal opposing sovereignties, because the constitution declares its supremacy, and that of the laws passed in pursuance thereof; and that which is not supreme must yield to that which is supreme....

The argument is that the power to control the manufacture of refined sugar is a monopoly over a necessary of life, to the enjoyment of which by a large part of the population of the United States interstate commerce is indispensable, and that, therefore, the general government, in the exercise of the power to regulate commerce, may repress such monopoly directly, and set aside the instruments which have created it. But this argument cannot be confined to necessaries of life merely, and must include all articles of general consumption. Doubtless the power to control the manufacture of a given thing involves, in a certain sense, the control of its disposition, but this is a secondary, and not the primary sense; and, although the exercise of that power may result in bringing the operation of commerce into play, it does not control it, and affects it only incidentally and indi-

Gibbons vodgen

rectly. Commerce succeeds to manufacture, and is not a part of it. The power to regulate commerce is the power to prescribe the rule by which commerce shall be governed, and is a power independent of the power to suppress monopoly. But it may operate in repression of monopoly whenever that comes within the rules by which commerce is governed, or whenever the transaction is itself a monopoly of commerce.

It is vital that the independence of the commercial power and of the police power, and the delimitation between them, however sometimes perplexing, should always be recognized and observed, for, while the one furnishes the strongest bond of union, the other is essential to the preservation of the autonomy of the states as required by our dual form of government; and acknowledged evils, however grave and urgent they may appear to be, had better be borne, than the risk be run, in the effort to suppress them, of more serious consequences by resort to expedients of even doubtful constitutionality.

It will be perceived how far reaching the proposition is that the power of dealing with a monopoly directly may be exercised by the general government whenever interstate or international commerce may be ultimately affected. The regulation of commerce applies to the subjects of commerce, and not to matters of internal police. Contracts to buy, sell, or exchange goods to be transported among the several states, the transportation and its instrumentalities, and articles bought, sold, or exchanged for the purposes of such transit among the states, or put in the way of transit, may be regulated; but this is because they form part of interstate trade or commerce. The fact that an article is

manufactured for export to another state does not of itself make it an article of interstate commerce, and the intent of the manufacturer does not determine the time when the article or product passes from the control of the state and belongs to commerce....

Slight reflection will show that if the national power extends to all contracts and combinations in manufacture, agriculture, mining, and other productive industries, whose ultimate result may affect external commerce, comparatively little of business operations and affairs would be left for state control....

The Circuit Court declined, upon the pleadings and proofs, to grant the relief prayed, and dismissed the bill, and we are of opinion that the Circuit Court of Appeals did not err in affirming the decree.

Decree affirmed.

HARLAN, J., DISSENTING

... The Court holds it to be vital in our system of government to recognize and give effect to both the commercial power of the nation and the police powers of the states, to the end that the union be strengthened and the autonomy of the states preserved. In this view I entirely concur.... But it is equally true that the preservation of the just authority of the general government is essential as well to the safety of the states as to the attainment of the important ends for which that government was ordained by the people of the United States; and the destruction of *that* authority would be fatal to the peace and well-being of the American people....

In my judgment, the citizens of the several states composing the Union are entitled of right to buy goods in the state where they are manufactured, or in any other state, without being confronted by an illegal combination whose business extends throughout the whole country, which, by the law everywhere, is an enemy to the public interests, and which prevents such buying, except at prices arbitrarily fixed by it.... Whatever improperly obstructs the free course of interstate intercourse and trade, as involved in the buying and selling of articles to be carried from one state to another, may be reached by Congress under its authority to regulate commerce among the states....

While the opinion of the court in this case does not declare the act of 1890 to be unconstitutional, it defeats the main object for which it was passed, for it is, in effect, held that the statute would be unconstitutional if interpreted as embracing such unlawful restraints upon the purchasing of goods in one state to be carried to another state as necessarily arise from the existence of combinations formed for the purpose and with the effect, not only of monopo-lizing the ownership of all such goods in every part of the country, but of controlling the prices for them in all the states. This view of the scope of the act leaves the public, so far as national power is concerned, entirely at the mercy of combinations which arbitrarily control the prices of articles purchased to be transported from one state to another state. I cannot assent to that view. In my judgment, the general government is not placed by the constitution in such a condition of helplessness that it must fold its arms and remain inactive while capital combines, under the name of a corporation, to destroy competition, not in one state only, but throughout the entire country, in the buying and selling of articles—especially the necessaries of life—that go into commerce among the states. The doctrine of the autonomy of the states cannot properly be invoked to justify a denial of power in the national government to meet such an emergency, involving, as it does, that freedom of commercial intercourse among the states which the constitution sought to attain....

COMMENTS

1. Antitrust lawyer Earl W. Kintner contends that in the late 1880s "opposition to the trusts was extremely widespread and was evidenced in Congress not only by the nearly unanimous final votes in favor of the Sherman Act's passage but also by the almost uniform recognition of the need for some type of regulatory legislation voiced during the debates" (Earl W. Kinter, ed., *The Legislative History of the Federal Antitrust Laws and Related Statutes*, 14 vols. [New York. NY: Chelsea House, 1978], I: 12). Despite such opposition, trusts proliferated. Historian David Gordon reports that "[f]rom 1879 to 1897 fewer than a dozen important [manufacturing] combinations had been formed, with a total capital of around one billion dollars. Before the century ended, nearly two hundred more combinations formed, with a total capital exceeding three billion dollars" (*Encyclopedia of the American Constitution*, 4 vols. [New York, NY: Macmillan, 1986], 3: 1107).

2. After the *Knight* decision, former railroad lawyer and corporation executive Attorney General Richard Olney, who was responsible for enforcing the Sherman Act, remarked, "You will have observed that the Govt has been defeated in the Supreme Court on the trust question. I have always supposed it would be and have taken the responsibility of not prosecuting under a law I believed to be no good." Between 1890 and 1900, the federal government prosecuted only eighteen cases under the Sherman Act.

QUESTIONS

1. Chief Justice Fuller distinguishes between "manufacture" and "commerce" in arriving at his conclusion in *Knight*. Is the distinction constitutionally relevant? Are the *Knight* distinctions between "manufacturing" and "commerce" and between "direct" and "indirect" effects on commerce any more useful than previous distinctions differentiating local from national subjects of regulation, or congressional commerce power from state police power?

2. The *Knight* court rejected congressional efforts to regulate the growth of monopolies on the basis of a conceptual framework that constitutional scholar Edward S. Corwin dubbed "dual federalism." Corwin defined dual federalism as a set of "postulates or axioms of constitutional interpretation":

   1. The national government is one of enumerated powers only;
   2. Also the purposes which it may constitutionally promote are few;
   3. Within their respective spheres the two centers of government are "sovereign" and hence "equal";
   4. The relation of the two centers with each other is one of tension rather than collaboration.

   ("The Passing of Dual Federalism," reprinted in Robert G. McCloskey, ed., *Essays in Constitutional Law* [New York, NY: Knopf, 1962], pp. 188–189)

   Previous cases in this chapter have suggested that the tension between the states and the national government is inevitable. Did *Knight* exacerbate the tension?

3. In a series of subsequent decisions handed down between 1897 and 1905, the Court eroded, without formally discarding, the distinction it made in *Knight* between manufacturing and commerce.

   Case: *United States v. Trans-Missouri Freight Association*, 166 U.S. 290 (1897)
   Vote: 5–4

Decision: Railroad companies are instruments of commerce whose business is commerce itself. A contract among competing railroads relating to traffic rates for the transportation of articles of commerce between the states that by its direct effect produces a restraint of trade or commerce is prohibited by the Sherman Anti-Trust Act.

Case: *Addyston Pipe and Steel Co. v. United States*, 175 U.S. 211 (1899)
Vote: 9–0

Decision: A conspiracy among six corporations engaged in the manufacture, sale, and transportation of iron pipe in four states to avoid competition is prohibited by the Sherman Anti-Trust Act. Nothing in the Constitution prevents Congress from prohibiting those private contracts that would directly and substantially regulate interstate commerce.

Case: *Northern Securities Company v. United States*, 193 U.S. 197 (1904)
Vote: 5–4

Decision: Creation of a trust company to facilitate a restraint of trade agreement between two railroads violates the Sherman Anti-Trust Act. A trust arrangement, entered into for the purpose of eliminating competition between railroads, is an illegal combination in restraint of interstate commerce and hence covered by the act.

Case: *Swift and Company v. United States*, 196 U.S. 375 (1905)
Vote: 9–0

Decision: A combination of a dominant proportion of the dealers in fresh meat throughout the United States to regulate prices, restrict shipments, establish uniform rules of credit, and get less than lawful rates from railroads to the exclusion of competitors with the intent to monopolize commerce among the states, is an illegal combination within the meaning of the Sherman Anti-Trust Act. The effect of such a combination on interstate commerce is direct and not accidental.

Are these subsequent developments consistent with *Knight*, or should the Court have overruled *Knight*?

4. In 1914, the Court formulated an alternative to the *Knight* analysis. Upholding congressional regulation of local, intrastate railroad rates under the Interstate Commerce Act of 1887, the Court, in a 7–2 vote, held that the interstate consequences of intrastate railroad rates justified national regulation. Justice Charles Evans Hughes wrote: "Whenever the interstate and intrastate operations of such carriers are so related that the government of the one involves the control of the other, it is Congress, and not the State, that is entitled to prescribe the final dominant rule, for otherwise Congress would be denied the exercise of its constitutional authority and the State, and not the Nation, would be supreme within the national field." *Houston E. & W. Texas Railway Co. v. United States* (*The Shreveport Rate Case*), 234 U.S. 342.

Throughout the 1920s and into the late 1930s, the Court clung to the *Knight* "logical nexus" analysis over the *Shreveport* "practical nexus" approach. Is one analysis more consistent with Article I, section 8, clause 3?

COMMENT

Like the Sugar Trust, major league baseball enjoys an antitrust exemption. In *Federal Baseball Club v. National League*, 259 U.S. 200 (1922), Justice Holmes held that "personal effort, not related to production, is not a subject of commerce." Relying on that opinion, the Court subsequently ruled that the reserve clause in baseball players' contracts is beyond the reach of antitrust laws. *Toolson v. New York Yankees*, 346 U.S. 356 (1953). Nineteen years later, despite its view that baseball's antitrust exemption is "an anomaly" and "an aberration," the Court adhered to both decisions in *Flood v. Kuhn*, 407 U.S. 258 (1972). (See Spencer Weber Waller, Neil B. Cohen, and Paul Finkelman, eds., *Baseball and the American Legal Mind* [New York, NY: Garland, 1995].)

THE AGE OF ENTERPRISE

Pollock v. Farmers' Loan & Trust Co.
158 U.S. 601 (1895)

SETTING

The Committee of Style at the Constitutional Convention introduced three kinds of taxes into the document: direct taxes; duties, imposts, and excises; and capitation taxes. When Massachusetts delegate Rufus King, a member of the Committee of Style, asked for the precise meaning of a direct tax, he received no answer. Nonetheless, Article I, section 9, of the Constitution provided that "No capitation, or other direct tax, shall be laid, unless in direct proportion to the census of enumeration herein before directed to be taken." Writing in *Federalist* No. 21, Alexander Hamilton defined direct taxes as those "which principally relate to land and buildings [and] may admit of a rule of apportionment."

In 1796, in *Hylton v. United States*, 3 Dallas 171, the Supreme Court upheld a federal tax on carriages as an excise tax (and therefore an indirect tax), stating that only head taxes and taxes on land were direct and, hence, required by the Constitution to be apportioned among the states. While *Hylton* suggested that Congress had the power to impose an income tax, Congress did not do so until the Civil War. In 1862, for the purpose of supporting the war effort, Congress levied a tax on individual incomes in excess of $600. The income tax law expired in 1872.

A major economic depression in 1893, a budget deficit caused by federal assumption of expenses associated with the Civil War, and Populist demands resulting from the shift from land as the primary source of wealth in the United States to wealth based on earnings, led Congress to include an income tax provision in the Tariff of 1894. The provision imposed a 2 percent tax on the gains, profits, and income of every person whose total income was over $4,000 per year (about 2 percent of the population), and a 2 percent tax on the entire net profits or incomes of most corporations. The tax reached income derived from any kind of property, rents, interest, dividends, salaries, and employment, and included income from all government securities except U.S. bonds, which by law were exempt from federal taxation.

The income tax law went into effect in August 1894. By December, parties were arranging lawsuits to test its constitutionality. Because an 1867 statute prohibited suits to restrain the assessment or collection of taxes, other methods for testing the constitutionality of the statute had to be devised. One "friendly" case was brought by Charles Pollock against the Farmers' Loan & Trust Co. Pollock, a citizen of New York, owned ten shares of stock (valued at about $5,000) in Farmers' Loan, a Massachusetts corporation and one of the country's largest trust companies. He requested that the company refrain from paying the tax required by the 1894 act. The board of directors declined his request, stating that they believed it was inexpedient to comply with Pollock's demand because of the costs of litigation and the risk of incurring penalties that could put a legal cloud over the title of the real estate that the company held in trust.

Pollock then filed suit in the Circuit Court of the United States for the Southern District of New York to prevent Farmers' Loan & Trust from wasting the funds entrusted to it by complying with the income tax law. The company demurred to the complaint. The circuit court sustained the company's demurrer. Pollock appealed directly to the Supreme Court of the United States as allowed by statute. The case was argued and decided twice.

Although technically the Court could have dismissed Pollock's lawsuit because the parties' interests were not adverse to one another, it accepted Pollock's appeal because of the importance of the issues. It ordered the case argued with two others challenging the constitutionality of the income tax. Approximately a month after argument, the Court announced its first decision. In *Pollock v. Farmers' Loan & Trust Co.*, 157 U.S. 429 (1895), the Court reversed the circuit court and entered a decree in favor of Pollock on two points. It held that taxing income from land was the same as taxing the land itself. The 1894 income tax law therefore violated the constitutional requirement that direct taxes be apportioned according to population. The Court also held that the tax on state and municipal bond interest was unconstitutional because it invaded the power of the states to borrow money. On three other issues raised by Pollock, the Court split 4–4 (Justice Howell Johnson did not participate because of illness):

First, was a tax on income from personal property a direct tax? Second, did the invalidity of the specific section on income from real property invalidate the entire income tax act? Third, if any part of the tax required by the act could be considered indirect, did it fail for want of uniformity?

Pollock filed a petition for rehearing in order to get an answer to those questions. The case was reheard in May 1895 with all nine justices participating. Each side was allotted five hours for argument.

HIGHLIGHTS OF SUPREME COURT ARGUMENTS

BRIEF FOR POLLOCK

◆ At the time the Constitution was adopted, income taxes were fully recognized as being direct taxes and hence subject to the apportionment requirement of Article I, section 9, of the Constitution.

◆ The Court's decision in *Hylton v. United States*, 3 Dallas 171 (1796), which gave a very narrow definition to direct taxes, is greatly weakened by the fact that it was decided before 1803 and the Court's assertion of the power of judicial review.

◆ The Constitution makes no distinction between real and personal property. Logic therefore dictates that if a tax on real property is a direct tax, as the Court held in the first *Pollock* case, a tax on personal property also is a direct tax.

◆ The income tax law is a single, comprehensive act. In construing a statute, the role of the Court is to determine Congress's intent. In this situation, Congress clearly stated that its intent was to tax all income, from whatever source derived. The Court already has declared two of the act's provisions unconstitutional. Since Congress's intent cannot be achieved, the entire income tax act must be declared unconstitutional.

◆ If the tax imposed under the income tax act is held to be indirect rather than direct, it is nonetheless unconstitutional because it is not imposed uniformly, as required by Article I, section 8. Individuals who earn less than $4,000, and certain businesses, associations, and corporations are treated differently under the act.

◆ Imposition of unequal and partial taxes also violates the Due Process Clause of the Fifth Amendment, because due process requires that the law operate on all alike.

BRIEF FOR FARMERS' LOAN & TRUST CO.

◆ A long line of precedents supports the income tax act questioned in this case. *Hylton v. United States*, 3 Dallas 171 (1796) should be given special weight. The Court in that case held that a specific personal property tax was a duty and came under the rule of uniformity. It overruled nearly all the arguments put forth immediately after the Constitutional Convention and upon which Pollock's counsel rely. Four members of the *Hylton* Court were delegates to the Constitutional Convention. A fifth was active in the North Carolina ratifying convention. Those justices' views of the meaning of a direct tax are entitled to special deference.

♦ In *Springer v. United States*, 102 U.S. 586 (1881) the Court directly decided that a general income tax is a duty or excise and not a direct tax. *Springer* is one of a wide array of precedents supporting Congress's power in this case.

♦ It is not necessary for the Court to declare the entire income tax provision of the act of 1894 invalid because of the earlier ruling that two of its provisions are invalid. The legislative history of the act shows that Congress considered exempting municipal bond interest. It cannot be inferred from the debates that Congress would not have adopted the income tax if income from municipal bonds had not been included.

♦ The "uniformity" requirement of Article I, section 8, is geographic in character: taxes in one state have to be the same as taxes in another state.

SUPREME COURT DECISION: 5–4

FULLER, C.J.

... [T]he constitution divided federal taxation into two great classes, the class of direct taxes, and the class of duties, imposts, and excises; and prescribed two rules which qualified the grant of power as to each class.

The power to lay direct taxes, apportioned among the several states in proportion to their representation in the popular branch of Congress—representation based on population as ascertained by the census—was plenary and absolute, but to lay direct taxes without apportionment was forbidden. The power to lay duties, imposts, and excises was subject to the qualification that the imposition must be uniform throughout the United States.

Our previous decision [in the first *Pollock* case, 157 U.S. 429 (1895), decided earlier this year] was confined to the consideration of the validity of the tax on the income from real estate, and on the income from municipal bonds. The question thus limited was whether such taxation was direct, or not, in the meaning of the constitution; and the court went no further, as to the tax on the income from real estate, than to hold that it fell within the same class as the source whence the income was derived,—that is, that a tax upon the realty and a tax upon the receipts therefrom were alike direct; while, as to the income from municipal bonds, that could not be taxed, because of want of power to tax the source, and no reference was made to the nature of the tax, as being direct or indirect.

We are now permitted to broaden the field of inquiry, and to determine to which of the two great classes a tax upon a person's entire income, whether derived from rents of products, or otherwise, of real estate, or from bonds, stocks, or other forms of personal property, belongs; and we are unable to conclude that the enforced subtraction from the yield of all the owner's real or personal property, in the manner prescribed, is so different from a tax upon the property itself that it is not a direct, but an indirect, tax, in the meaning of the constitution....

We know of no reason for holding otherwise than that the words "direct taxes," on the one hand, and "duties, imposts and excises," on the other, were used in the constitution in their natural and obvious sense. Nor, in arriving at what those terms embrace, do we perceive any ground for enlarging them beyond, or narrowing them within, their natural and obvious import at the time the constitution was framed and ratified....

The reasons for the clauses of the constitution in respect of direct taxation are not far to seek. The states, respectively possessed plenary powers of taxation.... They retained the power of direct taxation, and to that they looked as their chief resource; but even in respect of that they granted the concurrent power, and, if the tax were placed by both governments on the same subject, the claim of the United States had preference. Therefore they did not grant the power of direct taxation without regard to their own condition and resources as states, but they granted the power of apportioned direct taxation, a power just as efficacious to serve the needs of the general government, but securing to the states the opportunity to pay the amount apportioned, and to recoup from their own citizens in the most feasible way, and in harmony with their systems of local self-government. If, in the changes of wealth and population in particular states, apportionment produced inequality, it was an inequality stipulated for, just as the equal representation of the states, however small, in the senate, was stipulated for....

It is said that a tax on the whole income of property is not a direct tax in the meaning of the constitution, but a duty, and, as a duty, leviable without apportionment, whether direct or indirect. We do not think so. Direct taxation was not restricted in one breath, and the restriction blown to the winds in another....

The constitution prohibits any direct tax, unless in proportion to numbers as ascertained by the census, and, in the light of the circumstances to which we have referred, is it not an evasion of that prohibition to hold that a general unapportioned tax, imposed upon all property owners as a body for or in respect of their property, is not direct, in the meaning of the constitution, because confined to the income therefrom?

Whatever the speculative views of political economists or revenue reformers may be, can it be properly held that the constitution, taken in its plain and obvious sense, and with due regard to the circumstances attending the formation of the government, authorizes a general unapportioned tax on the products of the farm and the rents of real estate, although imposed merely because of ownership, and with no possible means of escape from payment, as belonging to a totally different class from that which includes the property from whence the income proceeds?

There can be but one answer, unless the constitutional restriction is to be treated as utterly illusory and futile, and the object of its framers defeated. We find it impossible to hold that a fundamental requisition deemed so important as to be enforced by two provisions, one affirmative and one negative, can be refined away by forced distinctions between that which gives value to property and the property itself.

Nor can we perceive any ground why the same reasoning does not apply to capital in personalty held for the purpose of income, or ordinarily yielding income, and to the income therefrom....

If it be true that the Constitution should have been so framed that a[n income] tax ... could be laid, the instrument defines the way for its amendment....

Our conclusions may therefore be summed up as follows:

First. We adhere to the opinion already announced, that, taxes on real estate being indisputably direct taxes, taxes on the rents or income of real estate are equally direct taxes.

Second. We are of opinion that taxes on personal property, or on the income of personal property, are likewise direct taxes.

Third. The tax imposed by sections 27 to 37, inclusive, of the act of 1894, so far as it falls on the income of real estate, and of personal property, being a direct tax, within the meaning of the constitution, and therefore unconstitutional and void, because not apportioned according to representation, all those sections, constituting one entire scheme of taxation, are necessarily invalid....

HARLAN, J., DISSENTING

... What are "direct taxes," within the meaning of the constitution? In the convention of 1787, Rufus King asked what was the precise meaning of "direct" taxation, and no one answered. The debates of that famous body do not show that any delegate attempted to give a clear, succinct definition of what, in his opinion, was a direct tax. Indeed, the report of those debates, upon the question now before us, is very meager and unsatisfactory....

A question so difficult to be answered by able statesmen and lawyers directly concerned in the organization of the present government can now, it seems, be easily answered, after a re-examination of documents, writings, and treatises on political economy, all of which, without any exception worth noting, have been several times directly brought to the attention of this court. And whenever that has been done the result always, until now, has been that a duty on incomes, derived from taxable subjects, of whatever nature, was held not to be a direct tax within the meaning of the constitution, to be apportioned among the states on the basis of population, but could be laid, according to the rule of uniformity, upon individual citizens, corporations, and associations, without reference to numbers in the particular states in which such citizens, corporations, or associations were domiciled....

From [the] history of legislation and of judicial decisions, it is manifest—

That in the judgment of the members of this court as constituted when the *Hylton* case [3 Dallas 171 (1796)] was decided—all of whom were statesmen and lawyers of distinction, two, Wilson and Paterson, being recognized as great leaders in the convention of 1787—the only taxes that could certainly be regarded as direct taxes, within the meaning of the Constitution, were capitation taxes and taxes on lands....

That from the foundation of the government, until 1861, congress, following the declarations of the judges in the *Hylton* Case, restricted direct taxation to real estate and slaves, and in 1861 to real estate exclusively, and has never, by any statute, indicated its belief that personal property, however assessed or valued, was the subject of "direct taxes" to be apportioned among the states....

That, in 1861 and subsequent years, Congress imposed, without apportionment among the states on the basis of numbers, but by the rule of uniformity, duties on income derived from every kind of property, real and personal, including income derived from rents, and from trades, professions, and employments, etc. And lastly—

That upon every occasion when it has considered the question whether a duty on incomes was a direct tax, within the meaning of the constitution, this court has, without a dissenting voice, determined it in the negative, always

proceeding on the ground that capitation taxes and taxes on land were the only direct taxes contemplated by the framers of the constitution....

The practical effect of the decision today is to give to certain kinds of property a position of favoritism and advantage inconsistent with the fundamental principles of our social organization, and to invest them with power and influence that may be perilous to that portion of the American people upon whom rests the larger part of the burdens of the government, and who ought not to be subjected to the dominion of aggregated wealth any more than the property of the country should be at the mercy of the lawless....

BROWN, J., DISSENTING [OMITTED]

JACKSON, J., DISSENTING [OMITTED]

WHITE J., DISSENTING [OMITTED]

QUESTIONS

1. During oral argument in the first *Pollock* case, 157 U.S. 429 (1895), attorney Joseph H. Choate attacked the 1894 income tax provision as "communistic in its purposes and tendencies and ... defended here upon principles as communistic, socialistic—what should I call them—populistic as ever have been addressed to any political assembly in the world." Did elements of Choate's argument work their way into Chief Justice Fuller's opinion?

2. One commentator on *Pollock* contended that no cases could be cited in support of the conclusion of the majority of the Court, and that for over a hundred years the term direct tax had been held to mean a tax on real estate only (Francis R. Jones, "*Pollock v. Farmers' Loan & Trust Co.*," 9 *Harvard Law Review* [1946]: 198, 203, 210). Assuming Jones's legal analysis is correct, what might account for the majority decision in *Pollock*?

3. On the day *Pollock* was announced, Justice Harlan declared from the bench, "On my conscience I regard this decision as a disaster!" Later, Charles Evans Hughes characterized the decision as a "self-inflicted

wound" comparable to the decision in *Dred Scott v. Sandford*. (See Carl B. Swisher, *History of the Supreme Court of the United States, vol. 5, The Taney Period, 1836–1864* [New York, NY: Macmillan Publishing Co., 1974], p. 631.)

Oregon Governor Sylvester Pennoyer wrote of *Pollock*: "We have during this time been living under a government not based upon the Federal Constitution, but under one created by the plausible sophistries of John Marshall. The Supreme Court has not contented itself with its undisputed judicial prerogative of declaring what the laws shall not be. Our constitutional government has been supplanted by a judicial oligarchy" (quoted in Charles Warren, *The Supreme Court in United States History*, 3 vols. [Boston, MA: Little, Brown and Company, 1923], 3: 425). To what "plausible sophistries" was Pennoyer was referring?

Can Congress's express power to tax in Article I, section 8, clause 1, be reconciled with the Supreme Court's authority to declare the constitutionality of congressional enactments?

COMMENTS

1. Taxing power can be exercised to serve a regulatory as well as a revenue-raising function. Only nine years after nullifying the revenue-raising income tax in *Pollock*, the Court upheld a regulatory tax in *McCray v. United States*, 195 U.S. 27 (1904). Congress enacted a tax of 10 cents per pound on oleomargarine that was colored to look like butter, but taxed uncolored oleomargarine at only 1/4 cent per pound. The tax clearly was designed to hinder competition between colored oleomargarine and butter. Rejecting both Tenth Amendment police powers and Fourteenth Amendment due process objections raised by colored oleomargarine producers, a 6–3 majority of the Supreme Court upheld the tax. Adopting a posture of restraint, Justice White said: "The right of Congress to tax within its delegated power being unrestrained, except as limited by the Constitution, it was within the authority conferred on Congress to select the objects upon which an excise should be laid."

2. The *Pollock* decision was overturned when the Sixteenth Amendment was ratified on February 3, 1913. That amendment provides that "The Congress shall have power to lay and collect taxes on incomes, from whatever source derived, without apportionment among the several States, and without regard to any census or enumeration." In the interim between *Pollock* and the Sixteenth Amendment, the Supreme Court held that a corporate tax assessed according to corporate income was not a direct tax but an excise on the privilege of doing business. *Flint v. Stone Tracy Co.*, 220 U.S. 107 (1911).

THE AGE OF ENTERPRISE

Hammer v. Dagenhart
247 U.S. 251 (1918)

Good will work harm Congress can forbid it goods (introdution)

SETTING

The *Setting* to *Hammer v. Dagenhart* (excerpted in Chapter 5, pp. 577–583) explains that child labor in the nineteenth century was at once a social scourge and an economic necessity. The Civil War sparked an industrial revolution in the manufacture of goods, but devastated the wages of workers, requiring all members of families, including young children, to work in mines, manufacturing plants, and on assembly lines. Thousands of children were robbed of their youth, their education, their health, and sometimes their lives by working long hours in unsafe and unhealthy conditions. Children were obliged to work because the meager wages they brought home were required to supplement household income. Many parents faced a tragic trade-off between sacrificing their children and family survival.

After the Civil War, reformers began to argue that child labor was a preventable evil. In the 1880s, labor unions, just beginning to organize, opposed child labor because cheap child labor undercut adult wages. By the turn of the century, the labor coalition gained passage of laws banning child labor in thirty-eight states. Those laws were mostly ineffective because of deficient enforcement, under-funded regulatory agencies, and inadequate staffing. Between 1879 and 1900 the number of children working in nonagricultural occupations tripled, reaching nearly 1.7 million. By 1900, 13 percent of all textile workers were under the age of sixteen. Although the numbers of children employed in industries began to decline due to child labor laws and automation in manufacturing, working children simply moved to "street trades," such as shining shoes and selling newspapers.

Encouraged by success in state legislatures, yet frustrated by the limitations and inconsistencies of those efforts, opponents of child labor sought federal legislation. With the support of the Wilson Administration, reformers persuaded Congress to enact the Keating-Owen Child Labor Act of 1916. The Child Labor Act made it a misdemeanor to ship in interstate commerce products from factories, canneries, or similar work places that employed children from fourteen to sixteen years of age for more than eight hours a day or more than six days a week. Congress grounded authority for Keating-Owen in its regulatory power under the Commerce Clause.

Supporters of the act were confident that, if challenged, the Child Labor Act would pass constitutional muster because the Supreme Court had interpreted the Commerce Clause as authorizing a wide variety of federal regulations. For instance, in *Hoke v. United States*, 227 U.S. 308 (1913), upholding the White Slave Traffic (Mann) Act that banned interstate prostitution, Justice McKenna wrote: "The power of Congress under the commerce clause is the ultimate determining question.... If the statute be a valid exercise of that power, how it may affect persons or States is not material to be considered. It is the supreme law of the land and persons and States are subject to it." In *Hammer v. Dagenhart*, however, the Court took a different view of congressional commerce powers.

Note: Read the *Setting* to and excerpt of *Hammer v. Dagenhart* in Chapter 5, pp. 577–583.

QUESTIONS

1. What intellectual common ground does *Hammer* share with *Knight*? Is the distinction between inherently "harmful" and "harmless" products any more defensible than the distinction between "manufacturing" and "commerce"?

2. To what extent does the Court's decision in *Hammer* reinforce Tocqueville's observation in the 1830s that "two distinct currents" were flowing in contrary directions in the same channel in the United States? What are the "currents" in *Hammer*?

SUGGESTIONS FOR FURTHER READING

Berger, Lawrence, and S. Rayan Johansson, "Child Health in the Workplace: The Supreme Court in *Hammer v. Dagenhart*," 5 *Journal of Health Politics, Policy and Law* (1980): 81.

Clinton, Robert Lowry, "Judicial Review, Nationalism, and the Commerce Clause: Contrasting Antebellum and Postbellum Supreme Court Decision Making," 47 *Political Research Quarterly* (1994): 857.

———, "John Marshall's Federalism: A Reply to Professor Gillman," 47 *Political Research Quarterly* (1994): 887.

Eichner, Alfred, *Emergence of Oligopoly: Sugar Refining as a Case Study* (Westport, CT: Greenwood Press, 1969).

Gillman, Howard, "The Struggle over Marshall and the Politics of Constitutional History," 47 *Political Research Quarterly* (1994): 877.

———, "More on the Origins of the Fuller Court's Jurisprudence: Reexamining the Scope of Federal Power over Commerce and Manufacturing in Nineteenth-Century Constitutional Law," 49 *Political Research Quarterly* (1996): 415.

Hovenkamp, Herbert, *Enterprise and American Law, 1836–1937* (Cambridge, MA: Harvard University Press, 1991).

_____, *Federal Antitrust Policy: The Law of Competition and Its Practice* (St. Paul, MN: West, 1994).

Hurst, J. Willard, *The Legitimacy of the Business Corporation in the Law of the United States, 1780–1970* (Charlottesville, VA: University of Virginia Press, 1968).

May, James, "Antitrust in the Formative Era: Political and Economic Theory in Constitutional and Antitrust Analysis, 1880–1918," 50 *Ohio State Law Journal* (1989): 257.

McCurdy, Charles W., "The *Knight* Sugar Decision of 1895 and the Modernization of American Corporation Law, 1896–1903," 53 *Business History Review* (1979): 304.

Mendelson, Wallace, "John Marshall and the Sugar Trust—A Reply to Professor Gillman," 49 *Political Research Quarterly* (1996): 405.

Paul, Arnold M., *Conservative Crisis and the Rule of Law: Attitudes of Bar and Bench, 1887–1895* (New York, NY: Harper, 1969).

Peritz, Rudolph J. R., *Competition Policy in America, 1888–1992: History, Rhetoric, Law* (New York, NY: Oxford University Press, 1996).

Urofsky, Melvin, "Myth and Reality: The Supreme Court and Protective Legislation in the Progressive Era," *Yearbook of the Supreme Court Historical Society* (1983).

Wood, Stephen B., *Constitutional Politics in the Progressive Era: Child Labor and the Law* (Chicago, IL: University of Chicago Press, 1968).

THE GREAT DEPRESSION AND THE NEW DEAL

A.L.A. Schechter Poultry Corp. v. United States
295 U.S. 495 (1935)

SETTING

The 1920s in America are fondly remembered as "roaring." This designation refers to both the social experimentation and the economic prosperity that seemed to characterize the period. Social strictures were changing and great wealth was created during the decade immediately after World War I. However, economic affluence was less widespread and social conventions were more conservative than is generally assumed. The decade saw deep contradictions.

This was the Jazz Age, the high point of the Harlem Renaissance, the time when flappers danced and movies talked. Americans spent more money on recreation and entertainment than ever before. The first million-dollar boxing match was staged, when ninety thousand people saw Jack Dempsey knock out Georges Carpentier in a New Jersey arena. Baseball's George Herman "Babe" Ruth was the Sultan of Swat. Headlines touting the antics of flag-pole sitters and marathon dancers grabbed wide attention. The world grew smaller as Charles Lindbergh ("Lucky Lindy") flew the first solo flight across the Atlantic Ocean.

The 1920s also saw Prohibition, the height of Ku Klux Klan activities and the Scopes trial, in which evangelical Christians challenged Darwin's theory of evolution. The 1920s was also a time of suspicion toward and resentment of "foreigners," both at home and abroad. Congress adopted three restrictive immigration laws, reducing quotas for eastern Europeans and virtually excluding Asians. Italian-Americans Nicola Sacco and Bartolomeo Vanzetti, immigrant anarchists, were tried, convicted, and executed for the alleged murder of a guard and paymaster during a Massachusetts robbery. The most damaging facts against them seemed to be their ethnic heritage and political views.

In a decade of unparalleled prosperity in the United States, between 1919 and 1929, the gross national product mushroomed by forty percent. Mass production brought consumer goods into nearly every home. Two-thirds of Americans had electricity by 1929. One-fourth owned vacuum cleaners. Automobile registration soared from eight million to twenty-three million during the decade. Perhaps symbolic of the period was a new magazine that began circulating in 1929: *Fortune Magazine*.

Not all sectors of the economy were healthy, however. Over-production in 1917–1918 to support World War I created what were known during the 1920s as "sick industries" in agriculture, coal mining, and textiles. The concentration of vast market power in a few trusts (described in the *Setting* to *E. C. Knight*, p. 244) skewed the distribution of wealth and income, and rendered industrial production vulnerable to a downturn in the business cycle. Legal and political obstacles to unions weakened workers' ability to act collectively.

In 1927, 1928, and most of 1929 the stock market rose to unprecedented heights. Almost two million Americans, just short of two percent of the population, "played the market." Stock prices climbed week after week until September 1929. In that month, stock prices stood at a dizzying 400 percent above their 1924 level. Then, between October 24 and October 29, the stock market collapsed.

On Tuesday, October 29th alone, almost sixteen-and-a-half-million shares were sold, driving prices down and creating panic as many Americans' life savings were wiped out. By the end of the day on October 29th almost all the paper profits of the entire year were gone. By early November, all the gains of 1928 had disappeared. The ensuing money panic caused banks outside of New York City to call back over two billion dollars. By the time the stock market stopped its free-fall in mid-November, the *New York Times* industrial average had fallen by half, from its September 3 high of 452, to 224. The market continued to drift downward. By the summer of 1930 all the profits of 1927 were erased. As of July 8, 1932, the *New York Times* industrial average was at 58.

The collapse of the financial markets was exacerbated by three underlying structural weaknesses in the American economy. First, key sectors of industry were already weak. Coal, railroads, and textiles were troubled before 1929. Two pillars of American economic growth, automobiles and construction, had foundered. Industrial production dropped by half between 1929 and 1932. By early 1933, unemployment had grown to more than 12 million people, about one-third of the labor force. (Many of these people were homeless, living on the roads and rails or in shanty towns dubbed "Hoovervilles" after the Republican president.) Second, production outstripped consumption. Due to inequalities in income distribution, workers and farmers who produced goods often could not afford to purchase them. In 1929, about sixty percent of America's families lived at or below the subsistence level. One percent of the population owned fifty-nine percent of the country's wealth. As unsold inventories grew, employers laid off workers who then had no income to sustain buying. Consequently, a sizeable nonconsuming population was growing in America before the Great Depression hit. Third, oligopolies dominated key industrial sectors. The top two hundred nonfinancial corporations controlled 49 percent of corporate wealth. Many of these companies speculated on the largely unregulated stock market. Those who speculated put up little cash, often trading in their own stock issues.

In 1932, as this social calamity unfolded, Franklin D. Roosevelt was elected president. Roosevelt had defeated Herbert Hoover in a campaign that had been a contest between Roosevelt's energetic optimism and Hoover's pessimism, Roosevelt's willingness to experiment and Hoover's cautious tentativeness, Roosevelt's anticipation of the future and Hoover's clinging to the past. Roosevelt was inaugurated on March 4, 1933, promising Americans a "New Deal." Five days later he called Congress into special session, halted transactions in gold, and declared a national bank holiday.

The New Deal approach to industrial recovery was a patchwork of programs intended to coordinate a number of historically hostile constituencies such as business and labor. Rough-and-tumble negotiations among several of President Roosevelt's key advisors in April and May 1933 resulted in a proposal for the National Industrial Recovery Act (NIRA). Shortly afterward, his administration submitted the NIRA to Congress. It would become the centerpiece of Roosevelt's first "One Hundred Days" (March 9–June 16, 1933).

Congress enacted the NIRA in June 1933. Section 1 announced several policies aimed at rehabilitating American industry, such as exemption from antitrust laws for trade associations. Section 2 gave the president authority to carry out the policies stated in Section 1 by establishing agencies and appointing employees as he saw fit. Section 3 gave the president authority to approve "codes of fair competition." With limited statutory exceptions, the NIRA gave the president complete discretion to determine the fairness of proposed codes based on his perception of the public interest. The NIRA also gave the president authority to grant exceptions to and exemptions from codes as he deemed fit. If members of trade associations or industries failed to propose a code, the president could prescribe a code to bind the industry. Once the president had approved of a code of fair competition, the NIRA provided that any violation was a misdemeanor punishable by a fine of not more than $500 for each offense, with each day the violation continued being deemed a separate offense.

In April 1934, pursuant to the authority given him under the NIRA, President Roosevelt approved by executive order the Code of Fair Competition for the Live Poultry Industry of the Metropolitan Area In and About the City of New York. The code was proposed by trade associations claiming to represent about 90 percent of the industry. Once approved, it became the standard of fair competition for the poultry industry. The poultry code for the New York area covered every person in the business of selling, transporting, handling, and/or slaughtering live poultry. Among other things, the code fixed the number of hours for workers at forty per week, established a minimum wage of fifty cents per hour, prohibited the employment of persons under sixteen years of age, gave employees freedom of choice regarding union membership, and prohibited unfair methods of competition.

Joseph Schechter operated the Schechter Live Poultry Market in Brooklyn, New York. Alexander, Martin, and Aaron Schechter operated the A.L.A. Schechter Poultry Corporation in the same city. Both corporations slaughtered and sold poultry for the local New York market. They purchased most of the poultry from markets outside the state of New York. The Schechters were indicted in U.S. District Court for the Eastern District of New York on sixty counts of conspiracy to violate the NIRA and the Code of Fair Competition for the Live Poultry Industry. They were accused of paying employees less than fifty cents per hour, permitting an employee to work more than forty hours per week, withholding sales reports, filing false reports, and committing unfair trade practices such as selling thousands of pounds of diseased chickens at four to eight cents per pound below the market price. The Schechters demurred to the indictment. The implicit contention of their demurrer was that the NIRA was unconstitutional.

The district court sustained the Schechters' demurrer to twenty-seven of the sixty counts in the indictment. Following trial on the remaining thirty-three counts, the Schechters were convicted on nineteen counts and acquitted on fourteen. The U.S. Court of Appeals for the Second Circuit affirmed the District Court on all but two of the counts. It reversed the Schechters' convictions for violation of the minimum wage and maximum hours provisions of the code.

The Schechters petitioned the Supreme Court of the United States for a writ of certiorari as to the counts on which the Court of Appeals affirmed their convictions. The United States petitioned for a writ of certiorari as to the counts on which the Court of Appeals reversed the Schechters' convictions.

HIGHLIGHTS OF SUPREME COURT ARGUMENTS

BRIEF FOR THE SCHECHTERS   — W i n

◆ The NIRA is unconstitutional because it delegates legislative authority to the president without establishing intelligible policies to govern him, without setting standards to guide and restrict his action, and without establishing an administrative procedure that guarantees due process of law. In past cases, delegation has been upheld when Congress has prescribed (1) a reasonably intelligible policy that was not to be effective at once or under all conditions; (2) a reasonably definite standard for administrative action in carrying out that policy when circumstances or conditions spelled out in the statute came into existence; and (3) an administrative procedure that follows rules and regulations adopted by the agency in accordance with the standard set down by Congress. The NIRA meets none of those conditions.

◆ In the past two years, the NIRA or its application has been struck down in seventeen federal cases as an improper regulation of commerce and as being inconsistent with America's dual system of government.

◆ The minimum wage and maximum hour provisions of the NIRA are beyond the purview of the commerce clause and violate the Fifth Amendment. The Court already has ruled that congressional regulation of wages and hours contravenes the Due Process Clause of the Fifth Amendment.

BRIEF FOR THE UNITED STATES

◆ The NIRA provides adequate standards to govern the president's actions. The statute requires the president to approve codes of fair competition after making prescribed findings of fact. The term "fair competition" sets a primary standard for presidential action and is no more vague than other standards that have been approved by the Court in the past. For example, "public convenience, interest or necessity," "public interest" and "purity, quality and fitness for consumption" have been held to give adequate guidance to the president in making rules and regulations. Under the NIRA, proposed codes are submitted for approval by representative groups in the industries affected by it. Business experience and judgment provide another standard for determining "fair competition." Finally, the meaning of "fair competition" as a standard to govern the president's action is given meaning by the policy statements in Section 1 of the NIRA, all of which point to industrial rehabilitation.

◆ In view of the emergency confronting Congress when the NIRA was passed, and the need for immediate action in many fields, the delegation contained in the statute is reasonable. If its policies are to be effective, a flexible procedure is needed to deal with the needs of different industries.

◆ Legislation respecting wages and hours of labor often has been upheld in the face of attacks under the Due Process Clause. The NIRA fully satisfies the requirements of Due Process in the Fifth Amendment.

SUPREME COURT DECISION: 9–0

HUGHES, C.J.

... We are told that the provision of the statute authorizing the adoption of codes must be viewed in the light of the grave national crisis with which Congress was confronted. Undoubtedly, the conditions to which power is addressed are always to be considered when the exercise of power is challenged. Extraordinary conditions may call for extraordinary remedies. But the argument necessarily stops short of an attempt to justify action which lies outside the sphere of constitutional authority. Extraordinary conditions do not create or enlarge constitutional power. The Constitution established a national government with powers deemed to be adequate, as they have proved to be both in war and peace, but these powers of the national government are limited by the constitutional grants. Those who act under these grants are not at liberty to transcend the imposed limits because they believe that more or different power is necessary. Such assertions of extra-constitutional authority were anticipated and precluded by the explicit terms of the Tenth Amendment—"The powers not delegated to the United States by the Constitution, nor prohibited by it to the States, are reserved to the States respectively, or to the people."

The further point is urged that the national crisis demanded a broad and intensive cooperative effort by those engaged in trade and industry, and that this necessary cooperation was sought to be fostered by permitting them to initiate the adoption of codes. But the statutory plan is not simply one for voluntary effort. It does not seek merely to endow voluntary trade or industrial associations or groups with privileges or immunities. It involves the coercive exercise of the lawmaking power. The codes of fair competition which the statute attempts to authorize are codes of laws. If valid, they place all persons within their reach under the obligation of positive law, binding equally those who assent and those who do not assent. Violations of the provisions of the codes are punishable as crimes....

If the codes have standing as penal statutes, this must be due to the effect of the executive action. But Congress cannot delegate legislative power to the President to exercise an unfettered discretion to make whatever he thinks may be needed or advisable for the rehabilitation and expansion of trade or industry.

Accordingly we turn to the Recovery Act to ascertain what limits have been set to the exercise of the President's discretion....

[T]he President in approving a code may impose his own conditions, adding to or taking from what is proposed, as "in his discretion" he thinks necessary "to effectuate the policy" declared by the act. Of course, he has no less liberty when he prescribes a code on his own motion or on complaint, and he is free to prescribe one if a code has not been approved. The Act provides for the creation by the President of administrative agencies to assist him, but the action or reports of such agencies, or of his other assistants—their recommendations and findings in relation to the making of codes—have no sanction beyond the will of the President, who may accept, modify or reject them as he pleases. Such recommendations or findings in no way limit the authority which Sec. 3 undertakes to vest in the President with no other conditions than those there specified. And this authority relates to a host of different trades and industries, thus extending the President's discretion to all the varieties of laws which he may deem to be beneficial in dealing with the vast array of commercial and industrial activities throughout the country....

Section 3 of the Recovery Act is without precedent.... We think that the code-making authority thus conferred is an unconstitutional delegation of legislative power....

The undisputed facts ... afford no warrant for the argument that the poultry handled by defendants at their slaughterhouse markets was in a "*current*" or "*flow*" of interstate commerce and was thus subject to congressional regulation. The mere fact that there may be a constant flow of commodities into a State does not mean that the flow continues after the property has arrived and has become commingled with the mass of property within the State and is there held solely for local disposition and use. So far as the poultry here in question is concerned, the flow in interstate commerce had ceased. The poultry had come to a permanent rest within the State. It was not held, used, or sold by defendants in relation to any further transactions in interstate commerce and was not destined for transportation to other States. Hence, decisions which deal with a stream of interstate commerce—where goods come to rest within a State temporarily and are later to go forward in interstate commerce—and with the regulations of transactions

involved in that practical continuity of movement, are not applicable here....

Did the defendants' transactions directly "*affect*" interstate commerce so as to be subject to federal regulation?...

[T]he distinction between direct and indirect effects of intrastate transactions upon interstate commerce must be recognized as a fundamental one, essential to the maintenance of our constitutional system. Otherwise, as we have said, there would be virtually no limit to the federal power and for all practical purposes we should have a completely centralized government....

The question of chief importance relates to the provisions of the Code as to the hours and wages of those employed in defendants' slaughterhouse markets. It is plain that these requirements are imposed in order to govern the details of defendants' management of their local business. The persons employed in slaughtering and selling in local trade are not employed in interstate commerce. Their hours and wages have no direct relation to interstate commerce. The question of how many hours these employees should work and what they should be paid differs in no essential respect from similar questions in other local businesses which handle commodities brought into a State and there dealt in as a part of its internal commerce....

The apparent implication [of the NIRA] is that the federal authority under the commerce clause should be deemed to extend to the establishment of rules to govern wages and hours in intrastate trade and industry generally throughout the country, thus overriding the authority of the States to deal with domestic problems arising from labor conditions in their internal commerce.

It is not the province of the Court to

consider the economic advantages or disadvantages of such a centralized system. It is sufficient to say that the Federal Constitution does not provide for it.... [T]he authority of the federal government may not be pushed to such an extreme as to destroy the distinction, which the commerce clause itself establishes, between commerce "among the several States" and the internal concerns of a State....

We are of the opinion that the attempt through the provisions of the Code to fix the hours and wages of employees of defendants in their intrastate business was not a valid exercise of federal power....

On both grounds we have discussed, the attempted delegation of legislative power, and the attempted regulation of intrastate transactions which affect interstate commerce only indirectly, we hold the code provisions here in question to be invalid and that the judgment of conviction must be reversed.

CARDOZO AND STONE, J.J., CONCURRING

The delegated power of legislation which has found expression in this code is not canalized within banks that keep it from overflowing. It is unconfined and vagrant....

This is delegation running riot....

To find immediacy or directness here is to find it almost everywhere. If centripetal forces are to be isolated to the exclusion of the forces that oppose and counteract them, there will be an end to our federal system....

COMMENT

Former Columbia University professor Raymond Moley, an important participant in Roosevelt's "Brain Trust," asked the president whether he realized that the NIRA took "an enormous step away from the philosophy of equalitarianism and laissez-faire." Roosevelt replied, "If that philosophy hadn't proven to be bankrupt, Herbert Hoover would be sitting here right now."

In an hour and twenty-five minute discourse before the White House press corps on May 31, 1935, four days after *Schechter* was announced, President Franklin D. Roosevelt said, among other things, "The implications of this decision are much more important than any other decision probably since the *Dred Scott* case.... We are the only nation in the world that has not solved [the] problem [of how to proceed in the area of economic regulation]. We thought we were solving it, and now it has been thrown right straight in our faces and we have been relegated to the horse-and-buggy definition of interstate commerce."

QUESTIONS

1. Does the result in *Schechter* turn predominantly on the constitutionality of Congress's power to delegate, or are other constitutional considerations involved? If there are other considerations, what are they?
2. Chief Justice Charles Evans Hughes, in an address to the American

Bar Association in 1931, decried the practice of delegating broad regulatory powers to administrative agencies. Justice Louis Brandeis, long a foe of industrial conglomerates, was less concerned in principle about delegation. Do the specific facts in *Schechter* help reconcile the fact that they joined the unanimous majority in *Schechter* despite their differences over delegation?

3. The federal government brought *Schechter* as a test case, hoping that a favorable Supreme Court ruling would encourage industry compliance with the NIRA codes of fair competition. Why did the facts of *Schechter* make it less than an ideal vehicle for the government to defend congressional commerce powers?

THE GREAT DEPRESSION AND THE NEW DEAL

United States v. Butler
297 U.S. 1 (1936)   *can trace tax $'s*

SETTING

The agricultural sector of the American economy was among those known as "sick industries" during the 1920s. Overproduction and inadequate postwar markets plagued farmers, and agriculture typified the country's economic problems. During this decade, some 450,000 farmers lost their farms, and farm income dropped from $16 billion to $11 billion. By 1932, farm income had dropped another $6 billion. In the twelve years between 1920 and 1932, the price of a bushel of wheat fell from $1.82 to 38 cents. Cotton went from 16 to 6 cents a pound. Those farmers who were able to hold onto their farms did so under the weight of heavy mortgages. The collapse of farm values affected farmers' mortgage holders as well as the farmers themselves.

By the time the Roosevelt administration took office in March 1933, most Americans realized that drastic action was required to alter the course of the depression. Within a few days of taking office, Roosevelt had called Congress into session, taken the United States off the gold standard, ordered banks to reopen, and begun a program of insuring bank deposits up to $5,000. Roosevelt also asked Congress to pass sweeping social and economic legislation, including the Agricultural Adjustment Act (AAA).

The fundamental purpose of the AAA was to reduce agricultural surplus by reducing production, thus restoring agricultural prices to a prewar parity level. Seven basic agricultural commodities were targeted by the act: cotton, wheat, corn, rice, tobacco, hogs, and milk. Farmers were paid to stop producing. Their compensation came from excise taxes (processing and floor stocks taxes) levied on the processors of those seven commodities. The AAA became law on May 12, 1933.

The Hoosac Mills Corporation, which operated cotton manufacturing plants in New Bedford, Taunton, and North Adams, Massachusetts, was one of the many companies during the depression that fell on hard times. On October 7, 1933, the Franklin Process Company filed suit in the U.S. District Court for the District of Massachusetts seeking appointment of a receiver in bankruptcy for Hoosac Mills. Ten days later, the court issued a decree appointing William M. Butler and James A. McDonough receivers. They issued a notice to all creditors to prove their claims against Hoosac Mills. Pursuant to that notice, on February 12, 1934, Joseph P. Carney, Collector of Internal Revenue for the district of Massachusetts, filed a claim for unpaid cotton processing and floor stocks taxes due from the Corporation pursuant to the AAA. Carney sought $43,486.09 plus a penalty of $286.30 in processing tax and $37,466.37 in floor stocks tax. The amount of the tax was computed based on regulations promulgated by the secretary of agriculture, as provided for by the AAA.

In their "First Report on Claims to the District Court," Butler and McDonough recommended that the government's claim be disallowed because they believed the AAA to be unconstitutional. However, the district court ruled that the processing and floor stocks taxes imposed by the AAA were constitutional and allowed the U.S. claim. The Court of Appeals for the First Circuit reversed, holding that the imposition and application of the processing and floor stocks taxes was beyond Congress's powers and an interference with the rights reserved to the states under the Tenth Amendment. The Supreme Court granted the U.S. petition for a writ of certiorari.

HIGHLIGHTS OF SUPREME COURT ARGUMENTS

BRIEF FOR THE UNITED STATES

◆ The taxes levied under the AAA are permitted by the power granted to Congress by the Constitution to lay and collect taxes. The processing tax is an excise on a particular use of a commodity. The floor stocks tax adjustment is a levy on the holding of manufactured goods for a particular purpose, a type of imposition that this court already has held to be a constitutional excise tax. Both taxes operate uniformly throughout the United States.

◆ There is no delegation of legislative authority with respect to the rate of the tax. Rates are fixed by a mathematical formula devised by Congress. Furthermore, Congress has expressly ratified the assessment and collection of these taxes.

◆ The taxes do not violate the Fifth Amendment because the taxing provisions of the AAA have a reasonable relation to the raising of revenue.

◆ The determination of what is for the general welfare is a matter for Congress to decide and this Court should not substitute its judgment for that of Congress.

◆ Since the taxes are imposed to provide for the general welfare, they also satisfy the requirement of public purpose.

◆ The AAA does not involve an attempt by Congress to exercise, contrary to the Tenth Amendment, powers reserved to the states or to the people.

AMICUS CURIAE BRIEFS SUPPORTING THE UNITED STATES

League for Economic Equality; American Farm Bureau Federation; Farmers National Grain Corporation; Texas Agricultural Association; National Beet Growers Association.

BRIEF FOR BUTLER

◆ Congress exceeded its limited powers and trespassed on the powers reserved to the states and to the people in authorizing and applying the taxes under the AAA. The connection between the AAA and commerce is tenuous because Congress is actually seeking to reduce the amount of agricultural products that go into interstate commerce.

◆ The processing and floor stocks taxes violate the Fifth Amendment by taking property from one class without compensation and giving to another class.

◆ Congress may not, under the guise of the taxing power, assert a power not delegated to it by the Constitution.

◆ The floor stocks taxes are direct taxes and are therefore void because they are not apportioned among the several states.

◆ The AAA impermissibly delegates legislative power to the secretary of agriculture.

AMICUS CURIAE BRIEFS SUPPORTING BUTLER

Joint brief of Hygrade Food Products Corporation, National Biscuit Company and P. Lorillard Company; National Association of Cotton Manufacturers; joint brief of Kingman Brewster and James Ivins; joint brief of the American Nut Company, General Candy Corporation, Peanut Specialty Company, Fisher Nut Company, The Warfield Company, Millard United Company, Nutrine Candy Company, Schutter-Johnson Candy Company, Williamson Candy Corporation and Purchasing Service Corporation; joint brief of twenty-four companies that had filed suits in federal district courts seeking restraining orders against the United States; Farmers' Independence Council of America; joint brief of General Mills, Inc., Pillsbury Flour Mills Co., Commander Larabee Corp, Russell Miller Milling Co., and International Milling Co.

SUPREME COURT DECISION: 6–3

ROBERTS, J.

... At the outset the United States contends that the respondents [Butler and McDonough] have no standing to question the validity of the tax.... It is said that what the respondents are endeavoring to do is to challenge the intended use of the money pursuant to Congressional appropriation when, by confession, that money will have become the property of the government and the taxpayer will no longer have any interest in it. *Massachusetts v. Mellon,* 262 U.S. 447 [(1923)], is claimed to foreclose litigation by the respondents or other taxpayers, as such, looking to restraint of the expenditure of government funds. That case might be an authority in the petitioners' favor if we were here concerned merely with a suit by a taxpayer to restrain the expenditure of the public moneys.... But here the respondents who are called upon to pay moneys as taxes, resist the exaction as a step in an unauthorized plan. This circumstance clearly distinguishes the case....

The tax can only be sustained by ignoring the avowed purpose and operation of the act, and holding it a measure merely laying an excise upon processors to raise revenue for the support of government. Beyond cavil the sole object of the legislation is to restore the purchasing power of agricultural products to a parity with that prevailing in an earlier day; to take money from the processor and bestow it upon farmers who will reduce their acreage for the accomplishment of the proposed end, and, meanwhile, to aid these farmers during the period required to bring the prices of their crops to the desired level.

The tax plays an indispensable part in the plan of regulation....

The statute not only avows an aim foreign to the procurement of revenue for the support of government, but by its operation shows the exaction laid upon processors to be the necessary means for the intended control of agricultural production....

It is inaccurate and misleading to speak of the exaction from processors prescribed by the challenged act as a tax, or to say that as a tax it is subject to no infirmity. A tax, in the general understanding of the term, and as used in the Constitution, signifies an exaction for the support of the government. The word has never been thought to connote the expropriation of money from one group for the benefit of another. We may concede that the latter sort of imposition is constitutional when imposed to effectuate regulation of a matter in which both groups are interested and in respect of which there is a power of legislative regulation. But manifestly no justification for it can be found unless as an integral part of such regulation. The exaction cannot be wrested out of its setting, denominated an excise for raising revenue, and legalized by ignoring its purpose as a mere instrumentality for bringing about a desired end....

We conclude that the act is one regulating agricultural production; that the tax is a mere incident of such regulation; and that the respondents have standing to challenge the legality of the exaction....

The government asserts that even if

the respondents may question the propriety of the appropriation embodied in the statute, their attack must fail because article 1, § 8 of the Constitution, authorizes the contemplated expenditure of the funds raised by the tax. This contention presents the great and the controlling question in the case....

There should be no misunderstanding as to the function of this court in such a case. It is sometimes said that the court assumes a power to overrule or control the action of the people's representatives. This is a misconception. The Constitution is the supreme law of the land ordained and established by the people. All legislation must conform to the principles it lays down. When an act of Congress is appropriately challenged in the courts as not conforming to the constitutional mandate, the judicial branch of the government has only one duty; to lay the article of the Constitution which is invoked beside the statute which is challenged and to decide whether the latter squares with the former. All the court does, or can do, is to announce its considered judgment upon the question. The only power it has, if such it may be called, is the power of judgment. This court neither approves nor condemns any legislative policy. Its delicate and difficult office is to ascertain and declare whether the legislation is in accordance with, or in contravention of, the provisions of the Constitution; and, having done that, its duty ends.

The question is not what power the federal government ought to have, but what powers in fact have been given by the people. It hardly seems necessary to reiterate that ours is a dual form of government; that in every state there are two governments; the state and the United States. Each state has all governmental powers save such as the people, by their Constitution, have conferred upon the United States, denied to the states, or reserved to themselves. The federal union is a government of delegated powers. It has only such as are expressly conferred upon it and such as are reasonably to be implied from those granted. In this respect we differ radically from nations where all legislative power, without restriction or limitation, is vested in a parliament or other legislative body subject to no restrictions except the discretion of its members....

The Congress is expressly empowered to lay taxes to provide for the general welfare. Funds in the Treasury as a result of taxation may be expended only through appropriation. Article 1, § 9, cl. 7. They can never accomplish the objects for which they were collected, unless the power to appropriate is as broad as the power to tax. The necessary implication from the terms of the grant is that the public funds may be appropriated "to provide for the general welfare of the United States." These words cannot be meaningless, else they would not have been used. The conclusion must be that they were intended to limit and define the granted power to raise and to expend money. How shall they be construed to effectuate the intent of the instrument?

Since the foundation of the nation, sharp differences of opinion have persisted as to the true interpretation of the phrase. Madison asserted it amounted to no more than a reference to the other powers enumerated in the subsequent clauses of the same section; that, as the United States is a government of limited and enumerated powers, the grant of power to tax and spend for the general national welfare must be confined to the enumerated legislative fields committed to the Congress. In this view the phrase is mere tautology, for taxation and appropriation are or may be necessary incidents of the exercise of any of the enumerated legislative powers. Hamilton, on the other hand, maintained the clause confers a power separate and distinct from those later enumerated, is not restricted in meaning by the grant of them, and Congress consequently has a substantive power to tax and to appropriate, limited only by the requirement that it shall be exercised to provide for the general welfare of the United States. Each contention has had the support of those whose views are entitled to weight....

But the adoption of the broader construction leaves the power to spend subject to limitations....

We are not now required to ascertain the scope of the phrase "general welfare of the United States" or to determine whether an appropriation in aid of agriculture falls within it. Wholly apart from that question, another principle embedded in our Constitution prohibits the enforcement of the Agricultural Adjustment Act. The act invades the reserved rights of the states. It is a statutory plan to regulate and control agricultural production, a matter beyond the powers delegated to the federal government. The tax, the appropriation of the funds raised, and the direction for their disbursement, are but parts of the plan. They are but means to an unconstitutional end.

From the accepted doctrine that the United States is a government of delegated powers, it follows that those not expressly granted, or reasonably to be implied from such as are conferred, are reserved to the states or to the people. To forestall any suggestion to the contrary, the Tenth Amendment was adopted. The same proposition, otherwise stated, is that powers not granted are prohibited. None to regulate agricultural production is given, and therefore legislation by Congress for that purpose is forbidden.

It is an established principle that the attainment of a prohibited end may not be accomplished under the pretext of the exertion of powers which are granted....

The power of taxation, which is expressly granted, may, of course, be adopted as a means to carry into operation another power also expressly granted. But resort to the taxing power to effectuate an end which is not legitimate, not within the scope of the Constitution, is obviously inadmissible....

If the taxing power may not be used as the instrument to enforce a regulation of matters of state concern with respect to which the Congress has no authority to interfere, may it, as in the present case, be employed to raise the money necessary to purchase a compliance which the Congress is powerless to command? The government asserts that whatever might be said against the validity of the plan, if compulsory, it is constitutionally sound because the end is accomplished by voluntary co-operation. There are two sufficient answers to the contention. The regulation is not in fact voluntary. The farmer, of course, may refuse to comply, but the price of such refusal is the loss of benefits. The amount offered is intended to be sufficient to exert pressure on him to agree to the proposed regulation....

But if the plan were one for purely voluntary co-operation it would stand no better so far as federal power is concerned. At best, it is a scheme for purchasing with federal funds submission to federal regulation of a subject reserved to the states....

Congress has no power to enforce its commands on the farmer to the ends sought by the Agricultural Adjustment Act. It must follow that it may not indirectly accomplish those ends by taxing and spending to purchase compliance. The Constitution and the entire plan of our government negative any such use of the power to tax and to spend as the act undertakes to authorize. It does not help to declare that local conditions throughout the nation have created a situation of national concern; for this is but to say that whenever there is a widespread similarity of local conditions, Congress may ignore constitutional limitations upon its own powers and usurp those reserved to the states. If, in lieu of compulsory regulation of subjects within the states' reserved jurisdiction, which is prohibited, the Congress could invoke the taxing and spending power as a means to accomplish the same end, clause 1 of section 8 of article 1 would become the instrument for total subversion of the governmental powers reserved to the individual states.

If the act before us is a proper exercise of the federal taxing power, evidently the regulation of all industry throughout the United States may be accomplished by similar exercises of the same power. It would be possible to exact money from one branch of an industry and pay it to another branch in every field of activity which lies within the province of the states. The mere threat of such a procedure might well induce the surrender of rights and the compliance with federal regulation as the price of continuance in business....

The expressions of the framers of the Constitution, the decisions of this court interpreting that instrument and the writings of great commentators will be searched in vain for any suggestion that there exists in the clause under discussion or elsewhere in the Constitution, the authority whereby every provision and every fair implication from that instrument may be subverted, the independence of the individual states obliterated, and the United States converted into a central government exercising uncontrolled police power in every state of the Union, superseding all local control or regulation of the affairs or concerns of the states....

The judgment is affirmed.

STONE, BRANDEIS, AND CARDOZO, J.J., DISSENTING

... The present stress of widely held and strongly expressed differences of opinion of the wisdom of the Agricultural Adjustment Act makes it important, in the interest of clear thinking and sound result, to emphasize at the outset certain propositions which should have controlling influence in determining the validity of the act. They are:

1. The power of courts to declare a statute unconstitutional is subject to two guiding principles of decision which ought never to be absent from judicial consciousness. One is that courts are concerned only with the power to enact statutes, not with their wisdom. The other is that while unconstitutional exercise of power by the executive and legislative branches of the government

is subject to judicial restraint, the only check upon our own exercise of power is our own sense of self-restraint. For the removal of unwise laws from the statute books appeal lies, not to the courts, but to the ballot and to the processes of democratic government.

2. The constitutional power of Congress to levy an excise tax upon the processing of agricultural products is not questioned. The present levy is held invalid, not for any want of power in Congress to lay such a tax to defray public expenditures, including those for the general welfare, but because the use to which its proceeds are put is disapproved.

3. As the present depressed state of agriculture is nation wide in its extent and effects, there is no basis for saying that the expenditure of public money in aid of farmers is not within the specifically granted power of Congress to levy taxes to "provide for the ... general welfare." The opinion of the Court does not declare otherwise.

4. No question of a variable tax fixed from time to time by fiat of the Secretary of Agriculture, or of unauthorized delegation of legislative power, is now presented. The schedule of rates imposed by the secretary in accordance with the original command of Congress has since been specifically adopted and confirmed by act of Congress, which has declared that it shall be the lawful tax....

It is with these preliminary and hardly controverted matters in mind that we should direct our attention to the pivot on which the decision of the Court is made to turn. It is that a levy unquestionably within the taxing power of Congress may be treated as invalid because it is a step in a plan to regulate agricultural production and is thus a forbidden infringement of state power....

The Constitution requires that public funds shall be spent for a defined purpose, the promotion of the general welfare. Their expenditure usually involves payment on terms which will insure use by the selected recipients within the limits of the constitutional purpose. Expenditures would fail of their purpose and thus lose their constitutional sanction if the terms of payment were not such that by their influence on the action of the recipients the permitted end would be attained. The power of Congress to spend is inseparable from persuasion to action over which Congress has no legislative control....

These effects upon individual action, which are but incidents of the authorized expenditure of government money, are pronounced to be themselves a limitation upon the granted power, and so the time-honored principle of constitutional interpretation that the granted power includes all those which are incident to it is reversed. "Let the end be legitimate," said the great Chief Justice, "let it be within the scope of the constitution, and all means which are appropriate, which are plainly adapted to that end, which are not prohibited, but consist with the letter and spirit of the constitution, are constitutional." *McCulloch v. Maryland.* This cardinal guide to constitutional exposition must now be rephrased so far as the spending power of the federal government is concerned. Let the expenditure be to promote the general welfare, still if it is needful in order to insure its use for the intended purpose to influence any action which Congress cannot command because within the sphere of state government, the expenditure is unconstitutional. And taxes otherwise lawfully levied are like-wise unconstitutional if they are appropriated to the expenditure whose incident is condemned....

That the governmental power of the purse is a great one is not now for the first time announced....

The suggestion that it must now be curtailed by judicial fiat because it may be abused by unwise use hardly rises to the dignity of argument. So may judicial power be abused....

A tortured construction of the Constitution is not to be justified by recourse to extreme examples of reckless congressional spending which might occur if courts could not prevent—expenditures which, even if they could be thought to effect any national purpose, would be possible only by action of a legislature lost to all sense of public responsibility. Such suppositions are addressed to the mind accustomed to believe that it is the business of courts to sit in judgment on the wisdom of legislative action. Courts are not the only agency of government that must be assumed to have capacity to govern. Congress and the courts both unhappily may falter or be mistaken in the performance of their constitutional duty....

QUESTIONS

1. In Justice Robert's opinion in *Butler*, which theory of limitations on congressional spending power appears to prevail: James Madison's view that the power to tax and spend for the general welfare is strictly limited to implementing those delegated legislative powers external to Article I, section 8, clause 1; or Alexander Hamilton's view that the power to tax and spend is merely limited by the general welfare language inherent in Article I, section 8, clause 1? What is the practical policy significance of the difference between these two views? Does Roberts somehow arrive at Madisonian conclusions on Hamiltonian grounds?

2. Justice Stone's statement in his *Butler* dissent—"... while unconstitutional exercise of power by the executive and legislative branches of the government is subject to judicial restraint, the only check upon our own exercise of power is our own sense of self-restraint..."—is a cogent formulation of the theory of judicial self-restraint. Did the majority or the dissenters in *Butler* show greater judicial self-restraint?

3. The League for Economic Equality argued in its *amicus curiae* brief that

   as far as constitutional law is concerned, only moderate reliance should be placed on judicial precedents, and that the Constitution itself should, at any given time, be matched against the problems of that time, with a view to ascertaining whether it is not susceptible of a reasonable interpretation rendering it equal to those prob-

lems.... No less in the realm of constitutional law than in that of politics or that of economics must realism prevail, and the Constitution
must be put to the test of pragmatism in every day and age of the
life of our country.

What are the strengths and weaknesses of such a theory of constitutional interpretation? Is it inevitable that such a theory would
arise in the context of a crisis the magnitude of the Great
Depression?

4. Counsel for Butler concluded his brief with the following observation:

> The form of government which may be erected upon the two words
> "general welfare," if this Act is approved, is now outlined: A central
> government with plenary and unlimited power, supreme in every
> sphere over the States and the people, with power to take property
> in any amount from any class for any purposes without accountabil-
> ity to the people or the restraints of a bill of rights; a central govern-
> ment in which the executive dominates, lays taxes, decides how
> they shall be spent and in short does what he desires by virtue of
> an unlimited power to tax and to purchase, while the representa-
> tives of the people are expected to give compliant approval to what
> the executive has done, and the judiciary is to be bound by decision
> made by subordinate executives.

If the justices had upheld the constitutionality of the AAA in
Butler, would the Supreme Court for all practical purposes have
conceded that Congress is the superior branch of government, entitled to construe the Constitution in light of contemporary exigencies?

COMMENT

United States v. Butler was handed down on January 6, 1936. It was the fifth in a
series of seven Supreme Court decisions, commencing with *Panama Refining
Company v. Ryan*, 293 U.S. 388 (1935) and ending with *Ashton v. Cameron
County District*, 298 U.S. 513 (1936), that gutted the First New Deal. On March 9,
1937, President Franklin D. Roosevelt delivered an historic radio "fireside
chat" to the nation. He declared that Americans had "reached the point as a
nation where we must take action to save the Constitution from the Court and
the Court from itself." The president criticized the Court's assumption of
power "to pass on the wisdom of [Acts of Congress like the Agricultural
Adjustment Act]—and to approve or disapprove the public policy written into
these laws." Roosevelt said next: "This is not only my accusation, it is the
accusation of *most* distinguished Justices of the present Supreme Court."
(Emphasis added.)

THE GREAT DEPRESSION AND THE NEW DEAL

National Labor Relations Board v. Jones & Laughlin Steel Corp. 301 U.S. 1 (1937)

SETTING

Only two major statutes passed during the First New Deal were sustained by the Supreme Court. A 5–4 Court upheld the emergency monetary statutes of 1933, particularly Congress's nullification of gold clauses in public and private contracts in *The Gold Clause Cases*, 294 U.S. 240. The statute authorizing establishment of the Tennessee Valley Authority was upheld in a divided opinion, 8–1 and 5–4, in *Ashwander v. Tennessee Valley Authority*, 297 U.S. 288 (1936).

Following Supreme Court decisions declaring the core of the First New Deal unconstitutional, prospects seemed slim that other regulations designed to ameliorate the suffering of the Great Depression and to redress imbalances in power between employers and employees would survive judicial review. In June 1936, for example, the Court, by a 5–4 vote, struck down a 1933 New York minimum wage statute for women and minors. *Morehead v. New York ex rel. Tipaldo*, 298 U.S. 587 (1936). Adhering to its earlier ruling in *Adkins v. Children's Hospital*, 261 U.S. 525 (1923), the majority held that the New York statute violated the right to make contracts, held to be part of the liberty protected by the Due Process Clause of the Fourteenth Amendment.

By the time *Morehead* was handed down, however, a bipartisan consensus had emerged among national policymakers. These officials agreed that governmental power must be exercised to respond to the depressed economic conditions that were fueling dangerously unstable social conditions. The Supreme Court—dubbed "The Nine Old Men" by the press—was seen as an obstacle, and *Morehead* was soundly criticized by members of both political parties.

New Deal advocates, frustrated with the Court's treatment of economic reform legislation, began exploring options for circumventing judicial review of federal statutes. One option that was considered was legislation withdrawing appellate jurisdiction from federal courts over a range of cases involving economic regulation. Another option was constitutional amendments that would clear the way for New Deal measures. A third was a detailed analysis of ways Congress might redraft invalid statutes to satisfy the Court's majority. All such options contained legal or political pitfalls.

Franklin Roosevelt was reelected by a landslide in November 1936. The president received 27.8 million votes to Republican Alf Landon's 16.7 million. Democrats carried every state except Maine and Vermont, electing decisive majorities in both the U.S. House of Representatives and the Senate. Early the next year, President Roosevelt and his attorney general, Homer Cummings, without consulting other members of the cabinet or Congress, concluded that the problem lay with an obstructionist Court, rather than with the Constitution or laws.

At Cummings' suggestion, they devised a plan for reforming the entire federal judiciary, based on the claim that the justices were overworked by their crowded docket. Central to the plan was the proposal that the president could appoint an additional justice to the Supreme Court for each one who had served ten years and had not retired within six months of his seventieth birthday. If the plan had met with congressional approval, Roosevelt would have been authorized to appoint six additional justices.

The president announced what would come to be known as his "Court-Packing Plan" on February 5, 1937. He discussed it during his fireside chat radio address of March 9, 1937. Neither he nor his attorney general was prepared for the vitriolic response. The *New York Herald-Tribune*, for example, commented, "The paper shell of American constitutionalism would continue if President Roosevelt secured passage of the law he now demands. But it would be only a shell." Although congressional reform of lower federal court procedures did result from President Roosevelt's confrontation with the Court, his proposal to add justices to the Supreme Court died when the Senate Judiciary Committee on June 14, 1937, recommended congressional rejection of the bill as a "needless, futile and utterly dangerous abandonment of constitutional principle."

Although Roosevelt lost the court-packing battle, he won the New Deal war. On March 29, 1937, the Supreme Court capitulated on the issue of government economic regulations in *West Coast Hotel v. Parrish*, 300 U.S. 379. (See Chapter 6, pp. 836–846.) In *Parrish*, the Court upheld a Washington state minimum wage law for women over the West Coast Hotel's argument that the law violated liberty of contract. Chief Justice Hughes wrote for a five-vote majority: "... the violation alleged by those attacking minimum wage regulation for women is deprivation of freedom of contract. What is this freedom? The Constitution does not speak of freedom of contracts." After *Parrish*, the Court gave increasing latitude to government economic regulation. One set of such regulations, a successor to the defunct National Industrial Recovery Act (NIRA), was in the works before the dramatic confrontation between Roosevelt and the Court.

Recall that the NIRA had been the centerpiece of the First Hundred Days. Over strong opposition from employer groups such as the National Association of Manufacturers (NAM) and the National Industrial Conference (NIC), organized labor successfully lobbied the Roosevelt administration to add § 7(a) to the NIRA. That section protected employees' right to organize and bargain collectively, free from "the interference, restraint, or coercion of employers of labor." Section 7(a) also outlawed yellow dog contracts. Having lost the political fight over § 7(a), employer groups attacked the "fair competition" required by the NIRA. Their goal was to blunt the effect of § 7(a) and thereby mitigate the potential for a shift in economic power to labor that NIRA created. Employers drafted codes in ways that perpetuated "open shops" and kept union organizers out of their factories. Their efforts effectively thwarted unionization drives in the automobile, newspaper, and steel industries. Early attempts to equalize power between employers and employees were scuttled judicially in 1935 when the Supreme Court overturned the NIRA in *Schechter Poultry Corp. v. United States*.

Even before *Schechter* was handed down, Senator Robert F. Wagner (D-NY) was leading a congressional initiative to resuscitate § 7(a) of the NIRA in an effort to obviate industrial strife. Senator Wagner introduced a labor relations bill that essentially reproduced the provisions of § 7(a) and strengthened the enforcement powers of the National Labor Relations Board (NLRB), which originally had been created in June 1934 under the NIRA. The Wagner bill grounded the NLRB's constitutional authority in carefully defined congressional commerce power. Wagner overcame lobbying efforts by the NAM to weaken the bill, and despite the tepid support of the Roosevelt administration—which sought to walk a line between business and labor—the Senate approved Wagner's proposal on May 16, 1935.

Following the May 27, 1935, *Schechter* decision's narrow reading of the Commerce Clause, Senator Wagner refined the bill's key terms before it was reported out of the House Labor Committee. The House committee defined commerce as "trade, traffic, commerce, transportation, or communication among the several States." Affecting commerce was defined as "in commerce, or burdening or obstructing commerce or the free flow of commerce, or having led to or tending to lead to a labor dispute burdening or obstructing commerce or the free flow of commerce." The House passed the Wagner Act on June 18, 1935. President Roosevelt signed it into law on July 5.

Officially known as the National Labor Relations Act (NLRA), the Wagner Act recognized the right of employees to organize and to bargain collectively through representatives of their own choosing. It created a new National Labor Relations Board, prescribed its organization, and defined "unfair labor practices." The revived NLRB was given authority to prevent unfair labor practices affecting commerce and received broad powers of investigation to carry out its mandate. The NLRB was also authorized to hold representative elections in companies whose workers petitioned for union elections and to certify the union selected by the majority of employees as their exclusive bargaining agent.

In January 1936, the Beaver Valley Lodge No. 200, Amalgamated Association of Iron, Steel, and Tin Workers of North America, filed a written charge against the Jones & Laughlin Steel Corporation, a Pennsylvania corporation, with the director of the sixth region of the NLRB. Jones & Laughlin, together with its nineteen subsidiaries, was the nation's fourth largest manufacturer and distributor of steel, pig iron, ores, and other materials. It employed over 22,000 persons in its two plants in Pittsburgh and Aliquippa, Pennsylvania. Approximately 75 per cent of Jones & Laughlin's products were shipped out of Pennsylvania to its subsidiaries in various parts of the country.

The Aliquippa works had been the site of union organizing efforts since 1933. Jones & Laughlin's previous antiunion tactics, which included forming a company union and intimidating Amalgamated union organizers, had led to a complaint being filed with the National Steel Labor Relations Board in October 1934. Union members who testified at the subsequent hearing required state police protection from Aliquippa police employed as security guards by Jones & Laughlin. Tom M. Girdler, assistant superintendent of the Aliquippa works, described life in that company town as a "benevolent dictatorship," but to union organizers, Aliquippa was known as "little Siberia."

The January 1936 Amalgamated charge alleged that Jones & Laughlin engaged in unfair labor practices affecting commerce by discouraging labor union membership at its Aliquippa works in two ways: interfering with, coercing, and restraining employees in their self-organization and free choice of representatives for purposes of collective bargaining or other aid or protection, and discharging twelve employees and demoting one other, all of whom were active union members. Jones & Laughlin admitted the discharges and demotion, but said that they had occurred because of inefficiency and violation of company rules. Jones & Laughlin also contended that the National Labor Relations Act was unconstitutional on several grounds, and that the company's activities were entirely intrastate and not subject to regulation by Congress or the NLRB.

After taking evidence at hearings, the NLRB sustained the union's charge. It found that the acts of Jones & Laughlin tended to cause labor disputes that burdened and obstructed the free flow of commerce. The NLRB ordered Jones & Laughlin to reinstate with back pay the ten employees whose dismissal led to the proceeding, to post notices that it would not discharge or discriminate against union membership, and to cease and desist from such discrimination and coercion. When Jones & Laughlin failed to comply, the NLRB petitioned the Court of Appeals for the Fifth Circuit for an enforcement order.

The Fifth Circuit Court of Appeals refused to enforce the NLRB's order, holding that the "Constitution does not vest in the federal government the power to regulate the relations as such of employer and employee in production or manufacturing." The NLRB petitioned the Supreme Court for a writ of certiorari.

HIGHLIGHTS OF SUPREME COURT ARGUMENTS

BRIEF FOR THE NLRB

◆ The NLRA is a valid exercise of Congress's commerce power, since its purpose is to prevent the kind of industrial strife that has been a recurrent problem in American history. A famous example was the steel strike of 1919–1920, which closed plants in more than seven states and affected more than 350,000 workers. Data compiled by NLRB economists demonstrate the impact of such strife in the steel and other industries on the American economy.

◆ Congress's action under the NLRA is narrow: rather than attempting to eliminate the causes of strife in all enterprises, it focuses on enterprises that affect interstate commerce. Past federal actions, ranging from mediation and conciliation, to dispatching troops to the area of a dispute, have been upheld.

◆ If Congress and the executive have the power to intervene to resolve industrial strife that affects commerce when it occurs, Congress has the power to prevent its occurrence.

◆ As to the extent of Congress's power to prevent industrial strife, the NLRA goes no further than has already been recognized as within Congress's authority. First, case law recognizes Congress's power over industrial strife in the manufacturing, producing, or processing divisions of an enterprise if the intent of a dispute is to affect interstate commerce. Second, case law recognizes the principle that an industrial dispute having the effect of substantially burdening commerce is within the control of Congress. Finally, case law indicates that Congress has the power to control recurring evils which in their totality constitutes a burden on interstate commerce. Since the NLRA does not go beyond these recognized powers, the only issue in the case is whether the NLRA applies constitutionally to Jones & Laughlin Corporation.

◆ The activities of Jones & Laughlin have a substantial impact on interstate commerce. The company is completely integrated economically, and about one hundred industries look to it for steel. It has warehouses throughout the country as part of its nationwide distribution system, and draws its raw materials from well-defined paths of commerce.

BRIEF FOR JONES & LAUGHLIN

◆ The NLRA is a regulation of labor relations, not of interstate commerce, and hence is beyond Congress's power to enact. Virtually every provision of the act expresses Congress's interest in establishing and promoting labor organizations. Regulation of employment relations is a power reserved to the states under the Tenth Amendment. The commerce clause cannot be used as a pretext for interfering with powers reserved to the states.

◆ Even if held to be a regulation of commerce, the NLRA is unconstitutional because it regulates production, which is not part of commerce. A long line of cases has held that manufacturing and production activities are not part of interstate commerce, even though they might precede or follow the movement of materials interstate. Supreme Court cases have held that even though a corporation receives raw materials through interstate commerce, its production activities, including employment relations, are not thereby subjected to Congress's jurisdiction.

◆ Application of the NLRA in this case violates Article III, section 2, of the Constitution and the Fifth and Seventh Amendments. The NLRB assumed that it had to show only a connection between strikes and the stoppage of commerce to justify its decision in this case. No strike or labor dispute existed, however, so the NLRB lacked authority to hear the case. The only dispute in the case was between the individual workers and Jones & Laughlin, over which the act gave jurisdiction to the NLRB. Depriving constitutional courts of their authority to try constitutional and jurisdictional issues violates Article III, section 2, of the Constitution.

◆ Allowing the NLRB to enter a money judgment without affording the company the benefit of a jury trial also violates the Seventh Amendment.

◆ The underlying philosophy of the NLRA is a threat to the corporation's management of its own business. The act sets up the NLRB as a higher court over the company's employment office. It gives the majority of employees an arbitrary and unfair power over the minority. The eventual impact of the NLRA will be to seriously disturb the discipline and morale of Jones & Laughlin's employees.

SUPREME COURT DECISION: 5–4

HUGHES, C.J.

… Contesting the ruling of the [National Labor Relations] Board, the respondent argues (1) that the act is in reality a regulation of labor relations and not of interstate commerce; (2) that the act can have no application to the respondent's relations with its production employees because they are not subject to regulation by the federal government; and (3) that the provisions of the act violate[s] … the Fifth … Amendment of the Constitution of the United States….

We turn to the questions of law which respondent urges in contesting the validity and application of the act.

First. The Scope of the Act.—The act is challenged in its entirety as an attempt to regulate all industry, thus invading the reserved powers of the States over their local concerns. It is asserted that the references in the act to interstate and foreign commerce are colorable at best; that the act is not a true regulation of such commerce or of matters which directly affect it, but on the contrary has the fundamental object of placing under the compulsory super-

vision of the federal government all industrial labor relations within the nation. The argument seeks support in the broad words of the preamble and in the sweep of the provisions of the act, and it is further insisted that its legislative history shows an essential universal purpose in the light of which its scope cannot be limited by either construction or by the application of the separability clause.

If this conception of terms, intent and consequent inseparability were sound, the act would necessarily fall by reason of the limitation upon the federal power which inheres in the constitutional grant, as well as because of the explicit reservation of the Tenth Amendment. *Schechter Corporation v. United States.* The authority of the federal government may not be pushed to such an extreme as to destroy the distinction, which the commerce clause itself establishes, between commerce "among the several States" and the internal concerns of a state. That distinction between what is national and what is local in the activities of commerce is vital to the maintenance of our federal system.

But we are not at liberty to deny effect to specific provisions, which Congress has constitutional power to enact, by superimposing upon them inferences from general legislative declarations of an ambiguous character, even if found in the same statute. The cardinal principle of statutory construction is to save and not to destroy. We have repeatedly held that as between two possible interpretations of a statute, by one of which it would be unconstitutional and by the other valid, our plain duty is to adopt that which will save the act....

We think it clear that the National Labor Relations Act may be construed so as to operate within the sphere of constitutional authority....

There can be no question that the commerce ... contemplated by the act ... is interstate and foreign commerce in the constitutional sense....

The grant of authority to the Board does not purport to extend to the relationship between all industrial employees and employers. Its terms do not impose collective bargaining upon all industry regardless of effects upon interstate or foreign commerce. It purports to reach only what may be deemed to burden or obstruct that commerce and, thus qualified, it must be construed as contemplating the exercise of control within constitutional bounds. It is a familiar principle that acts which directly burden or obstruct interstate or foreign commerce, or its free flow, are within the reach of the congressional power. Acts having that effect are not rendered immune because they grow out of labor disputes.... It is the effect upon commerce, not the source of the injury, which is the criterion....

Second. The Unfair Labor Practices in Question.—...

[I]n its present application, the statute goes no further than to safeguard the right of employees to self-organization and to select representatives of their own choosing for collective bargaining or other mutual protection without restraint or coercion by their employer.

That is a fundamental right. Employees have as clear a right to organize and select their representatives for lawful purposes as the respondent has to organize its business and select its own officers and agents. Discrimination and coercion to prevent the free exercise of the right of employees to self-organization and representation is a proper subject for condemnation by competent legislative authority. Long ago we stated the reason for labor organizations. We said that they were organized out of the necessities of the situation; that a single employee was helpless in dealing with an employer; that he was dependent ordinarily on his daily wage for the maintenance of himself and family; that, if the employer refused to pay him the wages that he thought fair, he was nevertheless unable to leave the employ and resist arbitrary and unfair treatment; that union was essential to give laborers opportunity to deal on an equality with their employer.... Fully recognizing the legality of collective action on the part of employees in order to safeguard their proper interests, we said that Congress was not required to ignore this right but could safeguard it. Congress could seek to make appropriate collective action of employees an instrument of peace rather than of strife. We said that such collective action would be a mockery if representation were made futile by interference with freedom of choice....

Third. The application of the Act to Employees Engaged in Production.—The Principle Involved.—Respondent says that, whatever may be said of employees engaged in interstate commerce, the industrial relations and activities in the manufacturing department of respondent's enterprise are not subject to federal regulation. The argument rests upon the proposition that manufacturing in itself is not commerce....

The congressional authority to protect interstate commerce from burdens and obstructions is not limited to transactions which can be deemed to be an essential part of a "flow" of interstate or foreign commerce. Burdens and obstructions may be due to injurious action springing from other sources. The fundamental principle is that the power to regulate commerce is the power to enact "all appropriate legislation" for its "protection or advancement." *The Daniel Ball*, 10 Wall[ace] 557 [(1871)]. Although activities may be intrastate in character when separately considered, if they have such a close and substantial relation to interstate commerce that their control is essential or appropriate to protect that commerce from burdens and obstructions, Congress cannot be denied the power to exercise that control. *Schechter Corporation v. United States*. Undoubtedly the scope of this power must be considered in the light of our dual system of government and may not be extended so as to embrace effects upon interstate commerce so indirect and remote that to embrace them, in view of our complex society, would effectually obliterate the distinction between what is national and what is local and create a completely centralized government. Id. The question is necessarily one of degree....

It is thus apparent that the fact that the employees here concerned were engaged in production is not determinative. The question remains as to the effect upon interstate commerce of the labor practice involved. In the *Schechter* Case, we found that the effect there was so remote as to be beyond the federal power. To find "immediacy or directness" there was to find it "almost everywhere," a result inconsistent with the maintenance of our federal system.... [This case is] not controlling here.

Fourth. Effects of the Unfair Labor Practice in Respondent's Enterprise.—Giving full weight to respondent's contention with respect to a break in the complete continuity of the "stream of commerce" by reason of respondent's manufacturing operations, the fact remains that the stoppage of those operations by industrial strife would have a most serious effect upon interstate commerce. In view of respondent's far-flung activities, it is idle to say that the effect would be indirect or remote. It is obvious that it would be immediate and might be catastrophic. We are asked to shut our eyes to the plainest facts of our national life and to deal with the question of direct and indirect effects in an intellectual vacuum. Because there may be but indirect and remote effects upon interstate commerce in connection with a host of local enterprises throughout the country, it does not follow that other industrial activities do not have such a close and intimate relation to interstate commerce as to make the presence of industrial strife a matter of the most urgent national concern. When industries organize themselves on a national scale, making their relation to interstate commerce the dominant factor in their activities, how can it be maintained that their industrial labor relations constitute a forbidden field into which Congress may not enter when it is necessary to protect interstate commerce from the paralyzing consequences of industrial war?...

Fifth. The Means Which the Act Employs.—Questions under the Due Process Clause and Other Constitutional Restrictions.—Respondent asserts its right to conduct its business in an orderly manner without being subjected to arbitrary restraints. What we have said points to the fallacy in the argument. Employees have their correlative right to organize for the purpose of securing the redress of grievances and to promote agreements with employers relating to rates of pay and conditions of work.... Restraint for the purpose of preventing an unjust interference with that right cannot be considered arbitrary or capricious....

The act has been criticized as one-sided in its application; that it subjects the employer to supervision and restraint and leaves untouched the abuses for which employees may be responsible; that it fails to provide a more comprehensive plan,—with better assurances of fairness to both sides and with increased chances of success in bringing about, if not compelling, equitable solutions of industrial disputes affecting interstate commerce. But we are dealing with the power of Congress, not with a particular policy or with the extent to which policy should go. We have frequently said that the legislative authority, exerted within its proper field, need not embrace all the evils within its reach....

The procedural provisions of the act are assailed. But these provisions, as we construe them, do not offend against the constitutional requirements governing the creation and action of administrative bodies.... The act establishes standards to which the Board must conform. There must be complaint, notice and hearing. The Board must receive evidence and make findings. The findings as to the facts are to be conclusive, but only if supported by evidence. The order of the Board is subject to review by the designated court, and only when sustained by the court may the order be enforced. Upon that review all questions of the jurisdiction of the Board and the regularity of its proceedings, all questions of constitutional right or statutory authority are open to examination by the court. We construe the procedural provisions as affording adequate opportunity to secure judicial protection against arbitrary action in accordance with the well-settled rules applicable to administrative agencies set up by Congress to aid in the enforcement of valid legislation. It is not necessary to repeat these rules which have frequently been declared. None of them appears to have been transgressed in the instant case. Respondent was notified and heard. It had opportunity to meet the charge of unfair labor practices upon the merits, and by withdrawing from the hearing it declined to avail itself of that opportunity. The facts found by the Board support its order and the evidence supports the findings. Respondent has no just ground for complaint on this score....

Our conclusion is that the order of the Board was within its competency and that the act is valid as here applied. The judgment of the Circuit Court of

Appeals is reversed and the cause is remanded for further proceedings in conformity with this opinion. It is so ordered.

Reversed and remanded.

MCREYNOLDS, VAN DEVANTER, SUTHERLAND, AND BUTLER, J.J., DISSENTING

… The Court as we think departs from well-established principles followed in *Schechter Poultry Corporation v. United States* and *Carter v. Carter Coal Co.*, 298 U.S. 238 (1936)….

The argument in support of the [National Labor Relations] Board affirms: "Thus the validity of any specific application of the preventive measures of this Act depends upon whether industrial strife resulting from the practices in the particular enterprise under consideration would be of the character which Federal power could control if it occurred. If strife in that enterprise could be controlled, certainly it could be prevented."

Manifestly that view of congressional power would extend it into almost every field of human industry.

In *Schechter*'s Case we said: "In determining how far the federal government may go in controlling intrastate transactions upon the ground that they 'affect' interstate commerce, there is a necessary and well-established distinction between direct and indirect effects. The precise line can be drawn only as individual cases arise, but the distinction is clear in principle…. But where the effect of intrastate transactions upon interstate commerce is merely indirect, such transactions remain within the domain of state power. If the commerce clause were construed to reach all enterprises and transactions which could be said to

have an indirect effect upon interstate commerce, the federal authority would embrace practically all the activities of the people, and the authority of the state over its domestic concerns would exist only by sufferance of the federal government. Indeed, on such a theory, even the development of the state's commercial facilities would be subject to federal control."…

Any effect on interstate commerce by the discharge of employees shown here would be indirect and remote in the highest degree, as consideration of the facts will show. In [this case] ten men out of ten thousand were discharged[.]… The immediate effect in the factor may be to create discontent among all those employed and a strike may follow, which, in turn, may result in reducing production, which ultimately may reduce the volume of goods moving in interstate commerce. By this chain of indirect and progressively remote events we finally reach the evil with which it is said the legislation under consideration undertakes to deal. A more remote and indirect interference with interstate commerce or a more definite invasion of the powers reserved to the states is difficult, if not impossible, to imagine.

The Constitution still recognizes the existence of states with indestructible powers; the Tenth Amendment was supposed to put them beyond controversy….

That Congress has power by appropriate means, not prohibited by the Constitution, to prevent direct and material interference with the conduct of interstate commerce is settled doctrine. But the interference struck at must be direct and material, not some mere possibility contingent on wholly uncertain events; and there must be no impairment of rights guaranteed....

The right to contract is fundamental and includes the privilege of selecting those with whom one is willing to assume contractual relations. This right is unduly abridged by the act now upheld. A private owner is deprived of power to manage his own property by freely selecting those to whom his manufacturing operations are to be entrusted. We think this cannot lawfully be done in circumstances like those here disclosed.

It seems clear to us that Congress has transcended the powers granted.

QUESTIONS

1. The decision in *Jones & Laughlin* reads as though Chief Justice Hughes resolved the case on the basis of the Commerce Clause, yet the effect of the decision was to uphold Congress's delegation of power to the NLRB. Can the Commerce Clause issues be separated from delegation issues in the case? Are the two necessarily related?

2. How is the Tenth Amendment implicated in *Jones & Laughlin*?

3. The Pennsylvania labor dispute that gave rise to the litigation in *Jones & Laughlin* was by no means isolated. Severe industrial strife, perhaps the inevitable consequence of the prolonged economic depression that left industrial workers not much better off than farmers, broke out in other parts of the country as well within a year of the Court's decision in *Schechter*. From September 1936 to March 1937, more than 484,000 workers engaged in sit-down strikes, closing plants where over one million workers were employed. The height of the conflict came when General Motors workers shut down the Flint, Michigan, plant. President Roosevelt was able to persuade General Motors executives to meet with workers on February 11, 1937, to attempt to negotiate a settlement. Those negotiations resulted in General Motors recognizing the United Automobile Workers Union of the Congress of Industrial Workers (CIO). Oral argument in *Jones & Laughlin* began on February 9.

   Did the facts and political climate in which *Jones & Laughlin* was litigated before the Supreme Court make it a better vehicle for the government to defend Congress's wide-reaching powers under the NLRA than the facts surrounding *Schechter*? What other forces might explain the result in *Jones & Laughlin*?

4. *Jones & Laughlin* was handed down with four companion Wagner Act cases. All four upheld the act as applied to smaller companies whose activities did not so clearly involve interstate commerce: *N.L.R.B. v. Fruehauf Trailer Co.*, 301 U.S. 49; *N.L.R.B. v. Friedman-Harry Marks Clothing Co.*, 301 U.S. 58; *Associated Press v. N.L.R.B.*, 301 U.S. 103; and *Washington, Virginia & Maryland Coach Co. v. N.L.R.B.*, 301 U.S. 142.

Political scientist Richard C. Cortner wrote that, taken together, these five cases

> mark the end of the "old Constitution" which was composed largely of doctrines protective of property rights as defined by classical economic theory and which had been erected through the reshaping of constitutional law by the forces of industrialism following the Civil War.... The Wagner Act cases opened the floodgates of national power and henceforth the conflict over its exercise would generally be resolved in the legislative and administrative processes. (*The Wagner Act Cases* [Knoxville, TN: University of Tennessee Press, 1964], p. 188)

Was the constitutional transition that Cortner describes an inevitable consequence of America's economic integration? Of the Great Depression?

COMMENT

Within four years of the *Jones & Laughlin* decision the four *Jones & Laughlin* dissenters were no longer on the Court: Hugo Black replaced Willis Van Devanter in 1937; Stanley Reed succeeded George Sutherland in 1938; Frank Murphy filled Pierce Butler's seat in 1940; James F. Byrnes succeeded James McReynolds in 1941. During this same four-year period, Franklin D. Roosevelt also appointed successors to three of the *Jones & Laughlin* majority: Felix Frankfurter replaced Benjamin Cardozo (1939); William O. Douglas replaced Louis Brandeis (1939); and Harlan Fiske Stone, an associate justice since 1925, was elevated to Chief Justice succeeding Charles Evans Hughes (1941).

THE GREAT DEPRESSION AND THE NEW DEAL

Steward Machine Co. v. Davis
301 U.S. 548 (1937)

SETTING

During the period of great industrial expansion in the United States between 1897 and 1926, unemployment in manufacturing, transportation, building, and mining averaged around 10 percent, but was never higher than 3 million. During the 1920s, unemployment in the nonagricultural sector fluctuated between 1.4 million and 4 million. Between 1929 and 1936, by contrast, unemployment fluctuated between 10 million and 16 million, touching as many as one-third of the nation's families. According to Congressional studies, the extraordinarily high rate of unemployment during the Great Depression had many consequences, including a decline in nutrition and health standards, the doubling up of displaced families in tenements, overcrowded hospitals, increases in mental illness and suicides, and increased crime rates. The problems associated with unemployment clearly transcended state lines. States were hesitant to adopt comprehensive unemployment acts because, among other things, they would burden local industries and discourage new industries from locating in the state, would attract unemployed workers from states that did not have unemployment programs, and might run afoul of laws prohibiting local taxes on industries engaged in interstate commerce.

The policy choices available to Congress in the light of the lengthy depression appeared to be threefold: establish a national unemployment compensation program, impose an excise tax and use the proceeds to fund a program set up by the national government but administered by the states, or impose an excise tax and allow credit against it for contribution to a state unemployment compensation system. Congress opted for the third alternative, which was reflected in the 1935 Social Security Act, consisting of eleven independent titles. Title IX provided for a tax to be collected from businesses that employed at least eight persons. The rate of the tax was 1 percent of total wages payable during the year 1936, 2 percent of those payable during the year 1937, and 3 percent thereafter, and Title IX permitted a deduction not to exceed 90 per cent of the tax if the employer paid into a state unemployment fund certified by the Social Security Board. The proceeds of the tax were earmarked for the Treasury of the United States. In short, Title IX imposed an excise tax on the receipt of services by an employer, but permitted a deduction, not to exceed 90 percent of the tax, for amounts paid by the employer pursuant to a state unemployment compensation law. Title III of the act permitted annual appropriations of $49 million to states to assist in the administration of their unemployment compensation laws. One effect of the act was to give the states strong incentives to establish unemployment programs consistent with national standards.

On March 2, 1937, the Charles C. Steward Machine Company of Birmingham, Alabama, which manufactured coal mining machinery, paid the sum of $46.14 as a tax imposed under the terms of the Social Security Act. The tax was one-tenth of one percent of the amount of wages paid by Steward Machine to its employees during the year 1936. On that same day, it filed a claim for a refund of the Social Security tax with the Commissioner of Internal Revenue. A week later, Commissioner Harwell G. Davis denied the claim. The next day, on March 10, Steward Machine filed suit against Davis in the U.S. District Court for the Northern District of Alabama seeking to recover the tax. Davis demurred to Steward Machine's contentions that the tax was unconstitutional. The district court sustained the demurrer and dismissed the suit. The Court of Appeals for the Fifth Circuit affirmed. The Supreme Court granted Steward Machine's petition for a writ of certiorari.

In an unusual move, the United States joined Steward Machine's petition for a writ of certiorari. According to Solicitor General Stanley Reed, "Delay in the determination of [the constitutionality of the Social Security Act] may result in a multitude of suits clogging the dockets of the courts, harassing the Government, and greatly overtaxing its facilities for the orderly handling of such litigation. For these reasons a final decision with respect to the validity of the tax here challenged would be in the public interest."

HIGHLIGHTS OF SUPREME COURT ARGUMENTS

BRIEF FOR STEWARD MACHINE

◆ The Social Security Act coerces the enactment by the states of unemployment compensation laws. Congress has seized on its taxing power as a pretext to provide a plan for unemployment.

◆ The act violates the Ninth and Tenth Amendments by setting up a federal system of unemployment compensation, by controlling the administration of state monies and intruding on the constitutional power and jurisdiction of the states.

◆ The act takes property away from employers without just compensation for the benefit of an arbitrarily defined class.

◆ The act constitutes an impermissible delegation of legislative authority in the Social Security Board, in violation of Article I, section I.

AMICUS CURIAE BRIEFS SUPPORTING STEWARD MACHINE

George P. Davis (counsel for Boston and Main Railroad, which raised the identical issues before the First Circuit Court of Appeals.)

BRIEF FOR THE UNITED STATES

◆ Title IX is a valid exercise of Congress's power to lay and collect taxes to provide for the general welfare.

◆ Title IX is consistent with the Fifth Amendment, because the proceeds of the tax are commingled in the U.S. Treasury and thus do not constitute the taking of property from one class of persons for the benefit of another.

◆ The act is not an attempt by Congress to regulate directly the relationship of employer and employee since Congress has not established an unemployment compensation system to operate in any state.

SUPREME COURT DECISION: 5–4

CARDOZO, J.

... The assault on the statute proceeds on an extended front. Its assailants take the ground that the tax is not an excise; that it is not uniform throughout the United States as excises are required to be; that its exceptions are so many and arbitrary as to violate the Fifth Amendment; that its purpose was not revenue, but an unlawful invasion of the reserved powers of the states; and that the states in submitting to it have yielded to coercion and have abandoned governmental functions which they are not permitted to surrender.

The objections will be considered seriatim with such further explanation as may be necessary to make their meaning clear.

First...

We are told that the relation of employment is one so essential to the pursuit of happiness that it may not be burdened with a tax. Appeal is made to history. From the precedents of colonial days, we are supplied with illustrations of excises common in the colonies. They are said to have been bound up with the enjoyment of particular commodities. Appeal is also made to principle or the analysis of concepts. An excise, we are told, imports a tax upon a privilege; employment, it is said, is a right, not a privilege, from which it follows that employment is not subject to an excise. Neither the one appeal nor the other leads to the desired goal.

As to the argument from history: Doubtless there were many excises in colonial days and later that were associated, more or less intimately, with the enjoyment or the use of property. This would not prove, even if no others were then known, that the forms then accepted were not subject to enlargement.... But in truth other excises were known, and known since early times....

The historical prop failing, the prop or fancied prop of principle remains. We learn that employment for lawful gain is a "natural" or "inherent" or "inalienable" right, and not a "privilege" at all. But natural rights, so called, are as much subject to taxation as rights of less importance. An excise is not limited to vocations or activities that may be prohibited altogether. It is not limited to those that are the outcome of a franchise. It extends to vocations or activities pursued as of common right. What the individual does in the operation of a business is amenable to taxation just as much as what he owns, at all events if the classification is not tyrannical or arbitrary.... Employment is a business relation, if not itself a business. It is a relation without which business could seldom be carried on effectively. The power to tax the activities and relations that constitute a calling considered as a unit is the power to tax any of them. The whole includes the parts....

The subject matter of taxation open to the power of the Congress is as comprehensive as that open to the power of the states, though the method of apportionment may at times be different. "The Congress shall have Power to lay and collect Taxes, Duties, Imposts and Excises." Article 1, § 8. If the tax is a direct one, it shall be apportioned according to the census or enumeration. If it is a duty, impost, or excise, it shall be uniform throughout the United States. Together, these classes include every form of tax appropriate to sovereignty.... Whether the tax is to be classified as an "excise" is in truth not of critical importance. If not that, it is an "impost" ... or a "duty."... A capitation or other "direct" tax it certainly is not....

The tax being an excise, its imposition must conform to the canon of uniformity. There has been no departure from this requirement. According to the settled doctrine, the uniformity exacted is geographical, not intrinsic....

Second: The excise is not invalid under the provisions of the Fifth Amendment by force of its exemptions.

The statute does not apply, as we have seen, to employers of less then eight. It does not apply to agricultural labor, or domestic service in a private home or to some other classes of less importance. Petitioner contends that the effect of these restrictions is an arbitrary discrimination vitiating the tax.

The Fifth Amendment unlike the Fourteenth has no equal protection clause.... But even the states, though subject to such a clause, are not confined to a formula of rigid uniformity in framing measures of taxation.... They may tax some kinds of property at one rate, and others at another, and exempt others altogether.... They may lay an excise on the operations of a particular kind of business, and exempt some other kind of business closely akin thereto.... If this latitude of judgment is lawful for the states, it is lawful, *a fortiori*, in legislation by the Congress, which is subject to restraints less narrow and confining....

The classifications and exemptions directed by the statute now in controversy have support in considerations of policy and practical convenience that cannot be condemned as arbitrary. The classifications and exemptions would therefore be upheld if they had been adopted by a state and the provisions of the Fourteenth Amendment were invoked to annul them....

Third: The excise is not void as involving the coercion of the states in contravention of the Tenth Amendment or of restrictions implicit in our federal form of government....

The case for the petitioner is built on the contention that here an ulterior aim is wrought into the very structure of the act, and what is even more important that the aim is not only ulterior, but essentially unlawful. In particular, the 90 per cent credit is relied upon as supporting that conclusion. But before the statute succumbs to an assault upon these lines, two propositions must be made out by the assailant.... There must be a showing in the first place that separated from the credit the revenue provisions are incapable of standing by themselves. There must be a showing in the second place that the tax and the credit in combination are weapons of coercion, destroying or impairing the autonomy of the states. The truth of each proposition being essential to the success of the assault, we pass for convenience to a consideration of the second, without pausing to inquire whether there has been a demonstration of the first.

To draw the line intelligently between duress and inducement, there is need to remind ourselves of facts as to the problem of unemployment that are now matters of common knowledge.... The relevant statistics are gathered in the brief of counsel for the government. Of the many available figures a few only will be mentioned. During the years 1929 to 1936, when the country was passing through a cyclical depression, the number of the unemployed mounted to unprecedented heights. Often the average was more than 10 million; at times a peak was attained of 16 million or more. Disaster to the breadwinner meant disaster to dependents. Accordingly the roll of the unemployed, itself formidable enough, was only a partial roll of the destitute or needy. The fact developed quickly that the states were unable to give the requisite relief. The problem had become national in area and dimensions. There was need of help from the nation if the people were not to starve. It is too late today for the argument to be heard with tolerance that in a crisis so extreme the use of the moneys of the nation to relieve the unemployed and their dependents is a use for any purpose narrower than the promotion of the general welfare....

In the presence of this urgent need for some remedial expedient, the question is to be answered whether the expedient adopted has overlept the bounds of power. The assailants of the statute say that its dominant end and aim is to drive the state Legislatures under the whip of economic pressure into the enactment of unemployment compensation laws at the bidding of the central government. Supporters of the statute say that its operation is not constraint, but the creation of a larger freedom, the states and the nation joining in a co-operative endeavor to avert a common evil. Before Congress acted, unemployment compensation insurance was still, for the most part, a project and no more.... But if states had been holding back before the passage of the federal law, inaction was not owing, for the most part, to the lack of sympathetic interest. Many held back through alarm lest in laying such a toll upon their industries, they would place themselves in a position of economic disadvantage as compared with neighbors or competitors.... Two consequences ensued. One was that the freedom of a state to contribute its fair share to the solution of a national problem was paralyzed by fear. The other was that in so far as there was failure by the states to contribute relief according to the measure of their capacity, a disproportionate burden, and a mountainous one, was laid upon the resources of the government of the nation.

The Social Security Act is an attempt to find a method by which all these public agencies may work together to a common end. Every dollar of the new taxes will continue in all likelihood to be used and needed by the nation as long as states are unwilling, whether through timidity or for other motives, to do what can be done at home. At least the inference is permissible that Congress so believed, though retaining undiminished freedom to spend the money as it pleased. On the other hand, fulfillment of the home duty will be lightened and encouraged by crediting the taxpayer upon his account with the Treasury of the nation to the extent that his contributions under the laws of the locality have simplified or diminished the problem of relief and the probable demand upon the resources of the fisc. Duplicated taxes, or burdens that approach them are recognized hardships that government, state or national, may properly avoid.... If Congress believed that the general welfare would better be promoted by relief through local units than by the system then in vogue, the co-operating localities ought not in all fairness to pay a second time....

Fourth: The statute does not call for a surrender by the states of powers essential to their quasi sovereign existence....

[T]he argument is made that by force of an agreement the moneys when withdrawn must be "paid through public employment offices in the State or such other agencies as the Board may approve." Section 903(a)(1), 42 U.S.C.A. § 1103(a)(1). But in truth there is no agreement as to the method of disbursement. There is only a condition which the state is free at pleasure to disregard or to fulfill. Moreover, approval is not requisite if public employment offices are made the disbursing instruments. Approval is to be a check upon resort to "other agencies" that may perchance, be irresponsible. A state looking for a credit must give assurance that her system has been organized upon a base of rationality....

All that the state has done is to say in effect through the enactment of a statute that her agents shall be authorized to deposit the unemployment tax receipts in the Treasury at Washington. Alabama Unemployment Act of September 14, 1935, section 10(i) (Gen. Acts Ala. 1935, p. 961). The statute may be repealed. Section 903(a)(6), 42 U.S.C.A. § 1103(a)(6). The consent may be revoked. The deposits may be withdrawn. The moment the state commission gives notice to the depositary that it would like the moneys back, the Treasurer will return them. To find state destruction there is to find it almost anywhere....

Fifth: Title III of the act is separable from title IX, and its validity is not at issue.

The essential provisions of that title have been stated in the opinion. As already pointed out, the title does not appropriate a dollar of the public moneys. It does no more than authorize appropriations to be made in the future for the purpose of assisting states in the administration of their laws, if Congress shall decide that appropriations are desirable. The title might be expunged, and title IX would stand intact. Without a severability clause we should still be led to that conclusion. The presence of such a clause (section 1103, 42 U.S.C.A. § 1303) makes the conclusion even clearer....

The judgment is affirmed.

MCREYNOLDS, J., DISSENTING

That portion of the Social Security legislation here under consideration, I think, exceeds the power granted to Congress. It unduly interferes with the orderly government of the state by her own people and otherwise offends the Federal Constitution....

No defense is offered for the legislation under review upon the basis of emergency. The hypothesis is that hereafter it will continuously benefit unemployed members of a class. Forever, so far as we can see, the states are expected to function under federal direction concerning an internal matter. By the sanction of this adventure, the door is open for progressive inauguration of others of like kind under which it can hardly be expected that the states will retain genuine independence of action. And without independent states a Federal Union as contemplated by the Constitution becomes impossible....

SUTHERLAND, VAN DEVANTER, J.J., DISSENTING

With most of what is said in the opinion just handed down, I concur....

[T]he question with which I have difficulty is whether the administrative provisions of the act invade the governmental administrative powers of the several states reserved by the Tenth Amendment. A state may enter into contracts; but a state cannot, by contract or statute, surrender the execution, or a share in the execution, of any of its governmental powers either to a sister state or to the federal government, any more than the federal government can surrender the control of any of its governmental powers to a foreign nation. The power to tax is vital and fundamental, and, in the highest degree, governmental in character. Without it, the state could not exist. Fundamental also, and no less important, is the governmental power to expend the moneys realized from taxation, and exclusively to administer the laws in respect of the character of the tax and the methods of laying and collecting it and expending the proceeds....

The precise question, therefore, which we are required to answer by an application of these principles is whether the congressional act contemplates a surrender by the state to the federal government, in whole or in part, of any state governmental power to administer its own unemployment law or the state payroll-tax funds which it has collected for the purposes of that law. An affirmative answer to this question, I think, must be made.

I do not, of course, doubt the power of the state to select and utilize a depository for the safe-keeping of its funds; but it is quite another thing to agree with the selected depository that the funds shall be withdrawn for certain stipulated purposes, and for no other. Nor do I doubt the authority of the federal government and a state government to co-operate to a common end, provided each of them is authorized to reach it. But such co-operation must be effectuated by an exercise of the powers which they severally possess, and not by an exercise, through invasion or surrender, by one of them of the governmental power of the other....

The force of what has been said is not broken by an acceptance of the view that the state is not coerced by the federal law. The effect of the dual distribution of powers is completely to deny to the states whatever is granted exclusively to the nation, and, conversely, to deny to the nation whatever is reserved exclusively to the states....

Nor may the constitutional objection suggested be overcome by the expectation of public benefit resulting from the federal participation authorized by the act. Such expectation, if voiced in support of a proposed constitutional enactment, would be quite proper for the consideration of the legislative body.... [E]verything which the act seeks to do for the relief of unemployment might have been accomplished, as is done by this same act for the relief of the misfortunes of old age, without obliging the state to surrender, or share with another government, any of its powers.

If we are to survive as the United States, the balance between the powers of the nation and those of the states must be maintained. There is grave danger in permitting it to dip in either direction, danger—if there were no other—in the precedent thereby set for further departures from the equipoise. The threat implicit in the present encroachment upon the administrative functions of the states is that greater encroachments, and encroachments upon other functions, will follow....

BUTLER, J., DISSENTING

... I am also of opinion that, in principle and as applied to bring about and to gain control over state unemployment compensation, the statutory scheme is repugnant to the Tenth Amendment[.]... The Constitution grants to the United States no power to pay unemployed persons or to require the states to enact laws or to raise or disburse money for that purpose. The provisions in question, if not amounting to coercion in a legal sense, are manifestly designed and intended directly to affect state action in the respects specified. And, if valid as so employed, this "tax and credit" device may be made effective to enable federal authorities to induce, if not indeed to compel, state enactments for any purpose within the realm of state power and generally to control state administration of state laws....

COMMENT

In *Helvering v. Davis*, 301 U.S. 619 (1937), a companion case to *Steward Machine*, the Court, 7–2, rejected a Tenth Amendment challenge to Titles II and VIII of the 1935 Social Security Act. Title II created the old age benefits program that has come to be called "social security." Title VIII required employers to take a payroll deduction from each employee's wages, match the deduction, and pay the total amount to the U.S. Treasury. Justice Cardozo defined the General Welfare Clause broadly: "... the concept of the general welfare [is not] static. Needs that were narrow or parochial a century ago may be interwoven in our day with the well-being of a nation."

QUESTIONS

1. Did *Steward Machine* effectively overrule *United States v. Butler*? If so, why did not the majority explicitly overrule it?

2. What, if anything, remains of the *Butler* "unconstitutional conditions" limitation on congressional taxing and spending power after *Steward Machine*? Compare the Court's statement in *United States v. Kahriger*, 345 U.S. 22 (1953): "Penalty provisions in tax statutes added for breach of a regulation concerning activities in themselves subject only to state regulation have caused this Court to declare the enactments invalid. Unless there are provisions extraneous to any tax need, courts are without authority to limit the exercises of the taxing power."

3. *Steward Machine* is often cited as one of the decisions marking the end of "dual federalism." Adherents to dual federalism view national and state powers in starkly opposing categorical terms, and view relations between the states and Washington, D.C. as an inherently conflictive contest, much like a tug of war. In Justice Cardozo's opinion, what presumptions about federalism undergird the 1935 Social Security Act?

SUGGESTIONS FOR FURTHER READING

Ackerman, Bruce, "Constitutional Politics/Constitutional Law," 99 *Yale Law Journal* (1989): 453.

Alsop, Joseph, and Turner Catledge, *The 168 Days* (Garden City, NY: Doubleday, 1938).

Baker, Leonard, *Back to Back: The Duel Between FDR and the Supreme Court* (New York, NY: Macmillan, 1967).

Barber, Sotirios A., *The Constitution and the Delegation of Congressional Power* (Chicago, IL: University of Chicago Press, 1975).

Burns, James MacGregor, *Roosevelt: The Lion and the Fox* (New York, NY: Harcourt Brace, 1956).

Cortner, Richard C., *The Wagner Act Cases* (Knoxville, TN: University of Tennessee Press, 1964).

_____, *The Jones & Laughlin Case* (New York, NY: Knopf, 1970).

Corwin, Edward S., *The Twilight of the Supreme Court: A History of Our Constitutional Theory* (New Haven, CT: Yale University Press, 1934.)

_____, *Constitutional Revolution, Ltd.* (Claremont, CA: Claremont Colleges Press, 1941).

Cushman, Robert E., "Social and Economic Control through Federal Taxation," 18 *Minnesota Law Review* (1934): 759.

Dodd, E. Merrick, "The Supreme Court and Organized Labor, 1941–1954," 58 *Harvard Law Review* (1945): 1018.

_____, "The Supreme Court and Fair Labor Standards, 1941–1945," 59 *Harvard Law Review* (1946): 321.

Forbath, William E., *Law and the Shaping of the American Labor Movement* (Cambridge, MA: Harvard University Press, 1991).

Freidel, Frank, "The Sick Chicken Case," in *Quarrels That Have Shaped the Constitution*, rev. ed., ed. John A. Garraty (New York, NY: Harper and Row, 1987).

Gillman, Howard, *The Constitution Besieged: The Rise and Demise of Lochner Era Police Powers Jurisprudence* (Durham, NC: Duke University Press, 1993).

Gross, James A., *The Making of the National Labor Relations Board: A Study in Economics, Politics, and the Law*, vol. 1 (1933–1946) (Albany, NY: State University of New York, 1974).

Hart, Henry M., "Processing Taxes and Protective Tariffs," 49 *Harvard Law Review* (1936): 610.

Horwitz, Morton J., *The Transformation of American Law 1870–1960: The Crisis of Legal Orthodoxy* (New York, NY: Oxford University Press, 1992).

Irons, Peter, *The New Deal Lawyers* (Princeton, NJ: Princeton University Press, 1982).

Jackson, Robert H., *The Struggle for Judicial Supremacy: A Study of A Crisis in American Power Politics* (New York, NY: Knopf, 1941).

Leuchtenberg, William E., *The Perils of Prosperity, 1914–32* (Chicago, IL: University of Chicago Press, 1958).

_____, "The Origins of Franklin D. Roosevelt's Court-Packing Plan," *The Supreme Court Review* (Chicago, IL: University of Chicago Press, 1966).

Linde, Hans A., "Justice Douglas on Freedom in the Welfare State," 39 *Washington Law Review* (1964): 4.

McCoy, Thomas, and Barry Friedman, "Conditional Spending: Federalism's Trojan Horse," *The Supreme Court Review* (Chicago, IL: University of Chicago Press, 1988).

Murphy, Paul L., "The New Deal Agricultural Program and the Constitution," 29 *Agricultural History* (1955): 160.

_____, *The Constitution in Crisis Times, 1918–1969* (New York, NY: Harper and Row, 1972)

Pearson, Drew, and Robert S. Allen, *The Nine Old Men* (Garden City, NY: Doubleday, 1937).

Pound, Roscoe, *The Formative Era of American Law* (Boston, MA: Little, Brown, 1938).

Pritchett, C. Herman, *The Roosevelt Court* (New York, NY: Macmillan, 1948).

Rosenthal, Albert, "Conditional Spending and the Constitution," 39 *Stanford Law Review* (1987): 1103.

Ross, William G., *A Muted Fury: Populists, Progressives, and Labor Unions Confront the Courts, 1890–1937* (Princeton, NJ: Princeton University Press, 1994).

Shapiro, Martin, *The Supreme Court and Administrative Agencies* (New York, NY: Free Press, 1968).

Schlesinger, Arthur M., *The New Deal in Action, 1933–1938* (New York, NY: Macmillan, 1939).

Stern, Robert L., "The Commerce Clause and the National Economy, 1933–1946" 59 *Harvard Law Review* (1946): 645.

Sullivan, Kathleen, "Unconstitutional Conditions," 10 *Harvard Law Review* (1989): 1413.

Sunstein, Cass R., "Constitutionalism after the New Deal," 101 *Harvard Law Review* (1987): 421.

Thayer, James Bradley, "The Origin and Scope of the American Doctrine of Constitutional Law," 7 *Harvard Law Review* (1893): 129.

Tomlins, Christopher L., *The State and the Unions: Labor Relations, Law, and the Organization of the American Labor Movement, 1880–1960* (New York, NY: Cambridge University Press, 1985).

MODERN VIEWS OF OLD CONTROVERSIES

United States v. Darby Lumber Co.
312 U.S. 100 (1941)

SETTING

Differences in working conditions among the states have been a source of controversy almost since the founding. In 1838, for example, an investigative committee in Pennsylvania observed that "any reduction in the hours of labor, or the prohibition of child labor, so long as it could apply only to Pennsylvania, must result disastrously to manufacturers in their competition with others not similarly restricted." In 1892 Congress investigated the sweatshop system, an employment system built on the need of semiskilled laborers to work long hours because of low wages (frequently in the clothing and cigar industries). The investigation concluded that "so long as interstate commerce in this regard is left free, the stamping out of the sweating system in any particular State is practically of no effect, except to impose peculiar hardship upon the manufacture of that State." By 1907, however, evils such as illness, infertility, and illiteracy caused by the labor of women and children were deemed a sufficiently serious national problem that Congress authorized another investigation, which led to passage of the Child Labor Act of 1916. Again, the conclusion was that "so long as there is a single State for which selfish or other reasons fails to enact effective child-labor legislation, it is beyond the power of every other State to protect effectively its own producers and manufacturers against ... unfair competition ... or to protect its consumers against unwittingly patronizing those who exploit the childhood of the country."

The prolonged economic depression of the 1930s produced an insistent demand for federal legislation establishing labor standards. The Fair Labor Standards Act (FLSA) of 1938 was one of a series of laws enacted to eliminate from the channels of interstate commerce goods produced under substandard labor conditions. Among other things, the FLSA required every employer whose employees were engaged in interstate commerce or in the production of goods for interstate commerce to pay a minimum wage of not less than twenty-five cents per hour and time-and-a-half for more than forty-four hours of work per week.

On November 2, 1939, Fred W. Darby, owner of the Darby Lumber Company of Statesboro, Georgia, was indicted in the U.S. District Court for the District of Georgia for various violations of the FLSA. The wages Darby paid in 1932 averaged 13.4¢/hour, "the lowest in that industry throughout the country," according to U.S. Attorney General Francis Biddle. Darby demurred to the indictment, asserting that the FLSA was unconstitutional because it did not fall within any of the powers granted to Congress in Article I, section 8, clause 3, of the Constitution, and because it violated the Fifth, Sixth, and Tenth Amendments.

The district court sustained Darby's demurrer and quashed the indictment. It ruled that the FLSA contravened the Commerce Cause in its application to a local lumberyard, and consequently did not reach Darby's Fifth Amendment claim. The United States appealed to the Supreme Court of the United States.

HIGHLIGHTS OF SUPREME COURT ARGUMENTS

BRIEF FOR THE UNITED STATES

◆ The FLSA is a valid exercise of Congress's commerce power. Individual states are helpless to remedy the problem of substandard working conditions, because they cannot forbid the importation of goods produced under such conditions.

◆ Congress made explicit findings in the FLSA that low labor standards are detrimental to the health and efficiency of workers, cause the channels of interstate commerce to spread those labor conditions among the states, burden commerce, lead to labor disputes that disrupt commerce, and constitute an unfair method of competition.

◆ *Hammer v. Dagenhart*, which distinguished between manufacture and commerce, is inconsistent with subsequent decisions of this Court. If it is reaffirmed, there will be a "no-man's-land" in which both the states and Congress are incompetent to act.

◆ Because the FLSA is a valid exercise of the power granted to Congress to regulate interstate commerce, there is no room for the Tenth Amendment to operate.

◆ The FLSA does not violate Due Process of the Fifth Amendment by unduly limiting liberty of contract. All evidence shows that the health and welfare of both the worker and the nation depend on the elimination of substandard working conditions.

BRIEF FOR DARBY

◆ The FLSA is an undisguised attempt on the part of the national government to establish minimum wages and maximum hours throughout industries in the entire nation.

◆ The government in this case seeks to establish the unrestricted power in the Federal Congress to legislate for the general welfare, in addition to the enumerated powers. The existence of such a power has been expressly denied in numerous cases.

◆ The grant of powers to the federal government by the Constitutional Convention was to be supplemental to and not destructive of the states. The

Tenth Amendment expressly safeguards the sovereignty of the states except as this sovereignty might be lessened by the powers delegated to the Federal Government.

◆ For more than fifty years it has been held that manufacturing, mining, agriculture, and the like are purely intrastate activities and subject to the exclusive control of the states under their police powers. It has never been held that Congress may regulate indiscriminately and directly the conditions of production of goods.

◆ Although the privilege of the individual to contract is not an absolute and unqualified right, it is imperative to recognize the distinction between minimum wage laws for women and minors and adult men. No statute has yet received judicial sanction by this Court which involved the establishment of minimum wages for men without regard to the circumstances.

SUPREME COURT DECISION: 9–0

STONE, J.

The two principal questions raised by the record in this case are, first, whether Congress has constitutional power to prohibit the shipment in interstate commerce of lumber manufactured by employees whose wages are less than a prescribed minimum or whose weekly hours of labor at that wage are greater than a prescribed maximum, and, second, whether it has power to prohibit the employment of workmen in the production of goods "for interstate commerce" at other than prescribed wages and hours. A subsidiary question is whether in connection with such prohibitions Congress can require the employer subject to them to keep records showing the hours worked each day and week by each of his employees including those engaged "in the production and manufacture of goods to wit, lumber, for 'interstate commerce.'"...

Section 15(a)(1) prohibits, and the indictment charges, the shipment in interstate commerce, of goods produced for interstate commerce by employees whose wages and hours of employment do not conform to the requirements of the Act. Since this section is not violated unless the commodity shipped has been produced under labor conditions prohibited by § 6 and § 7, the only question arising under the commerce clause with respect to such shipments is whether Congress has the constitutional power to prohibit them.

While manufacture is not of itself interstate commerce the shipment of manufactured goods interstate is such commerce and the prohibition of such shipment by Congress is indubitably a regulation of the commerce. The power to regulate commerce is the power "to prescribe the rule by which commerce is to be governed." *Gibbons v. Ogden.* It extends not only to those regulations which aid, foster and protect the commerce, but embraces those which prohibit it....

But it is said that the present prohibition ... is [a] regulation of wages and hours of persons engaged in manufacture, the control of which has been reserved to the states and upon which Georgia and some of the states of destination have placed no restriction....

The power of Congress over interstate commerce "is complete in itself, may be exercised to its utmost extent, and acknowledges no limitations, other than are prescribed by the constitution." *Gibbons v. Ogden*. That power can neither be enlarged nor diminished by the exercise or non-exercise of state power.... Congress, following its own conception of public policy concerning the restrictions which may appropriately be imposed on interstate commerce, is free to exclude from the commerce articles whose use in the states for which they are destined it may conceive to be injurious to the public health, morals or welfare, even though the state has not sought to regulate their use....

Such regulation is not a forbidden invasion of state power merely because either its motive or its consequence is to restrict the use of articles of commerce within the states of destination and is not prohibited unless by other Constitutional provisions. It is no objection to the assertion of the power to regulate interstate commerce that its exercise is attended by the same incidents which attend the exercise of the police power of the states....

The motive and purpose of the present regulation are plainly to make effective the Congressional conception of public policy that interstate commerce should not be made the instrument of competition in the distribution of goods produced under substandard labor conditions, which competition is injurious to the commerce and to the states from and to which the commerce flows. The motive and purpose of a regulation of

interstate commerce are matters for the legislative judgment upon the exercise of which the Constitution places no restriction and over which the courts are given no control.... Whatever their motive and purpose, regulations of commerce which do not infringe some constitutional prohibition are within the plenary power conferred on Congress by the Commerce Clause. Subject only to that limitation, presently to be considered, we conclude that the prohibition of the shipment interstate of goods produced under the forbidden substandard labor conditions is within the constitutional authority of Congress.

In the more than a century which has elapsed since the decision of *Gibbons v. Ogden*, these principles of constitutional interpretation have been so long and repeatedly recognized by this Court as applicable to the Commerce Clause, that there would be little occasion for repeating them now were it not for the decision of this Court twenty-two years ago in *Hammer v. Dagenhart*. In that case it was held by a bare majority of the Court over the powerful and now classic dissent of Mr. Justice Holmes setting forth the fundamental issues involved, that Congress was without power to exclude the products of child labor from interstate commerce. The reasoning and conclusion of the Court's opinion there cannot be reconciled with the conclusion which we have reached, that the power of Congress under the Commerce Clause is plenary to exclude any article from interstate commerce subject only to the specific prohibitions of the Constitution.

Hammer v. Dagenhart has not been followed. The distinction on which the decision was rested that Congressional power to prohibit interstate commerce is limited to articles which in themselves have some harmful or deleterious property—a distinction which was novel when made and unsupported by any provision of the Constitution—has long since been abandoned....

The conclusion is inescapable that *Hammer v. Dagenhart* was a departure from the principles which have prevailed in the interpretation of the commerce clause both before and since the decision and that such vitality, as a precedent, as it then had has long since been exhausted. It should be and now is overruled....

Section 15(a)(2) and §§ 6 and 7 require employers to conform to the wage and hour provisions with respect to all employees engaged in the production of goods for interstate commerce. As appellee's employees are not alleged to be "engaged in interstate commerce" the validity of the prohibition turns on the question whether the employment, under other than the prescribed labor standards, of employees engaged in the production of goods for interstate commerce is so related to the commerce and so affects it as to be within the reach of the power of Congress to regulate it.

To answer this question we must at the outset determine whether the particular acts charged in the counts which are laid under § 15(a)(2) as they were construed below, constitute "production for commerce" within the meaning of the statute. As the Government seeks to apply the statute in the indictment, and as the court below construed the phrase "produced for interstate commerce," it embraces at least the case where an employer engaged, as are appellees, in the manufacture and shipment of goods in filling orders of extrastate customers, manufactures his product with the intent or expectation that according to the normal course of his business all or some part of it will be selected for shipment to those customers.

Without attempting to define the precise limits of the phrase, we think the acts alleged in the indictment are within the sweep of the statute. The obvious purpose of the Act was not only to prevent the interstate transportation of the proscribed product, but to stop the initial step toward transportation, production with the purpose of so transporting it. Congress was not unaware that most manufacturing businesses shipping their product in interstate commerce make it in their shops without reference to its ultimate destination and then after manufacture select some of it for shipment interstate and some intrastate according to the daily demands of their business, and that it would be practically impossible, without disrupting manufacturing businesses, to restrict the prohibited kind of production to the particular pieces of lumber, cloth, furniture or the like which later move in interstate rather than intrastate commerce....

The recognized need of drafting a workable statute and the well known circumstances in which it was to be applied are persuasive of the conclusion, which the legislative history supports ... that the "production for commerce" intended includes at least production of goods, which, at the time of production, the employer, according to the normal course of his business, intends or expects to move in interstate commerce although, through the exigencies of the business, all of the goods may not thereafter actually enter interstate commerce.

There remains the question whether such restriction on the production of goods for commerce is a permissible exercise of the commerce power. The power of Congress over interstate commerce is not confined to the regulation of commerce among the states. It extends to those activities intrastate which so affect interstate commerce or the exercise of the power of Congress over it as to make regulation of them appropriate means to the attainment of a legitimate end, the exercise of the granted power of Congress to regulate interstate commerce....

While this Court has many times found state regulation of interstate commerce, when uniformity of its regulation is of national concern, to be incompatible with the Commerce Clause even though Congress has not legislated on the subject, the Court has never implied such restraint on state control over matters intrastate not deemed to be regulations of interstate commerce or its instrumentalities even though they affect the commerce.... In the absence of Congressional legislation on the subject state laws which are not regulations of the commerce itself or its instrumentalities are not forbidden even though they affect interstate commerce....

But it does not follow that Congress may not by appropriate legislation regulate intrastate activities where they have a substantial effect on interstate commerce....

Congress, having by the present Act adopted the policy of excluding from interstate commerce all goods produced for the commerce which do not conform to the specified labor standards, it may choose the means reasonably adapted to the attainment of the permitted end, even though they involve control of intrastate activities. Such legislation has often been sustained with respect to powers, other than the commerce power granted to the national government, when the means chosen, although not themselves within the granted power, were nevertheless deemed appropriate aids to the accomplishment of some purpose within an admitted power of the national government....

The means adopted by § 15(a)(2) for the protection of interstate commerce by the suppression of the production of the condemned goods for interstate commerce is so related to the commerce and so affects it as to be within the reach of the commerce power.... Congress, to attain its objective in the suppression of nationwide competition in interstate commerce by goods produced under substandard labor conditions, has made no distinction as to the volume or amount of shipments in the commerce or of production for commerce by any particular shipper or producer. It recognized that in present day industry, competition by a small part may affect the whole and that the total effect of the competition of many small producers may be great....

Our conclusion is unaffected by the Tenth Amendment[.]... The amendment states but a truism that all is retained which has not been surrendered. There is nothing in the history of its adoption to suggest that it was more than declaratory of the relationship between the national and state governments as it had been established by the Constitution before the amendment or that its purpose was other than to allay fears that the new national government might seek to exercise powers not granted, and that the states might not be able to exercise fully their reserved powers....

The requirement of records of wages and hours[,] § 15(a)(5) and § 11(c)[,] ... are incidental to those for the prescribed wages and hours, and hence validity of the former turns on validity of the latter. Since, as we have held, Congress may require production for interstate Commerce to conform to those conditions, it may require the employer, as a means of enforcing the valid law, to keep a record showing whether he has in fact complied with it. The requirement for records even of the intrastate transaction is an appropriate means to the legitimate end....

Validity of the wage and hour provisions under the Fifth Amendment. Both provisions are minimum wage require-ments compelling the payment of a minimum standard wage with a prescribed increased wage for overtime of "not less than one and one-half times the regular rate" at which the worker is employed. Since our decision in *West Coast Hotel Co. v. Parrish*, 300 U.S. 379 (1937), it is no longer open to question that the fixing of a minimum wage is within the legislative power and that the bare fact of its exercise is not a denial of due process under the Fifth more than under the Fourteenth Amendment. Nor is it any longer open to question that it is within the legislative power to fix maximum hours. *Holden v. Hardy*, 169 U.S. 366 [(1898)]....

Reversed.

QUESTIONS

1. By the time *Darby* was argued before the Supreme Court, one circuit court of appeals and eight federal district courts had already ruled that the FLSA was constitutional under the Commerce Clause. The District Court of Georgia was the only tribunal to declare the FLSA unconstitutional. What might explain such unanimity among the lower courts on a subject that, as previous cases in this chapter have demonstrated, has generated such controversy throughout American history?

2. At the Constitutional Convention, the Virginia Resolution directed that the national government be empowered "to legislate in all cases to which the separate states are incompetent." Counsel for the United States in *Darby* argued that the failure of the Committee of Detail at the Constitutional Convention to object to the Virginia Resolution is evidence that the Convention understood that Congress's enumerated powers, including the Commerce Clause, placed within the jurisdiction of the national government control over problems that are national in scope. Is counsel's argument an appropriate use of history as a guide to interpreting the Constitution?

3. Counsel for Darby concluded his argument with the following statement:

   This Court has ever been careful to restrict Federal control to matters which bear a close, substantial relationship to interstate commerce. Without exception any control over intrastate activities has been permitted only when the effect was incidental and secondary. To preserve this line of demarcation—which is a real and vital one—is of paramount importance to the preservation of our dual form of government. In attempting to obliterate the distinction between local and national spheres of power, the Fair Labor Standards Act breaks through and smashes the proper confines of Federal power which the Court has so carefully and painstakingly blazed.

Does counsel's statement accurately summarize the Court's Commerce Clause jurisprudence up to 1941? Compare *Perez v. United States*, 402 U.S. 146 (1971), where the Court upheld a conviction for "loan-sharking" under the federal Consumer Credit Protection Act of 1968, enacted under the authority of the Commerce Clause, against a challenge that the act illegitimately permitted prosecution of an intrastate activity, usually within the purview of local criminal law.

4. The Supreme Court's decision in *Darby* reflected a fundamental shift in the Supreme Court's attitude toward congressional regulation of the economy. Three years before *Darby*, in a footnote to another case involving economic regulation, the Court indicated that judicial scrutiny of congressional regulations of commerce was giving way to a different kind of judicial review. *United States v. Carolene Products, Co.*, 304 U.S. 144 (1938) involved the Filled Milk Act of 1923. The act defined filled milk as any milk to which any fat or oil other than milk fat had been added. The act prohibited and penalized by fine or imprisonment the shipping of filled milk in interstate commerce on the ground that filled milk was "an adulterated article of food, injurious to the public health, and its sale constitutes a fraud upon the public."

Carolene Products Company, an Illinois corporation, was indicted in 1935 on two counts of shipping filled milk to N. Comensky Grocery Company and General Company of St. Louis, Missouri, under the names of "Milnut" and "Carolene." Both products were compounds of condensed skimmed milk and coconut oil made to look like condensed milk or cream. Carolene Products demurred to the indictment.

The Court upheld the constitutionality of the Filled Milk Act by a vote of 6–1. In the course of his opinion upholding the statute, Justice Harlan Fiske Stone stated: "Even in the absence of [reports of legislative committees], the existence of facts supporting the legislative judgment is to be presumed, for regulatory legislation affecting ordinary commercial transactions is not to be pronounced unconstitutional unless in the light of the facts made known or generally assumed it is of such a character as to preclude the assumption that it rests upon some rational basis within the knowledge and experience of the legislators." To this sentence Stone appended footnote #4, which reads:

> There may be narrower scope for operation of the presumption of constitutionality when legislation appears on its face to be within a specific prohibition of the Constitution, such as those of the first ten amendments, which are deemed equally specific when held to be embraced within the Fourteenth. See *Stromberg v. California*, 283 U.S. 359 [1931], *Lovell v. Griffin*, 303 U.S. 444 [1938].
>
> It is unnecessary to consider now whether legislation which restricts those political processes which can ordinarily be expected to bring about repeal of undesirable legislation, is to be subjected to more exacting judicial scrutiny under the general prohibitions of the Fourteenth Amendment than are most other types of legislation. On restrictions upon the right to vote, see *Nixon v. Herndon*, 273 U.S. 536 [1927], *Nixon v. Condon*, 286 U.S. 73 [1932]; on restraints upon the dissemination of information, see *Near v. Minnesota*, 283 U.S. 697 [1931], *Grosjean v. American Press Co.*, 297 U.S. 233 [1936], *Lovell v. Griffin*; on interferences with political organizations, see *Stromberg v. California*, *Fiske v. Kansas*, 274 U.S. 380 [1927], *Whitney v. California*, 274 U.S. 357 [1927], *Herndon v. Lowry*, 301 U.S. 242 [1937], and see Holmes, J., in *Gitlow v. New York*, 268 U.S. 652 [1925]; as to prohibition of peaceable assembly, see *De Jonge* [sic] *v. Oregon*, 299 U.S. 353 [1937].
>
> Nor need we enquire whether similar considerations enter into the review of statutes directed at particular religious, *Pierce v. Society of Sisters*, 268 U.S. 510 [1925], or national, *Meyer v. Nebraska*, 262 U.S. 390 [1923], *Bartels v. Iowa*, 262 U.S. 404 [1923], *Farrington v. Tokushige*, 273 U.S. 284 [1927], or racial minorities. *Nixon v. Herndon*, *Nixon v. Condon*: whether prejudice against discrete and insular minorities may be a special condition, which tends seriously to curtail the operation of those political processes ordinarily to be relied upon to protect minorities, and which may call for a correspondingly more searching judicial inquiry. Compare *McCulloch v. Maryland*, 4 Wheat[on] 316 [1819]; *South Carolina State Highway Department v. Barnwell Bros.*, 303 U.S. 177 [1938], note 2, and cases cited.

The Court's decision and Footnote #4 in *Carolene Products* signaled some litigants to refrain from seeking judicial review, while inviting other litigants to seek access to courts. Of what relevance is Footnote #4 in *Carolene Products* to the issues in *Darby*?

5. In the wake of *Darby*, what constitutional limitations, if any, remain on congressional commerce power? Did the Court effectively disavow any judicial supervision of powers exercised under the Commerce Clause? Is the integrity of federalism dependent on active judicial scrutiny of the exercise of congressional power?

MODERN VIEWS OF OLD CONTROVERSIES

Wickard v. Filburn
317 U.S. 111 (1942)

SETTING

In response to *United States v. Butler*, Congress drafted a second Agricultural Adjustment Act (AAA) in 1938. In 1939, in *Mulford v. Smith*, 307 U.S. 38, the Court by a 7–2 vote upheld the second AAA as a valid exercise of Congress's power to regulate commerce. According to Justice Roberts's majority opinion, the production quotas authorized by the statute did not regulate agricultural production. Rather, the quotas reached interstate commerce at its "throat," where commodities entered the stream of commerce. *Mulford* left open the question of just how far the Court would be willing to extend its apparently flexible new attitude toward Congress's power to regulate commerce.

In February 1941, Congress amended the second AAA to impose marketing penalties on wheat farmers who planted wheat in excess of acreage allotments fixed by the secretary of agriculture. Like its predecessor, the purpose of the act was to regulate the volume of wheat moving in interstate and foreign commerce in order to mitigate fluctuations in supply, thereby minimizing the abnormally low and high prices that resulted from such surpluses and shortages. In May 1941, Secretary of Agriculture Claude Wickard imposed allotments on farmers when he determined that the total supply of American-grown wheat as of July 1, 1941, would exceed a normal year's domestic consumption plus exports by more than 35 per cent.

Roscoe Filburn, a Montgomery County, Ohio, farmer, maintained a herd of dairy cattle, raised poultry, and sold milk, poultry, and eggs. He devoted a small portion of his farm to growing winter wheat. It was his practice to dispose of each wheat crop in part by sale, in part by feeding grain to his poultry and livestock, by grinding some of the wheat into flour for home consumption, and by using part of the grain as seed for the following year's crop.

In the fall of 1940, Filburn planted 23 acres of winter wheat. In May 1941, the Department of Agriculture set his allotment at 11.1 acres. Filburn harvested approximately 462 bushels of wheat in July 1941, in excess of his market quota of 239 bushels. He refused to store the excess wheat, deliver it to the secretary of agriculture, or pay the prescribed penalty (49¢ a bushel or $117.11) for exceeding his allotment. Therefore, he received no marketing card.

On July 14, 1941, Filburn filed a complaint in the U.S. District Court for the Southern District of Ohio to enjoin Wickard from enforcing the marketing penalty imposed on Filburn for wheat planted in the fall of 1940.

A specially constituted three-judge federal district court panel granted the injunction on the grounds that Filburn's wheat was already under cultivation at the time the increased penalties were put into effect, and that Wickard had misled producers about the consequences of marketing wheat in excess of quota allotments. Wickard appealed the district court judgment to the Supreme Court, as allowed by statute.

The case was first argued during the October 1941 Term. The Court ordered reargument in 1942 on the following question: "Whether the act, insofar as it deals with wheat consumed on the farm of the producer, is within the power of Congress to regulate commerce."

HIGHLIGHTS OF SUPREME COURT ARGUMENTS

BRIEF FOR WICKARD

◆ Application of the increased penalties for wheat in excess of the 1941 crop quota available for marketing applied to a crop already planted and was not retroactive or in violation of due process because the amendment's restrictions did not apply until after the harvesting of the crop.

◆ The wheat provisions of the Agricultural Adjustment Act are a valid exercise of the federal commerce power. The act's purpose is to insure a balanced flow of basic agricultural commodities in interstate and foreign commerce. Congress has the power to attain that objective by any appropriate means under its power to regulate commerce.

◆ The Court's modern view of Congress's commerce power has been stated in *United States v. Darby*.

◆ Congress may regulate the totality of interstate and intrastate activities when they are so related that the regulation of the interstate activities alone would be ineffective or when persons subject to the interstate regulation would otherwise suffer discrimination.

◆ Regulating the amount of wheat produced for farm consumption is an appropriate means of achieving the goal of a balanced flow of commerce because of its effect on the overall supply and price structure.

BRIEF FOR FILBURN

◆ The allotment system violates due process of law in the Fifth Amendment because it is an invasion of a right of private property. Furthermore, it went into effect several months after Filburn had planted his fall 1940 crop of winter wheat.

◆ Two facts must be remembered in deciding this case. First, in many instances wheat farmers must consume a portion or all of the wheat they produce. Second, the 1941 amendments to the Agricultural Act proscribe the use

> by the producer of his own wheat, even though the product be used to feed himself, his family, livestock and poultry, and as seed for the next year's crop.

◆ Wheat produced by farmers for farm consumption never moves into the channels of intrastate or interstate commerce because it never is marketed. Wheat grown on the farm for feed, seed, and food is still under the control of the farmer, having not moved into any channel of trade. Congress cannot regulate this kind of production and consumption under its Commerce Clause power because commerce is in no way involved.

◆ If the Commerce Clause extended to the degree requested by the government, the United States would move toward a centralized government that eventually would lead to absolutism by successive nullifications of all Constitutional limitations.

SUPREME COURT DECISION: 9–0

JACKSON, J.

... It is urged that under the Commerce Clause of the Constitution, Article I, section 8, clause 3, Congress does not possess the power it has in this instance sought to exercise. The question would merit little consideration since our decision in *United States v. Darby*, sustaining the federal power to regulate production of goods for commerce, except for the fact that this Act extends federal regulations to production not intended in any part for commerce but wholly for consumption on the farm....

Appellee says that this is a regulation of production and consumption of wheat. Such activities are, he urges, beyond the reach of Congressional power under the Commerce Clause, since they are local in character, and their effects upon interstate commerce are at most "indirect."...

We believe that a review of the course of decision under the Commerce Clause will make plain ... that questions of the power of Congress are not to be decided by reference to any formula which would give controlling force to nomenclature such as "production" and "indirect" and foreclose consideration of the actual effects of the activity in question upon interstate commerce....

At the beginning Chief Justice Marshall described the federal commerce power with a breadth never yet exceeded. He made emphatic the embracing and penetrating nature of this power by warning that effective restraints on its exercise must proceed from political rather than judicial pronouncements....

The present Chief Justice has said in summary of the present state of the law: "The commerce power is not confined in its exercise to the regulation of commerce among the states. It extends to those activities intrastate which so affect interstate commerce, or the exertion of the power of Congress over it, as to make regulation of them appropriate means to the attainment of a legitimate end, the effective execution of the granted power to regulate interstate commerce.... The power of Congress over interstate commerce is plenary and complete in itself, may be exercised to its utmost extent, and acknowledges no limitations other than are prescribed in the Constitution.... It follows that no form of state activity can constitutionally thwart the regulatory power granted by the commerce clause to Congress. Hence the reach of that power extends to those intrastate activities which in a substantial way interfere with or obstruct the exercise of the granted power." *United States v. Wrightwood Dairy Co.*, 315 U.S. 110 (1942).

Whether the subject of the regulation in question was "production," "consumption," or "marketing" is, therefore, not material for purposes of deciding the question of federal power before us.... [E]ven if appellee's activity be local and though it may not be regarded as commerce, it may still, whatever its nature, be reached by Congress if it exerts a substantial economic effect on interstate commerce, and this irrespective of whether such effect is what might at some earlier time have been defined as "direct" or "indirect."...

Appellee's claim that the Act works a deprivation of due process even apart from its allegedly retroactive effect is not persuasive. Control of total supply, upon which the whole statutory plan is based, depends upon control of individual supply. Appellee's claim is not that his quota represented less than a fair share of the national quota, but that the Fifth Amendment requires that he be free from penalty for planting wheat and disposing of his crop as he sees fit.

We do not agree. In its effort to control total supply, the Government gave the farmer a choice which was, of course, designed to encourage cooperation and discourage non-cooperation. The farmer who planted within his allotment was in effect guaranteed a minimum return much above what his wheat would have brought if sold on a world market basis. Exemption from the applicability of quotas was made in favor of small producers. The farmer who produced in excess of his quota might escape penalty by delivering his wheat to the Secretary, or by storing it with the privilege of sale without penalty in a later year to fill out his quota, or irrespective of quotas if they are no longer in effect, and he could obtain a loan of 60 per cent of the rate for cooperators, or about 59 cents a bushel, on so much of his wheat as would be subject to penalty if marketed. Finally, he might make other disposition of his wheat, subject to the penalty. It is agreed that as the result of the wheat programs he is able to market his wheat at a price "far above any world price based on the natural reaction of supply and demand." We can hardly find a denial of due process in these circumstances, particularly since it is even doubtful that appellee's burdens under the program outweigh his benefits. It is hardly lack of due process for the Government to regulate that which it subsidizes....

Reversed.

Questions

1. *Wickard v. Filburn* rests on a plenary view of congressional powers over the regulation of commerce. Chief Justice Marshall also spoke of plenary congressional commerce power in *Gibbons v. Ogden*. Is

Wickard a defensible extension of or an unjustifiable break with *Gibbons*? In what ways are *Wickard* and *Darby* related?

2. Political scientist and constitutional historian C. Herman Pritchett referred to *Filburn* as the "high water mark of commerce clause expansionism" (*The American Constitution*, 3rd ed. [New York, NY: McGraw Hill, 1977], p. 198). Filburn's counsel predicted that if Congress's power to regulate were upheld in *Filburn*, the United States would approach a centralized government that would lead to absolutism by successive nullifications of Constitutional limitations. Counsel's argument implied that only courts could place limits on Congress.

   What constitutional limitations, if any, remain on Congress's power to regulate commerce in the wake of *Filburn*?

3. In a footnote (#27) to his majority opinion in *Maryland v. Wirtz*, 392 U.S. 183 (1968), Justice John Marshall Harlan wrote: "... [I]n *Wickard* ... the Court [did not declare] that Congress may use a relatively trivial impact on commerce as an excuse for broad general regulation of state or private activities. The Court ... said only that where a general regulatory statute bears a substantial relation to commerce, the *de minimis* character of individual instances arising under that statute is of no consequence." Is this an accurate reading of *Wickard*?

4. *Wickard* culminated the Court's rejection of the dichotomies between manufacturing and production and between direct and indirect effects on commerce, and of the doctrine of dual federalism. Under what circumstances might those distinctions be revived? Is an expansive reading of Congress's power to regulate commerce necessarily a death knell for the Tenth Amendment?

MODERN VIEWS OF OLD CONTROVERSIES

Heart of Atlanta Motel, Inc. v. United States
379 U.S. 241 (1964)

SETTING

President Roosevelt's eight appointments to the Supreme Court created a tribunal highly sympathetic to the exercise of federal power. *Wickard v. Filburn* significantly expanded congressional commerce powers. The *Wickard* Court quoted Chief Justice Hughes approvingly to the effect that: "The commerce power is not confined in its exercise to the regulation of commerce among the states. It extends to those activities intrastate which so affect interstate commerce, or the exertion of the power of Congress over it, as to make regulation of them appropriate means to the attainment of a legitimate end, the effective execution of the granted power to regulate interstate commerce." This sweeping statement created the possibility that, under Article I, section 8, clause 3, Congress could reach activities previously assumed beyond its Commerce Clause authority, including regulation of civil rights.

The modern civil rights movement was born in the 1950s, kindled by the Supreme Court's decision in *Brown v. Board of Education*, 347 U.S. 483 (1954), and fueled by struggles like the 1955 Montgomery, Alabama, bus boycott. By the early 1960s, blacks were growing impatient with the slow pace of integration and reluctant federal efforts to enforce civil rights. In February 1960, a sit-in demonstration at a Greensboro, North Carolina, Woolworth store lunch counter signaled the beginning of a wave of nonviolent civil disobedience. What began as peaceful demonstrations, however, often led to violent reactions throughout southern states. For example, Mississippi residents resisted so fiercely James Meredith's attempt to register as a student at the University of Mississippi in October 1962, that President Kennedy was obliged to send four hundred federal marshals and three thousand troops to enforce order. When the Reverend Martin Luther King Jr. led a campaign against racial discrimination in Birmingham, Alabama, in the spring of 1963, he and his followers were confronted with fire hoses, attack dogs, and electric cattle prods. In June 1963, Governor George Wallace blocked the doorway of the University of Alabama, shouting "Segregation now, segregation tomorrow, segregation forever!" Two months later, two hundred thousand mostly black demonstrators took part in a peaceful march in Washington, D.C., demanding government action to advance racial equality.

Lyndon Baines Johnson, who became president of the United States on the afternoon of November 22, 1963, following the assassination of President John F. Kennedy, was the first southern president since Andrew Johnson. As a tribute to Kennedy, Johnson asked Congress to enact a civil rights bill that was stalled in the House Rules Committee. A bipartisan effort mustered enough votes to invoke cloture (close debate and take a vote) and overcome a southern filibuster in the Senate, enabling Congress to pass the Civil Rights Act of 1964.

The act's far-reaching provisions strengthened federal voting rights (Title I) and facilitated school desegregation (Title IV). The act also prohibited discrimination on the basis of race, color, religion, or national origin in public accommodations if the discrimination was supported by state law or official action, if lodgings were provided to transient guests or if interstate travelers were served, or if a substantial portion of the goods sold or entertainment provided moved in interstate commerce (Titles II and III). The 1964 Civil Rights Act also prohibited discrimination in programs that received federal financial assistance (Title VI) and by employers, labor unions, and employment agencies (Title VII). President Johnson signed the Civil Rights Act into law on July 2, 1964.

Two hours after Johnson signed the Civil Rights Act, Moreton Rolleston Jr., a pugnacious segregationist and sole stockholder in the 216-room Heart of Atlanta Motel Corporation in downtown Atlanta, Georgia, filed suit in the U.S. District Court for the Northern District of Georgia. The suit attacked the constitutionality of Title II and sought an injunction against its enforcement. Title II prohibited, among other things, racial discrimination in places of public accommodation, including hotels and motels whose operation affected commerce.

Rolleston's complaint stated that the Heart of Atlanta Motel had never rented sleeping accommodations to members of the Negro race and that it intended to continue that practice. It claimed the motel would suffer irreparable damages and the loss of a large percentage of its customers, income, and good will if it obeyed the Civil Rights Act. The United States filed a counterclaim seeking an injunction restraining the motel from violating the act.

On July 22, 1964, a three-judge district court panel ruled for the United States and entered a permanent injunction against Heart of Atlanta Motel, restraining it from continuing to violate the Civil Rights Act. That court relied on *United States v. Darby*, which held that Congress's power to regulate commerce "extends to those activities *intrastate* which so affect *interstate* commerce ... as to make regulation of them appropriate means to ... the exercise of the granted power..." (emphasis added). The court stayed the injunction until August 11, 1964, however, to allow the Heart of Atlanta Motel an opportunity to prepare its record for appeal. Rolleston appealed to the Supreme Court of the United States.

HIGHLIGHTS OF SUPREME COURT ARGUMENTS

BRIEF FOR THE HEART OF ATLANTA MOTEL

◆ The commands of the 1964 Civil Rights Act are the same as those of the Civil Rights Act of 1875, a statute held unconstitutional by the Supreme Court in 1883 in the *Civil Rights Cases*.

◆ Congress had no authority to pass the 1964 Civil Rights Act because the discrimination prohibited by it is private rather than state sponsored. Neither the Constitution nor the Fourteenth Amendment prohibits discrimination by individuals on the basis of race.

◆ The Civil Rights Act violates the Fifth Amendment. By telling private property owners how their property can be used, the act results in a taking of private property without due process and without just compensation.

◆ The Civil Rights Act violates the Thirteenth Amendment. Forcing businesses to serve persons they choose not to serve constitutes involuntary servitude. The purpose of the Thirteenth Amendment was not merely to end slavery, but to create a system of free and voluntary labor throughout the United States.

◆ Congress, knowing of these objections, based the 1964 act on the commerce clause. The commerce clause was drafted to eliminate economic barriers between states. People are not a part of trade or commerce. The drafters of the Declaration of Independence and the Constitution never intended those documents to protect Negroes.

◆ The central issue in this case is whether Congress has the power to take away the personal liberty of an individual to run his business as he sees fit. If Congress's power in this case is upheld, there will be no limit to its power to appropriate and destroy individual liberty and property: it will be able to exercise its power to arrive at the full and complete socialistic state that the framers of the Constitution despised, dreaded, and detested.

AMICUS CURIAE BRIEF SUPPORTING THE HEART OF ATLANTA MOTEL, INC.

Attorneys general of Virginia and Florida.

BRIEF FOR THE UNITED STATES

◆ Congress had ample evidence of barriers to commerce created by racial discrimination in places of public accommodation when it framed the Civil Rights Act. Commerce in whole sections of the country is being impeded by boycotts, picketing, and mass demonstrations. Testimony before Congress showed that unavailability to Negroes of adequate lodging interferes significantly with interstate travel. Prohibiting discrimination against all Negroes is appropriate so they will not have to prove their "interstate status" when traveling.

◆ The motel's due process claim is answered by the Court's decision in *Ferguson v. Skrupa*, 372 U.S. 726 (1963), which held that due process grants no immunity from reasonable regulations of business and commercial activity.

◆ The motel's Thirteenth Amendment argument should be rejected, because the public accommodation provision in the 1964 act does no more than extend the common-law innkeeper rule, which requires service to all.

◆ The law offers no remedy for consequential losses or injuries resulting from lawful governmental action.

AMICUS CURIAE BRIEFS SUPPORTING THE UNITED STATES

Attorneys general of New York, California, and Massachusetts.

SUPREME COURT DECISION: 9–0

CLARK, J.

... The legislative history [of Title II of the Civil Rights Act of 1964] indicates that Congress based the Act on section 5 of the Equal Protection Clause of the Fourteenth Amendment as well as its power to regulate interstate commerce under Art. I, section 8, clause 3, of the Constitution....

The Senate Commerce Committee made it quite clear that the fundamental object of Title II was to vindicate "the deprivation of personal dignity that surely accompanies denials of equal access to public establishments." At the same time, however, it noted that such an objective has been and could be readily achieved "by congressional action based on the commerce power of the Constitution." Our study of the legislative record, made in the light of prior cases, has brought us to the conclusion that Congress possessed ample power in this regard, and we have therefore not considered the other grounds relied upon. This is not to say that the remaining authority upon which it acted was not adequate, a question upon which we do not pass, but merely that since the commerce power is sufficient for our decision here we have considered it alone....

While the Act as adopted carried no congressional findings the record of its passage through each house is replete with evidence of the burdens that discrimination by race or color places upon interstate commerce. This testimony included the fact that our people have become increasingly mobile with millions of people of all races traveling from State to State; that Negroes in particular have been the subject of discrimination in transient accommodations, having to travel great distances to secure the same; that often they have been unable to obtain accommodations and have had to call upon friends to put them up overnight; and that these conditions had become so acute as to require the listing of available lodging for Negroes in a special guidebook which was itself "dramatic testimony to the difficulties" Negroes encounter in travel. These exclusionary practices were found to be nationwide, the Under Secretary of commerce testifying that there is "no question that this discrimination in the North still exists to a large degree" and in the West and Midwest as well. This testimony indicated a qualitative as well as quantitative effect on interstate travel by Negroes. The former was the obvious impairment of the Negro traveler's pleasure and convenience that resulted when he continually was uncertain of finding lodging. As for the latter, there was evidence that this uncertainty stemming from racial discrimination had the effect of discouraging travel on the part of a substantial portion of the Negro community....

The power of Congress to deal with these obstructions depends on the meaning of the Commerce Clause. Its meaning was first enunciated 140 years ago by the great Chief Justice John Marshall in *Gibbons v. Ogden*....

[T]he determinative test of the exercise of power by the Congress under the Commerce Clause is simply whether the activity sought to be regulated is "commerce which concerns more States than one" and has a real and substantial relation to the national interest. Let us now turn to this facet of the problem.

That [commerce] ... included the movement of persons through more States than one was settled as early as 1849, in the *Passenger Cases* [7 Howard 283 (1849)]. Nor does it make any difference whether the transportation is commercial in character....

The same interest in protecting interstate commerce ... led Congress to deal with segregation in interstate carriers and the white-slave traffic has prompted it to extend the exercise of its power to gambling, to criminal enterprises, to deceptive practices in the sale of products, to fraudulent security transactions, to misbranding of drugs, ... and to racial discrimination by owners and managers of terminal restaurants.

That Congress was legislating against moral wrongs in many of these areas rendered its enactments no less valid. In framing Title II of this Act Congress was also dealing with what it considered a moral problem. But that fact does not detract from the overwhelming evidence of the disruptive effect that racial discrimination has had on commercial intercourse. It was this burden which empowered Congress to enact appropriate legislation, and, given this basis for the exercise of its power, Congress was not restricted by the fact that the particular obstruction to interstate commerce with which it was dealing was also deemed a moral and social wrong.

It is said that the operation of the motel here is of a purely local character. But, assuming this to be true, "[i]f it is interstate commerce that feels the pinch, it does not matter how local the operation which applies the squeeze." *United States v. Women's Sportswear Mgrs. Assn.*, 336 U.S. 460 (1949). As Chief Justice Stone put it in *United States v. Darby*,

> The power of Congress over interstate commerce is not confined to the regulation of commerce among the states. It extends to those activities intrastate which so affect interstate commerce or the exercise of the power of Congress over it as to make regulation of them appropriate means to the attainment of a legitimate end, the exercise of the granted power of Congress to regulate interstate commerce.

Thus, the power of Congress to promote interstate commerce also includes the power to regulate the local incidents thereof, including local activities in both the States of origin and destination, which might have a substantial and harmful effect upon that commerce. One need only examine the evidence which we have discussed above to see that Congress may—as it has—prohibit racial discrimination by motels serving travelers, however "local" their operations may appear.

Nor does the Act deprive appellant of liberty or property under the Fifth Amendment. The commerce power invoked here by the Congress is a specific and plenary one authorized by the Constitution itself. The only questions are: (1) whether Congress had a rational basis for finding that racial discrimination by motels affected commerce, and (2) if it had such a basis, whether the means it selected to eliminate that evil are reasonable and appropriate. If they are, appellant has no "right" to select its guests as it sees fit, free from governmental regulation....

Neither do we find any merit in the claim that the Act is a taking of property without just compensation. The cases are to the contrary.

We find no merit in the remainder of appellant's contentions, including that of "involuntary servitude."...

We, therefore, conclude that the action of the Congress in the adoption of the Act as applied here to a motel which concededly serves interstate travelers is within the power granted it by the Commerce Clause of the Constitution, as interpreted by this Court for 140 years. It may be argued that Congress could have pursued other methods to eliminate the obstructions it found in interstate commerce caused by racial discrimination. But this is a matter of policy that rests entirely with the Congress not with the courts. How obstructions in commerce may be removed—what means are to be employed—is within the sound and exclusive discretion of the Congress. It is subject only to one caveat—that the means chosen by it must be reasonably adapted to the end permitted by the Constitution. We cannot say that its choice here was not so adapted. The Constitution requires no more.

Affirmed.

DOUGLAS, J., CONCURRING

Though I join the Court's opinions, I am somewhat reluctant ... to rest solely on the Commerce Clause. My reluctance is not due to any conviction that Congress lacks power to regulate commerce in the interests of human rights. It is rather my belief that the right of people to be free of state action that discriminates against them because of race ..."occupies a more protected position in our constitutional system than does the movement of cattle, fruit, steel and coal across state lines." *Edwards v. California*, 314 U.S. 160 (1941)....

Hence I would prefer to rest on the assertion of legislative power contained in Section 5 of the Fourteenth Amendment which states: "The Congress shall have power to enforce, by appropriate legislation, the provisions of this article"—a power which the Court concedes was exercised at least in part in this Act....

The rights protected [by the Civil Rights Act] are clearly within the purview of our decisions under the Equal Protection Clause of the Fourteenth Amendment....

A decision based on the Fourteenth Amendment would have a more settling effect, making unnecessary litigation over whether a particular restaurant or inn is within the commerce definitions of the Act or whether a particular customer is an interstate traveler. Under my construction, the Act would apply to all customers in all the enumerated places of public accommodation. And that construction would put an end to all obstructionist strategies and finally close one door on a bitter chapter in American history....

BLACK, J., CONCURRING [OMITTED]

GOLDBERG, J., CONCURRING [OMITTED]

QUESTIONS

1. Identify the constitutional bases on which the Supreme Court could have upheld the 1964 Civil Rights Act. Which is the most defensible? Which is the least defensible?

2. In a June 5, 1964, letter to the Department of Justice, law professor Gerald Gunther wrote: "If a federal ban on discrimination in such businesses as stores and restaurants is to be enacted, it should rest on the obviously most relevant source of national power, the Fourteenth Amendment, rather than the tenuously related commerce clause. The proposed end run by way of the commerce clause seems to me ill-advised" (quoted in Gerald Gunther, *Constitutional Law*, 12th ed. [Westbury, NY: Foundation, 1991], p.148).

   Is Gunther correct? If so, why did Congress and the Court ignore his advice?

Concurring in *Heart of Atlanta*, Justice Douglas urged that the Civil Rights Act of 1964 be upheld on the basis of Congress's power to enforce the Equal Protection Clause of the Fourteenth Amendment. What language in the Fourteenth Amendment, as well as in existing precedents, suggests why the majority preferred the Commerce Clause? Compare *Edwards v. California*, 314 U.S. 160 (1941). What theory of state action is implied by Justice Douglas's position?

3. Legal scholar and attorney Robert L. Stern has observed that "[t]he few commerce clause cases of importance since [the 1940s] concerned the use of commerce power for noncommercial purposes: to combat racial segregation, crime, and environmental problems" (*Encyclopedia of the American Constitution*, 4 vols. [New York, NY: Macmillan, 1986], 1: 329). Summing up federal commerce power after 1937, political scientist Paul R. Benson Jr. writes: "Congress, under the Supreme Court's interpretation of the commerce clause, has the power to regulate all aspects of American economic life. This tremendous power extends also to matters of a social and/or moral nature if they embody some economic effect on commerce that *concerns more states than one*" (*Encyclopedia of the American Constitution*, 4 vols. [New York, NY: Macmillan, 1986], 3: 949) (emphasis added).

The words emphasized, of course, are John Marshall's from his definition of commerce among the states in *Gibbons v. Ogden*. Is *Heart of Atlanta* a legitimate extension of Marshall's interpretation of the Commerce Clause in *Gibbons*?

4. Moreton Rolleston Jr. argued his own case before the Supreme Court. In his brief for the Heart of Atlanta Motel, Rolleston took exception to Justice Douglas's concurring opinion in *Bell v. Maryland*, 378 U.S. 226 (1964), in which Douglas criticized Maryland's criminal trespass statute that had been used to convict twelve Baltimore demonstrators engaged in a "sit-in" to protest a segregated restaurant. Among other things, Douglas wrote, such use of trespass laws was unconstitutional because "*Apartheid* ... is barred by the common law as respects innkeepers and common carriers.... Why, then, even in the absence of a statute, should *apartheid* be given constitutional sanction in the restaurant field?" Furthermore, wrote Douglas, "The right of any person to travel *interstate* irrespective of race, creed, or color is protected by the Constitution.... Certainly his right to travel *intrastate* is as basic. Certainly his right to eat at public restaurants is as important in the modern setting as the right of mobility. In these times that right is, indeed, practically indispensable to travel interstate or intrastate." The United States cited Douglas's *Bell* opinion argument in its *Heart of Atlanta* brief.

Rolleston wrote:

> [I] must be old-fashioned and behind the times if [Douglas's views] are legal grounds upon which to determine the constitutionality of a statute. If these arguments were used by a young law student on his bar examination to practice law, [I submit] that he would never be granted a license.

How constitutionally far-fetched was Justice Douglas's opinion in *Bell*? Was it any more far-fetched than the Court's reading of the Commerce Clause in *Heart of Atlanta*? *ignore sec 5*

5. *Katzenbach v. McClung,* 379 U.S. 294 (1964), is a companion case to *Heart of Atlanta*. At issue was whether Ollie's Barbecue in Birmingham, Alabama, could confine service to blacks at its take-out counter. Ollie's Barbecue was a local eatery, serving few out-of-state customers. Nevertheless, Justice Clark held that the restaurant's discriminatory practices constituted a significant burden on commerce. Clark relied on the fact that 46 percent of the meat (worth $69,683) served annually by Ollie's Barbecue was supplied through interstate commerce and that that percentage, added to all other purchases of food through interstate commerce by proprietors who discriminated against blacks, was a burden on commerce. "We believe," Justice Clark wrote, "that [congressional] testimony afforded ample basis for the conclusion that established restaurants in such areas sold less interstate goods because of the discrimination, that interstate travel was obstructed directly by it, that business in general suffered and that many new businesses refrained from establishing there as a result."

How is *McClung* related to the *Wickard* "affecting commerce/cumulative effects" doctrine?

COMMENT

The more publicized case over the constitutionality of Section II of the 1964 Civil Rights Act involved Lester Maddox, who subsequently became governor of Georgia. Maddox owned an Atlanta fried chicken restaurant, the Pickrick, that refused to serve blacks. After the Civil Rights Act was signed, Maddox chased three blacks away from the Pickrick at gunpoint. The three sued in federal district court, seeking an injunction to restrain Maddox from further exclusion. The injunction was granted in *Willis and Kennedy v. Pickrick Restaurant*, 234 F. Supp. 179 (1964).

When Justice Hugo Black, presiding justice for the Fifth Circuit Court of Appeals, refused to stay the injunction pending Maddox's appeal to the Supreme Court, Maddox closed down the Pickrick. On the day he closed the restaurant, he referred to blacks standing outside as "you no-good dirty devils" and as "dirty Communists" (*New York Times*, August. 12, 1964, 1: 6).

MODERN VIEWS OF OLD CONTROVERSIES

United States v. Lopez
514 U.S. 549 (1995)

SETTING

After the Court's decision in cases like *Wickard v. Filburn* and *Heart of Atlanta*, it is without question that Congress's power under the authority of the Commerce Clause is extensive. Questions remained, however, about whether the Court would require Congress to show the link between the target of regulation and the Commerce Clause or if the Court would infer the link. In *United States v. Carolene Products*, 304 U.S. 1444 (1938), Justice Stone declared that "the existence of facts supporting the legislative judgment is to be presumed...." Justice Stone's comment amounted to a declaration that the only check on Congress's exercise of its Commerce Clause power would be a political one. Consequently, as the decision in *Heart of Atlanta* demonstrates, the Court for decades after *Carolene Products* upheld Congressional acts as valid exercises of its power under the Commerce Clause, whether or not Congress explicitly invoked its reliance on that provision.

Beginning in the late 1960s, the political climate began to change. Richard M. Nixon, for example, campaigned for president on a platform of "New Federalism" (returning power to the states) and promised to appoint justices to the Supreme Court who, as "strict constructionists," would again exert judicial control over Congress. In 1969, President Nixon appointed Warren E. Burger as chief justice to replace the retired Earl Warren. Between 1970 and 1991, three successive Republican presidents appointed nine Supreme Court associate justices: Harry Blackmun, Lewis F. Powell Jr., William Rehnquist, John Paul Stevens, Sandra Day O'Connor, Antonin Scalia, Anthony Kennedy, David Souter, and Clarence Thomas. By the mid-1970s, the Court was deeply divided on Commerce Clause questions involving states' rights, as *National League of Cities v. Usery*, 426 U.S. 833 (1976) (Chapter 5, pp. 586–596) demonstrates. This division had not been resolved a decade later. See *Garcia v. San Antonio Metropolitan Transit Authority*, 469 U.S. 528 (1985), Chapter 5, pp. 596–607. The Court also proved less deferential to Congress's presumed power to act under the authority of the Commerce Clause. Its review of the Gun-Free School Zones Act of 1990 is one example of the Court's more exacting standard of judicial review of congressional actions.

The goal of the Gun-Free School Zones Act was to "address the devastating tide of firearm violence in the nation's schools" and to "help prevent schools from becoming sanctuaries for armed criminals and drug gangs." The act was Congress's response to studies that showed that, in 1987, more than half a million students carried guns to school; more than one hundred thousand took a gun to school every day. In 1990, forty-two hundred teens were killed by guns. Section 922(q) of the act made it unlawful "for any individual knowingly to possess a firearm at a place that the individual knows, or has reasonable cause to believe, is a school zone." The act defined a school zone as the grounds of any public, private, or parochial school, or property within one thousand feet of such premises. Violators were subject to penalties of up to five years in prison and a $5,000 fine.

During congressional hearings on the Gun-Free School Zones Act, many witnesses testified about the impact of increasing firearms violence on the nation's educational system. However, none specifically discussed the effects on interstate commerce of firearm possession on or near school property. Neither the statute nor its legislative history contained express findings about the constitutional source of Congress's authority to enact the statute.

Alfonso Lopez Jr. was a twelfth-grade student at Edison High School in San Antonio, Texas. On March 10, 1992, he took a concealed .38 caliber handgun with five bullets to school. Acting on an anonymous tip, school authorities confronted Lopez, who admitted he was carrying the weapon. He explained that the gun had been given to him by "Gilbert" to deliver to another student after school for a "gang war." Lopez also told officials that he was to receive $40 for delivering the gun. Lopez was arrested and charged under Texas law with firearm possession on school premises. The following day, the state charges were dismissed after federal agents charged Lopez with violating the 1990 Gun-Free School Zones Act. He was subsequently indicted by a grand jury for violating the Gun-Free School Zones Act.

Lopez waived his right to a jury and was tried on stipulated facts in a bench trial before the U.S. District Court for the District of Western Texas. He was convicted and sentenced to six months in prison and two years of supervised release. The U.S. Court of Appeals for the Fifth Circuit reversed his conviction on the ground that the Gun-Free School Zones Act was unconstitutional. It ruled that "when Congress wishes to stretch its commerce power so far as to intrude on state prerogatives, it must express its intent in a perfectly clear fashion" and that no express findings regarding the effects on interstate commerce of guns in schools had been made.

The Supreme Court of the United States granted the U.S. petition for a writ of certiorari.

HIGHLIGHTS OF SUPREME COURT ARGUMENTS

BRIEF FOR THE UNITED STATES

◆ Congress is empowered under the Commerce Clause to regulate even intrastate, noncommercial activity that exerts a substantial impact on interstate commerce. Congress is not required to issue formal findings establishing a nexus between the regulated activity and interstate commerce, nor is it required to identify the Commerce Clause as the source of its power to act. The only question for the Court is whether Congress could rationally have concluded that gun possession on or near school premises affects interstate commerce.

◆ The conduct proscribed by section 922(q) of the Gun-Free School Zones Act affects commerce. Congress could find that guns spread the consequences of violent crime throughout the nation and that the presence of guns affects the willingness of individuals to travel to areas perceived as unsafe.

◆ Congress could find that the presence of guns near and in schools poses threats to the educational system and that disruption of the educational system would have deleterious effects on the national economy.

AMICUS CURIAE BRIEFS SUPPORTING THE UNITED STATES

Joint brief of the Center to Prevent Handgun Violence, American Federation of Teachers, Council of Great City Schools, National Association of Elementary School Principals, National Association of Secondary School Principals, National Education Association, National Parent Teacher Association, Major Cities Chiefs of Police, International Association of Chiefs of Police, National Association of Police Organizations, Fraternal Order of Police, Federal Law Enforcement Officers Association, Police Executives Research Forum, and National Organization of Black Police Enforcement Executives; joint brief of Children Now, Project on Children and Violence, Youth Alive, Children's Law Offices; Clarendon Foundation; joint brief of the National School Safety Center, National Crime Prevention Council, American Association of School Administrators, National Association of Secondary School Principals, National Crime Prevention Institute, National Association of School Research Officers, National Association of School Safety and Law Enforcement Officers, Superintendent of Los Angeles County Schools; joint brief of the states of Ohio, New York, District of Columbia; joint brief on behalf of sixteen members of the U.S. Senate and thirty-four members of the U.S. House of Representatives.

BRIEF FOR LOPEZ

◆ The Gun-Free School Zones Act intrudes into two areas traditionally regulated by the states—criminal law and education.

◆ Congress failed to make the link between the regulatory activity and commerce. Firearm possession is not a commercial activity.

◆ The Supreme Court has always required Congress to declare an activity's effect and to delineate the extent of the regulation it seeks to impose. The Gun-Free School Zones Act is bereft of any such findings or declarations. Where legislation intrudes on a traditional state prerogative, explicit findings are necessary to demonstrate the validity of the national legislation.

◆ Congress does not always intend to reach the full extent of its commerce power when it enacts legislation. Therefore, it must state its intent, because courts cannot make assumptions about the intended extent of its jurisdiction.

◆ Findings regarding the purpose of legislation are needed to safeguard federalism and maintain separation of powers among the branches. The lack of findings in this act is fatal.

◆ The Gun-Free School Zones Act interferes with the rights of law-abiding citizens to possess firearms, an intent that Congress has emphatically disclaimed in earlier legislation.

◆ The government's effort to link the act to commerce is little more than an argument for a general police power that the national government does not have.

AMICUS CURIAE BRIEFS SUPPORTING LOPEZ

Pacific Legal Foundation; joint brief of the National Conference of State Legislatures, National Governor's Association, National League of Cities, National Association of Counties, International City and County Managers Association, National Institute of Municipal Law Enforcement Officers, National School Boards Association; Texas Justice Foundation.

AMICUS CURIAE BRIEF SUPPORTING NEITHER PARTY

Joint brief of Academics for the Second Amendment, Second Amendment Foundation, Congress on Racial Equality, National Association of Chiefs of Police, and American Federation of Police.

SUPREME COURT DECISION: 5–4

REHNQUIST, C.J.

... We start with first principles. The Constitution creates a Federal Government of enumerated powers. As James Madison wrote, "[t]he powers delegated by the proposed Constitution to the federal government are few and defined. Those which are to remain in the State governments are numerous and indefinite." The *Federalist* No. 45....

The Constitution delegates to Congress the power "[t]o regulate Commerce with foreign Nations, and among the several States, and with the Indian Tribes." The Court, through Chief Justice Marshall, first defined the nature of Congress' commerce power in *Gibbons v. Ogden*.... The Gibbons Court, however, acknowledged that limitations on the commerce power are inherent in the very language of the Commerce Clause....

For nearly a century thereafter, the Court's Commerce Clause decisions dealt but rarely with the extent of Congress' power, and almost entirely with the Commerce Clause as a limit on state legislation that discriminated against interstate commerce.... Under this line of precedent, the Court held that certain categories of activity such as "production," "manufacturing," and "mining" were within the province of state governments, and thus were beyond the power of Congress under the Commerce Clause....

In 1887, Congress enacted the Interstate Commerce Act and in 1890, Congress enacted the Sherman Antitrust Act. These laws ushered in a new era of federal regulation under the commerce power. When cases involving these laws first reached this Court, we imported from our negative Commerce Clause cases the approach that Congress could not regulate activities such as "production," "manufacturing," and "mining."... Simultaneously, however, the Court held that, where the interstate and intrastate aspects of commerce were so mingled together that full regulation of interstate commerce required incidental regulation of intrastate commerce, the Commerce Clause authorized such regulation....

In *A.L.A. Schechter Poultry Corp. v. United States* the Court struck down regulations that fixed the hours and wages of individuals employed by an intrastate business because the activity being regulated related to interstate commerce only indirectly. In doing so, the Court characterized the distinction between direct and indirect effects of intrastate transactions upon interstate commerce as "a fundamental one, essential to the maintenance of our constitutional system." Activities that affected interstate commerce directly were within Congress' power; activities that affected interstate commerce indirectly were beyond Congress' reach. The justification for this formal distinction was rooted in the fear that otherwise "there would be virtually no limit to the federal power and for all practical purposes we

should have a completely centralized government."...

Jones & Laughlin Steel, *Darby*, and *Wickard*, [however,] ushered in an era of Commerce Clause jurisprudence that greatly expanded the previously defined authority of Congress under that Clause. In part, this was a recognition of the great changes that had occurred in the way business was carried on in this country. Enterprises that had once been local or at most regional in nature had become national in scope. But the doctrinal change also reflected a view that earlier Commerce Clause cases artificially had constrained the authority of Congress to regulate interstate commerce.

But even these modern-era precedents which have expanded congressional power under the Commerce Clause confirm that this power is subject to outer limits. In *Jones & Laughlin Steel*, the Court warned that the scope of the interstate commerce power "must be considered in the light of our dual system of government and may not be extended so as to embrace effects upon interstate commerce so indirect and remote that to embrace them, in view of our complex society, would effectually obliterate the distinction between what is national and what is local and create a completely centralized government."...

Consistent with this structure, we have identified three broad categories of activity that Congress may regulate under its commerce power.... First, Congress may regulate the use of the channels of interstate commerce.... Second, Congress is empowered to regulate and protect the instrumentalities of interstate commerce, or persons or things in interstate commerce, even though the threat may come only from intrastate activities.... Finally, Congress' commerce authority includes the power to regulate those activities having a substantial relation to interstate commerce....

Within this final category, admittedly, our case law has not been clear whether an activity must "affect" or "substantially affect" interstate commerce in order to be within Congress' power to regulate it under the Commerce Clause.... We conclude, consistent with the great weight of our case law, that the proper test requires an analysis of whether the regulated activity "substantially affects" interstate commerce.

We now turn to consider the power of Congress, in the light of this framework, to enact 922(q). The first two categories of authority may be quickly disposed of: 922(q) is not a regulation of the use of the channels of interstate commerce, nor is it an attempt to prohibit the interstate transportation of a commodity through the channels of commerce; nor can 922(q) be justified as a regulation by which Congress has sought to protect an instrumentality of interstate commerce or a thing in interstate commerce. Thus, if 922(q) is to be sustained, it must be under the third category as a regulation of an activity that substantially affects interstate commerce.

First, we have upheld a wide variety of congressional Acts regulating intrastate economic activity where we have concluded that the activity substantially affected interstate commerce.... [T]he pattern is clear. Where economic activity substantially affects interstate commerce, legislation regulating that activity will be sustained.

Even *Wickard*, which is perhaps the most far reaching example of Commerce Clause authority over intrastate activity, involved economic activity in a way that the possession of a gun in a school zone does not....

Section 922(q) is a criminal statute that by its terms has nothing to do with "commerce" or any sort of economic enterprise, however broadly one might define those terms. Section 922(q) is not an essential part of a larger regulation of economic activity, in which the regulatory scheme could be undercut unless the intrastate activity were regulated. It cannot, therefore, be sustained under our cases upholding regulations of activities that arise out of or are connected with a commercial transaction, which viewed in the aggregate, substantially affects interstate commerce.

Second, 922(q) contains no jurisdictional element which would ensure, through case-by-case inquiry, that the firearm possession in question affects interstate commerce....

Although as part of our independent evaluation of constitutionality under the Commerce Clause we of course consider legislative findings, and indeed even congressional committee findings, regarding effect on interstate commerce, ... the Government concedes that "[n]either the statute nor its legislative history contain[s] express congressional findings regarding the effects upon interstate commerce of gun possession in a school zone." We agree with the Government that Congress normally is not required to make formal findings as to the substantial burdens that an activity has on interstate commerce.... But to the extent that congressional findings would enable us to evaluate the legislative judgment that the activity in question substantially affected interstate commerce, even though no such substantial effect was visible to the naked eye, they are lacking here....

The Government's essential contention, *in fine*, is that we may determine here that 922(q) is valid because possession of a firearm in a local school zone does indeed substantially affect interstate commerce. The Government argues that possession of a firearm in a school zone may result in violent crime and that violent crime can be expected to affect the functioning of the national economy in two ways. First, the costs of violent crime are substantial, and, through the mechanism of insurance, those costs are spread throughout the population.... Second, violent crime reduces the willingness of individuals to travel to areas within the country that are perceived to be unsafe.... The Government also argues that the presence of guns in schools poses a substantial threat to the educational process by threatening the learning environment. A handicapped educational process, in turn, will result in a less productive citizenry. That, in turn, would have an adverse effect on the Nation's economic well-being. As a result, the Government argues that Congress could rationally have concluded that 922(q) substantially affects interstate commerce.

We pause to consider the implications of the Government's arguments. The Government admits, under its "costs of crime" reasoning, that Congress could regulate not only all violent crime, but all activities that might lead to violent crime, regardless of how tenuously they relate to interstate commerce. Similarly, under the Government's "national productivity" reasoning, Congress could regulate any activity that it found was related to the economic productivity of individual citizens: family law (including marriage, divorce, and child custody), for example.

Under the theories that the Government presents in support of 922(q), it is difficult to perceive any limitation on federal power, even in areas such as criminal law enforcement or education where States historically have been sovereign. Thus, if we were to accept the Government's arguments, we are hard-pressed to posit any activity by an individual that Congress is without power to regulate....

Admittedly, a determination whether an intrastate activity is commercial or noncommercial may in some cases result in legal uncertainty. But, so long as Congress' authority is limited to those powers enumerated in the Constitution, and so long as those enumerated powers are interpreted as having judicially enforceable outer limits, congressional legislation under the Commerce Clause always will engender "legal uncertainty."...

Congress has operated within this framework of legal uncertainty ever since this Court determined that it was the judiciary's duty "to say what the law is." *Marbury v. Madison.* Any possible benefit from eliminating this "legal uncertainty" would be at the expense of the Constitution's system of enumerated powers....

These are not precise formulations, and in the nature of things they cannot be. But we think they point the way to a correct decision of this case. The possession of a gun in a local school zone is in no sense an economic activity that might, through repetition elsewhere, substantially affect any sort of interstate commerce. Respondent was a local student at a local school; there is no indication that he had recently moved in interstate commerce, and there is no requirement that his possession of the firearm have any concrete tie to interstate commerce.

To uphold the Government's contentions here, we would have to pile inference upon inference in a manner that would bid fair to convert congressional authority under the Commerce Clause to a general police power of the sort retained by the States. Admittedly, some of our prior cases have taken long steps down that road, giving great deference to congressional action. The broad language in these opinions has suggested the possibility of additional expansion, but we decline here to proceed any further. To do so would require us to conclude that the Constitution's enumeration of powers does not presuppose something not enumerated ... and that there never will be a distinction between what is truly national and what is truly local.... This we are unwilling to do.

For the foregoing reasons the judgment of the Court of Appeals is
Affirmed.

KENNEDY AND O'CONNOR, J.J., CONCURRING

... The history of our Commerce Clause decisions contains at least two lessons of relevance to this case. The first ... is the imprecision of content-based boundaries used without more to define the limits of the Commerce Clause. The second, related to the first but of even greater consequence, is that the Court

as an institution and the legal system as a whole have an immense stake in the stability of our Commerce Clause jurisprudence as it has evolved to this point. *Stare decisis* operates with great force in counseling us not to call in question the essential principles now in place respecting the congressional power to regulate transactions of a commercial nature. That fundamental restraint on our power forecloses us from reverting to an understanding of commerce that would serve only an 18th-century economy, dependent then upon production and trading practices that had changed but little over the preceding centuries; it also mandates against returning to the time when congressional authority to regulate undoubted commercial activities was limited by a judicial determination that those matters had an insufficient connection to an interstate system. Congress can regulate in the commercial sphere on the assumption that we have a single market and a unified purpose to build a stable national economy.... It does not follow, however, that in every instance the Court lacks the authority and responsibility to review congressional attempts to alter the federal balance. This case requires us to consider our place in the design of the Government and to appreciate the significance of federalism in the whole structure of the Constitution.

Of the various structural elements in the Constitution, separation of powers, checks and balances, judicial review, and federalism, only concerning the last does there seem to be much uncertainty respecting the existence, and the content, of standards that allow the judiciary to play a significant role in maintaining the design contemplated by the Framers....

There is irony in this, because of the four structural elements in the Constitution just mentioned, federalism was the unique contribution of the Framers to political science and political theory.... Though on the surface the idea may seem counterintuitive, it was the insight of the Framers that freedom was enhanced by the creation of two governments, not one....

The theory that two governments accord more liberty than one requires for its realization two distinct and discernable lines of political accountability: one between the citizens and the Federal Government; the second between the citizens and the States. If, as Madison expected, the federal and state governments are to control each other, ... and hold each other in check by competing for the affections of the people, ... those citizens must have some means of knowing which of the two governments to hold accountable for the failure to perform a given function.... Were the Federal Government to take over the regulation of entire areas of traditional state concern, areas having nothing to do with the regulation of commercial activities, the boundaries between the spheres of federal and state authority would blur and political responsibility would become illusory.... The resultant inability to hold either branch of the government answerable to the citizens is more dangerous even than devolving too much authority to the remote central power....

The substantial element of political judgment in Commerce Clause matters leaves our institutional capacity to intervene more in doubt than when we decide cases, for instance, under the Bill of Rights even though clear and bright lines are often absent in the latter class

of disputes.... But our cases do not teach that we have no role at all in determining the meaning of the Commerce Clause....

The statute before us upsets the federal balance to a degree that renders it an unconstitutional assertion of the commerce power, and our intervention is required....

While it is doubtful that any State, or indeed any reasonable person, would argue that it is wise policy to allow students to carry guns on school premises, considerable disagreement exists about how best to accomplish that goal. In this circumstance, the theory and utility of our federalism are revealed, for the States may perform their role as laboratories for experimentation to devise various solutions where the best solution is far from clear....

The statute now before us forecloses the States from experimenting and exercising their own judgment in an area to which States lay claim by right of history and expertise, and it does so by regulating an activity beyond the realm of commerce in the ordinary and usual sense of that term....

For these reasons, I join in the opinion and judgment of the Court.

THOMAS, J., CONCURRING

... Although I join the majority, I write separately to observe that our case law has drifted far from the original understanding of the Commerce Clause. In a future case, we ought to temper our Commerce Clause jurisprudence in a manner that both makes sense of our more recent case law and is more faithful to the original understanding of that Clause....

At the time the original Constitution

was ratified, "commerce" consisted of selling, buying, and bartering, as well as transporting for these purposes....

[I]nterjecting a modern sense of commerce into the Constitution generates significant textual and structural problems. For example, one cannot replace "commerce" with a different type of enterprise, such as manufacturing. When a manufacturer produces a car, assembly cannot take place "with a foreign nation" or "with the Indian Tribes." Parts may come from different States or other nations and hence may have been in the flow of commerce at one time, but manufacturing takes place at a discrete site. Agriculture and manufacturing involve the production of goods; commerce encompasses traffic in such articles....

The Constitution not only uses the word "commerce" in a narrower sense than our case law might suggest, it also does not support the proposition that Congress has authority over all activities that "substantially affect" interstate commerce. The Commerce Clause does not state that Congress may "regulate matters that substantially affect commerce with foreign Nations, and among the several States, and with the Indian Tribes."...

Our construction of the scope of congressional authority has the additional problem of coming close to turning the Tenth Amendment on its head. Our case law could be read to reserve to the United States all powers not expressly prohibited by the Constitution. Taken together, these fundamental textual problems should, at the very least, convince us that the "substantial effects" test should be reexamined....

Apart from its recent vintage and its corresponding lack of any grounding in the original understanding of the

Constitution, the substantial effects test suffers from the further flaw that it appears to grant Congress a police power over the Nation....

If we wish to be true to a Constitution that does not cede a police power to the Federal Government, our Commerce Clause's boundaries simply cannot be "defined" as being "'commensurate with the national needs'" or self-consciously intended to let the Federal Government "'defend itself against economic forces that Congress decrees inimical or destructive of the national economy.'" Such a formulation of federal power is no test at all: it is a blank check....

STEVENS, J., DISSENTING [OMITTED]

SOUTER, J., DISSENTING

... The practice of deferring to rationally based legislative judgments "is a paradigm of judicial restraint." *FCC v. Beach Communications, Inc.*, 508 U.S. 307 (1993). In judicial review under the Commerce Clause, it reflects our respect for the institutional competence of the Congress on a subject expressly assigned to it by the Constitution and our appreciation of the legitimacy that comes from Congress's political accountability in dealing with matters open to a wide range of possible choices....

The modern respect for the competence and primacy of Congress in matters affecting commerce developed only after one of this Court's most chastening experiences, when it perforce repudiated an earlier and untenably expansive conception of judicial review in derogation of congressional commerce power....

[U]nder commerce, as under due process, adoption of rational basis review expressed the recognition that the Court had no sustainable basis for subjecting economic regulation as such to judicial policy judgments, and for the past half-century the Court has no more turned back in the direction of formalistic Commerce Clause review (as in deciding whether regulation of commerce was sufficiently direct) than it has inclined toward reasserting the substantive authority of *Lochner* due process (as in the inflated protection of contractual autonomy)....

There is today, however, a backward glance at both the old pitfalls, as the Court treats deference under the rationality rule as subject to gradation according to the commercial or noncommercial nature of the immediate subject of the challenged regulation.... The distinction between what is patently commercial and what is not looks much like the old distinction between what directly affects commerce and what touches it only indirectly. And the act of calibrating the level of deference by drawing a line between what is patently commercial and what is less purely so will probably resemble the process of deciding how much interference with contractual freedom was fatal. Thus, it seems fair to ask whether the step taken by the Court today does anything but portend a return to the untenable jurisprudence from which the Court extricated itself almost 60 years ago. The answer is not reassuring. To be sure, the occasion for today's decision reflects the century's end, not its beginning. But if it seems anomalous that the Congress of the United States has taken to regulating school yards, the act in question is still probably no more remarkable than state regulation of bake shops 90 years ago. In any event, there

is no reason to hope that the Court's qualification of rational basis review will be any more successful than the efforts at substantive economic review made by our predecessors as the century began....

Further glosses on rationality review, moreover, may be in the offing. Although this case turns on commercial character, the Court gestures toward two other considerations that it might sometime entertain in applying rational basis scrutiny (apart from a statutory obligation to supply independent proof of a jurisdictional element): does the congressional statute deal with subjects of traditional state regulation, and does the statute contain explicit factual findings supporting the otherwise implicit determination that the regulated activity substantially affects interstate commerce? Once again, any appeal these considerations may have depends on ignoring the painful lesson learned in 1937, for neither of the Court's suggestions would square with rational basis scrutiny....

Because Justice Breyer's opinion demonstrates beyond any doubt that the Act in question passes the rationality review that the Court continues to espouse, today's decision may be seen as only a misstep, its reasoning and its suggestions not quite in gear with the prevailing standard, but hardly an epochal case. I would not argue otherwise, but I would raise a caveat. Not every epochal case has come in epochal trappings. *Jones & Laughlin* did not reject the direct-indirect standard in so many words; it just said the relation of the regulated subject matter to commerce was direct enough. But we know what happened.

I respectfully dissent.

BREYER, STEVENS, SOUTER, AND GINSBURG, J.J., DISSENTING

The issue in this case is whether the Commerce Clause authorizes Congress to enact a statute that makes it a crime to possess a gun in, or near, a school. In my view, the statute falls well within the scope of the commerce power as this Court has understood that power over the last half-century....

In reaching this conclusion, I apply three basic principles of Commerce Clause interpretation. First, the power to "regulate Commerce ... among the several States," encompasses the power to regulate local activities insofar as they significantly affect interstate commerce.... As the majority points out, the Court, in describing how much of an effect the Clause requires, sometimes has used the word "substantial" and sometimes has not.... I use the word "significant" because the word "substantial" implies a somewhat narrower power than recent precedent suggests.... But, to speak of "substantial effect" rather than "significant effect" would make no difference in this case.

Second, in determining whether a local activity will likely have a significant effect upon interstate commerce, a court must consider, not the effect of an individual act (a single instance of gun possession), but rather the cumulative effect of all similar instances (i.e., the effect of all guns possessed in or near schools)....

Third, the Constitution requires us to judge the connection between a regulated activity and interstate commerce, not directly, but at one remove. Courts must give Congress a degree of leeway in determining the existence of a significant factual connection between the regulated activity and interstate commerce—both because the Constitution delegates the commerce power directly to Congress and because the determination requires an empirical judgment of a kind that a legislature is more likely than a court to make with accuracy. The traditional words "rational basis" capture this leeway.... Thus, the specific question before us, as the Court recognizes, is not whether the "regulated activity sufficiently affected interstate commerce," but, rather, whether Congress could have had "a rational basis" for so concluding....

Applying these principles to the case at hand, we must ask whether Congress could have had a *rational basis* for finding a significant (or substantial) connection between gun-related school violence and interstate commerce. Or, to put the question in the language of the *explicit* finding that Congress made when it amended this law in 1994: Could Congress rationally have found that "violent crime in school zones," through its effect on the "quality of education," significantly (or substantially) affects "interstate" or "foreign commerce"? As long as one views the commerce connection, not as a "technical legal conception," but as "a practical one," *Swift & Co. v. United States*, 196 U.S. 375 (1905), the answer to this question must be yes. Numerous reports and studies—generated both inside and outside government—make clear that Congress could reasonably have found the empirical connection that its law, implicitly or explicitly, asserts....

To hold this statute constitutional is not to "obliterate" the "distinction of what is national and what is local"; nor is it to hold that the Commerce Clause permits the Federal Government to "regulate any activity that it found was related to the economic productivity of individual citizens," to regulate "marriage, divorce, and child custody," or to regulate any and all aspects of education. For one thing, this statute is aimed at curbing a particularly acute threat to the educational process—the possession (and use) of life-threatening firearms in, or near, the classroom. The empirical evidence that I have discussed above unmistakably documents the special way in which guns and education are incompatible.... This Court has previously recognized the singularly disruptive potential on interstate commerce that acts of violence may have.... For another thing, the immediacy of the connection between education and the national economic well-being is documented by scholars and accepted by society at large in a way and to a degree that may not hold true for other social institutions. It must surely be the rare case, then, that a statute strikes at conduct that (when considered in the abstract) seems so removed from commerce, but which (practically speaking) has so significant an impact upon commerce....

[T]o find this legislation within the scope of the Commerce Clause would permit "Congress ... to act in terms of economic ... realities." *North American Co. v. SEC*, 327 U.S. [668 (1945)]. It would interpret the Clause as this Court has traditionally interpreted it, with the exception of one wrong turn subsequently corrected.... Upholding this legislation would do no more than simply recognize that Congress had a "rational basis" for finding a significant connection between guns in or near schools and (through their effect on education) the interstate and foreign commerce they threaten. For these reasons, I would reverse the judgment of the Court of Appeals. Respectfully, I dissent.

QUESTIONS

1. Is *Lopez* confined to judicial disciplining of inattentive congressional drafting, or does the decision have more far-reaching importance? What broader implications might it have for cases like *United States v. Darby*, *Wickard v. Filburn*, and *Heart of Atlanta*?

2. If Congress were to re-enact the Gun-Free School Zones Act adding only a statement of findings regarding the link between guns and commerce, would that cure the constitutional deficiencies cited by the majority in *Lopez*?

3. The Gun-Free School Zones Act did not amend federal juvenile delinquency laws that frequently shield young offenders from prosecution in federal courts. Does this, combined with Congress's failure to make factual findings linking gun possession to interstate commerce, suggest that the act was well-intentioned but not well thought through?

4. In its *amicus curiae* brief, the Pacific Legal Foundation argued that "If the Second and Tenth Amendments are ignored here, may the First and Fifth Amendments be ignored next?" Does it necessarily follow that a Supreme Court that is deferential to Congress in the realm of legislation justified under the Commerce Clause will also defer to the popularly elected branch if legislation trenches on civil rights?

5. Note the voting alignment in the *Lopez* majority. Chief Justice Rehnquist wrote only for himself and Justice Scalia. Three other Republican appointees—Kennedy, O'Connor, and Thomas—concurred, but for different reasons. Identify the various points of constitutional principle in the three opinions that netted the five vote majority. Are those differences significant? What of the differences among the dissenters?

SUGGESTIONS FOR FURTHER READING

Bogen, David S., "The Hunting of the Shark: An Inquiry into the Limits of Congressional Power under the Commerce Clause," 8 *Wake Forest Law Review* (1972): 187.

Brest, Paul, "The Conscientious Legislator's Guide to Constitutional Interpretation," 27 *Stanford Law Review* (1975): 585.

Corwin, Edward S., "The Passing of Dual Federalism," 36 *Virginia Law Review* (1950): 1.

Epstein, Richard, "The Proper Scope of the Commerce Power," 73 *Virginia Law Review* (1987): 1387.

Kramer, Larry, "Understanding Federalism," 45 *Vanderbilt Law Review* (1994): 1485.

Lee, Carol F., "The Political Safeguards of Federalism? Congress Responds to Supreme Court Decisions on State and Local Liability," 20 *Urban Lawyer* (1988): 301.

Myers, R. S., "The Burger Court and the Commerce Clause: An Evaluation of the Role of State Sovereignty," 60 *Notre Dame Lawyer* (1985): 1056.

Stern, Robert L., "The Commerce Clause and the National Economy, 1933–1946," 59 *Harvard Law Review* (1946): 901.

IMPLIED POWERS: DELEGATION OF LEGISLATIVE POWER

A.L.A. Schechter Poultry Corp. v. United States
295 U.S. 495 (1935)

SETTING

Article I of the Constitution begins: "All legislative Powers herein granted shall be vested in a Congress of the United States...." Interpreted strictly, this language precludes Congress from delegating any of its expressly authorized powers. A strict interpretation is known as the nondelegation doctrine. After the Civil War, as American society was transformed by industrialization, urbanization, immigration, and corporate integration the nondelegation doctrine became increasingly anachronistic, because Congress was forced to rely on executive agencies to implement congressional policies. The nondelegation doctrine was compromised further as the United States became a continental, then an international, power. Many argued that modern circumstances required that the black letter language of Article I, section 1, be read in conjunction with the language of Article I, section 8, clause 18, which grants Congress the power "To *make all Laws which shall be necessary and proper for carrying into Execution* the foregoing Powers, and all other Powers vested by this Constitution in the Government of the United States, or in any Department or Officer thereof" (emphasis added).

By the turn of the twentieth century, the Supreme Court acknowledged the practical necessity of modifying the strict nondelegation doctrine. While reaffirming the nondelegation doctrine, the Court upheld the Reciprocal Tariff Act of 1890 by a 7–2 vote. This legislation authorized the president to suspend certain articles (sugar, molasses, coffee, tea, and hides) from a duty-free list and impose tariffs on them if "he may deem" that other countries were treating those commodities "unequally." Justice Harlan wrote: "That Congress cannot delegate legislative power to the president is a principle universally recognized as vital to the integrity and maintenance of the system of government ordained by the Constitution." However, he concluded: "What the president was required to do was simply in execution of the act of Congress. It was not the making of law. He was the mere agent of the law-making department to ascertain and declare the event upon which its expressed will was to take effect." To deny the president this discretion "would be to stop the wheels of government." *Field v. Clark*, 143 U.S. 649 (1892).

The Court refined the *Clark* holding in *United States v. Grimaud*, 220 U.S. 506 (1911). That case involved a challenge to the Forest Reserve Act of 1897 as an unconstitutional delegation to the secretary of agriculture of power to make rules and regulations. Justice Lamar noted for a unanimous Court that "[i]n the nature of things it was impracticable for Congress to provide general regulations for [the] various and varying details of management." He continued, "Each reservation had its peculiar and special features; and in authorizing the Secretary of Agriculture to meet these local conditions, Congress was merely conferring administrative functions upon an agent, and not delegating to him legislative power." Regarding the distinction between legislative and administrative rule-making, Justice Lamar wrote:

> It must be admitted that it is difficult to define the line which separates legislative power to make laws, from administrative authority to make regulations.... But the authority to make administrative rules is not a delegation of legislative power, nor are such rules raised from an administrative to a legislative character because the violation thereof is punished as a public offense.

Seventeen years later, on the eve of the Great Depression, the Court formulated a standard to govern congressional delegation of rule-making authority to administrative agencies. *J. W. Hampton, Jr., & Co. v. United States*, 276 U.S. 394 (1928) involved a challenge to the so-called flexible tariff provision of the 1922 Tariff Act, which authorized the president to equalize duties charged on certain articles based on "differences in costs of production of articles wholly or in part the growth or product of the United States and of like or similar articles wholly or in part the growth or product of competing foreign countries." Upholding the congressional delegation of authority, Chief Justice Taft ruled:

> If Congress shall lay down by legislative act an intelligible principle to which the person or body authorized to fix such rates is directed to conform, such legislative action is not a forbidden delegation of legislative power. If it is thought wise to vary the customs duties according to changing conditions of production at home and abroad, it may authorize the Chief Executive to carry out this purpose, with the advisory assistance of a Tariff Commission appointed under congressional authority.

Such was the doctrinal status of legislative delegation when the American economy collapsed in autumn 1929. The social tragedy and governmental emergency that unfolded during the Great Depression is discussed in the *Setting* to *A.L.A. Schechter Poultry Corp. v. United States* on pp. 262–265. The Roosevelt administration responded energetically to the Great Depression. Among the initiatives proposed during the First Hundred Days was the June 1933 National Industrial Recovery Act (NIRA). F.D.R. characterized the National Recovery Administration (NRA) enabling act as "the most important and far-reaching legislation ever enacted by the American Congress." The heart of the NRA approach to rescuing the American economy was industry-wide codes of fair practices that, when signed by the president, had the force of federal law. Congress thus authorized the NRA to authorize specific businesses to draft their own regulations.

Roosevelt's advisors, known as his "brain trust," planned that a few major NRA codes would emerge to govern business practices. In practice, by February 1934, negotiations between representatives of industry, labor, and consumers had generated 557 basic codes and 208 supplementary codes. Sixty-two of those codes covered fewer than five hundred employees. Most of them were Byzantine in their intricacy.

A case in point was the Code of Fair Competition for the Live Poultry Industry of the New York Metropolitan Area. The wholesale poultry-slaughtering business in New York was plagued with criminal activity and fierce competition among butchers. Gangsters so dominated the poultry industry that the term "racket" had been coined to describe their nefarious activities. The New York wholesale poultry market had a national reputation for being a dumping ground for diseased poultry, spreading tuberculosis. The Live Poultry Code resulted from efforts of kosher wholesale poultry dealers to seek federal protection. The Code established a fifty cent per hour minimum wage and a maximum workweek of forty-eight hours, and it prohibited the sale of poultry that was unfit for human consumption. The code also prohibited "straight killing," a sales practice designed to force customers who purchased less than a full coop of birds to take merely the "run of the coop" instead of picking and choosing among chickens.

The four Schechter Brothers—Joseph, Alex, Martin, and Aaron—were charged with violating several provisions of the Live Poultry Code. Among the counts alleged were violations of the wages and hours provisions. Paradoxically, the Schechters were also charged with seeking to undercut their competition by allowing their customers to select the best chickens and by selling diseased poultry at four to eight cents per pound below the market price. The Schechters were convicted on seventeen counts of violating the Live Poultry Code and fined $7,425. When the Schechters' appeal eventually came before the Supreme Court in early May of 1935, it afforded the justices the opportunity to comment further on the delegation of legislative power.

Note: Review the *Setting* to and excerpt of *A.L.A. Schechter Poultry Corp. v. United States*, pp. 262–270.

QUESTIONS

1. Concurring in *Schechter*, Justice Cardozo wrote: "The delegated power of legislation which has found expression in this code is not canalized within banks that keep it from overflowing. It is unconfined and vagrant.... This is delegation running riot...." Identify the characteristics of the Live Poultry Code that support Cardozo's conclusion.

2. How might the NIRA have been drafted to bring it within the purview of the *Hampton* "intelligible principle" rule?

IMPLIED POWERS: DELEGATION OF LEGISLATIVE POWER

National Labor Relations Board v. Jones & Laughlin Steel Corp.
301 U.S. 1 (1937)

SETTING

As discussed in the *Setting* to *National Labor Relations Board v. Jones & Laughlin Steel Corp.* on pp. 280–283, in March 1937, five justices of the Supreme Court abandoned the liberty of contract doctrine that had functioned as an effective constitutional barrier, frustrating government efforts to regulate the wages and hours of workers. Whether or not this shift was the "Switch in Time That Saved Nine," as journalists dubbed it, the Court's jettisoning of aspects of one hundred and fifty years of jurisprudence in *West Coast Hotel v. Parrish*, 300 U.S. 379 (1937), was a sea change in constitutional interpretation. *Parrish* was one facet of the constitutional revolution that took place in the first year of President Roosevelt's second term. Another dimension was the Court's shelving of the *Schechter* nondelegation doctrine.

The National Labor Relations Act (NLRA), commonly known as the Wagner Act after its sponsor, New York Senator Robert Wagner, was adopted to replace the National Industrial Recovery Act (NIRA) that was declared unconstitutional in *Schechter*. Carefully drafted to address the constitutional flaw the *Schechter* Court found in the NIRA with respect to Congress's power under the Commerce Clause, the first section of the Wagner Act sought to tie injuries to commerce to employers' denial of employees' right to organize and employers' refusal to accept collective bargaining. The key provision of the NLRA guaranteed workers the right to self-organization and to bargain collectively through representatives of their own choosing. As explained previously, the Wagner Act also created the National Labor Relations Board (NLRB) and prescribed the NLRB's organization. It defined "unfair labor practices," empowered the NLRB to prevent unfair labor practices affecting commerce, and gave the NLRB broad powers of investigation.

Note: Review the *Setting* to and excerpt of *National Labor Relations Board v. Jones & Laughlin Steel Corp.*, pp. 280–291.

QUESTION

Law Professor William M. Wiecek contends that *Jones & Laughlin* "overruled" *Schechter* (*Liberty under Law: The Supreme Court in American Life* [Baltimore, MD: The Johns Hopkins University Press, 1988], p. 138). Some scholars and politicians agree. They also criticize *Jones & Laughlin* because they consider the *Schechter* decision a bulwark against Congress surrendering too much of its rule-making authority to administrative agencies and private commercial trade associations.

For example, in 1969 political scientist Theodore Lowi wrote:

> Delegation of power enjoys strong standing in the courts. The broadest applications of the doctrine have been accepted by the Supreme Court for over thirty years. The last major statute invalidated for involving too broad a delegation to either public agencies or private associations was the "sick chicken case" [*Schechter* decision] of 1935. The 1935 decision has never been reversed, but the Supreme Court has not seen fit to apply it since that time. Policy without law is what a broad delegation of power is. Policy without law is clearly constitutional, according to present judicial practice. (*The End of Liberalism: The Second Republic of the United States*, 2nd ed. [New York, NY: W. W. Norton, 1979], p. 93)

What are the constitutional dangers inherent in allowing Congress to delegate rule-making authority to executive agencies? Is such delegation an inevitable consequence of governmental regulation or does Congress have alternatives to delegation? Should the doctrine *delegata potestas non potest delegari*—powers delegated to Congress by the Constitution may not be redelegated—play a role at the national level of American government?

IMPLIED POWERS: DELEGATION OF LEGISLATIVE POWER

Immigration and Naturalization Service v. Chadha
462 U.S. 919 (1983)

SETTING

Formal executive administrative management—"bureaucracy"—has been a part of the American governmental process since the early days of the Republic. Notable early examples are the Departments of War, Navy, State, and Treasury, which were created by Congress in the eighteenth century. In the beginning, executive departments played the passive role of seeing to "executive details," just as Alexander Hamilton predicted in *Federalist* No. 72. By the end of the nineteenth century, however, as noted in the *Setting* to *A.L.A. Schechter Poultry Corp. v. United States* on pp. 262–265, executive departments and regulatory agencies had assumed a much more active policymaking role in American politics and the economy. For example, the Interstate Commerce Commission was created in 1887 and played an important role in regulating railroad rates. President Franklin Roosevelt's "New Deal" dramatically enlarged an already extensive federal administrative apparatus. Organizing American participation in World Wars I and II also required expanding greatly the administrative capacity of the federal government.

By the 1920s, Congress had created so many departments and agencies that representatives were increasingly concerned with their role as overseer of the executive branch. Passage of the Reorganization Act of 1939 gave formal recognition to a device called the legislative (or congressional) veto. Used in various forms since 1920, a legislative veto provision was first included in the Legislative Appropriations Act for fiscal 1933. The legislative veto required proposed agency and department rules and regulations to be submitted for some form of legislative approval or rejection before going into effect.

Legislative veto provisions took several forms over the years. On different occasions the veto power was vested in the whole Congress, in one house of Congress, in a particular committee, or even in a committee chairman. Sometimes legislation containing a legislative veto required that it be expressed in a negative vote in response to a particular agency proposal. At other times the veto was tied to the appropriations process. The majorities required to put the legislative veto into effect also varied over the years. Both simple and two-thirds majorities have been required to prevent rules and regulations from taking effect.

Intense debate about the constitutionality of the legislative veto surrounded adoption of the 1939 Reorganization Act and subsequent legislation containing the device. Despite the controversy, Congress made increasing use of the veto as the executive branch grew in size, complexity, and policy-making authority.

Though proposed initially by President Herbert Hoover, the legislative veto was never popular with the chief executive. Every president from Truman through Ford voiced concerns that its use gave the legislature too much discretion in how executive powers were exercised. A legislative veto provision in the Immigration and Naturalization Act (INA), originally passed in 1940, provided Justice Department officials with a case that finally tested the veto's constitutionality before the Supreme Court of the United States.

Section 244(a) of the INA authorized the attorney general to suspend the deportation of certain aliens who were otherwise deportable and to adjust their status to that of aliens lawfully admitted for permanent residence. To qualify, an alien had to have been physically present in the United States for a continuous period of not fewer than seven years, be of good moral character, and be a person whose deportation, in the attorney general's opinion, would result in extreme hardship. If the alien's deportation was suspended, Section 244(c)(1) required the attorney general to submit a complete and detailed statement of facts to the Congress explaining the suspension. Section 244(c)(2) provided that if, during the session of Congress in which a suspension was reported, or the next session, either the House or Senate passed a resolution stating that it did not approve of the suspension of such deportation, the attorney general was to deport the alien. Jagdish Rai Chadha, a Kenyan national who came to the United States on a student visa issued by Great Britain, was one of the aliens who felt the brunt of the statute.

Chadha was born in Kenya in 1944. In December 1963, Kenya became independent from Great Britain. The Kenyan government granted citizenship to all persons born in Kenya, with the exception of those whose parents were not Kenyan natives. The exception reflected a growing sense of Kenyan nationalism. Chadha's parents were from South Africa and India so Chadha had to apply to the Kenyan government for citizenship. In September 1966, while his application was pending, he obtained a British passport and came to the United States on a student visa that expired June 30, 1972. For five years Chadha studied at Bowling Green State University, earning a bachelor of science degree in business administration and a master of arts degree in political science and economics. He also became engaged to marry a U.S. citizen.

After graduation, Chadha began to look for a job. Because his student visa was about to expire, he inquired into possibilities for employment in Great Britain. He was advised by British authorities to apply to America for permission to remain in the United States indefinitely because of the dramatic increase in persons of East Asian descent seeking entry into Great Britain. Chadha went to an office of the Immigration and Naturalization Service (INS) to inquire into the prospects of remaining in the United States but was ordered to a hearing to show cause why he should not be deported because his student visa had expired.

During the deportation hearings that followed, Chadha filed for an application for suspension of deportation under INA Section 244. In June 1974, the immigration court ordered Chadha's deportation suspended because he had been in the United States for seven years, was of good moral character, and would face "extreme hardship" by reason of his Eastern Indian racial heritage if forced to return to Kenya or Great Britain.

As required by Section 244(c)(2), a report of Chadha's deportation suspension was transmitted to Congress. In December 1975, without debate or recorded vote, the House passed a resolution disapproving Chadha's deportation suspension and the suspension of five other aliens on the grounds that they had not satisfied the statutory requirements relating to hardship.

Following the House resolution, the INS reopened Chadha's deportation proceedings. Chadha contended that the provision in Section 244(c)(2) allowing congressional review of suspensions of deportation was unconstitutional because it violated the doctrine of separation of powers. The immigration court, concluding that it had no authority to rule on the constitutionality of an act of Congress, ordered Chadha deported to the United Kingdom. Chadha appealed to the Board of Immigration Appeals, which dismissed the appeal. Chadha then filed a petition for review of the deportation order with the U.S. Court of Appeals for the Ninth Circuit, again arguing that the "one-house veto" provision in Section 244(c)(2) violated separation of powers.

The INS agreed with Chadha that the Section 244(c)(2) "one-house veto" provision was unconstitutional and that Chadha's deportation order should be set aside. This agreement eliminated the adverse relationship between parties required for a case or controversy. To remedy this problem, the Ninth Circuit invited the House of Representatives and the Senate to appear as *amici curiae* to defend the constitutionality of Section 244(c)(2) procedures.

The Ninth Circuit ruled that Section 244(c)(2) was unconstitutional because it violated the doctrine of separation of powers by intruding on the executive function of enforcing the INA on a case-by-case basis. Furthermore, according to the Ninth Circuit, by assuming the task of correcting misapplications of the law through the "one-house veto," Section 244(c)(2) also interfered with a basic judicial function.

Following the Ninth Circuit's decision, the House and Senate were allowed to intervene in the proceedings to petition for rehearing and to petition the Supreme Court for writs of certiorari. Following denial of the request for a rehearing, the Senate and House filed petitions for writs of certiorari with the Supreme Court, and the INS filed an appeal. The Supreme Court consolidated the proceedings.

The case was argued in February 1982 and reargued in December 1982.

HIGHLIGHTS OF SUPREME COURT ARGUMENTS

BRIEF FOR THE INS

◆ The one-house veto is constitutionally infirm because it authorizes one house of Congress to pass a resolution that has the effect of law without the concurrence of the other house or presentation to the president. The Constitution explicitly requires all congressional actions involving exercise of legislative powers to receive the concurrence of both Houses and to be presented to the president for his approval.

◆ The veto provision is also defective for allowing one house of Congress to participate in the execution of previously enacted law. It thereby violates separation of powers and is unconstitutional under the rule of *Buckley v. Valeo*, 424 U.S. 1 (1976).

◆ Even if the Court were to mistakenly conclude that the court of appeals lacked jurisdiction to hear this case, the Supreme Court nonetheless is free to decide the constitutional question presented by the one-house veto because the constitutional issue is one of continuing and fundamental importance, presenting a question of law that has been fully argued by the parties.

BRIEF FOR CONGRESS

◆ *Senate* The Ninth Circuit should not have reached the constitutional issues in this case for two reasons. First, Chadha married a U.S. citizen in 1980, thus requiring the case to be resolved under a section of the INA statute that ordinarily provides for granting permanent residence to an alien spouse of a citizen. Second, the case should have been remanded to the INS for a hearing in light of the intervening Refugee Act of 1980, under which the attorney general can grant asylum and then permanent residence to any alien unable to return to his country out of fear of persecution on account of race.

◆ The legislative history of amendments to the INA show that Congress has repeatedly refused to give the executive branch exclusive authority to suspend deportations. The Ninth Circuit therefore erred in its conclusion that Section 244(c)(2) is severable from the rest of the statute and that the attorney general has complete and final power to adjust the status of deportable aliens.

◆ Section 244(c)(2), which has been in effect approximately forty years, is a constitutional exercise of congressional power. Courts have recognized that congressional power over the admission of aliens was complete. Congress has the discretion to share that function with the executive branch but is not obligated to delegate its authority completely. Neither does the section violate bicameralism, because the process of one-house review is not an act of lawmaking.

◆ *House of Representatives*   This case is nonjusticiable for two reasons. First, Chadha and the INS agreed that there are constitutional problems with Section 244(c)(2) and therefore are not adversary parties. Second, the separation of powers issues in the case are essentially political.

BRIEF FOR CHADHA

◆ The legislative veto provisions of Section 244(c)(2) are contrary to separation of powers because each of the three coordinate branches is limited to the powers assigned to it. The Constitution explicitly provides that all laws be made by the Congress, comprised of the Senate and House working in conjunction with the president. The INA statute delegates administration of the statute to the attorney general. While Congress could withdraw or alter its delegation through the regular legislative process, nothing in the Constitution recognizes a one-house veto power.

◆ The one-house veto violates the president's power to exercise his veto following congressional legislative enactments.

AMICUS CURIAE BRIEFS SUPPORTING CHADHA

The Counsel of Administrative Law of the Federal Bar Association; Nine members of the House of Representatives; the American Bar Association.

SUPREME COURT DECISION: 7–2

BURGER, C.J.

... Explicit and unambiguous provisions of the Constitution prescribe and define the respective functions of the Congress and of the Executive in the legislative process.... [We] find that the purposes underlying the Presentment Clauses, Art. I, Sec. 7, Cls. 2, 3, and the bicameral requirement of Art. I, Sec. 1 and Sec. 7, Cl. 2, guide our resolution of the important question presented in this case....

The records of the Constitutional Convention reveal that the requirement that all legislation be presented to the President before becoming law was uniformly accepted by the Framers.... The decision to provide the President with a limited and qualified power to veto was based on the profound conviction of the Framers that the powers conferred on Congress were the powers to be most carefully circumscribed. It is beyond doubt that lawmaking was a power to be shared by both Houses and the President....

The President's role in the lawmaking process also reflects the Framers' careful efforts to check whatever propensity a particular Congress might have to enact oppressive, improvident, or ill-considered measures....

The Bicameral requirement of Article I, Sec. 1, 7, was of scarcely less concern to the Framers than was the Presidential veto and indeed the two concepts are interdependent. By providing that no law could take effect without the concurrence of the prescribed majority of the Members of both Houses, the Framers reemphasized their belief, already remarked upon in connection with the Presentment Clauses, that legislation should not be enacted unless it has been carefully and fully considered by the Nation's elected officials....

This view was rooted in a general skepticism regarding the fallibility of human nature.... [The] Framers were also concerned, although not of one mind, over the apprehensions of the smaller states. Those states feared a commonality of interest among the larger states would work to their disadvantage; representatives of the larger states, on the other hand, were skeptical of a legislature that could pass laws favoring a minority of the people....

We therefore see that the Framers were acutely conscious that the bicameral requirement and the Presentment Clauses would serve essential constitutional functions. The President's participation in the legislative process was to protect the Executive Branch from Congress and to protect the whole people from improvident laws. The division of the Congress into two distinctive bodies assures that the legislative power would be exercised only after opportunity for full study and debate in separate settings. The President's unilateral veto power, in turn, was limited by the power of two thirds of both Houses of Congress to overrule a veto thereby precluding final arbitrary action of one person....

The Constitution sought to divide the delegated powers of the new federal government into three defined categories, legislative, executive and judicial, to assure, as nearly as possible, that each Branch of government would confine itself to its assigned responsibility....

The veto authorized by Sec. 244(c)(2) doubtless has been in many respects a convenient shortcut; the "sharing" with the Executive by Congress of its authority over aliens in this manner is, on its face, an appealing compromise. In purely practical terms, it is obviously easier for action to be taken by one House without submission to the President; but it is crystal clear from the records of the Convention, contemporaneous writings and debates, that the Framers ranked other values higher than efficiency. The records of the Convention and debates in the States preceding ratification underscore the common desire to define and limit the exercise of the newly created federal powers affecting the states and the people. There is unmistakable expression of a determination that legislation by the national Congress be a step-by-step, deliberate and deliberative process....

We hold that the Congressional veto provision in Sec. 244(c)(2) ... is unconstitutional.

POWELL, J., CONCURRING

The Court's decision, based on the Presentment Clauses, ... apparently will invalidate every use of the legislative veto. The breadth of this holding gives one pause. Congress has included the veto in literally hundreds of statutes, dating back to the 1930s. Congress clearly views this procedure as essential to controlling the delegation of power to administrative agencies. One reasonably may disagree with Congress' assessment of the veto's utility, but the respect due its judgment as a coordinate branch of Government cautions that our holding should be no more extensive than necessary to decide this case. In my view, the case may be decided on a narrower ground. When Congress finds that a particular person does not satisfy the statutory criteria for permanent residence in this country it has assumed a judicial function in violation of the principle of separation of powers. Accordingly, I concur only in the judgment.

WHITE, J., DISSENTING

Today the Court not only invalidates Sec. 244(c)(2) of the Immigration and Naturalization Act, but also sounds the death knell for nearly 200 other statutory provisions in which Congress has reserved a "legislative veto." For this reason, the Court's decision is of surpassing importance. And it is for this reason that the Court would have been well-advised to decide the case, if possible, on the narrower grounds of separation of powers, leaving for full consideration the constitutionality of other congressional review statutes operating on such varied matters as war powers and agency rulemaking, some of which concern the independent regulatory agencies.

The prominence of the legislative veto mechanism in our contemporary political system and its importance to Congress can hardly be overstated. It has become a central means by which Congress secures the accountability of executive and independent agencies. Without the legislative veto, Congress is faced with a Hobson's choice: either to refrain from delegating the necessary authority, leaving itself with a hopeless task of writing laws with the requisite specificity to cover endless special circumstances across the entire policy landscape, or in the alternative, to abdicate its lawmaking function to the executive branch and independent agencies. To choose the former leaves major national problems unresolved; to opt for the latter risks unaccountable policymaking by those not elected to fill that role. Accordingly, over the past five decades, the legislative veto has been placed in nearly 200 statutes. The device is known in every field of governmental concern: reorganization, budgets, foreign affairs, war powers, and regulation of trade, safety, energy, the environment and the economy....

If the legislative veto were as plainly unconstitutional as the Court strives to suggest, its broad ruling today would be more comprehensible. But, the constitutionality of the legislative veto is anything but clear cut. The issue divides scholars, courts, attorneys general, and the two other branches of the National Government. If the veto devices so flagrantly disregarded the requirements of Article I as the Court today suggests, I find it incomprehensible that Congress, whose members are bound by oath to uphold the Constitution, would have placed these mechanisms in nearly 200 separate laws over a period of 50 years....

The power to exercise a legislative

veto is not the power to write new law without bicameral approval or presidential consideration. The veto must be authorized by statute and may only negative what an Executive department or independent agency has proposed. On its face, the legislative veto no more allows one House of Congress to make law than does the presidential veto confer such power upon the President....

The Court's holding today that all legislative-type action must be enacted through the lawmaking process ignores that legislative authority is routinely delegated to the Executive branch, to the independent regulatory agencies, and to private individuals and groups.... This Court's decisions sanctioning such delegations make clear that Article I does not require all action with the effect of legislation to be passed as law....

I do not suggest that all legislative vetoes are necessarily consistent with separation of powers principles. A legislative check on an inherently executive function, for example that of initiating prosecutions, poses an entirely different question. But the legislative veto device here—and in many other settings—is far from an instance of legislative tyranny over the Executive. It is a necessary check on the unavoidably expanding power of the agencies, both executive and independent, as they engage in exercising authority delegated by Congress.

QUESTIONS

1. Sort out the differences between Chief Justice Burger's and Justice White's approaches to assessing the constitutionality of the legislative veto. Is it correct to term Burger's approach "formalist" and "categorical" while White's approach is "pragmatic" or "functionalist"? Is *Chadha* a throwback to *Schechter*?

2. The Supreme Court could have denied review in Chadha's case for at least two reasons. First, there was no case or controversy since the INS agreed with Chadha that the "one-house veto" provision of the INS legislation was unconstitutional. Second, the case became moot when Chadha married an American citizen. Should the Court have ignored its rules on justiciability and standing in order to render a decision in *Chadha*?

3. According to the *Congressional Quarterly Almanac*, one effect of *Chadha* was to invalidate legislative veto provisions contained in approximately 110 federal laws. In its entire history before 1983, the Court had not struck down so many laws (Washington, D.C.: Congressional Quarterly Press, 1983, p. 565). Is it surprising that such a far-reaching, "activist" decision would be written by Chief Justice Burger, an advocate of judicial self-restraint? Does the chief justice's legalistic interpretation of separation of powers doctrine compel such a result? Compare the chief justice's interpretation of separation of powers doctrine in *Chadha* with his rejection of Richard Nixon's legalistic argument in *United States v. Nixon*, Chapter 2, pp. 62–67.

4. Justice Antonin Scalia was an assistant attorney in the Office of Legal Counsel in 1975, and one of the members of the Justice Department eager to challenge the constitutionality of the legislative veto. According to Barbara Hinkson Craig, author of a book about *Chadha*, Scalia was instrumental in persuading the American Bar Association to file an *amicus curiae* brief, one that would "accomplish his purpose—which was to present a strong argument for the Court's ruling as broadly as possible" (*Chadha: The Story of an Epic Constitutional Struggle* [New York, NY: Oxford University Press, 1988], p. 185).

As a Supreme Court justice, Scalia wrote a biting dissent in *Morrison v. Olson*, 487 U.S. 654 (1988) (see Chapter 4, pp. 432–443), in which the Court upheld Congress's creation of the office of special prosecutor. What view of presidential and congressional powers is implied by Justice Scalia's opposition to both the legislative veto and the office of special prosecutor? Would Justice Scalia reject outcomes like *Jones & Laughlin* and embrace outcomes like *Schechter*?

5. Alan B. Morrison, the attorney who successfully argued *Chadha* before the Supreme Court, wrote: "The theory of the [one-house legislative] veto was that it improved accountability by ensuring that the elected representatives had a say in important regulatory decisions. In practice, it was quite different: in many cases Congress used the veto to prevent a rule from going into effect that was necessary to implement broad remedial statutes requiring specific agency action before they actually benefit the public" ("Close Reins on the Bureaucracy: Overseeing the Administrative Agencies," in *The Burger Years: Rights and Wrongs in the Supreme Court, 1969–1986*, ed. Herman Schwartz [New York, NY: Penguin, 1987], p. 200). Other critics of the legislative veto argue that it was used by members of Congress to protect special interests from the effects of regulatory legislation.

Do such practical drawbacks of the one-house veto invalidate its theoretical benefit of providing effective legislative oversight of the bureaucracy? What other constitutional checks on administrative agencies are available to Congress in the face of increasing socio-economic complexity requiring regulation? Does the Court's *Chadha* decision suggest that an inevitable consequence of the growth of governmental bureaucracy is loss of popular control of that apparatus?

6. In the sixteen months from the Court's decision to the close of the 98th Congress, 53 more legislative vetoes were included in legislation. The number of post-*Chadha* legislative vetoes grew to 102 by the close of the 99th Congress and to over 140 by the close of the 100th Congress. What other examples of the Supreme Court's decisions not being followed have been presented to this point? What do those examples demonstrate about the limits of the Supreme Court's exercise of its power of judicial review?

IMPLIED POWERS: DELEGATION OF LEGISLATIVE POWER

Bowsher v. Synar
478 U.S. 714 (1986)

SETTING

During the 1930s, policymakers who adhered to the theories of British econo-mist John Maynard Keynes advocated adjusting public spending upward on occasion, even at the risk of increasing budget deficits, in order to stimulate the economy and manage capitalist business cycles. The theory was that public works projects, combined with lower taxes, would generate jobs and give Americans more buying power, which in turn would stimulate economic growth and prosperity during periods of downward turns. Keynesian economic theory proved popular with New Dealers, as evidenced by the massive public works programs undertaken during the depression. Although President Roosevelt promised to balance the budget during his second term, he found it impossible to do so. World War II defense spending and the postwar building boom made it difficult to restore the balance between government revenues and expenditures. America's involvement in Vietnam exacerbated the problem. A federal budget deficit of some $3.8 billion in 1966 jumped to more than $25 billion by 1968 and to over $50 billion by 1975. By the mid-1970s, there was bipartisan agreement in Congress that the national deficit had become too large.

In 1974, Congress enacted the Congressional Budget and Impoundment Act to require Congress to consider the budget as a whole before turning to individual appropriations bills. Because individual spending bills came to the floor and were voted on separately, however, the 1974 act was not effective in curbing deficits. A proposed constitutional amendment in 1982 to require a bal-anced budget passed the Senate but failed in the House. In 1985, however, when the national debt exceeded $2 trillion, Senator Phil Gramm and twenty-three other senators introduced the Gramm-Rudman-Hollings bill. It was enacted as the Balanced Budget and Emergency Deficit Control Act.

The goal of the Gramm-Rudman Act was to achieve a balanced federal bud-get in six years through the establishment of progressively lower deficit targets, from $172 billion in 1986, to zero in 1991. The act delegated considerable fact-finding authority to the comptroller general, who is the head of the General Accounting Office, a position created by the Budget and Accounting Act of 1921. The comptroller general is appointed for a fifteen-year nonrenewable term by the president, with the advice and consent of the Senate. However, according to the 1921 law, the comptroller general may be removed by impeachment or, after a hearing, for cause by a joint resolution of Congress.

Under the Balanced Budget and Emergency Deficit Control Act, Charles A. Bowsher, who was comptroller general at the time, was to issue a report to the president and Congress each fiscal year containing an estimate of the size of the deficit and specifying the budget cuts, if any, that were necessary to meet the applicable deficit target. His report was to consider information prepared by the Director of the Office of Management and Budget (OMB) and the Director of the Congressional Budget Office (CBO), but was to involve "independent analysis," giving "due regard" to the data, assumptions, and methodologies used in the OMB/CBO reports and explaining fully "any differences between the contents" of his report and the OMB/CBO report. The Gramm-Rudman Act required the president to sequester federal funds in accordance with the comptroller general's report. If Congress did not act in a timely manner to trim budget allocations consistent with the comptroller general's report, the president's sequestration orders were to take effect automatically.

On December 12, 1985, the same day that President Reagan signed the Gramm-Rudman bill into law, Representative Mike Synar filed suit in the U.S. District Court for the District of Columbia seeking a declaratory judgment that portions of the act were unconstitutional. Eleven other members of the House of Representatives joined him as plaintiffs out of concern that the act would cripple valuable social programs. Bowsher, the comptroller general, the Senate, and the Speaker and Bipartisan Leadership Group of the House of Representatives were allowed to intervene as defendants. The National Treasury Employees Union brought a similar challenge on behalf of its members, who were retired federal employees and whose pension cost-of-living adjustments were subject to sequestration. Synar and his coplaintiffs contended that Congress unconstitutionally delegated its legislative power when it created an administrative mechanism to reduce the annual deficit, and that the Gramm-Rudman Act violated separation of powers by vesting executive power in the comptroller general who, according to the plaintiffs, is an officer of the legislative branch.

The cases were consolidated and heard by a three-judge panel. The district court upheld the Gramm-Rudman Act's delegation of power, but invalidated that part of the act specifying the comptroller general's participation in implementing automatic spending reductions. The judges reasoned that the law impermissibly conferred "executive power" on the comptroller general, because he is an officer removable by Congress. According to the district court, the removal provision gave the comptroller general a "presumed desire to avoid removal by pleasing Congress," thereby creating subservience to another branch that was impermissible in an officer performing administrative duties. Because the 1921 Budget and Accounting Act provided a congressional role in the removal of the comptroller general, Bowsher was constitutionally incapable of exercising the "executive powers" given to him by the Gramm-Rudman Act. Bowsher and the other defendants appealed to the Supreme Court of the United States.

HIGHLIGHTS OF SUPREME COURT ARGUMENTS

BRIEF FOR BOWSHER

◆ The district court erred in failing to examine the removal provision of the 1921 act. The legislative history of the 1921 act reveals Congress's intent that if the removal provision were invalid, it would be severed from the act. If the removal provision is unconstitutional, it should be severed and disregarded in determining the constitutionality of the 1985 act.

◆ The act of 1921 established the comptroller general as an independent auditor and watchdog, in contrast to the predecessor Treasury Department, which Congress regarded as subservient to the president because of the president's removal power.

◆ The district court's presumption that the removal provision makes the comptroller general "subservient to another branch" is unjustified in fact. The comptroller general consistently has demonstrated independence from both Congress and the president.

BRIEF FOR SYNAR

◆ The 1985 act unconstitutionally delegates legislative authority because its sole purpose is to create an administrative device to reduce spending without concomitant congressional responsibility for the decision to do so. The 1985 act was not motivated by the practical need to carry out legislative choices, but to foster legislative avoidance of difficult choices. Since the only justification for the delegation is the desire to avoid political accountability, the delegation is not proper.

◆ The 1985 act violates separation of powers, because it requires the participation of the director of the CBO, who is a legislative branch official.

AMICUS CURIAE BRIEFS SUPPORTING SYNAR

Joint brief of the American Federation of Labor and Congress of Industrial Organization, Public Employee Department, AFL-CIO; American Federation of Government Employees, AFL-CIO; American Postal Workers Union, AFL-CIO; and National Association of Letter Carriers, AFL-CIO.

SUPREME COURT DECISION: 7–2

BURGER, C.J.

The question presented by these appeals is whether the assignment by Congress to the Comptroller General of the United States of certain functions under the Balanced Budget and Emergency Deficit Control Act of 1985 violates the doctrine of separation of powers....

A threshold issue is whether the Members of Congress, members of the National Treasury Employees Union, or the Union itself have standing to challenge the constitutionality of the Act in question. It is clear that members of the Union, one of whom is an appellee here, will sustain injury by not receiving a scheduled increase in benefits.... This is sufficient to confer standing[.]...

The Constitution does not contemplate an active role for Congress in the supervision of officers charged with the execution of the laws it enacts. The President appoints "Officers of the United States" with the "Advice and Consent of the Senate...." Art. II, Sec. 2. Once the appointment has been made and confirmed, however, the Constitution explicitly provides for removal of Officers of the United States by Congress only upon impeachment by the House of Representatives and conviction by the Senate. An impeachment by the House and trial by the Senate can rest only on "Treason, Bribery or other high Crimes and Misdemeanors." Article II, Sec. 4. A direct congressional role in the removal of officers charged with the execution of the laws beyond this limited one is inconsistent with separation of powers....

Our decision in *INS v. Chadha* supports this conclusion. In *Chadha*, we struck down a one-House "legislative veto" provision by which each House of Congress retained the power to reverse a decision Congress had expressly authorized the Attorney General to make[.]...

To permit an officer controlled by Congress to execute the laws would be, in essence, to permit a congressional veto. Congress could simply remove, or threaten to remove, an officer for executing the laws in any fashion found to be unsatisfactory to Congress. This kind of congressional control over the execution of the laws, *Chadha* makes clear, is constitutionally impermissible.

The dangers of congressional usurpation of Executive Branch functions have long been recognized. "[T]he debates of the Constitutional Convention, and the *Federalist Papers*, are replete with expressions of fear that the Legislative Branch of the National Government will aggrandize itself at the expense of the other two branches." *Buckley v. Valeo*, 424 U.S. 1 (1976). Indeed, we also have observed only recently that "[t]he hydraulic pressure inherent within each of the separate Branches to exceed the outer limits of its power, even to accomplish desirable objectives, must be resisted." *Chadha*. With these principles in mind, we turn to consideration of whether the Comptroller General is controlled by Congress.

Appellants urge that the Comptroller General performs his duties independently and is not subservient to Congress. We agree with the District Court that this contention does not bear close scrutiny.

The critical factor lies in the provisions of the statute defining the Comptroller General's office relating to removability. Although the Comptroller General is nominated by the President from a list of three individuals recommended by the Speaker of the House of Representatives and the President *pro tempore* of the Senate, ... and confirmed by the Senate, he is removable only at the initiative of Congress. He may be removed not only by impeachment but also by joint resolution of Congress "at any time" resting on any one of the following bases:

(i) permanent disability;
(ii) inefficiency;
(iii) neglect of duty;
(iv) malfeasance; or
(v) a felony or conduct involving moral turpitude....

It is clear that Congress has consistently viewed the Comptroller General as an officer of the Legislative Branch. The Reorganization Acts of 1945 and 1949, for example, both stated that the Comptroller General and the GAO are "a part of the legislative branch of the Government." Similarly, in the Accounting and Auditing Act of 1950, Congress required the Comptroller General to conduct audits "as an agent of the Congress."...

[W]e see no escape from the conclusion that, because Congress has retained removal authority over the Comptroller General, he may not be entrusted with executive powers. The remaining question is whether the Comptroller General has been assigned such powers in the Balanced Budget and Emergency Deficit Control Act of 1985.

The primary responsibility of the Comptroller General under the instant Act is the preparation of a "report." This report must contain detailed estimates of projected federal revenues and expenditures. The report must also specify the reductions, if any, necessary to reduce the deficit to the target for the appropriate fiscal year. The reductions must be set forth on a program-by-program basis....

Appellants suggest that the duties assigned to the Comptroller General in the Act are essentially ministerial and mechanical so that their performance does not constitute "execution of the law" in a meaningful sense. On the contrary, we view these functions as plainly entailing execution of the law in constitutional terms. Interpreting a law enacted by Congress to implement the legislative mandate is the very essence of "execution" of the law. Under Sec. 251, the Comptroller General must exercise judgment concerning facts that affect the application of the Act. He must also interpret the provisions of the Act to determine precisely what budgetary calculations are required. Decisions of that kind are typically made by officers charged with executing a statute.

The executive nature of the Comptroller General's functions under the Act is revealed in Sec. 252(a)(3) which gives the Comptroller General the ultimate authority to determine the budget cuts to be made. Indeed, the Comptroller General commands the President himself to carry out, without the slightest variation (with exceptions not relevant to the constitutional issues presented), the directive of the Comptroller General as to the budget reductions[.]...

Congress of course initially determined the content of the Balanced Budget and Emergency Deficit Control Act; and undoubtedly the content of the Act determines the nature of the executive duty. However, as *Chadha* makes clear, once Congress makes its choice in enacting legislation, its participation ends. Congress can thereafter control the execution of its enactment only indirectly—by passing new legislation. By placing the responsibility for execution of the Balanced Budget and Emergency Deficit Control Act in the hands of an officer who is subject to removal only by itself, Congress in effect has retained control over the execution of the Act and has intruded into the executive function. The Constitution does not permit such intrusion.

We now turn to the final issue of remedy. Appellants urge that rather than striking down Sec. 251 and invalidating the significant power Congress vested in the Comptroller General to meet a national fiscal emergency, we should take the lesser course of nullifying the statutory provisions of the 1921 Act that authorizes Congress to remove the Comptroller General....

Severance at this late date of the removal provisions enacted 65 years ago would significantly alter the Comptroller General's office, possibly by making him subservient to the Executive Branch. Recasting the Comptroller General as an officer of the Executive Branch would accordingly alter the balance that Congress had in mind in drafting the Budget and Accounting Act of 1921 and the Balanced Budget and Emergency Deficit Control Act, to say nothing of the wide array of other tasks and duties Congress has assigned the Comptroller General in other statutes. Thus appellants' argument would require this Court to undertake a weighing of the importance Congress attached to the removal provisions in the Budget and Accounting Act of 1921 as well as in other subsequent enactments against the importance it placed on the Balanced Budget and Emergency Deficit Control Act of 1985.

Fortunately this is a thicket we need not enter. The language of the Balanced Budget and Emergency Deficit Control Act itself settles the issue. In Sec. 274(f), Congress has explicitly provided "fallback" provisions in the Act that take effect "[i]n the event ... *any* of the reporting procedures described in section 251 are invalidated." Sec. 274(f)(1) (emphasis added).... Assuming that appellants are correct in urging that this matter must be resolved on the basis of congressional intent, the intent appears to have been for Sec. 274(f) to be given

effect in this situation. Indeed, striking the removal provisions would lead to a statute that Congress would probably have refused to adopt....

Accordingly, rather than perform the type of creative and imaginative statutory surgery urged by appellants, our holding simply permits the fallback provisions to come into play....

We conclude that the District Court correctly held that the powers vested in the Comptroller General under Sec. 251 violate the command of the Constitution that the Congress play no direct role in the execution of the laws. Accordingly, the judgment and order of the District Court are affirmed.

Our judgment is stayed for a period not to exceed 60 days to permit Congress to implement the fallback provisions.

It is so ordered.

STEVENS AND MARSHALL, J.J., CONCURRING IN THE JUDGMENT

... I disagree with the Court ... on the reasons why the Constitution prohibits the Comptroller General from exercising the powers assigned to him by Sec. 251(b) and Sec. 251(c)(2) of the Act. It is not the dormant, carefully circumscribed congressional removal power that represents the primary constitutional evil. Nor do I agree with the conclusion of both the majority and the dissent that the analysis depends on a labeling of the functions assigned to the Comptroller General as "executive powers." Rather, I am convinced that the Comptroller General must be characterized as an agent of Congress because of his longstanding statutory responsibilities; that the powers assigned to him under the Gramm-Rudman-Hollings Act require him to make policy that will bind the Nation; and that, when Congress, or a component or an agent of Congress, seeks to make policy that will bind the Nation, it must follow the procedures mandated by Article I of the Constitution—through passage by both Houses and presentment to the President. In short, Congress may not exercise its fundamental power to formulate national policy by delegating that power to one of its two Houses, to a legislative committee, or to an individual agent of the Congress[.]... That principle, I believe, is applicable to the Comptroller General....

In assessing the role of the Comptroller General, it is appropriate to consider his already existing statutory responsibilities. Those responsibilities leave little doubt that one of the identifying characteristics of the Comptroller General is his statutorily required relationship to the Legislative Branch....

The powers delegated to the Comptroller General by Sec. 251 of the Act before us today have a ... chameleon-like quality. The District Court persuasively explained why they may be appropriately characterized as executive powers. But, when that delegation is held invalid, the "fallback provision" provides that the report that would otherwise be issued by the Comptroller General shall be issued by Congress itself. In the event that the resolution is enacted, the congressional report will have the same legal consequences as if it had been issued by the Comptroller General. In that event, moreover, surely no one would suggest that Congress had acted in any capacity other than "legislative." Since the District Court expressly recognized the validity of what it described as the "'fall-

back' deficit reduction process," *Synar v. United States*, 626 F.Supp. 1374, 1377 (DC 1986), it obviously did not doubt the constitutionality of the performance by Congress of the functions delegated to the Comptroller General....

The Gramm-Rudman-Hollings Act assigns to the Comptroller General the duty to make policy decisions that have the force of law. The Comptroller General's report is, in the current statute, the engine that gives life to the ambitious budget reduction process. It is the Comptroller General's report that "provide[s] for the determination of reductions" and that "contain[s] estimates, determinations, and specifications for all of the items contained in the report" submitted by the Office of Management and Budget and the Congressional Budget Office. Sec. 251(b). It is the Comptroller General's report that the President must follow and that will have conclusive effect. Sec. 252. It is, in short, the Comptroller General's report that will have a profound, dramatic, and immediate impact on the Government and on the Nation at large.

Article I of the Constitution specifies the procedures that Congress must follow when it makes policy that binds the Nation: its legislation must be approved by both of its Houses and presented to the President....

The distinction between the kinds of action that Congress may delegate to its own components and agents and those that require either compliance with Article I procedures or delegation to another branch pursuant to defined standards is reflected in the practices that have developed over the years regarding congressional resolutions. The joint resolution, which is used for "special purposes and ... incidental matters," 7 Deschler's *Precedents of the House of Representatives* 334 (1977), makes binding policy and "requires an affirmative vote by both Houses and submission to the President for approval" id., at 333—the full Article I requirements. A concurrent resolution, in contrast, makes no binding policy; it is "a means of expressing fact, principles, opinions, and purposes of the two Houses," Jefferson's *Manual and Rules of the House of Representatives* 176 (1983), and thus does not need to be presented to the President. It is settled, however, that if a resolution is intended to make policy that will bind the Nation and thus is "legislative in its character and effect," S. Rep. No. 1335, 54th Cong., 2d Sess., 8 (1897)—then the full Article I requirements must be observed. For "the nature or substance of the resolution, and not its form, controls the question of its disposition."

In my opinion, Congress itself could not exercise the Gramm-Rudman-Hollings functions through a concurrent resolution. The fact that the fallback provision in Sec. 274 requires a joint resolution rather than a concurrent resolution indicates that Congress endorsed this view. I think it equally clear that Congress may not simply delegate those functions to an agent such as the Congressional Budget Office. Since I am persuaded that the Comptroller General is also fairly deemed to be an agent of Congress, he too cannot exercise such functions....

I concur in the judgment.

WHITE, J., DISSENTING

The Court, acting in the name of separation of powers, takes upon itself to strike down the Gramm-Rudman-Hollings Act, one of the most novel and far-reaching legislative responses to a national crisis since the New Deal....

The Court's decision ... is based on a syllogism: the Act vests the Comptroller with "executive power"; such power may not be exercised by Congress or its agents; the Comptroller is an agent of Congress because he is removable by Congress; therefore the Act is invalid. I have no quarrel with the proposition that the powers exercised by the Comptroller under the Act may be characterized as "executive" in that they involve the interpretation and carrying out of the Act's mandate. I can also accept the general proposition that although Congress has considerable authority in designating the officers who are to execute legislation, the constitutional scheme of separated powers does prevent Congress from reserving an executive role for itself or for its "agents." ... I cannot accept, however, that the exercise of authority by an officer removable for cause by a joint resolution of Congress is analogous to the impermissible execution of the law by Congress itself, nor would I hold that the congressional role in the removal process renders the Comptroller an "agent" of the Congress, incapable of receiving "executive" power....

[T]he Court baldly mischaracterizes the removal provision when it suggests that it allows Congress to remove the Comptroller for "executing the laws in any fashion found to be unsatisfactory"; in fact, Congress may remove the Comptroller only for one or more of five specified reasons, which "although not so narrow as to deny Congress any leeway, circumscribe Congress' power to some extent by providing a basis for judicial review of congressional removal." *Ameron, Inc. v. United States Army Corps of Engineers*, 787 F.2d 875, 895 (CA3 1986).... [M]ore to the point, the Court overlooks or deliberately ignores the decisive difference between the congressional removal provision and the legislative veto struck down in *Chadha*: under the Budget and Accounting Act, Congress may remove the Comptroller only through a joint resolution, which by definition must be passed by both Houses and signed by the President.... In other words, a removal of the Comptroller under the statute satisfies the requirements of bicameralism and presentment laid down in *Chadha*....

The question to be answered is whether the threat of removal of the Comptroller General for cause through joint resolution as authorized by the Budget and Accounting Act renders the Comptroller sufficiently subservient to Congress that investing him with "executive" power can be realistically equated with the unlawful retention of such power by Congress itself[.]...

The statute does not permit anyone to remove the Comptroller at will; removal is permitted only for specified cause, with the existence of cause to be determined by Congress following a hearing. Any removal under the statute would presumably be subject to post-termination judicial review to ensure that a hearing had in fact been held and that the finding of cause for removal was not arbitrary.... These procedural and substantive limitations on the removal power militate strongly against the characterization of the Comptroller as a mere agent of Congress by virtue of the removal authority. Indeed, similarly qualified grants of removal power are generally deemed to protect the officers

to whom they apply and to establish their independence from the domination of the possessor of the removal power.... Removal authority limited in such a manner is more properly viewed as motivating adherence to a substantive standard established by law than as inducing subservience to the particular institution that enforces that standard....

More importantly, the substantial role played by the President in the process of removal through joint resolution reduces to utter insignificance the possibility that the threat of removal will induce subservience to the Congress....

The majority's contrary conclusion rests on the rigid dogma that, outside of the impeachment process, any "direct congressional role in the removal of officers charged with the execution of the laws ... is inconsistent with separation of powers." Reliance on such an unyielding principle to strike down a statute posing no real danger of aggrandizement of congressional power is extremely misguided and insensitive to our constitutional role. The wisdom of vesting "executive" powers in an officer removable by joint resolution may indeed be debatable—as may be the wisdom of the entire scheme of permitting an unelected official to revise the budget enacted by Congress—but such matters are for the most part to be worked out between the Congress and the President through the legislative process, which affords each branch ample opportunity to defend its interests....

I dissent.

BLACKMUN, J., DISSENTING

... [I]t seems to me that an attempt by Congress to participate directly in the removal of an executive officer—other than through the constitutionally prescribed procedure of impeachment—might well violate the principle of separation of powers by assuming for Congress part of the President's constitutional responsibility to carry out the laws.

In my view, however, that important and difficult question need not be decided in this litigation, because no matter how it is resolved the plaintiffs, now appellees, are not entitled to the relief they have requested. Appellees have not sought invalidation of the 1921 provision that authorizes Congress to remove the Comptroller General by joint resolution; indeed, it is far from clear they would have standing to request such a judgment. The only relief sought in this case is nullification of the automatic budget-reduction provisions of the Deficit Control Act, and that relief should not be awarded even if the Court is correct that those provisions are constitutionally incompatible with Congress' authority to remove the Comptroller General by joint resolution. Any incompatibility, I feel, should be cured by

refusing to allow congressional removal—if it ever is attempted—and not by striking down the central provisions of the Deficit Control Act. However wise or foolish it may be, that statute unquestionably ranks among the most important federal enactments of the past several decades. I cannot see the sense of invalidating legislation of this magnitude in order to preserve a cumbersome, 65-year-old removal power that has never been exercised and appears to have been all but forgotten until this litigation....

I do not claim that the 1921 removal provision is a piece of statutory deadwood utterly without contemporary significance. But it comes close. Rarely if ever invoked even for symbolic purposes, the removal provision certainly pales in importance beside the legislative scheme the Court strikes down today—an extraordinarily far-reaching response to a deficit problem of unprecedented proportions. Because I believe that the constitutional defect found by the Court cannot justify the remedy it has imposed, I respectfully dissent.

QUESTIONS

1. Did Chief Justice Burger resolve *Bowsher* on congressional delegation grounds, presidential removal grounds, or both?
2. Briefs were submitted by all the parties in this case, including the Speaker and Bipartisan Leadership Group of the House, the United States, and the National Treasury Employees Union. The United States adopted the position of the district court, contending that the Gramm-Rudman Act violated separation of powers because the comptroller general, an officer of the legislative branch subject to removal by Congress, cannot exercise "executive power." Compare the U.S. argument with the arguments made by Synar. Which argument is most constitutionally sound?

3. The Court in *Bowsher* based its invalidation of the automatic deficit reduction provision of the Gramm-Rudman Act solely on a statutory provision that had not been invoked and hence was not at issue in the case. That provision involved Congress's power to remove the comptroller general from office. What constitutional principles were at stake in *Bowsher* that would motivate an advocate of judicial self-restraint, like Chief Justice Burger, to adjudicate the constitutionality of a statutory provision that was not at issue in the case?

4. James Madison argued in the *Federalist* Nos. 47–51 that the effective separation of governmental powers requires the blending of those powers. Are the Court's holdings in *Chadha* and *Bowsher* consistent with Madison's theory, or is the Court in both cases seeking to draw bright-line, categorical distinctions among the branches? An alternative interpretation is: "Perhaps [*Bowsher*] is best understood as reaffirming the Framer's aversion to parliamentary government, with its 'mingling of the Executive and Legislative branches.' ... What our scheme of separation of powers forbids is an agency that is primarily dependent on one branch of government but that exercises the powers of another" (Laurence H. Tribe [quoting Madison], *American Constitutional Law*, 2nd ed. [Mineola, NY: Foundation Press, 1988], p. 253).

5. During the opinion-drafting process, five members of the Court—Justices Brennan, Marshall, O'Connor, Powell, and Stevens—voiced concern that Chief Justice Burger's initial draft, as Justice O'Connor put it, "cast doubt on the constitutionality of the independent [regulatory] agencies" (quoted in Walter F. Murphy, James E. Fleming, and Sotirios A. Barber, *American Constitutional Interpretation*, 2nd ed. [Westbury, NY: Foundation Press, 1995], p. 512). The five justices believed that, by suggesting that Congress can delegate only the power it sought to give the comptroller general to an official removable by the president, Burger's first draft of the opinion implicitly called into question congressional authority to create administrative agencies like the Federal Communications Commission and the Securities and Exchange Commission. In response, Chief Justice Burger rewrote his opinion. Did he respond adequately to his colleagues' concerns, or are those concerns voiced in Justice Stevens's concurrence?

COMMENT

Review *Bowsher* and *Chadha* as you read *Morrison v. Olson*, 487 U.S. 654 (1988), excerpted in Chapter 4, pp. 432–443.

IMPLIED POWERS: DELEGATION OF LEGISLATIVE POWER

Mistretta v. United States
488 U.S. 361 (1989)

SETTING

Throughout most of the twentieth century, the federal government and the states have employed a system of indeterminate sentencing for those convicted of crimes. Under an indeterminate sentencing system, statutes establish broad ranges of penalties for crimes, but give sentencing judges wide latitude in determining which offenders should be incarcerated and for how long, whether the offenders should pay a fine, and whether some lesser form of punishment—such as probation—should be imposed in lieu of incarceration or a fine. In addition to giving judges extensive latitude, the system of indeterminate sentencing permits probation and parole boards to determine which offenders can be returned to society under the supervision of probation or parole officers. Indeterminate sentencing is based on the assumption that the goal of the criminal justice system is to rehabilitate offenders and to return them to society as quickly as possible.

During the 1960s, America's population increased by 13 percent but violent crime went up about 150 percent. Public opinion polls indicated that most Americans believed that the criminal justice system pampered criminals, that rehabilitation of criminal offenders was neither a realistic nor a desirable goal, and that the wide disparities in sentences imposed by judges throughout the country sent the wrong message to criminals. Politicians at the state and national levels campaigned on platforms that promised to "get tough" on crime and to take away sentencing discretion from judges, who were perceived as too lenient when imposing criminal sentences. Congress, like many state legislatures, began to explore the possibility of a system of fixed or determinate sentences for criminal offenders.

Congress enacted the Sentencing Reform Act as part of the Comprehensive Crime Control Act of 1984. That act rejected the notion that one of the goals of imprisonment is to rehabilitate offenders, declaring instead that the function of imprisonment is punishment. The 1984 act also created the U.S. Sentencing Commission, which was to devise sentencing guidelines to be followed by federal district courts. Finally, the act authorized only limited appellate court review of sentences imposed under the guidelines. The overall effect of the Sentencing Reform Act was to constrain the discretion of judges and the Federal Parole Commission in deciding the punishment an offender should receive.

The U.S. Sentencing Commission was the centerpiece of the Sentencing Reform Act. It was designated a permanent "independent commission in the judicial branch of the United States" with seven voting members, three of whom must be federal judges. The act provided that commission members were to be appointed by the president with the advice and consent of the Senate. Judicial appointees were to be selected from a list of six judges recommended by the Judicial Conference of the United States. Members were to serve up to two six-year terms, and be removable by the president for good cause. As noted above, the principal mandate to the commission was the establishment of sentencing guidelines. Once adopted, the only way Congress could prevent guidelines from going into effect was to pass a law providing for different sentences for particular crimes. The Sentencing Reform Act also imposed on judges a mandate to impose sentences in accordance with the applicable guidelines. If a judge failed to do so, both the defendant and the United States could appeal the sentence. The first sentencing guidelines went into effect in November 1987, and applied to crimes committed on or after November 1, 1987.

John Mistretta was indicted in the U.S. District Court for the Western District of Missouri for three crimes arising out of the sale of cocaine to an undercover federal narcotics agent on December 3, 1987. Mistretta moved to have the sentencing guidelines held unconstitutional on the ground that the composition of the Sentencing Commission violated separation of powers principles and that Congress had delegated excessive authority to it to establish the guidelines. The district court rejected Mistretta's contentions. It ruled that the Sentencing Commission is an executive branch agency and that its guidelines are similar to the substantive rules commonly promulgated by other such agencies. The district court also held that the participation of three federal judges on the commission did not implicate separation of powers because "voluntary service of Article III judges in the Executive Branch is sanctioned by the history of judicial conduct as early as the Washington and Adams administrations...."

After the district court's ruling, Mistretta pleaded guilty to conspiracy to possess cocaine with intent to distribute it. Under the guidelines, he was sentenced to eighteen months in prison and three years of postprison supervision, and he was fined $1,000. Mistretta appealed to the U.S. Court of Appeals for the Eighth Circuit, then both he and the United States petitioned the Supreme Court of the United States for a writ of certiorari before judgment. According to the government, more than four hundred cases had been filed across the nation and district courts were sharply divided on the constitutionality of the Sentencing Guidelines Commission: twenty-one district courts had upheld it, while twenty-nine had declared it unconstitutional. Noting the importance of the issue and the uncertainty about the sentencing process, the Supreme Court granted the parties' petitions for certiorari before judgment.

HIGHLIGHTS OF SUPREME COURT ARGUMENTS

BRIEF FOR THE UNITED STATES

◆ Congress may delegate decisions about what sentences should be imposed for particular criminal offenses because sentencing is not a "core" legislative function that Congress itself must undertake. The Sentencing Reform Act provides sufficient guidance to the Sentencing Commission to avoid the charge of excessive delegation.

◆ Designating the Sentencing Commission as an entity in the judicial branch has no significance for separation of powers purposes. The label "judicial branch" would have relevance only if determining whether the laws applicable to the courts also apply to the commission.

◆ There is no problem created by a law authorizing the president to remove officers that he has appointed who exercise executive power. That three of the commissioners are federal judges does not call for a different result, because the act only authorizes the president to remove the judges from their positions as commissioners, not from their positions as Article III judges.

◆ The text of the Constitution does not prohibit judges from serving on a commission that exercises executive power.

AMICUS CURIAE BRIEFS SUPPORTING THE UNITED STATES

Joint brief of Joseph DiGenova, Kenneth Feinberg, Marvin Rankel, Gedney Howe III, Tommaso Rendino, Harold Tyler, and William Weld (all participated in the federal sentencing reform process); U.S. Senate; U.S. Sentencing Commission.

BRIEF FOR MISTRETTA

◆ The extraordinary blending of executive, legislative, and judicial functions in the Sentencing Commission creates a unique separation of powers problem. Congress made the commission part of the judicial branch and required three federal judges to serve on it, but assigned the commission the job of writing rules that bind the judicial and executive branches regarding criminal sentences.

◆ Even if a judicial body could issue sentencing guidelines, the president has too much control over it because of his reappointment and removal powers. The independence of the judicial branch is threatened because of the presence of presidential control of the kind forbidden by *Bowsher v. Synar.*

◆ Even if Congress could have delegated the guideline writing function to an executive branch body, the commission cannot be reassigned to that branch by this Court because Congress deliberately chose to put the commission in the judicial branch.

◆ The sentencing guidelines are unconstitutional because Congress has delegated too much power to make fundamental policy decisions to the commission. It has not given the commission sufficient direction to guide it in carrying out this lawmaking task.

AMICUS CURIAE BRIEF FOR MISTRETTA

National Association of Criminal Defense Lawyers.

SUPREME COURT DECISION: 8–1

BLACKMUN, J.

... Petitioner [first] argues that in delegating the power to promulgate sentencing guidelines for every federal criminal offense to an independent Sentencing Commission, Congress has granted the Commission excessive legislative discretion in violation of the constitutionally based nondelegation doctrine. We do not agree.

The nondelegation doctrine is rooted in the principle of separation of powers that underlies our tripartite system of Government.... [W]e long have insisted that "the integrity and maintenance of the system of government ordained by the Constitution" mandate that Congress generally cannot delegate its legislative power to another Branch. *Field v. Clark*, 143 U.S. 649 (1892). We also have recognized, however, that the separation-of-powers principle, and the nondelegation doctrine in particular, do not prevent Congress from obtaining the assistance of its coordinate Branches. In a passage now enshrined in our jurisprudence, Chief Justice Taft, writing for the Court, explained our approach to such cooperative ventures: "In determining what [Congress] may do in seeking assistance from another branch, the extent and character of that assistance must be fixed according to

common sense and the inherent necessities of the government co-ordination." *J. W. Hampton, Jr., & Co. v. United States,* 276 U.S. 394 (1928). So long as Congress "shall lay down by legislative act an intelligible principle to which the person or body authorized to [exercise the delegated authority] is directed to conform, such legislative action is not a forbidden delegation of legislative power." Id.

Applying this "intelligible principle" test to congressional delegations, our jurisprudence has been driven by a practical understanding that in our increasingly complex society, replete with ever changing and more technical problems, Congress simply cannot do its job absent an ability to delegate power under broad general directives....

In light of our approval of these broad delegations, we harbor no doubt that Congress' delegation of authority to the Sentencing Commission is sufficiently specific and detailed to meet constitutional requirements. Congress charged the Commission with three goals: to "assure the meeting of the purposes of sentencing as set forth" in the Act; to "provide certainty and fairness in meeting the purposes of sentencing, avoiding unwarranted sentencing disparities among defendants with similar records ... while maintaining sufficient flexibility to permit individualized sentences," where appropriate; and to "reflect, to the extent practicable, advancement in knowledge of human behavior as it relates to the criminal justice process." 28 U.S.C. Sec. 991(b)(1). Congress further specified four "purposes" of sentencing that the Commission must pursue in carrying out its mandate: "to reflect the seriousness of the offense, to promote respect for the law, and to provide just punishment for the offense"; "to afford adequate deterrence to criminal conduct"; "to protect the public from further crimes of the defendant"; and "to provide the defendant with needed ... correctional treatment." 18 U.S.C. Sec. 3553(a)(2).

In addition, Congress prescribed the specific tool—the guidelines system—for the Commission to use in regulating sentencing. More particularly, Congress directed the Commission to develop a system of "sentencing ranges" applicable "for each category of offense involving each category of defendant." 28 U.S.C. Sec. 994(b). Congress instructed the Commission that these sentencing ranges must be consistent with pertinent provisions of Title 18 of the United States Code and could not include sentences in excess of the statutory maxima. Congress also required that for sentences of imprisonment, "the maximum of the range established for such a term shall not exceed the minimum of that range by more than the greater of 25 percent or 6 months, except that, if the minimum term of the range is 30 years or more, the maximum may be life imprisonment." Sec. 994(b)(2). Moreover, Congress directed the Commission to use current average sentences "as a starting point" for its structuring of the sentencing ranges. Sec. 994(m).

To guide the Commission in its formulation of offense categories, Congress directed it to consider seven factors: the grade of the offense; the aggravating and mitigating circumstances of the crime; the nature and degree of the harm caused by the crime; the community view of the gravity of the offense; the public concern generated by the crime; the deterrent effect that a particular sentence may have on others; and the current incidence of the offense. Secs. 994(c)(1)-(7). Congress set forth 11 factors for the Commission to consider in establishing categories of defendants. These include the offender's age, education, vocational skills, mental and emotional condition, physical condition (including drug dependence), previous employment record, family ties and responsibilities, community ties, role in the offense, criminal history, and degree of dependence upon crime for a livelihood. Sec. 994(d)(1)-(11). Congress also prohibited the Commission from considering the "race, sex, national origin, creed, and socioeconomic status of offenders," Sec. 994(d), and instructed that the guidelines should reflect the "general inappropriateness" of considering certain other factors, such as current unemployment, that might serve as proxies for forbidden factors, Sec. 994(e).

In addition to these overarching constraints, Congress provided even more detailed guidance to the Commission about categories of offenses and offender characteristics. Congress directed that guidelines require a term of confinement at or near the statutory maximum for certain crimes of violence and for drug offenses, particularly when committed by recidivists. Sec. 994(h). Congress further directed that the Commission assure a substantial term of imprisonment for an offense constituting a third felony conviction, for a career felon, for one convicted of a managerial role in a racketeering enterprise, for a crime of violence by an offender on release from a prior felony conviction, and for an offense involving a substantial quantity of narcotics. Sec. 994(i). Congress also instructed "that the guidelines reflect ... the general appropriateness of imposing a term of imprisonment" for a crime of violence that resulted in serious bodily injury. On the other hand, Congress directed that guidelines reflect the general inappropriateness of imposing a sentence of imprisonment "in cases in which the defendant is a first offender who has not been convicted of a crime of violence or an otherwise serious offense." Sec. 994(j). Congress also enumerated various aggravating and mitigating circumstances, such as, respectively, multiple offenses or substantial assistance to the Government, to be reflected in the guidelines. Secs. 994(l) and (n). In other words, although Congress granted the Commission substantial discretion in formulating guidelines, in actuality it legislated a full hierarchy of punishment—from near maximum imprisonment, to substantial imprisonment, to some imprisonment, to alternatives—and stipulated the most important offense and offender characteristics to place defendants within these categories.

We cannot dispute petitioner's contention that the Commission enjoys significant discretion in formulating guidelines....

But our cases do not at all suggest that delegations of this type may not carry with them the need to exercise judgment on matters of policy....

We conclude that in creating the Sentencing Commission—an unusual hybrid in structure and authority—Congress neither delegated excessive legislative power nor upset the constitutionally mandated balance of powers among the coordinate Branches. The Constitution's structural protections do not prohibit Congress from delegating to an expert body located within the Judicial Branch the intricate task of formulating sentencing guidelines consistent with such significant statutory direction as is present here. Nor does our system of checked and balanced authority prohibit Congress from calling upon the accumulated wisdom and experience of the Judicial Branch in creating policy on a matter uniquely within the ken of judges. Accordingly, we hold that the Act is constitutional.

The judgment of United States District Court for the Western District of Missouri is affirmed.

It is so ordered.

SCALIA, J., DISSENTING

... I fully agree with the Court's rejection of petitioner's contention that the doctrine of unconstitutional delegation of legislative authority has been violated because of the lack of intelligible, congressionally prescribed standards to guide the Commission....

The focus of controversy, in the long line of our so-called excessive delegation cases, has been whether the *degree* of generality contained in the authorization for exercise of executive or judicial powers in a particular field is so unacceptably high as to *amount* to a delegation of legislative powers. I say "so-called excessive delegation" because although that convenient terminology is often used, what is really at issue is whether there has been *any* delegation of legislative power, which occurs (rarely) when Congress authorizes the exercise of executive or judicial power without adequate standards. Strictly speaking, there is no acceptable delegation of legislative power. As John Locke put it almost three hundred years ago, "[t]he power of the *legislative* being derived from the people by a positive voluntary grant and institution, can be no other, than what the positive grant conveyed, which being only to make *laws*, and not to make *legislators*, the *legislative* can have no power to transfer their authority of making laws, and place it in other hands." J. Locke, *Second Treatise of Government* 87 (emphasis added).... In the present case, however, a pure delegation of legislative power is precisely what we have before us. It is irrelevant whether the standards are adequate, because they are not standards related to the exercise of executive or judicial powers; they are, plainly and simply, standards for further legislation....

The delegation of lawmaking authority to the Commission is ... unsupported by any legitimating theory to explain why it is not a delegation of legislative power. To disregard structural legitimacy is wrong in itself—but since structure has purpose, the disregard also has adverse practical consequences. In this case ... the consequence is to facilitate and encourage judicially uncontrollable delegation....

By reason of today's decision, I anticipate that Congress will find delegation of its lawmaking powers much more attractive in the future. If rulemaking can be entirely unrelated to the exercise of judicial or executive powers, I foresee all manner of "expert" bodies, insulated from the political process, to which Congress will delegate various portions of its lawmaking responsibility. How tempting to create an expert Medical Commission (mostly M.D.'s, with perhaps a few Ph.D.'s in moral philosophy) to dispose of such thorny, "no-win" political issues as the withholding of life-support systems in federally funded hospitals, or the use of fetal tissue for research. This is an undemocratic precedent that we set—not because of the scope of the delegated power, but because its recipient is not one of the three Branches of Government. The only governmental power the Commission possesses is the power to make law; and it is not the Congress....

I think the Court errs ... not so much because it mistakes the degree of commingling, but because it fails to recognize that this case is not about commingling, but about the creation of a new Branch altogether, a sort of junior-varsity Congress....

QUESTIONS

1. Does the Court's opinion in *Mistretta* comport with Chief Justice Burger's attempts in *Chadha* and *Bowsher* to draw bright lines separating the three branches of government? Which approach is more constitutionally defensible: the categorical *Chadha/Synar* analysis or the functional *Mistretta* analysis? Which approach harkens back to *Schechter?*

2. Summarize Justice Scalia's dissent. Does it adhere to the categorical line of analysis in *Chadha* and *Synar*?

3. The *amicus* briefs submitted by the U.S. Senate and the Sentencing Commission argued in part that the Sentencing Reform Act of 1984 was "the most ambitious effort ever undertaken by Congress to reconsider the manner in which sentences are imposed on federal criminal defendants" and that it was the product of more than a decade of work reflecting a bipartisan effort. What is the constitutional significance, if any, of that argument? For purposes of constitutional analysis, does it make any difference whether a political solution to a problem is partisan, bipartisan, cooperative, or contentious? Compare *Seminole Tribe of Florida v. Florida*, 517 U.S. 1125 (1996), Chapter 5, pp. 620–633.

4. The Sentencing Commission argued in its brief that in order to win this appeal, Mistretta

> [m]ust demonstrate that *our* Constitution and *our* system of separated powers, viewed in the light of history and precedent, prohibit Congress from authorizing the Commission to perform a delegated function—the issuance of rules to govern sentencing within a congressionally-prescribed range—that the Constitution itself does not exclusively assign to any one branch. (Emphasis in original.)

The Sentencing Commission argued that the most striking feature of Mistretta's brief was that it was "wholly silent on the question of what *principles* govern the question whether a particular congressional design violates the separation of powers." (Emphasis in original.)

Did the Sentencing Commission correctly state Mistretta's burden? If so, what kind of evidence would Mistretta have needed in order to meet it?

5. The National Association of Defense Lawyers argued that the delegation to the Sentencing Commission of the traditional judicial sentencing role to be carried out by legislative rule-making and executive enforcement violates the constitutional principle of separation of powers. In an apparent paraphrase of Madison in *Federalist* No. 48, it argued, "The aggregation of power in one branch, or the exercise of non-branch authority by another, creates an imbalance which fosters constitutional crisis." Are any seeds of constitutional crisis sown in the Court's resolution of the issues in *Mistretta*?

COMMENT

Issues pertaining to the delegation of legislative powers are also addressed in *United States v. Curtiss-Wright Export Corp.*, 299 U.S. 304 (1936); *Youngstown Sheet and Tube Co. v. Sawyer*, 34 U.S. 579 (1952); *Myers v. United States*, 272 U.S.

52 (1926); *Humphrey's Executor v. United States*, 295 U.S. 602 (1935); and *Morrison v. Olson*, 487 U.S. 654 (1988), excerpted in Chapter 4.

SUGGESTIONS FOR FURTHER READING

Abourezk, James, "The Congressional Veto: A Contemporary Response to Executive Encroachment on Legislative Prerogative," 52 *Indiana Law Journal* (1977): 323.

Breyer, Stephen, "The Legislative Veto after *Chadha*," 72 *Georgia Law Review* (1984): 785.

Brubaker, Stanley, "Slouching toward Constitutional Duty: The Legislative Veto and the Delegation of Authority," 1 *Constitutional Commentary* (1984): 81.

Bruff, Harold H., and Ernest Gellhorn, "Congressional Control of Administrative Regulation: A Study of Legislative Vetoes, " 90 *Harvard Law Review* (1977): 1369.

_____, "Legislative Formality, Administrative Rationality," 63 *Texas Law Review* (1984): 207.

Craig, Barbara Hinkson, *The Legislative Veto: Congressional Control of Regulation* (Boulder, CO: Westview, 1983).

_____, Chadha*: The Story of An Epic Constitutional Struggle* (Berkeley, CA: University of California Press, 1988).

Dry, Murray, "The Congressional Veto and the Constitutional Separation of Powers," in *The Presidency in the Constitutional Order*, eds. Joseph M. Bessette and Jeffrey Tulis (Baton Rouge, LA: Louisiana University Press, 1981).

Elliott, Donald E., "Why Our Separation of Powers Jurisprudence Is So Abysmal," 57 *George Washington Law Review* (1989): 506.

_____, "*INS v. Chadha*: The Constitution, the Administrative Constitution, and the Legislative Veto," *The Supreme Court Review* (Chicago, IL: University of Chicago Press, 1983).

Fisher, Louis, "Judicial Misjudgments about the Lawmaking Process: The Legislative Veto Case," 45 *Public Administration Review* (1985): 705.

_____, "Constitutional Interpretation by Members of Congress," 63 *North Carolina Law Review* (1985): 707.

_____, "Legislative Vetoes, Phoenix Style," in *Courts, Judges, and Politics*, 4th ed., eds. Walter F. Murphy and C. Herman Pritchett (New York, NY: Random House, 1986).

_____, "The Legislative Veto Invalidated, It Survives," 56 *Law and Contemporary Problems* (1993): 273.

Froomkin, Michael, "In Defense of Agency Autonomy," 96 *Yale Law Journal* (1987): 787.

Javits, Jacob K., and Gary J. Klein, "Congressional Oversight and the Legislative Veto: A Constitutional Analysis," 52 *New York University Law Review* (1977): 455.

Levinson, J. Harold, "Legislative and Executive Veto of Rules of Administrative Agencies: Models and Alternatives," 24 *William & Mary Law Review* (1982): 79.

Miller, Geoffrey, "Independent Agencies," *The Supreme Court Review* (Chicago, IL: University of Chicago Press, 1986).

Ogul, Morris, "Congressional Oversight: Structures and Incentives," in *Congress Reconsidered*, 2nd ed., eds. Lawrence C. Dodd and Bruce I. Oppenheimer (Washington, D.C.: Congressional Quarterly, 1981).

Scalia, Antonin, "The Legislative Veto: A False Remedy for System Overload," 19 *Regulation* (November-December, 1979).

Skowronek, Stephen, *Building a New American State: The Expansion of National Administrative Capacities, 1877–1920* (New York, NY: Cambridge University Press, 1982).

Spann, Girardeau A., "Deconstructing the Legislative Veto," 68 *Minnesota Law Review* (1984): 473.

Strauss, Peter L., "Was There a Baby in the Bathwater? A Comment on The Supreme Court's Legislative Veto Decision," *Duke Law Journal* (1983): 789.

_____, "The Place of Agencies in Government," 84 *Columbia Law Review* (1984): 573.

_____, "Formal and Functional Approaches to Separation of Powers Questions—A Foolish Inconsistency?" 72 *Cornell Law Review* (1987): 488.

Tribe, Laurence, "The Legislative Veto Decision: A Law by Any Other Name?" 21 *Harvard Journal of Legislation* (1984): 7.

Vile, M. J. C., *Constitutionalism and the Separation of Powers* (Oxford: Clarendon Press, 1967).

Wood, Gordon S., *The Creation of the American Republic, 1776–1787* (New York, NY: Norton, 1972).

INVESTIGATIVE POWERS

Watkins v. United States
354 U.S. 178 (1957)

SETTING

Nothing in the Constitution expressly gives Congress the power to investigate. However, for years before the American Revolution, the English Parliament had exercised the investigatory power, and many of the colonial legislatures continued the practice. The first congressional investigation after the Constitution's adoption was in 1792, when the House appointed a committee to inquire into the fate of an expedition against the Indians. In 1885, Princeton University Professor Woodrow Wilson declared that "the informing function of Congress should be preferred even to its legislative function."

In 1881, in *Kilbourn v. Thompson*, 103 U.S. 168, the Supreme Court began to define the contours of Congress's implied power to investigate. It ruled that the right of inquiry was confined by the separation of powers, that an inquiry must deal with a subject on which Congress can validly legislate, and that the resolution setting up the investigation must indicate a congressional interest in legislating on that subject. In 1927, in *McGrain v. Daugherty*, 273 U.S. 135, the Court added a fourth condition: a witness may rightfully refuse to answer questions posed by an investigative committee "where the bounds of the power are exceeded or the questions are not pertinent to the matter under inquiry."

Despite judicial constraints imposed in the nineteenth and early twentieth centuries, political concerns over the worldwide spread of communism beginning shortly after World War I led to pressures to increase Congress's investigative powers. In 1919, for example, when approximately four million workers went on strike for higher wages, many believed that communists had been instrumental in fomenting the discontent. Race riots also broke out in 1919 and 1920, sparked by blacks who had migrated from the South to the North to work in war-related industries and to improve their economic condition. Although in retrospect those riots had nothing to do with communism, some attempted to link the upheavals with communist infiltration of any group desiring social change. Attorney General A. Mitchell Palmer fed the frenzy. He blamed urban race riots in Chicago on communist agitators. After a terrorist bombing on New York's Wall Street that killed thirty-eight and injured hundreds, Palmer declared that the country had been infiltrated by Bolsheviks and anarchists. He ordered raids on communist meetings all over the country. His "Palmer raids" resulted in thousands of arrests and record numbers of deportations. The largest raid occurred on January 1, 1920, when federal agents arrested between four and six thousand people in thirty-three different cities and detained them for months. Later that same January, the New York Assembly ousted five members of the Socialist Party, even though that party was legally recognized, the members had been popularly elected, and none had committed any offense. Fear of communists quickly became fear of foreigners and anyone else perceived to be "un-American"—including blacks, Jews, and Catholics.

In 1938, the House of Representatives adopted a resolution, Rule XI, which created the House Committee on Un-American Activities (HUAC) as a standing committee to be elected at the commencement of each Congress. Rule XI authorized the committee to investigate (1) the extent, character, and objects of un-American propaganda activities; (2) the diffusion of subversive and un-American propaganda; and (3) other questions in relation to the first two. From its inception, the committee asserted a separate and independent function, apart from investigation in aid of legislation. According to its chairman, Martin Dies, "Unlike most congressional committees, in addition to the legislative function we are required to make the American people aware if possible of the extent of the infiltration of Communism in all phases of our society."

After World War II, a second "Red Scare" breathed new life into HUAC. The cold war with Russia persuaded many Americans that there was a communist conspiracy to take over the country. In 1947, President Harry Truman issued an executive order requiring the Federal Bureau of Investigation and Civil Service Commission to look into the loyalty of all federal workers. Then Attorney General Tom Clark identified ninety organizations he believed to be disloyal to the United States. Membership in any of those groups was grounds for believing that the person was a communist. Congressman Richard M. Nixon helped to spearhead investigations by HUAC, which eventually led to passage of the 1950 Internal Security Act. That act required "communist front" organizations to register with the attorney general and forbade the employment of communists in defense plants. It also gave the president sweeping powers to round up suspected communists in times of emergency. President Truman vetoed the act, stating that it was "worse than the Sedition Act of 1798" and a "long step toward totalitarianism." Congress mustered the two-thirds majority required to override the president's veto.

A central focus of HUAC investigations during this period was communist infiltration of labor unions. One of the persons investigated was John T. Watkins, of Rock Island, Illinois, who became an organizer for the United Automobile Workers in 1953. Before that, Watkins was a labor organizer for the Farm Equipment Workers. He was identified as a member of the Communist Party in the period 1943–1946 by Donald O. Spencer, who testified before HUAC in Chicago in September 1952. When Walter Rumsey appeared before the committee in March 1954, Watkins was again identified as a member of the Communist Party in the early 1940s.

On April 29, 1954, Watkins was called to be a witness before a subcommittee of HUAC. At the time of Watkins's appearance, the committee was considering an amendment to the Internal Security Act, which would deny the "use of the National Labor Relations Board" to any labor organization that the Subversive Activities Control Board found to be a "Communist-controlled action group." In anticipation of his appearance, Watkins submitted a written statement informing the subcommittee that he would tell all about himself, but that he would not inform on past and reformed associates. During his testimony, Watkins admitted to the subcommittee that he cooperated with the Communist Party from 1942 until 1947, but denied that he was ever a member. However, Watkins refused to answer the subcommittee's questions about his knowledge of twenty-nine other people's Communist Party affiliations some ten years earlier.

Watkins was cited for contempt and subsequently was indicted in the U.S. District Court for the District of Columbia for refusing to answer. He moved to have the indictment dismissed on the grounds that it was invalid, because it violated his free speech rights and due process of law, and because eleven members of the grand jury were government employees who were subject to the government employees security program and therefore were biased. That motion was denied and he was convicted, given a suspended sentence of a year in prison, and fined $500. The Court of Appeals for the District of Columbia initially reversed Watkins's conviction, but subsequently affirmed it by a 6–2 margin. The Supreme Court of the United States granted his petition for a writ of certiorari.

HIGHLIGHTS OF SUPREME COURT ARGUMENTS

BRIEF FOR WATKINS

◆ When the sole or primary purpose of a congressional committee is to expose individuals to public scorn and retribution, the committee is engaging in a legislative trial in violation of the doctrine of separation of powers.

◆ The questions Watkins refused to answer were asked solely for the purpose of exposing him and his former associates to public scorn and ridicule. The information that the committee sought to elicit from Watkins was available to it from its own files.

◆ The resolution that authorized creation of HUAC did not authorize it to ask the questions that Watkins refused to answer. Whatever the scope and outer limits of the resolution, Congress did not give the committee a mandate to engage in exposure.

◆ The compelled disclosures sought by the committee abridge rights protected by the First Amendment. There is no pervasive congressional need for the information sought from Watkins that could justify the restraints on political liberties involved by the committee's questions.

AMICUS CURIAE BRIEFS SUPPORTING WATKINS

Robert M. Metcalf (under indictment in Ohio on similar facts) and the American Civil Liberties Union.

BRIEF FOR THE UNITED STATES

◆ The committee was acting pursuant to a valid legislative purpose when it questioned Watkins. Some forty-seven committee recommendations to the Congress have been acted on, including the Internal Security Act. The information the committee sought to elicit from Watkins was pertinent to its inquiry into the need for further legislation regarding communist infiltration into labor unions.

◆ The committee's inquiry would have been valid even if its purpose had been merely to inform Congress and the public of communist activities in labor unions.

◆ A witness before a congressional committee inquiring into the nature and extent of communist infiltration has no right under the First Amendment to decline to disclose whether he is or has been a member of the Communist Party. Congress has the right to inquire into possible membership in the Communist Party of leaders of labor unions and those active in union undertakings.

◆ Watkins was not entitled to dismissal of the indictment merely because of the presence of government employees on the grand jury.

AMICUS CURIAE BRIEF SUPPORTING THE UNITED STATES

American Bar Association.

SUPREME COURT DECISION: 6–1

(Burton, and Whittaker, J.J. did not participate.)

WARREN, C.J.

... We start with several basic premises on which there is general agreement. The power of the Congress to conduct investigations is inherent in the legislative process. That power is broad. It encompasses inquiries concerning the administration of existing laws as well as proposed or possibly needed statutes. It includes surveys of defects in our social, economic or political system for the purpose of enabling the Congress to remedy them. It comprehends probes into departments of the Federal Government to expose corruption, inefficiency or waste. But, broad as is this power of inquiry, it is not unlimited. There is no general authority to expose the private affairs of individuals without justification in terms of the functions of the Congress. This was freely conceded by the Solicitor General in his argument of this case. Nor is the Congress a law enforcement or trial agency. These are functions of the executive and judicial departments of government. No inquiry is an end in itself; it must be related to, and in furtherance of, a legitimate task of the Congress. Investigations conducted solely for the personal aggrandizement of the investigators or to 'punish' those investigated are indefensible.

It is unquestionably the duty of all citizens to cooperate with the Congress in its efforts to obtain the facts needed for intelligent legislative action. It is their unremitting obligation to respond to subpoenas, to respect the dignity of the Congress and its committees and to testify fully with respect to matters within the province of proper investigation. This, of course, assumes that the constitutional rights of witnesses will be respected by the Congress as they are in a court of justice. The Bill of Rights is applicable to investigations as to all forms of governmental action. Witnesses cannot be compelled to give evidence against themselves. They cannot be subjected to unreasonable search and seizure. Nor can the First Amendment freedoms of speech, press, religion, or political belief and association be abridged....

Abuses of the investigative process may imperceptibly lead to abridgment of protected freedoms. The mere summoning of a witness and compelling him to testify, against his will, about his beliefs, expressions or associations is a measure of governmental interference. And when those forced revelations concern matters that are unorthodox, unpopular, or even hateful to the general public, the reaction in the life of the witness may be disastrous. This effect is even more harsh when it is past beliefs, expressions or associations that are disclosed and judged by current standards rather than those contemporary with the matters exposed. Nor does the witness alone suffer the consequences. Those who are identified by witnesses and thereby placed in the same glare of publicity are equally subject to public stigma, scorn and obloquy. Beyond that, there is the more subtle and immeasurable effect upon those who tend to adhere to the most orthodox and uncontroversial views and associations in order to avoid a similar fate at some future time. That this impact is partly the result of non-governmental activity by private persons cannot relieve the investigators of their responsibility for initiating the reaction....

Accommodation of the congressional need for particular information with the individual and personal interest in privacy is an arduous and delicate task for any court. We do not underestimate the difficulties that would attend such an undertaking. It is manifest that despite the adverse effects which follow upon compelled disclosure of private matters, not all such inquiries are barred.... The critical element is the existence of, and the weight to be ascribed to, the interest of the Congress in demanding disclo-sures from an unwilling witness. We cannot simply assume, however, that every congressional investigation is justified by a public need that overbalances any private rights affected. To do so would be to abdicate the responsibility placed by the Constitution upon the judiciary to insure that the Congress does not unjustifiably encroach upon an individual's right to privacy nor abridge his liberty of speech, press, religion or assembly....

We have no doubt that there is no congressional power to expose for the sake of exposure. The public is, of course, entitled to be informed concerning the workings of its government. That cannot be inflated into a general power to expose where the predominant result can only be an invasion of the private rights of individuals. But a solution to our problem is not to be found in testing the motives of committee members for this purpose. Such is not our function. Their motives alone would not vitiate an investigation which had been instituted by a House of Congress if that assembly's legislative purpose is being served....

An essential premise in this situation is that the House or Senate shall have instructed the committee members on what they are to do with the power delegated to them. It is the responsibility of the Congress, in the first instance, to insure that compulsory process is used only in furtherance of a legislative purpose. That requires that the instructions to an investigating committee spell out that group's jurisdiction and purpose with sufficient particularity. Those instructions are embodied in the authorizing resolution. That document is the committee's charter. Broadly drafted and loosely worded, however, such resolutions can leave tremendous latitude to the discretion of the investigators. The more vague the committee's charter is, the greater becomes the possibility that the committee's specific actions are not in conformity with the will of the parent House of Congress....

It would be difficult to imagine a less explicit authorizing resolution [than that authorizing the House Committee on Un-American Activities]. Who can define the meaning of "un-American"? What is that single, solitary "principle of the form of government as guaranteed by our Constitution"? There is no need to dwell upon the language, however. At one time, perhaps, the resolution might have been read narrowly to confine the Committee to the subject of propaganda. The events that have transpired in the fifteen years before the interrogation of petitioner make such a construction impossible at this date.

The members of the Committee have clearly demonstrated that they did not feel themselves restricted in any way to propaganda in the narrow sense of the word. Unquestionably the Committee conceived of its task in the grand view of its name. Un-American activities were its target, no matter how or where manifested. Notwithstanding the broad purview of the Committee's experience, the House of Representatives repeatedly approved its continuation. Five times it extended the life of the special committee. Then it made the group a standing committee of the House. A year later, the Committee's charter was embodied in the Legislative Reorganization Act. On five occasions, at the beginning of sessions of Congress, it has made the authorizing resolution part of the rules of the House. On innumerable occasions, it has passed appropriation bills

to allow the Committee to continue its efforts.

Combining the language of the resolution with the construction it has been given, it is evident that the preliminary control of the Committee exercised by the House of Representatives is slight or non-existent. No one could reasonably deduce from the charter the kind of investigation that the Committee was directed to make. As a result, we are asked to engage in a process of retroactive rationalization. Looking backward from the events that transpired, we are asked to uphold the Committee's actions unless it appears that they were clearly not authorized by the charter. As a corollary to this inverse approach, the Government urges that we must view the matter hospitably to the power of the Congress—that if there is any legislative purpose which might have been furthered by the kind of disclosure sought, the witness must be punished for withholding it. No doubt every reasonable indulgence of legality must be accorded to the actions of a coordinate branch of our Government. But such deference cannot yield to an unnecessary and unreasonable dissipation of precious constitutional freedoms....

The consequences that flow from this situation are manifold.... The Committee is allowed, in essence, to define its own authority, to choose the direction and focus of its activities. In deciding what to do with the power that has been conferred upon them, members of the Committee may act pursuant to motives that seem to them to be the highest. Their decisions, nevertheless, can lead to ruthless exposure of private lives in order to gather data that is neither desired by the Congress nor useful to it. Yet it is impossible in this circumstance, with constitutional freedoms in jeopardy, to declare that the Committee has ranged beyond the area committed to it by its parent assembly because the boundaries are so nebulous.

More important and more fundamental than that, however, it insulates the House that has authorized the investigation from the witnesses who are subjected to the sanctions of compulsory process. There is a wide gulf between the responsibility for the use of investigative power and the actual exercise of that power. This is an especially vital consideration in assuring respect for constitutional liberties. Protected freedoms should not be placed in danger in the absence of a clear determination by the House or the Senate that a particular inquiry is justified by a specific legislative need.

It is, of course, not the function of this Court to prescribe rigid rules for the Congress to follow in drafting resolutions establishing investigating committees. That is a matter peculiarly within the realm of the legislature, and its decisions will be accepted by the courts up to the point where their own duty to enforce the constitutionally protected rights of individuals is affected. An excessively broad charter, like that of the House Un-American Activities Committee, places the courts in an untenable position if they are to strike a balance between the public need for a particular interrogation and the right of citizens to carry on their affairs free from unnecessary governmental interference. It is impossible in such a situation to ascertain whether any legislative purpose justifies the disclosures sought and, if so, the importance of that information to the Congress in furtherance of its legislative function. The reason no

court can make this critical judgment is that the House of Representatives itself has never made it. Only the legislative assembly initiating an investigation can assay the relative necessity of specific disclosures.

Absence of the qualitative consideration of petitioner's questioning by the House of Representatives aggravates a serious problem, revealed in this case, in the relationship of congressional investigating committees and the witnesses who appear before them. Plainly these committees are restricted to the missions delegated to them, i.e., to acquire certain data to be used by the House or the Senate in coping with a problem that falls within its legislative sphere. No witness can be compelled to make disclosures on matters outside that area. This is a jurisdictional concept of pertinency drawn from the nature of a congressional committee's source of authority. It is not wholly different from nor unrelated to the element of pertinency embodied in the criminal statute under which petitioner was prosecuted. When the definition of jurisdictional pertinency is as uncertain and wavering as in the case of the Un-American Activities Committee, it becomes extremely difficult for the Committee to limit inquiries to statutory pertinency....

The Government believes that the topic of inquiry before the Subcommittee concerned Communist infiltration in labor. In his introductory remarks, the Chairman made reference to a bill, then pending before the Committee, which would have penalized labor unions controlled or dominated by persons who were, or had been, members of a "Communist-action" organization, as defined in the Internal Security Act of

1950. The Subcommittee, it is contended, might have been endeavoring to determine the extent of such a problem.

This view is corroborated somewhat by the witnesses who preceded and followed petitioner before the Subcommittee. Looking at the entire hearings, however, there is strong reason to doubt that the subject revolved about labor matters. The published transcript is entitled: Investigation of Communist Activities in the Chicago Area, and six of the nine witnesses had no connection with labor at all.

The most serious doubts as to the Subcommittee's "question under inquiry," however, stem from the precise questions that petitioner has been charged with refusing to answer. Under the terms of the statute, after all, it is these which must be proved pertinent. Petitioner is charged with refusing to tell the Subcommittee whether or not he knew that certain named persons had been members of the Communist Party in the past. The Subcommittee's counsel read the list from the testimony of a previous witness who had identified them as Communists. Although this former witness was identified with labor, he had not stated that the persons he named were involved in union affairs. Of the thirty names propounded to petitioner, seven were completely unconnected with organized labor.... When almost a quarter of the persons on the list are not labor people, the inference becomes strong that the subject before the Subcommittee was not defined in terms of Communism in labor....

Having exhausted the several possible indicia of the "question under inquiry," we remain unenlightened as to the subject to which the questions asked petitioner were pertinent.

Certainly, if the point is that obscure after trial and appeal, it was not adequately revealed to petitioner when he had to decide at his peril whether or not to answer. Fundamental fairness demands that no witness be compelled to make such a determination with so little guidance. Unless the subject matter has been made to appear with undisputable clarity, it is the duty of the investigative body, upon objection of the witness on grounds of pertinency, to state for the record the subject under inquiry at that time and the manner in which the propounded questions are pertinent thereto. To be meaningful, the explanation must describe what the topic under inquiry is and the connective reasoning whereby the precise questions asked relate to it.

The statement of the Committee Chairman in this case, in response to petitioner's protest, was woefully inadequate to convey sufficient information as to the pertinency of the questions to the subject under inquiry. Petitioner was thus not accorded a fair opportunity to determine whether he was within his rights in refusing to answer, and his conviction is necessarily invalid under the Due Process Clause of the Fifth Amendment....

The judgment of the Court of Appeals is reversed, and the case is remanded to the District Court with instructions to dismiss the indictment.

It is so ordered.

FRANKFURTER, J., CONCURRING [OMITTED]

CLARK, J., DISSENTING

... It may be that at times the House Committee on Un-American Activities has, as the Court says, "conceived of its task in the grand view of its name." And, perhaps, as the Court indicates, the rules of conduct placed upon the Committee by the House admit of individual abuse and unfairness. But that is none of our affair. So long as the object of a legislative inquiry is legitimate and the questions propounded are pertinent thereto, it is not for the courts to interfere with the committee system of inquiry. To hold otherwise would be an infringement on the power given the Congress to inform itself, and thus a trespass upon the fundamental American principle of separation of powers. The majority has substituted the judiciary as the grand inquisitor and supervisor of congressional investigations. It has never been so....

The Court indicates that in this case the source of the trouble lies in the "tremendous latitude" given the Un-American Activities Committee in the Legislative Reorganization Act. It finds that the Committee "is allowed, in essence, to define its own authority (and) to choose the direction and focus of its activities." This, of course, is largely true of all committees within their respective spheres. And, while it is necessary that the "charter," as the opinion calls the enabling resolution, "spell out (its) jurisdiction and purpose," that must necessarily be in more or less general terms....

To restrain and limit the breadth of investigative power of this Committee necessitates the similar handling of all other committees. The resulting restraint imposed on the committee system appears to cripple the system beyond workability....

While ambiguity prevents exactness (and there is "vice in vagueness" the majority reminds), the sweep of the opinion seems to be that "preliminary

control" of the Committee must be exercised. The Court says a witness' protected freedoms cannot "be placed in danger in the absence of a clear determination by the House or the Senate that a particular inquiry is justified by a specific legislative need." Frankly I do not see how any such procedure as "preliminary control" can be effected in either House of the Congress. What will be controlled preliminarily? The plans of the investigation, the necessity of calling certain witnesses, the questions to be asked, the details of subpoenas *duces tecum*, etc? As it is now, Congress is hard pressed to find sufficient time to fully debate and adopt all needed legislation. The Court asserts that "the Congress has practically abandoned its original practice of utilizing the coercive sanction of contempt proceedings at the bar of the House." This was to be expected. It may be that back in the twenties and thirties Congress could spare the time to conduct contempt hearings, but that appears impossible now. The Court places a greater burden in the conduct of contempt cases before the courts than it does before "the bar of the House."...

Coming to the merits of Watkins' case, the Court reverses the judgment because: (1) The subject matter of the inquiry was not "made to appear with undisputable clarity" either through its "charter" or by the Chairman at the time of the hearing and, therefore, Watkins was deprived of a clear understanding of "the manner in which the propounded questions (were) pertinent thereto"; and (2) the present committee system of inquiry of the House, as practiced by the Un-American Activities Committee, does not provide adequate safeguards for the protection of the constitutional right of free speech. I subscribe to neither conclusion....

The Court condemns the long-established and long-recognized committee system of inquiry of the House because it raises serious questions concerning the protection it affords to constitutional rights. It concludes that compelling a witness to reveal his "beliefs, expressions or associations" impinges upon First Amendment rights.... I do not see how any First Amendment rights were endangered here. There is nothing in the First Amendment that provides the guarantees Watkins claims. That Amendment was designed to prevent attempts by law to curtail freedom of speech.... It guarantees Watkins' right to join any organization and make any speech that does not have an intent to incite to crime.... But Watkins was asked whether he knew named individuals and whether they were Communists. He refused to answer on the ground that his rights were being abridged. What he was actually seeking to do was to protect his former associates, not himself, from embarrassment. He had already admitted his own involvement. He sought to vindicate the rights, if any, of his associates. It is settled that one cannot invoke the constitutional rights of another....

We should afford to Congress the presumption that it takes every precaution possible to avoid unnecessary damage to reputations. Some committees have codes of procedure, and others use the executive hearing technique to this end. The record in this case shows no conduct on the part of the Un-American Activities Committee that justifies condemnation. That there may have been such occasions is not for us to consider here. Nor should we permit its past transgressions, if any, to lead to the rigid restraint of all congressional committees. To carry on its heavy responsibility the compulsion of truth that does not incriminate is not only necessary to the Congress but is permitted within the limits of the Constitution.

QUESTIONS

1. Summarize the *Watkins* rule. How much does the rule constrain the work of congressional investigative committees? If the power to investigate is inherent (i.e., not spelled out in the Constitution), on what basis does the Supreme Court impose limits on that power?

2. Is Justice Clark's dissenting opinion in *Watkins* predictable based on his communist-hunting role when he served as U.S. Attorney General?

3. The American Civil Liberties Union (ACLU) limited its *amicus* brief to the issue of "whether a legislative investigation into the nature and extent of Communist political propaganda can compel the petitioner to disclose his political associations on pain of imprisonment for refusal to do so." According to the ACLU, Watkins had a First Amendment right to remain silent in the face of HUAC's inquiries. Does the text of the First Amendment contain or imply a right to remain silent? Is the ACLU correct that the rights of free speech and assembly "are worthless if people can be compelled as was [Watkins] to account for their speech and assembly"?

4. The American Bar Association (ABA) argued on behalf of the United States as follows:

> Constitutional privileges must be ever preserved, so that no individual defendant will ever be denied the basic rights of American citizenship. Nevertheless those safeguards must not be over-extended to the point that enemies of our form of government be encouraged and aided in their subversive purposes.

Assuming that you agree with the ABA, what criteria would you use to determine whether to uphold or reverse Watkins's conviction?

5. Robert Metcalf, who submitted an *amicus curiae* brief on behalf of Watkins, was a stained glass artist and professor of art at Antioch College in Yellow Springs, Ohio. He was called to testify before the HUAC in September 1954, regarding his involvement in a Marxist discussion group on campus. Like Watkins, Metcalf told the committee about his own involvement, but refused to give the names of Antioch College students and faculty who also belonged to the group. Are the differences between Metcalf's and Watkins's professions of any relevance regarding the authority of HUAC to inquire into their political affiliations?

6. It is instructive to compare *Watkins* with *Sweezy v. New Hampshire*, 354 U.S. 234 (1957). Both were handed down the same day. *Sweezy* held that a state legislative investigation ran afoul of due process guarantees. Of particular interest is Justice Frankfurter's concurring opinion, in which he concludes that New Hampshire violated "the right of a citizen to political privacy, as protected by the Fourteenth Amendment." Does this suggest that state legislatures are more constrained by the Constitution in exercising their investigative powers than is Congress?

INVESTIGATIVE POWERS

Barenblatt v. United States
360 U.S. 109 (1959)

SETTING

Watkins v. United States was decidedly unpopular in Congress. June 17, 1957, the day the *Watkins* decision was announced, was dubbed "Red Monday" by the Court's critics. New Hampshire Senator Styles Bridges, Chair of the Republican Senate Policy Committee, attacked "this ultra-liberal policy motivated court." House Minority Leader Joe Martin of Massachusetts referred to *Watkins* on a national television program as having "crippled the investigating committees." Not surprisingly, Pennsylvania Representative Francis Walter, Chair of the House Un-American Activities Committee, rebuked the Court for its "invasion of the legislative field." Several members of Congress suggested impeaching every justice in the *Watkins* majority. Early in July 1957, Illinois Representative Noah Mason and Alabama Representative George W. Andrews announced that they were hiring "one of the best lawyers in America to prepare an impeachment resolution against all members of the High Court."

In addition to critical speeches and impeachment threats, several "court curbing" bills were introduced. The proposals adopted a variety of strategies, including giving the Senate appellate jurisdiction over the Supreme Court, allowing Congress to reverse Supreme Court constitutional interpretations, requiring a unanimous Court decision to invalidate a state law, and ordering lower federal courts to disregard Supreme Court decisions that conflicted with *stare decisis*. Other proposals sought to modify how justices were selected. A coalition of Democrats and liberal Republicans, led by Senate majority leader, Lyndon B. Johnson, managed to defeat these measures. Nevertheless, while these various legislative attacks were pending, the Court had another opportunity to consider Congress's power to investigate.

In February 1953, a subcommittee of the House Committee on Un-American Activities (HUAC) commenced public hearings into "Communist Methods of Infiltration—Education." Illinois Representative Harold H. Velde, the subcommittee chair, stated that because "Communism and Communist activities cannot be investigated in a vacuum," the investigation "must, of necessity, relate to individuals." The subcommittee's investigation continued into 1954. One of those subpoenaed to testify was Lloyd Barenblatt, a psychology instructor at Vassar College. Between 1947 and 1950, he was a graduate student at the University of Michigan studying for his Ph.D. in social psychology. During most of his stay at the University of Michigan he was a teaching fellow. Barenblatt appeared before the subcommittee on June 28, 1954. The purpose of the hearings involving Barenblatt was "to demonstrate to the people of Michigan the fields of concentration of the Communist Party in the Michigan area, and the identity of those individuals responsible for its success."

At the opening of the hearings, subcommittee counsel stated that the "field covered will be in the main communism in education and the experiences and background in the party by [ex-communist] Francis X. T. Crowley. It will deal with activities in Michigan, Boston, and in some small degree, New York."

Francis Crowley was the first witness to testify. He stated that he knew Barenblatt when Barenblatt was a student at the University of Michigan and that Barenblatt was a member of the Haldane Club of the Communist Party. The Haldane Club was a group of graduate students who engaged in intellectual discussions about Marxism, art, literature, and culture. According to Crowley, Barenblatt left the Communist Party in 1950.

Barenblatt was called to testify at 4:00. He had heard Crowley's testimony, admitted that he was a teaching fellow at the University of Michigan from 1948 to 1950, and that he knew Crowley. However, he refused to state whether he was then or had ever been a member of the Communist Party, whether he was a member of the Haldane Club, whether he knew Francis Crowley as a member of the Communist Party, and whether he was a member of the University of Michigan Council of Arts, Sciences, and Professions. Barenblatt contended that he had not been informed of the purpose of the inquiry and submitted to the committee a written statement of objections that constituted his reasons for refusing to answer the committee's questions. The list included an excerpt from *Jones v. Securities & Exchange Commission*, 298 U.S. 1 (1936), declaring that "The citizen when interrogated about his private affairs has a right before answering to know why the inquiry is made; and if the purpose disclosed is not a legitimate one, he may not be compelled to answer." Subcommittee chair Velde declared that the HUAC Subcommittee would not consider Barenblatt's objections and that it was interested only in knowing whether Barenblatt was asserting his privilege against self-incrimination.

Barenblatt subsequently was indicted and convicted in the District Court for the District of Columbia for contempt of Congress, arising from his refusal to answer certain questions posed by Velde's subcommittee of the House Committee on Un-American Activities. According to the district court, "There is no contention he was disrespectful or contumacious except in a legal sense. There is no doubt about that." The court ruled that Barenblatt was adequately notified about the purpose of the hearing by the opening statement made by the committee's counsel. Barenblatt's sentence was a $250 fine and six months in prison.

A three-judge panel of the D.C. Circuit Court of Appeals affirmed Barenblatt's conviction. It held that the law creating HUAC was constitutional and that "Courts must presume congressional investigations to have valid legislative purposes."

The Supreme Court granted Barenblatt's petition for a writ of certiorari and remanded the case for reconsideration in the light of *Watkins v. United States*. On remand, the court of appeals sustained the conviction by a 5–4 *en banc* vote. It held that the Court in *Watkins* had not intended to strike down the resolution creating HUAC. Two of the dissenting judges opined that *Watkins* did not authorize the committee to investigate in the field of education; two others maintained that the committee had no authority to compel testimony because Congress had given it no definite assignment. Barenblatt again petitioned the Supreme Court of the United States for a writ of certiorari.

HIGHLIGHTS OF SUPREME COURT ARGUMENTS

BRIEF FOR BARENBLATT

◆ On the basis of this court's decision in *Watkins*, it is clear that the language of the legislation granting investigative authority to the House Committee was not sufficiently definite and specific to constitute a delegation of power, and thus there is a complete lack of authority in the committee to investigate by compulsory process. The pervasive threat in the committee's free-wheeling power to compel testimony casts a restraint on free expression on all public issues and inhibits the expression of all nonconformist political thought.

◆ An investigation that imposes restraints on First Amendment rights is constitutional only if the restraints are justified by a compelling public need. Discussions that are purely intellectual do not pose a threat.

◆ If the purpose of the committee is to expose for the sake of exposure, that is not a legitimate legislative purpose.

◆ Congress did not authorize the committee to conduct by compulsory process an investigation into the field of education. Such inquiries infringe on the expression and exchange of ideas in the academic world.

◆ Governmental inquiry into private beliefs and associations is unconstitutional.

AMICUS CURIAE BRIEFS SUPPORTING BARENBLATT

American Association of University Professors; National Lawyers Guild.

BRIEF FOR THE UNITED STATES

◆ This court in *Watkins* criticized the committee's authorizing resolution but did not hold the resolution invalid. The committee is authorized to conduct by compulsory process an investigation of communism in the field of education.

◆ Barenblatt had no right under the First Amendment to refuse to tell the committee whether he was a member of the Communist Party. While Congress has no general power to inquire into political beliefs and associations, it does have the power to inquire into the nature, character, and activities of the Communist Party, because there is the strongest reason to believe that that organization, dominated and controlled by a foreign power, seeks to subvert and destroy the American form of government.

◆ There is no foundation for Barenblatt's claim that his conviction must be reversed because he was not sufficiently apprised of the pertinency of the questions asked by the committee. He did not object to the questions on the ground of pertinency and the pertinency of the questions was indisputably clear.

◆ It is untenable to assume that the Communist Party is merely another political party. Furthermore, Barenblatt was not questioned about his beliefs or opinions. He was asked about his membership.

◆ At the heart of *Watkins* is the requirement that the witness make an appropriate objection when called upon to answer a question. The purpose of that requirement is to give the committee the opportunity to explain to the witness the logical nexus between the answer sought and the subject of the inquiry. Barenblatt did not make appropriate objections to the committee's questions.

SUPREME COURT DECISION: 5–4

HARLAN, J.

Once more the Court is required to resolve the conflicting constitutional claims of congressional power and of an individual's right to resist its exercise....

In the present case congressional efforts to learn the extent of a nationwide, indeed worldwide, problem have brought one of its investigating committees into the field of education. Of course, broadly viewed, inquiries cannot be made into the teaching that is pursued in any of our educational institutions. When academic teaching-freedom and its corollary learning-freedom, so essential to the well-being of the Nation, are claimed, this Court will always be on the alert against intrusion by Congress into this constitutionally protected domain. But this does not mean that the Congress is precluded from interrogating a witness merely because he is a teacher. An educational institution is not a constitutional sanctuary from inquiry into matters that may otherwise be within the constitutional legislative domain merely for the reason that inquiry is made of someone within its walls....

Subcommittee's Authority to Compel Testimony

At the outset it should be noted that [House] Rule XI [the source of authority of the parent House Un-American Activities Committee] authorized this Subcommittee to compel testimony within the framework of the investigative authority conferred on the Un-American Activities Committee. Petitioner contends that *Watkins v. United States* nevertheless held the grant of this power in all circumstances ineffective because of the vagueness of Rule XI in delineating the Committee jurisdiction to which its exercise was to be appurtenant....

The *Watkins* case cannot properly be read as standing for such a proposition. A principal contention in *Watkins* was that the refusals to answer were justified because the [legal] requirement, under 2 U.S.C. § 192, that the questions asked be "pertinent to the question under inquiry" had not been satisfied. This Court reversed the conviction solely on that ground, holding that Watkins had not been adequately apprised of the subject matter of the Subcommittee's investigation or the pertinency thereto of the questions he refused to answer....

Petitioner also contends, independently of *Watkins*, that the vagueness of Rule XI deprived the Subcommittee of the right to compel testimony in this investigation into Communist activity. We cannot agree with this contention which in its furthest reach would mean that the House Un-American Activities Committee under its existing authority has no right to compel testimony in any circumstances. Granting the vagueness of the Rule, we may not read it in isolation from its long history in the House of Representatives. Just as legislation is often given meaning by the gloss of legislative reports, administrative interpretation, and long usage, so the proper meaning of an authorization to a congressional committee is not to be derived alone from its abstract terms unrelated to the definite content furnished them by the course of congressional actions. The Rule comes to us with a "persuasive gloss of legislative history," *United States v. Witkovich*, 353 U.S. 194 [(1957)], which shows beyond doubt that in pursuance of its legislative concerns in the domain of "national security" the House has clothed the Un-American Activities Committee with pervasive authority to investigate Communist activities in this country....

We are urged, however, to construe Rule XI so as at least to exclude the field of education from the Committee's compulsory authority.... We cannot follow that route here[.]...

[T]he legislative gloss on Rule XI is again compelling. Not only is there no indication that the House ever viewed the field of education as being outside the Committee's authority under Rule XI, but the legislative history affirmatively evinces House approval of this phase of the Committee's work....

In this framework of the Committee's history we must conclude that its legislative authority to conduct the inquiry presently under consideration is unassailable[.]...

Pertinency Claim   Undeniably a conviction for contempt ... cannot stand unless the questions asked are pertinent to the subject matter of the investigation. *Watkins v. United States*. But the factors which led us to rest decision on this ground in *Watkins* were very different from those involved here....

[P]etitioner in the case before us raised no objections on the ground of pertinency at the time any of the questions were put to him....

We need not, however, rest decision on petitioner's failure to object on this score, for here "pertinency" was made to appear "with undisputable clarity." [*Watkins.*] First of all, it goes without saying that the scope of the Committee's

authority was for the House, not a witness, to determine, subject to the ultimate reviewing responsibility of this Court. What we deal with here is whether petitioner was sufficiently apprised of "the topic under inquiry" thus authorized "and the connective reasoning whereby the precise questions asked relate(d) to it." Id. In light of his prepared memorandum of constitutional objections there can be no doubt that this petitioner was well aware of the Subcommittee's authority and purpose to question him as it did....

Petitioner's contentions on this aspect of the case cannot be sustained.

Constitutional Contentions   The Court's past cases establish sure guides to decision. Undeniably, the First Amendment in some circumstances protects an individual from being compelled to disclose his associational relationships. However, the protections of the First Amendment, unlike a proper claim of the privilege against self-incrimination under the Fifth Amendment, do not afford a witness the right to resist inquiry in all circumstances. Where First Amendment rights are asserted to bar governmental interrogation resolution of the issue always involves a balancing by the courts of the competing private and public interests at stake in the particular circumstances shown. These principles were recognized in the *Watkins* case[.]...

The first question is whether this investigation was related to a valid legislative purpose, for Congress may not constitutionally require an individual to disclose his political relationships or other private affairs except in relation to such a purpose....

That Congress has wide power to legislate in the field of Communist activity in this Country, and to conduct appropriate investigations in aid thereof, is hardly debatable. The existence of such power has never been questioned by this Court, and it is sufficient to say, without particularization, that Congress has enacted or considered in this field a wide range of legislative measures, not a few of which have stemmed from recommendations of the very Committee whose actions have been drawn in question here....

On these premises, this Court in its constitutional adjudications has consistently refused to view the Communist Party as an ordinary political party, and has upheld federal legislation aimed at the Communist problem which in a different context would certainly have raised constitutional issues of the gravest character....

We think that investigatory power in this domain is not to be denied Congress solely because the field of education is involved.... Indeed we do not understand petitioner here to suggest that Congress in no circumstances may inquire into Communist activity in the field of education. Rather, his position is in effect that this particular investigation was aimed not at the revolutionary aspects but at the theoretical classroom discussion of communism.

In our opinion this position rests on a too constricted view of the nature of the investigatory process, and is not supported by a fair assessment of the record before us. An investigation of advocacy of or preparation for overthrow certainly embraces the right to identify a witness as a member of the Communist Party ... and to inquire into the various manifestations of the Party's tenets.... Nor can it fairly be concluded

that this investigation was directed at controlling what is being taught at our universities rather than at overthrow. The statement of the Subcommittee Chairman at the opening of the investigation evinces no such intention, and so far as this record reveals nothing thereafter transpired which would justify our holding that the thrust of the investigation later changed. The record discloses considerable testimony concerning the foreign domination and revolutionary purposes and efforts of the Communist Party. That there was also testimony on the abstract philosophical level does not detract from the dominant theme of this investigation—Communist infiltration furthering the alleged ultimate purpose of overthrow. And certainly the conclusion would not be justified that the questioning of petitioner would have exceeded permissible bounds had he not shut off the Subcommittee at the threshold.

Nor can we accept the further contention that this investigation should not be deemed to have been in furtherance of a legislative purpose because the true objective of the Committee and of the Congress was purely "exposure." So long as Congress acts in pursuance of its constitutional power, the Judiciary lacks authority to intervene on the basis of the motives which spurred the exercise of that power....

Finally, the record is barren of other factors which in themselves might sometimes lead to the conclusion that the individual interests at stake were not subordinate to those of the state. There is no indication in this record that the Subcommittee was attempting to pillory witnesses. Nor did petitioner's appearance as a witness follow from indiscriminate dragnet procedures, lacking in probable cause for belief that he possessed information which might be helpful to the Subcommittee. And the relevancy of the questions put to him by the Subcommittee is not open to doubt.

We conclude that the balance between the individual and the governmental interests here at stake must be struck in favor of the latter, and that therefore the provisions of the First Amendment have not been offended.

We hold that petitioner's conviction for contempt of Congress discloses no infirmity, and that the judgment of the Court of Appeals must be affirmed.

Affirmed.

BLACK, J., WARREN, C.J., AND DOUGLAS, J., DISSENTING

... It goes without saying that a law to be valid must be clear enough to make its commands understandable. For obvious reasons, the standard of certainty required in criminal statutes is more exacting than in noncriminal statutes. This is simply because it would be unthinkable to convict a man for violating a law he could not understand. This Court has recognized that the stricter standard is as much required in criminal contempt cases as in all other criminal cases, and has emphasized that the "vice of vagueness" is especially pernicious where legislative power over an area involving speech, press, petition and assembly is involved.... For a statute broad enough to support infringement of speech, writings, thoughts and public assemblies, against the unequivocal command of the First Amendment necessarily leaves all persons to guess just what the law really means to cover, and fear of a wrong guess inevitably leads people to forego

the very rights the Constitution sought to protect above all others. Vagueness becomes even more intolerable in this area if one accepts, as the Court today does, a balancing test to decide if First Amendment rights shall be protected. It is difficult at best to make a man guess—at the penalty of imprisonment—whether a court will consider the State's need for certain information superior to society's interest in unfettered freedom. It is unconscionable to make him choose between the right to keep silent and the need to speak when the statute supposedly establishing the "state's interest" is too vague to give him guidance....

Measured by the foregoing standards, Rule XI cannot support any conviction for refusal to testify. In substance it authorizes the Committee to compel witnesses to give evidence about all "un-American propaganda," whether instigated in this country or abroad. The word "propaganda" seems to mean anything that people say, write, think or associate together about. The term "un-American" is equally vague....

The Court—while not denying the vagueness of Rule XI—nevertheless defends its application here because the questions asked concerned communism, a subject of investigation which had been reported to the House by the Committee on numerous occasions. If the issue were merely whether Congress intended to allow an investigation of communism, or even of communism in education, it may well be that we could hold the data cited by the Court sufficient to support a finding of intent. But that is expressly not the issue. On the Court's own test, the issue is whether Barenblatt can know with sufficient certainty, at the time of his interrogation, that there is so compelling a need for his replies that infringement of his rights of free association is justified. The record does not disclose where Barenblatt can find what that need is. There is certainly no clear congressional statement of it in Rule XI....

But even if Barenblatt could evaluate the importance to the Government of the information sought, Rule XI would still be too broad to support his conviction. For we are dealing here with governmental procedures which the Court itself admits reach to the very fringes of congressional power. In such cases more is required of legislatures than a vague delegation to be filled in later by mute acquiescence. If Congress wants ideas investigated, if it even wants them investigated in the field of education, it must be prepared to say so expressly and unequivocally. And it is not enough that a court through exhaustive research can establish, even conclusively, that Congress wished to allow the investigation. I can find no such unequivocal statement here.

For all these reasons, I would hold that Rule XI is too broad to be meaningful and cannot support petitioner's conviction....

[N]o matter how often or how quickly we repeat the claim that the Communist Party is not a political party, we cannot outlaw it, as a group, without endangering the liberty of all of us. The reason is not hard to find, for mixed among those aims of communism which are illegal are perfectly normal political and social goals. And muddled with its revolutionary tenets is a drive to achieve power through the ballot, if it can be done. These things necessarily make it a political party whatever other, illegal, aims it may have....

The fact is that once we allow any group which has some political aims or ideas to be driven from the ballot and from the battle for men's minds because some of its members are bad and some of its tenets are illegal, no group is safe. Today we deal with Communists or suspected Communists. In 1920, instead, the New York Assembly suspended duly elected legislators on the ground that, being Socialists, they were disloyal to the country's principles. In the 1830's the Masons were hunted as outlaws and subversives, and abolitionists were considered revolutionaries of the most dangerous kind in both North and South. Earlier still, at the time of the universally unlamented alien and sedition laws, Thomas Jefferson's party was attacked and its members were derisively called "Jacobins." Fisher Ames described the party as a "French faction" guilty of "subversion" and "officered, regimented and formed to subordination." Its members, he claimed, intended to "take arms against the laws as soon as they dare." History should teach us then, that in times of high emotional excitement minority parties and groups which advocate extremely unpopular social or governmental innovations will always be typed as criminal gangs and attempts will always be made to drive them out.... Today's holding, in my judgment, marks another major step in the progressively increasing retreat from the safeguards of the First Amendment....

Finally, I think Barenblatt's conviction violates the Constitution because the chief aim, purpose and practice of the House Un-American Activities Committee, as disclosed by its many reports, is to try witnesses and punish them because they are or have been

Communists or because they refuse to admit or deny Communist affiliations. The punishment imposed is generally punishment by humiliation and public shame. There is nothing strange or novel about this kind of punishment. It is in fact one of the oldest forms of governmental punishment known to mankind; branding, the pillory, ostracism and subjection to public hatred being but a few examples of it. Nor is there anything strange about a court's reviewing the power of a congressional committee to inflict punishment....

Ultimately all the questions in this case really boil down to one—whether we as a people will try fearfully and futilely to preserve democracy by adopting totalitarian methods, or whether in accordance with our traditions and our Constitution we will have the confidence and courage to be free.

I would reverse this conviction....

BRENNAN, J., DISSENTING [OMITTED]

COMMENT

Just as *Watkins* was accompanied by an opinion in a state legislative investigation case, *Barenblatt* was accompanied by *Uphaus v. Wyman*, 360 U.S. 72 (1959), also originating in New Hampshire. In that case, the Court affirmed a ruling of the New Hampshire Supreme Court that a 1940 federal sedition act (the Smith Act) did not strip the states of their powers to inquire into and prosecute for seditious activities against the state. The Court, by a 5–4 vote, upheld the conviction of Willard Uphaus for refusing to produce the list of guests at the World Fellowship, Inc., in 1954 and 1955, when he was asked to do so by a New Hampshire legislature investigative committee inquiring into subversive persons and organizations in that state.

QUESTIONS

1. Can *Watkins* and *Barenblatt* be reconciled? Is *Barenblatt* an example of judicial self-protection in the wake of opposition to *Watkins*? Should Supreme Court justices respond to threats to impeach them, or to curb the Court's jurisdiction?

2. The American Association of University Professors noted that between 1948 and 1954, nineteen members of college and university faculties had been dismissed or not reappointed as a consequence of investigations by congressional or state legislative committees. It argued that while academic freedom does not mean unqualified immunity from legislative investigations, the scope of legislative investigations of the academic community and its members must be carefully circumscribed in order to avoid conflict with the First and Fourteenth Amendments. Should legislative investigations be more carefully circumscribed when it comes to colleges and universities? What constitutional considerations, if any, influence your response?

3. The National Lawyers' Guild made the following argument as *amicus* in *Barenblatt*:

> The product of th[e] assumption [that security and freedom of thought are inherently incompatible] has been the technique of public exposure as a means of suppressing the idea of which [the investigative] bodies do not approve. Often there is no possible purpose to their activities except the instigation of black-lists, reprisals, and public hostility, of which these bodies then make pious disclaimers. There is scarcely any phase of the intellectual and cultural life of America which these bodies have considered beyond their reach, whether in politics, science, religion, philosophy, music, painting, literature, education, entertainment, or the professions. They have self-construed their vague grants of authority as sufficiently broad to permit investigation of any and every kind of organizational relationship, whether fraternal, social, political, economic, educational or otherwise, and of every kind of propaganda, including limitless inquiries into any and all ideas, opinions, beliefs and associations and any and all individuals and organizations.

Did the guild make generalized attack on legislative investigations *per se*, or only against some kinds of investigations? If the former, is it politically realistic? If the latter, what standards does the organization propose for distinguishing between acceptable and unacceptable investigations?

COMMENTS

1. In 1969, HUAC was renamed the Committee on Internal Security.
2. Since *Barenblatt*, Congress has had wide latitude to exercise its investigative powers. The only substantive standard governing such powers is that they be rationally related to some congressional objective. This does not mean that the Court imposes no controls, however. Procedurally, congressional investigations must respect the Fifth Amendment protection against self-incrimination, *Quinn v. United States*, 349 U.S. 155 (1955), the Fourth Amendment protection against unreasonable searches and seizures, *McPhaul v. United States*, 364 U.S. 372 (1960), and the due process requirement that state actors must comply with rules they have promulgated to regulate their own conduct, *Gojack v. United States*, 384 U.S. 702 (1966). In addition, *Watkins* defined due process as requiring Congress to state clearly a given committee's mandate when delegating investigatory authority, and as requiring that, when a witness challenges the pertinence of an investigation, the committee state for the record the subject under

inquiry as well as how any questions posed to the witness are pertinent to the subject under investigation.

In *Gibson v. Florida Legislative Investigation Committee*, 372 U.S. 539 (1963), the Court mixed a balancing approach that weighed legislative investigative powers against individual rights, and elements of strict scrutiny (requiring the government to demonstrate a relationship between the information sought and a compelling state interest), to overturn the contempt conviction of the president of the Miami branch of the National Association for the Advancement of Colored People (NAACP) for not producing NAACP membership lists and records at the request of a state legislative committee that was investigating "communist infiltration" of race relations.

SUGGESTIONS FOR FURTHER READING

Alfange, Dean Jr., "Congressional Investigations and the Fickle Court," 30 *University of Cincinnati Law Review* (1961): 113.

Barth, Alan, *Government by Investigation* (New York, NY: Viking Press, 1955).

Carr, Robert K., *The House Committee on Un-American Activities, 1945–1950* (Ithaca, NY: Cornell University Press, 1952).

"Court-Curb Proposals Stimulated by Controversial Decisions," in *Congress and the Nation* I (Washington, D.C.: Congressional Quarterly, Inc. 1965).

Fisher, Louis, *Constitutional Dialogues: Interpretation as Political Process* (Princeton, NJ: Princeton University Press, 1988).

Kalven, Harry, "Meiklejohn and the *Barenblatt* Opinion," 27 *University of Chicago Law Review* (1960): 315.

Landis, James M., "Constitutional Limitations of the Congressional Power of Investigation," 40 *Harvard Law Review* (1926): 153.

Maslow, Will, "Fair Procedure in Congressional Investigations: A Proposed Code," 54 *Columbia Law Review* (1954): 839.

Murphy, Walter F., *Congress and the Court: A Case Study in the American Political Process* (Chicago, IL: University of Chicago Press, 1962).

Nagel, Stuart S., "Court-Curbing Periods in American History," 18 *Vanderbilt Law Review* (1965): 925.

———, "Curbing the Court: The Politics of Congressional Reaction," in *The Legal Process from a Behavioral Perspective* (Beverly Hills, CA: Sage, 1969).

Symposium, "Congressional Investigations," 18 *University of Chicago Law Review* (1951): 421.

Taylor, Telford, *Grand Inquest: The Story of Congressional Investigations* (New York, NY: Simon & Schuster, 1955).

MEMBERSHIP AND PRIVILEGES

Powell v. McCormack
395 U.S. 486 (1969)

SETTING

The representatives of the twelve states that came together at the Constitutional Convention in 1787 (Rhode Island refused to participate) had little in common except their frustrations with government under the Articles of Confederation. Although the delegates to the Constitutional Convention were able to agree that a national government based on principles of representation was desirable, there were strong disagreements over who or what should be represented. Virginia delegates Edmund Randolph and James Madison proposed that population provide the basis of representation. William Paterson of New Jersey countered with a proposal that only states be represented. The Great Compromise, presented by Connecticut delegates Roger Sherman, William Samuel Johnson, and Oliver Ellsworth resolved the impasse of the Virginia and New Jersey plans, by providing that there would be two houses of Congress, one representing the states and one based on population.

Anticipating that the Congress would be the most powerful branch of the new government, the delegates expended great energy describing and circumscribing its membership, powers, and limits. Article I, the congressional article, is notable for its detail in comparison to Articles II and III, the executive and judicial articles. Article I, section 2, clause 2, for example, lists the qualifications of age, residency, and citizenship that must be met in order to serve in the House of Representatives. Article I, section 5, clause 1, specifies that "Each House shall be the Judge of the Elections, Returns and Qualifications of its own Members...."

Though seemingly uncontroversial, these organizational and housekeeping provisions have sparked significant political and constitutional debate. In 1862, Congress sought to expand on the requirements of Article I, section 2, clause 2, by enacting a law that required its members to take an oath declaring that they had never been disloyal to the national government. In 1870, the House excluded a member-elect for selling appointments to the military academy, and a member-elect was excluded from the House in 1899 for practicing polygamy. The provision in Article I, section 5, clause 1, that permits each House to judge the qualifications of its own members, has likewise provoked congressional action. In 1797, for example, the Senate expelled William Bount for encouraging an American Indian agent to neglect his duties and for negotiating for services for the British Government among the Indians.

Whether the qualifications for persons chosen to serve in Congress are defined and fixed by the Constitution, as Alexander Hamilton argued in *Federalist* No. 60, or are subject to alteration by Congress, remained unanswered until well into the twentieth century, when controversy surrounding New York Congressman Adam Clayton Powell Jr. erupted in the 90th Congress.

Powell was a charismatic, outspoken advocate of civil rights who served as pastor of New York City's Abyssinian Baptist Church (one of the largest congregations in the country) before being elected to Congress in 1944. He was consistently reelected and became chair of the House Committee on Education and Labor in 1961. The flamboyant Powell was considered to be the country's most powerful black legislator. However, his frequent run-ins with the law eventually led to his downfall. In 1958, for example, he was indicted for income tax evasion but a jury was unable to reach a verdict and the case ultimately was dismissed. Two years later he was convicted of libel and was held in contempt four times before he paid the judgment. He was also convicted of transferring property in order to avoid paying the libel judgment.

As a congressman, Powell went on several costly trips for pleasure, which he charged to the government. His wife was on the government payroll as a clerk while she lived in Puerto Rico, and the press had a heyday when it was discovered that Powell was accompanied by one of his female staff members when he vacationed on the Isle of Bimini in the Bahamas.

During the fall of 1966, the House Committee on House Administration conducted hearings regarding Powell's alleged misuse of funds. Although invited to testify, Powell declined. The committee concluded that Powell had violated House rules regarding the hiring of clerks and use of air travel credit cards. Nonetheless, in the November 8, 1966, general election Powell was reelected by an overwhelming margin. He was issued a certificate of election on December 15.

On January 9, 1967, the Democratic Caucus voted to remove Powell as chair of the House Education and Labor Committee. The 90th Congress opened the next day, after John McCormack was elected Speaker of the House. When McCormack announced that he was prepared to administer the oath of office to the members-elect, Representative Van Deerlin of California asked that Representative Powell stand aside. The allegations behind that request were that Powell was in contempt of court in the state of New York and in the Commonwealth of Puerto Rico and that he had committed official misconduct. McCormack granted the request. Following the swearing-in ceremony, House Resolution 1 was introduced and passed. It provided that the question of the right of Powell to be sworn in would be determined by a special committee. A Select Committee of nine lawyer-representatives, chaired by House Judiciary Committee Chairman Emanuel Celler, was created to investigate Powell's right to be sworn in.

Powell objected to the creation of the Select Committee, contending that it denied him due process of law without any of the traditional safeguards of an adversary proceeding. Powell, under protest, subsequently was interrogated by committee counsel, but limited his testimony to the constitutionally prescribed qualifications of age, citizenship, and inhabitancy.

The Select Committee concluded that although Powell met the qualifications of age, citizenship, and inhabitancy, and held a certificate of election from the State of New York, he had engaged in conduct that "reflected adversely on the integrity and reputation of the House and its Members." It recommended that he be seated, then censured and condemned, ordered to pay $40,000 to the Clerk of the House, and lose his seniority.

The House rejected the committee's recommendation and instead adopted Resolution 278, excluding Powell from membership in the 90th Congress. According to the resolution, Powell had improperly maintained his wife on the House payroll for two years even though she performed no official duties, had permitted and participated in improper expenditures of government funds for private purposes while chair of the Committee on Education and Labor, had engaged in contumacious conduct toward the courts of New York, and had failed to cooperate with the Select Committee.

Powell, along with thirteen of his constituents, then filed a class action suit in the U.S. District Court for the District of Columbia against McCormack, five members of the House, the clerk of the House, the sergeant-at-arms and the doorkeeper. They sought declaratory and injunctive relief and a writ of mandamus against the defendants. The suit alleged that Resolution 278 violated the Thirteenth, Fourteenth, and Fifteenth Amendments to the Constitution of the United States, and that, as to the female electors of Powell's district, it violated the Nineteenth Amendment as well. It further alleged that Resolution 278 constituted a bill of attainder and *ex post facto* law, inflicted cruel and unusual punishment in violation of the Eighth Amendment, and denied Powell his fundamental rights of due process in violation of the Fifth and Sixth Amendments.

The district court dismissed the complaint for want of subject matter jurisdiction. After a complex series of legal moves, the Court of Appeals for the District of Columbia affirmed the dismissal, on the grounds that the case presented a nonjusticiable political question and that the "Speech or Debate Clause" of Article I, section 6, barred the action. The Supreme Court of the United States granted Powell's petition for a writ of certiorari.

HIGHLIGHTS OF SUPREME COURT ARGUMENTS

BRIEF FOR POWELL

◆ The House of Representatives is required under the constitution to seat a duly qualified Congressman who meets all the qualifications for membership in the House. The history of the ratification period confirms that the Constitution would not have been adopted if it was intended to give the legislature the power to refuse to seat a representative of the people.

◆ Excluding Powell violated Article I, section 9, clause 3, which prohibits

Bills of Attainder. The House action is a classic example of a legislative act that inflicts punishment without a trial.

◆ The punishment of exclusion from membership violates due process of the Fifth Amendment. The Select Committee proceeded on the false premise that its inquiry was not "adversary" in nature.

◆ The exclusion of Powell was based at least in part on impermissible considerations of racism. The action perpetuates theories of black inferiority, implicating the Thirteenth, Fourteenth, and Fifteenth Amendments.

◆ Separation of powers requires, rather than prohibits, judicial intervention in this case. Courts cannot decline their constitutional responsibility out of a concern that the legislative branch might not respect their decision.

AMICUS CURIAE BRIEF SUPPORTING POWELL

American Civil Liberties Union.

BRIEF FOR MCCORMACK, ET AL.

◆ Separation of powers requires that each house of the legislative branch be free from interference by the other branches in the governance of its internal affairs.

◆ Article I, section 6, clause 1—the Speech or Debate Clause—bars any court from questioning members of the House of Representatives with respect to actions taken by them in connection with legitimate legislative activities such as exercise of their constitutional power to judge the qualifications of a member-elect or to punish or expel a member.

◆ The power to judge the qualifications of a member are exclusively committed to the House by Article I and may not be reviewed in any manner by a court acting under the authority of Article III.

◆ Powell's complaint represents an impermissible attempt to involve the federal courts in decision of a nonjusticiable political question. The nonjusticiability of this action is exposed by the inability of any court to grant the relief originally sought.

◆ Even if courts could review the action of the House, Powell has failed to state a cause of action. The House acted within its constitutional power in excluding him based on its uncontested findings that he had been contemptuous of the New York courts and had wrongfully misappropriated public funds while a member.

◆ This case may also be dismissed as moot. The 90th Congress is now history and Powell has been seated in the 91st Congress.

SUPREME COURT DECISION: 8–1

WARREN, C.J.

... Mootness After certiorari was granted, respondents filed a memoran-dum suggesting that two events which occurred subsequent to our grant of certiorari require that the case be dismissed as moot.... We conclude that

Powell's claim for back salary remains viable even though he has been seated in the 91st Congress and thus find it unnecessary to determine whether the other issues have become moot....

[E]ven if respondents are correct that petitioners' averments as to injunctive relief are not sufficiently definite, it does not follow that this litigation must be dismissed as moot. Petitioner Powell has not been paid his salary by virtue of an allegedly unconstitutional House resolution. That claim is still unresolved and hotly contested by clearly adverse parties....

Respondents further argue that Powell's "wholly incidental and subordinate" demand for salary is insufficient to prevent this litigation from becoming moot. They suggest that the "primary and principal relief" sought was the seating of petitioner Powell in the 90th Congress rendering his presumably secondary claims not worthy of judicial consideration. *Bond v. Floyd*, 385 U.S. 116 (1966), rejects respondents' theory that the mootness of a "primary" claim requires a conclusion that all "secondary" claims are moot....

Finally, respondents seem to argue that Powell's proper action to recover salary is a suit in the Court of Claims, so that, having brought the wrong action, a dismissal for mootness is appropriate. The short answer to this argument is that it confuses mootness with whether Powell has established a right to recover against the sergeant at arms, a question which it is inappropriate to treat at this stage of the litigation.

Speech or Debate Clause Respondents assert that the Speech or Debate Clause of the Constitution, Art. I, § 6, is an absolute bar to petitioners' action....

Our cases make it clear that the legislative immunity created by the Speech or Debate Clause performs an important function in representative government. It insures that legislators are free to represent the interests of their constituents without fear that they will be later called to task in the courts for that representation....

Legislative immunity does not, of course, bar all judicial review of legislative acts....

[A]lthough an action against a Congressman may be barred by the Speech or Debate Clause, legislative employees who participated in the unconstitutional activity are responsible for their acts....

That House employees are acting pursuant to express orders of the House does not bar judicial review of the constitutionality of the underlying legislative decision.... Respondents' suggestions ... ask us to distinguish between affirmative acts of House employees and situations in which the House orders its employees not to act or between actions for damages and claims for salary. We can find no basis in either the history of the Speech or Debate Clause or our cases for either distinction. The purpose of the protection afforded legislators is not to forestall judicial review of legislative action but to insure that legislators are not distracted from or hindered in the performance of their legislative tasks by being called into court to defend their actions. A legislator is no more or no less hindered or distracted by litigation against a legislative employee calling into question the employee's affirmative action than he would be by a lawsuit questioning the employee's failure to act. Nor is the distraction or hindrance increased because the claim is for salary rather than damages, or because the litigation questions action taken by the employee within rather than without the House. Freedom of legislative activity and the purposes of the Speech or Debate Clause are fully protected if legislators are relieved of the burden of defending themselves....

Exclusion or Expulsion   The resolution excluding petitioner Powell was adopted by a vote in excess of two-thirds of the 434 Members of Congress—307 to 116. Article I, § 5, grants the House authority to expel a member "with the Concurrence of two thirds." Respondents assert that the House may expel a member for any reason whatsoever and that, since a two-thirds vote was obtained, the procedure by which Powell was denied his seat in the 90th Congress should be regarded as an expulsion, not an exclusion....

Although respondents repeatedly urge this Court not to speculate as to the reasons for Powell's exclusion, their attempt to equate exclusion with expulsion would require a similar speculation that the House would have voted to expel Powell had it been faced with that question. Powell had not been seated at the time House Resolution No. 278 was debated and passed. After a motion to bring the Select Committee's proposed resolution to an immediate vote had been defeated, an amendment was offered which mandated Powell's exclusion. Mr. Celler, chairman of the Select Committee, then posed a parliamentary inquiry to determine whether a two-thirds vote was necessary to pass the resolution if so amended "in the sense that it might amount to an expulsion." The Speaker replied that "action by a majority vote would be in accordance

with the rules." Had the amendment been regarded as an attempt to expel Powell, a two-thirds vote would have been constitutionally required. The Speaker ruled that the House was voting to exclude Powell, and we will not speculate what the result might have been if Powell had been seated and expulsion proceedings subsequently instituted.

Nor is the distinction between exclusion and expulsion merely one of form. The misconduct for which Powell was charged occurred prior to the convening of the 90th Congress. On several occasions the House has debated whether a member can be expelled for actions taken during a prior Congress and the House's own manual of procedure applicable in the 90th Congress states that "both Houses have distrusted their power to punish in such cases."...

Members of the House having expressed a belief that such strictures apply to its own power to expel, we will not assume that two-thirds of its members would have expelled Powell for his prior conduct had the Speaker announced that House Resolution No. 278 was for expulsion rather than exclusion.

Finally, the proceedings which culminated in Powell's exclusion cast considerable doubt upon respondents' assumption that the two-thirds vote necessary to expel would have been mustered....

The Speaker ruled that House Resolution No. 278 contemplated an exclusion proceeding. We must reject respondents' suggestion that we overrule the Speaker and hold that, although the House manifested an intent to exclude Powell, its action should be tested by whatever standards may govern an expulsion....

Subject Matter Jurisdiction Respondents first contend that this is not a case "arising under" the Constitution within the meaning of Art. III. They emphasize that Art. I, § 5, assigns to each House of Congress the power to judge the elections and qualifications of its own members and to punish its members for disorderly behavior. Respondents also note that under Art. I, § 3, the Senate has the "sole power" to try all impeachments. Respondents argue that these delegations (to "judge," to "punish," and to "try") to the Legislative Branch are explicit grants of "judicial power" to the Congress and constitute specific exceptions to the general mandate of Art. III that the "judicial power" shall be vested in the federal courts. Thus, respondents maintain, the "power conferred on the courts by Article III does not authorize this Court to do anything more than declare its lack of jurisdiction to proceed."

We reject this contention. Article III, § 1, provides that the "judicial Power ... shall be vested in one supreme Court, and in such inferior Courts as the Congress may ... establish." Further, § 2 mandates that the "judicial Power shall extend to all Cases ... arising under this Constitution...." [T]his case clearly is one "arising under" the Constitution as the Court has interpreted that phrase. Any bar to federal courts reviewing the judgments made by the House or Senate in excluding a member arises from the allocation of powers between the two branches of the Federal Government (a question of justiciability), and not from the petitioners' failure to state a claim based on federal law....

Justiciability ... [W]e turn to the question whether the case is justiciable. Two determinations must be made in this regard. First, we must decide whether the claim presented and the relief sought are of the type which admit of judicial resolution. Second, we must determine whether the structure of the Federal Government renders the issue presented a "political question"—that is, a question which is not justiciable in federal court because of the separation of powers provided by the Constitution.

A. GENERAL CONSIDERATIONS In deciding generally whether a claim is justiciable, a court must determine whether "the duty asserted can be judicially identified and its breach judicially determined, and whether protection for the right asserted can be judicially molded." *Baker v. Carr.* Respondents do not seriously contend that the duty asserted and its alleged breach cannot be judicially determined. If petitioners are correct, the House had a duty to seat Powell once it determined he met the standing requirements set forth in the Constitution. It is undisputed that he met those requirements and that he was nevertheless excluded.

Respondents do maintain, however, that this case is not justiciable because, they assert, it is impossible for a federal court to "mold effective relief for resolving this case." Respondents emphasize that petitioners asked for coercive relief against the officers of the House, and, they contend, federal courts cannot issue mandamus or injunctions compelling officers or employees of the House to perform specific official acts. Respondents rely primarily on the Speech or Debate Clause to support this contention.

We need express no opinion about the appropriateness of coercive relief in this case, for petitioners sought a declaratory judgment, a form of relief the District Court could have issued.... We thus conclude that in terms of the general criteria of justiciability, this case is justiciable.

B. POLITICAL QUESTION DOCTRINE *1. Textually Demonstrable Constitutional Commitment* Respondents maintain that even if this case is otherwise justiciable, it presents only a political question....

Respondents' first contention is that this case presents a political question because under Art. I, § 5, there has been a "textually demonstrable constitutional commitment" to the House of the "adjudicatory power" to determine Powell's qualifications. Thus it is argued that the House, and the House alone, has power to determine who is qualified to be a member.

In order to determine whether there has been a textual commitment to a coordinate department of the Government, ... we must first determine what power the Constitution confers upon the House through Art. I, § 5, before we can determine to what extent, if any, the exercise of that power is subject to judicial review....

[W]hether there is a "textually demonstrable constitutional commitment of the issue to a coordinate political department" of government and what is the scope of such commitment are questions we must resolve for the first time in this case....

In order to determine the scope of any "textual commitment" under Art. I, § 5, we necessarily must determine the meaning of the phrase to "be the Judge of the Qualifications of its own Members."... Our examination of the relevant historical materials leads us to the conclusion that petitioners are correct and that the Constitution leaves the House without authority to exclude any person, duly elected by his constituents, who meets all the requirements for membership expressly prescribed in the Constitution....

Had the intent of the Framers emerged from these materials with less clarity, we would nevertheless have been compelled to resolve any ambiguity in favor of a narrow construction of the scope of Congress' power to exclude members-elect. A fundamental principle of our representative democracy is, in Hamilton's words, "that the people should choose whom they please to govern them." 2 Elliot's Debates 257. As Madison pointed out at the Convention, this principle is undermined as much by limiting whom the people can select as by limiting the franchise itself. In apparent agreement with this basic philosophy, the Convention adopted his suggestion limiting the power to expel. To allow essentially that same power to be exercised under the guise of judging qualifications, would be to ignore Madison's warning, ... against "vesting an improper & dangerous power in the Legislature." 2 Farrand 249. Moreover, it would effectively nullify the Convention's decision to require a two-thirds vote for expulsion. Unquestionably, Congress has an interest in preserving its institutional integrity, but in most cases that interest can be sufficiently safeguarded by the exercise of its power to punish its members for disorderly behavior and, in extreme cases, to expel a member with the concurrence of two-thirds. In short, both the intention of the Framers, to the extent it can be determined, and an examination of the basic principles of our democratic system persuade us that the Constitution does not vest in the

Congress a discretionary power to deny membership by a majority vote.

For these reasons, we have concluded that Art. I, § 5, is at most a "textually demonstrable commitment" to Congress to judge only the qualifications expressly set forth in the Constitution. Therefore, the "textual commitment" formulation of the political question doctrine does not bar federal courts from adjudicating petitioners' claims.

2. Other Considerations Respondents' alternate contention is that the case presents a political question because judicial resolution of petitioners' claim would produce a "potentially embarrassing confrontation between coordinate branches" of the Federal Government. But, as our interpretation of Art. I, § 5, discloses, a determination of petitioner Powell's right to sit would require no more than an interpretation of the Constitution. Such a determination falls within the traditional role accorded courts to interpret the law, and does not involve a "lack of the respect due (a) coordinate (branch) of government," nor does it involve an "initial policy determination of a kind clearly for nonjudicial discretion." *Baker v. Carr*. Our system of government requires that federal courts on occasion interpret the Constitution in a manner at variance with the construction given the document by another branch. The alleged conflict that such an adjudication may cause cannot justify the courts' avoiding their constitutional responsibility....

Nor are any of the other formulations of a political question "inextricable from the case at bar." *Baker v. Carr*. Petitioners seek a determination that the House was without power to exclude Powell from the 90th Congress, which, we have seen, requires an interpretation of the Constitution—a determination for which clearly there are "judicially ... manageable standards." Finally, a judicial resolution of petitioners' claim will not result in "multifarious pronouncements by various departments on one question." For, as we noted in *Baker v. Carr* it is the responsibility of this Court to act as the ultimate interpreter of the Constitution. *Marbury v. Madison*. Thus, we conclude that petitioners' claim is not barred by the political question doctrine, and, having determined that the claim is otherwise generally justiciable, we hold that the case is justiciable....

Conclusion ... [A]nalysis of the "textual commitment" under Art. I, § 5 ... has demonstrated that in judging the qualifications of its members Congress is limited to the standing qualifications prescribed in the Constitution. Respondents concede that Powell met these. Thus, there is no need to remand this case to determine whether he was entitled to be seated in the 90th Congress. Therefore, we hold that, since Adam Clayton Powell, Jr., was duly elected by the voters of the 18th Congressional District of New York and was not ineligible to serve under any provision of the Constitution, the House was without power to exclude him from its membership....

It is so ordered.

DOUGLAS, J.

While I join the opinion of the Court, I add a few words....

Contests may arise over whether an elected official meets the "qualifications" of the Constitution, in which event the House is the sole judge. But the House is not the sole judge when "qualifications" are added which are not specified in the Constitution.

A man is not seated because he is a Socialist or a Communist.

Another is not seated because in his district members of a minority are systematically excluded from voting.

Another is not seated because he has spoken out in opposition to the war in Vietnam.

The possible list is long. Some cases will have the racist overtones of the present one.

Others may reflect religious or ideological clashes.

At the root of all these cases, however, is the basic integrity of the electoral process....

STEWART, J., DISSENTING

I believe that events which have taken place since certiorari was granted in this case on November 18, 1968, have rendered it moot, and that the Court should therefore refrain from deciding the novel, difficult, and delicate constitutional questions which the case presented at its inception.

The essential purpose of this lawsuit by Congressman Powell and members of his constituency was to regain the seat from which he was barred by the 90th Congress. That purpose, however, became impossible of attainment on January 3, 1969, when the 90th Congress passed into history and the 91st Congress came into being. On that date, the petitioners' prayer for a judicial decree restraining enforcement of House Resolution No. 278 and commanding the respondents to admit

Congressman Powell to membership in the 90th Congress became incontestably moot.

The petitioners assert that actions of the House of Representatives of the 91st Congress have prolonged the controversy raised by Powell's exclusion and preserved the need for a judicial declaration in this case. I believe, to the contrary, that the conduct of the present House of Representatives confirms the mootness of the petitioners' suit against the 90th Congress. Had Powell been excluded from the 91st Congress, he might argue that there was a "continuing controversy" concerning the exclusion attacked in this case. And such an argument might be sound even though the present House of Representatives is a distinct legislative body rather than a continuation of its predecessor, and though any grievance caused by conduct of the 91st Congress is not redressable in this action. But on January 3, 1969, the House of Representatives of the 91st Congress admitted Congressman Powell to membership, and he now sits as the Representative of the 18th Congressional District of New York. With the 90th Congress terminated and Powell now a member of the 91st, it cannot seriously be contended that there remains a judicial controversy between these parties over the power of the House of Representatives to exclude Powell and the power of a court to order him reseated....

If any aspect of the case remains alive, it is only Congressman Powell's individual claim for the salary of which he was deprived by his absence from the 90th Congress. But even if that claim can be said to prevent this controversy from being moot, which I doubt, there is no need to reach the fundamental constitutional issues that the Court today undertakes to decide....

There are ... substantial questions as to whether, on his salary claim, Powell could obtain relief against any or all of [the] respondents. On the other hand, if he was entitled to a salary as a member of the 90th Congress, he has a certain and completely satisfactory remedy in an action for a money judgment against the United States in the Court of Claims. While that court could not have ordered Powell seated or entered a declaratory judgment on the constitutionality of his exclusion, it is not disputed that the Court of Claims could grant him a money judgment for lost salary on the ground that his discharge from the House violated the Constitution. I would remit Congressman Powell to that rem-

edy, and not simply because of the serious doubts about the availability of the one he now pursues. Even if the mandatory relief sought by Powell is appropriate and could be effective, the Court should insist that the salary claim be litigated in a context that would clearly obviate the need to decide some of the constitutional questions with which the Court grapples today, and might avoid them altogether. In an action in the Court of Claims for a money judgment against the United States, there would be no question concerning the impact of the Speech or Debate Clause on a suit against members of the House of Representatives and their agents, and questions of jurisdiction and justiciability would, if raised at all, be in a vastly different and more conventional form....

QUESTIONS

1. Counsel for McCormack argued that the Supreme Court should not grant certiorari in this case because

   [t]his case no longer involves a controversy between Mr. Powell and the House over his right to a seat or the right of his constituents to have him seated. Mr. Powell is now sitting in the House. This action, therefore, lacks those elements of a live case or controversy which are necessary to make it an appropriate framework for considering the delicate constitutional issues which petitioners tender—issues which involve the possibility of confrontation between coordinate branches of the Government.

   Does Chief Justice Warren's opinion adequately respond to this argument? If not, was the Court's grant of the writ of certiorari an example of judicial activism intruding on issues properly within Congress's province?

2. The American Civil Liberties Union argued as follows:

   If the choices of the voters duly expressed through orderly democratic procedures are allowed to be thwarted, those processes will soon no longer be looked to for the vindication of grievances. *Amici* believe therefore that a decision [for McCormack] would have effects beyond the repudiation of the rights of the individual parties herein involved and would constitute a threat to democratic government itself.

What evidence is there in Chief Justice Warren's opinion that he found this argument persuasive?

3. In what ways, if any, does the decision in *Powell* modify the political questions doctrine?

4. To what extent does the decision in *Powell* authorize judicial intrusion into the internal operations of Congress? If Powell had been expelled from Congress for misconduct, could the Supreme Court have reviewed the constitutionality of his expulsion? Does the Court's opinion suggest that all decisions of Congress, including impeachment, are reviewable?

COMMENT

Review *Powell* when you read *U.S. Term Limits, Inc. v. Thornton*, 514 U.S. 1218 (1995), excerpted in Chapter 5, pp. 607–620.

MEMBERSHIP AND PRIVILEGES

Gravel v. United States
408 U.S. 606 (1972)

SETTING

Article I, section 6, of the Constitution provides, in part, that senators and representatives are privileged from being questioned in any other place for "any speech of debate in either house." Known as the "Speech or Debate Clause," Article I, section 6, was approved by the Constitutional Convention without discussion or opposition. However, the clause is almost identical to the provision in the English Bill of Rights of 1689: "That the Freedom of Speech, and Debates or Proceedings in Parliament, ought not to be impeached or questioned in any Court or Place out of Parliament." The Speech or Debate Clause reflects a commitment to legislative supremacy, just as the provision in the English Bill of Rights reflected recognition of parliamentary supremacy.

The Supreme Court first interpreted the Speech or Debate Clause in *Kilbourn v. Thompson*, 103 U.S. 168 (1881), and concluded that it extends immunity to all "things generally done in a session of [Congress] by one of its members in relation to the business before it." It was not clear from *Kilbourn*, however, whether the Court would broadly or narrowly construe what constitutes the "business" before Congress. In *Tenney v. Brandhove*, 341 U.S. 367 (1972), the Court held that as long as legislators are "acting in the sphere of legitimate legislative activity" they are protected from lawsuits and "from the burden of defending themselves." The deep divisions caused by the Vietnam War in the 1960s and early 1970s provided the backdrop for the Court's consideration of the outer limits of the protection provided to a member of Congress by the Speech or Debate Clause.

On June 29, 1971, Alaska Senator Mike Gravel, an opponent of the administration's conduct of the Vietnam War, convened a hearing of the Subcommittee on Buildings and Grounds of the Public Works Committee of the U.S. Senate. At the outset of the hearing he stated that the conduct of U.S. foreign policy in Indochina was relevant to his subcommittee because of its effect on the domestic economy generally and specifically because it deprived the government of adequate funds to maintain public facilities.

During the course of the hearing, Gravel either read or had inserted into the congressional record portions of a classified study by the Department of Defense, popularly known as the "Pentagon Papers," which examined the history and causes of the conflict in Indochina. At the end of the hearing, he placed the entire study, comprising some seven thousand pages of material in forty-seven volumes and bearing a "top secret" classification, into the public subcommittee record. Gravel then arranged to have the Beacon Press, a nonprofit publishing division of the Unitarian Universalist Association, publish the subcommittee's record.

In August 1971, a federal grand jury sitting in Boston, Massachusetts, was investigating the release of the Pentagon Papers to the press. It subpoenaed Dr. Leonard Rodberg, a physicist and resident fellow at the Institute for Policy Studies in Washington, D.C., who had been a staff aide of Gravel's since June 29, to testify. Rodberg had assisted Gravel in negotiating with several publishing firms for the republication of the Pentagon Papers. Gravel moved to intervene and to quash the subpoena, on the grounds that the purpose of questioning Rodberg was to investigate Gravel himself, and that Gravel's activity was immune from judicial inquiry under the Speech or Debate Clause.

The U.S. District Court for the District of Massachusetts granted Gravel's motion to intervene but denied the motion to quash Rodberg's subpoena. It issued a Protective Order barring inquiry of any witness into Gravel's actions in holding the hearing and in preparing for it. It also ruled that Gravel's actions in securing the public distribution of the subcommittee's record "stands on a different footing" and was not protected by the Speech or Debate Clause.

Gravel appealed to the U.S. Court of Appeals for the First Circuit; the government cross-appealed. The appeals court affirmed the district court. It ruled that the Speech or Debate Clause does not extend to Gravel's exercise of the informing function in publishing the subcommittee's record and therefore did not bar the grand jury's investigation into Gravel's efforts to have the record published. It also ruled that the grand jury could interrogate everyone but Gravel and his aides about Gravel's actions preparing for the subcommittee's hearing, as long as the questioning was not directed to his motives for holding the hearing. Both Gravel and the United States petitioned the Supreme Court for a writ of certiorari. Justice William Brennan, acting as Circuit Justice, stayed the order of the court of appeals pending disposition of the case on the merits and the government's motion for an expedited schedule was granted.

HIGHLIGHTS OF SUPREME COURT ARGUMENTS

BRIEF FOR GRAVEL

◆ Although the scope of the privilege under the Speech or Debate Clause has never been fixed, it has consistently been construed broadly by the Supreme Court. The publication of committee records critical of executive conduct in foreign relations is a classic example of the informing function of Congress.

◆ The Justice Department concedes that the grand jury cannot question Gravel, but contends that everyone who assisted him in discharging his duties may be subject to unrestrained interrogation. Such an investigation would yield precisely the same information that the Speech or Debate Clause protects and implicates the same potential for intimidation, harassment, and distraction as if Gravel himself were questioned personally.

◆ Interrogation of Gravel's staff by the grand jury about privileged legislative activity violates separation of powers.

AMICUS CURIAE BRIEFS SUPPORTING GRAVEL

Unitarian Universalist Association; Leonard Rodberg; American Civil Liberties Union.

BRIEF FOR THE UNITED STATES

◆ The Speech or Debate Clause is precise in protecting only members of Congress. The privilege asserted by Gravel would reach a large number of congressional assistants and might be subject to abuse.

◆ The Speech or Debate Clause protects only speech or debate in either House; it does not provide immunity for private republication of such speech or debate. It should not be extended to cover the distribution of protected speech or debate through private republication that a member has undertaken without official approval.

◆ Even if the Speech or Debate Clause or legislative immunity permits a legislative aide to avoid testifying before a grand jury about republication of protected speech or debate, that immunity does not extend to third persons whose only possible connection with the legislative process was that they were negotiating for or handling the republication.

SUPREME COURT DECISION: 5–4

WHITE, J.

… Because the claim is that a Member's aide shares the Member's constitutional privilege, we consider first whether and to what extent Senator Gravel himself is exempt from process or inquiry by a grand jury investigating the commission of a crime. Our frame of reference is Art. I, § 6, cl. 1, of the Constitution[.]…

The last sentence of the Clause provides Members of Congress with two distinct privileges. Except in cases of "Treason, Felony and Breach of the Peace," the Clause shields Members from arrest while attending or traveling to and from a session of their House. History reveals, and prior cases so hold, that this part of the Clause exempts Members from arrest in civil cases only…. Nor does freedom from arrest confer immunity on a Member from service of process as a defendant in civil matters, … or as a witness in a criminal case…. It is, therefore, sufficiently plain that the constitutional freedom from arrest does not exempt Members of Congress from the operation of the ordinary criminal laws, even though imprisonment may prevent or interfere with the performance of their duties as Members….

In recognition, no doubt, of the force of this part of § 6, Senator Gravel disavows any assertion of general immunity from the criminal law. But he points out that the last portion of § 6 affords Members of Congress another vital privilege—they may not be questioned in any other place for any speech or debate in either House. The claim is not that while one part of § 6 generally permits prosecutions for treason, felony, and breach of the peace, another part nevertheless broadly forbids them. Rather, his insistence is that the Speech or Debate Clause at the very least protects him from criminal or civil liability and from questioning elsewhere than in the Senate, with respect to the events occurring at the subcommittee hearing at which the Pentagon Papers were introduced into the public record. To us this claim is incontrovertible. The Speech or Debate Clause was designed to assure a co-equal branch of the government wide freedom of speech, debate, and deliberation without intimidation or threats from the Executive Branch. It thus protects Members against prosecutions that directly impinge upon or threaten the legislative process. We have no doubt that Senator Gravel may not be made to answer—either in terms of questions or in terms of defending himself from prosecution—for the events that occurred at the subcommittee meeting. Our decision is made easier by the fact that the United States appears to have abandoned whatever position it took to the contrary in the lower courts.

Even so, the United States strongly urges that because the Speech or Debate Clause confers a privilege only upon "Senators and Representatives," Rodberg himself has no valid claim to constitutional immunity from grand jury inquiry. In our view, both courts below correctly rejected this position…. Both courts recognized what the Senate of the United States urgently presses here: that it is literally impossible, in view of the complexities of the modern legislative process, with Congress almost constantly in session and matters of legislative concern constantly proliferating, for Members of Congress to perform their legislative tasks without the help of aides and assistants; that the day-to-day work of such aides is so critical to the Members' performance that they must be treated as the latter's alter egos; and that if they are not so recognized, the central role of the Speech or Debate Clause—to prevent intimidation of legislators by the Executive and accountability before a possibly hostile judiciary—will inevitably be diminished and frustrated....

It is true that the Clause itself mentions only "Senators and Representatives," but prior cases have plainly not taken a literalistic approach in applying the privilege. The Clause also speaks only of "Speech or Debate," but the Court's consistent approach has been that to confine the protection of the Speech or Debate Clause to words spoken in debate would be an unacceptably narrow view. Committee reports, resolutions, and the act of voting are equally covered[.]...

The United States fears the abuses that history reveals have occurred when legislators are invested with the power to relieve others from the operation of otherwise valid civil and criminal laws. But these abuses, it seems to us, are for the most part obviated if the privilege applicable to the aide is viewed, as it must be, as the privilege of the Senator, and invocable only by the Senator or by the aide on the Senator's behalf, and if in all events the privilege available to the aide is confined to those services that would be immune legislative conduct if performed by the Senator himself. This view places beyond the Speech or Debate Clause a variety of services characteristically performed by aides for Members of Congress, even though within the scope of their employment. It likewise provides no protection for crim-

inal conduct threatening the security of the person or property of others, whether performed at the direction of the Senator in preparation for or in execution of a legislative act or done without his knowledge or direction. Neither does it immunize Senator or aide from testifying at trials or grand jury proceedings involving third-party crimes where the questions do not require testimony about or impugn a legislative act. Thus our refusal to distinguish between Senator and aide in applying the Speech or Debate Clause does not mean that Rodberg is for all purposes exempt from grand jury questioning.

We are convinced also that the Court of Appeals correctly determined that Senator Gravel's alleged arrangement with Beacon Press to publish the Pentagon Papers was not protected speech or debate within the meaning of Art. I, § 6, cl. 1, of the Constitution....

[It is true that] [p]rior cases have read the Speech or Debate Clause "broadly to effectuate its purposes," *United States v. Johnson*, 383 U.S. [169 (1966)]....

But the Clause has not been extended beyond the legislative sphere. That Senators generally perform certain acts in their official capacity as Senators does not necessarily make all such acts legislative in nature. Members of Congress are constantly in touch with the Executive Branch of the Government and with administrative agencies—they may cajole, and exhort with respect to the administration of a federal statute—but such conduct, though generally done, is not protected legislative activity....

Legislative acts are not all-encompassing. The heart of the Clause is speech or debate in either House. Insofar as the Clause is construed to reach other matters, they must be an integral part of the deliberative and communicative processes by which Members participate in committee and House proceedings with respect to the consideration and passage or rejection of proposed legislation or with respect to other matters which the Constitution places within the jurisdiction of either House....

Here, private publication by Senator Gravel through the cooperation of Beacon Press was in no way essential to the deliberations of the Senate; nor does questioning as to private publication threaten the integrity or independence of the Senate by impermissibly exposing its deliberations to executive influence. The Senator had conducted his hearings; the record and any report that was forthcoming were available both to his committee and the Senate. Insofar as we are advised, neither Congress nor the full committee ordered or authorized the publication. We cannot but conclude that the Senator's arrangements with Beacon Press were not part and parcel of the legislative process.

There are additional considerations. Article I, § 6, cl. 1, as we have emphasized, does not purport to confer a general exemption upon Members of Congress from liability or process in criminal cases. Quite the contrary is true. While the Speech or Debate Clause recognizes speech, voting, and other legislative acts as exempt from liability that might otherwise attach, it does not privilege either Senator or aide to violate an otherwise valid criminal law in preparing for or implementing legislative acts. If republication of these classified papers would be a crime under an Act of Congress, it would not be entitled to immunity under the Speech or Debate Clause. It also appears that the grand jury was pursuing this very subject in

the normal course of a valid investigation. The Speech or Debate Clause does not in our view extend immunity to Rodberg, as a Senator's aide, from testifying before the grand jury about the arrangement between Senator Gravel and Beacon Press or about his own participation, if any, in the alleged transaction, so long as legislative acts of the Senator are not impugned.

Similar considerations lead us to disagree with the Court of Appeals insofar as it fashioned, tentatively at least, a non-constitutional testimonial privilege protecting Rodberg from any questioning by the grand jury concerning the matter of republication of the Pentagon Papers.... [W]e cannot carry a judicially fashioned privilege so far as to immunize criminal conduct proscribed by an Act of Congress or to frustrate the grand jury's inquiry into whether publication of these classified documents violated a federal criminal statute. The so-called executive privilege has never been applied to shield executive officers from prosecution for crime, the Court of Appeals was quite sure that third parties were neither immune from liability nor from testifying about the republication matter, and we perceive no basis for conferring a testimonial privilege on Rodberg as the Court of Appeals seemed to do....

Neither do we perceive any constitutional or other privilege that shields Rodberg, any more than any other witness, from grand jury questions relevant to tracing the source of obviously highly classified documents that came into the Senator's possession and are the basic subject matter of inquiry in this case, as long as no legislative act is implicated by the questions....

The judgment of the Court of Appeals is vacated and the cases are remanded to that court for further proceedings consistent with this opinion.

So ordered.

DOUGLAS, J., DISSENTING

I would construe the Speech or Debate Clause to insulate Senator Gravel and his aides from inquiry concerning the Pentagon Papers, and Beacon Press from inquiry concerning publication of them, for that publication was but another way of informing the public as to what had gone on in the privacy of the Executive Branch concerning the conception and pursuit of the so-called "war" in Vietnam. Alternatively, I would hold that Beacon Press is protected by the First Amendment from prosecution or investigations for publishing or undertaking to publish the Pentagon Papers....

The introduction of a document into a record of the Committee or subcommittee by its Chairman certainly puts it in the public domain. Whether a particular document is relevant to the inquiry of the committee may be questioned by the Senate in the exercise of its power to prescribe rules for the governance and discipline of wayward members. But there is only one instance, as I see it, where supervisory power over that issue is vested in the courts, and that is where a witness before a committee is prosecuted for contempt and he makes the defense that the question he refused to answer was not germane to the legislative inquiry or within its permissible range....

Classification of documents is a concern of the Congress. It is, however, no concern of the courts, as I see it, how a document is stamped in an Executive Department or whether a committee of Congress can obtain the use of it. The federal courts do not sit as an ombudsman, refereeing the disputes between the other two branches. The federal courts do become vitally involved whenever their power is sought to be invoked either to protect the press against censorship as in *New York Times Co. v. United States*, 403 U.S. 713 [1971], or to protect the press against punishment for publishing "secret" documents or to protect an individual against his disclosure of their contents for any of the purposes of the First Amendment.

Forcing the press to become the Government's coconspirator in maintaining state secrets is at war with the objectives of the First Amendment....

When the press stands before the court as a suspected criminal, it is the duty of the court to disregard what the prosecution claims is the executive privilege and to acquit the press or overturn the ruling or judgment against it, if the First Amendment and the assertion of the executive privilege conflict. For the executive privilege—nowhere made explicit in the Constitution—is necessarily subordinate to the express commands of the Constitution....

Aside from the question of the extent to which publishers can be penalized for printing classified documents, surely the First Amendment protects against all inquiry into the dissemination of information which, although once classified, has become part of the public domain....

The story of the Pentagon Papers is a chronicle of suppression of vital decisions to protect the reputations and political hides of men who worked an amazingly successful scheme of deception on the American people. They were successful not because they were astute but because the press had become a frightened, regimented, submissive instrument, fattening on favors from those in power and forgetting the great tradition of reporting. To allow the press further to be cowed by grand jury inquiries and prosecution is to carry the concept of "abridging" the press to frightening proportions....

BRENNAN, DOUGLAS, AND MARSHALL, J.J., DISSENTING

... My concern is with the narrow scope accorded the Speech or Debate Clause by today's decision.... In my view, today's decision so restricts the privilege of speech or debate as to endanger the continued performance of legislative tasks that are vital to the workings of our democratic system.

In holding that Senator Gravel's alleged arrangement with Beacon Press to publish the Pentagon Papers is not shielded from extra-senatorial inquiry by the Speech or Debate Clause, the Court adopts what for me is a far too narrow view of the legislative function. The Court seems to assume that words spoken in debate or written in congressional reports are protected by the Clause, so that if Senator Gravel had recited part of the Pentagon Papers on the Senate floor or copied them into a Senate report, those acts could not be questioned "in any other Place." Yet because he sought a wider audience, to publicize information deemed relevant to matters pending before his own committee, the Senator suddenly loses his immunity and is exposed to grand jury investigation and possible prosecution for the republication. The explanation for this anomalous result is the Court's belief that "Speech or Debate" encompasses only acts necessary to the internal deliberations of Congress concerning proposed legisla-

tion. "Here," according to the Court, "private publication by Senator Gravel through the cooperation of Beacon Press was in no way essential to the deliberations of the Senate." Therefore, "the Senator's arrangements with Beacon Press were not part and parcel of the legislative process."

Thus, the Court excludes from the sphere of protected legislative activity a function that I had supposed lay at the heart of our democratic system. I speak, of course, of the legislator's duty to inform the public about matters affecting the administration of government....

There is substantial evidence that the Framers intended the Speech or Debate Clause to cover all communications from a Congressman to his constituents....

Whether the Speech or Debate Clause extends to the informing function is an issue whose importance goes beyond the fate of a single Senator or Congressman. What is at stake is the right of an elected representative to inform, and the public to be informed, about matters relating directly to the workings of our Government. The dialogue between Congress and people has been recognized, from the days of our founding, as one of the necessary elements of a representative system. We should not retreat from that view merely because, in the course of that dialogue, information may be revealed that is embarrassing to the other branches of government or violates their notions of necessary secrecy. A Member of Congress who exceeds the bounds of propriety in performing this official task may be called to answer by the other Members of his chamber. We do violence to the fundamental concepts of privilege, however, when we subject that same conduct to judicial scrutiny at the instance of the Executive....

Equally troubling in today's decision is the Court's refusal to bar grand jury inquiry into the source of documents received by the Senator and placed by him in the hearing record. The receipt of materials for use in a congressional hearing is an integral part of the preparation for that legislative act.... I would hold that Senator Gravel's receipt of the Pentagon Papers, including the name of the person from whom he received them, may not be the subject of inquiry by the grand jury.

I would go further, however, and also exclude from grand jury inquiry any knowledge that the Senator or his aides might have concerning how the source himself first came to possess the Papers. This immunity, it seems to me, is essential to the performance of the informing function. Corrupt and deceitful officers of government do not often post for public examination the evidence of their own misdeeds. That evidence must be ferreted out, and often is, by fellow employees and subordinates. Their willingness to reveal that information and spark congressional inquiry may well depend on assurances from their contact in Congress that their identities and means of obtaining the evidence will be held in strictest confidence. To permit the grand jury to frustrate that expectation through an inquiry of the Congressman and his aides can only dampen the flow of information to the Congress and thus to the American people. There is a similar risk, of course, when the Member's own House requires him to break the confidence. But the danger, it seems to me, is far less if the Member's colleagues, and not an "unfriendly executive" or "hostile judiciary," are charged with evaluating the propriety of his conduct. In any event, assuming that a Congressman can be required to reveal the sources of his information and the methods used to obtain that information, that power of inquiry, as required by the Clause, is that of the Congressman's House, and of that House only.

I respectfully dissent.

STEWART, J., DISSENTING IN PART

The Court today holds that the Speech or Debate Clause does not protect a Congressman from being forced to testify before a grand jury about sources of information used in preparation for legislative acts. This critical question was not embraced in the petitions for *certiorari*. It was not dealt with in the written briefs. It was addressed only tangentially during the oral arguments. Yet it is a question with profound implications for the effective functioning of the legislative process. I cannot join in the Court's summary resolution of so vitally important a constitutional issue....

I am not prepared to accept the Court's rigid conclusion that the Executive may always compel a legislator to testify before a grand jury about sources of information used in preparing for legislative acts. For that reason, I dissent from that part of the Court's opinion that so inflexibly and summarily decides this vital question.

QUESTIONS

1. According to Senator Gravel, in 1797, when a federal grand jury investigated the actions of Vermont Congressman Matthew Lyon, who sent out newsletters critical of the Adams administration's for-

eign policy and said to contain military secrets, Thomas Jefferson and James Madison wrote a comprehensive protest. They contended that the Speech or Debate Clause was designed to guarantee an absolute privilege to members of Congress from coercion by the coordinate branches of government and to communicate with the electorate. What, if any, precedential value should the *Gravel* Court have given to the 1797 incident?

2. In their briefs, the parties argued—and disagreed about—the historical development of the English parliamentary privilege for speech and debate in the long struggle for Parliamentary supremacy vis-a-vis the Crown. What, if any, relevance does English history have for understanding the Speech or Debate Clause of Article I?

3. The American Civil Liberties Union argued that although the precise issues in *Gravel* involved the reach of the Speech or Debate Clause, resolution implicated a clash between two larger contending values:

> On the one hand, there is the important societal interest in imposing upon public officials and their aides, be they legislative or executive, a substantial degree of accountability for their actions. On the other is the requirement, particularly important in our democratic society, that legislators have the independence and immunity which helps insure that representative government is a reality.

Does the majority or any of the dissenting opinions deal more adequately with the consequences of that potential clash?

COMMENT

In *United States v. Brewster*, 408 U.S. 501 (1972), decided the same term as *Gravel*, the Court held, 6–3, that the Speech or Debate Clause did not bar prosecution of former Senator David B. Brewer for accepting a bribe relating to his participation in action on postage rate regulation. A decade later, the Court refused to extend the *Gravel* immunity to White House aides in *Harlow v. Fitzgerald* 457 U.S. 800 (1982). Fitzgerald alleged that Bryce Harlow and Alexander Butterfield, aides to President Nixon, conspired to cause Fitzgerald's unlawful discharge as a civilian employee of the Air Force. Although the Court ruled that Harlow and Butterfield were not entitled to a blanket protection of immunity as presidential aides, they might enjoy qualified immunity from insubstantial claims.

SUGGESTIONS FOR FURTHER READING

Note, "The Bribed Congressman's Immunity from Prosecution," 75 *Yale Law Journal* (1965): 335.

Reinstein, Robert J., and Harvey A. Silverglate, "Legislative Privilege and the Separation of Power, 86 *Harvard Law Review* (1973): 1113.

Sandalow, Terrance, "Comments on *Powell v. McCormack*," 17 *University of California Los Angeles Law Review* (1969): 1.

CHAPTER 4

PRESIDENTIAL POWERS

APPOINTMENT AND REMOVAL POWERS

Myers v. United States
272 U.S. 52 (1926)

SETTING

Article I of the Constitution spells out in great detail the powers that are delegated to Congress and the restrictions on those powers. Article II, by contrast, provides only that "The executive Power shall be vested in a President of the United States of America (section 1)," and gives minimal explanation about the nature of presidential power and responsibilities (sections 2 and 3). In *Federalist* No. 70, Alexander Hamilton argued that the Constitution contemplates an "energetic executive," one who is capable of protecting the country against foreign attacks, providing steady administration of the laws, protecting property, and guarding against factionalism and anarchy. Hamilton rued the day when the United States might elect a "feeble executive," because that implied "a feeble execution of the government," which in Hamilton's view was synonymous with bad government.

Within the framework of Hamilton's views on executive power, two fundamental theories of presidential power have competed with one another over the years. One theory, which dominated the nineteenth century, is that the president can do only what the Constitution or statutes explicitly authorize. According to this theory, the president is a functionary whose role is to carry out the policies enacted by Congress. Faithful execution of the laws, not active involvement in their formation, is the watchword of this view of presidential power. Whether or not this theory and practice of the executive resulted in the "bad government" Hamilton feared, it produced few memorable presidents with the notable exceptions of Thomas Jefferson, Hamilton's nemesis, and Civil War president Abraham Lincoln.

Another theory, which became ascendant in the twentieth century in response to two world wars, a worldwide economic depression, a so-called cold war, and a permanent bureaucracy, dictated that the president should and must be the nation's political and moral leader. From this perspective, the Constitution's lack of precision in defining presidential power means that the person occupying the presidential office can shape it to meet the needs of the times in a way that reflects that president's personality. This theory of presidential leadership is consistent with Hamilton's notion that an effective chief executive must be "energetic." The threat inherent in this theory of presidential power is that, lacking constitutional boundaries, the executive will swallow up the legislative and judicial branches and subvert popular government.

One of the presidential powers left ambiguous by the Constitution is the power to remove presidential appointees. Article II, section 2, gives the president broad appointment power but is virtually silent—save for impeachment—about how and whether those appointees may be removed from office. Presidents who viewed their roles as passive functionaries who merely execute the laws gave little thought to removing their own or other presidents' appointees. Energetic presidents, on the other hand, became more tenacious in exploring the limits of their vague constitutional powers. Perhaps it is not surprising that it was not until the twentieth century that one of the fundamental questions about presidential removal power reached the Supreme Court, provoked by the actions of President Woodrow Wilson.

Students of the presidency generally rank Wilson among the handful of America's "great" presidents, one who brought extraordinary energy to the office. Once a professor of political economy and public law, he served as president of Princeton University from 1902 to 1910 and as governor of New Jersey from 1911 to 1913 before becoming president in 1913. Wilson campaigned for president on the promise of a New Freedom, by which he meant freedom from economic monopolies and the right of labor to bargain collectively regarding the terms and conditions of employment. He denounced the economic trusts of his time as "a great incubus on the productive part of American brains."

Wilson's greatest domestic achievements included creation of the Federal Reserve Board in 1913 (designed to make the nation's money supply more capable of responding to changing economic conditions and to curb bank abuses); the Federal Trade Commission in 1914 (created to end unfair methods of competition in interstate commerce); the Clayton Anti-Trust Act in 1914 (which, among other things, barred corporations from acquiring stock in competitor corporations); child labor laws in 1916 and 1919 (barring the shipment of child-made goods in interstate commerce and taxing the profits of companies that employed children); and a law limiting the workday of trainmen to eight hours (which paved the way for general acceptance of the eight-hour work day).

Wilson appointed Frank S. Myers postmaster at Portland, Oregon, in April 1913. Myers served his four-year term and was appointed to a second term, to run from July 1917 to July 1921. The appointments were made under an 1876 statute that provided, in part, that postmasters "shall be appointed and may be removed by the President by and with the advice and consent of the senate, and shall hold their offices for four years unless sooner removed or suspended according to law...." Myers's appointments were confirmed by the Senate.

On January 22, 1920, the first assistant postmaster general, acting on behalf of the president, asked Myers to resign. He refused. On January 31, without the advice or consent of the Senate, President Wilson removed Myers from office. Myers protested his removal, contending that it was contrary to law and that he was ready and willing to perform the duties of the office. On February 10, 1920, Myers asked the president to be told why he had been removed and protested the fact that he had been removed without a copy of charges or a hearing. Myers then took the position that he had not legally been removed from office, despite the fact that a successor was appointed and confirmed in 1920.

In April 1921, Myers petitioned the U.S. Court of Claims for $8,838.71, the amount of salary to which he would have been entitled if he had served out his term as postmaster. That court ruled that Myers's claim was barred by the doctrine of *laches*: he had delayed too long in filing his claim. Therefore it dismissed his petition. Myers appealed to the Supreme Court of the United States. While the appeal was pending, Myers died. The appeal was pursued by his wife, Lois P. Myers, the personal representative of his estate. The case was scheduled for argument on February 2, 1925, but it was rescheduled for April 13, because Pennsylvania Senator George Wharton Pepper requested permission to prepare an *amicus curiae* brief addressing the relationship between the legislative and executive branches regarding the appointment and removal power.

HIGHLIGHTS OF SUPREME COURT ARGUMENTS

BRIEF FOR MYERS

◆ The 1876 statute forbidding the removal of postmasters without the consent of the Senate is within the purview of the Constitution.

◆ Extensive case law establishes that Congress has the authority to require the president to have the advice and consent of the Senate before removing executive officers whose positions are established by statute.

AMICUS CURIAE BRIEF SUPPORTING MYERS

Senator George Wharton Pepper

BRIEF FOR THE UNITED STATES

◆ If the president, as part of his responsibility to see that the laws are faithfully executed, lacks the power to remove his subordinates in the executive department, Congress may take over the control of the whole civil service of the United States by making it impossible for the president to remove anyone except with its consent. In that case, the president is deprived of his power to see that the laws are faithfully executed.

◆ Congress, in creating an office, may limit the duration of the term thereof by abolishing the office. But when it provides that the president may not remove without concurrence of the Senate, it takes part of the president's constitutional power and divides it with the Senate. This Court can resolve this case by declaring the Act of 1867 unconstitutional, and thereby avoid addressing whether the president has absolute power to remove any executive officer.

◆ History, as well as debates at the Constitutional Convention, support the view that the president has removal power over executive officers independent of the Congress. It is intolerable to assume that if a minor executive official proves unworthy of the president's trust that he must retain him until the next session of the Senate or call Congress into extraordinary session for the purpose of obtaining its consent to remove the official.

SUPREME COURT DECISION: 6–3

TAFT, C.J.

... The question where the power of removal of executive officers appointed by the President by and with the advice and consent of the Senate was vested, was presented early in the first session of the First Congress....

In the House of Representatives of the First Congress, on Tuesday, May 18, 1789, Mr. Madison moved in the committee of the whole that there should be established three executive departments, one of Foreign Affairs, another of the Treasury, and a third of War, at the head of each of which there should be a Secretary, to be appointed by the President by and with the advice and consent of the Senate, and to be removable by the President. The committee agreed to the establishment of a Department of Foreign Affairs, but a discussion ensued as to making the Secretary removable by the President....

It is very clear ... that the exact ques-

tion which the House voted upon was whether it should recognize and declare the power of the President under the Constitution to remove the Secretary of Foreign Affairs without the advice and consent of the Senate. That was what the vote was taken for. Some effort has been made to question whether the decision carries the result claimed for it, but there is not the slightest doubt, after an examination of the record, that the vote was, and was intended to be, a legislative declaration that the power to remove officers appointed by the President and the Senate vested in the President alone, and until the Johnson impeachment trial in 1868 its meaning was not doubted, even by those who questioned its soundness....

The vesting of the executive power in the President was essentially a grant of the power to execute the laws. But the President alone and unaided could not execute the laws. He must execute them by the assistance of subordinates. This view has since been repeatedly affirmed by this court.... As he is charged specifically to take care that they be faithfully executed, the reasonable implication, even in the absence of express words, was that as part of his executive power he should select those who were to act for him under his direction in the execution of the laws. The further implication must be, in the absence of any express limitation respecting removals, that as his selection of administrative officers is essential to the execution of the laws by him, so must be his power of removing those for whom he cannot continue to be responsible....

The view of Mr. Madison and his associates [in 1789] was that not only did the grant of executive power to the President in the first section of article 2 carry with it the power of removal, but the express recognition of the power of appointment in the second section enforced this view on the well-approved principle of constitutional and statutory construction that the power of removal of executive officers was incident to the power of appointment....

The history of the clause by which the Senate was given a check upon the President's power of appointment makes it clear that it was not prompted by any desire to limit removals.... [T]he important purpose of those who brought about the restriction was to lodge in the Senate, where the small states had equal representation with the larger states, power to prevent the President from making too many appointments from the larger states....

Another argument urged against the constitutional power of the President alone to remove executive officers appointed by him with the consent of the Senate is that, in the absence of an express power of removal granted to the President, power to make provision for removal of all such officers is vested in the Congress by section 8 of article 1.

Mr. Madison, mistakenly thinking that an argument like this was advanced by Roger Sherman, took it up and answered it as follows:

> He [Roger Sherman] seems to think (if I understand him rightly) that the power of displacing from office is subject to legislative discretion, because, it having a right to create, it may limit or modify as it thinks proper. I shall not say but at first view this doctrine may seem to have some plausibility. But when I consider that the Constitution clearly intended to maintain a marked distinction between the legislative, executive and judicial powers of government, and when I consider that, if the Legislature has a power such as is contended for, they may subject and transfer at discretion powers from one department of our government to another, they may, on that principle, exclude the President altogether from exercising any authority in the removal of officers, they may give to the Senate alone, or the President and Senate combined, they may vest it in the whole Congress, or they may reserve it to be exercised by this house. When I consider the consequences of this doctrine, and compare them with the true principles of the Constitution, I own that I cannot subscribe to it....

The constitutional construction that excludes Congress from legislative power to provide for the removal of superior officers finds support in the second section of article 2. By it the appointment of all officers, whether superior or inferior, by the President is declared to be subject to the advice and consent of the Senate. In the absence of any specific provision to the contrary, the power of appointment to executive office carries with it, as a necessary incident, the power of removal. Whether the Senate must concur in the removal is aside from the point we now are considering. That point is that by the specific constitutional provision for appointment of executive officers with its necessary incident of removal, the power of appointment and removal is clearly provided for by the Constitution, and the legislative power of Congress in respect to both is excluded save by the specific exception as to inferior offices in the clause that follows....

It is argued that the denial of the legislative power to regulate removals in some way involves the denial of power to prescribe qualifications for office, or reasonable classification for promotion, and yet that has been often exercised. We see no conflict between the latter power and that of appointment and removal, provided of course that the qualifications do not so limit selection and so trench upon executive choice as to be in effect legislative designation....

[The President] must place in each member of his official family, and his chief executive subordinates, implicit faith. The moment that he loses confidence in the intelligence, ability, judgment, or loyalty of any one of them, he must have the power to remove him without delay. To require him to file charges and submit them to the consideration of the Senate might make impossible that unity and co-ordination in executive administration essential to effective action.

The duties of the heads of departments and bureaus in which the discretion of the President is exercised ... are the most important in the whole field of executive action of the government. There is nothing in the Constitution which permits a distinction between the removal of the head of a department or a bureau, when he discharges a political duty of the President or exercises his discretion, and the removal of executive officers engaged in the discharge of their other normal duties. The imperative reasons requiring an unrestricted power to remove the most important of his subordinates in their most important duties must therefore control the interpretation of the Constitution as to all appointed by him.

But this is not to say that there are not strong reasons why the President should have a like power to remove his appointees charged with other duties than those above described. The ordinary duties of officers prescribed by statute come under the general administrative control of the President by virtue of the general grant to him of the executive power, and he may properly supervise and guide their construction of the statutes under which they act in order to secure that unitary and uniform execution of the laws which article 2 of the Constitution evidently contemplated in vesting general executive power in the President alone. Laws are often passed with specific provision for adoption of regulations by a department or bureau head to make the law workable and effective. The ability and judgment manifested by the official thus empowered, as well as his energy and stimulation of his subordinates, are subjects which the President must consider and supervise in his administrative control. Finding such officers to be negligent and inefficient, the President should have the power to remove them. Of course there may be duties so peculiarly and specifically committed to the discretion of a particular officer as to raise a question whether the

President may overrule or revise the officer's interpretation of his statutory duty in a particular instance. Then there may be duties of a quasi judicial character imposed on executive officers and members of executive tribunals whose decisions after hearing affect interests of individuals, the discharge of which the President cannot in a particular case properly influence or control. But even in such a case he may consider the decision after its rendition as a reason for removing the officer, on the ground that the discretion regularly entrusted to that officer by statute has not been on the whole intelligently or wisely exercised. Otherwise he does not discharge his own constitutional duty of seeing that the laws be faithfully executed....

We come now to consider an argument, advanced and strongly pressed on behalf of the complainant, that this case concerns only the removal of a postmaster, that a postmaster is an inferior officer, and that such an office was not included within the legislative decision of 1789, which related only to superior officers to be appointed by the President by and with the advice and consent of the Senate. This, it is said, is the distinction which Chief Justice Marshall had in mind in *Marbury v. Madison* ... in respect to the President's power of removal of a District of Columbia justice of the peace appointed and confirmed for a term of years. We find nothing in *Marbury v. Madison* to indicate any such distinction. It cannot be certainly affirmed whether the conclusion there stated was based on a dissent from the legislative decision of 1789, or on the fact that the office was created under the special power of Congress exclusively to legislate for the District of Columbia, or on the fact that the office was a judicial one, or on the

circumstance that it was an inferior office. In view of the doubt as to what was really the basis of the remarks relied on and their *obiter dictum* character, they can certainly not be used to give weight to the argument that the 1789 decision only related to superior officers....

The fact seems to be that all departments of the government have constantly had in mind, since the passage of the Tenure of Office Act [of March 2, 1867], that the question of power of removal by the President of officers appointed by him with the Senate's consent has not been settled adversely to the legislative action of 1789, but, in spite of congressional action, has remained open until the conflict should be subjected to judicial investigation and decision....

What, then, are the elements that enter into our decision of this case? We have, first, a construction of the Constitution made by a [1789] Congress which was to provide by legislation for the organization of the government in accord with the Constitution which had just then been adopted, and in which there were, as Representatives and Senators, a considerable number of those who had been members of the convention that framed the Constitution and presented it for ratification. It was the Congress that launched the government. It was the Congress that rounded out the Constitution itself by the proposing of the first 10 amendments, which had in effect been promised to the people as a consideration for the ratification. It was the Congress in which Mr. Madison, one of the first in the framing of the Constitution, led also in the organization of the government under it. It was a Congress whose constitutional decisions have always been regarded, as they should be regarded, as of the greatest weight in the interpretation of that fundamental instrument. This construction was followed by the legislative department and the executive department continuously for 73 years, and this, although the matter in the heat of political differences between the executive and the Senate in President Jackson's time, was the subject of bitter controversy. This court has repeatedly laid down the principle that a contemporaneous legislative exposition of the Constitution, when the founders of our government and framers of our Constitution were actively participating in public affairs, acquiesced in for a long term of years, fixes the construction to be given its provisions....

We are now asked to set aside this construction thus buttressed and adopt an adverse view, because the Congress of the United States did so during a heated political difference of opinion between the then President and the majority leaders of Congress over the reconstruction measures adopted as a means of restoring to their proper status the states which attempted to withdraw from the Union at the time of the Civil War. The extremes to which the majority in both Houses carried legislative measures in that matter are now recognized by all who calmly review the history of that episode in our government leading to articles of impeachment against President Johnson and his acquittal. Without animadverting on the character of the measures taken, we are certainly justified in saying that they should not be given the weight affecting proper constitutional construction to be accorded to that reached by the First Congress of the United States during a political calm and acquiesced in by the

whole government for three-quarters of a century, especially when the new construction contended for has never been acquiesced in by either the executive or the judicial departments. While this court has studiously avoided deciding the issue until it was presented in such a way that it could not be avoided, in the references it has made to the history of the question, and in the presumptions it has indulged in favor of a statutory construction not inconsistent with the legislative decision of 1789, it has indicated a trend of view that we should not and cannot ignore. When on the merits we find our conclusion strongly favoring the view which prevailed in the First Congress, we have no hesitation in holding that conclusion to be correct; and it therefore follows that the Tenure of Office Act of 1867, in so far as it attempted to prevent ... President [Johnson] from removing executive officers who had been appointed by him by and with the advice and consent of the Senate, was invalid, and that subsequent legislation of the same effect was equally so.

For the reasons given, we must therefore hold that the provision of the law of 1876 by which the unrestricted power of removal of first-class postmasters is denied to the President is in violation of the Constitution and invalid. This leads to an affirmance of the judgment of the Court of Claims....

Judgment affirmed.

HOLMES, J., DISSENTING [OMITTED]

MCREYNOLDS, J., DISSENTING

... Nothing short of language clear beyond serious disputation should be held to clothe the President with authority wholly beyond congressional control arbitrarily to dismiss every officer whom he appoints except a few judges. There are no such words in the Constitution, and the asserted inference conflicts with the heretofore accepted theory that this government is one of carefully enumerated powers under an intelligible charter....

Constitutional provisions should be interpreted with the expectation that Congress will discharge its duties no less faithfully than the executive will attend to his. The Legislature is charged with the duty of making laws for orderly administration obligatory upon all. It possesses supreme power over national affairs and may wreck as well as speed them. It holds the purse; every branch of the government functions under statutes which embody its will; it may impeach and expel all civil officers. The duty is upon it "to make all laws which shall be necessary and proper for carrying into execution" all powers of the federal government. We have no such thing as three totally distinct and independent departments; the others must look to the legislative for direction and support. "In republican government the legislative authority necessarily predominates." The *Federalist* [57]. Perhaps the chief duty of the President is to carry into effect the will of Congress through such instrumentalities as it has chosen to provide. Arguments, therefore, upon the assumption that Congress may willfully impede executive action are not important....

Congress has long and vigorously asserted its right to restrict removals and there has been no common executive practice based upon a contrary view. The President has often removed, and it is admitted that he may remove,

with either the express or implied assent of Congress; but the present theory is that he may override the declared will of that body. This goes far beyond any practice heretofore approved or followed; it conflicts with the history of the Constitution, with the ordinary rules of interpretation, and with the construction approved by Congress since the beginning and emphatically sanctioned by this court. To adopt it would be revolutionary....

If the framers of the Constitution had intended "the executive power," in article 2, § 1, to include all power of an executive nature, they would not have added the carefully defined grants of section 2. They were scholarly men, and it exceeds belief "that the known advocates in the convention for a jealous grant and cautious definition of federal powers should have silently permitted the introduction of words and phrases in a sense rendering fruitless the restrictions and definitions elaborated by them." Why say, the President shall be commander-in-chief; may require opinions in writing of the principal officers in each of the executive departments; shall have power to grant reprieves and pardons; shall give information to Congress concerning the state of the union; shall receive ambassadors; shall take care that the laws be faithfully executed—if all of these things and more had already been vested in him by the general words? The Constitution is exact in statement....

Considering all these things, it is impossible for me to accept the view that the President may dismiss, as caprice may suggest, any inferior officer whom he has appointed with consent of the Senate, notwithstanding a positive inhibition by Congress. In the last analysis, that view has no substantial support, unless it be the polemic opinions expressed by Mr. Madison (and eight others) during the debate of 1789, when he was discussing questions relating to a "superior officer' to be appointed for an indefinite term. Notwithstanding his justly exalted reputation as one of the creators and early expounder of the Constitution, sentiments expressed under such circumstances ought not now to outweigh the conclusion which Congress affirmed by deliberate action while he was leader in the House and has consistently maintained down to the present year, the [*Marbury v. Madison*] opinion of this court solemnly announced through the great Chief Justice more than a century ago, and the canons of construction approved over and over again.

Judgment should go for the appellant.

BRANDEIS, J., DISSENTING

... The President's power of removal from statutory civil inferior offices, like the power of appointment to them, comes immediately from Congress. It is true that the exercise of the power of removal is said to be an executive act, and that when the Senate grants or withholds consent to a removal by the President, it participates in an executive act. But the Constitution has confessedly granted to Congress the legislative power to create offices, and to prescribe the tenure thereof; and it has not in terms denied to Congress the power to control removals. To prescribe the tenure involves prescribing the conditions under which incumbency shall cease. For the possibility of removal is a condition or qualification of the tenure. When Congress provides that the incumbent shall hold the office for four

years unless sooner removed with the consent of the Senate, it prescribes the term of the tenure.

It is also argued that the clauses in article 2, § 3, of the Constitution, which declare that the President "shall take Care that the Laws be faithfully executed, and shall Commission all the Officers of the United States" imply a grant to the President of the alleged uncontrollable power of removal. I do not find in either clause anything which supports this claim. The provision that the President "shall Commission all the Officers of the United States" clearly bears no such implication. Nor can it be spelled out of the direction that "he shall take Care that the Laws be faithfully executed." There is no express grant to the President of incidental powers resembling those conferred upon Congress by clause 18 of article 1, § 8....

To imply a grant to the President of the uncontrollable power of removal from statutory inferior executive offices involves an unnecessary and indefensible limitation upon the constitutional power of Congress to fix the tenure of the inferior statutory offices....

The separation of the powers of government did not make each branch completely autonomous. It left each in some measure, dependent upon the others, as it left to each power to exercise, in some respects, functions in their nature executive, legislative and judicial. Obviously the President cannot secure full execution of the laws, if Congress denies to him adequate means of doing so. Full execution may be defeated because Congress declines to create offices indispensable for that purpose; or because Congress, having created the office, declines to make the indispensable appropriation; or because Congress, having both created the office and made the appropriation, prevents, by restrictions which it imposes, the appointment of officials who in quality and character are indispensable to the efficient execution of the law. If, in any such way, adequate means are denied to the President, the fault will lie with Congress. The President performs his full constitutional duty, if, with the means and instruments provided by Congress and within the limitations prescribed by it, he uses his best endeavors to secure the faithful execution of the laws enacted....

Checks and balances were established in order that this should be "a government of laws and not of men."...

QUESTIONS

1. Summarize the views of Chief Justice Taft and the dissenters in *Myers* regarding the president's removal authority under Article II § 2, and the rationale each advances for his view. How do these different views comport with the two theories of presidential power outlined in the *Setting*; with relevant provisions of the Constitution?

2. Does Chief Justice Taft's view of presidential power in *Myers* push the theory of separation of powers to an extreme, effectively eliminating the concept of checks and balances explained by James Madison in the *Federalist* Nos. 47–51?

3. Senator Pepper, in his brief on behalf of Myers, contended that the questions before the Supreme Court were as follows:

   May the President, with the consent of the Senate, appoint to the office which the statute creates and may he later ignore that part of the creating statute which declares that the responsibility of removal shall be the joint responsibility of the President and Senate? May he ignore the statutory provision and assume the sole responsibility?

   Did Chief Justice Taft agree with Senator Pepper that *Myers* focused on these questions?

4. Would Chief Justice Taft have been wise to accept the government's invitation to avoid the broad question of presidential removal power and declare the Act of 1876 unconstitutional on the ground that it usurped power expressly delegated to the president? Would that have been a more narrow ground for resolving the controversy in *Myers*? Would Justice Brandeis have been satisfied with such a resolution?

5. As president, William Howard Taft adhered to the narrow theory that the president has only those powers given by the Constitution or by statute. As Chief Justice, Taft boldly articulated the Hamiltonian view of presidential powers. What might account for his change in perspective on this subject? Would it not seem more likely for Taft to have had the opposite views—Hamilton's while president, and the more restrained while chief justice?

6. Review Chief Justice Marshall's opinion in *Marbury v. Madison*. Does dictum in that opinion regarding presidential authority to revoke the commission of a justice of the peace shed light on the constitutional issue in *Myers*? If not, why not?

APPOINTMENT AND REMOVAL POWERS

Humphrey's Executor v. United States
295 U.S. 602 (1935)

SETTING

As noted in the *Setting* to *Myers*, Congress in 1914 created the Federal Trade Commission (FTC), as part of President Woodrow Wilson's attack on economic monopolies and trusts. The commission consisted of five members, each to be appointed by the president with the advice and consent of the Senate. Section 1 of the act provided, in part, that "Any commissioner may be removed by the President for inefficiency, neglect of duty, or malfeasance in office." During its early years, the FTC failed to become the active force its creators envisioned, because despite reformer's expectations, President Wilson's appointments to the FTC ranged from ineffective to incompetent. During the 1920s, the FTC was dominated by Republican appointees who were less than sympathetic to the commission's function as a watchdog of business. Although President Franklin Roosevelt understood the FTC's regulatory potential, it was still in the hands of Republican appointees when he assumed office in 1933.

One such appointee was William E. Humphrey, who had been appointed by President Herbert Hoover to a term of seven years that ended September 25, 1931. On June 30, 1931, during a Senate recess, Hoover reappointed Humphrey to serve until the end of the next session of Congress.

On January 27, 1932, President Hoover appointed Humphrey to a term that expired on September 25, 1938. Franklin Roosevelt became president in 1933, after a campaign that had focused on the Great Depression and the federal government's ineffective response to it. Roosevelt took office committed to invigorating agencies like the FTC. Between July 11, 1933, and October 7, 1933, the president repeatedly asked Humphrey to resign. Roosevelt stated that his request was made "without any reflection at all upon you personally, or upon the service you have rendered in your present capacity." Nonetheless, Roosevelt claimed "the aims and purposes of the Administration with respect to the work of the Commission can be carried out most effectively with personnel of my own choosing." In his letter to Humphrey the President stated:

> You will, I know, realize that I do not feel that your mind and my mind go along together on either the policies or the administering of the Federal Trade Commission, and, frankly, I think it is best for the people of this country that I should have a full confidence.

Humphrey refused to resign. Roosevelt removed him from office on October 8, 1933. Humphrey protested his removal to the president and to the FTC. Meanwhile, President Roosevelt appointed George C. Mathews to fill the vacancy created by Humphrey's removal and the Senate confirmed Mathews's appointment.

On October 27, 1933, Humphrey informed the president that he was still a member of the FTC and that he was entitled to his salary of $10,000 per year until the expiration of his term. Humphrey died four months later, on February 14, 1934. Samuel Rathbun was appointed executor of Humphrey's estate. On April 14, 1934, Rathbun filed suit against the United States in the U.S. Court of Claims for $3,043.06, plus interest, as salary for Humphrey from his removal on October 8, 1933, until his death. The United States filed a demurrer stating that the suit did not state a cause of action against the United States. The Court of Claims certified the case to the Supreme Court of the United States to answer two questions: (1) Do the provisions of section 1 of the FTC act, which states that "any commissioner may be removed by the President for inefficiency, neglect of duty, or malfeasance in office," restrict or limit the power of the president to remove a commissioner except for one of those named causes? (2) If the removal power of the president is limited, is such a restriction or limitation valid under the Constitution of the United States?

HIGHLIGHTS OF SUPREME COURT ARGUMENTS

BRIEF FOR HUMPHREY'S ESTATE

◆ The FTC act provides that commissioners may be removed for "inefficiency, neglect of duty or malfeasance in office." That language restricts the power of the president to remove for political purposes.

◆ The FTC was intended to be an independent regulatory body. The commission's independence is inconsistent with an unrestricted power of removal in the president.

◆ This case is distinguishable from *Myers v. United States*. Independent regulatory commissions are not purely executive offices. They exercise quasi-legislative and quasi-judicial functions as well. The *Myers* rule is applicable only to purely executive officers.

BRIEF FOR THE UNITED STATES

◆ If the FTC act is interpreted to limit the removal power of the president to the causes stated, it is an unconstitutional interference with the executive power of the president. The independence that Congress sought for independent regulatory commissions does not depend on an implied limitation of the president's power of removal.

◆ The functions of a quasi-legislative and quasi-judicial character that the commission performs are in no essential respects different from those committed to the heads of executive departments. *Myers* controls this case.

Supreme Court Decision: *9–0*

SUTHERLAND, J.

... The question first to be considered is whether, by the provisions of section 1 of the Federal Trade Commission Act ... the President's power is limited to removal for the specific causes enumerated therein. The negative contention of the government is based principally upon the decision of this court in *Shurtleff v. United States*, 189 U.S. 311 [(1903)].... In this court Shurtleff relied upon the maxim *expressio unius est exclusio alterius* [the expression of one thing means the exclusion of another]; but this court held that, while the rule expressed in the maxim was a very proper one and founded upon justifiable reasoning in many instances, it "should not be accorded controlling weight when to do so would involve the alteration of the universal practice of the government for over a century, and the consequent curtailment of the powers of the Executive in such an unusual manner." What the court meant by this expression appears from a reading of the opinion. That opinion—after saying that no term of office was fixed by the act and that, with the exception of judicial officers provided for by the Constitution, no civil officer had ever held office by life tenure since the foundation of the government—points out

that to construe the statute as contended for by Shurtleff would give the appraiser the right to hold office during his life or until found guilty of some act specified in the statute, the result of which would be a complete revolution in respect of the general tenure of office, effected by implication with regard to that particular office only....

The situation here presented is plainly and wholly different. The statute fixes a term of office, in accordance with many precedents. The first commissioners appointed are to continue in office for terms of three, four, five, six, and seven years, respectively; and their successors are to be appointed for terms of seven years—any commissioner being subject to removal by the President for inefficiency, neglect of duty, or malfeasance in office. The words of the act are definite and unambiguous.

The government says the phrase "continue in office" is of no legal significance and, moreover, applies only to the first Commissioners. We think it has significance. It may be that, literally, its application is restricted as suggested; but it, nevertheless, lends support to a view contrary to that of the government as to the meaning of the entire requirement in respect of tenure; for it is not easy to suppose that Congress intended to secure the first commissioners against removal except for the causes specified and deny like security to their successors. Putting this phrase aside, however, the fixing of a definite term subject to removal for cause, unless there be some countervailing provision or circumstance indicating the contrary, which here we are unable to find, is enough to establish the legislative intent that the term is not to be curtailed in the absence of such cause. But if the intention of Congress that no removal should be made during the specified term except for one or more of the enumerated causes were not clear upon the face of the statute, as we think it is, it would be made clear by a consideration of the character of the commission and the legislative history which accompanied and preceded the passage of the act.

The commission is to be nonpartisan; and it must, from the very nature of its duties, act with entire impartiality. It is charged with the enforcement of no policy except the policy of the law. Its duties are neither political nor executive, but predominantly quasi judicial and quasi legislative....

[T]he congressional intent [was] to create a body of experts who shall gain experience by length of service; a body which shall be independent of executive authority, except in its selection, and free to exercise its judgment without the leave or hindrance of any other official or any department of the government. To the accomplishment of these purposes, it is clear that Congress was of opinion that length and certainty of tenure would vitally contribute. And to hold that, nevertheless, the members of the commission continue in office at the mere will of the President, might be to thwart, in large measure, the very ends

which Congress sought to realize by definitely fixing the term of office.

We conclude that the intent of the act is to limit the executive power of removal to the causes enumerated, the existence of none of which is claimed here; and we pass to the second question.

To support its contention that the removal provision of section 1, as we have just construed it, is an unconstitutional interference with the executive power of the President, the government's chief reliance is *Myers v. United States*. That case has been so recently decided, and the prevailing and dissenting opinions so fully review the general subject of the power of executive removal, that further discussion would add little of value to the wealth of material there collected.... [T]he narrow point actually decided was only that the President had power to remove a postmaster of the first class, without the advice and consent of the Senate as required by act of Congress. In the course of the opinion of the court, expressions occur which tend to sustain the government's contention, but these are beyond the point involved and, therefore, do not come within the rule of *stare decisis*. In so far as they are out of harmony with the views here set forth, these expressions are disapproved....

The office of a postmaster is so essentially unlike the office now involved that the decision in the *Myers* Case cannot be accepted as controlling our decision here. A postmaster is an executive officer restricted to the performance of executive functions. He is charged with no duty at all related to either the legislative or judicial power. The actual decision in the *Myers* Case finds support in the theory that such an officer is merely one of the units in the executive department and, hence, inherently subject to the exclusive and illimitable power of removal by the Chief Executive, whose subordinate and aid he is. Putting aside dicta, which may be followed if sufficiently persuasive but which are not controlling, the necessary reach of the decision goes far enough to include all purely executive officers. It goes no farther; much less does it include an officer who occupies no place in the executive department and who exercises no part of the executive power vested by the Constitution in the President.

The Federal Trade Commission is an administrative body created by Congress to carry into effect legislative policies embodied in the statute in accordance with the legislative standard therein prescribed, and to perform other specified duties as a legislative or as a judicial *aid*. Such a body cannot in any proper sense be characterized as an arm or an eye of the executive. Its duties are performed without executive leave and, in the contemplation of the statute, must be free from executive control. In administering the provisions of the statute in respect of "unfair methods of competition," that is to say, in filling in and administering the details embodied by that general standard, the commission acts in part quasi legislatively and in part quasi judicially....

If Congress is without authority to prescribe causes for removal of members of the trade commission and limit executive power of removal accordingly, that power at once becomes practically all-inclusive in respect of civil officers with the exception of the judiciary provided for by the Constitution. The Solicitor General, at the bar, apparently recognizing this to be true, with commendable candor, agreed that his view in respect of the removability of members of the Federal Trade Commission necessitated a like view in respect of the Interstate Commerce Commission and the Court of Claims. We are thus confronted with the serious question whether not only the members of these quasi legislative and quasi judicial bodies, but the judges of the legislative Court of Claims, exercising judicial power continue in office only at the pleasure of the President.

We think it plain under the Constitution that illimitable power of removal is not possessed by the President in respect of officers of the character of those just named. The authority of Congress, in creating quasi legislative or quasi judicial agencies, to require them to act in discharge of their duties independently of executive control cannot well be doubted; and that authority includes, as an appropriate incident, power to fix the period during which they shall continue, and to forbid their removal except for cause in the meantime. For it is quite evident that one who holds his office only during the pleasure of another cannot be depended upon to maintain an attitude of independence against the latter's will.

The fundamental necessity of maintaining each of the three general departments of government entirely free from the control or coercive influence, direct or indirect, of either of the others, has often been stressed and is hardly open to serious question. So much is implied in the very fact of the separation of the powers of these departments by the Constitution; and in the rule which recognizes their essential coequality. The sound application of a principle that makes one master in his own house precludes him from imposing his control in the house of another who is master there....

The power of removal here claimed for the President falls within this principle, since its coercive influence threatens the independence of a commission, which is not only wholly disconnected from the executive department, but which, as already fully appears, was created by Congress as a means of carrying into operation legislative and judicial powers, and as an agency of the legislative and judicial departments....

The result of what we now have said is this: Whether the power of the President to remove an officer shall prevail over the authority of Congress to condition the power by fixing a definite term and precluding a removal except for cause will depend upon the charac-

ter of the office; the *Myers* decision, affirming the power of the President alone to make the removal, is confined to purely executive officers; and as to officers of the kind here under consideration, we hold that no removal can be made during the prescribed term for which the officer is appointed, except for one or more of the causes named in the applicable statute.

To the extent that, between the decision in the *Myers* Case, which sustains the unrestrictable power of the President to remove purely executive officers, and our present decision that such power does not extend to an office such as that here involved, there shall remain a field of doubt, we leave such cases as may fall within it for future consideration and determination as they may arise.

MCREYNOLDS, J., CONCURRING [OMITTED]

QUESTIONS

1. Notwithstanding Justice Sutherland's claims in *Humphrey's Executor*, is that opinion consistent with the Court's decision in *Myers*? Which decision is more consistent with Chief Justice Marshall's dictum about a president's removal powers in *Marbury v. Madison*?

2. Counsel for Humphrey's executor argued that the history of the FTC act shows that Congress intended that a president could remove a commissioner from office only for the reasons listed in the act—"inefficiency, neglect of duty or malfeasance"—and for no other cause. Is the Court's decision in *Humphrey's Executor* about Congress's intent or about the president's inherent powers of removal? Is the distinction important?

3. Congress apparently intended the FTC to perform quasi-legislative (rule making) and quasi-judicial (rule adjudication) functions even though it was located in the executive branch. What does the fact that the agency exercised all three governing functions add to the debate about the president's power to remove a commissioner? How persuasive is Justice Sutherland's declaration that there is a difference between members of independent regulatory commissions (which exercise quasi-legislative and judicial functions) and heads of

purely executive departments? Does Justice Sutherland's opinion in *Humphrey's Executor* effectively insulate independent regulatory agencies from all political influence?

4. What significance, if any, is there to the fact that the Senate confirmed President Roosevelt's nomination of George Mathews after Roosevelt had removed Humphrey? Does Matthews's confirmation suggest that the Senate acquiesced in, if not actually approved, the president's power to remove Humphrey? Should Justice Sutherland have taken that fact into account in his opinion?

5. Review *A.L.A. Schechter Poultry Corp. v. United States* (Chapter 3, pp. 262–270) and *NLRB v. Jones & Laughlin* (Chapter 3, pp. 280–291). Is the *Humphrey's Executor* doctrine a necessary response to the rise of administrative agencies and the abandonment of the nondelegation doctrine?

APPOINTMENT AND REMOVAL POWERS

Morrison v. Olson
487 U.S. 654 (1988)

SETTING

Article II, section 3, of the Constitution instructs the president to "take Care that the Laws be faithfully executed...." The instruction raises a potential conflict of interest when a given president's Department of Justice is required to investigate and consider prosecution against other executive branch officers. While the problem has occurred several times in American history, it surfaced in dramatic form during the Watergate investigation of the early 1970s. (See the *Setting* to *United States v. Nixon*, Chapter 2, pp. 58–61.) In what came to be known popularly as "The Saturday Night Massacre," President Richard Nixon ordered that Justice Department special prosecutor Archibald Cox be fired because Cox was seeking access to White House tapes that threatened to expose Nixon's personal involvement in the Watergate scandals. Although congressional investigations ultimately led to President Nixon's resignation, the firing of Cox renewed longstanding skepticism about whether the executive branch could successfully investigate its own high-ranking officials.

In response to the investigative and prosecutorial problems raised by Watergate, Congress enacted the Ethics in Government Act of 1978. The goal of the act was to "preserve and promote the accountability and integrity of public officers and of the institutions of the Federal Government and to invigorate the Constitutional separation of powers between [sic] the three branches of Government."

The Ethics in Government Act created a Special Division consisting of three judges of the D.C. Circuit Court of Appeals. If requested to do so by the attorney general after an investigation, the act gave the Special Division power to appoint an independent counsel to conduct certain criminal investigations and prosecutions of offenses against the United States. Appointment of an independent counsel by the Special Division suspended the prosecutorial authority that otherwise would reside with the Department of Justice. Under the act, an independent counsel could be removed from office only by impeachment or by the attorney general for "good cause," physical or mental incapacity, or any other condition that substantially impaired the independent counsel's performance.

In 1982, subcommittees of the House of Representatives were involved in investigations of the Environmental Protection Agency's (EPA) program of cleaning up hazardous wastes through a law called the "Superfund." The committees issued subpoenas directing the EPA to produce documents to facilitate the investigations. Based on advice from the Justice Department, President Ronald Reagan ordered Ann Burford, administrator of the EPA, to refuse to produce the documents on the ground that they contained "enforcement sensitive" information that could imperil ongoing administrative and judicial proceedings. When Burford followed the president's order, the House voted to hold her in contempt.

The Justice Department took no steps to prosecute the contempt. Instead, it filed suit against the House of Representatives seeking a declaration that Burford's claim of executive privilege was valid. The District Court for the District of Columbia dismissed the suit. It ruled that the dispute was between the legislative and executive branches, and therefore raised a nonjusticiable political question. Congress and the Reagan administration eventually resolved the controversy through an agreement that gave the House subcommittees limited access to the documents.

Angered by the role that the Department of Justice had played in the confrontation over Superfund information, the House Judiciary Committee initiated another investigation. In 1985, it issued a three-thousand page report that accused Thomas Olson, assistant attorney general for the Office of Legal Counsel, of giving the committee false testimony in March 1983. The report also contended that Edward Schmults, deputy attorney general, and Carol Dinkins, assistant attorney general for the Land and Natural Resources Division, had withheld handwritten notes and chronologies that obstructed the committee's investigation. In December 1985, the committee formally requested Attorney General Edwin Meese III to seek the appointment of an independent counsel under the Ethics in Government Act.

Four months after the Judiciary Committee's request, Meese asked the Special Division to appoint an independent counsel with jurisdiction to investigate whether Olson gave false testimony. In April 1986, the Special Division appointed James McKay to be independent counsel to investigate Olson's testimony and conduct. McKay resigned a month later and Alexia Morrison was appointed to take his place.

After a round of litigation on the scope of Morrison's prosecutorial jurisdiction under the Special Division's order, a federal grand jury issued subpoenas to Olson, Schmults, and Dinkins. Those three then filed suit in the U.S. District Court for the District of Columbia to quash the subpoenas. They claimed that the independent counsel provisions of the Ethics in Government Act were unconstitutional and that Morrison had no authority to proceed with her investigation of Olson.

The district court upheld the constitutionality of the independent prosecutor provision of the act and declared Olson, Schmults, and Dinkins in contempt of court for refusing to comply with the subpoenas. All three appealed to the Court of Appeals for the D.C. Circuit.

The Court of Appeals reversed the district court in a divided opinion, ruling that an independent counsel must be nominated by the president and confirmed by the Senate, consistent with Article II, section 2, clause 2. The court of appeals also held that the Ethics in Government Act unconstitutionally delegated power to a court to appoint an officer who performs executive functions, unconstitutionally restricted the attorney general's power to remove an independent counsel, and interfered with the president's responsibility to "take care that the Laws be faithfully executed."

Morrison appealed to the Supreme Court of the United States.

HIGHLIGHTS OF SUPREME COURT ARGUMENTS

BRIEF FOR MORRISON

◆ This case is not ripe for adjudication. Under the rule of *Blair v. United States*, 250 U.S. 273 (1919), a witness subpoenaed by a grand jury cannot challenge the constitutionality of the statute underlying the investigation, even after being held in contempt for failure to comply. The case will not be ripe for adjudication until Olson, Schmults, and Dinkins have appealed their contempt convictions.

◆ If the case is ripe for adjudication, the Court should hold that the independent prosecutor is an "inferior" officer for purposes of the Appointments Clause of Article II, because the position is temporary and its powers are severely limited in scope. The independent prosecutor is like a temporary U.S. Attorney, recognized by law as an "inferior officer." The Constitution, therefore, does not require that independent prosecutors be nominated by the president and confirmed by the Senate. Furthermore, nothing in the Appointments Clause limits Congress's choice of a particular appointing authority for any specific "inferior officer."

◆ The powers granted to the Special Division by the Ethics in Government Act do not violate the limits of Article III. The Special Division's role is limited to naming the independent counsel and defining the counsel's jurisdiction. These powers are not inconsistent with the supervisory powers of federal courts over the conduct of criminal proceedings.

◆ The independent counsel provision of the Ethics in Government Act does not violate the principle of separation of powers. It does not expand congressional or judicial power at the expense of the presidency. Even if the act does create some potential for disruption in the function of the executive, it is justified by the need to ensure that criminal laws be applied to high government officials in a fair and even-handed manner.

◆ The office of independent counsel is not a threat to individual liberties. Unjustified departure from Justice Department policy would constitute "good cause" for the attorney general to remove an independent counsel and could lead to judicial proceedings against the counsel. Independent counsels also are accountable to the Special Division through the requirement of a complete report following completion of activities.

AMICUS CURIAE BRIEFS SUPPORTING MORRISON

Lawrence Walsh (independent counsel in the "Iran/Contra" matter); Whitney North Seymour (independent counsel in the matter of Michael Deaver, former White House Deputy Chief of Staff); The American Bar Association; the U.S. Senate; the Speaker and Leadership Group of the House, the AFL/CIO; Common Cause; the Public Citizen Litigation Group; the Center for Constitutional Rights; three individuals claiming to have been wrongly convicted in actions involving the Departments of Justice and Treasury, and the Internal Revenue Service.

BRIEF FOR OLSON

◆ The Ethics in Government Act transfers the president's power to enforce criminal laws to a person totally outside the control of the attorney general, thereby displacing the executive from its discretionary law enforcement functions. Experience with independent counsels Seymour and Walsh demonstrates that the Special Division can grant jurisdiction to the counsels that differs substantially from the attorney general's recommendation.

◆ The independent counsel provision violates Article II's guarantee that executive power be vested in a unitary president who is required to see that the laws are faithfully executed. The act neither allows the president to select the independent counsel nor to supervise the conduct of a criminal investigation. The act also prevents the president from ensuring that criminal laws be enforced in a uniform manner because it created a separate system of justice for some persons.

◆ Under Article III, courts are limited to adjudicating cases in controversy and must abstain from exercising any power that is not strictly judicial in character. The independent counsel provision requires judges to perform nonjudicial functions, and thrusts them into an immediate, day-to-day supervisory function, which undermined the guarantee of an independent, impartial judiciary.

◆ The independent counsel is a principal, not inferior, officer of the government. If the position is to exist at all, it should be governed by the Appointments Clause of Article II.

BRIEF FOR SCHMULTS AND DINKINS

◆ The Ethics in Government Act vests in the independent counsel power and authority to prosecute offenses that belong exclusively to the executive.

◆ Giving ultimate responsibility for executive decisions in an officer appointed by a court violates Article II of the Constitution.

◆ The removal provisions of the act are unconstitutional. In *Bowsher v. Synar*, 478 U.S. 714 (1986), the Court ruled that Congress's only power of removal of an executive officer is by impeachment.

AMICUS CURIAE BRIEFS SUPPORTING OLSON

United States; former Attorneys General Edward H. Levi, Griffin B. Bell, and William French Smith; Michael Deaver (the first person to be indicted, tried, and convicted by an independent counsel).

SUPREME COURT DECISION: 7–1

(Kennedy, J., did not participate.)

REHNQUIST, C.J.

... The parties do not dispute that "[t]he Constitution for purposes of appointment ... divides all its officers into two classes." *United States v. Germaine*, 9 Otto 508 (1879). As we stated in *Buckley v. Valeo*, 424 U.S. 1 (1976), "[p]rincipal officers are selected by the President with the advice and consent of the Senate. Inferior officers Congress may allow to be appointed by the President alone, by the heads of departments, or by the Judiciary." The initial question is, accordingly, whether appellant is an "inferior" or a "principal" officer. If she is the latter, as the Court of Appeals concluded, then the Act is in violation of the Appointments Clause.

The line between "inferior" and "principal" officers is one that is far from clear, and the Framers provided little guidance into where it should be drawn.... We need not attempt here to decide exactly where the line falls between the two types of officers, because in our view appellant clearly falls on the "inferior officer" side of that line. Several factors lead to this conclusion.

First, [Morrison] is subject to removal by a higher Executive Branch official.... Second, appellant is empowered by the Act to perform only certain, limited duties. An independent counsel's role is restricted primarily to investigation and, if appropriate, prosecution for certain federal crimes....

Third, appellant's office is limited in jurisdiction.... Finally, appellant's office is limited in tenure. There is concededly no time limit on the appointment of a particular counsel. Nonetheless, the office of independent counsel is "temporary" in the sense that an independent counsel is appointed essentially to accomplish a single task, and when that task is over the office is terminated, either by the counsel herself or by action of the Special Division....

This does not, however, end our inquiry under the Appointments Clause. Appellees [Olson, Schmults and Dinkins] argue that even if appellant is an "inferior" officer, the Clause does not empower Congress to place the power to appoint such an officer outside the Executive Branch. They contend that the Clause does not contemplate congressional authorization of "interbranch appointments," in which an officer of one branch is appointed by officers of another branch. The relevant language of the Appointments Clause is worth repeating. It reads: "... but the Congress may by Law vest the Appointment of such inferior Officers, as they think proper, in the President alone, in the courts of Law, or in the Heads of Departments." On its face, the language of this "excepting clause" admits of no limitation on interbranch appointments. Indeed, the inclusion of "as they think proper" seems clearly to give Congress significant discretion to determine whether it is "proper" to vest the appointment of, for example, executive officials in the "courts of Law."...

We do not mean to say that Congress' power to provide for interbranch appointments of "inferior officers" is unlimited.... In this case, however, we do not think it impermissible for Congress to vest the power to appoint independent counsels in a specially created federal court. We thus disagree with the Court of Appeals' conclusion that there is an inherent incongruity about a court having the power to appoint prosecutorial officers....

Appellees next contend that the powers vested in the Special Division by the Act conflict with Article III of the Constitution. We have long recognized that by the express provision of Article III, the judicial power of the United States is limited to "Cases" and "Controversies." As a general rule, we have broadly stated that "executive or administrative duties of a nonjudicial nature may not be imposed on judges holding office under Art. III of the Constitution." The purpose of this limitation is to help ensure the independence of the Judicial Branch and to prevent the judiciary from encroaching into areas reserved for the other branches....

Appellees contend, however, that the Division's Appointments Clause powers do not encompass the power to define the independent counsel's jurisdiction. We disagree. In our view, Congress' power under the Clause to vest the "Appointment" of inferior officers in the courts may, in certain circumstances, allow Congress to give the courts some discretion in defining the nature and scope of the appointed official's authority. Particularly when, as here, Congress creates a temporary "office," the nature and duties of which will by necessity vary with the factual circumstances giving rise to the need for an appointment in the first place, it may vest the power to define the scope of the office in the court as an incident to the appointment of the officer pursuant to the

Appointments Clause. This said, we do not think that Congress may give the Division *unlimited* discretion to determine the independent counsel's jurisdiction. In order for the Division's definition of the counsel's jurisdiction to be truly "incidental" to its power to appoint, the jurisdiction that the court decides upon must be demonstrably related to the factual circumstances that gave rise to the Attorney General's investigation and request for the appointment of the independent counsel in the particular case....

We emphasize, nevertheless, that the Special Division has *no* authority to take any action or undertake any duties that are not specifically authorized by the Act. The gradual expansion of the authority of the Special Division might in another context be a bureaucratic success story, but it would be one that would have serious constitutional ramifications....

We now turn to consider whether the Act is invalid under the constitutional principle of separation of powers. Two related issues must be addressed: The first is whether the provision of the Act restricting the Attorney General's power to remove the independent counsel to only those instances in which he can show "good cause," taken by itself, impermissibly interferes with the President's exercise of his constitutionally appointed functions. The second is whether, taken as a whole, the Act violates the separation of powers by reducing the President's ability to control the prosecutorial powers wielded by the independent counsel....

Unlike both *Bowsher* [*v. Synar*, 478 U.S. 714 (1986)] and *Myers*, this case does not involve an attempt by Congress itself to gain a role in the removal of executive officials other than its established powers of impeachment and conviction. The Act instead puts the removal power squarely in the hands of the Executive Branch; an independent counsel may be removed from office, "only by the personal action of the Attorney General, and only for good cause." There is no requirement of congressional approval of the Attorney General's removal decision, though the decision is subject to judicial review. In our view, the removal provisions of the Act make this case more analogous to *Humphrey's Executor v. United States* ... than to *Myers or Bowsher*....

Considering for the moment the "good cause" removal provision in isolation from the other parts of the Act at issue in this case, we cannot say that the imposition of a "good cause" standard for removal by itself unduly trammels on executive authority. There is no real dispute that the functions performed by the independent counsel are "executive" in the sense that they are law enforcement functions that typically have been undertaken by officials within the Executive Branch....

Although the counsel exercises no small amount of discretion and judgment in deciding how to carry out her duties under the Act, we simply do not see how the President's need to control the exercise of that discretion is so central to the functioning of the Executive Branch as to require as a matter of constitutional law that the counsel be terminable at will by the President.

Nor do we think that the "good cause" removal provision at issue here impermissibly burdens the President's power to control or supervise the independent counsel, as an executive official, in the execution of her duties under the Act. This is not a case in which the power to remove an executive official has been completely stripped from the President, thus providing no means for the President to ensure the "faithful execution" of the laws. Rather, because the independent counsel may be terminated for "good cause," the Executive, through the Attorney General, retains ample authority to assure that the counsel is competently performing her statutory responsibilities in a manner that comports with the provisions of the Act....

The final question to be addressed is whether the Act, taken as a whole, violates the principle of separation of powers by unduly interfering with the role of the Executive Branch. Time and again we have reaffirmed the importance in our constitutional scheme of the separation of governmental powers into the three coordinate branches.... On the other hand, we have never held that the Constitution requires that the three Branches of Government "operate with absolute independence."...

We observe first that this case does not involve an attempt by Congress to increase its own powers at the expense of the Executive Branch.... The Act does empower certain members of Congress to request the Attorney General to apply for the appointment of an independent counsel, but the Attorney General has no duty to comply with the request, although he must respond within a certain time limit. Other than that, Congress' role under the Act is limited to receiving reports or other information and oversight of the independent counsel's activities, functions that we have recognized generally as being incidental to the legislative function of Congress.

Similarly, we do not think that the Act works any *judicial* usurpation of properly executive functions.... The Act does give a federal court the power to review the Attorney General's decision to remove an independent counsel, but in our view this is a function that is well within the traditional power of the judiciary.

Finally, we do not think the Act "impermissibly undermine[s]" the powers of the Executive Branch (*Commodity Futures Trading Comm'n v. Synar*, 478 U.S. 833 (1986)), or "disrupts the proper balance between the coordinate branches [by] prevent[ing] the Executive Branch from accomplishing its constitutionally assigned functions." *Nixon v. Administrator of General Services*, 433 U.S. 425 (1977). It is undeniable that the Act reduces the amount of control or supervision that the Attorney General and, through him, the President exercises over the investigation and prosecution of a certain class of alleged criminal activity. The Attorney General is not allowed to appoint the individual of his choice; he does not determine the counsel's jurisdiction; and his power to remove a counsel is limited. Nonetheless, the Act does give the Attorney General several means of supervising or controlling the prosecutorial powers that may be wielded by an independent counsel. Most importantly, the Attorney General retains the power to remove the counsel for "good cause," a power that we have already concluded provides the Executive with substantial ability to ensure that the laws are "faithfully executed" by an independent counsel. No independent counsel may be appointed without a specific request by the Attorney General, and the Attorney General's decision not to request appointment if he finds "no reasonable grounds to believe that further investigation is warranted" is committed to his unreviewable discretion. The Act thus gives the Executive a degree of control over the power to initiate an investigation by the independent counsel....

In sum, we conclude today that it does not violate the Appointments Clause for Congress to vest the appointment of independent counsels in the Special Division; that the powers exercised by the Special Division under the Act do not violate Article III; and that the Act does not violate the separation of powers principle by impermissibly interfering with the functions of the Executive Branch. The decision of the Court of Appeals is therefore reversed.

SCALIA, J., DISSENTING

... [I]t is ultimately irrelevant *how much* the statute reduces presidential control. The case is over when the Court acknowledges, as it must, that "[i]t is undeniable that the Act reduces the amount of control or supervision that the Attorney General and, through him, the President exercises over the investigation and prosecution of a certain class of alleged criminal activity." It effects a revolution in our constitutional jurisprudence for the Court, once it has determined that (1) purely executive functions are at issue here, and (2) those functions have been given to a person whose actions are not fully within supervision and control of the President, nonetheless to proceed further to sit in judgment of whether "the President's need to control the exercise of [the independent counsel's] discretion is *so central* to the functioning of the Executive Branch" as to require complete control, whether conferral of his powers upon someone else "*sufficiently* deprives the President of control over the indepen-

dent counsel to interfere impermissibly with [his] constitutional obligation to ensure the faithful execution of the laws," and whether "the Act give[s] the Executive branch *sufficient* control over the independent counsel to ensure that the President is able to perform his constitutionally assigned duties." It is not for us to determine, and we have never presumed to determine, how much of the purely executive powers of government must be within the full control of the President. The Constitution prescribes that they *all* are....

[T]he independent counsel is not an inferior officer because she is not *subordinate* to any officer in the Executive Branch (indeed, not even to the President)....

The Court essentially admits as much, noting that "appellant may not be 'subordinate' to the Attorney General (and the President) insofar as she possesses a degree of independent discretion to exercise the powers delegated under the Act." In fact, there is no doubt about it.... [T]he Act specifically grants her the "*full* power and *independent* authority to exercise *all* investigative and prosecutorial functions of the Department of Justice," and makes her removable only for "good cause," a limitation specifically intended to ensure that she be *independent* of, not *subordinate* to, the President and the Attorney General.

Because appellant is not subordinate to another officer, she is not an "inferior" officer and her appointment other than by the President with the advice and consent of the Senate is unconstitutional....

As far as I can discern from the Court's opinion, it is now open season upon the President's removal power for all executive officers.... The Court essentially says to the President "Trust us. We will make sure that you are able to accomplish your constitutional role." I think the Constitution gives the President—and the people—more protection than that....

I know and have the highest regard for the judges on the Special Division, and the independent counsel herself is a woman of accomplishment, impartiality and integrity. But the fairness of a process must be adjudged on the basis of what it permits to happen, not what it produced in a particular case....

A government of laws means a government of rules. Today's decision on the basic issue of fragmentation of executive power is ungoverned by rule, and hence ungoverned by law. It extends into the very heart of our most significant constitutional function the "totality of the circumstances" mode of analysis that this Court has in recent years become fond of. Taking all things into account, we conclude that the power

taken away from the President here is not really *too* much. The next time executive power is assigned to someone other than the President we may conclude, taking all things into account, that it *is* too much. That opinion, like this one, will not be confined by any rule.... This is not analysis; it is ad hoc judgment. And it fails to explain why it is not true that—as the text of the Constitution seems to require, as the Founders seemed to expect, and as our past cases have uniformly assumed—all purely executive power must be under the control of the President....

I prefer to rely upon the judgment of the wise men who constructed our system, and of the people who approved it, and of two centuries of history that have shown it to be sound. Like it or not, that judgment says, quite plainly, that "[t]he executive Power shall be vested in a President of the United States."

COMMENT

Review *Immigration and Naturalization Service v. Chadha* and *Bowsher v. Synar* (Chapter 3, pp. 342–361) as part of the analysis and discussion of *Morrison*.

QUESTIONS

1. Is *Morrison* an attack on presidential power, as Justice Scalia argues in his dissent, or a more theoretical opinion about the meaning of separation of powers? Can the two be separated? Does Chief Justice Rehnquist's opinion imply that *Morrison* shares common ground with *United States v. Nixon*, because in both cases the Supreme Court helped to maintain governmental stability by refusing to insulate high executive officers from criminal liability?

2. In an article entitled "Tuning Out the White House," Stuart Taylor Jr. characterized *Morrison* as "an historic decision, one of a handful over 200 years marking out the boundaries between the executive, legislative and judicial powers." Taylor quoted a Court insider as saying, "[*Morrison*] is not only the most important decision of this term but one of the most important cases in all of constitutional jurispru-

dence. It says that none of the three branches can ever again claim to be the absolute arbiter of anything" (*New York Times Magazine*, September 11, 1988, pp. 38, 41).

If Taylor's evaluation of *Morrison* is correct, did the decision in *Morrison* undermine *Marbury v. Madison*? Or did it reaffirm *Marbury* by reasserting the judiciary's role in policing the boundaries of executive authority?

3. Justice Scalia contended in his *Morrison* dissent that the Court worked a "constitutional revolution." Is Scalia's assertion grounded on the assumption that the executive branch should have exclusive control over federal criminal law enforcement, or does he suggest other grounds for his conclusion? Does Justice Scalia's dissent also suggest that he would disagree with Madison's claim in *Federalist* No. 48 that the legislative is the most important branch of government?

4. Historically, the Supreme Court has been unable to decide definitively between two distinct approaches when analyzing separation of powers claims. One approach (referred to as "structural" or "categorical") views the three branches of government as distinctly separate agencies that may not enter one another's domain. The other approach (referred to as "functional" or "pragmatic") balances the extent of one branch's intrusion into another against the goal sought to be achieved by the intrusion. Does Chief Justice Rehnquist take either approach in *Morrison*? If neither, what is his approach to separation of powers theory?

5. Writing in *Federalist* No. 48, James Madison contended that unless the legislative, executive, and judiciary departments "be so far connected and blended as to give to each a constitutional control over the others, the degree of separation ... essential to a free government, can never in practice be duly maintained."

Evaluate *Morrison* in light of Madison's contention that separation between government departments can be maintained only by blending their powers. Does Madison's theory embrace either the structural or functional analysis the Court traditionally has used in evaluating separation of powers arguments?

6. *Myers* and *Humphrey's Executor* seem to pull in opposing directions, with *Morrison* tending toward *Humphrey's Executor*. Does that mean that *Myers* is effectively overruled? Is it important for the Court to apply consistent theory in separation of powers cases?

COMMENT

Between 1974, when Richard Nixon resigned, and early 1993, when George Bush left office, thirteen special prosecutors were appointed. Reagan administration opposition to the Independent Counsel Reauthorization Act of 1987 (successor to the 1978 Ethics in Government Act), coupled with effective Republican efforts to block renewal of the statute, caused the act to lapse in 1992. Following President Clinton's election, Congress adopted the Independent Counsel Reauthorization Act in 1994. Under the 1994 reauthorization, Kenneth W. Starr was appointed special prosecutor to investigate possible criminal infractions arising from the president and Mrs. Clinton's participation in the Whitewater real estate venture. Starr obtained several indictments and convictions of Clinton associates.

SUGGESTIONS FOR FURTHER READING

Corwin, Edward S., "Tenure of Office and the Removal Power under the Constitution," 27 *Columbia Law Review* (1927): 353.

Fisher, Louis, *Constitutional Conflicts between Congress and the President* (Princeton, NJ: Princeton University Press, 1985).

Harriger, Katy J., *Independent Justice: The Federal Special Prosecutor in American Politics* (Lawrence, KS: University Press of Kansas, 1992).

Liberman, Lee, "*Morrison v. Olson*: A Formalistic Perspective on Why the Court Was Wrong," 38 *American University Law Review* (1989): 313.

Strauss, Peter, "The Place of Agencies in Government: Separation of Powers and the Fourth Branch," 84 *Columbia Law Review* (1984): 573.

Sunstein, Cass R., "Constitutionalism after the New Deal," 101 *Harvard Law Review* (1987): 421.

TREATY POWER

Missouri v. Holland
252 U.S. 416 (1920)

SETTING

As late as August 6, 1787, delegates to the Constitutional Convention, out of deference to the power of the states, worked on the assumption that treaties would be made by the Senate. (Before ratification of the Seventeenth Amendment in 1913, U.S. Senators were appointed directly by state legislatures.) Not until September 7, ten days before the convention adjourned, did the final treaty-making language of Article II, section 2, clause 2, emerge. The revised language gives the president the power to make treaties "provided two-thirds of the Senators present concur." Article VI, section 2, makes treaties, as well as laws of Congress, the supreme law of the land. As finally drafted, the treaty power created the potential for conflicts between the states and the President, notwithstanding the fact that the Senate theoretically represented the interests of the states in Congress and would consider state interests when ratifying treaties.

Conflicts between the president's treaty power and the rights of the states surfaced almost immediately. In 1783, for example, peace treaties were signed between Great Britain and its enemies France, Spain, and the United States. The Treaty of Paris, which ended the Revolutionary War, contained a provision that England acknowledge the United States as an independent nation. One of the most difficult provisions to negotiate involved the estates of British loyalists that had been confiscated by Americans during the war. The U.S. Congress was not willing to restore British property and the treaty could do no more than promise that Congress would "recommend" to the states that the states restore British property. However, the treaty did contain a provision that British creditors would not be impeded when seeking to collect debts in the former colonies. In 1796, in *Ware v. Hylton*, 3 Dallas 199, the Supreme Court ruled that that provision in the Treaty of Paris trumped a Virginia statute that allowed anyone owing a debt to a British creditor to discharge the debt by paying instead into the Virginia treasury.

The disputes that eventually led to the case of *Martin v. Hunter's Lessee* in 1816 (see Chapter 2, pp. 93–103) arose when the state of Virginia confiscated British property contrary to provisions of both the Treaty of Paris and the Jay Treaty of 1795 (negotiated in response to the war between Great Britain and France that grew out of the French Revolution and that almost involved the United States).

Conflicts between the president's treaty-making power and the rights of states continued into the nineteenth century and the Court continued to side with the president. In *Hauenstein v. Lynham*, 100 U.S. 483 (1880), for example, the Court ruled that a Virginia law, declaring that the property of aliens who died without wills devising the property would escheat (revert) to the state, had been superseded by an 1860 treaty with Switzerland.

All of the Court's early cases involving the treaty power demonstrated that that power can be used in a way that imposes limits on the exercise of state power. Another issue lurked in the background: could the treaty power be exercised in a way that would expand Congress's powers to regulate at the expense of states' prerogatives? That case came to the Court in the early decades of the twentieth century in the context of congressional attempts to protect migratory birds.

Shortly after the turn of the century, a coalition of groups—including state and national conservation organizations, progressive sportsmen's associations, state game officials, and members of the federal Department of Agriculture—began to lobby Congress for legislation to protect migratory birds. For many years, large-scale hunting during the spring breeding season threatened to eliminate many species of game birds as well as important insectivores like robins. Although various states had enacted statutes to protect migratory birds, their coverage varied widely. Furthermore, enforcement of state laws was undercut by pressure from hunters who wanted to be free to kill as many birds as possible during migratory periods.

Debates over federal protective legislation focused on the constitutionality of congressional regulation. Opponents argued that federal legislation would infringe on the reserved powers of the states, because migratory bird protection was one of the police powers of the states. Supporters countered that Congress could adopt protective legislation under the national government's "implied attributes of sovereignty." In 1913, Congress enacted the Migratory Bird Act. Shortly thereafter, two federal district courts declared the statute unconstitutional as beyond Congress's power.

In response, Senator Elihu Root introduced a resolution urging President Wilson to negotiate a treaty to protect migratory birds. In 1916, Wilson negotiated a convention with Great Britain, acting for Canada, for the protection of migratory birds. Early in July 1918, consistent with the U.S. obligation under the treaty, Congress enacted the Migratory Bird Treaty Act. The law prohibited the hunting, killing, or subsequent sale and shipment of the bird species covered by the treaty, except as allowed by regulations to be established by the secretary of agriculture.

President Wilson signed the law and in July 1918 he issued proclamations approving various regulations made by the secretary of agriculture to implement the Migratory Bird Treaty Act. Among other things, the regulations fixed the open hunting season in Missouri for most waterfowl at September 16 to December 31. Criminal penalties attached to hunting out of season. Under Missouri law, waterfowl hunting had been permitted from September 15 to the following April 30.

The state of Missouri brought suit in U.S. District Court for the Western District of Missouri against Ray P. Holland, U.S. Game Warden. The state requested an injunction to prevent the arrest and prosecution of two local citizens for violations of the Migratory Bird Treaty Act. The state claimed that the arrests and prosecutions invaded the sovereignty of the state of Missouri and interfered with the property rights of the people of Missouri to the wild game within its borders, held in trust by the state.

The District Court granted Holland's motion to dismiss the suit. It observed that although in the absence of a treaty the Migratory Bird Treaty Act would be unconstitutional, the existence of the treaty made the act constitutional. Missouri appealed to the Supreme Court of the United States.

HIGHLIGHTS OF SUPREME COURT ARGUMENTS

BRIEF FOR MISSOURI

◆ The authority of the state over wild game within its borders is paramount on either of two grounds. First, the state in its sovereign capacity as the representative of, and for the use and benefit of all its people in common, holds title to all wild game within its borders. Second, the Tenth Amendment reserves to the states or to the people those purely internal affairs that concern the people or the state. Without exception, wild game has been held to be part of the mass which is within the exclusive and absolute power of the state.

◆ Every treaty must be presumed to be made subject to the rightful powers of the governments concerned. Neither the treaty-making power alone, nor the treaty-making power in conjunction with any or all other departments of the government, can bind the government to do what the Constitution forbids. The powers reserved to the states or the people are as sacred as the power to make treaties.

AMICUS CURIAE BRIEF SUPPORTING MISSOURI

State of Kansas.

BRIEF FOR HOLLAND

◆ The Migratory Bird Act would be valid even if its provisions had not been enacted for the purpose of giving effect to a treaty. It is authorized by Article 4, section 3, of the Constitution, which gives Congress power to dispose of and make all needful rules and regulations respecting the territory or other property belonging to the United States; or by Article I, section 8, which gives Congress power to regulate commerce with foreign nations, among the several states, and with the Indian tribes.

◆ The Constitution expressly grants to Congress the power to enact such laws as may be necessary to give effect to treaties. The validity of such legislation cannot depend upon whether its subject matter is included within the general legislative powers of Congress. Rather, it depends on whether the treaty being enforced is within the treaty-making power of the United States.

◆ The power of the federal government to make and enforce treaties is not a limitation on the reserved powers of the states. It is the exercise of a power not reserved to the states, being both expressly granted to the United States and prohibited to the states. The treaty-making power embraces all such power as would have belonged to the several states if the Constitution had not been adopted. In the exercise of that power the federal government is the agent of both the people of the United States and the states themselves.

◆ The protection of migratory game is a proper subject of negotiations and treaties between the governments of the countries interested in such game.

AMICUS CURIAE BRIEF SUPPORTING HOLLAND

Association for the Protection of the Adirondacks.

SUPREME COURT DECISION: 7–2

HOLMES, J.

… [T]he question raised is the general one whether the treaty and statute are void as an interference with the rights reserved to the states….

If the treaty is valid, there can be no dispute about the validity of the statute under Article 1, Section 8, as a necessary and proper means to execute the powers of the government….

It is said that a treaty cannot be valid if it infringes the Constitution, that there are limits, therefore, to the treaty-making power, and that one such limit is that what an act of Congress could not do unaided, in derogation of the powers reserved to the States, a treaty cannot do….

Acts of Congress are the supreme law of the land only when made in pursuance of the Constitution, while treaties are declared to be so when made under the authority of the United States. It is open to question whether the authority of the United States means more than the formal acts prescribed to make the convention. We do not mean to imply that there are no qualifications to the treaty-making power; but they must be ascertained in a different way. It is obvious that there may be matters of the sharpest exigency for the national well-being that an act of Congress could not deal with, but that a treaty followed by such an act could, and it is not lightly to be assumed that, in matters requiring national action, "a power which must belong to and somewhere reside in every civilized government" is not to be found. *Andrews v. Andrews*, 188 U.S. 14 (1903)…. [W]hen we are dealing with words that also are a constituent act, like the Constitution of the United States, we must realize that they have called into life a being the development of which could not have been foreseen completely by the most gifted of its begetters. It was enough for them to realize or hope that they had created an organism; it has taken a century and has cost their successors much sweat and blood to prove that they created a nation. The case before us must be considered in the light of our whole experience, and not merely in that of what was said a hundred years ago. The treaty in question does not contravene any prohibitory words to be found in the Constitution. The only question is whether it is forbidden by some invisible radiation from the general terms of the 10th Amendment. We must consider what this country has become in deciding what that amendment has reserved….

Wild birds are not in the possession of anyone; and possession is the beginning of ownership. The whole foundation of the state's rights is the presence within their jurisdiction of birds that yesterday had not arrived, tomorrow may be in another state, and in a week a thousand miles away. If we are to be accurate, we cannot put the case of the state upon higher ground than that the treaty deals with creatures that for the moment are within the state borders, that it must be carried out by officers of the United States within the same territory, and that, but for the treaty, the state would be free to regulate this subject itself.

As most of the laws of the United States are carried out within the states, and as many of them deal with matters which, in the silence of such laws, the

State might regulate, such general grounds are not enough to support Missouri's claim.... No doubt the great body of private relations usually falls within the control of the State, but a treaty may override its power. We do not have to invoke the later developments of constitutional law for this proposition....

Here a national interest of very nearly the first magnitude is involved. It can be protected only by national action in concert with that of another power. The subject-matter is only transitorily within the state, and has no permanent habitat therein. But for the treaty and the statute, there soon might be no birds for any powers to deal with. We see nothing in the Constitution that compels the government to sit by while a food supply is cut off and the protectors of our forests and of our crops are destroyed. It is not sufficient to rely upon the States. The reliance is in vain, and were it otherwise, the question is whether the United States is forbidden to act. We are of opinion that the treaty and statute must be upheld.

Decree affirmed.

VAN DEVANTER AND PITNEY, J.J., DISSENTED WITHOUT OPINION

QUESTIONS

1. Does Justice Holmes's opinion in *Holland* mean that a president and Congress may use the treaty power as a vehicle for creating federal regulatory authority that otherwise would not exist under the Constitution? What are the practical checks on the exercise of such a power? What might explain why Justices Van Devanter and Pitney chose to merely record dissents in *Holland* rather than explaining the basis for their disagreement with Justice Holmes's opinion?

2. Justice Holmes's opinion in *Holland* generated extensive controversy, especially among adherents of states' rights. Historian Charles A. Lofgren fixes partial blame for the controversy on Justice Holmes's opinion: "... [Wh]ile resting on grounds which were well established and historically warranted, [the opinion] failed to explicate those grounds fully and carefully and failed as well to clarify sufficiently the limits to treaty power" ("*Missouri v. Holland* in Historical Perspective," *The Supreme Court Review* [Chicago, IL: University of Chicago Press, 1975], p. 121).

   How could Justice Holmes's opinion have been more carefully crafted?

3. Justice Holmes's theory in *Holland* about an "organic" constitution has been widely quoted. What are the implications of the "organic" theory of the Constitution for the exercise of executive power? Does Holmes's formulation suggest an activist or restrained role for judges in reviewing executive actions?

4. The Seventeenth Amendment provides for the direct popular election of senators, displacing the original constitutional structure

under which state legislatures elected senators. Does direct election of senators dilute the Senate's role as the guardian of states' rights in Congress? If so, have the states lost an effective check on the president's exercise of the treaty power or do the examples described in the *Setting* suggest that the Senate never was tenacious in protecting the rights of states when it considered ratifying treaties?

5. In *Federalist* No. 75, Alexander Hamilton characterized the shared Treaty Power in Article II, section 2, clause 2, as "one of best digested and most unexceptionable parts" of the Constitution. "With regard to the intermixture of powers," wrote Hamilton, "the joint possession of the power in question, by the President and Senate, ... afford[s] a greater prospect of security than the separate possession of it by either of them." Does the *Holland* decision bolster Hamilton's argument, or weaken it by illustrating how presidential and senatorial cooperation can expand the powers of the national government?

COMMENT

Opponents of the *Holland* decision saw it as providing the Senate with an incentive to ratify any treaty that might have the effect of enlarging Congress's powers at the expense of the states. After *Holland*, opponents of child labor in the United States, stymied by the Supreme Court's invalidation of the 1916 Keating-Owen Child Labor Act in *Hammer v. Dagenhart*, 247 U.S. 251 (1918) (see Chapter 5, pp. 577–583), discussed the possibility of having the president negotiate a treaty banning employment of underage children so that legislation then could be passed to implement that treaty. Those discussions never yielded results. The controversy provoked by *Holland* simmered for many years, however, heating up after World War II when the United States assumed a more active role in international affairs. In 1954 a constitutional amendment was proposed by *Holland* opponent, Republican Senator John W. Bricker of Ohio. It provided that "[a] treaty shall become effective as internal law only through legislation which would be valid in the absence of a treaty." The Bricker Amendment came within one vote of Senate passage.

In 1957, a plurality of the Supreme Court held that neither a treaty nor an executive agreement "can confer power on the Congress, or any other branch of Government, which is free from the restraints of the Constitution." *Reid v. Covert*, 354 U.S. 1. That decision was in contrast to *Woods v. Cloyd W. Miller Co.*, 333 U.S. 138 (1948), in which the Court held that the Housing and Rent Act of 1947, which provided for rent control, was a valid exercise of Congress's power "to cope with a current condition of which [World War II] was a direct and immediate cause."

Reid and *Woods* should be read in light of the Court's decisions in *United States v. Lopez*, 514 U.S. 549 (1995), Chapter 3, pp. 324–337, and *Seminole Tribe of Florida v. Florida*, 517 U.S. 1125 (1996), Chapter 5, pp. 620–633.

SUGGESTIONS FOR FURTHER READING

Henkin, Louis, "The Treaty Makers and the Law Makers: The Law of the Land and Foreign Relations," 107 *University of Pennsylvania Law Review* (1959): 903.

———, *Foreign Affairs and the Constitution* (Mineola, NY: Foundation Press, 1972).

———, *Constitutionalism, Democracy, and Foreign Affairs* (New York, NY: Columbia University Press, 1990).

Lofgren, Charles A., "*Missouri v. Holland* in Historical Perspective," *The Supreme Court Review* (Chicago, IL: University of Chicago Press, 1975).

Vose, Clement E., "State Against Nation: The Conservation Case of *Missouri v. Holland*," *Prologue* (Winter 1984): 233.

EXECUTIVE PRIVILEGE

United States v. Nixon
418 U.S. 683 (1974)

SETTING

As early as the administration of George Washington, presidents have claimed a constitutional privilege to withhold documents from the legislative and judicial branches, even though there is no textual support for such a privilege in the Constitution. In 1792, for example, President Washington refused to turn over papers requested by Congress regarding his knowledge of the defeat of General St. Clair by the Ohio Indians. Washington also refused to turn over to Congress papers relating to the negotiations of Jay's Treaty. President Thomas Jefferson defied a subpoena to testify at the treason trial of Aaron Burr, apparently relying on the claim of executive immunity. However, it was President Dwight Eisenhower who gave a name to the privilege presidents had asserted from the outset of government under the Constitution: executive privilege.

Until the twentieth century, claims of executive privilege were resolved through political accommodation and the power of the judiciary was not invoked. Even in this century, judicial intervention has not always been required to curb executive excesses and claims of executive privilege. President Lyndon Johnson, for example, who escalated the U.S. involvement in the undeclared war in Vietnam, bowed to antiwar forces in 1968 and declined to seek a second term as president. When courts have become engaged in controversies involving assertions of executive privilege, they have tended to be deferential to the chief executive, especially if the president invoked the privilege in the name of national security or foreign policy. In 1948, for example, Justice Robert Jackson wrote in *Chicago & Southern Airlines v. Waterman S.S. Co.*, 333 U.S. 103:

> The President, both as Commander-in-Chief and as the Nation's organ for foreign affairs, has available intelligence services whose reports neither are nor ought to be published to the world. It would be intolerable that courts, without the relevant information, should review and perhaps nullify actions of the Executive taken on information properly held secret.... But even if courts could require full disclosure, the very nature of executive decisions as to foreign policy is political, not judicial. Such decisions are wholly confided by our Constitution to the political departments of the government.... They are and should be undertaken only by those directly responsible to the people, whose welfare they advance or imperil. They are decisions of a kind for which the Judiciary has neither aptitude, facilities nor responsibility and have long been held to belong to the domain of political power not subject to judicial intrusion or inquiry.

However, the Court has rejected the notion that the president enjoys an absolute privilege to withhold information from the other branches. In *McGrain v. Daugherty*, 273 U.S. 135 (1927), for example, it ruled that the Senate could inquire into the failure of President Warren Harding's attorney general, Harry Daugherty, to prosecute persons, including Secretary of Interior Albert Fall, who had been implicated in the Teapot Dome scandal of the 1920s. That scandal involved government officials who gave federal oil reserves to private companies in return for huge monetary payoffs.

During the Watergate hearings of the early 1970s, described in the *Setting* to *United States v. Nixon* in Chapter 2, pp. 58–61, President Nixon's representatives frequently claimed executive privilege in refusing to produce documents. Discovery of tape-recorded conversations between the president and his subordinates, however, which would demonstrate conclusively whether there was a connection between the president and the Watergate burglary, gave rise to the constitutional crisis over executive privilege at issue in *Nixon*.

Note: Review the *Setting* to and excerpt of *United States v. Nixon* in Chapter 2, pp. 58–67.

QUESTIONS

1. What privilege did President Nixon claim: the privilege against disclosing sensitive military or diplomatic information; the privilege of confidentiality of files and records of the executive branch; a general privilege protecting internal executive discussions and deliberations;

the privilege of immunity from judicial process? All of these? Does it make a difference to the outcome in *Nixon*?

2. During the 1968 presidential campaign, candidate Nixon was highly critical of the Warren Court and emphasized the need for "law and order" justices on the Supreme Court. He subsequently was able to make four appointments to the Court: Chief Justice Burger (1969), and Justices Blackmun (1971), Powell (1972), and Rehnquist (1972). Justice Rehnquist did not participate in *Nixon*, because he had been an assistant attorney in the Office of Legal Counsel from 1969–1971 and wished to avoid the appearance of a conflict of interest. The Court's opinion in *United States v. Nixon* was unanimous, written by the president's friend, Chief Justice Burger. Is the Court's opinion in *Nixon* any more persuasive because of the agreement of the three Nixon appointees? If any or all had dissented, would President Nixon have been able to declare some kind of victory over the judicial branch?

3. If the Supreme Court had accepted the president's argument for absolute executive privilege, would it also be forced to accept an argument that Congress alone may determine what legislation it is authorized to enact? Compare the language of Articles I and II in thinking about this question.

4. Under the Court's ruling in *Myers v. United States*, was not President Nixon within his rights to remove the Watergate prosecutor, as an employee of the executive branch, from office? What facts might have persuaded the *Nixon* Court that the *Myers* rule did not apply?

COMMENT

Among the several legal issues resulting from the Watergate scandal arose the question of whether presidents enjoy absolute immunity from payment of damages or only qualified immunity. The Court first addressed the issue in a case brought by a discharged Pentagon management analyst who was a "whistle-blower."

> **Case:** *Nixon v. Fitzgerald*, 457 U.S. 731 (1982)
> **Vote:** 5–4
> **Decision:** Presidents are entitled to absolute immunity from damages liability predicated on official acts. In light of the special nature of the president's constitutional office and functions, absolute presidential immunity exists from damages liability for acts within the "outer perimeter" of the president's official responsibilities. There remains the constitutional remedy of impeachment, as well as the deterrent effects of constant scrutiny by the press, oversight by Congress, a desire to earn re-election, the need to maintain prestige as an element of presidential influence, and a president's concern for historical stature.

Case: *Clinton v. Jones*, ____ U.S. ____ (1997)
Vote: 9–0
Decision: The president is not entitled to immunity from suit for the duration of his presidency when he is sued for his unofficial actions. The concern expressed in *Nixon v. Fitzgerald*, 457 U.S. 731 (1982)—that denying immunity might induce the president to make official decisions that are not in the best interests of the nation in order to avoid litigation—is inapplicable where only personal, private conduct by a president is at issue. Jones may proceed immediately with her suit, which alleges that in 1991, when Clinton was governor of Arkansas and she was a state employee, he conspired with a state trooper to lure her to a hotel room, where he sexually harassed and assaulted her, then later defamed her by denying that he had ever met her and calling her a liar.

SUGGESTIONS FOR FURTHER READING

Berger, Raoul, *Executive Privilege: A Constitutional Myth* (Cambridge, MA: Harvard University Press, 1974).

Cox, Archibald, "Watergate and the Constitution of the United States," *University of Toronto Law Journal* (1976): 125.

Kurland, Philip B., *Watergate and the Constitution* (Chicago, IL: University of Chicago Press, 1978).

Symposium, "*United States v. Nixon*," 22 *University of California Los Angeles Law Review* (1974): 1.

Symposium, "*United States v. Nixon*," 9 *Loyola of Los Angeles Law Review* (1975): 11.

EMERGENCY AND FOREIGN POLICY POWERS

Prize Cases
2 Black 635 (1863)

SETTING

The 1858 debates between Abraham Lincoln and Stephen A. Douglas during their race for the Illinois Senate gave sharp focus to the growing slavery controversy throughout the United States. Lincoln and Douglas debated the national, rather than the local, implications of whether slavery could be extended into the territories, the status of blacks in the light of the 1857 Supreme Court decision in *Dred Scott v. Sandford* that blacks were not citizens of the United States, and whether territorial residents had the power to regulate the institution of slavery. In the next few years, increased Republican Party strength in Congress was matched by threats of southern secession. South Carolina made good on the threat in December 1860, when the state learned that Lincoln had been elected president. Mississippi, Florida, Alabama, Georgia, and Louisiana followed South Carolina's lead and formed the Confederate States of America. They were eventually joined by Texas, Virginia, North Carolina, Arkansas, and Tennessee. If sectional divisions over slavery made civil war probable, secession made it inevitable. War broke out in April 1861.

The onset of civil war creates particularly difficult constitutional questions, not the least of which are what powers it gives to a chief executive. Faced with imminent dissolution of the Union, President Lincoln had to decide whether to call Congress into special session, or whether to assume responsibility for making unprecedented policy decisions himself. He opted for the latter. On April 15, 1861, he issued a call for seventy-five thousand militia. Subsequently, he suspended the privilege of the writ of habeas corpus and took other drastic actions to protect the internal security of the Union. On April 19, 1861, Lincoln ordered a blockade of Confederate ports to prevent the seceded states from receiving war munitions and supplies from foreign nations. He declared that any person who interfered with a vessel of the United States would "be held amenable to the laws of the United States for the prevention and punishment of piracy."

On April 27, Lincoln extended the blockade to the recently seceded states of Virginia and North Carolina. Lincoln took these actions by presidential proclamation. The blockade was troubling legally for many reasons, one of which was that under international law the right to establish a blockade exists only under conditions of war, which implies at least two belligerent parties. The president's position was paradoxical. On the one hand, he insisted that the federal government and the Confederacy were not belligerents because the seceded states were engaged in an illegitimate insurrection. Therefore, he objected strongly when foreign nations issued proclamations of neutrality between belligerents, designed to protect their ships entering U.S. ports. On the other hand, he claimed that a blockade enforced against all ships entering southern ports was legitimate because the federal government was under attack and blockades are a prerogative of war.

When he could no longer avoid calling Congress into session, Lincoln ordered members to convene on July 4, 1861. In his message to the Congress he stated that he believed the blockade was legal even though Congress had not formally declared war. Congress continued to decline to declare war on the seceded states, but, on July 13, it authorized Lincoln to declare that a state of insurrection existed and for all practical purposes ratified the blockade, by declaring that foreign ships found entering any closed ports would be forfeited to the United States. On August 6, Congress ratified all of the president's previous unilateral actions.

Cases involving the legality of the blockade quickly appeared on the dockets of federal courts. The *Prize Cases* were selected to be the test cases to go to the Supreme Court of the United States. They involved the status of four ships and their cargoes that had been seized before Congress acted on July 13. All four ships had been captured by public vessels of the United States for violating the blockade and had been claimed as prize. One ship, the *Amy Warwick*, contained coffee and was captured en route to Richmond, Virginia. The *Hiawatha* was a British ship that was unable to leave Richmond when the Civil War began and was unable to employ a tow boat until a few days after the blockade had become effective. The *Brilliante* was a Mexican ship that was seized when it entered New Orleans more than a month after the blockade went into effect. The *Crenshaw* was owned by citizens of Richmond and was captured as it attempted to take tobacco to England. The owners of the ships, called claimants, brought suit to have their ships and cargoes restored to them.

The cases were tried in U.S. District Courts in Massachusetts, all of which held that the ships had been lawfully taken as prize. The cases were appealed to the Circuit Court of the United States for the District of Massachusetts. Justice Nelson, sitting as the circuit court judge, affirmed. However, he stated in his opinion that he did not necessarily agree with the lower courts on the merits, and was affirming their decisions only to allow swift review by the Supreme Court. Nonetheless, the cases did not appear on that Court's docket until the 1863 Term.

HIGHLIGHTS OF SUPREME COURT ARGUMENTS

BRIEF FOR THE SHIPS' CLAIMANTS

◆ Only international wars invest property and persons with enemy character. This is merely a war by a part of the people of this country against its regular government and international prize rules do not apply. The government's goal in a civil war is not to damage and destroy; it is to restore the body politic with the least damage.

◆ In this situation it is unsound to apply international war doctrines of prize.

◆ The Constitution does not contain the word "necessity;" therefore, the president cannot claim necessity as the basis for his imposition of the blockade. None of the express and enumerated powers in the Constitution gives him the power to impose the blockade.

◆ The president is to act as commander-in-chief, not as legislator or emperor.

◆ The Act of July 13 cannot legalize and validate the earlier presidential proclamations.

BRIEF FOR THE UNITED STATES

◆ When these ships were captured, the United States was engaged in a civil war and had engaged its entire military power to win that war. The rights of war include blockade and maritime capture as prize.

◆ It is absurd to argue that only Congress can declare war and that the belligerent parties must be independent nations. Such an argument aids and abets rebellion and paralyzes government.

◆ It is immaterial in prize cases whether the owner of the property has or has not taken part in the war.

SUPREME COURT DECISION: 5–4

GRIER, J.

There are certain propositions of law which must necessarily affect the ultimate decision of these cases[.]...

They are, 1st. Had the President a right to institute a blockade of ports in possession of persons in armed rebellion against the Government, on the principles of international law, as known and acknowledged among civilized States?

2d. Was the property of persons domiciled or residing within those States a proper subject of capture on the sea as "enemies' property?"...

That a blockade de facto actually existed, and was formally declared and notified by the President on the 27th and 30th of April, 1861, is an admitted fact in these cases.

That the President, as the Executive Chief of the Government and Commander-in-chief of the Army and Navy, was the proper person to make such notification, has not been, and cannot be disputed....

The right of prize and capture has its origin in the "*jus belli*," [the law of war] and is governed and adjudged under the law of nations. To legitimate the capture of a neutral vessel or property on the high seas, a war must exist de facto, and the neutral must have a knowledge or notice of the intention of one of the parties belligerent to use this mode of coercion against a port, city, or territory, in possession of the other.

Let us enquire whether, at the time this blockade was instituted, a state of war existed which would justify a resort to these means of subduing the hostile force.

War has been well defined to be, "That state in which a nation prosecutes its right by force."

The parties belligerent in a public war are independent nations. But it is not necessary to constitute war, that both parties should be acknowledged as independent nations or sovereign States. A war may exist where one of the belligerents claims sovereign rights as against the other.

Insurrection against a government may or may not culminate in an organized rebellion, but a civil war always begins by insurrection against the lawful authority of the Government. A civil war is never solemnly declared; it becomes such by its accidents—the number, power, and organization of the persons who originate and carry it on. When the party in rebellion occupy and hold in a hostile manner a certain portion of territory; have declared their independence; have cast off their allegiance; have organized armies; have commenced hostilities against their former sovereign, the world acknowledges them as belligerents, and the contest a war. They claim to be in arms to establish their liberty and independence, in order to become a sovereign State, while the sovereign party treats them as insurgents and rebels who owe allegiance, and who should be punished with death for their treason.

The laws of war, as established among nations, have their foundation in reason, and all tend to mitigate the cruelties and misery produced by the scourge of war. Hence the parties to a civil war usually concede to each other belligerent rights. They exchange prisoners, and adopt the other courtesies and rules common to public or national wars....

As a civil war is never publicly proclaimed, *eo nomine*, [by that name] against insurgents, its actual existence is a fact in our domestic history which the Court is bound to notice and to know....

By the Constitution, Congress alone has the power to declare a national or foreign war. It cannot declare war against a State, or any number of States, by virtue of any clause in the Constitution. The Constitution confers on the President the whole Executive power. He is bound to take care that the laws be faithfully executed. He is Commander-in-chief of the Army and Navy of the United States, and of the militia of the several States when called into the actual service of the United States. He has no power to initiate or declare a war either against a foreign nation or a domestic State. But by the Acts of Congress of February 28th, 1795, and 3d of March, 1807, he is authorized to call out the militia and use the military and naval forces of the United States in case of invasion by foreign nations, and to suppress insurrection against the government of a State or of the United States.

If a war be made by invasion of a foreign nation, the President is not only authorized but bound to resist force by force. He does not initiate the war, but is bound to accept the challenge without waiting for any special legislative authority. And whether the hostile party be a foreign invader, or States organized in rebellion, it is none the less a war, although the declaration of it be "unilateral."...

Whether the President in fulfilling his duties, as Commander-in-chief, in suppressing an insurrection, has met with such armed hostile resistance, and a civil war of such alarming proportions as will compel him to accord to them the character of belligerents, is a question to be decided by him, and this Court must be governed by the decisions and acts of the political department of the Government to which this power was entrusted....

Without admitting that such an act was necessary under the circumstances, it is plain that if the President had in any manner assumed powers which it was necessary should have the authority or sanction of Congress, that on the well known principle of law, "*omnis ratihabitio retrotrahitur et mandato equiparatur,*" [every ratification relates back and is equivalent to a prior authority] this ratification has operated to perfectly cure the defect....

The objection made to this act of ratification, that it is *ex post facto*, and therefore unconstitutional and void, might possibly have some weight on the trial of an indictment in a criminal Court. But precedents from that source cannot be received as authoritative in a tribunal administering public and international law.

On this first question therefore we

are of the opinion that the President had a right, *jure belli*, to institute a blockade of ports in possession of the States in rebellion, which neutrals are bound to regard.

II. We come now to the consideration of the second question. What is included in the term "enemies' property?"

Is the property of all persons residing within the territory of the States now in rebellion, captured on the high seas, to be treated as "enemies' property" whether the owner be in arms against the Government or not?

The right of one belligerent not only to coerce the other by direct force, but also to cripple his resources by the seizure or destruction of his property, is a necessary result of a state of war. Money and wealth, the products of agriculture and commerce, are said to be the sinews of war, and as necessary in its conduct as numbers and physical force. Hence it is, that the laws of war recognize the right of a belligerent to cut these sinews of the power of the enemy, by capturing his property on the high seas.

The appellants contend that the term "enemy" is properly applicable to those only who are subjects or citizens of a foreign State at war with our own....

They insist, moreover, that the President himself, in his proclamation, admits that great numbers of the persons residing within the territories in possession of the insurgent government, are loyal in their feelings, and forced by compulsion and the violence of the rebellious and revolutionary party and its "de facto government" to submit to their laws and assist in their scheme of revolution; that the acts of the usurping government cannot legally

sever the bond of their allegiance; they have, therefore, a co-relative right to claim the protection of the government for their persons and property, and to be treated as loyal citizens, till legally convicted of having renounced their allegiance and made war against the Government by treasonably resisting its laws.

They contend, also, that insurrection is the act of individuals and not of a government or sovereignty; that the individuals engaged are subjects of law. That confiscation of their property can be effected only under a municipal law. That by the law of the land such confiscation cannot take place without the conviction of the owner of some offence, and finally that the secession ordinances are nullities and ineffectual to release any citizen from his allegiance to the national Government, and consequently that the Constitution and Laws of the United States are still operative over persons in all the States for punishment as well as protection.

This argument rests on the assumption of two propositions, each of which is without foundation on the established law of nations. It assumes that where a civil war exists, the party belligerent claiming to be sovereign, cannot, for some unknown reason, exercise the rights of belligerents, although the revolutionary party may. Being sovereign, he can exercise only sovereign rights over the other party. The insurgent may be killed on the battle-field or by the executioner; his property on land may be confiscated under the municipal law; but the commerce on the ocean, which supplies the rebels with means to support the war, cannot be made the subject of capture under the laws of war, because it is "*unconstitutional!!!*" Now, it is a proposition never doubted, that the belligerent party who claims to be sovereign, may exercise both belligerent and sovereign rights. Treating the other party as a belligerent and using only the milder modes of coercion which the law of nations has introduced to mitigate the rigors of war, cannot be a subject of complaint by the party to whom it is accorded as a grace or granted as a necessity. We have shown that a civil war such as that now waged between the Northern and Southern States is properly conducted according to the humane regulations of public law as regards capture on the ocean.

Under the very peculiar Constitution of this Government, although the citizens owe supreme allegiance to the Federal Government, they owe also a qualified allegiance to the State in which they are domiciled. Their persons and property are subject to its laws.

Hence, in organizing this rebellion, they have acted as States claiming to be sovereign over all persons and property within their respective limits, and asserting a right to absolve their citizens from their allegiance to the Federal Government. Several of these States have combined to form a new confederacy, claiming to be acknowledged by the world as a sovereign State. Their right to do so is now being decided by wager of battle. The ports and territory of each of these States are held in hostility to the General Government. It is no loose, unorganized insurrection, having no defined boundary or possession. It has a boundary marked by lines of bayonets, and which can be crossed only by force—south of this line is enemies' territory, because it is claimed and held in possession by an organized, hostile and belligerent power.

All persons residing within this territory whose property may be used to increase the revenues of the hostile power are, in this contest, liable to be treated as enemies, though not foreigners. They have cast off their allegiance and made war on their Government, and are none the less enemies because they are traitors....

Whether property be liable to capture as "enemies' property" does not in any manner depend on the personal allegiance of the owner....

The produce of the soil of the hostile territory, as well as other property engaged in the commerce of the hostile power, as the source of its wealth and strength, are always regarded as legitimate prize, without regard to the domicil of the owner, and much more so if he reside and trade within their territory.

We now proceed to notice the facts peculiar to the several cases submitted for our consideration. The principles which have just been stated apply alike to all of them....

The judgment[s] [are] therefore affirmed.

NELSON, CATRON, AND CLIFFORD, J.J., AND TANEY, C.J., DISSENTING

... The legal consequences resulting from a state of war between two countries at this day are well understood, and will be found described in every approved work on the subject of international law....

This power [to declare war] in all civilized nations is regulated by the fundamental laws or municipal constitution of the country.

By our constitution this power is lodged in Congress. Congress shall have power "to declare war, grant letters of marque and reprisal, and make rules concerning captures on land and water."...

But we are asked, what would become of the peace and integrity of the Union in case of an insurrection at home or invasion from abroad if this power could not be exercised by the President in the recess of Congress, and until that body could be assembled?

The framers of the Constitution fully comprehended this question, and provided for the contingency. Indeed, it would have been surprising if they had not, as a rebellion had occurred in the State of Massachusetts while the Convention was in session, and which had become so general that it was quelled only by calling upon the military power of the State. The Constitution declares that Congress shall have power "to provide for calling forth the militia to execute the laws of the Union, suppress insurrections, and repel invasions." Another clause, "that the President shall be Commander-in-chief of the Army and Navy of the United States, and of the militia of the several States when called into the actual service of the United States;" and, again: "He shall take care that the laws shall be faithfully executed."...

Congress assembled on the call for an extra session the 4th of July, 1861, and among the first acts passed was one in which the President was authorized by proclamation to interdict all trade and intercourse between all the inhabitants of States in insurrection and the rest of the United States, subjecting vessel and cargo to capture and condemnation as prize, and also to direct the capture of any ship or vessel belonging in whole or in part to any inhabitant of a State whose inhabitants are declared by the proclamation to be in a state of insurrection, found at sea or in any part of the rest of the United States. The 4th section also authorized the President to close any port in a Collection District obstructed so that the revenue could not be collected, and provided for the capture and condemnation of any vessel attempting to enter....

This Act of Congress, we think, recognized a state of civil war between the Government and the Confederate States, and made it territorial....

Congress on the 6th of August, 1862, passed an Act confirming all acts, proclamations, and orders of the President, after the 4th of March, 1861, respecting the army and navy, and legalizing them, so far as was competent for that body, and it has been suggested, but scarcely argued, that this legislation on the subject had the effect to bring into existence an *ex post facto* civil war with all the rights of capture and confiscation, *jure belli*, from the date referred to....

Upon the whole, after the most careful consideration of this case which the pressure of other duties has admitted, I am compelled to the conclusion that no civil war existed between this Government and the States in insurrection till recognized by the Act of Congress 13th of July, 1861; that the President does not possess the power under the Constitution to declare war or recognize its existence within the meaning of the law of nations, which carries with it belligerent rights, and thus change the country and all its citizens from a state of peace to a state of war; that this power belongs exclusively to the Congress of the United States, and, consequently, that the President had no power to set on foot a blockade under the law of nations, and that the capture of the vessel and cargo in this case, and in all cases before us in which the capture occurred before the 13th of July, 1861, for breach of blockade, or as enemies' property, are illegal and void, and that the decrees of condemnation should be reversed and the vessel and cargo restored.

QUESTIONS

1. According to Justice Grier's majority opinion, is the existence of war a question of law or a question of fact? What difference does it make? Does the Constitution give Congress the authority to declare war on a state or states?

2. The *Prize Cases* were argued for twelve days before the Court, between February 10 and 25, 1863. Multiple counsel appeared on each side of the issue. The Court handed down its opinion on March 10. Does the speed of the justices' response to the lengthy oral argument suggest that the issues were well understood and that the justices' minds were already made up? Might it suggest that the Court was sensitive to the political need for speedy resolution of the issues?

3. William Evarts, one of the counsel for the United States, took the position that, legally, the Civil War was like a war between belligerent nations and that the four ships, therefore, were properly taken as prize under the principles of international law. That position seems contradictory to President Lincoln's political stance that states had no right to secede and, hence, the Union was still intact. Are the two positions reconcilable? Was the character of the war relevant to the justices' resolution of the *Prize Cases*?

4. If Justice Nelson's dissent had been the majority opinion, could ships legally be taken as prize after July 13, 1861? Does Nelson's dissent take the position that the Civil War was a war in law as well as in fact after July 13, 1862?

5. In 1973, in response to growing domestic opposition to the Vietnam War, Congress enacted the War Powers Resolution over President Richard Nixon's veto. It provided the following:

THE WAR POWERS RESOLUTION

Joint Resolution Concerning the War Powers of Congress and the President Resolved by the Senate and House of Representatives of the United States of America in Congress assembled, That:...

Purpose and Policy

Sec. 2 (a) It is the purpose of this joint resolution to fulfill the intent of the framers of the Constitution of the United States and insure that the collective judgment of both the Congress and the President will apply to the introduction of U.S. Armed Forces into hostilities, or into situations where imminent involvement in hostilities is clearly indicated by the circumstances, and to the continued use of such forces in hostilities or in such situations.

(b) Under article 1, section 8, of the Constitution, it is specifically provided that the Congress shall have the power to make all laws necessary and proper for carrying into execution, not only its own powers but also all other powers vested by the Constitution in the Government of the United States, or in any department or officer thereof.

(c) The constitutional powers of the President as Commander-in-Chief to introduce U.S. Armed Forces into hostilities, or into situations where imminent involvement in hostilities indicated by the circumstances, are exercised only pursuant to (1) a declaration of war, (2) specific statutory authorization, or (3) a national emergency created by attack upon the United States, its territories or possessions or its armed forces.

Consultation

Sec. 3. The President in every possible instance shall consult with Congress before introducing U.S. Armed Forces into hostilities or into situations where imminent involvement in hostilities is clearly indicated by the circumstances, and after every such introduction shall consult regularly with the Congress until U.S. Armed Forces are no longer engaged in hostilities or have been removed from such situations.

Sec. 4 (a) In the absence of a declaration of war, in any case in which U.S. Armed Forces are introduced—

(1) into hostilities or into situations where imminent involvement in hostilities is clearly indicated by the circumstances;

(2) into the territory, airspace or waters of a foreign nation, while equipped for combat, except for deployments which related solely to supply, replacement, repair, or training of such forces; or

(3) in numbers which substantially enlarge U.S. Armed Forces equipped for combat already located in a foreign nation; the President shall submit within 48 hours to the speaker of the House of Representatives and to the president pro tempore of the Senate a report, in writing, setting forth—

(A) the circumstances necessitating the introduction of U.S. Armed Forces;

(B) the constitutional and legislative authority under which such introduction took place; and

(C) the estimated scope and duration of the hostilities or involvement.

(b) The President shall provide such other information as the Congress may request in the fulfillment of its constitutional responsibilities with respect to committing the Nation to war and to the use of U.S. Armed Forces abroad.

(c) Whenever U.S. Armed Forces are introduced into hostilities or into any situation described in subsection (a) of this section, the President shall, so long as such armed forces continue to be engaged in such hostilities or situation, report to Congress periodically on the status of such hostilities or situation as well as on the scope and duration of such hostilities or situation, but in no event shall he report to the Congress less often than once every six months.

Congressional Action

Sec 5. (a) Each report submitted pursuant to section 4(a)(1) shall be transmitted to the Speaker of the House of Representatives and to the President pro tempore of the Senate on the same calendar day. Each report so transmitted shall be referred to the Committee on Foreign Affairs of the House of Representatives and to the Committee on Foreign Relations of the Senate for appropriate action. If, when the report is transmitted, the Congress has adjourned sine die or has adjourned for any period in excess of three calendar days, the Speaker of the House of Representatives and the President pro tempore of the Senate, if they deem it advisable (or if petitioned by at least 30 percent of the membership of their respective Houses) shall jointly request the President to convene Congress in order that it may consider the report and take appropriate action pursuant to this section.

(b) Within sixty calendar days after a report is submitted or is required to be submitted pursuant to section 4 (a)(1), whichever is earlier, the President shall terminate any use of U.S. Armed Forces with respect to which such report was submitted (or required to be submitted), unless the Congress (1) has declared war or has enacted a specific authorization for such use of U.S. Armed Forces, (2) has extended by law such sixty-day period, or (3) is physically unable to meet as a result of an armed attack upon the United States. Such sixty-day period shall be extended for not more than an additional thirty days if the President determines and certifies to the Congress in writing that unavoidable military necessity respecting the safety of U.S. Armed Forces requires the continued use of such armed forces in the course of bringing about a prompt removal of such forces.

(c) Notwithstanding subsection (b), at any time that U.S. Armed Forces are engaged in hostilities outside the territory of the United States, its possessions and territories without a declaration of war or specific statutory authorization, such forces shall be removed by the president if the Congress so directs by concurrent resolution.

Interpretation of Joint Resolution

Sec. 8. (a) Authority to introduce U.S. Armed Forces into hostilities or into situations wherein involvement in hostilities is clearly indicated by the circumstances shall be inferred-

(1) from any provision of law (whether or not in effect before the date of the enactment of this joint resolution), including any provision contained in any appropriation Act, unless such provision

specifically authorizes the introduction of U.S. Armed Forces into hostilities or into such situations and states that it is intended to constitute specific statutory authorization within the meaning of this joint resolution; or

(2) from any treaty heretofore or hereafter ratified unless such treaty is implemented by legislation specifically authorizing the introduction of U.S. Armed Forces into hostilities or into such situations and stating that it is intended to constitute specific statutory authorization within the meaning of this joint resolution.

(b) Nothing in this joint resolution shall be construed to require any further specific statutory authorization to permit members of U.S. Armed Forces to participate jointly with members of the armed forces of one or more foreign countries in the headquarters operations or high-level military commands which were established prior to the date of enactment of this joint resolution and pursuant to the United Nations Charter or any treaty ratified by the United States prior to such date.

(c) For purposes of this joint resolution, the term "introduction of U.S. Armed Forces" includes the assignment of members of such armed forces to command, coordinate, participate in the movement of, or accompany the regular or irregular military forces of any foreign country or government when such military forces are engaged, or there exists an imminent threat that such forces will become engaged, in hostilities.

(d) Nothing in this joint resolution-

(1) is intended to alter the constitutional authority of the Congress or of the President, or the provisions of existing treaties; or

(2) shall be construed as granting any authority to the President with respect to the introduction of U.S. Armed Forces into hostilities or into situations wherein involvement in hostilities is clearly indicated by the circumstances which authority he would not have had in the absence of this joint resolution.

Separability Clause

Sec. 9. if any provision of this joint resolution or the application thereof to any person or circumstances is held invalid, the remainder of the joint resolution and the application of such provision to any other person or circumstance shall not be affected thereby...

President Nixon particularly objected to sections 5(b) and 5(c), claiming that they infringed unconstitutionally on the president's authority as Commander-in-Chief. Do the *Prize Cases* shed any light on whether the War Powers Resolution is constitutional?

EMERGENCY AND FOREIGN POLICY POWERS

Ex parte Milligan
4 Wallace 2 (1866)

SETTING

As explained previously, one of President Lincoln's earliest strategies for subduing the states that had seceded from the Union was to order an April 19,
1861, blockade of southern ports. The constitutionality of that action was
decided in the *Prize Cases*.

In September 1862, Lincoln issued a proclamation declaring that

> during the existing insurrection and as a necessary means for suppressing
> the same, all rebels and insurgents, their aiders and abettors within the
> United States, and all persons discouraging volunteer enlistments, resisting
> militia drafts, or guilty of any disloyal practice, affording aid and comfort to
> rebels against the authority of the United States, shall be subject to martial
> law, and liable to trial and punishment by courts-martial or military com-
> missions.

On March 3, 1863, Congress ratified Lincoln's proclamation of martial law
by enacting a statute that declared that, during the rebellion, the president
was "authorized" to suspend the writ of habeas corpus whenever he deemed
public safety to require that it be suspended. The act also provided that political prisoners in nonrebel states would be discharged from custody if they
took an oath of allegiance after a federal grand jury had convened and failed
to issue indictments against them.

On October 5, 1864, Major General Alvin Hovey, Military Commandant of
the District of Indiana, ordered that Lambdin P. Milligan, a civilian citizen of
the United States and Indiana, be arrested and taken to a military prison in
Indianapolis. As a "Peace Democrat," Milligan advocated that the Union recognize the Confederate States of America and end the war. Milligan was accused
of being part of a conspiracy to seize U.S. arsenals, release prisoners of war,
arm them, and march with them into Kentucky and Missouri in order to cooperate with rebel forces that were invading Kentucky, Indiana, and Illinois.
Milligan pleaded not guilty to the charges.

On October 21, 1864, Milligan went on trial before a military commission
on charges of conspiracy against the United States, affording aid and comfort
to rebels against the United States, inciting insurrection, disloyal practices,
and violating the laws of war. Milligan objected to the military commission's
jurisdiction over the case. Nonetheless, he was found guilty on all charges and
sentenced to be hanged.

In January 1865, a federal grand jury was empaneled to consider whether Milligan had violated the laws of the United States and whether an indictment should issue against him in federal court. The grand jury adjourned without taking action.

In May 1865, Milligan's sentence from the military commission was approved by the War Department and President Andrew Johnson, who had become president after Lincoln's assassination in April, and his execution was ordered to be carried out without delay. At the last moment, however, President Johnson commuted Milligan's sentence to life in prison.

Milligan filed a petition for a writ of habeas corpus in the Circuit Court of the United States for the District of Indiana. He claimed that under the habeas corpus statute of March 1863, he was entitled to be turned over to the proper civil tribunal or to be discharged from custody altogether. He renewed his argument that the military commission had no jurisdiction over him because he had not been a resident in any of the rebellious states and contended that he had been denied his constitutional right to trial by jury.

The judges of the Circuit Court could not agree whether the military commission had jurisdiction over Milligan, whether the habeas corpus writ should issue, and whether Milligan should be discharged from custody. The judges therefore certified those questions to the Supreme Court of the United States.

Milligan's case was consolidated on appeal with *Ex parte Bowles*, and *Ex parte Horsey*, which raised the same questions.

HIGHLIGHTS OF SUPREME COURT ARGUMENTS

BRIEF FOR THE UNITED STATES

◆ The Supreme Court lacks jurisdiction to hear this case. The 1802 statute allowing questions to be certified to the Court contemplated a dispute between two parties and their agreement on the questions certified. The U.S. attorney took no part in the discussion of the questions to certify.

◆ The military commission that convicted Milligan derived its authority from the president's declaration of martial law in 1862 and his suspension of the writ of habeas corpus. The president acted under his authority as commander-in-chief. He needed no congressional authorization. Congress nonetheless expressly ratified the proclamation in March 1863. The proclamation and supporting legislation were in effect throughout the proceedings involving Milligan.

◆ Martial law and its tribunals have been recognized as necessary since the Revolutionary period because of the inadequacy of peacetime tribunals to deal with the problem of organized rebellion. Proceedings by military commissions should be judged by the standards of martial law and military authority.

◆ The military commission had jurisdiction over Milligan despite his civilian status because the acts for which he was found guilty were military as well as civil offenses, committed within a military district of a geographical military department.

◆ Even if the Court rules that the military commission lacked jurisdiction over Milligan, he is not entitled to freedom. He can be held as a prisoner captured in war until hostilities end. Then he will be turned over to civil authorities for judicial action in civilian courts.

BRIEF FOR MILLIGAN

◆ During Milligan's military trial, the courts of Indiana were open and the laws had their full effect. Those courts remain open. No judicial processes have been interrupted. Judicial proceedings against Milligan should have taken place in civilian courts because any person not in the military or naval service cannot be punished until he has a fair, open, public trial before an impartial jury, in a court created by Congress for the purpose of trying specific offenses.

◆ The military tribunal lacked jurisdiction for several reasons: First, the president's proclamation of martial law in 1862 is void because it was not authorized by any act of Congress. Even if it is valid, martial law operates only in places where military force has suspended the civilian functions of government.

◆ Second, the president's power under martial law can suspend the rights of citizens only temporarily. It cannot abrogate them.

◆ Third, laws creating military commissions limited the reach of those laws to those in military service and to spies. Milligan is a civilian.

◆ Finally, the president, upon his own will and judgment, lacks authority to bring any person in the land before military officers and subject him to trial, punishment, and even death. The executive power is limited to that directly specified in some part of the Constitution or by an act of Congress.

SUPREME COURT DECISION

(9–0 on result, 5–4 on who has power to decide when martial law is necessary)

DAVIS, J.

... The controlling question in the case is this: Upon the facts stated in Milligan's petition, and the exhibits filed, had the military commission mentioned in it jurisdiction, legally, to try and sentence him?...

No graver question was ever considered by this court, nor one which more nearly concerns the rights of the whole people; for it is the birthright of every American citizen when charged with crime, to be tried and punished according to law.... The provisions of [the constitution] on the administration of criminal justice are too plain and direct, to leave room for misconstruction or doubt of their true meaning. Those applicable to this case are found in that clause of the original Constitution which says that ["]the trial of all crimes, except in case of impeachment, shall be by jury;" and in the fourth, fifth, and sixth articles of the amendments....

The Constitution of the United States is a law for rulers and people, equally in war and in peace, and covers with the shield of its protection all classes of men, at all times, and under all circumstances. No doctrine, involving more pernicious consequences, was ever invented by the wit of man than that any of its provisions can be suspended during any of the great exigencies of government. Such a doctrine leads directly to anarchy or despotism, but the theory of necessity on which it is based is false; for the government, within the Constitution, has all the powers granted to it, which are necessary to preserve its existence; as has been happily proved by the result of the great effort to throw off its just authority....

One of the plainest constitutional provisions was, therefore, infringed when Milligan was tried by a court not ordained and established by Congress, and not composed of judges appointed during good behavior....

It is claimed that martial law covers with its broad mantle the proceedings of this Military Commission. The proposition is this: That in a time of war the commander of an armed force (if in his opinion the exigencies of the country demand it, and of which he is to judge), has the power, within the lines of his military district, to suspend all civil rights and their remedies, and subject citizens as well as soldiers to the rule of *his will*; and in the exercise of his lawful authority cannot be restrained, except by his superior officer or the President of the United States.

If this position is sound to the extent claimed, then when war exists, foreign or domestic, and the country is subdivided into military departments for mere convenience, the commander of one of them can, if he chooses, within his limits, on the plea of necessity, with the approval of the Executive, substitute military force for and to the exclusion of the laws, and punish all persons, as he thinks right and proper, without fixed or certain rules.

The statement of this proposition shows its importance; for, if true, republican government is a failure, and there is an end of liberty regulated by law. Martial law, established on such a basis, destroys every guarantee of the Constitution, and effectually renders the "military independent of and superior to the civil power"—the attempt to do which by the King of Great Britain was deemed by our fathers such an offence, that they assigned it to the world as one of the causes which impelled them to declare their independence. Civil liberty and this kind of martial law cannot endure together; the antagonism is irreconcilable; and, in the conflict, one or the other must perish....

It is essential to the safety of every government that, in a great crisis, like the one we have just passed through, there should be a power somewhere of suspending the writ of habeas corpus.... In the emergency of the times, an immediate public investigation according to law may not be possible; and yet, the peril to the country may be too imminent to suffer such persons to go at large....

It follows, from what has been said on this subject, that there are occasions when martial rule can be properly applied. If, in foreign invasion or civil war, the courts are actually closed, and it is impossible to administer criminal justice according to law, then, on the theatre of active military operations, where war really prevails, there is a necessity to furnish a substitute for the civil authority, thus overthrown, to preserve the safety of the army and society; and as no power is left but the military, it is allowed to govern by martial rule until the laws can have their free course. As necessity creates the rule, so it limits its duration; for, if this government is continued after the courts are reinstated, it is a gross usurpation of power. Martial rule can never exist where the courts are open, and in the proper and unobstructed exercise of their jurisdiction. It is also confined to the locality of actual war....

The two remaining questions in this case must be answered in the affirmative. The suspension of the privilege of the writ of habeas corpus does not suspend the writ itself. The writ issues as a matter of course; and on the return made to it the court decides whether the party applying is denied the right of proceeding any further with it.

If the military trial of Milligan was contrary to law, then he was entitled, on the facts stated in his petition, to be discharged from custody by the terms of the act of Congress of March 3d, 1863....

But it is insisted that Milligan was a prisoner of war, and, therefore, excluded from the privileges of the statute. It is not easy to see how he can be treated as a prisoner of war, when he lived in Indiana for the past twenty years, was arrested there, and had not been, during the late troubles, a resident of any of the states in rebellion. If

in Indiana he conspired with bad men to assist the enemy, he is punishable for it in the courts of Indiana; but, when tried for the offence, he cannot plead the rights of war; for he was not engaged in legal acts of hostility against the government, and only such persons, when captured, are prisoners of war. If he cannot enjoy the immunities attaching to the character of a prisoner of war, how can he be subject to their pains and penalties?...

CHASE, C.J. AND WAYNE, SWAYNE, AND MILLER, J.J., CONCURRING IN PART AND DISSENTING IN PART

... [I]t is more important to the country and to every citizen that [Milligan] should not be punished under an illegal sentence, sanctioned by this court of last resort, than that he should be punished at all....

[T]he opinion ... asserts not only that the Military Commission held in Indiana was not authorized by Congress, but that it was not in the power of Congress to authorize it; from which it may be thought to follow, that Congress has no power to indemnify the officers who composed the commission against liability in civil courts for acting as members of it.

We cannot agree to this....

We think that Congress had power, though not exercised, to authorize the Military Commission which was held in Indiana....

The Constitution itself provides for military government as well as for civil government. And we do not understand it to be claimed that the civil safeguards of the Constitution have application in cases within the proper sphere of the former.

What, then, is that proper sphere?...

Congress has the power not only to raise and support and govern armies, but to declare war. It has, therefore, the power to provide by law for carrying on war with vigor and success, except such as interferes with the command of the forces and conduct of campaigns. That power and duty belong to the President as Commander-in-Chief....

The power to make the necessary laws is in Congress; the power to execute in the President. Both powers imply many subordinate and auxiliary powers. Each includes all authorities essential to its due exercise. But neither can the President, in war more than in peace, intrude upon the proper authority of Congress, nor Congress upon the proper authority of the President. Both are servants of the people, whose will is expressed in the fundamental law. Congress cannot direct the conduct of campaigns, nor can the President, or any commanded under him, without the sanction of Congress, institute tribunals for the trial and punishment of offenses, either of soldiers or civilians, unless in cases of controlling necessity, which justifies what it compels, or at least insures acts of indemnity from the justice of the legislature.

We by no means assert that Congress can establish and apply the laws of war where no war has been declared or exists.

Where peace exists the laws of peace must prevail. What we do maintain is, that when the nation is involved in war, and some portions of the country are invaded, and all are exposed to invasion, it is within the power of Congress to determine in what states or districts such great and imminent public danger exists as justifies the authorization of military tribunals for the trial of crimes and offenses against the discipline or security of the army or against the public safety....

The fact that the Federal courts were open was regarded by Congress as a sufficient reason for not exercising the power; but that fact could not deprive Congress of the right to exercise it....

QUESTIONS

1. Justice Samuel Miller, in a private letter written the day before *Milligan* was argued before the Supreme Court, said about U.S. Attorney General James Speed, "[T]he session of the Court has developed his utter want of ability as a lawyer—He is certainly one of the feeblest men who has addressed the Court this term" (Charles Fairman, *History of the Supreme Court of the United States, vol. 6: Reconstruction and Reunion, 1864–88* Part I [New York, NY: Macmillan, 1971], p. 201).

   What constitutional arguments might have been more persuasive in justifying the exercise of executive power defended in *Ex parte Milligan* than those Attorney General Speed offered on the government's behalf?

2. The majority opinion in *Milligan* was written by Justice David Davis, a close personal friend of President Lincoln and one of the managers of Lincoln's 1864 presidential campaign. Justice Davis's dim view of the

president's suspension of constitutional guarantees was shared by Chief Justice Taney, who had conveyed his thoughts to Lincoln in May 1861. Why would the president act counter to the advice that his order to suspend the writ of habeas corpus was not constitutional?

3. If Congress had exercised its power to authorize military commissions, might the outcome in *Milligan* have been different?

4. Identify the differences between *Milligan* and the *Prize Cases* that led the Court to uphold the exercise of executive power in one but not the other.

5. John P. Frank, in an article entitled, "*Ex parte Milligan*," contended that "*Ex parte Milligan* is one of the truly great documents of the American Constitution, a bulwark for the protection of the civil liberties of every American citizen. It is the pledge of the Supreme Court to the people of the United States that the constitutional right of freedom from arrest and punishment at the caprice of the executive branch of the Government, particularly the military, and the right of trial by jury can never be taken away so long as the courts are open and can function. There are no more important constitutional rights than these" (44 *Columbia Law Review* [1944]: 639). Is Frank correct?

EMERGENCY AND FOREIGN POLICY POWERS

United States v. Curtiss-Wright Export Corp.
299 U.S. 204 (1936)

SETTING

Following a war with Chile in the late nineteenth century, the South American Republic of Bolivia ceded its appreciable land holdings on the Pacific coast, which left Bolivia completely landlocked. The country was forced to turn eastward to seek an outlet to the Atlantic Ocean. One possibility was through the Paraguay River, which reaches the Atlantic through the Parana River and the Rio de la Plata. The Paraguay River formed the eastern boundary of a large and relatively unknown area between Bolivia and Paraguay known as the Chaco Boreal. In the 1920s, oil was discovered in the Chaco Boreal, giving both Bolivia and Paraguay additional incentive to claim the area. Such disputes were not uncommon in South America because of the vagueness of boundaries between Spanish administrative districts in the days before independence.

In 1932, Bolivian troops were dispatched to the wilderness of the Chaco Boreal to secure it for Bolivia. They were met by Paraguayan troops. While no war was ever declared, a three-year battle between Bolivia and Paraguay threatened to draw in other countries. Both belligerents looked abroad to purchase arms and munitions. American arms suppliers welcomed orders from abroad because of the depressed domestic economy.

At the urging of the League of Nations, the United States, Mexico, Cuba, Columbia, and Uruguay declared neutrality and attempted to bring pressure on Bolivia and Paraguay to stop fighting. In an effort to cut off the arms trade that threatened American neutrality, Congress passed a joint resolution on May 24, 1934. It provided:

> That if the President finds that the prohibition of the sale of arms and munitions of war in the United States to those countries now engaged in armed conflict in the Chaco may contribute to the reestablishment of peace between those countries, and if after consultation with the governments of other American Republics and with their cooperation, as well as that of such other governments as he may deem necessary, he makes a proclamation to that effect, it shall be unlawful to sell, except under such limitations and exceptions as the President prescribes, any arms or munitions of war in any place in the United States to the countries now engaged in that armed conflict, or to any person, company, or association acting in the interest of either country, until otherwise ordered by the President or Congress.

Violation of the resolution was punishable by a fine of up to $10,000, two years imprisonment, or both.

On the day the resolution was passed, President Franklin Roosevelt issued a proclamation prohibiting the sale of arms and munitions of war produced in the United States to countries engaged in armed conflict in the Chaco. The proclamation remained in force until November 14, 1935, when a truce between Bolivia and Paraguay arranged by the neutral countries went into effect.

In January 1936, the U.S. District Court for the Southern District of New York issued an indictment against the Curtiss-Wright Export Corporation, Curtiss Aeroplane and Motor Company, Barr Shipping Corporation, John Allard, Clarence Webster, Samuel Abelow, and Robert Barr. They were charged with conspiring to sell fifteen machine guns to Bolivia between May 28, 1934, and November 14, 1935, in violation of the joint resolution and the president's proclamation. The defendants demurred to the first count. Among other things, they contended that the joint resolution was an invalid delegation of legislative power to the executive.

The District Court sustained the demurrer and dismissed the indictment. The United States took direct appeal to the Supreme Court of the United States as allowed under the Criminal Appeals Act of 1907. The central issue on appeal was whether the joint resolution was an invalid delegation of legislative power to the executive.

Highlights of Supreme Court Arguments

BRIEF FOR THE UNITED STATES

◆ The Joint Resolution of May 28, 1934, was a valid constitutional delegation of legislative power to the president. Since 1794, similar delegations of power have been made in the field of foreign affairs. The joint resolution contained a clear statement of congressional policy and established a definite standard by which the president was to base his actions. The joint resolution did not allow the president to issue a proclamation on the basis of vague opinion. He was to rely on facts that were peculiarly available to him as president.

◆ The discretion given to the president by the joint resolution was much less broad than has been allowed by other statutes that have been sustained by the Court. The discretion under this resolution is distinguishable from *Schechter Corp. v. United States*, in which the Court criticized Congress for delegating legislative power without declaring any policy or establishing any standards for the president to follow.

BRIEF FOR CURTISS-WRIGHT

◆ The joint resolution invalidly delegated legislative power for at least four reasons. First, the resolution did not go into effect unless the president decided that prohibiting arms sales would help to reestablish peace in the Chaco. Making or not making a law is a legislative function that Congress cannot surrender. Second, the resolution did not take effect until after an optional proclamation that the president might never have made. The president was under no obligation to proclaim anything. The resolution thus gave the president unfettered discretion of the kind the Court struck down in *Schechter Poultry*. Third, the resolution gave the president coordinate power to repeal it, thus giving him legislative power. Fourth, the resolution gave the president unlimited discretion to determine exceptions to any proclamation he might issue. The resolution provided no standards or rules for the president to follow in making exceptions.

BRIEF FOR THE OTHER DEFENDANTS

◆ The government is incorrect that similar delegations of power in the field of foreign relations have been commonplace throughout history. With only three exceptions, all the legislative precedents relied on by the government were examples of legislation that became operative only if a prescribed event occurred. None left it to the president to determine whether the event had happened.

◆ The acts charged in the indictment no longer constitute an offense against the United States. Therefore, the prosecutions must fail.

Supreme Court Decision: 7–1

(Stone, J., did not participate.)

SUTHERLAND, J.

... The determination which we are called to make ... is whether the Joint Resolution ... is vulnerable to attack under the rule that forbids a delegation of the law-making power. In other words, assuming (but not deciding) that the challenged delegation, if it were confined to internal affairs, would be invalid, may it nevertheless be sustained on the ground that its exclusive aim is to afford a remedy for a hurtful condition within foreign territory?

It will contribute to the elucidation of the question if we first consider the differences between the powers of the Federal government in respect of foreign or external affairs and those in respect of domestic or internal affairs. That there are differences between them, and that these differences are fundamental, may not be doubted.

The two classes of powers are different, both in respect of their origin and their nature. The broad statement that the federal government can exercise no powers except those specifically enumerated in the Constitution, and such implied powers as are necessary and proper to carry into effect the enumerated powers, is categorically true only in respect of our internal affairs. In that field, the primary purpose of the Constitution was to carve from the general mass of legislative powers *then possessed by the states* such portions as it was thought desirable to vest in the Federal government, leaving those not included in the enumeration still in the states. That this doctrine applies only to powers which the states had, is self evi-

dent. And since the states severally never possessed international powers, such powers could not have been carved from the mass of state powers but obviously were transmitted to the United States from some other source....

As a result of the separation from Great Britain by the colonies, acting as a unit, the powers of external sovereignty passed from the Crown not to the colonies severally, but to the colonies in their collective and corporate capacity as the United States of America. Even before the Declaration, the colonies were a unit in foreign affairs, acting through a common agency—namely the Continental Congress, composed of delegates from the thirteen colonies.... Rulers come and go; governments end and forms of government change; but sovereignty survives. A political society cannot endure without a supreme will somewhere. Sovereignty is never held in suspense. When, therefore, Great Britain in respect of the colonies ceased, it immediately passed to the Union. That fact was given practical application almost at once. The treaty of peace, made on September 3, 1783, was concluded between his Brittanic Majesty and the "United States of America."

The Union existed before the Constitution, which was ordained and established among other things to form "a more perfect Union." Prior to that event, it is clear that the Union, declared by the Articles of Confederation to be "perpetual," was the sole possessor of external sovereignty, and in the Union it remained without change save in so far as the

Constitution in express terms qualified its exercise....

[T]he investment of the Federal government with the powers of external sovereignty did not depend upon the affirmative grants of the Constitution. The powers to declare and wage war, to conclude peace, to make treaties, to maintain diplomatic relations with other sovereignties, if they had never been mentioned in the Constitution, would have vested in the Federal government as necessary concomitants of nationality....

Not only, as we have shown, is the Federal power over external affairs in origin and essential character different from that over internal affairs, but participation in the exercise of the power is significantly limited. In this vast external realm, with its important, complicated, delicate and manifold problems, the President alone has the power to speak or listen as a representative of the nation. He *makes* treaties with the advice and consent of the Senate; but he alone negotiates. Into the field of negotiation the Senate cannot intrude; and Congress itself is powerless to invade it....

It is important to bear in mind that we are here dealing not alone with an authority vested in the President by an exertion of legislative power, but with such an authority plus the very delicate, plenary and exclusive power of the President as the sole organ of the Federal government in the field of international relations—a power which does not require as a basis for its exercise an act of Congress, but which, of course, like every other governmental power, must be exercised in subordination to the applicable provisions of the Constitution. It is quite apparent that if, in the maintenance of our international relations, embarrassment—perhaps

serious embarrassment—is to be avoided and success for our aims achieved, congressional legislation which is to be made effective through negotiation and inquiry within the international field must often accord to the President a degree of discretion and freedom from statutory restriction which would not be admissible were domestic affairs alone involved. Moreover, he, not Congress, has the better opportunity of knowing the conditions which prevail in foreign countries, and especially is this true in time of war. He has his confidential sources of information. He has his agents in the form of diplomatic, consular and other officials. Secrecy in respect of information gathered by them may be highly necessary, and the premature disclosure of it productive of harmful results....

In the light of the foregoing observations, it is evident that this court should not be in haste to apply a general rule which will have the effect of condemning legislation like that under review as constituting an unlawful delegation of legislative power. The principles which justify such legislation find overwhelming support in the unbroken legislative practice which has prevailed almost from the inception of the national government to the present day....

Practically every volume of the United States Statutes contains one or more acts or joint resolutions of Congress authorizing action by the President in respect of subjects affecting foreign relations, which either leave the exercise of the power to his unrestricted judgment, or provide a standard far more general than that which has always been considered requisite with regard to domestic affairs....

The result of holding that the joint

resolution here under attack is void and unenforceable as constituting an unlawful delegation of legislative power would be to stamp this multitude of comparable acts and resolutions as likewise invalid. And while this court may not, and should not, hesitate to declare acts of Congress, however many times repeated, to be unconstitutional if beyond all rational doubt it finds them to be so, an impressive array of legislation ... enacted by nearly every Congress from the beginning of our national existence to the present day, must be given unusual weight in the process of reaching a correct determination of the problem....

The uniform, long-continued and undisputed legislative practice just disclosed rests upon an admissible view of the Constitution which, even if the practice found far less support in principle than we think it does, we should not feel at liberty at this late day to disturb....

It is enough to summarize by saying that, both upon principle and in accordance with precedent, we conclude there is sufficient warrant for the broad discretion vested in the President to determine whether the enforcement of the statute will have a beneficial effect upon the reestablishment of peace in the affected countries; whether he shall make proclamation to bring the resolution into operation; whether and when the resolution shall cease to operate and to make proclamation accordingly; and to prescribe limitations and exceptions to which the enforcement of the resolution shall be subject....

The judgment of the court below must be reversed and the cause remanded for further proceedings in accordance with the foregoing opinion....

MCREYNOLDS, J., DISSENTING

Mr. Justice McReynolds does not agree. He is of opinion that the court below reached the right conclusion and its judgment ought to be affirmed.

QUESTIONS

1. Because Congress's Joint Resolution explicitly authorized the president's actions in prohibiting the sale of arms, it was not necessary for Justice Sutherland to reach the more fundamental question posed by *Curtiss-Wright* concerning the character of presidential authority over foreign relations. What concerns might have led him to do so? Can Sutherland's opinion in *Curtiss-Wright* be reconciled with his vote in the unanimous *Schechter Poultry* decision?

2. State the doctrine announced in *Curtiss-Wright*. Political scientist David Gray Adler contends that in fashioning the "radical, pathbreaking" *Curtiss-Wright* doctrine, the Court misinterpreted and converted the president's exclusive authority to communicate with foreign nations into exclusive policy-making authority. "Thus, it was Sutherland who infused a purely communicative role with a substantive policy-making function and thereby manufactured a great power of [John Marshall's] sole-organ doctrine" ("Foreign Policy and the Separation of Powers: The Influence of the Judiciary," in *Judging the*

Constitution, eds. Michael McCann and Gerald L. Houseman [Glenview, IL: Scott, Foresman, 1989], p. 160). Another commentator found the Court's reasoning in *Curtiss-Wright* "so novel as to afford room for much speculation as to the precise effect and possible future importance of the decision" (Note, 1 *Maryland Law Review* [1936]: 167).

Are these criticisms warranted? What guidance did Justice Sutherland receive from Article II in fashioning his opinion in *Curtiss-Wright*? Lacking constitutional guidance, was Justice Sutherland justified in relying on political reality regarding the nature of executive authority in foreign affairs? Are the lack of practical alternatives an explanation for Justice McReynolds's decision not to write a dissenting opinion?

3. Consider the view of presidential powers announced in *Curtiss-Wright* in light of these remarks by Justice Robert H. Jackson in *Woods v. Cloyd W. Miller Co.*, 333 U.S. 138, 147 (1948):

> No one will question that [the war power] is the most dangerous one to free government in the whole catalogue of powers. It usually is invoked in haste and excitement when calm legislative consideration of constitutional limitation is difficult. It is executed in a time of patriotic fervor that makes moderation unpopular. And, worst of all, it is interpreted by the Judges under the influence of the same passions and pressures.

Is there a constitutional remedy for this dilemma?

4. In February 1942, President Franklin Roosevelt issued Executive Order No. 9066, which authorized the secretary of war to issue orders regulating the activities and movement of over 112,000 people of Japanese descent living on the Pacific coast, 70,000 of whom were American citizens. Congress ratified the president's order in legislation passed the next month. The law made it a misdemeanor for anyone to violate restrictions imposed by the secretary of war, punishable by a fine up to $5,000 and one year in prison for each offense. In May 1942, Lt. Gen. John L. DeWitt, Military Commander of the Western Defense Command, issued an "exclusion order" that required all persons of Japanese ancestry to evacuate an area of California and to report to relocation camps. In *Korematsu v. United States*, 323 U.S. 214 (1944), the Supreme Court, acknowledging that legal restrictions that curtail the civil rights of a single racial group are "immediately suspect," nonetheless upheld the validity of the exclusion order. Justice Black, writing for the 6–3 majority, stated that in upholding the exclusion order

> … we are not unmindful of the hardships imposed by it upon a large group of American citizens. But hardships are part of war, and war is an aggregation of hardships. All citizens alike, both in and out of

uniform, feel the impact of war in greater or lesser measure. Citizenship has its responsibilities as well as its privileges, and in time of war the burden is always heavier.

Is the Court's reasoning in *Korematsu* an inevitable extension of its reasoning in *Curtiss-Wright*? Or was the Court's deference to executive authority in *Korematsu*, notwithstanding *Korematsu*'s racial implications, predictable because World War II was a declared war? If President Bush had issued exclusion orders affecting Iraqi nationals during the Persian Gulf War, would the *Curtiss-Wright* and *Korematsu* reasoning have supported his orders?

5. The Court's expansive view of presidential powers in the international arena has not changed in the years since *Curtiss-Wright*. Whatever its merits at the time, have events like the Korean conflict, U.S. involvement in the war in Southeast Asia, the Iran-Contra affair, the Persian Gulf War and Bosnia challenged the wisdom of the *Curtiss-Wright* decision? How, if at all, should *Curtiss-Wright* be rewritten in light of such events?

EMERGENCY AND FOREIGN POLICY POWERS

Youngstown Sheet & Tube Co. v. Sawyer
343 U.S. 579 (1952)

SETTING

In June 1950, North Korean forces equipped with Soviet-made weapons invaded South Korea. Responding to a call from the United Nations Security Council to member nations to furnish assistance, President Harry S Truman sent air and naval forces to Korea. At this time, American soldiers in Korea had much more sophisticated equipment than in the past. The fire power of combat units, for example, was 50 percent greater in the Korean conflict than it had been in World War II. Airplanes and ships also were much more technologically advanced. All depended on steel—the basic commodity used in the manufacture of military weapons, munitions, and equipment—but one sector of the steel industry was having labor problems.

On December 31, 1951, several contracts expired between a major steel producer, the Youngstown Sheet & Tube Company and the United Steelworkers Union. When negotiations stalemated over new contracts covering wages, hours, and terms and conditions of employment, the president of the union issued an ultimatum stating that at 12:10 A.M. on April 9, 1952, all employees working at the iron and steel producing and manufacturing plants in the United States would initiate an organized strike against Youngstown Sheet & Tube. Neither mandatory mediation nor an inquiry and report by the Federal Wage Stabilization Board was able to salvage the negotiations.

According to several administrative officials, even a brief interruption in the production of steel would have dire consequences for the military effort in Korea. The administrator of the Defense Production Administration, for example, claimed that the total supply of steel normally available to the United States was substantially less than the estimated requirements of civilian and defense production. Secretary of Defense Robert A. Lovett reported that 84 percent of all super-alloy steel, 36.6 percent of all alloy steel, and 32.4 percent of all stainless steel produced in the United States was required for direct military purposes.

On April 8, 1952, President Truman issued Executive Order 10340 to his secretary of commerce, Charles Sawyer. The order commanded Sawyer to take possession of the country's steel mills and to operate them so that the critical need for steel in the Korean military effort would be satisfied. The president stated that a work stoppage in the nation's steel mills would "immediately jeopardize and imperil our national defense and the defense of those joined with us in resisting aggression, and would add to the continuing danger of our soldiers, sailors and airmen engaged in combat in the field." The order designated the president of each company to act as operating manager for the United States until further notice.

On April 9, 1952, President Truman sent a message to Congress explaining his action in "seizing" the steel mills. He expressed his willingness to cooperate with instructions from Congress, but indicated that if Congress did not respond, he would see to it that the steel industry kept operating. Congress did not respond.

The Youngstown Sheet & Tube Company, four other steel companies, and a ferromanganese company included in the seizure order sought preliminary and permanent injunctions from the U.S. District Court for the District of Columbia to restrain Secretary Sawyer from implementing the executive order. They argued that seizure of their plants was an unconstitutional invasion of their property rights, exposing them to injuries for which monetary damages would afford inadequate compensation. Solicitor General Philip Perlman argued against the injunctions, claiming that the president possessed inherent prerogative power under the circumstances and that his action was not reviewable by the courts. According to Perlman, the president was subject only to the judgment of the people, speaking through impeachment proceedings, or at the polls.

The district court issued a preliminary injunction in favor of the steel companies, restraining Sawyer from continuing the seizures he had undertaken on authority of the executive order. The government appealed the decision to the U.S. Court of Appeals for the District of Columbia. It also petitioned the Supreme Court of the United States for a writ of certiorari, allowed under a federal statute providing for the granting of certiorari prior to judgment by a court of appeals. The Court of Appeals then issued a stay of the district court's order until the Supreme Court could act on the government's petition.

HIGHLIGHTS OF SUPREME COURT ARGUMENTS

BRIEF FOR YOUNGSTOWN SHEET & TUBE

◆ No one challenges the importance of the uninterrupted production of steel. Congress, however, provided a mechanism in the 1947 Labor Management Relations Act for assuring continued production in times of national emergency. The president has not availed himself of this mechanism. His executive order therefore violates the Due Process Clause of the Fifth Amendment.

◆ There is no valid reason for the president's failure to follow the procedure established by Congress, and to adopt instead a procedure that is inconsistent with it. The only justification for the president's action is the theory of unlimited executive power in times of emergency. This theory of "Crown prerogative" was rejected in the American Revolution. The written Constitution of the United States is the American response to the theory.

◆ The taking of private property for public use under the power of eminent domain is a legislative, not executive, power.

◆ Nothing in the Constitution gives the president the executive power he claims. Seizure of the steel mills conflicts with laws enacted by Congress. Courts have held that the president as commander-in-chief has the power to control civilian activity only where an emergency is so imminent and the threat of military danger to the nation so pressing that the slightest delay would lead to disaster. No one contends that those conditions are present in this case.

AMICUS CURIAE BRIEFS SUPPORTING YOUNGSTOWN

The Brotherhood of Locomotive Engineers, the Brotherhood of Locomotive Firemen and Enginemen, and the Order of Railway Conductors.

BRIEF FOR SAWYER

◆ Article II of the Constitution gives the president power to deal with critical emergencies. Section 1 vests the executive power in the president. That section should be read as a grant of all the executive powers of which the government is capable. Unlike a parliamentary form of government, the American system presupposes a vigorous executive. The grave crisis facing the country in the face of the threatened production stoppage in the steel industry demands a strong executive power.

◆ Article II, section 2, which makes the president commander in chief, was specifically invoked by President Truman in issuing his executive order. No one can deny the place of steel at the heart of the defense industry.

◆ Article II, section 3, which directs the president to take care that the laws be faithfully executed, has been given broad scope by the Court in prior decisions. Seizure of the steel mills was implied as part of the president's obligation to carry out the national policy of deterring and repelling aggression.

◆ From the beginning of the republic the president's power to act on a particular occasion has been understood to derive from more than one of the grants contained in Article II. Examples from the Revolution, the War of 1812, and the administrations of Presidents Lincoln, Wilson, and Roosevelt demonstrate the president's broad powers to deal with emergencies.

◆ Nothing in the Labor Management Relations Act precluded the president from taking the action he did. Debates during consideration of the act made it clear that Congress recognized seizure as a routine, acceptable remedy for crises in the collective bargaining field. The mechanism provided for in the statute cannot be read as a prohibition of the action taken by the president in this case.

AMICUS CURIAE BRIEF SUPPORTING SAWYER

United Steelworkers of America.

SUPREME COURT DECISION: 6–3

BLACK, J.

... The President's power, if any, to issue the order must stem either from an act of Congress or from the Constitution itself. There is no statute that expressly authorizes the President to take possession of property as he did here. Nor is there any act of Congress to which our attention has been directed from which such a power can fairly be implied....

Moreover, the use of the seizure technique to solve labor disputes in order to prevent work stoppages was not only unauthorized by any congressional enactment; prior to this controversy, Congress had refused to adopt that method of settling labor disputes. When the Taft-Hartley [Labor Management Relations] Act was under consideration in 1947, Congress rejected an amendment which would have authorized such governmental seizures in cases of emergency. Apparently, it was thought that the technique of seizure, like that of compulsory arbitration, would interfere with the process of collective bargaining. Consequently, the plan Congress adopted in that Act did not provide for seizure under any circumstances. Instead, the plan sought to bring about settlements by use of the customary devices of mediation, conciliation, investigation by boards of inquiry, and public reports. In some instances temporary injunctions were authorized to provide cooling-off periods. All this failing, unions were left free to strike after a secret vote by employees as to whether they wished to accept their employer's final settlement offer.

It is clear that if the President had authority to issue the order he did, it must be found in some provisions of the Constitution. And it is not claimed that express constitutional language grants this power to the President. The contention is that presidential power should be implied from the aggregate of his powers under the Constitution. Particular reliance is placed on provisions of Article II which say that "the executive Power shall be vested in a President..."; that he "shall take Care that the Laws be faithfully executed"; and that he "shall be Commander in Chief of the Army and Navy of the United States."

The order cannot properly be sustained as an exercise of the President's military power as Commander in Chief of the Armed Forces. The Government attempts to do so by citing a number of cases upholding broad powers in military commanders engaged in day-to-day fighting in a theater of war. Such cases need not concern us here. Even though "theater of war" be an expanding concept, we cannot with faithfulness to our constitutional system hold that the Commander in Chief of the Armed Forces has the ultimate power as such to take possession of private property in order to keep labor disputes from stopping production. This is a job for the Nation's lawmakers, not for its military authorities.

Nor can the seizure order be sustained because of the several constitutional provisions that grant executive power to the President. In the framework of our Constitution, the President's power to see that the laws are faithfully executed refutes the idea that he is to be a lawmaker. The Constitution limits his functions in the lawmaking process to the recommending of laws he thinks wise and the vetoing of laws he thinks bad. And the Constitution is neither silent nor equivocal about who shall make laws which the President is to execute. The first section of the first article says that "All legislative Powers herein granted shall be vested in a Congress of the United States...." After granting many powers to the Congress, Article I goes on to provide that Congress may "make all Laws which shall be necessary and proper for carrying into Execution the foregoing Powers and all other Powers vested by this Constitution in the Government of the United States, or in any Department of Officer thereof."

The President's order does not direct that a congressional policy be executed in a manner prescribed by Congress—it directs that a presidential policy be executed in a manner prescribed by the President.... The power of Congress to adopt such public policies as those proclaimed by the order is beyond question.... The Constitution did not subject this law-making power of Congress to presidential or military supervision or control.

It is said that other Presidents without congressional authority have taken possession of private business enterprises in order to settle labor disputes. But even if this be true, Congress has not thereby lost its exclusive constitutional authority to make laws necessary and proper to carry out the powers vested by the Constitution "in the

Government of the United States, or in any Department or Officer thereof."...

The judgment of the District Court is affirmed.

FRANKFURTER, J., CONCURRING

... By the Labor Management Relations Act of 1947, Congress said to the President, "You may not seize. Please report to us and ask for seizure power if you think it is needed in a specific situation." ... The utmost that the Korean conflict may imply is that it may have been desirable to have given the President further authority, a freer hand in these matters. Absence of authority in the President to deal with a crisis does not imply a want of power in the Government. Conversely the fact that power exists in the Government does not vest it in the President. The need for new legislation does not enact it. Nor does it repeal or amend existing law....

DOUGLAS, J., CONCURRING

... The legislative nature of the action taken by the President seems to me to be clear. When the United States takes over an industrial plant to settle a labor controversy, it is condemning property. The seizure of the plant is a taking in the constitutional sense. A permanent taking would amount to the nationalization of the industry. A temporary taking falls short of that goal. But though the seizure is only for a week or a month, the condemnation is complete and the United States must pay compensation for the temporary possession....

The command of the Fifth Amendment is that no "private property be taken for public use, without just compensation." That constitutional requirement has an important bearing on the present case.

The President has no power to raise revenues. That power is in the Congress by Article I, Section 8 of the Constitution. The President might seize and the Congress by subsequent action might ratify the seizure. But until and unless Congress acted, no condemnation would be lawful....

We pay a price for our system of checks and balances, for the distribution of power among the three branches of government. It is a price that today may seem exorbitant to many. Today a kindly President uses the seizure power to effect a wage increase and to keep the steel furnaces in production. Yet tomorrow another President might use the same power to prevent a wage increase, to curb trade-unionists, to regiment labor as oppressively as industry thinks it has been regimented by this seizure.

JACKSON, J., CONCURRING

... A judge, like an executive adviser, may be surprised at the poverty of really useful and unambiguous authority applicable to concrete problems of executive power as they actually present themselves. Just what our forefathers did envision, or would have envisioned had they foreseen modern conditions, must be divined from materials almost as enigmatic as the dreams Joseph was called upon to interpret for Pharaoh. A century and a half of partisan debate and scholarly speculation yields no net result but only supplies more or less apt quotations from respected sources on each side of any question. They largely cancel each other. And court decisions are indecisive because of the judicial practice of dealing with the largest questions in the most narrow way....

Presidential powers are not fixed but fluctuate, depending upon their disjunction or conjunction with those of Congress. We may begin by a somewhat over-simplified grouping of practical situations in which a President may doubt, or others may challenge, his powers, and by distinguishing roughly the legal consequences of this factor of relativity.

1. When the President acts pursuant to an express or implied authorization of Congress, his authority is at its maximum, for it includes all that he possesses in his own right plus all that Congress can delegate. In these circumstances, and in these only, may he be said (for what it is worth), to personify the federal sovereignty. If his act is held unconstitutional under these circumstances, it usually means that the Federal Government as an undivided whole lacks power....

2. When the President acts in absence of either a congressional grant or denial of authority, he can only rely upon his own independent powers, but there is a zone of twilight in which he and Congress may have concurrent authority, or in which its distribution is uncertain. Therefore, congressional inertia, indifference or quiescence may sometimes, at least as a practical matter, enable, if not invite, measures on independent presidential responsibility. In this area, any actual test of power is likely to depend on the imperatives of events and contemporary imponderables rather than on abstract theories of law.

3. When the President takes measures incompatible with the expressed or implied will of Congress, his power is at its lowest ebb, for then he can rely only upon his own constitutional powers minus any constitutional powers of Congress over the matter. Courts can sustain exclusive Presidential control in such a case only by disabling the Congress from acting upon the subject....

Into which of these classifications does this executive seizure of the steel industry fit?...

[T]he current seizure [could] be justified only by the severe tests under the third grouping where it can be supported only by any remainder of executive power after subtraction of such powers as Congress may have over the subject.... Thus, this Court's first review of such seizures occurs under circumstances which leave Presidential power most vulnerable to attack and in the least favorable of possible constitutional postures....

In view of the ease, expedition and safety with which Congress can grant and has granted large emergency powers, certainly ample to embrace this crisis, I am quite unimpressed with the argument that we should affirm possession of them without statute. Such power either has no beginning or it has no end....

But I have no illusion that any decision by this Court can keep power in the hands of Congress if it is not wise and timely in meeting its problems. A crisis that challenges the President equally, or perhaps primarily, challenges Congress....

BURTON, J., CONCURRING

... The present situation is not comparable to that of an imminent invasion or threatened attack. We do not face the issue of what might be the President's constitutional power to meet such cata-strophic situations. Nor is it claimed that the current seizure is in the nature of a military command addressed by the President, as Commander-in-Chief, to a mobilized nation waging, or imminently threatened with, total war.

The controlling fact here is that Congress, within its constitutionally delegated power, has prescribed for the President specific procedures, exclusive of seizure, for his use in meeting the present type of emergency.... Under these circumstances, the President's order of April 8 invaded the jurisdiction of Congress....

CLARK, J., CONCURRING

... [T]he hard fact [is] that neither the Defense Production Act nor Taft-Hartley authorized the seizure challenged here, and the Government made no effort to comply with the procedures established by the Selective Service Act of 1948, a statute which expressly authorizes seizures when producers fail to supply necessary defense material....

VINSON, C.J., REED, AND MINTON, J.J., DISSENTING

... Some members of the Court are of the view that the President is without power to act in time of crisis in the absence of express statutory authorization. Other members of the Court affirm on the basis of their reading of certain statutes. Because we cannot agree that affirmance is proper on any ground, and because of the transcending importance of the questions presented not only in this critical litigation but also to the power of the President and of future Presidents to act in time of crisis, we are compelled to register this dissent....

Those who suggest that this is a case involving extraordinary powers should be mindful that these are extraordinary times. A world not yet recovered from the devastation of World War II has been forced to face the threat of another and more terrifying global conflict....

A review of executive action demonstrates that our Presidents have on many occasions exhibited the leadership contemplated by the Framers when they made the President Commander in Chief, and imposed upon him the trust to "take Care that the Laws be faithfully executed." With or without explicit statutory authorization, Presidents have at such times dealt with national emergencies by acting promptly and resolutely to enforce legislative programs, at least to save those programs until Congress could act. Congress and the courts have responded to such executive initiative with consistent approval....

There is no question that the possession was other than temporary in character and subject to congressional direction—either approving, disapproving or regulating the manner in which the mills were to be administered and returned to the owners. The President immediately informed Congress of his action and clearly stated his intention to abide by the legislative will. No basis for claims of arbitrary action, unlimited powers or dictatorial usurpation of congressional power appears from the facts of this case. On the contrary, judicial, legislative and executive precedents throughout our history demonstrate that in this case the President acted in full conformity with his duties under the Constitution. Accordingly, we would reverse the order of the District Court....

COMMENT

The immediate result of the *Youngstown* decision was to trigger a strike in the steel industry that lasted fifty-three days. However, the shortages predicted by the government never materialized. A government study after the strike explained, "The enormous inventory of steel on hand at the beginning of the strike became a source of amazement to the entire country, a supply which permitted steel-using industries to operate substantially at full levels for nearly two months with new production virtually shut off" (quoted in Maeva Marcus, *Truman and the Steel Seizure Case: The Limits of Presidential Power* [New York, NY: Columbia University Press, 1977], p. 252).

QUESTIONS

1. Does the fact that the prevailing justices delivered their opinions *seriatim* in *Youngstown*, the consequence being that there was no majority opinion, undermine the force of the result in the case? Which opinion is most persuasive? Which would constitutional scholars and advocates be most likely to quote?

2. In *Youngstown* the Court addressed a direct conflict between those who believe that the Constitution imposes limits on the Article II powers of the president, and those who believe that the Constitution creates a strong national executive capable of responding to national emergencies such as the threatened closure of the steel mills. If there had been a congressional declaration of war in the Korean conflict, would the outcome of *Youngstown* have been different? Is it troubling that five justices seemed to interpret congressional silence as congressional disapproval of the president's action?

3. Justice Black's opinion in *Youngstown* emphasizes principles, while Chief Justice Vinson's opinion emphasizes pragmatism. Which consideration should have been given deference in the circumstances posed by *Youngstown*? Are Justice Jackson's analytical categories useful in resolving constitutional problems relating to presidential actions?

4. In addition to the fundamental views of presidential power described in the *Setting* to *Myers v. United States*, three theories have developed along with the office. President William Howard Taft saw executive power as constrained by specific constitutional grants of power. (See William H. Taft, *Our Chief Magistrate and His Powers* [New York, NY: Columbia University Press, 1916].) Theodore Roosevelt subscribed to a "stewardship theory" of the presidency that views the chief executive as having authority to act on behalf of public welfare. (See Theodore Roosevelt, *An Autobiography* [New York, NY: Macmillan, 1913].) Franklin D. Roosevelt adhered to the theory of executive pre-

rogative, under which the president's obligation to the public good might require him to act outside the specific provisions of law.

Which of those theories is most constitutionally defensible?

5. Reread *United States v. Curtiss-Wright Export Corp.* Summarize the nature of presidential power in light of *Curtiss-Wright* and *Youngstown*.

EMERGENCY AND FOREIGN POLICY POWERS

New York Times v. United States
403 U.S. 713 (1971)

SETTING

At least as early as the presidency of John Adams, presidents have relied on emergencies to justify silencing political dissent. Adams and other Federalists, for example, pushed for adoption of the Alien and Sedition Acts of 1798, which sought to punish those who opposed or wrote critically about the government in the face of the threat of war with France. The Sedition Act made it a high misdemeanor for anyone to write, print, or publish "any false, scandalous and malicious writing" against the government of the United States, Congress or the president "with intent to defame ... or to bring them, or either of them, into contempt or disrepute; or to excite against them ... the hatred of the good people of the United States." The Sedition Act led to several seditious libel trials and several of those trials resulted in convictions. No cases under the Sedition Act reached the Supreme Court, however, and the act was allowed to expire when the Federalist Party lost control of the presidency and Congress to Jeffersonian Republicans in 1800.

Nonetheless, the Sedition Act posed serious constitutional problems because of the First Amendment. Federalists had argued that the First Amendment merely incorporated the English common-law guarantee against "prior restraint." Prior restraint occurs when the government requires that publishers obtain government approval before publication. William Blackstone stated the traditional English view of prior restraint in his *Commentaries on the Laws of England*, published in the late 1760s. According to Blackstone, liberty of the press consists "in laying no *previous* restraints on publications...." Significantly, Blackstone conceded that government was authorized to penalize publishers for material they printed.

American revolutionary leaders like Thomas Jefferson were concerned that the threat of postpublication punishment would result in press self-censorship. Taking his cue from one of Blackstone's contemporaries who had criticized Blackstone as "an anti-republican lawyer," Jefferson argued on several occasions that those interested in human liberty would find Blackstone no model. Nevertheless, Blackstone's two-part understanding of press freedom continued to influence American judicial interpretations of the First Amendment throughout most of the nineteenth century.

In 1916, Harvard law professor and First Amendment scholar Zechariah Chafee Jr. renewed the attack on the common law approach to prior restraint. He argued that the Blackstonian formulation was "... wholly out of accord with a common-sense view of the relations of state and citizen," and that a common-sense view would neither bar prior restraint absolutely nor permit publishers to be penalized for exercising freedom of expression.

Nonetheless, not until *Near v. Minnesota*, 283 U.S. 697 (1931), did the Supreme Court, by a 5–4 vote, strike down a statute allowing injunctions to ban publication of any "malicious, scandalous, and defamatory newspaper." Chief Justice Charles Evans Hughes's opinion incorporated the First Amendment's guarantee of press freedom against the states and held that "liberty of the press, historically considered and taken up by the Federal Constitution, has meant, principally, although not exclusively, immunity from previous restraint or censorship...." The Court's ruling did not end debate over the issue of prior restraint, however. Publication of politically sensitive information has remained unpopular with those who wield power.

On June 17, 1967, Secretary of Defense Robert McNamara commissioned a top-secret historical analysis of the U.S. involvement in Indochina. The forty-seven-volume study, *History of the U.S. Decision-Making Process on Vietnam Policy*, became popularly known as the "Pentagon Papers." Its contents were so candid and sensitive that only fifteen copies of the original report were produced.

Daniel Ellsberg, one of the authors of the Pentagon Papers, became so alienated from the government's conduct during the Vietnam War that, in the spring of 1971, he decided to release copies of the papers to the *New York Times* and the *Washington Post* newspapers as an act of resistance. The document was still classified "Top Secret-Sensitive" when Ellsberg released a large portion of it to the press.

The Pentagon Papers appeared at a time when the American public's support for President Nixon and his conduct of the Vietnam War was eroding. A March 1971 poll revealed that Nixon's approval rating had slid to 50 percent. The same poll showed that support for the president's conduct of the war had declined to 34 percent. Another survey found that 51 percent of Americans were persuaded that the war was "morally wrong." In April 1971, massive street protests against the war took place, for the first time spearheaded by Vietnam veterans. After examining the Pentagon Papers for several months and debating whether or not to print them, the *New York Times* commenced installment publication on June 13, 1971. The Nixon administration had asked the *Times* to cease publishing the papers but the newspaper refused. On June 15, the U.S. Department of Justice requested a temporary restraining order to halt further publication by the *Times*. Three days later, the Justice Department requested a temporary restraining order against the *Washington Post*, which had begun publishing the Pentagon Papers on June 18.

In the *New York Times* case, the District Court for the Southern District of New York refused the government's request for a temporary restraining order. The government appealed to the Court of Appeals for the Second Circuit. The appellate court issued a temporary restraining order and remanded the case to the district court for further hearings. The *New York Times* petitioned the Supreme Court for a writ of certiorari.

In the *Washington Post* case, the District Court for the District of Columbia refused to issue a temporary restraining order. On appeal by the government, the Court of Appeals for the District of Columbia temporarily restrained the *Post* from continuing its series and ordered the district court to hear the government's request for an injunction. On remand, the district court refused the government's request for an injunction but extended the restraining order to give the government time to appeal. The Court of Appeals for the District of Columbia affirmed. The government petitioned the Supreme Court for a writ of certiorari.

The Supreme Court agreed to accept both cases on June 25, 1971, and stayed further publication of the Pentagon Papers by the *Times* and the *Post*. It heard arguments the next day.

HIGHLIGHTS OF SUPREME COURT ARGUMENTS

BRIEF FOR *NEW YORK TIMES*

◆ To the extent that exceptions exist to the rule of no prior restraints they are in connection with the redress of individual or private wrongs, not debate over an issue of public policy.

◆ The government rests its claim of inherent authority in this case not on extreme emergency but on ordinary circumstances. The question that looms in the background of this case is whether in extraordinary circumstances of the gravest emergency the president may have inherent authority to act for the public interest, either by proclamation or executive order or by availing himself of judicial process.

◆ If the government's claim to inherent presidential authority cannot stand, its claim must have a statutory basis. None exists in this case. No statutory provisions prohibit the dissemination of sensitive government information.

◆ The Court should define the conditions for applying for an injunction very narrowly so that prior restraint by litigation does not become the government's strategy for restraining or postponing publication of unpopular materials.

AMICUS CURIAE BRIEFS SUPPORTING *NEW YORK TIMES* AND *WASHINGTON POST*

American Civil Liberties Union; National Emergency Civil Liberties Committee; Twenty-seven Members of Congress.

BRIEF FOR THE UNITED STATES

◆ Whatever the classification of the material (whether "top secret" or "secret"), and however the newspapers may have come into possession of it, the First Amendment does not preclude the issuing of an injunction preventing publication. Courts have authorized prior restraints in many situations, including under cease-and-desist orders and in enforcing statutory copyrights.

◆ A court may enjoin a newspaper from publishing material whose disclosure poses a grave and immediate danger to national security. The authority of the Executive Department to protect the nation against publication of information whose disclosure would endanger the national security stems from the constitutional power of the president over the conduct of foreign affairs and his authority as commander in chief.

◆ Congress has recognized the authority of the president to protect the secrecy of information relating to foreign affairs and national defense. The first exception to the Freedom of Information Act is for matters that "are specifically required by Executive order to be kept secret in the interest of the national defense or foreign policy."

SUPREME COURT DECISION

(per curiam)

We granted certiorari ... in these cases in which the United States seeks to enjoin the *New York Times* and the *Washington Post* from publishing the contents of a classified study entitled *History of U.S. Decision-Making Process on Vietnam Policy.*

"Any system of prior restraint of expression comes to this Court bearing a heavy presumption against its constitutional validity." *Bantam Books, Inc. v. Sullivan,* 372 U.S. 58 (1963).... The government "thus carries a heavy burden of showing justification for the imposition of such a restraint." *Organization for a Better Austin v. Keefe,* 402 U.S. 415 (1971).... The District Court for the Southern District of New York in the *New York Times* case ... and the District Court for the District of Columbia and the Court of Appeals for the District of Columbia Circuit ... in the *Washington Post* case held that the Government had not met that burden. We agree.

The judgment of the Court of Appeals for the District of Columbia Circuit is therefore affirmed. The order of the Court of Appeals for the Second circuit is reversed ... and the case is remanded with directions to enter a judgment affirming the judgment of the District Court for the Southern District of New York. The stays entered June 25, 1971, by the Court are vacated. The judgments shall issue forthwith.

So ordered.

BLACK AND DOUGLAS, J.J., CONCURRING

... In seeking injunctions against these newspapers and in its presentation to the Court, the Executive Branch seems to have forgotten the essential purpose and history of the First Amendment. When the Constitution was adopted, many people strongly opposed it because the document contained no Bill of Rights to safeguard certain basic freedoms. They especially feared that the new powers granted to a central government might be interpreted to permit the government to curtail freedom of religion, press, assembly, and speech.... The Bill of Rights changed the original Constitution into a new charter under which no branch of government could abridge the people's freedoms of press, speech, religion, and assembly. Yet the Solicitor General argues and some members of the Court appear to agree that the general powers of the Government adopted in the original Constitution should be interpreted to limit and restrict the specific and emphatic guarantees of the Bill of Rights adopted later. I can imagine no greater perversion of history....

In the First Amendment the Founding Fathers gave the free press the protection it must have to fulfill its essential role in our democracy.... In my view, far from deserving condemnation for their courageous reporting, the *New York Times*, the *Washington Post*, and other newspapers should be commended for serving the purpose that the Founding Fathers saw so clearly. In revealing the workings of government that led to the Viet Nam war, the newspapers nobly did precisely that which the Founders hoped and trusted they would do....

[W]e are asked to hold that despite the First Amendment's emphatic command, the Executive Branch, the Congress, and the Judiciary can make laws enjoining publication of current news and abridging freedom of the press in the name of "national security." The Government does not even attempt to rely on any act of Congress. Instead it makes the bold and dangerously far-reaching contention that the courts should take it upon themselves to "make" a law abridging freedom of the press in the name of equity, presidential power and national security, even when the representative of the people in Congress have adhered to the command of the First Amendment and refused to make such a law.... To find that the President has "inherent power" to halt the publication of news by resort to the courts would wipe out the First Amendment and destroy the fundamental liberty and security of the very people the Government hopes to make "secure."...

DOUGLAS AND BLACK, J.J., CONCURRING [OMITTED]

BRENNAN, J., CONCURRING

... I write separately in these cases only to emphasize what should be apparent: that our judgment in the present cases may not be taken to indicate the propriety, in the future, of issuing temporary stays and restraining orders to block the publication of material sought to be suppressed by the Government.... [E]ven if it be assumed that some of the interim restraints were proper in the two cases before us, that assumption has no bearing upon the propriety of similar judicial action in the future. To begin with, there has now been ample time for reflection and judgment; whatever values there may be in the preservation of novel questions for appellate review may not support any restraints in the future. More important, the First Amendment stands as an absolute bar to the imposition of judicial restraints in circumstances of the kind presented by these cases....

Our cases, it is true, have indicated that there is a single, extremely narrow class of cases in which the First

Amendment's ban on prior judicial restraint may be overridden. Our cases have thus far indicated that such cases may arise only when the Nation "is at war." *Schenck v. United States*, 294 U.S. 47 (1919)....

Unless and until the Government has clearly made out its case, the First Amendment commands that no injunction may issue.

STEWART AND WHITE, J.J., CONCURRING

In the governmental structure created by our Constitution, the Executive is endowed with enormous power in the two related areas of national defense and international relations. This power, largely unchecked by the Legislative and Judicial branches, has been pressed to the very hilt since the advent of the nuclear missile age. For better or worse, the simple fact is that a President of the United States possesses vastly greater constitutional independence in these two vital areas of power than does, say, a prime minister of a country with a parliamentary form of government.

In the absence of the governmental checks and balances present in other areas of our national life, the only effective restraint upon executive policy and power in the areas of national defense and international affairs may lie in an enlightened citizenry—in an informed and critical public opinion which alone can here protect the values of democratic government. For this reason, it is perhaps here that a press that is alert, aware, and free most vitally serves the basic purpose of the First Amendment. For without an informed and free press there cannot be an enlightened people.

Yet it is elementary that the successful conduct of international diplomacy and the maintenance of an effective national defense requires both confidentiality and secrecy. Other nations can hardly deal with this Nation in an atmosphere of mutual trust unless they can be assured that their confidences will be kept. And within our own executive departments, the development of considered and intelligent international policies would be impossible if those charged with their formulation could not communicate with each other freely, frankly, and in confidence. In the area of basic national defense the frequent need for absolute secrecy is, of course, self-evident.

I think there can be but one answer to this dilemma, if dilemma it be. The responsibility must be where the power is. If the Constitution gives the Executive a large degree of unshared power in the conduct of foreign affairs and the maintenance of our national defense, then under the Constitution the Executive must have the largely unshared duty to determine and preserve the degree of internal security necessary to exercise that power successfully....

[I]n the cases before us we are asked neither to construe specific regulations nor to apply specific laws. We are asked, instead, to perform a function that the Constitution gave to the Executive, not the Judiciary. We are asked, quite simply, to prevent the publication by two newspapers that the Executive Branch insists should not, in the national interest, be published. I am convinced that the Executive is correct with respect to some of the documents involved. But I cannot say that disclosure of any of them will surely result in direct, immediate, and irreparable damage to our Nation or its people. That being so, there can under the First Amendment be but one judicial resolution to the issues before us. I join the judgments of the Court.

WHITE AND STEWART, J.J., CONCURRING

... [A]fter examining the materials the Government characterizes as the most sensitive and destructive [I cannot] deny that revelation of these documents will do substantial damage to public interests. Indeed, I am confident that their disclosure will have that result....

Prior restraints require an unusually heavy justification under the First Amendment; but failure by the Government to justify prior restraints does not measure its constitutional entitlement to a conviction for criminal publication. That the Government mistakenly chose to proceed by injunction does not mean that it could not successfully proceed in another way....

[T]he newspapers are presumably now on full notice of the position of the United States and must face the consequences if they publish. I would have no difficulty in sustaining convictions under [the Espionage Act of 1917 and the U.S. criminal code] on facts that would not justify the intervention of equity and the imposition of a prior restraint....

MARSHALL, J., CONCURRING

... The problem here is whether in these particular cases the Executive Branch has authority to invoke the equity jurisdiction of the courts to protect what it believes to be the national interest....

It would ... be utterly inconsistent with the concept of separation of powers for this Court to use its power of contempt to prevent behavior that Congress has specifically declined to prohibit. There would be a similar damage to the basic concept of these co-equal branches of Government if when the Executive Branch has adequate authority granted by Congress to protect "national security" it can choose instead to invoke the contempt power of a court to enjoin the threatened conduct. The Constitution provides that Congress shall make laws, the President execute laws, and courts interpret laws. It did not provide for government by injunction in which the courts and the Executive Branch can "make law" without regard to the action of Congress....

Even if it is determined that the Government could not in good faith bring prosecutions against the *New York Times* and the *Washington Post*, it is clear that Congress has specifically rejected passing legislation that would have clearly given the President the power he seeks here and made the current activity of the newspapers unlawful. When Congress specifically declines to make conduct unlawful it is not for the Court to redecide those issues—to overrule Congress. See *Youngstown Sheet & Tube v. Sawyer*....

Either the Government has the power under statutory grant to use traditional criminal law to protect the country or, if there is no basis for arguing that Congress has made the activity a crime, it is plain that Congress has specifically refused to grant the authority the Government seeks from this Court. In either case this Court does not have authority to grant the requested relief. It is not for this Court to fling itself into every breach perceived by some Government official nor is it for this Court to take on itself the burden of enacting law, especially a law that Congress has refused to pass....

BURGER, C.J., DISSENTING [OMITTED]

HARLAN AND BLACKMUN, J.J., AND
BURGER, C.J., DISSENTING

These cases forcefully call to mind the wise admonitions of Mr. Justice Holmes dissenting in *Northern Securities Co. v. United States*, 193 U.S. 197 (1904): "Great cases, like hard cases, make bad law. For great cases are called great, not by reason of their real importance in shaping the law of the future, but because of some accident of immediate overwhelming interest which appeals to the feelings and distorts the judgment.". . With all respect, I consider that the Court has been almost irresponsibly feverish in dealing with these cases....

Due regard for the extraordinarily important and difficult questions involved in these litigations should have led the Court to shun such a precipitate timetable. In order to decide the merits of these cases properly, some or all of the following questions should have been faced:

1. Whether the Attorney General is authorized to bring these suits in the name of the United States....

2. Whether the First Amendment permits the federal courts to enjoin publication of stories which would present a serious threat to national security....

3. Whether the threat to publish highly secret documents is of itself a sufficient implication of national security to justify an injunction on the theory that regardless of the contents of the documents harm enough results simply from the demonstration of such a breach of secrecy.

4. Whether the unauthorized disclosure of any of these particular documents would seriously impair the national security.

5. What weight should be given to the opinion of high officers in the Executive Branch of the Government with respect to questions 3 and 4.

6. Whether the newspapers are entitled to retain and use the documents notwithstanding the seemingly uncontested facts that the documents, or the originals of which they are duplicates, were purloined from the Government's possession and that the newspapers received them with the knowledge that they had been feloniously acquired....

7. Whether the threatened harm to the national security or the Government's possessory interest in the documents justifies the issuance of an injunction against publication in light of—

a. The strong First Amendment policy against prior restraints on publication;

b. The doctrine against enjoining conduct in violation of criminal statutes; and

c. The extent to which the materials at issue have apparently already been otherwise disseminated.

These are difficult questions of fact, of law, and of judgment; the potential consequences of erroneous decision are enormous. The time which has been available to us, to the lower courts, and to the parties has been wholly inadequate for giving these cases the kind of consideration they deserve....

Forced as I am to reach the merits of these cases, I dissent from the opinion and judgments of the Court....

BLACKMUN, J., DISSENTING

... I hope that damage already has not been done [resulting from publication of these papers]. If, however, damage has been done, and if, with the Court's action today, these newspapers proceed to publish the critical documents and there results therefrom "the death of soldiers, the destruction of alliances, the greatly increased difficulty of negotiations with our enemies, the inability of our diplomats to negotiate," to which list I might add the factors of prolongation of the war and of further delay in the freeing of United States prisoners, then the Nation's people will know where the responsibility for these sad consequences rests.

QUESTIONS

1. In the aftermath of the *New York Times* decision, describe the president's authority to protect national security using prior restraint. Under what set of circumstances, if any, would a majority of the justices have upheld the government's censorship attempt in the *New York Times* case?

2. A mere seventeen days elapsed between publication of the first installment of the *Pentagon Papers* in the *New York Times* and the Supreme Court's decision in *New York Times*. Is Justice Harlan correct that the Court was "irresponsibly feverish" in dealing with the *New York Times* decision? Is a hidden premise of his opinion that the president should be virtually unfettered in his role as guardian of the national security?

3. Are there parallels between the Court's decisions in *Youngstown Sheet & Tube* and *New York Times*? Do the cases suggest that the Court is retreating from its decision in *Curtiss-Wright* or are the cases distinguishable on their facts?

4. In a February 15, 1989, *Washington Post* article entitled "Secrets Not Worth Keeping," Erwin N. Griswold, who had argued the government's case against the *New York Times* and the *Washington Post* as solicitor general, wrote that "the principal concern of the classifiers is not with national security, but rather with governmental embarrassment of one sort or another." Is there any situation where avoiding embarrassment to the president might justify limiting publication of information?

5. In *Snepp v. United States*, 444 U.S. 507 (1980), the Court upheld the right of the Central Intelligence Agency (CIA) to require its employees to sign secrecy agreements promising not to publish information about the agency without the Director's prior approval. In 1977, former CIA agent Frank Snepp wrote *Decent Interval: An Insider's Account of Saigon's Indecent End* (New York, NY: Random House, 1977). The book painted a highly critical picture of the last days of American involvement in Vietnam but it contained no classified information. Nevertheless, the Supreme Court held that Snepp had violated his position of trust and had caused the United States irreparable harm. The Court ordered him to "disgorge the benefits of his

faithlessness" by forfeiting all present and future profits from the book to the government and to submit all future writings to the CIA for its approval. Compare *CIA v. Simms*, 471 U.S. 159 (1985), in which the Court held that Congress has given the CIA a broad statutory exemption from disclosing information under the Freedom of Information Act.

Do these cases suggest a resurgence of judicial deference to the executive branch? Or are they better understood as judicial reluctance to enforce the First Amendment's guarantees of free speech and press in the context of national security?

EMERGENCY AND FOREIGN POLICY POWERS

United States v. United States District Court
407 U.S. 297 (1972)

SETTING

In April 1969, the United States had more than 543,000 troops in Vietnam. Although never a declared war, the Vietnam conflict had been going on since the 1950s as the United States and other nations sharing a cold war commitment to rooting out communism in Asia battled against North Vietnamese communist forces. By the early 1960s, there was growing sentiment in the United States that the war in Vietnam could not be won. Some believed that the war had been a mistake in the first place, while others believed that the government had lied to Americans about the purposes and costs of the war, which eventually left more than 58,000 Americans dead, 304,000 wounded, and carried a price tag of some $110 billion.

Opposition to the Vietnam war became violent in 1969, especially among college and university student protesters, and the following year was marked by civil unrest throughout the country. In response to the unrest, President Richard Nixon claimed authority to use electronic surveillance to monitor American citizens if the Justice Department believed that those citizens were involved in "subversive" activities associated with Vietnam protests. According to the president, because the nation's security was at stake, he was not bound by the requirement of the Fourth Amendment to the Constitution that requires a judicial magistrate to issue a search warrant based on probable cause before the government engages in electronic surveillance.

One of the targets of anti-Vietnam protestors was the Central Intelligence

Agency (CIA). On October 7, an office of the CIA in Ann Arbor, Michigan, was dynamited. Soon after the Ann Arbor bombing, Lawrence Plamondon, John Sinclair, and John Forrest were indicted by a federal grand jury in the Eastern District of Michigan for the crime of conspiracy to destroy U.S. government property in association with that bombing. Plamondon (but not Sinclair or Forrest) also was indicted for the crime of destruction of government property for actually detonating the bomb. All three pleaded not guilty to the crimes.

On October 5, 1970, Plamondon, Sinclair, and Forrest filed pretrial motions to compel the United States to disclose "any and all logs, records, and memoranda of any electronic or other surveillance directed at any of the defendants herein or at unindicted co-conspirator herein...." that the government intended to offer at trial. The government acknowledged that its agents had overheard conversations that had involved Plamondon and admitted that Attorney General John Mitchell had ordered electronic surveillance (wiretaps) "to gather intelligence information deemed necessary to protect the nation for attempts of domestic organizations to attack and subvert the existing structure of the Government." The government offered to file the logs of the surveillance with the trial judge for his *in camera* (in chambers, in secret) inspection. However, the government argued that its warrantless wiretaps were authorized on one of two grounds: by Title III of the Omnibus Crime Control and Safe Streets Act of 1968 or by the president's inherent power to secure the intelligence necessary to preserve the national security.

The trial court rejected the government's argument. It held that the surveillance of Plamondon violated the Fourth Amendment and ordered the government to make full disclosure to Plamondon of the conversations that had been overheard illegally.

Because the trial court's pretrial order was neither final nor appealable, the United States petitioned the U.S. Court of Appeals for the Sixth Circuit to issue a writ of mandamus instructing the trial court to set aside its order. The appellate court refused to issue the writ. It held that the trial court was correct that the government surveillance violated the Fourth Amendment's prohibition against unreasonable searches and seizures and that the proper remedy for the violation was disclosure to Plamondon of the overheard conversations. The Supreme Court granted the U.S. petition for a writ of certiorari.

HIGHLIGHTS OF SUPREME COURT ARGUMENTS

BRIEF FOR THE UNITED STATES

◆ The Fourth Amendment prohibits only unreasonable warrantless searches. Determining whether a particular search is reasonable requires balancing the need to search against the invasion that the search entails.

◆ The president, as chief executive, is responsible for assuring that our system of government is viable and for safeguarding it against overthrow by unlawful means. For the past thirty years presidents have authorized electronic surveillance in national security cases without a warrant.

◆ In order to obtain a warrant in national security cases, the government would have to disclose sensitive and highly secret information, which would significantly reduce the chances of the surveillance being effective.

◆ If national security surveillance without a warrant is unlawful, automatic disclosure nonetheless should not be required. In *Alderman v. United States*, 394 U.S. 165 (1969), the Court ruled that conversations overheard by illegal surveillance, to which defendants have standing to object, must be disclosed for the purpose of an adversary hearing on relevance. That holding should be modified to permit a trial court to make an initial *in camera* determination whether the information obtained by the surveillance is arguably relevant to a prosecution before turning the material over to a defendant.

BRIEF FOR UNITED STATES DISTRICT COURT

◆ This case is controlled by *Katz v. United States*, 389 U.S. 347 (1967), which held that searches conducted without prior approval by a judge or magistrate are *per se* unreasonable under the Fourth Amendment, subject only to a few well-delineated exceptions. None of the exceptions applies here.

◆ In this case, the government bears a heavy burden to justify creating a new exception to the warrant requirement. Its burden is to show both the need for the search, and the need to search without benefit of a warrant.

◆ Whatever power the president may have to use warrantless electronic surveillance with respect to foreign powers cannot be invoked to support a domestic search. Special powers in foreign affairs are recognized only where domestic rights can be protected.

BRIEF FOR PLAMONDON, SINCLAIR, AND FORREST

◆ The government seeks this Court's approval for the power to engage in wholesale wiretapping of American citizens without regard for the commands of the Fourth Amendment.

◆ The "standard" that the attorney general has used to exercise vast power in this case—"attempts of domestic organizations to attack and subvert the existing structure of the Government"—fails to meet the most elementary tests of the Fourth Amendment as to precision and particularity.

◆ The Court should not retreat from its recent holding in *Alderman*.

AMICUS CURIAE BRIEFS SUPPORTING THE DISTRICT COURT AND DEFENDANTS PLAMONDON, SINCLAIR, AND FORREST

American Civil Liberties Union of Michigan; International Union, United Automobile, Aerospace and Agricultural Implement Workers of America (UAW).

SUPREME COURT DECISION: 8–0

(Rehnquist, J., did not participate.)

POWELL, J.

[The Court first considered and rejected the government's argument that the warrantless surveillance of Plamondon was authorized by Title III of the Omnibus Crime Control and Safe Streets Act of 1968.]

... [This] case requires no judgment on the scope of the President's surveillance power with respect to the activities of foreign powers, within or without his country. The Attorney General's affidavit in this case states that the surveillance were "deemed necessary to protect the nation from attempts of *domestic organizations* to attack and subvert the existing structure of Government (emphasis supplied). There is no evidence of any involvement, directly, or indirectly, of a foreign power....

Our present inquiry, though important, is therefore a narrow one. It addresses a question left open by *Katz v. United States*, 389 U.S. 347 (1967):

Whether safeguards other than prior authorization by a magistrate would satisfy the Fourth Amendment in a situation involving the national security.

The determination of this question requires the essential Fourth Amendment inquiry into the "reasonableness" of the search and seizure in question, and the way in which that "reasonableness" derives content and meaning through reference to the warrant clause....

Our decision in *Katz* refused to lock the Fourth Amendment into instances of actual physical trespass. Rather, the Amendment governs "not only the seizure of tangible items, but extends as well to the recording of oral statements ... without any technical trespass under ... local property law." That decision implicitly recognized that the broad and unsuspected governmental incursions into conversational privacy which electronic surveillance entails necessitate the application of Fourth Amendment safeguards.

National security cases, moreover, often reflect a convergence of First and Fourth Amendment values not present in cases of "ordinary" crime. Though the investigative duty of the executive may be stronger in such cases, so also is there greater jeopardy to constitutionally protected speech....

The price of lawful public dissent must not be a dread of subjection to an unchecked surveillance power. Nor must the fear of unauthorized official eavesdropping deter vigorous citizen dissent and discussion of Government action in private conversation. For private dissent, no less than open public discourse, is essential to our free society.

As the Fourth Amendment is not absolute in its terms, our task is to examine and balance the basic values at stake in this case: the duty of Government to protect the domestic security, and the potential danger posed by unreasonable surveillance to individual privacy and free expression. If the legitimate need of Government to safeguard domestic security requires the use of electronic surveillance, the question is whether the needs of citizens for privacy and the free expression may not be better protected by requiring a warrant before such surveillance is undertaken. We must also ask whether a warrant requirement would unduly frustrate the efforts of Government to protect itself from acts of subversion and overthrow directed against it.

Though the Fourth Amendment speaks broadly of "unreasonable searches and seizures," the definition of "reasonableness" turns, at least in part, on the more specific commands of the warrant clause....

Fourth Amendment freedoms cannot properly be guaranteed if domestic security surveillance may be conducted solely within the discretion of the Executive Branch. The Fourth Amendment does not contemplate the executive officers of Government as neutral and disinterested magistrates. Their duty and responsibility are to enforce the laws, to investigate, and to prosecute. But those charged with this investigative and prosecutorial duty should not be the sole judges of when to utilize constitutionally sensitive means in pursuing their tasks. The historical judgment, which the Fourth Amendment accepts, is that unreviewed executive discretion may yield too readily to pressures to obtain incriminating evidence and overlook potential invasions of privacy and protected speech....

The Fourth Amendment contemplates a prior judicial judgment, not the risk that executive discretion may be reasonably exercised. This judicial role accords with our basic constitutional doctrine that individual freedoms will best be preserved through a separation of powers and division of functions among the different branches and levels of Government.... The independent check upon executive discretion is not

satisfied, as the Government argues, by "extremely limited" post-surveillance judicial review. Indeed, post-surveillance review would never reach the surveillance which failed to result in prosecutions. Prior review by a neutral and detached magistrate is the time-tested means of effectuating Fourth Amendment rights.

It is true that there have been some exceptions to the warrant requirement.... But those exceptions are few in number and carefully delineated; in general, they serve the legitimate needs of law enforcement officers to protect their own well-being and preserve evidence from destruction. Even while carving out those exceptions, the Court has reaffirmed the principle that the "police must, whenever practicable, obtain advance judicial approval of searches and seizures through the warrant procedure." *Terry v. Ohio*, 392 U.S. 1 (1968).

The Government argues that the special circumstances applicable to domestic security surveillance necessitate a further exception to the warrant requirement. It is urged that the requirement of prior judicial review would obstruct the President in the discharge of his constitutional duty to protect domestic security. We are told further that these surveillance are directed primarily to the collecting and maintaining of intelligence with respect to subversive forces, and are not an attempt to gather evidence for specific criminal prosecutions. It is said that this type of surveillance should not be subject to traditional warrant requirements which were established to govern investigation of criminal activity, not ongoing intelligence gathering.

The Government further insists that courts "as a practical matter would have neither the knowledge nor the techniques necessary to determine whether there was probable cause to believe that surveillance was necessary to protect national security." These security problems, the Government contends, involve "a large number of complex and subtle factors" beyond the competence of courts to evaluate.

As a final reason for exemption from a warrant requirement, the Government believes that disclosure to a magistrate of all or even a significant portion of the information involved in domestic security surveillance "would create serious potential dangers to the national security and to the lives of informants and agents.... Secrecy is the essential ingredient in intelligence gathering; requiring prior judicial authorization would create a greater danger of leaks ... because in addition to the judge, you have the clerk, the stenographer and some other officer like a law assistant or bailiff who may be apprised of the nature of the surveillance."

These contentions in behalf of a complete exemption from the warrant requirement, when urged on behalf of the President and the national security in its domestic implications, merit the most careful consideration. We certainly do not reject them lightly, especially at a time of worldwide ferment and when civil disorders in this country are more prevalent than in the less turbulent periods of our history. There is, no doubt, pragmatic force to the Government's position.

But we do not think a case has been made for the requested departure from Fourth Amendment standards. The circumstances described do not justify complete exemption of domestic security surveillance from prior judicial

scrutiny. Official surveillance, whether its purpose be criminal investigation or ongoing intelligence gathering, risks infringement of constitutionally protected privacy of speech. Security surveillance are especially sensitive because of the inherent vagueness of the domestic security concept, the necessarily broad and continuing nature of intelligence gathering, and the temptation to utilize such surveillance to oversee political dissent. We recognize, as we have before, the constitutional basis of the President's domestic security role, but we think it must be exercised in a manner compatible with the Fourth Amendment. In this case we hold that this requires an appropriate prior warrant procedure.

We cannot accept the Government's argument that internal security matters are too subtle and complex for judicial evaluation. Courts regularly deal with the most difficult issues of our society. There is no reason to believe that federal judges will be insensitive to or uncomprehending of the issues involved in domestic security cases. Certainly courts can recognize that domestic security surveillance involves different considerations from the surveillance of "ordinary crime." If the threat is too subtle or complex for our senior law enforcement officers to convey its significance to a court, one may question whether there is probable cause for surveillance.

Nor do we believe prior judicial approval will fracture the secrecy essential to official intelligence gathering. The investigation of criminal activity has long involved imparting sensitive information to judicial officers who have respected the confidentialities involved. Judges may be counted upon to be espe-

cially conscious of security requirements in national security cases....

As the surveillance of Plamondon's
conversations was unlawful, because
conducted without prior judicial
approval, the courts below correctly
held that *Alderman v. United States*, 394
U.S. 165 (1969), is controlling and that it

requires disclosure to the accused of
his own impermissibly intercepted conversations.

The judgment of the Court of Appeals
is hereby affirmed.

Affirmed.

DOUGLAS, J., CONCURRING [OMITTED]

QUESTIONS

1. Is there evidence in Justice Powell's opinion that the result in *United
   States District Court* might have been different under a different set of
   facts? Under what set of facts might the government's warrantless
   wiretaps have been upheld as constitutional?

2. In what respect is *United States District Court* a victory for the judicial
   branch as much as a defeat for the executive branch? Reread *United
   States v. Nixon*. With respect to the issue of executive versus judicial
   power, are the two opinions similar?

3. In the summer of 1967, President Lyndon Johnson, acting pursuant to
   a federal statute, sent federal troops to Detroit, Michigan, to assist
   local authorities in quelling the riots that broke out after the assassination of civil rights leader Dr. Martin Luther King Jr. That experience convinced army authorities that it needed a data-gathering system to help it prepare to respond to civil unrest. The army
   subsequently put into operation a program of collecting information
   about public activities that might have the potential for civil disorder. The primary source of information for the data bank it created
   at Fort Holabird, Maryland, was the news media and publications in
   general circulation. Other information came from reports of army
   agents who attended public meetings and from information provided
   by local law enforcement agencies. By the early 1970s, Congress
   became concerned about the scope of the army's domestic surveillance system and held hearings, which resulted in the army destroying a considerable amount of the information in the data bank.
   Nonetheless, Arlo Tatum and others filed a class action suit against
   Secretary of Defense Melvin Laird claiming that the existence of even
   a limited surveillance system by the army had a chilling effect on the
   exercise of their First Amendment freedoms, that maintenance of the
   surveillance system was not an appropriate activity for the army,
   and that the army might misuse the information in the future.

   In *Laird v. Tatum*, 408 U.S. 1 (1972), the Supreme Court ruled 5–4
   that the suit did not present a justiciable controversy and that
   Tatum and the other plaintiffs had not established the requisite

standing to sue because they had alleged no actual harm, merely a "subjective chill" on the exercise of their First Amendment rights.

Is the Court's decision in *Laird* consistent with its decision in *United States District Court?* Identify a set of facts that might have persuaded the Supreme Court to reach the merits in *Laird*. Does *United States District Court* provide a hint about how the justices might have ruled in *Laird* if the plaintiffs had presented a justiciable controversy?

4. The brief for the UAW in *United States District Court* stated:

> The UAW and its members know from bitter experience what it is to be spied upon. In the not-too-distant past, political and economic opponents were labeling the UAW "subversive," "dangerous" and "a threat to national security;" then using these labels as an excuse to ride roughshod over our precious civil liberties.... Present officers of the UAW have lived through surveillance and other denials of their basic rights. They know full well that the activities of the Justice Department in this case have a chilling effect on the First Amendment rights of the members of the UAW. We submit that we are in a position to help this Court more realistically to evaluate the true dangers of the government's position. And we fear that, unless those dangers are fully appreciated, the UAW and Americans generally may yet be forced to repeat some of the saddest chapters in this nation's history.

If the Supreme Court had agreed with the government in *United States District Court*, what contemporary groups or organizations might be subject to surveillance today? Would it make any difference whether the governmental surveillance of those groups was justified on grounds of foreign policy, national security, or emergency powers?

COMMENTS

1. On June 17, 1972, two days before the Court issued its opinion in *United States District Court*, five men were arrested for breaking and entering at the Democratic National Committee Headquarters located in the Watergate housing and office complex in Washington, D.C. They were attempting to plant electronic surveillance devices. Their arrest was an early episode in what came to be known as "Watergate," which led to the Court's decision in *United States v. Nixon* and eventually resulted in President Nixon's resignation on August 9, 1974.

2. In 1978, Congress adopted the Foreign Intelligence Surveillance Act. The act reaffirmed the ruling in *United States District Court* that federal agents cannot undertake warrantless surveillance and wiretapping without prior judicial approval and that agents seeking a warrant must produce evidence of criminal activity.

EMERGENCY AND FOREIGN POLICY POWERS

Dames and Moore v. Regan
453 U.S. 654 (1981)

SETTING

On February 1, 1979, the Shiite Muslim leader Ayatollah Ruholla Khomeini returned to Teheran, Iran, after fifteen years in exile. After ten days of fighting with government troops, backers of the Ayatollah drove Shah Mohammed Reza Pahlevi from power. Thousands were killed in the months of rioting that followed and many supporters of the Shah were killed in mass executions. Khomeini and other Iranian leaders labeled the United States "The Great Satan." Among their grievances was the fact that the U.S. Central Intelligence Agency had staged a 1953 coup against the elected government of Iran, restoring the Shah to power and shipping over $19 billion worth of arms to the Shah's military between 1973 and 1978.

The deposed Shah fled to Morocco, then to the Bahamas and to Mexico. On October 22, 1979, the Shah was permitted to enter the United States at the insistence of Secretary of State Henry Kissinger and Chase Manhattan bank president David Rockefeller. Ill with cancer, the Shah was immediately hospitalized in New York. The U.S. ambassador in Teheran had warned against admitting the Shah to the United States, predicting that doing so would foment more civil discord and increase Iranian hatred of Americans.

The ambassador's fears proved correct. On November 4, 1979, Iranian students seized the U.S. Embassy in Teheran and took as hostages the sixty-six embassy personnel in the compound. The students demanded that the United States return the Shah to Iran to stand trial. A few days later, at the order of Ayatollah Khomeini, the students released five women, eight black people and one very ill hostage.

Following the seizure of the embassy, President Jimmy Carter undertook massive diplomatic and economic efforts to win the release of the hostages. The president suspended oil imports from Iran, expelled all 183 Iranian diplomats from the United States, and began to impose other economic sanctions. One of the economic measures was to freeze Iranian assets in the United States. On November 14, 1979, acting under the authority of the International Emergency Economic Powers Act (IEEPA), Carter declared a national emergency and blocked the removal or transfer of all Iranian property subject to U.S. jurisdiction. He declared:

> The President has today acted to block all official Iranian assets in the United States, including deposits in United States banks and their foreign branches and subsidiaries. This order is in response to reports that the

> Government of Iran is about to withdraw its funds. The purpose of this order is to ensure that claims on Iran by the United States and its citizens are provided for in an orderly manner.

The President then authorized a limited number of judicial proceedings, including prejudgment attachments, against Iran, but did not allow the entry of any judgment or decree.

On December 19, 1979, Dames and Moore, a partnership, filed suit in the U.S. District Court for the Central District of California against the government of Iran, the Atomic Energy Organization of Iran (AEOI), and a number of Iranian banks that, according to Dames and Moore, had been nationalized by the government of Iran. Its complaint alleged that it was under contract with the AEOI to conduct site studies for a proposed nuclear power plant in Iran. The AEOI eventually canceled the contract, but Dames and Moore contended that the AEOI owed it $3,436,694.30 for services it had performed under the contract before cancellation.

In February 1981, the district court granted Dames and Moore's motion for summary judgment against AEOI and the government of Iran for the full amount, plus interest. It issued orders of attachment against the defendants' property to secure the judgment.

In January 1981, during his last days in office, President Carter negotiated with the government of Iran an executive agreement known as the "Algerian Declarations." Under the declarations, the president agreed to terminate legal proceedings in American courts involving claims by American nationals against Iran, to nullify attachments against Iranian property entered by American courts to secure judgments against Iran, and to transfer those claims from American courts to an arbitration tribunal called the Iran-United States Claims Tribunal. In return, the government of Iran agreed to release the hostages. On January 20, 1981, President Carter implemented the Algerian Declarations through a series of Executive Orders and Treasury Department regulations.

In response to the president's actions, the district court stayed execution of the judgment against the Iranian defendants that it previously had granted to Dames and Moore. Dames and Moore then filed suit against Secretary of the Treasury Donald Regan for declaratory and injunctive relief to prevent enforcement of the Executive Orders and Treasury Department regulations in a way that would adversely affect its action against the Iranian defendants for breach of contract. The district court dismissed the motion for failure to state a claim. Dames and Moore appealed to the U.S. Circuit Court of Appeals for the Ninth Circuit. The district court then entered an injunction pending appeal, to prevent the U.S. government from transferring any Iranian property in the United States (estimated to be over $4 billion) that was subject to any writ of attachment, garnishment, judgment, levy, or lien issued in any court in favor of Dames and Moore. Dames and Moore and the U.S. government both petitioned the Supreme Court of the United States for a writ of certiorari before judgment. The government of Iran filed a motion to intervene, also urging the Supreme Court to issue a writ of certiorari even though the Ninth Circuit Court of Appeals had not yet entered judgment in the case.

HIGHLIGHTS OF SUPREME COURT ARGUMENTS

BRIEF FOR DAMES AND MOORE

◆ The president's actions have extinguished statutory rights of American citizens to litigate in U.S. courts commercial claims against a foreign state and its instrumentalities. They have also nullified judicial liens securing commercial claims. No such presidential action is authorized by the IEEPA.

◆ When Congress enacted the Foreign Sovereign Immunities Act, pursuant to its Article I powers, it removed the president from his role in the resolution of commercial claims by U.S. citizens against foreign states.

◆ The president lacks inherent authority to settle or remove Americans' enforceable claims that are properly before courts created under Article III of the Constitution.

◆ The IEEPA does not authorize the president to permanently transfer foreign property away from American creditors and back to a hostile power.

◆ Even if the president's acts were authorized, they have the consequence of taking private property for a public purpose. Under the Fifth Amendment, Dames and Moore is entitled to reasonable compensation.

BRIEF FOR THE UNITED STATES

◆ The president's actions were clearly authorized by the language of the IEEPA. That statute authorizes him to "regulate, direct and compel, nullify, void, prevent or prohibit, any … transfer" with respect to foreign property when he has declared a national emergency. The only issue in this case is the extent and nature of the president's powers under the IEEPA in situations where the act has been properly invoked.

◆ The president's actions do not infringe on the jurisdiction of the courts. The president's actions, taken in conjunction with Congressional authorization, effect a substantive change in the law that courts in the proper exercise of their jurisdiction are obliged to follow.

◆ Dames and Moore's Fifth Amendment argument is premature. It is entirely possible that the Claims Tribunal will afford them complete relief.

SUPREME COURT DECISION: 8–1

REHNQUIST, J.

The questions presented by this case touch fundamentally upon the manner in which our Republic is to be governed. Throughout the nearly two centuries of our Nation's existence under the Constitution, this subject has generated considerable debate….

Our decision today will not dramatically alter this situation, for the Framers "did not make the judiciary the overseer of our government." *Youngstown Sheet & Tube v. Sawyer* (Frankfurter, J., concurring). We are confined to a resolution of the dispute presented to us. That dispute involves various Executive Orders and regulations by which the President nullified attachments and liens on Iranian assets in the United States, directed that these assets be transferred to Iran, and suspended claims against Iran that may be presented to an International Claims Tribunal. This action was taken in an effort to comply with an Executive Agreement between the United States and Iran....

[W]e stress that the expeditious treatment of the issues involved by all of the courts which have considered the President's actions makes us acutely aware of the necessity to rest decision on the narrowest possible ground capable of deciding the case.... We attempt to lay down no general "guidelines" covering other situations not involved here, and attempt to confine the opinion only to the very questions necessary to decision of the case....

The parties and the lower courts, confronted with the instant questions, have all agreed that much relevant analysis is contained in *Youngstown Sheet & Tube Co. v. Sawyer*.... Justice Jackson's concurring opinion elaborated in a general way the consequences of different types of interaction between the two democratic branches in assessing Presidential authority to act in any given case. When the President acts pursuant to an express or implied authorization from Congress, he exercises not only his powers but also those delegated by Congress. In such a case the executive action "would be supported by the strongest of presumptions and the widest latitude of judicial interpreta-

tion, and the burden of persuasion would rest heavily upon any who might attack it." When the President acts in the absence of congressional authorization he may enter "a zone of twilight in which he and Congress may have concurrent authority, or in which its distribution is uncertain." In such a case the analysis becomes more complicated, and the validity of the President's action, at least so far as separation-of-powers principles are concerned, hinges on a consideration of all the circumstances which might shed light on the views of the Legislative Branch toward such action, including "congressional inertia, indifference or quiescence." Finally, when the President acts in contravention of the will of Congress, "his power is at its lowest ebb," and the Court can sustain his actions "only by disabling the Congress from acting upon the subject."...

Justice Jackson ... recognized that his three categories represented "a somewhat over-simplified grouping," and it is doubtless the case that executive action in any particular instance falls, not neatly in one of three pigeonholes, but rather at some point along a spectrum running from explicit congressional authorization to explicit congressional prohibition. This is particularly true as respects cases such as the one before us, involving responses to international crises the nature of which Congress can hardly have been expected to anticipate in any detail.

In nullifying post-November 14, 1979, attachments and directing those persons holding blocked Iranian funds and securities to transfer them to the Federal Reserve Bank of New York for ultimate transfer to Iran, President Carter cited five sources of express or inherent power. The Government, however, has principally relied on Sec. 203 of the [International Emergency Economic Powers Act] as authorization for these actions. Section 1702(a)(1) provides in part:

> At the times and to the extent specified in section 1701 of this title, the President may, under such regulations as he may prescribe, by means of instructions, licenses, or otherwise—
> (A) investigate, regulate, or prohibit—
> (i) any transactions in foreign exchange,
> (ii) transfers of credit or payments between, by, through, or to any banking institution, to the extent that such transfers or payments involve any interest of any foreign country or a national thereof,
> (iii) the importing or exporting of currency or securities, and
> (B) investigate, regulate, direct and compel, nullify, void, prevent or prohibit, any acquisition, holding, withholding, use, transfer, withdrawal, transportation, importation or exportation of, or dealing in, or exercising any right, power, or privilege with respect to, or transactions involving, any property in which any foreign country or a national thereof has any interest;
> by any person, or with respect to any property, subject to the jurisdiction of the United States....

Because the President's action in nullifying the attachments and ordering the transfer of the assets was taken pursuant to specific congressional authorization, it is "supported by the strongest of presumptions and the widest latitude of judicial interpretation, and the burden of persuasion would rest heavily upon any who might attack it." *Youngstown*. Under the circumstances of this case, we cannot say

that petitioner has sustained that heavy burden....

Although we have concluded that the IEEPA constitutes specific congressional authorization to the President to nullify the attachments and order the transfer of Iranian assets, there remains the question of the President's authority to suspend claims pending in American courts. Such claims have, of course, an existence apart from the attachments which accompanied them. In terminating these claims through Executive Order No. 12294 the President purported to act under authority of both the IEEPA and 22 U.S.C. Sec. 1732, the so-called "Hostage Act."

We conclude that although the IEEPA authorized the nullification of the attachments, it cannot be read to authorize the suspension of the claims. The claims of American citizens against Iran are not in themselves transactions involving Iranian property or efforts to exercise any rights with respect to such property. An in personam lawsuit, although it might eventually be reduced to judgment and that judgment might be executed upon, is an effort to establish liability and fix damages and does not focus on any particular property within the jurisdiction. The terms of the IEEPA therefore do not authorize the President to suspend claims in American courts....

The Hostage Act, passed in 1868, provides:

> Whenever it is made known to the President that any citizen of the United States has been unjustly deprived of his liberty by or under the authority of any foreign government, it shall be the duty of the President forthwith to demand of that government the reasons of such imprisonment; and if it appears to be wrongful and in violation

of the rights of American citizenship, the President shall forthwith demand the release of such citizen, and if the release so demanded is unreasonably delayed or refused, the President shall use such means, not amounting to acts of war, as he may think necessary and proper to obtain or effectuate the release; and all the facts and proceedings relative thereto shall as soon as practicable be communicated by the President to Congress.

We are reluctant to conclude that this provision constitutes specific authorization to the President to suspend claims in American courts. Although the broad language of the Hostage Act suggests it may cover this case, there are several difficulties with such a view. The legislative history indicates that the Act was passed in response to a situation unlike the recent Iranian crisis. Congress in 1868 was concerned with the activity of certain countries refusing to recognize the citizenship of naturalized Americans traveling abroad, and repatriating such citizens against their will.... These countries were not interested in returning the citizens in exchange for any sort of ransom. This also explains the reference in the Act to imprisonment "in violation of the rights of American citizenship." Although the Iranian hostage-taking violated international law and common decency, the hostages were not seized out of any refusal to recognize their American citizenship—they were seized precisely because of their American citizenship. The legislative history is also somewhat ambiguous on the question whether Congress contemplated Presidential action such as that involved here or rather simply reprisals directed against the offending foreign country and its citizens.... Concluding that neither the IEEPA

nor the Hostage Act constitutes specific authorization of the President's action suspending claims, however, is not to say that these statutory provisions are entirely irrelevant to the question of the validity of the President's action. We think both statutes highly relevant in the looser sense of indicating congressional acceptance of a broad scope for executive action in circumstances such as those presented in this case....

Although we have declined to conclude that the IEEPA or the Hostage Act directly authorizes the President's suspension of claims for the reasons noted, we cannot ignore the general tenor of Congress' legislation in this area in trying to determine whether the President is acting alone or at least with the acceptance of Congress. As we have noted, Congress cannot anticipate and legislate with regard to every possible action the President may find it necessary to take or every possible situation in which he might act.... [T]he enactment of legislation closely related to the question of the President's authority in a particular case which evinces legislative intent to accord the President broad discretion may be considered to "invite" "measures on independent presidential responsibility." *Youngstown.*

Crucial to our decision today is the conclusion that Congress has implicitly approved the practice of claim settlement by executive agreement. This is best demonstrated by Congress' enactment of the International Claims Settlement Act of 1949. The Act had two purposes: (1) to allocate to United States nationals funds received in the course of an executive claims settlement with Yugoslavia, and (2) to provide a procedure whereby funds resulting from future settlements could be distributed. To achieve these ends Congress created the International Claims Commission, now the Foreign Claims Settlement Commission, and gave it jurisdiction to make final and binding decisions with respect to claims by United States nationals against settlement funds. By creating a procedure to implement future settlement agreements, Congress placed its stamp of approval on such agreements. Indeed, the legislative history of the Act observed that the United States was seeking settlements with countries other than Yugoslavia and that the bill contemplated settlements of a similar nature in the future.

Over the years Congress has frequently amended the International Claims Settlement Act to provide for particular problems arising out of settlement agreements, thus demonstrating Congress' continuing acceptance of the President's claim settlement authority....

In addition to congressional acquiescence in the President's power to settle claims, prior cases of this Court have also recognized that the President does have some measure of power to enter into executive agreements without obtaining the advice and consent of the Senate....

Petitioner raises two arguments in opposition to the proposition that Congress has acquiesced in this longstanding practice of claims settlement by executive agreement. First, it suggests that all pre-1952 settlement claims, and corresponding court cases ... should be discounted because of the evolution of the doctrine of sovereign immunity. Petitioner observes that prior to 1952 the United States adhered to the doctrine of absolute sovereign immunity, so that absent action by the Executive there simply would be no

remedy for a United States national against a foreign government. When the United States in 1952 adopted a more restrictive notion of sovereign immunity ... it is petitioner's view that United States nationals no longer needed executive aid to settle claims and that, as a result, the President's authority to settle such claims in some sense "disappeared." Though petitioner's argument is not wholly without merit, it is refuted by the fact that since 1952 there have been at least 10 claims settlements by executive agreement. Thus, even if the pre-1952 cases should be disregarded, congressional acquiescence in settlement agreements since that time supports the President's power to act here.

Petitioner next asserts that Congress divested the President of the authority to settle claims when it enacted the Foreign Sovereign Immunities Act of 1976 (hereinafter FSIA). The FSIA granted personal and subject-matter jurisdiction in the federal district courts over commercial suits brought by claimants against those foreign states which have waived immunity.... Petitioner thus insists that the President, by suspending its claims, has circumscribed the jurisdiction of the United States courts in violation of Art. III of the Constitution.

We disagree. In the first place, we do not believe that the President has attempted to divest the federal courts of jurisdiction. Executive Order No. 12294 purports only to "suspend" the claims, not divest the federal court of "jurisdiction."... The President has exercised the power, acquiesced in by Congress, to settle claims and, as such, has simply effected a change in the substantive law governing the lawsuit. Indeed, the very example of sovereign immunity belies petitioner's argument. No one would suggest that a determination of sovereign immunity divests the federal courts of "jurisdiction." Yet, petitioner's argument, if accepted, would have required courts prior to the enactment of the FSIA to reject as an encroachment on their jurisdiction the President's determination of a foreign state's sovereign immunity.

Petitioner also reads the FSIA much too broadly. The principal purpose of the FSIA was to codify contemporary concepts concerning the scope of sovereign immunity and withdraw from the President the authority to make binding determinations of the sovereign immunity to be accorded foreign states.... The FSIA was thus designed to remove one particular barrier to suit, namely sovereign immunity, and cannot be fairly read as prohibiting the President from settling claims of United States nationals against foreign governments....

In light of all of the foregoing—the inferences to be drawn from the character of the legislation Congress has enacted in the area, such as the IEEPA and the Hostage Act, and from the history of acquiescence in executive claims settlement—we conclude that the President was authorized to suspend pending claims pursuant to Executive Order No. 12294....

Our conclusion is buttressed by the fact that the means chosen by the President to settle the claims of American nationals provided an alternative forum, the Claims Tribunal, which is capable of providing meaningful relief....

Just as importantly, Congress has not disapproved of the action taken here. Though Congress has held hearings on the Iranian Agreement itself, Congress has not enacted legislation, or even passed a resolution, indicating its dis-

pleasure with the Agreement. Quite the contrary, the relevant Senate Committee has stated that the establishment of the Tribunal is "of vital importance to the United States." We are thus clearly not confronted with a situation in which Congress has in some way resisted the exercise of Presidential authority.

Finally, we [emphasize] the narrowness of our decision. We do not decide that the President possesses plenary power to settle claims, even as against foreign governmental entities....

We do not think it appropriate at the present time to address petitioner's contention that the suspension of claims, if authorized, would constitute a taking of property in violation of the Fifth Amendment to the United States Constitution in the absence of just compensation. Both petitioner and the Government concede that the question whether the suspension of the claims constitutes a taking is not ripe for review....

The judgment of the District Court is accordingly affirmed, and the mandate shall issue forthwith.

It is so ordered.

STEVENS, J., CONCURRING IN PART

In my judgment the possibility that requiring this petitioner to prosecute its claim in another forum will constitute an unconstitutional "taking" is so remote that I would not address the jurisdictional question.... However, I join the remainder of the opinion.

POWELL, J., CONCURRING AND DISSENTING IN PART

I join the Court's opinion except its decision that the nullification of the attachments did not effect a taking of property interests giving rise to claims for just compensation. The nullification of attachments presents a separate question from whether the suspension and proposed settlement of claims against Iran may constitute a taking. I would leave both "taking" claims open for resolution on a case-by-case basis in actions before the Court of Claims. The facts of the hundreds of claims pending against Iran are not known to this Court and may differ from the facts in this case. I therefore dissent from the Court's decision with respect to attachments. The decision may well be erroneous, and it certainly is premature with respect to many claims.

I agree with the Court's opinion with respect to the suspension and settlement of claims against Iran and its instrumentalities. The opinion makes clear that some claims may not be adjudicated by the Claims Tribunal and that others may not be paid in full. The Court holds that parties whose valid claims are not adjudicated or not fully paid may bring a "taking" claim against the United States in the Court of Claims, the jurisdiction of which this Court acknowledges. The Government must pay just compensation when it furthers the Nation's foreign policy goals by using as "bargaining chips" claims lawfully held by a relatively few persons and subject to the jurisdiction of our courts. The extraordinary powers of the President and Congress upon which our decision rests cannot, in the circumstances of this case, displace the Just Compensation Clause of the Constitution.

COMMENT

The fifty-two remaining hostages were held captive in Iran for more than a year. When President Carter's diplomatic and economic efforts failed, the president dispatched a military force to rescue the hostages. Three helicopters malfunctioned and the commander was forced to abort the rescue effort. Then two aircraft collided, killing eight American servicemen. In order to prevent subsequent rescue efforts, the Iranians scattered the hostages through the country. Despite the death of the Shah in Cairo in July 1980, the hostage crisis did not abate. Instead, Ayatollah Khomeini demanded return of the Shah's assets to Iran and made other demands as conditions for the hostages' release.

When war broke out between Iraq and Iran in 1980, Iran became more vulnerable to American economic pressure. With Algeria acting as intermediary, a deal for the hostages' release was negotiated. Khomeini dropped all of his demands except for unfreezing Iranian assets in the United States and the hostages were released on January 20, 1981. Meanwhile, President Carter was defeated by Ronald Reagan in the November 1980 elections. Carter's failure to end the hostage crisis was a successful campaign issue for Reagan.

QUESTIONS

1. The introduction to Justice Rehnquist's opinion suggests that in his view it may be impossible for the judiciary to set clear constitutional

boundaries for the exercise of executive authority. Does that mean that the judicial branch is relegated to the role of determining whether Congress has succeeded in circumscribing the president's authority? If so, has statutory construction been substituted for constitutional analysis in cases like *Dames and Moore*?

2. According to Justice Rehnquist, Justice Robert H. Jackson's concurring opinion in *Youngstown Sheet & Tube v. Sawyer* provided the analytical framework for resolving *Dames and Moore*. Review Justice Jackson's *Youngstown* concurrence on pp. 483–484 to see if you agree.

3. Counsel for the United States observed that during the hostage crisis, the government of Iran threatened to remove all of its assets from the United States. Such an action would have resulted in there being no assets against which American claimants in lawsuits—over four hundred at the time of the executive orders—could secure their legal recoveries. What, if any, weight should the Supreme Court have given to that threat in evaluating the president's action?

4. The Islamic Republic of Iran and the Bank Markazi Iran submitted briefs as intervenors. Among the arguments made by the Republic of Iran was that, as a matter of international law, the Algerian Declarations obligated the United States to terminate all litigation in U.S. courts based on claims of U.S. nationals against Iran and to remove judicial impediments to the promised transfer of Iranian assets. In the light of the Algerian Declarations, would the Supreme Court have been well advised to resolve *Dames and Moore* on the basis of international law?

5. On the question of how to interpret congressional silence regarding executive branch actions, *Dames and Moore* seems to represent a point somewhere between *Youngstown Sheet & Tube v. Sawyer* and *Haig v. Agee*, 453 U.S. 280 (1981). In *Youngstown*, the Court read congressional silence as meaning no explicit authorization for presidential seizure of steel mills. By contrast, in *Haig*, the Court read congressional silence as implicit approval of the president's order that revoked certain passports on national security grounds. Compare *Kent v. Dulles*, 357 U.S. 116 (1958), where the Court held that Congress could not "silently grant" the secretary of state the authority to deny passports on the basis of an applicant's Communist Party membership.

What standard, if any, for weighing the significance of congressional silence in the face of claims of executive power emerges from these cases? In considering this question, read *United States v. Belmont*, 301 U.S. 324 (1937) and *United States v. Pink*, 315 U.S. 203 (1942). Both of those cases arose out of claims resulting from the Bolshevik Revolution in Russia in the context of agreements reached when the United States extended diplomatic recognition to the Soviet

Union. The Court ruled that in the context of international compacts and agreements, "complete power over international affairs is in the national government and is not and cannot be subject to any curtailment or interference on the part of the several states."

6. What does *Dames and Moore* add to the other cases in this section regarding the president's foreign policy and emergency powers? Which cases appear to state general rules, and which seem to involve exceptions based on the facts?

SUGGESTIONS FOR FURTHER READING

Adler, David G., "The Constitution and Presidential Warmaking," 103 *Political Science Quarterly* (1988): 1.

_____, and Larry N. George, eds., *The Constitution and the Conduct of American Foreign Policy* (Lawrence, KS: University Press of Kansas, 1996).

Allison, Graham, "Making War," 40 *Law and Contemporary Problems* (1976): 86.

Berger, Raoul, "The Presidential Monopoly of Foreign Affairs," 71 *Michigan Law Review* (1972): 1

Bernath, Stewart L., *Squall across the Atlantic: American Civil War* Prize Cases *and Diplomacy* (Berkeley, CA: University of California Press, 1970).

Carter, Stephen, "The Constitutionality of the War Powers Resolution," 70 *Virginia Law Review* (1984): 101.

Charns, Alexander, *Cloak and Gavel: FBI Wiretaps, Bugs, Informers, and the Supreme Court* (Urbana, IL: University of Illinois Press, 1991).

Chemerinsky, Edward, "Controlling Inherent Presidential Power: Providing a Framework for Judicial Review," 56 *Southern California Law Review* (1983): 863.

Comment, "Congressional Control of Presidential War-Making under the War Powers Act: The Status of a Legislative Veto after *Chadha*," 132 *University of Pennsylvania Law Review* (1984): 1217.

Corwin, Edward S., *Total War and the Constitution* (New York, NY: Knopf, 1947).

_____, "The Steel Seizure Case: A Judicial Brick without Straw," 53 *Columbia Law Review* (1953): 53.

_____, *The President: Office and Powers, 1787–1957: Historical Analysis of Practice and Opinion*, 4th rev. ed. (New York, NY: New York University Press, 1957).

Dahl, Robert A., *Congress and Foreign Policy* (New York, NY: Harcourt Brace, 1950).

Divine, Robert A., "The Case of the Smuggled Bombers," in *Quarrels That Have Shaped the Constitution*, rev. ed., ed. John A. Garraty (New York, NY: Harper, 1987).

Ely, John Hart, "The American War in Indochina, Part I: The (Troubled)

Constitutionality of the War They Told Us About," 42 *Stanford Law Review* (1980): 877.

———, "Suppose Congress Wanted a War Powers Act That Worked," 88 *Columbia Law Review* (1988): 1379.

———, "The American War in Indochina, Part II: The Unconstitutionality of the War They Didn't Tell Us About," 42 *Stanford Law Review* (1990): 1093.

———, *War and Responsibility: Constitutional Lessons of Vietnam and Its Aftermath* (Princeton, NJ: Princeton University Press, 1993).

Eskridge Jr., William N., "Interpreting Legislative Inaction," 87 *Michigan Law Review* (1988): 67.

Fisher, Louis, *Constitutional Conflicts between Congress and the President* (Princeton, NJ: Princeton University Press, 1985).

———, *Presidential War Power* (Lawrence, KS: University of Kansas Press, 1995).

Frost, David, "Interview with Richard M. Nixon," transcript, *New York Times*, May 20, 1977, A16.

Gambione, Joseph G., "*Ex parte Milligan*: The Restoration of Judicial Prestige?" 16 *Civil War History* (1970): 246.

Glennon, Michael J., *Constitutional Diplomacy* (Princeton, NJ: Princeton University Press, 1990).

Grabow, John, "Congressional Silence and the Search for Legislative Intent: A Venture into 'Speculative Unrealities,'" 64 *Buffalo University Law Review* (1984): 737.

Henken, Louis, "The Right to Know and the Duty to Withhold: The Case of the Pentagon Papers," 120 *University of Pennsylvania Law Review* (1971): 271.

Horack, John, "Congressional Silence: A Tool of Judicial Supremacy," 25 *Texas Law Review* (1947).

Junger, Peter, "Down Memory Lane: The Case of the Pentagon Papers," 23 *Western Reserve Law Review* (1971): 3.

Kalven Jr., Harry, "Foreword: Even When a Nation Is at War," 85 *Harvard Law Review* (1971): 3.

Kauper, Paul, "The Steel Seizure Case: Congress, the President, and the Supreme Court," 51 *Michigan Law Review* (1952): 141.

Koh, Harold Hongju, *The National Security Constitution: Sharing Power after the Iran-Contra Affair* (New Haven, CT: 1990).

Kutler, Stanley I., *Judicial Power and Reconstruction Politics* (Chicago, IL: University of Chicago Press, 1968).

Levitan, David M., "The Foreign Relations Power: An Analysis of Mr. Justice Sutherland's Theory," 55 *Yale Law Journal* (1946): 467.

Lofgren, Charles A., "War-Making under the Constitution: The Original Understanding," 81 *Yale Law Journal* (1972): 672.

Lofgren, Charles A., *United States v. Curtiss-Wright Corporation*: An Historical Reassessment," 83 *Yale Law Journal* (1973): 1.

———, *"Government from Reflection and Choice": Constitutional Essays on War, Foreign Relations and Federalism* (New York, NY: Oxford University Press, 1986).

Marcus, Maeva, *Truman and the Steel Seizure Case: The Limits of Presidential Power* (New York, NY: Columbia University Press, 1977).

———, "Separation of Powers in the Early National Period," 30 *William & Mary Law Review* (1989): 269.

Marks, Lee R., and John C. Grabow, "The President's Foreign Economic Powers after *Dames & Moore v. Regan*: Legislation by Acquiescence," 68 *Cornell Law Review* (1982): 68.

McConnell, Grant, *The Steel Seizure Case of 1952* (Tuscaloosa, AL: University of Alabama Press, 1960).

Miller, Arthur S., "*Dames & Moore v. Regan*: A Political Decision by a Political Court," 29 *University of California Los Angeles Law Review* (1982): 1104.

Monaghan, Henry P., Presidential War-Making," 50 *Boston University Law Review* (1970): 19.

Nevins, Allan, "The Case of the Copperhead Conspirator," in *Quarrels That Have Shaped the Constitution*, rev. ed., ed. John A. Garraty (New York, NY: Harper, 1987).

Note, "The Future of the War Powers Resolution," 36 *Stanford Law Review* (1984): 1407.

Osgood, Russell, "Early Versions and Practices of Separation of Powers: A Comment," 30 *William & Mary Law Review* (1989): 279.

Pyle, Christopher H., and Richard Pious, eds., *The President, Congress, and the Constitution* (New York, NY: Free Press, 1984).

Randall, James G., *Constitutional Problems under Lincoln*, rev. ed. (Glouscester, MA: Peter Smith, 1963).

Ratner, Leonard, "The Coordinated Warmaking Power—Legislative, Executive, and Judicial Roles," 44 *Southern California Law Review* (1971): 461.

Reveley, W. Taylor, *War Powers of the President and Congress: Who Holds the Arrows and Olive Branch* (Charlottesville, VA: University of Virginia Press, 1981).

Rossiter, Clinton, *Constitutional Dictatorship* (Princeton, NJ: Princeton University Press, 1948).

———, *The Supreme Court and the Commander in Chief*, expanded ed. (Ithaca, NY: Cornell University Press, 1976).

Rostow, Eugene, "Great Cases Make Bad Law: The War Powers Act," 50 *Texas Law Review* (1972): 833.

Rudenstein, David, *The Day the Presses Stopped: A History of the Pentagon Papers Case* (Berkeley, CA: University of California Press, 1996).

Scigliano, Robert, *The Supreme Court and the Presidency* (New York, NY: Free Press, 1971).

_____, "The War Powers Resolution and the War Powers," in *The Presidency in the Constitutional Order*, eds. Jeffrey M. Bessette and Jeffrey Tulis (Baton Rouge, LA: Louisiana State University Press, 1981).

Shapiro, Martin, ed., *The Pentagon Papers and the Courts: A Study in Foreign Policy-Making Versus Freedom of the Press* (San Francisco, CA: Chandler, 1972).

Sofaer, Abraham D., *War, Foreign Affairs and Constitutional Powers: The Origins* (Cambridge, MA: Ballinger, 1976).

Symposium, "*Dames & Moore v. Regan*," 29 *University of California Los Angeles Law Review* (1981): 977.

Tribe, Laurence, "Toward a Syntax of the Unsaid: Construing the Sounds of Congressional and Constitutional Silence," 57 *Indiana Law Journal* (1982): 515.

Trimble, Phillip R., "Foreign Policy Frustrated—*Dames & Moore*, Claims Court Jurisdiction and a New Raid on the Treasury," 84 *Columbia Law Review* (1984): 317.

Ungar, Sanford J., *The Papers and the Papers: An Account of the Legal and Political Battle over the Pentagon Papers* (New York, NY: Columbia University Press, 1989).

Van Alstyne, William, "Congress, the President, and the Power to Declare War," 121 *University of Pennsylvania Law Review* (1972): 1.

Westin, Alan F., *The Anatomy of a Constitutional Law Case:* Youngstown Sheet & Tube v. Sawyer, *The Steel Seizure Decisions* (New York, NY: Columbia University Press, 1990, originally published 1958).

CHAPTER 5

FEDERALISM: ONGOING DEBATES OVER DIVIDED POWER

SUPREMACY CLAUSE AND FEDERALISM

Martin v. Hunter's Lessee
1 Wheaton 304 (1816)

SETTING

Perhaps the most striking feature of government in the United States is that it is not a single entity, but two—national and state. The states came into being after the Revolutionary War. The national government was not created for another decade, following the failure of the Articles of Confederation under which the states attempted unsuccessfully to govern the nation as coequal sovereigns. In structure, the national and state governments resemble one another: Both have legislative, executive, and judicial branches, both are governed by constitutions, and both have well-defined spheres of responsibility. Citizens owe allegiance to both the national government and the government of the state in which they reside. However, the respective powers of and boundaries between the national and state governments have never been definitively established. Whether the two governments are dual sovereigns operating exclusively within their separate spheres, whether one is superior to the other, or whether the two are destined to be locked in a perpetual struggle for power, are questions that have never been finally resolved. The term that describes nation-state relations in the United States is federalism.

The Supremacy Clause of the Constitution of the United States has been one source of debate over federalism. Article VI, section 2, provides that the laws of the United States made pursuant to the Constitution "... shall be the supreme Law of the Land," notwithstanding "any Thing in the Constitution or Laws of any State to the Contrary...." As Alexander Hamilton observed in *Federalist* No. 33, the Supremacy Clause was the source of "much virulent invective and petulant declamation against the proposed Constitution," because advocates of states' rights perceived it, along with the Necessary and Proper Clause of Article I, section 8, as a "pernicious engine by which their local governments were to be destroyed and their liberties exterminated." Hamilton predicted that it would be the responsibility of the national government to judge the proper reach of its own powers, and that if it exceeded those bounds, the people would take political measures to restrain it. In fact, the practical consequences of the Supremacy Clause on federalism have been worked out through the Supreme Court's exercise of the power of judicial review.

As explained in Chapter 1, in fleshing out the bare bones outline of Article III the first Congress organized the judicial branch through enactment of a judiciary act. The bill that eventually became the Judiciary Act of 1789 was controversial. James Monroe wrote to James Madison that the bill

> to embrace the Judiciary will occasion more difficulty, I apprehend, than any other, as it will form an exposition of the powers of the Government itself, and show in the opinion of those who organize it, how far it can discharge its own functions, or must depend for that purpose on the aid of those of the States.

Monroe's prediction proved correct. The most controversial provision was Section 25, which authorized writs of error to the Supreme Court of the United States from judgments in state courts where federal statutes or treaties were involved, or when a state statute or common law rule had been upheld against a challenge under the Constitution of the United States. James Jackson of Georgia contended that Section 25 "swallows up every shadow of a State judiciary," while its defenders contended that Section 25 was necessary "to guard the rights of the Union against the invasion of the States."

The Judiciary Act was finally passed on September 24, 1789, containing the controversial Section 25. The question of the constitutionality of Section 25 reached the Supreme Court in 1816 in a complicated case involving land claims in Virginia.

Note: Review the *Setting* to and excerpt of *Martin v. Hunter's Lessee* in Chapter 2, pp. 93–103.

QUESTIONS

1. Explain the relationship between Section 25 of the Judiciary Act of 1789 and the Supremacy Clause in Article VI. What are the implications of that relationship for federalism?
2. Do Articles III and VI of the Constitution require that state judges defer to the U.S. Supreme Court's interpretation of the Constitution of the United States?

COMMENT

Justice Story's decision in *Martin* fanned the flames of sectional discord. To states' rights supporters, the Court's assertion of judicial power symbolized Federalist, then Whig, efforts to achieve national supremacy. Courts in seven states refused to recognize the jurisdiction of federal courts over state cases raising federal questions. In 1821 and 1832, Supreme Court opponents in Congress, led by South Carolina Senator John C. Calhoun, sought unsuccessfully to repeal Section 25 of the Judiciary Act of 1789.

Although the Court's decision in *Martin* held that the Supreme Court may review state Supreme Court decisions that raise federal questions, it did not resolve the issue of what constitutes a "federal question." Consequently, in addition to fueling the fires of sectional discord early in the country's history, the decision virtually guaranteed protracted litigation on the subject of "federal questions."

SUPREMACY CLAUSE AND FEDERALISM

McCulloch v. Maryland
4 Wheaton 304 (1819)

SETTING

The nation's first president, George Washington, appointed Alexander Hamilton as his secretary of the treasury. Hamilton's view of government was reflected in a comment he made at the Constitutional Convention:

> All communities divide themselves into the few and the many. The first are the rich and well-born; the other the mass of the people ... turbulent and changing, they seldom judge or determine right. Give therefore to the first class a distinct, permanent share in the Government.

Hamilton brought that philosophy to his position as secretary of the treasury, which was reflected in several major reports that he prepared on subjects ranging from the nation's credit to a report on manufactures. His January 1791 Report on the Bank proposed that the United States create a national bank. One of the functions of a national bank would be to serve as the government's financial agent. Another would be to issue paper bank notes to supplement the gold and silver coins (specie) that were in short supply, thus fostering commerce. Yet another function of the bank would be to assist new businesses. A national bank would foster the loyalty of groups like public creditors, financiers, merchant-shippers and those with established wealth. According to Hamilton's proposal, the United States would put up $2 million of the bank's $10 million capital and appoint one-fifth of its directors. Private investors would be invited to provide the rest of the capital and to elect the other directors.

Hamilton was confident that Congress had the authority under the Constitution to charter a national bank. However, his proposal ran into a firestorm of opposition. Secretary of State Thomas Jefferson viewed a national bank as an instrument of commerce, the wealthy, and cities, which would destroy America's agrarian values. When President Washington asked Jefferson for his opinion on the constitutionality of Hamilton's bank proposal, Jefferson replied that the Constitutional Convention had created a compact among the states and had intended to "lace up" Congress "straightly within the enumerated powers." James Madison, by then a member of Congress, agreed. Madison argued that Congress had no authority to charter a national bank. In Madison's view, Congress's only powers were those explicitly enumerated in the Constitution and the authority to charter a national bank could not be derived from any of the enumerated powers.

After conferring with national bank opponents like Jefferson and Madison, President Washington asked Hamilton to prepare an explanation of why Congress had authority under the Constitution to charter a bank. Hamilton responded with his "Opinion on the Constitutionality of an Act to Establish a Bank." In it, he argued that the powers granted to Congress by the Constitution "ought to be construed liberally in advancement of the public good." Although President Washington was not entirely persuaded by Hamilton's defense of the bank, he nonetheless signed into law on February 25, 1791, the bill that created the First National Bank. The private capital required for the bank was subscribed within a matter of four hours of the offer.

In 1811, the First National Bank's charter expired and Congress, by one vote, failed to renew it. Without a national bank, it was very difficult for the United States to pay for the debts it had incurred in the War of 1812. In the absence of a national bank, state legislatures had chartered many state banks, each having the authority to issue paper money. At that time there was no one national currency in the United States and holders of state bank notes found it virtually impossible to convert the notes into specie. As a consequence, the value of state notes declined, the national debt soared, and the United States slipped into an economic depression.

By the time Congress debated chartering a second national bank in 1816, Jeffersonian Republicans understood the need for it and President James Monroe supported the proposal. Even Madison argued in favor of the bank, contending that the constitutional issues raised when the first bank had been chartered had been resolved "by repeated recognitions ... of the validity of such an institution in acts of the legislative, executive and judicial branches of the Government ... accompanied by ... a concurrence of the general will of the nation."

Congress chartered the Second Bank of the United States for twenty-three years, capitalizing it at $35 million, which made it the largest corporation in the country. The Bank's home office was located in Philadelphia. By the time *McCulloch v. Maryland* came before the Supreme Court, the Bank operated eighteen branch offices throughout what was then the United States: as far north as Portsmouth, New Hampshire; as far south as New Orleans, Louisiana, and Louisville, Kentucky; and to Cincinnati, Ohio, in the west.

Note: Review the *Setting* to and excerpt of *McCulloch v. Maryland* in Chapter 3, pp. 211–222.

QUESTIONS

1. Explain Chief Justice Marshall's theory of the Union, the powers of the national government, and the relationship between the national government and the states. Are his views mandated by the Constitution or are they imposed on the Constitution? Did Marshall's opinion rubber-stamp Hamilton's reading of the Constitution?

2. Is Chief Justice Marshall correct that Article I marks only the "great outlines" of congressional power? What are the practical implications of that position?

3. In a letter to Thomas Ritchie, written in 1820, Thomas Jefferson characterized the national judiciary as: "the subtle core of sappers and miners constantly working under ground to undermine the foundations of our confederated fabric. They are construing our Constitution from a coordination of general [that is, national] and special [that is, state] government to a general and supreme one alone. This will lay all things at their feet" (quoted in Dumas Malone, *Thomas Jefferson and His Time*, 6 vols. [Boston, MA: Little, Brown, 1981], 6: 356). Is *McCulloch v. Maryland* an example of such undermining?

SUGGESTIONS FOR FURTHER READING

Berger, Raoul, *Federalism: The Founder's Design* (New York, NY: St Martin's, 1987).

Hammond, Bray, "The Bank Cases," in *Quarrels That Have Shaped the Constitution*, rev. ed., ed. John A. Garraty (New York, NY: Harper, 1988).

Plous, Harold J., and Gordon E. Baker, "*McCulloch v. Maryland*: Right Principle, Wrong Case," 9 *Stanford Law Review* (1957): 710.

Warren, Charles, "Legislative and Judicial Attacks on the Supreme Court of the United States—A History of the Twenty-Fifth Section of the Judiciary Act," 47 *American Law Review* (1913): 1.

White, G. Edward, *The Marshall Court and Cultural Change, 1815–1835*, abridged ed. (New York, NY: Oxford University Press, 1991).

NATIONAL PREEMPTION

Prigg v. Pennsylvania
16 Peters 539 (1842)

SETTING

Before the Civil War, debates over slavery were often fought out in terms of nation-state relations. One recurring question was whether state and federal laws regarding slavery could coexist or whether national laws would trump state provisions. In legal terms, would national laws preempt state laws? The controversy traced back to one of the compromises made at the Constitutional Convention.

The Fugitive Slave Clause of Article 4, section 2, was one of the major concessions made to the South by northern and northeastern states. The clause declared that a slave's (the euphemism "Person held to Service or Labour" was used) escape did not discharge that person from "Service or Labour" and required that fugitive slaves be delivered up to their owners. In 1793, under the authority of Article 4, section 2, a Congress composed of many members of the Constitutional Convention passed the first Fugitive Slave Act. The act required the owner of fugitive slaves to appear in a federal court and to receive a certificate authorizing removal of the slaves from the fugitive state to the state of escape. The law was difficult to implement because there were too few federal judges at the time and federal magistrates were slow to act.

For almost forty years the North and South coexisted in an uneasy peace based on the Fugitive Slave Clause and the Fugitive Slave Act. By the 1830s, however, there were indications that the peace could not last. Antislavery sentiment was fanned by abolitionists such as Boston publisher William Lloyd Garrison, who, in January 1831, published the first issue of *The Liberator*. The front page of the first *Liberator* proclaimed:

> I shall strenuously contend for the immediate franchisement of our slave population…. On this subject I do not wish to think, or speak, or write, with moderation…. I am in earnest—I will not equivocate—I will not excuse—I will not retreat a single inch—AND I WILL BE HEARD.

Although very few copies of *The Liberator* made it below the Mason-Dixon Line, southerners believed that Garrison's virulent castigation of slavery fomented rebellion. Prominent southerners blamed Garrison for the 1831 Nat Turner slave rebellion in Virginia. Turner had enlisted other blacks in a revolt that resulted in the deaths of fifty-seven whites. Upwards of a hundred blacks were killed as the rebellion was put down, and Turner was hanged. This uprising caused southern states to demand even more restrictive fugitive slave laws.

Pennsylvania was a focal point of renewed debate over fugitive slaves because some Pennsylvanians were instrumental in the operation of several "underground railroad" routes. The underground railroad was a network of safe havens and transportation routes by means of which a few fugitive slaves escaped to Canada by traveling from one abolitionist's home to another.

Responding to charges from Maryland that Pennsylvania residents were aiding and abetting fugitive slaves, the Pennsylvania legislature in 1826 passed "An Act to give effect to the provisions of the Constitution of the United States relative to fugitives from labor, for the protection of people of color, and to prevent kidnapping" of persons assumed to be fugitive slaves. Also known as the Pennsylvania Personal Liberty Law, the act was intended both to aid slave owners in recovering their property and to protect free blacks against kidnapping. Like the federal Fugitive Slave Act, it required slave owners to appear before a magistrate, prove ownership of fugitive slaves, and obtain a certificate of removal.

Prigg v. Pennsylvania involved Margaret Morgan, who was a slave of Margaret Ashmore under the laws of Maryland. In 1832, Morgan escaped with her children into Pennsylvania, a free state, to live with her husband. In 1833, she gave birth to another child. In 1837, Edward Prigg, Ashmore's agent and attorney, along with Nathan Bemis, Jacob Forward, and Stephen Lewis, residents of Maryland, apprehended Morgan as a fugitive from labor and took her before a magistrate in York County, Pennsylvania, to get a certificate of removal. The magistrate refused to issue the certificate. Nonetheless, Prigg and the others took Morgan and her children back to Maryland and delivered them to the custody of Ashmore.

Prigg and his cohorts subsequently were indicted in a York County, Pennsylvania, court for the crime of kidnapping Morgan. The governor of Pennsylvania demanded that the governor of Maryland have the slave catchers returned to Pennsylvania for trial. Following extensive political maneuvering between officials in the two states, Maryland agreed to return Prigg to Pennsylvania in order to test the constitutionality of Pennsylvania's 1826 law. He pleaded "not guilty" to the indictment.

Following a jury trial in the court of Oyer and Terminer for York County, the jury issued a special verdict, on which the court entered judgment against Prigg. The case was removed to the Pennsylvania Supreme Court, which affirmed Prigg's conviction. Prigg appealed to the Supreme Court of the United States.

HIGHLIGHTS OF SUPREME COURT ARGUMENTS

BRIEF FOR PRIGG

◆ Under Article 4, section 2, Congress has exclusive jurisdiction over the subject of fugitive slaves. The constitutionality of the Fugitive Slave Act has been recognized by courts in three nonslaveholding states (Massachusetts,

New York, and Pennsylvania), and by all federal courts in cases involving fugitive slaves.

◆ Congress's power in this area must be exclusive if the purposes of Article 4, section 2, are to be achieved. If states have concurrent authority over fugitive slaves, the Constitutional guarantee signifies nothing.

◆ If Congress's power over fugitive slaves is not exclusive, any concurrent powers residing with the states are suspended by the actual exercise of federal power.

BRIEF FOR PENNSYLVANIA

◆ The Pennsylvania law of 1826 is consistent with Article 4, section 2, of the Constitution, which was merely a guarantee that states be prohibited from passing laws declaring slaves to be free within their jurisdictions. Beyond prohibiting states from setting fugitive slaves free, the Constitution left the states at liberty to exercise their own judgment in passing laws on the redelivery of slaves to their owners.

◆ The Fugitive Slave Act of 1793 exceeded Congress's authority over the return of fugitive slaves. Article 4, section 2, gave no authority to the national government; it simply prohibited the states from passing laws or regulations liberating fugitive slaves. Congress's power is limited to legislating on the subject of fugitives from justice. There is not the remotest connection between the power to render up fugitives from justice and fugitive slaves.

◆ The Constitution did not aim to abridge any state sovereignty on the subject of fugitive slaves beyond prohibiting them from setting fugitive slaves at liberty. The states are the best judges of the mode of delivering up fugitive slaves most acceptable to their citizens.

◆ Assuming that Congress did have authority to enact the Fugitive Slave Act, the Pennsylvania law is consistent with it. Together, the two laws form a harmonious system by recognizing the rights of the slaveholder while reflecting the feelings, sympathies, and sovereign power of the states.

SUPREME COURT DECISION: 9–0

(on invalidity of Pennsylvania law)

STORY, J.

... Before proceeding to discuss the very important and interesting questions involved in this record, it is fit to say, that the cause has been conduced in the court below, and has been brought here by the co-operation and sanction, both of the State of Maryland, and the State of Pennsylvania, in the most friendly and courteous spirit, with a view to have those questions finally disposed of by the adjudication of this court; so that the agitations on this subject, in both states, which have had a tendency to interrupt the harmony between them, may subside, and the conflict of opinion be put at rest. It should also be added, that the statute of Pennsylvania of 1826, was (as has been suggested at the bar) passed with a view of meeting the supposed wishes of Maryland on the subject of fugitive slaves; and that, although it has failed to produce the good effects intended in its practical construction, the result was unforeseen and undesigned....

There are two clauses in the Constitution upon the subject of fugitives, which stand in juxtaposition with each other, and have been thought mutually to illustrate each other. They are both contained in the second section of the fourth article, and are in the following words: "A person charged in any State with treason, felony or other crime, who shall flee from justice, and be found in another State, shall, on demand of the executive authority of the State, from which he fled, be delivered up, to be removed to the State having jurisdiction of the crime." "No person held to service or labor in one State, under the laws thereof, escaping into another, shall, in consequence of any law or regulation therein, be discharged from such service or labor; but shall be delivered up, on claim of the party to whom such service or labor may be due."

The last clause is that, the true interpretation whereof is directly in judgment before us. Historically, it is well known, that the object of this clause was to secure to the citizens of the slaveholding States the complete right and title of ownership in their slaves, as property, in every State in the Union into which they might escape from the State where they were held in servitude. The full recognition of this right and title was indispensable to the security of this species of property in all the slaveholding States; and, indeed, was so vital

to the preservation of their domestic interests and institutions, that it cannot be doubted, that it constituted a fundamental article, without the adoption of which the Union could not have been formed. Its true design was, to guard against the doctrines and principles prevalent in the non-slaveholding States, by preventing them from intermeddling with, or obstructing, or abolishing the rights of the owners of slaves....

How, then, are we to interpret the language of the clause? The true answer is, in such a manner as, consistently with the words, shall fully and completely effectuate the whole objects of it.... No court of justice can be authorized so to construe any clause of the Constitution as to defeat its obvious ends, when another construction, equally accordant with the words and sense thereof, will enforce and protect them....

[T]he clause contains a positive and unqualified recognition of the right of the owner in the slave, unaffected by any State law or legislation whatsoever, because there is no qualification or restriction of it to be found therein; and we have no right to insert any, which is not expressed, and cannot be fairly implied. Especially, are we estopped from so doing, when the clause puts the right to the service or labor upon the same ground, and to the same extent, in every other State as in the State from which the slave escaped, and in which he was held to the service or labor. If this be so, then all the incidents to that right attach also. The owner must, therefore, have the right to seize and repossess the slave, which the local laws of his own state confer upon him, as property; and we all know that this right of seizure and recaption is universally acknowledged in all the slaveholding States. Indeed, this is not more than a mere affirmance of the principles of the common law applicable to this very subject.... Upon this ground, we have not the slightest hesitation in holding, that under and in virtue of the Constitution, the owner of a slave is clothed with entire authority, in every State in the Union, to seize and recapture his slave, whenever he can do it, without any breach of the peace or any illegal violence. In this sense, and to this extent, this clause of the Constitution may properly be said to execute itself, and to require no aid from legislation, State or national....

And this leads us to the consideration of the other part of the clause, which implies at once a guarantee and a duty. It says, "but he (the slave) shall be delivered up, on claim of the party to whom such service or labor may be due." Now, we think it exceedingly difficult, if not impracticable, to read this language, and not to feel, that it contemplated some further remedial redress than that which might be administered at the hands of the owner himself. A claim is to be made! What is a claim? It is, in a just juridical sense, a demand of some matter as of right, made by one person upon another, to do or to forbear to do some act or thing as a matter of duty....

It is plain, then, that where a claim is made by the owner, out of possession, for the delivery of a slave, it must be made, if at all, against some other person; and inasmuch as the right is a right of property, capable of being recognized and asserted by proceedings before a court of justice, between parties adverse to each other, it constitutes, in the strictest sense, a controversy between the parties, and a case "arising under the Constitution" of the United States, within the express delegation of judicial power given by that instrument. Congress, then, may call that power into activity, for the very purpose of giving effect to that right; and if so, then it may prescribe the mode and extent in which it shall be applied, and how, and under what circumstances, the proceedings shall afford a complete protection and guarantee to the right....

The remaining question is, whether the power of legislation upon this subject is exclusive in the national government, or concurrent in the States, until it is exercised by congress. In our opinion, it is exclusive; and we shall now proceed briefly to state our reasons for that opinion. The doctrine stated by this court, in *Sturges v. Crowninshield*, 4 Wheat[on] 122 [(1819), contains the true, although not the sole, rule or consideration, which is applicable to this particular subject. "Wherever," said Mr. Chief Justice Marshall, in delivering the opinion of the court, "the terms in which a power is granted to congress, or the nature of the power, require, that it should be exercised exclusively by congress, the subject is as completely taken from the state legislatures, as if they had been forbidden to act." The nature of the power, and the true objects to be attained by it, are then as important to be weighed, in considering the question of its exclusiveness, as the words in which it is granted.

In the first place, it is material to state … that the right to seize and retake fugitive slaves and the duty to deliver them up, in whatever state of the Union they may be found, and, of course, the corresponding power in Congress to use the appropriate means to enforce the right and duty, derive their whole validity and obligation exclusively from the Constitution of the United States, and are there, for the first time, recognised and established in that peculiar character. Before the adoption of the Constitution, no State had any power whatsoever over the subject, except within its own territorial limits, and could not bind the sovereignty or the legislation of other States. Whenever the right was acknowledged, or the duty enforced, in any State, it was as a matter of comity, and not as a matter of strict moral, political or international obligation or duty. Under the Constitution, it is recognised as an absolute, positive right and duty, pervading the whole Union with an equal and supreme force, uncontrolled and uncontrollable by State sovereignty or State legislation....

In the next place, the nature of the provision and the objects to be attained by it, require that it should be controlled by one and the same will, and act uniformly by the same system of regulations throughout the Union. If, then, the States have a right, in the absence of legislation by congress, to act upon the subject, each State is at liberty to prescribe just such regulations as suit its own policy, local convenience and local feelings. The legislation of one State may not only be different from, but utterly repugnant to and incompatible with, that of another. The time and mode, and limitation of the remedy, the proofs of the title, and all other incidents applicable thereto, may be prescribed in one state, which are rejected or disclaimed in another. One State may require the owner to sue in one mode, another, in a different mode. One State may make a statute of limitations as to the remedy, in its own tribunals, short and summary; another may prolong the period, and yet

restrict the proofs. Nay, some States may utterly refuse to act upon the subject at all; and others may refuse to open its courts to any remedies in rem, because they would interfere with their own domestic policy, institutions or habits. The right, therefore, would never, in a practical sense, be the same in all the States. It would have no unity of purpose, or uniformity of operation. The duty might be enforced in some States; retarded or limited in others; and denied, as compulsory, in many, if not in all. Consequences like these must have been foreseen as very likely to occur in the non-slave-holding States, where legislation, if not silent on the subject, and purely voluntary, could scarcely be presumed to be favorable to the exercise of the rights of the owner.

It is scarcely conceivable, that the slave-holding States would have been satisfied with leaving to the legislation of the non-slave-holding States, a power of regulation, in the absence of that of Congress, which would or might practically amount to a power to destroy the rights of the owner. If the argument, therefore, of a concurrent power in the States to act upon the subject-matter, in the absence of legislation by Congress, be well founded; then, if Congress had never acted at all, or if the act of Congress should be repealed, without providing a substitute, there would be a resulting authority in each of the States to regulate the whole subject, at its pleasure, and to dole out its own remedial justice, or withhold it, at its pleasure, and according to its own views of policy and expediency. Surely, such a state of things never could have been intended, under such a solemn guarantee of right and duty. On the other hand, construe the right of legislation as exclusive in

Congress, and every evil and every danger vanishes. The right and the duty are then co-extensive and uniform in remedy and operation throughout the whole Union. The owner has the same security, and the same remedial justice, and the same exemption from state regulation and control, through however many States he may pass with his fugitive slave in his possession, *in transitu* [in transit] to his own domicile....

Upon these grounds, we are of opinion, that the act of Pennsylvania upon which this indictment is founded, is unconstitutional and void. It purports to punish as a public offence against that State, the very act of seizing and removing a slave, by his master, which the Constitution of the United States was designed to justify and uphold....

TANEY, C.J., DISSENTING IN PART

... [A]s I understand the opinion of the court, it ... decides that the power to provide a remedy for [the right of a master to arrest his fugitive slave] is vested exclusively in Congress; and that all laws upon the subject passed by a State, since the adoption of the Constitution of the United States, are null and void; even although they were intended, in good faith, to protect the owner in the exercise of his rights of property, and do not conflict in any degree with the act of Congress....

I think the States are not prohibited; and that, on the contrary, it is enjoined

upon them as a duty to protect and support the owner when he is endeavoring to obtain possession of his property found within their respective territories.

The language used in the Constitution does not, in my judgment, justify the construction given to it by the court. It contains no words prohibiting the several States from passing laws to enforce this right. They are in express terms forbidden to make any regulation that shall impair it. But there the prohibition stops....

THOMPSON, BALDWIN, WAYNE, AND DANIEL, J.J., CONCURRING [OMITTED]

MCLEAN, J., CONCURRING IN PART AND DISSENTING IN PART

... The presumption, in a non-slave-holding State, is against the right of the master, and in favor of the freedom of the person he claims. This presumption may be rebutted, but until it is rebutted by the proof required in the act of 1793, and also, in my judgment, by the constitution, must not the law of the state be respected and obeyed?...

My opinion ... does not rest so much upon the particular law of Pennsylvania, as upon the inherent and sovereign power of a State to protect its jurisdiction and the peace of its citizens, in any and every mode which its discretion shall dictate, which shall not conflict with a defined power of the federal government.

QUESTIONS

1. Summarize Justice Story's opinion in *Prigg*. Does his opinion stand for the proposition that all state laws that interfere with enforcement of the Fugitive Slave Act are unconstitutional? In Justice Story's view,

did state officials have authority to enforce the Fugitive Slave Act? Could federal officials force them to do so?

2. Does Chief Justice Taney's dissent in *Prigg* stand for the proposition that under the Constitution the states retain whatever powers are not explicitly denied to them? Is that view consistent with the view that Congress has only those powers explicitly delegated to it by some provision of the Constitution? Under Taney's reading, how would other conflicts between national and state laws be resolved?

3. Is it significant that the Court could not arrive at a unanimous opinion in *Prigg* concerning the relative powers of the national government and the states? Does the Court's inability to do so suggest that there is something intractable about defining precisely the nature of the respective powers of the national government and the states?

4. Justice Story noted at the outset of his opinion in *Prigg* that both Maryland and Pennsylvania approached the litigation with a "friendly and courteous spirit." Put another way, *Prigg* was a trumped up case. Officials in Maryland and Pennsylvania agreed to bring the case in order to test the constitutionality of the Pennsylvania Personal Liberty Law. As explained in Chapter 1, the Supreme Court could have refused to hear the case because the parties were not strictly adverse to one another and therefore had no actual case in controversy. Was the principle regarding national preemption stated in *Prigg* so important that the justices were warranted in overlooking their own rule against deciding "friendly" cases?

5. In 1842, when he had returned to Massachusetts, Justice Story told his family and friends that *Prigg* was a "triumph of freedom" (R. Kent Newmeyer, *Supreme Court Justice Joseph Story* [Chapel Hill, NC: University of North Carolina Press, 1985], p. 372). On what basis could Justice Story make such a claim, given that his opinion upheld the Fugitive Slave Act over the Pennsylvania law that opposed rendition of fugitive slaves? Does Story's statement suggest that *Prigg* must be understood in terms of principles that transcended the actual controversy in that case?

COMMENT

The fugitive slave issue implicated many aspects of federalism, not all of which were resolved by *Prigg*. Between 1842 and the Civil War, the Court also handed down the following decisions:

Case: *Jones v. VanZandt*, 5 Howard 215 (1847)
Vote: 9–0

Decision: The Fugitive Slave Act of 1793, authorizing slave holders to seize or arrest fugitive slaves, and making it a crime to obstruct or hinder reclamation, is a valid exercise of Congress's power under Article 4, section 2, clause 3, and is not repugnant to the Northwest Ordinance of 1787, which outlawed slavery in American territories. The act was passed merely to render effective the guaranty of the Constitution itself.

Case: *Strader v. Graham*, 10 Howard 82 (1851)
Vote: 9–0
Decision: State law alone must decide the question whether slaves who were permitted by their master to pass occasionally from a slave state (in this case, Kentucky), to a free state (in this case, Ohio), thereby acquire a right to freedom after their return to Kentucky. The Northwest Ordinance of 1787, governing the territory out of which the state of Ohio was carved, does not confer jurisdiction on federal courts to decide such issues.

Case: *Moore v. Illinois*, 14 Howard 13 (1853)
Vote: 7–1
Decision: An Illinois statute making it a misdemeanor to harbor or secrete any negro, mulatto, or person of color does not conflict with Article 4, Section 2, Clause 3, of the Constitution because it does not conflict with the right of the owner or claimant to arrest and recapture his slave. The statute is a valid exercise of the state's police power to define offenses and punish offenders of its laws.

Case: *Ableman v. Booth*, 21 Howard 506 (1859)
Vote: 9–0
Decision: The federal Fugitive Slave Act of 1850 is a constitutional exercise of Congress's powers despite a contrary ruling by the Wisconsin Supreme Court on the ground that the act violated a state guarantee of a jury trial for a state resident. For the sake of uniformity in application of the law, federal courts have exclusive jurisdiction over cases arising under the act. States also lack authority to release by habeas corpus persons in custody pursuant to federal authority.

Case: *Kentucky v. Dennison*, 24 Howard 66 (1861)
Vote: 8–0
Decision: The Fugitive Slave Law of 1793, making it a duty for the chief executive of a state to render up a fugitive from justice upon demand of the chief executive of the state from which the fugitive fled, does not impose a constitutional duty of compliance and hence is not enforceable in federal courts. State governors have only a "moral duty" to render up fugitives from justice. Under the Constitution, the federal government has no power to impose on a state officer any duty whatever and compel him to perform it.

NATIONAL PREEMPTION

Pennsylvania v. Nelson
350 U.S. 497 (1956)

SETTING

Governments have always enacted laws to protect themselves against the threat—real or perceived—of destruction from within. In 1798, for example, the Federalist Party enacted a series of laws called the Alien and Sedition Acts to suppress Republican opposition to Federalist programs. The Sedition Act imposed heavy fines and imprisonment on anyone found guilty of "combining and conspiring to oppose the execution of the laws, or publishing false, scandalous, or malicious writings against the President, Congress, or the government of the United States." The Sedition Act was used to suppress critics of the Adams administration and, although only ten Republicans were ever convicted under its provisions, many were put on trial and the threat of prosecution had a chilling effect on free speech. The Alien and Sedition Acts expired before the Supreme Court could determine their constitutionality.

Sedition acts are particularly popular in times of war and national emergency. In 1917, in response to World War I, Congress enacted the Espionage Act, and a year later, reacting both to the war and to the Communist Revolution of 1917, it passed the Sedition Act of 1918. The 1918 law penalized anyone who used "disloyal, profane, scurrilous, or abusive" language about the U.S. government, the American flag, or military uniforms. In 1919, the state of Pennsylvania, like more than thirty other states, also adopted a Sedition Act to protect the state from internal subversion. The law was reenacted in 1939. Under the Pennsylvania law, it was a crime, among other things,

> to make or cause to be made any outbreak … of violence against this state or against the United States; to encourage any person … to engage in any conduct with the view of overthrowing or destroying … by any force or show or threat of force, the government of this state or of the United States."

In 1940, Congress enacted the Smith Act, which made it a crime to advocate, abet, advise, or teach the violent overthrow of the U.S. government or to publish or distribute printed matter that advocated violent overthrow, or to join any society that advocated violent overthrow of the U.S. government. The Smith Act was one of a series of acts aimed at preventing the spread of Communism. Conflicts between national and state sedition acts inevitably led to litigation that raised preemption questions.

In early 1950, Matthew Cvetic testified before a hearing of the U.S. House

Committee on Un-American Activities (the Committee is described in Chapter 3, pp. 372–373) investigating the Communist Party in Pittsburgh, Pennsylvania. Cvetic identified Steve Nelson, Andrew Onda, and James Dolsen as spies, saboteurs, gangsters, traitors, atheists, and communists. Nelson, an admitted member of the Communist Party, subsequently was indicted on twelve counts of violating the 1939 Pennsylvania Sedition Act by encouraging people to engage in activities aimed at overthrowing and destroying the governments of Pennsylvania and the United States, and by publishing and distributing printed matter encouraging government overthrow.

Nelson was unable to retain local counsel to represent him at trial because of his political unpopularity. His motion for a continuance to permit him to engage out-of-state counsel was denied and he was compelled to proceed to trial without counsel. While his Pennsylvania trial was underway, Nelson was also indicted for violation of the 1940 Smith Act.

Following his trial in the Court of Quarter Sessions of Allegheny County, Pennsylvania, Nelson was convicted and sentenced to prison for twenty years and fined $10,000. He appealed to the Superior Court of Pennsylvania, which affirmed. Nelson then appealed to the Supreme Court of Pennsylvania, which reversed the conviction and quashed the indictment against him. Although on appeal Nelson had alleged many trial errors and violation of his due process rights, the Pennsylvania Supreme Court reversed his conviction on the narrow ground that the Smith Act superseded the Pennsylvania Sedition Act. The Supreme Court granted Pennsylvania's petition for a writ of certiorari.

HIGHLIGHTS OF SUPREME COURT ARGUMENTS

BRIEF FOR PENNSYLVANIA

◆ Decisions of this Court firmly establish the power of the state to make it a crime to commit acts advocating the overthrow of the government of the United States by force or violence.

◆ The rights of states to enact their own sedition laws is part of the right of self-preservation that is essential to state sovereignty.

◆ The police power gives the state the inherent right to suppress insurrection and to enact laws for the punishment of offenders. The national government has no police organization to protect lives and property.

◆ No language in the Smith Act expresses an intent to supersede the Pennsylvania Sedition Act and there is no conflict between the two acts.

AMICUS CURIAE BRIEFS SUPPORTING PENNSYLVANIA

State of Texas; Commonwealth of Massachusetts; joint brief of New Hampshire, Arizona, Connecticut, Florida, Georgia, Indiana, Kansas, Louisiana, Maine, Maryland, Massachusetts, Michigan, Mississippi, Nebraska, Nevada, New Mexico, New York, North Carolina, Ohio, South Carolina, Tennessee,

Virginia, Washington, and Wisconsin; State of Illinois; The American Legion; United States.

BRIEF FOR NELSON

◆ Nelson was tried under the Pennsylvania statute proscribing sedition against the United States and was convicted on that charge. He was not convicted of sedition against the state of Pennsylvania. The only issue in this case is whether the state can enact or enforce a law making sedition against the United States a crime when there is an identical federal law on the same subject.

◆ The power exercised by the federal government in enacting the Smith Act springs from the very roots of political sovereignty. The subject matter of sedition against the United States is not within the traditional authority reserved to the states under the Constitution.

◆ Even though state and federal powers are concurrent and equal, where Congress has passed specific legislation in the exercise of a power delegated to it, that legislation must be deemed to supersede identical state law on the same subject in the absence of clear indication to the contrary.

◆ Double or even multiple punishment for the commission of the identical crime would be inflicted if both state and federal laws were permitted to stand. Guarantees against double jeopardy would thereby be implicated.

AMICUS CURIAE BRIEFS SUPPORTING NELSON

Joint brief of individuals who have been indicted or subjected to interrogation pursuant to laws in Massachusetts, New Hampshire, Kentucky, and Florida; Civil Liberties Committee of the Philadelphia Yearly Meeting of the Religious Society of Friends.

SUPREME COURT DECISION: 6–3

WARREN, C.J.

... Because of the important question of federal-state relationship involved, we granted *certiorari.*

It should be said at the outset that the decision in this case does not affect the right of States to enforce their sedition laws at times when the Federal Government has not occupied the field and is not protecting the entire country from seditious conduct. The distinction between the two situations was clearly recognized by the court below. Nor does it limit the jurisdiction of the States where the Constitution and Congress have specifically given them concurrent jurisdiction[.]... Neither does it limit the right of the State to protect itself at any time against sabotage or attempted violence of all kinds. Nor does it prevent the State from prosecuting where the same act constitutes both a federal offense and a state offense under the police power[.]...

Where, as in the instant case,

Congress has not stated specifically whether a federal statute has occupied a field in which the States are otherwise free to legislate, different criteria have furnished touchstones for decision....

In this case, we think that each of several tests of supersession is met.

First, "(t)he scheme of federal regulation (is) so pervasive as to make reasonable the inference that Congress left no room for the States to supplement it." (*Rice v. Santa Fe Elevator Corp.*, 331 U.S. 218 (1947).) The Congress determined in 1940 that it was necessary for it to re-enter the field of antisubversive legislation, which had been abandoned by it in 1921. In that year, it enacted the Smith Act which proscribes advocacy of the overthrow of any government—federal, state or local—by force and violence and organization of and knowing membership in a group which so advocates.... The Internal Security Act of 1950 is aimed more directly at Communist organizations. It distinguishes between "Communist-action organizations" and "Communist-front organizations," requiring such organizations to register and to file annual reports with the Attorney General giving complete details as to their officers and funds. Members of Communist-action organizations who have not been registered by their organization must register as individuals.... And the Act imposes certain sanctions upon both "action" and "front" organizations and their members. The Communist Control Act of 1954 declares "that the Communist Party of the United States, although purportedly a political party, is in fact an instrumentality of a conspiracy to overthrow the Government of the United States" and that "its role as the agency of a hostile foreign power ren-

ders its existence a clear present and continuing danger to the security of the United States." It also contains a legislative finding that the Communist Party is a "Communist-action organization" within the meaning of the Internal Security Act of 1950 and provides that "knowing" members of the Communist Party are "subject to all the provisions and penalties" of that Act. It furthermore sets up a new classification of "Communist-infiltrated organizations" and provides for the imposition of sanctions against them.

We examine these Acts only to determine the congressional plan. Looking to all of them in the aggregate, the conclusion is inescapable that Congress has intended to occupy the field of sedition. Taken as a whole, they evince a congressional plan which makes it reasonable to determine that no room has been left for the States to supplement it. Therefore, a state sedition statute is superseded regardless of whether it purports to supplement the federal law....

Second, the federal statutes "touch a field in which the federal interest is so dominant that the federal system (must) be assumed to preclude enforcement of state laws on the same subject." *Rice.* Congress has devised an all-embracing program for resistance to the various forms of totalitarian aggression. Our external defenses have been strengthened, and a plan to protect against internal subversion has been made by it. It has appropriated vast sums, not only for our own protection, but also to strengthen freedom throughout the world. It has charged the Federal Bureau of Investigation and the Central Intelligence Agency with responsibility for intelligence concerning Communist seditious activities against our Government, and has denominated such activities as part of a world conspiracy. It accordingly proscribed sedition against all government in the nation—national, state and local....

Third, enforcement of state sedition acts presents a serious danger of conflict with the administration of the federal program. Since 1939, in order to avoid a hampering of uniform enforcement of its program by sporadic local prosecutions, the Federal Government has urged local authorities not to intervene in such matters, but to turn over to the federal authorities immediately and unevaluated all information concerning subversive activities....

[T]he Pennsylvania Statute presents a peculiar danger of interference with the federal program. For, as the court below observed:

> Unlike the Smith Act, which can be administered only by federal officers acting in their official capacities, indictment for sedition under the Pennsylvania statute can be initiated upon an information made by a private individual. The opportunity thus present for the indulgence of personal spite and hatred or for furthering some selfish advantage or ambition need only be mentioned to be appreciated....

In his brief, the Solicitor General states that forty-two States plus Alaska and Hawaii have statutes which in some form prohibit advocacy of the violent overthrow of established government. These statutes are entitled anti-sedition statutes, criminal anarchy laws, criminal syndicalist laws, etc. Although all of them are primarily directed against the overthrow of the United States Government, they are in no sense uniform. And our attention has not been called to any case where the prosecution has been successfully directed against an attempt to destroy state or local government. Some of these Acts are studiously drawn and purport to protect fundamental rights by appropriate definitions, standards of proof and orderly procedures in keeping with the avowed congressional purpose "to protect freedom from those who would destroy it, without infringing upon the freedom of all our people." Others are vague and are almost wholly without such safeguards. Some even purport to punish mere membership in subversive organizations which the federal statutes do not punish where federal registration requirements have been fulfilled.

When we were confronted with a like situation in the field of labor-management relations, Mr. Justice Jackson wrote:

> A multiplicity of tribunals and a diversity of procedures are quite as apt to produce incompatible or conflicting adjudications as are different rules of substantive law. [*Garner v. Teamsters, Chauffeurs and Helpers Local Union No. 776*, 346 U.S. 485 (1953)]

Should the States be permitted to exercise a concurrent jurisdiction in this area, federal enforcement would encounter not only the difficulties mentioned by Mr. Justice Jackson, but the added conflict engendered by different criteria of substantive offenses....

The judgment of the Supreme Court of Pennsylvania is affirmed.

Affirmed.

REED, BURTON, AND MINTON, J.J., DISSENTING

The problems of governmental power may be approached in this case free from the varied viewpoints that focus on the problems of national security. This is a jurisdictional problem of general importance because it involves an asserted limitation on the police power of the States when it is applied to a crime that is punishable also by the Federal Government. As this is a recurring problem, it is appropriate to explain our dissent.

Congress has not, in any of its statutes relating to sedition, specifically barred the exercise of state power to punish the same Acts under state law. And, we read the majority opinion to assume for this case that, absent federal legislation, there is no constitutional bar to punishment of sedition against the United States by both a State and the Nation. The majority limits to the federal courts the power to try charges of sedition against the Federal Government.

First, the Court relies upon the pervasiveness of the antisubversive legislation embodied in the Smith Act of 1940, ... the Internal Security Act of 1950, ... and the Communist Control Act of 1954. It asserts that these Acts in the aggregate mean that Congress has occupied the "field of sedition" to the exclusion of the States. The "occupation of the field" argument has been developed by this Court for the Commerce Clause and legislation thereunder to prevent partitioning of this country by locally erected trade barriers. In those cases this Court has ruled that state legislation is superseded when it conflicts with the comprehensive regulatory scheme and purpose of a federal plan....

But the federal sedition laws are distinct criminal statutes that punish willful advocacy of the use of force against "the government of the United States or the government of any State." These criminal laws proscribe certain local activity without creating any statutory or administrative regulation. There is, consequently, no question as to whether some general congressional regulatory scheme might be upset by a coinciding state plan. In these circumstances the conflict should be clear and direct before this Court reads a congressional intent to void state legislation into the federal sedition acts.... We cannot agree that the federal criminal sanctions against sedition directed at the United States are of such a pervasive character as to indicate an intention to void state action.

Secondly, the Court states that the federal sedition statutes touch a field "in which the federal interest is so dominant" they must preclude state laws on the same subject....

We are citizens of the United States and of the State wherein we reside and are dependent upon the strength of both to preserve our rights and liberties. Both may enact criminal statutes for mutual protection unless Congress has otherwise provided....

Thirdly, the Court finds ground for abrogating Pennsylvania's antisedition statute because, in the Court's view, the State's administration of the Act may hamper the enforcement of the federal law.... We find no suggestion from any official source that state officials should be less alert to ferret out or punish subversion. The Court's attitude as to interference seems to us quite contrary to that of the Legislative and Executive Departments. Congress was advised of the existing state sedition legislation when the Smith Act was enacted and has been kept current with its spread. No declaration of exclusiveness followed....

Finally, and this one point seems in and of itself decisive, there is an independent reason for reversing the Pennsylvania Supreme Court. The Smith Act appears in Title 18 of the United States Code, 18 U.S.C.A., which Title codifies the federal criminal laws. Section 3231 of that Title provides:

Nothing in this title shall be held to take away or impair the jurisdiction of the courts of the several States under the laws thereof.

That declaration springs from the federal character of our Nation. It recognizes the fact that maintenance of order and fairness rests primarily with the States....

QUESTIONS

1. The *amicus* brief for the state of New Hampshire and other states contended that Representative Howard Smith of Virginia, the sponsor of the Smith Act "never had the faintest notion that Congress was nullifying the concurrent jurisdiction of the sovereign states" and that the debates surrounding adoption of the Smith Act made it clear that that was not the intent of the law. The *amicus* brief for the United States agreed. It contended that congressional nullification of important parts of the basic criminal laws of most of the states "requires the clearest sort of showing that such was the purpose of Congress" and that both the Smith Act and its legislative history "are barren of any suggestion that supersedure of similar state laws was intended."

   Is Chief Justice Warren's opinion in *Nelson* responsive to the concerns of *amici*? Is there evidence in the opinion that the Court reviewed Congress's intent in adopting the Smith Act to determine whether it was intended to supersede state legislation regarding sedition against the national government? Should it have?

2. In the *amicus* brief submitted on behalf of individuals who had been prosecuted or interrogated under other state sedition laws, counsel contended that if the Supreme Court reversed the Pennsylvania Supreme Court's opinion, "the already perilous weapon of prevention [of sedition] would be given a double barrel and be handed over to the notoriously unrestrained and uncritical hands of state prosecutors. The implications of a sanction of such a dual system can hardly be overstated." Does any language in Chief Justice Warren's opinion in *Nelson* indicate that one of the federalism issues that prompted the Court to grant certiorari in *Nelson* was the Court's concern with the quality of justice administered by the states?

3. After the decision in *Nelson*, the state of Pennsylvania petitioned for rehearing, on the ground that the Court's opinion did not state clearly that it was not intended to inhibit a state in prosecutions for sedition against the state as such. The Court denied the petition. Was counsel for Pennsylvania correct that *Nelson* could and should have been more clear about the reach of federal preemption in the field of sedition?

COMMENT

Nelson was one of the nine cases, along with *Watkins v. United States*, cited in unsuccessful congressional legislation, introduced in 1958, as among four categories of cases requiring that the Supreme Court's power be curbed. One aspect of congressional anger at the Supreme Court was the view that decisions like *Nelson* violated states' rights. (See "Court-Curb Proposals Stimulated by Controversial Decisions," in *Congress and the Nation I* [Washington, D.C.: Congressional Quarterly, Inc. 1965].)

NATIONAL PREEMPTION

Cipollone v. Liggett Group, Inc.
505 U.S. 504 (1992)

SETTING

Not all national preemption issues have come to the Supreme Court in contexts like *Prigg* and *Nelson* in which both the national government and a state government have enacted legislation seeking to regulate particular conduct. Another context that raises preemption questions is exemplified by Congress's efforts to regulate cigarette advertising: Do federal regulations with which the tobacco industry has complied shield the industry from suits brought under state laws for damages suffered by cigarette smokers?

Responding to increasing scientific evidence linking tobacco smoking to public health problems, Congress in 1965 enacted the Federal Cigarette Labeling and Advertising Act. Section 4 of the act required that conspicuous labels be placed on every package of cigarettes sold in the United States, warning that cigarette smoking may be hazardous to health. Section 5, entitled "Preemption," provided that no statement relating to smoking and health other than the statement required by section 4 could be required on any cigarette package. In 1969, Congress enacted the Public Health Cigarette Smoking Act to require label warnings that said, in effect, "WARNING: THE SURGEON GENERAL HAS DETERMINED THAT CIGARETTE SMOKING IS DANGEROUS TO YOUR HEALTH." The 1969 law also amended section 5 to specify that

> No requirement or prohibition based on smoking and health shall be imposed under State law with respect to the advertising or promotion of any cigarettes the packages of which are [lawfully] labeled.

Over twenty years before adoption of this congressional legislation, Rose Cipollone became a smoker. The daughter of Italian immigrants, she was born in 1925 and reared in Queens, New York. As a girl, she idolized female movie stars, admiring their glamorous gowns and sophistication. Cipollone began to smoke Chesterfield Cigarettes (manufactured by Liggett) in 1942, at the age of 16, because it was a "cool, glamorous and grown-up" thing to do. She smoked Chesterfields because she was attracted by the advertisements of movie stars and pretty girls smoking them and because the ads stated that the cigarettes were "mild," which she interpreted to mean safe. By 1943, she was smoking a pack of Chesterfields a day. In 1955, in her desire to smoke a safe cigarette, Cipollone switched to the "miracle tip" filtered L&M Cigarettes, also manufactured by Liggett.

In 1964, the Surgeon General's Report on Smoking and Health reported links between smoking, cancer, and heart disease. Cipollone did not believe the reports because, "Tobacco companies wouldn't do anything that was going to kill you so I figured, ah, until they proved it to me to be real, I didn't take it seriously." She was certain that "if there was anything that [was] dangerous, that the tobacco people wouldn't allow it and the government wouldn't let them do that." Impressed by the images of glamorous, liberated women in the Virginia Slims ads, Cipollone switched to Virginia Slims in 1968. She later switched to Parliaments because she thought they were safer, based on their advertisements about being lower in tar and nicotine with a recessed filter.

In 1981, Cipollone was diagnosed with lung cancer but was unable to quit smoking. Even after one lung was removed in 1982, she continued to smoke clandestinely.

In August 1983, Cipollone and her husband, Antonio, filed a complaint against the Liggett Group, Inc., Lorillard, Inc., and Philip Morris, Inc., three of the leading firms in the tobacco industry. The prime defendant was the Liggett Group, whose cigarettes Cipollone had smoked from 1942 to 1968. The Cipollones filed their suit in the Federal District Court for the District of New Jersey, invoking its diversity jurisdiction. Their complaint alleged that Cipollone developed lung cancer because she smoked cigarettes manufactured and sold by Liggett. Following Rose's death in 1984, Antonio Cipollone filed an amended complaint, but he, too, died while the case was in progress. The litigation was continued by their son, Thomas, as the executor of his parents' estates. According to Thomas Cipollone's complaint, the defendant cigarette manufacturers failed to inform consumers adequately of the health risks of smoking, intentionally neutralized the effect of the congressionally-mandated health warnings through their advertising and public relations campaigns, knowingly misrepresented the health hazards of smoking, and ignored and withheld from the public medical and scientific evidence of the dangers of smoking.

All of Cipollone's claims were based on New Jersey law. One of Liggett's defenses was that it was protected against litigation in state court by the 1965 and 1969 federal statutes for conduct after 1965. In other words, it contended that Cipollone's state litigation had been preempted by the federal statutes.

The district court ruled that the federal statutes did not by their express terms or by implication preempt state common law actions and struck the preemption defense. Liggett took an interlocutory appeal to the Court of Appeals for the Third Circuit, which held that under the federal statutes state-law damages actions relating to smoking and health were preempted to the extent that the actions challenged the adequacy of the warning on cigarette labels or the propriety of the advertising and promotion of cigarettes. The case was remanded to the district court.

On remand, the trial court ruled that Cipollone's claims that Liggett failed to warn, expressly warranted, fraudulently misrepresented, and conspired, were preempted to the extent that they relied on post-1965 advertising and public relations activities. After a four-month trial, the jury awarded Cipollone $400,000 in damages on the pre-1966 express warranty claim against Liggett, the manufacturer of the cigarettes Rose had smoked before 1965. The jury also found that Liggett had a duty to warn of the hazards of smoking before 1966, that it failed to do so, and that its failure to warn was the proximate cause of Rose's lung cancer and death. The jury also returned a verdict in favor of Liggett on the failure to warn claim because of its findings regarding the comparative fault of Rose Cipollone and Liggett. The jury rejected Cipollone's fraudulent misrepresentation and conspiracy claims.

Both sides appealed. The Court of Appeals for the Third Circuit affirmed the district court's preemption rulings, but remanded for a new trial on other grounds. The Supreme Court of the United States granted Cipollone's petition for a writ of certiorari.

HIGHLIGHTS OF SUPREME COURT ARGUMENTS

BRIEF FOR CIPOLLONE

◆ Under the Supremacy Clause, state law tort claims may be preempted by federal law if Congress has stated explicitly that the state law claims are displaced; if Congress has exclusively occupied a particular field with the intent to supplant state law claims; or state law actually conflicts with the federal statute. None of those conditions is met in this case.

◆ Preemption of traditional state common law tort claims is an extraordinary occurrence, particularly of common law personal injury actions where the federal law provides no alternative remedy. The effect of preemption in this situation would leave the citizens of the several states without a remedy and would provide a shield for those guilty of tortious conduct.

◆ The presumption against preemption has served as a gatekeeper for traditional rights and remedies defined by state common law. Congressional intent to override this presumption must be expressed with drastic clarity, especially if preemption would leave a legal vacuum where state common law once stood.

AMICUS CURIAE BRIEFS SUPPORTING CIPOLLONE

Joint brief of the states of Minnesota, Alabama, Arizona, Connecticut, Idaho, Maine, Nevada, New Jersey, New Mexico, North Dakota, Ohio, and Washington; American College of Chest Physicians; Association of Trial Lawyers of America; American Medical Association; Trial Lawyers for Public Justice; joint brief of the National League of Cities, National Conference of State Legislatures, National Association of Counties, Council of State Governments, International City Management Association, and U.S. Conference of Mayors; joint brief of six former Surgeons General of the United States, The American Council for Science and Health, and the Tobacco Products Liability Project.

BRIEF FOR THE LIGGETT GROUP, INC., ET AL.

◆ Cipollone's claims are preempted because the Labeling and Advertising Act declares a federal policy demanding uniform federal standards in a prescribed area, creates a regulatory scheme that the Act declares comprehensive, and includes an express preemption provision. The state tort law duties Cipollone alleges conflict with the declared federal policy and intrude on the field occupied by the Act.

◆ The claims in this case are premised on a theory of failure to warn. That is an implicit attack on the adequacy of the federal warning, because they seek to establish a state-law duty to provide additional warnings regarding smoking and health.

◆ The federal Labeling and Advertising Act marks out a carefully defined field for exclusive federal control: any health-based obligations imposed with respect to warnings or on advertising and promotional activities.

◆ Cipollone's suggestion that a tort "duty" is not a "requirement" fails as a matter of plain English. A duty is a course of action that is required because of one's position; a requirement is something that is obligatory. The two terms are one and the same.

AMICUS CURIAE BRIEFS SUPPORTING LIGGETT GROUP, ET AL.

Product Liability Advisory Council; Association of National Advertisers, Inc.; National Association of Manufacturers

SUPREME COURT DECISION: 4–3–2

STEVENS, J.

... Article VI of the Constitution provides that the laws of the United States "shall be the supreme Law of the Land; ... any Thing in the Constitution or Laws of any state to the Contrary notwithstanding." Thus, since our decision in *McCulloch v. Maryland* it has been settled that state law that conflicts with federal law is "without effect."... Consideration of issues arising under the Supremacy Clause "start[s] with the assumption that the historic police powers of the States [are] not to be superseded by ... Federal Act unless that [is] the clear and manifest purpose of Congress." *Rice v. Santa Fe Elevator Corp.*, 331 U.S. 218 (1947). Accordingly, "'[t]he purpose of Congress is the ultimate touchstone'" of pre-emption analysis. *Malone v. White Motor Corp.*, 435 U.S. 497 (1978) (quoting *Retail Clerks v. Schermerhorn*, 375 U.S. 96 (1963))....

In our opinion, the pre-emptive scope of the 1965 Act and the 1969 Act is governed entirely by the express language in Sec. 5 of each Act. When Congress has considered the issue of pre-emption and has included in the enacted legislation a provision explicitly addressing that issue, and when that provision provides a "reliable indicium of congressional intent with respect to state authority," *Malone*, "there is no need to infer congressional intent to pre-empt state laws from the substantive provisions" of the legislation. *California Federal Savings & Loan Assn. v. Guerra*, 479 U.S. 272 (1987).... In this case, the other provisions of the 1965 and 1969 Acts offer no cause to look beyond Sec. 5 of each Act. Therefore, we need only identify the domain expressly pre-empted by each of those sections. As the 1965 and 1969 provisions differ substantially, we consider each in turn.

In the 1965 pre-emption provision regarding advertising (Sec. 5(b)), Congress spoke precisely and narrowly: "No statement relating to smoking and health shall be required in the advertising of [properly labeled] cigarettes." Section 5(a) used the same phrase ("No statement relating to smoking and

health") with regard to cigarette labeling. As Sec. 5(a) made clear, that phrase referred to the sort of warning provided for in Sec. 4, which set forth verbatim the warning Congress determined to be appropriate. Thus, on their face, these provisions merely prohibited state and federal rule-making bodies from mandating particular cautionary statements on cigarette labels (Sec. 5(a)) or in cigarette advertisements (Sec. 5(b)).

Beyond the precise words of these provisions, this reading is appropriate for several reasons. First, ... we must construe these provisions in light of the presumption against the pre-emption of state police power regulations. This presumption reinforces the appropriateness of a narrow reading of Sec. 5. Second, the warning required in Sec. 4 does not by its own effect foreclose additional obligations imposed under state law. That Congress requires a particular warning label does not automatically pre-empt a regulatory field....

This reading comports with the 1965 Act's statement of purpose, which expressed an intent to avoid "diverse, nonuniform, and confusing labeling and advertising regulations with respect to any relationship between smoking and health." Read against the backdrop of regulatory activity undertaken by state legislatures and federal agencies in response to the Surgeon General's report, the term "regulation" most naturally refers to positive enactments by those bodies, not to common law damages actions....

For these reasons, we conclude that Sec. 5 of the 1965 Act only pre-empted state and federal rulemaking bodies from mandating particular cautionary statements and did not pre-empt state law damages actions.

Compared to its predecessor in the 1965 Act, the plain language of the pre-emption provision in the 1969 Act is much broader. First, the later Act bars not simply "statements" but rather "requirement[s] or prohibition[s] ... imposed under State law." Second, the later Act reaches beyond statements "in the advertising" to obligations "with respect to the advertising or promotion" of cigarettes.

Notwithstanding these substantial differences in language, both petitioner and respondents contend that the 1969 Act did not materially alter the pre-emptive scope of federal law. Their primary support for this contention is a sentence in a Committee Report which states that the 1969 amendment "clarified" the 1965 version of Sec. 5(b). We reject the parties' reading as incompatible with the language and origins of the amendments....

Petitioner next contends that Sec. 5(b), however broadened by the 1969 Act, does not pre-empt common law actions. He offers two theories for limiting the reach of the amended Sec. 5(b). First, he argues that common law damages actions do not impose "requirement[s] or prohibition[s]" and that Congress intended only to trump "state statute[s], injunction[s], or executive pronouncement[s]." We disagree; such an analysis is at odds both with the plain words of the 1969 Act and with the general understanding of common law damages actions. The phrase "[n]o requirement or prohibition" sweeps broadly and suggests no distinction between positive enactments and common law; to the contrary, those words easily encompass obligations that take the form of common law rules....

Petitioner's second argument for

excluding common law rules from the reach of Sec. 5(b) hinges on the phrase "imposed under State law." This argument fails as well.... Although the presumption against pre-emption might give good reason to construe the phrase "state law" in a pre-emption provision more narrowly than an identical phrase in another context, in this case such a construction is not appropriate. As explained above, the 1965 version of Sec. 5 was precise and narrow on its face; the obviously broader language of the 1969 version extended that section's pre-emptive reach....

That the pre-emptive scope of Sec. 5(b) cannot be limited to positive enactments does not mean that that section pre-empts all common law claims. For example, as respondents concede, Sec. 5(b) does not generally pre-empt "state-law obligations to avoid marketing cigarettes with manufacturing defects or to use a demonstrably safer alternative design for cigarettes." For purposes of Sec. 5(b), the common law is not of a piece....

We therefore ... must fairly but—in light of the strong presumption against pre-emption—narrowly construe the precise language of Sec. 5(b) and we must look to each of petitioner's common law claims to determine whether it is in fact pre-empted. The central inquiry in each case is straightforward: we ask whether the legal duty that is the predicate of the common law damages action constitutes a "requirement or prohibition based on smoking and health ... imposed under State law with respect to ... advertising or promotion," giving that clause a fair but narrow reading....

We consider each category of damages actions in turn. In doing so, we express no opinion on whether these actions are viable claims as a matter of state law; we assume *arguendo* [for the sake of argument] that they are.

Failure to Warn   To establish liability for a failure to warn, petitioner must show that "a warning is necessary to make a product ... reasonably safe, suitable and fit for its intended use," that respondents failed to provide such a warning, and that that failure was a proximate cause of petitioner's injury. In this case, petitioner offered two closely related theories concerning the failure to warn: first, that respondents "were negligent in the manner [that] they tested, researched, sold, promoted, and advertised" their cigarettes; and second, that respondents failed to provide "adequate warnings of the health consequences of cigarette smoking." Petitioner's claims are pre-empted to the extent that they rely on a state law "requirement or prohibition ... with respect to ... advertising or promotion." Thus, insofar as claims under either failure to warn theory require a showing that respondents' post-1969 advertising or promotions should have included additional, or more clearly stated, warnings, those claims are pre-empted. The Act does not, however, pre-empt petitioner's claims that rely solely on respondents' testing or research practices or other actions unrelated to advertising or promotion.

Breach of Express Warranty   Petitioner's claim for breach of an express warranty arises under N.J. Stat. Ann. Sec. 12A:2-313(1)(a) (West 1991), which provides:

> Any affirmation of fact or promise made by the seller to the buyer which

relates to the goods and becomes part of the basis of the bargain creates an express warranty that the goods shall conform to the affirmation or promise.

Petitioner's evidence of an express warranty consists largely of statements made in respondents' advertising....

A manufacturer's liability for breach of an express warranty derives from, and is measured by, the terms of that warranty. Accordingly, the "requirements" imposed by an express warranty claim are not "imposed under State law," but rather imposed by the warrantor.... While the general duty not to breach warranties arises under state law, the particular "requirement ... based on smoking and health ... with respect to the advertising or promotion [of] cigarettes" in an express warranty claim arises from the manufacturer's statements in its advertisements. In short, a common law remedy for a contractual commitment voluntarily undertaken should not be regarded as a "requirement ... imposed under State law " within the meaning of Sec. 5(b).

That the terms of the warranty may have been set forth in advertisements rather than in separate documents is irrelevant to the pre-emption issue (though possibly not to the state law issue of whether the alleged warranty is valid and enforceable) because although the breach of warranty claim is made "with respect to advertising" it does not rest on a duty imposed under state law. Accordingly, to the extent that petitioner has a viable claim for breach of express warranties made by respondents, that claim is not pre-empted by the 1969 Act.

Fraudulent Misrepresentation
Petitioner alleges two theories of fraudulent misrepresentation. First, peti-

tioner alleges that respondents, through their advertising, neutralized the effect of federally mandated warning labels. Such a claim is predicated on a state-law prohibition against statements in advertising and promotional materials that tend to minimize the health hazards associated with smoking. Such a prohibition, however, is merely the converse of a state law requirement that warnings be included in advertising and promotional materials. Section 5(b) of the 1969 Act pre-empts both requirements and prohibitions; it therefore supersedes petitioner's first fraudulent misrepresentation theory.

Regulators have long recognized the relationship between prohibitions on advertising that downplays the dangers of smoking and requirements for warnings in advertisements…. In this light it seems quite clear that petitioner's first theory of fraudulent misrepresentation is inextricably related to petitioner's first failure to warn theory, a theory that we have already concluded is largely pre-empted by Sec. 5(b).

Petitioner's second theory, as construed by the District Court, alleges intentional fraud and misrepresentation both by "false representation of a material fact [and by] conceal[ment of] a material fact." The predicate of this claim is a state law duty not to make false statements of material fact or to conceal such facts. Our pre-emption analysis requires us to determine whether such a duty is the sort of requirement or prohibition proscribed by Sec. 5(b).

Section 5(b) pre-empts only the imposition of state law obligations "with respect to the advertising or promotion" of cigarettes. Petitioner's claims that respondents concealed material facts are therefore not pre-empted insofar as those claims rely on a state law duty to disclose such facts through channels of communication other than advertising or promotion….

Moreover, petitioner's fraudulent misrepresentation claims that do arise with respect to advertising and promotions (most notably claims based on allegedly false statements of material fact made in advertisements) are not pre-empted by Sec. 5(b). Such claims are not predicated on a duty "based on smoking and health" but rather on a more general obligation—the duty not to deceive….

Conspiracy to Misrepresent or Conceal Material Facts   Petitioner's final claim alleges a conspiracy among respondents to misrepresent or conceal material facts concerning the health hazards of smoking. The predicate duty underlying this claim is a duty not to conspire to commit fraud. For the reasons stated in our analysis of petitioner's intentional fraud claim, this duty is not pre-empted by Sec. 5(b) for it is not a prohibition "based on smoking and health" as that phrase is properly construed. Accordingly, we conclude that the 1969 Act does not pre-empt petitioner's conspiracy claim.

To summarize our holding: The 1965 Act did not pre-empt state law damages actions; the 1969 Act pre-empts petitioner's claims based on a failure to warn and the neutralization of federally mandated warnings to the extent that those claims rely on omissions or inclusions in respondents' advertising or promotions; the 1969 Act does not pre-empt petitioner's claims based on express warranty, intentional fraud and misrepresentation, or conspiracy.

The judgment of the Court of Appeals is accordingly reversed in part and affirmed in part, and the case is remanded for further proceedings consistent with this opinion.

It is so ordered.

BLACKMUN, KENNEDY, AND SOUTER, J.J., CONCURRING IN PART, CONCURRING IN THE JUDGMENT IN PART, AND DISSENTING IN PART

The Court today would craft a compromise position concerning the extent to which federal law pre-empts persons injured by cigarette manufacturers' unlawful conduct from bringing state common-law damages claims against those manufacturers. I, however, find the Court's divided holding with respect to the original and amended versions of the federal statute entirely unsatisfactory. Our precedents do not allow us to infer a scope of pre-emption beyond that which clearly is mandated by Congress' language. In my view, *neither* version of the federal legislation at issue here provides the kind of unambiguous evidence of congressional intent necessary to displace state common-law damages claims....

The principles of federalism and respect for state sovereignty that underlie the Court's reluctance to find pre-emption where Congress has not spoken directly to the issue apply with equal force where Congress has spoken, though ambiguously. In such cases, the question is not *whether* Congress intended to pre-empt state regulation, but to what *extent*. We do not, absent unambiguous evidence, infer a scope of pre-emption beyond that which clearly is mandated by Congress' language. I therefore agree with the Court's unwill-

ingness to conclude that the state common-law damages claims at issue in this case are pre-empted unless such result is "'the clear and manifest purpose of Congress.'"

I also agree with the Court's application of the foregoing principles ... where it concludes that none of petitioner's common-law damages claims are pre-empted by the 1965 Act....

My agreement with the Court ceases at this point. Given the Court's proper analytical focus on the scope of the express pre-emption provisions at issue here and its acknowledgement that the 1965 Act does not pre-empt state common-law damages claims, I find the Court's conclusion that the 1969 Act pre-empts at least some common-law damages claims little short of baffling. In my view, the modified language of Sec. 5(b), 15 U.S.C. Sec. 1334(b) ("No requirement or prohibition based on smoking and health shall be imposed under State law with respect to the advertising or promotion of any cigarettes the packages of which are labeled in conformity with the provisions of this Act"), no more "clearly" or "manifestly" exhibits an intent to pre-empt state common-law damages actions than did the language of its predecessor in the 1965 Act. Nonetheless, the Court reaches a different conclusion, and its reasoning warrants scrutiny.

The Court premises its pre-emption ruling on what it terms the "substantial changes" wrought by Congress in Sec. 5(b)[.]... As an initial matter, I do not disagree with the Court that the phrase "State law," in an appropriate case, can encompass the common law as well as positive enactments such as statutes and regulations.... I do disagree, however, with the Court's conclusion that

"State law" as used in Sec. 5(b) represents such an all-inclusive reference....

Although the Court flatly states that the phrase "no requirement or prohibition" "sweeps broadly" and "easily encompass[es] obligations that take the form of common law rules," those words are in reality far from unambiguous and cannot be said clearly to evidence a congressional mandate to pre-empt state common-law damages actions....

More important, the question whether common-law damages actions exert a regulatory effect on manufacturers analogous to that of positive enactments—an assumption crucial to the Court's conclusion that the phrase "requirement or prohibition" encompasses common-law actions—is significantly more complicated than the [Court suggests].

The effect of tort law on a manufacturer's behavior is necessarily indirect. Although an award of damages by its very nature attaches additional consequences to the manufacturer's continued unlawful conduct, no particular course of action (e.g., the adoption of a new warning label) is required. A manufacturer found liable on, for example, a failure-to-warn claim may respond in a number of ways....

Stepping back from the specifics of the Court's pre-emption analysis to view the result the Court ultimately reaches, I am further disturbed. Notwithstanding the Court's ready acknowledgement that "'[t]he purpose of Congress is the ultimate touchstone' of pre-emption analysis," the Court proceeds to create a crazy quilt of pre-emption from among the common-law claims implicated in this case, and in so doing reaches a result that Congress surely could not have intended.

The most obvious problem with the Court's analysis is its frequent shift in the level of generality at which it examines the individual claims....

In short, I can perceive no principled basis for many of the Court's asserted distinctions among the common-law claims, and I cannot believe that Congress intended to create such a hodge-podge of allowed and disallowed claims when it amended the pre-emption provision in 1970....

SCALIA, AND THOMAS, J.J., CONCURRING IN THE JUDGMENT IN PART AND DISSENTING IN PART

Today's decision announces what, on its face, is an extraordinary and unprecedented principle of federal statutory construction: that express pre-emption provisions must be construed narrowly, "in light of the presumption against the pre-emption of state police power regulations." The life-span of this new rule may have been blessedly brief, inasmuch as the opinion that gives it birth ... proceeds to ignore it ... by adjudging at least some of the common-law tort claims at issue here pre-empted. In my view, there is no merit to this newly crafted doctrine of narrow construction. Under the Supremacy Clause, U.S. Const., Art. VI, cl. 2, our job is to interpret Congress's decrees of pre-emption neither narrowly nor broadly, but in accordance with their apparent meaning. If we did that job in the present case, we would find, under the 1965 Act, pre-emption of the petitioner's failure-to-warn claims; and under the 1969 Act, we would find pre-emption of the petitioner's claims complete....

With much of what the plurality says [about pre-emption] I agree—that "the language of the [1969] Act plainly reaches beyond [positive] enactments," that the general tort-law duties petitioner invokes against the cigarette companies can, as a general matter, impose "requirement[s] or prohibition[s]" within the meaning of Sec. 5(b) of the 1969 Act, and that the phrase "State law" as used in that provision embraces state common law. I take issue with the plurality, however, on its application of these general principles to the present case. Its finding that they produce only partial pre-emption of petitioner's common-law claims rests upon three misperceptions that I shall discuss in turn, under headings indicating the erroneously permitted claims to which they apply.

Pre-1969 Failure-to-Warn Claims
According to the Court, Sec. 5(b) of the 1965 Act "is best read as having superseded only positive enactments by legislatures or administrative agencies that mandate *particular* warning labels" (emphasis added). In essence, the Court reads Sec. 5(b)'s critical language "No *statement* relating to smoking and health shall be required" to mean "No *particular* statement relating to smoking and health shall be required." The Court reasons that because common-law duties do not require cigarette manufacturers to include any *particular* statement in their advertising, but only *some* statement warning of health risks, those duties survive the 1965 Act. I see no basis for this element of "particularity."...

To the extent petitioner's claims are premised specifically on respondents' failure (during the period in which the 1965 Act was in force) to include in their advertising any statement relating to

smoking and health, I would find those claims, no less than the similar post-1969 claims, pre-empted. In addition, ... I would find pre-emption even of those claims based on respondents' failure to make health-related statements to consumers *outside* their advertising. However, since Sec. 5(b) of the 1965 Act enjoins only those laws that require "statement[s]" in cigarette advertising, those of petitioner's claims that, if accepted, would penalize statements voluntarily made by the cigarette companies must be deemed to survive. As these would appear to include petitioner's breach-of-express-warranty and intentional fraud and misrepresentation claims, I concur in the Court's judgment in this respect.

Post-1969 Breach-of-Express-Warranty Claims
In the context of this case, petitioner's breach-of-express-warranty claim necessarily embodies an assertion that respondents' advertising and promotional materials made statements to the effect that cigarette smoking is not unhealthy. Making such statements civilly actionable certainly constitutes an advertising "requirement or prohibition ... based on smoking and health." The plurality appears to accept this, but finds that liability for breach of express warranty is not "imposed under State law" within the meaning of Sec. 5(b) of the 1969 Act. "[R]ather," it says, the duty "is best understood as undertaken by the manufacturer itself." I cannot agree.

When liability attaches to a particular promise or representation, it attaches by law. For the making of a voluntary promise or representation, no less than for the commission of an intentional tort, it is the background law against which the act occurs, and not the act itself, that supplies the element of legal obligation…. Of course, New Jersey's law of express warranty attaches legal consequences to the cigarette manufacturer's voluntary conduct in making the warranty, and in that narrow sense, I suppose, the warranty obligation can be said to be "undertaken by the manufacturer." But on that logic it could also be said that the duty to warn about the dangers of cigarettes is undertaken voluntarily by manufacturers when they choose to sell in New Jersey; or, more generally, that *any* legal duty imposed on volitional behavior is not one imposed by law.

Post-1969 Fraud and Misrepresentation Claims
According to the plurality, at least one of petitioner's intentional fraud and misrepresentation claims survives Sec. 5(b) of the 1969 Act because the common-law duty underlying that claim is not "based on smoking and health" within the meaning of the Act. If I understand the plurality's reasoning, it proceeds from the implicit assumption that only duties deriving from laws that are specifically directed to "smoking and health," or that are uniquely crafted to address the relationship between cigarette companies and their putative victims, fall within Sec. 5(b) of the Act, as amended. Given that New Jersey's tort-law "duty not to deceive," is a general one, applicable to all commercial actors and all kinds of commerce, it follows from this assumption that Sec. 5(b) does not pre-empt claims based on breaches of that duty.

This analysis is suspect, to begin with, because the plurality is unwilling to apply it consistently…. [I]f New Jersey's common-law duty to avoid false statements of material fact—as applied to the cigarette companies' behavior—is not "based on smoking and health," the same must be said of New Jersey's common-law duty to warn about a product's dangers. *Each* duty transcends the relationship between the cigarette companies and cigarette smokers; *neither* duty was specifically crafted with an eye toward "smoking and health." None of the arguments the plurality advances to support its distinction between the two is persuasive….

Once one is forced to select a *consistent* methodology for evaluating whether a given legal duty is "based on smoking and health," it becomes obvious that the methodology must focus not upon the ultimate source of the duty (e.g., the common law) but upon its proximate application. Use of the "ultimate source" approach (i.e., a legal duty is not "based on smoking and health" unless the law from which it derives is directed only to smoking and health) would gut the statute, inviting the very "diverse, nonuniform, and confusing cigarette … advertising regulations" Congress sought to avoid. And the problem is not simply the common law: Requirements could be imposed by state executive agencies as well, so long as they were operating under a *general* statute authorizing their supervision of "commercial advertising" or "unfair trade practices."…

I would apply to all petitioner's claims what I have called a "proximate application" methodology for determining whether they invoke duties "based on smoking and health"—I would ask, that is, whether, whatever the source of the duty, it imposes an obligation in this case because of the effect of smoking upon health. On that basis, I would find petitioner's failure-to-warn and misrepresentation claims both pre-empted.

Finally, there is an additional flaw in the plurality's opinion, a systemic one that infects even its otherwise correct disposition of petitioner's post-1969 failure-to-warn claims. The opinion states that, since Sec. 5(b) proscribes only "requirement[s] or prohibition[s] ... *'with respect to ... advertising or promotion,'*" (emphasis added) state-law claims premised on the failure to warn consumers "through channels of communication other than advertising or promotion" are not covered. This preserves not only the (somewhat fanciful) claims based on duties having no relation to the advertising and promotion (one could imagine a law requiring manufacturers to disclose the health hazards of their products to a state public-health agency), but also claims based on duties that can be complied with by taking action *either* within the advertising and promotional realm or *elsewhere*. Thus, if—as appears to be the case in New Jersey—a State's common law requires manufacturers to advise consumers of their products' dangers, but the law is indifferent as to *how* that requirement is met (i.e., through "advertising or promotion" or otherwise), the plurality would apparently be unprepared to find pre-emption as long as the jury were instructed not to zero in on deficiencies in the manufacturers' advertising or promotion.

I think that is inconsistent with the law of pre-emption. Advertising and promotion are the normal means by which a manufacturer communicates required product warnings to prospective customers, and by far the most economical means. It is implausible that Congress meant to save cigarette companies from being compelled to convey such data to consumers through that means, only to allow them to be compelled to do so through means more onerous still. As a practical matter, such a "tell-the-consumers-any-way-you-wish" law compels manufacturers to relinquish the advertising and promotion immunity accorded them by the Act. The test for pre-emption in this setting should be one of practical compulsion, i.e., whether the law practically compels the manufacturers to engage in behavior that Congress has barred the States from prescribing directly.... Though the hypothetical law requiring disclosure to a state regulatory agency would seem to survive this test, I would have no difficulty finding that test met with respect to state laws that require the cigarette companies to meet general standards of "fair warning" regarding smoking and health....

Questions

1. In *Cipollone*, the Court ruled that some, but not all, state common law damages claims with respect to cigarette smoking are preempted by the federal legislation that mandated warning labels on cigarette packaging. Most states have enacted measures to restrict cigarette smoking in public places, restrict cigarette sales to minors, restrict the distribution of cigarette samples, impose requirements on the sales of cigarettes in vending machines, and have licensing requirements for cigarette sales. Does the Court's decision in *Cipollone*

undermine any of these state regulatory activities based on the theory of federal preemption?

2. The National Association of Manufacturers (NAM) argued as follows:

> [T]his Court should reject [Cipollone's] invitation to adopt a broad and inflexible rule that preemption cannot occur unless either Congress expresses its intent "with drastic clarity" or there is no sense, however farfetched, in which state and federal law can co-exist. Such a rigid approach would require the Court to abandon its long-established and highly appropriate practice of deciding preemption questions by fact-specific inquiries into the purpose, structure, and language of particular pieces of legislation and particular conflicts between state and federal law.

To what extent did the Court in *Cipollone* accept or reject the NAM's argument? What principles did the Court provide for deciding whether federal legislation has preempted state causes of action?

3. If you were a justice, how clear and explicit would you require Congress to be in declaring its intent to preempt state common law or state statutory law with federal legislation? Does the answer depend on your views of federalism? Having read *Cipollone*, what advice would you give to Congress about stating its intent to preempt state law when it enacts legislation?

4. Arguing on behalf of the Liggett Group, the Product Liability Advisory Council contended that the sole question in *Cipollone* was "who decides what communications are appropriate" regarding the relationship between smoking and health. The Association of National Advertisers argued that *Cipollone* also raised issues of commercial speech:

> When speakers seeking to communicate with a national audience are forced to comply with a series of overlapping and, often, conflicting state and local rules, two adverse speech consequences inevitably follow. First, the duty to comply with differing local speech regulations impedes effective communication by complicating and, often, precluding the use of uncluttered uniform messages and nationwide media that are the most effective means of mass communication. Second, the cost of local tailoring imposes a significant and wholly unnecessary economic burden on the commercial speech process.

What other Constitutional concerns might be implicated in a case involving federal preemption of state laws?

5. If you were a judge in a lower federal court or a state court, what principles in *Cipollone* would guide you in deciding whether a particular state cause of action had been preempted by federal regulatory legislation? Could *Cipollone* have been written more clearly to provide guidance to lower court judges, or does the nature of American federalism mean that preemption determinations can never be made with precision?

SUGGESTIONS FOR FURTHER READING

Ausness, Richard C., "Cigarette Company Liability: Preemption, Public Policy, and Alternative Compensation Schemes," 39 *Syracuse Law Review* (1988): 897.

Cover, Robert, *Justice Accused: Antislavery and The Judicial Process* (New Haven, CT: Yale University Press, 1975).

Finkelman, Paul, "*Prigg v. Pennsylvania* and Northern State Courts: Anti-Slavery Use of a Pro-Slavery Decision," 25 *Civil War History* (1979): 5.

Hoke, S. Candice, "Preemption Pathologies and Civic Republican Values," 71 *Boston University Law Review* (1991): 685.

Note, "Pre-emption as a Preferential Ground: A New Canon of Construction," 12 *Stanford Law Review* (1959): 208.

Note, "Third Circuit Review: *Cipollone v. Liggett Group, Inc.*" 32 *Villanova Law Review* (1987): 875.

Swisher, Carl Brent, *History of the Supreme Court of the United States: The Taney Period 1836–1864* (New York, NY: Macmillan, 1974), p. 546.

Tribe, Laurence H., "Anti-Cigarette Suits: Federalism with Smoke and Mirrors," *The Nation*, June 7, 1986, p. 788.

STATES' RIGHTS

Mayor of the City of New York v. Miln
11 Peters 102 (1837)

SETTING

During the early decades of the American Republic, conflicts over regulation of the nation's rapidly expanding commerce played a salient role in debates over federalism. In *Gibbons v. Ogden* (1824), recall, Chief Justice John Marshall delivered a ringing endorsement of economic nationalism. While entrepreneurs cheered Marshall's liberation of commerce from state-chartered monopolies and parochial regulation, advocates of states' rights worried that the chief justice's broad definition of congressional commerce powers could swallow state prerogatives. Southerners were particularly concerned that Congress would use its commerce power to regulate slavery, an institution that they believed was best left to the states. When Maryland native Roger Brooke Taney became chief justice in 1836, southern hopes were raised that the Supreme Court might restore at least some ground that the states had lost to the central government while John Marshall was chief justice.

The hopes of states' rights advocates were grounded in Taney's credentials. For example, in 1832, as attorney general in Andrew Jackson's administration, Taney had played an important role in getting the president to veto legislation rechartering the Second National Bank of the United States, which many southerners and westerners called "The Monster." Taney wrote Jackson's veto message and, in a pointed reference to John Marshall's opinion in *McCulloch v. Maryland*, he stated that "the opinion of judges has no more authority over Congress than the opinion of Congress has over the judges, and on that point the President is independent of both." Despite Jackson's veto, however, the Bank's original charter ran until 1836. When successive secretaries of the treasury refused to destroy the bank by transferring its assets to state banks that were controlled by Jackson supporters, Jackson appointed Taney treasury secretary, who then shifted all the bank's resources into state "pet banks."

Taney became chief justice in 1837, as the abolition movement was gaining momentum in the North. Five of the Supreme Court's seven justices, however, were southerners. Three cases on the Court's docket were carryovers from Marshall's tenure. In *Briscoe v. the Bank of Kentucky*, 11 Peters 257 (1837), the post-Marshall Court ignored Marshall's decision in *Craig v. Missouri*, 4 Peters 410 (1830), that state-issued bank notes were constitutionally prohibited bills of credit. The Taney Court ruled that paper money issued by the Bank of the Commonwealth of Kentucky was valid. In *Charles River Bridge v. Warren Bridge*, 11 Peters 420 (1837) (Chapter 6, pp. 741–750), the Court abandoned Marshall's vested rights theory of contracts in lieu of a flexible, more entrepreneurial view of state power more in tune with expanding commercial and transportation needs. *New York v. Miln* gave the justices the chance to rethink the relationship of the Commerce Clause and the Tenth Amendment.

Note: Review the *Setting* to and excerpt of *New York v. Miln* in Chapter 3, pp. 230–237.

QUESTIONS

1. What theory of the Tenth Amendment is reflected in *Miln*? Under that theory, is the Tenth Amendment a limitation on Congress's powers under the Commerce Clause?

2. How does Justice Barbour's view of federalism in *Miln* differ from John Marshall's view of federalism in *Gibbons*? (See Chapter 3, pp. 222–229.)

3. Justice Joseph Story dissented in *Briscoe*, *Charles River* and *Miln*. In *Miln*, Story wrote: "I have the consolation to know, that I had the entire concurrence ... of that great constitutional jurist, the late Chief Justice Marshall.... [H]is deliberate opinion was, that the act of New

York [contested in *Miln*] was unconstitutional; and that the present case fell directly within the principles established in the case of *Gibbons v. Ogden.*" Which view comports better with the constitutional division of powers between the states and the national government: the Marshall/Story view, or the Barbour/Taney view? Can this question be answered in absolute terms, or does it depend on the facts of each case?

4. *Miln* stands for the proposition that, under the Tenth Amendment, states may restrict people's freedom of movement based on their economic status. That holding was overruled in *Edwards v. California*, 314 U.S. 160 (1941). Are there political issues in contemporary American society that suggest that *Edwards* may be in jeopardy and that the reasoning in *Miln* might again gain favor?

STATES' RIGHTS

Cooley v. Board of Wardens
12 Howard (1851)

SETTING

In the context of rapid mid-nineteenth century commercial expansion and spreading controversies over slavery, the Taney Court's reaffirmation of states' police power, while not rejecting the Marshall Court's *Gibbons* framework, raised divisive questions: Where is the constitutional line between congressional power to regulate commerce under Article I, section 8, clause 3, and states' inherent powers to regulate that are reserved in the Tenth Amendment? Can a single line be drawn on a principled basis that is capable of general applicability? Or should shifting lines be drawn on an ad hoc, case-by-case basis? For almost fifteen years after *Miln*, the Court gave conflicting answers to these questions, which only compounded the doctrinal confusion.

Cooley v. Board of Wardens arose in this muddled doctrinal context at a time when sectional tensions over slavery were growing worse. *Cooley* provided the Court an opportunity to resolve doctrinal disorder in the realm of commercial regulation and was potentially a vehicle for bringing some stability to the increasingly inflamed debate over slavery.

Note: Review the *Setting* to and excerpt of *Cooley v. Board of Wardens* in Chapter 3, pp. 237–243.

QUESTIONS

1. Does Justice Curtis's opinion in *Cooley* either limit congressional commerce power or enlarge state police power? If it does neither, what are the practical effects of the "Locality Rule"?

2. Did *Cooley* answer the question about the respective powers of the national and state governments to regulate the commercial aspects of slavery? Should it have?

3. Professors Alfred H. Kelly, Winfred A. Harbison, and Herman Belz claim that: "The [*Cooley*] rule was an eloquent statement of indefiniteness. Yet, as Professor [Carl B.] Swisher has observed, with the statement, the indefiniteness seemed more manageable" (*The American Constitution: Its Origins and Development*, 6th ed. [New York, NY: W. W. Norton, 1983], p. 241). Is "indefiniteness" part of the nature of American federalism? If so, is it naive to expect the Supreme Court to develop coherent constitutional doctrine regarding federalism?

4. Historian Melvin I. Urofsky writes of the tangled web the *Cooley* Court wove from strands of federalism, commerce, and transportation policy: "The intense competition between railroads and water navigation did not abate until after the Civil War[.]... In those instances where Congress had authorized construction, railroads would usually win; but where states had acted on their own, judges sympathetic to water traffic would, on occasion, still declare [rail structures that impeded navigation] nuisances. *Cooley* provided a rough rule of thumb, but so long as the economic issues remained unresolved, so too did the legal questions" (*A March of Liberty: A Constitutional History of the United States* [New York, NY: Knopf, 1988], pp. 330–331). What insights into the intricacies of constitutional interpretation does Urofsky's observation provide?

STATES' RIGHTS

Texas v. White
7 Wallace 700 (1869)

SETTING

General Robert E. Lee's surrender at Appomattox on April 9, 1865, brought an end to the Civil War and to the Confederate States of America. The Union victory settled the practical question of whether or not states could secede from the Union. Victory by federal forces, however, did not resolve the legal debate about the character of the Union and the constitutional status of the states that had formed the Confederate States of America. Neither did it settle the matter of the character of relations between the national government and the states.

Before the Civil War, two theories of the Union vied for support. They are generally called the "compact theory" and the "central supremacy theory."

Compact theorists, whose early advocates included Thomas Jefferson and James Madison, argued that the United States was created by a compact among the states. According to this theory, articulated in the Virginia and Kentucky Resolutions in 1798–99, the central government can exercise only those powers delegated to it by the states. The Tenth Amendment reserves to the states (or to the people) all powers that are not delegated by the Constitution to the national government nor prohibited by the Constitution to the states. States retain the right to decide whether the central government violates the compact and retain the power to nullify acts of the central government believed to be contrary to the compact. Before the Civil War, John C. Calhoun was perhaps the most prominent exponent of this view. To Jefferson's and Madison's argument, Calhoun added the right of sovereign states to withdraw from the compact at will.

Central supremacy theorists, such as John Marshall and Daniel Webster, contended that the people, not the states, established the United States and that the Union they created is perpetual. Marshall stated the theory clearly in *McCulloch v. Maryland.* Abraham Lincoln put his own mark on the central supremacy position in his March 4, 1861, First Inaugural Address:

> [T]he proposition that, in legal contemplation, the Union is perpetual [is] confirmed by the history of the Union itself....
>
> It follows from these views that no State, upon its own mere motion, can lawfully get out of the Union—that *resolves* and *ordinances* to that effect are legally void; and that acts of violence, within any State or States, against the authority of the United States, are insurrectionary or revolutionary.

The Civil War did not silence the debate between compact and central supremacy theorists. After the war, however, that debate shifted to the Supreme Court. The issue that framed the debate was a convoluted financial transaction that was affected by the Civil War.

Texas was admitted to the Union in 1845 amidst disputes over the location of its northern and western boundaries. Texas claimed as part of its territory land including the state of New Mexico and the future states of Kansas, Oklahoma, Colorado, and Wyoming. Included in its claims were lands north of 36 degrees, 30 minutes, which in turn were related to the divisive issue of slavery in the territories. State officials were willing to compromise on the border location issue if the United States would assume some $10 million of Texas's indebtedness. In 1851, in partial settlement of the border dispute, the United States issued $5 million worth of gold indemnity bonds, payable to the State of

Texas or bearer, at an interest rate of 5 percent. The Texas legislature authorized the state comptroller to sell the bonds (for the purpose of supporting schools for the education of children of the poor, and aiding railroads), provided they were endorsed in Austin, Texas, by the state's governor. Most were endorsed, sold, and paid on presentation to the United States before 1860. Some of the 782 unendorsed bonds, however, were still in the Texas treasury when the Civil War broke out. On February 1, 1861, delegates to a state convention adopted an ordinance "To Dissolve the Union between the State of Texas and the Other States United under the Compact styled 'The Constitution of the United States of America.'" The next month the convention established a rebel government, adopted a new constitution, and joined other southern states in making war on the United States.

On January 11, 1862, the confederate Texas legislature repealed the act requiring endorsement of the indemnity bonds by the governor. It also created a military board and authorized it to sell up to $1 million of any bonds that remained in the treasury for the purpose of defraying the costs of the war. The next day, the Military Board sold 135 unendorsed bonds to George W. White and John Chiles. In return for the bonds, White and Chiles were to deliver to the military board a large quantity of medicine and tools for carding cotton. White and Chiles were prevented from making the delivery when the goods were plundered by disbanded soldiers on their way to Austin. The deal that White and Chiles had made with the financially desperate rebel state of Texas smacked of swindle, because White and Chiles accepted the gold bonds on the condition that, if they failed to deliver on their contract, they could repay the military board in relatively worthless bonds of the Confederate States of America. At the time that White and Chiles's deal was concluded, Texas state bonds were worth a mere eight cents to the federal dollar.

After the Civil War, while Texas was still undergoing reconstruction, its provisional government invoked the Supreme Court's original jurisdiction in an effort to recover the gold bonds from White and Chiles. Texas contended that the bond sale by the rebel government to White and Chiles had been illegal and was void.

Texas's case against White and Chiles was argued with similar cases against six other individuals and the Commercial Bank of Kentucky.

HIGHLIGHTS OF SUPREME COURT ARGUMENTS

BRIEF FOR TEXAS

♦ The state of Texas, as a state, could not and did not rebel against the United States during the Civil War. The actions of the state's magistrates, including the legislature, were void and should be treated as though they did not occur. From the date of the Ordinance of Secession to the adoption of the present Texas constitution, no competent public authority existed in Texas capable of entering into a contract.

◆ White and Chiles can stand in no better position with respect to the bonds than the government that conveyed them. They should be treated as constructive bailees of the trust fund.

BRIEF FOR CHILES

◆ Texas is not recognized as one of the United States because it is not permitted to have a voice in the election of the president and vice president, nor to have representatives in Congress. It is held and governed by the other states as a conquered province. Therefore, it is not competent to sue in U.S. courts.

◆ If the Court determines that Texas is still a state in the Union, the acts of the military board in selling the bonds must be recognized as valid. It was not contrary to the laws of Texas at the time to sell the bonds.

◆ The Court should reject the humiliating argument of the state that it can repudiate a contract entered into by its chosen and trusted officers while they were engaged in a war for independence.

BRIEF FOR WHITE

◆ Texas, by the course of rebellion during the Civil War, so changed her status as to be disqualified from suing in the Supreme Court.

◆ The State of Texas, whether acting as a matter of law or as a matter of fact during the Civil War, authorized the military board to act for it. A state can act only through its agents. There was an absolute sale and delivery of the bonds. Texas should be estopped from denying the validity of the board's acts.

◆ The validity of other contracts entered into during the period of the rebel government—including contracts of marriage—have been sustained. The contract between the state and White and Chiles should be treated no differently.

◆ If the action can be maintained on the assumption that Texas is a state, it is the same state that existed when the contract with White and Chiles was entered into. The state has no standing in court to assert the invalidity of its own agreement.

SUPREME COURT DECISION: 6–3

CHASE, C.J.

... It is not to be questioned that this court has original jurisdiction of suits by States against citizens of other States, or that the States entitled to invoke this jurisdiction must be States of the Union. But, it is equally clear that no such jurisdiction has been conferred upon this court of suits by any other political communities than such States.

If, therefore, it is true that the State of Texas was not at the time of filing this bill, or is not now, one of the United States, we have no jurisdiction of this suit, and it is our duty to dismiss it....

A state, in the ordinary sense of the Constitution, is a political community of free citizens, occupying a territory of defined boundaries, and organized under a government sanctioned and limited by a written constitution, and established by the consent of the governed. It is the union of such states, under a common constitution, which forms the distinct and greater political unit, which that Constitution designates as the United States, and makes of the people and states which compose it one people and one country....

Having thus ascertained the [sense] in which the word "state" is employed in the Constitution, we will proceed to consider the proper application of what has been said.

The Republic of Texas was admitted into the Union, as a State, on the 27th of December, 1845. By this act the new State, and the people of the new State, were invested with all the rights, and became subject to all the responsibilities and duties of the original States under the Constitution.

From the date of admission, until 1861, the State was represented in the Congress of the United States by her senators and representatives, and her relations as a member of the Union remained unimpaired. In that year, acting upon the theory that the rights of a State under the Constitution might be renounced, and her obligations thrown off at pleasure, Texas undertook to sever the bond thus formed, and to break up her constitutional relations with the United States....

Did Texas, in consequence of these acts, cease to be a State? Or, if not, did the State cease to be a member of the Union?

It is needless to discuss, at length, the question whether the right of a State to withdraw from the Union for any cause, regarded by herself as sufficient, is consistent with the Constitution of the United States.

The Union of the States never was a purely artificial and arbitrary relation. It began among the Colonies, and grew out of common origin, mutual sympathies, kindred principles, similar interests and geographical relations. It was confirmed and strengthened by the necessities of war, and received definite form, character, and sanction from the Articles of Confederation. By these the Union was solemnly declared to "be perpetual." And when these articles were found to be inadequate to the exigencies of the country, the Constitution was ordained "to form a more perfect Union." It is difficult to convey the idea of indissoluble unity more clearly than by these words. What can be indissoluble if a perpetual Union, made more perfect, is not?

But the perpetuity and indissolubility of the Union by no means implies the loss of distinct and individual existence, or of the right of self government by the States.... Under the Constitution, though the powers of the States were much restricted, still, all powers not delegated to the United States, nor prohibited to the States, are reserved to the States respectively, or to the people. And we have already had occasion to remark at this term, that "the people of each State compose a State, having its own government, and endowed with all the functions essential to separate and independent existence," and that "without the States in Union, there could be no such political body as the United States." Not only, therefore, can there be no loss of separate and independent autonomy to the States, through their union under the Constitution, but it may be not unreasonably said that the preservation of the States, and the maintenance of their governments, are as much within the design and care of the Constitution as the preservation of the Union and the maintenance of the National government. The Constitution, in all its provisions, looks to an indestructible Union, composed of indestructible States.

When, therefore, Texas became one of the United States, she entered into an indissoluble relation. All the obligations of perpetual union, and all the guaranties of republican government in the Union, attached at once to the State. The act which consummated her admission into the Union was something more than a compact; it was the incorporation of a new member into the political body. And it was final. The union between Texas and the other States was as complete, as perpetual, and as indissoluble as the union between the original States. There was no place for reconsideration, or revocation, except through revolution, or through consent of the States.

Considered, therefore, as transactions under the Constitution, the Ordinance of Secession, adopted by the convention and ratified by a majority of the citizens of Texas, and all the Acts of her legislature intended to give effect to that ordinance, were absolutely null. They were utterly without operation in law. The obligations of the State as a member of the Union, and of every citizen of the State, as a citizen of the United States, remained perfect and unimpaired. It certainly follows that the State did not cease to be a State, nor her citizens to be citizens of the Union. If this were otherwise, the State must have become foreign, and her citizens foreigners. The war must have ceased to be a war for the suppression of rebellion, must have become a war for conquest and subjugation.

Our conclusion therefore is, that Texas continued to be a State, and a State of the Union, notwithstanding the transactions to which we have referred. And this conclusion, in our judgment, is not in conflict with any act or declaration of any department of the National government, but entirely in accordance with the whole series of such acts and declarations since the first outbreak of the rebellion.

But in order [for] ... a State ... to sue in this court, there needs to be a State Government, competent to represent the State in its relations with the National Government, so far at least as the institution and prosecution of a suit is concerned.

And it is by no means a logical conclusion, from the premises which we have endeavored to establish, that the governmental relations of Texas to the Union remained unaltered. Obligations often remain unchanged, while relations are greatly changed.... All admit that during [the] time of civil war, the rights of the State as a member, and of her people as citizens of the Union, were suspended. The government and citizens of the State, refusing to recognize their constitutional obligations, assumed the character of enemies, and incurred the consequences of rebellion.

These new relations imposed new duties upon the United States. The first was that of suppressing the rebellion. The next was that of re-establishing the broken relations of the State with the Union....

[T]he case of Texas furnishes a striking illustration. When the war closed there was no government in the State except that which had been organized for the purpose of waging war against the United States....

[W]hile the war yet smoldered in Texas, the President of the United States issued his Proclamation appointing a provisional Governor for the State, and providing for the assembling of a convention, with a view to the re-establishment of a republican government, under an amended Constitution and to the restoration of the State to her proper constitutional relations....

A provisional Governor of the State was appointed by the President in 1865; in 1866 a Governor was elected by the people under the constitution of that year; at a subsequent date a Governor was appointed by the commander of the district [under Reconstruction]. Each of the three exercised executive functions and actually represented the State in the Executive Department.

In the case before us each has given his sanction to the prosecution of the suit, and we find no difficulty ... in holding that the sanction thus given sufficiently warranted the action of the solicitor and counsel in behalf of the State. The necessary conclusion is that the suit was instituted and is prosecuted by competent authority....

[On the merits,] the title of the State is not devested [sic] by the act of the insurgent government in entering into this contract....

[Furthermore, it] is impossible ... to hold the defendants protected by absence of notice of the want of title in White and Chiles. As these persons acquired no right to payment of these bonds as against the State, purchasers could acquire none through them.

On the whole case, therefore, our conclusion is that the State of Texas is entitled to the relief sought by her bill, and a decree must be made accordingly.

GRIER, J., DISSENTING

... The original jurisdiction of this court can be invoked only by one of the United States. The Territories have no such right conferred on them by the Constitution, nor have the Indian tribes who are under the protection of the military authorities of the government.

Is Texas one of these United States? Or was she such at the time this bill was filed, or since?

This is to be decided as a *political fact*, not as a *legal fiction*. This court is bound to know and notice the public history of the nation.

If I regard the truth of history for the last eight years, I cannot discover the State of Texas as one of these United States....

SWAYNE, AND MILLER J.J., DISSENTING

I concur with my brother Grier as to the incapacity of the State of Texas, in her present condition, to maintain an original suit in this court. The question, in my judgment, is one in relation to which this court is bound by the action of the legislative department of the government....

COMMENT

George Paschal, one of the attorneys for Texas, argued a version of the central supremacy theory during the oral argument of *Texas v. White*. Paschal was a leading attorney in Texas, but a prominent Union loyalist during the Civil War. The theory that many of Paschal's fellow Texans rejected when they voted to secede is the very theory on which Texas prevailed in *Texas v. White*.

QUESTIONS

1. What are the implications for federalism of Chief Justice Chase's sweeping statement: "The Constitution, in all its provisions, looks to an indestructible Union, composed of indestructible States"? Did Chase adopt either the compact theory or the central supremacy theory in his opinion? If the Civil War was fought in part to determine whether the national government or the states possess ultimate governing authority in the United States, what answer to that question was provided by the Court in *Texas v. White*?

2. In *Federalist* No. 46, James Madison discussed "the disposition and the faculty" the federal and state governments "may respectively possess to resist and frustrate the measure of each other." Is the elusive nature of federalism one of the elements of that resistance and frustration? See Justice Rehnquist's dissent in *Nevada v. Hall*, 440 U.S. 410 (1979), where he refers to the "tacit postulates" of the constitutional scheme that, in addition to explicit constitutional provisions, protect states' semiautonomous status. Is federalism one of those "tacit postulates"?

3. Is it fair to say that defining the nature of federalism in *Texas v. White* was of greater concern to the Supreme Court than the protection of private property? Could the Court have resolved the federalism issue the way it did while at the same time allowing White and Chiles to benefit from the terms of their contract?

STATES' RIGHTS

Collector v. Day
78 U.S. 113 (1871)

SETTING

Congress has explored a variety of means for financing the operatio[...] national government. It has imposed tariffs and excises on goods, so[...] lands, and imposed duties. During the Civil War, it enacted the coun[...]

federal income tax, but exempted annual incomes of $600 or less. The first federal income tax law expired a few years after the war. In 1864, Congress enacted the country's first graduated income tax: 5 percent on incomes up to $5,000, 7 1/2 percent on the excess over $5,000 up to $10,000 and 10 percent on the excess over $10,000. Clearly, the graduated income tax fell heavily on the wealthy.

Judges were among those vehemently opposed to the income tax. Chief Justice Taney, for example, contended that the income tax on his salary was unconstitutional because of the guarantee in Article III of the Constitution that judges' salaries will not be diminished during their terms in office. Despite the objection of the chief justice and many other federal judges, no cases were filed dealing with the constitutionality of the federal income tax as applied to federal judges' salaries. However, the income tax also was collected on the salaries of state judges, which led to an important case in the area of intergovernmental tax immunity. The immunity doctrine, which rests on no specific constitutional language, was first articulated by the Court in *McCulloch v. Maryland* to protect the national government from taxes imposed by the states.

Joseph M. Day, a probate judge for Barnstable, Massachusetts, paid his income taxes for the years 1866 and 1867 under protest. He subsequently filed suit in the Circuit Court of the United States for the District of Massachusetts against James Buffington, collector of the Internal Revenue Service, to recover $61.51 plus interest that he had paid, claiming that the federal income tax on his salary had been collected in violation of the Constitution. The case was submitted to the court on stipulated facts, which ruled in favor of Judge Day. Collector Buffington petitioned the Supreme Court of the United States for a writ of error.

HIGHLIGHTS OF SUPREME COURT ARGUMENTS

BRIEF FOR COLLECTOR BUFFINGTON

◆ The Constitution gives Congress the power to tax for certain purposes—the common debts, the common defense, and the general welfare—for which the states are no longer responsible. In the exercise of its granted powers, the national government is supreme.

◆ If state officers are exempt from federal taxation of their salaries, the effect of an income tax would be to raise their salaries as compared to other citizens of the state.

◆ The income tax in question imposes no tax on the office or the officer; it falls on the salary earned by a citizen of Massachusetts.

◆ Judge Day's salary is taxable by the state of Massachusetts. The inference is unavoidable that it is equally taxable by the United States.

◆ In *Veazie Bank v. Fenno*, 75 U.S. 533 (1896), this court held that the United States could lawfully tax the operations of a state bank, even with the purpose of driving its issues of notes out of circulation. It follows that the United States can lawfully tax the salary of a state employee.

BRIEF FOR DAY

◆ The national government and the state governments exist as two separate and distinct sovereignties, each restricted in its powers, and each exempt from the interference or control of the other.

◆ This case poses the precise opposite of *Dobbins v. Erie Co.*, 16 Peters 435 (1842), where this Court ruled that a state has no power to tax the office or the emoluments of the office of an officer of the United States.

◆ The power of one government to tax in any way the functions, instrumentalities, or revenues of another, or the compensation paid by another government to its public officers, is wholly incompatible with any power of self-preservation or right of independent existence on the part of the government liable to such taxation.

SUPREME COURT DECISION: 8–1

NELSON, J.

The case presents the question whether it is competent for Congress, under the Constitution of the United States, to impose a tax upon the salary of a judicial officer of a State?

In *Dobbins v. The Commissioners of Erie County* [16 Peters 435 (1842)], it was decided that it was not competent for the legislature of a State to levy a tax upon the salary or emoluments of an officer of the United States. The decision was placed mainly upon the ground that the officer was a means or instrumentality employed for carrying into effect some of the legitimate powers of the government, which could not be interfered with by taxation or otherwise by the States, and that the salary or compensation for the service of the officer was inseparably connected with the office; that if the officer, as such, was exempt, the salary assigned for his support or maintenance while holding the

office was also, for like reasons, equally exempt....

It is conceded in the case of *McCulloch v. Maryland*, that the power of taxation by the States was not abridged by the grant of a similar power to the government of the Union; that it was retained by the States, and that the power is to be concurrently exercised by the two governments; and also that there is no express constitutional prohibition upon the States against taxing the means or instrumentalities of the general government. But, it was held, and, we agree properly held, to be prohibited by necessary implication; otherwise, the States might impose taxation to an extent that would impair, if not wholly defeat, the operations of the Federal authorities when acting in their appropriate sphere.

These views, we think, abundantly establish the soundness of the decision of the case of *Dobbins v. The Commissioners of Erie*, which determined that the States were prohibited, upon a proper construction of the Constitution, from taxing the salary or emoluments of an officer of the government of the United States. And we shall now proceed to show that, upon the same construction of that instrument, and for like reasons, that government is prohibited from taxing the salary of the judicial officer of a State.

It is a familiar rule of construction of the Constitution of the Union, that the sovereign powers vested in the State governments by their respective constitutions, remained unaltered and unimpaired, except so far as they were granted to the government of the United States. That the intention of the framers of the Constitution in this respect might not be misunderstood, this rule of interpretation is expressly declared in the tenth article of the amendments, namely: "The powers not delegated to the United States are reserved to the States respectively, or to the people." The government of the United States, therefore, can claim no powers which are not granted to it by the Constitution, and the powers actually granted must be such as are expressly given, or given by necessary implication.

The general government, and the States, although both exist within the same territorial limits, are separate and distinct sovereignties, acting separately and independently of each other, within their respective spheres. The former in its appropriate sphere is supreme; but the States within the limits of their powers not granted, or, in the language of the tenth amendment, "reserved," are as independent of the general government as that government within its sphere is independent of the States....

Upon looking into the Constitution it will be found that but a few of the articles in that instrument could be carried into practical effect without the existence of the States.

Two of the great departments of the government, the executive and legislative, depend upon the exercise of the powers, or upon the people of the States. The Constitution guarantees to the States a republican form of government, and protects each against invasion or domestic violence. Such being the separate and independent condition of the States in our complex system, as recognized by the Constitution, and the existence of which is so indispensable, that, without them, the general government itself would disappear from the family of nations, it would seem to follow, as a reasonable, if not a necessary consequence, that the means and instrumentalities employed for carrying on the operations of their governments, for preserving their existence, and fulfilling the high and responsible duties assigned to them in the Constitution, should be left free and unimpaired, should not be liable to be crippled, much less defeated by the taxing power of another government, which power acknowledges no limits but the will of the legislative body imposing the tax. And, more especially, those means and instrumentalities which are the creation of their sovereign and reserved rights, one of which is the establishment of the judicial department, and the appointment of officers to administer their laws. Without this power, and the exercise of it, we risk nothing in saying that no one of the States under the form of government guaranteed by the Constitution could long preserve its existence. A despotic government might. We have said that one of the reserved powers was that to establish a judicial department; it would have been more accurate, and in accordance with the existing state of things at the time, to have said the power to maintain a judicial department. All of the thirteen States were in the possession of this power, and had exercised it at the adoption of the Constitution; and it is not pretended that any grant of it to the general government is found in that instrument. It is, therefore, one of the sovereign powers vested in the States by their constitutions, which remained unaltered and unimpaired, and in respect to which the State is as independent of the general government as that government is independent of the States.

The supremacy of the general government, therefore, so much relied on in the argument of the counsel for the plaintiff in error, in respect to the question before us, cannot be maintained. The two governments are upon an equality, and the question is whether the power "to lay and collect taxes" enables the general government to tax the salary of a judicial officer of the State, which officer is a means or instrumentality employed to carry into execution one of its most important functions, the administration of the laws, and which concerns the exercise of a right reserved to the States?

We do not say the mere circumstance of the establishment of the judicial department, and the appointment of officers to administer the laws, being among the reserved powers of the State, disables the general government from levying the tax, as that depends upon the express power "to lay and collect taxes," but it shows that it is an original inherent power never parted with, and, in respect to which, the supremacy of that government does not exist, and is

of no importance in determining the question; and further, that being an original and reserved power, and the judicial officers appointed under it being a means or instrumentality employed to carry it into effect, the right and necessity of its unimpaired exercise, and the exemption of the officer from taxation by the general government stand upon as solid a ground, and are maintained by principles and reasons as cogent as those which led to the exemption of the Federal officer in *Dobbins* from taxation by the State; for, in this respect, that is, in respect to the reserved powers, the State is as sovereign and independent as the general government. And if the means and instrumentalities employed by that government to carry into operation the powers granted to it are, necessarily, and, for the sake of self-preservation, exempt from taxation by the States, why are not those of the States depending upon their reserved powers, for like reasons, equally exempt from Federal taxation? Their unimpaired existence in the one case is as essential as in the other. It is admitted that there is no express provision in the Constitution that prohibits the general government from taxing the means and instrumentalities of the States, nor is there any prohibiting the States from taxing the means and instrumentalities of that government. In both cases the exemption rests upon necessary implication, and is upheld by the great law of self-preservation; as any government, whose means employed in conducting its operations, if subject to the control of another and distinct government, can exist only at the mercy of that government. Of what avail are these means if another power may tax them at discretion?...

Judgment Affirmed.

BRADLEY, J., DISSENTING

I dissent from the opinion of the court in this case, because, it seems to me that the general government has the same power of taxing the income of officers of the State governments as it has of taxing that of its own officers. It is the common government of all alike; and every citizen is presumed to trust his own government in the matter of taxation. No man ceases to be a citizen of the United States by being an officer under the State government. I cannot accede to the doctrine that the general government is to be regarded as in any sense foreign or antagonistic to the State governments, their officers, or people; nor can I agree that a presumption can be admitted that the general government will act in a manner hostile to the existence or functions of the State governments, which are constituent parts of the system or body politic forming the basis on which the general government is founded. The taxation by the State governments of the instruments employed by the general government in the exercise of its powers, is a very different thing. Such taxation involves an interference with the powers of a government in which other States and their citizens are equally interested with the State which imposes the taxation. In my judgment, the limitation of the power of taxation in the general government, which the present decision establishes, will be found very difficult of control. Where are we to stop in enumerating the functions of the State governments, which will be interfered with by Federal taxation? If a State incorporates a railroad to carry out its purposes of internal improvement, or a bank to aid its financial arrangements, reserving, perhaps, a percentage on the stock or profits, for the supply of its own treasury, will the bonds or stock of such an institution be free from Federal taxation? How can we now tell what the effect of this decision will be? I cannot but regard it as founded on a fallacy, and that it will lead to mischievous consequences. I am as much opposed as any one can be to any interference by the general government with the just powers of the State governments. But no concession of any of the just powers of the general government can easily be recalled....

QUESTIONS

1. In *Collector v. Day*, did the Court declare an act of Congress unconstitutional, or did it hold that the income tax law could not be applied to a salary paid to a state official? Is the distinction significant? What role does the Tenth Amendment play in your response?

2. Supreme Court historian Charles Warren reports the following commentary in the *Cincinnati Enquirer* regarding the decision in *Collector v. Day*:

    > [It demonstrates] that the States have rights which are as sovereign as those of the General Government, and that the maintenance of their political dignity and sovereignty is as essential to good order and the perpetuity of free institutions as is the maintenance of the

political dignity and sovereignty of the Federal Government, [and] knocks the pins from under the trestle work the Republicans have been erecting, and over which they hoped to march the people from a land of freedom to one of despotism" (*The Supreme Court in United States History*, 2 vols. [Boston, MA: Little Brown and Co., 1926], II: 535).

Why was the sovereignty of state governments associated with political liberty and the assertion of national authority was considered an act of despotism in the 1870s? Are similar concerns present even to this day?

Political scientist C. Herman Pritchett contends that *Collector v. Day* "must be considered ... in the light of the times." He maintains that the opinion came from a Court that "was uneasy about the dominance of the Radical Reconstructionists" following the Civil War, and their plans for the expansion of the national government (*The American Constitution* [New York, NY: McGraw-Hill, 1959], pp. 215–216). Does any language in *Collector v. Day* support or refute Pritchett's theory?

3. Counsel for Day contended that under the Constitution the national and state governments exist as "two separate and distinct sovereignties." Did the Court in Day reject that proposition without completely embracing its opposite?

4. The intergovernmental immunity doctrine announced in *Collector v. Day* traces back to Chief Justice Marshall's opinion in *McCulloch v. Maryland* and appears to be the logical reciprocal of the 1842 *Dobbins v. Erie Co.* decision (16 Peters 435), in which the Court ruled that a federal official is exempt from taxation by a state. Accordingly, doctrine announced in *Day* might be described as (among other things) "what's sauce for the goose is sauce for the gander," meaning that if the states may not tax federal officials, the federal government may not tax state officials. Is such reciprocity compelled by the Constitution? Is reciprocity good constitutional policy?

COMMENT

In *South Carolina v. Baker*, 485 U.S. 505 (1988), the Supreme Court declared: "state [tax] immunity arises from the constitutional structure and a concern for protecting state sovereignty whereas the federal [tax] immunity arises from the Supremacy Clause." For a useful summary of the reciprocal tax immunity doctrine see *Massachusetts v. United States*, 435 U.S. 444 (1978). The high-water mark of the reciprocal tax immunity doctrine came in *Indian Motorcycle Co. v. United States*, 283 U.S. 570 (1931), where the Court exempted a private manufacturer of motorcycles from federal sales taxes on vehicles purchased by a municipal police department.

STATES' RIGHTS

Champion v. Ames
188 U.S. 321 (1903)

SETTING

Lotteries have a lengthy, checkered history in the United States. The 1612 charter from King James to the Virginia Company of London, for example, included powers to establish one or more lotteries. During the colonial period, states used lotteries as a method of funding public works such as streets, wharves, schools, and hospitals. In 1776, the Continental Congress authorized a national lottery to raise money for the army, and later relied on lotteries to help fund the construction of public buildings in Washington, D.C.

Beginning in the mid-1800s, lotteries came under attack from religious and secular sources. Some wished them outlawed because they were contrary to Christian morals. Others cited financial mismanagement and fraud. In 1842, Congress outlawed lotteries in the District of Columbia. By the late 1800s virtually all state laws contained statutory or constitutional prohibitions on lotteries.

In 1890, as part of an attempt to support state antilottery laws, Congress passed a law forbidding the use of the U.S. mails for the purpose of advertising lottery schemes. The constitutionality of that law was challenged in *In re Rapier*, 143 U.S. 110 (1892). The *Rapier* decision upheld the federal statute but did not address the complex question whether the legislation had invaded the police powers of the states. The explanation for this omission appears to be the death of Justice Bradley, to whom the opinion was assigned after conference, but who died before completing it. The Court subsequently issued a short decision upholding the statute, stating that Congress's power to establish post offices and post roads embraces regulation of the entire postal system.

The 1890 legislation was easily evaded, especially by lottery companies that were organized in other countries but did business in the United States. At the urging of the postmaster general, <u>Congress</u> in 1895 attempted to close the channels of interstate commerce in lottery tickets by <u>making it a crime for anyone to bring into the United States, or cause to be carried from one state to another, any lottery ticket or lottery ticket equivalent</u>. Violation was punishable by a fine, imprisonment, or both.

In May 1899, a complaint was filed against Charles Champion (alias W. W. Ogden), W. F. Champion, and Charles B. Park for conspiracy to violate the 1895 statute by depositing lottery tickets of the Pan-American Lottery Company of Paraguay with the Wells Fargo Express Company in Dallas, Texas, to be sent to Fresno, California. The three subsequently were indicted by the Grand Jury for the Northern District of Texas. Charles Champion was arrested in Chicago, committed to the custody of U.S. Marshal John Ames when he failed to post a $1,000 bond, and was ordered to stand trial in the U.S. District Court of Texas in January 1890.

While in Ames's custody, Champion filed a petition for a writ of habeas corpus ordering Ames to release him. Champion was released on bail between the time he filed the petition and when Ames responded. The judge of the Circuit Court for the Northern District of Illinois denied the writ and remanded Champion to Ames's custody. Champion appealed to the Supreme Court of the United States.

The case was first argued at the October 1900 Term. The Court ordered reargument in 1901, consolidating Champion's appeal with *Francis v. United States*, a case from Ohio raising similar issues. The Court ordered a third argument at its October 1902 Term.

HIGHLIGHTS OF SUPREME COURT ARGUMENTS

BRIEF FOR CHAMPION *regulation of morals is police power*

◆ The test of the validity of a statute is its real, not its apparent, object. Congress's real object in the antilottery legislation is to regulate the morals of the people and in the process to control and destroy the lottery business. The power to regulate commerce does not include the power to regulate morals. Regulation of the public morals is a police power deliberately reserved to the states by the Tenth Amendment. Congress possesses no police power.

◆ Lottery tickets and lottery advertisements are not articles of commerce. Lottery tickets are more like railroad tickets and insurance policies, which the courts repeatedly have ruled are not articles of commerce. A lottery ticket is nothing more than evidence of title to an intangible interest in the drawing of a lottery. *lottery tickets aren't commerce*

◆ Congress cannot conclusively determine what is or is not an article of commerce. That inquiry is essentially judicial. The Constitution neither changes with time, not does it in theory bend to the force of circumstances.

◆ The antilottery statute violates the First Amendment's guarantee of a free press. Under Article I, Section 8, Congress could prohibit the use of the U.S. mails for the transportation of lottery tickets and advertisements. Closing all channels of interstate commerce, however, impinges on Champion's right to a free press.

BRIEF FOR AMES

◆ Any article bought or sold is an article of commerce and within Congress's power of regulation. The only test as to whether something is an article of commerce is whether it is or customarily has been the subject of purchase and sale. The history of the purchase and sale of lottery tickets is lengthy and worldwide. Understood in common sense terms, lottery tickets have as much intrinsic value as other articles of commerce, and clearly fall within the broad definition of commerce articulated in *Gibbons v. Ogden* and subsequent cases. *Gibbons* also is authority for the proposition that the power to regulate includes the power to prohibit.

◆ The protection of a free press extends only to the expression and circulation of opinions. Lottery tickets are purely commercial instruments and in no sense express an opinion. The First Amendment cannot be construed to protect that which in the legislative discretion of the country has been found to be indecent or immoral.

SUPREME COURT DECISION: 5–4

HARLAN, J.

… The appellant insists that the carrying of lottery tickets from one state to another state by an express company engaged in carrying freight and packages from state to state, although such tickets may be contained in a box or package, does not constitute, and cannot by any act of Congress be legally made to constitute, *commerce* among the states; … consequently, that Congress cannot make it an offense to cause such tickets to be carried from one state to another.

The government insists that express companies, when engaged, for hire, in the business of transportation from one state to another, are instrumentalities of commerce among the states; that the carrying of lottery tickets from one state to another is commerce which Congress may regulate; and that as a means of executing the power to regulate interstate commerce Congress may make it an offense against the United States to cause lottery tickets to be carried from one state to another….

[A review of prior cases shows that] commerce among the States embraces

navigation, intercourse, communication, traffic, the transit of person, and the transmission of messages by telegraph. They also show that the power to regulate commerce among the several States is vested in Congress as absolutely as it would be in a single government, having in its constitution the same restrictions on the exercise of the power as are found in the Constitution of the United States; that such power is plenary, complete in itself, and may be exerted by Congress to its utmost extent, subject *only* to such limitations as the Constitution imposes upon the exercise of the powers granted by it; and that in determining the character of the regulations to be adopted Congress has a large discretion which is not to be controlled by the courts, simply because, in their opinion, such regulations may not be the best or most effective that could be employed.

We come then to inquire whether there is any solid foundation upon which to rest the contention that Congress may not regulate the carrying of lottery tickets from one State to another, at least by corporations or companies whose business it is, for hire, to carry tangible property from one State to another.

It was said in argument that lottery tickets are not of any real or substantial value in themselves, and therefore are not subjects of commerce. If that were conceded to be the only legal test as to what are to be deemed subjects of the commerce that may be regulated by Congress, we cannot accept as accurate the broad statement that such tickets are of no value. Upon their face they showed that the lottery company offered a large capital prize, to be paid to the holder of the ticket winning the prize at the drawing advertised to be held at Asuncion, Paraguay. Money was placed on deposit in different banks in the United States to be applied by the agents representing the lottery company to the prompt payment of prizes. These tickets were the subject of traffic; they could have been sold; and the holder was assured that the company would pay to him the amount of the prize drawn. That the holder might not have been able to enforce his claim in the courts of any country making the drawing of lotteries illegal, and forbidding the circulation of lottery tickets, did not change the fact that the tickets issued by the foreign company represented so much money payable to the person holding them and who might draw the prizes affixed to them. Even if a holder did not draw a prize, the tickets, before the drawing, had a money value in the market among those who chose to sell or buy lottery tickets. In short, a lottery ticket is a subject of traffic and is so designated in the act of 1895....

We are of opinion that lottery tickets are subjects of traffic and therefore are subjects of commerce, and the regula-tion of the carriage of such tickets from state to state, at least by independent carriers, is a regulation of commerce among the several states....

Are we prepared to say that a provision which is, in effect, a *prohibition* of the carriage of such articles from state to state is not a fit or appropriate mode for the *regulation* of that particular kind of commerce?...

If a state, when considering legislation for the suppression of lotteries within its own limits, may properly take into view the evils that inhere in the raising of money, in that mode, why may not Congress, invested with the power to regulate commerce among the several States, provide that such commerce shall not be polluted by the carrying of lottery tickets from one State to another? In this connection it must not be forgotten that the power of Congress to regulate commerce among the States is plenary, is complete in itself, and is subject to no limitations except such as may be found in the Constitution. What provision in that instrument can be regarded as limiting the exercise of the power granted? What clause can be cited which, in any degree, countenances the suggestion that one may, of right, carry or cause to be carried from one State to another that which will harm the public morals? We cannot think of any clause of that instrument that could possibly be invoked by those who assert their right to send lottery tickets from State to State except the one providing that no person shall be deprived of his liberty without due process of law. We have said that the liberty protected by the Constitution embraces the right to be free in the enjoyment of one's faculties; "to be free to use them in all lawful ways; to live and work where he will; to earn his livelihood by any lawful calling; to pursue any livelihood or avocation, and for that purpose to enter into all contracts that may be proper." *Allgeyer v. Louisiana* [165 U.S. 578 (1897)]. But surely it will not be said to be a part of any one's liberty, as recognized by the supreme law of the land, that he shall be allowed to introduce into commerce among the States an element that will be confessedly injurious to the public morals.

If it be said that the act of 1895 is inconsistent with the Tenth Amendment, reserving to the States respectively or to the people the powers not delegated to the United States, the answer is that the power to regulate commerce among the States has been expressly delegated to Congress.

Besides, Congress, by that act, does not assume to interfere with traffic or commerce in lottery tickets carried on exclusively within the limits of any State, but has in view only commerce of that kind among the several States. It has not assumed to interfere with the completely internal affairs of any State, and has only legislated in respect of a matter which concerns the people of the United States. As a State may, for the purpose of guarding the morals of its own people, forbid all sales of lottery tickets within its limits, so Congress, for the purpose of guarding the people of the United States against the "widespread pestilence of lotteries" and to protect the commerce which concerns all the States, may prohibit the carrying of lottery tickets from one State to another. In legislating upon the subject of the traffic in lottery tickets, as carried on through interstate commerce, Congress only supplemented the action of those States—perhaps all of them—

which, for the protection of the public morals, prohibit the drawing of lotteries, as well as the sale or circulation of lottery tickets, within their respective limits.... We should hesitate long before adjudging that an evil of such appalling character, carried on through interstate commerce, cannot be met and crushed by the only power competent to that end. We say competent to that end, because Congress alone has the power to occupy, by legislation, the whole field of interstate commerce....

The present case does not require the court to declare the full extent of the power that Congress may exercise in the regulation of commerce among the States. We may, however, repeat, in this connection, what the court has heretofore said, that the power of Congress to regulate commerce among the States, although plenary, cannot be deemed arbitrary, since it is subject to such limitations or restrictions as are prescribed by the Constitution....

FULLER, C.J., BREWER, SHIRAS, AND PECKHAM, J.J., DISSENTING

... When Chief Justice Marshall said that commerce embraced intercourse, he added, commercial intercourse, and this was necessarily so, since, as Chief Justice Taney pointed out, if intercourse were a word of larger meaning than the word commerce, it could not be substituted for the word of more limited meaning contained in the Constitution.

Is the carriage of lottery tickets from one State to another commercial intercourse?

The lottery ticket purports to create contractual relations and to furnish the means of enforcing a contractual right....

These contracts are not commerce in any proper meaning of the word. They are not subjects of trade and barter offered in the market as something having an existence and value independent of the parties to them....

An invitation to dine, or to take a drive, or a note of introduction, all become articles of commerce under the ruling in this case, by being deposited with an express company for transportation. This in effect breaks down all the differences between that which is, and that which is not, an article of commerce, and the necessary consequence is to take from the States all jurisdiction over the subject so far as interstate communication is concerned. It is a long step in the direction of wiping out all traces of state lines, and the creation of a centralized Government....

I regard this decision as inconsistent with the views of the framers of the Constitution, and of Marshall, its great expounder. Our form of government may remain notwithstanding legislation or decision, but, as long ago observed, it is with governments as it is with religions: the form may survive the substance of the faith....

QUESTIONS

1. *Champion* was decided on Commerce Clause grounds. Identify other constitutional provisions that arguably could have been the source of Congress's power to regulate lottery tickets. If you had argued *Champion* for the United States, would you have relied on the Commerce Clause or one of those other sources? Which constitutional source is most deferential to considerations of federalism?

2. *Champion v. Ames* had the practical effect of creating a federal police power, even though such power is not spelled out in any provision of the Constitution. Should exercise of such a power be limited to situations where Congress (as it did in *Champion*) exercises it to aid the states in suppressing activities that states have identified as contrary to the public health, welfare, safety, and morals? Or should Congress exercise its police power to foster federal policies? What theory of federalism informs your response?

3. In *McCulloch v. Maryland* Chief Justice John Marshall wrote:

   > Should congress, in the execution of its powers, adopt measures which are prohibited by the constitution; or should congress, under the pretext of executing its powers, pass laws for the accomplishment of objects not intrusted to the government; it would become the painful duty of this tribunal, should a case requiring such a decision come before it, to say, that such an act was not the law of the land.

   Champion's attorney argued the traditional understanding that "Regulation of the public morals is a police power deliberately reserved to the states by the Tenth Amendment." Why did the Court not follow Marshall's lead and declare the federal lottery legislation unconstitutional?

4. Law professor Robert E. Cushman contended that in its efforts to protect the national health, morals, and general welfare—in short, to exercise a national police power—Congress was compelled to "use a process of indirection and has had to do good not merely by stealth but by subterfuge" ("The National Police Power Under the Commerce Clause of the Constitution," 3 *Minnesota Law Review* 381 [1918–19]). Does the fact that Congress established its "police power" by enacting legislation to which the states (as represented in the Senate) unanimously agreed undermine Cushman's theory?

5. Soon after *Champion* was decided, Michigan lawyer Alfred Russell predicted that the legal profession would approve of the result because it was based on the Commerce Clause expressly granting power to Congress. (See William Sutherland, "Is Congress a Conservator of the Public Morals?" 38 *American Law Review* 194 [1904].) Instead, the legal profession was almost as divided as the Court. In a reply to Russell, California attorney William Sutherland attacked *Champion* as a usurpation of states' police power, which he claimed was "essentially exclusive" to the states (Id., at 207–208). Why would practicing lawyers have reacted so strongly to a decision that involves American federalism?

COMMENT

Congress's protective conditions legislation has not been confined to lotteries. In the early years of the twentieth century, the Court upheld congressional bans on interstate transportation of diseased cattle, *Reid v. Colorado*, 187 U.S. 137 (1902); interstate transportation of impure food, *Hipolite Egg Co. v. United States*, 220 U.S. 45 (1911); interstate transportation of women for immoral purposes, *Hoke v. United States*, 227 U.S. 308 (1913), and *Caminetti v. United States*, 242 U.S. 470 (1917); interstate transportation of pictorial representations of prize fights destined for public display, *Weber v. Freed*, 239 U.S. 325 (1916); interstate transportation of alcoholic beverages into states where intoxicants had been prohibited, *Clark Distilling Co. v. Western Maryland Railway Co.*, 242 U.S. 311 (1917); and interstate transportation of stolen automobiles, *Brooks v. United States*, 267 U.S. 432 (1925).

STATES' RIGHTS

Hammer v. Dagenhart
247 U.S. 251 (1918)

SETTING

Child labor in America antedates the Revolution. Demand for workers in the colonies was so high that a brisk trade in recruiting laborers developed in England. So-called "crimps," agents of colonial planters and British merchants, scoured the English countryside signing up emigrant workers, including children. Following Alexander Hamilton's advice that they would find women's and children's labor "more useful, and the latter more early useful than they would otherwise be," American manufacturers hired mostly women and children. By 1820, upwards of half the workers in many American factories were girls and boys below the age of eleven. Despite sporadic legislative efforts to ban child labor in the first half of the nineteenth century, such as a Connecticut law in 1813, child labor did not become a political issue of any magnitude until after the Civil War. The economy of the "New South," which developed in the 1880s, featured a rapidly growing textile industry. Mill workers were mostly poor, white women, and children between the ages of ten and fifteen. They lived and worked in "mill villages" owned entirely by companies. Other occupations dominated by child labor around the turn of the century were agriculture, glass manufacturing, street trades such as vending and hawking, and industrial homework like cigar manufacturing in private kitchens and living rooms.

Among the reforms enacted during the Progressive Era, 1900–1916, were child labor laws placing restrictions on the age at which children could be employed, limiting their hours of work, and otherwise safeguarding their health and safety. Thirty-eight states passed such laws by 1912. Because of the diversity in state laws, as well as the inadequate enforcement of these state statutes, the National Child Labor Committee lobbied Congress for a federal law.

In 1916, Congress passed the Keating-Owen Child Labor Act over the objections of southern textile mills and organizations like the National Association of Manufacturers. The act did not prohibit child labor outright. Rather, it prohibited the shipment in interstate commerce of any products made in factories or mines that employed children under fourteen years of age, allowed children between the ages of fourteen and sixteen to work more than eight hours per day or six days per week, or employed children between 7 P.M. and 6 A.M. These provisions covered about one in fourteen of the nation's 2 million child laborers. The act gave the secretary of labor authority to enter and inspect work places covered by the act. The U.S. attorney in each district was authorized to prosecute violators.

Seven-year-old Reuben Dagenhart and his fourteen-year-old brother John were employed by the Fidelity Manufacturing Company, a Charlotte, North Carolina, cotton mill. In August 1917, shortly before the Keating-Owen Act went into effect, the "Southern Textile Bulletin" proclaimed that it would challenge the law's validity in court. In a test case contrived by the executive committee of Southern Cotton Manufacturers, Fidelity employee Roland Dagenhart, father of Rueben and John, filed suit in the U.S. District Court for the Western District of North Carolina to enjoin enforcement of the Keating-Owen Child Labor Act and to prevent the cotton mill from discharging one of his sons and limiting the working hours of the other. Dagenhart's suit stated that he was a man of small means with a large family, that the compensation arising from the services of his minor sons was essential, and that the statute invaded his property rights in the labor and wages of his sons.

The district court, without opinion, declared the Child Labor Act unconstitutional and enjoined William Hammer, U.S. Attorney for the Western District of North Carolina, from enforcing it. Hammer appealed to the Supreme Court of the United States.

HIGHLIGHTS OF SUPREME COURT ARGUMENTS

BRIEF FOR HAMMER

◆ The Child Labor Law is a valid exercise of Congress's power to regulate interstate commerce. The law does not prohibit the manufacture of child-made goods. Its effect is limited to the shipment of such goods through channels of interstate commerce. *not regulating*

◆ Many evils are associated with child labor in factories, including stunted growth, decreased resistance to disease, inadequate education, and high accident rates. Although several states have legislated on the subject of child labor, the legislation is not uniform. States authorizing the use of child labor are able to compete unfairly in interstate commerce, making it difficult for manufacturers in states with child labor laws to survive economically. Congress's thorough investigation of the subject convinced it that a uniform rule for the conduct of interstate commerce is necessary. In this light, the Child Labor Act does not violate the Due Process Clause of the Fifth Amendment.

◆ The Due Process Clause limits Congress in the same way that the Fourteenth Amendment limits states. If states can bar the facilities of intrastate commerce to child-made goods, Congress can do likewise for interstate commerce.

◆ That Congress has no power to prohibit the use of child labor in factories and mines is conceded. Congress's power to regulate interstate commerce, however, is plenary. In *Hoke v. United States*, 227 U.S. 308 (1913), the *prostitutes Harm*

Court ruled that if a statute is a valid exercise of the commerce power, its effect on persons or states is not material. The Child Labor Act's effect on the state's police power, therefore, is not a consideration.

BRIEF FOR DAGENHART

◆ Determination of the kinds of employment and the conditions of that employment suitable for children is a matter for local control. Nothing in the Constitution delegated determination of such matters to Congress. The purpose and effect of the Child Labor Act is to prevent the employment of children. Rather than a regulation of commerce, therefore, the act is an impermissible regulation of the internal affairs of the states.

◆ It is true that case law recognizes the authority of Congress to prevent the use of interstate commerce as an instrument of evil, giving it authority to prevent the movement of bad eggs, obscene literature, and prostitutes through interstate commerce. No claim is made, however, that the products produced by child labor are an evil. They are harmless and useful articles of commerce. The Child Labor Law establishes no legitimate relationship between the thing prohibited and the object to be obtained by the enactment.

◆ The Child Labor Law deprives Dagenhart of property without due process. Similar regulations, if enacted by a state, would not offend due process because of the states' recognized police powers under the Tenth Amendment. Congress's creation of a privileged class of citizens who may engage in interstate commerce, and its creation of a class of citizens of whom it does not approve, however, does violate due process. The central question in the case is whether those who earnestly favor an absolutely nationalized control of every function and activity of life, and the complete elimination of the States as political entities, have hit upon a new and yet unused tool to accomplish their purposes.

SUPREME COURT DECISION: 5–4

DAY, J.

… The power essential to the passage of this act, the government contends, is found in the commerce clause of the Constitution which authorizes Congress to regulate commerce with foreign nations and among the States….

In each of [the prior cases upholding prohibitions on transportation of a particular commodity in interstate commerce] the use of interstate transportation was necessary to the accomplishment of a harmful result. In other words, although the power over interstate transportation was to regulate, that could only be accomplished by prohibiting the use of the facilities of interstate commerce to effect the evil intended.

This element is wanting in the present case. The thing intended to be accomplished by this statute is the denial of the facilities of interstate commerce to those manufacturers in the States who employ children within the prohibited ages. The act in its effect does not regulate transportation among the states, but aims to standardize the ages at which children may be employed in mining and manufacturing within the states. The goods shipped are of themselves harmless. The act permits them to be freely shipped after thirty days from the time of their removal from the factory. When offered for shipment, and before transportation begins, the labor of their production is over, and the mere fact that they were intended for interstate commerce transportation does not make their production subject to federal control under the commerce power.... *Knight*

Over interstate transportation, or its incidents, the regulatory power of Congress is ample, but the production of articles, intended for interstate commerce, is a matter of local regulation.... If it were otherwise, all manufacture intended for interstate shipment would be brought under federal control to the practical exclusion of the authority of the states, a result certainly not contemplated by the framers of the Constitution when they vested in Congress the authority to regulate commerce among the States....

The grant of authority over a purely federal matter was not intended to destroy the local power always existing and carefully reserved to the states in the Tenth Amendment to the Constitution....

A statute must be judged by its natural and reasonable effect.... The control by Congress over interstate commerce cannot authorize the exercise of authority not entrusted to it by the Constitution.... The maintenance of the authority of the states over matters purely local is as essential to the preservation of our institutions as is the conservation of the supremacy of the federal power in all matters entrusted to the nation by the federal Constitution.

In interpreting the Constitution it must never be forgotten that the nation is made up of states to which are entrusted the powers of local government. And to them and to the people the powers not expressly delegated to the national government are reserved....

In our view the necessary effect of this act is, by means of a prohibition against the movement in interstate commerce of ordinary commercial commodities to regulate the hours of labor of children in factories and mines within the states, a purely state authority. Thus the act in a two-fold sense is repugnant to the Constitution. It not only transcends the authority delegated to Congress over commerce but also exerts a power as to a purely local matter to which the federal authority does not extend. The far reaching result of upholding the act cannot be more plainly indicated than by pointing out that if Congress can thus regulate matters entrusted to local authority by prohibition of the movement of commodities in interstate commerce, all freedom of commerce will be at an end, and the power of the states over local matters may be eliminated, and thus our system of government be practically destroyed. *extreme Dual Fed.*

For these reasons we hold that this law exceeds the constitutional authority of Congress. It follows that the decree of the District Court must be Affirmed.

Marshall opinion

HOLMES, MCKENNA, BRANDEIS, AND CLARKE, J.J., DISSENTING

... The question is ... whether the exercise of its otherwise constitutional power by Congress can be pronounced unconstitutional because of its possible reaction upon the conduct of the States in a matter upon which I have admitted that they are free from direct control. I should have thought that matter had been disposed of so fully as to leave no room for doubt. I should have thought that the most conspicuous decisions of this Court had made it clear that the power to regulate commerce and other constitutional powers could not be cut down or qualified by the fact that it might interfere with the carrying out of the domestic policy of any State....

It does not matter whether the supposed evil precedes or follows the transportation. It is enough that in the opinion of Congress the transportation encourages the evil. I may add that in the cases on the so-called White Slave Act [*Hoke v. United States*, 227 U.S. 308 (1913); *Caminetti v. United States*, 242 U.S. 470 (1917)] it was established that the means adopted by Congress as convenient to the exercise of its power might have the character of police regulations....

The notion that prohibition is any less prohibition when applied to things now thought evil I do not understand. But if there is any matter upon which civilized countries have agreed—far more unanimously than they have with regard to intoxicants and some other matters over which this country is now emotionally aroused—it is the evil of premature and excessive child labor. I should have thought that if we were to introduce our own moral conceptions where in my opinion they do not belong, this was preeminently a case for upholding the exercise of all its power by the United States.

But I had thought that the propriety of the exercise of a power admitted to exist in some cases was for the consideration of Congress alone and that this Court always had disavowed the right to intrude its judgment upon questions of policy or morals. It is not for this Court to pronounce when prohibition is necessary to regulation if it ever may be necessary—to say that it is permissible as against strong drink but not as against the product of ruined lives....

COMMENT

Professor Stanley I. Kutler wrote: "The most poignant historical commentary on *Hammer* came from the supposed victor, Rueben Dagenhart, whose father had sued in order to sustain his 'freedom' to allow his ... boy to work in a textile mill. Six years later, Rueben, a 105-pound man, recalled that his victory had earned him a soft drink, some automobile rides from his employer, and a salary of one dollar a day; he had lost his education and his health" (*Encyclopedia of the American Constitution* [New York, NY: Macmillan, 1986], p. 894).

QUESTIONS

1. The underpinning of Justice Day's decision in *Hammer* is the statement that: "In interpreting the Constitution it must never be forgotten that the nation is made up of states to which are entrusted the

powers of local government. And to them and to the people the powers not *expressly delegated* to the national government are reserved"
(emphasis added). Is Justice Day's statement of the Tenth
Amendment's language and meaning correct?

Compare Article II of the Articles of Confederation: "Each state
retains its sovereignty, freedom and independence and every Power,
Jurisdiction and right, which is not by this confederation expressly
delegated to the United States, in Congress assembled." Are the differences in wording between the Tenth Amendment and Article II of
the Articles of Confederation significant for purposes of understanding American federalism?

2. "Dual federalism" is a term coined by constitutional scholar Edward
S. Corwin ("The Passing of Dual Federalism," 36 *Virginia Law Review*
[1950]; *The Twilight of the Supreme Court* [New Haven, CT: Yale
University Press, 1934]; and *Liberty against Government: The Rise,
Flowering and Decline of a Famous Juridical Concept* [Baton Rouge,
LA: Louisiana State University Press, 1948]), to describe a constitutional doctrine created by the Court. According to the doctrine of
dual federalism, states and the national government are separate
sovereigns, and Congress may not exercise powers to achieve ends
that have not been specifically delegated to it, because powers not
delegated are categorically reserved to the States under the Tenth
Amendment. What aspects of the *Hammer* decision exemplify dual
federalism?

3. U.S. Solicitor General John W. Davis argued before the Court:

> The shipment of child-made goods outside of one State directly
> induces similar employment of children in competing states. It is
> not enough to answer that each State theoretically may regulate
> conditions of manufacturing within its own borders. As Congress
> saw the situation, the States were not entirely free agents. For salu-
> tary statutes had been repealed, legislative action on their part
> defeated and postponed time and again, solely by reason of the
> argument (valid or not) that interstate competition would not be
> withstood.

Is Davis's statement an indication that realistically dual federalism is
a nullity in a commercially united country?

4. Before its decision in *Hammer* the Court had let stand several congressional interstate commerce prohibitions banning adulterated
foods and impure drugs, stolen cars, prostitutes, prize fight films,
and liquor. (See *Comment*, p. 576.) Can *Hammer* be reconciled with
Champion v. Ames and other "federal police power" cases? What role
should the test of the "harmfulness" of the thing excluded from interstate commerce play in determining the constitutionality of exercises
of federal power?

COMMENT

After *Hammer v. Dagenhart*, Congress enacted the 1918 Child Labor Tax Law, which imposed a 10 percent tax on the annual net profits on every employer of child labor in businesses covered by the act. In *Bailey v. Drexel Furniture Company*, 259 U.S. 20 (1922), the Court, 8–1, held that the statute was an unconstitutional exercise of the taxing power under Article I, section 8. The Court stated that Congress might enact a tax with the combined purposes of raising revenue and restraining unwanted activities, but that it had no authority "to give such magic to the word 'tax' as to impose a levy whose exclusive object was to penalize."

STATES' RIGHTS

Missouri v. Holland
252 U.S. 416 (1920)

SETTING

Supporters of federal legislation banning child labor, like that challenged successfully in *Hammer v. Dagenhart*, argued that such employment practices created a social problem nationwide in scope. Hence the problem was not susceptible to state or local regulation. Likewise, conservationists argued that protecting migratory birds was a federal concern because wild fowl knew neither state nor international borders.

Opponents replied that both the 1916 Keating-Owen Child Labor Act and the Migratory Bird Act of 1918 impinged on states' reserved powers. To states' rights advocates, the statute at issue in *Missouri v. Holland* posed a greater danger to the Tenth Amendment because it derived its authority from a treaty. They noted that the predecessor 1913 Migratory Bird Act had been held unconstitutionally beyond the power of Congress by two federal district courts. *United States v. Shauver*, 214 F. 154 E.D. Ark. (1914); *United States v. McCullagh*, 221 F 288 D. Kans. (1915).

Note: Review the *Setting* to and excerpt of *Missouri v. Holland* in Chapter 4, pp. 443–449.

QUESTIONS

1. Under *Holland*, what limitations, if any, are there on what Congress can regulate pursuant to implementing a treaty? Are these limitations more of a political than a legal nature?

2. Given the *Holland* reading of congressional powers, do Article II, section 2, and Article VI together circumvent Article V? The Tenth Amendment?

3. If you were an opponent of the North American Free Trade Agreement, what strategies would be available to you, in the light of *Holland*, to stop Congress from, for example, requiring the automobile industry to out-source production of major components used in assembling passenger vehicles and trucks?

STATES' RIGHTS

NLRB v. Jones & Laughlin
301 U.S. 1 (1937)

SETTING

Dual federalism, as exemplified by the Court's decision in *Hammer v. Dagenhart* and explained in question #2, p. 582, following that case, was one of several judicially fashioned doctrines deployed to defeat federal oversight of labor/management relations before and during the Great Depression. A second, complementary doctrine was the proposition stated in *United States v. E. C. Knight* (Chapter 3, pp. 244–252), that manufacturing is separate from commerce. The *Knight* Court held that Congress could regulate commerce but it had no authority to regulate manufacture. A third doctrine was nondelegation. As articulated in *A.L.A. Schechter Poultry Corp. v. United States*, Chapter 3, pp. 262–270, the nondelegation doctrine holds that Congress may not legitimately delegate legislative authority to an administrative agency operating in the executive branch. Until 1937, dual federalism, the *Knight* distinction, and the nondelegation doctrine operated to curtail the authority of Congress to regulate commerce and, consequently, to restrict congressional efforts to govern relations between employers and their employees.

The Court heard arguments in *NLRB v. Jones & Laughlin* in a highly charged political atmosphere. The United States was in the depths of the Great Depression. Oral arguments in *Jones & Laughlin* began on February 9, 1937. Four days earlier, President Franklin D. Roosevelt had sent to Congress his plan to reform the federal courts. One part of his so-called "Court packing" plan would have allowed the president to appoint one justice to the Supreme Court for every justice who had at least ten years service and who had waited more than six months past his seventieth birthday to resign or retire. *Jones & Laughlin* was also argued in the midst of a labor strike in which General Motors workers had shut down the Flint, Michigan, plant.

Note: Review the *Setting* to and excerpt of *NLRB v. Jones & Laughlin* in Chapter 3, pp. 280–291.

QUESTIONS

1. Compare the Court's interpretation of federalism in *Jones & Laughlin* with its interpretation in *Collector v. Day* and *Hammer v. Dagenhart*. How extensive a revolution in federalism did *Jones & Laughlin* represent?

2. Justice McReynolds wrote in his *Jones & Laughlin* dissent: "A more remote and indirect interference with interstate commerce or a more definite invasion of the powers reserved to the states is difficult, if not impossible, to imagine." After *Jones & Laughlin*, what remedies are available to the states for such invasions?

3. The same day that the Court handed down *Jones & Laughlin*, it decided *NLRB v. Friedman-Harry Marks Clothing Co.*, 301 U.S. 58 (1937). This case involved a small Virginia manufacturer, most of whose raw materials came from, and most of whose finished products were sold in, other states. The Court upheld application of the National Labor Relations Act to the company. Should the size of a manufacturing establishment figure in determining whether Congress or a state ought to regulate its operation?

STATES' RIGHTS

United States v. Darby
312 U.S. 100 (1941)

SETTING

Jones & Laughlin was decided by a deeply divided Court, as indicated by the 5–4 vote. Within four years of *Jones & Laughlin*, however, President Franklin Roosevelt was transforming the Supreme Court, even without the benefit of his defeated Court-packing plan. By 1941, the four *Jones & Laughlin* dissenters, disparagingly termed "The Four Horsemen of the Apocalypse" by New Deal supporters, were gone. Hugo Black replaced Willis Van Devanter (July 1937), Stanley Reed replaced George Sutherland (January 1938), Frank Murphy replaced Pierce Butler (November 1940), and James Byrnes replaced James McReynolds (February 1941). At the same time, several justices who had voted with the *Jones & Laughlin* majority were succeeded by New Dealers. Benjamin Cardozo's seat was taken by Felix Frankfurter. Louis Brandeis was followed by William O. Douglas. When Harlan Fiske Stone became chief justice upon Charles Evans Hughes's retirement, Robert Jackson was appointed associate justice.

Roosevelt's seven appointments solidified support for a profound constitutional switch that had been initiated by the *Jones & Laughlin* majority. The post-*Jones & Laughlin* Court understood federalism and the Court's role in supervising nation-state relationships much differently. *United States v. Darby*, decided without dissent a mere four years after *Jones & Laughlin*, demonstrates how thoroughly the Court had rejected dual federalism by 1941.

Note: Review the *Setting* to and excerpt of *United States v. Darby* in Chapter 3, pp. 302–310.

QUESTIONS

1. According to the *Darby* Court, what is the nature of American federalism. What is the status of the Tenth Amendment? Does the Court no longer see itself as having a constitutional obligation to police the line between national and state powers?

2. Chief Justice Stone wrote in *Darby* that Congress could "regulate intrastate activities where they have substantial effect on interstate commerce." What standard does Chief Justice Stone suggest for assessing how "substantial" an effect must be to justify federal regulation of intrastate commerce?

STATES' RIGHTS

National League of Cities v. Usery
426 U.S. 883 (1976)

[handwritten] Supports 10th amendment
— rules in states favor

SETTING

Following the Great Depression and World War II, a number of factors combined to increase the scope of the national government's domestic operations. One was the growth of the federal administrative machinery necessary to implement the New Deal programs of President Franklin Roosevelt and the Great Society programs of President Lyndon Johnson. Another was the perception that only national policies and programs could remedy problems such as racial injustice, poverty, decline in educational standards, and urban blight. Still another was the belief of many Americans, particularly civil rights groups and the poor, that Congress was more responsive to domestic problems than state legislatures and in a better position financially to address them.

By the late 1960s, however, the size and cost of the national government had become a political issue. Presidential candidate Richard Nixon campaigned on a platform of decentralizing power and restoring the vigor of state and local governments. In his State of the Union Address in 1971, President Nixon proposed a "New Federalism," the purpose of which was to reverse the concentration of power in Washington. Nixon administration programs, like revenue sharing and block grants, were designed to give states and localities easier access to monies raised by the national government and greater discretion over the use of those monies to meet local problems.

Nixon's New Federalism rekindled legal controversies that many thought had been settled by the judicial revolution initiated by the Court's decisions in *NLRB v. Jones & Laughlin* in 1937 and completed by *United States v. Darby* in 1941. Darby explicitly stated that the Tenth Amendment "... states but a truism that all is retained which has not been surrendered." It was widely believed that the federal government could regulate virtually all local activities under the authority of the Commerce Clause by simply showing that the activities affected interstate commerce. Federal regulatory legislation grounded in Congress's commerce power proliferated in the years after *Jones & Laughlin*. President Nixon's New Federalism, and his promise to appoint justices to the Supreme Court of the United States who were more sympathetic to the rights of states, provided litigants with new incentives to challenge the reach of Congress's power under the Commerce Clause.

The Fair Labor Standards Act (FLSA) of 1938 set minimum wage and overtime pay requirements for employees engaged in commerce or the production of goods for commerce, and prohibited the shipment in interstate commerce of any goods manufactured in violation of those requirements. In *Darby*, recall, the Supreme Court upheld the FLSA as a valid exercise of Congress's plenary power over commerce. In doing so, the Court overruled *Hammer v. Dagenhart*, one of the last vestiges of pre-*Jones & Laughlin* jurisprudence in the field of interstate commerce.

In 1961, Congress amended the FLSA, extending its coverage to persons employed in "enterprises" engaged in commerce or in the production of goods for commerce. In 1966, it changed the definition of "employers" under the act and extended its coverage to state hospitals, institutions, and schools. Two years later, the Supreme Court upheld both amendments as valid exercises of Congress's commerce power. *Maryland v. Wirtz*, 392 U.S. 183 (1968).

In 1974, Congress again amended the FLSA. This time Congress extended the minimum wage and overtime provisions of the FLSA to virtually all state and local government employees. In addition, overtime exceptions for drivers, operators, and conductors of mass transit facilities were phased out. Opponents of the amendments—including the National League of Cities,

National Governors' Conference, eighteen states, one metropolitan government, and three cities—filed suit in U.S. District Court for the District of Columbia against Secretary of Labor Peter Brennan seeking an injunction against enforcement of the 1974 amendments and a declaration that they violated the Fifth, Tenth, and Eleventh Amendments to the Constitution and could not be justified as an exercise of Congress's commerce power.

A three-judge federal district court panel dismissed the suit. Although the judges were "troubled" by contentions that the 1974 FLSA amendments would intrude on the states' performance of essential governmental functions, they believed that the amendments were required to apply the principles of *Maryland v. Wirtz*, 392 U.S. 183 (1968), and dismissed the case. The National League of Cities and the other plaintiffs appealed to the Supreme Court of the United States.

The case was first argued in April 1975. It was reargued in March 1976, at which time the name of William Usery, then secretary of labor, was substituted for Brennan.

HIGHLIGHTS OF SUPREME COURT ARGUMENTS

BRIEF FOR THE NATIONAL LEAGUE OF CITIES, ET AL.

◆ No legislation before the FLSA amendments has so permeated the whole of state and local government. Because these governments operate through their employees, and the act imposes regulatory controls on all employees, the act effectively intrudes into every function of every state and local government.

◆ The major purpose of the Constitutional Convention was to create a workable system of federalism, involving a sharing of governmental powers between the national and state levels. Preventing centralized power was a major part of the constitutional design. The 1974 FLSA amendments overstep constitutional federalism because they reflect an attempt by Congress to centralize power by regulating the terms and conditions of state and local government employees. Unique local concepts like volunteerism and compensatory time off in lieu of overtime pay are wiped out by the statute and replaced by rigid, nationwide uniform rules.

◆ *Maryland v. Wirtz*, 392 U.S. 183 (1968), does not control this case, because it was based on the assumption that the 1961 and 1966 FLSA amendments involved no real federal interference with the states. While it condoned regulation of hospital and school employees, it did not provide any serious analysis of the ultimate impact on federalism. If the Court does find *Wirtz* to be controlling it should be overruled.

◆ The Tenth Amendment did not create the federal system of government; the federal system is embedded in the entire structure of the Constitution. The Tenth Amendment, however, protects the states' governmental powers. In *United States v. Carolene Products*, 304 U.S. 144 (1938), the

Court stated that the presumption of constitutionality of a federal statute weakens as the legislation affects a fundamentally protected right "within a specific prohibition of the Constitution, such as those of the first ten amendments." Congress, therefore, is required to meet a higher standard than mere "rationality" in justifying the 1974 FLSA amendments. It failed to meet that standard.

STATE OF CALIFORNIA AS INTERVENOR

◆ The state of California is not included under the FLSA because as a state it is not an "enterprise."

◆ Application of the FLSA to all state employees is not supported by a compelling national interest.

◆ The 1974 FLSA amendments touch the very heart of state sovereignty. The operations of state government are not in competition with and have no relationship to interstate commerce.

STATE OF MARYLAND, ON A SEPARATE BRIEF

◆ The Court must understand the negative impact of the 1974 FLSA amendments on state budgetary practices.

AMICUS CURIAE BRIEFS SUPPORTING NATIONAL LEAGUE OF CITIES, ET AL.

The National Association of Counties, the National Institute of Municipal Law Officers.

BRIEF FOR USERY

◆ The issues in this case were resolved by *Wirtz*, because the schools and hospitals covered by the 1966 amendments are just as essential government services as any of the public agencies covered by the 1974 amendments. The 1974 amendments do not threaten state sovereignty or displace state policy. They require only that in pursuit of state policy, states satisfy wage and hour minimum standards.

◆ The activities of state and local governments have a significant affect on interstate commerce. Substandard labor conditions could lead to labor disputes which would burden the flow of goods in interstate commerce. In 1973, for example, over four hundred thousand state and local government employees were paid less than $1.90 per hour, while poverty-level income for a non-farm family was approximately $2.27 per hour. Under the Commerce Clause, Congress has the power to deal with the economic consequences of substandard labor conditions.

◆ Extension of the FLSA to state and local governments does not violate any constitutional immunity of the states. The Court said in *Wirtz*, reflecting other decisions, that Congress may regulate state activities that have a substantial affect on commerce. Because the 1974 amendments are within Congress's delegated power to regulate commerce, they are not precluded by the Tenth Amendment's reservation to the states of "powers not delegated."

◆ The argument that the Tenth Amendment is an affirmative limitation on congressional power was rejected by Chief Justice Marshall in *Gibbons v. Ogden*.

AMICUS CURIAE BRIEFS SUPPORTING USERY

Florida Police Benevolent Association; the International Conference of Police Associations; the AFL-CIO; the National Education Association; the Coalition of American Public Employees; two U.S. Senators; and the states of Alabama, Colorado, Michigan, and Minnesota.

SUPREME COURT DECISION: 5–4

REHNQUIST, J.

... This Court has never doubted that there are limits upon the power of Congress to override state sovereignty, even when exercising its otherwise plenary powers to tax or to regulate commerce which are conferred by Art. I of the Constitution.... In *Fry v. United States*, 421 U.S. 542 (1975), the Court recognized that an express declaration of this limitation is found in the Tenth Amendment:

> While the Tenth Amendment has been characterized as a 'truism,' stating merely that 'all is retained which has not been surrendered,' it is not without significance. The Amendment expressly declares the constitutional policy that Congress may not exercise power in a fashion that impairs the States' integrity or their ability to function effectively in a federal system."

We have repeatedly recognized that there are attributes of sovereignty attaching to every state government which may not be impaired by

Congress, not because Congress may lack an affirmative grant of legislative authority to reach the matter, but because the Constitution prohibits it from exercising the authority in that manner....

One undoubted attribute of state sovereignty is the States' power to determine the wages which shall be paid to those whom they employ to carry out their governmental functions, what hours those persons will work, and what compensation will be provided where these employees may be called upon to work overtime. The question we must resolve here, then, is whether these determinations are "'functions essential to separate and independent existence'" so that Congress may not abrogate the States' otherwise plenary authority to make them....

In their complaint appellants advanced estimates of substantial costs which will be imposed upon them by the 1974 amendments [to the FLSA].... Judged solely in terms of increased costs in dollars, these allegations show a significant impact on the functioning of the governmental bodies involved....

Quite apart from the substantial costs imposed upon the States and their political subdivisions, the Act displaces state policies regarding the manner in which they will structure delivery of those governmental services which their citizens require. The Act, speaking directly to the States qua States, requires that they shall pay all but an extremely limited minority of their employees the minimum wage rates currently chosen by Congress. It may well be that as a matter of economic policy it would be desirable that States, just as private employers, comply with these minimum wage requirements. But it cannot be gainsaid that the federal requirement directly supplants the considered policy choices of the States' elected officials and administrators as to how they wish to structure pay scales in state employment. The State might wish to employ persons with little or no training, or those who wish to work on a casual basis, or those who for some other reason do not possess minimum employment requirements, and pay them less than the federally prescribed minimum wage. It may wish to offer part-time or summer employment to teenagers at a figure less than the minimum wage, and if unable to do so may decline to offer such employment at all. But the Act would forbid such choices by the States. The only "discretion" left to them under the Act is either to attempt to increase their revenue to meet the additional financial burden imposed upon them by paying congressionally prescribed wages to their existing complement of employees, or to reduce that complement to a number which can be paid the federal minimum wage without increasing revenue.

This dilemma presented by the minimum wage restrictions may seem not immediately different from that faced by private employers, who have long been covered by the Act and those who must find ways to increase their gross income if they are to pay higher wages while maintaining current earnings. The difference, however, is that a State is not merely a factor in the "shifting economic arrangements" of the private sector of the economy, ... but is itself a coordinate element in the system established by the Framers for governing our Federal Union....

Our examination of the effect of the 1974 amendments, as sought to be extended to the States and their political subdivisions, satisfies us that both the minimum wage and the maximum hour provisions will impermissibly interfere with the integral governmental functions of these bodies.... [E]ven if we accept appellee's assessments concerning the impact of the amendments, their application will nonetheless significantly alter or displace the States' abilities to structure employer-employee relationships in such areas as fire prevention, police protection, sanitation, public health, and parks and recreation. These activities are typical of those performed by state and local governments in discharging their dual functions of administering the public law and furnishing public services. Indeed, it is functions such as these which governments are created to provide, services such as these which the States have traditionally afforded their citizens. If Congress may withdraw from the States the authority to make those fundamental employment decisions upon which their systems for performance of these functions must rest, we think there would be little left of the States' "'separate and independent existence.'" *Coyle v. Oklahoma*, 221 U.S. 559 (1911).... We hold that insofar as the challenged amendments operate to directly displace the States' freedom to structure integral operations in areas of traditional governmental functions, they are not within the authority granted Congress by Art. I, Sec. 8, cl. 3....

[W]e have reaffirmed today that the States as States stand on a quite different footing from an individual or a corporation when challenging the exercise of Congress' power to regulate commerce.... We agree that such assertions of power, if unchecked, would indeed, as Mr. Justice Douglas cautioned in his dissent in *Wirtz*, allow "the National Government [to] devour the essentials of state sovereignty" and would therefore transgress the bounds of the authority granted Congress under the Commerce Clause. *Maryland v. Wirtz*, 392 U.S. (1968). While there are obvious differences between the schools and hospitals involved in *Wirtz* and the fire and police departments affected here, each provides an integral portion of those governmental services which the States and their political subdivisions have traditionally afforded their citizens. We are therefore persuaded that *Wirtz* must be overruled. The judgment of the District Court is accordingly reversed, and the cases are remanded for further proceedings consistent with this opinion.

So ordered.

BLACKMUN, J., CONCURRING

The Court's opinion and the dissents indicate the importance and significance of this litigation as it bears upon the relationship between the Federal Government and our States. Although I am not untroubled by certain possible implications of the Court's opinion— some of them suggested by the dissents—I do not read the opinion so despairingly as does my Brother Brennan. In my view, the result with respect to the statute under challenge here is necessarily correct. I may misinterpret the Court's opinion, but it seems to me that it adopts a balancing approach, and does not outlaw federal power in areas such as environmental protection, where the federal interest is demonstrably greater and where state facility compliance with imposed federal standards would be essential.... With this understanding on my part of the Court's opinion, I join it.

BRENNAN, WITH WHOM WHITE, AND MARSHALL, J.J., JOIN, DISSENTING

The Court concedes, as of course it must, that Congress enacted the 1974 amendments pursuant to its exclusive power under Art I, Sec. 8, cl 3, of the Constitution "[t]o regulate Commerce ... among the several States." It must therefore be surprising that my Brethren should choose this bicentennial year of our independence to repudiate principles governing judicial interpretation of our Constitution settled since the time of Mr. Chief Justice John Marshall, discarding his postulate that the Constitution contemplates that restraints upon exercise by Congress of its plenary commerce power lie in the political process and not in the judicial process. For 152 years ago Mr. Chief Justice Marshall enunciated that principle to which, until today, his successors on this Court have been faithful....

Gibbons v. Ogden. Only 34 years ago, *Wickard v. Filburn* reaffirmed that "[a]t the beginning Chief Justice Marshall ... made emphatic the embracing and penetrating nature of [Congress's commerce] power by warning that effective restraints on its exercise must proceed from political rather than from judicial processes."

My Brethren do not successfully obscure today's patent usurpation of the role reserved for the political process by their purported discovery in the Constitution of a restraint derived from sovereignty of the States on Congress' exercise of the commerce power....

We said in *United States v. California*, 297 U.S. 175 (1936)[:]... "The sovereign power of the states is necessarily diminished to the extent of the grants of power to the federal government in the Constitution.... [T]he power of the state is subordinate to the constitutional exercise of the granted federal power."...

My Brethren thus have today manufactured an abstraction without substance, founded neither in the words of the Constitution nor on precedent. An abstraction having such profoundly pernicious consequences is not made less so by characterizing the 1974 amendments as legislation directed at the "States *qua* States." Of course, regulations that this Court can say are not regulations of "commerce" cannot stand, and in this sense "[t]he Court has ample power to prevent ... 'the utter destruction of the State as a political entity.'" But my Brethren make no claim that the 1974 amendments are not regulations of "commerce"; rather they overrule *Wirtz* in disagreement with historic principles that *United States v. California* reaf-

firmed.... Clearly, therefore, my Brethren are also repudiating the long line of our precedents holding that a judicial finding that Congress has not unreasonably regulated a subject matter of "commerce" brings to an end the judicial role. "Let the end be legitimate, let it be within the scope of the constitution, and all means which are appropriate, which are plainly adapted to that end, which are not prohibited, but consist with the letter and spirit of the constitution, are constitutional." *McCulloch v. Maryland.*

The reliance of my Brethren upon the Tenth Amendment as "an express declaration of [a state sovereignty] limitation," ... not only suggests that they overrule governing decisions of this Court that address this question but must astound scholars of the Constitution....

Today's holding patently is in derogation of the sovereign power of the Nation to regulate interstate commerce. Can the States engage in businesses competing with the private sector and then come to the courts arguing that withdrawing the employees of those businesses from the private sector evades the power of the Federal Government to regulate commerce?...

My Brethren do more than turn aside longstanding constitutional jurisprudence that emphatically rejects today's conclusion. More alarming is the startling restructuring of our federal system, and the role they create therein for the federal judiciary. This Court is simply not at liberty to erect a mirror of its own conception of a desirable governmental structure....

It is unacceptable that the judicial process should be thought superior to the political process in this area. Under the Constitution the Judiciary has no role to play beyond finding that Congress has not made an unreasonable legislative judgment respecting what is "commerce." My Brother Blackmun suggests that controlling judicial supervision of the relationship between the States and our National Government by use of a balancing approach diminishes the ominous implications of today's decision. Such an approach, however, is a thinly veiled rationalization for judicial supervision of a policy judgment that our system of government reserves to Congress.

Judicial restraint in this area merely recognizes that the political branches of our Government are structured to protect the interests of the States, as well as the Nation as a whole, and that the States are fully able to protect their own interests in the premises. Congress is constituted of representatives in both the Senate and House elected from the States.... There is no reason whatever to suppose that in enacting the 1974 amendments Congress, even if it might extensively obliterate state sovereignty by fully exercising its plenary power respecting commerce, had any purpose to do so. Surely the presumption must be to the contrary. Any realistic assessment of our federal political system,

dominated as it is by representatives of the people *elected from the States*, yields the conclusion that it is highly unlikely that those representatives will ever be motivated to disregard totally the concerns of these States.... Certainly this was the premise upon which the Constitution, as authoritatively explicated in *Gibbons v. Ogden*, was founded. Indeed, though the States are represented in the National Government, national interests are not similarly represented in the States' political processes. Perhaps my Brethren's concern with the Judiciary's role in preserving federalism might better focus on whether Congress, not the States, is in greater need of this Court's protection....

STEVENS, J., DISSENTING

The Court holds that the Federal Government may not interfere with a sovereign State's inherent right to pay a substandard wage to the janitor at the state capitol. The principle on which the holding rests is difficult to perceive.... Since I am unable to identify a limitation on ... federal power that would not also invalidate federal regulation of state activities that I consider unquestionably permissible, I am persuaded that this statute is valid....

QUESTIONS

1. Does Justice Rehnquist's opinion in *National League of Cities* derive from his reading of the Tenth Amendment or from a structural analysis of the workings of the federal system? Is the difference significant?

2. What guidelines does Justice Rehnquist's opinion in *National League of Cities* provide for distinguishing between "traditional" and "nontraditional" state governmental functions for purposes of determining the applicability of federal laws? Is the distinction workable? Is there a better test? Consider the statement in *Atascadero State Hospital v.*

Scanlan, 473 U.S. 234 (1985), that the "Eleventh Amendment implicates the fundamental constitutional balance between the Federal Government and the States."

3. Harvard law school professor Laurence Tribe contended in an article written shortly after the Court's decision in *National League of Cities* that the decision "may be taken to have established new 'rights' of states as against the national government—rights beyond those derived simply from the constitutional requirement of a meaningful existence for states as separate entities" ("Unraveling *National League of Cities*: The New Federalism and Affirmative Rights to Essential Government Services," 90 *Harvard Law Review* [1977]: 1065).

If professor Tribe is correct does *National League of Cities* signal a return to the pre-*Jones & Laughlin* approach to Commerce Clause questions?

4. *National League of Cities* was decided by a 5–4 vote. It was the first time in almost forty years that a Court majority had held unconstitutional an act of Congress for reasons pertaining to federalism. Justice Blackmun joined the majority, but his concurring opinion indicated that he had several reservations about the decision. What were those reservations? Can you hypothesize a set of facts that might persuade Justice Blackmun that the majority erred in *National League of Cities*?

COMMENT

The Court's decision in *National League of Cities* revived litigation over federalism that had been virtually dormant since 1941. The following cases typify the Court's approach to federalism questions between 1976 and 1985, when it revisited the *National League of Cities* doctrine in *Garcia v. San Antonio Metropolitan Transit Authority*, 469 U.S. 528 (1985), the next excerpted case.

Case: *Hodel v. Virginia Surface Mining & Reclamation Association*, 452 U.S. 264 (1981)

Vote: 9–0

Decision: A federal strip mining law that allows states to maintain regulatory authority over strip mining on nonfederal lands only if they enforce federally imposed environmental standards, and prove that they have the resources to do so, does not displace the states' traditional right to regulate land use. A successful challenge relying on *National League of Cities* must show that the challenged statute regulates the states as states; must address matters that are indisputably attributes of state sovereignty; and must impair the state's ability to structure integral operations of traditional governmental functions. Even if these conditions are met, a state challenge will fail if the federal interest advanced is such that it justifies state submission.

Case: *United Transportation Union v. Long Island Rail Road Co.*, 455 U.S. 678 (1982)

Vote: 9–0

Decision: A state cannot claim Tenth Amendment immunity under the doctrine in *National League of Cities* for a state-owned railroad that is engaged in interstate commerce. Operating a railroad in interstate commerce is not a "traditional" state function.

Case: *Federal Energy Regulatory Commission v. Mississippi*, 456 U.S. 742 (1982)

Vote: 5–4

Decision: The Public Utility Regulatory Policies Act of 1978, requiring state utility regulatory commissions to follow federally imposed procedures when considering federally suggested standards, does not violate the Tenth Amendment doctrine in *National League of Cities*. Congress could have preempted state regulation of utilities altogether and directly imposed its own standards.

Case: *Equal Employment Opportunity Commission v. Wyoming*, 460 U.S. 226 (1983)

Vote: 5–4

Decision: Extension of the federal Age Discrimination in Employment Act of 1967 to state and local governments—prohibiting employers from discriminating among persons between forty and seventy on the basis of age unless age is shown to be a "bona fide occupational qualification"—does not interfere with the activities of states as public employers. Neither does it displace the states' freedom to structure integral operations in areas of traditional governmental functions.

STATES' RIGHTS

Garcia v. San Antonio Metropolitan Transit Authority
469 U.S. 528 (1985)

SETTING

To many scholars, *National League of Cities* was a surprising bellwether of a policy change in Commerce Clause jurisprudence. The Tenth Amendment, moribund since the Court's rejection of dual federalism in the late 1930s, suddenly was brought back to life as an affirmative limitation on Congress's power to regulate commerce. However, as the summary of decisions after *National League of Cities* illustrates, in none of the cases brought in the wake of *National League of Cities* did the Court muster a majority to limit congressional power because of state authority. In 1982, Justice Blackmun, whose concurrence had given Justice Rehnquist the crucial fifth vote in *National League of Cities*, began siding with Justices Brennan, White, Marshall, and Stevens as they called into question the workability of the *National League of Cities* standards.

As a practical matter, *National League of Cities* seemed to create a constitutional "gray area" because it did not specify all of the state activities that were protected from the reach of the Fair Labor Standards Act (FLSA). It listed, by way of example, "fire protection, police protection, sanitation, public health, and parks and recreation." By overruling *Maryland v. Wirtz*, 392 U.S. 183 (1968), *National League of Cities* also prevented the FLSA from reaching public schools and hospitals. The only activity specifically mentioned as not immune from the FLSA was a state-operated railroad.

In 1979, the secretary of labor issued regulations under which the wage and hour administrator of the Department of Labor was to determine the state and local government operations against which he would seek to enforce the FLSA. The deputy wage and hour administrator subsequently declared that the municipally owned San Antonio Transit System of San Antonio, Texas, was not protected by the Tenth Amendment from application of the FLSA's minimum wage and overtime provisions. This administrative declaration gave rise to litigation that would prove to be the next test of the Supreme Court's commitment to the doctrine underlying *National League of Cities*.

In November 1979, the San Antonio Metropolitan Transit Authority (SAMTA), a regional transit authority created to serve the San Antonio metropolitan area, filed a complaint in U.S. District Court for the Western District of Texas. It sought a declaratory judgment that its operations were an integral part of a political subdivision of the state of Texas and therefore were exempt from the minimum wage and overtime provisions of the FLSA under the ruling in *National League of Cities*. F. Ray Marshall, the secretary of labor, filed a counterclaim against SAMTA for back pay and injunctive relief. The American Public Transit Association (APTA) and Joe Garcia, a SAMTA employee, were permitted to intervene in the litigation.

The district court held that local publicly owned mass transit systems like SAMTA were integral operations in the areas of traditional governmental functions under *National League of Cities* and entered summary judgment for SAMTA and APTA. Marshall and Garcia appealed to the Supreme Court of the United States, which vacated the district court's decision and remanded the case for further consideration in light of the Court's intervening decision in *United Transportation Union v. Long Island Rail Road*, 455 U.S. 678 (1982). In that case, the Court had rejected a "static historical view of state functions" and upheld application of the Railway Labor Act to the state-owned railroad, because of the importance to the national economy of preventing disruptions in rail service due to labor disputes.

On remand, the district court again entered summary judgment for SAMTA and APTA. It held that while states had not always owned and operated mass-transit systems, they had engaged in a long-standing pattern of public regulation and that this regulatory tradition gave rise to an "inference of sovereignty." The secretary of labor and Garcia again appealed.

HIGHLIGHTS OF SUPREME COURT ARGUMENTS

After initial argument by the parties and several *amici* about whether SAMTA was exempt from the provisions of the FLSA, the Court ordered reargument on the following question: "Whether or not the principles of the Tenth Amendment as set forth in *National League of Cities v. Usery* should be reconsidered."

BRIEF FOR GARCIA

◆ *National League of Cities* should be reconsidered and overruled because it is based on two erroneous assumptions: First, that the framers of the Tenth Amendment intended federal sovereignty to be subordinate to state sovereignty. Second, that the framers intended to enforce this affirmative limitation by vesting the judiciary with power to invalidate laws which the judiciary finds unduly intrusive on state sovereignty. Nothing in the text and structure of the Constitution, the records of the Convention, or the *Federalist Papers* supports the theory that powers delegated to the national government are subject to limitation on a case-by-case review in the interest of preserving state sovereignty.

◆ The era in which the Court narrowly construed Congress's commerce power based on the Tenth Amendment was relatively short-lived. It began with *Hammer v. Dagenhart* in 1918 and ended with *United States v. Darby* in 1941 and the Court's declaration that the Tenth Amendment states a "truism" that all was retained by the states that was not surrendered.

◆ The Court's decision in *National League of Cities* failed to treat adequately the abundance of precedents that were contrary to its conclusion. It relied on language from earlier decisions that provided no support for its holding. For example, *National League of Cities* cited *Texas v. White* for the proposition that the Constitution looks to an "indestructible Union, composed of indestructible States." The *White* Court made that point in the context of declaring that under the Constitution no state has a right to withdraw from the Union.

◆ If the Court holds that *National League of Cities* was correct in holding that state sovereignty limits Congress's commerce power, the decision nonetheless erred by equating state sovereignty with a state's provision of goods and services (as opposed to making and enforcing laws), and by equating states with their political subdivisions. Defining state sovereignty to include economic activities unnecessarily hobbles Congress's power to regulate commerce.

◆ It is impermissible to treat the Tenth Amendment as giving the word "state" a broader meaning than it has under the Eleventh Amendment, or to hold that political subdivisions share state sovereign immunity for Tenth Amendment purposes but not for Eleventh Amendment purposes.

BRIEF FOR SECRETARY OF LABOR RAYMOND DONOVAN

◆ The key principle in *National League of Cities* is sound; namely, that the federal commerce power cannot be exercised to regulate state activity in a way that would hamper the state government's ability to fulfill its role in the union and endanger its separate and independent existence. At least two points, however, need clarification. First is the role of the courts in defining federalism relationships. The proper role is limited, to be exercised only when Congress ignores the values behind federalism and nullifies state prerogatives in performing core functions. Second is the standard to be used in determining whether particular state activities are protected. The standard essentially should be historical. The appropriate test is whether at the time the federal government first entered the field with regulatory legislation, the states had generally established themselves with fixed patterns of organization as providers of the particular service.

◆ *National League of Cities* need not be overruled, but the decision of the district court should be reversed. There is no serious claim that states had generally undertaken to provide public transit service before enactment of federal legislation governing employment relations.

BRIEF FOR SAMTA

◆ *National League of Cities* embodies a sound and enduring constitutional doctrine that is the necessary consequence of the structure of the American federal system. There can be no doubt that the founders intended to preserve state sovereignty in the new nation. They could have had no idea that the Commerce Clause would give the federal government unlimited regulatory authority over the internal commerce of the states or over the states as states. All eight states that proposed amendments to the Constitution at the first Congress in 1789 recommended a provision reserving powers to the states.

◆ The Supreme Court has decided an almost unbroken line of cases recognizing that states must be left to function within their spheres as sovereigns free from the tentacles of the Commerce Clause.

◆ The Court's decision in *Darby* limited only the private sector's ability to rely on concepts of federalism to avoid Commerce Clause regulation. The Court has never ruled that the federal commerce power over states is limitless. Such a ruling would be a formula for destruction of the states as governing authorities in modern society.

AMICUS CURIAE BRIEFS SUPPORTING SAMTA

The attorneys general of twenty-four states; the National Institute of Municipal Law Officers, Colorado Public Employees' Retirement Association and the National Employer Labor Relations Association, the National League of Cities; the Legal Foundation of America.

SUPREME COURT DECISION: 5–4

BLACKMUN, J.

We revisit in [this] case an issue raised in *National League of Cities v. Usery*. In that litigation, this Court, by a sharply divided vote, ruled that the Commerce Clause does not empower Congress to enforce the minimum-wage and overtime provisions of the Fair Labor Standards Act (FLSA) against the States "in areas of traditional governmental functions." Although National League of Cities supplied some examples of "traditional governmental functions," it did not offer a general explanation of how a "traditional" function is to be distinguished from a "nontraditional" one. Since then, federal and state courts have struggled with the task, thus imposed, of identifying a traditional function for purposes of state immunity under the Commerce Clause....

Our examination of this "function" standard applied in [this] and other cases over the last eight years now persuades us that the attempt to draw the boundaries of state regulatory immunity in terms of "traditional governmental functions" is not only unworkable but is also inconsistent with established principles of federalism and, indeed, with those very federalism principles on which *National League of Cities* purported to rest. That case, accordingly, is overruled....

Were SAMTA a privately owned and operated enterprise, it could not credibly argue that Congress exceeded the bounds of its Commerce Clause powers in prescribing minimum wages and overtime rates for SAMTA's employees. Any constitutional exemption from the requirements of the FLSA therefore must rest on SAMTA's status as a governmental entity rather than on the "local" nature of its operations....

Thus far, this Court ... has made little headway in defining the scope of the governmental functions deemed protected under *National League of Cities*. In that case the Court set forth examples of protected and unprotected functions, but provided no explanation of how those examples were identified....

Many constitutional standards involve "undoubte[d] ... grey areas," and despite the difficulties that this Court and other courts have encountered so far, it normally might be fair to venture the assumption that case-by-case development would lead to a workable standard for determining whether a particular governmental function should be immune from federal regulation under the Commerce Clause....

We rejected the possibility of making immunity turn on a purely historical standard of "tradition," ... and properly so.... The most obvious defect of a historical approach to [defining] state immunity is that it prevents a court from accommodating changes in the historical functions of States, changes that have resulted in a number of once-private functions like education being assumed by the States and their subdivisions. At the same time, the only apparent virtue of a rigorous historical standard, namely, its promise of a reasonably objective measure for state immunity, is illusory. Reliance on history as an organizing principle results in linedrawing of the most arbitrary sort; the genesis of state governmental functions stretches over a historical continuum from before the Revolution to the present, and courts would have to decide by fiat precisely how longstanding a pattern of state involvement had to be for federal regulatory authority to be defeated.

A nonhistorical standard for selecting immune governmental functions is likely to be just as unworkable as a historical standard. The goal of identifying "uniquely" governmental functions, for example, has been rejected by the Court in the field of government tort liability in part because the notion of a "uniquely" governmental function is unmanageable. Another possibility would be to confine immunity to "necessary" governmental services, that is, services that would be provided inadequately or not at all unless the government provided them. The set of services that fits into this category, however, may well be negligible....

We believe, however, that there is a more fundamental problem at work here.... The problem is that neither the governmental/proprietary distinction nor any other that purports to separate out important governmental functions can be faithful to the role of federalism in a democratic society. The essence of our federal system is that within the realm of authority left open to them under the Constitution, the States must be equally free to engage in any activity that their citizens choose for the common weal, no matter how unorthodox or unnecessary anyone else—including the judiciary—deems state involvement to be. Any rule of state immunity that looks to the "traditional," "integral," or "necessary" nature of governmental functions inevitably invites an unelected federal judiciary to make decisions about which state policies it favors and which ones it dislikes....

We therefore now reject, as unsound in principle and unworkable in practice, a rule of state immunity from federal regulation that turns on a judicial appraisal of whether a particular governmental function is "integral" or "traditional."... We accordingly return to the underlying issue that confronted this Court in *National League of Cities*—the manner in which the Constitution insulates States from the reach of Congress' power under the Commerce Clause.

The central theme of *National League of Cities* was that the States occupy a special position in our constitutional system and that the scope of Congress' authority under the Commerce Clause must reflect that position....

What has proved problematic is not the perception that the Constitution's federal structure imposes limitations on the Commerce Clause, but rather the nature and content of those limitations.

We doubt that courts ultimately can identify principled constitutional limitations on the scope of Congress' Commerce Clause powers over the States merely by relying on *a priori* definitions of state sovereignty. In part, this is because of the elusiveness of objective criteria for "fundamental" elements of state sovereignty, a problem we have witnessed in the search for "traditional governmental functions." There is, however, a more fundamental reason: the sovereignty of the States is limited by the Constitution itself....

The States unquestionably do "retai[n] a significant measure of sovereign authority." They do so, however, only to the extent that the Constitution has not divested them of their original powers and transferred those powers to the Federal Government....

[T]o say that the Constitution assumes the continued role of the States is to say little about the nature of that role....

[T]he Framers chose to rely on a federal system in which special restraints on federal power over the States inhered principally in the workings of the National Government itself, rather than in discrete limitations on the objects of federal authority. State sovereign interests, then, are more properly protected by procedural safeguards inherent in the structure of the federal government than by judicially created limitations on federal power....

The fact that some federal statutes such as the FLSA extend general obligations to the States cannot obscure the extent to which the political position of the States in the federal system has served to minimize the burdens that the States bear under the Commerce Clause.

We realize that changes in the structure of the Federal Government have taken place since 1789, not the least of which has been the substitution of popular election of Senators by the adoption of the Seventeenth Amendment in 1913, and that these changes may work to alter the influence of the States in the federal political process. Nonetheless, against this background, we are convinced that the fundamental limitation that the constitutional scheme imposes on the Commerce Clause to protect the "States as States" is one of process rather than one of result....

Of course, we continue to recognize that the States occupy a special and specific position in our constitutional system and that the scope of Congress' authority under the Commerce Clause must reflect that position. But the principal and basic limit on the federal commerce power is that inherent in all congressional action—the built-in restraints that our system provides through state participation in federal governmental action. The political process ensures that laws that unduly burden the States will not be promulgated....

Though the separate concurrence providing the fifth vote in *National League of Cities* was "not untroubled by certain possible implications" of the decision, the Court in that case attempted to articulate affirmative limits on the Commerce Clause power in terms of core governmental functions and fundamental attributes of state sovereignty. But the model of democratic decisionmaking the Court there identified underestimated, in our view, the solicitude of the national political process for the continued vitality of the States. Attempts by other courts since then to draw guidance from this model have proved it both impracticable and doctrinally barren. In sum, in *National League of Cities* the Court tried to repair what did not need repair.

We do not lightly overrule recent precedent. We have not hesitated, however, when it has become apparent that a prior decision has departed from a proper understanding of congressional power under the Commerce Clause. Due respect for the reach of congressional power within the federal system mandates that we do so now.

National League of Cities v. Usery is overruled. The judgment of the District Court is reversed, and these cases are remanded to that court for further proceedings consistent with this opinion.

It is so ordered.

POWELL, REHNQUIST, AND O'CONNOR, J.J., AND BURGER, C.J., DISSENTING

... Whatever effect the Court's decision may have in weakening the application of *stare decisis*, it is likely to be less important than what the Court has done to the Constitution itself. A unique feature of the United States is the *federal* system of government guaranteed by the Constitution and implicit in the very name of our country. Despite some genuflecting in the Court's opinion to the concept of federalism, today's decision effectively reduces the Tenth Amendment to meaningless rhetoric when Congress acts pursuant to the Commerce Clause....

In our federal system the States have a major role that cannot be pre-empted by the National Government. As contemporaneous writings and the debates at the ratifying conventions make clear, the States' ratification of the Constitution was predicated on this understanding of federalism. Indeed, the Tenth Amendment was adopted specifically to ensure that the important role promised the States by the proponents of the Constitution was realized.

Much of the initial opposition to the Constitution was rooted in the fear that the National Government would be too powerful and eventually would eliminate the States as viable political entities. This concern was voiced repeatedly until proponents of the Constitution made assurances that a Bill of Rights, including a provision explicitly reserving powers in the States, would be among the first business of the new Congress....

This history, which the Court simply ignores, documents the integral role of the Tenth Amendment in our constitutional theory. It exposes as well, I believe, the fundamental character of the Court's error today. Far from being "unsound in principle," judicial enforcement of the Tenth Amendment is essential to maintaining the federal system so

carefully designed by the Framers and adopted in the Constitution....

[T]he harm to the States that results from federal overreaching under the Commerce Clause is not simply a matter of dollars and cents. Nor is it a matter of the wisdom or folly of certain policy choices. Rather, by usurping functions traditionally performed by the States, federal overreaching under the Commerce Clause undermines the constitutionally mandated balance of power between the States and the Federal Government, a balance designed to protect our fundamental liberties....

As I view the Court's decision today as rejecting the basic precepts of our federal system and limiting the constitutional role of judicial review, I dissent.

REHNQUIST, J., DISSENTING

I join both Justice Powell's and Justice O'Connor's thoughtful dissents. Justice Powell's reference to the "balancing test" approved in *National League of Cities* is not identical with the language in that case, which recognized that Congress could not act under its commerce power to infringe on certain fundamental aspects of state sovereignty that are essential to "the States' separate and independent existence." Nor is either test, or Justice O'Connor's suggested approach, precisely congruent with Justice Blackmun's views in 1976, when he spoke of a balancing approach which did not outlaw federal power in areas "where the federal interest is demonstrably greater." But under any one of these approaches the judgment in these cases should be affirmed, and I do not think it incumbent on those of us in dissent to spell out further the fine points of a principle that will, I am confident, in time again command the support of a majority of this Court.

O'CONNOR, DISSENTING

… The problems of federalism in an integrated national economy are capable of more responsible resolution than holding that the States as States retain no status apart from that which Congress chooses to let them retain. The proper resolution, I suggest, lies in weighing state autonomy as a factor in the balance when interpreting the means by which Congress can exercise its authority on the States as States. It is insufficient, in assessing the validity of congressional regulation of a State pursuant to the commerce power, to ask only whether the same regulation would be valid if enforced against a private party….

It has been difficult for this Court to craft bright lines defining the scope of the state autonomy protected by *National League of Cities*. Such difficulty is to be expected whenever constitutional concerns as important as federalism and the effectiveness of the commerce power come into conflict. Regardless of the difficulty, it is and will remain the duty of this Court to reconcile these concerns in the final instance. That the Court shuns the task today by appealing to the "essence of federalism" can provide scant comfort to those who believe our federal system requires something more than a unitary, centralized government. I would not shirk the duty acknowledged by *National League of Cities* and its progeny, and I share Justice Rehnquist's belief that this Court will in time again assume its constitutional responsibility.

I respectfully dissent.

QUESTIONS

1. The British newspaper, *The Economist*, expressed puzzlement over *Garcia*, claiming that the decision partly repudiated *Marbury v. Madison*: "Since 1803 the court has claimed the authority … to invalidate actions of the federal government if they conflict with the constitution. The *Garcia* decision seems to suggest that the principle of judicial review does not apply to questions of federalism when congress acts under the commerce clause. [T]he Supreme Court seems to have declared that judicial enforcement of the constitutional position on federalism is at an end." (Quoted in William W. Van Alstyne, "The Second Death of Federalism," 83 *Michigan Law Review* 1709 [1985].)

   Does *Garcia* partially abdicate the power of judicial review claimed in *Marbury v. Madison*?

2. Parties on both sides of the issue in *Garcia* claimed support for their position from the debates at the Constitutional Convention, the *Federalist Papers* and Supreme Court precedents. Is it simply impossible to arrive at one lasting meaning of federalism in the American political system? If so, what is the proper role of judicial review in cases involving federalism?

3. Justice Blackmun wrote in *Garcia*: "[T]he principal and basic limit on

the federal commerce power is that inherent in all congressional action—the built-in restraints that our system provides through state participation in federal governmental action. The political process ensures that laws that unduly burden the States will not be promulgated."

Garcia was handed down on February 19, 1985. Nine months later, on November 13, 1985, President Ronald Reagan signed a bill into law that lifted the time-and-a-half overtime pay requirement for state and local government employees under the Fair Labor Standards Act. According to the *Congressional Quarterly Weekly Report*, passage of the law was "one of the faster actions on major legislation in recent years" (43 *Congressional Quarterly Weekly Report*, November 16, 1985, p. 2379). Does Congress's swift action demonstrate the truth of Justice Blackmun's observation in *Garcia*?

4. The Court's decisions in *National League of Cities* and *Garcia*, respectively, represent the extreme of judicial intervention to protect state interests against national encroachment and the extreme of judicial reluctance to scrutinize the expansion of national powers. Is there a middle ground between the two approaches? What would a middle ground look like?

5. Why did Justice Blackmun change his position between *National League of Cities* and *Garcia*? Were the reservations he expressed in his *National League of Cities* concurring opinion a harbinger? An interview with Justice Blackmun in the *New York Times Magazine*, February 20, 1983, p. 20, sheds some light on the issue.

STATES' RIGHTS

United States v. Lopez
514 U.S. 549 (1995)

Setting

In *New York v. United States*, 505 U.S. 144 (1992), Justice Sandra Day O'Connor summarized the two approaches that the Supreme Court has taken in cases raising questions of federalism:

> These questions can be viewed in either of two ways. In some cases the Court has inquired whether an Act of Congress is authorized by one of the powers delegated to Congress in Article I of the Constitution.... In other

cases the Court has sought to determine whether an Act of Congress invades the province of state sovereignty reserved by the Tenth Amendment.

The issue in *New York v. United States* was whether Congress has the authority to require states to dispose of radioactive wastes generated within their borders. Justice O'Connor continued:

> In a case like this one, involving the division of authority between federal and state government, the two inquiries are mirror images of each other. If a power is delegated to Congress in the Constitution, the Tenth Amendment expressly disclaims any reservation of that power to the States; if a power is an attribute of state sovereignty reserved by the Tenth Amendment, it is necessarily a power the Constitution has not conferred on Congress.

In an otherwise fragmented decision, all of the justices were able to agree in *New York v. United States* that while Congress has the power to encourage states to provide for the disposal of radioactive wastes generated within their borders, Congress cannot compel the states to do so.

The act being contested in *United States v. Lopez*, the 1990 Gun-Free School Zones Act, banned firearms from public, private, or parochial school grounds. Like the Low-Level Radioactive Waste Policy Act at issue in *New York v. United States*, the 1990 law implicated both federal commerce power and state police power. *Lopez* required the Court again to enter the debate over divided power.

Note: Review the *Setting* to and excerpt of *United States v. Lopez* in Chapter 3, pp. 324–337.

QUESTIONS

1. According to the majority in *Lopez*, how are Commerce Clause and federalism questions interrelated?

2. Does *Lopez* represent a return to pre-*Darby* conceptions of federalism or did Congress merely fail to jump through the hoops of identifying the link between guns in schools and the Commerce Clause?

3. Justice Breyer argued in his *Lopez* dissent that the Court should

> apply three basic principles of Commerce Clause interpretation. First, the power to "regulate Commerce … among the several States," encompasses the power to regulate local activities insofar as they significantly affect interstate commerce….
>
> Second, in determining whether a local activity will likely have a significant effect upon interstate commerce, a court must consider, not the effect of an individual act (a single instance of gun possession), but rather the cumulative effect of all similar instances (i.e., the effect of all guns possessed in or near schools)….

Third, the Constitution requires ... [c]ourts [to] give Congress a degree of leeway in determining the existence of a significant factual connection between the regulated activity and interstate commerce....

What, if anything, does Justice Breyer's identification of these three basic principles add to the understanding of the relationship between federalism and the Commerce Clause?

STATES' RIGHTS

U.S. Term Limits, Inc. v. Thornton
514 U.S. 1218 (1995)

SETTING

Three sections of Article I of the Constitution of the United States deal with the qualifications and elections of members of the House of Representatives and Senate. Article I, section 2, states that a representative must be at least 25 years of age, a citizen of the United States for at least seven years, and an inhabitant of the state he or she represents. Section 3 requires that a Senator be at least thirty years of age, a citizen of the United States for at least nine years, and an inhabitant of the state he or she represents. Section 4 provides that "the times, places and manner of holding elections for Senators and Representatives, shall be prescribed in each state by the legislature thereof."

Article I does not place limits on the number of terms a representative or senator can serve. However, the idea of term limits is not of recent origin. For example, the Virginia Plan (so called because it was submitted to the Philadelphia Convention by the Virginia delegation), which shaped significantly the 1787 Constitution, suggested that members of the federal legislature would be "incapable of re-election for the space of ____ [left blank] after the expiration of their term of service." That proposal was rejected. Nonetheless, shortly after ratification of the Constitution, states began placing restrictions on access to the printed ballot, including districting and residency requirements, and prohibiting certain classes of felons from holding office.

Since World War II, the reelection advantages of incumbents has grown. In 1992, 88 percent of the House and 82 percent of the Senate comprised incumbents who ran and were reelected. Even in the 1994 midterm elections, when Republicans gained control of both the House and Senate for the first time since 1952, over 84 percent of House Democratic incumbents and over 87 percent of Senate Democratic incumbents were reelected.

Public frustration with Congress, and with the apparent permanence of its membership, led to a grass-roots movement to impose congressional term limitations. In 1990, Colorado was the first state to enact congressional term limits. By 1994, twenty-two other states had done likewise. Advocates of term limits found legal support for their efforts from the Supreme Court's decision in *Storer v. Brown*, 415 U.S. 724 (1974). The *Storer* Court upheld a California law that barred appearance on a printed ballot of independent candidates for the House or Senate who had been affiliated with a political party within a year of the preceding primary election or had voted in the primary. In footnote 16 to *Storer*, the Court observed that the contention that the law violated Article I, Section 2, clause 2, was "wholly without merit."

At the November 3, 1992, general election, Arkansas voters joined the ranks of states imposing term limits on members of Congress by adopting Amendment Seventy-three—a "Term Limitation Amendment"—to the Arkansas Constitution. It passed by a 60–40 percent margin. The preamble to the amendment stated that "elected officials who remain in office too long become preoccupied with re-election and ignore their duties as representatives of the people." It maintained that "[e]ntrenched incumbency has reduced voter participation" and has resulted in an "electoral system that is less free, less competitive, and less representative than the system established by the Founding Fathers." Pursuant to Amendment 73, a member of Congress who had served three or more terms in the House of Representatives or two or more terms in the Senate could not have his or her name appear on the ballot. However, that person could retain office through a write-in campaign.

Shortly after the enactment of Amendment Seventy-three, Bobbie E. Hill, on behalf of the League of Women Voters, joined with others to seek a declaratory judgment that the Arkansas constitutional amendment violates Articles I and IV, as well as the First and Fourteenth Amendments, to the Constitution of the United States. Hill's complaint named as defendants "all persons who have or claim any interest which would be affected by the declaration," including then-Governor Bill Clinton and Ray Thornton, an Arkansas representative in Congress. The State of Arkansas intervened as a defendant through its attorney general, J. Winston Bryant, as did organizations such as U.S. Term Limits, Inc., Arkansans for Governmental Reform, and Americans for Term Limits.

The Circuit Court for Pulaski County, Arkansas, granted Hill's motion for summary judgment on the ground that § 3 of Amendment Seventy-three violated Article I, § 2, clause 2, and § 3, clause 3, of the Constitution of the United States. The Arkansas Supreme Court affirmed, in a 5–2 decision, issuing five separate opinions. A plurality of three justices ruled that Amendment Seventy-three superimposed an additional qualification for office on the exclusive list in Article I. It concluded that the "glimmer of opportunity" through the write-in was too "faint" to "salvage Amendment Seventy-three from constitutional attack." Two justices concurred separately, on the ground that Amendment Seventy-three violated the Qualifications Clause. Two justices dissented, contending that the Tenth Amendment gives states the right to structure the government and to set qualifications for office as long as those qualifications do not violate the Qualifications Clause. According to the dissent, the Qualifications Clause sets only minimum requirements for congressional office.

Arkansas and the other intervenors, U.S. Term Limits, Inc., Arkansans for Governmental Reform, and Americans for Term Limits, petitioned the Supreme Court of the United States for writs of certiorari. Both petitions were granted and consolidated.

HIGHLIGHTS OF SUPREME COURT ARGUMENTS

BRIEF FOR U.S. TERM LIMITS, INC.

◆ Amendment Seventy-three does not set a qualification for office. It was advocated by supporters of turnover in elective offices and was designed to lessen the overwhelming advantages enjoyed by multiterm incumbents. It does so only by not printing the names of incumbents on ballots. It does not disqualify anyone from running, being elected or serving.

◆ Equating a state ballot regulation with disqualification from office would open to Article I challenges state primary laws and hundreds of other provisions by which the fifty states tightly regulate Congressional elections.

◆ Even if Amendment Seventy-three adds qualifications for holding office, Article I still is not violated. Sections 2 and 44 explicitly assign states broad power over congressional elections. The disqualifications in §§ 2 and 3 set minimums but contain no restrictions on state laws.

◆ This Court has repeatedly declined to imply from the Constitution's silence prohibitions on the exercise of state powers. The Tenth Amendment further confirms that constitutional limits on state power are normally not expressed.

◆ At least half the states added qualifications for Congress promptly after the Constitution was adopted, including districting, nominating and screening processes, residency and property ownership requirements, and laws forbidding large groups of government officials and employees from running for Congress. For over two hundred years there have been disqualifications for persons convicted of certain crimes.

◆ No federal function is threatened by state disqualification statutes. The ability of the people of the states to choose who is to make federal laws for them is a practical and essential regulator of the federal balance.

BRIEF FOR ARKANSAS

◆ The framers envisioned frequent turnover for legislative offices, especially in the House of Representatives, whose members must stand for election biennially.

◆ States have broad power under Article I and the Tenth Amendment to regulate federal elections. Term limits and ballot access laws are legitimate, historically based, judicially approved regulations designed to even the playing field between incumbents and challengers and ultimately to enhance the responsiveness of delegates to Congress.

◆ States can regulate voting processes even if the regulations exclude some candidates from office. The Qualification Clauses do not guarantee anyone the right to campaign for office. Neither are they exclusive. In *Powell v. McCormack* this court said only that each house of Congress cannot add qualifications, not that states are barred from doing so.

AMICUS CURIAE BRIEFS SUPPORTING U.S. TERM LIMITS, INC., AND ARKANSAS

Joint brief of Alaska Committee for Limited Congress, Idahoans for Term Limits, Nevadans for Term Limits, and Northwest Legal Foundation; State of Washington; joint brief of the Mountain States Legal Foundation, Wyoming Citizens for Responsible Government, South Dakotans for Term Limits, Montanans for Limited Terms, Arizona Citizens for Limited Terms, and Americans Back in Charge; joint brief of Virginians for Term Limits, North Carolina Term Limits Coalition, South Carolinians for Term Limits, Louisianans for Term Limits, Eight is Enough; joint brief of Congressional Term Limits Coalition of Maine, Maryland for Term Limits, Vermont Term Limits, Connecticut Term Limits, New Hampshire Citizens for Term Limits, and New Jersey Term Limits Coalition, Inc.; Citizens United Foundation; U.S. Justice Foundation; Michigan Governor John Engler; joint brief of the Washington Legal Foundation, Senator Kay Bailey Hutchison and Representatives Robert Dornan, Dana Rohrabacher, Tillie Fowler, Gerald Soloman, Peter Blote, Bob Franks, Martin Hoke, Bill Baker, Scott McInnis, Dan Miller, Bob McCollum, Bob Inglis, Jim Ramsford, Scott Klug, Jay Kim, Nick Smith; New Yorkers for Term Limits; Allied Education Foundation.

BRIEF FOR THORNTON

◆ Although Article I grants states the authority to prescribe the qualifications of electors, it delegates no similar authority to states or to Congress concerning the qualifications of who may be elected. Article I gives Congress extraordinary authority to make or alter state election laws. The text and structure of Article I leave no room for states to establish additional qualifications for membership in Congress. Article I's comprehensive regulation completely preempts state authority to prescribe the characteristics of federal legislators.

◆ The history surrounding the drafting, ratification, and early interpretation of the Constitution shows that the framers intended that the qualifications listed in Article I be exclusive. The framers explicitly rejected term limit and rotation in office proposals. They considered but did not adopt proposals to delegate to states the power to prescribe certain types of qualifications. Early Congresses considered and rejected constitutional amendments to provide for term limits.

◆ Amendment Seventy-three establishes an additional and therefore unconstitutional qualification for members of Congress. The argument that Amendment Seventy-three is permissible because it does not bar from Congress an incumbent who manages to win a write-in election overlooks the principle that the door to the national legislature should be open to all and voters should be allowed to vote for whomever they please.

◆ Amendment Seventy-three manipulates election procedures in order to disable an identifiable class of persons from service in the federal legislature. It is, therefore, outside the authority of the Time, Place and Manner Clause of Article I.

AMICUS CURIAE BRIEFS SUPPORTING THORNTON

Joint brief of the American Civil Liberties Union (ACLU) and ACLU of Washington State; League of Women Voters; United States; Representative Henry Hyde III.

SUPREME COURT DECISION: 5–4

STEVENS, J.

... [T]he constitutionality of Amendment 73 depends critically on the resolution of two distinct issues. The first is whether the Constitution forbids States from adding to or altering the qualifications specifically enumerated in the Constitution. The second is, if the Constitution does so forbid, whether the fact that Amendment 73 is formulated as a ballot access restriction rather than as an outright disqualification is of constitutional significance. Our resolution of these issues draws upon our prior resolution of a related but distinct issue: whether Congress has the power to add to or alter the qualifications of its Members.

Twenty-six years ago, in *Powell v. McCormack* we reviewed the history and text of the Qualifications Clauses in a case involving an attempted exclusion of a duly elected Member of Congress. The principal issue was whether the power granted to each House in Art. I, § 5, to judge the "Qualifications of its own Members" includes the power to impose qualifications other than those set forth in the text of the Constitution. In an opinion by Chief Justice Warren for eight Members of the Court, we held that it does not....

We ultimately ... [concluded] that the House of Representatives has no "authority to *exclude* any person, duly elected by his constituents, who meets all the requirements for membership expressly prescribed in the Constitution." *Powell* (emphasis in original).... In reaching that conclusion, we undertook a detailed historical review to determine the intent of the Framers. Though recognizing that the Constitutional Convention debates themselves were inconclusive, ... we determined that the "relevant historical materials" reveal that Congress has no power to alter the qualifications in the text of the Constitution....

We thus conclude now, as we did in *Powell*, that history shows that, with respect to Congress, the Framers intended the Constitution to establish fixed qualifications....

Powell ... establishes two important propositions: first, that the "relevant historical materials" compel the conclusion that, at least with respect to qualifications imposed by Congress, the Framers intended the qualifications listed in the Constitution to be exclusive; and second, that that conclusion is equally compelled by an understanding of the "fundamental principle of our representative democracy ... 'that the people should choose whom they please to govern them.'"...

In sum, ... we reaffirm that the qualifications for service in Congress set forth in the text of the Constitution are "fixed," at least in the sense that they may not be supplemented by Congress.

Our reaffirmation of *Powell* does not necessarily resolve the specific questions presented in these cases. For petitioners argue that whatever the constitutionality of additional qualifications for membership imposed by Congress, the historical and textual materials discussed in *Powell* do not support the conclusion that the Constitution prohibits additional qualifications imposed by States. In the absence of such a constitutional prohibition, petitioners argue, the Tenth Amendment and the principle of reserved powers require that States be allowed to add such qualifications....

We disagree for two independent reasons. First, we conclude that the power to add qualifications is not within the "original powers" of the States, and thus is not reserved to the States by the Tenth Amendment. Second, even if States possessed some original power in this area, we conclude that the Framers intended the Constitution to be the exclusive source of qualifications for members of Congress, and that the Framers thereby "divested" States of any power to add qualifications....

Contrary to petitioners' assertions, the power to add qualifications is not part of the original powers of sovereignty that the Tenth Amendment reserved to the States. Petitioners' Tenth Amendment argument misconceives the nature of the right at issue because that Amendment could only "reserve" that which existed before....

With respect to setting qualifications for service in Congress, no such right existed before the Constitution was ratified. The contrary argument overlooks the revolutionary character of the government that the Framers conceived. Prior to the adoption of the Constitution, the States had joined together under the Articles of Confederation. In that system, "the States retained most of their sovereignty, like independent nations bound together only by treaties." *Wesberry v. Sanders*, 376 U.S. 1 (1964). After the Constitutional Convention convened, the Framers were presented with, and eventually adopted a variation of, "a plan not merely to amend the Articles of Confederation but to create an entirely new National Government with a National Executive, National Judiciary, and a National Legislature." In adopting that plan, the Framers envisioned a uniform national system, rejecting the notion that the Nation was a collection of States, and instead creating a direct link between the National Government and the people of the United States.... In that National Government, representatives owe primary allegiance not to the people of a State, but to the people of the Nation.... Representatives and Senators are as much officers of the entire union as is the President. States thus "have just as much right, and no more, to prescribe new qualifications for a representative, as they have for a president.... It is no original prerogative of state power to appoint a representative, a senator, or president for the union."...

This conclusion is consistent with our previous recognition that, in certain limited contexts, the power to regulate the incidents of the federal system is not a reserved power of the States, but rather is delegated by the Constitution. Thus, we have noted that "[w]hile, in a loose sense, the right to vote for representatives in Congress is sometimes spoken of as a right derived from the states, ... this statement is true only in the sense that the states are authorized by the Constitution, to legislate on the subject as provided by § 2 of Art. I." *United States v. Classic*, 313 U.S. 299 (1941)....

In short, as the Framers recognized, electing representatives to the National Legislature was a new right, arising from the Constitution itself. The Tenth Amendment thus provides no basis for concluding that the States possess reserved power to add qualifications to those that are fixed in the Constitution. Instead, any state power to set the qualifications for membership in Congress must derive not from the reserved powers of state sovereignty, but rather from

the delegated powers of national sovereignty. In the absence of any constitutional delegation to the States of power to add qualifications to those enumerated in the Constitution, such a power does not exist....

Congress' subsequent experience with state-imposed qualifications provides further evidence of the general consensus on the lack of state power in this area....

We recognize, as we did in *Powell*, that "congressional practice has been erratic" and that the precedential value of congressional exclusion cases is "quite limited." Nevertheless, those incidents lend support to the result we reach today....

Additional qualifications pose the same obstacle to open elections whatever their source. The egalitarian ideal, so valued by the Framers, is thus compromised to the same degree by additional qualifications imposed by States as by those imposed by Congress.

Similarly, we believe that state-imposed qualifications, as much as congressionally imposed qualifications, would undermine the second critical idea recognized in *Powell*: that an aspect of sovereignty is the right of the people to vote for whom they wish. Again, the source of the qualification is of little moment in assessing the qualification's restrictive impact.

Finally, state-imposed restrictions, unlike the congressionally imposed restrictions at issue in *Powell*, violate a third idea central to this basic principle: that the right to choose representatives belongs not to the States, but to the people....

Permitting individual States to formulate diverse qualifications for their representatives would result in a patchwork of state qualifications, undermining the uniformity and the national character that the Framers envisioned and sought to ensure.... Such a patchwork would also sever the direct link that the Framers found so critical between the National Government and the people of the United States....

Petitioners argue that, even if States may not add qualifications, Amendment 73 is constitutional because it is not such a qualification, and because Amendment 73 is a permissible exercise of state power to regulate the "Times, Places and Manner of Holding Elections." We reject these contentions.

Unlike §§ 1 and 2 of Amendment 73, which create absolute bars to service for long-term incumbents running for state office, § 3 merely provides that certain Senators and Representatives shall not be certified as candidates and shall not have their names appear on the ballot. They may run as write-in candidates and, if elected, they may serve. Petitioners contend that only a legal bar to service creates an impermissible qualification, and that Amendment 73 is therefore consistent with the Constitution....

We need not decide whether petitioners' narrow understanding of qualifications is correct because, even if it is, Amendment 73 may not stand. As we have often noted, "'[c]onstitutional rights would be of little value if they could be ... indirectly denied.'" *Harman v. Forssenius*, 380 U.S. 528 (1965), quoting *Smith v. Allwright*, 321 U.S. 649 (1944). The Constitution "nullifies sophisticated as well as simple-minded modes" of infringing on Constitutional protections. *Lane v. Wilson*, 307 U.S. 268 (1939).

In our view, Amendment 73 is an indirect attempt to accomplish what the Constitution prohibits Arkansas from accomplishing directly. As the plurality opinion of the Arkansas Supreme Court recognized, Amendment 73 is an "effort to dress eligibility to stand for Congress in ballot access clothing," because the "intent and the effect of Amendment 73 are to disqualify congressional incumbents from further service." We must, of course, accept the State Court's view of the purpose of its own law: we are thus authoritatively informed that the sole purpose of § 3 of Amendment 73 was to attempt to achieve a result that is forbidden by the Federal Constitution. Indeed, it cannot be seriously contended that the intent behind Amendment 73 is other than to prevent the election of incumbents. The preamble of Amendment 73 states explicitly: "[T]he people of Arkansas ... herein limit the terms of elected officials." Sections 1 and 2 create absolute limits on the number of terms that may be served. There is no hint that § 3 was intended to have any other purpose....

Petitioners make the ... argument that Amendment 73 merely regulates the "Manner" of elections, and that the Amendment is therefore a permissible exercise of state power under Article I, § 4, cl. 1 (the Elections Clause) to regulate the "Times, Places and Manner" of elections. We cannot agree.

A necessary consequence of petitioners' argument is that Congress itself would have the power to "make or alter" a measure such as Amendment 73. Art. I, § 4, cl. 1.... That the Framers would have approved of such a result is unfathomable. As our decision in Powell and our discussion above make clear, the Framers were particularly concerned that a grant to Congress of the authority to set its own qualifications would lead inevitably to congressional self-aggrandizement and the upsetting of the delicate constitutional balance.... We refuse to adopt an interpretation of the Elections Clause that would so cavalierly disregard what the Framers intended to be a fundamental constitutional safeguard.

Moreover, petitioners' broad construction of the Elections Clause is fundamentally inconsistent with the Framers' view of that Clause. The Framers intended the Elections Clause to grant States authority to create procedural regulations, not to provide States with license to exclude classes of candidates from federal office....

The judgment is affirmed.

It is so ordered.

KENNEDY, J., CONCURRING

... In my view ... it is well settled that the whole people of the United States asserted their political identity and unity of purpose when they created the federal system. The dissent's course of reasoning suggesting otherwise might be construed to disparage the republican character of the National Government, and it seems appropriate to add these few remarks to explain why that course of argumentation runs counter to fundamental principles of federalism.

Federalism was our Nation's own discovery. The Framers split the atom of sovereignty. It was the genius of their idea that our citizens would have two political capacities, one state and one federal, each protected from incursion by the other. The resulting Constitution created a legal system unprecedented in form and design, establishing two orders of government, each with its own direct relationship, its own privity, its own set of mutual rights and obligations to the people who sustain it and are governed by it. It is appropriate to recall these origins, which instruct us as to the nature of the two different governments created and confirmed by the Constitution.

A distinctive character of the National Government, the mark of its legitimacy, is that it owes its existence to the act of the whole people who created it. It must be remembered that the National Government too is republican in essence and in theory.... Once the National Government was formed under our Constitution, the same republican principles continued to guide its operation and practice....

In one sense it is true that "the people of each State retained their separate political identities," for the Constitution takes care both to preserve the States and to make use of their identities and structures at various points in organizing the federal union. It does not at all follow from this that the sole political identity of an American is with the State of his or her residence. It denies the dual character of the Federal Government which is its very foundation to assert that the people of the United States do not have a political identity as well, one independent of, though consistent with, their identity as citizens of the State of their residence.... It must be recognized that "'[f]or all the great purposes for which the Federal government was formed, we are one people, with one common country.'" *Shapiro v. Thompson*, 394 U.S. 618 (1969)....

Of course, because the Framers recognized that state power and identity were essential parts of the federal balance ... the Constitution is solicitous of the prerogatives of the States, even in an otherwise sovereign federal province. The Constitution uses state boundaries to fix the size of congressional delegations, U.S. Const[itution], Art. I, § 2, cl. 3, ensures that each State shall have at least one representative, *ibid.*, grants States certain powers over the times, places, and manner of federal elections (subject to congressional revision), Art. I, § 4, cl. 1, requires that when the President is elected by the House of Representatives, the delegations from each State have one vote, Art. II, § 1, cl. 3, and [Amendment] 12, and allows States to appoint electors for the President, Art. II, § 1, cl. 2. Nothing in the Constitution or The Federalist Papers, however, supports the idea of state interference with the most basic relation between the National Government and its citizens, the selection of legislative representatives. Indeed, even though the Constitution uses the qualifications for voters of the most numerous branch of the States' own legislatures to set the qualifications of federal electors, Art. I, § 2, cl. 1, when these electors vote, we have recognized that they act in a federal capacity and exercise a federal right....

Not the least of the incongruities in the position advanced by Arkansas is the proposition, necessary to its case, that it can burden the rights of resident voters in federal elections by reason of the manner in which they earlier had exercised it. If the majority of the voters had been successful in selecting a candidate, they would be penalized from exercising that same right in the future. Quite apart from any First Amendment

concerns, ... neither the law nor federal theory allows a State to burden the exercise of federal rights in this manner.... Indeed, as one of the "right[s] of the citizen[s] of this great country, protected by implied guarantees of its Constitution," the Court identified the right "'to come to the seat of government ... to share its offices, to engage in administering its functions.'" *Slaughter-House Cases* [16 Wallace 36 (1873)]. This observation serves to illustrate the extent of the State's attempted interference with the federal right to vote (and the derivative right to serve if elected by majority vote) in a congressional election, rights that do not derive from the state power in the first instance but that belong to the voter in his or her capacity as a citizen of the United States....

THOMAS, O'CONNOR, AND SCALIA, J.J., AND REHNQUIST, C.J., DISSENTING

It is ironic that the Court bases today's decision on the right of the people to "choose whom they please to govern them."...

To be sure, when the Tenth Amendment uses the phrase "the people," it does not specify whether it is referring to the people of each State or the people of the Nation as a whole. But the latter interpretation would make the Amendment pointless: there would have been no reason to provide that where the Constitution is silent about whether a particular power resides at the state level, it might or might not do so. In addition, it would make no sense to speak of powers as being reserved to the undifferentiated people of the Nation as a whole, because the Constitution does not contemplate that those people will either exercise power or delegate it. The Constitution simply does not recognize any mechanism for action by the undifferentiated people of the Nation. Thus, the amendment provision of Article V calls for amendments to be ratified not by a convention of the national people, but by conventions of the people in each State or by the state legislatures elected by those people. Likewise, the Constitution calls for Members of Congress to be chosen State by State, rather than in nationwide elections. Even the selection of the President—surely the most national of national figures—is accomplished by an electoral college made up of delegates chosen by the various States, and candidates can lose a Presidential election despite winning a majority of the votes cast in the Nation as a whole....

In short, the notion of popular sovereignty that undergirds the Constitution does not erase state boundaries, but rather tracks them. The people of each State obviously did trust their fate to the people of the several States when they consented to the Constitution; not only did they empower the governmental institutions of the United States, but they also agreed to be bound by constitutional amendments that they themselves refused to ratify.... At the same time, however, the people of each State retained their separate political identities. As Chief Justice Marshall put it, "[n]o political dreamer was ever wild enough to think of breaking down the lines which separate the States, and of compounding the American people into one common mass." *McCulloch v. Maryland*....

The import of this structure is the same as the import of the Tenth Amendment: if we are to invalidate Arkansas' Amendment 73, we must point to something in the Federal Constitution that deprives the people of Arkansas of the power to enact such measures....

The majority's essential logic is that the state governments could not "reserve" any powers that they did not control at the time the Constitution was drafted. But it was not the state governments that were doing the reserving. The Constitution derives its authority instead from the consent of the people of the States. Given the fundamental principle that all governmental powers stem from the people of the States, it would simply be incoherent to assert that the people of the States could not reserve any powers that they had not previously controlled....

The majority is ... quite wrong to conclude that the people of the States cannot authorize their state governments to exercise any powers that were unknown to the States when the Federal Constitution was drafted. Indeed, the majority's position frustrates the apparent purpose of the Amendment's final phrase. The Amendment does not preempt any limitations on state power found in the state constitutions, as it might have done if it simply had said that the powers not delegated to the Federal Government are reserved to the States. But the Amendment also does not prevent the people of the States from amending their state constitutions to remove limitations that were in effect when the Federal Constitution and the Bill of Rights were ratified....

[W]hile the majority is correct that the Framers expected the selection process to create a "direct link" between members of the House of Representatives and the people, the link was between the Representatives from each State and the people of that State; the people of Georgia have no say over whom the people of Massachusetts select to represent them in Congress. This arrangement must baffle the majority, whose understanding of Congress would surely fit more comfortably within a system of nationwide elections. But the fact remains that when it comes to the selection of Members of Congress, the people of each State have retained their independent political identity. As a result, there is absolutely nothing strange about the notion that the people of the States or their state legislatures possess "reserved" powers in this area....

The majority settles on "the Qualifications Clauses" as the constitutional provisions that Amendment 73 violates.... Because I do not read those provisions to impose any unstated prohibitions on the States, it is unnecessary for me to decide whether the majority is correct to identify Arkansas' ballot-access restriction with laws fixing true term limits or otherwise prescribing "qualifications" for congressional office.... [T]he Qualifications Clauses are merely straightforward recitations of the minimum eligibility requirements that the Framers thought it essential for every Member of Congress to meet. They restrict state power only in that they prevent the States from abolishing all eligibility requirements for membership in Congress....

It is radical enough for the majority to hold that the Constitution implicitly precludes the people of the States from prescribing any eligibility requirements for the congressional candidates who seek their votes. This holding, after all, does not stop with negating the term limits

that many States have seen fit to impose on their Senators and Representatives. Today's decision also means that no State may disqualify congressional candidates whom a court has found to be mentally incompetent, ... who are currently in prison, ... or who have past vote-fraud convictions.... Likewise, after today's decision, the people of each State must leave open the possibility that they will trust someone with their vote in Congress even though they do not trust him with a vote in the election for Congress....

In order to invalidate § 3 of Amendment 73, however, the majority must go farther. The bulk of the majority's analysis ... addresses the issues that would be raised if Arkansas had prescribed "genuine, unadulterated, undiluted term limits." But as the parties have agreed, Amendment 73 does not actually create this kind of disqualification.... It does not say that covered candidates may not serve any more terms in Congress if reelected, and it does not indirectly achieve the same result by barring those candidates from seeking reelection. It says only that if they are to win reelection, they must do so by write-in votes.

One might think that this is a distinction without a difference. As the majority notes, "[t]he uncontested data submitted to the Arkansas Supreme Court" show that write-in candidates have won only six congressional elections in this century. But while the data's accuracy is indeed "uncontested," petitioners filed an equally uncontested affidavit challenging the data's relevance....

The majority responds that whether "the Arkansas amendment has the likely effect of creating a qualification" is "simply irrelevant to our holding today." But the majority—which, after all, bases its holding on the asserted exclusivity of the Qualifications Clauses—never adequately explains how it can take this position and still reach its conclusion....

The voters of Arkansas evidently believe that incumbents would not enjoy such overwhelming success if electoral contests were truly fair—that is, if the government did not put its thumb on either side of the scale. The majority offers no reason to question the accuracy of this belief. Given this context, petitioners portray § 3 of Amendment 73 as an effort at the state level to offset the electoral advantages that congressional incumbents have conferred upon themselves at the federal level....

I do not mean to suggest that States have unbridled power to handicap particular classes of candidates, even when those candidates enjoy federally conferred advantages that may threaten to skew the electoral process. But laws that allegedly have the purpose and effect of handicapping a particular class of candidates traditionally are reviewed under the First and Fourteenth Amendments rather than the Qualifications Clauses....

To analyze such laws under the Qualifications Clauses may open up whole new vistas for courts. If it is true that "the current congressional campaign finance system ... has created an electoral system so stacked against challengers that in many elections voters have no real choices," are the Federal Election Campaign Act Amendments of 1974 unconstitutional under (of all things) the Qualifications Clauses?... If it can be shown that nonminorities are at a significant disadvantage when they seek election in districts dominated by minority voters, would the intentional creation of "majority-minority districts" violate the Qualifications Clauses even if it were to survive scrutiny under the Fourteenth Amendment?... More generally, if "[d]istrict lines are rarely neutral phenomena" and if "districting inevitably has and is intended to have substantial political consequences," ... will plausible Qualifications Clause challenges greet virtually every redistricting decision?...

The majority's opinion may not go so far, although it does not itself suggest any principled stopping point.... Rather, I would read the Qualifications Clauses to do no more than what they say. I respectfully dissent.

COMMENT

In analyzing and discussing *Term Limits*, review *Powell v. McCormack*, Chapter 3, pp. 394–405.

QUESTIONS

1. What would have been the result in *Term Limits* if the Court had analyzed the issues under the Tenth Amendment interpretation urged by U.S. Term Limits, Inc. and Arkansas?
2. Justice Thomas in dissent in *Term Limits* wrote: "The Federal

Government and the States … face different default rules: where the Constitution is silent about the exercise of a particular power—that is, where the Constitution does not speak either expressly or by necessary implication—the Federal Government lacks that power and the States enjoy it." Is Justice Thomas hinting that the Court should return to the days of dual federalism where the justices police the boundaries between national and state powers?

3. Some have called the quest for term limits the greatest grassroots movement of the twentieth century. Will the Court's decision in *Term Limits* put an end to that movement, or might it supply fuel? If the term limits movement persists, will it in turn fuel a resurrected states' rights movement and help revitalize debate over the Tenth Amendment?

4. *Term Limits* nullified congressional term limitation provisions that had been adopted in twenty-three states. Consequently, seventy-two House members from seven states, who would have been banned from running for reelection after 1996, may now do so. Only a federal constitutional term limit amendment could stand in the way of incumbents running for office as long as they please. Does this situation appear to present term limit proponents with a Catch-22 situation similar to that confronting supporters of reapportionment before *Baker v. Carr* (Chapter 2, pp. 172–182)?

STATES' RIGHTS

Seminole Tribe of Florida v. Florida
517 U.S. 1125 (1996)

SETTING

As explained in Chapter 2, in *Chisholm v. Georgia* (see pp. 83–93) the Supreme Court accepted jurisdiction over a suit against Georgia by a citizen of South Carolina. The Court's action so threatened the concept of state sovereignty that only two days after its decision was made public a bill was introduced into the Senate proposing to amend the Constitution to prevent individuals from suing states in federal courts. Both houses of Congress overwhelmingly voted to adopt the Eleventh Amendment. It was swiftly ratified (1795) and provides that

> The Judicial power of the United States shall not be construed to extend to any suit in law or equity, commenced or prosecuted against one of the United States by Citizens of another State, or by Citizens or Subjects of any Foreign State.

The text of the Eleventh Amendment complicated the debate about the meaning of federalism and whether ultimate governing sovereignty resides with the states or with the national government. By the 1880s, the Court had established that in determining whether a suit was prosecuted against a state, it would "look behind and through the nominal parties on the record to ascertain who are the real parties to the suit." *In re Ayers*, 123 U.S. 443 (1887).

Throughout the years, the Court has taken inconsistent views about whether the Eleventh Amendment immunizes states from suit in federal court. The high-water mark in the Court's states' rights interpretation of the Eleventh Amendment came in *Hans v. Louisiana*, 134 U.S. 1 (1890), when it ruled that, although not directly required by its text, the Amendment also bars federal court suits brought by citizens of the same state being sued. In 1904, by contrast, the Court ruled that when they ratified the Constitution, states consented to federal court suits initiated by other states. *South Dakota v. North Carolina*, 192 U.S. 286 (1904). Four years later, in *Ex parte Young*, 209 U.S. 123 (1908), the Court ruled that the Eleventh Amendment does not extend to federal court actions seeking to enjoin state officials from enforcing state laws that conflict with the Constitution.

Like the Tenth Amendment, the potential for conflict between the Eleventh Amendment and other constitutional provisions is great. Article I, section 8, clause 3, for example, grants the federal government authority over Indian as well as interstate commerce. Known in one context as the Indian Commerce Clause, Article I, section 8, clause 3, was the product of colonial history and ambiguous language in the Articles of Confederation that had failed to resolve the relationship between the emerging national government, the states, and the Indian tribes. Pursuant to the Indian commerce clause, and in response to a Supreme Court decision in 1987, *California v. Cabazon Band of Mission Indians*, 480 U.S. 202—declaring that California had no authority to regulate poker and other gaming activities on Indian reservations in its state—Congress in 1988 enacted the Indian Gaming Regulatory Act. The act, and the litigation that led to it, reflected controversy over the role of gaming—called by some the "new buffalo"—that had become a major economic activity on many Indian reservations beginning in the 1970s.

By the mid-1990s, gaming on Indian land had become a multibillion-dollar-a-year business. The Indian Gaming Act divides gaming on Indian lands into three categories and provides regulatory schemes for each category. Class III gaming includes such things as slot machines, casino games, banking card games, dog racing, and lotteries. It is the most heavily regulated category and is allowed only if it is adopted by ordinance or resolution of the governing body of the tribe, is located in a state that permits gaming for any purpose by any person, organization, or entity, and is conducted "in conformance with a Tribal-State compact entered into by the Indian tribe and the State." The act imposes on states the duty to negotiate in good faith toward the formation of a compact and gives tribes the power to sue in federal district court to compel a state to perform that duty.

A tribe that brings an action to ensure the formation of a compact must show that no compact has been agreed to and that the state has failed to respond in good faith to the tribe's request to negotiate. Such a showing shifts the burden to the state to prove that it did in fact negotiate in good faith with the tribe. If the trial court finds that the state did not negotiate in good faith, it is required to "order the State and Indian tribe to conclude such a compact within a 60-day period." If no agreement is reached, both sides submit a proposed compact that represents their last best offer to a mediator appointed by the court. The mediator chooses the proposal that "best comports" with the terms of the act and any other applicable federal law. The state then has sixty days to consent and, if it fails to do so, the secretary of the interior prescribes the procedures under which class III gaming may be conducted on the tribe's lands.

In September 1991, the Seminole Tribe, a federally recognized Indian tribe that occupies five separate reservations in Florida, filed suit in the U.S. District Court for the Southern District of Florida alleging that the state and its governor, Lawton Chiles, had violated the act's requirement of good faith negotiation, which the tribe had requested in January of that year. Florida moved to dismiss the suit on the ground that it violated the state's sovereign immunity from suit in federal court. The district court denied the motion. It based its decision on *Pennsylvania v. Union Gas Co.*, 491 U.S. 1 (1989), in which the Court held that the Eleventh Amendment does not protect a state against suits in federal court that have been authorized by Congress under its power to regulate interstate commerce. According to the court, the Indian Commerce Clause similarly gives Congress the power to abrogate states' immunity from suit in federal court so long as Congress, as it did in enacting the Indian Gaming Act, clearly relied on that clause as the source of its power to authorize federal lawsuits against the states. Florida took an interlocutory appeal to the Court of Appeals for the Eleventh Circuit, which reversed. That court held that the Eleventh Amendment barred the tribe's action. According to the Eleventh Circuit, Congress's power to regulate interstate commerce is more extensive than its authority to regulate Indian commerce, and the Indian Gaming Act exceeds Congress's power under the Indian Commerce Clause. Consequently, it held that it had no jurisdiction over the tribe's suit against Florida. It remanded the case to the district court with directions to dismiss the tribe's suit. The Supreme Court granted the Seminole Tribe's petition for a writ of certiorari.

HIGHLIGHTS OF SUPREME COURT ARGUMENTS

BRIEF FOR THE SEMINOLE TRIBE

◆ While states retain some authority to regulate interstate commerce under Article I, section 8, clause 3, they retain no such authority under that clause to regulate affairs with Indians. Congress has sole authority over relations with the Indian tribes, which includes the power to limit state sovereignty and abrogate Eleventh Amendment immunity if necessary.

◆ This Court's decision in *Pennsylvania v. Union Gas*, 491 U.S. 1 (1989), was correctly decided. It should be followed here.

◆ *Ex parte Young*, 209 U.S. 123 (1908), is applicable to the facts in this case, even though the Indian Gaming Act does not mention a designation such as governor. It was error for the Eleventh Circuit to fail to apply it. Under *Young*, a federal court may require a governor to negotiate in good faith pursuant to the Indian Gaming Act.

◆ The Eleventh Amendment does not extend immunity beyond its text. The 1890 case of *Hans v. Louisiana*, 134 U.S. 1 (1890), extended immunity beyond the text of the amendment and should be interpreted narrowly.

◆ This Court should reject any invitation to apply the Tenth Amendment in this case. It was not raised before the district court and the Eleventh Circuit refused to address the argument because it was not preserved.

AMICUS CURIAE BRIEFS SUPPORTING THE SEMINOLE TRIBE

The United States; joint brief of the Spokane Tribe of Indians, Shakopee Mdewakanton Dakota Community, Coquille Indian Tribe, Shoalwater Bay Indian Tribe, Winnebago Tribe of Nebraska, Yakima Indian Nation, Confederated Salish and Kootenai Tribes of the Flathead Reservation and Confederated Tribes of the Colville Reservation; the Miccosukee Tribe of Florida; joint brief of the National Indian Gaming Association, Minnesota Indian Gaming Association and California-Nevada Indian Gaming Association; joint brief of the Tohono O'Odham Nation, White Mountain Apache Tribe, and Pascua Yaqui Tribe; joint brief of the Poarch Band of Creek Indians and Ponca Tribe of Oklahoma; joint brief of the San Manuel Band of Mission Indians, Rumsey Indian Rancheria of Wintun Indians, Jackson Rancheria Band of Miwuk Indians, Table Mountain Rancheria of California, Table Bluff Reservation of Wiyot Indians of California, Guidiville Band of Pomo Indians of the Guidiville Rancheria, and Viejas Band of Kumeyaay Indians; joint brief of the Stockbridge-Munsee Indian Community, the Oneida Indian Nation of Wisconsin, the Tonawanda Band of Senacas, and the Tunica-Biloxi Tribe.

BRIEF FOR FLORIDA

◆ The Eleventh Amendment does not permit a suit by an Indian tribe against a state or its governor based on the alleged failure of the state to negotiate a gaming compact in good faith. The Eleventh Amendment embodies the concept of sovereign immunity in its entirety and Florida has not consented to this suit.

◆ The result in *Pennsylvania v. Union Gas*, 491 U.S. 1 (1989), is narrow and should not be extended, because the Indian Commerce Clause gives Congress complete authority over Indian tribes, not over states. *Union Gas* should be overruled if it cannot be limited to its facts and to the context of regulations of interstate commerce.

◆ *Ex parte Young*, 209 U.S. 123 (1908), is inapplicable in this case, because all obligations under the Indian Gaming Act are imposed on the state, not on the state's governor.

◆ If the Indian Gaming Act does not grant a state the discretion to negotiate with respect to a compact with a tribe, it is a violation of the Tenth Amendment's prohibition against legislation that requires states to administer federal programs.

◆ A tribal exception to *Hans v. Louisiana*, 134 U.S. 1 (1890), should not be allowed. Such an exception would abrogate the states' sovereign immunity in favor of Indian tribes.

AMICUS CURIAE BRIEFS SUPPORTING FLORIDA

Joint brief of the National Governors' Association, Council of State Governments, National Conference of State Legislatures, National Association of Counties, International City/County Management Association, National League of Cities and U.S. Conference of Mayors; joint brief of California, Washington, Alabama, Arizona, Arkansas, Colorado, Connecticut, Hawaii, Idaho, Kansas, Louisiana, Maine, Massachusetts, Michigan, Mississippi, Missouri, Montana, Nebraska, Nevada, New Hampshire, New York, North Carolina, Ohio, Oklahoma, Pennsylvania, Rhode Island, South Dakota, Texas, Vermont, Virginia, and West Virginia.

SUPREME COURT DECISION: 5–4

REHNQUIST, C.J.

I

[W]e granted certiorari in order to consider two questions: (1) Does the Eleventh Amendment prevent Congress from authorizing suits by Indian tribes against States for prospective injunctive relief to enforce legislation enacted pursuant to the Indian Commerce Clause? and (2) Does the doctrine of *Ex parte Young*, 209 U.S. 123 (1908) permit suits against a State's governor for prospective injunctive relief to enforce the good faith bargaining requirement of the Act? We answer the first question in the affirmative, the second in the negative, and

we therefore affirm the Eleventh Circuit's dismissal of petitioner's suit....

II

In order to determine whether Congress has abrogated the States' sovereign immunity, we ask two questions: first, whether Congress has "unequivocally expresse[d] its intent to abrogate the immunity," *Green v. Mansour*, 474 U.S. 64, 68 (1985); and second, whether Congress has acted "pursuant to a valid exercise of power." Ibid.

Congress' intent to abrogate the States' immunity from suit must be obvious from "a clear legislative statement." *Blatchford v. Native Village of Noatak*,

501 U.S. 775, 786 (1991). This rule arises from a recognition of the important role played by the Eleventh Amendment and the broader principles that it reflects....

Here, we agree with the parties, with the Eleventh Circuit in the decision below and with virtually every other court that has confronted the question that Congress has ... provided an "unmistakably clear" statement of its intent to abrogate.... Congress intended through the Act to abrogate the States' sovereign immunity from suit....

[W]e turn now to consider whether the Act was passed "pursuant to a valid exercise of power." *Green v. Mansour*, 474 U.S. 64 (1985).... [O]ur inquiry into whether Congress has the power to abrogate unilaterally the States' immunity from suit is narrowly focused on one question: Was the Act in question passed pursuant to a constitutional provision granting Congress the power to abrogate? Previously, in conducting that inquiry, we have found authority to abrogate under only two provisions of the Constitution. In *Fitzpatrick v. Bitzer*, 427 U.S. 445 (1976), we recognized that the Fourteenth Amendment, by expanding federal power at the expense of state autonomy, had fundamentally altered the balance of state and federal power struck by the Constitution. We noted that Section(s) 1 of the Fourteenth Amendment contained prohibitions expressly directed at the States and that Section(s) 5 of the Amendment expressly provided that "The Congress shall have the power to enforce, by appropriate legislation, the provisions of this article." We held that through the Fourteenth Amendment, federal power extended to intrude upon the province of the Eleventh Amendment and therefore that Section(s) 5 of the Fourteenth Amendment allowed Congress to abrogate the immunity from suit guaranteed by that Amendment.

In only one other case has congressional abrogation of the states' Eleventh Amendment immunity been upheld. In *Pennsylvania v. Union Gas Co.*, 491 U.S. 1 (1989), a plurality of the Court found that the Interstate Commerce Clause, Art. I, Section(s) 8, cl. 3, granted Congress the power to abrogate state sovereign immunity, stating that the power to regulate interstate commerce would be "incomplete without the authority to render States liable in damages."

[In this case, we must] consider whether [the Indian Commerce Clause] grants Congress the power to abrogate the States' sovereign immunity.... Following the rationale of the *Union Gas* plurality, our inquiry is limited to determining whether the Indian Commerce Clause, like the Interstate Commerce Clause, is a grant of authority to the Federal Government at the expense of the States. The answer to that question is obvious. If anything, the Indian Commerce Clause accomplishes a greater transfer of power from the States to the Federal Government than does the Interstate Commerce Clause. This is clear enough from the fact that the States still exercise some authority over interstate trade but have been divested of virtually all authority over Indian commerce and Indian tribes. Under the rationale of *Union Gas*, if the States' partial cession of authority over a particular area includes cession of the immunity from suit, then their virtually total cession of authority over a different area must also include cession of the immunity from suit.... [T]he plurality opinion in *Union Gas* allows no principled distinction in favor of the States to be drawn between the Indian Commerce Clause and the Interstate Commerce Clause....

[However], the Court in *Union Gas* reached a result without an expressed rationale agreed upon by a majority of the Court.... Since it was issued, *Union Gas* has created confusion among the lower courts that have sought to understand and apply the deeply fractured decision....

The plurality's rationale also deviated sharply from our established federalism jurisprudence and essentially eviscerated our decision in *Hans* [*v. Louisiana*], 134 U.S. 1 (1890). It was well established in 1989 when *Union Gas* was decided that the Eleventh Amendment stood for the constitutional principle that state sovereign immunity limited the federal courts' jurisdiction under Article III.... And our decisions since *Hans* had been equally clear that the Eleventh Amendment reflects "the fundamental principle of sovereign immunity [that] limits the grant to judicial authority in Article III." *Pennhurst State School and Hospital v. Halderman*, 465 U.S. 89 (1984)....

Never before the decision in *Union Gas* had we suggested that the bounds of Article III could be expanded by Congress operating pursuant to any constitutional provision other than the Fourteenth Amendment. Indeed, it had seemed fundamental that Congress could not expand the jurisdiction of the federal courts beyond the bounds of Article III. *Marbury v. Madison*....

In the five years since it was decided, *Union Gas* has proven to be a solitary departure from established law. Reconsidering the decision in *Union Gas*, we conclude that none of the policies underlying *stare decisis* require our con-

tinuing adherence to its holding.... The case involved the interpretation of the Constitution and therefore may be altered only by constitutional amendment or revision by this Court. Finally, both the result in *Union Gas* and the plurality's rationale depart from our established understanding of the Eleventh Amendment and undermine the accepted function of Article III. We feel bound to conclude that *Union Gas* was wrongly decided and that it should be, and now is, overruled....

For over a century, we have grounded our decisions in the oft-repeated understanding of state sovereign immunity as an essential part of the Eleventh Amendment.... It is true that we have not had occasion previously to apply established Eleventh Amendment principles to the question whether Congress has the power to abrogate state sovereign immunity (save in *Union Gas*). But consideration of that question must proceed with fidelity to this century-old doctrine.

The dissent, to the contrary, disregards our case law in favor of a theory cobbled together from law review articles and its own version of historical events.... In putting forward a new theory of state sovereign immunity, the dissent develops its own vision of the political system created by the Framers, concluding with the statement that "[t]he Framer's principal objectives in rejecting English theories of unitary sovereignty ... would have been impeded if a new concept of sovereign immunity had taken its place in federal question cases, and would have been substantially thwarted if that new immunity had been held untouchable by any congressional effort to abrogate it." This sweeping statement ignores the fact that the Nation survived for nearly two centuries without the question of the existence of such power ever being presented to this Court. And Congress itself waited nearly a century before even conferring federal question jurisdiction on the lower federal courts.

In overruling *Union Gas* today, we reconfirm that the background principle of state sovereign immunity embodied in the Eleventh Amendment is not so ephemeral as to dissipate when the subject of the suit is an area, like the regulation of Indian commerce, that is under the exclusive control of the Federal Government. Even when the Constitution vests in Congress complete law-making authority over a particular area, the Eleventh Amendment prevents congressional authorization of suits by private parties against unconsenting States. The Eleventh Amendment restricts the judicial power under Article III, and Article I cannot be used to circumvent the constitutional limitations placed upon federal jurisdiction. Petitioner's suit against the State of Florida must be dismissed for a lack of jurisdiction.

III

Petitioner argues that we may exercise jurisdiction over its suit to enforce Section(s) 2710(d)(3) against the Governor notwithstanding the jurisdictional bar of the Eleventh Amendment. Petitioner notes that since our decision in *Ex parte Young*, 209 U.S. 123 (1908), we often have found federal jurisdiction over a suit against a state official when that suit seeks only prospective injunctive relief in order to "end a continuing violation of federal law." *Green v. Mansour*, 474 U.S. at 68. The situation presented here, however, is sufficiently different from that giving rise to the traditional *Ex parte Young* action so as to preclude the availability of that doctrine.

Here, the "continuing violation of federal law" alleged by petitioner is the Governor's failure to bring the State into compliance with [the act's requirement that the state negotiate in good faith]. But the duty to negotiate imposed upon the State by that statutory provision does not stand alone....

Where Congress has created a remedial scheme for the enforcement of a particular federal right, we have, in suits against federal officers, refused to supplement that scheme with one created by the judiciary. Here, of course, the question is not whether a remedy should be created, but instead is whether the Eleventh Amendment bar should be lifted, as it was in *Ex parte Young*, in order to allow a suit against a state officer. Nevertheless, we think that the same general principle applies: therefore, where Congress has prescribed a detailed remedial scheme for the enforcement against a State of a statutorily created right, a court should hesitate before casting aside those limitations and permitting an action against a state officer based upon *Ex parte Young*....

We hold that *Ex parte Young* is inapplicable to petitioner's suit against the Governor of Florida, and therefore that suit is barred by the Eleventh Amendment and must be dismissed for a lack of jurisdiction.

IV

The Eleventh Amendment prohibits Congress from making the State of Florida capable of being sued in federal court. The narrow exception to the Eleventh Amendment provided by the *Ex parte Young* doctrine cannot be used [in this situation], because Congress enacted a remedial scheme ... specifically designed for the enforcement of [the right of good-faith bargaining]. The Eleventh Circuit's dismissal of petitioner's suit is hereby affirmed.

It is so ordered.

STEVENS, J., DISSENTING

… The importance of the majority's decision to overrule the Court's holding in *Pennsylvania v. Union Gas Co.* cannot be overstated. The majority's opinion does not simply preclude Congress from establishing the rather curious statutory scheme under which Indian tribes may seek the aid of a federal court to secure a State's good faith negotiations over gaming regulations. Rather, it prevents Congress from providing a federal forum for a broad range of actions against States, from those sounding in copyright and patent law, to those concerning bankruptcy, environmental law, and the regulation of our vast national economy.

There may be room for debate over whether, in light of the Eleventh Amendment, Congress has the power to ensure that such a cause of action may be enforced in federal court by a citizen of another State or a foreign citizen. There can be no serious debate, however, over whether Congress has the power to ensure that such a cause of action may be brought by a citizen of the State being sued. Congress' authority in that regard is clear….

The majority appears to acknowledge that one cannot deduce from either the text of Article III or the plain terms of the Eleventh Amendment that the judicial power does not extend to a congressionally created cause of action against a State brought by one of that State's citizens. Nevertheless, the majority asserts that precedent compels that same conclusion. I disagree….

The fundamental error that continues to lead the Court astray is its failure to acknowledge that its modern embodiment of the ancient doctrine of sovereign immunity "has absolutely nothing to do with the limit on judicial power contained in the Eleventh Amendment." It rests rather on concerns of federalism and comity that merit respect but are nevertheless, in cases such as the one before us, subordinate to the plenary power of Congress….

In this country the sovereignty of the individual States is subordinate both to the citizenry of each State and to the supreme law of the federal sovereign. For that reason, Justice Holmes' explanation for a rule that allows a State to avoid suit in its own courts does not even speak to the question whether Congress should be able to authorize a federal court to provide a private remedy for a State's violation of federal law. In my view, neither the majority's opinion today, nor any earlier opinion by any Member of the Court, has identified any acceptable reason for concluding that the absence of a State's consent to be sued in federal court should affect the power of Congress to authorize federal courts to remedy violations of federal law by States or their officials in actions not covered by the Eleventh Amendment's explicit text….

Fortunately, and somewhat fortuitously, a jurisdictional problem that is unmentioned by the Court may deprive its opinion of precedential significance. The Indian Gaming Regulatory Act establishes a unique set of procedures for resolving the dispute between the Tribe and the State. If each adversary adamantly adheres to its understanding of the law, if the District Court determines that the State's inflexibility constitutes a failure to negotiate in good faith, and if the State thereafter continues to insist that it is acting within its rights, the maximum sanction that the Court can impose is an order that refers the controversy to a member of the Executive Branch of the Government for resolution. As the Court of Appeals interpreted the Act, this final disposition is available even though the action against the State and its Governor may not be maintained. (The Court does not tell us whether it agrees or disagrees with that disposition.) In my judgment, it is extremely doubtful that the obviously dispensable involvement of the judiciary in the intermediate stages of a procedure that begins and ends in the Executive Branch is a proper exercise of judicial power. It may well follow that the misguided opinion of today's majority has nothing more than an advisory character. Whether or not that be so, the better reasoning in Justice Souter's far wiser and far more scholarly opinion will surely be the law one day.

For these reasons, as well as those set forth in Justice Souter's opinion, I respectfully dissent.

SOUTER, GINSBURG, AND BREYER J.J., DISSENTING

... The fault I find with the majority today is not in its decision to reexamine *Union Gas*, for the Court in that case produced no majority for a single rationale supporting congressional authority. Instead, I part company from the Court because I am convinced that its decision is fundamentally mistaken, and for that reason I respectfully dissent.

It is useful to separate three questions: (1) whether the States enjoyed sovereign immunity if sued in their own courts in the period prior to ratification of the National Constitution; (2) if so, whether after ratification the States were entitled to claim some such immunity when sued in a federal court exercising jurisdiction either because the suit was between a State and a non-state litigant who was not its citizen, or because the issue in the case raised a federal question; and (3) whether any state sovereign immunity recognized in federal court may be abrogated by Congress.

The answer to the first question is not clear, although some of the Framers assumed that States did enjoy immunity in their own courts. The second question was not debated at the time of ratification, except as to citizen-state diversity jurisdiction; there was no unanimity, but in due course the Court in *Chisholm v. Georgia* answered that a state defendant enjoyed no such immunity. As to federal question jurisdiction, state sovereign immunity seems not to have been debated prior to ratification, the silence probably showing a general understanding at the time that the States would have no immunity in such cases.

The adoption of the Eleventh Amendment soon changed the result in *Chisholm*, not by mentioning sovereign immunity, but by eliminating citizen-state diversity jurisdiction over cases with state defendants....

The Court's answer today to the third question is ... at odds with the Founders' view that common law, when it was received into the new American legal systems, was always subject to legislative amendment. In ignoring the reasons for this pervasive understanding at the time of the ratification, and in holding that a nontextual common-law rule limits a clear grant of congressional power under Article I, the Court follows a course that has brought it to grief before in our history, and promises to do so again....

Whatever the scope of sovereign immunity might have been in the Colonies ... or during the period of Confederation, the proposal to establish a National Government under the Constitution drafted in 1787 presented a prospect unknown to the common law prior to the American experience: the States would become parts of a system in which sovereignty over even domestic matters would be divided or parceled out between the States and the Nation, the latter to be invested with its own judicial power and the right to prevail against the States whenever their respective substantive laws might be in conflict. With this prospect in mind, the 1787 Constitution might have addressed state sovereign immunity by eliminating whatever sovereign immunity the States previously had, as to any matter subject to federal law or jurisdiction; by recognizing an analogue to the old immunity in the new context of federal jurisdiction, but subject to abrogation as to any matter within that jurisdiction; or by enshrining a doctrine of inviolable state sovereign immunity in the text, thereby giving it constitutional protection in the new federal jurisdiction.

The 1787 draft in fact said nothing on the subject, and it was this very silence that occasioned some, though apparently not widespread, dispute among the Framers and others over whether ratification of the Constitution would preclude a State sued in federal court from asserting sovereign immunity as it could have done on any matter of nonfederal law litigated in its own courts. As it has come down to us, the discussion gave no attention to congressional power under the proposed Article I but focused entirely on the limits of the judicial power provided in Article III. And although the jurisdictional bases together constituting the judicial power of the national courts under section 2 of Article III included questions arising under federal law and cases between States and individuals who are not citizens, it was only upon the latter citizen-state diversity provisions that preratification questions about state immunity from suit or liability centered....

The argument among the Framers and their friends about sovereign immunity in federal citizen-state diversity cases, in any event, was short lived and ended when this Court, in *Chisholm v. Georgia* chose between the constitutional alternatives of abrogation and recognition of the immunity enjoyed at common law....

The Eleventh Amendment, of course, repudiated *Chisholm* and clearly divested federal courts of some jurisdiction as to cases against state parties:

> The Judicial power of the United States shall not be construed to extend to any suit in law or equity, commenced or prosecuted against one of the United States by Citizens of another State, or by Citizens or Subjects of any Foreign State.

There are two plausible readings of this provision's text. Under the first, it simply repeals the Citizen-State Diversity Clauses of Article III for all cases in which the State appears as a defendant. Under the second, it strips the federal courts of jurisdiction in any case in which a state defendant is sued by a citizen not its own, even if jurisdiction might otherwise rest on the existence of a federal question in the suit. Neither reading of the Amendment, of course, furnishes authority for the Court's view in today's case....

The history and structure of the Eleventh Amendment convincingly show that it reaches only to suits subject to federal jurisdiction exclusively under the Citizen-State Diversity Clauses....

It should accordingly come as no surprise that the weightiest commentary following the amendment's adoption described it simply as constricting the scope of the Citizen-State Diversity Clauses....

Reading the Eleventh Amendment solely as a limit on citizen-state diversity jurisdiction has the virtue of coherence with this Court's practice, with the views of John Marshall, with the history of the Amendment's drafting, and with its allusive language....

Given the Framers' general concern with curbing abuses by state governments, it would be amazing if the scheme of delegated powers embodied in the Constitution had left the National Government powerless to render the States judicially accountable for violations of federal rights. And of course the Framers did not understand the scheme to leave the government powerless.... The Framers' principal objectives in rejecting English theories of unitary sovereignty, moreover, would have been impeded if a new concept of sovereign immunity had taken its place in federal question cases, and would have been substantially thwarted if that new immunity had been held to be untouchable by any congressional effort to abrogate it.

Today's majority discounts this concern. Without citing a single source to the contrary, the Court dismisses the historical evidence regarding the Framers' vision of the relationship between national and state sovereignty, and reassures us that "the Nation survived for nearly two centuries without the ques-

tion of the existence of [the abrogation] power ever being presented to this Court." But we are concerned here not with the survival of the Nation but the opportunity of its citizens to enforce federal rights in a way that Congress provides.

There is, finally, a response to the Court's rejection of *Ex parte Young* that ought to go without saying. Our longstanding practice is to read ambiguous statutes to avoid constitutional infirmity. This practice alone (without any need for a clear statement to displace *Young*) would be enough to require *Young*'s application. So, too, would the application of another rule, requiring courts to choose any reasonable construction of a statute that would eliminate the need to confront a contested constitutional issue (in this case, the place of state sovereign immunity in federal question cases and the status of *Union Gas*). Construing the statute to harmonize with *Young*, as it readily does, would have saved an act of Congress and rendered a discussion on constitutional grounds wholly unnecessary. This case should be decided on this basis alone....

There is an even more fundamental "clear statement" principle ... that the Court abandons today. John Marshall recognized it over a century and a half ago in the very context of state sovereign immunity in federal question cases:

The jurisdiction of the Court, then, being extended by the letter of the constitution to all cases arising under it, or under the laws of the United States, it follows that those who would withdraw any case of this description from that jurisdiction, must sustain the exemption they claim on the spirit and true meaning of the constitution, which spirit and true meaning must be so apparent as to overrule the words which its framers have employed. *Cohens v. Virginia.*

Because neither text, precedent, nor history supports the majority's abdication of our responsibility to exercise the jurisdiction entrusted to us in Article III, I would reverse the judgment of the Court of Appeals.

QUESTIONS

1. To what extent does *Seminole Tribe* pose the same kinds of federalism dilemmas examined in the cases decided under the Tenth Amendment? What insights into the nature of American federalism does the Court's ongoing disagreement provide regarding the relationship between the national government and the states?

2. Before passage of the Indian Gaming Act, states had virtually no role in regulating Indian gaming. Only forceful lobbying in Congress won them the right to participate, through the requirement of good faith negotiations with tribes, in regulating Indian gaming. Giving states a role in regulating Indian gaming, however, created the possibility that states could effectively veto class III gaming on Indian reservations by bargaining to impasse. The solution Congress chose to prevent that from happening was federal court supervision if negotiations stalled. In the light of that political resolution, consider the argument of California and the thirty states that joined in its *amicus* brief:

   This case is more about federalism than about Indian tribes... The sovereign interests of all the States of the Union—those with Indian lands within their borders *as well as* those without—are seriously jeopardized by the method chosen by the Congress to implement this legislation. The statute here directly commands the States to do certain acts, as if the States were mere subdivisions of a national government. No choice, incentive or acceptable alternative is given a State under this legislation. States must comply or face federal court orders." (Emphasis in original.)

   Did Chief Justice Rehnquist adopt this view in his majority opinion in *Seminole Tribe*? Should he have taken into account the political realities of nation-state-tribal relations reflected in the Indian Gaming Act in analyzing the constitutionality of the statute?

3. Justice Souter's dissent in *Seminole Tribe* is a sixty-seven-page exegesis on the common law, the intention of the founders, and judicial precedent on the subject of federal judicial power. What reasons can you give for why Chief Justice Rehnquist's opinion in *Seminole Tribe* would elicit such a thoroughgoing analysis and criticism? In Justice Souter's opinion, what constitutional values were at stake in *Seminole Tribe*?

4. What do Chief Justice Rehnquist's majority opinion in *Seminole Tribe* and the dissents by Justices Stevens and Souter reveal about the contemporary Court's view of the proper role of federal judicial

power in the American system of government? Provide examples of how those competing views could affect the resolution of other controversial issues of public policy.

5. In the wake of the Court's decision in *Seminole Tribe*, what recourse is available to Congress to insure that states negotiate in good faith with tribes to enter into a compact with those that wish to conduct gaming activities on Indian reservations? Is Justice Stevens' dissenting observation correct that the impact of the Court's decision may be only marginal because of the involvement of the executive branch if a state refuses to bargain in good faith?

6. Chief Justice Rehnquist could have resolved *Seminole Tribe* solely on the basis of *Ex parte Young*, 209 U.S. 123 (1908), thereby avoiding the necessity of overruling *Pennsylvania v. Union Gas*, 491 U.S. 1 (1989). Why might he have chosen the more judicially active approach of reaching an issue it was not necessary to reach in order to decide the case? Does the overruling of *Union Gas* make *Seminole Tribe* a more substantial victory for states' rights? Was such an approach predictable in the light of the federalism controversy in *National League of Cities v. Usery* and *Garcia v. San Antonio Metropolitan Transit Authority*?

COMMENT

In *Idaho v. Coeur d'Alene Tribe of Idaho*, _____ U.S. _____ (1997), the Supreme Court held, 5–4, that federal courts are barred by the Eleventh Amendment from hearing cases against state officers for injunctive and declaratory relief, if granting such relief would require adjudication of the state's title to disputed waters and submerged lands, or would deprive the state of all the practical benefits of such ownership. The U.S. District Court for the district of Idaho did not err in dismissing the Indian tribe's complaint for failure to state a claim.

STATES' RIGHTS

Printz v. United States
_____ U.S. _____ (1997)

SETTING

Handguns are pervasive throughout contemporary American society. In the 1950s handguns accounted for one-fifth of all gun sales. By 1992, roughly half of all new guns purchased in the United States were handguns. Of the estimated two hundred twenty million guns owned by Americans in the early 1990s, sixty to seventy million—about one-third—were handguns. Handgun violence is also pervasive. Although handguns account for one-third of all guns owned, they were used in 75 percent of all homicides and 80 percent of robberies involving firearms committed in the early 1990s.

Three decades ago, public shock and outrage at the 1968 assassinations by gunshot of Martin Luther King Jr. and Robert F. Kennedy prompted Congress to enact a Gun Control Act. This statute established a comprehensive federal scheme governing the manufacture, importation, and distribution of firearms in interstate commerce. Among other things, the act made it unlawful for certain persons—such as convicted felons—to receive or possess firearms in or affecting interstate commerce.

On March 30, 1981, would-be assassin John Hinckley shot President Ronald Reagan and three others with a handgun. The president's press secretary, James Brady, suffered permanent brain damage from the shot that hit him. In 1985, responding to attempts by the National Rifle Association (NRA) to weaken the 1968 Gun Control Act, James Brady's wife, Sarah, joined the board of Handgun Control, Inc. (HCI), a group committed to limiting access to handguns. The Bradys and HCI tirelessly pressed Congress for legislation regulating the acquisition and ownership of handguns. Their efforts were consistently frustrated by effective NRA lobbying. Meanwhile, gun violence escalated. Between 1988 and 1992, for example, handgun murders in the United States increased by 41 percent.

By 1993, members of Congress acknowledged the national "epidemic of gun violence." Congress adopted what was popularly known as the Brady Handgun Violence Prevention Act, which amended the 1968 Gun Control Act by requiring the attorney general to establish a national instant criminal background check system by November 30, 1998. As an interim measure—effective February 28, 1994—the Brady Act made it unlawful for a federally licensed firearms dealer to sell a handgun without first providing the chief law enforcement officer of a recipient's residence (defined as the chief of police, sheriff, or equivalent officer or designee of such official) with the recipient's name, address, and date of birth. The act prohibited the firearms dealer from making the transfer for five business days after providing the notice to the law enforcement officer unless, within that period, the officer informs the dealer that the officer has no information that the recipient is not entitled to have the handgun. The law imposed three duties on the chief law enforcement officer during that five-day waiting period. First:

> A chief law enforcement officer ... shall make a *reasonable effort* to ascertain ... whether receipt or possession would be a violation of the law, including research in whatever State and local record keeping systems are available and in a national system designated by the [U.S.] Attorney General. (Emphasis supplied.)

Second:

> Unless the chief law enforcement officer to whom a statement is transmitted … determines that a transaction would violate Federal, State, or local law, … the officer shall, within 20 business days after the date the transferee made the statement on the basis of which the notice was provided, destroy the statement, any record containing information derived from the statement, and any record created as a result of the notice required….

Third:

> If a chief law enforcement officer determines that an individual is ineligible to receive a handgun and the individual requests the officer to provide the reason for such determination, the officer shall provide the reasons to the individual in writing within 20 business days after receipt of the request.

The legislation also provided that if a person was denied the opportunity to purchase a firearm because of erroneous information provided by a chief law enforcement officer, the person could sue the jurisdiction for which the officer worked.

Soon after the Brady Act was adopted, the Bureau of Alcohol, Tobacco, and Firearms issued an open letter to chief law enforcement officers providing them guidance about the meaning of "reasonable effort" in the act. The letter stated that law enforcement officers were in the "best position to determine" the meaning of a "reasonable effort" and that officers were allowed to set their own standards, based on their own circumstances, including "the availability of resources, access to records, and taking into account the law enforcement priorities of the jurisdiction."

Ray Printz is the sheriff of Ravalli County, Montana. He filed suit in the U.S. District Court for the District of Montana seeking a declaration that several of the interim requirements under the Brady Act are unconstitutional and an injunction against their enforcement. Printz was joined by Richard Mack, the sheriff of Graham County, Arizona. Specifically, they contended that the requirement that chief law enforcement officials make a "reasonable effort" to ascertain if there is a legal impediment to a handgun sale violates the Tenth Amendment and exceeds Congress's power under the Commerce Clause. Printz and Mack claimed that they had limited resources and that implementing the requirements of the Brady Act would require them to shift staff and financial resources from enforcement of state law to enforcement of the federal legislation. The two sheriffs relied on the Supreme Court's decision in *New York v. United States*, 505 U.S. 144 (1992) (see pp. 605–606), for the argument that "the federal government is now flatly precluded from commanding state officers to assist in carrying out a federal program." The district court agreed with Printz and Mack that *New York* prohibited Congress from commanding state law enforcement officers to make a "reasonable effort" to inquire into the legality of handgun sales under the Brady Act. However, it ruled that the other interim requirements do not violate the Tenth Amendment, and that the "reasonable effort" provision could be severed from the rest of the act, so that the five-day waiting period for handgun sales remained intact.

The U.S. Court of Appeals for the Ninth Circuit affirmed in part and reversed in part. It ruled that all of the provisions of the Brady Act are constitutional. The Supreme Court granted Printz and Mack's petition for a writ of certiorari.

HIGHLIGHTS OF SUPREME COURT ARGUMENTS

BRIEF FOR PRINTZ AND MACK

◆ Congress has no power under the Commerce Clause to issue commands that violate the Tenth Amendment. The power to regulate interstate commerce does not include the power to conscript law enforcement agencies of the states.

◆ In *New York v. United States*, 505 U.S. 144 (1992), this court held that Congress cannot order states to enact or administer a federal regulatory program.

◆ The duties of the states enumerated in the Constitution do not include execution of federal criminal law.

◆ The Brady Act makes handgun transfers a state investigative priority, forcing law enforcement officials to shift scarce resources away from other enforcement activities.

◆ The president and the executive branch of the federal government—not the states—are responsible for executing federal law.

◆ This Court's decision in *United States v. Lopez* also explains why the Brady Act is an unconstitutional imposition on the states: "Under our federal system the administration of criminal justice rests with the States...." The Brady Act usurps the most fundamental element of state sovereignty, which is administration of criminal justice.

◆ The "reasonable effort" requirement cannot be severed from the rest of the Brady Act. This Court must declare the entire act unconstitutional, including the five-day waiting period.

AMICUS CURIAE BRIEFS SUPPORTING PRINTZ AND MACK

Law Enforcement Alliance of America; joint brief of the Council of State Governments and National Conference of State Legislatures; National Rifle Association; Gun Owners Foundation; joint brief of the states of Colorado, Idaho, Kansas, Montana, Nebraska, South Dakota, Virginia, and Wyoming.

BRIEF FOR THE UNITED STATES

◆ The interim provisions of the Brady Act require temporary, limited, nonpolicymaking assistance by chief law enforcement officers in giving effect to the federal scheme pending the establishment of a national instant background check system. The officers are not required to establish any new legal restrictions, only to ascertain whether an already existing restriction is applicable to a particular case.

◆ This Court must reject the absolutist position taken by Printz and Mack, which is that Congress may not, under any circumstances, require local officials to assist in the application of federal law to private persons. There is no basis in this Court's jurisprudence of federalism to support that contention.

◆ To the extent that federalism constrains Congress's ability to impose duties under federal law on local officials, the limits must be found in the Tenth Amendment and the obligation imposed by Congress must be closely examined to determine whether the federal obligation impairs that interest in a serious and substantial way. The constitutional line is crossed only when Congress compels the states to make law in their sovereign capacities, not when Congress requires the assistance of state or local officials in carrying out a broadly applicable federal law.

◆ This case is distinguishable from *New York v. United States*, 505 U.S. 144 (1992), because in that case the portions of the federal statute held to be unconstitutional required the states to enact certain policies regarding the collection and disposal of radioactive waste. Under the Brady Act, the states are not required to make any substantive policy decisions about who should or should not be eligible to receive a handgun.

◆ The burden imposed on the states to implement the interim requirements of the Brady Act does not threaten the states' separate and independent existence. Consequently, *Garcia v. San Antonio Metropolitan Transit Authority* is not implicated. Assistance by chief law enforcement officials in enforcing the Brady Act also accords with this country's longstanding tradition against a national police force.

◆ This Court should not reach the question of the validity of the five-day waiting period even if the "reasonable effort" provisions are invalidated, because law enforcement officials lack standing to challenge the validity of the waiting periods.

AMICUS CURIAE BRIEFS SUPPORTING THE UNITED STATES

American Federation of Labor and Congress of Industrial Organizations; joint brief of Handgun Control, Inc., Center to Prevent Handgun Violence, the U.S. Conference of Mayors, Federal Law Enforcement Officers' Association, Fraternal Order of Police, International Association of Chiefs of Police, Major Cities Chiefs, National Association of Police Organizations, National Organization of Black Law Enforcement Executives, National Troopers' Coalition, and Police Executive Research Forum; joint brief of the states of Maryland, Connecticut, Florida, Hawaii, Iowa, Michigan, Minnesota, Mississippi, Nevada, North Carolina, Oregon, Rhode Island, and Wisconsin; Association of the Bar of the City of New York; joint brief of U.S. Senators Herb Kohl, Paul Simon, John Chafee, Edward M. Kennedy, Dianne Feinstein, John Kerry, Frank Lautenberg, Tom Harkin, Bill Bradley, Carol Moseley-Braun, and Bob Kerrey.

SUPREME COURT DECISION: 5–4

SCALIA, J.

... [I]t is apparent that the Brady Act purports to direct state law enforcement officers to participate, albeit only temporarily, in the administration of a federally enacted regulatory scheme....

The petitioners here object to being pressed into federal service, and contend that congressional action compelling state officers to execute federal laws is unconstitutional. Because there is no constitutional text speaking to this precise question, the answer to the [chief law enforcement officers' (CLEOs')] challenge must be sought in historical understanding and practice, in the structure of the Constitution, and in the jurisprudence of this Court....

[E]arly laws establish, at most, that the Constitution was originally understood to permit imposition of an obligation on state *judges* to enforce federal prescriptions, insofar as those prescriptions related to matters appropriate for the judicial power. That assumption was perhaps implicit in one of the provisions of the Constitution, and was explicit in another. In accord with the so-called Madisonian Compromise, Article III, § 1, established only a Supreme Court, and made the creation of lower federal courts optional with the Congress— even though it was obvious that the Supreme Court alone could not hear all federal cases throughout the United States.... And the Supremacy Clause, Art. VI, cl. 2, announced that "the Laws of the United States ... shall be the supreme Law of the Land; and the Judges in every State shall be bound thereby." It is understandable why courts should have been viewed distinctively in this regard; unlike legislatures and executives, they applied the law of other sovereigns all the time. The principle underlying so-called "transitory" causes of action was that laws which operated elsewhere created obligations in justice that courts of the forum state would enforce.... The Constitution itself, in the Full Faith and Credit Clause, Art. IV, § 1, generally required such enforcement with respect to obligations arising in other States....

For these reasons, we do not think the early statutes imposing obligations on state courts imply a power of Congress to impress the state executive into its service....

Not only do the enactments of the early Congresses, as far as we are aware, contain no evidence of an assumption that the Federal Government may command the States' executive power in the absence of a particularized constitutional authorization, they contain some indication of precisely the opposite assumption....

In addition to early legislation, the Government also appeals to other sources we have usually regarded as indicative of the original understanding of the Constitution.... But none of these statements necessarily implies—what is the critical point here—that Congress could impose these responsibilities *without the consent of the States*. They appear to rest on the natural assumption that the States would consent to allowing their officials to assist the Federal Government[.]...

To complete the historical record, we must note that there is not only an absence of executive-commandeering statutes in the early Congresses, but there is an absence of them in our later history as well, at least until very recent years....

The Government points to a number of federal statutes enacted within the past few decades that require the participation of state or local officials in implementing federal regulatory schemes. Some of these are connected to federal funding measures, and can perhaps be more accurately described as conditions upon the grant of federal funding than as mandates to the States; others, which require only the provision of information to the Federal Government, do not involve the precise issue before us here, which is the forced participation of the States' executive in the actual administration of a federal program. We of course do not address these or other currently operative enactments that are not before us; it will be time enough to do so if and when their validity is challenged in a proper case. For deciding the issue before us here, they are of little relevance. Even assuming they represent assertion of the very same congressional power challenged here, they are of such recent vintage that they are no more probative than the statute before us of a constitutional tradition that lends meaning to the text. Their persuasive force is far outweighed by almost two centuries of apparent congressional avoidance of the practice....

[C]onstitutional practice ... tends to negate the existence of the congressional power asserted here, but is not conclusive. We turn next to consideration of the structure of the Constitution, to see if we can discern among its "essential postulate[s]," *Principality of Monaco v. Mississippi*, 292 U.S. 313, 322 (1934), a principle that controls the present cases.

It is incontestable that the Constitution established a system of "dual sovereignty." *Gregory v. Ashcroft*, 501 U.S. 452, 457 (1991).... Although the States surrendered many of their powers to the new Federal Government, they retained "a residuary and inviolable sovereignty," The *Federalist* No. 39. This is reflected throughout the Constitution's text[.]...

The Framers' experience under the Articles of Confederation had persuaded them that using the States as the instruments of federal governance was both ineffectual and provocative of federal-state conflict.... "The Framers explicitly chose a Constitution that confers upon Congress the power to regulate individuals, not States." [*New York v. United States*, 505 U.S. 144 (1992).] The great innovation of this design was that "our citizens would have two political capacities, one state and one federal, each protected from incursion by the other"—"a legal system unprecedented in form and design, establishing two orders of government, each with its own direct relationship, its own privity, its own set of mutual rights and obligations to the people who sustain it and are governed by it." *U.S. Term Limits, Inc. v. Thornton.* The Constitution thus contemplates that a State's government will represent and remain accountable to its own citizens....

This separation of the two spheres is one of the Constitution's structural protections of liberty.... The power of the Federal Government would be augmented immeasurably if it were able to impress into its service—and at no cost to itself—the police officers of the 50 States.... The Constitution does not leave to speculation who is to administer the laws enacted by Congress[: it is the President.]... The Brady Act effectively transfers this responsibility to thousands of CLEOs in the 50 States, who are left to implement the program without meaningful Presidential control (if indeed meaningful Presidential control is possible without the power to appoint and remove). The insistence of the Framers upon unity in the Federal Executive—to insure both vigor and accountability—is well known.... That unity would be shattered, and the power of the President would be subject to reduction, if Congress could act as effectively without the President as with him, by simply requiring state officers to execute its laws....

Finally, and most conclusively in the present litigation, we turn to the prior jurisprudence of this Court....

[O]pinions of ours have made clear that the Federal Government may not compel the States to implement, by legislation or executive action, federal regulatory programs....

When we were ... confronted squarely with a federal statute that unambiguously required the States to enact or administer a federal regulatory program, our decision should have come as no surprise. At issue in *New York v. United States* were the so-called "take title" provisions of the Low-Level Radioactive Waste Policy Amendments Act of 1985, which required States either to enact legislation providing for the disposal of radioactive waste generated within their borders, or to take title to, and possession of the waste—effectively requiring the States either to legislate pursuant to Congress's directions, or to implement an administrative solution. We concluded that Congress could constitutionally require the States to do neither....

The Government contends that *New York* is distinguishable on the following ground: unlike the "take title" provisions invalidated there, the background-check provision of the Brady Act does not require state legislative or executive officials to make policy, but instead issues a final directive to state CLEOs. It is permissible, the Government asserts, for Congress to command state or local officials to assist in the implementation of federal law so long as "Congress itself devises a clear legislative solution that regulates private conduct" and requires state or local officers to provide only "limited, nonpolicymaking help in enforcing that law." "[T]he constitutional line is crossed only when Congress compels the States to make law in their sovereign capacities."... This Court has not been notably successful in describing the latter line; indeed, some think we have abandoned the effort to do so.... We are doubtful that the new line the Government proposes would be any more distinct....

Even assuming, moreover, that the Brady Act leaves no "policymaking" discretion with the States, we fail to see how that improves rather than worsens the intrusion upon state sovereignty....

The Government also maintains that requiring state officers to perform discrete, ministerial tasks specified by Congress does not violate the principle of *New York* because it does not diminish the accountability of state or federal officials. This argument fails even on its own terms. By forcing state governments to absorb the financial burden of implementing a federal regulatory program, Members of Congress can take credit for "solving" problems without having to ask their constituents to pay for the solutions with higher federal taxes. And even when the States are not forced to absorb the costs of implementing a federal program, they are still put in the position of taking the blame for its burdensomeness and for its defects....

Finally, the Government puts forward a cluster of arguments that can be grouped under the heading: "The Brady Act serves very important purposes, is most efficiently administered by CLEOs during the interim period, and places a minimal and only temporary burden upon state officers." There is considerable disagreement over the extent of the burden, but we need not pause over that detail. Assuming *all* the mentioned factors were true, they might be relevant if we were evaluating whether the incidental application to the States of a federal law of general applicability excessively interfered with the functioning of state governments.... But where, as here, it is the whole *object* of the law to direct the functioning of the state executive, and hence to compromise the structural framework of dual sovereignty, such a "balancing" analysis is inappropriate. It is the very *principle* of separate state sovereignty that such a law offends, and no comparative assessment of the various interests can overcome that fundamental defect....

We held in *New York* that Congress cannot compel the States to enact or enforce a federal regulatory program. Today we hold that Congress cannot circumvent that prohibition by conscripting the State's officers directly. The Federal Government may neither issue directives requiring the States to address particular problems, nor command the States' officers, or those of their political subdivisions, to administer or enforce a federal regulatory program. It matters not whether policymak-

ing is involved, and no case-by-case weighing of the burdens or benefits is necessary; such commands are fundamentally incompatible with our constitutional system of dual sovereignty. Accordingly, the judgment of the Court of Appeals for the Ninth Circuit is reversed.

It is so ordered.

O'CONNOR, J., CONCURRING [OMITTED]

THOMAS, J., CONCURRING

... I write separately to emphasize that the Tenth Amendment affirms the undeniable notion that under our Constitution, the Federal Government is one of enumerated, hence limited, powers.... Accordingly, the Federal Government may act only where the Constitution authorizes it to do so.... The Constitution, in addition to delegating certain enumerated powers to Congress, places whole areas outside the reach of Congress' regulatory authority.... [For instance, t]he Second Amendment ... appears to contain an express limitation on the government's authority.... This Court has not had recent occasion to consider the nature of the substantive right safeguarded by the Second Amendment. If, however, the Second Amendment is read to confer a *personal* right to "keep and bear arms," a colorable argument exists that the Federal Government's regulatory scheme, at least as it pertains to the purely intrastate sale or possession of firearms, runs afoul of that Amendment's protections. As the parties did not raise this argument, however, we need not consider it here. Perhaps, at some future date, this Court will have the opportunity to determine whether Justice [Joseph] Story was correct when he wrote that the right to bear arms "has justly been considered, as the palladium of the liberties of a republic."...

STEVENS, SOUTER, GINSBURG, AND BREYER, J.J., DISSENTING

When Congress exercises the powers delegated to it by the Constitution, it may impose affirmative obligations on executive and judicial officers of state and local governments as well as ordinary citizens. This conclusion is firmly supported by the text of the Constitution, the early history of the Nation, decisions of this Court, and a correct understanding of the basic structure of the Federal Government.

These cases do not implicate the more difficult questions associated with congressional coercion of state legislatures addressed in *New York v. United States*. Nor need we consider the wisdom of relying on local officials rather than federal agents to carry out aspects of a federal program, or even the question whether such officials may be required to perform a federal function on a permanent basis. The question is whether Congress, acting on behalf of the people of the entire Nation, may require local law enforcement officers to perform certain duties during the interim needed for the development of a federal gun control program. It is remarkably similar to the question, heavily debated by the Framers of the Constitution, whether the Congress could require state agents to collect federal taxes. Or the question whether Congress could impress state judges into federal service to entertain and decide cases that they would prefer to ignore.

Indeed, since the ultimate issue is one of power, we must consider its implications in times of national emergency. Matters such as the enlistment of air raid wardens, the administration of a military draft, the mass inoculation of children to forestall an epidemic, or perhaps the threat of an international terrorist, may require a national response before federal personnel can be made available to respond. If the Constitution empowers Congress and the President to make an appropriate response, is there anything in the Tenth Amendment, "in historical understanding and practice, in the structure of the Constitution, [or] in the jurisprudence of this Court," that forbids the enlistment of state officers to make that response effective? More narrowly, what basis is there in any of those sources for concluding that it is the Members of this Court, rather than the elected representatives of the people, who should determine whether the Constitution contains the unwritten rule that the Court announces today?

Perhaps today's majority would suggest that no such emergency is presented by the facts of these cases. But such a suggestion is itself an expression of a policy judgment. And Congress' view of the matter is quite different from that implied by the Court today....

Unlike the First Amendment, which prohibits the enactment of a category of laws that would otherwise be authorized by Article I, the Tenth Amendment imposes no restriction on the exercise of delegated powers.... The Amendment confirms the principle that the powers of the Federal Government are limited to those affirmatively granted by the Constitution, but it does not purport to limit the scope or the effectiveness of the exercise of powers that are delegated to Congress.... [T]he Amendment provides no support for a rule that immunizes local officials from obligations that might be imposed on ordinary citizens. Indeed, it would be more reasonable to infer that federal law may impose greater duties on state officials than on private citizens because another provision of the Constitution requires that "all executive and judicial Officers, both of the United States and of the several States, shall be bound by Oath or Affirmation, to support this Constitution."...

There is not a clause, sentence, or paragraph in the entire text of the Constitution of the United States that supports the proposition that a local police officer can ignore a command contained in a statute enacted by Congress pursuant to an express delegation of power enumerated in Article I....

Indeed, the historical materials strongly suggest that the Founders intended to enhance the capacity of the federal government by empowering it—as a part of the new authority to make demands directly on individual citizens—to act through local officials....

The Court's response to this powerful historical evidence is weak. The majority suggests that "none of these statements necessarily implies ... Congress could impose these responsibilities without the consent of the States." No fair reading of these materials can justify such an interpretation....

Bereft of support in the history of the founding, the Court rests its conclusion on the claim that there is little evidence the National Government actually exercised such a power in the early years of the Republic. This reasoning is misguided in principle and in fact.... [W]e

have never suggested that the failure of the early Congresses to address the scope of federal power in a particular area or to exercise a particular authority was an argument against its existence....

More importantly, the fact that Congress did elect to rely on state judges and the clerks of state courts to perform a variety of executive functions is surely evidence of a contemporary understanding that their status as state officials did not immunize them from federal service. The majority's description of these early statutes is both incomplete and at times misleading....

We are far truer to the historical record by applying a functional approach in assessing the role played by these early state officials. The use of state judges and their clerks to perform executive functions was, in historical context, hardly unusual.... And, of course, judges today continue to perform a variety of functions that may more properly be described as executive.... The majority's insistence that this evidence of federal enlistment of state officials to serve executive functions is irrelevant simply because the assistance of "judges" was at issue rests on empty formalistic reasoning of the highest order....

[T]he majority's opinion consists almost entirely of arguments *against* the substantial evidence weighing in opposition to its view; the Court's ruling is strikingly lacking in affirmative support. Absent even a modicum of textual foundation for its judicially crafted constitutional rule, there should be a presumption that if the Framers had actually intended such a rule, at least one of them would have mentioned it.

The Court's "structural" arguments

are not sufficient to rebut that presumption. The fact that the Framers intended to preserve the sovereignty of the several States simply does not speak to the question whether individual state employees may be required to perform federal obligations, such as registering young adults for the draft, creating state emergency response commissions designed to manage the release of hazardous substances, collecting and reporting data on underground storage tanks that may pose an environmental hazard, and reporting traffic fatalities and missing children to a federal agency....

Perversely, the majority's rule seems more likely to damage than to preserve the safeguards against tyranny provided by the existence of vital state governments. By limiting the ability of the Federal Government to enlist state officials in the implementation of its programs, the Court creates incentives for the National Government to aggrandize itself. In the name of State's rights, the majority would have the Federal Government create vast national bureaucracies to implement its policies. This is exactly the sort of thing that the early Federalists promised would not occur, in part as a result of the National Government's ability to rely on the magistracy of the states....

[T]here [is no] force to the assumption undergirding the Court's entire opinion that if this trivial burden on state sovereignty is permissible, the entire structure of federalism will soon collapse. [This case does] not involve any mandate to state legislatures to enact new rules. When legislative action, or even administrative rule-making, is at issue, it may be appropriate for Congress either to pre-empt the State's

lawmaking power and fashion the federal rule itself, or to respect the State's power to fashion its own rules. But this case, unlike any precedent in which the Court has held that Congress exceeded its powers, merely involves the imposition of modest duties on individual officers. The Court seems to accept the fact that Congress could require private persons, such as hospital executives or school administrators, to provide arms merchants with relevant information about a prospective purchaser's fitness to own a weapon; indeed, the Court does not disturb the conclusion that flows directly from our prior holdings that the burden on police officers would be permissible if a similar burden were also imposed on private parties with access to relevant data.... A structural problem that vanishes when the statute affects private individuals as well as public officials is not much of a structural problem.

Far more important than the concerns that the Court musters in support of its new rule is the fact that the Framers entrusted Congress with the task of creating a working structure of intergovernmental relationships around the framework that the Constitution authorized. Neither explicitly nor implicitly did the Framers issue any command that forbids Congress from imposing federal duties on private citizens or on local officials. As a general matter, Congress has followed the sound policy of authorizing federal agencies and federal agents to administer federal programs. That general practice, however, does not negate the existence of power to rely on state officials in occasional situations in which such reliance is in the national interest. Rather, the occasional exceptions confirm the wisdom of

Justice Holmes' reminder that "the machinery of government would not work if it were not allowed a little play in its joints." *Bain Peanut Co. of Tex. v. Pinson*, 282 U.S. 499 (1931)....

The provision of the Brady Act that crosses the Court's newly defined constitutional threshold is more comparable to a statute requiring local police officers to report the identity of missing children to the Crime Control Center of the Department of Justice than to an offensive federal command to a sover-eign state. If Congress believes that such a statute will benefit the people of the Nation, and serve the interests of cooperative federalism better than an enlarged federal bureaucracy, we should respect both its policy judgment and its appraisal of its constitutional power.

Accordingly, I respectfully dissent.

SOUTER, J., DISSENTING [OMITTED]

BREYER, J., DISSENTING [OMITTED]

COMMENTS

1. As of June 27, 1997, when *Printz* was handed down, twenty-seven states were exempt from the Brady Act because they already carried out screening measures of their own. (Ohio suspended its background checks in the wake of the *Printz* decision.) Twenty-three states performed background checks on prospective gun buyers only because the Brady Act required them to do so. Law enforcement officials have identified several of those twenty-three states, such as South Carolina, Mississippi, and Texas, as major sources for the guns used in crimes in other states with stricter laws, like states in the Northeast. Attorney General Janet Reno estimated that the Brady Act has prevented two hundred fifty thousand convicted felons, fugitives, and people with mental illness from buying guns since the law went into effect.

2. As noted in the *Setting*, starting November 30, 1998, the Brady Act requires gun dealers to check the names of prospective buyers against a computerized list of offenders currently being compiled by the Federal Bureau of Investigation. On that date, the portion of the Brady Act the Court voided in *Printz* will become inoperative through congressional mandate.

3. In a rare bench speech, Justice John Paul Stevens responded to Justice Scalia's announcement of the *Printz* majority opinion. Stevens occasionally read from a memorandum containing excerpts from his dissenting opinion, but often he spoke off-the-cuff, making points that his written opinion omitted. For example, Justice Stevens said that in its lack of textual support in the Constitution itself, the *Printz* majority opinion reminded him of Justice William Douglas's opinion in *Griswold v. Connecticut*, 381 U.S. 479 (1965), where Douglas extrapolated a right to privacy from "emanations" and "penumbras" of specific constitutional provisions. *Griswold v. Connecticut* has been criti-

cized for over thirty years by judicial conservatives, like Justice Scalia, as epitomizing judicial activism (Linda Greenhouse, "Court Restricts Brady Gun Law as Intrusion on States," [http://www.nytimes.com/], June 28, 1997).

QUESTIONS

1. What is the rule of *Printz*? Is the rule consistent with *Garcia*? How does the Court distinguish *Printz* from *New York v. United States*?

2. In what ways does the *Printz* decision refine understandings of American federalism? In its brief, the United States characterized Printz and Mack's position on federalism as "absolutist." Is this an accurate description of the *Printz* majority's view of the Tenth Amendment? How does the majority's view compare with the understanding of federalism articulated by Justice Thomas in his concurrence? Does either the majority's reading of the Tenth Amendment or Justice Thomas's view resemble the "dual federalism" approach to states' rights that prevailed in much nineteenth- and early-twentieth-century constitutional jurisprudence?

3. Federal laws require state and local law enforcement agencies to report cases of missing children, traffic fatalities, data collection regarding hazardous substances releases, plans for asbestos abatement, inventories of state hazardous waste sites, and inventories of underground storage tanks. How, if at all, are those requirements different from the interim requirements imposed on chief law enforcement officials under the Brady Act? In light of *Printz*, are statutes requiring participation by state and local officials in implementing federal regulatory schemes in jeopardy?

4. The National Rifle Association argued in its brief that:

   > If the Ninth Circuit's holding is upheld, then the federal government will be given a green light to commandeer the states to perform federal tasks for free, and the states will eventually be robbed of their funds, their resources and their independence; a pattern that will ultimately result in the destruction of federalism.

   Identify other instances in American history in which a similar federalism argument has been made. Does the Court respond to that argument in *Printz*?

5. Note the alignment of parties *amici* in *Printz*. What factors might account for the U.S. Conference of Mayors lending its support to the United States while the Council of State Governments supported Printz and Mack? What might account for some states' support for the United States and other states' support for Printz and Mack?

6. In 1992, the year before the Brady Act, the Federal Bureau of Investigation reported that "handguns were used to murder 36 people in Sweden, 97 in Switzerland, 60 in Japan, 128 in Canada, 33 in Great Britain, 13 in Australia and 13,495 in the United States." The House Report accompanying the Brady Act claimed that firearms injuries exacted $41.4 billion in medical costs and $19 billion in lost productivity each year. Do these statistics have any relevance for the federalism concerns in *Printz*? Should they?

SUGGESTIONS FOR FURTHER READING

Barber, Sotirios, "*National League of Cities v. Usery*: New Meaning for the Tenth Amendment," *Supreme Court Review* (Chicago, IL: University of Chicago Press, 1976).

Berger, Lawrence, and S. Rayan Johansson, "Child Health in the Workplace: The Supreme Court in *Hammer v. Dagenhart*," 5 *Journal of Health Politics, Policy, and Law* (1980): 81.

Braeman, John, *Change and Continuity in Twentieth Century America: The 1920s* (Columbus, OH: The Ohio State University Press, 1968).

Choper, Jesse H., *Judicial Review and the National Political Process: A Functional Analysis of the Role of the Supreme Court* (Chicago, IL: University of Chicago Press, 1982).

Cohen, William, "Congressional Power to Validate Unconstitutional State Laws: A Forgotten Solution to an Old Enigma," 35 *Stanford Law Review* (1985): 387.

Corwin, Edward S., "Congress's Powers to Prohibit Commerce," 18 *Cornell Law Quarterly* (1933): 477.

Cushman, Robert E., "The National Police Power under the Commerce Clause of the Constitution," 3 *Minnesota Law Review* (1919): 289.

Field, Martha, "*Garcia v. San Antonio Municipal Transit Authority*: The Demise of a Misguided Doctrine," 99 *Harvard Law Review* (1985): 84.

Flax, Karen, "In the Wake of *National League of Cities v. Usery*: A Derelict Makes Waves," 34 *South Carolina Law Review* (1983): 649.

Freund, Ernst, *The Police Power: Public Policy and Constitutional Rights* (Buffalo, NY: W. S. Hein, 1940).

Frickey, Philip, "Lawnet: The Case of the Missing (Tenth) Amendment," 75 *Minnesota Law Review* (1991): 755.

Hall, Kermit L., ed., *Federalism: A Nation of States—Major Historical Interpretations* (New York, NY: Garland, 1987).

Jones, William Carey, "The Child Labor Decision," 6 *California Law Review* (1918): 45.

Kaden, Lewis, "Politics, Money, and State Sovereignty," 79 *Columbia Law Review* (1979): 847.

Konefsky, Samuel J., *Chief Justice Stone and the Supreme Court* (New York, NY: Macmillan, 1946).

LaPierre, D. Bruce, "Political Accountability in the National Political Process— The Alternative to Judicial Review of Federalism Issues," 80 *Northwestern University Law Review* (1985): 577.

Lipner, Joseph, "Imposing Federal Business on Officers of the States: What the Tenth Amendment Might Mean," 57 *George Washington Law Review* (1989): 907.

Lofgren, Charles A., "*National League of Cities v. Usery*, Dual Federalism Reborn," 4 *Claremont Journal of Public Affairs* (1977): 19.

_____, "The Origins of the Tenth Amendment: History, Sovereignty, and the Problem of Constitutional Intention," in *Constitutional Government in America*, ed. Ronald K. L. Collins (Durham, NC: Carolina Academic Press, 1980).

Merritt, Deborah Jones, "The Guarantee Clause and State Autonomy: Federalism for a Third Century," 88 *Columbia Law Review* (1988): 1.

Michelman, Frank I., "States' Rights and States' Roles: The Permutations of 'Sovereignty' in *National Leagues of Cities v. Usery*," 86 *Yale Law Journal* (1977): 1165.

Murphy, Paul L., *The Constitution in Crisis, 1918–1969* (New York, NY: Harper and Row, 1972).

Nagel, Robert, "Federalism as a Fundamental Value: *National League of Cities* in Perspective," *Supreme Court Review* (Chicago, IL: University of Chicago Press, 1981).

Powell, Thomas Reed, "Intergovernmental Tax Immunities," 8 *George Washington Law Review* (1940): 1213.

Pritchett, C. Herman, *Constitutional Law of the Federal System* (Englewood Cliffs, NJ: Prentice Hall, 1984).

Redish, Martin H., *The Constitution as Political Structure* (New York, NY: Oxford University Press, 1995).

Redish, Martin H., and Karen Drizin, "Constitutional Federalism and Judicial Review: The Role of Textual Analysis," 62 *New York University Law Review* (1987): 1.

Scheiber, Harry N., "American Federalism and the Diffusion of Power," 9 *University of Toledo Law Review* (1978): 619.

_____, "Federalism and Legal Process: Historical and Contemporary Analysis of the American System," 10 *Law and Society Review* (1980): 663.

_____, "Public Rights and the Rule of Law in American Legal History," 72 *California Law Review* (1984): 217.

Scheiber, Harry N., and Malcolm M. Feeley, eds., *Power Divided: Essays on the Theory and Practice of Federalism* (Berkeley, CA: Institute of Governmental Studies, University of California, 1988).

Schwartz, Bernard, *From Confederation to Nation: The American Constitution, 1837–1877* (Baltimore, MD: The Johns Hopkins University, 1973).

‾‾‾‾‾‾, *"National League of Cities* Again—R.I.P. or a Ghost That Still Walks?" 54 *Fordham Law Review* (1985): 141.

Spitzer, Robert J., *The Politics of Gun Control* (Chatham, NJ: Chatham House, 1995).

Stern, Robert L., "The Commerce Clause Revisited: Federalization of Intrastate Crime," 14 *Arizona Law Review* (1973): 271.

Sutherland, William, "The Child Labor Cases & the Constitution," 8 *Cornell Law Quarterly* (1923): 338.

Swindler, William E., *Court and Constitution in the Twentieth Century, Vol 1., The Old Legality, 1889–1932* (Indianapolis, IN: Bobbs-Merrill, 1969).

‾‾‾‾‾‾, *Court and Constitution in the Twentieth Century, Vol. 2, The New Legality, 1932–1968* (Indianapolis, IN: Bobbs-Merrill, 1970).

Symposium, "Federalism," 86 *Yale Law Journal* (1977): 1018.

Tribe, Laurence H., "Unraveling *National League of Cities*," 90 *Harvard Law Review* (1977): 1065.

Urofsky, Melvin, "Myth and Reality: The Supreme Court and Protective Legislation in the Progressive Era," *Yearbook of the Supreme Court Historical Society* (1983).

Van Alstyne, William W., "The Second Death of Federalism," 83 *Michigan Law Review* (1985): 1709.

Wechsler, Herbert, "The Political Safeguards of Federalism: The Role of the States in the Composition and Selection of the National Government," 54 *Columbia Law Review* (1954): 543.

Wood, Stephen, *Constitutional Politics in the Progressive Era: Child Labor and the Law* (Chicago, IL: University of Chicago Press, 1968).

THE BILL OF RIGHTS AND THE STATES

Barron v. Baltimore
7 Peters 243 (1833)

SETTING

The Constitutional Convention did not consider including a bill of r
Constitution until late in its deliberations. In August, and again in
the question was raised, debated only briefly, and defeated. Th

bill of rights did not die, however. During ratification debates in the states, the lack of a bill of rights was a rallying cry for those opposed to the Constitution. Anti-Federalists urged states to either condition ratification on the addition of a bill of rights, or to include recommendations for a bill of rights as part of the ratification process. In an effort to win approval for the Constitution, Federalists in five states—Virginia, Massachusetts, South Carolina, New Hampshire, and New York—pledged to add a bill of rights to the Constitution after its adoption.

On June 8, 1789, James Madison made good on the bill of rights pledge by submitting to the House of Representatives a list of proposed amendments "in order to quiet that anxiety which prevails in the public mind." Congress made several changes in the list proposed by Madison but in September 1789 it submitted twelve amendments to the states for ratification. One, dealing with congressional apportionment, was not ratified. Another, prohibiting changes in levels of compensation for senators and representatives without an intervening election, was ratified belatedly, becoming the Twenty-seventh Amendment in 1992. The other ten became part of the Constitution in December 1791.

Despite its brevity, the Bill of Rights is a complex document. The First Amendment protects freedom of speech, religion, the press, peaceable assembly, and petition. The First Amendment is the only one that begins with the phrase, "Congress shall make no law...." The Second Amendment assures states of the right to maintain militias and, in the context of that right, the right of the people to keep and bear arms. The Third Amendment restricts the government's power to quarter soldiers in people's homes. The Fourth, Fifth, and Sixth Amendments have been called a "mini-code of criminal procedure," because they explain rights of the criminally accused. The Fifth Amendment also contains a Due Process Clause and the guarantee that private property will not be taken for public use without just compensation. The Seventh Amendment guarantees the right of trial by jury in common law suits involving more than $20, while the Eighth Amendment again focuses on the rights of the criminally accused and convicted by forbidding excessive bails and fines and prohibiting cruel and unusual punishments. The Ninth and Tenth Amendments do not contain guarantees of specific rights. The Ninth provides that the mention in the Constitution of certain rights should not be interpreted to "deny or disparage others retained by the people," but it does not indicate what other rights retained by the people might be. The Tenth Amendment, which Madison had proposed appear first, addresses federalism: "The powers not delegated to the United States by the Constitution, nor prohibited by it to the States, are reserved to the States respectively, or to the people."

The phrasing of the protections contained in the Bill of Rights, as well as the political climate in which it was adopted, raised the question of whether the Bill of Rights places limitations only on the actions of the national government, or whether it places limitations on the actions of state governments as well. The Supreme Court provided the first response near the end of Chief Justice Marshall's tenure in the case of *Barron v. Baltimore*.

John Barron and John Craig owned a highly profitable wharf on the Patapsco River in Baltimore, Maryland. When they built their wharf it was in the deepest water in the harbor, easily accessible to a variety of vessels. Between 1815 and 1821, the city, exercising power delegated to it by the state of Maryland, undertook a series of public works projects that included paving several Baltimore streets and diverting streams from beds that flowed from the hills bordering the city.

During rainy seasons, the new water courses created by the public works projects deposited large quantities of sand and dirt into the water in front of Barron and Craig's wharf. The deposits made the water so shallow that vessels eventually could not operate in their wharf. By 1822, Barron and Craig's property was of little or no value as a wharf.

City of Baltimore officials acknowledged that the consequences of the improvements were ruinous for Barron and Craig, but offered no compensation. They claimed that their actions were justified by authority they deduced from the city's charter, granted by the Maryland legislature, and by various acts of the legislature that gave the city authority to grade and pave streets and regulate the harbor and its waters for the health of the city. In 1822, Barron, as survivor of Craig, sued the mayor, the city council of Baltimore, and the state of Maryland in Baltimore County Court for the taking of their property without compensation, contrary to the requirements of the Fifth Amendment.

The Baltimore County Court awarded Barron $4,500 in damages. The Maryland Court of Appeals, the highest court of the state, reversed the county court's decision. Barron petitioned the Supreme Court of the United States for a writ of error.

HIGHLIGHTS OF SUPREME COURT ARGUMENTS

BRIEF FOR BARRON

◆ Barron and Craig's right and profit of wharfage, and use of the water at the wharf for navigation, is a vested interest, inviolable even by the state, except upon just compensation.

◆ Even though Baltimore is a municipal corporation, it is liable for the torts it commits and for actual misfeasance.

◆ Baltimore's action destroying Barron and Craig's wharf was repugnant to the Fifth Amendment of the Constitution, which states that "private property shall not be taken for public use without just compensation." This amendment regulates the legislation of the states for the protection of the people in each and all of the states, regarded as citizens of the United States.

◆ The Supreme Court has appellate jurisdiction over the constitutionality of state actions that infringe on a right in the Constitution of the United States.

Note: The Court did not permit the city of Baltimore or the attorney general of Maryland to present an argument.

SUPREME COURT DECISION: 7–0

MARSHALL, C.J.

The judgment brought up by this writ of error having been rendered by the court of a State, this tribunal can exercise no jurisdiction over it unless it be shown to come within the provisions of the twenty-fifth section of the [Judiciary Act of 1789].

The plaintiff in error contends ... that [the Fifth Amendment to the Constitution] being in favor of the liberty of the citizen, ought to be so construed as to restrain the legislative power of a State, as well as that of the United States. If this proposition be untrue, the court can take no jurisdiction of the cause.

The question thus presented is, we think, of great importance, but not of much difficulty.

The Constitution was ordained and established by the people of the United States for themselves, for their own government, and not for the government of the individual States. Each State established a Constitution for itself, and in that Constitution, provided such limitations and restrictions on the powers of its particular government, as its judgment dictated. The people of the United States framed such a government for the United States as they supposed best adapted to their situation and best calculated to promote their interests. The powers they conferred on this government were to be exercised by itself; and the limitations on power, if expressed in general terms, are naturally, and, we think, necessarily applicable to the government created by the instrument. They are limitations of power granted in the instrument itself; not of distinct governments, framed by different persons and for different purposes.

If these propositions be correct, the fifth amendment must be understood as restraining the power of the general government, not as applicable to the States....

Had the people of the several States, or any of them, required changes in their constitutions; had they required additional safeguards to liberty from the apprehended encroachments of their particular governments; the remedy was in their own hands, and would have been applied by themselves. A convention would have been assembled by the discontented State, and the required improvements would have been made by itself. The unwieldy and cumbrous machinery of procuring a recommendation from two-thirds of Congress, and the assent of three-fourths of their sister States, could never have occurred to any human being, as a mode of doing that which might be effected by the State itself. Had the framers of these amendments intended them to be limitations on the powers of the State governments, they would have imitated the framers of the original Constitution, and have expressed that intention. Had Congress engaged in the extraordinary occupation of improving the constitutions of the several States, by affording the people additional protection from the exercise of power by their own governments, in matters which concerned themselves alone, they would have declared this purpose in plain and intelligible language.

But it is universally understood, it is a part of the history of the day, that the great revolution which established the Constitution of the United States, was not effected without immense opposition. Serious fears were extensively entertained, that those powers which the patriot statesmen, who then watched over the interests of our country, deemed essential to union, and to the attainment of those invaluable objects for which union was sought, might be exercised in a manner dangerous to liberty. In almost every convention by which the Constitution was adopted, amendments to guard against the abuse of power were recommended. These amendments demanded security against the apprehended encroachments of the general government—not against those of the local governments.

In compliance with a sentiment thus generally expressed, to quiet fears thus extensively entertained, amendments were proposed by the required majority in Congress, and adopted by the States. These amendments contain no expression indicating an intention to apply them to the State governments. This court cannot so apply them.

We are of opinion, that the provision in the fifth amendment to the Constitution, declaring that private property shall not be taken for public use, without just compensation, is intended solely as a limitation on the exercise of power by the government of the United States, and is not applicable to the legislation of the States. We are therefore of the opinion that there is no repugnancy between the several acts of the General Assembly of Maryland, given in evidence by the defendants at the trial of this case in the court of that State, and the Constitution of the United States.

This court, therefore, has no jurisdiction of the cause, and [it] is dismissed.

QUESTIONS

1. The Supreme Court's refusal to allow counsel for the city of Baltimore or Roger B. Taney, the Maryland attorney general, to put on an argument suggests that in the Court's view the result was, as Chief Justice Marshall put it, "not of too much difficulty." Why was the *Barron* result so open-and-shut? Under what constitutional theory might the Court have found an argument for applying the Takings Clause of the Fifth Amendment against the states?

2. Does *Barron* mean that, as of 1833, the Bill of Rights does not protect individuals against state action?

3. James Madison proposed that most of the bills of right he submitted to the House of Representatives in June 1789 be inserted into Article I, Section 9, of the original Constitution. If Madison's suggestion had been followed, would the outcome in *Barron* have been different? What does Madison's proposal about the location of most of the bills of right indicate about his intention regarding the scope of those rights? Does the language of the Bill of Rights itself suggest anything

about the applicability of its guarantees to the states? (For instance, compare the language of the First Amendment with the language of the Seventh Amendment.)

4. In introducing the Bill of Rights, Madison declared the following proposal, to be located in Article I, Section 10, more important than all the others: "The equal rights of conscience, the freedom of speech or of the press, and the right of trial by jury in criminal cases, shall not be infringed by any State." The Senate declined to include this proposal in the Bill of Rights. Does the Senate's action provide any additional insight into its intention about the scope of the Bill of Rights? Should the Supreme Court have taken congressional intent into account in deciding *Barron*? (For insight into the framers' intentions, read Hamilton's *Federalist* No. 28, *The Federalist Papers*, ed. Clinton Rossiter [New York, NY: Mentor, 1961].)

5. Constitutional historian Charles Warren wrote of the *Barron* decision: "It is a striking fact that this last of Marshall's opinions on this branch of law should have been delivered in limitation of the operation of the Constitution, whose undue extension he had been so long charged with seeking" (Charles Warren, *The Supreme Court in United States History*, 3 vols. [Boston, MA: Little, Brown and Company, 1923], I: 240–241). Is *Barron* consistent with Chief Justice Marshall's prior decisions? In what ways? What insights does the *Barron* decision provide into Chief Justice Marshall's view of federalism?

THE BILL OF RIGHTS AND THE STATES

Slaughter-House Cases
16 Wallace 36 (1873)

SETTING

After the Civil War, Ku Klux Klan terror tactics and the Black Codes demonstrated that the states of the former Confederacy were committed to nullifying the rights of America's former slaves. In response, Congress passed the Civil Rights Act of 1866. It set national standards for the protection of freed blacks. The act overruled *Dred Scott v. Sandford* (Chapter 2, pp. 150–158) by declaring that all persons born or naturalized in the United States ("excluding Indians not taxed") are citizens of the United States, and gave blacks the same benefit of the laws as whites. President Andrew Johnson vetoed the Civil Rights Act on the ground that it violated states' rights. Congress overrode the veto.

Despite the veto override, there were nationwide debates over whether the Civil Rights Act stripped the states of too much power. Radical Republicans concluded that they should incorporate the bill's provisions into a new constitutional amendment in order to guarantee federal enforcement powers regarding civil rights. On April 30, 1866, the Joint Committee on Reconstruction proposed an amendment that was, in the words of Joint Committee member Iowa Senator James W. Grimes, "a plan of reconstruction." As such, the Fourteenth Amendment was Congress's most concise formulation of its Reconstruction policy. Section One of the final draft of the Fourteenth Amendment contains three important clauses guaranteeing privileges or immunities, due process, and equal protection of the laws. Each of those guarantees manifested the Radical Republicans' intention to use the power of the national government to protect the rights of ex-slaves.

Section One of the Fourteenth Amendment was drafted by Ohio Representative John A. Bingham. According to Congressman Bingham, the purpose of the Privileges or Immunities Clause was to make the guarantees of the Bill of Rights a limitation on the states as well as on the national government. Bingham said that he had drafted the Privileges or Immunities Clause in response to Chief Justice John Marshall's "suggestion," as Bingham put it, in *Barron v. Baltimore* that "Had the framers of [the first eight amendments to the Constitution] intended them to be limitations on the powers of the State governments, they would have imitated the framers of the original constitution and have expressed that intention." Referring to the Privileges or Immunities Clause in the Fourteenth Amendment, Bingham observed in 1871: "I did imitate the framers of the original Constitution."

The Slaughter-House Cases gave the Supreme Court an opportunity to put its interpretive stamp on the meaning of the Privileges or Immunities Clause of Section One of the Fourteenth Amendment. The particular origins of *The Slaughter-House Cases* trace to March 1869, when the Louisiana legislature passed Act 118 entitled, "An act to protect the health of the city of New Orleans, to locate the stock-landings and slaughter-houses, and to incorporate the Crescent City Live Stock Landing and Slaughter-House Company." The new company consisted of seventeen incorporators. Act 118 gave the Crescent City Company a monopoly over slaughterhouses in the city of New Orleans and the parishes of Orleans, Jefferson, and St. Bernard for a period of twenty-five years. Crescent City was authorized to construct one "grand slaughter-house," capable of slaughtering five hundred animals per day, and was given the duty of permitting any person to slaughter animals in its facilities, under penalty of a fine for each refusal. All other stock handling companies and slaughterhouses were ordered closed by June 1, 1869.

New York City, Boston, Milwaukee, and San Francisco had earlier passed statutes similar to Act 118 to protect the public health. The goal of the statutes was to control the dumping of carcasses into municipal water supplies. The New Orleans law, though presented as a public health act, in fact was a spoils scheme. The incorporators had distributed cash and stock to

New Orleans municipal officials, members of both houses of the Louisiana legislature, and the state governor as bribes to ensure passage of Act 118.

By June 1869, approximately two hundred suits were instituted for and
against the Crescent City Live-Stock Company in six district courts in
Louisiana. Crescent City sought to enjoin an estimated one thousand other
butchers from operating slaughterhouses in violation of the act. Other butchers sued Crescent City and the state of Louisiana in an effort to have the act
declared unconstitutional.

By agreement of the parties, all but six cases, selected because they contained all the points at issue between the slaughterhouse and its opponents,
were dropped. The six cases were litigated in the district courts in which they
were filed. Under the agreement, they were appealed as a whole to the
Louisiana Supreme Court. That court ruled for Crescent City. Opponents of
the slaughterhouse petitioned the Supreme Court for a writ of error.

In March 1871, some of the parties claimed to have settled the issues and
moved for dismissal. Three of the parties, however, objected to having their
cases dismissed, claiming they had given no authority to settle their cases.
Following argument and decision on the motion to dismiss, the three cases
were set for argument on the merits. One involved the Butchers' Benevolent
Association of New Orleans against the Crescent City Company.

The three cases were argued together in January 1872. Justice Samuel
Nelson did not participate. Following argument, the Justices split 4–4 on the
result. They ordered the case reargued at the next Term. The second argument occurred in February 1873, by which time Justice Ward Hunt had
replaced Justice Samuel Nelson.

HIGHLIGHTS OF SUPREME COURT ARGUMENTS

BRIEF FOR THE BUTCHERS' BENEVOLENT ASSOCIATION OF NEW ORLEANS

◆ Act 118 is described as an act of police, adopted by the state to promote salubrity, security, and public order. But laws of police, like other state
laws, are valid only if they do not violate the limits of the Constitution.

◆ Act 118 violates the Fourteenth Amendment's Privileges or Immunities
Clause. Limiting a man's choice of a trade, depriving him of a business he has
pursued, and giving others the exclusive right to practice that trade violate
rights of national citizenship declared by the Amendment. The purpose of the
Fourteenth Amendment was to assure all men the rights of life, liberty, and
property, the right to labor freely, and the enjoyment of the fruits of their own
industry.

BRIEF FOR LOUISIANA AND CRESCENT CITY COMPANY

◆ The Privileges or Immunities Clause is not used for the first time in the
Fourteenth Amendment. The original Constitution provided that "the citizens

of each state shall be entitled to all privileges and immunities of citizenship in the several states." The privileges and immunities contemplated there are those that are fundamental, such as the right of going into any state for the purpose of residing therein; the right of taking up one's residence therein; becoming a citizen; the right of free entrance and exit and passage through; and the protection of laws affecting personal liberty.

◆ The Privileges or Immunities Clause of the Fourteenth Amendment added no privileges or immunities to the Constitution that citizens of the United States did not enjoy before its adoption. If Act 118 would have been constitutional before adoption of the Fourteenth Amendment, it is constitutional now. If the complaining butchers' argument is accepted, states will lose their ability to impose licenses and license fees, regulate dangerous trades or articles, restrain the manufacture of alcohol and lotteries, enact Sunday closing laws and child labor laws.

SUPREME COURT DECISION: 5–4

MILLER, J.

… This statute is denounced not only as creating a monopoly and conferring odious and exclusive privileges upon a small number of persons at the expense of the great body of the community of New Orleans, but it is asserted that it deprives a large and meritorious class of citizens—the whole of the butchers of the city—of the right to exercise their trade, the business to which they have been trained and on which they depend for the support of themselves and their families; and that the unrestricted exercise of the business of butchering is necessary to the daily subsistence of the population of the city.

But a critical examination of the act hardly justifies these assertions.

It is true that it grants, for a period of twenty-five years, exclusive privileges…. But it is not true that it deprives the butchers of the right to exercise their trade, or imposes upon them any restriction incompatible with its successful pursuit, or furnishing the people

of the city with the necessary daily supply of animal food….

The wisdom of the monopoly granted by the legislature may be open to question, but it is difficult to see a justification for the assertion that the butchers are deprived of the right to labor in their occupation, or the people of their daily service in preparing food, or how this statute, with the duties and guards imposed upon the company, can be said to destroy the business of the butcher, or seriously interfere with its pursuit.

The power here exercised by the legislature of Louisiana is, in its essential nature, one which has been, up to the present period in the constitutional history of this country, always conceded to belong to the States, however it may *now* be questioned in some of its details….

Unless, therefore, it can be maintained that the exclusive privilege granted by this charter to the corporation is beyond the power of the legislature of Louisiana, there can be no just exception to the validity of the statute.

And in this respect we are not able to see that these privileges are especially odious or objectionable....

It cannot be denied that the statute under consideration is aptly framed to remove from the more densely populated part of the city, the noxious slaughter-houses, and large and offensive collections of animals necessarily incident to the slaughtering business of a large city, and to locate them where the convenience, health, and comfort of the people require they shall be located. And it must be conceded that the means adopted by the act for this purpose are appropriate, are stringent, and effectual....

The proposition is, therefore, reduced to these terms: Can any exclusive privileges be granted to any of its citizens, or to a corporation, by the legislature of a State?

It may ... be considered as established, that the authority of the legislature of Louisiana to pass the present statute is ample, unless some restraint in the exercise of that power be found in the Constitution of that state or in the amendments to the Constitution of the United States adopted since the date of [previous] decisions....

The plaintiffs in error accepting this issue, allege that the statute is a violation of the Constitution of the United States [in that] ... it abridges the privileges and immunities of citizens of the United States.

This court is thus called upon for the first time to give construction to [this article]....

The first section of the fourteenth article ... opens with a definition of citizenship—not only citizenship of the United States, but citizenship of the States. No such definition was previously found in the Constitution, nor had any attempt been made to define it by act of Congress....

The first observation we have to make on this clause is, ... it declares that persons may be citizens of the United States without regard to their citizenship of a particular State, and it overturns the *Dred Scott* decision by making *all persons* born within the United States and subject to its jurisdiction citizens of the United States. That its main purpose was to establish the citizenship of the negro can admit of no doubt....

The next observation is more important in view of the arguments of counsel in the present case. It is that the distinction between citizenship of the United States and citizenship of a state is clearly recognized and established. Not only may a man be a citizen of the United States without being a citizen of a state, but an important element is necessary to convert the former into the latter. He must reside within the state to make him a citizen of it, but it is only necessary that he should be born or naturalized in the United States to be a citizen of the Union.

It is quite clear, then, that there is a citizenship of the United States, and a citizenship of a State, which are distinct from each other, and which depend upon different characteristics or circumstances in the individual.

We think this distinction and its explicit recognition in this amendment of great weight in this argument, because the next paragraph of the same section, which is the one mainly relied on by the plaintiffs in error, speaks only of privileges and immunities of citizens of the several States. The argument, however, in favor of the plaintiffs rests wholly on the assumption that citizenship is the same, and the privileges and immunities guaranteed by the clause are the same.

The language is, "No State shall make or enforce any law which shall abridge the privileges or immunities of citizens of *the United States*." It is a little remarkable, if this clause was intended as a protection to the citizen of a State against the legislative power of his own State, that the word citizen of the State should be left out when it is so carefully used, and used in contradistinction to citizens of the United States, in the very sentence which precedes it. It is too clear for argument that the change in phraseology was adopted understandingly and with a purpose.

Of the privileges and immunities of the citizen of the United States, and of the privileges and immunities of the citizen of the State, and what they respectively are, we will presently consider; but we wish to state here that it is only the former which are placed by this clause under the protection of the Federal Constitution, and that the latter, whatever they may be, are not intended to have any additional protection by this paragraph of the amendment.

If, then, there is a difference between the privileges and immunities belonging to a citizen of the United States as such, and those belonging to the citizen of the State as such, the latter must rest for their security and protection where they have heretofore rested; for they are not embraced by this paragraph of the amendment....

The first occurrence of the words "privileges and immunities" in our constitutional history is to be found in the fourth of the Articles of the old Confederation.

It declares "That, the better to secure and perpetuate mutual friendship and intercourse among the people of the different states in this Union, the free inhabitants of each of these states, paupers, vagabonds, and fugitives from justice excepted, shall be entitled to all the privileges and immunities of free citizens in the several states; and the people of each state shall enjoy therein all the privileges of trade and commerce, subject to the same duties, impositions, and restrictions as the inhabitants thereof respectively."

In the Constitution of the United States ... the corresponding provision is found in section two of the 4th article, in the following words: The citizens of each state shall be entitled to all the privileges and immunities of citizens of the several states....

Fortunately we are not without judicial construction of this clause of the Constitution....

Its sole purpose was to declare to the several States, that whatever those rights, as you grant or establish them to your own citizens, or as you limit or qualify, or impose restrictions on their exercise, the same, neither more nor less, shall be the measure of the rights of citizens of other States within your jurisdiction.

It would be the vainest show of learning to attempt to prove by citations of authority, that up to the adoption of the recent amendments, no claim or pretence was set up that those rights depended on the Federal government for their existence or protection, beyond the very few express limitations which the Federal Constitution imposed upon the States—such, for instance, as the prohibition against ex post facto laws, bills of attainder, and laws impairing the obligation of contracts. But with the exception of these and a few other restrictions, the entire domain of the privileges and immunities of citizens of the States, as above defined, lay within the constitutional and legislative power of the States, and without that of the Federal government. Was it the purpose of the fourteenth amendment ... to transfer the security and protection of all the civil rights which we have mentioned, from the States to the Federal government?...

We are convinced that no such results were intended by the Congress which proposed these amendments, nor by the legislatures of the States which ratified them.

Having shown that the privileges and immunities relied on in the argument are those which belong to citizens of the States as such, and that they are left to the State governments for security and protection, and not by this article placed under the special care of the Federal government, we may hold ourselves excused from defining the privileges and immunities of citizens of the United States which no State can abridge, until some case involving those privileges may make it necessary to do so.

But lest it should be said that no such privileges and immunities are to be found if those we have been considering are excluded, we venture to suggest some which owe their existence to the Federal government, its National character, its Constitution, or its laws.

One of these is well described in the case of *Crandall v. Nevada* [6 Wallace 35 (1868)]. It is said to be the right of the citizen of this great country, protected by implied guarantees of its Constitution, "to come to the seat of government to assert any claim he may have upon that government, to transact any business he may have with it, to seek its protection, to share its offices, to engage in administering its functions. He has the right of free access to its seaports, through which all operations of foreign commerce are conducted, to the sub-treasuries, land offices, and courts of justice in the several States." And quoting from the language of Chief Justice Taney in another case, it is said "*that for all the great purposes for which the Federal government was established*, we are one people, with one common country, *we are all citizens of the United States*;" and it is, as such citizens, that their rights are supported in this court in *Crandall v. Nevada.*

Another privilege of a citizen of the United States is to demand the care and protection of the Federal government over his life, liberty, and property when on the high seas or within the jurisdiction of a foreign government. Of this there can be no doubt, nor that the right depends upon his character as a citizen of the United States. The right to peaceably assemble and petition for redress of grievances, the privilege of the writ of *habeas corpus*, are rights of the citizen guaranteed by the Federal Constitution. The right to use the navigable waters of the United States, however they may penetrate the territory of the several States, all rights secured to our citizens by treaties with foreign nations are dependent upon citizenship of the United States, and not citizenship of a State. One of these privileges is conferred by the very article under consideration. It is that a citizen of the United States can, of his own volition, become a citizen of any State of the Union by a *bona fide* residence therein, with the same rights as other citizens of that State. To these may be added the rights secured by the thirteenth and fifteenth articles of amendment, and by the other clause of the fourteenth, next to be considered.

But it is useless to pursue this branch of the inquiry, since <u>we are of opinion that the rights claimed by these plaintiffs in error, if they have any existence, are not privileges and immunities of citizens of the United States within the meaning of the clause of the fourteenth amendment under consideration</u>....

The judgments of the Supreme Court of Louisiana in those cases are affirmed.

FIELD, J., CHASE, C.J., SWAYNE AND BRADLEY, J.J., DISSENTING

... No one will deny the abstract justice which lies in the position of the plaintiffs in error; and I shall endeavor to show that the position has some support in the fundamental law of the country.

It is contended in justification for the act in question that it was adopted in the interest of the city, to promote its cleanliness and protect its health, and was the legitimate exercise of what is termed the <u>police power of the State</u>. That power undoubtedly extends to all regulations affecting the health, good order, morals, peace, and safety of society, and is exercised on a great variety of subjects, and in almost numberless ways. <u>All sorts of restrictions and burdens are imposed under it, and when these are not in conflict with any constitutional prohibitions, or fundamental principles, they cannot be successfully assailed in a judicial tribunal.</u> With this power of the State and its legitimate exercise I shall not differ from the majority of the court. But under the pretence of prescribing a police regulation the State cannot be permitted to encroach upon any of the just rights of

the citizen, which the Constitution intended to secure against abridgment....

The act of Louisiana presents the naked case, unaccompanied by any public considerations, where a right to pursue a lawful and necessary calling, previously enjoyed by every citizen, and in connection with which a thousand persons were daily employed, is taken away and vested exclusively for twenty-five years, for an extensive district and a large population, in a single corporation, or its exercise is for that period restricted to the establishments of the corporation, and there allowed only upon onerous conditions....

The question presented is, therefore, one of the gravest importance, not merely to the parties here, but to the whole country. <u>It is nothing less than the question</u> whether the recent amendments to the Federal Constitution protect the citizens of the United States against the deprivation of their common rights by State legislation. In my judgment the fourteenth amendment does afford such protection, and was so intended by the Congress which framed and the States which adopted it....

The amendment does not attempt to confer any new privileges or immunities upon citizens, or to enumerate or define those already existing. It assumes that there are such privileges and immunities which belong of right to citizens as such, and ordains that they shall not be abridged by State legislation. If this inhibition has no reference to privileges and immunities of this character, but only refers, as held by the majority of the court in their opinion, to such privileges and immunities as were before its adoption specially designated in the Constitution or necessarily implied as belonging to citizens of the United States, it was a vain and idle enactment, which accomplished nothing, and most unnecessarily excited Congress and the people on its passage. With privileges and immunities thus designated or implied no State could ever have interfered by its laws, and no new constitutional provision was required to inhibit such interference. The supremacy of the Constitution and the laws of the United States always controlled any State legislation of that character. But if the amendment refers to the natural and inalienable rights which belong to all citizens, the inhibition has a profound significance and consequence.

What, then, are the privileges and immunities which are secured against abridgment by State legislation?...

The privileges and immunities designated in the second section of the fourth article of the Constitution are ... those which of right belong to the citizens of all free governments, and they can be enjoyed under that clause by the citizens of each State in the several States upon the same terms and conditions as they are enjoyed by the citizens of the latter States. No discrimination can be made by one State against the citizens of other States in their enjoyment, nor can any greater imposition be levied than such as is laid upon its own citizens. It is a clause which insures equality in the enjoyment of these rights between citizens of the several States whilst in the same State....

BRADLEY, J., DISSENTING

... Every citizen ... being primarily a citizen of the United States, and, secondarily, a citizen of the State where he resides, what, in general, are the privileges and immunities of a citizen of the United States? Is the right, liberty, or privilege of choosing any lawful employment one of them?

If a State legislature should pass a law prohibiting the inhabitants of a particular township, county, or city, from tanning leather or making shoes, would such a law violate any privileges or immunities of those inhabitants as citizens of the United States, or only their privileges and immunities as citizens of that particular State? Or if a State legislature should pass a law of caste, making all trades and professions, or certain enumerated trades and professions, hereditary, so that no one could follow any such trades or professions except that which was pursued by his father, would such a law violate the privileges and immunities of the people of that State as citizens of the United States, or only as citizens of the State? Would they have no redress but to appeal to the courts of that particular State?

This seems to me to be the essential question before us for consideration. And, in my judgment, the right of any citizen to follow whatever lawful employment he chooses to adopt (submitting himself to all lawful regulations) is one of his most valuable rights, and one which the legislature of a State cannot invade, whether restrained by its own constitution or not.

The right of a State to regulate the conduct of its citizens is undoubtedly a very broad and extensive one, and not to be lightly restricted. But there are certain fundamental rights which this right of regulation cannot infringe. It may prescribe the manner of their exercise, but it cannot subvert the rights themselves.... I speak now of the rights of citizens of any free government....

[E]ven if the Constitution were silent, the fundamental privileges and immunities of citizens, as such, would be no less real and no less inviolable than they now are. It was not necessary to say in words that the citizens of the United States should have and exercise all the privileges of citizens; the privilege of buying, selling, and enjoying property; the privilege of engaging in any lawful employment for a livelihood; the privilege of resorting to the laws for redress of injuries, and the like. Their very citizenship conferred these privileges, if they did not possess them before. And these privileges they would enjoy whether they were citizens of any State or not. Inhabitants of Federal territories and new citizens, made such by annexation of territory or naturalization, though without any status as citizens of a State, could, nevertheless, as citizens of the United States, lay claim to every one of the privileges and immunities which have been enumerated; and among these none is more essential and fundamental than the right to follow such profession or employment as each one may choose, subject only to uniform regulations equally applicable to all....

SWAYNE, J., DISSENTING [OMITTED]

COMMENT

Historian Charles Fairman describes the irony of *The Slaughter-House Cases*:

> One might have supposed that it would be a case on behalf of Negroes, or the suit of some citizen from the North complaining of treatment in the South, that first raised the Fourteenth Amendment at the bar of the Supreme Court. Instead it was a suit by Southern whites, complaining against Carpetbag legislation; the right they would vindicate was not a political but an economic liberty—namely, to carry on the business of slaughtering cattle, free from a monopoly conferred by the legislature upon a favored group of incorporators. This was all out of accord with what the members of Congress had in mind in their debates. (*History of the Supreme Court of the United States, Vol. 6: Reconstruction and Reunion 1864–88*, Part I [New York, NY: Macmillan, 1971], p. 1308)

QUESTIONS

1. What does Justice Miller's *Slaughter-House* interpretation of the Privileges or Immunities Clause imply for the view that the Fourteenth Amendment incorporates the Bill of Rights against the states? Are there similarities between Miller's *Slaughter-House* opinion and *Barron v. Baltimore*?

2. The Butchers' Benevolent Association of New Orleans was represented by former Supreme Court Justice John Campbell. Campbell argued that the concept of citizenship protected by the Fourteenth Amendment "was based on the [Lockean] commitment to securing fundamental rights against all threats, including any from the states. High among these rights, as 'property of a sacred kind,' was the

'right to labor ... and to the product of one's faculties'" (quoted in Rogers Smith, "'One United People': Second-Class Female Citizenship and the American Quest for Community," 1 *Yale Journal of Law & Humanities* [1989]: 229). What privileges or immunities of citizenship pertain to "free labor"?

3. Attorneys for the Butchers' Benevolent Association cited the Thirteenth and Fourteenth Amendments in support of their argument against the monopoly. What principles in those amendments support legal opposition to monopoly? Is it surprising that residents of the former Confederacy would deploy a theory premised on federal supervision of state legislation?

4. Historian Charles Warren observed that between 1870 and 1873 the Court "was receding somewhat from the almost unvaried support which it had theretofore given to Congressional power..." (*The Supreme Court in United States History*, 3 vols. [Boston, MA: Little, Brown and Company, 1923], 3: 255). Warren singled out *The Slaughter-House Cases* as indicating when "the change in the attitude of the Court became most marked" (Ibid., p. 257). What elements in the *Slaughter-House Cases* are "[s]igns of a reaction in favor of the State powers" (Ibid., pp. 255–256)?

COMMENT

The *Slaughter-House Cases* also addressed, for the first time, the meaning of the Fourteenth Amendment Due Process and Equal Protection Clauses. See Volume II, Chapter 5.

THE BILL OF RIGHTS AND THE STATES

Hurtado v. California
110 U.S. 516 (1884)

SETTING

During the 1789 debates in the House of Representatives, James Madison was floor manager for the amendments that eventually were adopted and ratified as the Bill of Rights. Madison argued that aspects of those amendments ought to apply to the states as well as to the national government. In particular, he advocated that "[n]o state violate the equal rights of conscience, of the free-dom of the press, or the trial by jury in criminal cases." In his opinion, the states "are as liable to attack these invaluable privileges as the General Government." Madison's views did not prevail.

After disappointments in cases like *Barron v. Baltimore* and the *Slaughter-House Cases*, advocates of incorporation of the Bill of Rights shifted their focus to the Due Process Clause of the Fourteenth Amendment. Supporters of incorporation argued that the language of the Fourteenth Amendment stating that no State shall "deprive any person of life, liberty, or property, without due process of law" authorized federal courts to "nationalize" specific guaran-tees of the Bill of Rights.

The concept of due process of law traces back to the Magna Charta of 1215. "Chapter 39" of Magna Charta—originally the Articles of the Barons—sealed by King John at Runnymede, England, read: "No free man shall be seized or imprisoned, or stripped of his rights or possessions, or outlawed or exiled, or deprived of his standing in any other way, nor will we proceed with force against him, or send others to do so, except by the lawful judgment of his equals or by the law of the land."

Although Magna Charta did not contain the specific phrase, "due process of law," its underlying norm that government not act arbitrarily served as an inspiration for the American War of Independence, and as one important point of departure for the Fifth Amendment. James Madison, who drafted the Bill of Rights, wrote that no person shall be "deprived of life, liberty, or property, without due process of law." As noted, the Fourteenth Amendment duplicates the language of the Fifth Amendment, requiring the states as well as the national government to adhere to due process of law.

Despite its deep roots in Anglo-American constitutionalism, and its appearance in two constitutional amendments, the meaning and requirements of due process of law have always been ambiguous. In 1878, the Supreme Court held that due process was not derived from a fixed set of procedures, but that its meaning would be determined "by the gradual process of judicial inclusion and exclusion, as the cases presented for decision shall require...." *Davidson v. New Orleans*, 96 U.S. 97. An appeal from a conviction in a California murder case provided the Court with an opportunity to clarify the meaning of due process of law.

Article I, section 8, of the 1879 California constitution provided that "Offenses heretofore required to be prosecuted by indictment, shall be prose-cuted by information, after examination and commitment by a magistrate, or by indictment, with or without such examination and commitment, as may be prescribed by law." An information is a written accusation filed by a prosecu-tor against a person for an alleged criminal offense without a formal grand jury indictment. Several sections of the 1880 California Penal Code were designed to implement that constitutional provision.

In February 1882, the district attorney of Sacramento County filed an infor-mation in the Superior Court of Sacramento County against Joseph Hurtado for the murder of Jose Antonio Stuardo. Hurtado was arraigned and pleaded not guilty. He was tried before a jury, convicted of first-degree murder, and sentenced to death. The Supreme Court of California affirmed his conviction.

In July 1883, the Superior Court of Sacramento County ordered a hearing to set the date for Hurtado's execution. Hurtado's lawyer objected to the carrying out of the judgment against Hurtado on the ground that Hurtado had never been legally indicted. Indictment by information, he argued, violates the Fifth and Fourteenth Amendments.

The Superior Court overruled Hurtado's objections and fixed a date for his execution. Hurtado appealed to the California Supreme Court, which held that his objection to the order fixing his execution was not appealable. Hurtado petitioned the Supreme Court of the United States for a writ of error.

HIGHLIGHTS OF SUPREME COURT ARGUMENTS

BRIEF FOR HURTADO

◆ The Constitution is silent on the method of trial. Therefore, common law principles govern. Historically, the common law has required indictment by grand jury in felony cases. Indictment by information has been allowed only in misdemeanor cases.

◆ The concept of due process could not have been put in the Constitution with the idea that its meaning be subject to the process of expansion and contraction according to the varying judgments of different legislators and judges.

◆ The goal of the Fourteenth Amendment is to guarantee equality of rights under the law and to prevent arbitrary administration of the law. Indictment by grand jury has been recognized for hundreds of years as one of the shields to the liberties of citizens. States should not be permitted to part with institutions founded on the experience of ages granted to the people for their self-protection.

BRIEF FOR CALIFORNIA

◆ The Fifth Amendment is a restriction on the federal government and not on the states.

◆ Due process guarantees no more than a timely procedure to judgment and execution. Due process cannot be said to be the equivalent of guarantees spelled out in the Fifth, Sixth, and Seventh Amendments without rendering those clauses superfluous.

◆ The right to indictment by grand jury was not secured by seventeen states when the Fourteenth Amendment was adopted. The method of indictment traditionally has been a matter of legislative discretion. Indictment by grand jury is not a sacred right, denial of which constitutes a violation of due process of law.

SUPREME COURT DECISION: 7–1

(Field, J., did not participate.)

MATTHEWS, J.

… The question … involves a consideration of what additional restrictions upon the legislative policy of the States has been imposed by the Fourteenth Amendment to the Constitution of the United States….

It is urged upon us … that the claim made in behalf of the plaintiff in error is supported by the decision of this court in *Murray's Lessee v. Hoboken Land & Imp. Co.*, 18 How[ard] 272 [(1856)]. There, Mr. Justice Curtis, delivering the opinion of the court, after showing that due process of law must mean something more than the actual existing law of the land, for otherwise it would be no restraint upon legislative power, proceeds as follows: "To what principle, then, are we to resort to ascertain whether this process, enacted by Congress, is due process? To this the answer must be twofold. We must examine the constitution itself to see whether this process be in conflict with any of its provisions. If not found to be so, we must look to those settled usages and modes of proceeding existing in the common and statute law of England before the emigration of our ancestors, and which are shown not to have been unsuited to their civil and political condition by having been acted on by them after the settlement of this country." This, it is argued, furnishes an indispensable test of what constitutes "due process of law;" that any proceeding otherwise authorized by law, which is not thus sanctioned by usage, or which supersedes and displaces one that is, cannot be regarded as due process of law. But this inference is unwarranted. The real syllabus of the passage quoted is that a process of law, which is not otherwise forbidden, must be taken to be due process of law, if it can show the sanction of settled usage both in England and in this country; but it by no means follows, that nothing else can be due process of law…. [T]o hold that ["settled usage"] is essential to due process of law, would be to deny every quality of the law but its age, and to render it incapable of progress or improvement. It would be to stamp upon our jurisprudence the unchangeableness attributed to the laws of the Medes and Persians….

[F]lexibility and capacity for growth and adaptation is the peculiar boast and excellence of the common law….

The Constitution of the United States was ordained, it is true, by descendants of Englishmen, who inherited the traditions of the English law and history; but it was made for an undefined and expanding future, and for a people gathered, and to be gathered, from many nations and of many tongues; and while we take just pride in the principles and institutions of the common law, we are not to forget that in lands where other systems of jurisprudence prevail, the ideas and processes of civil justice are also not unknown…. There is nothing in *Magna Charta*, rightly construed as a broad charter of public right and law, which ought to exclude the best ideas of all systems and of every age; and as it was the characteristic principle of the common law to draw its inspiration from every fountain of justice, we are not to assume that the sources of its supply have been exhausted. On the contrary, we should expect that the new and various experiences of our own situation and system will mould and shape it into new and not less useful forms....

In this country written constitutions were deemed essential to protect the rights and liberties of the people against the encroachments of power delegated to their governments, and the provisions of *Magna Charta* were incorporated into bills of rights. They were limitations upon all the powers of government, legislative as well as executive and judicial. It necessarily happened, therefore, that as these broad and general maxims of liberty and justice held in our system a different place and performed a different function from their position and office in English constitutional history and law, they would receive and justify a corresponding and more comprehensive interpretation. Applied in England only as guards against executive usurpation and tyranny, here they have become bulwarks also against arbitrary legislation; but in that application, as it would be incongruous to measure and restrict them by the ancient customary English law, they must be held to guaranty, not particular forms of procedure, but the very substance of individual rights to life, liberty, and property. Restraints that could be fastened upon executive authority with precision and detail, might prove obstructive and injurious when imposed on the just and necessary discretion of legislative power; and while, in every instance, laws that violated express and specific injunctions and prohibitions might without embarrassment be judicially declared to be void, yet any general principle or maxim founded on the essential nature of law,

as a just and reasonable expression of the public will, and of government as instituted by popular consent and for the general good, can only be applied to cases coming clearly within the scope of its spirit and purpose, and not to legislative provisions merely establishing forms and modes of attainment....

Such is the often repeated doctrine of this court. In *Munn v. Illinois*, 94 U.S. 113 [(1877)] the chief justice, delivering the opinion of the court, said: "A person has no property, no vested interest, in any rule of the common law. That is only one of the forms of municipal law, and is no more sacred than any other. Rights of property which have been created by the common law cannot be taken away without due process; but the law itself, as a rule of conduct, may be changed at the will or even at the whim of the Legislature, unless prevented by constitutional limitations. Indeed, the great office of statutes is to remedy defects in the common law as they are developed, and to adapt it to the changes of time and circumstances." ... And Mr. Justice Miller, in *Davidson v. New Orleans*, 96 U.S. 97 [(1878)], after showing the difficulty, if not the impossibility, of framing a definition of this constitutional phrase which should be "at once perspicuous, comprehensive, and satisfactory," and thence deducing the wisdom "in the ascertaining of the intent and application of such an important phrase in the federal constitution, by the gradual process of judicial inclusion and exclusion, as the cases presented for decision shall require," says, however, that "it is not possible to hold that a party has, without due process of law, been deprived of his property, when, as regards the issues affecting it, he has by the laws of the state fair trial in a court of justice, according to the modes of proceeding applicable to such a case."...

The same words ["due process of law"] are contained in the Fifth Amendment. That article makes specific and express provision for perpetuating the institution of the grand jury, so far as relates to prosecutions for the more aggravated crimes under the laws of the United States. It declares that "No person shall be held to answer for a capital or otherwise infamous crime, unless on a presentment or indictment of a grand jury, except in cases arising in the land or naval forces, or in the militia when in actual service in time of war or public danger; nor shall any person be subject for the same offense to be twice put in jeopardy of life or limb; nor shall he be compelled in any criminal case to be a witness against himself." It then immediately adds: "nor be deprived of life, liberty, or property without due process of law." According to a recognized canon of interpretation, especially applicable to formal and solemn instruments of constitutional law, we are forbidden to assume, without clear reason to the contrary, that any part of this most important amendment is superfluous. The natural and obvious inference is that, in the sense of the constitution, "due process of law" was not meant or intended to include, ex vi termini, [by force of the term] the institution and procedure of a grand jury in any case. The conclusion is equally irresistible, that when the same phrase was employed in the 14th Amendment to restrain the action of the States, it was used in the same sense and with no greater extent; and that if in the adoption of that amendment it had been part of its purpose to perpetuate the institution of the grand jury in all

the States, it would have embodied, as did the Fifth Amendment, express declarations to that effect....

But it is not to be supposed that ... legislative powers are absolute and despotic, and that the Amendment prescribing due process of law is too vague and indefinite to operate as a practical restraint. It is not every Act, legislative in form, that is law.... Arbitrary power, enforcing its edicts to the injury of the persons and property of its subjects, is not law, whether manifested as the decree of a personal monarch or of an impersonal multitude. And the limitations imposed by our constitutional law upon the action of the governments, both state and national, are essential to the preservation of public and private rights, notwithstanding the representative character of our political institutions. The enforcement of these limitations by judicial process is the device of self-governing communities to protect the rights of individuals and minorities, as well against the power of numbers, as against the violence of public agents transcending the limits of lawful authority, even when acting in the name and wielding the force of the government....

"It must be conceded," said this court, speaking by Mr. Justice Miller, in *Loan Ass'n v. Topeka*, 20 Wall[ace] 655 [(1875)] "that there are such rights in every free government beyond the control of the state. A government which recognized no such rights,—which held the lives, the liberty, and the property of its citizens subject at all times to the absolute disposition and unlimited control of even the most democratic depository of power,—is after all but a despotism."...

It follows that any legal proceeding enforced by public authority, whether sanctioned by age and custom, or newly devised in the discretion of the legislative power in furtherance of the general public good, which regards and preserves these principles of liberty and justice, must be held to be due process of law....

Tried by these principles, we are unable to say that the substitution for a presentment or indictment by a grand jury of the proceeding by information after examination and commitment by a magistrate, certifying to the probable guilt of the defendant, with the right on his part to the aid of counsel, and to the cross-examination of the witnesses produced for the prosecution, is not due process of law....

For these reasons, finding no error therein, the judgment of the supreme court of California is affirmed.

HARLAN, J., DISSENTING

... "Due process of law," within the meaning of the National Constitution, does not import one thing with reference to the powers of the States and another with reference to the powers of the General Government. If particular proceedings, conducted under the authority of the General Government, and involving life, are prohibited because not constituting that due process of law required by the Fifth Amendment of the constitution of the United States, similar proceedings, conducted under the authority of a State, must be deemed illegal, as not being due process of law within the meaning of the Fourteenth Amendment. What, then, is the meaning of the words "due process of law," in the latter amendment?

In seeking that meaning we are, fortunately, not left without authoritative directions as to the source, and the only source, from which the necessary information is to be obtained....

[A]ccording to the settled usages and modes of proceeding existing under the common and statute law of England at the settlement of this country, information in capital cases was not consistent with the "law of the land" or with "due process of law." Such was the understanding of the patriotic men who established free institutions upon this continent. Almost the identical words of *Magna Charta* were incorporated into most of the State Constitutions before the adoption of our National Constitution. When they declared, in substance, that no person shall be deprived of life, liberty, or property except by the judgment of his peers or the law of the land, they intended to assert his right to the same guaranties that were given in the mother country by the great charter and the laws passed in furtherance of its fundamental principles....

[T]he reasoning of the opinion indubitably leads to the conclusion that but for the specific provisions made in the constitution for the security of the personal rights enumerated, the general inhibition against deprivation of life, liberty, and property without due process of law would not have prevented congress from enacting a statute in derogation of each of them.

Still further; it results from the doctrines of the opinion, if I do not misapprehend its scope, that the clause of the Fourteenth Amendment forbidding the deprivation of life or liberty without due process of law would not be violated by a state regulation dispensing with petit juries in criminal cases, and permitting a person charged with a crime involving life to be tried before a single judge, or even a justice of the peace, upon a rule to show cause why he should not be hanged....

It seems to me that too much stress is put upon the fact that the framers of the Constitution made express provision for the security of those rights which at common law were protected by the requirement of due process of law, and, in addition, declared, generally, that no person shall "be deprived of life, liberty, or property without due process of law." The rights, for the security of which these express provisions were made, were of a character so essential to the safety of the people that it was deemed wise to avoid the possibility that Congress, in regulating the processes of law, would impair or destroy them. Hence, their specific enumeration in the earlier amendments of the constitution, in connection with the general requirement of due process of law, the latter itself being broad enough to cover every right of life, liberty, or property secured by the settled usages and modes of proceedings existing under the common and statute law of England at the time our government was founded....

It is said by the court that the Constitution of the United States was made for an undefined and expanding future, and that its requirement of due process of law, in proceedings involving life, liberty, and property, must be so interpreted as not to deny to the law the capacity of progress and improvement; that the greatest security for the fundamental principles of justice resides in the right of the people to make their own laws and alter them at pleasure. It is difficult, however, to perceive anything in the system of prosecuting human beings for their lives, by information, which suggests that the State which adopts it has entered upon an era of progress and improvement in the law of criminal procedure.... Under the local statutes in question, even the district attorney of the county is deprived of any discretion in the premises; for if in the judgment of the magistrate before whom the accused is brought—and, generally, he is only a justice of the peace—a public offense has been committed, it becomes the duty of the district attorney to proceed against him, by information, for the offense indicated by the committing magistrate. Thus, in California nothing stands between the citizen and prosecution for his life except the judgment of a justice of the peace....

When the Fourteenth Amendment was adopted all the States of the Union, some in terms, all substantially, declared, in their Constitutions, that no person shall be deprived of life, liberty, or property otherwise than "by the judgment of his peers or the law of the land," or "without due process of law."... Now, it is a fact of momentous interest in this discussion, that, when the Fourteenth Amendment was submitted and adopted, the Bill of Rights and the Constitutions of twenty-seven states expressly forbade criminal prosecutions, by information, for capital cases; while in the remaining ten States such prosecutions were impliedly forbidden by a general clause declaring that no person should be deprived of life otherwise than by "the judgment of his peers or the law of the land," or "without due process of law." It may be safely affirmed that, *when that amendment was adopted*, a criminal prosecution, by information, for a crime involving life, was not permitted in any one of the States composing the Union. So that the court, in this case, while conceding that the requirement of due process of law protects the fundamental principles of liberty and justice, adjudges, in effect, that an immunity or right, recognized at the common law to be essential to personal security, jealously guarded by our National Constitution against violation by any tribunal or body exercising authority under the general government, and expressly or impliedly recognized, when the Fourteenth Amendment was adopted, in the Bill of Rights or Constitution of every State in the Union, is yet not a fundamental principle in governments established, as those of the States of the Union are, to secure to the citizen liberty and justice, and therefore is not involved in due process of law as required by that amendment in proceedings conducted under the sanction of a State. My sense of duty constrains me to dissent from this interpretation of the supreme law of the land.

QUESTIONS

1. In *Hurtado*, Justice Matthews held that, because the Fifth Amendment expressly includes both the grand jury requirement and the due process guarantee, the grand jury requirement cannot be included (incorporated) as one element of the Fourteenth Amendment Due Process Clause. His position exemplifies a rule of judicial construction referred to as the "doctrine of nonsuperfluousness." According to that doctrine, judges should not interpret language to include an enumerated guarantee within a more general protection, because to do so renders the enumerated guarantee superfluous. Is Justice Matthews's opinion or Justice Harlan's dissenting view more persuasive on the subject of how to read the requirements of the Due Process Clause of the Fourteenth Amendment?

2. Counsel for Hurtado argued that, because the Fifth Amendment to the Constitution of the *United States* grants persons a specific protection, such as indictment by grand jury, the Constitution of the United States prohibits *states* from discarding such practices. Why does it follow that the Constitution of the United States binds the states? How does the concept of "due process" figure in Hurtado's position?

3. Arguing for state innovation in criminal procedures, Justice Matthews maintained that "to deny every quality of the law but its age ... [stamps] our jurisprudence [with] unchangeableness...." Where do the limits of state innovation end and the beginning of arbitrary state power begin? Does Matthews use due process to abdicate judicial responsibility?

4. Does Justice Matthews's opinion in *Hurtado* contain the rudiments of a doctrinal basis for federal courts declaring that some guarantees of the Bill of Rights bind the States but that others do not?

5. In *Chicago, Burlington, & Quincy Railroad v. City of Chicago*, 166 U.S.

226 (1897), the Court applied the Takings Clause of the Fifth Amendment against the states, thereby overruling one aspect of *Barron v. Baltimore*. Three years later, the Court reaffirmed *Hurtado* in *Maxwell v. Dow*, 176 U.S. 581 (1900), upholding a state court conviction reached by an eight-person jury. The justices ruled that the right to be tried by a jury of twelve persons is not guaranteed by the Due Process Clause of the Fourteenth Amendment. Justice Harlan dissented in *Maxwell*: "If ... the 'due process of law' required by the Fourteenth Amendment does not allow a state to take private property without just compensation, but does allow the life or liberty of the citizen to be taken in a mode that is repugnant to the settled usages and the modes of proceeding authorized at the time the Constitution was adopted and which was expressly forbidden in the national Bill of Rights, it would seem that the protection of private property is of more consequence than the protection of the life and liberty of the citizen."

Is Harlan correct that the Court's due process of law jurisprudence in this era was characterized by a double standard?

THE BILL OF RIGHTS AND THE STATES

Palko v. Connecticut
302 U.S. 319 (1937)

SETTING

Even though the Court in *Hurtado v. California* refused to hold that the Due Process Clause of the Fourteenth Amendment incorporated against the states the Fifth Amendment guarantee of indictment by a grand jury, the *Hurtado* opinion did declare that "[a]bitrary power ... is not law," and that constitutional limitations "are essential to the preservation of public and private rights." Justice Matthews wrote: "The enforcement of these limitations by judicial process is the device of self-governing communities to protect the rights of individuals and minorities, as well against the power of numbers, as against the violence of public agents...."

Nonetheless, in the early twentieth century, the Court continued to follow *Hurtado*, refraining from taking jurisdiction in cases involving criminal justice guarantees derived from the Bill of Rights. As noted in question #5 following *Hurtado*, the Court reaffirmed that opinion in 1900 in upholding a Utah law that provided for an eight-person jury despite the traditional federal requirement that the Sixth Amendment right to trial "by an impartial jury" meant a jury of twelve. *Maxwell v. Dow*, 176 U.S. 581. Eight years later, the Court refused to censure a state trial judge's remark that ran counter to the guarantee in the Fifth Amendment that no person be compelled to be a witness against himself. The trial judge had called attention to the fact that criminal defendants had refused to testify at trial in their own behalf. *Twining v. New Jersey*, 211 U.S. 78 (1908). If a federal judge had made such a comment, it probably would have been held to violate the Fifth Amendment protection against self- incrimination.

Despite rejecting the specific claims in *Hurtado*, *Maxwell* and *Twining*, the Court in these and other cases adhered to the principle that due process requires "fairness." By the end of the nineteenth century, the court had by implication ruled that the Eighth Amendment applies against the states, because it held that execution by electrocution is not a form of "cruel and unusual punishment." *In re Kemmler*, 135 U.S. 436 (1890). In 1897, recall, the Court applied the Fifth Amendment's Takings Clause against the states in *Chicago, Burlington, & Quincy Railroad v. City of Chicago*, 166 U.S. 226 (see pp. 672–673). In 1925, the Court ruled that some First Amendment "rights and 'liberties,'" including speech and press, are so "fundamental" that they are protected by the Fourteenth Amendment from impairment by the states. *Gitlow v. New York*, 268 U.S. 652, a view repeated in *Near v. Minnesota*, 283 U.S. 697, 1931. In 1932, the Court held that in some circumstances—such as a criminal trial for a capital offense in a racially hostile environment—the need for legal counsel is so great that failure of a trial court to appoint effective counsel violates due process. *Powell v. Alabama*, 287 U.S. 45 (1932).

The doctrinal confusion resulting from holdings such as these virtually invited litigants to bring cases in an effort to force the Court to articulate the standards that govern the determination of which (if not all) of the provisions of the Bill of Rights apply against the states through the Due Process Clause of the Fourteenth Amendment. Criminal cases from state courts were likely candidates because so many provisions of the Bill of Rights relate to the conduct of criminal proceedings.

Frank Palko was indicted by a grand jury for the 1935 premeditated murder of Thomas Kearney in Bridgeport, Connecticut. He was charged with first-degree murder but, following a jury trial in Fairfield County Superior Court, was convicted of second-degree murder and sentenced to life in prison. A Connecticut statute adopted in 1886 allowed the state, with the permission of the trial judge, to appeal all questions of law arising in the trial of criminal cases.

The state appealed to the Connecticut Supreme Court of Errors, claiming that the trial judge in Palko's case erred by (1) excluding testimony about a confession that Palko allegedly had made; (2) excluding testimony on cross-examination of Palko to impeach his credibility; and (3) imprecisely instructing the jury about the difference between first- and second-degree murder.

These errors, Connecticut contended, led to Palko's conviction for second-degree murder rather than first-degree murder. The Supreme Court of Errors agreed that the trial judge had committed reversible errors prejudicial to the prosecution and ordered a new trial.

Before the commencement of his second trial, Palko moved to have the indictment dismissed on the ground that the second trial subjected him to double jeopardy in violation of the Fourteenth Amendment of the Constitution of the United States. His motion was denied. Palko was convicted of first-degree murder at his second trial and sentenced to death by electrocution. He appealed his conviction to the Supreme Court of Errors, which affirmed. Palko appealed to the Supreme Court of the United States.

HIGHLIGHTS OF SUPREME COURT ARGUMENTS

BRIEF FOR PALKO

◆ The Connecticut statute that allows Palko to be tried twice for the same offense placed him twice in jeopardy. The verdict in Palko's first trial was an acquittal on the first-degree murder charge. Forcing Palko to stand trial a second time on the same charge exposed him to double jeopardy, which is prohibited by the Fifth Amendment.

◆ The right against double jeopardy is such a fundamental and immutable principle of law that it falls within the protection of both the Due Process and Privileges or Immunities Clauses of the Fourteenth Amendment.

◆ The Court should consider the historical analysis in Horace Edgar Flack's book, *The Adoption of the Fourteenth Amendment* (Baltimore, MD: The Johns Hopkins University Press, 1908), showing that the drafters of the Fourteenth Amendment intended to make the first eight amendments to the federal constitution applicable to the states.

BRIEF FOR CONNECTICUT

◆ The definition of double jeopardy in a criminal prosecution is a matter of judicial construction by state courts. Little will be left to the powers of the states to administer criminal law if any ruling by state courts becomes a federal question.

◆ Rights under the common law—such as those embodied in the first ten amendments to the Constitution—are not privileges relating to national citizenship referred to in the Fourteenth Amendment. The fact that the rule against double jeopardy was established at common law does not mean that the right is a fundamental principle of justice for due process purposes. Other rights recognized at common law, including the right to presentment by a grand jury and right to a jury trial in civil cases, have not been made applicable against the states by the Fourteenth Amendment.

SUPREME COURT DECISION: 8–1

CARDOZO, J.

The argument for appellant is that whatever is forbidden by the Fifth Amendment is forbidden by the Fourteenth also....

His thesis is even broader. Whatever would be a violation of the original bill of rights (Amendments 1 to 8) if done by the federal government is now equally unlawful by force of the Fourteenth Amendment if done by a state. There is no such general rule.

The Fifth Amendment provides, among other things, that no person shall be held to answer for a capital or otherwise infamous crime unless on presentment or indictment of a grand jury. This court has held that, in prosecutions by a state, presentment or indictment by a grand jury may give way to informations at the instance of a public officer.... The Fifth Amendment provides also that no person shall be compelled in any criminal case to be a witness against himself. This court has said that, in prosecutions by a state, the exemption will fail if the state elects to end it.... The Sixth Amendment calls for a jury trial in criminal cases and the Seventh for a jury trial in civil cases at common law where the value in controversy shall exceed $20. This court has ruled that consistently with those amendments trial by jury may be modified by a state or abolished altogether....

On the other hand, the due process clause of the Fourteenth Amendment may make it unlawful for a state to abridge by its statutes the freedom of speech which the First Amendment safeguards against encroachment by the Congress, ... or the like freedom of the press, ... or the free exercise of religion, ... or the right of peaceable assembly, without which speech would be unduly trammeled, ... or the right of one accused of crime to the benefit of counsel.... In these and other situations immunities that are valid as against the federal government by force of the specific pledges of particular amendments have been found to be implicit in the concept of ordered liberty, and thus, through the Fourteenth Amendment, become valid as against the states.

The line of division may seem to be wavering and broken if there is a hasty catalogue of the cases on the one side and the other. Reflection and analysis will induce a different view. There emerges the perception of a rationalizing principle which gives to discrete instances a proper order and coherence. The right to trial by jury and the immunity from prosecution except as the result of an indictment may have value and importance. Even so, they are not of the very essence of a scheme of ordered liberty. To abolish them is not to violate a "principle of justice so rooted in the traditions and conscience of our people as to be ranked as fundamental." *Snyder v. Massachusetts*, 291 U.S. 97 [(1934)].... Few would be so narrow or provincial as to maintain that a fair and enlightened system of justice would be impossible without them. What is true of jury trials and indictments is true also, as the cases show, of the immunity from compulsory self-incrimination.... This too might be lost, and justice still be done. Indeed, today as in the past there are students of our penal system who look upon the immunity as a mischief rather than a benefit, and who would limit its scope, or destroy it altogether. No doubt there would remain the need to give protection against torture, physical or mental.... Justice, however, would not perish if the accused were subject to a duty to respond to orderly inquiry. The exclusion of these immunities and privileges from the privileges and immunities protected against the action of the States has not been arbitrary or casual. It has been dictated by a study and appreciation of the meaning, the essential implications, of liberty itself.

We reach a different plane of social and moral values when we pass to the privileges and immunities that have been taken over from the earlier articles of the Federal Bill of Rights and brought within the Fourteenth Amendment by a process of absorption. These in their origin were effective against the federal government alone. If the Fourteenth Amendment has absorbed them, the process of absorption has had its source in the belief that neither liberty nor justice would exist if they were sacrificed.... This is true, for illustration, of freedom of thought and speech. Of that freedom one may say that it is the matrix, the indispensable condition, of nearly every other form of freedom. With rare aberrations a pervasive recognition of that truth can be traced in our history, political and legal. So it has come about that the domain of liberty, withdrawn by the Fourteenth Amendment from encroachment by the states, has been enlarged by latter-day judgments to include liberty of the mind as well as liberty of action....

Is that kind of double jeopardy to which the statute has subjected [appellant] a hardship so acute and shocking that our policy will not endure it? Does it violate those "fundamental principles of liberty and justice which lie at the base of all our civil and political institutions"?... The answer surely must be "no." What the answer would have to be if the state were permitted after a trial free from error to try the accused over again or to bring another case against him, we have no occasion to consider. We deal with the statute before us and no other. The state is not attempting to wear the accused out by a multitude of cases with accumulated trials. It asks no more than this, that the case against him shall go on until there shall be a trial free from the corrosion of substantial legal error.... This is not cruelty at all, nor even vexation in any immoderate degree. If the trial had been infected with error adverse to the accused, there might have been review at his instance, and as often as necessary to purge the vicious taint. A reciprocal privilege, subject at all times to the discretion of the presiding judge, has now been granted to the state. There is here no seismic innovation. The edifice of justice stands, its symmetry, to many, greater than before....

The judgment is affirmed.

BUTLER, J., DISSENTED WITHOUT OPINION

QUESTIONS

1. Justice Cardozo ruled in *Palko* that criminal procedural guarantees are not so essential to "a scheme of ordered liberty" as to be subject to federal court jurisdiction. What criteria should justices use in deciding which guarantees in the Bill of Rights are "essential" or

"nonessential?" Are not all rights in the Bill of Rights equally "essential" or "nonessential"?

2. Does the Court in *Palko* adopt a prudential rule designed to protect judicial authority, does it fashion a constitutional rule required by the Fourteenth Amendment, or both?

3. In what ways does the Court's view of due process in *Palko* resemble its view in *Hurtado v. California*? Does the Court's reluctance to formulate predictable federal procedural rules advance state interests?

4. Dissenting in *Griswold v. Connecticut*, 381 U.S. 479 (1965), Justice Hugo Black wrote: "[o]ne of the most effective ways of diluting or expanding a constitutionally guaranteed right is to substitute for the crucial word or words of a constitutional guarantee another word or words, more or less flexible and more or less restricted in meaning...." Does Black's criticism of justices substituting their own formulation(s) in lieu of undertaking constitutional analysis apply to *Palko*? To *Hurtado*?

5. In footnote #4 to *United States v. Carolene Products*, 304 U.S. 144 (1938), the Court declared:

> There may be narrower scope for operation of the presumption of constitutionality when legislation appears on its face to be within a specific prohibition of the Constitution, such as those of the first ten amendments, which are deemed equally specific when held to be embraced within the Fourteenth. See *Stromberg v. California*, 283 U.S. 359 [1931]; *Lovell v. Griffin*, 303 U.S. 444 [1938].
>
> It is unnecessary to consider now whether legislation which restricts those political processes which can ordinarily be expected to bring about repeal of undesirable legislation, is to be subjected to more exacting judicial scrutiny under the general prohibitions of the Fourteenth Amendment than are most other types of legislation. On restrictions upon the right to vote, see *Nixon v. Herndon*, 273 U.S. 536 [1927], *Nixon v. Condon*, 286 U.S. 73 [1932]; on restraints upon the dissemination of information, see *Near v. Minnesota*, 283 U.S. 697 [1931], *Grosjean v. American Press Co.*, 297 U.S. 233 [1936], *Lovell v. Griffin*; on interferences with political organizations, see *Stromberg v. California*, *Fiske v. Kansas*, 274 U.S. 380 [1927], *Whitney v. California*, 274 U.S. 357 [1927], *Herndon v. Lowry*, 301 U.S. 242 [1937], and see Holmes, J., in *Gitlow v. New York*, 268 U.S. 652 [1925]; as to prohibition of peaceable assembly, see *De Jonge* [sic] *v. Oregon*, 299 U.S. 353 [1937].
>
> Nor need we enquire whether similar considerations enter into the review of statutes directed at particular religious, *Pierce v. Society of Sisters*, 268 U.S. 510 [1925], or national, *Meyer v. Nebraska*, 262 U.S. 390 [1923], *Bartels v. Iowa*, 262 U.S. 404 [1923], *Farrington v. Tokushige*, 273 U.S. 284 [1927], or racial minorities. *Nixon v. Herndon*, *Nixon v. Condon*: whether prejudice against discrete and insular minorities may be a special condition, which tends seriously to curtail the operation of those political processes ordinarily to be relied upon to protect minorities, and which may call for a corre-

spondingly more searching judicial inquiry. Compare *McCulloch v. Maryland*, 4 Wheat[on] 316 [1819]; *South Carolina State Highway Department v. Barnwell Bros.*, 303 U.S. 177 [1938], note 2, and cases cited.

This *Carolene Products* footnote is often cited as the origin of the "preferred position" approach to the Bill of Rights. The preferred position holds that because the First Amendment's guarantees are so essential to "those political processes" required to maintain democracy, laws infringing on rights such as freedom of speech and press must be shown not merely to have a rational basis, but also to be justified by overwhelmingly conclusive considerations. Is the reasoning in *Palko* consistent with footnote #4?

COMMENT

Thirty-one years after Frank Palko was executed by the state of Connecticut, the Supreme Court incorporated the right against double jeopardy against the states in *Benton v. Maryland*, 395 U.S. 784 (1969).

THE BILL OF RIGHTS AND THE STATES

Adamson v. California
332 U.S. 46 (1947)

SETTING

On August 24, 1944, a black male named Admiral Dewey Adamson was arrested in Los Angeles, California and charged with the murder of sixty-four-year-old Stella Blauvelt, a white female. Blauvelt's body had been found on the floor of her Los Angeles apartment about a month before Adamson's arrest. Her body was face upward covered with two bloodstained pillows and a lamp cord was wrapped tightly around the neck three times and tied in a knot. Bruises on the hands and face indicated that Blauvelt had been severely beaten before her death. Testing revealed that she had been murdered the day before, in broad daylight.

Adamson was charged by information with first-degree murder and burglary. The charging instrument also stated that Adamson had been convicted in the 1920s for burglary, larceny, and robbery. Adamson admitted to the earlier convictions, which under California law barred the prosecution from mentioning those convictions at his trial for Blauvelt's murder. However, Article I, section 13, of the California Constitution provided:

> But in any criminal case, whether the defendant testifies or not, his failure to explain or to deny by his testimony any evidence or facts in the case against him may be commented upon by the court and by counsel and may be considered by the court or by the jury.

Thus, Adamson faced a dilemma: If he took the stand during the murder trial, evidence of his prior convictions could be used to impeach the credibility of his testimony; if he did not take the stand in his own defense, California law allowed the prosecution to comment on his silence.

Adamson was tried in a California Superior Court. At trial, an expert testified that scotch tape that he had removed from a door to the garbage compartment of the kitchen of Blauvelt's apartment contained six latent fingerprints that corresponded with Adamson's fingerprints. The door was found unhinged, leaning against the kitchen sink. Adamson could have entered the apartment through the garbage compartment. Testimony also revealed that during the investigation of the murder, the tops of three women's stockings were found in and on the dresser in Adamson's room. The stockings were not all the same color, and each was knotted. Blauvelt's body did not have any shoes or stockings on it. However, it appeared that on the day she was murdered, Blauvelt had been wearing stockings and the lower part of a silk stocking with the top torn off was laying on the floor under her body. None of the stocking tops found in Adamson's room matched that piece of stocking.

Testimony at trial also revealed that Blauvelt was in the habit of wearing large diamond rings and that she was wearing them on the day she died. None of them was found. A witness for the state positively identified Adamson, stating that at some time between August 10 and 14, 1944, she overheard Adamson ask an unidentified person if he was interested in buying a diamond ring. However, no testimony directly linked Adamson to Blauvelt's murder, none of her belongings was found in his possession, and no one saw a black man in her apartment or in her apartment house on the day of the murder.

Although he consistently denied murdering Blauvelt, Adamson did not take the witness stand at his trial and rested his case without putting on any evidence. During closing argument to the jury, the prosecutor commented at least seven times about Adamson's failure to testify. Among his comments were:

> The defendant has not taken the stand; he has not denied that [he was identified as having offered a diamond ring for sale]; it is uncontradicted in the testimony. There he sits, not getting on the stand, not giving you what his version of the situation is. You have got the right, members of this jury, to consider the fact and consider that four hundred and some odd pages of testimony are uncontradicted from the lips of this defendant.

At the close of his argument, the prosecutor stated:

> In conclusion, I am going to just make this one statement to you: Counsel asks you to find this defendant not guilty. But does the defendant get on the stand and say, under oath, 'I am not guilty'? Not one word from him, and not one word from a single witness.

The judge's jury instructions included the comment that "It is the right of court and counsel to comment on the failure of defendant to explain or deny any evidence against him, and to comment on the evidence, the testimony and credibility of any witness...."

The jury convicted Adamson of first-degree murder and of first-degree burglary. He was sentenced to death. He moved for a new trial on the ground that Article I, section 13, of the California Constitution was an unconstitutional infringement on his rights under the Due Process Clause of the Fifth Amendment to the Constitution of the United States, and the Privileges or Immunities Clause of the Fourteenth Amendment. That motion was denied. Adamson then appealed to the California Supreme Court, which affirmed his conviction and rejected his federal constitutional challenge to the state constitution. Adamson appealed to the Supreme Court of the United States.

HIGHLIGHTS OF SUPREME COURT ARGUMENTS

BRIEF FOR ADAMSON

◆ Article I, section 13, of the California Constitution violates due process under the Constitution of the United States because it amounts to testimonial compulsion and that silence in court is tantamount to an admission of guilt. The right not to be compelled to testify against one's self is fundamental.

◆ Article I, section 13, offends the procedural safeguards guaranteed by the Fourteenth Amendment to fair public trials.

◆ The stockings found in Adamson's apartment were improperly admitted at trial. The prosecution conceded that they were not part of the stocking found under the body and their introduction furnished an additional motive for the crime—a sexual one. The mere suggestion of such a motive was calculated to excite the prejudices of the jury, because Adamson is black and Blauvelt was white.

BRIEF FOR CALIFORNIA

◆ It is true that the Constitution of the United States and most state constitutions guarantee that no person in a criminal trial shall be compelled to testify against himself. However, the right given to prosecutors and judges to comment on a defendant's failure to explain or deny evidence or facts against him does not violate the Fourteenth Amendment and is a right recognized in many states.

◆ California courts have ruled that it was not the intent of Article I, section 13, to shift the burden of proof in a criminal case. The prosecution still must prove guilt beyond a reasonable doubt.

◆ This Court in *Twining v. New Jersey*, 211 U.S. 78 (1908) rejected the proposition that the privilege against self-incrimination was incorporated against the states by the Fourteenth Amendment. That case is controlling here.

◆ The Fourteenth Amendment Due Process Clause does not guarantee that the decisions of state courts shall be free of error or that every ruling during a trial shall be correct. In this case, the highest court of the state concluded that admission of portions of women's stockings found in Adamson's room was competent evidence and that it was not introduced to inflame the passions of the jury.

SUPREME COURT DECISION: 5–4

REED, J.

... We shall assume, but without any intention thereby of ruling upon the issue, that state permission by law to the court, counsel and jury to comment upon and consider the failure of defendant "to explain or to deny by his testimony any evidence or facts in the case against him" would infringe defendant's privilege against self-incrimination under the Fifth Amendment if this were a trial in a court of the United States under a similar law. Such an assumption does not determine appellant's rights under the Fourteenth Amendment. It is settled law that the clause of the Fifth Amendment, protecting a person against being compelled to be a witness against himself, is not made effective by the Fourteenth Amendment as a protection against state action on the ground that freedom from testimonial compulsion is a right of national citizenship, or because it is a personal privilege or immunity secured by the Federal Constitution as one of the rights of man that are listed in the Bill of Rights....

After declaring that state and national citizenship co-exist in the same person, the Fourteenth Amendment forbids a state from abridging the privileges and immunities of citizens of the United States. As a matter of words, this leaves a state free to abridge, within the limits of the due process clause, the privileges and immunities flowing from state citizenship. This reading of the Federal Constitution has heretofore found favor with the majority of this Court as a natural and logical interpretation. It accords with the constitutional doctrine of federalism by leaving to the states the responsibility of dealing with the privileges and immunities of their citizens except those inherent in national citizenship. It is the construction placed upon the amendment by justices whose own experience had given them contemporaneous knowledge of the purposes that led to the adoption of the Fourteenth Amendment. This construction has become embedded in our federal system as a functioning element in preserving the balance between national and state power. We reaffirm the conclusion of the *Twining* [*v. New Jersey*, 211 U.S. 78 (1908)] and *Palko* [*v. Connecticut*] cases that protection against self-incrimination is not a privilege or immunity of national citizenship.

Appellant ... contends that if the privilege against self-incrimination is not a right protected by the privileges and immunities clause of the Fourteenth Amendment against state action, this privilege, to its full scope under the Fifth Amendment, inheres in the right to a fair trial. A right to a fair trial is a right admittedly protected by the due process clause of the Fourteenth Amendment. Therefore, appellant argues, the due process clause of the Fourteenth Amendment protects his privilege against self-incrimination. The due process clause of the Fourteenth Amendment, however, does not draw all the rights of the federal Bill of Rights under its protection. That contention was made and rejected in *Palko v. Connecticut*....

For a state to require testimony from an accused is not necessarily a breach of a state's obligation to give a fair trial. Therefore, we must examine the effect of the California law applied in this trial to see whether the comment on failure to testify violates the protection against state action that the due process clause does grant to an accused. The due process clause forbids compulsion to testify by fear of hurt, torture or exhaustion. It forbids any other type of coercion that falls within the scope of due process. California follows Anglo-American legal tradition in excusing defendants in criminal prosecutions from compulsory testimony.... That is a matter of legal policy and not because of the requirements of due process under the Fourteenth Amendment. So our inquiry is directed, not at the broad question of the constitutionality of compulsory testimony from the accused under the due process clause, but to the constitutionality of the provision of the

California law that permits comment upon his failure to testify. It is, of course, logically possible that while an accused might be required, under appropriate penalties, to submit himself as a witness without a violation of due process, comment by judge or jury on inferences to be drawn from his failure to testify, in jurisdictions where an accused's privilege against self-incrimination is protected, might deny due process. For example, a statute might declare that a permitted refusal to testify would compel an acceptance of the truth of the prosecution's evidence.

Generally, comment on the failure of an accused to testify is forbidden in American jurisdictions. This arises from state constitutional or statutory provisions similar in character to the federal provisions. California, however, is one of a few states that permit limited comment upon a defendant's failure to testify. That permission is narrow. The California law ... authorizes comment by court and counsel upon the "failure of the defendant to explain or to deny by his testimony any evidence or facts in the case against him." This does not involve any presumption, rebuttable or irrebuttable, either of guilt or of the truth of any fact, that is offered in evidence.... It allows inferences to be drawn from proven facts. Because of this clause, the court can direct the jury's attention to whatever evidence there may be that a defendant could deny and the prosecution can argue as to inferences that may be drawn from the accused's failure to testify.... There is here no lack of power in the trial court to adjudge and no denial of a hearing. California has prescribed a method for advising the jury in the search for truth. However sound may be the legislative conclusion that an accused should not be compelled in any criminal case to be a witness against himself, we see no reason why comment should not be made upon his silence. It seems quite natural that when a defendant has opportunity to deny or explain facts and determines not to do so, the prosecution should bring out the strength of the evidence by commenting upon defendant's failure to explain or deny it. The prosecution evidence may be of facts that may be beyond the knowledge of the accused. If so, his failure to testify would have little if any weight. But the facts may be such as are necessarily in the knowledge of the accused. In that case a failure to explain would point to an inability to explain....

The purpose of due process is not to protect an accused against a proper conviction but against an unfair conviction. When evidence is before a jury that threatens conviction, it does not seem unfair to require him to choose between leaving the adverse evidence unexplained and subjecting himself to impeachment through disclosure of former crimes....

We find no other error that gives ground for our intervention in California's administration of criminal justice.

Affirmed.

FRANKFURTER, J., CONCURRING

... Between the incorporation of the Fourteenth Amendment into the Constitution and the beginning of the present membership of the Court—a period of 70 years—the scope of that Amendment was passed upon by 43 judges. Of all these judges, only one, who may respectfully be called an eccentric exception, ever indicated the belief that the Fourteenth Amendment was a shorthand summary of the first eight Amendments theretofore limiting only the Federal Government, and that due process incorporated those eight Amendments as restrictions upon the powers of the States. Among these judges were not only those who would have to be included among the greatest in the history of the Court, but—it is especially relevant to note—they included those whose services in the cause of human rights and the spirit of freedom are the most conspicuous in our history. It is not invidious to single out Miller, Davis, Bradley, Waite, Matthews, Gray, Fuller, Holmes, Brandeis, Stone, and Cardozo (to speak only of the dead) as judges who were alert in safeguarding and promoting the interests of liberty and human dignity through law. But they were also judges mindful of the relation of our federal system to a progressively democratic society and therefore duly regardful of the scope of authority that was left to the States even after the Civil War. And so they did not find that the Fourteenth Amendment, concerned as it was with matters fundamental to the pursuit of justice, fastened upon the States' procedural arrangements which, in the language of Mr. Justice Cardozo, only those who are "narrow or provincial" would deem essential to "a fair and enlightened system of justice." *Palko v. Connecticut*....

The short answer to the suggestion that the provision of the Fourteenth Amendment, which ordains "nor shall any State deprive any person of life, liberty, or property, without due process of law," was a way of saying that every State must thereafter initiate prosecutions through indictment by a grand jury, must have a trial by a jury of 12 in criminal cases, and must have trial by such a jury in common law suits where the amount in controversy exceeds $20, is that it is a strange way of saying it. It would be extraordinarily strange for a Constitution to convey such specific commands in such a roundabout and inexplicit way.... Arguments that may now be adduced to prove that the first eight Amendments were concealed within the historic phrasing of the Fourteenth Amendment were not unknown at the time of its adoption. A surer estimate of their bearing was possible for judges at the time than distorting distance is likely to vouchsafe. Any evidence of design or purpose not contemporaneously known could hardly have influenced those who ratified the Amendment. Remarks of a particular proponent of the Amendment, no matter how influential, are not to be deemed part of the Amendment. What was submitted for ratification was his proposal, not his speech. Thus, at the time of the ratification of the Fourteenth Amendment the constitutions of nearly half of the ratifying States did not have the rigorous requirements of the Fifth Amendment for instituting criminal proceedings through a grand jury. It could hardly have occurred to these States that by ratifying the Amendment they uprooted their established methods for prosecuting crime and fastened upon themselves a new prosecutorial system.

Indeed, the suggestion that the Fourteenth Amendment incorporates the first eight Amendments as such is not unambiguously urged. Even the boldest innovator would shrink from suggesting to more than half the States that they may no longer initiate prose-

cutions without indictment by grand jury, or that thereafter all the States of the Union must furnish a jury of 12 for every case involving a claim above $20. There is suggested merely a selective incorporation of the first eight Amendments into the Fourteenth Amendment. Some are in and some are out, but we are left in the dark as to which are in and which are out. Nor are we given the calculus for determining which go in and which stay out. If the basis of selection is merely that those provisions of the first eight Amendments are incorporated which commend themselves to individual justices as indispensable to the dignity and happiness of a free man, we are thrown back to a merely subjective test....

It may not be amiss to restate the pervasive function of the Fourteenth Amendment in exacting from the States observance of basic liberties.... The Amendment neither comprehends the specific provisions by which the founders deemed it appropriate to restrict the federal government nor is it confined to them. The Due Process Clause of the Fourteenth Amendment has an independent potency, precisely as does the Due Process Clause of the Fifth Amendment in relation to the Federal Government. It ought not to require argument to reject the notion that due process of law meant one thing in the Fifth Amendment and another in the Fourteenth. The Fifth Amendment specifically prohibits prosecution of an "infamous crime" except upon indictment; it forbids double jeopardy; it bars compelling a person to be a witness against himself in any criminal case; it precludes deprivation of 'life, liberty, or property, without due process of law.' Are Madison and his contemporaries in the framing of the Bill of Rights to be charged with writing into it a meaningless clause? To consider 'due process of law' as merely a shorthand statement of other specific clauses in the same amendment is to attribute to the authors and proponents of this Amendment ignorance of, or indifference to, a historic conception which was one of the great instruments in the arsenal of constitutional freedom which the Bill of Rights was to protect and strengthen.

A construction which gives to due process no independent function but turns it into a summary of the specific provisions of the Bill of Rights would, as has been noted, tear up by the roots much of the fabric of law in the several States, and would deprive the States of opportunity for reforms in legal process designed for extending the area of freedom. It would assume that no other abuses would reveal themselves in the course of time than those which had become manifest in 1791. Such a view not only disregards the historic meaning of "due process." It leads inevitably to a warped construction of specific provisions of the Bill of Rights to bring within their scope conduct clearly condemned by due process but not easily fitting into the pigeon-holes of the specific provisions. It seems pretty late in the day to suggest that a phrase so laden with historic meaning should be given an improvised content consisting of some but not all of the provisions of the first eight Amendments, selected on an undefined basis, with improvisation of content for the provisions so selected.

And so, when, as in a case like the present, a conviction in a State court is here for review under a claim that a right protected by the Due Process Clause of the Fourteenth Amendment

has been denied, the issue is not whether an infraction of one of the specific provisions of the first eight Amendments is disclosed by the record. The relevant question is whether the criminal proceedings which resulted in conviction deprived the accused of the due process of law to which the United States Constitution entitled him. Judicial review of that guaranty of the Fourteenth Amendment inescapably imposes upon this Court an exercise of judgment upon the whole course of the proceedings in order to ascertain whether they offend those canons of decency and fairness which express the notions of justice of English-speaking peoples even toward those charged with the most heinous offenses. These standards of justice are not authoritatively formulated anywhere as though they were prescriptions in a pharmacopoeia. But neither does the application of the Due Process Clause imply that judges are wholly at large. The judicial judgment in applying the Due Process Clause must move within the limits of accepted notions of justice and is not to be based upon the idiosyncrasies of a merely personal judgment. The fact that judges among themselves may differ whether in a particular case a trial offends accepted notions of justice is not disproof that general rather than idiosyncratic standards are applied. An important safeguard against such merely individual judgment is an alert deference to the judgment of the State court under review.

MURPHY AND RUTLEDGE, J.J., DISSENTING

... I agree [with Justice Black] that the specific guarantees of the Bill of Rights should be carried over intact into the first section of the Fourteenth Amendment. But I am not prepared to say that the latter is entirely and necessarily limited by the Bill of Rights. Occasions may arise where a proceeding falls so far short of conforming to fundamental standards of procedure as to warrant constitutional condemnation in terms of a lack of due process despite the absence of a specific provision in the Bill of Rights....

BLACK AND DOUGLAS, J.J., DISSENTING

... This decision reasserts a constitutional theory spelled out in *Twining v. New Jersey* that this Court is endowed by the Constitution with boundless power under "natural law" periodically to expand and contract constitutional standards to conform to the Court's conception of what at a particular time constitutes "civilized decency" and "fundamental principles of liberty and justice." Invoking this *Twining* rule, the Court concludes that although comment upon testimony in a federal court would violate the Fifth Amendment, identical comment in a state court does not violate today's fashion in civilized decency and fundamentals and is therefore not prohibited by the Federal Constitution as amended.

The *Twining* case was the first, as it is the only decision of this Court, which has squarely held that states were free, notwithstanding the Fifth and Fourteenth Amendments, to extort evidence from one accused of crime. I agree that if *Twining* be reaffirmed, the result reached might appropriately follow. But I would not reaffirm the *Twining* decision. I think that decision and the "natural law" theory of the Constitution upon which it relies,

degrade the constitutional safeguards of the Bill of Rights and simultaneously appropriate for this Court a broad power which we are not authorized by the Constitution to exercise....

The first 10 amendments were proposed and adopted largely because of fear that Government might unduly interfere with prized individual liberties. The people wanted and demanded a Bill of Rights written into their Constitution. The amendments embodying the Bill of Rights were intended to curb all branches of the Federal Government in the fields touched by the amendments— Legislative, Executive, and Judicial. The Fifth, Sixth, and Eighth Amendments were pointedly aimed at confining exercise of power by courts and judges within precise boundaries, particularly in the procedure used for the trial of criminal cases. Past history provided strong reasons for the apprehensions which brought these procedural amendments into being and attest the wisdom of their adoption. For the fears of arbitrary court action sprang largely from the past use of courts in the imposition of criminal punishments to suppress speech, press, and religion. Hence the constitutional limitations of courts' powers were, in the view of the Founders, essential supplements to the First Amendment, which was itself designed to protect the widest scope for all people to believe and to express the most divergent political, religious, and other views.

But these limitations were not expressly imposed upon state court action. In 1833, *Barron v. Baltimore* was decided by this Court. It specifically held inapplicable to the states that provision of the Fifth Amendment which declares: "nor shall private property be taken for public use, without just compensation." In deciding the particular point raised, the Court there said that it could not hold that the first eight amendments applied to the states. This was the controlling constitutional rule when the Fourteenth Amendment was proposed in 1866.

My study of the historical events that culminated in the Fourteenth Amendment, and the expressions of those who sponsored and favored, as well as those who opposed its submission and passage, persuades me that one of the chief objects that the provisions of the Amendment's first section, separately, and as a whole, were intended to accomplish was to make the Bill of Rights, applicable to the states. With full knowledge of the import of the *Barron* decision, the framers and backers of the Fourteenth Amendment proclaimed its purpose to be to overturn the constitutional rule that case had announced. This historical purpose has never received full consideration or exposition in any opinion of this Court interpreting the Amendment....

[T]he Court ... today declines, to appraise the relevant historical evidence of the intended scope of the first section of the Amendment. Instead it [has] relied upon previous cases, none of which had analyzed the evidence showing that one purpose of those who framed, advocated, and adopted the Amendment had been to make the Bill of Rights applicable to the States. None of the cases relied upon by the Court today made such an analysis.

For this reason, I am attaching to this dissent, an appendix [omitted] which contains a resume, by no means complete, of the Amendment's history. In my judgment that history conclusively demonstrates that the language of the first section of the Fourteenth Amendment, taken as a whole, was thought by those responsible for its submission to the people, and by those who opposed its submission, sufficiently explicit to guarantee that thereafter no state could deprive its citizens of the privileges and protections of the Bill of Rights. Whether this Court ever will, or whether it now should, in the light of past decisions, give full effect to what the Amendment was intended to accomplish is not necessarily essential to a decision here. However that may be, our prior decisions, including *Twining*, do not prevent our carrying out that purpose, at least to the extent of making applicable to the states, not a mere part, as the Court has, but the full protection of the Fifth Amendment's provision against compelling evidence from an accused to convict him of crime. And I further contend that the "natural law" formula which the Court uses to reach its conclusion in this case should be abandoned as an incongruous excrescence on our Constitution. I believe that formula to be itself a violation of our Constitution, in that it subtly conveys to courts, at the expense of legislatures, ultimate power over public policies in fields where no specific provision of the Constitution limits legislative power....

At the same time that the *Twining* decision held that the states need not conform to the specific provisions of the Bill of Rights, it consolidated the power that the Court had assumed under the due process clause by laying even broader foundations for the Court to invalidate state and even federal regulatory legislation. For under the *Twining* formula, which includes nonregard for the first eight amendments, what are "fundamental rights" and in accord with "canons of decency," as the Court said in *Twining*, and today reaffirms, is to be independently "ascertained from time to time by judicial action."... Thus the power of legislatures became what this Court would declare it to be at a particular time independently of the specific guarantees of the Bill of Rights such as the right to freedom of speech, religion and assembly, the right to just compensation for property taken for a public purpose, the right to jury trial or the right to be secure against unreasonable searches and seizures. Neither the contraction of the Bill of Rights safeguards nor the invalidation of regulatory laws by this Court's appraisal of "circumstances" would readily be classified as the most satisfactory contribution of this Court to the nation....

Conceding the possibility that this Court is now wise enough to improve on the Bill of Rights by substituting natural law concepts for the Bill of Rights, I think the possibility is entirely too speculative to agree to take that course. I would therefore hold in this case that the full protection of the Fifth Amendment's proscription against compelled testimony must be afforded by California. This I would do because of reliance upon the original purpose of the Fourteenth Amendment....

COMMENT

After the Supreme Court issued its opinion, Adamson's attorney, Morris Lavine, filed a petition for rehearing that emphasized the unfairness of Adamson's trial and implored the majority to "join now in the parade toward one more liberty preserved and protected for all peoples under the Constitution." Adamson's petition was denied. After several other failed appeals, Adamson was executed in the gas chamber at San Quentin on December 9, 1949.

QUESTIONS

1. If Adamson had been tried in a federal court, instead of in a state court, and the prosecutor or judge had commented on his failure to testify, Adamson's conviction would have been reversed on Fifth Amendment grounds. On what principle does Justice Reed conclude that it is not reversible error for the same comments to be made in state court? Does a particular theory of federalism support his conclusion?

2. Justice Black excoriated his colleagues for perpetuating "an incongruous excrescence on our Constitution," an approach to constitutional interpretation that "subtly conveys to courts, at the expense of legislatures, ultimate power over public policies" by means of subjective terms such as notions of "civilized standards," "canons of decency," and "fundamental justice." Assume, for the sake of argument, that the Court had adopted Black's "total incorporation" approach to the Bill of Rights. Would that eliminate the possibility of judicial subjectivity?

3. Justice Black added a thirteen-page appendix to his dissent that con-

sisted of an historical review that he believed "conclusively demonstrates that the language of the first section of the Fourteenth Amendment, taken as a whole, was thought by those responsible for its submission to the people, and by those who opposed its submission, sufficiently explicit to guarantee that thereafter no state could deprive its citizens of the privileges and protections of the Bill of Rights." Professor Charles Fairman took issue with Black's conclusion in his article "Does the Fourteenth Amendment Incorporate the Bill of Rights? The Original Understanding," 2 *Stanford Law Review* (1949): 5.

Does the fact that Black and Fairman, two careful, thoughtful students of the intentions of the drafters of the Fourteenth Amendment, come to divergent conclusions suggest that the quest for "original understanding" is chimerical?

4. Review the dissents by Justices Field and Bradley in the *Slaughter-House Cases* (pp. 661–663) and Justice Cardozo's majority opinion in *Palko* (pp. 676–677) in the context of Justice Black's dissent in *Adamson*. Which reading of the Fourteenth Amendment is most persuasive?

5. Justice Frankfurter noted in his *Adamson* concurrence: "Between the incorporation of the Fourteenth Amendment into the Constitution and the beginning of the present membership of the Court—a period of 70 years—the scope of that Amendment was passed upon by forty-three judges. Of all these judges, only one, who may respectfully be called an *eccentric exception*, ever indicated the belief that the Fourteenth Amendment was a shorthand summary of the first eight Amendments theretofore limiting only the Federal Government, and that due process incorporated those eight Amendments as restrictions upon the powers of the States" (emphasis added). The "eccentric exception" was John Marshall Harlan. What, if anything, is eccentric about believing that all the guarantees in the Bill of Rights are limitations on state powers as well as on national powers?

THE BILL OF RIGHTS AND THE STATES

Rochin v. California
342 U.S. 165 (1952)

SETTING

On July 1, 1949, at about 9:00 A.M., three Los Angeles County deputy sheriffs assigned to the Narcotics Detail entered a two-story dwelling house in which Antonio Richard Rochin resided with his common-law wife, Margarita

Hernandez, his mother, and his brothers and sisters. The sheriffs entered through an unlocked door and went upstairs, followed by Rochin's mother. The door to Rochin's room had a small hook on it, which was broken when the officers kicked the door. In the room they found Rochin seated on a bed, next to Hernandez. On a bedside table Deputy Sheriff Jones noticed two capsules. He asked Rochin, "Whose stuff is this?" Rochin leaned over, grabbed the capsules and placed them in his month. Jones then grabbed Rochin by the throat and squeezed. Rochin screamed and struggled. The two other officers then jumped on Rochin, seeking unsuccessfully to extract the capsules. The deputy sheriffs then ordered Rochin to get dressed, placed him in handcuffs, and took him to a local hospital. At the hospital, Rochin was strapped down to an operating table and a doctor was asked to pump his stomach. The doctor inserted a foot-long tube down Rochin's throat into his stomach and suctioned the contents into a pail. The contents included two objects that one of the deputy sheriffs said looked like capsules of heroin. Chemical analysis revealed that the capsules contained morphine.

Rochin was subsequently accused by information of the felony of unlawful possession of morphine. Rochin waived his right to a jury trial and was tried before a judge of a California Superior Court. Although Rochin objected to their introduction, the two capsules extracted during the pumping of his stomach were received into evidence. He was convicted and sentenced to jail for sixty days. The District Court of Appeal affirmed, even though it found that the deputy sheriffs "were guilty of unlawfully breaking into and entering [Rochin's] room and were guilty of unlawfully assaulting and battering defendant while in the room," and were also guilty of "unlawfully assaulting, battering, torturing and falsely imprisoning [Rochin] at the alleged hospital." The California Supreme Court denied review, two justices dissenting. The Supreme Court granted Rochin's petition for a writ of certiorari.

HIGHLIGHTS OF SUPREME COURT ARGUMENTS

BRIEF FOR ROCHIN

◆ Rochin's arrest and seizure, as well as the search and his battering and false imprisonment violated substantial rights guaranteed him by the Fourth, Fifth, and Fourteenth Amendments to the Constitution of the United States.

◆ The extortion of testimony from a criminal defendant by physical torture and the use and receipt of such evidence in trial proceedings violates the privileges or immunities guaranteed by the Fourth, Fifth, and Fourteenth Amendments.

◆ The state's use of evidence illegally obtained violates the Fourth, Fifth, and Fourteenth Amendments. Thirty states have adopted rules excluding evidence obtained in violation of constitutional guarantees. States should be required to do so as a constitutional mandate.

AMICUS CURIAE **BRIEF SUPPORTING ROCHIN**

The American Civil Liberties Union.

BRIEF FOR CALIFORNIA

◆ It is well established under California law that otherwise competent evidence is not rendered inadmissible by the fact that it might have been obtained by improper or illegal means.

◆ The Fourth and Fifth Amendments to the Constitution of the United States are not limitations on the states. The Fourteenth Amendment did not incorporate and make operative in state courts the entire Bill of Rights.

◆ The privilege against self-incrimination in the Fifth Amendment to the Constitution of the United States and Article I, section 13, of the California Constitution, is limited to testimonial compulsion and does not include forced physical disclosures. The privilege does not empower a person to use his body to conceal or secrete evidence that already has been observed by police officers.

SUPREME COURT DECISION: 8–0

(Minton, J., did not participate.)

FRANKFURTER, J.

… In our federal system the administration of criminal justice is predominantly committed to the care of the States. The power to define crimes belongs to Congress only as an appropriate means of carrying into execution its limited grant of legislative powers. U.S. Const. Art. I, § 8, cl. 18. Broadly speaking, crimes in the United States are what the laws of the individual States make them, subject to the limitations of Art. I, § 10, cl. 1, in the original Constitution, prohibiting bills of attainder and ex post facto laws, and of the Thirteenth and Fourteenth Amendments.

These limitations, in the main, concern not restrictions upon the powers of the States to define crime, except in the restricted area where federal authority has pre-empted the field, but restrictions upon the manner in which the States may enforce their penal codes. Accordingly, in reviewing a State criminal conviction under a claim of right guaranteed by the Due Process Clause of the Fourteenth Amendment, from which is derived the most far reaching and most frequent federal basis of challenging State criminal justice, "we must be deeply mindful of the responsibilities of the States for the enforcement of criminal laws, and exercise with due humility our merely negative function in subjecting convictions from state courts to the very narrow scrutiny which the Due Process Clause of the Fourteenth Amendment authorizes." *Malinski v. People of State of New York*, 324 U.S. 401 (1945)….

However, this Court too has its responsibility. Regard for the requirements of the Due Process Clause "inescapably imposes upon this Court an exercise of judgment upon the whole course of the proceedings (resulting in a conviction) in order to ascertain whether they offend those canons of decency and fairness which express the notions of justice of English-speaking peoples even toward those charged with the most heinous offenses." *Malinski*. These standards of justice are not authoritatively formulated anywhere as though they were specifics. Due process of law is a summarized constitutional guarantee of respect for those personal immunities which, as Mr. Justice Cardozo twice wrote for the Court, are "so rooted in the traditions and conscience of our people as to be ranked as fundamental," *Snyder v. Commonwealth of Massachusetts*, 291 U.S. 97 (1934), or are "implicit in the concept of ordered liberty." *Palko v. State of Connecticut*.

The Court's function in the observance of this settled conception of the Due Process Clause does not leave us without adequate guides in subjecting State criminal procedures to constitutional judgment. In dealing not with the machinery of government but with human rights, the absence of formal exactitude, or want of fixity of meaning, is not an unusual or even regrettable attribute of constitutional provisions. Words being symbols do not speak without a gloss. On the one hand the gloss may be the deposit of history, whereby a term gains technical content. Thus the requirements of the Sixth and Seventh Amendments for trial by jury in the federal courts have a rigid meaning. No changes or chances can alter the content of the verbal symbol of "jury"—a body of twelve men who must reach a unanimous conclusion if the verdict is

to go against the defendant. On the other hand, the gloss of some of the verbal symbols of the Constitution does not give them a fixed technical content. It exacts a continuing process of application.

When the gloss has thus not been fixed but is a function of the process of judgment, the judgment is bound to fall differently at different times and differently at the same time through different judges. Even more specific provisions, such as the guaranty of freedom of speech and the detailed protection against unreasonable searches and seizures, have inevitably evoked as sharp divisions in this Court as the least specific and most comprehensive protection of liberties, the Due Process Clause.

The vague contours of the Due Process Clause do not leave judges at large. We may not draw on our merely personal and private notions and disregard the limits that bind judges in their judicial function. Even though the concept of due process of law is not final and fixed, these limits are derived from considerations that are fused in the whole nature of our judicial process.... These are considerations deeply rooted in reason and in the compelling traditions of the legal profession. The Due Process Clause places upon this Court the duty of exercising a judgment, within the narrow confines of judicial power in reviewing State convictions, upon interests of society pushing in opposite directions.

Due process of law thus conceived is not to be derided as resort to a revival of "natural law." To believe that this judicial exercise of judgment could be avoided by freezing "due process of law' at some fixed stage of time or thought is to suggest that the most important aspect of constitutional adjudication is a function for inanimate machines and not for judges, for whom the independence safeguarded by Article III of the Constitution was designed and who are presumably guided by established standards of judicial behavior. Even cybernetics has not yet made that haughty claim. To practice the requisite detachment and to achieve sufficient objectivity no doubt demands of judges the habit of self-discipline and self-criticism, incertitude that one's own views are incontestable and alert tolerance toward views not shared. But these are precisely the presuppositions of our judicial process. They are precisely the qualities society has a right to expect from those entrusted with ultimate judicial power.

Restraints on our jurisdiction are self-imposed only in the sense that there is from our decisions no immediate appeal short of impeachment or constitutional amendment. But that does not make due process of law a matter of judicial caprice. The faculties of the Due Process Clause may be indefinite and vague, but the mode of their ascertainment is not self-willed. In each case "due process of law" requires an evaluation based on a disinterested inquiry pursued in the spirit of science, on a balanced order of facts exactly and fairly stated, on the detached consideration of conflicting claims, on a judgment not ad hoc and episodic but duly mindful of reconciling the needs both of continuity and of change in a progressive society.

Applying these general considerations to the circumstances of the present case, we are compelled to conclude that the proceedings by which this conviction was obtained do more than offend some fastidious squeamishness

or private sentimentalism about combatting crime too energetically. This is conduct that shocks the conscience. Illegally breaking into the privacy of the petitioner, the struggle to open his mouth and remove what was there, the forcible extraction of his stomach's contents—this course of proceeding by agents of government to obtain evidence is bound to offend even hardened sensibilities. They are methods too close to the rack and the screw to permit of constitutional differentiation....

On the facts of this case the conviction of the petitioner has been obtained by methods that offend the Due Process Clause. The judgment below must be reversed.

Reversed.

BLACK, J., CONCURRING

Adamson v. People of State of California sets out reasons for my belief that state as well as federal courts and law enforcement officers must obey the Fifth Amendment's command that "No person ... shall be compelled in any criminal case to be a witness against himself." I think a person is compelled to be a witness against himself not only when he is compelled to testify, but also when as here, incriminating evidence is forcibly taken from him by a contrivance of modern science....

In the view of a majority of the Court, however, the Fifth Amendment imposes no restraint of any kind on the states. They nevertheless hold that California's use of this evidence violated the Due Process Clause of the Fourteenth Amendment. Since they hold as I do in this case, I regret my inability to accept their interpretation without protest. But I believe that faithful adherence to the specific guarantees in the Bill of Rights insures a more permanent protection of individual liberty than that which can be afforded by the nebulous standards stated by the majority.

What the majority hold is that the Due Process Clause empowers this Court to nullify any state law if its application "shocks the conscience," offends "a sense of justice" or runs counter to the "decencies of civilized conduct." The majority emphasize that these statements do not refer to their own consciences or to their senses of justice and decency. For we are told that "we may not draw on our merely personal and private notions"; our judgment must be grounded on "considerations deeply rooted in reason and in the compelling traditions of the legal profession." We are further admonished to measure the validity of state practices, not by our reason, or by the traditions of the legal profession, but by "the community's sense of fair play and decency"; by the "traditions and conscience of our people"; or by "those canons of decency and fairness which express the notions of justice of English-speaking peoples." These canons are made necessary, it is said, because of "interests of society pushing in opposite directions."

If the Due Process Clause does vest this Court with such unlimited power to invalidate laws, I am still in doubt as to why we should consider only the notions of English-speaking peoples to determine what are immutable and fundamental principles of justice. Moreover, one may well ask what avenues of investigation are open to discover "canons" of conduct so universally favored that this Court should write them into the Constitution? All we are told is that the discovery must be made by an "evaluation based on a disinterested inquiry pursued in the spirit of science, on a balanced order of facts."....

I long ago concluded that the accordion-like qualities of this [mode of analysis] must inevitably imperil all the individual liberty safeguards specifically enumerated in the Bill of Rights....

DOUGLAS, J., CONCURRING

... As an original matter it might be debatable whether the provision in the Fifth Amendment that no person "shall be compelled in any criminal case to be a witness against himself" serves the ends of justice. Not all civilized legal procedures recognize it. But the choice was made by the Framers, a choice which sets a standard for legal trials in this country. The Framers made it a standard of due process for prosecutions by the Federal Government. If it is a requirement of due process for a trial in the federal courthouse, it is impossible for me to say it is not a requirement of due process for a trial in the state courthouse.... I think that words taken from his lips, capsules taken from his stomach, blood taken from his veins are all inadmissible provided they are taken from him without his consent. They are inadmissible because of the command of the Fifth Amendment.

That is an unequivocal, definite and workable rule of evidence for state and federal courts. But we cannot in fairness free the state courts from that command and yet excoriate them for flouting the "decencies of civilized conduct" when they admit the evidence. That is to make the rule turn not on the Constitution but on the idiosyncrasies of the judges who sit here....

QUESTIONS

1. Justice Frankfurter concluded that "the proceedings by which [Rochin's] conviction was obtained do more than offend some fastidious squeamishness or private sentimentalism about combatting crime too energetically. This is conduct that shocks the conscience." Is the rule of *Rochin* that if police engage in conduct that shocks the Supreme Court's conscience the Court will apply a relevant provision of the Bill of Rights against the states to prevent such conduct? If that is the rule of *Rochin*, is it workable? To which of the guarantees in the Bill of Rights would the rule not apply?

2. Counsel for California, future Governor Edmund G. Brown, concluded the state's brief as follows:

   > [The State of California] requests that this Court continue to recognize the right of the state to formulate its own policy for its own courts based on its own experience, and the right of such state after balancing the opposing interests represented by the necessity for individual protection plus the possibility of other redress for the violation of such individual right against the social need that crime must be repressed, to adopt either the admissibility rule or the exclusionary rule as it deems best for the interests of all of its people.

   Does making the Bill of Rights apply against the states via the Fourteenth Amendment Due Process Clause jeopardize states' rights? Is California's plea any less cogent today?

3. The American Civil Liberties Union argued that exclusion at trial of the illegally obtained evidence was the only sufficient remedy for the police illegality in *Rochin*. Is that true? What other remedies might be available to the justices that would be more protective of states' rights?

THE BILL OF RIGHTS AND THE STATES

Duncan v. Louisiana
391 U.S. 145 (1968)

SETTING

In 1966, more than a decade after the Supreme Court in *Brown v. Board of Education*, 347 U.S. 483 (1954), declared racially segregated schools unconstitutional, a federal district court ordered that black students be allowed to transfer to the formerly all-white Boothville-Venice School in Plaquemines Parrish, Louisiana. Pursuant to that order, two cousins of Gary Duncan, a nineteen-year-old black man, transferred to the school in September 1966. One cousin, Bert Grant, was fourteen years of age; the other, Bernard St. Ann, was sixteen.

After they transferred to Boothville-Venice School, Grant and St. Ann were repeatedly assaulted, threatened, and harassed by white students. On October 18, 1966, Duncan was driving past the school and saw four white fourteen-year-old boys confronting his cousins. It was approximately 3:30 P.M. and school had just let out. Duncan stopped his car to see what was happening, got out and approached the group. He exchanged words with his cousins and the white boys, then told his cousins to get into his car. Herman Landry Jr., one of the white boys, muttered to Duncan, "You must think you're tough." At that point, Duncan either touched Landry on the elbow or slapped him on the arm. Duncan then got into his car and he and his cousins drove away.

On December 5, 1996, Duncan was charged in the Twenty-Fifth Judicial District Court of Louisiana (Plaquemines Parish) with the misdemeanor offense of simple battery against Landry. Simple battery was defined by the Louisiana Revised Statutes as a battery committed without a dangerous weapon. The offense was punishable by a maximum of two years in prison and a fine of $300. Duncan pleaded "not guilty" and filed a formal demand for a jury trial. His demand was rejected, because Article 779 of the Louisiana Code of Criminal Procedure denied a jury trial on misdemeanor charges, consistent with Louisiana tradition that the right to a trial by jury depended on whether the court could impose a sentence "at hard labor."

Duncan's case was tried by the trial court without a jury. Duncan and his cousins testified that Duncan had not slapped Landry, but had merely touched him on the elbow while telling him that it would be best if he went home. The white boys and a shopkeeper who witnessed the episode from approximately 250 feet away testified that Duncan had slapped Landry on the arm. The trial judge resolved the factual dispute against Duncan and found him guilty. He sentenced Duncan to sixty days in prison and fined him $150.

Duncan filed an application for a writ of certiorari in the Louisiana Supreme Court, on the ground that Article 779 denied him the right of trial by jury, contrary to the commands of the Sixth and Fourteenth Amendments. That court denied the application, stating in a memorandum decision that there was "No error of law in the ruling complained of." Duncan appealed to the Supreme Court of the United States.

HIGHLIGHTS OF SUPREME COURT ARGUMENTS

BRIEF FOR DUNCAN

◆ This Court's decision in *Maxwell v. Dow*, 176 U.S. 581 (1900), holding that the Fourteenth Amendment does not make applicable to the states any of the specific guarantees of the Bill of Rights, is at odds with recent decisions.

◆ In recent decisions, apart from the right to trial by jury, this Court has held every guarantee of the Sixth Amendment applicable to state criminal proceedings.

◆ Trial by jury is the only procedural right included in the body of the Constitution and reiterated in the Bill of Rights.

◆ The overwhelming majority of states guarantee a jury trial right in criminal cases as broad as that secured in federal courts by the Sixth Amendment.

◆ The decision to apply a particular guarantee of the Bill of Rights to state criminal proceedings has depended on the Court's determination as to whether the right is so fundamental and essential to a fair trial that it is incorporated in the Due Process Clause of the Fourteenth Amendment. Denial of trial by jury lessens the state's burden of persuasion in a criminal proceeding.

BRIEF FOR LOUISIANA

◆ The Sixth Amendment was intended only as an iron-clad restriction to prevent Congress from making changes in jury trials in federal courts. The states reserved to themselves the unrestricted power to change their own constitutional and statutory provisions regarding jury trials. The Fourteenth Amendment did not take this reserved power away from the states.

◆ Even if the Sixth Amendment right to a jury trial applies to the state, Duncan's conviction without a jury is proper because this Court has held that a jury trial is not required in the prosecution of petty offenses.

◆ This Court consistently has held that a jury trial is not essential to due process and that a fair trial may be had without a jury.

◆ If the Sixth Amendment is held to be applicable to the states, many states will be required to change their criminal jury procedures to conform with that of the federal courts. That result was not intended by the Due Process Clause of the Fourteenth Amendment.

AMICUS CURIAE BRIEF SUPPORTING LOUISIANA

State of New York.

SUPREME COURT DECISION

(7–2 on result, 4–3–2 on rule)

WHITE, J.

… The test for determining whether a right extended by the Fifth and Sixth Amendments with respect to federal criminal proceedings is also protected against state action by the Fourteenth Amendment has been phrased in a variety of ways in the opinions of this Court…. The claim before us is that the right to trial by jury guaranteed by the Sixth Amendment meets these tests. The position of Louisiana, on the other hand, is that the Constitution imposes upon the States no duty to give a jury trial in any criminal case, regardless of the seriousness of the crime or the size of the punishment which may be imposed. Because we believe that trial by jury in criminal cases is fundamental to the American scheme of justice, we hold that the Fourteenth Amendment guarantees a right of jury trial in all criminal cases which—were they to be tried in a federal court—would come within the Sixth Amendment's guarantee. Since we consider the appeal before us to be such a case, we hold that the Constitution was violated when appellant's demand for jury trial was refused....

The guarantees of jury trial in the Federal and State Constitutions reflect a profound judgment about the way in which law should be enforced and justice administered. A right to jury trial is granted to criminal defendants in order to prevent oppression by the Government. Those who wrote our constitutions knew from history and experience that it was necessary to protect against unfounded criminal charges brought to eliminate enemies and against judges too responsive to the voice of higher authority. The framers of the constitution strove to create an independent judiciary but insisted upon further protection against arbitrary action. Providing an accused with the right to be tried by a jury of his peers gave him an inestimable safeguard against the corrupt or overzealous prosecutor and against the compliant, biased, or eccentric judge. If the defendant preferred the common-sense judgment of a jury to the more tutored but perhaps less sympathetic reaction of the single judge, he was to have it. Beyond this, the jury trial provisions in the Federal and State Constitutions reflect a fundamental decision about the

exercise of official power—a reluctance to entrust plenary powers over the life and liberty of the citizen to one judge or to a group of judges. Fear of unchecked power, so typical of our State and Federal Governments in other respects, found expression in the criminal law in this insistence upon community participation in the determination of guilt or innocence. The deep commitment of the Nation to the right of jury trial in serious criminal cases as a defense against arbitrary law enforcement qualifies for protection under the Due Process Clause of the Fourteenth Amendment, and must therefore be respected by the States.

Of course jury trial has "its weaknesses and the potential for misuse," *Singer v. United States*, 380 U.S. 24 (1965). We are aware of the long debate, especially in this century, among those who write about the administration of justice, as to the wisdom of permitting untrained laymen to determine the facts in civil and criminal proceedings. Although the debate has been intense, with powerful voices on either side, most of the controversy has centered on the jury in civil cases. Indeed, some of the severest critics of civil juries acknowledge that the arguments for criminal juries are much stronger. In addition, at the heart of the dispute have been express or implicit assertions that juries are incapable of adequately understanding evidence or determining issues of fact, and that they are unpredictable, quixotic, and little better than a roll of dice. Yet, the most recent and exhaustive study of the jury in criminal cases concluded that juries do understand the evidence and come to sound conclusions in most of the cases presented to them and that when juries differ with the result at which the judge would have arrived, it is usually because they are serving some of the very purposes for which they were created and for which they are now employed.

The State of Louisiana urges that holding that the Fourteenth Amendment assures a right to jury trial will cast doubt on the integrity of every trial conducted without a jury. Plainly, this is not the import of our holding. Our conclusion is that in the American States, as in the federal judicial system, a general grant of jury trial for serious offenses is a fundamental right, essential for preventing miscarriages of justice and for assuring that fair trials are provided for all defendants. We would not assert, however, that every criminal trial—or any particular trial—held before a judge alone is unfair or that a defendant may never be as fairly treated by a judge as he would be by a jury. Thus we hold no constitutional doubts about the practices, common in both federal and state courts, of accepting waivers of jury trial and prosecuting petty crimes without extending a right to jury trial. However, the fact is that in most places more trials for serious crimes are to juries than to a court alone; a great many defendants prefer the judgment of a jury to that of a court. Even where defendants are satisfied with bench trials, the right to a jury trial very likely serves its intended purpose of making judicial or prosecutorial unfairness less likely.

Louisiana's final contention is that even if it must grant jury trials in serious criminal cases, the conviction before us is valid and constitutional because here the petitioner was tried for simple battery and was sentenced to only 60 days in the parish prison. We are not persuaded. It is doubtless true that there is a category of petty crimes or offenses which is not subject to the Sixth Amendment jury trial provision and should not be subject to the Fourteenth Amendment jury trial requirement here applied to the States. Crimes carrying possible penalties up to six months do not require a jury trial if they otherwise qualify as petty offenses[.]... But the penalty authorized for a particular crime is of major relevance in determining whether it is serious or not and may in itself, if severe enough, subject the trial to the mandates of the Sixth Amendment.... In the case before us the Legislature of Louisiana has made simple battery a criminal offense punishable by imprisonment for up to two years and a fine. The question, then, is whether a crime carrying such a penalty is an offense which Louisiana may insist on trying without a jury.

We think not.... Of course the boundaries of the petty offense category have always been ill-defined, if not ambulatory. In the absence of an explicit constitutional provision, the definitional task necessarily falls on the courts, which must either pass upon the validity of legislative attempts to identify those petty offenses which are exempt from jury trial or, where the legislature has not addressed itself to the problem, themselves face the question in the first instance. In either case it is necessary to draw a line in the spectrum of crime, separating petty from serious infractions. This process, although essential, cannot be wholly satisfactory, for it requires attaching different consequences to events which, when they lie near the line, actually differ very little....

We need not, however, settle in this case the exact location of the line between petty offenses and serious crimes. It is sufficient for our purposes to hold that a crime punishable by two years in prison is, based on past and contemporary standards in this country, a serious crime and not a petty offense. Consequently, appellant was entitled to a jury trial and it was error to deny it.

The judgment below is reversed and the case is remanded for proceedings not inconsistent with this opinion.

Reversed and remanded.

BLACK AND DOUGLAS, J.J., CONCURRING

The Court today holds that the right to trial by jury guaranteed defendants in criminal cases in federal courts by Art. III of the United States Constitution and by the Sixth Amendment is also guaranteed by the Fourteenth Amendment to defendants tried in state courts. With this holding I agree for reasons given by the Court. I also agree because of reasons given in my dissent in *Adamson v. People of State of California....*

I am very happy to support this selective process through which our Court has since the *Adamson* case held most of the specific Bill of Rights' protections applicable to the States to the same extent they are applicable to the Federal Government....

While I do not wish at this time to discuss at length my disagreement with Brother Harlan's forthright and frank restatement of the now discredited *Twining* doctrine, I do want to point out what appears to me to be the basic difference between us. His view, as was indeed the view of *Twining*, is that "due process is an evolving concept" and therefore that it entails a "gradual process of judicial inclusion and exclusion" to ascertain those "immutable principles ... of free government which

no member of the Union may disregard." Thus the Due Process Clause is treated as prescribing no specific and clearly ascertainable constitutional command that judges must obey in interpreting the Constitution, but rather as leaving judges free to decide at any particular time whether a particular rule or judicial formulation embodies an "immutable principl(e) of free government" or is "implicit in the concept of ordered liberty," or whether certain conduct "shocks the judge's conscience" or runs counter to some other similar, undefined and undefinable standard. Thus due process, according to my Brother Harlan, is to be a phrase with no permanent meaning, but one which is found to shift from time to time in accordance with judges' predilections and understandings of what is best for the country. If due process means this, the Fourteenth Amendment, in my opinion, might as well have been written that "no person shall be deprived of life, liberty or property except by laws that the judges of the United States Supreme Court shall find to be consistent with the immutable principles of free government." It is impossible for me to believe that such unconfined power is given to judges in our Constitution that is a written one in order to limit governmental power.

Another tenet of the *Twining* doctrine as restated by my Brother Harlan is that "due process of law requires only fundamental fairness." But the "fundamental fairness" test is one on a par with that of shocking the conscience of the Court. Each of such tests depends entirely on the particular judge's idea of ethics and morals instead of requiring him to depend on the boundaries fixed by the written words of the Constitution.

Nothing in the history of the phrase "due process of law" suggests that constitutional controls are to depend on any particular judge's sense of values....

Finally I want to add that I am not bothered by the argument that applying the Bill of Rights to the States "according to the same standards that protect those personal rights against federal encroachment," interferes with our concept of federalism in that it may prevent States from trying novel social and economic experiments. I have never believed that under the guise of federalism the States should be able to experiment with the protections afforded our citizens through the Bill of Rights....

It seems to me totally inconsistent to advocate on the one hand, the power of this Court to strike down any state law or practice which it finds "unreasonable" or "unfair" and, on the other hand, urge that the States be given maximum power to develop their own laws and procedures. Yet the due process approach of my Brothers Harlan and Fortas does just that since in effect it restricts the States to practices which a majority of this Court is willing to approve on a case-by-case basis. No one is more concerned than I that the States be allowed to use the full scope of their powers as their citizens sees fit. And that is why I have continually fought against the expansion of this Court's authority over the States through the use of a broad, general interpretation of due process that permits judges to strike down state laws they do not like....

FORTAS, J., CONCURRING

... [A]lthough I agree with the decision of the Court, I cannot agree with the implication that the tail must go with the hide: that when we hold, influenced by the Sixth Amendment, that "due process" requires that the States accord the right of jury trial for all but petty offenses, we automatically import all of the ancillary rules which have been or may hereafter be developed incidental to the right to jury trial in the federal courts. I see no reason whatever, for example, to assume that our decision today should require us to impose federal requirements such as unanimous verdicts or a jury of 12 upon the States. We may well conclude that these and other features of federal jury practice are by no means fundamental—that they are not essential to due process of law—and that they are not obligatory on the States....

The draftsmen of the Fourteenth Amendment intended what they said, not more or less: that no State shall deprive any person of life, liberty, or property without due process of law. It is ultimately the duty of this Court to interpret, to ascribe specific meaning to this phrase. There is no reason whatever for us to conclude that, in so doing, we are bound slavishly to follow not only the Sixth Amendment but all of its bag and baggage, however securely or insecurely affixed they may be by law and precedent to federal proceedings....

HARLAN AND STEWART, J.J., DISSENTING

... The Court's approach to this case is an uneasy and illogical compromise among the views of various Justices on how the Due Process Clause should be interpreted. The Court does not say that those who framed the Fourteenth Amendment intended to make the Sixth Amendment applicable to the States. And the Court concedes that it finds nothing unfair about the procedure by which the present appellant was tried. Nevertheless, the Court reverses his conviction: it holds, for some reason not apparent to me, that the Due Process Clause incorporates the particular clause of the Sixth Amendment that requires trial by jury in federal criminal cases—including, as I read its opinion, the sometimes trivial accompanying baggage of judicial interpretation in federal contexts. I have raised my voice many times before against the Court's continuing undiscriminating insistence upon fastening on the States federal notions of criminal justice, and I must do so again in this instance. With all respect, the Court's approach and its reading of history are altogether topsy-turvy.

I believe I am correct in saying that every member of the Court for at least the last 135 years has agreed that our Founders did not consider the requirements of the Bill of Rights so fundamental that they should operate directly against the States. They were wont to believe rather that the security of liberty in America rested primarily upon the dispersion of governmental power across a federal system. The Bill of Rights was considered unnecessary by some but insisted upon by others in order to curb the possibility of abuse of power by the strong central government they were creating.

The Civil War Amendments dramatically altered the relation of the Federal Government to the States. The first section of the Fourteenth Amendment imposes highly significant restrictions on state action. But the restrictions are couched in very broad and general terms: citizenship; privileges and immunities; due process of law; equal protection of the laws.... The question [thus] has been, Where does the Court properly look to find the specific rules that define and give content to such terms as "life, liberty, or property" and "due process of law"?

A few members of the Court have taken the position that the intention of those who drafted the first section of the Fourteenth Amendment was simply, and exclusively, to make the provisions of the first eight Amendments applicable to state action. This view has never been accepted by this Court. In my view, often expressed elsewhere, the first section of the Fourteenth Amendment was meant neither to incorporate, nor to be limited to, the specific guarantees of the first eight Amendments....

Although I therefore fundamentally disagree with the total incorporation view of the Fourteenth Amendment, it seems to me that such a position does at least have the virtue, lacking in the Court's selective incorporation approach, of internal consistency: we look to the Bill of Rights, word for word, clause for clause, precedent for precedent because, it is said, the men who wrote the Amendment wanted it that way. For those who do not accept this "history," a different source of "intermediate premises" must be found. The Bill of Rights is not necessarily irrelevant to the search for guidance in interpreting the Fourteenth Amendment, but the reason for and the nature of its relevance must be articulated.

Apart from the approach taken by the absolute incorporationists, I can see only one method of analysis that has any internal logic. That is to start with the words "liberty" and "due process of law" and attempt to define them in a way that accords with American traditions and our system of government....

Since, as I see it, the Court has not even come to grips with the issues in this case, it is necessary to start from the beginning. When a criminal defendant contends that his state conviction lacked "due process of law," the question before this Court, in my view, is whether he was denied any element of fundamental procedural fairness. Believing, as I do, that due process is an evolving concept and that old principles are subject to re-evaluation in light of later experience, I think it appropriate to deal on its merits with the question whether Louisiana denied appellant due process of law when it tried him for simple assault without a jury....

[E]ven if I were persuaded that trial by jury is a fundamental right in some criminal cases, I could see nothing fundamental in the rule, not yet formulated by the Court, that places the prosecution of appellant for simple battery within the category of "jury crimes" rather than "petty crimes."...

There is no obvious reason why a jury trial is a requisite of fundamental fairness when the charge is robbery, and not a requisite of fairness when the same defendant, for the same actions, is charged with assault and petty theft. The reason for the historic exception for relatively minor crimes is the obvious one: the burden of jury trial was thought to outweigh its marginal advantages. Exactly why the States should not be allowed to make continuing adjustments, based on the state of their criminal dockets and the difficulty of summoning jurors, simply escapes me....

QUESTIONS

1. Louisiana's brief in *Duncan* contained the following historical information:

   > Unique among her sister states, Louisiana under the dominion of France and Spain until the early nineteenth Century, inherited a continental legal system derived from Rome through the systems of France and Spain.
   >   As a territory for nine years in the early nineteenth century, Louisiana was under the exclusive jurisdiction of the United States, and its court procedure came directly under the operation of the Sixth Amendment.
   >   The people of Louisiana were dissatisfied with the territorial law affecting them. Among other things, they objected to jury trials because having been instilled by their French heritage with respect for superior training, they were at a loss to understand how a jury of unschooled men could dispense justice.

   Should the Court have paid deference to Louisiana's historical traditions in analyzing whether the Sixth Amendment's right to a jury trial applies to the states? Is there a principled basis on which different states could be treated differently for purposes of application of the Bill of Rights?

2. In 1833, in *Democracy in America*, Alexis de Tocqueville maintained that

> The institution of the jury ... places the real direction of society in the hands of the governed, or a portion of the governed[.]... He who punishes infractions of the law, is therefore the real master of society. (*Democracy in America*, 2 vols. [New York, NY: Schocken, 1974], I: 333–334)

What are the constitutional ramifications of Tocqueville's argument in the context of the incorporation debate?

3. Louisiana petitioned the Supreme Court for rehearing following the decision in *Duncan*. It claimed that the plurality opinion, holding that the Sixth Amendment guarantees the right to a jury trial in "serious criminal cases" failed to identify the criteria a state must use to determine what is a serious criminal case as distinguished from a petty offense for which a jury trial is not an entitlement. Louisiana also contended that the plurality left in doubt "whether a twelve-man unanimous jury is necessary for the trial of 'serious criminal cases.'" The Supreme Court denied the petition for rehearing. Why would the plurality have chosen to leave unanswered such important questions in *Duncan*? Was the Court's refusal to confront the question a sign of judicial deference to the states?

COMMENT

No majority of the Supreme Court has accepted the argument that the Fourteenth Amendment incorporated all of the provisions of the Bill of Rights against the states. Instead, the Court has taken a path of "selective incorporation." Its basic approach has been that some rights are so fundamental that they must apply against the states as well as the national government. The following list of incorporated provisions is adapted from the Congressional Research Service's *The Constitution of the United States: Analysis and Interpretation* (Washington, D.C.: Government Printing Office, 1982), pp. 956–958, n. 12:

FIRST AMENDMENT

Religion

Free Exercise: *Hamilton v. Regents*, 293 U.S. 245 (1934); *Cantwell v. Connecticut*, 310 U.S. 296 (1940).

Establishment: *Everson v. Board of Education*, 330 U.S. 1 (1947); *Illinois ex rel McCollum v. Board of Education*, 333 U.S. 203 (1948).

Speech

Gitlow v. New York, 268 U.S. 652 (1925); *Fiske v. Kansas*, 274 U.S. 380 (1927); *Stromberg v. California*, 283 U.S. 359 (1931).

Press

Near v. Minnesota, 283 U.S. 697 (1931).

Assembly

Association: *DeJonge v. Oregon*, 299 U.S. 353 (1937); *NAACP v. Alabama*, 357 U.S. 449 (1958).

Petition: *DeJonge v. Oregon*, 299 U.S. 353 (1937); *Hague v. CIO*, 307 U.S. 496 (1939); *Bridges v. California*, 314 U.S. 252 (1941).

FOURTH AMENDMENT

Wolf v. Colorado, 338 U.S. 25 (1949); *Mapp v. Ohio*, 367 U.S. 643 (1961).

FIFTH AMENDMENT

Double Jeopardy: *Benton v. Maryland*, 395 U.S. 784 (1969); *Ashe v. Swenson*, 397 U.S. 436 (1970).

Self-Incrimination: *Malloy v. Hogan*, 378 U.S. 1 (1964); *Griffin v. California*, 380 U.S. 609 (1965).

Just Compensation: *Chicago, B & Q Railroad v. City of Chicago*, 166 U.S. 226 (1897).

SIXTH AMENDMENT

Speedy Trial: *Klopfer v. North Carolina*, 386 U.S. 213 (1967).

Public Trial: *In re Oliver*, 333 U.S. 257 (1948).

Jury Trial: *Duncan v. Louisiana*, 391 U.S. 145 (1968).

Impartial Jury: *Irvin v. Dowd*, 366 U.S. 717 (1961); *Turner v. Louisiana*, 379 U.S. 466 (1965); *Parker v. Gladden*, 385 U.S. 363 (1966)

Notice of Charges: *In re Oliver,* 333 U.S. 257 (1948).

Confrontation: *Pointer v. Texas*, 380 U.S. 400 (1965); *Douglas v. Alabama*, 380 U.S. 415 (1965).

Compulsory Process: *Washington v. Texas*, 338 U.S. 14 (1967).

Counsel: *Powell v. Alabama*, 287 U.S. 45 (1932); *Gideon v. Wainwright*, 372 U.S. 335 (1963); *Argersinger v. Hamlin*, 407 U.S. 25 (1972).

EIGHTH AMENDMENT

Louisiana ex rel Francis v. Resweber, 329 U.S. 459 (1947); *Robinson v. California*, 370 U.S. 660 (1962).

NOT INCORPORATED

Second Amendment, Third Amendment, Grand Jury Indictment Clause of Fifth Amendment, Seventh Amendment.

SUGGESTIONS FOR FURTHER READING

Benedict, Michael Les, "Preserving Federalism: Reconstruction and the Waite Court," *The Supreme Court Review* (Chicago, IL: University of Chicago Press, 1978).

Beth, Loren P., "The *Slaughter-House Cases*—Revisited," 23 *Louisiana Law Review* (1963): 587.

Cortner, Richard C., *The Supreme Court and the Second Bill of Rights: The*

Fourteenth Amendment and the Nationalization of Civil Liberties (Madison, WI: University of Wisconsin Press, 1981).

Corwin, Edward S., "The Doctrine of Due Process of Law Before the Civil War," 24 *Harvard Law Review* (1911): 460.

_____, *The "Higher Law" Background of American Constitutional Law* (Ithaca, NY: Cornell University Press, 1929).

Crosskey, William W., "Charles Fairman, 'Legislative History,' and the Constitutional Limitations on State Authority," 22 *University of Chicago Law Review* (1954): 1.

Curtis, Michael Kent, *No State Shall Abridge: The Fourteenth Amendment and the Bill of Rights* (Durham, NC: Duke University Press, 1986).

Ely, John Hart, *Democracy and Distrust: A Theory of Judicial Review* (Cambridge, MA: Harvard University Press, 1980).

Fairman, Charles A., "Does the Fourteenth Amendment Incorporate the Bill of Rights? The Original Understanding," 2 *Stanford Law Review* (1949): 5.

_____, "A Reply to Professor Crosskey," 22 *University of Chicago Law Review* (1954): 144.

Hamilton, Walton H., "The Path of Due Process of Law," in *The Constitution Reconsidered*, ed. Conyers Read (New York, NY: Columbia University Press, 1938).

Henkin, Louis, "Selective Incorporation in the Fourteenth Amendment," 73 *Yale Law Journal* (1963): 74.

Hyman, Harold M., *A More Perfect Union: The Impact of the Civil War and Reconstruction on the Constitution* (New York, NY: Knopf, 1973).

Israel, Jerold, "Selective Incorporation Revisited," 71 *Michigan Law Review* (1982): 253.

Kaczorowski, Robert, *The Politics of Judicial Interpretation: The Federal Courts, Department of Justice and Civil Rights, 1866–1876* (Dobbs Ferry, NY: Oceana, 1985).

_____, *Nationalization of Civil Rights: Constitutional Theory and Practice in a Racist Society, 1866–1883* (New York, NY: Garland, 1987).

Kadish, Sanford, "Methodology and Criteria in Due Process Analysis—Survey and Criticism," 66 *Yale Law Journal* (1957): 319.

Murphy, Walter F., "*Slaughter-House*, Civil Rights, and Limits on Constitutional Change," 32 *American Journal of Jurisprudence* (1987): 1

Nelson, William E., *The Fourteenth Amendment: From Political Principle to Judicial Doctrine* (Cambridge, MA: Harvard University Press, 1988).

tenBroek, Jacobus, *Equal under Law*, new enlarged ed. (New York, NY: Collier, 1965).

Walker, Frank H., "Constitutional Law—Was It Intended that the Fourteenth Amendment Incorporates the Bill of Rights?" 42 *North Carolina Law Review* (1964): 925.

THE SUPREME COURT AND STATE CONSTITUTIONS

PruneYard Shopping Center v. Robins
447 U.S. 74 (1980)

SETTING

In 1776, following their declaration of independence from Great Britain, the thirteen states began to set up new governments. Most of the states drafted and adopted their own constitutions, although in states like Connecticut and Rhode Island, where the colonial charters had been so liberal, all that was required was to strike mention of the king. State constitutions were drawn up in a climate of opinion that emphasized popular sovereignty and the existence of certain fundamental rights with which government cannot interfere. The pattern in all state constitutions, before describing the government and its powers, was to declare the rights that the citizens reserved to themselves, such as freedom of the press, freedom from unreasonable searches and seizures, the right to trial by jury, and the requirement that state government follow proper legal procedures in conducting its business. State bills of right, in short, appeared at the beginning of a constitution, rather than as an appendage to it. The presence of a bill of rights in a state constitution provides citizens with a vehicle for litigating in state courts whether government has infringed improperly on particular rights.

As previous cases in this chapter have demonstrated, state courts were not always vigilant in protecting individual rights and liberties, which led to a movement to incorporate the guarantees of the first eight amendments to the Constitution of the United States against the states. Emphasis on state constitutional protections was eclipsed by what is frequently called the nationalization of the Bill of Rights, discussed in a previous section of this chapter.

Beginning in the 1970s, the Supreme Court became increasingly restrictive in its interpretation of the guarantees in the federal Bill of Rights. In response, litigants and some state judges began to refocus on state constitutional guarantees. Whether the Supreme Court of the United States would defer to states that declared that their state constitutions grant greater protections to individuals than the federal Bill of Rights as construed by the Supreme Court became an important subject of litigation by the 1980s.

A lead case during the period of "rediscovery" of state constitutional guarantees involved the relationship between freedom of speech and private property rights. The case arose out of the efforts of a group of American Jews to seek access to a privately owned shopping mall in Santa Clara County, California, to circulate petitions in an effort to mobilize the U.S. government to support Israel in an ongoing confrontation with Syria.

PruneYard Shopping Center is a twenty-one-acre shopping center in Santa Clara County, California, owned by Fred Sahadi. In 1975, the shopping center contained sixty-five shops, ten restaurants, and a movie theater. It is bordered on two sides by public sidewalks and street. Although the shopping center is open to the public and encourages the public to patronize its commercial establishments, Sahadi had a policy of prohibiting all hand billing and circulation of petitions within the center.

On November 17, 1975, Michael Robbins and Ira Marcus, high-school age students in the 1976 confirmation class of Temple Emanu-El, located in San Jose, California, went to the PruneYard Shopping Center, where they set up a table in the central courtyard and solicited signatures in support of petitions condemning Syria for refusing to allow Jews to leave the country. The students were accompanied by their teacher, Roberta Bell-Kliger. The petitions also condemned a United Nations resolution on Zionism. The group planned to send the petitions to President Gerald Ford and to members of Congress. The reason the group went to the shopping center was because of the scarcity of people on the publicly owned areas of downtown San Jose. The students' self-imposed policy was to treat all people courteously, not to block entrances to the center or to stores, and to remain orderly.

Approximately five minutes after they began to collect signatures, security personnel for the shopping center told them that their conduct was prohibited by shopping center regulations and that they would have to leave, but that they could continue to circulate their petitions on the public sidewalks outside the center. The students left. The small volume of foot traffic on the public sidewalks made their signature-gathering efforts pointless. They went to another privately owned shopping center in Santa Clara County, but again were denied access for petitioning purposes.

The students subsequently contacted Sahadi and offered to submit to any reasonable regulations to allow them to continue their petition project. Sahadi stated that their activity would not be allowed under any circumstances. The students then filed for an injunction against the shopping center requiring it to permit the students to gather signatures in the common areas of the PruneYard Shopping Center. The Santa Clara County Superior Court refused to grant the injunction, finding that the students had other adequate avenues of communication available to them. The California Court of Appeal affirmed.

The California Supreme Court reversed and ordered the trial court to issue the injunction. In doing so, the court relied on the free speech and petitioning provisions of Article I, sections 2 and 3, of the California Constitution. Section 2(a) provides that: "Every person may freely speak, write and publish his or her sentiments on all subjects, being responsible for the abuse of this right. A law may not restrain or abridge liberty of speech or press." According to the state high court, shopping centers in California are essential and invaluable forums and are the gathering places for California communities. Furthermore, it found that private shopping centers have replaced traditional public forums. The court concluded that the definitive protection of speech and petitioning in the California Constitution could be vindicated only by permitting peaceful hand billing and solicitation of signatures at shopping centers under appropriate time, place, and manner restrictions. Sahadi and PruneYard Shopping Center appealed to the Supreme Court of the United States.

HIGHLIGHTS OF SUPREME COURT ARGUMENTS

BRIEF FOR PRUNEYARD

◆ In compelling him to make his property available as a forum for petitioning, the California Supreme Court failed to balance Sahadi's First, Fifth, and Fourteenth Amendment rights against the state-created right to enter on private property to solicit petition signatures from shopping center patrons. Under this Court's decision in *Lloyd Corp. v. Tanner*, 407 U.S. 551 (1972), such a balance must be struck before a state may constitutionally require access to private property for speech purposes.

◆ The California courts were required to determine whether Sahadi's federal constitutional rights superseded a right of access grounded on the free speech and petitioning provisions of the California Constitution. Because this is a case in which resolution of the federal question was necessary to the judgment below, this Court has jurisdiction.

◆ Resolution of this case is controlled by *Lloyd Corp. v. Tanner*, which upheld the right of a privately owned shopping center to prohibit the distribution of handbills on its property. Sahadi's First (speech), Fifth (property), and Fourteenth Amendment rights are superior to the state right of access created by the California Supreme Court.

◆ When adequate alternative channels of communication are available, as the trial court found in this case, the federal constitutional rights of shopping center owners outweigh any state-created right of access.

AMICUS CURIAE BRIEFS SUPPORTING PRUNEYARD

Homart Development Company; International Council of Shopping Centers; joint brief of The Taubman Company, Inc. and California Business Properties Association.

BRIEF FOR ROBBINS, MARCUS, AND BELL-KLIGER

◆ Supreme Court review in this case is inappropriate because the California Supreme Court's decision rests on adequate and independent state grounds.

◆ This Court's decision in *Lloyd Corp. v. Tanner*, 407 U.S. 551 (1972), did not diminish the power of the states to regulate property and resolve disputes between its citizens under state law. It merely established the limits of the First Amendment as a basis of such regulation. It said nothing about what the outcome would be under state constitutional provisions that are more protective of individual rights than the Constitution of the United States.

◆ The rights of petition and incidental speech are inherent in a democratic society and are fundamental in California, where they are expressly guaranteed by the state constitution.

◆ California's restrictions on PruneYard's power to control its property does not amount to a taking of property under the Fifth Amendment: Sahadi had no right to silence his patrons and suffers no loss by their noninterfering speech and petitioning.

◆ The owner of land that serves the general public is subject to reasonable regulations imposed for the public welfare.

AMICUS CURIAE BRIEFS SUPPORTING ROBBINS, MARCUS, AND BELL-KLIGER

United States; joint brief of The American Civil Liberties Union of Northern California, The ACLU Foundation of Southern California, and the American Civil Liberties Union; The American Federation of Labor and the Congress of Industrial Organization.

SUPREME COURT DECISION: 9–0

REHNQUIST, J.

Our reasoning in *Lloyd* [*Corp. v. Tanner*, 407 U.S. 551 (1972)] ... does not *ex proprio vigore* [by its own force] limit the authority of the State to exercise its police power or its sovereign right to adopt in its own Constitution individual liberties more expansive than those conferred by the Federal Constitution.... In *Lloyd* there was no state constitutional or statutory provision that had been construed to create rights to the use of private property by strangers, comparable to those found to exist by the California Supreme Court here. It is, of course, well established that a State in the exercise of its police power may adopt reasonable restrictions on private property so long as the restrictions do not amount to a taking without just compensation or contravene any other federal constitutional provision....

Appellants ... contend that a right to exclude others underlies the Fifth Amendment guarantee against the taking of property without just compensation and the Fourteenth Amendment guarantee against the deprivation of property without due process of law.

It is true that one of the essential sticks in the bundle of property rights is the right to exclude others.... And here there has literally been a "taking" of that right to the extent that the California Supreme Court has interpreted the State Constitution to entitle its citizens to exercise free expression and petition rights on shopping center property. But it is well established that "not every destruction or injury to property by governmental action has been held to be a 'taking' in the constitutional sense." *Armstrong v. United States*, 364 U.S. 40 (1960). Rather, the determination whether a state law unlawfully infringes a landowner's property in violation of the Taking Clause requires an examination of whether the restriction on private property "forc[es] some people alone to bear public burdens which, in all fairness and justice, should be borne by the public as a whole." Id. This examination entails inquiry into such factors as the character of the governmental action, its economic impact, and its interference with reasonable investment-backed expectations....

Here the requirement that appellants permit appellees to exercise state-protected rights of free expression and petition on shopping center property clearly does not amount to an unconstitutional infringement of appellants' property rights under the Taking Clause. There is nothing to suggest that preventing appellants from prohibiting this sort of activity will unreasonably impair the value or use of their property as a shopping center. The PruneYard is a large commercial complex that covers several city blocks, contains numerous separate business establishments, and is open to the public at large. The decision of the California Supreme Court makes it clear that the PruneYard may restrict expressive activity by adopting time, place, and manner regulations that will minimize any interference with its commercial functions. Appellees were orderly, and they limited their activity to the common areas of the shopping center. In these circumstances, the fact that they may have "physically invaded" appellants' property cannot be viewed as determinative....

There is also little merit to appellants' argument that they have been denied their property without due process of law. In *Nebbia v. New York*, 291 U.S. 502 (1934), this Court stated:

[N]either property rights nor contract rights are absolute ... Equally fundamental with the private right is that of the public to regulate it in the common interest....

... [T]he guaranty of due process, as has often been held, demands only that the law shall not be unreasonable, arbitrary or capricious, and that the means selected shall have a real and substantial relation to the objective sought to be attained.

Appellants have failed to provide sufficient justification for concluding that this test is not satisfied by the State's asserted interest in promoting more expansive rights of free speech and petition than conferred by the Federal Constitution.

Appellants finally contend that a private property owner has a First Amendment right not to be forced by the State to use his property as a forum for the speech of others....

[T]he shopping center by choice of its owner is not limited to the personal use of appellants. It is instead a business establishment that is open to the public to come and go as they please. The views expressed by members of the public in passing out pamphlets or seeking signatures for a petition thus will not likely be identified with those of the owner. Second, no specific message is dictated by the State to be displayed on appellants' property. There consequently is no danger of governmental discrimination for or against a particular message. Finally, as far as appears here appellants can expressly disavow any connection with the message by simply posting signs in the area where the speakers or handbillers stand. Such signs, for example, could disclaim any sponsorship of the message and could explain that the persons are communicating their own messages by virtue of state law....

We conclude that neither appellants' federally recognized property rights nor their First Amendment rights have been infringed by the California Supreme Court's decision recognizing a right of appellees to exercise state-protected rights of expression and petition on appellants' property. The judgment of the Supreme Court of California is therefore

Affirmed.

BLACKMUN, J. CONCURRING [OMITTED]

MARSHALL, J., CONCURRING

... I applaud the court's decision, which is a part of a very healthy trend of affording state constitutional provisions a more expansive interpretation than this Court has given to the Federal Constitution....

I join the opinion of the Court.

WHITE, J., CONCURRING IN PART AND CONCURRING IN THE JUDGMENT [OMITTED]

POWELL AND WHITE, J.J., CONCURRING IN PART AND IN THE JUDGMENT

Although I join the judgment, I do not agree with all of the reasoning[.]...

[T]he Court rejects appellants' contention that "a private property owner has a First Amendment right not to be forced by the State to use his property as a forum for the speech of others." I agree that the owner of this shopping center has failed to establish a cognizable First Amendment claim in this case. But some of the language in the Court's opinion is unnecessarily and perhaps confusingly broad. In my view, state action that transforms privately owned property into a forum for the expression

of the public's views could raise serious First Amendment questions....

As the Court observes, this case involves only a state-created right of limited access to a specialized type of property. But even when no particular message is mandated by the State, First Amendment interests are affected by state action that forces a property owner to admit third-party speakers. In many situations, a right of access is no less intrusive than speech compelled by the State itself.... If a state law mandated public access to the bulletin board of a free-standing store, hotel, office, or small shopping center, customers might well conclude that the messages reflect the view of the proprietor. The same would be true if the public were allowed to solicit or distribute pamphlets in the entrance area of a store or in the lobby of a private building. The property owner or proprietor would be faced with a choice: he either could permit his customers to receive a mistaken impression or he could disavow the messages. Should he take the first course, he effectively has been compelled to affirm someone else's belief. Should he choose the second, he had been forced to speak when he would prefer to remain silent. In short, he has lost control over his freedom to speak or not to speak on certain issues....

A property owner also may be faced with speakers who wish to use his premises as a platform for views that he finds morally repugnant....

One easily can identify other circumstances in which a right of access to commercial property would burden the owner's First and Fourteenth Amendment right to refrain from speaking. But appellants have identified no such circumstance....

On the record before us, I cannot say

that customers of this vast center would be likely to assume that appellees' limited speech activity expressed the views of the PruneYard or of its owner....

QUESTIONS

1. In *PruneYard* the Court upheld a state court's interpretation of the California Constitution's guarantee of speech and petition rights that is more protective of those rights than the Constitution of the United States has been interpreted to be. What is the effect of that holding on a private property owner's rights under the Constitution of the United States? Can they be reconciled, or is the decision in *PruneYard* another example of the inchoate nature of American federalism?

2. Does *PruneYard* stand for the proposition that states retain considerable latitude under their own constitutions to secure the rights of their citizens? If so, does this mean that the Constitution of the United States provides only minimum guarantees of rights?

3. What are the ramifications for federal/state relations of the *PruneYard* opinions by Justices Rehnquist and Powell, respectively?

4. The *amicus* brief of the United States, supporting respondents Robbins, Marcus, and Bell-Kliger in *PruneYard*, argued that state protection of the reasonable exercise of speech and petition rights in privately owned shopping centers is consistent with the First and Fifth Amendments to the Constitution of the United States. For what reasons would the United States take this position? What insights, if any, into federal/state relations does its position provide?

THE SUPREME COURT AND STATE CONSTITUTIONS

Michigan v. Long
463 U.S. 1032 (1983)

SETTING

Although the Fourth Amendment to the Constitution of the United States prohibits warrantless searches and seizures, the Supreme Court of the United States has fashioned a number of exceptions to the warrant requirement. One such exception is the so-called "stop and frisk" rule announced in 1968 in *Terry v. Ohio*, 392 U.S. 1, designed to assure police officer safety in some encounters with criminal suspects. Under *Terry*, an officer may conduct a warrantless pat-down or "frisk" of the outer clothing of a suspect in an attempt to discover weapons that could endanger the officer. Any object that the officer believes provides reasonable suspicion of its being a weapon may be removed from the suspect and introduced as evidence at trial. (See Volume II, Chapter 8.)

A criminal case from the state of Michigan raised the question of whether the *Terry* exception should be extended to include "frisks" of objects as well as individuals in the name of officer safety. The answer to that question was complicated by Article I, section 11, of the Michigan Constitution, which provides:

> The person, houses, papers and possessions of every person shall be secure from unreasonable searches and seizures. No warrant to search any place or to seize any person or things shall issue without describing them, nor without probable cause, supported by oath or affirmation. The provisions of this section shall not be construed to bar from evidence in any criminal proceedings any narcotic drug, firearm, bomb, explosive or any other dangerous weapon, seized by a peace officer outside the curtilage of any dwelling house in this state.

The issue in *Michigan v. Long* involved the so-called "independent and adequate state ground" doctrine: Does the Constitution of the United States or a state constitution provide the appropriate framework for determining whether a criminal defendant's rights have been violated?

Long arose out of the following facts: Just after midnight on the morning of August 25, 1977, Deputies Howell and Lewis of the Barry County, Michigan, Sheriff's Department observed a car drive past them in the opposite direction. They clocked the speed on a radar gun at seventy-one miles per hour. They turned around and pursued the car without turning on their vehicle's flashing lights. The officers lost the speeding car, then saw it make a left turn, drive down the side of the road, swerve into a ditch and stop. David Long, the driver and sole occupant, was still sitting in the driver's seat when the deputies drove up behind it. As they walked toward the car, Long got out and met them near the rear fender. Deputy Howell asked Long to produce his driver's license. Long stared at Howell but made no response. Howell asked again. Long waited a few seconds, then produced his license. Howell then asked for a certificate of registration and proof of insurance. Long again neither moved nor responded. Then, without saying anything, Long turned around and walked back to the open door on the driver's side. Howell concluded that Long "was on something" and the two deputies followed him.

As they approached the open car door, the deputies saw a large folded knife lying on the floorboard in front of the driver's seat near the open door. Long was instructed to "hold it" and to put his hands on the roof of the car. Howell frisked Long for weapons, while Lewis retrieved a large folding Browning knife.

After seizing the knife, Howell told Long that he was not under arrest, but that he was not free to leave because Howell "still wanted to talk to him." Howell then shined his flashlight into the front seat of the car to search for more weapons. He saw something leather-like sticking out from under the folded-down front-seat armrest. Howell kneeled in the car, raised the armrest and saw an open leather pouch, which was large enough to contain a weapon. Before touching the pouch, however, Howell also saw a clear plastic bag containing a grass-like material protruding from one side of the pouch. Howell believed the material was marijuana. He removed the pouch and plastic baggie and showed them to Deputy Lewis and to Long. Long confirmed that the baggie contained marijuana. Howell then felt a solid object in the pouch and discovered that it contained a bottle filled with white powder, a tin foil wrapped pill, and a package of cigarette papers.

Long was arrested for possession of marijuana and the deputies decided to impound his car. As they awaited arrival of the tow truck, they searched the car's interior for additional contraband and the glove box for a vehicle registration. They found neither. Howell then asked Long for the key to the trunk and Long responded that he did not have one. Howell walked to the rear of the car and observed that the trunk lock had been punched out, leaving a hole. He also observed two hand prints in the layer of dust on the car. He inserted his pocketknife into the hole, raised the trunk lid, and saw two large bags of marijuana with a split in them. (The bags were subsequently weighed and determined to contain about 75 pounds of marijuana.) Long was then handcuffed, placed in the squad car, and taken to the sheriff's department.

Long was charged with possession of marijuana with intent to deliver. He moved pretrial to suppress the marijuana taken from the car's interior and its trunk. A jury trial in the Barry County Circuit Court commenced on August 28, 1978, and, following an improper opening statement by the prosecutor, the charges were reduced to possession of marijuana. Long's subsequent motions to exclude the contraband were denied. Following a brief trial and an hour of deliberation, the jury convicted Long of possession of marijuana. He was placed on probation for two years and fined $1,000.

Long appealed his conviction to the Michigan Court of Appeals, which affirmed. The Michigan Supreme Court reversed, stating that the case did not come within the narrowly drawn exceptions to the warrant requirements of either Article I, section 11, of the Michigan Constitution or the Fourth Amendment to the Constitution of the United States. It held that because Long was outside the car with an officer between him and the door, the frisk of the car for weapons was not justified on the grounds of officer safety. The Supreme Court of the United States granted Michigan's petition for a writ of certiorari.

HIGHLIGHTS OF SUPREME COURT ARGUMENTS

BRIEF FOR MICHIGAN

◆ The search of Long's car was valid because of the deputies' concern that there might be more weapons in the car. The resulting "frisk" of the armrest was justified by a reasonable suspicion that the situation was dangerous. Under the rule of *Terry v. Ohio*, 392 U.S. 1 (1968), lifting the armrest of the car to investigate the leather-like article protruding from under the armrest was reasonable.

◆ This Court should permit a protective frisk of that part of Long's car that was reasonably accessible to him when he sought to re-enter the car to obtain needed identification.

AMICUS CURIAE BRIEF SUPPORTING MICHIGAN

Joint brief of Gulf and Great Plains Legal Foundation of America and Americans for Effective Law Enforcement, Inc.; United States.

BRIEF FOR LONG

◆ Certiorari was improvidently granted in this case. The decision of the Michigan Supreme Court rests on an adequate state law ground; namely, Article I, section 11, of the Michigan Constitution. Michigan courts have consistently imposed a higher standard under the state constitution relating to search and seizure than this Court has imposed under the Fourth Amendment. Because of the independent state ground for decision, this court lacks jurisdiction.

◆ The limited, narrowly construed exceptions to the Fourth Amendment's warrant requirement should not be expanded. Expansion of *Terry v. Ohio*, 392 U.S. 1 (1968), would result in the scope of protective searches being broader than searches made incident to arrest and is not justified by the dangers of police work.

◆ A potentially dangerous, but ordinarily innocent, object in the vicinity of investigating officers is not alone reason to believe that a traffic violator nearby is dangerous.

SUPREME COURT DECISION

(8–1 on jurisdiction, 6–3 on merits)

O'CONNOR, J.

... Before reaching the merits, we must consider Long's argument that we are without jurisdiction to decide this case because the decision below rests on an adequate and independent state ground. The court below referred twice to the state constitution in its opinion, but otherwise relied exclusively on federal law. Long argues that the Michigan courts have provided greater protection from searches and seizures under the state constitution than is afforded under the Fourth Amendment, and the references to the state constitution therefore establish an adequate and independent ground for the decision below.

It is, of course, "incumbent upon this Court ... to ascertain for itself ... whether the asserted non-federal ground independently and adequately supports the judgment." *Abie State Bank v. Bryan*, 282 U.S. 765 (1931). Although we have announced a number of principles in order to help us determine whether various forms of references to state law constitute adequate and independent state grounds, we openly admit that we have thus far not developed a satisfying and consistent approach for resolving this vexing issue. In some instances, we have taken the strict view that if the ground of decision was at all unclear, we would dismiss the case…. In other instances, we have vacated, … or continued a case, … in order to obtain clarification about the nature of a state court decision…. In more recent cases, we have ourselves examined state law to determine whether state courts have used federal law to guide their application of state law or to provide the actual basis for the decision that was reached….

This ad hoc method of dealing with cases that involve possible adequate and independent state grounds is antithetical to the doctrinal consistency that is required when sensitive issues of federal-state relations are involved. Moreover, none of the various methods of disposition that we have employed thus far recommends itself as the preferred method that we should apply to the exclusion of others, and we therefore determine that it is appropriate to reexamine our treatment of this jurisdictional issue in order to achieve the consistency that is necessary.

The process of examining state law is unsatisfactory because it requires us to interpret state laws with which we are generally unfamiliar, and which often, as in this case, have not been discussed at length by the parties. Vacation and continuance for clarification have also been unsatisfactory both because of the delay and decrease in efficiency of judicial administration … and, more important, because these methods of disposition place significant burdens on state courts to demonstrate the presence or absence of our jurisdiction…. Finally, outright dis-

missal of cases is clearly not a panacea because it cannot be doubted that there is an important need for uniformity in federal law, and that this need goes unsatisfied when we fail to review an opinion that rests primarily upon federal grounds and where the independence of an alleged state ground is not apparent from the four corners of the opinion….

Respect for the independence of state courts, as well as avoidance of rendering advisory opinions, have been the cornerstones of this Court's refusal to decide cases where there is an adequate and independent state ground. It is precisely because of this respect for state courts, and this desire to avoid advisory opinions, that we do not wish to continue to decide issues of state law that go beyond the opinion that we review, or to require state courts to reconsider cases to clarify the grounds of their decisions. Accordingly, when, as in this case, a state court decision fairly appears to rest primarily on federal law, or to be interwoven with the federal law, and when the adequacy and independence of any possible state law ground is not clear from the face of the opinion, we will accept as the most reasonable explanation that the state court decided the case the way it did because it believed that federal law required it to do so. If a state court chooses merely to rely on federal precedents as it would on the precedents of all other jurisdictions, then it need only make clear by a plain statement in its judgment or opinion that the federal cases are being used only for the purpose of guidance, and do not themselves compel the result that the court has reached. In this way, both justice and judicial administration will be greatly improved. If the state court decision indicates clearly and expressly that it is alternatively based on bona fide separate, adequate, and independent grounds, we, of course, will not undertake to review the decision.

This approach obviates in most instances the need to examine state law in order to decide the nature of the state court decision, and will at the same time avoid the danger of our rendering advisory opinions. It also avoids the unsatisfactory and intrusive practice of requiring state courts to clarify their decisions to the satisfaction of this Court. We believe that such an approach will provide state judges with a clearer opportunity to develop state jurisprudence unimpeded by federal interference, and yet will preserve the integrity of federal law. "It is fundamental that state courts be left free and unfettered by us in interpreting their state constitutions. But it is equally important that ambiguous or obscure adjudications by state courts do not stand as barriers to a determination by this Court of the validity under the federal constitution of state action." [*Minnesota v.*] *National Tea Co.*, 309 U.S. [551 (1940)].

The principle that we will not review judgments of state courts that rest on adequate and independent state grounds is based, in part, on "the limitations of our own jurisdiction." *Herb v. Pitcairn*, 324 U.S. 117 (1945). The jurisdictional concern is that we not "render an advisory opinion, and if the same judgment would be rendered by the state court after we corrected its views of federal laws, our review could amount to nothing more than an advisory opinion." Id. Our requirement of a "plain statement" that a decision rests upon adequate and independent state grounds does not in any way authorize the rendering of advisory opinions.

Rather, in determining, as we must, whether we have jurisdiction to review a case that is alleged to rest on adequate and independent state grounds ... we merely assume that there are no such grounds when it is not clear from the opinion itself that the state court relied upon an adequate and independent state ground and when it fairly appears that the state court rested its decision primarily on federal law.

Our review of the decision below under this framework leaves us unconvinced that it rests upon an independent state ground. Apart from its two citations to the state constitution, the court below relied exclusively on its understanding of *Terry* [*v. Ohio*, 392 U.S. 1 (1968)] and other federal cases. Not a single state case was cited to support the state court's holding that the search of the passenger compartment was unconstitutional.... The references to the state constitution in no way indicate that the decision below rested on grounds in any way independent from the state court's interpretation of federal law. Even if we accept that the Michigan constitution has been interpreted to provide independent protection for certain rights also secured under the Fourth Amendment, it fairly appears in this case that the Michigan Supreme Court rested its decision primarily on federal law.

Rather than dismissing the case, or requiring that the state court reconsider its decision on our behalf solely because of a mere possibility that an adequate and independent ground supports the judgment, we find that we have jurisdiction in the absence of a plain statement that the decision below rested on an adequate and independent state ground....

[On the merits, the Court held that the protective search of the passenger compartment of David Long's car was reasonable under *Terry v. Ohio*. If, while conducting a protective search of an automobile, police officers discover contraband other than weapons, they cannot be required to ignore the contraband, and the Fourth Amendment does not require its suppression under such circumstances.]

The decision of the Michigan Supreme Court is reversed, and the case is remanded for further proceedings not inconsistent with this opinion.

It is so ordered.

BLACKMUN, CONCURRING IN PART AND CONCURRING IN THE JUDGMENT [OMITTED]

BRENNAN AND MARSHALL, J.J., DISSENTING. [OMITTED]

STEVENS, J., DISSENTING

The jurisprudential questions presented in this case are far more important than the question whether the Michigan police officer's search of respondent's car violated the Fourth Amendment. The case raises profoundly significant questions concerning the relationship between two sovereigns—the State of Michigan and the United States of America.

The Supreme Court of the State of Michigan expressly held "that the deputies' search of the vehicle was proscribed by the Fourth Amendment of the United States Constitution and art. 1, Sec. 11 of the Michigan Constitution." The state law ground is clearly adequate to support the judgment, but the question whether it is independent of the Michigan Supreme Court's understanding of federal law is more difficult. Four possible ways of resolving that question present themselves: (1) asking the Michigan Supreme Court directly, (2) attempting to infer from all possible sources of state law what the Michigan Supreme Court meant, (3) presuming that adequate state grounds are independent unless it clearly appears otherwise, or (4) presuming that adequate state grounds are not independent unless it clearly appears otherwise. This Court has, on different occasions, employed each of the first three approaches; never until today has it even hinted at the fourth. In order to "achieve the consistency that is necessary," the Court today undertakes a reexamination of all the possibilities. It rejects the first approach as inefficient and unduly burdensome for state courts, and rejects the second approach as an inappropriate expenditure of our resources. Although I find both of those decisions defensible in themselves, I cannot accept the Court's decision to choose the fourth approach over the third—to presume that adequate state grounds are intended to be dependent on federal law unless the record plainly shows otherwise. I must therefore dissent.

If we reject the intermediate approaches, we are left with a choice between two presumptions: one in favor of our taking jurisdiction, and one against it. Historically, the latter presumption has always prevailed....

The Court today points out that in several cases we have weakened the traditional presumption by using the other two intermediate approaches identified above. Since those two approaches are now to be rejected, however, I would think that *stare decisis* would call for a return to historical principle. Instead, the Court seems to conclude that because some precedents are to be rejected, we must overrule them all.

Even if I agreed with the Court that we are free to consider as a fresh proposition whether we may take presumptive jurisdiction over the decisions of sovereign states, I could not agree that an expansive attitude makes good sense. It appears to be common ground that any rule we adopt should show "respect for state courts, and [a] desire to avoid advisory opinions." And I am confident that all members of this Court agree that there is a vital interest in the sound management of scarce federal judicial resources. All of those policies counsel against the exercise of federal jurisdiction. They are fortified by my belief that a policy of judicial restraint—one that allows other decisional bodies to have the last word in legal interpretation until it is truly necessary for this Court to intervene—enables this Court to make its most effective contribution to our federal system of government....

In this case the State of Michigan has arrested one of its citizens and the Michigan Supreme Court has decided to turn him loose. The respondent is a United States citizen as well as a Michigan citizen, but since there is no claim that he has been mistreated by the State of Michigan, the final outcome of the state processes offended no federal interest whatever. Michigan simply provided greater protection to one of its citizens than some other State might provide or, indeed, than this Court might require throughout the country.

I believe that in reviewing the decisions of state courts, the primary role of this Court is to make sure that persons who seek to vindicate federal rights have been fairly heard....

The Court offers only one reason for asserting authority over cases such as the one presented today: "an important need for uniformity in federal law [that] goes unsatisfied when we fail to review an opinion that rests primarily upon federal grounds and where the independence of an alleged state ground is not apparent from the four corners of the opinion." Of course, the supposed need to "review an opinion" clashes directly with our oft-repeated reminder that "our power is to correct wrong judgments, not to revise opinions." *Herb v. Pitcairn*, 324 U.S. 117 (1945). The clash is not merely one of form: the "need for uniformity in federal law" is truly an ungovernable engine. That same need is no less present when it is perfectly clear that a state ground is both independent and adequate. In fact, it is equally present if a state prosecutor announces that he believes a certain policy of nonenforcement is commanded by federal law. Yet we have never claimed jurisdiction to correct such errors, no matter how egregious they may be, and no matter how much they may thwart the desires of the state electorate. We do not sit to expound our understanding of the Constitution to interested listeners in the legal community; we sit to resolve disputes. If it is not apparent that our views would affect the outcome of a particular case, we cannot presume to interfere.

Finally, I am thoroughly baffled by the Court's suggestion that it must stretch its jurisdiction and reverse the judgment of the Michigan Supreme Court in order to show "[r]espect for the independence of state courts." Would we show respect for the Republic of Finland by convening a special sitting for the sole purpose of declaring that its decision to release an American citizen was based upon a misunderstanding of American law?

I respectfully dissent.

Questions

1. Summarize the doctrine of "independent and adequate state grounds" explained in *Michigan v. Long*. How does the majority's interpretation of this doctrine differ from Justice Stevens' reading of it? What are the federalism implications of each interpretation?

2. Is the Court's holding in *Long* consistent with *PruneYard*?

3. How persuasive is Justice O'Connor's rejection of Long's argument that the Supreme Court of the United States lacked jurisdiction because the Michigan Supreme Court's decision was based on an independent state constitutional ground? If the justices believed that the applicability of state law was uncertain in *Long*, should they have remanded the case to the Michigan Supreme Court for clarification of the ground on which its judgment rested rather than deciding the case on federal constitutional grounds? Justice O'Connor is an advocate of states' rights. Is her opinion in *Long* consistent with her commitment to a decentralized system of justice?

4. Given the fact that states are primarily responsible for administering the criminal justice system, is it appropriate for the Supreme Court to presume state dependence on federal law when a state court decision "fairly appears to rest primarily on federal law, or to be interwoven with federal law and when the adequacy and independence of any possible state law ground is not clear from the face of the opinion"? In America's system of federalism, should not the presumption cut in favor of the states?

5. The *amicus* brief submitted by the Gulf and Great Plains Legal Foundation on behalf of Michigan argued that a "frisk" of a car's interior for weapons should be allowed because traffic stops are a leading cause of police officer fatalities and that officers may not always be able to physically interpose their own bodies between a stopped person and the person's vehicle. Furthermore, police training manuals emphasize that every situation and every suspect must be regarded as "unpredictable." The Michigan Supreme Court's analysis, according to the Foundation, "would prevent officers from using consistent, systematic procedures to minimize the effects of this unpredictability."

   Does the Court's analysis in *Long* suggest that it agrees with the practical concerns expressed in the *amicus* brief and that the justices disagree with states whose constitutions grant criminal defendants more extensive rights than have been recognized under the Constitution of the United States?

Suggestions for Further Reading

Brennan Jr., William J., "State Constitutions and the Protection of Individual Rights," 90 *Harvard University Law Review* (1977): 489.

Brennan Jr., William J., "The Bill of Rights and the States: The Revival of State Constitutions as Guardians of Individual Rights," 61 *New York University Law Review* (1986): 535.

Falk Jr., Jerome B., "Foreword: The State Constitution: A More Than 'Adequate' Nonfederal Ground," 61 *California Law Review* (1973): 273.

Force, Robert, "State 'Bills of Rights': A Case of Neglect and the Need for a Renaissance," 3 *Valparaiso University Law Review* (1969): 125.

Graves, W. Brookes, "State Constitutional Law: A Twenty-Five-Year Summary," 8 *William & Mary Law Review* (1966): 1.

Howard, A. E. Dick, "State Courts and Constitutional Rights in the Day of the Burger Court," 62 *Virginia Law Review* (1976): 873.

Linde, Hans A., "Without 'Due Process': Unconstitutional Law in Oregon," 49 *Oregon Law Review* (1970): 125.

————, "First Things First: Rediscovering the States' Bills of Rights," 9 *University of Baltimore Law Review* (1980): 379.

Nagel, Robert F., *Intellect and Craft: The Contributions of Justice Hans Linde to American Constitutionalism* (Boulder, CO: Westview Press, 1995).

Newman, Jon O., "The 'Old Federalism': Protection of Individual Rights by State Constitutions in an Era of Federal Court Passivity," 15 *Connecticut Law Review* (1982): 21.

Note, "Freedom of Expression under State Constitutions," 20 *Stanford Law Review* (1968): 318.

Note, "Rediscovering the California Declaration of Rights," 26 *Hastings Law Journal* (1974): 481.

Note, "State Constitutional Guarantees of Adequate State Ground: Supreme Court Review and Problems of Federalism," 13 *American Criminal Law Review* (1976): 737.

Note, "Of Laboratories and Liberties: State Court Protection of Political and Civil Rights," 10 *Georgia Law Review* (1976): 533.

Note, "The New Federalism: Toward a Principled Interpretation of the State Constitution," 29 *Stanford Law Review* (1977): 297.

Symposium: "The Emergence of State Constitutional Law," 63 *Texas Law Review* (1985): 959.

Tarr, G. Alan, "Understanding State Constitutions," 65 *Temple Law Review* (1992): 1169.

Wilkes Jr., Donald E., "The New Federalism in Criminal Procedure: State Court Evasion of the Burger Court," 62 *Kentucky Law Journal* (1974): 421.

————, "More on the New Federalism in Criminal Procedure," 63 *Kentucky Law Journal* (1975): 873.

————, "The New Federalism in Criminal Procedure Revisited," 64 *Kentucky Law Journal* (1976): 729.

CHAPTER 6

—⟶⟵—

PROPERTY RIGHTS
VERSUS GOVERNMENTAL POWERS

CONTRACTS CLAUSE

Fletcher v. Peck
6 Cranch 87 (1810)

SETTING

Among the central features of constitutional government—some would argue *the* central feature—are limitations on governmental powers. As James Madison wrote in *Federalist* No. 51, "In framing a government ... the great difficulty lies in this: you must first enable the government to control the governed, and in the next place *oblige it to control itself*." (Emphasis added.) Much of American constitutional history has involved the quest for effective ways of obliging state and federal governments to refrain from infringing on property rights. The search began early on, in *Calder v. Bull*, 3 Dallas 386 (1789) (excerpted on pp. 772–777), where litigants sought to use the *Ex Post Facto Clause* of Article I, section 10, clause 1, to prevent a state legislature from enacting laws that retroactively affected property rights. After the *Calder* Court declared that the Constitution's two *Ex Post Facto* clauses pertain solely to criminal statutes, champions of property rights turned to the Contracts Clause, Article I, section 1, clause 1, in the effort to establish constitutional checks on state governments.

The Contracts Clause was added to the Constitution toward the end of the Philadelphia Convention. In late August 1787, delegate Rufus King of Massachusetts tried to persuade the delegates that the Convention should adopt the language of the Northwest Ordinance of 1787 that prohibited states from passing laws impairing the obligation of contracts. Gouverneur Morris of Pennsylvania responded that the proposal went "too far" and succeeded in having King's motion defeated. King, however, was subsequently able to persuade the Committee of Style, of which he was a member, to add the Contracts Clause. Language prohibiting states from impairing the obligation of contracts provoked little debate when the Committee reported to the

Convention on September 12. Two days later, however, another Massachusetts delegate, Elbridge Gerry, failed in his effort to include a similar prohibition against the national government.

In the limited debates about the Contracts Clause that occurred during the state ratifying conventions, Luther Martin of Maryland opposed the clause on the ground that it would prevent states from giving relief to debtors in economic hard times. James Madison defended the provision as a way of protecting private property, one of the "first principles" of government.

The scope of the Contracts Clause, and whether it prohibits only states from impairing the obligations of private contracts, was not settled by the Constitutional Convention. *Fletcher v. Peck* gave the Marshall Court an opportunity to give the first definitive interpretation of the clause. The case grew out of a political scandal in the state of Georgia.

In 1795, the Georgia legislature authorized the sale of some 35 million acres of land in territory known as the Yazoo tracts (located in the present states of Mississippi and Alabama) to the Georgia Company, the Georgia Mississippi Company, the Upper Mississippi Company, and the Tennessee Company. The selling price was $500,000, or about one and one-half cents an acre. The companies had promised to give legislators a share of the lands amounting to approximately $1,000 each in return for authorizing the sale.

An outraged Georgia electorate turned the bribed legislators out of office at the next election. In 1796, the new legislature repealed the year-old land grant and voided all the property rights the land grant had created. The rescinding law stated that since the 1795 law

> was made without constitutional authority, and fraudulently obtained, it is hereby declared of no binding force or effect on this state, or the people thereof, but is, and are to be considered, both law and grant, as they ought to be, *ipso facto*, of themselves, void, and the territory therein mentioned is also hereby declared to be the sole property of the state, subject only to the right of treaty of the United States to enable the state to purchase under its pre-emption right, the Indian title to the same.

Between the time of the original and rescinding acts of the legislature, the four land companies sold off as many parcels of the Yazoo tract as possible. Purchasers, many of whom were unaware of the fraud behind the original land grants, claimed that the 1796 rescinding act was null and void. In 1802, the U.S. government agreed to assume responsibility for resolving the confusion involving land titles created by the Yazoo incident. That agreement transferred the controversy from the state legislature to Congress. Congress struggled with the problem of compensation for six years. Meanwhile, some claimants decided to test the validity of the land titles in federal courts. John Peck and Robert Fletcher were among them.

Peck and Fletcher were shareholders in the New England Mississippi Company, which had acquired a parcel of the land conveyed to the Georgia Company under the 1795 grant. In 1803, Peck, a Massachusetts resident, sold fifteen thousand acres of the Yazoo land to Fletcher, a citizen of New Hampshire, for $3,000. The purpose of the sale was to arrange a case in federal court to determine the validity of the land titles acquired by the Georgia Company under the 1795 grant. In his suit for breach of contract, Fletcher relied on two theories. The first theory was that the Georgia legislature had no authority to sell the Yazoo lands in 1795. The second theory was that, assuming the validity of the original grant, the Georgia Company's title was invalidated by the 1796 Georgia rescinding act. Under either theory, Fletcher claimed, Peck could not convey clear title to the land to him.

The circuit court for the district of Massachusetts declared the 1795 act valid and the rescinding act of 1796 invalid. Peck, therefore, was held to have acquired clear title from the Georgia Company, which he conveyed to Fletcher. Fletcher appealed to the Supreme Court of the United States.

The case was first argued in 1809 and decided on a point of pleading. It was reargued on the merits in 1810.

Highlights of Supreme Court Arguments

BRIEF FOR FLETCHER

◆ Peck's defenses in the case are legally inadequate because they do not respond to the allegations of breach of contract.

◆ The Yazoo tract in contention originally belonged to the British crown. After the Revolution, the land devolved upon the United States, not the state of Georgia. Therefore, Georgia had no authority to sell the tract under the 1795 act.

BRIEF FOR PECK

◆ Any interest the United States has in the Yazoo lands derives from Georgia. This is because following the Revolution the several states were free, sovereign, independent entities. The Articles of Confederation made clear that no state was to be deprived of its territory for the benefit of the United States.

◆ There is nothing in the Constitution that can give the United States title to the lands in question. Article 4, section 3, of the Constitution explicitly states that the claims of states will not be prejudiced by Congress in disposing of and making rules for the territories and other properties of the United States.

◆ Assuming that the Georgia legislature had authority to dispose of the land in 1795, the legislature had no right to declare the law void the following year. Declaring the validity of a law is a judicial, not a legislative, function.

◆ A grant is an executed contract. An executed contract creates an implied executory contract, which is that the grantee shall continue to enjoy the thing granted according to the terms of the grant. The Constitution prohibits states from passing any law impairing the obligation of a contract.

◆ Both Fletcher and Peck are innocent of the fraud involving the Georgia legislature. They were bona fide purchasers, for value, without notice of fraud, and therefore are not affected by it.

SUPREME COURT DECISION: 7–0

MARSHALL, C.J.

... That the legislature of Georgia, unless restrained by its own constitution, possesses the power of disposing of the unappropriated lands within its own limits, in such a manner as its own judgment shall dictate, is a proposition not to be controverted. The only question, then, presented [in this regard] ... for the consideration of the court, is this, did the then constitution of the state of Georgia prohibit the legislature to dispose of the lands, which were the subject of this contract, in the manner stipulated by the contract?

The question, whether a law be void for its repugnancy to the constitution, is at all times, a question of much delicacy, which ought seldom, if ever, to be decided in the affirmative in a doubtful case. The court, when impelled by duty to render such a judgment, would be unworthy of its station, could it be unmindful of the solemn obligations which that station imposes....

[I]n the constitution of Georgia, adopted in the year 1789, the court can perceive no restriction on the legislative power, which inhibits the passage of the act of 1795. The court cannot say that, in passing that act, the legislature has transcended its powers, and violated the constitution....

That corruption should find its way into the governments of our infant republics, and contaminate the very source of legislation, or that impure motives should contribute to the passage of a law, or the formation of a legislative contract, are circumstances most deeply to be deplored. How far a court of justice would, in any case, be competent, on proceedings instituted by the state itself, to vacate a contract thus formed, and to annul rights acquired, under that contract, by third persons having no notice of the improper means by which it was obtained, is a question which the court would approach with much circumspection. It may well be doubted how far the validity of a law depends upon the motives of its framers, and how far the particular inducements, operating on members of the supreme sovereign power of a state, to the formation of a contract by that power, are examinable in a court of justice....

If the majority of the legislature be corrupted, it may well be doubted, whether it be within the province of the judiciary to control their conduct, and, if less than a majority act from impure motives, the principle by which judicial interference would be regulated, is not clearly discerned.

Whatever difficulties this subject might present, when viewed under aspects of which it may be susceptible, this court can perceive none in the particular pleadings now under consideration.

This is not a bill brought by the state of Georgia, to annul the contract, nor does it appear to the court … that the state of Georgia is dissatisfied with the sale that has been made. The case, as made out in the pleadings, is simply this: One individual who holds lands in the state of Georgia, under a deed covenanting that the title of Georgia was in the grantor, brings an action of covenant upon this deed, and assigns, as a breach, that some of the members of the legislature were induced to vote in favour of the law, which constituted the contract, by being promised an interest in it, and that therefore the act is a mere nullity.

… It would be indecent in the extreme, upon a private contract between two individuals, to enter into an inquiry respecting the corruption of the sovereign power of a state. If the title be plainly decided from a legislative act, which the legislature might constitutionally pass, if the act be clothed with all the requisite forms of a law, a court, sitting as a court of law, cannot sustain a suit brought by one individual against another founded on the allegation that the act is a nullity, in consequence of the impure motives which influenced certain members of the legislature which passed the law….

The lands in controversy vested absolutely in James Gunn and others [of the Georgia Company], the original grantees, by the conveyance of the governor, made in pursuance of an act of assembly to which the legislature was fully competent. Being thus in full possession of the legal estate, they, for a valuable consideration, conveyed portions of the land to those who were willing to purchase. If the original transaction was infected with fraud, these purchasers did not participate in it, and had no notice of it. They were innocent. Yet the legislature of Georgia has involved them in the fate of the first parties to the transaction, and, if the act be valid, has annihilated their rights also.

The legislature of Georgia was a party to this transaction; and for a party to pronounce its own deed invalid, whatever cause may be assigned for its invalidity, must be considered as a mere act of power which must find its vindication in a train of reasoning not often heard in courts of justice….

If a suit be brought to set aside a conveyance obtained by fraud, and the fraud be clearly proved, the conveyance will be set aside, as between the parties; but the parties of third persons, who are purchasers without notice, for a valuable consideration, cannot be disregarded. Titles which, according to every legal test, are perfect, are acquired with that confidence which is inspired by the opinion that the purchaser is safe. If there be any concealed defect, arising from the conduct of those who had held the property long before he acquired it, of which he had no notice, that concealed defect cannot be set up against him. He has paid his money for a title good at law, he is innocent, whatever may be the guilt of others, and equity will not subject him to the penalties attached to that guilt. All titles would be insecure, and the intercourse between man and man would be very seriously obstructed, if this principle be overturned….

In this case the legislature may have had ample proof that the original grant was obtained by practices which can never be too much reprobated, and which would have justified its abrogation so far as respected those to whom crime was imputable. But the grant, when issued, conveyed an estate in fee-simple to the grantee, clothed with all the solemnities which law can bestow. This estate was transferable; and those who purchased parts of it were not stained by that guilt which infected the original transaction. Their case is not distinguishable from the ordinary case of purchasers of a legal estate without knowledge of any secret fraud which might have led to the emanation of the original grant. According to the well known course of equity, their rights could not be affected by such fraud. Their situation was the same, their title was the same, with that of every other member of the community who holds land by regular conveyances from the original patentee.

Is the power of the legislature competent to the annihilation of such title, and to a resumption of the property thus held?

The principle asserted is, that one legislature is competent to repeal any act which a former legislature was competent to pass; and that one legislature cannot abridge the powers of a succeeding legislature.

The correctness of this principle, so far as respects general legislation, can never be controverted. But, if an act be done under a law, a succeeding legislature cannot undo it. The past cannot be recalled by the most absolute power. Conveyances have been made; those conveyances have vested legal estates, and, if those estates may be seized by the sovereign authority, still, that they originally vested is a fact, and cannot cease to be a fact.

When, then, a law is in its nature a contract, when absolute rights have vested under that contract; a repeal of the law cannot devest those rights; and the act of annulling them, if legitimate, is

rendered so by a power applicable to the case of every individual in the community....

The constitution of the United States declares that no state shall pass any bill of attainder, *ex post facto* law or law impairing the obligation of contracts.

Does the case now under consideration come within this prohibitory section of the constitution?

In considering this very interesting question, we immediately ask ourselves what is a contract? Is a grant a contract?

A contract is a compact between two or more parties, and is either executory or executed. An executory contract is one in which a party binds himself to do, or not to do, a particular thing; such was the law under which the conveyance was made by the [Georgia] governor. A contract executed is one in which the object of contract is performed; and this, says Blackstone, differs in nothing from a grant. The contract between Georgia and the purchasers was executed by the grant. A contract executed, as well as one which is executory, contains obligations binding on the parties. A grant, in its own nature, amounts to an extinguishment of the right of the grantor, and implies a contract not to re-assert that right. A party is, therefore, always estopped by his own grant.

Since, then, in fact, a grant is a contract executed, the obligation of which still continues, and since the constitution uses the general term contract, without distinguishing between those which are executory and those which are executed, it must be construed to comprehend the latter as well as the former. A law annulling conveyances between individuals, and declaring that the grantors should stand seised of their former estates, notwithstanding those grants, would be as repugnant to the constitution as a law discharging the vendors of property from the obligation of executing their contracts by conveyances. It would be strange if a contract to convey was secured by the constitution, while an absolute conveyance remained unprotected.

If, under a fair construction of the constitution, grants are comprehended under the term contracts, is a grant from the state excluded from the operation of the provision? Is the clause to be considered as inhibiting the state from impairing the obligation of contracts between two individuals, but as excluding from that inhibition contracts made with itself?

The words themselves contain no such distinction. They are general, and are applicable to contracts of every description. If contracts made with the state are to be exempted from their operation, the exception must arise from the character of the contracting party, not from the words which are employed.

Whatever respect might have been felt for the state sovereignties, it is not to be disguised that the framers of the constitution viewed, with some apprehension, the violent acts which might grow out of the feelings of the moment; and that the people of the United States, in adopting that instrument, have manifested a determination to shield themselves and their property from the effects of those sudden and strong passions to which men are exposed. The restrictions on the legislative power of the states are obviously founded in this sentiment; and the constitution of the United States contains what may be deemed a bill of rights for the people of each state....

It is, then, the unanimous opinion of the court, that, in this case, the estate having passed into the hands of a purchaser for a valuable consideration, without notice, the state of Georgia was restrained, either by general principles which are common to our free institutions, or by the particular provisions of the constitution of the United States, from passing a law whereby the estate of the plaintiff in the premises so purchased could be constitutionally and legally impaired and rendered null and void....

Judgment affirmed with costs.

JOHNSON, J., CONCURRING

... I do not hesitate to declare that a state does not possess the power of revoking its own grants. But I do it on a general principle, on the reason and nature of things: a principle which will impose laws even on the deity....

When the legislature have once conveyed their interest or property in any subject to the individual, they have lost all control over it; have nothing to act upon; it has passed from them; is vested in the individual; becomes intimately blended with his existence, as essentially so as the blood that circulates through his system. The government may indeed demand of him the one or the other, not because they are not his, but because whatever is his is his country's....

I have thrown out these ideas that I may have it distinctly understood that my opinion on this point is not founded on the provision in the constitution of the United States, relative to laws impairing the obligation of contracts. It is much to be regretted that words of less equivocal signification, had not been adopted in that article of the constitution. There is reason to believe, from the letters of Publius [in the *Federalist*], which are well-known to be entitled to the highest respect, that the object of the convention was to afford a general protection to individual rights against the acts of the state legislatures. Whether the words, "acts impairing the obligation of contracts," can be construed to have the same force as must have been given to the words "obligation and effect of contracts," is the difficulty in my mind....

I have been very unwilling to proceed to the decision of this cause at all. It appears to me to bear strong evidence, upon the face of it, of being a mere feigned case. It is our duty to decide on the rights, but not on the speculations of parties. My confidence, however, in the respectable gentlemen who have been engaged for the parties, has induced me to abandon my scruples, in the belief that they would never consent to impose a mere feigned case upon this court.

QUESTIONS

1. Alexander Hamilton, then a New York attorney, was consulted by one of the Yazoo purchasers about the constitutionality of the Georgia Rescinding Act. In 1796 he prepared a pamphlet expressing the view that Article I, section 10, "must be equivalent to saying that no State shall pass a law revoking, invalidating, or altering a contract," and that the Georgia rescinding act was "contrary to the Constitution and therefore null" (quoted in Charles Warren, *The Supreme Court in United States History*, 3 vols. [Boston, MA: Little, Brown and Company, 1923], I: 396–397).

   Marshall's interpretation of the Contracts Clause in *Fletcher* clearly paralleled Hamilton's opinion. Nevertheless, there are other interpretations of the Contracts Clause. Most historians believe that the Contracts Clause was included in the Constitution in response to cries for debt relief during the depressed economic conditions following the Revolution and that the primary purpose of the clause was to prevent states from passing bankruptcy and other laws to relieve debtors of their legal obligations to creditors. Should Marshall have deferred to the original understanding of the Contracts Clause? What views about property rights informed Hamilton's and Marshall's interpretations of the Contracts Clause?

2. A grant and a contract are different legal concepts. To grant means to bestow or to confer. A contract requires bargained-for consideration and imposes duties on the parties to the agreement. The 1795 Georgia land grant created no obligations. Whose interests were benefited, and whose impaired, by Chief Justice Marshall defining a grant as a contract?

3. *Fletcher* marks the first time the Supreme Court declared a state law unconstitutional. Subsequently, the Contracts Clause became the basis on which the Supreme Court invalidated state laws in half of the

instances before 1890 where it declared state laws unconstitutional. One hundred and thirteen years after *Fletcher*, Justice Oliver Wendell Holmes Jr. wrote: "I do not think that the United States would come to an end if we lost our power to declare an Act of Congress void. I do think the Union would be imperilled [sic] if we could not make that declaration as to the laws of the several states" (*Collected Legal Papers* [New York, NY: Harcourt Brace, 1920], pp. 295–296).

From the perspective of private property rights, is the Court's power over state laws so essential? Without such a check, might state legislatures run roughshod over the rights of property owners? Are there institutional reasons why state legislatures might be more inclined to do so than Congress?

4. Chief Justice Marshall concluded in *Fletcher* that the state of Georgia was limited, "*either* by general principles which are common to our free institutions, *or* by the particular provisions of the constitution of the United States" (emphasis added). By contrast, Justice Johnson argued that his view that Georgia "does not possess the power of revoking its own grants ... is not founded on the provision in the constitution of the United States, relative to laws impairing the obligation of contracts [but because of] *a general principle*, on the reason and nature of things: a principle which will impose laws even on the deity" (emphasis added). On which foundations should limitations on state governmental power over private property be based: general principles of natural law, implied restrictions, and/or express constitutional provisions?

Compare *Terrett v. Taylor*, 9 Cranch 43 (1815). In that case, Justice Story held that Virginia could not divest the Episcopal Church of its property, because doing so would transgress "principles of natural justice," "fundamental laws of every free government," and the "spirit and letter" of the Constitution. Does this language suggest that the Court in 1815 had established itself as the guardian of private property on both constitutional and extra-constitutional grounds?

5. Justice Story, who served as co-counsel for Peck during the second argument of *Fletcher*, was appointed to the Supreme Court the year after *Fletcher* was decided. Was Story culpable for bringing a "mere feigned case," as Justice Johnson suggests, to the Supreme Court? Compare *Fletcher* with *Prigg v. Pennsylvania*, Chapter 5, pp. 523–531. Do those two opinions suggest that the Court will wink at case in controversy (justiciability) requirements if the justices think an issue is sufficiently important? What principles in *Fletcher* and *Prigg* did the justices think were important enough to warrant Supreme Court intervention despite the lack of actual cases in controversy?

6. The *Fletcher* decision had important practical consequences for the

rapid westward migration of settlers during this era. Constitutional historian Melvin Urofsky writes:

> With settlers streaming westward, land changed hands frequently, and clear title depended on the validity of original grants. Virginia, for example, had granted large tracts of lands in what later became Kentucky, and the original grantees moved quickly to sell off the lots. The lack of decent survey maps, the absence of local land offices to register the deeds, the shortage of qualified conveyancers, and the large number of squatters would clog federal and state courts in Kentucky with property cases for decades to come. *Fletcher* at least provided a rule by which the courts could try, even if not always successfully, to clear away the morass of disputed claims. (*A March of Liberty* [New York, NY: Alfred A. Knopf, 1988], p. 228)

In the context described by Urofsky, *Fletcher* can be read as both protecting the *status quo* in property relations and fostering a dramatic change in those relations. Which did Marshall intend?

COMMENT

Two years after *Fletcher v. Peck*, Chief Justice Marshall had an opportunity to decide whether states were bound by the terms of colonial grants. In 1758, the New Jersey legislature gave tax immunity to lands owned by the Delaware Indians. The Delawares sold the land to white purchasers. In 1804, after that sale, the legislature rescinded the tax exemption. In *New Jersey v. Wilson*, 7 Cranch 164 (1812), Marshall held that because the purchasers believed in good faith that they had acquired the tax exemption with their title, the state legislature could not repeal the exemption. Although defeated in court, New Jersey ignored the decision and continued to collect taxes on the land. In 1886, the Supreme Court held that the tax exemption had lapsed because the landowners had acquiesced to the imposition of the taxes. *Given v. Wright*, 117 U.S. 649.

CONTRACTS CLAUSE

Dartmouth College v. Woodward
4 Wheaton 518 (1819)

SETTING

Political parties are not mentioned in the Constitution, and were criticized by many in the Founding generation. Nonetheless, by the early nineteenth century, political parties had become crucial institutions for mobilizing and organizing political participation. The line of division between the first American political parties, Federalists and Republicans, was becoming increasingly sharp over the extent to which private property rights should be free from state legislative interference under the Contracts Clause. Federalists regarded property as a vested (absolute) right with which state legislatures cannot interfere. Republicans were more solicitous of the rights of legislatures. *Fletcher v. Peck* was a clear triumph for the Federalist Party in this debate. *Fletcher*, however, dealt only with the property rights of private individuals. It did not address the property rights of corporate entities or whether Article I, section 10, clause 1, gave state legislatures more latitude to alter corporate charters than they had to alter private grants. The Supreme Court confronted that question in *Dartmouth College v. Woodward*, a case whose origins preceded the American Revolution.

In 1754, at his own expense, Eleazar Wheelock established an Indian charity school on his estate located in Lebanon in the Connecticut colony. The purpose of Wheelock's school was to educate Indians "with a view to their carrying the gospel in their own language, and spreading the knowledge of the Great Redeemer among their savage tribes." After several years of operation, Wheelock gave Rev. Nathaniel Whitaker broad power of attorney on behalf of his school and sent him and Samson Occom, an Indian who had been converted by Wheelock, to England to solicit "worthy and generous contributors." Whitaker contacted several individuals who offered to make contributions, including the Right Honorable William Earl of Dartmouth. Based on their pledges of support, Whitaker named the Earl of Dartmouth and eight others as trustees of Wheelock's school.

Wheelock subsequently gave a different power of attorney to the trustees to relocate the school at a place they deemed appropriate to carry out the Christian education of Indians. The trustees selected a site in New Hampshire on the Connecticut River. In 1769, King George III granted the school a corporate charter under the name of Dartmouth College, gave it "perpetual succession and continuance forever," fixed the number of trustees at twelve, and named the first twelve trustees. By 1816, the college had acquired valuable lands in Vermont and New Hampshire and enjoyed an annual income of over $25,000.

On June 27, 1816, the newly elected Jeffersonian Republican legislature of New Hampshire passed a law entitled, "An act to amend the charter, and enlarge and improve the corporation of Dartmouth College." The legislation created a new corporation, Dartmouth University, to which it transferred all the property, rights, powers, liberties, and privileges of Dartmouth College. The act increased the number of trustees for Dartmouth University to twenty-one and created a board of twenty-five overseers.

However, at the annual meeting of the trustees of Dartmouth College, the trustees, most of whom were members of the Federalist Party, adopted a resolution not to accept, or act under, the Republican legislation of June 27. In September, 1817, they removed Judge William H. Woodward as secretary and treasurer because of his support of the university and his refusal to turn over to them the records and seal of the college. The following month, the college's new secretary, Mills Olcott, again demanded from Woodward two books of records containing all of the activities of the college from its founding until that date; the original corporate charter; the seal of the college; and four volumes of accounting books. Woodward again refused, claiming to hold them for the use of the rightful trustees and subject to their orders.

On December 18, 1816, the New Hampshire legislature amended the act of June 27. The amendment authorized the governor of New Hampshire to call a meeting of the trustees and overseers of Dartmouth University. It also reduced the number of trustees required to transact business. Eight days later, the legislature passed another amendment to the June 27 act. It imposed a fine of $500 for each offense on anyone who failed to perform duties under the amended charter.

The trustees of Dartmouth University organized on February 4, 1817. One of their first acts was to appoint Judge Woodward secretary and treasurer of the university. On February 8, the trustees of Dartmouth College filed suit in the Court of Common Pleas to recover the college records, books, and seal, and damages of $50,000. Since Judge Woodward was the presiding judge of that court, the action was transferred to the Superior Court.

The jury to which the case was tried returned a special verdict, stating its findings of fact in the case and requesting the court to declare the law. The New Hampshire Superior Court found for the new trustees, upholding the legislation of June 27, December 18 and 26, 1816. Since the Superior Court was the highest court in New Hampshire, Dartmouth College petitioned the Supreme Court for a writ of error.

Highlights of Supreme Court Arguments

BRIEF FOR DARTMOUTH COLLEGE

◆ Dartmouth College is a private charity created by a grant from the Crown to the trustees. The grant included all the elements of a valid contract, giving the trustees a vested right under article two of the bill of rights of the state of New Hampshire. The state constitution contains prohibitions and a bill of rights that were intended to limit the legislative power and protect the rights and property of citizens.

◆ The grant of corporate powers and privileges is as much a contract as a grant of land.

◆ The trustees of Dartmouth College possess vested liberties, privileges, and immunities under the charter from the Crown. Once vested, such liberties, privileges, and immunities are as inviolable as any vested rights of property whatever. The legislation of June 27, 1816, created a second corporation which effectively destroyed the original Dartmouth College. The 1816 legislation amounts to an impairment of the obligation of a contract by a state, a direct violation of the Contracts Clause. The acts of June 27 and December 18 and 26, therefore, are not binding on Dartmouth College.

◆ The privilege of being a member of a corporation under a lawful grant, and exercising the rights and powers of such member, is a privilege, liberty, or franchise that has been the object of legal protection from the time of Magna Charta to present. The claim of Dartmouth University, that all property of which the use may be beneficial to the public belongs therefore to the public, is a new doctrine. It has no precedent and is supported by no known principle.

◆ When Dr. Wheelock established his school and accepted the corporate charter from the Crown, he never supposed that the charter secured to him and his successors no legal rights. If the legislature may treat Dartmouth College this way, then the various academies in New England, all created the same way and including Harvard College and Yale College, are not secure.

◆ The effect of the 1816 acts is to take rights of property and franchises from one party and give them to another. This is not a valid exercise of a legislative power. The taking away of vested rights requires a forfeiture, which in turn requires judicial action.

BRIEF FOR WOODWARD

◆ The Crown charter to Dartmouth College created a public, not a private, corporation. The legal elements required for a transaction to be a contract were not present. The charter was issued for the benefit of the people, not the benefit of the trustees. The charter conferred no personal, private, individual benefit on the trustees in return for the payment of legal consideration. Since the charter to the college was not a contract, the state retained the power to modify it in the public interest.

◆ If, by a technical fiction, the grant of the charter can be considered a contract between the Crown (or state) and the trustees of Dartmouth College, the 1816 legislation did not impair any obligations under it. The legislation merely modified the charter to adapt it to the new government and to changes in New Hampshire's civil institutions following the Revolution. No rights were devested by the legislation; the old corporation was not abolished; the former trustees were continued in office.

◆ The constitutional convention did not intend to interfere with the exercise of powers reserved to the states. Education of youth, and encouragement of the arts and sciences, are police powers retained by the states.

◆ The Contracts Clause does not extend to grants of political power, to contracts concerning the internal government and police of a sovereign state, nor to contracts which relate merely to matters of civil institution, even of a private nature. The purpose of the charter to Dartmouth College was to educate youth, a recognized responsibility of the state.

◆ Even when first granted under the colonial government, the charter to Dartmouth College was subject to the authority of the British parliament over all charters containing grants of political power. It might have been revoked or modified by an act of Parliament. The Revolution did not destroy that supreme authority which every political society has over its public institutions. The authority was simply transferred to the people of New Hampshire. They have not relinquished it.

SUPREME COURT DECISION: 6–1

MARSHALL, C.J.

... The single question now to be considered is, do the acts to which the [special] verdict refers violate the constitution of the United States?

This court can be insensible neither to the magnitude nor delicacy of this question. The validity of a legislative act is to be examined; and the opinion of the highest law tribunal of a state is to be revised.... On more than one occasion this court has expressed the cautious circumspection with which it approaches the consideration of such questions; and has declared that, in no doubtful case would it pronounce a legislative act to be contrary to the constitution. But the American people have said, in the constitution of the United States, that "no state shall pass any bill of attainer, ex post facto law, or law impairing the obligation of contracts." In the same instrument they have also said, "that the judicial power shall extend to all cases in law and equity arising under the constitution." On the judges of this court, then, is imposed the high and solemn duty of protecting, from even legislative violation, those contracts which the constitution of our country has placed beyond legislative control....

It can require no argument to prove, that the circumstances of this case constitute a contract. An application is made to the crown for a charter to incorporate a religious and literary institution.... The charter is granted, and on its faith the property is conveyed. Surely, in this transaction every ingredient of a complete and legitimate contract is to be found.

The points for consideration are,

1. Is this contract protected by the constitution of the United States? 2. Is it impaired by the acts under which the defendant holds?...

That the framers of the constitution did not intend to restrain the states in the regulation of their civil institutions, adopted for internal government, and that the instrument they have given us, is not to be so construed, may be admitted. The provision of the constitution [Article I, Sec. 10] never has been understood to embrace other contracts, than those which respect property, or some object of value, and confer rights which may be asserted in a court of justice....

The parties in this case differ less on general principles, less on the true construction of the constitution in the abstract, than on the application of those principles to this case, and on the true construction of the charter of 1769. This is the point on which the cause essentially depends. If the act of incorporation be a grant of political power, if it create a civil institution, to be employed in the administration of the government, or if the funds of the college be public property, or if the state of New Hampshire, as a government, be alone interested in its transactions, the subject is one in which the legislature of the state may act according to its own judgment, unrestrained by any limitation of its power imposed by the constitution of the United States.

But if this be a private eleemosynary institution, endowed with a capacity to take property for objects unconnected with government, whose funds are bestowed by individuals, on the faith of the charter; if the donors have stipulated for the future disposition and management of those funds, in the manner prescribed by themselves; there may be more difficulty in the case, although neither the persons who have made these stipulations, nor those for whose benefit they were made, should be parties to the cause....

[From whence] can be derived the idea that Dartmouth College [became] a public institution, and its trustees public officers, exercising powers conferred by the public for public objects?... Is it from the act of incorporation? Let this subject be considered.

A corporation is an artificial being, invisible, intangible, and existing only in contemplation of law. Being the mere creature of law, it possesses only those properties which the charter of its creation confers upon it, either expressly, or as incidental to its very existence.... Among the most important are immortality, and if the expression may be allowed, individuality; properties, by which a perpetual succession of many persons are considered as the same, and may act as a single individual.... It is chiefly for the purpose of clothing bodies of men, in succession, with these qualities and capacities, that corporations were invented, and are in use. By these means, a perpetual succession of

individuals are capable of acting for the promotion of the particular object, like one immortal being. But this being does not share in the civil government of the country, unless that be the purpose for which it was created. Its immortality no more confers on it political power, or a political character, than immortality would confer such power or character on a natural person. It is no more a state instrument than a natural person exercising the same powers would be....

There can be no reason for implying in a charter, given for a valuable consideration, a power which is not only not expressed, but is in direct contradiction to its express stipulations.

From the fact, then, that a charter of incorporation has been granted, nothing can be inferred which changes the character of the institution, or transfers to the government any new power over it....

[From a review of its charter,] it appears that Dartmouth College is an eleemosynary institution, incorporated for the purpose of perpetuating the application of the bounty of the donors, to the specified objects of that bounty; that its trustees or governors were originally named by the founder, and invested with the power of perpetuating themselves; that they are not public officers, nor is it a civil institution, participating in the administration of government; but a charity-school, or a seminary of education, incorporated for the preservation of its property, and the perpetual application of that property to the objects of its creation....

Dr. Wheelock, acting for himself, and for those who, at his solicitation, had made contributions to his school, applied for this charter, as the instrument which should enable him and them, to perpetuate their beneficent intention. It was granted. An artificial, immortal being, was created by the crown, capable of receiving and distributing forever, according to the will of the donors, the donations which should be made to it.... What has since occurred, to strip it of its inviolability? Circumstances have not changed it. In reason, in justice, and in law, it is now, what it was in 1769.

This is plainly a contract to which the donors, the trustees and the crown (to whose rights and obligations New Hampshire succeeds) were the original parties. It is a contract made on a valuable consideration. It is a contract for the security and disposition of property. It is a contract, on the faith of which real and personal estate has been conveyed to the corporation. It is then a contract within the letter of the constitution, and within its spirit also, unless the fact that the property is invested by the donors in trustees for the promotion of religion and education ... shall create a particular exception, taking this case out of the prohibition contained in the constitution.

It is more than possible that the preservation of rights of this description was not particularly in the view of the framers of the constitution, when the clause under consideration was introduced into that instrument. It is probable that interferences of more frequent recurrence, to which the temptation was stronger, and of which the mischief was more extensive, constituted the great motive for imposing this restriction on the state legislatures. But although a particular and a rare case may not, in itself, be of sufficient magnitude to induce a rule, yet it must be governed by the rule, when established,

unless some plain and strong reason for excluding it can be given. It is not enough to say, that this particular case was not in the mind of the convention, when the article was framed, nor of the American people, when it was adopted. It is necessary to go further, and to say that, had this particular case been suggested, the language would have been so varied, as to exclude it, or it would have been made a special exception....

Almost all eleemosynary corporations, those which are created for the promotion of religion, or charity, or of education, are of the same character. The law of this case is the law of all....

The opinion of the Court, after mature deliberation, is, that this is a contract, the obligation of which cannot be impaired, without violating the constitution of the United States....

We next proceed to the inquiry, whether its obligation has been impaired by those acts of the legislature of New Hampshire, to which the special verdict refers....

On the effect of this law, two opinions cannot be entertained.... The will of the state is substituted for the will of the donors, in every essential operation of the college.... Th[e] system is totally changed. The charter of 1769 exists no longer.... This may be for the advantage of this college in particular, and may be for the advantage of literature in general; but it is not according to the will of the donors, and is subversive of that contract, on the fact of which their property was given....

It results from this opinion, that the acts of the legislature of New Hampshire, which are stated in the special verdict found in this cause, are repugnant to the constitution of the United States; and that the judgment on this special verdict ought to have been for the plaintiffs. The judgment of the State Court must, therefore, be reversed.

STORY, J., CONCURRING

... In my judgment it is perfectly clear that any act of a legislature which takes away any powers or franchises vested by its charter in a private corporation or its corporate officers, or which restrains or controls the legitimate exercise of them, or transfers them to other persons, without its assent, is a violation of the obligations of that charter. If the legislature mean to claim such an authority, it must be reserved in the grant. The charter of Dartmouth College contains no such reservation; and I am therefore bound to declare that the acts of the legislature of New Hampshire, now in question, do impair the obligations of that charter, and are, consequently, unconstitutional and void.

WASHINGTON, J., CONCURRING [OMITTED]

DUVALL, J., DISSENTED WITHOUT OPINION

QUESTIONS

1. Is *Dartmouth College* the logical extension of *Fletcher v. Peck* or does it break new legal ground in the area of property rights? Does any language in Chief Justice Marshall's *Dartmouth College* opinion indicate that he was sensitive to the political implications of his opinion? Is such sensitivity appropriate or inappropriate for a judge whose duty is to declare the law?

2. According to natural rights philosophers like John Locke, vested rights are individual entitlements that are intrinsic to human existence and require protection from the reach of government. In Locke's view, vested rights are "pre-political" in the sense that they exist before the creation of civil society. A primary obligation of government, according to Locke's social contract theory, is to protect vested rights.

   The Framers of the Constitution were profoundly influenced by natural rights philosophers such as Locke. For the Framers, the primary justification for constitutional government was limiting legislative interference with private individuals' vested rights to possess and use property. As James Madison put it in *Federalist* No. 10, property rights originate from "[t]he diversity of faculties of men.... The protection of these faculties is the first object of government."

   Is Marshall's opinion in *Dartmouth College* consistent with the concept of vested rights? What language in his opinion supports your conclusion?

3. Criticizing Chief Justice Marshall's opinion in *Dartmouth College*, constitutional historian Melvin Urofsky writes that Marshall "ignored the strong argument of counsel for the new trustees, that gratuitous charters lacked consideration, a universally recognized element of any contract" (*A March of Liberty* [New York, NY: Alfred Knopf, 1988], p. 237).

What reasons might explain why Chief Justice Marshall would cavalierly ignore established legal doctrine, with his claim that: "It can require no argument to prove that the circumstances of this case constitute a contract"?

4. In the wake of the *Dartmouth College* decision, if you were a member of a state legislature, how would you write charters of incorporation in order to retain legislative authority to regulate corporate activity? Does Justice Story's concurring opinion provide any clues?

COMMENT

In *Sturges v. Crowninshield*, 4 Wheaton 122 (1819), the Court decided that states could not pass legislation cancelling debts contracted before enactment of a bankruptcy statute. Chief Justice Marshall held that such legislation impaired the obligation of contracts. Comprehensive federal bankruptcy legislation was stalled in Congress at the time. Compare *Green v. Biddle*, 8 Wheaton 1 (1821), where the Court invalidated the Kentucky Occupying Claimants Law that had been adopted to make it more difficult for landowners to evict "squatters" who had settled western lands in good faith and had made improvements on the land. *Sturges* overturned the New York bankruptcy statute because it operated retroactively. When a prospective debt relief statute came before the Court in *Ogden v. Saunders*, 12 Wheaton 213 (1827), the Court upheld its constitutionality, 4–3, over Marshall's vigorous opposition. Failing to command a majority in a constitutional case for the first and only time during his thirty-four-year tenure, Marshall dissented, insisting that the words of the Contracts Clause "admit of a prospective, as well as of a retrospective, operation." One aspect of the disagreement in *Ogden* was a debate between Marshall, who adhered to his natural law view of contract rights, and the majority, which saw contractual obligations as created by positive legislative enactments.

CONTRACTS CLAUSE

Charles River Bridge v. Warren Bridge
11 Peters 420 (1837)

SETTING

By the time Chief Justice John Marshall died on July 6, 1835, the Supreme Court's interpretation of the Contracts Clause had retreated from the high-water mark of vested rights jurisprudence represented by his opinion in *Dartmouth*

College v. Woodward. Late in his career, even Marshall himself agreed that courts should not read implied grants of privilege against a state into a corporate charter. In *Providence Bank v. Billings*, 4 Peters 514 (1830), for example, a bank claimed that immunity from state taxation was implied in its charter. Marshall held that no tax exemption could ever be assumed to be part of a contract, grant, or charter, ruling that corporate charters must be strictly construed to favor the public interest, and that courts should not read implied grants of privilege against a state into a charter. The *Charles River Bridge* case, which appeared on the Court's docket early in the tenure of Chief Justice Roger Brooke Taney, gave the Court an opportunity to further erode the Contracts Clause as a barrier against legislative regulation of property and its use.

Charles River Bridge had its origins in the partnership between state legislatures and private corporations, commonplace in the early days of the American republic, to develop economic infrastructure. Before the nineteenth century, it was routine for state legislatures to incorporate business corporations and grant them charters to build public facilities such as bridges. In this respect, corporations were arms of the state. They derived their existence, powers, and guarantees of profit from special legislative acts.

In 1785, the Massachusetts legislature passed a law that incorporated the Charles River Bridge Company and gave it authority to build a bridge over the Charles River between Boston and Charlestown. The bridge was to replace a toll ferry between the two cities that had been operated since 1640 by Harvard College under a charter from the colonial legislature. Under its charter, the Charles River bridge was to be a toll bridge, and the company was required to pay Harvard College an annual stipend for forty years to compensate it for the loss of revenues that Harvard would suffer when people used the bridge instead of the ferry.

The Charles River Bridge Company built the bridge and opened it in 1786. A legislative amendment in 1792 provided that the bridge would become the property of Massachusetts in 1856. Until then, the company would operate it as a toll bridge. By 1827, the Charles River Bridge Company was collecting annual tolls of $30,000, reflecting increased traffic caused by burgeoning populations in Boston and Charlestown. The situation in those two cities was by no means unique. Rapid changes in transportation were occurring throughout the country. The steam locomotive, for example, invented in 1826, quickly displaced the stagecoach as a means of moving goods and people. Toll roads gave way to canals.

In 1828, responding to the increasing pressures of urban congestion, the Jacksonian-dominated Massachusetts legislature incorporated the Warren Bridge Company to construct a second bridge across the Charles River from Boston to Charlestown. The second bridge was to be essentially parallel to the Charles River Bridge. The Warren Bridge charter provided that the bridge would become the property of the state and operate as a free bridge as soon as the company's expenses in constructing it had been recovered and it had earned a specified return. Until then, but not to exceed six years, the Warren Bridge was to operate as a toll bridge.

Soon after passage of the legislation chartering the Warren Bridge, the Charles River Bridge Company sought an injunction from the Supreme Judicial Court for the County of Suffolk, Massachusetts, against construction of the Warren Bridge. It argued that the charter of the Warren Bridge Company violated the Contracts Clause because it impaired the obligation of the contract between Massachusetts and the Charles River Bridge Company.

Before the Suffolk County court issued its decision, the Warren Bridge was constructed and had commenced operation. The Charles River Bridge Company filed a supplemental suit seeking reimbursement of the tolls that already had been diverted from the Charles River Bridge and an injunction against use of the Warren Bridge as a public way.

The Massachusetts court dismissed the Charles River Bridge Company's request for an injunction, holding that the act incorporating the Warren Bridge Company did not impair the obligation of the contract between Massachusetts and the Charles River Bridge Company. The Charles River Bridge Company petitioned the Supreme Court for a writ of error. The case was first argued at the Court's 1831 Term, but only six justices were present and they split on the result. Justice Story drafted an opinion reversing the Massachusetts court, but he was unable to muster a majority. The case was reargued in 1832, and again split with only six justices present.

By the time the case was argued at the 1837 Term, the Warren River Bridge had become the property of Massachusetts and was operating as a free bridge. The Charles River Bridge had closed.

Highlights of Supreme Court Arguments

BRIEF FOR THE CHARLES RIVER BRIDGE COMPANY

◆ The owners of the ferry crossing the Charles River had an exclusive franchise which passed to the Charles River Bridge Company under the 1785 charter and 1792 amendment. Under the rule of *Fletcher v. Peck*, the charter was a contract that vested the company with rights of property for the duration of its charter, including the right to collect tolls in return for the company's risk and hazard in constructing the bridge. The subsequent grant of a charter to the Warren Bridge Company destroyed the Charles River Bridge Company's ability to collect those tolls, and thus impaired the obligation of the contract between the company and the state. The Constitution explicitly prohibits states from impairing the obligation of contracts.

◆ In *Fletcher v. Peck*, the Court held that once a grant is given, it is exclusive and cannot be withdrawn by the state; the rights of the grantor are forever extinguished. The grant to the Warren Bridge Company, depriving the Charles River Bridge of its tolls, was analogous to the Georgia legislature's rescinding of the land grants at issue in *Fletcher*, and is constitutionally invalid for the same reasons.

◆ By granting a charter to the competing bridge company, the

Massachusetts legislature confiscated private property of the Charles River Bridge Company for which it provided no compensation. The fact that the grant to the Charles River Bridge Company was an executed contract gives the Supreme Court jurisdiction to resolve the case.

BRIEF FOR THE WARREN BRIDGE COMPANY

◆ The Supreme Court cannot issue the equitable relief sought by the Charles River Bridge Company, because the Warren Bridge is the property of the state of Massachusetts. No injunction can issue against the state, because it was not a party to the action.

◆ Whatever the rights of the owners of the ferry had been, those rights were extinguished when the ferry was taken for public use. Nothing in the grant to the Charles River Bridge Company conveyed to it an exclusive right or monopoly. The settled law has been declared by the Massachusetts court: in public grants, no rights pass by implication. In the grant to the Charles River Bridge Company, the legislature said nothing about restraining its power to authorize the construction of new bridges.

◆ No property was taken from the Charles River Bridge Company by the 1828 charter to the Warren Bridge Company. The initial investment by stockholders in the Charles River Bridge of about $46,000 yielded a return of over $1,200,000 before the Warren Bridge became state property and began operation as a free bridge.

◆ If the Court holds for the Charles River Bridge Company it will uphold the rights of monopolists over the rights of the people expressed through their state legislatures.

SUPREME COURT DECISION: 4–3

TANEY, C.J.

... [It is] to the Act of the Legislature of Massachusetts, of 1785, by which the plaintiffs were incorporated by the name of "The Proprietors of the Charles River Bridge," and ... in the law of 1792, prolonging their charter, that we must look for the extent and nature of the franchise conferred upon plaintiffs.

Much has been said in the argument of the principles of construction by which this law is to be expounded, and what undertakings, on the part of the state, may be implied. The court think

there can be no serious difficulty on that head. It is the grant of certain franchises, by the public, to a private corporation, and in a matter where the public interest is concerned. The rule of construction in such cases is well settled, both in England, and by the decisions of our own tribunals.... [I]n the case of *The Proprietors of the Stourbridge Canal v. Wheeley et al.* [2 Barn. & Adol. 793], the court [said], ... "This, like many other cases, is a bargain between a company of adventurers and the public, the terms of which are expressed in the statute; and the rule of construction in all such cases, is now fully established to be this—that any ambiguity in the terms of the contract, must operate against the adventurers, and in favor of the public, and the plaintiffs can claim nothing that is not clearly given them by the act.".…

Borrowing, as we have done, our system of jurisprudence from the English law; and having adopted, in every other case, civil and criminal, its rules for the construction of statutes; is there anything in our local situation, or in the nature of our political institutions, which should lead us to depart from the principle, where corporations are concerned?… Can any good reason be assigned, for excepting this particular class of cases from the operation of the general principle; and for introducing a new and adverse rule of construction known to the English common law, in every other case, without exception? We think not; and it would present a singular spectacle, if, while the courts in England are restraining, within the strictest limits, the spirit of monopoly, and exclusive privileges in the nature of monopolies, and confining corporations to the privileges plainly given to them in their charter; the courts of this country should be found enlarging these privileges by implication; and construing a statute more unfavorably to the public, and to the rights of the community, than would be done in a like case in an English court of justice.…

[T]he object and end of all government is to promote the happiness and prosperity of the community by which it is established; and it can never be assumed, that the government intended to diminish its power of accomplishing the end for which it was created. And in a country like ours, free, active and enterprising, continually advancing in numbers and wealth, new channels of communication are daily found necessary, both for travel and trade, and are essential to the comfort, convenience and prosperity of the people. A state ought never to be presumed to surrender this power, because, like the taxing power, the whole community have an interest in preserving it undiminished. And when a corporation alleges, that a state has surrendered, for seventy years, its power of improvement and public accommodation, in a great and important line of travel, along which a vast number of its citizens must daily pass, the community have a right to insist, in the language of this court … "that its abandonment ought not to be presumed, in a case, in which the deliberate purpose of the state to abandon it does not appear." *Providence Bank v. Billings and Pittman*, 4 Peters 514 (1830). The continued existence of a government would be of no great value, if, by implications and presumptions, it was disarmed of the powers necessary to accomplish the ends of its creation, and the functions it was designed to perform, transferred to the hands of privileged corporations.… No one will question, that the interests of the great body of the people of the state, would, in this instance, be affected by the surrender of this great line of travel to a single corporation, with the right to exact toll, and exclude competition, for seventy years. While the rights of private property are sacredly guarded, we must not forget, that the community also have rights, and that the happiness and well-being of every citizen depends on their faithful preservation.

Adopting the rule of construction above stated as the settled one, we proceed to apply it to the charter of 1785, to the proprietors of the Charles River bridge.... There is no exclusive privilege given to them over the waters of Charles River, above or below their bridge; no right to erect another bridge themselves, nor to prevent other persons from erecting one, no engagement from the state, that another shall not be erected; and no undertaking not to sanction competition, nor to make improvements that may diminish the amount of its income.... No words are used, from which an intention to grant any of these rights can be inferred; if the plaintiff is entitled to them, it must be implied, simply, from the nature of the grant; and cannot be inferred, from the words by which the grant is made.

The relative position of the Warren bridge has already been described. It does not interrupt the passage over the Charles River bridge, nor make the way to it, or from it, less convenient.... But its income is destroyed by the Warren bridge; which, being free, draws off the passengers and property which would have gone over it, and renders their franchise of no value. This is the gist of the complainant; for it is not pretended, that the erection of the Warren bridge would have done them any injury, or in any degree affected their right of property, if it had not diminished the amount of their tolls. In order, then, to entitle themselves to relief, it is necessary to show, that the legislature contracted not to do the act of which they complain; and that they impaired, or in other words, violated, that contract, by the erection of the Warren bridge.

The inquiry, then, is, does the charter contain such a contract on the part of the state? Is there any such stipulation to be found in that instrument? It must be admitted on all hands, that there is none; no words that even relate to another bridge, or to the diminution of their tolls, or to the line of travel. If a contract on that subject can be gathered from the charter, it must be by implication; and cannot be found in the words used. Can such an agreement be implied? The rule of construction before stated is an answer to the question: in charters of this description, no rights are taken from the public, or given to the corporation, beyond those which the words of the charter, by their natural and proper construction, purport to convey....

Indeed, the practice and usage of almost every state in the Union, old enough to have commenced the work of internal improvement, is opposed to the doctrine contended for on the part of the plaintiffs in error. Turnpike roads have been made in succession, on the same line of travel; the later ones interfering materially with the profits of the first. These corporations have, in some instances, been utterly ruined by the introduction of newer and better modes of transportation and travelling. In some cases, railroads have rendered the turnpike roads on the same line of travel so entirely useless, that the franchise of the turnpike corporation is not worth preserving. Yet in none of these cases have the corporation supposed that their privileges were invaded, or any contract violated on the part of the state. Amid the multitude of cases which have occurred, and have been daily occurring, for the last forty or fifty years, this is the first instance in which such an implied contract has been contended for, and this court called upon to infer it, from an ordinary act of incorporation, containing nothing more than the usual stipulations and provisions to be found in every such law. The absence of any such controversy, when there must have been so many occasions to give rise to it, proves, that neither states, nor individuals, nor corporations, ever imagined that such a contract could be implied from such charters. It shows, that the men who voted for these laws, never imagined that they were forming such a contract; and if we maintain that they have made it, we must create it by a legal fiction, in opposition to the truth of the fact, and the obvious intention of the party. We cannot deal thus with the rights reserved to the states; and by legal intendments and mere technical reasoning, take away from them any portion of that power over their own internal police and improvement, which is so necessary to their well-being and prosperity....

The judgment of the supreme judicial court of the commonwealth of Massachusetts, dismissing the plaintiff's bill, must therefore, be affirmed, with costs.

MCLEAN, J., WOULD HAVE DISMISSED THE CASE FOR WANT OF JURISDICTION

STORY AND THOMPSON, J.J., DISSENTING

... [I]t has been argued ... that if grants of this nature are to be construed liberally, as conferring any exclusive rights on the grantees, it will interpose an effectual barrier against all general improvements of the country.... For my own part, I can conceive of no surer plan to arrest all public improvements, founded on private capital and enterprise, than to make the outlay of that capital uncertain and questionable, both as to security and as to productiveness. No man will hazard his capital in any enterprise, in which, if there be a loss, it must be borne exclusively by himself; and if there be success, he has not the slightest security of enjoying the rewards of that success, for a single moment. If the government means to invite its citizens to enlarge the public comforts and conveniences, to establish bridges, or turnpikes, or canals, or railroads, there must be some pledge, that the property will be safe; that the enjoyment will be co-extensive with the grant; and that success will not be the signal of a general combination to overthrow its rights and to take away its profits. The very agitation of a question of this sort is sufficient to alarm every stockholder in every public enterprise of this sort, throughout the whole country....

But if there were any foundation for the argument itself, in a general view, it would totally fail in its application to the present case. Here, the grant, however exclusive, is but for a short and limited period, more than two-thirds of which have already elapsed; and when it is gone, the whole property and franchise are to revert to the state. The legislature exercised a wholesome foresight on the subject; and within a reasonable period, it will have an unrestricted authority to do whatever it may choose, in the appropriation of the bridge and its tolls. There is not, then, under any fair aspect of the case, the slightest reason to presume that public improvements either can, or will, be injuriously retarded by a liberal construction of the present grant.

... Now I put it to the common sense of every man, whether if, at the moment of granting the charter, the legislature had said to the proprietors; you shall build the bridge; you shall bear the burdens; you shall be bound by the charges; and your sole reimbursement shall be from the tolls of forty years: and yet we will not even guaranty you any certainty of receiving any tolls; on the contrary; we reserve to ourselves the full power and authority to erect other bridges, toll or free bridges, according to our own free will and pleasure, contiguous to yours, and having the same termini with yours; and if you are successful, we may thus supplant you, divide, destroy your profits, and annihilate your tolls, without annihilating your burdens: if, I say, such had been the language of the legislature, is there a man living, of ordinary discretion or prudence, who would have accepted such a charter, upon such terms? I fearlessly answer, no. There would have been such a gross inadequacy of consideration, and such a total insecurity of all the rights of property, under such circumstances, that the project would have been dropped still-born. And I put the question further, whether any legislature, meaning to promote a project of permanent, public utility (such as this confessedly was), would ever have dreamed of such a qualification of its own grant, when it sought to enlist private capital and private patronage to insure the accomplishment of it?...

[I]t is most important to remember, that in the construction of all legislative grants, the common law must be taken into consideration; for the legislature must be presumed to have in view the general principles of construction which are recognized by the common law.

Now, no principle is better established, than the principle, that when a thing is given or granted, the law giveth, impliedly, whatever is necessary for the taking and enjoying the same....

Wherever any other bridge or ferry is so near, that it injures the franchise, or diminishes the toll, in a positive and essential degree, there it is a nuisance, and is actionable. It invades the franchise, and ought to be abated. But whether there be such injury or not, is a matter, not of law, but of fact....

I maintain, that, upon the principles of common reason and legal interpretation, the present grant carries with it a necessary implication, that the legislature shall do no act to destroy or essentially to impair the franchise; that (as one of the learned judges of the state court expressed it) there is an implied agreement that the state will not grant another bridge between Boston and Charlestown, so near as to draw away the custom from the old one; and (as another learned judge expressed it) that there is an implied agreement of the state to grant the undisturbed use of the bridge and its tolls, so far as respects any acts of its own, or of any persons acting under its authority. In other words, the state impliedly contracts not to resume its grant, or to do any act to the prejudice or destruction of its grant. I maintain, that there is no authority or principle established in relation to the construction of crown grants, or legislative grants, which does not concede and justify this doctrine....

QUESTIONS

1. Chief Justice Taney's majority opinion in *Charles River Bridge* and Justice Story's dissent represent significantly different approaches to questions of property, commerce, and contracts. How did each jus-

tice understand the fundamental constitutional principles of protecting property and promoting commerce? Which was the more important principle to each justice? Would Chief Justice John Marshall have agreed with Justice Story?

2. Contemporary reaction to *Charles River Bridge* divided along party lines. Whigs, the successors to the Federalist Party, decried the decision as eroding vested rights and removing the constitutional protection of contracts. Democrats applauded the decision as dissolving monopolies and promoting free enterprise. Their responses reflected what historian Carl Swisher called the "competing values of stability and change" that were in tension during this era in the field of transportation. Advances in transportation required venture capital, which in turn depended on investments that could be attracted only if property rights were secure (Carl B. Swisher, *History of the Supreme Court of the United States, vol. 5, The Taney Period, 1836–1864* [New York, NY: Macmillan, 1974], pp. 74–75).

   Is the constitutional doctrine underlying *Dartmouth College* or the doctrine underlying *Charles River Bridge* more likely to promote capitalist economic development in the United States? Or were both required?

3. Daniel Webster believed that *Charles River Bridge* "completely overturned ... a great provision of the Constitution." Webster, a graduate of Dartmouth College, had argued his alma mater's case before the Supreme Court and staked his reputation as a lawyer that Taney's opinion in *Charles River Bridge* could not stand. He wrote to Justice Story that "the intelligent part of the [legal] profession will all be with you" (Carl Brent Swisher, *Roger B. Taney* [New York, NY: Macmillan Co., 1935], p. 377).

   What does Webster's conclusion suggest about the commitments of what he considered to be intelligent lawyers in mid-nineteenth-century America? Were Webster's "intelligent lawyers" synonymous with conservative elite lawyers? Alexis de Tocqueville's observations on the "temper" of the American legal profession, based on his travels and conversations in the United States during this period, shed light on the issue raised by this question (*Democracy in America*, 2 vols., ed. Phillips Bradley [New York, NY: Vintage Books, 1945], 2: 282–291).

4. Writing about the transformation in the understanding of property from a static, agricultural conception, to a dynamic conception more instrumental to financial and industrial capitalism, legal historian Morton Horwitz argues that there were two competing "ideological tendencies" at work after the American Revolution. One was the spirit of economic development and the use of the state to foster low-cost growth. The other was the desire to protect the economic

status quo and to use the law as a vehicle to prevent redistribution of wealth. "While the first tendency underlined and acknowledged the malleable—and hence political—character of law, the second sought to depoliticize the law and to insist upon its objective, neutral, and facilitative character" (*The Transformation of American Law* [Cambridge, MA: Harvard University Press, 1977], pp. 254–255. Compare A. W. B. Simpson, "The Horwitz Thesis and the History of Contracts," 46 *University of Chicago Law Review* [1979]: 533).

Professor Horwitz contends that *Charles River Bridge* represents "the last great contest in America" between these competing ideologies (Ibid, p. 143). Is it accurate to characterize *Charles River Bridge* as "antibusiness," or "antiproperty"?

CONTRACTS CLAUSE

Stone v. Mississippi
11 Otto 814 (1880)

SETTING

Although frequently discomforting to students of constitutional law, it is not uncommon for appellate courts to allow doctrine to evolve in seemingly inconsistent ways. The coexistence of *Dartmouth College v. Woodward* and *Charles River Bridge v. Warren Bridge* is an example of seemingly contradictory doctrinal development at the Supreme Court level. *Dartmouth College* was a triumph for *status quo* vested property rights and implied judicial antipathy toward state-supported economic growth. *Charles River Bridge* enhanced the power of state legislatures. That decision authorized states to exercise their police powers, to modify corporate charters in order to facilitate economic development. *Charles River Bridge* thus was a triumph for those who saw state legislatures as having a legitimate role in shaping economic activities. Significantly, *Charles River Bridge* did not overrule *Dartmouth College*. Consequently, both decisions were precedents for purposes of the Contracts Clause litigation that inevitably followed. Another important chapter in the conflict over vested property rights and state police powers played out soon after the Civil War.

On January 16, 1867, the post-Civil War Mississippi provisional legislature enacted a law that incorporated the Mississippi Agricultural, Educational and Manufacturing Society, a lottery company, with which John B. Stone was associated. The legislature granted the company a twenty-five-year charter to conduct a lottery. In consideration for the grant, the company paid the state $5,000, in addition to an annual tax of $1,000 and half of one percent of its revenues. The provisional legislature's act was significant: between 1822 and 1867, the Mississippi legislature had consistently prohibited lotteries in the state, declaring them inconsistent with the rules of social morality.

On December 1, 1869, the state of Mississippi ratified its first post-Civil War constitution. Article XII, section 15, of that constitution contained a provision that prohibited the legislature from authorizing lotteries, the sale of lottery tickets, or the drawing of lottery tickets. The constitutional provision was intended to be retroactive.

Pursuant to the new constitution, the Mississippi legislature in July 1870 enacted a law that made it illegal to conduct a lottery within the state. Stone continued to sell lottery tickets, nonetheless. The Mississippi attorney general filed an information in the Circuit Court of Warren County requiring Stone and the corporation to show by what authority it exercised the privilege of issuing and selling lottery tickets. Stone set up as his defense the act of January 16, 1867, that granted the charter and gave him and the corporation authority to conduct lotteries. He argued that he was complying with all the conditions imposed by the charter, that the 1869 constitution and 1870 statute interfered with rights that had vested under the corporate grant, and that the constitutional provision and statute impermissibly attempted to impair the obligation of a contract.

The circuit court ruled against Stone and the corporation. The Mississippi Supreme Court affirmed. Stone petitioned the Supreme Court of the United States for a writ of error.

HIGHLIGHT OF SUPREME COURT ARGUMENTS

Note: Supreme Court arguments were not reported.

SUPREME COURT DECISION: 9–0

WAITE, C.J.

It is now too late to contend that any contract which a State actually enters into when granting a charter to a private corporation is not within the protection of the clause in the Constitution of the United States that prohibits States from passing laws impairing the obligation of contracts. Art. 1, sect. 10. The doctrines of *Trustees of Dartmouth College v.*

Woodward announced by this court more than sixty years ago, have become so imbedded in the jurisprudence of the United States as to make them to all intents and purposes a part of the Constitution itself. In this connection, however, it is to be kept in mind that it is not the charter which is protected, but only any contract the charter may contain. If there is no contract, there is nothing in the grant on which the

Constitution can act. Consequently, the first inquiry in this class of cases always is, whether a contract has in fact been entered into, and if so, what its obligations are.

In the present case the question is whether the State of Mississippi, in its sovereign capacity, did by the charter now under consideration bind itself irrevocably by a contract[.]... There can be no dispute but that ... the legislature of the State chartered a lottery company[.]... If the legislature that granted this charter had the power to bind the people of the State and all succeeding legislatures to allow the corporation to continue its corporate business during the whole term of its authorized existence, there is no doubt about the sufficiency of the language employed to effect that object, although there was an evident purpose to conceal the vice of the transaction by the phrases that were used. Whether the alleged contract exists, therefore, or not, depends on the authority of the legislature to bind the State and the people of the State in that way.

All agree that the legislature cannot bargain away the police power of a State.... Many attempts have been made in this court and elsewhere to define the police power, but never with entire success. It is always easier to determine whether a particular case comes within the general scope of the power, than to give an abstract definition of the power itself which will be in all respects accurate. No one denies, however, that it extends to all matters affecting the public health or the public morals.... Neither can it be denied that lotteries are proper subjects for the exercise of this power.... [T]his court said, more than thirty years ago, speaking through Mr. Justice Grier, in *Phalen v. Virginia*, 8

How[ard] 163 [(1850)], that "experience has shown that the common forms of gambling are comparatively innocuous when placed in contrast with the widespread pestilence of lotteries."...

If lotteries are to be tolerated at all, it is no doubt better that they should be regulated by law, so that the people may be protected as far as possible against the inherent vices of the system[.]... When the government is untrammelled by any claim of vested rights or chartered privileges, no one has ever supposed that lotteries could not lawfully be suppressed, and those who manage them punished severely as violators of the rules of social morality....

The question is therefore directly presented, whether, in view of these facts, the legislature of a State can, by the charter of a lottery company, defeat the will of the people, authoritatively expressed, in relation to the further continuance of such business in their midst. We think it cannot. No legislature can bargain away the public health or the public morals. The people themselves cannot do it, much less their servants. The supervision of both these subjects of governmental power is continuing in its nature, and they are to be dealt with as the special exigencies of the moment may require. Government is organized with a view to their preservation, and cannot divest itself of the power to provide for them. For this purpose the largest legislative discretion is allowed, and the discretion cannot be parted with any more than the power itself....

[T]he power of governing is a trust committed by the people to the government, no part of which can be granted away. The people, in their sovereign capacity, have established their agencies for the preservation of the public health and the public morals, and the protection of public and private rights. These several agencies can govern according to their discretion, if within the scope of their general authority, while in power; but they cannot give away nor sell the discretion of those that are to come after them, in respect to matters the government of which, from the very nature of things, must "vary with varying circumstances." They may create corporations, and give them, so to speak, a limited citizenship; but as citizens, limited in their privileges, or otherwise, these creatures of the government creation are subject to such rules and regulations as may from time to time be ordained and established for the preservation of health and morality.

The contracts which the Constitution protects are those that relate to property rights, not governmental. It is not always easy to tell on which side of the line which separates governmental from property rights a particular case is to be put; but in respect to lotteries there can be no difficulty. They are not, in the legal acceptation of the term, *mala in se* [wrongs in themselves], but, as we have just seen, may properly be made *mala prohibita* [prohibited wrongs].... Any one, therefore, who accepts a lottery charter does so with the implied understanding that the people, in their sovereign capacity, and through their properly constituted agencies, may resume it at any time when the public good shall require, whether it be paid for or not. All that one can get by such a charter is a suspension of certain governmental rights in his favor, subject to withdrawal at will. He has in legal effect nothing more than a license to enjoy the privilege on the terms named for the specified time, unless it be sooner abrogated by the sovereign power of the State. It is a permit, good as against existing laws, but subject to future legislative and constitutional control or withdrawal.

[Affirmed.]

QUESTIONS

1. Despite Chief Justice Waite's protestations, does *Stone* effectively overrule *Dartmouth College*? Or can *Stone* be read as merely narrowing the application of the Contracts Clause to public contracts?

2. Chief Justice Waite observed in *Stone* that "the legislature cannot bargain away the police power of a State." What insights into the meaning of the police power are provided by his opinion? How extensive a reservation of state power does *Stone v. Mississippi* contemplate?

3. Are the distinctions that Chief Justice Waite makes in *Stone* among licenses, privileges, and contracts persuasive? Do the distinctions have constitutional significance?

4. *Stone* holds that a state cannot prohibit itself contractually from exercising its police powers. In *West River Bridge Company v. Dix*, 6 Howard 507 (1848), the Court held that a state cannot contract away its power to seize specific property in return for payment of just compensation. By comparison, in *Georgia Railway Co. v. Redwine*,

342 U.S. 299 (1952), the Court held that a state may bind itself contractually never to tax a person or organization. Can these various readings of the Contracts Clause be reconciled? What if they cannot be? What insight into constitutional interpretation follows?

5. Chief Justice Waite asserted: "The doctrines of *Trustees of Dartmouth College v. Woodward* announced by this court more than sixty years ago, have become so imbedded in the jurisprudence of the United States as to make them to all intents and purposes a part of the Constitution itself." What does Waite's contention reveal about his view of the relationship between the authority of the Supreme Court and the authority of the Constitution? Is Waite's view consistent with Chief Justice Marshall's theory of constitutional interpretation in *Marbury v. Madison*?

CONTRACTS CLAUSE

Home Building & Loan Association v. Blaisdell
290 U.S. 398 (1934)

SETTING

The cry for debt relief has been a recurrent theme in American history. The Constitution, itself, was adopted in the midst of an economic crisis that motivated state legislators to pass stay laws, valuation laws, legal tender laws, and other statutes designed to relieve the debts of their constituents. Subsequent periods of economic downturn in 1812, 1837, and surrounding the Civil War; the economic panics of 1873, 1893, and 1907; and the deflation accompanying World War I yielded a variety of state debt relief laws. In all cases, the question was whether debt relief laws violated the Contracts Clause, which appeared to favor creditors by prohibiting states from passing laws impairing the obligations of contracts. In most instances, courts struck down debt relief statutes, citing Contracts Clause violations. The conflict between the Contracts Clause and legislative actions to mitigate suffering resulting from periodic downturns in the business cycle arose again during the Great Depression that began in the late 1920s.

As explained in Chapter 3, only the manufacturing sector of the American economy prospered after World War I. In 1920, an income of $2,000 was considered the bare minimum for survival, yet sixty per cent of Americans earned less than that. The farm economy was in dire straits. Already plagued by dismally low prices, falling incomes, and vanishing top soil, farmers faced loss of their farms to banks or loan associations. Between 1927 and 1932, about ten per cent of the country's total farm property had been foreclosed at auction. By 1933, more than 750,000 farmers had lost their land. Mortgage foreclosures were perhaps the most poignant of the Great Depression's many devastating consequences. In some rural areas, farmers rioted against bankers and threatened judges' lives.

The Great Depression touched not only farmers. Between 1929 and 1932, the total value of outstanding urban and rural mortgages declined by $3 billion. National income dropped over fifty per cent, from $85 billion in 1929 to $36 billion in 1932. In 1932, over 250,000 home mortgages were foreclosed. By early 1933, foreclosures were occurring at a rate of more than a thousand per day.

State legislatures responded by enacting a variety of mortgage relief statutes. Arkansas, for example, extended the time for pleading. Iowa, Montana, Nebraska, Oklahoma, and Illinois stayed foreclosure proceedings. Arkansas, Montana, New Hampshire, North Carolina, Texas, and Wisconsin postponed the day of sale. In April 1933, the Minnesota legislature joined Iowa, Kansas, New Hampshire, North Dakota, Vermont, and Wisconsin in passing legislation that prolonged the period of redemption from foreclosure. Declaring an emergency to exist because of economic depression in virtually all sectors of the economy, the Minnesota Mortgage Moratorium Act authorized owners of homes and small businesses to petition local courts to extend the period of redemption from foreclosure sales for up to two years (May 1, 1935).

Validity of the Minnesota statute and, by implication, of similar statutes in other states, was tested by John and Rosella Blaisdell, who had purchased a fourteen-room house in Minneapolis, Minnesota, in 1926. They lived in three rooms of the house and rented out the remaining eleven. They financed the purchase through a loan of $3,800 from the Home Building & Loan Association. The loan agreement provided that if the Blaisdells failed for a period of two months to make payments when due, they would be in default and the entire amount of the debt would then become due. If they failed to pay the entire amount, the agreement gave Home Building & Loan authority to sell the property at public auction.

In May 1932, the Blaisdell's house was sold at a public auction to Home Building & Loan for $3,700, the full amount of outstanding mortgage debt. The sale was held because the Blaisdells had defaulted for two months in their payments. Under Minnesota law prior to the Moratorium Act, the Blaisdells had only one year from the sale to redeem themselves under the contract. If they failed to make redemption in that time, Home Building's sheriff's certificate of sale would convert into fee simple ownership of the property. In April 1933, fourteen days before their redemption period expired, the Blaisdells applied to the District Court of Hennepin County for an order extending the period of redemption from the foreclosure sale on their property, based on the Minnesota Mortgage Moratorium Act. Home Building & Loan objected to introduction of the Mortgage Moratorium Law as evidence, claiming that it violated the Minnesota constitution and the Contracts, Equal Protection, and Due Process Clauses of the Constitution of the United States.

The district court sustained Home Building & Loan's objection and dismissed the proceeding. The Blaisdells appealed to the Supreme Court of Minnesota. That court reversed and remanded the case for trial. Following a trial in July 1933, the court ordered that the Blaisdell's time to redeem from the foreclosure sale be extended until May 1, 1935. During that period the Blaisdells were ordered to pay Home Building $40 per month. Home Building & Loan again appealed to the Minnesota Supreme Court, repeating its claims about the unconstitutionality of the Mortgage Moratorium Law. The state high court affirmed the trial court's order. Home Building & Loan then appealed to the Supreme Court of the United States.

Highlights of Supreme Court Arguments

BRIEF FOR HOME BUILDING & LOAN

◆ The Mortgage Moratorium Law impairs the obligation of a contract and violates due process because it arbitrarily changes the agreed remedy of private foreclosure into foreclosure by action in the courts.

◆ The Minnesota law is not a valid exercise of the state's police power. The relationship between a mortgagor and mortgagee arising out of the borrowing and lending of money is a private matter not affected by the public interest. The economic depression the legislature claimed as justification for the law is not an emergency capable of suspending the limitations of the federal Constitution.

◆ Even the war power of the federal government is not without limitations. An actual emergency does not suspend constitutional limitations and guarantees.

BRIEF FOR THE BLAISDELLS

◆ Every contract is entered into subject to the implied limitation that in an emergency its terms can be varied in a reasonable manner by a state exercising its police power. Under normal times and conditions, the Mortgage Moratorium Law would be unconstitutional. Economic conditions in Minnesota, however, are such that if foreclosures are allowed to continue, a large portion of the homes and farms of the state will become the property of trust companies, banks, insurance companies, and other mortgagees. So many breaches of the peace occurred at foreclosure sales prior to passage of the law that the Governor had been forced to direct sheriffs not to hold such sales until the legislature could pass a measure dealing with the emergency.

◆ In the 1920s, the Supreme Court upheld laws in the District of Columbia and the state of New York fundamentally similar to the Minnesota law, even though the economic emergency then was not as dire as the one facing Minnesota in the 1930s.

AMICUS CURIAE BRIEF SUPPORTING BLAISDELLS

Vernon Vrooman (Des Moines, Iowa, attorney).

SUPREME COURT DECISION: 5–4

HUGHES, C.J.

...The [Minnesota Mortgage Moratorium Act] does not impair the integrity of the mortgage indebtedness. The obligation for interest remains. The [Minnesota Mortgage Moratorium Act] does not affect the validity of the sale or the right of a mortgagee-purchaser to title in fee, or his right to obtain a deficiency judgment, if the mortgagor fails to redeem within the prescribed period. Aside from the extension of time, the other conditions of redemption are unaltered. While the mortgagor remains in possession, he must pay the rental value as that value has been determined, upon notice and hearing, by the court. The rental value so paid is devoted to the carrying of the property by the application of the required payments to taxes, insurance, and interest on the mortgage indebtedness. While the mortgagee-purchaser is debarred from actual possession, he has, so far as rental value is concerned, the equivalent of possession during the extended period.

In determining whether the provision for this temporary and conditional relief exceeds the power of the state by reason of the clause in the Federal Constitution prohibiting impairment of the obligations of contracts, we must consider the relation of emergency to constitutional power, the historical setting of the contract clause, the development of the jurisprudence of this Court in the construction of that clause, and the principles of construction which we may consider to be established.

Emergency does not create power. Emergency does not increase granted power or remove or diminish the restrictions imposed upon power granted or reserved. The Constitution was adopted in a period of grave emergency. Its grants of power to the federal government and its limitations of the power of the States were determined in the light of emergency, and they are not altered by emergency. What power was thus granted and what limitations were thus imposed are questions which have always been, and always will be, the subject of close examination under our constitutional system.

While emergency does not create power, emergency may furnish the occasion for the exercise of power.... The constitutional question presented in the light of an emergency is whether the power possessed embraces the particular exercise of it in response to particular conditions.... When the provisions of the Constitution, in grant or restriction, are specific, so particularized as not to admit of construction, no question is presented. Thus, emergency would not permit a state to have more than two

Senators in the Congress, or permit the election of President by a general popular vote without regard to the number of electors to which the States are respectively entitled, or permit the States to "coin money" or to "make anything but gold and silver coin a tender in payment of debts." But, where constitutional grants and limitations of power are set forth in general clauses, which afford a broad outline, the process of construction is essential to fill in the details. That is true of the contract clause. The necessity of construction is not obviated by the fact that the contract clause is associated in the same section with other and more specific prohibitions....

Not only is the [Contracts Clause] qualified by the measure of control which the state retains over remedial processes, but the state also continues to possess authority to safeguard the vital interests of its people.... Not only are existing laws read into contracts in order to fix obligations as between the parties, but the reservation of essential attributes of sovereign power is also read into contracts as a postulate of the legal order. The policy of protecting contracts against impairment presupposes the maintenance of a government by virtue of which contractual relations are worthwhile—a government which retains adequate authority to secure the peace and good order of society....

The economic interests of the state may justify the exercise of its continuing and dominant protective power notwithstanding interference with contracts....

Undoubtedly, whatever is reserved of state power must be consistent with the fair intent of the constitutional limitation of that power.... But it does not follow that conditions may not arise in which a temporary restraint of enforcement may be consistent with the spirit and purpose of the constitutional provision and thus be found to be within the range of the reserved power of the state to protect the vital interests of the community....

[T]here has been a growing appreciation of public needs and of the necessity of finding ground for a rational compromise between individual rights and public welfare. The settlement and consequent contraction of the public domain, the pressure of a constantly increasing density of population, the interrelation of the activities of our people and the complexity of our economic interests, have inevitably led to an increased use of the organization of society in order to protect the very bases of individual opportunity. Where, in earlier days, it was thought that only the concerns of individuals or of classes were involved, and that those of the state itself were touched only remotely, it has later been found that the fundamental interests of the state are directly affected; and that the question is no longer merely that of one party to a contract as against another, but of the use of reasonable means to safeguard the economic structure upon which the good of all depends.

It is no answer to say that this public need was not apprehended a century ago, or to insist that what the provision of the Constitution meant to the vision of that day it must mean to the vision of our time. If by the statement that what the Constitution meant at the time of its adoption it means to-day, it is intended to say that the great clauses of the Constitution must be confined to the interpretation which the framers, with the conditions and outlook of their time, would have placed upon them, the statement carries its own refutation. It was to guard against such a narrow conception that Chief Justice Marshall uttered the memorable warning: "We must never forget, that it is a *constitution* we are expounding," ... "a constitution intended to endure for ages to come, and, consequently, to be adapted to the various *crises* of human affairs." (*McCulloch v. Maryland*)....

Applying the criteria established by our decisions, we conclude:

1. An emergency existed in Minnesota which furnished a proper occasion for the exercise of the reserved power of the state to protect the vital interests of the community. The declarations of the existence of this emergency by the Legislature and by the Supreme Court of Minnesota cannot be regarded as a subterfuge or as lacking in adequate basis....

2. The legislation was addressed to a legitimate end; that is, the legislation was not for the mere advantage of particular individuals but for the protection of a basic interest of society.

3. In view of the nature of the contracts in question—mortgages of unquestionable validity—the relief afforded and justified by the emergency, in order not to contravene the constitutional provision, could only be of a character appropriate to that emergency, and could be granted only upon reasonable conditions.

4. The conditions upon which the period of redemption is extended do not appear to be unreasonable. The initial extension of the time of redemption for thirty days from the approval of the act was obviously to give a reasonable opportunity for the authorized application to the court. As already noted, the integrity of the mortgage indebtedness

is not impaired; interest continues to run; the validity of the sale and the right of a mortgagee-purchaser to title or to obtain a deficiency judgment, if the mortgagor fails to redeem within the extended period, are maintained; and the conditions of redemption, if redemption there be, stand as they were under the prior law....

5. The legislation is temporary in operation. It is limited to the exigency which called it forth....

We are of the opinion that the Minnesota statute as here applied does not violate the contract clause of the Federal Constitution. Whether the legislation is wise or unwise as a matter of policy is a question with which we are not concerned....

The judgment of the Supreme Court of Minnesota is affirmed....

SUTHERLAND, MCREYNOLDS, VAN DEVANTER, AND BUTLER, J.J., DISSENTING

A provision of the Constitution, it is hardly necessary to say, does not admit of two distinctly opposite interpretations. It does not mean one thing at one time and an entirely different thing at another time....

... The whole aim of construction, as applied to a provision of the Constitution, is to discover the meaning, to ascertain and give effect to the intent of its framers and the people who adopted it.... The necessities which gave rise to the provision, the controversies which preceded, as well as the conflicts of opinion which were settled by its adoption, are matters to be considered to enable us to arrive at a correct result.... The history of the times, the state of things existing when the provision was framed and adopted should be looked to in order to ascertain the mischief and the remedy.... As nearly as possible we should place ourselves in the condition of those who framed and adopted it.... And, if the meaning be at all doubtful, the doubt should be resolved, wherever reasonably possible to do so, in a way to forward the evident purpose with which the provision was adopted....

An application of these principles to the question under review removes any doubt, if otherwise there would be any, that the contract impairment clause denies to the several states the power to mitigate hard consequences resulting to debtors from financial or economic exigencies by an impairment of the obligation of contracts of indebtedness....

The present exigency is nothing new. From the beginning of our existence as a nation, periods of depression, of industrial failure, of financial distress, of unpaid and unpayable indebtedness, have alternated with years of plenty.... [T]he attempt by legislative devices to shift the misfortune of the debtor to the shoulders of the creditor without coming into conflict with the contract impairment clause has been persistent and oft-repeated....

It is quite true that an emergency may supply the occasion for the exercise of power, depending upon the nature of the power and the intent of the Constitution with respect thereto. The emergency of war furnishes an occasion for the exercise of certain of the war powers. This the Constitution contemplates, since they cannot be exercised upon any other occasion. The existence of another kind of emergency authorizes the United States to protect each of the states of the Union against domestic violence.... But we are here dealing not with a power granted by the Federal Constitution, but with the state police power, which exists in its own right. Hence the question is, not whether an emergency furnishes the occasion for the exercise of that police power, but whether an emergency furnishes an occasion for the relaxation of the restrictions upon the power imposed by the contract impairment clause; and the difficulty is that the contract impairment clause forbids state action under any circumstances, if it have the effect of impairing the obligation of contracts. That clause restricts every state power in the particular specified, no matter what may be the occasion. It does not contemplate that an emergency shall furnish an occasion for softening the restriction or making it any the less a restriction upon state action in that contingency than it is under strictly normal conditions.

The Minnesota statute either impairs the obligation of contracts or it does not....

A statute which materially delays enforcement of the mortgagee's contractual right of ownership and possession does not modify the remedy merely; it destroys, for the period of delay, *all* remedy so far as the enforcement of that right is concerned....

QUESTIONS

1. Chief Justice Hughes wrote in *Blaisdell*: "Not only are existing laws read into contracts in order to fix obligations as between the parties, but the reservation of essential attributes of sovereign power is also

read into contracts as a postulate of the legal order." Does this passage mean that all contracts are subject to change if a state legislature decides to do so? In the wake of *Blaisdell*, what does the Contracts Clause mean?

2. A distinction between "modifying" and "impairing" the obligations of a contract is central to the majority's opinion in *Blaisdell*. Is the distinction meaningful? Does the answer depend on whether one answers from the perspective of a debtor or a creditor?

3. Writing in May, 1934, about the distinction that the *Blaisdell* majority drew between emergency not creating power, on the one hand, and powers reserved to the states that may be exercised in emergencies, on the other, University of Minnesota law professor William L. Prosser observed: "The distinction, while it has an air of legerdemain, is of no small importance. If the contract clause may be suspended in an emergency, then likewise other clauses of the Constitution may be suspended, and—provided only that the emergency be great enough—there will be no Constitution left. Such reasoning forgets the lesson of *Ex parte Milligan*. But there is ample precedent ... for the principle that contracts when made are subject to the expectation that the State, in a reasonable exercise of its police power, may change or affect the contract itself" ("The Minnesota Mortgage Moratorium," 7 *Southern California Law Review* [1934]: 365).

   Did the majority in *Blaisdell* suspend the Contracts Clause in an emergency, or merely permit Minnesota to exercise reserve police powers in an emergency? What difference does it make constitutionally?

4. Compare *Blaisdell* with *Fletcher v. Peck* and *Dartmouth College v. Woodward*. Is Chief Justice Hughes's reading in *Blaisdell* as flimsy as Chief Justice Marshall's reading in *Fletcher v. Peck* and *Dartmouth College v. Woodward*? If so, do these thinly authoritative readings cast doubt on the legitimacy of judicial review?

5. Justice Benjamin Cardozo drafted an unpublished concurring opinion to *Blaisdell*. He wrote, in part:

   > Looking back over the century, one perceives ... how the court in its interpretation of the contract clause has been feeling its way toward a rational compromise between private rights and public welfare. From the beginning it was seen that something must be subtracted from the words of the Constitution in all their literal and stark significance.... [This rational compromise holds that] [c]ontracts were still to be preserved. There was to be no arbitrary destruction of their binding force, nor any arbitrary impairment.... But a promise exchanged between individuals was not to paralyze the state in its endeavor in times of direful crisis to keep its lifeblood flowing.

(Professor Alpheus Thomas Mason found this draft among the private papers of Justice Harlan Fiske Stone. It is quoted in Walter F. Murphy, James E. Fleming, and Sotirios A. Barber, *American Constitutional Interpretation*, 2nd ed. [Westbury, New York: Foundation Press, 1995], p. 213.) Is Justice Cardozo's reading of the Contracts Clause a reflection of political reality? Should he have published the opinion?

6. In his *Blaisdell* opinion, Chief Justice Hughes quoted from John Marshall in *McCulloch v. Maryland*: "We must never forget, that it is *a constitution* we are expounding, ... a constitution intended to endure for ages to come, and, consequently, to be adapted to the various *crises* of human affairs." In dissent, Justice Sutherland wrote: "A provision of the Constitution, it is hardly necessary to say, does not admit of two distinctly opposite interpretations. It does not mean one thing at one time and an entirely different thing at another time."

Are the two views of constitutional interpretation reflected in these quotations as mutually exclusive as they appear? Compare Hughes's and Sutherland's views with Justice Holmes's description of the Constitution in *Missouri v. Holland*, Chapter 4, pp. 443–449.

CONTRACTS CLAUSE

Allied Structural Steel v. Spannaus
438 U.S. 234 (1978)

SETTING

Many jurists and constitutional commentators believed that *Blaisdell* effectively rendered the Contracts Clause a "dead letter." Lamenting this occurrence, Justice Hugo Black said bluntly in dissent in a 1965 case involving the Contracts Clause:

> To subvert the protection of the Contract Clause ... the Court has imported into this constitutional field what I believe to be a constitutionally insupportable due process "balancing" technique[.]... Otherwise stated, a person can make a good deal with a State but if it turns out to be a very good deal for him or a very bad deal for the State, the State is free to renege at any time.... Thus this Court's judgment as to "reasonableness" of a law impairing or even repudiating a valid contract becomes the measure of the Contract Clause's protection. *City of El Paso v. Simmons*, 379 U.S. 497.

Twelve years after *City of El Paso*, however, the Court seemed to resuscitate the Contracts Clause. In *United States Trust Company of New York v. State of New Jersey*, 431 U.S. 1 (1977), it held that "private contracts are not subject to unlimited modification under the police power." For the majority, Justice Blackmun rejected the invitation "to engage in a utilitarian comparison of pubic benefit and private loss." The following year, another case from Minnesota provided the Court with the chance to revisit the Contracts Clause.

Allied Structural Steel, a private company in the business of fabricating and erecting steel structures such as bridges, had its principal place of business in Illinois, but for many years it maintained an office in Minnesota. In August 1963, Allied instituted a qualified pension plan for its employees, under Section 401 of the Internal Revenue Code. Contributions to the plan were not earmarked for, nor allocated to, specific employees but were paid in a gross amount that actuaries calculated would be sufficient to meet the obligations of the contract to the covered group. The actuarial calculations assumed that not all employees would remain in Allied's employ long enough to obtain vested benefits. Under the plan, an employee's benefits vested if the employee was fifty-five years or older and his or her age, added to years of service, totaled at least seventy-five years. If the employee was younger than fifty-five, his or her years of service with the company added to age must total at least eighty. Hence, if an employee started working for Allied at age twenty-six, retirement benefits would vest at age fifty-four.

On April 10, 1974, the Minnesota legislature enacted the Private Pension Protection Act. It imposed guaranteed, retroactive vested pension benefits after ten years of service if the employer substantially closed a plant. Under the act, if Allied decided to close its Minnesota plant, an employee who began working for Allied at age twenty-six would have retirement benefits vest at age thirty-six, or seventeen years sooner than under the employee's contract with Allied. The consequence for Allied was dramatic: Under the state law Allied would be required to pay an employee retirement benefits from $114,171 to $185,751 more than it had contracted to pay.

The Minnesota Act contained a so-called "self-destruct" provision: It would become null and void if a federal law was passed that guaranteed the payment of a substantial portion of an employee's vested pension benefits. Such a law was enacted—the Employee Retirement Income Security Act of 1974 (ERISA)—and was signed into law on September 2, 1974.

During the summer of 1974, Allied began to phase out its Minnesota office. On July 31, it discharged eleven of its thirty Minnesota employees and in August it notified the Minnesota Commissioner of Labor that it was closing its office. At least nine of the discharged employees did not have vested pension rights under the company's plan, but had worked for Allied for ten years or more and thus qualified as pension obligees of the company under the Minnesota Private Pension Protection Act. On August 18, the state notified Allied that it owed a pension funding charge of approximately $185,000 under the provisions of the act.

Allied filed suit against Minnesota attorney general Warren Spannaus in the U.S. District Court for the Northern District of Illinois to have the Minnesota Act declared unconstitutional and its enforcement enjoined. The action was transferred to the District Court of Minnesota. A three-judge panel of that court upheld the constitutionality of the Private Pension Protection Act, on the ground that the Contracts Clause was limited to protection of public contracts. The district court cited *United States Trust Company v. New Jersey* as the authority for its ruling that legislation impairing private contracts was entitled to "considerable deference." Allied appealed directly to the Supreme Court of the United States, as allowed by statute from decisions of three-judge district court panels.

HIGHLIGHTS OF SUPREME COURT ARGUMENTS

BRIEF FOR ALLIED STRUCTURAL STEEL

◆ The Minnesota act forces Allied retroactively to spend money to fulfill new pension contracts that the legislature created. This impairment goes far beyond what this Court upheld in *Home Building & Loan v. Blaisdell*.

◆ The theory that private contracts are less protected by the Constitution than public contracts has never been the law in this country. The district court's distorted reading of *United States Trust Company* should be corrected.

◆ If Minnesota can take money away from pension plan employers to help a segment of senior citizens, it can invade or re-make contracts concerning any citizen or group of citizens for the aid of any other identifiable group of citizens.

◆ The Minnesota act should be compared with ERISA, which did not force any employers to change their contracts with their employees.

AMICUS CURIAE BRIEF SUPPORTING ALLIED STEEL

U.S. Chamber of Commerce.

BRIEF FOR SPANNAUS

◆ The Minnesota Pension Act is a valid exercise of the state's police power. It is directed at obvious public purposes and, under any appropriate degree of deference to Minnesota legislative judgments, is aimed at achieving those purposes in a necessary and reasonable manner. Even if a statute impairs contract obligations, it will be sustained if it serves a legitimate public purpose and does so in a necessary and reasonable manner.

◆ This case is controlled by the Court's decision in *Home Building & Loan v. Blaisdell*. The proper focus is on whether the legislation is addressed to a legitimate end and whether the measures taken are reasonable and appropriate to that end.

◆ The state's pension act is directed to the protection of the economic welfare of employees and senior citizens by assuring them the receipt of earned and expected pension benefits and therefore falls within the broad police power of the state.

SUPREME COURT DECISION: 5–3

(Blackmun, J., did not participate.)

STEWART, J.

... There can be no question of the impact of the Minnesota Private Pension Benefits Protection Act upon the company's contractual relationships with its employees. The Act substantially altered those relationships by superimposing pension obligations upon the company conspicuously beyond those that it had voluntarily agreed to undertake. But it does not inexorably follow that the Act, as applied to the company, violates the Contract Clause of the Constitution....

Although it was perhaps the strongest single constitutional check on state legislation during our early years as a Nation, the Contract Clause receded into comparative desuetude with the adoption of the Fourteenth Amendment, and particularly with the development of the large body of jurisprudence under the Due Process Clause of that Amendment in modern constitutional history. Nonetheless, the Contract Clause remains part of the Constitution. It is not a dead letter. And its basic contours are brought into focus by several of this Court's 20th-century decisions.

First of all, it is to be accepted as a commonplace that the Contract Clause does not operate to obliterate the police power of the States....

If the Contract Clause is to retain any meaning at all, however, it must be understood to impose some limits upon the power of a State to abridge existing contractual relationships, even in the exercise of its otherwise legitimate police power. The existence and nature of those limits were clearly indicated in a series of cases in this Court arising from the efforts of the States to deal with the unprecedented emergencies brought on by the severe economic depression of the early 1930's.

In *Home Building & Loan Assn. v. Blaisdell*, the Court upheld against a Contract Clause attack a mortgage moratorium law that Minnesota had enacted to provide relief for homeowners threatened with foreclosure. Although the legislation conflicted directly with lenders' contractual foreclosure rights, the Court there acknowledged that, despite the Contract Clause, the States retain residual authority to enact laws "to safeguard the vital interests of [their] people." Id. In upholding the state mortgage moratorium law, the Court found five factors significant. First, the state legislature had declared in the Act itself that an emergency need for the protection of homeowners existed. Second, the state law was enacted to protect a basic societal interest, not a favored group. Third, the relief was appropriately tailored to the emergency that it was designed to meet. Fourth, the imposed conditions were reasonable. And, finally, the legislation was limited to the duration of the emergency.

The *Blaisdell* opinion thus clearly implied that if the Minnesota moratorium legislation had not possessed the characteristics attributed to it by the Court, it would have been invalid under the Contract Clause of the Constitution....

In applying these principles to the present case, the first inquiry must be whether the state law has, in fact, operated as a substantial impairment of a contractual relationship. The severity of the impairment measures the height of the hurdle the state legislation must clear. Minimal alteration of contractual obligations may end the inquiry at its first stage. Severe impairment, on the other hand, will push the inquiry to a careful examination of the nature and purpose of the state legislation....

The effect of Minnesota's Private Pension Benefits Protection Act on this contractual obligation was severe. The company was required in 1974 to have made its contributions throughout the pre-1974 life of its plan as if employees' pension rights had vested after 10 years, instead of vesting in accord with the terms of the plan. Thus a basic term of the pension contract—one on which the company had relied for 10 years—was substantially modified. The result was that, although the company's past contributions were adequate when made, they were not adequate when computed under the 10-year statutory vesting requirement. The Act thus forced a current recalculation of the past 10 years' contributions based on the new, unanticipated 10-year vesting requirement.

Not only did the state law thus retroactively modify the compensation that the company had agreed to pay its employees from 1963 to 1974, but also it did so by changing the company's obligations in an area where the element of reliance was vital—the funding of a pension plan....

Moreover, the retroactive state-imposed vesting requirement was applied only to those employers who terminated their pension plans or who, like the company, closed their Minnesota offices. The company was thus forced to make all the retroactive changes in its contractual obligations at one time. By simply proceeding to close its office in Minnesota, a move that had been planned before the passage of the Act, the company was assessed an immediate pension funding charge of approximately $185,000.

Thus, the statute in question here nullifies express terms of the company's contractual obligations and imposes a completely unexpected liability in potentially disabling amounts. There is not even any provision for gradual applicability or grace periods.... Yet there is no showing in the record before us that this severe disruption of contractual expectations was necessary to meet an important general social problem....

[W]hether or not the legislation was aimed largely at a single employer, it clearly has an extremely narrow focus. It applies only to private employers who have at least 100 employees, at least one of whom works in Minnesota, and who have established voluntary private pension plans, qualified under Sec. 401 of the Internal Revenue Code. And it applies only when such an employer closes his Minnesota office or terminates his pension plan. Thus, this law can hardly be characterized, like the law at issue in the *Blaisdell* case, as one enacted to protect a broad societal interest rather than a narrow class.

Moreover, in at least one other important respect the Act does not resemble the mortgage moratorium legislation whose constitutionality was upheld in the *Blaisdell* case. This legislation, imposing a sudden, totally unanticipated, and substantial retroactive obligation upon the company to its employees, was not enacted to deal with a situation remotely approaching the broad and desperate emergency economic conditions of the early 1930's— conditions of which the Court in *Blaisdell* took judicial notice.

Entering a field it had never before sought to regulate, the Minnesota Legislature grossly distorted the company's existing contractual relationships with its employees by superimposing retroactive obligations upon the company substantially beyond the terms of its employment contracts. And that burden was imposed upon the company only because it closed its office in the State.

This Minnesota law simply does not possess the attributes of those state laws that in the past have survived challenge under the Contract Clause of the Constitution. The law was not even purportedly enacted to deal with a broad, generalized economic or social problem.... It did not operate in an area already subject to state regulation at the time the company's contractual obligations were originally undertaken, but invaded an area never before subject to regulation by the State.... It did not effect simply a temporary alteration of the contractual relationships of those within its coverage, but worked a severe, permanent, and immediate change in those relationships—irrevocably and retroactively.... And its narrow aim was leveled, not at every Minnesota employer, not even at every Minnesota employer who left the State, but only at those who had in the past been sufficiently enlightened as voluntarily to agree to establish pension plans for their employees.

[W]e ... hold that if the Contract Clause means anything at all, it means that Minnesota could not constitutionally do what it tried to do to the company in this case.

The judgment of the District Court is reversed.

It is so ordered.

BRENNAN, J., AND WHITE AND MARSHALL, J.J., DISSENTING

... Today's decision greatly expands the reach of the [Contracts] Clause. The Minnesota Private Pension Benefits Protection Act (Act) does not abrogate or dilute any obligation due a party to a private contract; rather, like all positive social legislation, the Act imposes new, additional obligations on a particular class of persons. In my view, any constitutional infirmity in the law must therefore derive, not from the Contract Clause, but from the Due Process Clause of the Fourteenth Amendment. I perceive nothing in the Act that works a denial of due process and therefore I dissent....

The primary question in this case is whether the Contract Clause is violated by state legislation enacted to protect employees covered by a pension plan by requiring an employer to make outlays—which, although not in this case, will largely be offset against future savings—to provide terminated employees with the equivalent of benefits reasonably to be expected under the plan.... The basic fallacy of today's decision is its mistaken view that the Contract Clause protects all contract-based expectations, including that of an employer that his obligations to his employees will not be legislatively enlarged beyond those explicitly provided in his pension plan.

Historically, it is crystal clear that the Contract Clause was not intended to embody a broad constitutional policy of protecting all reliance interests grounded in private contracts.... [T]he Framers never contemplated that the Clause would limit the legislative power of States to enact laws creating duties that might burden some individuals in order to benefit others....

Although the debates in the Constitutional Convention and the subsequent public discussion of the Constitution are not particularly enlightening in determining the scope of the Clause, they support the view that the sole evil at which the Contract Clause was directed was the theretofore rampant state legislative interference with the ability of creditors to obtain the payment or security provided for by contract.... The Framers regarded the Contract Clause as simply an adjunct to the currency provisions of Art. I, Sec. 10, which operated primarily to bar legislation depriving creditors of the payment of the full value of their loans....

The terms of the Contract Clause negate any basis for its interpretation as protecting all contract-based expectations from unjustifiable interference. It applies, as confirmed by consistent judicial interpretations, only to state legislative Acts.... Its inapplicability to impair-

ments by state judicial acts or by national legislation belies interpretation of the Clause as intended broadly to make all contract expectations inviolable. Rather, the only possible interpretation of its terms, especially in view of its history, is as a limited prohibition directed at a particular, narrow social evil, likely to occur only through state legislative action. This evil is identified with admirable precision: "Law[s] *impairing* the Obligation of Contracts." (Emphasis supplied.) It is nothing less than an abuse of the English language to interpret, as does the Court, the term "impairing" as including laws which create new duties. While such laws may be conceptualized as "enlarging" the obligation of a contract when they add to the burdens that had previously been imposed by a private agreement, such laws cannot be prohibited by the Clause because they do not dilute or nullify a duty a person had previously obligated himself to perform....

The Court seems to attempt to justify its distortion of the meaning of the Contract Clause on the ground that imposing new duties on one party to a contract can upset his contract-based expectations as much as can laws that effectively relieve the other party of any duty to perform. But it is no more anomalous to give effect to the term "impairment" and deny a claimant protection under the Contract Clause when new duties are created than it is to give effect to the Clause's inapplicability to acts of the National Government and deny a Contract Clause remedy when an Act of Congress denies a creditor the ability to enforce a contract right to payment. Both results are simply consequences of the fact that the clause does not protect all contract-based expectations.

More fundamentally, the Court's distortion of the meaning of the Contract Clause creates anomalies of its own and threatens to undermine the jurisprudence of property rights developed over the last 40 years. The Contract Clause, of course, is but one of several clauses in the Constitution that protect existing economic values from governmental interference. The Fifth Amendment's command that "private property [shall not] be taken for public use, without just compensation" is such a clause. A second is the Due Process Clause, which during the heyday of substantive due process ... largely supplanted the Contract Clause in importance and operated as a potent limitation on government's ability to interfere with economic expectations.... Decisions over the past 50 years have developed a coherent, unified interpretation of all the constitutional provisions that may protect economic expectations and these decisions have recognized a broad latitude in States to effect even severe interference with existing economic values when reasonably necessary to promote the general welfare.... At the same time the prohibition of the Contract Clause, consistently with its wording and historic purposes, has been limited in application to state laws that diluted, with utter indifference to the legitimate interests of the beneficiary of a contract duty, the existing contract obligation[.]...

Today's conversion of the Contract Clause into a limitation on the power of States to enact laws that impose duties additional to obligations assumed under private contracts must inevitably produce results difficult to square with any rational conception of a constitutional order. Under the Court's opinion, any law that may be characterized as "superimposing" new obligations on those provided for by contract is to be regarded as creating "sudden, substantial, and unanticipated burdens" and then to be subjected to the most exacting scrutiny. The validity of such a law will turn upon whether judges see it as a law that deals with a generalized social problem, whether it is temporary (as few will be) or permanent, whether it operates in an area previously subject to regulation, and, finally, whether its duties apply to a broad class of persons. The necessary consequence of the extreme malleability of these rather vague criteria is to vest judges with broad subjective discretion to protect property interests that happen to appeal to them.

To permit this level of scrutiny of laws that interfere with contract-based expectations is an anomaly. There is nothing sacrosanct about expectations rooted in contract that justify according them a constitutional immunity denied other property rights. Laws that interfere with settled expectations created by state property law (and which impose severe economic burdens) are uniformly held constitutional where reasonably related to the promotion of the general welfare....

QUESTIONS

1. The Minnesota Private Pension Act contained no statement or findings of any emergency existing in the state, nor threats to the welfare of any substantial segment of the Minnesota population. According

to *Allied*, the legislature effectively declared, "If you substantially close a plant in Minnesota and have a pension plan, you must pay pension benefits that we ordain rather than those you contracted to pay." Do these facts sufficiently distinguish *Allied* from *Blaisdell* to justify the different outcomes in the two cases?

2. Summarize Contracts Clause jurisprudence as stated in *Allied*. What, if anything, did the *Allied* Court add to Contracts Clause analysis?

3. Constitutional scholar Edward S. Corwin maintained that "the 'obligations of contracts' clause is today of negligible importance…" (*The Constitution and What It Means Today*, 12th ed. [Princeton, NJ: Princeton University Press, 1958], p. 85). By contrast, writing for the Court in *Allied*, Justice Potter Stewart noted, "[i]f the Contract Clause is to retain any meaning at all … it must be understood to impose *some* limits upon the power of a state to abridge existing contractual relationships, even in the exercise of its otherwise legitimate police power." *Allied* seems to reside somewhere between Corwin's conclusion and Marshall's ruling in *Dartmouth College*. But where? What are the limits that Justice Stewart refers to as "some" limits?

4. Does the *Allied* majority, in effect, apply a "heightened scrutiny" test to the Minnesota law; that is, that if a law operates to impair contractual obligations, the state must show a "compelling state interest" and "necessary means" in order for the statute to pass constitutional muster?

5. Three cases decided after *Allied* suggest that the Court may not yet be ready to apply the sweeping language of that opinion in ways that limit state regulatory authority. In *Energy Reserves Group v. Kansas Power & Light Co.*, 459 U.S. 400 (1983), the Court unanimously rejected a contract-impairment challenge to a state natural gas regulation. In *Exxon Corp. v. Eagerton*, 462 U.S. 176 (1983), another unanimous Court rejected a Contracts Clause challenge to a state-imposed oil and gas severance tax. *Keystone Bituminous Coal Association v. DeBenedictis*, 480 U.S. 470 (1987), rejected a Contracts Clause challenge to the Pennsylvania Subsidence Act, holding that despite acknowledged "substantial impairment of a contractual relationship," "the impairment of petitioners' right to enforce the damage waiver is amply justified by the public purposes served by the Subsidence Act." However, none of these three cases jettisons the *Allied* reasoning. Should the Court do so; or should it extend *Allied* and thereby reinvigorate the Contracts Clause as a substantive constraint on legislation in order to protect property?

COMMENT

Many of the cases in the following section employ the Due Process Clauses of the Fifth and Fourteenth Amendments, respectively, as means to insulate economic rights from government regulation. As you read those cases, keep in mind the efforts to use the Contracts Clause in a similar manner, and think about the ways in which the Court's Contracts Clause jurisprudence is related to, and distinct from, what is conventionally called economic substantive due process jurisprudence.

SUGGESTIONS FOR FURTHER READING

Baker, Jonathan B., "Has the Contract Clause Counter-Revolution Halted? "Rhetoric, Rights, and Markets in Constitutional Analysis," 12 *Hastings Constitutional Law Quarterly* (1984): 71.

Corwin, Edward S., "The Basic Doctrine of American Constitutional Law," 12 *Michigan Law Review* (1914): 247.

————, "The 'Higher Law' Background of American Constitutional Law," 42 *Harvard Law Review* (1928-29): 149.

Current, Richard N., "The Dartmouth College Case," in *Quarrels that Have Shaped the Constitution*, rev. ed., ed. John A. Garraty (New York, NY: Harper, 1987).

Ely Jr., James W., *The Guardian of Every Other Right: A Constitutional History of Property Rights* (New York, NY: Oxford University Press, 1992).

Epstein, Richard A., "Toward a Revitalization of the Contract Clause," 51 *University of Chicago Law Review* (1984): 703.

Friendly, Henry J., *The Dartmouth College Case and the Public—Private Penumbra* (Austin, TX: University of Texas Press, 1969).

Graff, Henry F., "The Charles River Bridge Case," in *Quarrels that Have Shaped the Constitution*, rev. ed., ed. John A. Garraty (New York, NY: Harper, 1987).

Hale, Robert L., "The Supreme Court and the Contract Clause," 57 *Harvard Law Review* (1944): 512.

Horwitz, Morton J., *The Transformation of American Law, 1780–1860* (Cambridge, MA: Harvard University Press, 1977).

Hurst, J. Willard, *Law and the Conditions of Freedom in the Nineteenth Century United States* (Madison, WI: University of Wisconsin Press, 1956).

Kutler, Stanley I., *Privilege and Creative Destruction: The Charles River Bridge Case*, rev. ed. (New York, NY: Norton, 1977).

Magrath, C. Peter, *Yazoo: The Case of* Fletcher v. Peck (New York, NY: Norton, 1967).

Miller, Charles A., *The Supreme Court and the Uses of History* (Cambridge, MA: Harvard University Press, 1969).

Mullett, Charles, *Fundamental Law and the American Revolution, 1760–1776* (New York, NY: Columbia University Press, 1933).

Nedelsky, Jennifer, *Private Property and the Limits of American Constitutionalism: The Madisonian Framework and Its Legacy* (Chicago, IL: University of Chicago Press, 1990).

Newmyer, R. Kent, *The Supreme Court under Marshall and Taney* (Arlington Heights, IL: Harlan Davidson, 1968).

_____, *Supreme Court Justice Joseph Story: Statesman of the Old Republic* (Chapel Hill, NC: University of North Carolina Press, 1985).

Note, "A Process-Oriented Approach to the Contract Clause," 89 *Yale Law Journal* (1980): 1623.

Note, "Rediscovering the Contract Clause," 97 *Harvard Law Review* (1984): 1414.

Schwartz, Bernard, "Old Wine in New Bottles? The Renaissance of the Contracts Clause," *The Supreme Court Review* (Chicago, IL: University of Chicago Press, 1979).

Shirley, John M., *The* Dartmouth College *Causes and the Supreme Court* (New York, NY: Da Capo, 1971, originally published 1879).

Siegel, Stephen A., "Understanding the Nineteenth Century Contract Clause: The Role of the Property-Privilege Distinction and "Takings" Clause Jurisprudence," 60 *Southern California Law Review* (1986): 1.

Stites, Francis N., *Private Interest and Public Gain: The* Dartmouth College *Case, 1819* (Amherst, MA: University of Massachusetts Press, 1972).

Sunstein, Cass R., "Naked Preferences and the Constitution," 84 *Columbia Law Review* (1984): 1689.

Sterk, Stewart E., "The Continuity of Legislatures: Of Contracts and the Contracts Clause," 88 *Columbia Law Review* (1988): 647.

Wood, Gordon S., *The Creation of the American Republic, 1776–1787* (New York, NY: Norton, 1972).

Wright, Benjamin Fletcher, *The Contract Clause of the Constitution* (Cambridge, MA: Harvard University Press, 1938).

JUDICIAL PROTECTION OF PROPERTY INTERESTS

Calder v. Bull
3 Dallas 386 (1798)

SETTING

Natural rights philosophy, which was dominant during the Revolutionary period, contains a theory that some rights are so fundamental to an individual that they are beyond government control. Among rights considered to be "vested" in the individual is the right to be secure in the possession of private property. A consequence of the so-called vested rights theory is that government cannot interfere with private property. In the late seventeenth and early eighteenth centuries, American society was essentially agrarian. Property was understood primarily as land and slaves, and property rights were understood as guaranteeing absolute, undisturbed dominion over territory and chattel. The Federalist Party took the position that it was the duty of the courts to declare invalid state or federal statutes that violated property rights. In carrying out that task, many jurists did not perceive themselves as confined to invoking specific provisions in the federal or state constitutions. Instead, they considered themselves free to invoke abstract principles of justice in order to declare invalid laws that violated the rights of private property.

Article I, section 9, clause 3, of the Constitution of the United States explicitly prohibits Congress from passing *ex post facto* laws, which are laws that retroactively alter rights or obligations. Article I, section 10, places the same prohibition on the states. The prohibition against *ex post facto* laws is closely related to the doctrine of vested rights, and, at the time the Constitution was adopted, there was some question about whether the *ex post facto* prohibitions embraced all laws, whether of a civil or criminal nature, because they helped to assure that rights that had vested could not be taken away or altered. Responding to the criticism of those who opposed ratification of the Constitution of the United States because it did not contain a bill of rights, Alexander Hamilton, in *Federalist* No. 84, related the *ex post facto* protections solely to criminal laws. He wrote:

> The creation of crimes after the commission of the fact, or, in other words, the subjecting of men to punishment for things which, when they were done, were breaches of no law ... have been in all ages the favorite and most formidable instruments of tyranny.

Constitutional prohibitions against *ex post facto* laws were in potential conflict with the practice of several New England states, which for many years had ordered new trials by legislative resolve, thereby creating and imposing new law on cases that had already been decided. A decedent's will contested in *Calder v. Bull* was one example of the exercise of legislative power to overturn a court decision.

On March 21, 1793, the probate court of Hartford, Connecticut, issued a decree disapproving of and refusing to record the will of the late physician Normand Morrison, which he had made on August 21, 1779. Under his will, Morrison devised his estate to his grandparents, Caleb Bull and his wife. Without the will, John Calder's wife claimed the estate as Morrison's heiress. The probate court's action was not the last word on who inherited Morrison's estate, however, because in May 1795, the Connecticut legislature passed a resolution that set aside the probate court's decree and ordered a new probate hearing. Based on that resolution, the probate court on July 27, 1795, approved Morrison's will and ordered it to be recorded. The Calders sought judicial review, but the Connecticut Superior Court affirmed the second decree of the probate court, as did the Connecticut Supreme Court of Errors. Because more than eighteen months had elapsed from the March 1793 decree, the Calders were barred by a Connecticut statute from obtaining a new hearing or trial in the probate court. They sought a writ of error from the Supreme Court of the United States.

HIGHLIGHTS OF SUPREME COURT ARGUMENTS

Note: *Calder v. Bull* was argued during the February 1795 Term of the Court, but there is no record of the argument.

SUPREME COURT DECISION: 4–0

(Delivered *seriatim*; Ellsworth, C.J., and Washington, J., did not participate.)

CHASE, J.

... The sole enquiry [in the present dispute] is, whether this resolution or law of Connecticut ... is an *ex post facto* law, within the prohibition of the Federal Constitution?...

The people of the United States erected their Constitutions, or forms of government, to establish justice, to promote the general welfare, to secure the blessings of liberty; and to protect their persons and property from violence. The purposes for which men enter into society will determine the nature and terms of the social compact; and as they are the foundation of the legislative power, they will decide what are the proper objects of it: The nature, and ends of legislative power will limit the exercise of it. This fundamental principle flows from the very nature of our free Republican governments, that no man should be compelled to do what the laws do not require; nor to refrain from acts which the laws permit. There are acts which the Federal, or State, Legislature cannot do, without exceeding their authority. There are certain vital principles in our free Republican governments, which will determine and over-rule an apparent and flagrant abuse of legislative power; as to authorize manifest injustice by positive law; or to take away that security for personal liberty, or private property, for the protection whereof the government was established. An ACT of the Legislature (for I cannot call it a law) contrary to the great first principles of the social compact, cannot be considered a rightful exercise of legislative authority. The obligation of a law in governments established on express compact, and on republican principles, must be determined by the nature of the power, on which it is founded. A few instances will suffice to explain what I mean. A law that punished a citizen for an innocent action, or, in other words, for an act, which, when done, was in violation of no existing law; a law that destroys, or impairs, the lawful private contracts of citizens; a law that makes a man a Judge in his own cause; or a law that takes property from A. and gives it to B: It is against all reason and justice, for a people to entrust a Legislature with SUCH powers; and, therefore, it cannot be presumed that they have done it....

I will state what laws I consider *ex post facto* laws, within the words and the intent of the prohibition. 1st. Every law that makes an action, done before the passing of the law, and which was innocent when done, criminal; and punishes such action. 2nd. Every law that aggravates a crime, or makes it greater than it was, when committed. 3rd. Every law that changes the punishment, and inflicts a greater punishment, than the law annexed to the crime, when committed. 4th. Every law that alters the legal rules of evidence, and receives less, or different, testimony, than the law required at the time of the commission of the offence, in order to convict the offender. All these, and similar laws, are manifestly unjust and oppressive. In my opinion, the true distinction is between *ex post facto laws*, and retrospective laws. Every *ex post facto* law must necessarily be retrospective; but every retrospective law is not an *ex post facto* law: the former, only, are prohibited....

In the present case, there is no fact done by Bull and wife Plaintiffs in Error, that is in any manner affected by the law or resolution of Connecticut: It does not concern, or relate to, any act done by them. The decree of the Court of Probate of Hartford (on the 21st, March) in consequence of which Calder and wife claim a right to the property in question, was given before the said law or resolution, and in that sense, was affected and set aside by it; and in consequence of the law allowing a hearing and the decision in favor of the will, they have lost, what they would have

been entitled to, if the Law or resolution, and the decision in consequence thereof, had not been made. The decree of the Court of probate is the only fact, on which the law or resolution operates. In my judgment the case of the Plaintiffs in Error, is not within the letter of the prohibition; and, for the reasons assigned, I am clearly of opinion, that it is not within the intention of the prohibition[.]...

I am of opinion, that the decree of the Supreme Court of Errors of Connecticut be affirmed, with costs.

PATERSON, J.

... The question ... which arises on the pleadings in this cause, is, whether the resolution of the Legislature of Connecticut, be an *ex post facto* law, within the meaning of the Constitution of the United States? I am of opinion, that it is not. The words, *ex post facto*, when applied to a law, have a technical meaning, and, in legal phraseology, refer to crimes, pains, and penalties....

I had an ardent desire to have extended the provision in the Constitution to retrospective laws in general. There is neither policy nor safety in such laws; and, therefore, I have always had a strong aversion against them. It may, in general, be truly observed of retrospective laws of every description, that they neither accord with sound legislation, nor the fundamental principles of the social compact. But on full consideration, I am convinced, that *ex post facto* laws must be limited in the manner already expressed; they must be taken in their technical, which is also their common and general, acceptation, and are not to be understood in their literal sense.

IREDELL, J.

... If ... a government, composed of Legislative, Executive and Judicial departments, were established, by a Constitution, which imposed no limits on the legislative power, the consequence would inevitably be, that whatever the legislative power chose to enact, would be lawfully enacted, and the judicial power could never interpose to pronounce it void....

In order, therefore, to guard against so great an evil, it has been the policy of all the American states, which have, individually, framed their state constitutions since the revolution, and of the people of the United States, when they framed the Federal Constitution, to define with precision the objects of the legislative power, and to restrain its exercise within marked and settled boundaries. If any act of Congress, or of the Legislature of a state, violates those constitutional provisions, it is unquestionably void; though, I admit, that as the authority to declare it void is of a delicate and awful nature, the Court will never resort to that authority, but in a clear and urgent case. If, on the other hand, the Legislature of the Union, or the Legislature of any member of the Union, shall pass a law, within the general scope of their constitutional power, the Court cannot pronounce it to be void, merely because it is, in their judgment, contrary to the principles of natural justice. The ideas of natural justice are regulated by no fixed standard: the ablest and the purest men have differed upon the subject; and all that the Court could properly say, in such an event, would be, that the Legislature (possessed of an equal right of opinion) had passed an act which, in the opinion of the judges, was inconsistent with the abstract principles of natural justice. There are then but two lights, in which the subject can be viewed: 1st. If the Legislature pursue the authority delegated to them, their acts are valid. 2nd. If they transgress the boundaries of that authority, their acts are invalid. In the former case, they exercise the discretion vested in them by the people, to whom alone they are responsible for the faithful discharge of their trust: but in the latter case, they violate a fundamental law, which must be our guide, whenever we are called upon as judges to determine the validity of a legislative act.

Still, however, in the present instance, the act or resolution of the Legislature of Connecticut, cannot be regarded as an *ex post facto* law; for, the true construction of the prohibition extends to criminal, not to civil, cases....

CUSHING, J. [OMITTED]

QUESTIONS

1. Although *Calder v. Bull* has long been accepted as the authority regarding the meaning of the *ex post facto* clauses of the Constitution, scholars have questioned the soundness of the decision. University of Minnesota law professor Oliver P. Field, for example, analyzed the records of the Constitutional Convention and concluded: "One can hardly feel that the term *ex post facto* was intended to be limited to criminal cases when it was embodied in that text of

the Constitution." Rather, the clause was believed to be a "promising weapon against special legislation" ("*Ex Post Facto* in the Constitution," 20 *Michigan Law Review* (1921–22): 315).

In the wake of *Calder*, what other "promising weapons" are there in the Constitution to fend off laws that, in Justice Chase's language, "[take] property from A. and [give] it to B"?

2. James Madison argued in *Federalist* No. 44 that bills of attainder, *ex post facto* laws, and laws impairing the obligation of contracts "are contrary to the first principles of the social compact and to every principle of sound legislation." What did Madison mean? How does his observation relate to the protection of property rights? What language in the justices' various opinions in *Calder* reflects Madison's view?

3. Justice Chase in *Calder* states that there are some principles transcending the Constitution that limit what a legislature can do. His two examples are making a person both judge and party in her own case, and taking a person's property without compensation and giving it to another. Are there other principles that can or should be added to Chase's list? Is Chase's list an example of judicial activism?

4. *Calder v. Bull* is the first case in American constitutional history to cite the *Federalist* Papers as authority. The *Federalist* Papers, written during the controversy surrounding adoption of the Constitution, were clearly a partisan effort on behalf of ratification, and were written pseudonymously. Was it appropriate for the Court in 1795, or now, to cite the papers as an authoritative source of Constitutional interpretation?

JUDICIAL PROTECTION OF PROPERTY INTERESTS

Slaughter-House Cases
16 Wallace 36 (1873)

SETTING

Due process is an extremely flexible concept. Nonetheless, the concept of due process is deeply embedded in the Anglo-American legal tradition. The concept of due process traces back to Norman England after 1066 and is embodied in Chapter 39 of Magna Charta in 1215. English jurist Sir Edward Coke made frequent reference to the concept in the 1600s and James Madison included the guarantee of due process in the Fifth Amendment in 1791. The guarantee was restated in the Fourteenth Amendment in 1868.

Originally, due process guaranteed that no person would be deprived of life, liberty, or property except according to fair legal proceedings. Stated in the language of Magna Charta, Chapter 39, due process meant that: "No freemen … [will be] in any way destroyed … except by … the law of the land." In *Murray v. The Hoboken Land and Improvement Company*, 18 Howard 272 (1855), Justice Benjamin Curtis characterized due process this way:

> The words, "due process of law," were undoubtedly intended to convey the same meaning as the words, "by the law of the land," in Magna Charta. Lord Coke, in his commentary on those words, says they mean due process of law….
> The constitution contains no description of those *processes* which [due process] was intended to allow or forbid. It does not even declare what principles are to be applied to ascertain whether it be due process. It is manifest that it was not left to the legislative power to enact any *process* which might be devised. The article is a restraint on the legislative as well as on the executive and judicial powers of the government, and cannot be so construed as to leave congress free to make any process "due process of law," by its mere will. (Emphasis added)

In 1856, the New York Court of Appeals offered a different interpretation of due process. It held that due process prohibits government from infringing on vested rights to life, liberty, and property. Called "substantive due process," this understanding shifts the focus from requiring the government to follow specified procedures to precluding government from infringing on specified rights. "The true interpretation of these constitutional phrases is, that where rights are acquired by the citizen under the existing law, there is no power in any branch of the government to take them away[.]" *Wynehamer v. The People*, 13 N.Y. 378 (1856).

After the Fourteenth Amendment was ratified in 1868, property rights advocates seized on the Due Process Clause as a check on state governmental regulatory authority. The *Slaughter-House Cases* were the first attempt to persuade federal judges to read the Fourteenth Amendment Due Process Clause as containing substantive restraints on state regulatory power.

Note: Review the *Setting* to and excerpt of *Slaughter-House Cases* in Chapter 5, pp. 654–664. Regarding due process, Justice Miller wrote:

> The argument has not been much pressed in these cases that the defendant's charter deprives the plaintiffs of their property without due process of law, or that it denies to them the equal protection of the law. The first of these paragraphs has been in the Constitution since the adoption of the 5th Amendment, as a restraint upon the federal power. It is also to be found in some form of expression in the constitutions of nearly all the States, as a restraint upon the power of the States. This law then, has practically been the same as it now is during the existence of the government, except so far as the present Amendment may place the restraining power over the States in this matter in the hands of the Federal Government.
> We are not without judicial interpretation, therefore, both state and national, of the meaning of this clause. And it is sufficient to say that under no construction of that provision that we have ever seen, or any, that we

deem admissible, can the restraint imposed by the State of Louisiana upon the exercise of their trade by the butchers of New Orleans be held to be a deprivation of property within the meaning of that provision.

QUESTIONS

1. Louisiana Act 118 could be unconstitutional for two reasons. First, the monopoly deprived some butchers of their rights to property and liberty without due process of law. Second, the state did not exercise its police powers neutrally because it bestowed a privilege on the Crescent City Company that was not bestowed on other butchers. Are both understandings in the *Slaughter-House* dissents? Is either more prominent?

2. In 1874, the Court ruled that the right to sell intoxicating liquors is not one of the privileges or immunities of citizens of the United States that the states are forbidden to abridge. It affirmed the conviction of Bartemeyer, a bartender, who had sold a glass of whisky to a customer contrary to the 1860 Iowa Act for the Suppression of Intemperance. However, Justice Miller observed:

   > [I]f it were true, and it was fairly presented to us, that [Bartemeyer] was the owner of the glass of intoxicating liquor which he sold to [the customer], at the time that the State of Iowa first imposed an absolute prohibition on the sale of such liquors, then we concede that two very grave questions would arise, namely: 1. Whether this would be a statute depriving him of his property without due process of law; and secondly, whether if it were so, it would be so far a violation of the fourteenth Amendment in that regard as would call for judicial action by this Court?" *Bartemeyer v. Iowa*, 18 Wallace 129 (1874).

   Is *Bartemeyer* at odds with *Slaughter-House*?

JUDICIAL PROTECTION OF PROPERTY INTERESTS

Munn v. Illinois
94 U.S. 113 (1877)

SETTING

Munn v. Illinois is another early example of property owners asking the Supreme Court to rule that certain fundamental rights are beyond the reach of government. *Munn* pitted farmers against railroads.

Until the 1870s, the development of the railroad was considered an unmixed blessing in the United States. The national government fostered railroad construction by granting some 155 million acres of public lands for rail beds. States and municipalities contributed hundreds of millions of dollars for the same purpose. The prevailing assumption was that competition would provide any regulation that might be necessary to assure that railroads served the public interest.

Farmers were among the first to challenge the assumption that railroads should be free from governmental regulation. After the Civil War, the agricultural sector of the American economy faced a fairly steady depression. Although there were several explanations for the economic plight of farmers—including failure to diversify crops and high tariffs favoring manufacturing—many farmers traced their problems to monopolistic practices among railroads, which kept transportation rates high. Railroads also controlled the elevators in which grain farmers had to store their commodities as they awaited opportunities to move them to market. The Patrons of Husbandry—commonly known as the Grange—grew out of the economic plight and political frustrations of farmers in the late 1860s.

Tensions between farmers and railroads were played out in the context of local circumstances. In most localities, agrarian political alliances developed in support of regulation. In some, railroad regulation was not perceived as advantageous. By the mid-1870s, state laws regulating railroads, known as "Granger laws," were either proposed or in effect in Illinois, Iowa, Minnesota, and Wisconsin. Drafters of the Illinois Constitution of 1870 sought to protect farmers against railroad practices such as mixing different varieties and strains of grain at storage elevators and keeping shipping rates high. Article 13 of the 1870 Illinois Constitution declared all grain elevators to be public warehouses, specified rules for their operation, and directed the legislature to pass laws for the protection of producers, shippers, and receivers of grain and produce.

The Illinois legislature passed the Railroad and Warehouse Law of 1871 to implement Article 13. The law divided public warehouses into three classes. Class A included elevators located in cities having not fewer than one hundred thousand population. Proprietors of Class A warehouses were required to obtain operating licenses from the clerk of the circuit court. The law also established maximum rates that could be charged for storing and handling grain: two cents per bushel for the first thirty days and one-half cent per bushel for each succeeding period of fifteen days or part thereof. Two grain elevator proprietors ran afoul of this law in 1872.

Ira Munn and George Scott operated the Northwestern Grain Elevator in Chicago. Built in 1862 at the North Branch of the Chicago River, the elevator received, stored, and delivered grain primarily from and to the Chicago and Northwestern Railway in transit to eastern markets. In June 1872, Munn and Scott were indicted in the Criminal Court of Cook County for conducting business without having obtained a license from the circuit court and for charging more for storing and handling grain than allowed by the 1871 statute. They pleaded not guilty to the indictment. However, following trial, Munn and Scott were found guilty and fined $100. Their conviction was affirmed by the Illinois Supreme Court. They petitioned the Supreme Court of the United States for a writ of error.

HIGHLIGHTS OF SUPREME COURT ARGUMENTS

BRIEF FOR MUNN AND SCOTT

◆ The Illinois rate regulation violates the Fourteenth Amendment because it takes property from Munn and Scott without due process. Munn and Scott's property rights were in existence at the time Section 13 and the subsequent legislation were passed. Due process requires a judicial proceeding before they can be deprived of those rights.

◆ In the United States, the use of private property is protected as well as property itself. Every person is entitled to follow the pursuits or occupations he pleases and to use his property as he desires.

◆ The Illinois law violates equal protection of the laws by treating the owners of certain kinds of grain warehouses differently as a class than owners of other grain warehouses. Chicago is the only city in Illinois with a population greater than one hundred thousand. The warehouses in Chicago are owned by approximately thirty persons. To satisfy the Fourteenth Amendment's equal protection clause, all owners must be treated alike.

◆ The Illinois law is not a valid exercise of the state's police powers. No one contends that the warehouses are public nuisances, jeopardize the public health, are operated in an offensive manner, or disturb the public peace. The rate regulations amount to punishments even though no unlawful conduct has occurred.

BRIEF FOR ILLINOIS

◆ States have the power to regulate the inspection and storage of grain in public warehouses as part of their power to regulate intrastate commerce. In both *Gibbons v. Ogden* and *The Slaughter-House Cases* the Court gave its approval to state regulations of internal commerce.

◆ Setting maximum rates warehouses can charge for the storage of grain is not a taking of property. Munn and Scott are not put out of business by the rate requirements, nor are they compelled to use their property as a warehouse. The law simply requires that persons who use their property for a specific purpose conform to regulations deemed essential by the legislature for the protection of public interests.

◆ Warehousemen for the storage of grain in Chicago are engaged in a public employment distinguished from ordinary business pursuits. They occupy a status similar to that of common carriers. Common carriers have long been held by the law to exercise a kind of public office in the carrying on of their business activities.

◆ Illinois laws regulating grain warehouses are a legitimate exercise of the state's police power. The purpose of the rate provisions is to prevent extortion and an abuse of position by those engaged in public employments. The legislature of Illinois was the competent and proper body to determine all questions about the validity or expediency of the act in question.

SUPREME COURT DECISION: 7–2

WAITE, C.J.

... Every statute is presumed to be constitutional. The courts ought not to declare one to be unconstitutional, unless it is clearly so. If there is doubt, the expressed will of the legislature should be sustained.

The Constitution contains no definition of the word "deprive," as used in the Fourteenth Amendment. To determine its signification, therefore, it is necessary to ascertain the effect which usage has given it, when employed in the same or a like connection.

While this provision of the amendment is new in the Constitution of the United States, as a limitation upon the powers of the States, it is old as a principle of civilized government. It is found in Magna Charta, and, in substance if not in form, in nearly or quite all the constitutions that have been from time to time adopted by the several States of the Union. By the Fifth Amendment, it was introduced into the Constitution of the United States as a limitation upon the powers of the national government, and by the Fourteenth, as a guaranty against any encroachment upon an acknowledged right of citizenship by the legislatures of the States....

When one becomes a member of society, he necessarily parts with some rights or privileges which, as an individual not affected by his relations to others, he might retain. "A body politic," as aptly defined in the preamble of the Constitution of Massachusetts, "is a social compact by which the whole people covenants with each citizen, and each citizen with the whole people, that all shall be governed by certain laws for the common good." This does not confer power upon the whole people to control rights which are purely and exclusively private ... but it does authorize the establishment of laws requiring each citizen to so conduct himself, and so use his own property, as not unnecessarily to injure another. This is the very essence of government, and has found expression in the maxim *sic utere tuo ut alienum non laedas* [use your own property in such a manner as to not injure that of another].... Under these powers the government regulates the conduct of its citizens one towards another, and the manner in which each shall use his own property, when such regulation becomes necessary for the public good....

[D]own to the time of the adoption of the Fourteenth Amendment, it was not supposed that statutes regulating the use, or even the price of the use, of private property necessarily deprived an owner of his property without due process of law. Under some circumstances they may, but not under all. The amendment does not change the law in this particular: it simply prevents the States from doing that which will operate as such a deprivation.

This brings us to inquire as to the principles upon which this power of regulation rests, in order that we may determine what is within and what without its operative effect. Looking, then, to the common law, from whence came the right which the Constitution protects, we find that when private property is "affected with a public interest, it ceases to be *juris privati* [of private right] only." This was said by Lord Chief Justice Hale more than two hundred years ago, in his treatise *De Portibus Maris*, 1 Harg. Law Tracts, 78, and has been accepted without objection as an essential element in the law of property ever since. Property does become clothed with a public interest when used in a manner to make it of public consequence, and affect the community at large. When, therefore, one devotes his property to a use in which the public has an interest, he, in effect, grants to the public an interest in that use, and must submit to be controlled by the public for the common good, to the extent of the interest he has thus created. He may withdraw his grant by discontinuing the use; but, so long as he maintains the use, he must submit to the control....

It remains only to ascertain whether the warehouses of these plaintiffs in error, and the business which is carried on there, come within the operation of this principle.

For this purpose we accept as true the statements of fact contained in the elaborate brief of one of the counsel of the plaintiffs in error. From these it appears that ... "The quantity [of grain] received in Chicago has made it the greatest grain market in the world. This business has created a demand for means by which the immense quantity of grain can be handled or stored, and these have been found in grain warehouses, which are commonly called elevators[.]... The grain warehouses or elevators in Chicago are immense structures, holding from 300,000 to 1,000,000 bushels at one time, according to size. They are divided into bins of large capacity and great strength.... This mode of conducting the business was inaugurated more than twenty years ago, and has grown to immense proportions. The railways have found it impracticable to own such elevators, and public policy forbids the transaction of such business by the carrier; the ownership has, therefore, been by private individuals, who have embarked their capital and devoted their industry to such business as a private pursuit."

In this connection it must also be borne in mind that, although in 1874 there were in Chicago fourteen warehouses adapted to this particular business, and owned by about thirty persons, nine business firms controlled them, and that the prices charged and received for storage were such "as have been from year to year agreed upon and established by the different elevators or warehouses in the city of Chicago, and which rates have been annually published in one or more newspapers printed in said city, in the month of January in each year, as the established rates for the year then next ensuing such publication." Thus it is apparent that all the elevating facilities through which these vast productions "of seven or eight great States of the West" must pass on the way "to four or five of the

States on the seashore" may be a "virtual" monopoly.

Under such circumstances it is difficult to see why, if the common carrier, or the miller, or the ferryman, or the innkeeper, or the wharfinger, or the baker, or the cartman, or the hackney-coachman, pursues a public employment and exercises "a sort of public office," these plaintiffs in error do not. They stand, to use again the language of their counsel, in the very "gateway of commerce," and take toll from all who pass. Their business most certainly "tends to a common charge, and is become a thing of public interest and use."... Certainly, if any business can be clothed "with a public interest, and cease to be *juris privati* only," this has been. It may not be made so by the operation of the Constitution of Illinois or this statute, but it is by the facts....

It matters not in this case that these plaintiffs in error had built their warehouses and established their business before the regulations complained of were adopted. What they did was from the beginning subject to the power of the body politic to require them to conform to such regulations as might be established by the proper authorities for the common good. They entered upon their business and provided themselves with the means to carry it on subject to this condition. If they did not wish to submit themselves to such interference, they should not have clothed the public with an interest in their concerns....

It is insisted, however, that the owner of property is entitled to a reasonable compensation for its use, even though it be clothed with a public interest, and that what is reasonable is a judicial and not a legislative question....

In countries where the common law prevails, it has been customary from time immemorial for the legislature to declare what shall be a reasonable compensation under such circumstances, or, perhaps more properly speaking, to fix a maximum beyond which any charge made would be unreasonable. Undoubtedly, in mere private contracts, relating to matters in which the public has no interest, what is reasonable must be ascertained judicially. But this is because the legislature has no control over such a contract. So, too, in matters which do affect the public interest, and as to which legislative control may be exercised, if there are no statutory regulations upon the subject, the courts must determine what is reasonable. The controlling fact is the power to regulate at all. If that exists, the right to establish the maximum of charge, as one of the means of regulation, is implied. In fact, the common-law rule, which requires the charge to be reasonable, is itself a regulation as to price. Without it the owner could make his rates at will, and compel the public to yield to his terms, or forego the use.

But a mere common-law regulation of trade or business may be changed by statute. A person has no property, no vested interest, in any rule of the common law. That is only one of the forms of municipal law, and is no more sacred than any other. Rights of property which have been created by the common law cannot be taken away without due process; but the law itself, as a rule of conduct, may be changed at the will, or even at the whim, of the legislature, unless prevented by constitutional limitations. Indeed, the great office of statutes is to remedy defects in the common law as they are developed, and to adapt it to the changes of time and circumstances. To limit the rate of charge for services rendered in a public employment, or for the use of property in which the public has an interest, is only changing a regulation which existed before. It establishes no new principle in the law, but only gives a new effect to an old one.

We know that this is a power which may be abused; but that is no argument against its existence. For protection against abuses by legislatures the people must resort to the polls, not to the courts....

Judgment affirmed.

FIELD AND STRONG, J.J. DISSENTING

... The principle upon which the opinion of the majority proceeds is, in my judgment, subversive of the rights of private property, heretofore believed to be protected by constitutional guaranties against legislative interference[.]...

The question presented, therefore, is one of the greatest importance,—whether it is within the competency of a State to fix the compensation which an individual may receive for the use of his own property in his private business, and for his services in connection with it....

The declaration of the [Illinois] Constitution of 1870, that private buildings used for private purposes shall be deemed public institutions, does not make them so. The receipt and storage of grain in a building erected by private means for that purpose does not constitute the building a public warehouse. There is no magic in the language, though used by a constitutional convention, which can change a private business into a public one, or alter the character of the building in which the business is transacted....

But it would seem from its opinion

that the court holds that property loses something of its private character when employed in such a way as to be generally useful. The doctrine declared is that property "Becomes clothed with a public interest when used in a manner to make it of public consequence, and affect the community at large;" and from such clothing the right of the Legislature is deduced to control the use of the property, and to determine the compensation which the owner may receive for it. When Sir Matthew Hale, and the sages of the law in his day, spoke of property as affected by a public interest, and ceasing from that cause to be *juris privati* solely, that is, ceasing to be held merely in private right, they referred to property dedicated by the owner to public uses, or to property the use of which was granted by the government, or in connection with which special privileges were conferred. Unless the property was thus dedicated, or some right bestowed by the government was held with the property, either by specific grant or by prescription of so long a time as to imply a grant originally, the property was not affected by any public interest so as to be taken out of the category of property held in private right. But it is not in any such sense that the terms "clothing property with a public interest" are used in this case. From the nature of the business under consideration—the storage of grain—which, in any sense in which the words can be used, is a private business, in which the public are interested only as they are interested in the storage of other products of the soil, or in articles of manufacture, it is clear that the court intended to declare that, whenever one devotes his property to a business which is useful to the public, "affects the community at large," the Legislature can regulate the compensation which the owner may receive for its use, and for his own services in connection with it. "When, therefore," says the court, "one devotes his property to a use in which the public has an interest, he, in effect, grants to the public an interest in that use, and must submit to be controlled by the public for the common good, to the extent of the interest he has thus created. He may withdraw his grant by discontinuing the use; but, so long as he maintains the use, he must submit to the control."...

If this be sound law, if there be no protection, either in the principles upon which our republican government is founded, or in the prohibitions of the Constitution against such invasion of private rights, all property and all business in the State are held at the mercy of a majority of its legislature. The public has no greater interest in the use of buildings for the storage of grain than it has in the use of buildings for the residences of families, nor, indeed, any thing like so great an interest; and, according to the doctrine announced, the Legislature may fix the rent of all tenements used for residences, without reference to the cost of their erection. If the owner does not like the rates prescribed, he may cease renting his houses....

The doctrine of the State court, that no one is deprived of his property, within the meaning of the constitutional inhibition, so long as he retains its title and possession, and the doctrine of this court, that, whenever one's property is used in such a manner as to affect the community at large, it becomes by that fact clothed with a public interest, and ceases to be *juris privati* only, appear to me to destroy, for all useful purposes, the efficacy of the constitutional guaranty. All that is beneficial in property

arises from its use, and the fruits of that use; and whatever deprives a person of them deprives him of all that is desirable or valuable in the title and possession. If the constitutional guaranty extends no further than to prevent a deprivation of title and possession, and allows a deprivation of use, and the fruits of that use, it does not merit the encomiums it has received. Unless I have misread the history of the provision now incorporated into all our State constitutions, and by the Fifth and Fourteenth Amendments into our Federal Constitution, and have misunderstood the interpretation it has received, it is not thus limited in its scope, and thus impotent for good. It has a much more extended operation that either court, State, or Federal has given to it. The provision, it is to be observed, places property under the same protection as life and liberty. Except by due process of law, no State can deprive any person of either. The provision has been supposed to secure to every individual the essential conditions for the pursuit of happiness; and for that reason has not been heretofore, and should never be, construed in any narrow or restricted sense.

No State "shall deprive any person of life, liberty, or property without due process of law," says the 14th Amendment to the Constitution. By the term "life," as here used, something more is meant than mere animal existence. The inhibition against its deprivation extends to all those limbs and faculties by which life is enjoyed. The provision equally prohibits the mutilation of the body by the amputation of an arm or leg, or the putting out of an eye, or the destruction of any other organ of the body through which the soul communicates with the outer world. The deprivation not only of life, but of whatever God has given to every one with life, for its growth and enjoyment, is prohibited by the provision in question, if its efficacy be not frittered away by judicial decision.

By the term "liberty," as used in the provision, something more is meant than mere freedom from physical restraint or the bounds of a prison. It means freedom to go where one may choose, and to act in such manner, not inconsistent with the equal rights of others, as his judgment may dictate for the promotion of his happiness; that is, to pursue such callings and avocations as may be most suitable to develop his capacities, and give to them their highest enjoyment.

The same liberal construction which is required for the protection of life and liberty, in all particulars in which life and liberty are of any value, should be applied to the protection of private property....

The power of the State over the property of the citizen under the constitutional guaranty is well defined. The State may take his property for public uses, upon just compensation being made therefor. It may take a portion of his property by way of taxation for the support of the government. It may control the use and possession of his property, so far as may be necessary for the protection of the rights of others, and to secure to them the equal use and enjoyment of their property. The doctrine that each one must so use his own as not to injure his neighbor—*sic utere tuo ut alienum non laedas*—is the rule by which every member or society must possess and enjoy his property; and all legislation essential to secure this common and equal enjoyment is a legitimate exercise of State authority. Except in cases where property may be destroyed to arrest a conflagration or the ravages of pestilence, or be taken under the pressure of an immediate and overwhelming necessity to prevent a public calamity, the power of the State over the property of the citizen does not extend beyond such limits....

There is nothing in the character of the business of the defendants as warehousemen which called for the interference complained of in this case. Their buildings are not nuisances; their occupation of receiving and storing grain infringes upon no rights of others, disturbs no neighborhood, infects not the air, and in no respect prevents others from using and enjoying their property as to them may seem best. The legislation in question is nothing less than a bold assertion of absolute power by the State to control at its discretion the property and business of the citizen, and fix the compensation he shall receive. The will of the legislature is made the condition upon which the owner shall receive the fruits of his property and the just reward of his labor, industry, and enterprise....

QUESTIONS

1. Summarize the "affected with a public interest" doctrine announced in *Munn*. If you were a state legislator attempting to draft regulatory legislation, of what practical guidance would you find that doctrine?

2. Summarize the majority's reading of the Fourteenth Amendment Due Process Clause guarantee in *Munn* and the dissenters' reading of it. Despite the Court's deference to the legislature in *Munn*, is there a suggestion in Chief Justice Waite's opinion that in some circumstances the court might be willing to substitute its judgment for a legislature's? What might those conditions be?

3. Did the *Munn* majority effectively refute Justice Field's dissenting argument that if the legislature constitutionally may regulate the storage of grain it may regulate any economic activity?

4. Another example of the efforts of property rights advocates to persuade the Court to interpret due process in substantive terms was decided the same year as *Munn v. Illinois*. In *Davidson v. New Orleans*, 6 Otto 97 (1877), the Supreme Court was asked to overturn a tax assessment on various parcels of real estate, valued at $50,000, to fund draining swamp lands within the Louisiana parishes of Carroll and Orleans. The assessments were attacked as depriving the plaintiff of property without due process of law. Writing for the majority, Justice Samuel Miller wrote: "the constitutional meaning or value of the phrase 'due process of law,' remains to-day without that satisfactory precision of definition which judicial decisions have given to nearly all the other guarantees of personal rights found in the constitutions of the several States and of the United States." Nevertheless, Miller continued:

> But while it has been a part of the Constitution, as a restraint upon the power of the States, only a very few years, the docket of this court is crowded with cases in which we are asked to hold that State courts and State legislatures have deprived their own citizens of life, liberty, or property without due process of law. There is here abundant evidence that there exists some strange misconception of the scope of this provision as found in the fourteenth amendment. In fact, it would seem, from the character of many of the cases before us, and the arguments made in them, that the clause under consideration is looked upon as a means of bringing to the test of the decision of this court the abstract opinions of every unsuccessful litigant in a State court of the justice of the decision against him, and of the merits of the legislation on which such a decision may be founded.

Justice Miller's opinion suggests that the Fourteenth Amendment Due Process Clause was shifting political lobbying efforts from legislatures to the courts. Could (and should) the Supreme Court have construed the guarantee of due process to avoid that result?

COMMENTS

1. Legal writer Robert Lingo characterized the political dynamics behind *Munn* and four other Granger cases decided the same Term as follows: "The railroads themselves ... assumed an uncompromis-

ing attitude, and shielded behind their private charters they denied the right of the public, the states, or the nation to regulate or in any other way interfere with their operations. Opposed to this view, put forward by the farm organizations, was the belief that no private individual or group should be above the power of the state and people, and that the state must be able to regulate private businesses and the use of private property for the good of the general public" (Robert Lingo, "The Abiding Influence of *Munn v. Illinois*," in *Legal and Economic Influence of the Grange, 1867–1967* [Washington, D.C.: The National Grange, 1967], p. 36).

2. Thirteen years after *Munn*, the Court decided *Chicago, Milwaukee & St. Paul Railway Co. v. Minnesota* (*Minnesota Rate Cases*), 134 U.S. 418 (1890). In the intervening period, the appointment of a new chief justice, Melville W. Fuller, and several new associate justices had rendered the Court's membership more amenable to protecting corporate property rights. Only Justices Stephen J. Field, Joseph P. Bradley, and Samuel F. Miller remained from the *Munn* Court. Justice Field's dissenting view in *Munn* now commanded a six-vote majority. The Court overturned railroad rates such as those that had been set by the Railroad and Warehouse Commission of the State of Minnesota. The Commission had set substitute rates following an investigation in which it found that the Chicago, Milwaukee, and St. Paul Railway Company was charging unequal and unreasonable rates for transporting milk from the cities of Farmington, Northfield, Faribault, and Owatonna, Minnesota, to St. Paul and Minneapolis. Writing for the Court, Justice Blatchford held:

> The question of the reasonableness of a rate of charge for transportation by a railroad company, involving as it does the element of reasonableness both as regards the company and as regards the public, is eminently a question for judicial investigation, requiring due process of law for its determination. If the company is deprived of the power of charging reasonable rates for the use of its property, and such deprivation takes place in the absence of an investigation by judicial machinery, it is deprived of the lawful use of its property, and thus, in substance and effect, of the property itself, without due process of law[.]...

In dissent, Justice Bradley claimed that the decision: "practically overrules *Munn v. Illinois*, and the several railroad cases that were decided at the same time. The governing principle of those cases was that the regulation and settlement of the fares of railroads and other public accommodations is a legislative prerogative and not a judicial one."

A transitional case, illustrating the shift in judicial reading of the Fourteenth Amendment Due Process Clause from *Munn* to the

Minnesota Rate Cases, is *Mugler v. Kansas*, 123 U.S. 623 (1887). In *Mugler*, the Court upheld a Kansas statute that prohibited the manufacture or sale of liquor without a license. Nonetheless, Justice John Marshall Harlan said:

> It does not at all follow that every statute enacted ostensibly for the promotion of [public health, safety or morality] is to be accepted as a legitimate exertion of the police powers of the state. There are, of necessity, limits beyond which legislation cannot rightfully go. While every possible presumption is to be indulged in favor of the validity of a statute ... the courts must obey the constitution rather than the law-making department of government, and must, upon their own responsibility, determine whether, in any particular case, these limits have been passed.... The courts are not bound by mere forms, nor are they to be misled by mere pretenses. They are at liberty, indeed, are under a solemn duty, to look at the substance of things, whenever they enter upon the inquiry whether the legislature has transcended the limits of its authority. If, therefore, a statute purporting to have been enacted to protect the public health, the public morals, or the public safety, has no real or substantial relation to those objects, or is a palpable invasion of rights secured by the fundamental law, it is the duty of the courts to so adjudge, and thereby give effect to the constitution.

Scholars have identified several factors that contributed to the Court's eventual recognition of economic substantive due process. They include:

> (1) The origins of the Fourteenth Amendment's Due Process Clause, which a few think was intended to protect economic rights, and some think was designed to protect fundamental rights more generally.
>
> (2) The writings of nineteenth century legal academics such as Thomas M. Cooley, Christopher G. Tiedeman, and John F. Dillon, who argued that private property is the preeminent vested right in the American constitutional order, which courts should protect from legislative incursions.
>
> (3) Effective arguments supporting judicial intervention, brought before the Court by elite business lawyers who represented clients who would benefit from judicial protection of economic rights.
>
> (4) The ideas of classical political economy and social Darwinism that briefly prevailed in parts of the American intellectual community and then were belatedly adopted by the judicial community.
>
> (5) The conservative predilections of the members of the Supreme Court.

JUDICIAL PROTECTION OF PROPERTY INTERESTS

Santa Clara County
v. Southern Pacific Railroad
118 U.S. 394 (1886)

Setting

Although the corporation has always played an important role in American society, the business corporation is a relatively modern device. In early American history most corporations were eleemosynary, that is, charitable, organizations such as churches, schools, or municipal entities, incorporated by state legislatures to perform a public service. Corporate charters also were granted to private franchises, but with the stipulation that the franchise engage in an activity related to the public interest, such as constructing a bridge, a turnpike, or a canal. In order to carry out these public improvements, corporations were frequently given exclusive legal privileges such as the power of eminent domain and shelter from competition. (See *Charles River Bridge v. Warren Bridge*, pp. 744–748.)

Early in the nineteenth century, the Supreme Court recognized the corporation's special status as a device for serving the public interest. In *Dartmouth College v. Woodward* (pp. 733–741), Chief Justice Marshall described the qualities of the corporation, saying, "Among the most important are immortality, and if the expression may be allowed, individuality; properties, by which a perpetual succession of many persons are considered as the same, and may act as a single individual."

In the nineteenth century the private business corporation became increasingly common. By the 1840s, general incorporation laws began replacing individual charters. Originally a highly regulated and protected device to serve the public interest, the corporation was transformed into an instrument of corporate capitalism. One of the main beneficiaries of the new corporate form was the railroad, a transportation innovation central to the success of the industrial revolution. States and the national government pursued aggressive policies to encourage the spread of this new technology throughout the country.

In 1852, the California legislature granted a right-of-way through the state for the purpose of constructing a railroad from the Atlantic to the Pacific. The legislature deemed a transcontinental railroad necessary to promoting the "highest commercial interests of the Republic." By the late 1860s, however, public attitudes toward railroads had hardened. Consolidation of railroad ownership and practices of some of the more unscrupulous railroad financiers, including Daniel Drew, Jay Gould, and James Fisk, led the California legislature to enact stringent regulations. Some of those efforts assumed constitutional proportions during the constitutional convention of 1878–79. An otherwise divided group of delegates had in common a desire to rein in railroad corporations under a system of control.

Delegates to the California constitutional convention created a Board of Equalization to levy taxes on railroads in a manner that would force them to bear their full share of the burden of state taxation. As a concession to property owners who were badly in debt, the delegates also created a provision specifying that persons who owned mortgaged property had to pay taxes only on the value of the property less the amount of the mortgages, with the mortgaged value assessed to creditors. However, the constitution contained an exception to the general rule of taxation: railroads, most of which were heavily mortgaged, did not have the right to deduct the amount of their mortgage debts from the value of their taxable property.

When the new constitution went into effect, the railroads refused to pay the taxes assessed against them. In 1883, Santa Clara County, San Bernardino County, and the state of California brought actions in California courts against the Southern Pacific, Central Pacific, and Northern Pacific Railroad Companies for nonpayment of taxes claimed due under assessments made by the State Board of Equalization. The cases came to be known as the California Railroad Tax Cases. The litigation involved the validity of California's constitution and statutes relating to the taxation of railroads.

On the motion of the railroads, the California Railroad Tax Cases, of which the Santa Clara County litigation was one, were removed to the Circuit Court of the United States, Ninth Circuit, District of California. The railroads waived the right to trial by jury. Following trial, the circuit court entered judgment for the railroads. The counties and the state petitioned the Supreme Court of the United States for a writ of error.

HIGHLIGHTS OF SUPREME COURT ARGUMENTS

[Omitted]

Before oral argument in the case, Chief Justice Waite made the following statement:

> The court does not wish to hear argument on the question whether the provision in the Fourteenth Amendment to the Constitution, which forbids a State to deny to any person within its jurisdiction the equal protection of the laws, applies to these corporations. We are all of opinion that it does.

SUPREME COURT DECISION: 9–0

[Opinion omitted]

QUESTIONS

1. Given the change in the character and purpose of corporations, from eleemosynary entities chartered to serve a public interest, to profit-making entities, was it appropriate social policy for the Court to extend the shelter of the Fourteenth Amendment to business corporations without benefit of argument or an explanation of its action? Does such an exercise of judicial review undermine the court's legitimacy?

2. Railroad corporations had sought the status of persons under the Fourteenth Amendment a year before *Santa Clara* was decided, in a case that was declared moot before the Supreme Court could act. However, in his argument on behalf of the railroad in *San Mateo County v. Southern Pacific Railroad Co.*, 116 U.S. 138 (1885), Roscoe Conkling, who had been a member of the Joint Committee on Reconstruction that drafted the Fourteenth Amendment, hinted that the Committee intended the word "persons" in the amendment to include corporations. Conkling's recollection of the Committee's intent apparently was not widely shared.

   What role, if any, should claims about the intent of the drafters play in constitutional interpretation? How might intent be authoritatively determined?

3. William M. Evarts was one of Southern Pacific Railroad's counsel on the brief in *Santa Clara*. Evarts was a very influential lawyer who had served as president of the New York State and American Bar Associations, as a Republican senator from New York, secretary of state, and U.S. attorney general. As a litigator on behalf of corporate business interests, one of Evarts's greatest successes was persuading the New York Court of Appeals to adopt a substantive reading of due process in *In re Jacobs*, 98 N.Y. 98 (1885). Political scientist Benjamin R. Twiss characterizes Evarts's argument in the *Jacobs* case as "the most powerful collection of precedents for laissez-faire in both judicial decisions and philosophical and economic theory that had yet been submitted to a court" (*Lawyers and the Constitution: How Laissez Faire Came to the Supreme Court* [Princeton, NJ: Princeton University Press, 1942], p. 99).

   In what ways did the Court's declaration that corporations are "persons" for Fourteenth Amendment purposes contribute to Evarts's theory of economic liberty? Did the Court's pronouncement in *Santa Clara* effectively prohibit the states from exercising their police powers to regulate corporations?

4. Law professor Morton J. Horwitz wrote: "[T]he real significance of the Supreme Court's decision in *Santa Clara* may be precisely that it [went] beyond Justice Miller's *Slaughterhouse* effort to confine the

scope of the equal protection clause" (*The Transformation of American Law, 1870–1960* [New York, NY: Oxford University Press, 1992], p. 69). Explain how *Santa Clara* is a crucial aspect of the evolution of economic substantive due process.

5. Dissenting in *Connecticut General Life Insurance Company v. Johnson*, 303 U.S. 77 (1938), Justice Hugo Black wrote: "[The Fourteenth Amendment] sought to prevent discrimination by the states against classes of races.... Yet, of the cases in this Court in which the Fourteenth Amendment was applied during the first fifty years after its adoption [in 1868], less than one-half of one per cent invoked it in protection of the negro race, and more than 50 per cent asked that its benefits be extended to corporations." Justice Black believed that the Court should overrule *Santa Clara* and focus on the Fourteenth Amendment as a source of protection for blacks. Compare Justice Douglas's dissent in *Wheeling Steel Corp. v. Glander*, 337 U.S. 562 (1949), where he also argued that *Santa Clara* should be overruled.

If you were a justice, how would you construe the word "person" in the Fourteenth Amendment? Can the Court's reading of the word "person" in the Fourteenth Amendment Due Process Clause in *Santa Clara* be reconciled with the protection of life in that same clause?

JUDICIAL PROTECTION OF PROPERTY INTERESTS

Pollock v. Farmers' Loan & Trust Co.
158 U.S. 601 (1895)

SETTING

The American economy and society underwent dramatic changes in the eighteenth and nineteenth centuries. With those changes came new understandings of property. Pre-Revolutionary America had been primarily agrarian and antientrepreneurial. As noted previously, in those days property was understood to encompass primarily land and slaves. Consistent with the natural rights philosophy of John Locke, property also was understood as a natural or vested right with which government could not interfere.

The expansive economic development that characterized the early decades of the nineteenth century eroded the narrow, pre-Revolutionary understanding of property. Property came to encompass anything that was subject to being owned, whether it was tangible, like land, or intangible, like a contract right. Soon property was understood to include every species of valuable right and interest.

Before the Civil War, state judges, in particular, fashioned common law rules of law that advanced business, industrial, and financial interests. In the field of personal injury law, for example, judges developed rules such as the assumption of the risk doctrine that barred injured workers from recovering damages from their employers for injuries they suffered on the job. The fields of contracts, property, and bankruptcy likewise witnessed the development of legal rules and doctrines that fostered economic growth and development.

The Supreme Court was also instrumental in fostering economic growth. In cases like *Charles River Bridge v. Warren Bridge*, for example, the Court rejected a static interpretation of the Contracts Clause in favor of an interpretation that fostered entrepreneurial development in transportation.

After the Civil War, a paradoxical situation existed: Despite the rapid changes in the understanding of property that accompanied American economic development and geographic expansion, the ideology of absolute vested rights remained vital. Decisions such as *Calder v. Bull*, *Fletcher v. Peck*, and *Dartmouth College v. Woodward* remained standing and demonstrated that although the meaning of property had changed dramatically in the nineteenth century and had come to be identified with forms of wealth that could be used to produce more wealth, underlying legal rules designed to protect the rights of property owners changed hardly at all. Consequently, while some legal doctrine, such as in *Charles River Bridge*, facilitated the production of wealth during the nineteenth century, other doctrine, such as in *Calder*, made it difficult for state legislatures and Congress to regulate or redistribute that wealth.

In 1893, a series of bank failures and industrial collapses resulted in a major economic panic. The panic led to depletion of the nation's gold reserves and massive budget deficits. An 1894 tariff act, which became law without President Grover Cleveland's signature, contained a 2 percent tax on incomes above $4,000. In addition to federal budget deficits that required new sources of revenue, the income tax of 1894 was part of the reform policy of Democrats, who controlled the presidency and both houses of Congress, designed to modify the regressive tax structure that had been created in the two decades after the Civil War. The growth of Populist Party support in the West and South, fueled by tax protests, spurred efforts to adopt a graduated income tax. To its opponents, the Income Tax of 1894 was anathema. In the words of influential legal treatise writer and railroad lawyer, John F. Dillon, the tax was:

> a forced contribution from the rich for the benefit of the poor, and as a means of distributing the rich man's property among the rest of the community ... is class legislation of the most pronounced and vicious type ... violative of the constitutional rights of the property owner, subversive of the existing social policy, and essentially revolutionary.

Note: Review the *Setting* to and excerpt of *Pollock v. Farmers' Loan & Trust Co.* in Chapter 3, pp. 752–759.

QUESTIONS

1. Summarize the defense of property rights in the *Pollock* majority opinion. Is Justice Harlan's dissent "anti-property rights"?

2. Legal historian Morton J. Horwitz writes: "In progressive constitutional historiography, the decision of the Supreme Court of the United States in *Pollock v. Farmers' Loan & Trust Co.* has always stood for the essence of judicial usurpation.... [F]ar from marking a sharp break with the past, the decision in *Pollock* instead exemplified the crystallization and culmination of ideas that had been gathering strength in American constitutional thought for over fifty years. *Pollock* simply represented one of the most dramatic applications of a recent convergence of constitutional doctrines that would restrict the power of the state to redistribute wealth" (*The Transformation of American Law, 1870–1960* [New York, NY: Oxford University Press, 1992], p. 19).

   Based on the decisions earlier in this chapter, is Horwitz correct? What language in *Pollock* illustrates the convergence of the entrepreneurial and vested-rights constitutional doctrines discussed in both *Settings* to *Pollock*?

JUDICIAL PROTECTION OF PROPERTY INTERESTS

Lochner v. New York
198 U.S. 45 (1905)

SETTING

Industrial capitalism profoundly transformed workplace relationships following the Civil War. Mechanization and creation of large-scale corporate organizations gave rise to factory work in an impersonal urban setting. Formerly skilled craftsmen became assembly line workers doing routinized work. Previously self-employed farmers and small business owners became employees bound to their work by contract. Economic self-sufficiency was replaced by dependency and labor market vulnerability. However, under the double standard that prevailed during the seventy-five years spanning the mid-1860s to the mid-1930s, combinations of capital were accepted as natural while combinations of labor were attacked as socialistic. Propertied interests also staunchly opposed economic regulations as infringements on their fundamental rights.

Workers themselves were deeply divided over the legitimacy of capitalism, government's role in a market economy, the social bases of labor organization, and attitudes toward laborers who were not White, Anglo-Saxon Protestants. The United States lagged far behind other Western industrial nations in adopting statutes regulating wages, hours, and working conditions of employees. Nevertheless, workers lobbied state legislatures for protective legislation. The limited social legislation that existed in America before the 1930s was adopted by the states under the authority of their police powers. Massachusetts, New York, Oregon, and Washington were pioneers in the state regulatory field.

In the last decade of the nineteenth century, state court judges, and eventually federal jurists, embraced a substantive reading of due process. Viewing regulatory statutes as infringing arbitrarily on fundamental ecomonic rights, they were reluctant to accept state legislative responses to the social changes wrought by industrial capitalism. For example, New York passed a law in 1882 outlawing the manufacture of cigars in tenement houses. The law's aim was to ban the notorious "sweating" system that required employees to work tediously for long hours, under unhealthy conditions, at low wages. The New York Court of Appeals struck down the law as depriving the cigar manufacturer of liberty and property. Judge Robert Earl wrote:

> It is … plain that this law interferes with the profitable and free use of his property by the owner or lessee of a tenement-house who is a cigarmaker, and trammels him in the application of his industry and the disposition of his labor, and thus, in a strictly legitimate sense, it arbitrarily deprives him of his property and of some portion of his personal liberty. *In re Jacobs*, 98 N.Y. 98 (1885).

Jacobs also illustrated a doctrine that complemented economic substantive due process. Many judges opposed exercises of the police power that they perceived as favoring one particular social group or class over others. Thus, many judges not only held regulatory statutes to a substantive due process standard, they required regulatory legislation to be "neutral," and to serve a "public purpose." Judge Earl also complained of the New York cigar manufacturing law:

> What does this act attempt to do? In form, it makes it a crime for a cigar-maker in New York and Brooklyn, the only cities in the State having a population exceeding 500,000, to carry on a perfectly lawful trade in his own home.… [H]e will become a criminal for doing that which is perfectly lawful outside of the two cities named—everywhere else, so far as we are able to learn, in the whole world. *In re Jacobs*, 98 N.Y. 98 (1885).

✱ President Theodore Roosevelt remarked that the *Jacobs* decision demonstrated that its authors "… knew legalism, but not life." *Jacobs* also was a precursor of another case from the Empire State, *Lochner v. New York*.

Throughout the 1880s, New York state bakers had struggled to unionize their industry. At the center of those efforts was a drive to reduce their typical sixteen- to eighteen-hour work day to ten hours. Conditions in the bakeries were oppressive. As one New York baker described them: "It is nothing unusual for a man to do his night's work and then have to work three or four hours with the day hands. Our trade is the worst paid trade in New York.... This means eight dollars for ninety hours of hard work. Is it any wonder there are so many coffins?" On April 23, 1887, a mass meeting of bakers adopted a resolution supporting reduced work hours. The bakers' organizing efforts were only partially successful, however. Many bakeries remained nonunion. In order to bring nonunion bakeries into line with those bound by collective bargaining agreements, the Baker's Progressive Union lobbied the state legislature to pass a ten-hour work law for bakers.

The union argued that long hours spent in hot shops damaged bakers' health and jeopardized the production of wholesome bread. An 1892 study, conducted by the New York Commissioner of Labor Statistics with the aid of the organization of Journeymen Bakers, fed agitation for shorter hours. The study found that union bakers in New York City averaged ten-and-one-half hours daily, including Sundays, while bakers working in nonunion shops averaged twelve-and-one-half hours. The bakers' lobbying campaign was fruitful: New York's 1897 Labor Law provided that no employee should be "required or permitted to work in a biscuit, bread or cake bakery or confectionery establishment more than sixty hours in any one week, or more than ten hours in any one day on the last day of the week." Violation of the law was a misdemeanor.

Compliance with the 1897 statute was low, and it was poorly enforced. The Master Bakers' Association, a bakery owners' organization, urged outright noncompliance. In the year it was passed, the Labor Law's ten-hour day provision was implemented in only 312 of 855 baking establishments inspected by state officials. Among those refusing to comply with the law was Utica, New York, bakery owner Joseph Lochner. He was arrested when one of his employees complained to the Factory Inspection Department that Lochner violated the law by permitting Amam Schmitter, another employee, to work more than 60 hours during the week of April 19–April 26, 1901, at Lochner's nonunion bakery. Lochner demurred to the charge.

Lochner's demurrer was overruled. He was tried and convicted in the County Court of Oneida County and fined $50. Lochner had been convicted of a similar offense in 1899 and fined $20. His conviction was affirmed by a divided Appellate Division and the New York Court of Appeals.

On behalf of Lochner, the Master Bakers' Association petitioned the Supreme Court of the United States for a writ of error. *reversed*

HIGHLIGHTS OF SUPREME COURT ARGUMENTS

BRIEF FOR LOCHNER

◆ The New York labor law is not a reasonable exercise of the state's police power. The contention that flour dust is unhealthful is disputed by medical authorities. Furthermore, modern baking factories are models of cleanliness and healthfulness. Proper enforcement of the state's health laws will protect bakers working in unsanitary conditions.

◆ The police powers of the state were never intended by the people adopting state and federal constitutions to be so paternal as to take away the treasured freedoms of the individual and his right to pursue life, liberty, and happiness. State and federal courts have consistently upheld personal liberties against attempted police power regulations.

◆ The New York law was never intended as a health provision. It is purely a labor law. It reflects the success of almost a decade of lobbying by bakers for ten-hour days. It prohibits absolutely the employment of bakers for more than sixty hours per week without regard to loss of property or other emergencies that might arise, the desire of employees to contract for overtime work, or the willingness of employers to pay for extra work in emergencies. No other statute in the United States is so restrictive.

◆ The New York law is distinguishable from other hours limitations laws that had been upheld by the Court. *Holden v. Hardy*, 169 U.S. 366 (1898), for example, which upheld a Utah law limiting working hours of miners, was justified because working in underground mines has always been recognized as hazardous and unhealthful. The baking trade is not.

BRIEF FOR NEW YORK

◆ The Supreme Court lacks jurisdiction to examine the judgments of the lower courts because Lochner did not raise the federal constitutional issues there. According to Supreme Court precedents, the Court's jurisdiction over judgments of state courts extends only to those cases in which it is clear that the party bringing the case to the Court intends to assert a federal right.

◆ If the Court does claim jurisdiction over the case, the New York law must be recognized as a valid exercise of the state's police power. The police power is necessarily elastic, so as to meet the new and changing conditions of civilization. New York has become a great commercial and manufacturing state. Police power regulations that might have been invalid fifty years ago are required to meet modern conditions, including urban crowding, specialization of labor, and the growth of the factory. Review of the entire statute, of which limitations on hours of labor in bakeries and confectionery establishments is only a small element, eliminates any doubt about its purpose as a public health regulation. If there are differences of opinion about the wisdom of particular police power enactments, those differences should be resolved by legislatures, not courts.

SUPREME COURT DECISION: 5–4

PECKHAM, J.

… The statute necessarily interferes with the right of contract between the employer and employees, concerning the number of hours in which the latter may labor in the bakery of the employer. The general right to make a contract in relation to his business is part of the liberty of the individual protected by the

14th Amendment of the Federal Constitution. *Allgeyer v. Louisiana* [165 U.S. 578 (1897)]. Under that provision no state can deprive any person of life, liberty, or property without due process of law. The right to purchase or to sell labor is part of the liberty protected by this amendment, unless there are circumstances which exclude the right. There are, however, certain powers, existing in the sovereignty of each state in the Union, somewhat vaguely termed police powers, the exact description and limitation of which have not been attempted by the courts. Those powers, broadly stated, and without, at present, any attempt at a more specific limitation, relate to the safety, health, morals, and general welfare of the public. Both property and liberty are held on such reasonable conditions as may be imposed by the governing power of the state in the exercise of those powers, and with such conditions the 14th Amendment was not designed to interfere....

The state, therefore, has power to prevent the individual from making certain kinds of contracts, and in regard to them the Federal Constitution offers no protection. If the contract be one which the state, in the legitimate exercise of its police power, has the right to prohibit, it is not prevented from prohibiting it by the 14th Amendment.... Therefore, when the state, by its legislature, in the assumed exercise of its police powers, has passed an act which seriously limits the right to labor or the right of contract in regard to their means of livelihood between persons who are *sui juris* [possessing full social and civil rights] (both employer and employee), it becomes of great importance to determine which shall prevail,—the right of the individual to labor for such time as he may choose, or the right of the state to prevent the individual from laboring, or from entering into any contract to labor, beyond a certain time prescribed by the state.

This court has recognized the existence and upheld the exercise of the police powers of the states in many cases which might fairly be considered as border ones, and it has, in the course of its determination of questions regarding the asserted invalidity of such statutes, on the ground of their violation of the rights secured by the Federal Constitution, been guided by rules of a very liberal nature, the application of which has resulted, in numerous instances, in upholding the validity of state statutes thus assailed....

It must, of course, be conceded that there is a limit to the valid exercise of the police power by the state. There is no dispute concerning this general proposition. Otherwise the 14th Amendment would have no efficacy and the legislatures of the states would have unbounded power, and it would be enough to say that any piece of legislation was enacted to conserve the morals, the health, or the safety of the people; such legislation would be valid, no matter how absolutely without foundation the claim might be. The claim of the police power would be a mere pretext,—become another and delusive name for the supreme sovereignty of the state to be exercised free from constitutional restraint. This is not contended for. In every case that comes before this court, therefore, where legislation of this character is concerned, and where the protection of the Federal Constitution is sought, the question necessarily arises: Is this a fair, reasonable, and appropriate exercise of the police power of the state, or is it an unreasonable, unnecessary, and arbitrary inter-ference with the right of the individual to his personal liberty, or to enter into those contracts in relation to labor which may seem to him appropriate or necessary for the support of himself and his family? Of course the liberty of con-tract relating to labor includes both par-ties to it. The one has as much right to purchase as the other to sell labor.

This is not a question of substituting the judgment of the court for that of the legislature. If the act be within the power of the state it is valid, although the judgment of the court might be totally opposed to the enactment of such a law. But the question would still remain: Is it within the police power of the state? and that question must be answered by the court.

The question whether this act is valid as a labor law, pure and simple, may be dismissed in a few words. There is no reasonable ground for interfering with the liberty of person or the right of free contract, by determining the hours of labor, in the occupation of a baker. There is no contention that bakers as a class are not equal in intelligence and capacity to men in other trades or man-ual occupations, or that they are not able to assert their rights and care for themselves without the protecting arm of the state, interfering with their inde-pendence of judgment and of action. They are in no sense wards of the state. Viewed in the light of a purely labor law, with no reference whatever to the ques-tion of health, we think that a law like the one before us involves neither the safety, the morals, nor the welfare, of the public, and that the interest of the public is not in the slightest degree affected by such an act. The law must be upheld, if at all, as a law pertaining to

the health of the individual engaged in the occupation of a baker. It does not affect any other portion of the public than those who are engaged in that occupation. Clean and wholesome bread does not depend upon whether the baker works but ten hours per day or only sixty hours a week. The limitation of the hours of labor does not come within the police power on that ground.

It is a question of which of two pow-ers or rights shall prevail,—the power of the state to legislate or the right of the individual to liberty of person and free-dom of contract. The mere assertion that the subject relates, though but in a remote degree, to the public health, does not necessarily render the enact-ment valid. The act must have a more direct relation, as a means to an end, and the end itself must be appropriate and legitimate, before an act can be held to be valid which interferes with the general right of an individual to be free in his person and in his power to con-tract in relation to his own labor....

We think the limit of the police power has been reached and passed in this case. There is, in our judgment, no rea-sonable foundation for holding this to be necessary or appropriate as a health law to safeguard the public health, or the health of the individuals who are fol-lowing the trade of a baker. If this statute be valid, and if, therefore, a proper case is made out in which to deny the right of an individual, *sui juris*, as employer or employee, to make con-tracts for the labor of the latter under the protection of the provisions of the Federal Constitution, there would seem to be no length to which legislation of this nature might not go....

We think that there can be no fair doubt that the trade of a baker, in and of itself, is not an unhealthy one to that degree which would authorize the legislature to interfere with the right to labor, and with the right of free contract on the part of the individual, either as employer or employee. In looking through statistics regarding all trades and occupations, it may be true that the trade of a baker does not appear to be as healthy as some other trades, and is also vastly more healthy than still others. To the common understanding the trade of a baker has never been regarded as an unhealthy one. Very likely physicians would not recommend the exercise of that or of any other trade as a remedy for ill health. Some occupations are more healthy than others, but we think there are none which might not come under the power of the legislature to supervise and control the hours of working therein, if the mere fact that the occupation is not absolutely and perfectly healthy is to confer that right upon the legislative department of the government. It might be safely affirmed that almost all occupations more or less affect the health....

[The] interference on the part of the legislatures of the several states with the ordinary trades and occupations of the people seems to be on the increase....

It is impossible for us to shut our eyes to the fact that many of the laws of this character, while passed under what is claimed to be the police power for the purpose of protecting the public health or welfare, are, in reality, passed from other motives. We are justified in saying so when, from the character of the law and the subject upon which it legislates, it is apparent that the public health or welfare bears but the most remote relation to the law. The purpose of a statute must be determined from the natural and legal effect of the language

employed; and whether it is or is not repugnant to the Constitution of the United States must be determined from the natural effect of such statutes when put into operation, and not from their proclaimed purpose....

It is manifest to us that the limitation of the hours of labor as provided for in this section of the statute under which the indictment was found, and the plaintiff in error convicted, has no such direct relation to, and no such substantial effect upon, the health of the employee, as to justify us in regarding the section as really a health law. It seems to us that the real object and purpose were simply to regulate the hours of labor between the master and his employees (all being men, *sui juris*), in a private business, not dangerous in any degree to morals, or in any real and substantial degree to the health of the employees. Under such circumstances the freedom of master and employee to contract with each other in relation to their employment, and in defining the same, cannot be prohibited or interfered with, without violating the Federal Constitution....

Reversed.

HOLMES, J., DISSENTING

... This case is decided upon an economic theory which a large part of the country does not entertain. If it were a question whether I agreed with that theory, I should desire to study it further and long before making up my mind. But I do not conceive that to be my duty, because I strongly believe that my agreement or disagreement has nothing to do with the right of a majority to embody their opinions in law. It is settled by various decisions of this court that state constitutions and state laws may regulate life in many ways which we as legislators might think as injudicious, or if you like as tyrannical, as this, and which, equally with this, interfere with the liberty to contract.... The 14th Amendment does not enact Mr. Herbert Spencer's *Social Statics [or the Conditions Essential to Human Happiness Specified and the First of Them Developed* (New York, NY: D. Appleton, 1888)].... [A] Constitution is not intended to embody a particular economic theory, whether of paternalism and the organic relation of the citizen to the state or of laissez faire. It is made for people of fundamentally differing views, and the accident of our finding certain opinions natural and familiar, or novel, and even shocking, ought not to conclude our judgment upon the question whether statutes embodying them conflict with the Constitution of the United States.

General propositions do not decide concrete cases. The decision will depend on a judgment or intuition more subtle than any articulate major premise. But I think that the proposition just stated, if it is accepted, will carry us far toward the end. Every opinion tends to become a law. I think that the word "liberty," in the 14th Amendment, is perverted when it is held to prevent the natural outcome of a dominant opinion, unless it can be said that a rational and fair man necessarily would admit that the statute proposed would infringe fundamental principles as they have been understood by the traditions of our people and our law. It does not need research to show that no such sweeping condemnation can be passed upon the statute before us. A reasonable man might think it a proper measure on the score of health. Men whom I certainly could not pronounce unreasonable would uphold it as a first instalment of a general regulation of the hours of work. Whether in the latter aspect it would be open to the charge of inequality I think it unnecessary to discuss.

HARLAN, WHITE, AND DAY, J.J., DISSENTING

... Speaking generally, the state, in the exercise of its powers, may not unduly interfere with the right of the citizen to enter into contracts that may be necessary and essential in the enjoyment of the inherent rights belonging to everyone, among which rights is the right "to be free in the enjoyment of all his faculties, to be free to use them in all lawful ways, to live and work where he will, to earn his livelihood by any lawful calling, to pursue any livelihood or avocation." This was declared in *Allgeyer v. Louisiana*, 165 U.S. 578 (1897). But in the same case it was conceded that the right to contract in relation to persons and property, or to do business, within a state, may be "regulated, and sometimes prohibited, when the contracts or business conflict with the policy of the state as contained in its statutes."...

I take it to be firmly established that what is called the liberty of contract may, within certain limits, be subjected to regulations designed and calculated to promote the general welfare, or to guard the public health, the public morals, or the public safety....

Granting, then, that there is a liberty of contract which cannot be violated even under the sanction of direct legislative enactment, but assuming, as according to settled law we may assume, that such liberty of contract is subject to such regulations as the state may reasonably prescribe for the common good and the well-being of society, what are the conditions under which the judiciary may declare such regulations to be in excess of legislative authority and void? Upon this point there is no room for dispute; for the rule is universal that a legislative enactment, Federal or state, is never to be disregarded or held invalid unless it be, beyond question, plainly and palpably in excess of legislative power.... If there be doubt as to the validity of the statute, that doubt must therefore be resolved in favor of its validity, and the courts must keep their hands off, leaving the legislature to meet the responsibility for unwise legislation. If the end which the legislature seeks to accomplish be one to which its power extends, and if the means employed to that end, although not the wisest or best, are yet not plainly and palpably unauthorized by law, then the court cannot interfere....

Let these principles be applied to the present case....

It is plain that this statute was enacted in order to protect the physical well-being of those who work in bakery and confectionery establishments. It may be that the statute had its origin, in part, in the belief that employers and employees in such establishments were not upon an equal footing, and that the necessities of the latter often compelled them to submit to such exactions as unduly taxed their strength. Be this as it may, the statute must be taken as expressing the belief of the people of New York that, as a general rule, and in the case of the average man, labor in excess of sixty hours during a week in such establishments may endanger the health of those who thus labor. Whether or not this be wise legislation it is not the province of the court to inquire. Under our systems of government the courts are not concerned with the wisdom or policy of legislation. So that, in determining the question of power to interfere with liberty of contract, the court may inquire whether the means devised by the state are germane to an end which may be lawfully accomplished and have a real or substantial relation to the protection of health, as involved in the daily work of the persons, male and female, engaged in bakery and confectionery establishments. But when this inquiry is entered upon I find it impossible, in view of common experience, to say that there is here no real or substantial relation between the means employed by the state and the end sought to be accomplished by its legislation.... Therefore I submit that this court will transcend its functions if it assumes to annul the statute of New York....

I take leave to say that the New York statute, in the particulars here involved, cannot be held to be in conflict with the 14th Amendment, without enlarging the scope of the amendment far beyond its original purpose, and without bringing under the supervision of this court matters which have been supposed to belong exclusively to the legislative departments of the several states when exerting their conceded power to guard the health and safety of their citizens by such regulations as they in their wisdom deem best....

QUESTIONS

1. At the federal level, the precursor to *Lochner* was *Allgeyer v. Louisiana*, 165 U.S. 578 (1897). In *Allgeyer* the Court unanimously struck down a Louisiana statute that made it illegal for its citizens to

buy insurance from out-of-state companies. The ostensible purpose of the statute was to protect the public from questionable insurance practices. Justice Peckham's *Allgeyer* opinion stated that the statute violated due process under the Fourteenth Amendment by denying what he termed "liberty of contract." According to Justice Peckham, due process included "the right of the citizen ... to live and work where he will; to earn his livelihood by any lawful calling; to pursue any livelihood or avocation, and for that purpose to enter into all contracts which may be proper, necessary, and essential to his carrying out to a successful conclusion the purposes above mentioned." *Allgeyer* thus deployed due process of law under the Fourteenth Amendment as a substantive limitation on government's power to limit economic liberty.

Consistent with *In re Jacobs*, *Allgeyer* also held government to a standard of even-handed treatment. Justice Peckham quoted favorably Justice Harlan's opinion in *Powell v. Pennsylvania*, 127 U.S. 678 (1888): "... enjoyment upon terms of equality with all others in similar circumstances of the privilege of pursuing an ordinary calling or trade, and of acquiring, holding, and selling property, is an essential part of [a person's] rights of liberty and property, as guarantied by the fourteenth amendment."

Political scientist Howard Gillman contends that the Court in *Lochner*, *Allgeyer* and similar cases developed a "master principle of neutrality," which Gillman explains as follows:

> [I]t was illegitimate for government to single out for special treatment and attending certain groups or classes simply to improve their position in relation to competing classes; government could impose special burdens and benefits only if it could be demonstrated that the special treatment would advance public health, safety, or morality. (*The Constitution Besieged: The Rise and Demise of Lochner Era Police Powers Jurisprudence* [Durham, NC: Duke University Press, 1993], p. 125)

What language in *Lochner* illustrates the complementary standards of economic substantive due process and the notion that legislatures cannot act to benefit particular classes of persons?

2. Law professor William M. Wiecek cites *Lochner* as an example of what legal theorist G. Edward White called "the oracular theory of judging." Wiecek describes this theory as presupposing "the existence of timeless principles of justice embodied in the Constitution of the United States. The judges' function was chiefly to restrain the coercive power of government in order to protect the liberty of the individual. Judges discovered and applied these principles in the suprapolitical act of judging, a process marked by reason rather than by will" (*Liberty under Law: The Supreme Court in American Life*

[Baltimore, MD: The Johns Hopkins Press, 1988], pp. 132–133). What elements of the oracular theory are reflected in Justice Peckham's *Lochner* opinion? What timeless principles did he identify?

3. The legal fiction that employers and employees possess equal rights when entering into labor contracts—termed a "mental prepossession" by Louis D. Brandeis in 1916—underlay the majority opinion in *Lochner*. Historically, which social interests benefited from this fiction? Which were disadvantaged?

4. Eight years after his dissent in *Lochner*, Justice Holmes observed: "When twenty years ago a vague terror went over the earth and the word socialism began to be heard, I thought and still think that fear was translated into doctrines that had no proper place in the Constitution or the common law."

   Is it correct to read *Lochner* as the Supreme Court's attempt to protect industrial capitalism from the evils of regulatory socialism via the doctrine of *laissez-faire*?

5. Many critics of the *Lochner* decision argue that the majority cast itself in the role of a "super-legislature," second-guessing the judgment of New York's elected representatives that prolonged exposure to flour dust was harmful to bakery workers' health, and defeating progressive legislation. Even though the Supreme Court invalidated over two hundred economic regulations, typically on due process grounds, the Court upheld as many regulations as it rejected between 1905 and 1935. (See *The Constitution of the United States: Analysis and Interpretation* [Washington, D.C.: U.S. Government Printing Office, 1987], pp. 1883–2114.)

   Under what circumstances, if any, should courts trump legislatures on matters of public policy? If the Court does overturn legislation, on what grounds should it do so?

COMMENT

In *Lochner*, Justice Peckham concluded: "It seems to us that the real object and purpose [of the New York law] were simply to regulate the hours of labor between the master and his employees (*all being men, sui juris*), in a private business, not dangerous in any degree to morals, or in any real and substantial degree to the health of the employees" (emphasis added). *Sui juris* translates literally as "of his or her own rights." It means to have the mental and physical capability to manage one's own affairs and to possess full social and political rights.

In 1908, the justices were asked to decide whether the liberty of contract doctrine applied to women as well as to men. *Muller v. Oregon*, 208 U.S. 412 (1908) arose out of reform efforts to enhance the status of working women by protecting them from dangerous workplaces. Around the turn of the century, women's rights advocates supported women entering the work place. They viewed wage labor as providing women the potential opportunity for financial independence and social advancement, and as changing the structure of domestic responsibilities. Women's rights advocates also struggled to reform conditions at the work place. Under the leadership of Josephine C. Goldmark and Florence Kelley, the National Consumers' League (NCL) was in the fore-front of this movement. The NCL argued for the abolition of sweatshops and lobbied for equal pay for equal work, shorter work days, minimum wages, and other basic employees' rights. After its organization in 1903, the National Women's Trade Union was also instrumental in obtaining protective legislation.

In the early years of the twentieth century, the political climate in Oregon was favorable to social reform. Progressive governor W.S. U'Ren and his Direct Legislation League succeeded in passing initiative and referendum bills in 1902, the direct primary in 1904, an effective corrupt practices act in 1908, and the recall in 1910. This period also saw adoption of a series of progressive labor laws guaranteeing workers the right to join unions, regulating child labor, and making it easier for railroad employees to sue for job-related injuries. In 1912 the state constitution had been amended to give women the vote. As part of these progressive reforms, on February 19, 1903, Oregon adopted a law providing that no female be employed in any mechanical establishment, factory, or laundry more than ten hours a day. Violation of the statute was a misdemeanor.

The Supreme Court upheld the Oregon statute, 9–0. "[W]ithout questioning in any respect the decision in *Lochner v. New York*," Justice David J. Brewer wrote for the Court:

> That woman's physical structure and the performance of maternal functions place her at a disadvantage in the struggle for subsistence is obvious. This is especially true when the burdens of motherhood are upon her. Even when they are not, by abundant testimony of the medical fraternity continuance for a long time on her feet at work, repeating this from day to day, tends to injurious effects upon the body, and, as healthy mothers are essential to vigorous offspring, the physical well-being of woman becomes an object of public interest and care in order to preserve the strength and vigor of the race.
>
> Still again, history discloses the fact that woman has always been dependent upon man. He established his control at the outset by superior physical strength, and this control in various forms, with diminishing intensity, has continued to the present. As minors, though not to the same extent, she has been looked upon in the courts as needing especial care that her rights may be preserved. Education was long denied her, and while now the doors of the school room are opened and her opportunities for acquiring knowledge are great, yet even with that and the consequent increase of capacity for business affairs it is still true that in the struggle for subsistence she is not an equal competitor with her brother. Though limitations upon personal and contractual rights may be removed by legislation, there

is that in her disposition and habits of life which will operate against a full assertion of those rights. She will still be where some legislation to protect her seems necessary to secure a real equality of right. Doubtless there are individual exceptions, and there are many respects in which she has an advantage over him; but looking at it from the viewpoint of the effort to maintain an independent position in life, she is not upon an equality. Differentiated by these matters from the other sex, she is properly placed in a class by herself, and legislation designed for her protection may be sustained, even when like legislation is not necessary for men and could not be sustained.... [H]aving in view not merely her own health, but the well-being of the race ... legislation [is justified] to protect her from the greed as well as the passion of man. The limitations which this statute places upon her contractual powers, upon her right to agree with her employer as to the time she shall labor, are not imposed solely for her benefit, but also largely for the benefit of all....

JUDICIAL PROTECTION OF PROPERTY INTERESTS

Adair v. United States
208 U.S. 161 (1908)

SETTING

Before the Civil War, American workers made only sporadic efforts at self-organization. After the War, however, several factors combined to spawn unionization. One was the technological and organizational changes accompanying the industrial revolution that swept the country during the last quarter of the nineteenth century, leading to huge capitalist empires in such fields as rail transportation, steel, and oil. By the turn of the century, some twenty-five per cent of wage earners in the United States were working for corporations. A second factor that contributed to unionization was the erosion of economic self-sufficiency for workers that resulted from the evolution of industrial capitalism. A third factor was growth of cities, which made workers dependent on their wages for survival. Gone were the days when workers could survive periods of unemployment by maintaining a garden and a few animals. A fourth factor that fostered unionization among skilled workers was the arrival of large numbers of immigrants who offered a pool of cheap, unskilled labor to employers. Industrial workers's efforts to obtain regulations of wages, hours, and working conditions provided yet another source of unionization. Union solidarity and collective bargaining complemented the efforts of labor lobbyists to obtain protective legislation like the statute struck down in *Lochner v. New York.*

The growth in union membership from 868,500 in 1900 to over 2,000,000 in 1904, frightened corporate employers. Led by such organizations as the National Civic Federation, the Citizens' Industrial Association, and the National Association of Manufacturers, employers undertook an aggressive antiunion campaign. Their most potent weapon was the "iron-clad oath," which union members called contemptuously the "yellow-dog" contract. Such contracts required workers to agree that, as a condition of employment, they would not join any union, thus maintaining an "open shop." Yellow-dog contracts were most widely used in the bituminous coal fields in West Virginia, Kentucky, and Tennessee. They were also employed to hinder unionization in the shoe, glass, hosiery, clothing, metal trades, and commercial printing industries.

In the last decade of the nineteenth century, in response to frequently violent confrontations between labor and management, fifteen states enacted laws that prohibited employers from firing employees for joining a union, or from making the yellow-dog contract a condition of employment. A strike called by the Railway Union in 1894 against the Pullman Company, following the company's announcement of a 20 percent wage cut, made clear the need for federal legislation. The Pullman Strike was bloody and disruptive. It paralyzed rail service in twenty-seven states, primarily in the northeast and midwest. Over the objections of Illinois Governor John P. Atgeld and union president Eugene V. Debs, President Grover Cleveland sent federal troops to Chicago to support the railroads. State and federal courts were also accomplices in employers' antiunion drives. In the case of *In re Debs*, 158 U.S. 564 (1895), for example, the Supreme Court sustained the use of injunctions by the national government to prevent workers from interfering with the transportation of the mails. Justice Brewer wrote for the unanimous *Debs* Court: "[I]t is a lesson which cannot be learned too soon or too thoroughly that under this government of and by the people the means of redress of all wrongs are through the courts and at the ballot box, and that no wrong, real or fancied, carries with it legal warrant to invite as a means of redress the co-operation of a mob, with its accompanying acts of violence."

In 1898, Congress passed the Erdman Act. The act sought to promote interstate commerce by eliminating the antiunion practices of discharging union members and enforcing yellow-dog contracts. The rationale underlying the Act was that by eliminating these impediments to workers' self-organization, strikes like those against the Pullman Company could be avoided. Section 10 of the Erdman Act made it a crime to threaten any employee with loss of employment, or to unjustly discriminate against any employee because of membership in a labor organization. The statute provided for fines from $100 to $1,000.

In 1906 William Adair, a master mechanic for the Louisville and Nashville Railroad Company, threatened to discharge and then did discharge O. B. Coppage, another employee of the railroad, because of Coppage's membership in the Order of Locomotive Firemen. Adair was subsequently indicted in the District Court of the Eastern District of Kentucky for violation of Section 10 of the Erdman Act.

Adair entered a demurrer to the indictment, challenging the constitutionality of Section 10 of the Act.

The District Court for the Eastern District of Kentucky overruled Adair's demurrer and ordered the case to trial. Adair was tried by a jury, found guilty, and fined $100. He petitioned the Supreme Court of the United States for a writ of error.

HIGHLIGHTS OF SUPREME COURT ARGUMENTS

BRIEF FOR ADAIR

◆ Section 10 violates due process of law guaranteed by the Fifth Amendment by destroying valuable property rights of contract. On many occasions the Court has declared restrictions on the right to contract to be unconstitutional. Statutes in at least four states that are similar to the Erdman Act have already been held to be unconstitutional.

◆ Section 10 is impermissible class legislation. It confers benefits on union labor that are not conferred on nonunion labor.

BRIEF FOR THE UNITED STATES

◆ The Court has held on several occasions that the right of individuals to make contracts is subservient to the power of Congress to protect the public health, safety, or convenience.

◆ Only Congress has authority to determine questions of policy. The Court should not second-guess Congressional determinations.

SUPREME COURT DECISION: 6–2

(Moody, J., did not participate.)

HARLAN, J.

... The first inquiry is whether the part of the 10th section of the act of 1898 upon which the first count of the indictment was based is repugnant to the 5th Amendment of the Constitution, declaring that no person shall be deprived of liberty or property without due process of law. In our opinion that section, in the particular mentioned, is an invasion of the personal liberty, as well as of the right of property, guaranteed by that Amendment. Such liberty and right embrace the right to make contracts for the purchase of the labor of others, and equally the right to make contracts for the sale of one's own labor; each right, however, being subject to the fundamental condition that no contract, whatever its subject-matter, can be sustained which the law, upon reasonable grounds, forbids as inconsistent with the public interests, or as hurtful to the public order, or as detrimental to the common good....

Without stopping to consider what would have been the rights of the railroad company under the 5th Amendment, had it been indicted under the act of Congress, it is sufficient in this case to say that, as agent of the railroad company, and, as such, responsible for the conduct of the business of one of its departments, it was the defendant Adair's right—and that right inhered in his personal liberty, and was also a right of property—to serve his employer as best he could, so long as he did nothing that was reasonably forbidden by law as injurious to the public interests. It was the right of the defendant to prescribe the terms upon which the services of Coppage would be accepted, and it was the right of Coppage to become or not, as he chose, an employee of the railroad company upon the terms offered to him....

While, as already suggested, the right of liberty and property guaranteed by the Constitution against deprivation without due process of law is subject to such reasonable restraints as the common good or the general welfare may require, it is not within the functions of government—at least, in the absence of contract between the parties—to compel any person, in the course of his business and against his will, to accept or retain the personal services of another, or to compel any person, against his will, to perform personal services for another. The right of a person to sell his labor upon such terms as he deems proper is, in its essence, the same as the right of the purchaser of labor to prescribe the conditions upon which he will accept such labor from the person offering to sell it. So the right of the employee to quit the service of the employer, for

whatever reason, is the same as the right of the employer, for whatever reason, to dispense with the services of such employee. It was the legal right of the defendant, Adair,—however unwise such a course might have been,—to discharge Coppage because of his being a member of a labor organization, as it was the legal right of Coppage, if he saw fit to do so,—however unwise such a course on his part might have been,—to quit the service in which he was engaged, because the defendant employed some persons who were not members of a labor organization. In all such particulars the employer and the employee have equality of right, and any legislation that disturbs that equality is an arbitrary interference with the liberty of contract which no government can legally justify in a free land.... In the absence, however, of a valid contract between the parties controlling their conduct towards each other and fixing a period of service, it cannot be, we repeat, that an employer is under any legal obligation, against his will, to retain an employee in his personal service any more than an employee can be compelled, against his will, to remain in the personal service of another....

As the relations and the conduct of the parties towards each other was not controlled by any contract other than a general employment on one side to accept the services of the employee and a general agreement on the other side to render services to the employer,—no term being fixed for the continuance of the employment,—Congress could not, consistently with the 5th Amendment, make it a crime against the United States to discharge the employee because of his being a member of a labor organization.

But it is suggested that the authority

[handwritten margin note: congress' commercial powers don't extend to internal commerce, esp. individual contracts of labor]

to make it a crime for an agent or officer of an interstate carrier, having authority in the premises from his principal, to discharge an employee from service to such carrier, simply because of his membership in a labor organization, can be referred to the power of Congress to regulate interstate commerce, without regard to any question of personal liberty or right of property arising under the 5th Amendment. This suggestion can have no bearing in the present discussion unless the statute, in the particular just stated, is, within the meaning of the Constitution, a regulation of commerce among the states. If it be not, then clearly the government cannot invoke the commerce clause of the Constitution as sustaining the indictment against Adair.

Let us inquire what is commerce, the power to regulate which is given to Congress?

This question has been frequently propounded in this court, and the answer has been—and no more specific answer could well have been given—that commerce among the several states comprehends traffic, intercourse, trade, navigation, communication, the transit of persons, and the transmission of messages by telegraph,—indeed, every species of commercial intercourse among the several states,—but not that commerce "completely internal, which is carried on between man and man, in a state, or between different parts of the same state, and which does not extend to or affect other states."... But what possible legal or logical connection is there between an employee's membership in a labor organization and the carrying on of interstate commerce? Such relation to a labor organization cannot have, in itself and in the eye of the law, any bearing upon the commerce with

which the employee is connected by his labor and services. Labor associations, we assume, are organized for the general purpose of improving or bettering the conditions and conserving the interests of its members as wage-earners,—an object entirely legitimate and to be commended rather than condemned. But surely those associations, as labor organizations, have nothing to do with interstate commerce, as such. One who engages in the service of an interstate carrier will, it must be assumed, faithfully perform his duty, whether he be a member or not a member of a labor organization. His fitness for the position in which he labors and his diligence in the discharge of his duties cannot, in law or sound reason, depend in any degree upon his being or not being a member of a labor organization. It cannot be assumed that his fitness is assured, or his diligence increased, by such membership, or that he is less fit or less diligent because of his not being a member of such an organization. It is the employee as a man, and not as a member of a labor organization, who labors in the service of an interstate carrier. Will it be said that the provision in question had its origin in the apprehension, on the part of Congress, that, if it did not show more consideration for members of labor organizations than for wage-earners who were not members of such organizations, or if it did not insert in the statute some such provision as the one here in question, members of labor organizations would, by illegal or violent measures, interrupt or impair the freedom of commerce among the states? We will not indulge in any such conjectures, nor make them, in whole or in part, the basis of our decision. We could not do so consistently with the respect due to a coordinate department of the government. We could not do so without imputing to Congress the purpose to accord to one class of wage-earners privileges withheld from another class of wage-earners, engaged, it may be, in the same kind of labor and serving the same employer. Nor will we assume, in our consideration of this case, that members of labor organizations will, in any considerable numbers, resort to illegal methods for accomplishing any particular object they have in view.

Looking alone at the words of the statute for the purpose of ascertaining its scope and effect, and of determining its validity, we hold that there is no such connection between interstate commerce and membership in a labor organization as to authorize Congress to make it a crime against the United States for an agent of an interstate carrier to discharge an employee because of such membership on his part....

It results, on the whole case, that the provision of the statute under which the defendant was convicted must be held to be repugnant to the 5th Amendment, and as not embraced by nor within the power of Congress to regulate interstate commerce, but, under the guise of regulating interstate commerce, and as applied to this case, it arbitrarily sanctions an illegal invasion of the personal liberty as well as the right of property of the defendant, Adair....

MCKENNA, J., DISSENTING

The opinion of the court proceeds upon somewhat narrow lines and either omits or does not give adequate prominence to the considerations which, I think, are determinative of the questions in the case. The principle upon which the opinion is grounded is, as I understand it, that a labor organization has no legal or logical connection with interstate commerce, and that the fitness of an employee has no dependence or relation with his membership in such organization. It is hence concluded that to restrain his discharge merely on account of such membership is an invasion of the liberty of the carrier guaranteed by the 5th Amendment of the Constitution of the United States. The conclusion is irresistible if the propositions from which it is deduced may be viewed as abstractly as the opinion views them. May they be so viewed?...

I may assume at the outset that the liberty guaranteed by the 5th Amendment is not a liberty free from all restraints and limitations, and this must be so or government could not be beneficially exercised in many cases. Therefore, in judging of any legislation which imposes restraints or limitations, the inquiry must be, What is their purpose, and is the purpose within one of the powers of government? Applying this principle immediately to the present case, without beating about in the abstract, the inquiry must be whether Sec. 10 of the act of Congress has relation to the purpose which induced the act, and which it was enacted to accomplish, and whether such purpose is in aid of interstate commerce, and not a mere restriction upon the liberty of carriers to employ whom they please, or to have business relations with whom they please....

The provisions of the act are explicit and present a well co-ordinated plan for the settlement of disputes between carriers and their employees, by bringing the disputes to arbitration and accommodation, and thereby prevent strikes and the public disorder and derangement of business that may be consequent upon them. I submit no worthier purpose can engage legislative attention or be the object of legislative action[.]...

We are told that labor associations are to be commended. May not, then Congress recognize their existence? yes, and recognize their power as conditions to be counted with in framing its legislation? Of what use would it be to attempt to bring bodies of men to agreement and compromise of controversies if you put out of view the influences which move them or the fellowship which binds them,—maybe controls and impels them, whether rightfully or wrongfully, to make the cause of one the cause of all? And this practical wisdom Congress observed,—observed, I may say, not in speculation or uncertain prevision of evils, but in experience of evils,—an experience which approached to the dimensions of a national calamity. The facts of history should not be overlooked nor the course of legislation....

But it is said it cannot be supposed that labor organizations will, "by illegal or violent measures, interrupt or impair the freedom of commerce," and to so suppose would be disrespect to a co-ordinate branch of the government, and to impute to it a purpose "to accord to one class of wage-earners privileges withheld from another class of wage-earners, engaged, it may be, in the same kind of labor and serving the same employer." Neither the supposition nor the disrespect is necessary, and, it may be urged, they are no more invidious than to impute to Congress a careless or deliberate or purposeless violation of the constitutional rights of the carriers. Besides, the legislation is to be accounted for. It, by its letter, makes a difference between members of labor

organizations and other employees of carriers. If it did not, it would not be here for review....

I have said that it is not necessary to suppose that labor organizations will violate the law, and it is not. Their power may be effectively exercised without violence or illegality, and it cannot be disrespect to Congress to let a committee of the Senate speak for it and tell the reason and purposes of its legislation. The committee on education, in its report, said of the bill: "The measure under consideration may properly be called a voluntary arbitration bill, having for its object the settlement of disputes between capital and labor, as far as the interstate transportation companies are concerned. The necessity for the bill arises from the calamitous results in the way of ill-considered strikes arising from the tyranny of capital or the unjust demands of labor organizations, whereby the business of the country is brought to a standstill and thousands of employees, with their helpless wives and children, are confronted with starvation." And, concluding the report, said: "It is our opinion that this bill, should it become a law, would reduce to a minimum labor strikes which affect interstate commerce, and we therefore recommend its passage."...

Counsel ... makes a great deal of the difference between direct and indirect effect upon interstate commerce, and assert that Sec. 10 is an indirect regulation at best, and not within the power of Congress to enact.... [I]t is enough to say that [this contention] gives too much isolation to Sec. 10. The section is part of the means to secure and make effective the scheme of arbitration set forth in the statute....

I think the judgment should be affirmed.

HOLMES, J., DISSENTING

... The ground on which this particular law is held bad is not so much that it deals with matters remote from commerce among the states, as that it interferes with the paramount individual rights secured by the 5th Amendment. The section is, in substance, a very limited interference with freedom of contract, no more. It does not require the carriers to employ anyone. It does not forbid them to refuse to employ anyone, for any reason they deem good, even where the notion of a choice of persons is a fiction and wholesale employment is necessary upon general principles that it might be proper to control. The section simply prohibits the more powerful party to exact certain undertakings, or to threaten dismissal or unjustly discriminate on certain grounds against those already employed. I hardly can suppose that the grounds on which a contract lawfully may be made to end are less open to regulation than other terms. So I turn to the general question whether the employment can be regulated at all. I confess that I think that the right to make contracts at will that has been derived from the word "liberty" in the Amendments has been stretched to its extreme by the decisions; but they agree that sometimes the right may be restrained. Where there is, or generally is believed to be, an important ground of public policy for restraint, the Constitution does not forbid it, whether this court agrees or disagrees with the policy pursued. It cannot be doubted that to prevent strikes, and, so far as possible, to foster its scheme of arbitration, might be deemed by Congress an important point of policy, and I think it impossible to say that Congress might not reasonably think that the provision in question would help a good deal to carry its policy along. But suppose the only effect really were to tend to bring about the complete unionizing of such railroad laborers as Congress can deal with, I think that object alone would justify the act. I quite agree that the question what and how much good labor unions do, is one on which intelligent people may differ; I think that laboring men sometimes attribute to them advantages, as many attribute to combinations of capital disadvantages, that really are due to economic conditions of a far wider and deeper kind; but I could not pronounce it unwarranted if Congress should decide that to foster a strong union was for the best interest, not only of the men, but of the railroads and the country at large.

QUESTIONS

1. Justice Harlan, author of the *Adair* opinion, dissented in *Lochner v. New York.* How can his support of legislation mandating maximum hours for bakers be reconciled with his opposition to legislation outlawing yellow-dog contracts?

2. Many critics of the Court's early twentieth-century due process jurisprudence have linked *Adair* with two other decisions in this period to form what is termed pejoratively the "*Allgeyer-Lochner-Adair*" line of cases. What doctrinal characteristics do the decisions share? On what grounds are they open to criticism?

3. Writing about labor conflicts and law around the turn of the century, legal historian Lawrence M. Friedman notes:

> Forced to choose sides, legal institutions necessarily reflected the wants of their basic constituencies. This meant that legislatures swung back and forth, depending on the strength of interests, blocs, parties and lobbies, or compromised. The courts were more independent of short-run swings of opinion. Partly for this reason, courts could afford to indulge in principles and ideologies. These were usually on the conservative side, because judges were solid, independent men of middle class. They were terrified of class struggle, mob rule, the anarchists and their bombs, railroad strikers, and the collapse of the social system as they knew it." (*A History of American Law*, 2nd ed. [New York, NY: Simon and Schuster, 1985], p. 555)

What "principles and ideologies" are reflected in Justice Harlan's opinion in *Adair*? What social interests were advantaged and disadvantaged by those principles and ideologies?

4. Some critics of the Court's decisions involving social reform legislation between 1890 and the middle 1930s argue that they often exemplified "judicial formalism." Judicial formalism is a mode of legal reasoning whereby a court judges the constitutionality of a statute in terms of abstract legal concepts and distinctions without regard for the social circumstances to which a statute was meant to apply. With its emphasis on "equality of right" between employers and employees, in isolation from the social reality of the asymmetrical bargaining power characteristic of labor relations between workers and management in the industrial era, the *Lochner/Adair* doctrine is a species of judicial formalism.

Compare Court's reading of "liberty of contract" in *Lochner* and *Adair* with the Court's distinction between "manufacturing" and "commerce" in *E.C. Knight*, Chapter 3, pp. 245–252. Is *Knight* another example of judicial formalism?

5. As previously noted, in *In re Debs*, 158 U.S. 564 (1895), the Court held that the national government could use injunctions to remove obstructions to interstate commerce and transportation of the mail. By contrast, in *Adair*, the Court stated that the national government did not have authority to outlaw yellow-dog contracts as part of its power to regulate commerce. What principles help to reconcile the apparent inconsistency between the *Debs* and *Adair* interpretations of governmental powers?

COMMENT

In the early decades of the twentieth century, the labor movement generated additional litigation. Some of this litigation involved liberty of contract, exercises of the police power, and the regulation of interstate commerce. Other cases focused on strike practices of unions under the 1890 Sherman Anti-Trust

Act. The following decisions are a sample of the Court's approach to labor issues in the first two decades of the twentieth century:

Case: *Loewe v. Lawlor*, 208 U.S. 275 (1908)

Vote: 9–0

Decision: A combination of labor organizations to compel a manufacturer to unionize his shops, or to boycott his goods if he refuses to, is a combination in restraint of trade under the Sherman Anti-Trust Act. Organizations of farmers and laborers are not exempt from the operation of the Act. Any combination that essentially obstructs the free flow of commerce between the states, or restricts the liberty of a trader to engage in business, violates the Act.

Case: *Coppage v. Kansas*, 236 U.S. 1 (1915)

Vote: 7–2

Decision: A Kansas statute outlawing the yellow-dog contract and prohibiting discharge of union employees is not "a legitimate object for the exercise of the police power," and violates the Due Process Clause of the Fourteenth Amendment. *Note: Coppage* and *Adair* were overruled in *Phelps Dodge v. NLRB*, 313 U.S. 177 (1941).

Case: *Hitchman Coal & Coke Company v. Mitchell*, 245 U.S. 229 (1917)

Vote: 6–3

Decision: Entering into an employment contract is a liberty interest that is entitled to protection by the court from union interference. Employers are entitled to injunctions to enforce labor contracts.

Case: *Duplex Printing Press Company v. Deering*, 254 U.S. 433 (1921)

Vote: 6–3

Decision: The Sherman Anti-Trust Act, as amended by the Clayton Act of 1914, prohibits combinations and conspiracies by employees against employers to restrain interstate commerce. Threats of a secondary boycott to force unionization, an eight-hour day, and union wage scales violate the act and may be enjoined.

Case: *Coronado Coal Company v. United Mine Workers*, 268 U.S. 295 (1925)

Vote: 9–0

Decision: Tortious destruction of mines by union laborers to stop the production of non-union coal and prevent its shipment through interstate commerce violates the Sherman Anti-Trust Act. The mere reduction in the supply of an article to be shipped in interstate commerce by illegal or tortious prevention of its manufacture or production ordinarily is an indirect and remote obstruction to that commerce. When the intent is to restrain or control the supply entering and moving in interstate commerce, however, or the price in interstate markets, there is a direct violation of the act.

Case: *Bedford Cut Stone Company v. Journeymen Stone Cutters*, 274 U.S. 37 (1927)

Vote: 7–2

Decision: Union rules requiring members in other states not to build with limestone produced by labor eligible for membership in unions, thereby coercing local employers from purchasing such limestone, violate the Sherman Anti-Trust Act. Upon showing of an intent to restrain interstate commerce, the act authorizes granting of injunctive relief.

JUDICIAL PROTECTION OF PROPERTY INTERESTS

Adkins v. Children's Hospital
261 U.S. 525 (1923)

SETTING

Legislation that establishes the hours or working conditions of industrial employees imposes governmental restraints on market freedom. Such freedom, declared Chief Justice William Howard Taft in *Wolff Packing Co. v. Court of Industrial Relations*, 262 U.S. 522 (1923), "is the general rule, and restraint the exception." As *Lochner v. New York* illustrates, the Supreme Court held that labor legislation both deprived persons of substantive rights and was an illegitimate exercise of state police powers because it favored employees over employers in contractual bargaining. Legislation that set minimum wages for industrial employees was even more suspect than maximum hours or health and safety statutes: Minimum wage laws cut to the heart of the wage/labor bargain.

By 1922, thirteen states and the District of Columbia had enacted minimum wage laws in response to lobbying efforts on behalf of workers. The District of Columbia Minimum Wage Law was enacted in September 1918, following hearings in both houses of Congress. It focused on protecting women and minors from detrimental health conditions resulting from inadequate wages. Wages were particularly low among hotel, hospital, and restaurant employees. According to the investigation, women's wages were not enough to pay for room and board, to say nothing of life's other essentials.

The District Minimum Wage Law created a three-member Minimum Wage Board to determine minimum wages for women in any occupation within the District and to enforce those wages. The Board subsequently ordered that no woman or minor girl could be employed in any hospital, hotel, lodging house, apartment house, club, restaurant, cafeteria, or other place where food was sold at a wage rate less than 34½¢ per hour, $16.50 per week, or $71.50 per month. The law allowed a deduction of 30¢ for each meal provided by the employer.

Jesse C. Adkins, representing the Minimum Wage Board, sought to enforce the Board's orders against Children's Hospital and the Congress Hall Hotel Company. Willie Lyons, a 21-year-old elevator operator for the hotel, was informed by her employer that she would be laid off if the company was compelled to pay her the new minimum wage. Lyons then declared that she was willing to work at her existing wage of $35 per month plus two meals per day, and joined Children's Hospital in a suit filed in the Supreme Court of the District of Columbia to enjoin enforcement of the Minimum Wage Law. Lyons and Children's Hospital argued that the law deprived them of liberty and property without due process of law, in violation of the Fifth Amendment. The trial court agreed and vacated the order of the Minimum Wage Board. The Court of Appeals for the District of Columbia initially reversed the Supreme Court of the District of Columbia but, on rehearing, it affirmed, declaring the District of Columbia Minimum Wage Law unconstitutional. Adkins, on behalf of the Board, appealed to the Supreme Court of the United States.

HIGHLIGHTS OF SUPREME COURT ARGUMENTS

BRIEF FOR ADKINS

◆ The proper analysis of this case is controlled by Chief Justice's Marshall's canon of constitutional construction in *McCulloch v. Maryland*: "Let the end be legitimate, let it be within the scope of the Constitution, and all means which are appropriate, which are plainly adapted to that end, which are not prohibited, but consist with the letter and spirit of the Constitution, are constitutional." A law passed by Congress is to be presumed constitutional unless shown to be otherwise beyond a rational doubt.

◆ The Minimum Wage Law is aimed at a legitimate end. Congress is charged with the responsibility of safeguarding the welfare of the District of Columbia.

◆ The means chosen by Congress—a minimum wage law—are clearly appropriate and plainly adapted to accomplish the legitimate end of preventing women and minors from living in poverty.

◆ The burden is on Children's Hospital and the Congress Hall Hotel to show that the Constitution denies Congress the power to enact and enforce the Minimum Wage Law for the District.

AMICUS CURIAE BRIEFS SUPPORTING ADKINS

State of Wisconsin; Industrial Welfare Commission of California; Industrial Welfare Commission of Oregon; state of Kansas; state of New York.

BRIEF FOR CHILDREN'S HOSPITAL AND LYONS

◆ The Minimum Wage Law is pure price fixing. It does not regulate business or working conditions. It was not enacted as an emergency measure to prevent the stoppage or interruption of pubic business. It is a permanent policy of wage fixing.

◆ From the standpoint of the woman who desires employment, the Minimum Wage Law may prevent her from working in admittedly healthy and moral surroundings.

◆ The Minimum Wage Law violates the protection of liberty and property guaranteed in the Fifth and Fourteenth Amendments, which includes freedom of contract for personal services. This Court consistently has so held. A law fixing wages in private employment is beyond the exercise of legislative power.

◆ The central issue in this case is whether a law fixing the price of labor is within the police power at all. The question is not whether it is a proper exercise of that power.

SUPREME COURT DECISION: 5–3

(Brandeis, J., did not participate.)

SUTHERLAND, J.

... The statute now under consideration is attacked upon the ground that it authorizes an unconstitutional interference with the freedom of contract included within the guaranties of the due process clause of the Fifth Amendment. That the right to contract about one's affairs is a part of the liberty of the individual protected by this clause is settled by the decisions of this court and is no longer open to question.... Within this liberty are contracts of employment of labor. In making such contracts, generally speaking, the parties have an equal right to obtain from each other the best terms they can as the result of private bargaining....

There is, of course, no such thing as absolute freedom of contract. It is subject to a great variety of restraints. But freedom of contract is, nevertheless, the general rule and restraint the exception, and the exercise of legislative authority to abridge it can be justified only by the existence of exceptional circumstances. Whether these circumstances exist in the present case constitutes the question to be answered....

In ... [*Muller v. Oregon*, 208 U.S. 412 (1908)], the validity of an Oregon statute, forbidding the employment of any female in certain industries more than ten hours during any one day was upheld. The decision proceeded upon the theory that the difference between the sexes may justify a different rule respecting hours of labor in the case of women than in the case of men.... But the ancient inequality of the sexes, otherwise than physical, as suggested in the *Muller* Case has continued "with diminishing intensity." In view of the great—not to say revolutionary—changes which have taken place since that utterance, in the contractual, political, and civil status of women, culminating in the Nineteenth Amendment, it is not unreasonable to say that these differences have now come almost, if not quite, to the vanishing point. In this aspect of the matter, while the physical differences must be recognized in appropriate cases, and legislation fixing hours or conditions of work may properly take them into account, we cannot accept the doctrine that women of mature age, *sui juris*, require or may be subjected to restrictions upon their liberty of contract which could not lawfully be imposed in the case of men under similar circumstances. To do so would be to ignore all the implications to be drawn from the present day trend of legislation, as well as that of common thought and usage, by which woman is accorded emancipation from the old doctrine that she must be given special protection or be subjected to special restraint in her contractual and civil relationships....

The essential characteristics of the statute now under consideration, which differentiate it from the laws fixing hours of labor, will be made to appear as we proceed. It is sufficient now to point out that the latter ... deal with incidents of the employment having no necessary effect upon the heart of the contract; that is, the amount of wages to be paid and received. A law forbidding work to continue beyond a given number of hours leaves the parties free to contract about wages and thereby equalize whatever additional burdens may be imposed upon the employer as a result of the restrictions as to hours, by an adjustment in respect of the amount of wages. Enough has been said to show that the authority to fix hours of labor cannot be exercised except in respect of those occupations where work of long continued duration is detrimental to health. This court has been careful in every case where the question has been raised, to place its decision upon this limited authority of the Legislature to regulate hours of labor and to disclaim any purpose to uphold the legislation as fixing wages, thus recognizing an essential difference between the two. It seems plain that these decisions afford no real support for any form of law establishing minimum wages.

If now, in the light furnished by the foregoing exceptions to the general rule forbidding legislative interference with freedom of contract, we examine and analyze the statute in question, we shall see that it differs from them in every material respect. It is not a law dealing with any business charged with a public interest or with public work, or to meet and tide over a temporary emergency. It has nothing to do with the character, methods, or periods of wage payments. It does not prescribe hours of labor or conditions under which labor is to be done. It is not for the protection of persons under legal disability or for the prevention of fraud. It is simply and exclusively a price-fixing law, confined to adult women ... who are legally as capable of contracting for themselves as men. It forbids two parties having lawful capacity—under penalties as to the employer—to freely contract with one another in respect of the price for which one shall render service to the other in a purely private employment where both are willing, perhaps anxious, to agree, even though the consequence may be to oblige one to surrender a desirable engagement and the other to dispense with the services of a desirable employee. The price fixed by the board need have no relation to the capacity or earning power of the employee, the number of hours which may happen to constitute the day's work, the character of the place where the work is to be done, or the circumstances or surroundings of the employment, and, while it has no other basis to support its validity than the assumed necessities of the employee, it takes no account of any independent resources she may have. It is based wholly on the opinions of the members of the board and their advisers—perhaps an average of their opinions, if they do not precisely agree—as to what will be necessary to provide a living for a woman, keep her in health and preserve her morals. It applies to any and every occupation in the District, without regard to its nature or the character of the work.

The standard furnished by the statute for the guidance of the board is so vague as to be impossible of practical application with any reasonable degree of accuracy. What is sufficient to supply the necessary cost of living for a woman worker and maintain her in good health and protect her morals is obviously not a precise or unvarying sum—not even approximately so. The amount will depend upon a variety of circumstances: The individual temperament, habits of thrift, care, ability to buy necessaries intelligently, and whether the woman live alone or with her family....

The law takes account of the necessities of only one party to the contract. It ignores the necessities of the employer by compelling him to pay not less than a certain sum, not only whether the employee is capable of earning it, but irrespective of the ability of his business to sustain the burden, generously leaving him, of course, the privilege of abandoning his business as an alternative for going on at a loss.... It compels him to pay at least the sum fixed in any event, because the employee needs it, but requires no service of equivalent value from the employee. It therefore undertakes to solve but one-half of the problem. The other half is the establishment of a corresponding standard of efficiency, and this forms no part of the policy of the legislation.... The law ... embraces those whose bargaining power may be as weak as that of the employee.... To the extent that the sum fixed exceeds the fair value of the services rendered,

it amounts to a compulsory exaction from the employer for the support of a partially indigent person, for whose condition there rests upon him no peculiar responsibility, and therefore, in effect, arbitrarily shifts to his shoulders a burden which, if it belongs to anybody, belongs to society as a whole.

The feature of this statute, which perhaps more than any other, puts upon it the stamp of invalidity, is that it exacts from the employer an arbitrary payment for a purpose and upon a basis having no causal connection with his business, or the contract or the work the employee engages to do.... The ethical right of every worker, man or woman, to a living wage may be conceded. One of the declared and important purposes of trade organizations is to secure it. And with that principle and with every legitimate effort to realize it in fact, no one can quarrel; but the fallacy of the proposed method of attaining it is that it assumes that every employer is bound at all events to furnish it....

Finally, it may be said that if, in the interest of the public welfare, the police power may be invoked to justify the fixing of a minimum wage, it may, when the public welfare is thought to require it, be invoked to justify a maximum wage. The power to fix high wages connotes, by like course of reasoning, the power to fix low wages. If, in the face of the guaranties of the Fifth Amendment, this form of legislation shall be legally justified, the field for the operation of the police power will have been widened to a great and dangerous degree....

It follows, from what has been said, that the act in question passes the limit prescribed by the Constitution, and accordingly the decrees of the court below are

Affirmed.

TAFT, C.J., AND SANFORD, J., DISSENTING

... The boundary of the police power beyond which its exercise becomes an invasion of the guaranty of liberty under the Fifth and Fourteenth Amendments to the Constitution is not easy to mark. Our court has been laboriously engaged in pricking out a line in successive cases. We must be careful, it seems to me, to follow that line as well as we can, and not to depart from it by suggesting a distinction that is formal rather than real....

Legislatures which adopt a requirement of maximum hours or minimum wages may be presumed to believe that when sweating employers are prevented from paying unduly low wages by positive law they will continue their business, abating that part of their profits, which were wrung from the necessities of their employees, and will concede the better terms required by the law, and that while in individual cases, hardship may result, the restriction will inure to the benefit of the general class of employees in whose interest the law is passed, and so to that of the community at large....

Without ... expressing an opinion that a minimum wage limitation can be enacted for adult men, it is enough to say that the case before us involves only the application of the minimum wage to women. If I am right in thinking that the Legislature can find as much support in experience for the view that a sweating wage has as great and as direct a tendency to bring about an injury to the health and morals of workers, as for the

view that long hours injure their health, then I respectfully submit that *Muller v. Oregon*[, 208 U.S. 412 (1908)] controls this case....

I am not sure from a reading of the opinion whether the court thinks the authority of *Muller v. Oregon* is shaken by the adoption of the Nineteenth Amendment. The Nineteenth Amendment did not change the physical strength or limitations of women upon which the decision in *Muller v. Oregon* rests. The amendment did give women political power and makes more certain that legislative provisions for their protection will be in accord with their interests as they see them. But I do not think we are warranted in varying constitutional construction based on physical differences between men and women, because of the amendment.

But for my inability to agree with some general observations in the forcible opinion of Mr. Justice Holmes ... I should be silent and merely record my concurrence in what he says. It is perhaps wiser for me, however, in a case of this importance separately to give my reasons for dissenting.

HOLMES, J., DISSENTING

The question in this case is the broad one, Whether Congress can establish minimum rates of wages for women in the District of Columbia with due provision for special circumstances, or whether we must say that Congress had no power to meddle with the matter at all. To me, notwithstanding the deference due to the prevailing judgment of the court, the power of Congress seems absolutely free from doubt. The end—to remove conditions leading to ill health, immorality and the deterioration of the race—no one would deny to be within the scope of constitutional legislation. The means are means that have the approval of Congress, of many states, and of those governments from which we have learned our greatest lessons. When so many intelligent persons, who have studied the matter more than any of us can, have thought that the means are effective and are worth the price, it seems to me impossible to deny that the belief reasonably may be held by reasonable men. If the law encountered no other objection than that the means bore no relation to the end or that they cost too much I do not suppose that anyone would venture to say that it was bad. I agree, of course, that a law answering the foregoing requirements might be invalidated by specific provisions of the Constitution. For instance, it might take private property without just compensation. But, in the present instance, the only objection that can be urged is found within the vague contours of the Fifth Amendment, prohibiting the depriving any person of liberty or property without due process of law. To that I turn.

The earlier decisions upon the same words in the Fourteenth Amendment began within our memory and went no farther than an unpretentious assertion of the liberty to follow the ordinary callings. Later that innocuous generality was expanded into the dogma, Liberty of Contract. Contract is not specially mentioned in the text that we have to construe. It is merely an example of doing what you want to do, embodied in the word liberty. But pretty much all law consists in forbidding men to do some things that they want to do, and contract is no more exempt from law than other acts....

I confess that I do not understand the principle on which the power to fix a minimum for the wages of women can be denied by those who admit the power to fix a maximum for their hours of work. I fully assent to the proposition that here as elsewhere the distinctions of the law are distinctions of degree, but I perceive no difference in the kind or degree of interference with liberty, the only matter with which we have any concern, between the one case and the other. The bargain is equally affected whichever half you regulate. *Muller v. Oregon*, I take it, is as good law today as it was in 1908. It will need more than the Nineteenth Amendment to convince me that there are no differences between men and women, or that legislation cannot take those differences into account. I should not hesitate to take them into account if I thought it necessary to sustain this act.... But after *Bunting v. Oregon* [, 243 U.S. 426 (1917)], I had supposed that it was not necessary, and that *Lochner v. New York* would be allowed a deserved repose.

This statute does not compel anybody to pay anything. It simply forbids employment at rates below those fixed as the minimum requirement of health and right living. It is safe to assume that women will not be employed at even the lowest wages allowed unless they earn them, or unless the employer's business can sustain the burden. In short the law in its character and operation is like hundreds of so-called police laws that have been upheld. I see no greater objection to using a board to apply the standard fixed by the act than there is to the other commissions with which we have become familiar or than there is to the requirement of a license in other cases. The fact that the statute warrants classification, which like all classifications may bear hard upon some individuals, or in exceptional cases, notwithstanding the power given to the Board to issue a special license, is no greater infirmity than is incident to all law. But the ground on which the law is held to fail is fundamental and therefore it is unnecessary to consider matters of detail.

The criterion of constitutionality is not whether we believe the law to be for the public good.... If a legislature should adopt what he thinks the doctrine of modern economists of all schools, that "freedom of contract is a misnomer as applied to a contract between an employer and an ordinary individual employee," I could not pronounce an opinion with which I agree impossible to be entertained by reasonable men. If the same legislature should accept his further opinion that industrial peace was best attained by the device of a Court having the above powers, I should not feel myself able to contradict it, or to deny that the end justified restrictive legislation quite as adequately as beliefs concerning Sunday or exploded theories about usury. I should have my doubts, as I have them about this statute—but they would be whether the bill that has to be paid for every gain, although hidden as interstitial detriments, was not greater than the gain was worth: a matter that it is not for me to decide....

QUESTIONS

1. The *amicus* brief submitted by the state of Wisconsin noted that all state supreme courts that had considered minimum wage legislation had upheld the laws. The California brief contended that in the ten years that its minimum wage act had been in effect it had been viewed consistently as essential for the protection of women and children in industry. The Oregon brief pointed out that that state's 1913 minimum wage law had been passed without a single dissenting vote in the legislature, had been upheld by a unanimous Oregon supreme court, and that the law had become an established part of the industrial life of Oregon. What accounts for the difference of opinion between state courts and the Supreme Court of the United States on the subject of the constitutionality of stautory minimum wages for women and children?

2. As noted earlier, in *Wolff Packing* Chief Justice Taft observed that economic freedom "is the general rule, and restraint the exception." Justice Sutherland for the majority reiterated that point in *Adkins*: "... freedom of contract is ... the general rule and restraint the exception...." Chief Justice Taft claimed in dissent that the Minimum Wage Board's "restraint" was an acceptable "exception" to that rule. Is Taft correct that the result in *Adkins* was controlled by *Muller v. Oregon*, 208 U.S. 412 (1908)? According to the majority in *Adkins*, what is the difference between regulating maximum hours and minimum wages?

3. *Adkins*, along with *Lochner*, has been called "one of the landmarks in the Supreme Court's losing battle against economic regulation" (C.

Hermann Pritchett, *The American Constitution* [New York, NY: McGraw-Hill Book Company, 1959], p. 576). Why were those two cases losing battles? What forces were at work that were more powerful than the Supreme Court's exercise of its power of judicial review?

4. The brief submitted to the Court by Felix Frankfurter, counsel for Adkins, adopted a format pioneered by Louis D. Brandeis several years before. In 1905, the same year *Lochner* was decided, Brandeis told the Harvard Ethical Society: "Out of the facts grows the law: that is, propositions are not considered abstractly, but always with reference to the facts." Brandeis argued that legislators and judges should base their judgments on social scientific knowledge of conditions gleaned from evidence, statistics, and expert testimony. The so-called "Brandeis Brief" evolved out of Brandeis's speech at Harvard.

The "Brandeis Brief" was first employed to support the Oregon maximum hours statute contested in *Muller v. Oregon*, 208 U.S. 412 (1908), discussed on pp. 806–808. Josephine Goldmark, Brandeis's sister-in-law, supervised compilation of data from the Columbia University and New York Public libraries for the *Muller* brief. Law professor Howard Hovenkamp, describes the brief submitted in *Muller* as

> an odd assortment of information: domestic and foreign statutes, tracts, writings of clergymen, and reports of regulatory agencies. Much of the information it contained was not "social science" at all, at least not as we understand that term today.... Rather, the brief contained a record of 'the world's experience upon which the legislation limiting the hours of women is based.' The "world's experience" turned out to be that women had less endurance than men, that their reproductive systems were more easily damaged, and that they had less capacity than men to enter into sound business agreements that adequately protected their own interests. ("The Political Economy of Substantive Due Process," 40 *Stanford Law Review* [1988]: 443)

Although the Brandeis/Goldmark litigation strategy of arguing social scientific "data" as much as precedents and rules succeeded in *Muller*, Justice Peckham had ignored completely Justice Harlan's previous effort to do much the same in his *Lochner* dissent, and the majority dismissed Felix Frankfurter's subsequent efforts as counsel to Adkins, saying that it found such facts "interesting but only mildly persuasive." In fact, Chief Justice Edward D. White responded to a Brandeis brief submitted to the Court in *Adams v. Tanner*, 244 U.S. 590 (1917), by saying: "I could compile a brief twice as thick to prove that the legal profession ought to be abolished" (quoted in Leo Pfeffer, *This Honorable Court* [Boston, MA: Beacon, 1965], p. 259).

For what reasons did the Brandeis/Goldmark litigation strategy succeed in *Muller* but not in *Lochner*, *Adams*, and *Adkins*?

JUDICIAL PROTECTION OF PROPERTY INTERESTS

Nebbia v. New York
291 U.S. 502 (1934)

SETTING

The Great Depression of the late 1920s and 1930s set the stage for a dramatic clash between supporters of the New Deal and "The Nine Old Men" of the Supreme Court, as critics had caricatured that institution. As seen in Chapter 3, the Court repeatedly interpreted the Constitution to limit government's regulatory powers and to require that police powers be exercised in ways that did not benefit "special interests." Thus, economic substantive due process dictated that the government that governed "best" governed with the *least* interference with fundamental rights, such as liberty and property. *Lochner* era police powers jurisprudence also required that the government that governed "best" must govern in wholly *neutral* terms, not on behalf of discrete classes like labor. These twin doctrines, combined with notions of dual federalism that defined the powers of the national and state governments in rigidly categorical terms, helped to insulate the justices in a cocoon of legal formalism. The harsh realities of the Great Depression intruded into that world like thunder on a clear day.

The Great Depression hit the dairy industry with the same violent force as the rest of the nation's agricultural sector. The effects were particularly great in New York, where the dairy industry affected more people than any other business in the state. Between March 1929 and March 1933, the producers' price for fluid milk was reduced by 61 percent. During 1932, the price paid to New York state farmers for milk was less than the cost of production. In the spring of 1933, the price paid to New York farmers for milk was the lowest since 1896. Milk distribution tended toward monopoly; in New York during that period, only three companies handled approximately two-thirds of the state's total milk supply. Indebted dairy farmers and those who had fixed costs were destroyed economically. Foreclosures and tax sales were commonplace in every dairy community in the state. Despite declining prices, milk supply did not diminish. In March 1933, the dire economic conditions resulted in a milk producers' strike, as had occurred in previous eras of economic depression in New York—1883, 1916, and 1919. In the 1933 strike, a state trooper and a striker were killed and much property was destroyed. In August 1933 a more violent and widespread strike broke out.

For eight weeks in 1933 the New York legislature debated how to respond to the crisis in the milk industry. It concluded that, as an emergency measure, it was necessary to control milk prices in the state and that a milk control board should be established "to regulate and stabilize the milk indus-try as well as may be done under the circumstances." It then adopted the Agriculture and Markets Law, popularly known as the Milk Control Law, which created the Milk Control Board.

On April 14, 1933, the Board issued an order setting minimum prices for sales of milk and cream in all cities and villages of more than one thousand population, except for New York City and three neighboring counties. The order required milk dealers to charge the consumer at least nine cents per quart of milk. The order defined "dealer" as any person who purchased or handled milk in the state, or who sold milk in the state, except for on-site con-sumption. The effect of the order was that store keepers and milk delivery operations were required to charge the same minimum price for milk.

Leo Nebbia was a "cash-and-carry" storekeeper in Rochester, New York. On April 19, 1933, he sold two quarts of milk to Jedo Del Signore for eighteen cents. As an inducement to Del Signore to purchase milk from his store instead of having it delivered to his home for the same price, Nebbia gave Del Signore a loaf of bread worth five cents. Nebbia was subsequently charged by informa-tion in Rochester City Court with violation of the Milk Control Law. He pleaded not guilty. At the opening of his trial in County Court, his counsel argued that the indictment should be dismissed because the Milk Control Law was uncon-stitutional under the Fourteenth Amendment to the Constitution of the United States. Nebbia was tried, convicted, and fined five dollars. He paid the fine under protest and appealed to the Monroe County Court, which affirmed. The New York Court of Appeals, that state's highest appellate court, also affirmed. Nebbia then appealed to the Supreme Court of the United States.

HIGHLIGHTS OF SUPREME COURT ARGUMENTS

BRIEF FOR NEBBIA

◆ This case is controlled by a long line of Supreme Court cases including *Adkins v. Children's Hospital*. Like other statutes held to be unconstitutional, the New York Milk Control Law violates due process rights under the Fourteenth Amendment.

◆ The Milk Control Law unfairly discriminates against Nebbia as a cash and carry dealer, thereby violating his rights to equal protection of the laws.

◆ The economic depression affecting New York dairy farmers does not suspend the Fourteenth Amendment.

BRIEF FOR NEW YORK

◆ The Milk Control Law is a valid exercise of the state's police power. The determination of the necessity for a particular exercise of the police power is a matter to be determined by the state legislature.

◆ Fixing minimum prices to consumers is an important and desirable feature of the Milk Control Law. It is directly related to the protection of the public interest.

> ◆ Fixing minimum prices is a recognized and common form of utility regulation.

AMICUS CURIAE BRIEFS SUPPORTING NEW YORK

Attorney General of Connecticut; Attorney General of Ohio.

SUPREME COURT DECISION: 5–4

ROBERTS, J.

... *First*. The appellant urges that the order of the Milk Control Board denies him the equal protection of the laws.... We think the contention that the discrimination deprives the appellant of equal protection is not well founded....

Second. The more serious question is whether, in the light of the conditions disclosed, the enforcement of section 312(e) denied the appellant the due process secured to him by the Fourteenth Amendment....

Under our form of government the use of property and the making of contracts are normally matters of private and not of public concern. The general rule is that both shall be free of governmental interference. But neither property rights nor contract rights are absolute; for government cannot exist if the citizen may at will use his property to the detriment of his fellows, or exercise his freedom of contract to work them harm. Equally fundamental with the private right is that of the public to regulate it in the common interest....

[T]his court from the early days affirmed that the power to promote the general welfare is inherent in government. Touching the matters committed to it by the Constitution the United States possesses the power, as do the states in their sovereign capacity touching all subjects jurisdiction of which is not surrendered to the federal government, as shown by the quotations above given. These correlative rights, that of the citizen to exercise exclusive dominion over property and freely to contract about his affairs, and that of the state to regulate the use of property and the conduct of business, are always in collision. No exercise of the private right can be imagined which will not in some respect, however slight, affect the public; no exercise of the legislative prerogative to regulate the conduct of the citizen which will not to some extent abridge his liberty or affect his property. But subject only to constitutional restraint the private right must yield to the public need.

The Fifth Amendment, in the field of federal activity, and the Fourteenth, as respects State action, do not prohibit governmental regulation for the public welfare. They merely condition the exertion of the admitted power, by securing that the end shall be accomplished by methods consistent with due process. And the guaranty of due process, as has often been held, demands only that the law shall not be unreasonable, arbitrary, or capricious, and that the means selected shall have a real and substantial relation to the object sought to be attained. It results that a regulation valid for one sort of business, or in given circumstances, may be invalid for another sort, or for the same business under other circumstances, because the reasonableness of each regulation depends upon the relevant facts....

The Constitution does not guarantee the unrestricted privilege to engage in a business or to conduct it as one pleases....

The milk industry in New York has been the subject of long-standing and drastic regulation in the public interest. The legislative investigation of 1932 was persuasive of the fact that for this and other reasons unrestricted competition aggravated existing evils and the normal law of supply and demand was insufficient to correct maladjustments detrimental to the community. The inquiry disclosed destructive and demoralizing competitive conditions and unfair trade practices which resulted in retail price cutting and reduced the income of the farmer below the cost of production. We do not understand the appellant to deny that in these circumstances the legislature might reasonably consider further regulation and control desirable for protection of the industry and the consuming public. That body believed conditions could be improved by preventing destructive price-cutting by stores which, due to the flood of surplus milk, were able to buy at much lower prices than the larger distributors and to sell without incurring the delivery costs of the latter. In the order of which complaint is made the Milk Control Board fixed a price of ten cents per quart for sales by a distributor to a consumer, and nine cents by a store to a consumer,

thus recognizing the lower costs of the store, and endeavoring to establish a differential which would be just to both. In the light of the facts the order appears not to be unreasonable or arbitrary, or without relation to the purpose to prevent ruthless competition from destroying the wholesale price structure on which the farmer depends for his livelihood, and the community for an assured supply of milk.

But we are told that because the law essays to control prices it denies due process. Notwithstanding the admitted power to correct existing economic ills by appropriate regulation of business, even though an indirect result may be a restriction of the freedom of contract or a modification of charges for services or the price of commodities, the appellant urges that direct fixation of prices is a type of regulation absolutely forbidden. His position is that the Fourteenth Amendment requires us to hold the challenged statute void for this reason alone. The argument runs that the public control of rates or prices is *per se* unreasonable and unconstitutional, save as applied to businesses affected with a public interest; that a business so affected is one in which property is devoted to an enterprise of a sort which the public itself might appropriately undertake, or one whose owner relies on a public grant or franchise for the right to conduct the business, or in which he is bound to serve all who apply; in short, such as is commonly called a public utility; or a business in its nature a monopoly. The milk industry, it is said, possesses none of these characteristics, and, therefore, not being affected with a public interest, its charges may not be controlled by the state. Upon the soundness of this contention the appellant's case against the statute depends.

We may as well say at once that the dairy industry is not, in the accepted sense of the phrase, a public utility. We think the appellant is also right in asserting that there is in this case no suggestion of any monopoly or monopolistic practice. It goes without saying that those engaged in the business are in no way dependent upon public grants or franchises for the privilege of conducting their activities. But if, as must be conceded, the industry is subject to regulation in the public interest, what constitutional principle bars the state from correcting existing maladjustments by legislation touching prices? We think there is no such principle. The due process clause makes no mention of sales or of prices any more than it speaks of business or contracts or buildings or other incidents of property. The thought seems nevertheless to have persisted that there is something peculiarly sacrosanct about the price one may charge for what he makes or sells, and that, however able to regulate other elements of manufacture or trade, with incidental effect upon price, the state is incapable of directly controlling the price itself. This view was negatived many years ago. *Munn v. Illinois*. The appellant's claim is, however, that this court, in there [sic] sustaining a statutory prescription of charges for storage by the proprietors of a grain elevator, limited permissible legislation of that type to businesses affected with a public interest, and he says no business is so affected except it have one or more of the characteristics he enumerates. But this is a misconception. Munn and Scott held no franchise from the state. They owned the property upon which their elevator was situated and conducted their business as private citizens. No doubt they felt at liberty to deal with whom they pleased and on such terms as they might deem just to themselves. Their enterprise could not fairly be called a monopoly, although it was referred to in the decision as a "virtual monopoly." This meant only that their elevator was strategically situated and that a large portion of the public found it highly inconvenient to deal with others. This court concluded the circumstances justified the legislation as an exercise of the governmental right to control the business in the public interest; that is, as an exercise of the police power. It is true that the court cited a statement from Lord Hale's *De Portibus Maris*, to the effect that when private property is "affected with a public interest, it ceases to be *juris privati* only"; but the court proceeded at once to define what it understood by the expression, saying: "Property does become clothed with a public interest when used in a manner to make it of public consequence, and affect the community at large." Thus understood, "affected with a public interest" is the equivalent of "subject to the exercise of the police power"; and it is plain that nothing more was intended by the expression. The court had been at pains to define that power ending its discussion in these words: "From this it is apparent that, down to the time of the adoption of the Fourteenth Amendment, it was not supposed that statutes regulating the use, or even the price of the use, of private property necessarily deprived an owner of his property without due process of law. Under some circumstances they may, but not under all. The amendment does not change the law in this particular; it simply prevents the States from doing that which will operate as such a deprivation."

In the further discussion of the principle it is said that when one devotes his property to a use, "in which the public has an interest," he in effect "grants to the public an interest in that use" and must submit to be controlled for the common good. The conclusion is that if Munn and Scott wished to avoid having their business regulated they should not have embarked their property in an industry which is subject to regulation in the public interest.

The true interpretation of the court's language is claimed to be that only property voluntarily devoted to a known public use is subject to regulation as to rates. But obviously Munn and Scott had not voluntarily dedicated their business to a public use. They intended only to conduct it as private citizens, and they insisted that they had done nothing which gave the public an interest in their transactions or conferred any right of regulation. The statement that one has dedicated his property to a public use is, therefore, merely another way of saying that if one embarks in a business which public interest demands shall be regulated, he must know regulation will ensue....

The touchstone of public interest in any business, its practices and charges, clearly is not the enjoyment of any franchise from the state, *Munn v. Illinois*. Nor is it the enjoyment of a monopoly[.]...

Many other decisions show that the private character of a business does not necessarily remove it from the realm of regulation of charges or prices....

It is clear that there is no closed class or category of businesses affected with a public interest, and the function of

courts in the application of the Fifth and Fourteenth Amendments is to determine in each case whether circumstances vindicate the challenged regulation as a reasonable exertion of governmental authority or condemn it as arbitrary or discriminatory.... The phrase "affected with a public interest" can, in the nature of things, mean no more than that an industry, for adequate reason, is subject to control for the public good.... [T]here can be no doubt that upon proper occasion and by appropriate measures the state may regulate a business in any of its aspects, including the prices to be charged for the products or commodities it sells.

So far as the requirement of due process is concerned, and in the absence of other constitutional restriction, a state is free to adopt whatever economic policy may reasonably be deemed to promote public welfare, and to enforce that policy by legislation adapted to its purpose. The courts are without authority either to declare such policy, or, when it is declared by the legislature, to override it. If the laws passed are seen to have a reasonable relation to a proper legislative purpose, and are neither arbitrary nor discriminatory, the requirements of due process are satisfied, and judicial determination to that effect renders a court *functus officio* [a task performed].... And it is equally clear that if the legislative policy be to curb unrestrained and harmful competition by measures which are not arbitrary or discriminatory it does not lie with the courts to determine that the rule is unwise. With the wisdom of the policy adopted, with the adequacy or practicability of the law enacted to forward it, the courts are both incompetent and unauthorized to deal....

Tested by these considerations we find no basis in the due process clause of the Fourteenth Amendment for condemning the provisions of the Agriculture and Markets Law here drawn into question.

The judgment is affirmed.

MCREYNOLDS, VAN DEVANTER, SUTHERLAND, AND BUTLER, J.J., DISSENTING

… The Fourteenth Amendment wholly disempowered the several states to "deprive any person of life, liberty, or property, without due process of law." The assurance of each of these things is the same. If now liberty or property may be struck down because of difficult circumstances, we must expect that hereafter every right must yield to the voice of an impatient majority when stirred by distressful exigency. Amid the turmoil of civil war Milligan was sentenced: happily, this Court intervened. Constitutional guaranties are not to be "thrust to and fro and carried about with every wind of doctrine." They were intended to be immutable so long as within our charter. Rights shielded yesterday should remain indefeasible today and tomorrow. Certain fundamentals have been set beyond experimentation; the Constitution has released them from control by the state. Again and again this Court has so declared….

If validity of the enactment depends upon emergency, then to sustain this conviction we must be able to affirm that an adequate one has been shown by competent evidence of essential facts. The asserted right is federal. Such rights may demand and often have received affirmation and protection here. They do not vanish simply because the power of the state is arrayed against them. Nor are they enjoyed in subjection to mere legislative findings.

If she relied upon the existence of emergency, the burden was upon the State to establish it by competent evidence. None was presented at the trial. If necessary for appellant to show absence of the asserted conditions, the little grocer was helpless from the beginning—the practical difficulties were too great for the average man.

What circumstances give force to an "emergency" statute? In how much of the State must they obtain? Everywhere, or will a single county suffice? How many farmers must have been impoverished or threatened violence to create a crisis of sufficient gravity? If three days after this act became effective another "very grievous murrain" had descended and half of the cattle had died, would the emergency then have ended, also the prescribed rates? If prices for agricultural products become high can consumers claim a crisis exists and demand that the Legislature fix less ones? Or are producers alone to be considered, consumers neglected? To these questions we have no answers. When emergency gives potency, its subsidence must disempower; but no test for its presence or absence has been offered. How is an accused to know when some new rule of conduct arrived, when it will disappear?…

The exigency is of the kind which inevitably arises when one set of men continue to produce more than all others can buy. The distressing result to the producer followed his ill-advised but voluntary efforts. Similar situations occur in almost every business. If here we have an emergency sufficient to empower the Legislature to fix sales prices, then whenever there is too much or too little of an essential thing—whether of milk or grain or pork or coal or shoes or clothes—constitutional provisions may be declared inoperative and the "anarchy and despotism" prefigured in Milligan's Case are at the door....

Is the milk business so affected with public interest that the Legislature may prescribe prices for sales by stores? This Court has approved the contrary view; has emphatically declared that a State lacks power to fix prices in similar private businesses....

Regulation to prevent recognized evils in business has long been upheld as permissible legislative action. But fixation of the price at which A, engaged in an ordinary business, may sell, in order to enable B, a producer, to improve his condition, has not been regarded as within legislative power. This is not regulation, but management, control, dicta-tion—it amounts to the deprivation of the fundamental right which one has to conduct his own affairs honestly and along customary lines. The argument advanced here would support general prescription of prices for farm products, groceries, shoes, clothing, all the necessities of modern civilization, as well as labor, when some Legislature finds and declares such action advisable and for the public good. This Court has declared that a State may not by legislative fiat convert a private business into a public utility.... And if it be now ruled that one dedicates his property to public use whenever he embarks on an enterprise which the Legislature may think it desirable to bring under control, this is but to declare that rights guaranteed by the Constitution exist only so long as supposed public interest does not require their extinction. To adopt such a view, of course, would put an end to liberty under the Constitution....

QUESTIONS

1. Counsel for the state of New York summarized the issue and economic principle in *Nebbia* as follows:

   > "[Nebbia's] position is that it is the constitutional right of every tradesman, at all times and under all conditions, to fix the price for his commodities. This, he says, is a supreme good which cannot be set aside even upon the clearest demonstration that a temporary exigency calls for different treatment. Undoubtedly, self-regulation of business through free competition is a good worthy of considerable sacrifice, but it is not always the preponderant value.... Public utilities are businesses in which free competition works out badly, and accordingly they are controlled upon a different principle."

   Does this statement capture the essence of the debate over due process and state police powers?

2. The attorneys general of Connecticut and Ohio offered several grounds for upholding the New York Milk Control Law: as a health measure to stabilize availability and quality of milk, as a public

safety measure in the face of strikes and riots, and as a temporary emergency measure in the light of the Depression. Should the Court have decided *Nebbia* on one of those alternatives (or another that you might think of)? Would doing so have been more of an exercise of judicial restraint than Justice Roberts's approach?

3. Under the American system of federalism should states be given more deference when they regulate under the authority of their reserved police powers than Congress is given when it regulates under the authority of one of its enumerated powers? Or is the constitutional source of the regulatory power irrelevant to the question of government's authority to affect business at all?

4. Political scientist Howard Gillman writes of *Nebbia* that, conventionally, it "has been taken to mean that the Court had decided to defer to the legislature's judgment with respect to the wisdom of economic policies regarding price-fixing.... A more likely interpretation of the result in *Nebbia* is that a few justices who were more or less committed to the public purpose limit on legislative power concluded that there was a good reason to think that the law promoted the health of the community as a whole, and was not merely designed to enrich milk producers and large milk dealers" (*The Constitution Besieged: The Rise and Demise of Lochner Era Police Powers Jurisprudence* [Durham, NC: Duke University Press, 1993], pp. 180–181).

Is Gillman correct in stating that the result in *Nebbia* is best explained in terms of a debate over the New York Milk Control Board order as an acceptable public health measure versus an illegitimate grant of special benefit? Or did the outcome result from a debate over whether the Milk Board order was an act reasonably related to the goal of promoting public welfare versus a forbidden deprivation of property rights? Are the two explanations mutually exclusive?

5. Reread *Home Building & Loan Association v. Blaisdell*, pp. 754–762. *Nebbia* and *Blaisdell* were decided the same Term by identical 5–4 votes. Are the two decisions "bellwethers" in the sense that, signaling rejection of central tenets of economic substantive due process and *Lochner* era police powers jurisprudence, they are precursors of a new constitutionalism? Or are the two cases an acknowledgement that in time of economic crisis, legal formalism can yield to limited government regulations?

6. Do the Contracts Clause and the Fourteenth Amendment Due Process Clause impose substantive prohibitions on the exercise of state police powers, drawing lines around activities into which government may never intrude, or do they merely limit certain particular exercises of those powers?

JUDICIAL PROTECTION OF PROPERTY INTERESTS

West Coast Hotel v. Parrish
300 U.S. 379 (1937)

SETTING

The Supreme Court's 1934 Term suggested that the justices were increasingly receptive to *state* economic regulatory laws. *Blaisdell* and *Nebbia* seemed to signal that the Roosevelt administration's innovative and wide-ranging government economic interventions undertaken during the "First Hundred Days" of the New Deal might survive judicial review, albeit by a narrow majority. In its 1935 Term, however, the Court was less than receptive to *federal* regulatory measures. First, the Court overturned the petroleum codes promulgated under the National Industrial Recovery Act (NIRA). *Panama Refining Co. v. Ryan*, 293 U.S. 388 (1935). Later that year, the Court invalidated a law establishing a mandatory retirement and pension plan for all carriers subject to the Interstate Commerce Act. *Railroad Retirement Board v. Alton Railroad Co.*, 295 U.S. 330 (1935). *Alton* was a harbinger of hardening judicial opposition to the New Deal, because the Court typically had deferred to congressional authority to regulate railroads under the Commerce Clause. Three weeks later, on May 27, 1935, came "Black Monday," when *Schechter, Louisville Bank v. Radford*, 295 U.S. 555 (1935), and *Humphrey's Executor* were handed down. (See Chapter 4, pp. 436–442.)

Those decisions were soon followed by *Carter v. Carter Coal Co.*, 298 U.S. 238 (1936), in which the Court declared unconstitutional the central provisions of the 1935 Bituminous Coal Conservation Act. Then came *United States v. Butler*, declaring unconstitutional the Agricultural Adjustment Act. In June 1936, the Court returned to its attack on state regulation, striking down a 1933 New York minimum wage statute for women and minors. *Morehead v. New York ex rel. Tipaldo*, 298 U.S. 587 (1936). Citing as controlling precedent its 1923 decision in *Adkins v. Children's Hospital*, the majority held that the New York statute violated the right to make contracts, which it held to be part of the liberty protected by the Due Process Clause of the Fourteenth Amendment. Justice Pierce Butler wrote for the *Morehead* majority: "The *Adkins* Case, unless distinguishable, requires affirmance of the judgment below.... No application has been made for reconsideration of the constitutional question there decided. The validity of the principles upon which that decision rests is not challenged."

As explained in the *Setting* to *National Labor Relations Board v. Jones & Laughlin* (Chapter 3, pp. 280–291), by the time *Morehead* was handed down, a bipartisan political consensus had emerged that governmental power must be exercised to respond to the depressed economic conditions that were fueling dangerously unstable social conditions. The Supreme Court was perceived by many as obstructing urgent reforms. In early 1937, after his resounding reelection as president, Franklin Roosevelt and his attorney general, Homer Cummings, made a proposal that was quickly labeled the "Court-Packing Plan." The core of their plan was that the president could appoint an additional justice to the Supreme Court for each one who had served ten years and had not retired within six months of his seventieth birthday. If their proposal had met with congressional approval, Roosevelt would have been authorized to appoint six additional justices.

One of the reasons the Senate gave for rejecting Roosevelt's proposal was a Supreme Court decision announced March 29, 1937. Unbeknownst to the president, the fate of his Court-packing plan and his New Deal legislation, as well as the doctrine of economic substantive due process and *Lochner* era police powers jurisprudence, were tied to a Wenatchee, Washington, chambermaid whose case had worked its way to the Supreme Court from Washington courts late in 1936.

Elsie Parrish worked intermittently for the West Coast Hotel from August 1933 to May 1935. Her salary during that time was less than the $14.50 per forty-eight hour week set by the Industrial Welfare Committee, created in 1913 by the Washington legislature as part of the "Minimum Wages for Women Act." When Parrish's employment ended she sued the hotel for $216.19, the difference between the wages she had received and the sum to which she was entitled according to the Industrial Welfare Committee. Her suit (joined in by her husband in order to comply with Washington's community property laws) also asked for $17 that the hotel admitted she was due, but which she had refused to accept because it had been offered to her as complete satisfaction of the hotel's debt.

The Superior Court of the State of Washington for Chelan County ruled for the hotel. The trial judge said the case was controlled by *Adkins v. Children's Hospital* and that the Minimum Wages for Women Act violated the Fourteenth Amendment.

The Washington Supreme Court reversed the trial court. It held that *Adkins* was not controlling because the Washington case involved a state statute rather than an act of Congress, and the statute was enacted in the public interest. West Coast Hotel appealed to the Supreme Court of the United States.

HIGHLIGHTS OF SUPREME COURT ARGUMENTS

BRIEF FOR WEST COAST HOTEL

◆ The Washington statute is an unconstitutional attempt to regulate the wages of women without due process. Passed in 1913, ten years before the decision in *Adkins*, it cannot be justified as an emergency measure.

◆ The Washington statute also deprives the hotel of its right to freedom of contract. The issues in this case have been repeatedly litigated in *Adkins* and since. The results consistently have favored the hotel's position.

◆ If states could deprive persons of their rights through the police power, the Constitution would be a nullity. Liberty of contract is one such right.

BRIEF FOR THE PARRISHES

◆ The Washington statute is a reasonable exercise of the police power and therefore does not violate the Fourteenth Amendment. It is the province of the legislature to determine which situations pertaining to the public interest require exercise of the police power. Courts are not in a position to second-guess the wisdom of such laws.

◆ The *Adkins* decision does not control this case because the Washington law was passed by a state legislature exercising its police power and received the approval of the highest court of the state. *Adkins* involved a federal statute that had been declared unconstitutional by the highest court of the District of Columbia.

◆ There are no cases where a decision of the highest court of a state on a minimum wage regulation has been reversed by the Supreme Court.

AMICUS CURIAE BRIEF SUPPORTING THE PARRISHES

State of Washington.

SUPREME COURT DECISION: 5–4

HUGHES, C.J.

… The appellant relies upon the decision of this Court in *Adkins v. Children's Hospital*…. On the argument at bar, counsel for the appellees attempted to distinguish the *Adkins* Case upon the ground that the appellee was employed in a hotel and that the business of an innkeeper was affected with a public interest. That effort at distinction is obviously futile, as it appears that in one of the cases ruled by the *Adkins* opinion the employee was a woman employed as an elevator operator in a hotel….

The recent case of *Morehead v. New York ex rel. Tipaldo* came here on *certiorari* to the New York court which had held the New York minimum wage act for women to be invalid. A minority of this Court thought that the New York statute was distinguishable in a material feature from that involved in the *Adkins* Case and that for that and other reasons the New York statute should be sustained. But the Court of Appeals of New York had said that it found no material difference between the two statutes and this Court held that the "meaning of the statute" as fixed by the decision of the state court "must be accepted here as if the meaning had been specifically expressed in the enactment." That view led to the affirmance by this Court of the judgment in the *Morehead* Case, as the Court considered that the only question before it was whether the *Adkins* Case was distinguishable and that reconsideration of that decision had not been sought....

We think that the question which was not deemed to be open in the *Morehead* Case is open and is necessarily presented here. The Supreme Court of Washington has upheld the minimum wage statute of that state. It has decided that the statute is a reasonable exercise of the police power of the state. In reaching that conclusion, the state court has invoked principles long established by this Court in the application of the Fourteenth Amendment. The state court has refused to regard the decision in the *Adkins* Case as determinative and has pointed to our decisions both before and since that case as justifying its position. We are of the opinion that this ruling of the state court demands on our part a re-examination of the *Adkins* Case. The importance of the question, in which many states having similar laws are concerned, the close division by which the decision in the *Adkins* Case was reached, and the economic conditions which have supervened, and in the light of which the reasonableness of the exercise of the protective power of the state must be considered, make it not only appropriate, but we think imperative, that in deciding the present case the subject should receive fresh consideration....

The principle which must control our decision is not in doubt. The constitutional provision invoked is the due process clause of the Fourteenth Amendment governing the states, as the due process clause invoked in the *Adkins* Case governed Congress. In each case the violation alleged by those attacking minimum wage regulation for women is deprivation of freedom of contract. What is this freedom? The Constitution does not speak of freedom of contract. It speaks of liberty and prohibits the deprivation of liberty without due process of law. In prohibiting that deprivation, the Constitution does not recognize an absolute and uncontrollable liberty. Liberty in each of its phases has its history and connotation. But the liberty safeguarded is liberty in a social organization which requires the protection of law against the evils which menace the health, safety, morals, and welfare of the people. Liberty under the Constitution is thus necessarily subject to the restraints of due process, and regulation which is reasonable in relation to its subject and is adopted in the interests of the community is due process....

The point that has been strongly stressed that adult employees should be deemed competent to make their own contracts was decisively met nearly forty years ago in *Holden v. Hardy*, 169 U.S. 366 (1898), where we pointed out the inequality in the footing of the parties. We said:

> The legislature has also recognized the fact, which the experience of legislators in many states has corroborated, that the proprietors of these establishments and their operatives do not stand upon an equality, and that their interests are, to a certain extent, conflicting. The former naturally desire to obtain as much labor as possible from their employees, while the latter are often induced by the fear of discharge to conform to regulations which their judgment, fairly exercised, would pronounce to be detrimental to their

health or strength. In other words, the proprietors lay down the rules, and the laborers are practically constrained to obey them. In such cases self-interest is often an unsafe guide, and the legislature may properly interpose its authority....

It is manifest that this established principle is peculiarly applicable in relation to the employment of women in whose protection the state has a special interest. That phase of the subject received elaborate consideration in *Muller v. Oregon*, where the constitutional authority of the state to limit the working hours of women was sustained. We emphasized the consideration that "woman's physical structure and the performance of maternal functions place her at a disadvantage in the struggle for subsistence" and that her physical well being "becomes an object of public interest and care in order to preserve the strength and vigor of the race." We emphasized the need of protecting women against oppression despite her possession of contractual rights. We said that "though limitations upon personal and contractual rights may be removed by legislation, there is that in their disposition and habits of life which will operate against a full assertion of those rights. She will still be where some legislation to protect her seems necessary to secure a real equality of right." Hence she was "properly placed in a class by herself, and legislation designed for her protection may be sustained, even when like legislation is not necessary for men, and could not be sustained." We concluded that the limitations which the statute there in question "places upon her contractual powers, upon her right to agree with her employer, as to the time she shall labor'

were 'not imposed solely for her benefit, but also largely for the benefit of all.'"...

This array of precedents and the principles they applied were thought by the dissenting Justices in the *Adkins* Case to demand that the minimum wage statute be sustained. The validity of the distinction made by the Court between a minimum wage and a maximum of hours in limiting liberty of contract was especially challenged. That challenge persists and is without any satisfactory answer....

One of the points which was pressed by the Court in supporting its ruling in the *Adkins* Case was that the standard set up by the District of Columbia Act did not take appropriate account of the value of the services rendered. In the *Morehead* Case, the minority thought that the New York statute had met that point in its definition of a "fair wage" and that it accordingly presented a distinguishable feature which the Court could recognize within the limits which the *Morehead* petition for certiorari was deemed to present. The Court, however, did not take that view and the New York Act was held to be essentially the same as that for the District of Columbia. The statute now before us is like the latter, but we are unable to conclude that in its minimum wage requirement the state has passed beyond the boundary of its broad protective power.

The minimum wage to be paid under the Washington statute is fixed after full consideration by representatives of employers, employees, and the public. It may be assumed that the minimum wage is fixed in consideration of the services that are performed in the particular occupations under normal conditions. Provision is made for special licenses at less wages in the case of women who are incapable of full ser-

[handwritten left margin: women placed in a class by themselves]

vice. The statement of Mr. Justice Holmes in the *Adkins* Case is pertinent: "This statute does not compel anybody to pay anything. It simply forbids employment at rates below those fixed as the minimum requirement of health and right living. It is safe to assume that women will not be employed at even the lowest wages allowed unless they earn them, or unless the employer's business can sustain the burden. In short the law in its character and operation is like hundreds of so-called police laws that have been up-held."...

We think that the views thus expressed are sound and that the decision in the *Adkins* Case was a departure from the true application of the principles governing the regulation by the state of the relation of employer and employed.... Those principles have been reenforced by our subsequent decisions.... In *Nebbia v. New York*, dealing with the New York statute providing for minimum prices for milk, the general subject of the regulation of the use of private property and of the making of private contracts received an exhaustive examination, and we again declared that if such laws "have a reasonable relation to a proper legislative purpose, and are neither arbitrary nor discriminatory, the requirements of due process are satisfied"; that "with the wisdom of the policy adopted, with the adequacy or practicability of the law enacted to forward it, the courts are both incompetent and unauthorized to deal"; that "times without number we have said that the legislature is primarily the judge of the necessity of such an enactment, that every possible presumption is in favor of its validity, and that though the court may hold views inconsistent with the wisdom of the law, it may not

be annulled unless palpably in excess of legislative power."

With full recognition of the earnestness and vigor which characterize the prevailing opinion in the *Adkins* Case, we find it impossible to reconcile that ruling with these well-considered declarations. What can be closer to the public interest than the health of women and their protection from unscrupulous and overreaching employers? And if the protection of women is a legitimate end of the exercise of state power, how can it be said that the requirement of the payment of a minimum wage fairly fixed in order to meet the very necessities of existence is not an admissible means to that end? The legislature of the State was clearly entitled to consider the situation of women in employment, the fact that they are in the class receiving the least pay, that their bargaining power is relatively weak, and that they are the ready victims of those who would take advantage of their necessitous circumstances. The legislature was entitled to adopt measures to reduce the evils of the "sweating system," the exploiting of workers at wages so low as to be insufficient to meet the bare cost of living, thus making their very helplessness the occasion of a most injurious competition. The legislature had the right to consider that its minimum wage requirements would be an important aid in carrying out its policy of protection. The adoption of similar requirements by many states evidences a deepseated conviction both as to the presence of the evil and as to the means adapted to check it. Legislative response to that conviction cannot be regarded as arbitrary or capricious and that is all we have to decide. Even if the wisdom of the policy be regarded as debatable and its effects uncertain, still the legislature is entitled to its judgment.

There is an additional and compelling consideration which recent economic experience has brought into a strong light. The exploitation of a class of workers who are in an unequal position with respect to bargaining power and are thus relatively defenseless against the denial of a living wage is not only detrimental to their health and well being, but casts a direct burden for their support upon the community. What these workers lose in wages the taxpayers are called upon to pay. The bare cost of living must be met. We may take judicial notice of the unparalleled demands for relief which arose during the recent period of depression and still continue to an alarming extent despite the degree of economic recovery which has been achieved. It is unnecessary to cite official statistics to establish what is of common knowledge through the length and breadth of the land. While in the instant case no factual brief has been presented, there is no reason to doubt that the state of Washington has encountered the same social problem that is present elsewhere. The community is not bound to provide what is in effect a subsidy for unconscionable employers. The community may direct its law-making power to correct the abuse which springs from their selfish disregard of the public interest. The argument that the legislation in question constitutes an arbitrary discrimination, because it does not extend to men, is unavailing. This Court has frequently held that the legislative authority, acting within its proper field, is not bound to extend its regulation to all cases which it might possibly reach....

Our conclusion is that the case of

Adkins v. Children's Hospital should be, and it is, overruled. The judgment of the Supreme Court of the state of Washington is affirmed.

Affirmed.

SUTHERLAND, VAN DEVANTER, MCREYNOLDS, AND BUTLER, J.J., DISSENTING

... Under our form of government, where the written Constitution, by its own terms, is the supreme law, some agency, of necessity, must have the power to say the final word as to the validity of a statute assailed as unconstitutional. The Constitution makes it clear that the power has been intrusted to this court when the question arises in a controversy within its jurisdiction; and so long as the power remains there, its exercise cannot be avoided without betrayal of the trust....

The suggestion that the only check upon the exercise of the judicial power, when properly invoked, to declare a constitutional right superior to an unconstitutional statute is the judge's own faculty of self-restraint, is both ill considered and mischievous. Self-restraint belongs in the domain of will and not of judgment. The check upon the judge is that imposed by his oath of office, by the Constitution, and by his own conscientious and informed convictions; and since he has the duty to make up his own mind and adjudge accordingly, it is hard to see how there could be any other restraint. This Court acts as a unit. It cannot act in any other way; and the majority (whether a bare majority or a majority of all but one of its members), therefore, establishes the controlling rule as the decision of the court, binding, so long as it remains unchanged, equally upon those who disagree and upon those who subscribe to it. Otherwise, orderly administration of justice would cease. But it is the right of those in the minority to disagree, and sometimes, in matters of grave importance, their imperative duty to voice their disagreement at such length as the occasion demands—always, of course, in terms which, however forceful, do not offend the proprieties or impugn the good faith of those who think otherwise.

It is urged that the question involved should now receive fresh consideration, among other reasons, because of "the economic conditions which have supervened"; but the meaning of the Constitution does not change with the ebb and flow of economic events. We frequently are told in more general words that the Constitution must be construed in the light of the present. If by that it is meant that the Constitution is made up of living words that apply to every new condition which they include, the statement is quite true. But to say, if that be intended, that the words of the Constitution mean today what they did not mean when written—that is, that they do not apply to a situation now to which they would have applied then—is to rob that instrument of the essential element which continues it in force as the people have made it until they, and not their official agents, have made it otherwise....

The judicial function is that of interpretation; it does not include the power of amendment under the guise of interpretation. To miss the point of difference between the two is to miss all that the phrase "supreme law of the land" stands for and to convert what was intended as inescapable and enduring mandates into mere moral reflections.

If the Constitution, intelligently and reasonably construed in the light of these principles, stands in the way of desirable legislation, the blame must rest upon that instrument, and not upon the court for enforcing it according to its terms. The remedy in that situation—and the only true remedy—is to amend the Constitution....

Coming, then, to a consideration of the Washington statute, it first is to be observed that it is in every substantial respect identical with the statute involved in the *Adkins* Case. Such vices as existed in the latter are present in the former. And if the *Adkins* Case was properly decided, as we who join in this opinion think it was, it necessarily follows that the Washington statute is invalid....

That the clause of the Fourteenth Amendment which forbids a state to deprive any person of life, liberty, or property without due process of law includes freedom of contract is so well settled as to be no longer open to question. Nor reasonably can it be disputed that contracts of employment of labor are included in the rule....

We [have] pointed out that minimum wage legislation such as that here involved does not deal with any business charged with a public interest, or with public work, or with a temporary emergency, or with the character, methods, or periods of wage payments, or with hours of labor, or with the protection of persons under legal disability, or with the prevention of fraud. It is, simply and exclusively, a law fixing wages for adult women who are legally as capable of contracting for themselves as men, and cannot be sustained unless upon principles apart from those involved in cases already decided by the court....

Neither the statute involved in the Adkins Case nor the Washington statute, so far as it is involved here, has the slightest relation to the capacity or earning power of the employee, to the number of hours which constitute the day's work, the character of the place where the work is to be done, or the circumstances or surroundings of the employment. The sole basis upon which the question of validity rests is the assumption that the employee is entitled to receive a sum of money sufficient to provide a living for her, keep her in health and preserve her morals....

The Washington statute, like the one for the District of Columbia, fixes minimum wages for adult women. Adult men and their employers are left free to bargain as they please; and it is a significant and an important fact that all state statutes to which our attention has been called are of like character. The common-law rules restricting the power of women to make contracts have, under our system, long since practically disappeared. Women today stand upon a legal and political equality with men. There is no longer any reason why they should be put in different classes in respect of their legal right to make contracts; nor should they be denied, in effect, the right to compete with men for work paying lower wages which men may be willing to accept. And it is an arbitrary exercise of the legislative power to do so....

An appeal to the principle that the legislature is free to recognize degrees of harm and confine its restrictions accordingly, is but to beg the question, which is—Since the contractual rights of men and women are the same, does the legislation here involved, by restricting only the rights of women to make contracts as to wages, create an arbitrary discrimination? We think it does. Difference of sex affords no reasonable ground for making a restriction applicable to the wage contracts of all working women from which like contracts of all working men are left free. Certainly a suggestion that the bargaining ability of the average woman is not equal to that of the average man would lack substance. The ability to make a fair bargain, as every one knows, does not depend upon sex.

If, in the light of the facts, the state legislation, without reason or for reasons of mere expediency, excluded men from the provisions of the legislation, the power was exercised arbitrarily. On the other hand, if such legislation in respect of men was properly omitted on the ground that it would be unconstitutional, the same conclusion of unconstitutionality is inescapable in respect of similar legislative restraint in the case of women....

Finally, it may be said that a statute absolutely fixing wages in the various industries at definite sums and forbidding employers and employees from contracting for any other than those designated would probably not be thought to be constitutional. It is hard to see why the power to fix minimum wages does not connote a like power in respect of maximum wages. And yet, if both powers be exercised in such a way that the minimum and the maximum so nearly approach each other as to become substantially the same, the right to make any contract in respect of wages will have been completely abrogated....

COMMENTS

1. Conventionally, Justice Owen Roberts is cast as playing the central role in the clash between "The Nine Old Men" and the Roosevelt administration. He is seen as the focal point of the so-called "switch in time that saved nine." This simplistic view holds that an indecisive Justice Roberts caved in to pressure generated, in part, by Roosevelt's Court-packing plan and switched positions, abandoning his *Morehead* vote against the New York minimum wage statute, to favor the Washington law contested in *West Coast Hotel*. The historical record provides a picture of a less irresolute jurist. A memorandum written by Justice Roberts shows that he had made up his mind to support the Washington law weeks before Roosevelt's judicial reform proposal was announced. More importantly, Roberts explained his "deviation" in *Morehead* as a vote dictated by the restrictive terms of the petition for *certiorari* that did not ask the Court to reconsider and possibly reverse *Adkins*, but merely to distinguish the New York statute from the District of Columbia order negated in *Adkins*.

2. So complete was the Court's abandonment of economic substantive due process and *Lochner* era police powers jurisprudence, that in only a single case after *Parrish* did it overturn a state statute pertaining to business on substantive due process grounds. *Connecticut General Life Insurance Company v. Johnson*, 303 U.S. 77 (1938). Justice Douglas summarized the Court's post-*Parrish* approach:

   > The day is gone when this Court uses the Due Process Clause of the Fourteenth Amendment to strike down state laws, regulatory of business and industrial conditions, because they may be unwise, improvident, or out of harmony with a particular school of thought.... We emphasize again what Chief Justice Waite said in *Munn v. Illinois*: "For protection against abuses by legislatures the people must resort to the polls, not to the courts." *Williamson v. Lee Optical Company*, 384 U.S. 483 (1955).

QUESTIONS

1. To what extent are the differences between Chief Justice Hughes's majority and Justice Sutherland's dissenting opinions in *Parrish* a function of disagreements over the Court's duty in interpreting the Constitution, of differing views of appropriate relations between government and the economy, or both? How does one controversy bear on the other?

2. Is the Court's opinion in *Parrish* more or less intellectually and constitutionally defensible than the Court's opinions in *Adkins* and *Lochner*?

3. Does the language of *Parrish* indicate any grounds on which statutes guaranteeing minimum wages for men could be treated differently from statutes guaranteeing minimum wages for women?

4. The statute at issue in *Parrish* was enacted in 1913, the same year that Oregon adopted an almost identical minimum wage statute. In 1917, the Supreme Court affirmed state court rulings declaring the Oregon statute constitutional. *Stettler v. O'Hara*, 243 U.S. 629 (1917). The Court's vote was 4–4, however, and therefore established no precedent. Justice Brandeis did not participate in *Stettler* because he had participated as an advocate in *Muller v. Oregon* before his appointment to the Court. If Brandeis had participated, the decision undoubtedly would have been 5–4 in favor of the constitutionality of the Oregon statute.

   Similarly, if *Adkins* had followed a normal course through the courts of the District of Columbia to the Supreme Court it would have been heard during the 1921 Term. Given the Court's personnel at that time, it is likely that the justices would have sustained the District of Columbia legislation.

   Law professor J. Kennard Cheadle observed, "It seems fantastic that decisions on important matters of government should hinge on events so irrelevant to the issues at stake. It is fantastic. It is also a reality" ("The Parrish Case," 11 *University of Cincinnati Law Review* [1937]: 307, 309–312, 314).

   What perspectives on judicial review are provided by the historical facts described above and by Cheadle's observation?

5. Law professor Laurence H. Tribe writes:

   > [W]hat was wrong with [the] *Lochner* [approach to constitutional analysis] was the Court's overconfidence, both in its own factual notions about working conditions and perhaps also in its own normative convictions about the meaning of liberty[.]... But it would be wrong to make too much of the point[.]... At most, [the Court has] a duty not to be pigheaded, *too* certain of all of one's premises, and a solemn duty to connect one's decisions to an intelligible view of the Constitution. (*American Constitutional Law*, 2nd ed. [Mineola, NY: Foundation Press, 1988] p. 586)

   Is there a difference between the obligation to have an "intelligible" constitutional view inform one's judicial decisions, and possessing a "correct" constitutional answer? On what basis can it be said that *Lochner* era constitutionalism was wrong or right?

SUGGESTIONS FOR FURTHER READING

Benedict, Michael Les, "Laissez-Faire and Liberty: A Re-evaluation of the Meaning and Origins of Laissez-Faire Constitutionalism," 3 *Law and History Review* (1985): 293.

Commons, John R., *Legal Foundations of Capitalism* (Madison, WI: University of Wisconsin Press, 1968, originally published 1924).

Corwin, Edward S., "The Doctrine of Due Process of Law before the Civil War," 24 *Harvard Law Review* (1911): 366.

_____, *Court over Constitution* (Princeton, NJ: Princeton University Press, 1932).

_____, *Liberty against Government: The Rise, Flowering, and Decline of a Famous Juridical Concept* (Baton Rouge, LA: Louisiana University Press, 1948).

Ely, James W. Jr., ed., *Property Rights in American History*, 6 vols. (New York, NY: Garland, 1997).

Fairman, Charles, "The So-Called *Granger Cases*, Lord Hale, and Justice Bradley," 5 *Stanford Law Review* (1953): 587.

Fine, Sidney, *Laissez Faire and the General Welfare State* (Ann Arbor, MI: University of Michigan Press, 1956).

Field, Oliver P., "Ex Post Facto in the Constitution," 20 *Michigan Law Review* (1922): 315.

Foster, James C., *The Ideology of Apolitical Politics: Elite Lawyers' Response to the Legitimation Crisis of American Capitalism, 1870–1920* (New York, NY: Garland, 1990).

Frankfurter, Felix, "Hours of Labor and Realism in Constitutional Law," 23 *Harvard Law Review* (1916): 353.

_____, "Mr. Justice Roberts," 104 *University of Pennsylvania Law Review* (1955): 311.

Gillman, Howard, *The Constitution Besieged: The Rise and Demise of Lochner Era Police Powers Jurisprudence* (Durham, NC: Duke University Press, 1993).

Goldstein, Leslie F., "Popular Sovereignty, the Origins of Judicial Review, and the Revival of Unwritten Law," 48 *Journal of Politics* (1986): 51.

Goldwin, Robert A., and William A. Schambra, eds., *How Capitalistic Is the Constitution?* (Washington, D.C.: American Enterprise Institute, 1982).

Graham, Howard Jay, "The 'Conspiracy Theory' of the Fourteenth Amendment," 47 *Yale Law Journal* (1938): 371; 48 *Yale Law Journal* (1938): 171; reprinted in *Everyman's Constitution: Historical Essays on the Fourteenth Amendment, the "Conspiracy Theory," and American Constitutionalism* (Madison, WI: State Historical Society of Wisconsin, 1968).

Grey, Thomas, "Do We Have an Unwritten Constitution?" 27 *Stanford Law Review* (1975): 703.

_____, "Origins of the Unwritten Constitution: Fundamental Law in American Revolutionary Thought", 30 *Stanford Law Review* (1978): 843.

Goldsmith, Irving B., and Gordon W. Winks, "Price-Fixing from *Nebbia* to

Guffey," in *Selected Essays on Constitutional Law*, ed. Douglas B. Maggs (Chicago, IL: Association of American Law Schools, 1938).

Hand, Learned, "Due Process of Law and the Eight-Hour Day," 21 *Harvard Law Review* (1908): 495.

_____, *The Spirit of Liberty*, 3rd ed. (New York, NY: Knopf, 1960).

Horwitz, Morton J., "*Santa Clara* Revisited: The Development of Corporate Theory," 88 *West Virginia Law Review* (1985–86): 173.

_____, *The Transformation of American Law, 1870–1960: The Crisis of Legal Orthodoxy* (New York, NY: Oxford University Press, 1992).

Hovenkamp, Howard, "The Political Economy of Substantive Due Process," 40 *Stanford Law Review* (1988): 443.

_____, *Enterprise and American Law, 1836–1937* (Cambridge, MA: Harvard University Press, 1991).

Hurst, J. Willard, *The Legitimacy of the Business Corporation in the Law of the United States, 1780–1970* (Charlottesville, VA: University of Virginia Press, 1970).

Jacobs, Clyde E., *Law Writers and the Courts* (Berkeley, CA: University of California Press, 1954).

Kennedy, Duncan, "Toward an Historical Understanding of Legal Consciousness: The Case of Classical Legal Thought in America, 1850–1940," in *Research in Law and Sociology*, vol. 3, ed. Steven Spitzer (Greenwich, CT: JAI Press, 1980).

Kens, Paul, *Judicial Power and Reform Politics: The Anatomy of Lochner v. New York* (Lawrence, KS: University of Kansas Press, 1990).

Kessler-Harris, Alice, *Out to Work: A History of Wage-Earning Women in the United States* (New York, NY: Oxford University press, 1982).

Leonard, Charles A., *A Search for a Judicial Philosophy: Mr. Justice Roberts and the Constitutional Revolution of 1937* (Port Washington, NY: Kennikat Press, 1971).

Leuchtenburg, William E., "The Case of the Wenatchee Chambermaid," in *Quarrels that Have Shaped the Constitution*, rev. ed., ed. John A. Garraty (New York, NY: Harper and Row, 1987).

Lieberman, Elias, *Unions before the Bar* (New York, NY: Harper and Row, 1950).

Linde, Hans A., "Without Due Process," 40 *Oregon Law Review* (1970): 125.

_____, "Due Process of Lawmaking," 55 *Nebraska Law Review* (1976): 197.

Magrath, C. Peter, "The Case of the Unscrupulous Warehouseman," in *Quarrels That Have Shaped the Constitution*, rev. ed., ed. John A. Garraty (New York, NY: Harper and Row, 1987).

Mason, Alpheus Thomas, *Brandeis: A Free Man's Life* (New York, NY: Viking, 1946).

_____, "The Case of the Overworked Laundress," in *Quarrels that Have*

Shaped the Constitution, rev. ed., ed. John A. Garraty (New York, NY: Harper and Row, 1987).

McCann, Michael W., "Resurrection and Reform: Perspectives on Property in the American Constitutional Tradition," 13 *Politics & Society* (1984): 143.

McCloskey, Robert G., *American Conservatism in the Age of Enterprise, 1865–1910* (New York, NY: Harper and Row, 1964).

Mendelson, Wallace, "A Missing Link in the Evolution of Due Process," 10 *Vanderbilt Law Review* (1956): 125.

————, *Capitalism, Democracy, and the Supreme Court* (New York, NY: Appleton-Century-Crofts, 1960).

Miller, Arthur Selwyn, *The Supreme Court and American Capitalism* (New York, NY: Free Press, 1968).

Miller, George L., *Railroads and the Granger Laws* (Madison, WI: University of Wisconsin Press, 1971).

Nelson, William E., "The Impact of the Antislavery Movement upon Styles of Judicial Reasoning in Nineteenth Century America," 87 *Harvard Law Review* (1974): 513.

————, *The Fourteenth Amendment: From Political Principle to Judicial Doctrine* (Cambridge, MA: Harvard University Press, 1988).

Noonan Jr., John T., *Persons and Masks of the Law: Cardozo, Holmes, Jefferson, and Wythe as Makers of the Masks* (New York, NY: Farrar, Straus & Giroux, 1976).

Note, "Ex Post Facto Limitations on Legislative Power," 73 *Michigan Law Review* (1975): 1491.

Paul, Arnold, *Conservative Crisis and the Rule of Law* (New York, NY: Harper and Row, 1960).

Peller, Gary, "The Metaphysics of American Law," 73 *California Law Review* (1985): 1151.

Phillips, Michael J., "Another Look at Economic Substantive Due Process," *Wisconsin Law Review* (1987): 265.

Porter, Mary Cornelia, "*Lochner* and Company: Revisionism Revisited," in *Liberty, Property, and Government: Constitutional Interpretation before the New Deal*, ed. Ellen Frankel and Paul and Howard Dickman (Albany, NY: State University of New York Press, 1989).

Powell, Thomas Reed, "The Judiciality of Minimum Wage Legislation," 37 *Harvard Law Review* (1924): 545.

Scheiber, Harry N., "The Road to *Munn*: Eminent Domain and the Concept of Public Purpose in the State Courts," 5 *Perspectives in American History* (1971): 329.

Sherry, Suzanna, "The Founder's Unwritten Constitution," 54 *University of Chicago Law Review* (1987): 1127.

Siegan, Bernard H., "Rehabilitating *Lochner*," *San Diego Law Review* (1985): 453.

Strum, Philippa, *Louis D. Brandeis: Justice for the People* (Cambridge, MA: Harvard University Press, 1984).

Sunstein, Cass R., "Interest Groups in American Public Law," 38 *Stanford Law Review* (1985): 29.

_____, "*Lochner*'s Legacy," 87 *Columbia Law Review* (1987): 873.

Sutherland, Arthur, *Constitutionalism in America: The Origin and Evolution of Its Fundamental Ideas* (New York, NY: Blaisdell, 1965).

Swindler, William F., *Court and Constitution in the Twentieth Century: The Old Legality, 1889–1932* (Indianapolis, IN: Bobbs-Merrill, 1969).

Tarrow, Sidney, "*Lochner v. New York*: A Political Analysis," 5 *Labor History* (1964): 277.

Twiss, Benjamin, *Lawyers and the Constitution: How Laissez Faire Came to the Supreme Court* (Princeton, NJ: Princeton University Press, 1942).

Vining, Jacob, *Legal Identity: The Coming of Age of Public Law* (New Haven, CT: Yale University Press, 1978).

Warren, Charles, "The New 'Liberty' under the Fourteenth Amendment," 39 *Harvard Law Review* (1926): 431.

Vose, Clement E., "The National Consumers' League and the Brandeis Brief," 1 *Midwest Journal of Political Science* (1957): 267.

Yudof, Mark G., "Equal Protection, Class Legislation, and Sex Discrimination: One Small Cheer for Mr. Herbert Spencer's *Social Statics*," 88 *Michigan Law Review* (1990):1366.

TAKINGS

Barron v. Baltimore
7 Peters 243 (1833)

SETTING

Although ownership of private property is one of the natural rights that many believe the Constitution was adopted to protect, nothing in the Constitution prohibits government's exercise of the power of eminent domain, which is the power to take private property for public use. In *Van Horne's Lessee v. Dorrance*, 2 U.S. 304 (1795), Justice William Patterson explained the power of eminent domain this way:

The despotic power, as it is aptly called by some writers, of taking property, when state necessity requires, exists in every government; the existence of such power is necessary; government could not subsist without it....

Three years later, in *Calder v. Bull*, Justice James Iredell noted that "private rights must yield to public exigencies" and that public projects "are necessarily sometimes built upon the soil owned by individuals."

The Fifth Amendment places a qualification on government's exercise of the power of eminent domain. It provides that private property shall not "be taken for public use, without just compensation." The principle underlying the Fifth Amendment's Takings Clause is that private property owners should not be forced to bear a burden that should be borne by the public as a whole.

Two kinds of issues commonly arise in Takings Clause litigation. The first is whether government has "taken" private property for public use or whether, in the exercise of its police power, it has merely imposed a regulation or condition on the use of that property for which the owner is not entitled to compensation. This issue often forces courts to balance the rights of government against the rights of property owners. The second issue is how much compensation the property owner is entitled to receive when property is taken for public use.

Barron v. Baltimore involved a threshold question: when property is taken by a state government or one of its subdivisions, does the Takings Clause of the Fifth Amendment compel the state to provide compensation?

Note: Review the *Setting* to and excerpt of *Barron v. Baltimore* in Chapter 5, pp. 649–654.

QUESTIONS

1. The City of Baltimore conceded that its public improvement project had the effect of rendering Barron and Craig's property worthless, yet the city refused to offer the men compensation. What does that refusal suggest about the city's understanding of its police powers relative to private property rights?

2. Chief Justice Marshall's opinion in *Barron* rejected the argument that the Takings Clause of the Fifth Amendment imposes a compensation requirement on the city of Baltimore, a political subdivision of the state of Maryland. If the Takings Clause is not available as a remedy, what remedy does Marshall's opinion suggest is available to litigants like Barron and Craig whose property is destroyed by a public works project? Is it a practical remedy?

3. In *Barron*, Chief Justice Marshall refused the invitation to hold that the Takings Clause is a limitation on state governments as well as a limitation on the national government. Review his opinions in

Fletcher v. Peck and *Dartmouth College v. Woodward.* Are there lines of reasoning in those opinions that would have supported a ruling that the Takings Clause does limit the state as well as the national government? Does Marshall's opinion in *Barron* suggest a deference to states' rights? If so, might that deference have something to do with the fact that in 1833 slavery (which at core involved property ownership) was primarily a state issue?

4. The Takings Clause did not play a major role in constitutional law before the Civil War. Might it be that the Court's decisions involving the Contracts Clause helped to obviate the need for litigants to focus the Court on the Takings Clause? Legal historian J. Willard Hurst offers another explanation: Until the later years of the nineteenth century, economic growth (which he refers to as "the release of energy") took precedence over compensating property owners (*Law and the Conditions of Freedom in the Nineteenth-Century United States* [Madison, WI: University of Wisconsin Press, 1956]). Does Hurst's theory suggest that private property ownership is not a "natural right," but is merely instrumental to some other goal such as economic growth? What are the constitutional ramifications of such a theory?

5. The Takings Clause was the first provision of the Bill of Rights to be "incorporated" against the states; that is, to be held to be a limitation on the states as well as the national government. *Chicago, Burlington, and Quincy Railroad Co. v. City of Chicago*, 166 U.S. 226 (1897). Review the chart of Bill of Rights incorporation in Chapter 5, pp. 705–706, following *Duncan v. Louisiana*. What, if anything, does that chronology reveal about the Court's priorities regarding constitutional protections for property and individual liberty? What, if anything, does it reveal about the Court's view of the authority of the states?

TAKINGS

Pennsylvania Coal Co. v. Mahon
260 U.S. 393 (1922)

SETTING

The Fifth Amendment provides that private property shall not be taken for public use without just compensation. The amendment's command is straightforward when government confiscates or condemns land for public use. It becomes problematic when government imposes regulations on the use of private property. In those circumstances, the issue is whether a regulation is the equivalent of a taking. Many land use regulations are imposed in the name of public health, safety, welfare, and morals. It falls to the courts to balance the state's exercise of its police power against the rights of property owners to just compensation.

Before 1922, the Court showed substantial deference to the states' regulatory powers regarding property. In 1887, for example, in *Mugler v. Kansas*, 123 U.S. 623, the Court upheld a statewide prohibition law on the grounds that the social effects of the excessive use of alcohol were so notorious that their regulation justified state action. One consequence of upholding the Kansas law was to prohibit Peter Mugler from using the building on his property as a brewery, even though the building had no other use. The Court declared that state regulations enacted on the basis of the police power do not constitute takings, because they do not interfere with an owner's right to use or dispose of property legally; they merely forbid uses that are "prejudicial" to the public interest. According to the *Mugler* Court, only governmental acquisition or physical invasion constitutes an unconstitutional taking.

In 1915, the Court again rejected two Takings Clause challenges. In *Reinman v. Little Rock*, 237 U.S. 171, it upheld a Little Rock, Arkansas, ordinance that terminated a preexisting land use by prohibiting horse stables in parts of the city that were zoned for commercial uses only. In *Hadacheck v. Sebastian*, 239 U.S. 394, it upheld a Los Angeles ordinance that prohibited the operation of brickyards within a three-square-mile area of the city.

Despite this strong tradition of judicial deference to state regulation, Takings Clause litigation did not abate. In 1922, Justice Oliver Wendell Holmes rewrote constitutional law in this area in a case that arose out of conflicts between coal miners and city dwellers in Pennsylvania.

The anthracite coal field of northeastern Pennsylvania covers approximately five thousand square miles of territory, underlaid by coal of depths varying from zero to twenty-two hundred feet. Mining operations in the area began in the early 1800s and continued into the twentieth century. For most of this period, coal removal had little effect on the surface, because "first mining" operations were conducted in a way that left coal pillars for surface support. Cities, towns, highways, railroads, public improvements such as sewer and water pipes, gas lines, and electric wires developed on land overlaying coal mines.

"Second mining" involved the removal of the coal pillars left by first mining. As second mining progressed, various areas in the anthracite region began to experience surface subsidence, or cave-ins. By 1920, cave-ins had become so serious and extensive that the Pennsylvania legislature began drafting legislation to prohibit the owners of mineral rights from exercising those rights under houses and schools. In 1921, the legislature unanimously enacted the Kohler Act. The preamble of the act stated that:

> [T]he anthracite coal industry in this Commonwealth has been and is being carried on in populous communities in such manner as to remove the natural support of the surface of the soil to such an extent as to result in

wrecked and dangerous streets and highways, collapsed public buildings, churches, schools, factories, stores and private dwellings, broken gas, water and sewer systems, the loss of human life, and in general so as to threaten and seriously endanger the lives and safety of large numbers of the people of the Commonwealth.

The act made it a crime to cause the caving in, collapse, or subsidence of any dwelling house used for human habitation, regardless of negligence, and in spite of any mining rights a coal company might own. The act also gave courts power to issue injunctions to prevent violations of the act. When signing the Kohler Act into law, the governor stated:

> I regard the enactment of this mine cave legislation as a great progressive step. For half a century thoughtful people have realized that something must ultimately be done to prevent the complete desolation of the anthracite region and for a generation the appeal to the Commonwealth to save the situation has been heard here at the capital.

The Kohler Act faced almost immediate legal challenge, because it took away from coal companies mining rights that they had explicitly retained by contract when selling parcels of land. The first case to reach the Supreme Court of the United States involved Pittston, Pennsylvania, attorney H. J. Mahon and his wife, Margaret Craig Mahon.

In 1917, Mrs. Mahon inherited a two-story frame house in Pittston from her father, Alexander Craig. The Mahons began living in the house shortly after Mrs. Mahon inherited it. The house was located on land that Alexander Craig had purchased from the Pennsylvania Coal Company in 1878. The deed conveying the property from the coal company to Craig expressly reserved the right of the company to remove all the coal under the parcel and provided that Craig or his assigns would waive all claims for damages that might arise from mining out the coal from under it or from under adjacent parcels.

On September 1, 1921, W. A. May, president of Pennsylvania Coal, wrote to the Mahons as follows:

> You are hereby notified that the mining operations of the Pennsylvania Coal Company beneath your premises will, by September 15, have reached a point which will then or shortly thereafter cause subsidence and disturbance to the surface of your lot.
>
> Although in the deed to Alexander Craig, under which you hold, we expressly reserved the right to remove the coal under your lot without liability for damages which might be caused thereby, we desire to notify you of the situation so as to enable you to take proper steps for the protection of your dwelling and for the safety of yourselves and the members of your household during the period when the disturbance will continue.

The Mahons filed suit in the Court of Common Pleas of Luzerne County. They invoked the Kohler Act in seeking an injunction to restrain Pennsylvania Coal from removing the coal from under their house. That court found that "if not restrained, [Pennsylvania Coal] will ... cause the caving-in, collapse and subsidence of the surface, together with the dwelling, entailing injury upon [the Mahons].'' Nonetheless, it denied the injunction and dismissed the action, because "the owner of the coal has an absolute right [under the contract of sale] to remove the whole of the same, free from all liability for injury thereby inflicted'' and that no interest "except the private interest of the [Mahons]'' was at stake.

The Pennsylvania Supreme Court, with one justice dissenting, reversed, ruling that the Kohler Act was a valid exercise of the state's police power. The Supreme Court of the United States granted Pennsylvania Coal's petition for a writ of error.

Highlights of Supreme Court Arguments

BRIEF FOR PENNSYLVANIA COAL

◆ The Kohler Act impairs the obligation of the contract between Pennsylvania Coal and the Mahons.

◆ The Kohler Act is not a valid exercise of the police power. It is a fraud perpetrated by private owners and politicians on the owners of minerals because, in the guise of police regulation, it seeks to recapture for surface owners rights of support they have bargained away. It was intended solely for a favored and restricted class of private citizens.

◆ The Kohler Act takes away property without compensation, in violation of the Fifth Amendment's guarantee of Due Process of Law. The act is not a regulation, but amounts to a transfer of a property right from one citizen to another. If surface support in the anthracite district is necessary for public use, it can constitutionally be acquired only by condemnation with just compensation.

BRIEF FOR MAHON

◆ The Kohler Act does not impair the obligation of contract, because that right is subject to the essential authority of government to maintain peace and security and to enact laws for the promotion of the health, safety, morals, and welfare of those subject to its jurisdiction.

◆ The Kohler Act does not deprive Pennsylvania Coal of its property without due process, because it permits the company to continue mining. It merely restricts the company to mining in a manner that does not cause the caving in, collapse, or subsidence of certain properties.

◆ That mining is a dangerous business and therefore subject to regulation is well settled.

◆ The Kohler Act is a bona fide exercise of the police power. It is a matter of common knowledge that great loss of life and irreparable damage and uncompensated loss of property have attended the unregulated and unrestricted business of anthracite coal mining in the populous communities of Pennsylvania.

AMICUS CURIAE BRIEF SUPPORTING MAHON

Pennsylvania Attorney General.

SUPREME COURT DECISION: 8–1

HOLMES, J.

… Government hardly could go on if to some extent values incident to property could not be diminished without paying for every such change in the general law. As long recognized some values are enjoyed under an implied limitation and must yield to the police power. But obviously the implied limitation must have its limits or the contract and due process clauses are gone. One fact for consideration in determining such limits is the extent of the diminution. When it reaches a certain magnitude, in most if not in all cases there must be an exercise of eminent domain and compensation to sustain the act. So the question depends upon the particular facts. The greatest weight is given to the judgment of the legislature but it always is open to interested parties to contend that the legislature has gone beyond its constitutional power….

It is our opinion that the act cannot be sustained as an exercise of the police power, so far as it affects the mining of coal under streets or cities in places where the right to mine such coal has been reserved…. What makes the right to mine coal valuable is that it can be exercised with profit. To make it commercially impracticable to mine certain coal has very nearly the same effect for constitutional purposes as appropriating or destroying it. This we think that we are warranted in assuming that the statute does….

The rights of the public in a street purchased or laid out by eminent domain are those that it has paid for. If in any case its representatives have been so short sighted as to acquire only surface rights without the right of support we see no more authority for supplying the latter without compensation than there was for taking the right of way in the first place and refusing to pay for it because the public wanted it very much. The protection of private property in the 5th Amendment presupposes that it is wanted for public use, but provides that it shall not be taken for such use without compensation. A similar assumption is made in the decisions upon the 14th Amendment…. When this seemingly absolute protection is found to be qualified by the police power, the natural tendency of human nature is to extend the qualification more and more until at last private property disappears. But that cannot be accomplished in this way under the Constitution of the United States.

The general rule at least is that while property may be regulated to a certain extent, if regulation goes too far it will be recognized as a taking. It may be doubted how far exceptional cases, like the blowing up of a house to stop a conflagration, go—and if they go beyond the general rule, whether they do not stand as much upon tradition as upon principle. We are in danger of forgetting that a strong public desire to improve the public condition is not enough to warrant achieving the desire by a shorter cut than the constitutional way of paying for the change….

We assume, of course, that the statute was passed upon the conviction that an exigency existed that would warrant it, and we assume that an exigency exists that would warrant the exercise of eminent domain. But the question at bottom is upon whom the loss of the changes desired should fall. So far as private persons or communities have seen fit to take the risk of acquiring only surface rights, we cannot see that the fact that their risk has become a danger warrants the giving to them greater rights than they bought.

Decree reversed.

BRANDEIS, J., DISSENTING

... Coal in place is land, and the right of the owner to use his land is not absolute. He may not so use it as to create a public nuisance, and uses, once harmless, may, owing to changed conditions, seriously threaten the public welfare. Whenever they do, the legislature has power to prohibit such uses without paying compensation; and the power to prohibit extends alike to the manner, the character and the purpose of the use. Are we justified in declaring that the legislature of Pennsylvania has, in restricting the right to mine anthracite, exercised this power so arbitrarily as to violate the 14th Amendment?

Every restriction upon the use of property imposed in the exercise of the police power deprives the owner of some right theretofore enjoyed, and is, in that sense, an abridgment by the state of rights in property without making compensation. But restriction imposed to protect the public health, safety, or morals from dangers threatened is not a taking. The restriction here in question is merely the prohibition of a noxious use. The property so restricted remains in the possession of its owner. The state does not appropriate it or make any use of it. The state merely prevents the owner from making a use which interferes with paramount rights of the public. Whenever the use prohibited ceases to be noxious—as it may because of further change in local or social conditions—the restriction will have to be removed and the owner will again be free to enjoy his property as heretofore.

The restriction upon the use of this property cannot, of course, be lawfully imposed, unless its purpose is to protect the public. But the purpose of a restriction does not cease to be public, because incidentally some private persons may thereby receive gratuitously valuable special benefits.... Furthermore, a restriction, though imposed for a public purpose, will not be lawful, unless the restriction is an appropriate means to the public end. But to keep coal in place is surely an appropriate means of preventing subsidence of the surface; and ordinarily it is the only available means. Restriction upon use does not become inappropriate as a means, merely because it deprives the owner of the only use to which the property can then be profitably put.... Nor is a restriction imposed through exercise of the police power inappropriate as a means, merely because the same end might be effected through exercise of the power of eminent domain, or otherwise at public expense.... If by mining anthracite coal the owner would necessarily unloose poisonous gases, I suppose no one would doubt the power of the state to prevent the mining, without buying his coal fields. And why may not the state, likewise, without paying compensation, prohibit one from digging so deep or excavating so near the surface, as to expose the community to like dangers? In the latter case, as in the former, carrying on the business would be a public nuisance.

It is said that one fact for consideration in determining whether the limits of the police power have been exceeded is the extent of the resulting diminution in value, and that here the restriction destroys existing rights of property and contract. But values are relative. If we are to consider the value of the coal kept in place by the restriction, we should compare it with the value of all other parts of the land. That is, with the value not of the coal alone, but with the value of the whole property. The rights of an owner as against the public are not increased by dividing the interests in his property into surface and subsoil. The sum of the rights in the parts can not be greater than the rights in the whole....

QUESTIONS

1. Summarize the law of regulatory takings expressed in *Pennsylvania Coal*. Is the question of whether a regulation effects a taking a question of fact or of law? Almost all government actions like zoning statutes, minimum wage and maximum hour legislation, and environmental laws affect the value of property. Such actions can be more-or-less redistributive, or more-or-less costly, depending on where one draws the line distinguishing regulations from takings.

2. The attorney general of Pennsylvania argued that *Pennsylvania Coal* was before the Supreme Court in too narrow a posture and that it would be erroneous for the Court to view the questions presented as being limited only to the private property rights of the Mahons. The Pennsylvania brief urged the Court to consider the impact of the case on the larger population of Pennsylvania and the broad geographic areas affected by anthracite coal mining. Is there any evidence in Justice Holmes's opinion that the majority of the Court was persuaded to view the case in broader perspective? What of Justice Brandeis's dissent? During the sixteen years that they served on the Court together, Justice Holmes and Brandeis usually agreed on major constitutional issues. What issues divided them in *Pennsylvania Coal*?

3. The City of Scranton, Pennsylvania, and the Scranton Gas and Water Company intervened on behalf of the Mahons in *Pennsylvania Coal*. The Gas and Water Company argued that courts should take judicial notice (accept as true without the production of evidence) of the history of the disastrous results to property and the safety and lives of public of second mining. Is there any evidence that the majority of justices did so? Should they have? Should the justices have given any weight to the fact that the Kohler Act was passed unanimously as necessary for the protection of the life and health of Pennsylvania

citizens and was declared by the government to be necessary to eliminate a great public crisis?

4. In 1962, in *Goldblatt v. Town of Hempstead*, 369 U.S. 590, the Supreme Court held that a stringent antidredging ordinance that effectively prohibited continuation of a sand and gravel business did not constitute a taking. Can that holding be reconciled with *Pennsylvania Coal*? Should *Pennsylvania Coal* have been overruled? Or was the Court wise to preserve its prerogative to declare when a regulation has gone "too far"?

TAKINGS

Euclid v. Ambler Realty Co.
272 U.S. 365 (1926)

SETTING

In *Pennsylvania Coal* Justice Holmes held that Pennsylvania went "too far" when it passed the Kohler Act regulating the removal of anthracite coal. A more traditional form of land use regulation is zoning, which separates parcels of land into categories and specifies the uses that are allowed in each category. Zoning can be controversial, because it has a significant impact on the economic return an owner can get from a parcel of land. Zoning became commonplace in the United States with the urbanization that accompanied the industrial revolution and World War I. Four years after its *Pennsylvania Coal* decision, the Court addressed the question of whether a municipal zoning ordinance went "too far." The case originated in the village of Euclid, Ohio, a suburb of Cleveland.

The city of Cleveland, Ohio, was founded in 1796 on a small area of land at the mouth of the Cuyahoga River. With the beginning of its large industrial and commercial development, the city expanded to a larger flat plane thirty to fifty feet above the waters of Lake Erie. The village of Euclid, a residential suburb that lies east of Cleveland, was originally developed as a residential district by people seeking refuge from the noise and smoke of the big city. Shortly after the turn of the century, three main highways traversed the village from east to west and two railroads passed through it just north of Euclid Avenue, one of the highways and a main business artery of Cleveland. Recognizing the potential for industrial development in the village, the Ambler Realty Company of Cleveland purchased sixty-eight acres in the west end, abutting Euclid Avenue on the south and the Nickel Plate Railroad on the north, but did not develop it. Instead, it held the land vacant for speculative purposes. On both the east and west sides of Ambler Realty's property were residential subdivisions.

World War I stimulated considerable factory development in the greater Cleveland area and contributed to a real estate boom in all vacant land adjacent to railroads, including the vacant lands abutting railroad lines that passed through the village of Euclid. Despite the boom, however, no commercial, factory, or industrial structure or store was built in the three-and-a-half mile strip adjoining Euclid Avenue. Ambler Realty did not sell or develop its sixty-eight-acre parcel during this period.

By the early 1920s, it was evident that industrial development in Cleveland, which followed the railroad lines that passed through the village of Euclid, would expand into and eventually absorb the village. In an effort to restrain that occurrence, and following the lead of New York City (which adopted the first zoning ordinance in 1916), the village of Euclid adopted Ordinance No. 2812 in 1923, which established a comprehensive zoning plan for the village to regulate and restrict the location of trades, industries, apartments, duplexes, and single family residences. Under the ordinance, the village was divided into six use districts (U-1 to U-6), three height districts (H-1 to H-3), and four area districts (A-1 to A-4). The U-1 district was the only district in which buildings were restricted to those enumerated in the ordinance. In the other districts, the uses were cumulative: uses in U-2 included those enumerated in U-1, while uses in U-3 included uses enumerated in U-2 and U-1 and so forth.

The sixty-eight-acres owned by Ambler Realty came under three zones—U-2, U-3, and U-6. Only the U-6 category, which affected the northerly five hundred feet of the real estate company's property, allowed unrestricted manufacturing and industrial operations.

Soon after the zoning ordinance was adopted, Ambler Realty Company filed suit in the U.S. District Court for the Northern District of Ohio, alleging that the zoning ordinance lessened the value of its property, restricted and limited the uses to which it could be devoted, and imposed limitations and restrictions that violated the Ohio constitution and the Fifth Amendment to the Constitution of the United States. It sought to have enforcement of the ordinance permanently enjoined.

At trial, expert witnesses for Ambler Realty testified that the sixty-eight acres as a whole had a value of approximately $9,000 per acre if uses were unrestricted, but that if restricted to residential uses, the land had a value of only $3,000 per acre. Witnesses for the village of Euclid disagreed with the valuation figures and testified that safety and public health were the primary purposes of the ordinance.

The district court granted the injunction, stating, in part, that "the evidence clearly shows that the normal and reasonably to be expected use and development of [Ambler Realty's] land along Euclid Avenue is for general trade and commercial purposes...." The village of Euclid appealed to the Supreme Court of the United States.

HIGHLIGHTS OF SUPREME COURT ARGUMENTS

BRIEF FOR THE VILLAGE OF EUCLID

◆ Before Euclid's zoning ordinance may be declared unconstitutional, it must be found that it bears no relationship to the health, safety, public convenience, public comfort, or prosperity or general welfare.

◆ This Court previously has held that where the police power has been validly exercised, even a tremendous financial loss cannot stand in the way of the public welfare.

◆ Regulations adopted pursuant to the police power must be interpreted in the light of the conditions, circumstances, and particular needs and situation of a given community. If in the light of those circumstances the legislation has a relationship to the public health, safety, and general welfare, the legislation must be sustained as valid. The validity of a police power regulation must be determined by the general purpose of the ordinance, not its effect on one particular piece of property.

◆ Even though there is unquestionably a "taking" when a local government exercises its police power, it is not of such a nature that requires compensation under the Fifth Amendment.

◆ Comprehensive zoning ordinances have already been held to be constitutional exercises of the police power and, as of January 1, 1925, are in effect in some 320 municipalities across the United States.

AMICUS CURIAE BRIEF SUPPORTING THE VILLAGE OF EUCLID

Joint brief of The National Conference on City Planning, the Ohio State Conference on City Planning, the National Housing Association, and the Massachusetts Federation of Town Planning Boards.

BRIEF FOR AMBLER REALTY

◆ The belief that municipal authorities can assert some sort of communal control over privately owned land is at variance with the fundamental nature of private ownership and in derogation of the protection offered private property ownership by the Constitution.

◆ A municipality may not use the police power as an excuse to arbitrarily divert property from its appropriate and most economical uses, or diminish its value by imposing restrictions that have no basis other than the momentary tastes of public authorities.

◆ Regulations on the alienation and use of private property are looked upon with disfavor and must be construed strictly in the interest of the free transfer and use of property.

SUPREME COURT DECISION: 6–3

SUTHERLAND, J.

... The ordinance is assailed on the grounds that it is in derogation of section 1 of the Fourteenth Amendment to the federal Constitution in that it deprives appellee of liberty and property without due process of law and denies it the equal protection of the law[.]...

Before proceeding to a consideration of the case, it is necessary to determine the scope of the inquiry....

The record goes no farther than to show ... that the normal and reasonably to be expected use and development of that part of appellee's land adjoining Euclid avenue is for general trade and commercial purposes, particularly retail stores and like establishments, and that the normal and reasonably to be expected use and development of the residue of the land is for industrial and trade purposes. Whatever injury is inflicted by the mere existence and threatened enforcement of the ordinance is due to restrictions in respect of these and similar uses, to which perhaps should be added—if not included in the foregoing—restrictions in respect of apartment houses. Specifically there is nothing in the record to suggest that any damage results from the presence in the ordinance of those restrictions relating to churches, schools, libraries, and other public and semipublic buildings. It is neither alleged nor proved that there is or may be a demand for any part of appellee's land for any of the last-named uses, and we cannot assume the existence of facts which would justify an injunction upon this record in respect to this class of restrictions. For present purposes the provisions of the ordinance in respect of these uses may therefore be put aside as unnecessary to be considered. It is also unnecessary to consider the effect of the restrictions in respect of U-1 districts, since none of appellee's land falls within that class....

Building zone laws are of modern origin. They began in this country about twenty-five years ago. Until recent years, urban life was comparatively simple; but, with the great increase and concentration of population, problems have developed, and constantly are developing, which require, and will continue to require, additional restrictions in respect of the use and occupation of private lands in urban communities. Regulations, the wisdom, necessity, and validity of which, as applied to existing conditions, are so apparent that they are now uniformly sustained, a century ago, or even half a century ago, probably would have been rejected as arbitrary and oppressive. Such regulations are sustained, under the complex conditions of our day, for reasons analogous to those which justify traffic regulations, which, before the advent of automobiles and rapid transit street railways, would have been condemned as fatally arbitrary and unreasonable. And in this there is no inconsistency, for, while the meaning of constitutional guaranties never varies, the scope of their application must expand or contract to meet the new and different conditions which are constantly coming within the field of their operation. In a changing world it is impossible that it should be otherwise. But although a degree of elasticity is thus imparted, not to the meaning, but to the application of constitutional principles, statutes and ordinances, which, after giving due weight to the new conditions, are found clearly not to conform to the Constitution, of course, must fall.

The ordinance now under review, and all similar laws and regulations, must find their justification in some aspect of the police power, asserted for the public welfare. The line which in this field separates the legitimate from the illegitimate assumption of power is not capable of precise delimitation. It varies with circumstances and conditions. A regulatory zoning ordinance, which would be clearly valid as applied to the great cities, might be clearly invalid as applied to rural communities. In solving doubts, the maxim "*sic utere tuo ut alienum non laedas*," which lies at the foundation of so much of the common law of nuisances, ordinarily will furnish a fairly helpful clew. And the law of nuisances, likewise, may be consulted, not for the purpose of controlling, but for the helpful aid of its analogies in the process of ascertaining the scope of, the power. Thus the question whether the power exists to forbid the erection of a building of a particular kind or for a particular use, like the question whether a particular thing is a nuisance, is to be determined, not by an abstract consideration of the building or of the thing considered apart, but by considering it in connection with the circumstances and the locality.... A nuisance may be merely a right thing in the wrong place, like a pig in the parlor instead of the barnyard. If the validity of the legislative classification for zoning purposes be fairly debatable, the legislative judgment must be allowed to control....

There is no serious difference of opinion in respect of the validity of laws and regulations fixing the height of buildings within reasonable limits, the character of materials and methods of construction, and the adjoining area which must be left open, in order to minimize the danger of fire or collapse, the evils of overcrowding and the like, and excluding from residential sections offensive trades, industries and structures likely to create nuisances....

Here, however, the exclusion is in general terms of all industrial establishments, and it may thereby happen that not only offensive or dangerous industries will be excluded, but those which are neither offensive nor dangerous will share the same fate. But this is no more than happens in respect of many practice-forbidding laws which this court has upheld, although drawn in general terms so as to include individual cases that may turn out to be innocuous in themselves.... The inclusion of a reasonable margin, to insure effective enforcement, will not put upon a law, otherwise valid, the stamp of invalidity. Such laws may also find their justification in the fact that, in some fields, the bad fades into the good by such insensible degrees that the two are not capable of being readily distinguished and separated in terms of legislation. In the light of these considerations, we are not prepared to say that the end in view was not sufficient to justify the general rule of the ordinance, although some industries of an innocent character might fall within the proscribed class....

We find no difficulty in sustaining restrictions of the kind thus far reviewed. The serious question in the case arises over the provisions of the ordinance excluding from residential districts apartment houses, business houses, retail stores and shops, and other like establishments. This question involves the validity of what is really the crux of the more recent zoning legislation, namely, the creation and maintenance of residential districts, from which business and trade of every sort, including hotels and apartment houses, are excluded. Upon that question this court has not thus far spoken. The decisions of the state courts are numerous and conflicting; but those which broadly sustain the power greatly outnumber those which deny it altogether or narrowly limit it, and it is very apparent that there is a constantly increasing tendency in the direction of the broader view....

[These] decisions ... agree that the exclusion of buildings devoted to business, trade, etc., from residential districts, bears a rational relation to the health and safety of the community....

It is true that when, if ever, the provisions set forth in the ordinance in tedious and minute detail, come to be concretely applied to particular premises, including those of the appellee, or to particular conditions, or to be considered in connection with specific complaints, some of them, or even many of them, may be found to be clearly arbitrary and unreasonable. But

where the equitable remedy of injunction is sought, as it is here, not upon the ground of a present infringement or denial of a specific right, or of a particular injury in process of actual execution, but upon the broad ground that the mere existence and threatened enforcement of the ordinance, by materially and adversely affecting values and curtailing the opportunities of the market, constitute a present and irreparable injury, the court will not scrutinize its provisions, sentence by sentence, to ascertain by a process of piecemeal dissection whether there may be, here and there, provisions of a minor character, or relating to matters of administration, or not shown to contribute to the injury complained of, which, if attacked separately, might not withstand the test of constitutionality. In respect of such provisions, of which specific complaint is not made, it cannot be said that the landowner has suffered or is threatened with an injury which entitles him to challenge their constitutionality....

Decree reversed.

VAN DEVANTER, MCREYNOLDS, AND BUTLER, J.J., DISSENTED WITHOUT OPINION

QUESTIONS

1. According to the Court in *Euclid*, what is the relationship between the state's police power and the individual's right to compensation for a public taking of property? How is the *Euclid* view different from the view in *Pennsylvania Coal*? Is *Euclid* a departure from *Pennsylvania Coal*, or can the two decisions be reconciled?

2. In all likelihood, Euclid's zoning ordinances were motivated by the community's desire to exclude ethnic eastern Europeans from moving from nearby Cleveland. At one point in his opinion, Justice Sutherland refers to an apartment house as "a mere parasite." Is such a motive a valid exercise of the police power? Should the Court inquire into a community's motives in adopting zoning ordinances?

Compare *Euclid* with *Nectow v. Cambridge*, 277 U.S. 183 (1928). In *Nectow* the Court unanimously invalidated a particular application of the zoning ordinances of the city of Cambridge, Massachusetts. Justice Sutherland wrote:

> The governmental power to interfere by zoning regulations with the general rights of the land owner by restricting the character of his use, is not unlimited, and, other questions aside, such restriction cannot be imposed if it does not bear a substantial relation to the public health, safety, morals, or general welfare. Here, the express finding of the [special judicial] master, ... confirmed by the court below, is that the health, safety, convenience, and general welfare of the inhabitants of the part of the city affected will not be promoted by the disposition made by the ordinance of the locus in question.

Should the Court have made a similar finding in *Euclid*?

3. The three justices who dissented from the majority in *Euclid* provided no reasons for their dissent. Why might they choose to dissent without articulating their reasoning?

4. In *Euclid*, Ambler Realty company complained that the Euclid zoning ordinance diminished the value of its land because it could not develop most of its property at manufacturing and industrial levels. Assume that the company had purchased the property with the intent of building homes on it and the zoning ordinance designated the area for manufacturing/industrial uses but prohibited housing. Could Ambler Realty have relied on the Fifth Amendment under those facts?

TAKINGS

Penn Central Transportation Company v. City of New York
438 U.S. 104 (1978)

SETTING

During the 1950s, state, federal, and municipal governments became increasingly concerned with the preservation of buildings and sites that have historic, aesthetic, or cultural significance. By 1965, all fifty states and at least fifty-one cities had enacted some form of historic preservation laws. In 1966, Congress passed the National Historical Preservation Act. In 1969, the National Environmental Policy Act made historic preservation an integral part of the nation's environmental goals. A year later, the Urban Transportation Act required that planning for mass transit projects include consideration of the effects on "historical and cultural assets."

A century before passage of the National Environmental Policy Act, in 1869, Cornelius Vanderbilt received permission from the New York legislature to build a railroad station in New York City. The Grand Central Depot opened in 1871, but quickly became inadequate. In 1903, the city authorized construction of a new terminal. Ten years later, the new Grand Central Terminal was opened to the public. It was considered a masterpiece of architecture and comprehensive urban design, serving as a gateway to New York City. Because of the terminal and the uses surrounding it, Park Avenue became the most prestigious residential district in the nation. The terminal was eight stories high, with a Beaux Arts facade, magnificent columns, carefully sculptured details, paintings of the constellations by Paul Helleu, and was topped by statuary of Mercury, Hercules, and Minerva around the clock on the 42nd Street side.

In August 1967, over the objection of Penn Central Transportation Company (the 95 percent shareholder in the New York Harlem Railroad Company that owned Grand Central Station), the Landmarks Preservation Commission of the City of New York entered an order designating Grand Central Terminal and its site a "landmark" and a "landmark site." In making the designation the Commission stated:

> Grand Central Station, one of the great buildings of America, evokes a spirit that is unique in this City. It combines distinguished architecture with a brilliant engineering solution, wedded to one of the most fabulous railroad terminals of our time. Monumental in scale, this great building functions as well today as it did when it was built. In style it represents the best of the French Beaux Arts.

The effect of the landmark designation was to bar any construction on the site and any alteration of the exterior appearance of the building without prior approval of the Landmarks Commission. The designation also required Penn Central to keep the building in "good repair" and imposed criminal sanctions for violation of the Landmark Commission's order.

In 1970, Penn Central's precarious financial situation forced it into bankruptcy reorganization. In 1969, as part of its plan to improve its financial condition, Penn Central entered into an agreement with UGP Properties, Inc., under which UGP either would tear down Grand Central Station and construct a new office building, or construct a fifty-five-story office tower above the existing building. The agreement guaranteed Penn Central an income of $1 million a year during construction, and minimum rental of $3 million per year for at least fifty years thereafter.

UGP hired the architectural firm of Marcel Breuer and Associates to design the proposed office building. It submitted the Breuer design to the Landmarks Commission, which rejected both the proposal to tear down the building and the proposal to construct an office tower above it. The

Commission reasoned that tearing down an historic building was no way to preserve it and that constructing a fifty-six-story modern office building over an eight-story building with a flamboyant Beaux-Arts facade was an "aesthetic joke" because the new building would overwhelm the terminal by its sheer mass and "would reduce the landmark itself to the status of a curiosity." However, pursuant to a New York city ordinance that allowed property owners to transfer unused development rights to other lots, Penn Central was given transferred development rights (TDRs) that it was entitled to use in developing property it owned across the street from Grand Central Station. The TDRs allowed Penn Central to develop another parcel with 20 percent more floor space than it otherwise would have been entitled to do.

Penn Central did not develop other plans after the Commission rejected its proposals. Instead, it filed suit in New York Supreme Court claiming that application of the preservation law to its property was a taking of property under the Fifth Amendment and an arbitrary deprivation of property under the Fourteenth Amendment. It sought to have the city enjoined from using the Landmarks Law to impede construction above Grand Central Station, and to be compensated monetarily.

The New York Supreme Court, Trial Term, granted declaratory and injunctive relief, but severed the question of damages. The Appellate Division reversed, holding that Penn Central had shown only that it had lost the most profitable use of its property, not that it had been deprived unconstitutionally of its property. The Court of Appeals affirmed. Penn Central appealed to the Supreme Court of the United States.

Highlights of Supreme Court Arguments

Brief for Penn Central

◆ Penn Central's right to construct an office building over Grand Central Terminal is a property right, fully protected by the Constitution. The Landmarks Law clearly operates to "take" that property. This Court has previously held that an owner is constitutionally entitled to compensation for the taking of air space above land.

◆ The Due Process Clause prevents the public from forcing private owners to bear burdens that should properly be borne by the public as a whole. The claim that the action taken is justified under the police power of the state cannot justify disregard of constitutional prohibitions against taking of private property.

◆ It is wrong to force the property owner to bear the burden of proving that it is incapable of earning a reasonable return on its remaining property if air rights are taken without compensation.

◆ The determination of just compensation for particular property is a judicial function. The property owner is entitled to receive as compensation an amount equal to whatever is determined to be the property's value. Diminution of the value of property is sufficient to require compensation.

AMICUS CURIAE BRIEFS SUPPORTING PENN CENTRAL

Real Estate Board of New York; Pacific Legal Foundation.

BRIEF FOR NEW YORK CITY

◆ It has been recognized since *Euclid v. Ambler Realty Co.* that federal, state, and local governments may regulate the use of private property. When a land-use regulation is within the state's police power, the burden is on the property owner to establish that property has been confiscated. It is insufficient to show merely that the regulation has deprived the owner of the most profitable use of the property.

◆ The validity of a land-use regulation requires the balancing of three factors: the importance of the regulation to the public good; the reasonableness with which the regulation attempts to achieve that good; and how substantially the regulation affects the economic viability of the particular parcel.

◆ Treating buildings with historical significance differently from buildings that are not landmarks is a legitimate state interest.

◆ Penn Central is not entitled to compensation for the regulation imposed on the use of the terminal. There has been no exercise of the power of eminent domain in this case.

AMICUS CURIAE BRIEFS SUPPORTING NEW YORK CITY

United States; joint brief of the National Trust for Historic Preservation, cities of New Orleans, Boston, and San Antonio, National Conference of State Historic Preservation Officers, Don't Tear It Down, National Institute of Municipal Law Officers, National League of Cities, and Sierra Club; Committee to Save Grand Central Station; State of New York; State of California.

SUPREME COURT DECISION: 6–3

BRENNAN, J.

... [W]e must decide whether the application of New York City's Landmarks Preservation Law to the parcel of land occupied by Grand Central Terminal has "taken" its owners' property in violation of the Fifth and Fourteenth Amendments....

The New York City law is typical of many urban landmark laws in that its primary method of achieving its goals is not by acquisitions of historic properties, but rather by involving public entities in land-use decisions affecting these properties and providing services, standards, controls, and incentives that will encourage preservation by private owners and users. While the law does place special restrictions on landmark properties as a necessary feature to the attainment of its larger objectives, the major theme of the law is to ensure the owners of any such properties both a "reasonable return" on their investments and maximum latitude to use their parcels for purposes not inconsistent with the preservation goals....

Before considering appellants' specific contentions, it will be useful to review the factors that have shaped the jurisprudence of the Fifth Amendment injunction "nor shall private property be taken for public use, without just compensation." The question of what constitutes a "taking" for purposes of the Fifth Amendment has proved to be a problem of considerable difficulty. While this Court has recognized that the "Fifth Amendment's guarantee ... [is] designed to bar Government from forcing some people alone to bear public burdens which, in all fairness and justice, should be borne by the public as a whole," *Armstrong v. United States*, 364 U.S. 40 (1960), this Court, quite simply, has been unable to develop any "set formula" for determining when "justice and fairness" require that economic injuries caused by public action be compensated by the government, rather than remain disproportionately concentrated on a few persons....

In engaging in these essentially ad hoc, factual inquiries, the Court's decisions have identified several factors that have particular significance. The economic impact of the regulation on the claimant and, particularly, the extent to which the regulation has interfered with distinct investment-backed expectations are, of course, relevant considerations.... So, too, is the character of the governmental action. A "taking" may more readily be found when the interference with property can be characterized as a physical invasion by government ... than when interference arises from some public program adjusting the ben-

efits and burdens of economic life to promote the common good.

"Government hardly could go on if to some extent values incident to property could not be diminished without paying for every such change in the general law," *Pennsylvania Coal Co. v. Mahon*, and this Court has accordingly recognized, in a wide variety of contexts, that government may execute laws or programs that adversely affect recognized economic values. Exercises of the taxing power are one obvious example. A second are the decisions in which this Court has dismissed "taking" challenges on the ground that, while the challenged government action caused economic harm, it did not interfere with interests that were sufficiently bound up with the reasonable expectations of the claimant to constitute "property" for Fifth Amendment purposes....

More importantly for the present case, in instances in which a state tribunal reasonably concluded that "the health, safety, morals, or general welfare" would be promoted by prohibiting particular contemplated uses of land, this Court has upheld land-use regulations that destroyed or adversely affected recognized real property interests....

Zoning laws generally do not affect existing uses of real property, but "taking" challenges have also been held to be without merit in a wide variety of situations when the challenged governmental actions prohibited a beneficial use to which individual parcels had previously been devoted and thus caused substantial individualized harm....

Pennsylvania Coal Co. v. Mahon is the leading case for the proposition that a state statute that substantially furthers important public policies may so frustrate distinct investment-backed expectations as to amount to a "taking."...

Finally, government actions that may be characterized as acquisitions of resources to permit or facilitate uniquely public functions have often been held to constitute "takings."...

In contending that the New York City law has "taken" their property in violation of the Fifth and Fourteenth Amendments, appellants make a series of arguments, which, while tailored to the facts of this case, essentially urge that any substantial restriction imposed pursuant to a landmark law must be accompanied by just compensation if it is to be constitutional....

They first observe that the airspace above the Terminal is a valuable property interest[.]... They urge that the Landmarks Law has deprived them of any gainful use of their "air rights" above the Terminal and that, irrespective of the value of the remainder of their parcel, the city has "taken" their right to this superadjacent airspace, thus entitling them to "just compensation" measured by the fair market value of these air rights.

Apart from our own disagreement with appellants' characterization of the effect of the New York City law the submission that appellants may establish a "taking" simply by showing that they have been denied the ability to exploit a property interest that they heretofore had believed was available for development is quite simply untenable.... "Taking" jurisprudence does not divide a single parcel into discrete segments and attempt to determine whether rights in a particular segment have been entirely abrogated. In deciding whether a particular governmental action has effected a taking, this Court focuses rather both on the character of the action and on the nature and extent of the interference with rights in the parcel as a whole—here, the city tax block designated as the "landmark site."

Secondly, appellants, focusing on the character and impact of the New York City law, argue that it effects a "taking" because its operation has significantly diminished the value of the Terminal site....

Stated baldly, appellants' position appears to be that the only means of ensuring that selected owners are not singled out to endure financial hardship for no reason is to hold that any restriction imposed on individual landmarks pursuant to the New York City scheme is a "taking" requiring the payment of "just compensation." Agreement with this argument would, of course, invalidate not just New York City's law, but all comparable landmark legislation in the Nation. We find no merit in it....

Equally without merit is the related argument that the decision to designate a structure as a landmark "is inevitably arbitrary or at least subjective, because it is basically a matter of taste" thus unavoidably singling out individual landowners for disparate and unfair treatment. The argument has a particularly hollow ring in this case. For appellants not only did not seek judicial review of either the designation or of the denials of the certificates of appropriateness and of no exterior effect, but do not even now suggest that the Commission's decisions concerning the Terminal were in any sense arbitrary or unprincipled. But, in any event, a landmark owner has a right to judicial review of any Commission decision, and, quite simply, there is no basis whatsoever for a conclusion that courts will have any greater difficulty identifying arbitrary or discriminatory action in the context of landmark regulation than in the context of classic zoning or indeed in any other context.

Next, appellants observe that New York City's law differs from zoning laws and historic-district ordinances in that the Landmarks Law does not impose identical or similar restrictions on all structures located in particular physical communities. It follows, they argue, that New York City's law is inherently incapable of producing the fair and equitable distribution of benefits and burdens of governmental action which is characteristic of zoning laws and historic-district legislation and which they maintain is a constitutional requirement if "just compensation" is not to be afforded. It is, of course, true that the Landmarks Law has a more severe impact on some landowners than on others, but that in itself does not mean that the law effects a "taking." Legislation designed to promote the general welfare commonly burdens some more than others.... For example, the property owner in *Euclid* who wished to use its property for industrial purposes was affected far more severely by the ordinance than its neighbors who wished to use their land for residences.

In any event, appellants' repeated suggestions that they are solely burdened and unbenefited is factually inaccurate. This contention overlooks the fact that the New York City law applies to vast numbers of structures in the city in addition to the Terminal—all the structures contained in the 31 historic districts and over 400 individual landmarks, many of which are close to the Terminal....

Appellants' final broad-based attack would have us treat the law as an instance ... in which government, acting in an enterprise capacity, has appropriated part of their property for some strictly governmental purpose.... [T]he Landmarks Law neither exploits appellants' parcel for city purposes nor facilitates nor arises from any entrepreneurial operations of the city.... The Landmarks Law's effect is simply to prohibit appellants or anyone else from occupying portions of the airspace above the Terminal, while permitting appellants to use the remainder of the parcel in a gainful fashion....

Rejection of appellants' broad arguments is not, however, the end of our inquiry, for all we thus far have established is that the New York City law is not rendered invalid by its failure to provide "just compensation" whenever a landmark owner is restricted in the exploitation of property interests, such as air rights, to a greater extent than provided for under applicable zoning laws. We now must consider whether the interference with appellants' property is of such a magnitude that "there must be an exercise of eminent domain and compensation to sustain [it]." *Pennsylvania Coal Co. v. Mahon.* That inquiry may be narrowed to the question of the severity of the impact of the law on appellants' parcel, and its resolution in turn requires a careful assessment of the impact of the regulation on the Terminal site.

[T]he New York City law does not interfere in any way with the present uses of the Terminal. Its designation as a landmark not only permits but contemplates that appellants may continue to use the property precisely as it has been used for the past 65 years: as a railroad terminal containing office space and concessions. So the law does not interfere with what must be regarded as Penn Central's primary expectation concerning the use of the parcel. More importantly, on this record, we must regard the New York City law as permitting Penn Central not only to profit from the Terminal but also to obtain a "reasonable return" on its investment....

Affirmed.

REHNQUIST AND STEVENS, J.J., AND BURGER, C.J., DISSENTING

... The question in this case is whether the cost associated with the city of New York's desire to preserve a limited number of "landmarks" within its borders must be borne by all of its taxpayers or whether it can instead be imposed entirely on the owners of the individual properties....

Because the Taking Clause of the Fifth Amendment has not always been read literally, however, the constitutionality of appellees' actions requires a closer scrutiny of this Court's interpretation of the three key words in the Taking Clause—"property," "taken," and "just compensation."

Appellees do not dispute that valuable property rights have been destroyed. And the Court has frequently emphasized that the term "property" as used in the Taking Clause includes the entire "group of rights inhering in the citizen's [ownership]." *United States v. General Motors Corp.*, 323 U.S. 373 (1945)....

While neighboring landowners are free to use their land and "air rights" in any way consistent with the broad boundaries of New York zoning, Penn Central, absent the permission of appellees, must forever maintain its property in its present state. The prop-

erty has been thus subjected to a nonconsensual servitude not borne by any neighboring or similar properties.

Appellees have thus destroyed—in a literal sense, "taken"—substantial property rights of Penn Central. While the term "taken" might have been narrowly interpreted to include only physical seizures of property rights, "the construction of the phrase has not been so narrow. The courts have held that the deprivation of the former owner rather than the accretion of a right or interest to the sovereign constitutes the taking." Id.... Because "not every destruction or injury to property by governmental action has been held to be a 'taking' in the constitutional sense," *Armstrong v. United States* [364 U.S. 40 (1960)], however, this does not end our inquiry. But an examination of the two exceptions where the destruction of property does not constitute a taking demonstrates that a compensable taking has occurred here.

[T]he Court [has] recognized that the government can prevent a property owner from using his property to injure others without having to compensate the owner for the value of the forbidden use....

The nuisance exception to the taking guarantee is not coterminous with the police power itself. The question is whether the forbidden use is dangerous to the safety, health, or welfare of others....

Appellees are not prohibiting a nuisance. The record is clear that the proposed addition to the Grand Central Terminal would be in full compliance with zoning, height limitations, and other health and safety requirements. Instead, appellees are seeking to preserve what they believe to be an outstanding example of beaux-arts architecture. Penn Central is prevented from further developing its property basically because too good a job was done in designing and building it. The city of New York, because of its unadorned admiration for the design, has decided that the owners of the building must preserve it unchanged for the benefit of sightseeing New Yorkers and tourists.

Even where the government prohibits a noninjurious use, the Court has ruled that a taking does not take place if the prohibition applies over a broad cross section of land and thereby "secure[s] an average reciprocity of advantage." *Pennsylvania Coal Co. v. Mahon*. It is for this reason that zoning does not constitute a "taking." While zoning at times reduces individual property values, the burden is shared relatively evenly and it is reasonable to conclude that on the whole an individual who is harmed by one aspect of the zoning will be benefited by another.

Here, however, a multimillion dollar loss has been imposed on appellants; it is uniquely felt and is not offset by any benefits flowing from the preservation of some 400 other "landmarks" in New York City. Appellees have imposed a substantial cost on less than one one-tenth of one percent of the buildings in New York City for the general benefit of all its people. It is exactly this imposition of general costs on a few individuals at which the "taking" protection is directed....

Appellees, apparently recognizing that the constraints imposed on a landmark site constitute a taking for Fifth Amendment purposes, do not leave the property owner empty-handed.... [T]he property owner may theoretically "transfer" his previous right to develop the landmark property to adjacent properties if they are under his control. Appellees have coined this system "Transfer Development Rights," or TDRs.

Of all the terms used in the Taking Clause, "just compensation" has the strictest meaning. The Fifth Amendment does not allow simply an approximate compensation but requires "a full and perfect equivalent for the property taken." *Monongahela Navigation Co. v. United States*, 148 U.S. 312 [(1893)]....

Because the record on appeal is relatively slim, I would remand to the Court of Appeals for a determination of whether TDRs constitute a "full and perfect equivalent for the property taken."

Over 50 years ago, Mr. Justice Holmes, speaking for the Court, warned that the courts were "in danger of forgetting that a strong public desire to improve the public condition is not enough to warrant achieving the desire by a shorter cut than the constitutional way of paying for the change." *Pennsylvania Coal Co. v. Mahon*. The Court's opinion in this case demonstrates that the danger thus foreseen has not abated....

QUESTIONS

1. In the wake of the Court's decision in *Penn Central*, what is the difference between the noncompensable regulations of property pursuant to the police power, and the taking of property for public use under the Fifth and Fourteenth Amendments? Does *Penn Central* resolve the conflict between *Mugler* and *Pennsylvania Coal*?

2. Although Penn Central objected to having Grand Central Station designated as an historic landmark, it did not seek judicial review of the designation. Neither did it seek judicial review of the Commission's rejection of its plans to construct the fifty-six-story office tower. Having failed to pursue legal challenges at those stages, should the Penn Central Transportation Company have been barred from pursuing the issues in *Penn Central*?

3. Does the Court's decision in *Penn Central* have the effect of shifting the burden of preserving historic monuments for the good of society to the private property owner? Is Justice Brennan correct that designation of property as an historic landmark "enhances the economic position of the landowner" because of the system of transferable development rights? If it were not for the transferable development rights awarded to Penn Central, would Justice Brennan have decided *Penn Central* differently?

   What factors should be taken into consideration in determining whether all reasonable use of property has been denied as a result of regulatory activity? How should "reasonable return" on investment property be determined?

4. If the Supreme Court had accepted Penn Central's argument that depriving it of its air rights—and, consequently, of considerable income—was a taking for which compensation must be paid, would historic preservation in the United States be virtually impossible? What role, if any, should that potential consequence have played in the Court's analysis of the constitutional issues in *Penn Central*?

TAKINGS

Lucas v. South Carolina Coastal Council
505 U.S. 1003 (1992)

SETTING

In *Penn Central*, the Court announced three criteria for evaluating takings claims: (1) the economic impact of the regulation on the claimant; (2) the extent to which the regulation interferes with distinct investment-backed expectations; (3) the character of the government action. Despite upholding the designation of Grand Central Station as an historic site, the fact that the vote was 6–3 with a strong dissent suggested to some that the Court's deferential attitude toward state regulation of property was on the wane. Furthermore, the Court held that a governmental action having the character of a "physical invasion" was more likely to constitute a "taking" than an action having the effect of "adjusting the benefits and burdens of economic life to promote the common good." Not surprisingly, takings litigation did not diminish.

In *Agins v. Tiburon*, 447 U.S. 255 (1980), the Court upheld a city zoning ordinance that imposed severe density restrictions on scenic property overlooking San Francisco Bay, and that prevented a developer from building as many houses on the land as were allowed when he purchased the property. Despite its unanimous holding, the Court set forth the following test: if an ordinance either fails to "substantially advance legitimate state interests," or denies an owner of the "economically viable use of his land," a general zoning law will constitute a taking for which compensation is required. Such language put cities and states on notice that the justices might not remain as deferential to zoning and land use regulations as they had been. That message was reinforced in 1987 in *First English Evangelical Lutheran Church v. County of Los Angeles*, 482 U.S. 304 (1987). The Court declared that the Fifth Amendment guarantee was designed "not to limit the governmental interference with property rights *per se*, but rather to secure compensation in the event of otherwise proper interference amounting to a taking."

These hints that the Supreme Court might be more willing to intercede against the states on behalf of the rights of private property owners were an encouraging sign to those whose property had been affected by land use regulations. One such owner was South Carolina real estate developer David H. Lucas.

In December 1986, Lucas purchased two beach lots for $975,000 in the Wild Dunes Development on the Isle of Palms in Charleston County, South Carolina. Both lots were zoned single-family residential. They were separated by a lot on which a home had been built in the 1980s and there were homes on either side of each lot. Lucas intended to build two homes—one for himself and one for resale. At the time that he purchased the property no state, county, or municipal regulations prevented him from building the homes. Before Lucas's purchases, however, the lots suffered from severe episodic erosion. Between 1981 and 1983, the erosion was so serious that the mayor of Isle of Palms issued twelve emergency orders for sand scraping and sandbagging to protect pre-existing homes that were close to Lucas's property. In 1983, the South Carolina Coastal Council issued an erosion control permit to construct an 850-foot rock revetment immediately west of Lucas's lots, and a 1,300-foot rock revetment to the east of the property.

In July 1988, nineteen months after Lucas purchased the two lots, the South Carolina Beachfront Management Act went into effect. That act was aimed at "discouraging new construction in close proximity to the beach/dune system and encouraging those who have erected structures too close to the system to retreat from it." The act directed the South Carolina Coastal Council to implement a forty-year retreat policy by drawing setback lines along the coast. No new construction or reconstruction was to be allowed seaward of the setback line. The Council drew a setback line behind Lucas's property based on historical evidence of severe erosion in the area during the previous forty years.

Lucas did not challenge the location of the setback line. Instead he filed suit in the Court of Common Pleas of Charleston County, claiming that the Act so restricted his ownership rights that it violated the South Carolina constitution and the Takings Clause of the Fifth Amendment.

The trial court found that the act worked a total and permanent loss in the value of Lucas's property and awarded him $1,232,387.50 in damages. It further ordered that Lucas turn over title to the lots to the state. The Coastal Council appealed to the South Carolina supreme court.

In 1990, while the case was on appeal, the South Carolina legislature enacted amendments to the Beachfront Management Act. The amendments allowed property owners to seek a special permit from the Council if their planned construction or reconstruction was not on a primary ocean-front sand dune or on the active beach. The amendments also stipulated that in applying for a special permit, property owners agreed to remove offending structures if the Council found them "detrimental to the public health, safety, or welfare."

After adoption of the amendments, the Coastal Council petitioned the state supreme court to consider the impact of the amendments on Lucas's claim that there had been a taking of his property. The court denied the petition. On the merits, however, it reversed the court of common pleas. It held that Lucas had erroneously relied on the legal position that he had lost "all economically viable use" of his property. It also held that a legitimate use of a state's police power makes the object of a land-use regulation a nuisance and thus immune from compensation under the Takings Clause. The South Carolina supreme court denied Lucas's petition for rehearing. He petitioned the Supreme Court of the United States for a writ of certiorari.

Highlights of Supreme Court Arguments

BRIEF FOR LUCAS

◆ This case is ripe for adjudication because the trial court found that Lucas's property had been permanently taken as a result of application of the 1988 legislation.

◆ The South Carolina supreme court's application of the nuisance exception to the Takings Clause short-circuits any attempt to balance private rights and public interests. At the time several of this Court's decisions regarding the nuisance exception were decided, the concept of taking property by regulation had not been recognized.

◆ Although this Court has applied a variety of tests to determine if just compensation is due under the Fifth Amendment, it has remained true to the

Pennsylvania Coal principle that private rights cannot be ignored, even in the face of legitimate state interests.

◆ There is no precedent for the proposition asserted by the South Carolina Supreme Court that just compensation can be denied in cases where the value of property is virtually eliminated by the application of a land-use regulation. There is no public policy justification for recognizing a nuisance exception in cases where the value of property is totally eliminated by regulation.

◆ If South Carolina is intent on promoting tourism and recreation along its shore, it must be prepared to compensate land owners if it insists they not develop their property and must leave it in its natural state. The burden of confiscatory environmental regulation should fall on society and not on individual property owners.

◆ To the extent this Court wishes to recognize a nuisance exception to the Takings Clause, it must be narrowly drawn. The Court should also articulate an objective federal definition of nuisance-like harms for purposes of Takings Clause litigation.

AMICUS CURIAE BRIEFS SUPPORTING LUCAS

United States; Defenders of Property Rights, American Sheep Industries Association, Inc., Environmental Conservation Organization, Land Improvement Contractors Association, and Outdoor Advertising Association of America, Inc.; U.S. Senators Steve Symms, Larry Craig, Don Nickles, and Conrad Burns; National Association of Realtors; Pacific Legal Foundation; The Nemours Foundation, Inc.; National Association of Home Builders, and International Council of Shopping Centers; Mountain States Legal Foundation; the National Cattlemen's Association.

BRIEF FOR THE SOUTH CAROLINA COASTAL COUNCIL

◆ Lucas's claim of a permanent taking is not ripe, because the 1990 amendments allow him the opportunity to apply for a permit to construct homes seaward of the baseline and he has not done so. This Court has consistently held that a land-use challenge is not ripe if the property owner has failed to apply for a variance or to seek a determination of whether a permit would be issued by the regulatory agency.

◆ If the Court nonetheless concludes that the case is ripe for adjudication, it should reject Lucas's extreme position that the economic impact of a state's restriction on the use of property is the sole factor in determining whether a regulation amounts to a taking. The character of the government action, whether it was aimed at preventing injury to public health and safety and other property, and the extent to which it interferes with reasonable investment-backed expectations, also needs to be considered. This Court has always relied on *ad hoc*, factual inquiries into the circumstances of each case.

It has never adopted a legal formula for identifying when a taking has occurred.

    ◆ The economic impacts, even severe ones, on Lucas's property are justified because of the serious injury to public health and safety and physical damage to nearby properties that undoubtedly occur without the regulations. Recent hurricanes in the area graphically demonstrate this problem.

    ◆ Governments do not owe compensation in situations in which a petitioner's investment-back expectations in property are unreasonable. Lucas has been associated with the property at issue in this case since the early 1980s and knew the lots were in an area marked by shifting sands and subject to ongoing serious threats of erosion. He had reason to know at the time of purchase that government could validly restrict uses of the land.

    ◆ Lucas has not lost all use of his property. At a minimum, he retains the right to make passive and recreational use of the parcels. The property remains extremely valuable for purposes short of permanent, residential development.

AMICUS CURIAE BRIEFS SUPPORTING THE SOUTH CAROLINA COASTAL COUNCIL

National Growth Management Leadership Project; Broward County, Leon County, Manatee County, and the city of North Miami Beach, Florida; State of California; National Trust for Historic Preservation in the United States; Nueces County, Texas; Scituate, Massachusetts Conservation Commission; American Littoral Society; Chesapeake Bay Foundation; Coast Alliance; Environmental Defense Fund; National Audubon Society; National Resources Defense Council; National Wildlife Federation; South Carolina Wildlife Federation; joint brief of Dr. Joseph F. Donoghue, Dr. Paul T. Gayes, Dr. Joseph T. Kelly, Dr. Orrin Pilke, Dr. Rutherford H. Platt, and Dr. Stan Riggs; joint brief of States of Florida, Alabama, Connecticut, Delaware, Georgia, Hawaii, Iowa, Maine, Maryland, Massachusetts, Michigan, Minnesota, Nevada, New Jersey, New Mexico, New Hampshire, New York, North Carolina, Oregon, Pennsylvania, Rhode Island, Utah, Vermont, Virginia, Wisconsin, and Texas; Guam and Puerto Rico; joint brief of Sierra Club, the Humane Society of the United States, and the American Institute of Biological Sciences.

Supreme Court Decision: 6–3

SCALIA, J.

... As a threshold matter, we must briefly address the Council's suggestion that this case is inappropriate for plenary review. After briefing and argument before the South Carolina Supreme Court, but prior to issuance of that court's opinion, the Beachfront Management Act was amended to authorize the Council, in certain circumstances, to issue "special permits" for the construction or reconstruction of habitable structures seaward of the baseline. According to the Council, this amendment renders Lucas's claim of a permanent deprivation unripe, as Lucas may yet be able to secure permission to build on his property.... Because petitioner "has not yet obtained a final decision regarding how [he] will be allowed to develop [his] property," *Williamson County Regional Planning Comm'n of Johnson City v. Hamilton Bank*, 473 U.S. 190 (1985), the Council argues that he is not yet entitled to definitive adjudication of his takings claim in this Court.

We think these considerations would preclude review had the South Carolina Supreme Court rested its judgment on ripeness grounds, as it was (essentially) invited to do by the Council. The South Carolina Supreme Court shrugged off the possibility of further administrative and trial proceedings, however, preferring to dispose of Lucas's takings claims on the merits. This unusual disposition does not preclude Lucas from applying for a permit under the 1990 amendment for *future* construction, and challenging, on takings grounds, any denial. But it does preclude, both practically and legally, any takings claim with respect to Lucas's *past* deprivation, *i.e.*, for his having been denied construction rights during the period before the 1990 amendment....

In these circumstances, we think it would not accord with sound process to insist that Lucas pursue the late-created "special permit" procedure before his takings claim can be considered ripe. Lucas has properly alleged Article III injury-in-fact in this case, with respect to both the pre-1990 and post-1990 constraints placed on the use of his parcels by the Beachfront Management Act....

Prior to Justice Holmes' exposition in *Pennsylvania Coal Co. v. Mahon*, it was generally thought that the Takings Clause reached only a "direct appropriation" of property, or the functional equivalent of a "practical ouster of [the owner's] possession." *Transportation Co. v. Chicago*, 99 U.S. 642 (1879).... Justice Holmes recognized in *Mahon*, however, that if the protection against physical appropriation of private property was to be meaningfully enforced, the government's power to redefine the range of interests included in the ownership of property was necessarily constrained by constitutional limits. These considerations gave birth in that case to the oft-cited maxim that, "while property may be regulated to a certain extent, if regulation goes too far it will be recognized as a taking." *Mahon.*

Nevertheless, our decision in *Mahon* offered little insight into when, and under what circumstances, a given regulation would be seen as going "too far" for purposes of the Fifth Amendment. In 70-odd years of succeeding "regulatory taking" jurisprudence, we have generally eschewed any "'set formula'" for determining how far is too far, preferring to "engag[e] in ... essentially ad hoc, factual inquiries." *Penn Central Transportation Co. v. New York City* (quoting *Goldblatt v. Hempstead*, 369 U.S. [590] (1962)). We have, however, described at least two discrete categories of regulatory action as compensable without case-specific inquiry into the public interest advanced in support of the restraint. The first encompasses regulations that compel the property owner to suffer a physical "invasion" of his property. In general (at least with regard to permanent invasions), no matter how minute the intrusion, and no matter how weighty the public purpose behind it, we have required compensation....

The second situation in which we have found categorical treatment appropriate is where regulation denies all economically beneficial or productive use of land....

We have never set forth the justification for this rule. Perhaps it is simply, as Justice Brennan suggested, that total deprivation of beneficial use is, from the landowner's point of view, the equivalent of a physical appropriation. Surely, at least, in the extraordinary circumstances when *no* productive or economically beneficial use of land is permitted, it is less realistic to indulge our usual assumption that the legislature is simply "adjusting the benefits and burdens of economic life," *Penn Central Transportation Co.*, in a manner that secures an "average reciprocity of advantage" to everyone concerned. Id. And the *functional* basis for permitting the government, by regulation, to affect property values without compensation—that "Government hardly could go on if to some extent values incident to property could not be diminished without paying for every such change in the general law," ... id.—does not apply to the relatively rare situations where the government has deprived a landowner of all economically beneficial uses.

On the other side of the balance, affirmatively supporting a compensation requirement, is the fact that regulations that leave the owner of land without economically beneficial or productive options for its use—typically, as here, by requiring land to be left substantially in its natural state—carry with them a heightened risk that private property is being pressed into some form of public service under the guise of mitigating serious public harm....

We think, in short, that there are good reasons for our frequently expressed belief that when the owner of real property has been called upon to sacrifice *all* economically beneficial uses in the name of the common good, that is, to leave his property economically idle, he has suffered a taking.

The trial court found Lucas's two beachfront lots to have been rendered valueless by respondent's enforcement of the coastal-zone construction ban. Under Lucas's theory of the case, which rested upon our "no economically viable use" statements, that finding entitled him to compensation. Lucas believed it unnecessary to take issue with either the purposes behind the Beachfront Management Act, or the means chosen by the South Carolina Legislature to effectuate those purposes. The South Carolina Supreme Court, however, thought otherwise. In its view, the Beachfront Management Act was no ordinary enactment, but involved an exercise of South Carolina's "police powers" to mitigate the harm to the public interest that petitioner's use of his land might occasion. By neglecting to dispute the findings enumerated in the Act or otherwise to challenge the legislature's purposes, petitioner "concede[d] that the beach/dune area of South Carolina's shore is an extremely valuable public resource, that the erection of new construction, *inter alia*, contributes to the erosion and destruction of this public resource; and that discouraging new construction in close proximity to the beach/dune area is necessary to prevent a great public harm." In the court's view, these concessions brought petitioner's challenge within a long line of this Court's cases sustaining against Due Process and Takings Clause challenges the State's use of its "police powers" to enjoin a property owner from activities akin to public nuisances.

It is correct that many of our prior opinions have suggested that "harmful or noxious uses" of property may be proscribed by government regulation without the requirement of compensation. For a number of reasons, however, we think the South Carolina Supreme Court was too quick to conclude that principle decides the present case. The "harmful or noxious uses" principle was the Court's early attempt to describe in theoretical terms why government may, consistent with the Takings Clause, affect property values by regulation without incurring an obligation to compensate—a reality we nowadays acknowledge explicitly with respect to the full scope of the State's police power....

"Harmful or noxious use" analysis was, in other words, simply the progenitor of our more contemporary statements that "land-use regulation does not effect a taking if it 'substantially advance[s] legitimate state interests'...." *Nollan v. California Coastal Commission*, 483 U.S. 825 (1987) (quoting *Agins v. Tiburon*, 447 U.S. at 260).

The transition from our early focus on control of "noxious" uses to our contemporary understanding of the broad realm within which government may regulate without compensation was an easy one, since the distinction between "harm-preventing" and "benefit-conferring" regulation is often in the eye of the beholder....

When it is understood that "prevention of harmful use" was merely our early formulation of the police power justification necessary to sustain (without compensation) *any* regulatory diminution in value; and that the distinc-

tion between regulation that "prevents harmful use" and that which "confers benefits" is difficult, if not impossible, to discern on an objective, value-free basis, it becomes self-evident that noxious-use logic cannot serve as a touchstone to distinguish regulatory "takings"—which require compensation—from regulatory deprivations that do not require compensation. A *fortiori* the legislature's recitation of a noxious-use justification cannot be the basis for departing from our categorical rule that total regulatory takings must be compensated. If it were, departure would virtually always be allowed....

Where the State seeks to sustain regulation that deprives land of all economically beneficial use, we think it may resist compensation only if the logically antecedent inquiry into the nature of the owner's estate shows that the proscribed use interests were not part of his title to begin with. This accords, we think, with our "takings" jurisprudence, which has traditionally been guided by the understandings of our citizens regarding the content of, and the State's power over, the "bundle of rights" that they acquire when they obtain title to property. It seems to us that the property owner necessarily expects the uses of his property to be restricted, from time to time, by various measures newly enacted by the State in legitimate exercise of its police power; "[a]s long recognized, some values are enjoyed under an implied limitation and must yield to the police power." *Pennsylvania Coal Co. v. Mahon*. And in the case of personal property, by reason of the State's traditionally high degree of control over commercial dealings, he ought to be aware of the possibility that new regulation might even render his property economically worthless (at least if the property's only economically productive use is sale or manufacture for sale). In the case of land, however, we think the notion pressed by the Council that title is somehow held subject to the "implied limitation" that the State may subsequently eliminate all economically valuable use is inconsistent with the historical compact recorded in the Takings Clause that has become part of our constitutional culture.

Where "permanent physical occupation" of land is concerned, we have refused to allow the government to decree it anew (without compensation), no matter how weighty the asserted "public interests" involved,—though we assuredly *would* permit the government to assert a permanent easement that was a pre-existing limitation upon the landowner's title. We believe similar treatment must be accorded confiscatory regulations, *i.e.*, regulations that prohibit all economically beneficial use of land: Any limitation so severe cannot be newly legislated or decreed (without compensation), but must inhere in the title itself, in the restrictions that background principles of the State's law of property and nuisance already place upon land ownership. A law or decree with such an effect must, in other words, do no more than duplicate the result that could have been achieved in the courts—by adjacent landowners (or other uniquely affected persons) under the State's law of private nuisance, or by the State under its complementary power to abate nuisances that affect the public generally, or otherwise....

The "total taking" inquiry we require today will ordinarily entail (as the application of state nuisance law ordinarily entails) analysis of, among other things,

the degree of harm to public lands and resources, or adjacent private property, posed by the claimant's proposed activities, the social value of the claimant's activities and their suitability to the locality in question, and the relative ease with which the alleged harm can be avoided through measures taken by the claimant and the government (or adjacent private landowners) alike. The fact that a particular use has long been engaged in by similarly situated owners ordinarily imparts a lack of any common-law prohibition (though changed circumstances or new knowledge may make what was previously permissible no longer so.[)] So also does the fact that other landowners, similarly situated, are permitted to continue the use denied to the claimant.

It seems unlikely that common-law principles would have prevented the erection of any habitable or productive improvements on petitioner's land; they rarely support prohibition of the "essential use" of land. *Curtin v. Benson*, 222 U.S. 86 (1911). The question, however, is one of state law to be dealt with on remand. We emphasize that to win its case South Carolina must do more than proffer the legislature's declaration that the uses Lucas desires are inconsistent with the public interest, or the conclusory assertion that they violate a common-law maxim such as *sic utere tuo ut alienum non laedas* [so use your own property as to not harm that of another]. As we have said, a "State, by *ipse dixit* [on it's own authority], may not transform private property into public property without compensation...." Instead, as it would be required to do if it sought to restrain Lucas in a common-law action for public nuisance, South Carolina must identify background principles of nuisance and property law that prohibit the uses he now intends in the circumstances in which the property is presently found. Only on this showing can the State fairly claim that, in proscribing all such beneficial uses, the Beachfront Management Act is taking nothing.

The judgment is reversed and the cause remanded for proceedings not inconsistent with this opinion.

So ordered.

KENNEDY, J., CONCURRING IN THE JUDGMENT

... The finding of no value must be considered under the Takings Clause by reference to the owner's reasonable investment-backed expectations. The Takings Clause, while conferring substantial protection on property owners, does not eliminate the police power of the State to enact limitations on the use of their property. The rights conferred by the Takings Clause and the police power of the State may coexist without conflict. Property is bought and sold, investments are made, subject to the State's power to regulate. Where a taking is alleged from regulations which deprive the property of all value, the test must be whether the deprivation is contrary to reasonable, investment-backed expectations.

There is an inherent tendency towards circularity in this synthesis, of course; for if the owner's reasonable expectations are shaped by what courts allow as a proper exercise of governmental authority, property tends to become what courts say it is. Some circularity must be tolerated in these matters, however, as it is in other spheres. The definition, moreover, is not circular in its entirety. The expectations protected by the Constitution are based on objective rules and customs that can be understood as reasonable by all parties involved.

In my view, reasonable expectations must be understood in light of the whole of our legal tradition. The common law of nuisance is too narrow a confine for the exercise of regulatory power in a complex and interdependent society. The State should not be prevented from enacting new regulatory initiatives in response to changing conditions, and courts must consider all reasonable expectations whatever their source. The Takings Clause does not require a static body of state property law; it protects private expectations to ensure private investment. I agree with the Court that nuisance prevention accords with the most common expectations of property owners who face regulation, but I do not believe this can be the sole source of state authority to impose severe restrictions. Coastal property may present such unique concerns for a fragile land system that the State can go further in regulating its development and use than the common law of nuisance might otherwise permit. The Supreme Court of South Carolina erred, in my view, by reciting the general purposes for which the state regulations were enacted without a determination that they were in accord with the owner's reasonable expectations and therefore sufficient to support a severe restriction on specific parcels of property....

BLACKMUN, J., DISSENTING

Today the Court launches a missile to kill a mouse.... [T]he Court ... ignores its jurisdictional limits, remakes its traditional rules of review, and creates simultaneously a new categorical rule and an exception (neither of which is rooted in our prior case law, common law, or common sense.)...

My fear is that the Court's new policies will spread beyond the narrow confines of the present case. For that reason, I, like the Court, will give far greater attention to this case than its narrow scope suggests—not because I can intercept the Court's missile, or save the targeted mouse, but because I hope perhaps to limit the collateral damage....

If the state legislature is correct that the prohibition on building in front of the setback line prevents serious harm, then, under this Court's prior cases, the Act is constitutional.... The Court consistently has upheld regulations imposed to arrest a significant threat to the common welfare, whatever their economic effect on the owner....

My disagreement with the Court begins with its decisions to review this case. This Court has held consistently that a land-use challenge is not ripe for review until there is a final decision about what uses of the property will be permitted....

Even if I agree with the Court that there were no jurisdictional barriers to deciding this case, I still would not try to decide it. The Court creates its new taking jurisprudence on the trial court's finding that the property had lost all economic value. That finding is almost certainly erroneous. Petitioner still can enjoy other attributes of ownership, such as the right to exclude others ... Petitioner can picnic, swim, camp in a tent, or live on the property in a movable trailer.... Petitioner also retains the right to alienate the land, which would have value for neighbors and for those prepared to enjoy proximity to the ocean without a house....

The Court's willingness to dispense with precedent in its haste to reach a result is not limited to its initial jurisdictional decision....

The Court also alters the long-settled rules of review....

The South Carolina Supreme Court's decision to defer to legislative judgments in the absence of a challenge from petitioner comports with one of this Court's oldest maxims: "the existence of facts supporting the legislative judgment is to be presumed." *United States v. Carolene Products*, 304 U.S. 144 (1938)....

[T]his Court always has required plaintiffs challenging the constitutionality of an ordinance to provide "some factual foundation of record" that contravenes the legislative findings. *O'Gorman & Young v. Hartford Ins. Co.*, 282 U.S. 258 (1931). In the absence of such proof, "the presumption of constitutionality must prevail." Id.

Rather than invoking these traditional rules, the Court decides the State has the burden to convince the courts that its legislative judgments are correct. Despite Lucas' complete failure to contest the legislature's findings of serious harm to life and property if a permanent structure is built, the Court decides that the legislative findings are not sufficient to justify the use prohibitions. Instead, the Court "emphasize[s]" the State must do more than merely proffer its legislative judgments to avoid invalidating its law. In this case, apparently, the State now has the burden of showing the regulation is not a taking. The Court offers no justification for its sudden hostility toward state legislation, and I doubt that it could....

Until today, the Court explicitly had rejected the contention that the government's power to act without paying compensation turns on whether the prohibited activity is a common-law nuisance.... Instead the Court has relied in the past, as the South Carolina Court has done here, on legislative judgments of what constitutes a harm.

The Court rejects the notion that the State always can prohibit uses it deems a harm to the public without granting compensation because "the distinction between 'harm-preventing' and 'benefit-conferring' regulation is often in the eye of the beholder." Since the characterization will depend "primarily upon one's evaluation of the worth of competing uses of real estate," the Court decides a legislative judgment of this kind no longer can provide the desired "objective, value-free basis" for upholding a regulation. The Court, however, fails to explain how its proposed common law alternative escapes the same trap.

The threshold inquiry for imposition of the Court's new rule, "deprivation of all economically valuable use," itself cannot be determined objectively. As the Court admits, whether the owner has been deprived of all economic value of his property will depend on how "property" is defined....

Even more perplexing, however, is the Court's reliance on common-law principles of nuisance in its quest for a value-free taking jurisprudence. In determining what is a nuisance at common law, state courts make exactly the decision that the Court finds so troubling when made by the South Carolina General Assembly today: they determine whether the use is harmful.... There simply is no reason to believe that new interpretations of the hoary

common law nuisance doctrine will be particularly "objective" or "value-free." Once one abandons the level of generality of *sic utere tuo ut alienum non laedas*, one searches in vain, I think, for anything resembling a principle in the common law of nuisance.

Finally, the Court justifies its new rule that the legislature may not deprive a property owner of the only economically valuable use of his land, even if the legislature finds it to be a harmful use, because such action is not part of the "long recognized" understandings of our citizens. These "understandings" permit such regulation only if the use is a nuisance under the common law. Any other course is "inconsistent" with the historical compact recorded in the Takings Clause." It is not clear from the Court's opinion where our "historical compact" or "citizens' understanding" comes from, but it does not appear to be history....

I find no clear and accepted "historical compact" or "understanding of our citizens" justifying the Court's new taking doctrine. Instead, the Court seems to treat history as a grab-bag of principles, to be adopted where they support the Court's theory, and ignored where they do not.... What makes the Court's analysis unworkable is its attempt to package the law of two incompatible eras and peddle it as historical fact....

I dissent.

STEVENS, J., DISSENTING

Today the Court restricts one judge-made rule and expands another. In my opinion it errs on both counts. Proper application of the doctrine of judicial restraint would avoid the premature adjudication of an important constitutional question. Proper respect for our precedents would avoid an illegal expansion of the concept of "regulatory takings."...

Cavalierly dismissing the doctrine of judicial restraint, the Court today tersely announces that "we do not think it prudent to apply that prudential requirement here." I respectfully disagree and would save consideration of the merits for another day. Since, however, the Court has reached the merits, I shall do so as well.

In its analysis of the merits, the Court starts from the premise that this Court has adopted a "categorical rule that total regulatory takings must be compensated," and then sets itself to the task of identifying the exceptional cases in which a State may be relieved of this categorical obligation. The test the Court announces is that the regulation must do no more than duplicate the result that could have been achieved under a State's nuisance law. Under this test the categorical rule will apply unless the regulation merely makes explicit what was otherwise an implicit limitation on the owner's property rights.

In my opinion, the Court is doubly in error. The categorical rule the Court establishes is an unsound and unwise addition to the law and the Court's formulation of the exception to that rule is too rigid and too narrow....

In addition to lacking support in past decisions, the Court's new rule is wholly arbitrary. A landowner whose property is diminished in value 95% recovers nothing, while an owner whose property is diminished 100% recovers the land's full value. The case at hand illustrates this arbitrariness well. The Beachfront Management Act not only prohibited the

building of new dwellings in certain areas, it also prohibited the rebuilding of houses that were "destroyed beyond repair by natural causes or by fire."...

On the other hand, developers and investors may market specialized estates to take advantage of the Court's new rule. The smaller the estate, the more likely that a regulatory change will effect a total taking.... To my mind, neither of these results is desirable or appropriate, and both are distortions of our takings jurisprudence.

Finally, the Court's justification for its new categorical rule is remarkably thin....

[T]he Court's new rule is unsupported by prior decisions, arbitrary and unsound in practice, and theoretically unjustified. In my opinion, a categorical rule as important as the one established by the Court today should be supported by more history or more reason than has yet been provided....

Under our reasoning in *Mugler*, a state's decision to prohibit or to regulate certain uses of property is not a compensable taking just because the particular uses were previously lawful. Under the Court's opinion today, however, if a state should decide to prohibit the manufacture of asbestos, cigarettes, or concealable firearms, for example, it must be prepared to pay for the adverse economic consequences of its decisions. One must wonder if Government will be able to "go on" effectively if it must risk compensation "for every such thing in the general law." *Mahon*.

The Court's holding today effectively freezes the State's common law, denying the legislature much of its traditional power to revise the law governing the rights and uses of property. Until today, I had thought that we had long abandoned this approach to constitutional law. More than a century ago we recognized that "the great office of statutes is to remedy defects in the common law as they are developed, and to adapt it to the changes of time and circumstances." *Munn v. Illinois*.... Arresting the development of the common law is not only a departure from our prior decisions; it is also profoundly unwise....

Of course, some legislative redefinition of property will effect a taking and must be compensated—but it certainly cannot be the case that every movement away from common law does so. There is no reason, and less sense, in such an absolute rule. We live in a world in which changes in the economy and the environment occur with increasing frequency and importance. If it was wise a century ago to allow Government "'the largest legislative discretion'" to deal with "the special exigencies of the moment," *Mugler*, it is imperative to do so today. The rule that should govern a decision in a case of this kind should focus on the future, not the past.

The Court's categorical approach rule will, I fear, greatly hamper the efforts of local officials and planners who must deal with increasingly complex problems in land-use and environmental regulation. As this case—in which the claims of an *individual* property owner exceed $1 million—well demonstrates, these officials face both substantial uncertainty because of the ad hoc nature of takings law and unacceptable penalties if they guess incorrectly about that law.

Viewed more broadly, the Court's new rule and exception conflict with the very character of our takings jurisprudence. We have frequently and consistently recognized that the definition of a

taking cannot be reduced to a "set formula" and that determining whether a regulation is a taking is "essentially [an] ad hoc, factual inquir[y]."...

It is well established that a takings case "entails inquiry into [several factors:] the character of the governmental action, its economic impact, and its interference with reasonable investment-backed expectations." The Court's analysis today focuses on the last two of these three factors: the categorical rule addresses a regulation's "economic impact," while the nuisance exception recognizes that ownership brings with it only certain "expectations." Neglected by the Court today is the first, and in some way, the most important factor in takings analysis: the character of the regulatory action....

In analyzing takings claims, courts have long recognized the difference between a regulation that targets one or two parcels of land and a regulation that enforces a state-wide policy....

In considering Lucas' claim, the generality of the Beachfront Management Act is significant. The Act does not target particular landowners, but rather regulates the use of the coastline of the entire state. Indeed, South Carolina's Act is best understood as part of a national effort to protect the coastline, one initiated by the Federal Coastal Zone Management Act of 1972.... In short, the South Carolina Act imposed substantial burdens on owners of developed and undeveloped land alike. This generality indicates that the Act is not an effort to expropriate owners of undeveloped land.

Admittedly, the economic impact of this regulation is dramatic and petitioner's investment-backed expectations are substantial. Yet, if anything, the costs to and expectations of the owners of developed land are even greater. I doubt, however, that the cost to owners of developed land of renourishing the beach and allowing their seawalls to deteriorate effects a taking. The costs imposed on the owners of undeveloped land, such as petitioner, differ from those costs only in degree, not in kind....

In view of all of these factors, even assuming that petitioner's property was rendered valueless, the risk inherent in investments of the sort made by petitioner, the generality of the Act, and the compelling purpose motivating the South Carolina Legislature persuade me that the Act did not effect a taking of petitioner's property.

Accordingly, I respectfully dissent.

STATEMENT OF SOUTER, J.

I would dismiss the writ of certiorari in this case as having been granted improvidently. After briefing and argument it is abundantly clear that an unreviewable assumption on which this case comes to us is both questionable as a conclusion of Fifth Amendment law and sufficient to frustrate the Court's ability to render certain the legal premises on which its holding rests.

The petition for review was granted on the assumption that the state by regulation had deprived the owner of his entire economic interest in the subject property. Such was the state trial court's conclusion, which the state supreme court did not review. It is apparent now that in light of our prior cases, the trial court's conclusion is highly questionable. While the respondent now wishes to contest the point, the Court is certainly right to refuse to take up the issue, which is not fairly included within the question presented, and has received only the most superficial and one-sided treatment before us.

Because the questionable conclusion of total deprivation cannot be reviewed, the Court is precluded from attempting to clarify the concept of total (and, in the Court's view, categorically compensable) taking on which it rests....

The upshot is that the issue of what constitutes a total deprivation is being addressed by indirection, and with uncertain results, in the Court's treatment of defenses to compensation claims. While the issue of what constitutes total deprivation deserves the Court's attention, as does the relationship between nuisance abatement and such total deprivation, the Court should confront these matters directly. Because it can neither do so in this case, nor skip over those preliminary issues and deal independently with defenses to the Court's categorical compensation rule, the Court should dismiss the instant writ and await an opportunity to face the total deprivation question squarely....

QUESTIONS

1. The effect of Justice Scalia's opinion in *Lucas* is to substitute a "categorical rule" for the Court's prior *ad hoc* approach to deciding regulatory takings cases. What are the legal and political consequences of the shift in approach? Is the most significant aspect of

Lucas how it shifts the burden of proof to government to defend its land use regulations?

2. As a practical matter, is the categorical rule announced in *Lucas* workable? In how many situations does a land use regulation deprive an owner of "all economically beneficial use" of land? Is Justice Blackmun correct that the restrictions imposed by the South Carolina Costal Commission on Lucas's property did not deprive him of "all economically beneficial use" of his property?

3. The United States entered *Lucas* as *amicus* on behalf of *Lucas*. Is the federal government's posture in *Lucas* consistent with the 1972 federal Coastal Zone Management Act that provided states with money and incentives to protect the public from shoreline erosion and coastal hazards?

4. Celebrating the outcome in *Lucas*, columnist George F. Will wrote: "Surrounded by the rubble of socialist regimes, we seek the lessons of this century. One is this: There is an indissoluble connection between private property and individual freedom.... Government is not yet inhibited enough. Arguably, it should be required to compensate property owners when its actions directly and substantially diminish the value of property" (*The Sunday Oregonian*, July 5, 1992, B3).

   What are the consequences of Will's view for land use planning and environmental protection? Can either be left to the private sector?

5. Lawyer and land use regulation expert Jerold S. Kayden claims that *Lucas* "could have the effect of increasing the role for state courts" (*New York Times*, June 30, 1992, A10). Do the various opinions in *Lucas* support that conclusion? Will *Lucas* also increase the role of economists as expert witnesses in Takings Clause litigation, or is the *Lucas* rule only apparently based on economic considerations?

6. In *Yee v. City of Escondido*, 503 U.S. 519 (1992), a unanimous Court ruled that an Escondido, California, rent control ordinance setting mobile home rents back to their 1986 levels and prohibiting rent increases in mobile home parks without the city council's approval, is not a "taking" and hence no compensation is due the mobile home park owner. The ordinance, said the Court, does not authorize an unwanted physical occupation of the property, and therefore it does not amount to a *per se* taking. According to the Court, the government effects a compensable physical taking only where it requires a land owner to submit to the material occupation of his land and the Escondido ordinance merely regulates the use of the land by regulating the relationship between landlord and tenant.

   Is *Lucas* consistent with *Escondido*?

TAKINGS

Dolan v. City of Tigard
512 U.S. 374 (1994)

SETTING

In 1987, in *Nollan v. California Coastal Commission*, 483 U.S. 825, the Court announced a so-called "nexus test" for evaluating whether property regulations amount to takings for purposes of the Fifth Amendment. In that case, James Nollan, the prospective purchaser of a beachfront lot in Ventura County, California, planned to demolish a small bungalow on the property and replace it with a three-bedroom house. He sought a building permit from the California Coastal Commission, as required by California law. The Commission granted the permit, conditioned on the requirement that Nollan give the public an easement to pass across the portion of the property that lay between the mean high tide line and a concrete seawall that separated the beach portion of the Nollan property from the rest of the lot. Nollan protested the requirement and eventually sued to invalidate it.

Justice Scalia, writing for a 5–4 majority when the issue reached the Supreme Court, held that conditioning the issuance of a building permit on the requirement that Nollan grant the public an easement across his property did not substantially advance the legitimate state interests that the Coastal Commission had cited as the reason for imposing the condition. Scalia wrote:

> the lack of nexus between the condition and the original purpose of the building restriction converts that purpose to something other than what it was. The purpose then becomes, quite simply, the obtaining of an easement to serve some valid governmental purpose, but without payment of compensation. Whatever may be the outer limits of "legitimate state interests" in the takings and land-use context, this is not one of them. In short, unless the permit condition serves the same governmental purpose as the development ban, the building restriction is not a valid regulation of land use but "an out-and-out plan of extortion.

Under the *Nollan* test, a nexus must exist between the impacts created by development and any condition on development imposed by the government. If the purpose and effect do not "fit," the regulation will be held to be a taking.

Dolan v. City of Tigard provided the Court a chance to expand on its *Nollan* ruling. *Dolan* also provided some members of the Court the opportunity to rethink both the burden of proof and the presumption of constitutionality in Takings Clause cases.

In 1973, the State of Oregon adopted a statute requiring cities and counties to adopt comprehensive land use plans in compliance with statewide land use goals developed by the state's Land Conservation and Development Commission (LCDC), an administrative agency created to administer the state's land use regulatory system. Cities and counties are required to adopt land use regulations to implement local comprehensive plans that are made in conformity with state land use goals.

In 1975, LCDC adopted Goal 5 to conserve open space and protect natural and scenic resources. It also adopted Goal 12 to provide and encourage a safe, convenient, and economic transportation system.

The city of Tigard is a rapidly growing community that abuts Portland's southwest boundary. Tigard's 1983 comprehensive plan, adopted in conformity with the state land use goals, contained a finding that the city would develop policies to retain "a vegetative buffer along streams and drainageways, to reduce runoff and flood damage and provide erosion and siltation control." The policy the city adopted was to require the dedication of all undeveloped land within the hundred-year floodplain along a small creek called Fanno Creek. The policy also called for easements or dedications to construct pedestrian and bicycle pathways.

In 1989, the city revised its zoning ordinance to implement its comprehensive plan. Section 18.120.180.A.8 of the Community Development Code provided that the city would "require the dedication of sufficient open land area for greenway adjoining and within the floodplain. This area shall include portions at a suitable elevation for the construction of pedestrian/bicycle pathway within the floodplain in accordance with the adopted pedestrian/bicycle plan."

Florence and John Dolan are the owners of a chain of A-Boy Electric Plumbing and Supply stores in the Portland metropolitan area. One of their stores is located on a 1.67-acre commercial lot on Main Street in Tigard. The lot is contiguous to Fanno Creek and part of it is within the creek's hundred-year floodplain. The Dolans proposed to tear down the old 9,700-square-foot building and to construct in its place a 17,600-square-foot structure to better meet the needs of their business. They also proposed to establish a paved parking area with 39 parking spaces.

When the Dolans applied for approval to build their new building, the city, pursuant to zoning ordinance section 18.120.180.A.8, conditioned its approval on the requirement that the Dolans dedicate to the city all of the portions of their lot lying within the hundred-year floodplain for use as a greenway and that they dedicate an additional fifteen-foot strip of property adjacent to and above the hundred-year floodplain for reconstruction of a storm drainage channel. The fifteen-foot strip was also to be used as a public pedestrian and bicycle pathway, which the Dolans were required to construct. The dedication requirement consisted of approximately seven thousand square feet, or about 10 percent of the 1.67 acre parcel.

The Dolans contended that the exactions required by the city as a condition of building their new store were unconstitutional. They appealed the city's requirement to the Oregon Land Use Board of Appeals (LUBA), a three-attorney administrative hearings body appointed by the Oregon governor, which has exclusive jurisdiction over appeals of land use decisions made by local governments. LUBA held that the Dolans's constitutional claim was not ripe because they had failed to seek a variance. The Dolans then reapplied to the city, seeking a variance. It was denied, and the Dolans again appealed to LUBA, reasserting their federal constitutional claim.

LUBA held that the city's exactions were not an unconstitutional taking because the federal takings standard of scrutiny did not require a substantial relationship between the adverse impacts of the proposed use and government-imposed exactions, and that the exactions imposed by the city were reasonably related to the adverse impacts of the Dolans's new store. The Dolans petitioned for appellate review from the Oregon Court of Appeals.

The Oregon Court of Appeals affirmed LUBA, as did the Oregon Supreme Court. The Oregon high court reasoned that both the pedestrian-bicycle pathway condition and the storm drainage dedication had an essential nexus to the development of the proposed new store, and that the conditions therefore were reasonably related to the impact of the expansion of the Dolans's business. John Dolan died soon after the Oregon supreme court's ruling. Florence Dolan petitioned the Supreme Court of the United States for a writ of certiorari.

HIGHLIGHTS OF SUPREME COURT ARGUMENTS

BRIEF FOR THE DOLANS

◆ This case squarely presents the question of when this Court's opinion in *Nollan* permits a local government to demand that real property be dedicated to the public by the owner of land as a condition of the government allowing the land owner to secure a building permit.

◆ A government may not impose a dedication requirement unless there is evidence in the record that the building's adverse impacts on municipal recreation, storm water disposal, and transportation services are directly, substantially, and proportionately linked in both character and degree to the dedications.

◆ The city of Tigard failed to establish the required "essential nexus" of a reasonably direct and proportional relationship both in character and degree between the effects of the Dolans' proposed store improvements and the exaction of seven thousand square feet of their private property.

◆ This Court mandated in *Nollan* that the imposition of dedications on development permits is one context in which heightened judicial scrutiny of the means-ends relationship is in order. The Oregon Supreme Court's use of the "reasonably related" level of review failed to follow *Nollan*.

AMICUS CURIAE BRIEFS SUPPORTING THE DOLANS

Northwest Legal Foundation; joint brief of the Mountain States Legal Foundation, The Alliance for America, and The Fairness to Land Owners Committee; joint brief of The Washington Legal Foundation and Allied Educational Foundation; joint brief of the Georgia Public Policy Foundation and Southeastern Legal Foundation; joint brief of the Pacific Legal Foundation,

Richard Ehrlich, and Building Industry Association of Washington, The Urban Land Council of Oregon; joint brief of the National Association of Home Builders, International Council of Shopping Centers, National Association for Commercial Real Estate, National Realty Committee, National Multi-Housing Council, National Apartment Association, American Seniors Housing Association; joint brief of the National Association of Realtors and the Oregon Association of Realtors; joint brief of the Washington Legal Foundation, Pennsylvania Landowners' Association, Inc. and The Allied Educational Foundation; joint brief of Defenders of Property Rights, Alliance for America, American Environmental Foundation, American Loggers Solidarity, Arizona Citizens Coalition on Resource Decisions, Appalachian Forest Management Group, Citizens for Constitutional Property Rights, Council on Property Rights; Institute for Justice; Terrence and Tamara Wellner; American Farm Bureau Federation; Oregon Farm Bureau Federation; Thomas and Esther Nelson.

BRIEF FOR THE CITY OF TIGARD

◆ The city of Tigard could have denied the Dolans's permit application outright because of the traffic congestion and drainage concerns it raised and would not have been required to pay compensation. A municipality does not take private property in violation of the Fifth and Fourteenth Amendments when, instead of denying a development application based on legitimate public concerns, it acts far less harshly by addressing those concerns through conditions such as the ones imposed here.

◆ The conditions that a municipality imposes as a condition of receiving a building permit is not subject to strict judicial scrutiny under the Takings Clause. The Dolans's reliance on *Nollan* is misplaced. That case did not mark a dramatic shift in this Court's takings jurisprudence. It did not eliminate the presumption of constitutionality that this Court has long applied to legislative decisions, and it did not require the government to prove the precise extent of the burdens that a policy power regulation was designed to alleviate.

◆ The Takings Clause does not require a municipality to demonstrate a mathematically equivalent relationship between an exaction and the impacts of a proposed development.

◆ The Dolans are asking this Court to return to the *Lochnerian* days of heightened judicial review of economic regulation, this time under the guise of takings analysis rather than through the already-discredited substantive due process analysis.

◆ The conditions imposed on the Dolans's property substantially advanced a legitimate state interest and was reasonably related to the projected impacts of the Dolans's proposed development.

AMICUS CURIAE BRIEFS SUPPORTING THE CITY OF TIGARD

United States; City of New York; Oregon; Broward County, Florida; joint brief of The Bicycle-Pedestrian Pathway Dedication by the Rails-To-Trains

Conservancy, the League of American Bicyclists, the Bicycle Federation of Oregon; National Wildlife Federation; the American Society of Landscape Architects; State of New Jersey; joint brief of National Association of Counties, Council of State Governments, National League of Cities, International City/County Management Association, National Institute of Municipal Law Officers, and U.S. Conference of Mayors; joint brief of 1000 Friends of Oregon, Oregon Chapter of American Planning Association, American Planning Association, and National Trust for Historic Preservation; Association of State Floodplain Managers; American Federation of Labor and Congress of Industrial Organizations; National Audubon Society.

SUPREME COURT DECISION: 5–4

REHNQUIST, C.J.

... We granted certiorari to resolve a question left open by our decision in *Nollan v. California Coastal Commission* [, 483 U.S. 825 (1987)], of what is the required degree of connection between the exactions imposed by the city and the projected impacts of the proposed development....

One of the principal purposes of the Takings Clause is "to bar Government from forcing some people alone to bear public burdens which, in all fairness and justice, should be borne by the public as a whole." *Armstrong v. United States*, 364 U.S. 40 (1960). Without question, had the city simply required petitioner to dedicate a strip of land along Fanno Creek for public use, rather than conditioning the grant of her permit to redevelop her property on such a dedication, a taking would have occurred. Such public access would deprive petitioner of the right to exclude others, "one of the most essential sticks in the bundle of rights that are commonly characterized as property." *Kaiser Aetna v. United States*, 444 U.S. 164 (1979).

On the other side of the ledger, the authority of state and local governments to engage in land use planning has been

sustained against constitutional challenge as long ago as our decision in *Euclid v. Ambler Realty Co....*

Petitioner contends that the city has forced her to choose between the building permit and her right under the Fifth Amendment to just compensation for the public easements. Petitioner does not quarrel with the city's authority to exact some forms of dedication as a condition for the grant of a building permit, but challenges the showing made by the city to justify these exactions. She argues that the city has identified "no special benefits" conferred on her, and has not identified any "special quantifiable burdens" created by her new store that would justify the particular dedications required from her which are not required from the public at large.

In evaluating petitioner's claim, we must first determine whether the "essential nexus" exists between the "legitimate state interest" and the permit condition exacted by the city.... If we find that a nexus exists, we must then decide the required degree of connection between the exactions and the projected impact of the proposed development. We were not required to reach this question in *Nollan*, because we concluded that the connection did not meet even the loosest standard....

Undoubtedly, the prevention of flooding along Fanno Creek and the reduction of traffic congestion in the Central Business District qualify as the type of legitimate public purposes we have upheld. It seems equally obvious that a nexus exists between preventing flooding along Fanno Creek and limiting development within the creek's 100-year flood plain. Petitioner proposes to double the size of her retail store and to pave her now-gravel parking lot, thereby expanding the impervious surface on the property and increasing the amount of stormwater run-off into Fanno Creek.

The same may be said for the city's attempt to reduce traffic congestion by providing for alternative means of transportation. In theory, a pedestrian/bicycle pathway provides a useful alternative means of transportation for workers and shoppers....

The second part of our analysis requires us to determine whether the degree of the exactions demanded by the city's permit conditions bear the required relationship to the projected impact of petitioner's proposed development.... Here the Oregon Supreme Court deferred to what it termed the "city's unchallenged factual findings" supporting the dedication conditions and found them to be reasonably related to the impact of the expansion of petitioner's business....

The question for us is whether these findings are constitutionally sufficient to justify the conditions imposed by the city on petitioner's building permit....

We think a term such as "rough proportionality" best encapsulates what we hold to be the requirement of the Fifth Amendment. No precise mathematical calculation is required, but the city must make some sort of individualized determination that the required dedication is related both in nature and extent to the impact of the proposed development....

Justice Stevens' dissent relies upon a law review article for the proposition that the city's conditional demands for part of petitioner's property are "a species of business regulation that heretofore warranted a strong presumption of constitutional validity." But simply denominating a governmental measure as a "business regulation" does not immunize it from constitutional challenge on the grounds that it violates a provision of the Bill of Rights.... We see no reason why the Takings Clause of the Fifth Amendment, as much a part of the Bill of Rights as the First Amendment or Fourth Amendment, should be relegated to the status of a poor relation in these comparable circumstances. We turn now to analysis of whether the findings relied upon by the city here, first with respect to the floodplain easement, and second with respect to the pedestrian/bicycle path, satisfied these requirements.

It is axiomatic that increasing the amount of impervious surface will increase the quantity and rate of stormwater flow from petitioner's property. Therefore, keeping the floodplain open and free from development would likely confine the pressures on Fanno Creek created by petitioner's development. In fact, because petitioner's property lies within the Central Business District, the Community Development Code already required that petitioner leave 15% of it as open space and the undeveloped floodplain would have nearly satisfied that requirement. But the city demanded more—it not only wanted petitioner not to build in the floodplain, but it also wanted petitioner's property along Fanno

Creek for its Greenway system. The city has never said why a public greenway, as opposed to a private one, was required in the interest of flood control.

The difference to petitioner, of course, is the loss of her ability to exclude others. As we have noted, this right to exclude others is "one of the most essential sticks in the bundle of rights that are commonly characterized as property." *Kaiser Aetna.* It is difficult to see why recreational visitors trampling along petitioner's floodplain easement are sufficiently related to the city's legitimate interest in reducing flooding problems along Fanno Creek, and the city has not attempted to make any individualized determination to support this part of its request....

[T]he city wants to impose a permanent recreational easement upon petitioner's property that borders Fanno Creek. Petitioner would lose all rights to regulate the time in which the public entered onto the Greenway, regardless of any interference it might pose with her retail store. Her right to exclude would not be regulated, it would be eviscerated....

With respect to the pedestrian/bicycle pathway, we have no doubt that the city was correct in finding that the larger retail sales facility proposed by petitioner will increase traffic on the streets of the Central Business District.... But on the record before us, the city has not met its burden of demonstrating that the additional number of vehicle and bicycle trips generated by the petitioner's development reasonably relate to the city's requirement for a dedication of the pedestrian/bicycle pathway easement. The city simply found that the creation of the pathway "could offset some of the traffic demand ... and lessen the increase in traffic congestion."...

No precise mathematical calculation is required, but the city must make some effort to quantify its findings in support of the dedication for the pedestrian/bicycle pathway beyond the conclusory statement that it could offset some of the traffic demand generated.

Cities have long engaged in the commendable task of land planning, made necessary by increasing urbanization particularly in metropolitan areas such as Portland. The city's goals of reducing flooding hazards and traffic congestion, and providing for public greenways, are laudable, but there are outer limits to how this may be done. "A strong public desire to improve the public condition [will not] warrant achieving the desire by a shorter cut than the constitutional way of paying for the change." *Pennsylvania Coal.*

It is so ordered.

STEVENS, BLACKMUN AND GINSBURG, J.J., DISSENTING

... The city of Tigard has demonstrated that its plan is rational and impartial and that the conditions at issue are "conducive to fulfillment of authorized planning objectives." Dolan, on the other hand, has offered no evidence that her burden of compliance has any impact at all on the value or profitability of her planned development. Following the teaching of the cases on which it purports to rely, the Court should not isolate the burden associated with the loss of the power to exclude from an evaluation of the benefit to be derived from the permit to enlarge the store and the parking lot.

The Court's assurances that its "rough proportionality" test leaves ample room for cities to pursue the "commendable task of land use planning,"—even twice avowing that "[n]o precise mathematical calculation is required,"—are wanting given the result that test compels here. Under the Court's approach, a city must not only "quantify its findings," and make "individualized determination[s]" with respect to the nature and the extent of the relationship between the conditions and the impact, but also demonstrate "proportionality." The correct inquiry should instead concentrate on whether the required nexus is present and venture beyond considerations of a condition's nature or germaneness only if the developer establishes that a concededly germane condition is so grossly disproportionate to the proposed development's adverse effects that it manifests motives other than land use regulation on the part of the city. The heightened requirement the Court imposes on cities is even more unjustified when all the tools needed to resolve the questions presented by this case can be garnered from our existing case law.

Applying its new standard, the Court finds two defects in the city's case. First, while the record would adequately support a requirement that Dolan maintain the portion of the floodplain on her property as undeveloped open space, it does not support the additional requirement that the floodplain be dedicated to the city. Second, while the city adequately established the traffic increase that the proposed development would generate, it failed to quantify the offsetting decrease in automobile traffic that the bike path will produce. Even under the Court's new rule, both defects are, at most, nothing more than harmless error....

The Court has made a serious error by abandoning the traditional presumption of constitutionality and imposing a novel burden of proof on a city implementing an admittedly valid comprehensive land use plan. Even more consequential than its incorrect disposition of this case, however, is the Court's resurrection of a species of substantive due process analysis that it firmly rejected decades ago.

The Court begins its constitutional analysis by citing *Chicago, B. & Q. R. Co. v. Chicago*, [166 U.S. 226 (1897)] for the proposition that the Takings Clause of the Fifth Amendment is "applicable to the States through the Fourteenth Amendment." That opinion, however, contains no mention of either the Takings Clause or the Fifth Amendment; it held that the protection afforded by the Due Process Clause of the Fourteenth Amendment extends to matters of substance as well as procedure, and that the substance of "the due process of law enjoined by the Fourteenth Amendment required compensation to be made or adequately secured to the owner of private property taken for public use under the authority of the state." It applied the same kind of substantive due process analysis more frequently identified with a better known case that accorded similar substantive protection to a baker's liberty interest in working 60 hours a week and 10 hours a day. See *Lochner v. New York*.

Later cases have interpreted the Fourteenth Amendment's substantive protection against uncompensated deprivations of private property by the States as though it incorporated the text of the Fifth Amendment's Takings Clause.... There was nothing problematic about that interpretation in cases enforcing the Fourteenth Amendment against state action that involved the actual physical invasion of private property.... Justice Holmes charted a significant new course, however, when he opined that a state law making it "commercially impracticable to mine certain coal" had "very nearly the same effect for constitutional purposes as appropriate or destroying it." *Pennsylvania Coal Co. v. Mahon.* The so-called "regulatory takings" doctrine that the Holmes dictum kindled has an obvious kinship with the line of substantive due process cases that *Lochner* exemplified. Besides having similar ancestry, both doctrines are potentially open-ended sources of judicial power to invalidate state economic regulations that Members of this Court view as unwise or unfair.

This case inaugurates an even more recent judicial innovation than the regulatory takings doctrine: the application of the "unconstitutional conditions" label to a mutually beneficial transaction between a property owner and a city....

Dolan has no right to be compensated for a taking unless the city acquires the property interests that she has refused to surrender. Since no taking has yet occurred, there has not been any infringement of her constitutional right to compensation....

Even if Dolan should accept the city's conditions in exchange for the benefit that she seeks, it would not necessarily follow that she has been denied "just compensation" since it would be appropriate to consider the receipt of that benefit in any calculation of "just compensation." ... But even if that discretionary benefit were so trifling that it could not be considered just compensation when it has "little or no relationship" to the property, the Court fails to explain why the same value would suffice when the required nexus is present. In this respect, the Court's reliance on the "unconstitutional conditions" doctrine is assuredly novel, and arguably incoherent....

The Court has decided to apply its heightened scrutiny to a single strand—

the power to exclude—in the bundle of rights that enables a commercial enterprise to flourish in an urban environment....

In its application of what is essentially the doctrine of substantive due process, the Court confuses the past with the present.... Today's majority should heed the words of Justice Sutherland:

> ... while the meaning of constitutional guaranties never varies, the scope of their application must expand or contract to meet the new and different conditions which are constantly coming within the field of their operation. In a changing world, it is impossible that it should be otherwise. *Euclid v. Ambler Co.*

In our changing world one thing is certain: uncertainty will characterize predictions about the impact of new urban developments on the risks of floods, earthquakes, traffic congestion, or environmental harms. When there is doubt concerning the magnitude of those impacts, the public interest in averting them must outweigh the private interest of the commercial entrepreneur. If the government can demonstrate that the conditions it has imposed in a land-use permit are rational, impartial and conducive to fulfilling the aims of a valid land-use plan, a strong presumption of validity should attach to those conditions. The burden of demonstrating that those conditions have unreasonably impaired the economic value of the proposed improvement belongs squarely on the shoulders of the party challenging the state action's constitutionality. That allocation of burdens has served us well in the past. The Court has stumbled badly today by reversing it.

SOUTER, J., DISSENTING

This case, like *Nollan*, invites the Court to examine the relationship between conditions imposed by development permits, requiring landowners to dedicate portions of their land for use by the public, and governmental interests in mitigating the adverse effects of such development. Nollan declared the need for a nexus between the nature of an exaction of an interest in land (a beach easement) and the nature of governmental interests. The Court treats this case as raising a further question, not about the nature, but about the degree, of connection required between such an exaction and the adverse effects of development. The Court's opinion announces a test to address this question, but as I read the opinion, the Court does not apply that test to these facts, which do not raise the question the Court addresses.

First, as to the floodplain and Greenway, the Court acknowledges that an easement of this land for open space (and presumably including the five feet required for needed creek channel improvements) is reasonably related to flood control, but argues that the "permanent recreational easement" for the public on the Greenway is not so related.... [T]he city of Tigard never sought to justify the public access portion of the dedication as related to flood control. It merely argued that whatever recreational uses were made of the bicycle path and the one foot edge on either side, were incidental to the permit condition requiring dedication of the 15-foot easement for an 8-foot-wide bicycle path and for flood control, including open space requirements and relocation of the bank of the river by some five feet. It seems to me such incidental recreational use can

stand or fall with the bicycle path, which the city justified by reference to traffic congestion. As to the relationship the Court examines, between the recreational easement and a purpose never put forth as a justification by the city, the Court unsurprisingly finds a recreation area to be unrelated to flood control.

Second, as to the bicycle path, the Court again acknowledges the "theor[etically]" reasonable relationship between "the city's attempt to reduce traffic congestion by providing [a bicycle path] for alternative means of transportation" and the "correct" finding of the city that "the larger retail sales facility proposed by petitioner will increase traffic on the streets of the Central Business District." The Court only faults the city for saying that the bicycle path "could" rather than "would" offset the increased traffic from the store. That again, as far as I can tell, in an application of *Nollan*....

I cannot agree that the application of *Nollan* is a sound one here, since it appears that the Court has placed the burden of producing evidence of relationship on the city, despite the usual rule in cases involving the police power that the government is presumed to have acted constitutionally. Having thus assigned the burden, the Court concludes that the City loses based on one word ("could" instead of "would"), and despite the fact that this record shows the connection the Court looks for. Dolan has put forward no evidence that the burden of granting a dedication for the bicycle path is unrelated in kind to the anticipated increase in traffic congestion, nor, if there exists a requirement that the relationship be related in degree, has Dolan shown that the exaction fails any such test. The city, by contrast, calculated the increased traffic flow that would result from Dolan's proposed development to be 435 trips per day, and its Comprehensive Plan, applied here, relied on studies showing the link between alternative modes of transportation, including bicycle paths, and reduced street traffic congestion.... *Nollan*, therefore, is satisfied, and on that assumption the city's conditions should not be held to fail a further rough proportionality test

or any other that might be devised to given meaning to the constitutional limits....

In any event, on my reading, the Court's conclusions about the city's vulnerability carry the Court no further than *Nollan* has gone already, and I do not view this case as a suitable vehicle for taking the law beyond that point....

QUESTIONS

1. Chief Justice Rehnquist writes in *Dolan*:

   [S]imply denominating a governmental measure as a "business regulation" does not immunize it from constitutional challenge on the grounds that it violates a provision of the Bill of Rights.... We see no reason why the Takings Clause of the Fifth Amendment, as much a part of the Bill of Rights as the First Amendment or Fourth Amendment, should be relegated to the status of a poor relation in these comparable circumstances.

   Does this statement suggest that the contemporary Court is on the verge of a return to some variant of *Pennsylvania Coal* with respect to judicial protection of private property rights?

2. Is the city of Tigard correct that *Dolan* invited the Court to return to "*Lochnerian*" economic substantive due process analysis in the guise of the Takings Clause, a claim apparently buttressed by Justice Stevens's dissent? How did the Court respond to that invitation, if indeed it was extended?

3. The United States, arguing in favor of the city of Tigard, contended that many federal programs further their regulatory objectives by imposing conditions on a permit applicant's use of his or her property. Does *Dolan* portend restrictions on federal programs such as clean air and water, transportation, and highway beautification? The United States argued on behalf of the property owner in *Lucas*. How could it argue for the city of Tigard in *Dolan*?

4. The National Association of Home Builders and International Council of Shopping Centers offered the following characterization of the issue in *Dolan*:

   That a bike path and greenway system along a river are legitimate and worthwhile public desires is not the question. The question is whether the land for and construction of these public amenities must be contributed by individual private property owners, without payment therefor, who happen to own and wish to improve land that is within the government's chosen path of such facilities.

Is this an accurate statement of the principle at issue in *Dolan* or was the controversy more complicated?

5. One possible reading of *Dolan* is that it pits a private property owner, clinging to the Constitution in the name of profit, against a local government, hamstrung by budget constraints that make it impossible to purchase every piece of property it needs to maintain the urban environment. While property owners and municipalities are on a collision course, the big loser is the environment because it is vulnerable, without an effective advocate. Is this a problem for which there is an adequate constitutional solution?

Suggestions for Further Reading

Ackerman, Bruce A., *Private Property and the Constitution* (New Haven, CT: Yale University Press, 1977).

Brownstein, Alan E., "The Takings Clause and the Iranian Claims Settlement," 29 *University of California Los Angeles Law Review* (1982): 984.

Byrne, Peter, "Green Property," 7 *Constitutional Commentary* (1990): 239.

"Economic Affairs as Human Affairs," in *Scalia v. Epstein: Two Views of Judicial Activism* (Washington, D.C.: Cato Institute, 1985).

Epstein, Richard A., *Takings: Private Property and Eminent Domain* (Cambridge, MA: Harvard University Press, 1985).

Hohfeld, Wesley, "Some Fundamental Legal Conceptions as Applied in Legal Reasoning," 23 *Yale Law Journal* (1919): 16.

Michelman, Frank, "Property, Utility, and Fairness: Comments on the Ethical Foundations of 'Just Compensation' Law," 80 *Harvard Law Review* (1967): 1165.

———, "Property as a Constitutional Right," 38 *Washington & Lee Law Review* (1981): 1097.

Note, "The Origins and Original Significance of the Just Compensation Clause of the Fifth Amendment," 94 *Yale Law Journal* (1985): 694.

Rose, Carol, "*Mahon* Reconstructed: Why the Takings Issues Is Still a Muddle," 57 *Southern California Law Review* (1984): 561.

Sax, Joseph L., "Takings and the Police Power," 74 *Yale Law Journal* (1964): 36.

———, "Takings, Private Property and Public Rights," 81 *Yale Law Journal* (1971): 149.

APPENDIX A

> ⸺◦⸺

CONSTITUTION
OF THE UNITED STATES

[handwritten: 78 says, gover cannot be trusted — courts are well suited to keep government from violating peoples rights — supreme court stands]

We the People of the United States, in Order to form a more perfect Union, establish Justice, insure domestic Tranquility, provide for the common defence, promote the general Welfare, and secure the Blessings of Liberty to ourselves and our Posterity, do ordain and establish this Constitution for the United States of America.

Article I

Section 1. All legislative Powers herein granted shall be vested in a Congress of the United States, which shall consist of a Senate and House of Representatives.

Section 2. The House of Representatives shall be composed of Members chosen every second Year by the People of the several States, and the Electors in each State shall have the Qualifications requisite for Electors of the most numerous Branch of the State Legislature.

No Person shall be a Representative who shall not have attained to the Age of twenty five Years, and been seven Years a Citizen of the United States, and who shall not, when elected, be an Inhabitant of that State in which he shall be chosen.

[Representatives and direct Taxes shall be apportioned among the several States which may be included within this Union, according to their respective Numbers, which shall be determined by adding to the whole Number of free Persons, including those bound to Service for a Term of Years, and excluding Indians not taxed, three fifths of all other Persons.] (*Modified by Section 2 of Amendment XIV.*) The actual Enumeration shall be made within three Years after the first Meeting of the Congress of the United States, and within every subsequent Term of ten Years, in such Manner as they shall by Law direct. The Number of Representatives shall not exceed one for every thirty Thousand, but each State shall have at Least one Representative; and until such enumeration shall be made, the State of New Hampshire shall be entitled to chuse three, Massachusetts eight, Rhode-Island and Providence Plantations one, Connecticut five, New-York six, New Jersey four, Pennsylvania eight, Delaware one, Maryland six, Virginia ten, North Carolina five, South Carolina five, and Georgia three.

When vacancies happen in the Representation from any State, the Executive Authority thereof shall issue Writs of Election to fill such Vacancies.

The House of Representatives shall chuse their Speaker and other Officers; and shall have the sole Power of Impeachment.

Section 3. The Senate of the United States shall be composed of two Senators from each State, [chosen by the Legislature thereof] (*Modified by Amendment XVII*), for six Years; and each Senator shall have one Vote.

Immediately after they shall be assembled in Consequence of the first Election, they shall be divided as equally as may be into three Classes. The Seats of the Senators of the first Class shall be vacated at the Expiration of the second Year, of the second Class at the Expiration of the fourth Year, and of the third Class at the Expiration of the sixth Year, so that one third may be chosen every second Year; [and if Vacancies happen by Resignation, or otherwise, during the Recess of the Legislature of any State, the Executive thereof may make temporary Appointments until the next Meeting of the Legislature, which shall then fill such Vacancies.] (*Modified by Amendment XVII.*)

No Person shall be a Senator who shall not have attained to the Age of thirty Years, and been nine Years a Citizen of the United States, and who shall not, when elected, be an Inhabitant of that State for which he shall be chosen.

The Vice President of the United States shall be President of the Senate, but shall have no Vote, unless they be equally divided.

The Senate shall chuse their other Officers, and also a President pro tempore, in the Absence of the Vice President, or when he shall exercise the Office of President of the United States.

The Senate shall have the sole Power to try all Impeachments. When sitting for that Purpose, they shall be on Oath or Affirmation. When the President of the United States is tried, the Chief Justice shall preside: And no Person shall be convicted without the Concurrence of two thirds of the Members present.

Judgment in Cases of Impeachment shall not extend further than to removal from Office, and disqualification to hold and enjoy any Office of honor, Trust or Profit under the United States: but the Party convicted shall nevertheless be liable and subject to Indictment, Trial, Judgment and Punishment, according to Law.

Section 4. The Times, Places and Manner of holding Elections for Senators and Representatives, shall be prescribed in each State by the Legislature thereof; but the Congress may at any time by Law make or alter such Regulations, except as to the Places of chusing Senators.

The Congress shall assemble at least once in every Year, and such Meeting shall be [on the first Monday in December] (*Modified by Section 2 of Amendment XX*) unless they shall by Law appoint a different Day.

Section 5. Each House shall be the Judge of the Elections, Returns and Qualifications of its own Members, and a Majority of each shall constitute a Quorum to do Business; but a smaller Number may adjourn from day to day, and may be authorized to compel the Attendance of absent Members, in such Manner, and under such Penalties as each House may provide.

Each House may determine the Rules of its Proceedings, punish its Members for disorderly Behaviour, and, with the Concurrence of two thirds, expel a Member.

Each House shall keep a Journal of its Proceedings, and from time to time publish the same, excepting such Parts as may in their Judgment require Secrecy; and the Yeas and Nays of the Members of either House on any question shall, at the Desire of one fifth of those Present, be entered on the Journal.

Neither House, during the Session of Congress, shall, without the Consent of the other, adjourn for more than three days, nor to any other Place than that in which the two Houses shall be sitting.

Section 6. The Senators and Representatives shall receive a Compensation for their Services, to be ascertained by Law, and paid out of the Treasury of the United States. They shall in all Cases, except Treason, Felony and Breach of the Peace, be privileged from Arrest during their Attendance at the Session of their respective Houses, and in going to and returning from the same; [and for any Speech or Debate in either House, they shall not be questioned in any other Place.]

No Senator or Representative shall, during the Time for which he was elected, be appointed to any civil Office under the Authority of the United States, which shall have been created, or the Emoluments whereof shall have been encreased during such time; and no Person holding any Office under the United States, shall be a Member of either House during his Continuance in Office.

Section 7. All Bills for raising Revenue shall originate in the House of Representatives; but the Senate may propose or concur with Amendments as on other Bills.

Every Bill which shall have passed the House of Representatives and the Senate, shall, before it become a Law, be presented to the President of the United States: If he approve he shall sign it, but if not he shall return it, with his Objections to that House in which it shall have originated, who shall enter the Objections at large on their Journal, and

proceed to reconsider it. If after such Reconsideration two thirds of that House shall agree to pass the Bill, it shall be sent, together with the Objections, to the other House, by which it shall likewise be reconsidered, and if approved by two thirds of that House, it shall become a Law. But in all such Cases the Votes of both Houses shall be determined by Yeas and Nays, and the Names of the Persons voting for and against the Bill shall be entered on the Journal of each House respectively. If any Bill shall not be returned by the President within ten Days (Sundays excepted) after it shall have been presented to him, the Same shall be a Law, in like Manner as if he had signed it, unless the Congress by their Adjournment prevent its Return, in which Case it shall not be a Law.

Every Order, Resolution, or Vote to which the Concurrence of the Senate and House of Representatives may be necessary (except on a question of Adjournment) shall be presented to the President of the United States; and before the Same shall take Effect, shall be approved by him, or being disapproved by him, shall be repassed by two thirds of the Senate and House of Representatives, according to the Rules and Limitations prescribed in the Case of a Bill.

Section 8. The Congress shall have Power To lay and collect Taxes, Duties, Imposts and Excises, to pay the Debts and provide for the common Defence and general Welfare of the United States; but all Duties, Imposts and Excises shall be uniform throughout the United States;

To borrow Money on the credit of the United States;

To regulate Commerce with foreign Nations, and among the several States, and with the Indian Tribes;

To establish an uniform Rule of Naturalization, and uniform Laws on the subject of Bankruptcies throughout the United States;

To coin Money, regulate the Value thereof, and of foreign Coin, and fix the Standard of Weights and Measures;

To provide for the Punishment of counterfeiting the Securities and current Coin of the United States;

To establish Post Offices and post Roads;

To promote the Progress of Science and useful Arts, by securing for limited Times to Authors and Inventors the exclusive Right to their respective Writings and Discoveries;

To constitute Tribunals inferior to the supreme Court;

To define and punish Piracies and Felonies committed on the high Seas, and Offences against the Law of Nations;

To declare War, grant Letters of Marque and Reprisal, and make Rules concerning Captures on Land and Water;

To raise and support Armies, but no Appropriation of Money to that Use shall be for a longer Term than two Years;

To provide and maintain a Navy;

To make Rules for the Government and Regulation of the land and naval Forces;

To provide for calling forth the Militia to execute the Laws of the Union, suppress Insurrections and repel Invasions;

To provide for organizing, arming, and disciplining, the Militia, and for governing such Part of them as may be employed in the Service of the United States, reserving to the States respectively, the Appointment of the Officers, and the Authority of training the Militia according to the discipline prescribed by Congress;

To exercise exclusive Legislation in all Cases whatsoever, over such District (not exceeding ten Miles square) as may, by Cession of particular States, and the Acceptance of Congress, become the Seat of the Government of the United States, and to exercise like Authority over all Places purchased by the Consent of the Legislature of the State in which the Same shall be, for the Erection of Forts, Magazines, Arsenals, dock-Yards, and other needful Buildings;—And

To make all Laws which shall be necessary and proper for carrying into Execution the foregoing Powers, and all other Powers vested by this Constitution in the Government of the United States, or in any Department or Officer thereof.

Section 9. The Migration or Importation of such Persons as any of the States now existing shall think proper to admit, shall not be prohibited by the Congress prior to the Year one thousand eight hundred and eight, but a Tax or duty may be imposed on such Importation, not exceeding ten dollars for each Person.

The Privilege of the Writ of Habeas Corpus shall not be suspended, unless when in Cases of Rebellion or Invasion the public Safety may require it.

No Bill of Attainder or ex post facto Law shall be passed.

[No Capitation, or other direct, Tax shall be laid, unless in Proportion to the Census or Enumeration herein before directed to be taken.] (*Modified by Amendment XVI.*)

No Tax or Duty shall be laid on Articles exported from any State.

No Preference shall be given by any Regulation of Commerce or Revenue to the Ports of one State over those of another; nor shall Vessels bound to, or from, one State, be obliged to enter, clear, or pay Duties in another.

No Money shall be drawn from the Treasury, but in Consequence of Appropriations made by Law; and a regular Statement and Account of the Receipts and Expenditures of all public Money shall be published from time to time.

No Title of Nobility shall be granted by the United States: And no Person holding any Office of Profit or Trust under them, shall, without the Consent of the Congress, accept of any present, Emolument, Office, or Title, of any kind whatever, from any King, Prince, or foreign State.

Section 10. No State shall enter into any Treaty, Alliance, or Confederation; grant Letters of Marque and Reprisal; coin Money; emit Bills of Credit; make any Thing but gold and silver Coin a Tender in Payment of Debts; pass any Bill of Attainder, ex post facto Law, or Law impairing the Obligation of Contracts, or grant any Title of Nobility.

No State shall, without the Consent of the Congress, lay any Imposts or Duties on Imports or Exports, except what may be absolutely necessary for executing its inspection Laws; and the net Produce of all Duties and Imposts, laid by any State on Imports or Exports, shall be for the Use of the Treasury of the United States; and all such Laws shall be subject to the Revision and Controul of Congress.

No State shall, without the Consent of Congress, lay any Duty of Tonnage, keep Troops, or Ships of War in time of Peace, enter into any Agreement or Compact with another State, or with a foreign Power, or engage in War, unless actually invaded, or in such imminent Danger as will not admit of delay.

Article II

Section 1. The executive Power shall be vested in a President of the United States of America. He shall hold his Office during the Term of four Years, and, together with the Vice President, chosen for the same Term, be elected, as follows

Each State shall appoint, in such Manner as the Legislature thereof may direct, a Number of Electors, equal to the whole Number of Senators and Representatives to which the State may be entitled in the Congress: but no Senator or Representative, or Person holding an Office of Trust or Profit under the United States, shall be appointed an Elector.

[The Electors shall meet in their respective States, and vote by Ballot for two Persons, of whom one at least shall not be an Inhabitant of the same State with themselves. And they shall make a List of all the Persons voted for, and of the Number of Votes for each; which List they shall sign and certify, and transmit sealed to the Seat of the Government of the United States, directed to the President of the Senate. The President of the Senate shall, in the Presence of the Senate and House of Representatives, open all the Certificates, and the Votes shall then be counted. The Person having the greatest Number of Votes shall be the President, if such Number be a Majority of the whole Number of Electors appointed; and if there be more than one who have such Majority, and have an equal Number of Votes, then the House of Representatives shall immediately chuse by Ballot one of them for President; and if no Person have a Majority, then from the five highest on the List the said House shall in like

Manner chuse the President. But in chusing the President, the Votes shall be taken by States, the Representation from each State having one Vote; a quorum for this Purpose shall consist of a Member or Members from two thirds of the States, and a Majority of all the States shall be necessary to a Choice. In every Case, after the Choice of the President, the Person having the greatest Number of Votes of the Electors shall be the Vice President. But if there should remain two or more who have equal Votes, the Senate shall chuse from them by Ballot the Vice President.] (*Modified by Amendment XII.*)

The Congress may determine the Time of chusing the Electors, and the Day on which they shall give their Votes; which Day shall be the same throughout the United States.

No Person except a natural born Citizen, or a Citizen of the United States, at the time of the Adoption of this Constitution, shall be eligible to the Office of President; neither shall any Person be eligible to that Office who shall not have attained to the Age of thirty five Years, and been fourteen Years a Resident within the United States.

[In Case of the Removal of the President from Office, or of his Death, Resignation, or Inability to discharge the Powers and Duties of the said Office, the Same shall devolve on the Vice President, and the Congress may by Law provide for the Case of Removal, Death, Resignation or Inability, both of the President and Vice President, declaring what Officer shall then act as President, and such Officer shall act accordingly, until the Disability be removed, or a President shall be elected.] (*Modified by Amendment XXV.*)

The President shall, at stated Times, receive for his Services, a Compensation, which shall neither be increased nor diminished during the Period for which he shall have been elected, and he shall not receive within that Period any other Emolument from the United States, or any of them.

Before he enter on the Execution of his Office, he shall take the following Oath or Affirmation:—"I do solemnly swear (or affirm) that I will faithfully execute the Office of President of the United States, and will to the best of my Ability, preserve, protect and defend the Constitution of the United States."

Section 2. The President shall be Commander in Chief of the Army and Navy of the United States, and of the Militia of the several States, when called into the actual Service of the United States; he may require the Opinion, in writing, of the principal Officer in each of the executive Departments, upon any Subject relating to the Duties of their respective Offices, and he shall have Power to grant Reprieves and Pardons for Offences against the United States, except in Cases of Impeachment.

He shall have Power, by and with the Advice and Consent of the Senate, to make Treaties, provided two thirds of the Senators present concur; and he shall nominate, and by and with the Advice and Consent of the Senate, shall appoint Ambassadors, other public Ministers and Consuls, Judges of the supreme Court, and all other Officers of the United States, whose Appointments are not herein otherwise provided for, and which shall be established by Law: but the Congress may by Law vest the Appointment of such inferior Officers, as they think proper, in the President alone, in the Courts of Law, or in the Heads of Departments.

The President shall have Power to fill up all Vacancies that may happen during the Recess of the Senate, by granting Commissions which shall expire at the End of their next Session.

Section 3. He shall from time to time give to the Congress Information of the State of the Union, and recommend to their Consideration such Measures as he shall judge necessary and expedient; he may, on extraordinary Occasions, convene both Houses, or either of them, and in Case of Disagreement between them, with Respect to the Time of Adjournment, he may adjourn them to such Time as he shall think proper; he shall receive Ambassadors and other public Ministers; he shall take Care that the Laws be faithfully executed, and shall Commission all the Officers of the United States.

Section 4. The President, Vice President and all civil Officers of the United States, shall be removed from Office on Impeachment for, and Conviction of, Treason, Bribery, or other high Crimes and Misdemeanors.

Article III

Section 1. The judicial Power of the United States shall be vested in one supreme Court, and in such inferior Courts as the Congress may from time to time ordain and establish. The Judges, both of the supreme and inferior Courts, shall hold their Offices during good Behaviour, and shall, at stated Times, receive for their Services a Compensation, which shall not be diminished during their Continuance in Office.

Section 2. The judicial Power shall extend to all Cases, in Law and Equity, arising under this Constitution, the Laws of the United States, and Treaties made, or which shall be made, under their Authority;—to all Cases affecting Ambassadors, other public Ministers and Consuls;—to all Cases of admiralty and maritime Jurisdiction;—to Controversies to which the United States shall be a Party;—to Controversies between two or more States;—[between a State and Citizens of another State] (*Modified by Amendment XI*);—between Citizens of different States;—between Citizens of the same State claiming Lands under Grants of different States, [and between a State, or the Citizens thereof, and foreign States, Citizens or Subjects.] (*Modified by Amendment XI.*)

In all Cases affecting Ambassadors, other public Ministers and Consuls, and those in which a State shall be Party, the supreme Court shall have original Jurisdiction. In all the other Cases before mentioned, the supreme Court shall have appellate Jurisdiction, both as to Law and Fact, with such Exceptions, and under such Regulations as the Congress shall make.

The Trial of all Crimes, except in Cases of Impeachment, shall be by Jury; and such Trial shall be held in the State where the said Crimes shall have been committed; but when not committed within any State, the Trial shall be at such Place or Places as the Congress may by Law have directed.

Section 3. Treason against the United States shall consist only in levying War against them, or in adhering to their Enemies, giving them Aid and Comfort. No Person shall be convicted of Treason unless on the Testimony of two Witnesses to the same overt Act, or on Confession in open Court.

The Congress shall have Power to declare the Punishment of Treason, but no Attainder of Treason shall work

Anti- dis likes idea of states being

Corruption of Blood, or Forfeiture except during the Life of the Person attainted.

Article IV

Section 1. Full Faith and Credit shall be given in each State to the public Acts, Records, and judicial Proceedings of every other State. And the Congress may by general Laws prescribe the Manner in which such Acts, Records and Proceedings shall be proved, and the Effect thereof.

Section 2. The Citizens of each State shall be entitled to all Privileges and Immunities of Citizens in the several States.

A Person charged in any State with Treason, Felony, or other Crime, who shall flee from Justice, and be found in another State, shall on Demand of the executive Authority of the State from which he fled, be delivered up, to be removed to the State having Jurisdiction of the Crime.

[No Person held to Service or Labour in one State, under the Laws thereof, escaping into another, shall, in Consequence of any Law or Regulation therein, be discharged from such Service or Labour, but shall be delivered up on Claim of the Party to whom such Service or Labour may be due.] (*Modified by Amendment XIII.*)

Section 3. New States may be admitted by the Congress into this Union; but no new State shall be formed or erected within the Jurisdiction of any other State; nor any State be formed by the Junction of two or more States, or Parts of States, without the Consent of the Legislatures of the States concerned as well as of the Congress.

The Congress shall have Power to dispose of and make all needful Rules and Regulations respecting the Territory or other Property belonging to the United States; and nothing in this Constitution shall be so construed as to Prejudice any Claims of the United States, or of any particular State.

Section 4. The United States shall guarantee to every State in this Union a Republican Form of Government, and shall protect each of them against Invasion; and on Application of the Legislature, or of the Executive (when the Legislature cannot be convened), against domestic Violence.

Article V

The Congress, whenever two thirds of both Houses shall deem it necessary, shall propose Amendments to this Constitution, or, on the Application of the Legislatures of two thirds of the several States, shall call a Convention for proposing Amendments, which, in either Case, shall be valid to all Intents and Purposes, as Part of this Constitution, when ratified by the Legislatures of three fourths of the several States, or by Conventions in three fourths thereof, as the one or the other Mode of Ratification may be proposed by the Congress; Provided that no Amendment which may be made prior to the Year One thousand eight hundred and eight shall in any Manner affect the first and fourth Clauses in the Ninth Section of the first Article; and that no State, without its Consent, shall be deprived of its equal Suffrage in the Senate.

Article VI

All Debts contracted and Engagements entered into, before the Adoption of this Constitution, shall be as valid against the

United States under this Constitution, as under the Confederation.

This Constitution, and the Laws of the United States which shall be made in Pursuance thereof; and all Treaties made, or which shall be made, under the Authority of the United States, shall be the supreme Law of the Land; and the Judges in every State shall be bound thereby, any Thing in the Constitution or Laws of any State to the Contrary notwithstanding.

The Senators and Representatives before mentioned, and the Members of the several State Legislatures, and all executive and judicial Officers, both of the United States and of the several States, shall be bound by Oath or Affirmation, to support this Constitution;

but no religious Test shall ever be required as a Qualification to any Office or public Trust under the United States.

Article VII

The Ratification of the Conventions of nine States, shall be sufficient for the Establishment of this Constitution between the States so ratifying the Same.

done in Convention by the Unanimous Consent of the States present the Seventeenth Day of September in the Year of our Lord one thousand seven hundred and Eighty seven and of the Independence of the United States of America the Twelfth In witness whereof We have hereunto subscribed our Names,

Gº. WASHINGTON—
Presidᵗ. and deputy from Virginia

New Hampshire

John Langdon
Nicholas Gilman

Massachusetts

Nathaniel Gorham
Rufus King

Connecticut

Wm. Saml. Johnson
Roger Sherman

New York

Alexander Hamilton

New Jersey

Wil: Livingston
David Brearley
Wm. Paterson
Jona: Dayton

Pennsylvania

B Franklin
Thomas Mifflin
Robt Morris
Geo. Clymer
Thos. FitzSimons
Jared Ingersoll
James Wilson
Gouv Morris

Delaware

Geo: Read
Gunning Bedford jun
John Dickinson
Richard Bassett
Jaco: Broom

Maryland

James McHenry
Dan of St. Thos. Jenifer
Danl Carroll

Virginia

John Blair
James Madison

North Carolina

Wm. Blount
Richd. Dobbs Spaight
Hu Williamson

South Carolina

J. Rutledge
Charles Cotesworth
    Pinckney
Charles Pinckney
Pierce Butler

Georgia

William Few
Abr Baldwin

Attest William Jackson, Secretary

In Convention Monday, September 17th 1787.
Present
The States of

New Hampshire, Massachusetts, Connecticut, Mr. Hamilton from New York, New Jersey, Pennsylvania, Delaware, Maryland, Virginia, North Carolina, South Carolina and Georgia.

Resolved,

That the preceeding Constitution be laid before the United States in Congress assembled, and that it is the Opinion of this Convention, that it should afterwards be submitted to a Convention of Delegates, chosen in each State by the People thereof, under the Recommendation of its Legislature, for their Assent and Ratification; and that each Convention assenting to, and ratifying the Same, should give Notice thereof to the United States in Congress assembled. Resolved, That it is the Opinion of this Convention, that as soon as the Conventions of nine States shall have ratified this Constitution, the United States in Congress assembled should fix a Day on which Electors should be appointed by the States which have ratified the same, and a Day on which the Electors should assemble to vote for the President, and the Time and Place for commencing Proceedings under this Constitution.

That after such Publication the Electors should be appointed, and the Senators and Representatives elected: That the Electors should meet on the Day fixed for the Election of the President, and should transmit their Votes certified, signed, sealed and directed, as the Constitution requires, to the Secretary of the United States in Congress assembled, that the Senators and Representatives should convene at the Time and Place assigned; that the Senators should appoint a President of the Senate, for the sole purpose of receiving, opening and counting the Votes for President; and, that after he shall be chosen, the Congress, together with the President, should, without Delay, proceed to execute this Constitution.

By the Unanimous Order of the Convention

Gº. WASHINGTON—Presidᵗ.
W. Jackson, Secretary.

Amendments to The Constitution of the United States of America, proposed by Congress, and ratified by the Legislatures of the several States, pursuant to the fifth Article of the original Constitution

Amendment I[1]

Congress shall make no law respecting an establishment of religion, or prohibiting the free exercise thereof; or abridging the freedom of speech, or of the press; or the right of the people peaceably to assemble, and to petition the Government for a redress of grievances.

Amendment II

A well regulated Militia, being necessary to the security of a free State, the

---

[1] The first ten amendments to the Constitution were ratified effective December 15, 1791.

right of the people to keep and bear Arms, shall not be infringed.

Amendment III

No Soldier shall, in time of peace be quartered in any house, without the consent of the Owner, nor in time of war, but in a manner to be prescribed by law.

Amendment IV

The right of the people to be secure in their persons, houses, papers, and effects, against unreasonable searches and seizures, shall not be violated, and no Warrants shall issue, but upon probable cause, supported by Oath or affirmation, and particularly describing the place to be searched, and the persons or things to be seized.

Amendment V

No person shall be held to answer for a capital, or otherwise infamous crime, unless on a presentment or indictment of a Grand Jury, except in cases arising in the land or naval forces, or in the Militia, when in actual service in time of War or public danger; nor shall any person be subject for the same offence to be twice put in jeopardy of life or limb; nor shall be compelled in any criminal case to be a witness against himself, nor be deprived of life, liberty, or property, without due process of law; nor shall private property be taken for public use, without just compensation.

Amendment VI

In all criminal prosecutions, the accused shall enjoy the right to a speedy and public trial, by an impartial jury of the State and district wherein the crime shall have been committed, which district shall have been previously ascertained by law, and to be informed of the nature and cause of the accusation; to be confronted with the witnesses against him; to have compulsory process for obtaining witnesses in his favor, and to have the Assistance of Counsel for his defence.

Amendment VII

In Suits at common law, where the value in controversy shall exceed twenty dollars, the right of trial by jury shall be preserved, and no fact tried by a jury, shall be otherwise re-examined in any Court of the United States, than according to the rules of the common law.

Amendment VIII

Excessive bail shall not be required, nor excessive fines imposed, nor cruel and unusual punishments inflicted.

Amendment IX

The enumeration in the Constitution, of certain rights, shall not be construed to deny or disparage others retained by the people.

Amendment X

The powers not delegated to the United States by the Constitution, nor prohibited by it to the States, are reserved to the States respectively, or to the people.

Amendment XI[2]

The Judicial power of the United States shall not be construed to extend to any suit in law or equity, commenced or prosecuted against one of the United States by Citizens of another State, or by Citizens or Subjects of any Foreign State.

---

[2] Ratified February 7, 1795.

Amendment XII[3]

The Electors shall meet in their respective states, and vote by ballot for President and Vice-President, one of whom, at least, shall not be an inhabitant of the same state with themselves; they shall name in their ballots the person voted for as President, and in distinct ballots the person voted for as Vice-President, and they shall make distinct lists of all persons voted for as President, and of all persons voted for as Vice-President, and of the number of votes for each, which lists they shall sign and certify, and transmit sealed to the seat of the government of the United States, directed to the President of the Senate;— The President of the Senate shall, in the presence of the Senate and House of Representatives, open all the certificates and the votes shall then be counted;— The person having the greatest number of votes for President, shall be the President, if such number be a majority of the whole number of Electors appointed; and if no person have such majority, then from the persons having the highest numbers not exceeding three on the list of those voted for as President, the House of Representatives shall choose immediately, by ballot, the President. But in choosing the President, the votes shall be taken by states, the representation from each state having one vote; a quorum for this purpose shall consist of a member or members from two-thirds of the states, and a majority of all the states shall be necessary to a choice. [And if the House of Representatives shall not choose a President whenever the right of choice shall devolve upon them, before the fourth day of March next following, then the Vice-President shall act as President, as in the case of the death or other constitutional disability of the President.—] (*Superseded by Section 3 of Amendment XX.*) The person having the greatest number of votes as Vice-President, shall be the Vice-President, if such number be a majority of the whole number of Electors appointed, and if no person have a majority, then from the two highest numbers on the list, the Senate shall choose the Vice-President; a quorum for the purpose shall consist of two-thirds of the whole number of Senators, and a majority of the whole number shall be necessary to a choice. But no person constitutionally ineligible to the office of President shall be eligible to that of Vice-President of the United States.

Amendment XIII[4]

Section 1. Neither slavery nor involuntary servitude, except as a punishment for crime whereof the party shall have been duly convicted, shall exist within the United States, or any place subject to their jurisdiction.

Section 2. Congress shall have power to enforce this article by appropriate legislation.

Amendment XIV[5]

Section 1. All persons born or naturalized in the United States, and subject to the jurisdiction thereof, are citizens of the United States and of the State wherein they reside. No State shall make or enforce any law which shall abridge the privileges or immunities of citizens of the United States; nor shall any State deprive any person of life, liberty, or

---

[3] Ratified June 15, 1804.

[4] Ratified December 6, 1865.

[5] Ratified July 9, 1868.

property, without due process of law; nor deny to any person within its jurisdiction the equal protection of the laws.

Section 2. Representatives shall be apportioned among the several States according to their respective numbers, counting the whole number of persons in each State, excluding Indians not taxed. But when the right to vote at any election for the choice of electors for President and Vice President of the United States, Representatives in Congress, the Executive and Judicial officers of a State, or the members of the Legislature thereof, is denied to any of the male inhabitants of such State, being twenty-one years of age, and citizens of the United States, or in any way abridged, except for participation in rebellion, or other crime, the basis of representation therein shall be reduced in the proportion which the number of such male citizens shall bear to the whole number of male citizens twenty-one years of age in such State.

Section 3. No person shall be a Senator or Representative in Congress, or elector of President and Vice President, or hold any office, civil or military, under the United States, or under any State, who, having previously taken an oath, as a member of Congress, or as an officer of the United States, or as a member of any State legislature, or as an executive or judicial officer of any State, to support the Constitution of the United States, shall have engaged in insurrection or rebellion against the same, or given aid or comfort to the enemies thereof. But Congress may by a vote of two-thirds of each House, remove such disability.

Section 4. The validity of the public debt of the United States, authorized by law, including debts incurred for payment of pensions and bounties for ser-

vices in suppressing insurrection or rebellion, shall not be questioned. But neither the United States nor any State shall assume or pay any debt or obligation incurred in aid of insurrection or rebellion against the United States, or any claim for the loss or emancipation of any slave; but all such debts, obligations and claims shall be held illegal and void.

Section 5. The Congress shall have power to enforce, by appropriate legislation, the provisions of this article.

Amendment XV[6]

Section 1. The right of citizens of the United States to vote shall not be denied or abridged by the United States or by any State on account of race, color, or previous condition of servitude.

Section 2. The Congress shall have power to enforce this article by appropriate legislation.

Amendment XVI[7]

The Congress shall have power to lay and collect taxes on incomes, from whatever source derived, without apportionment among the several States, and without regard to any census or enumeration.

Amendment XVII[8]

The Senate of the United States shall be composed of two Senators from each State, elected by the people thereof, for six years; and each Senator shall have one vote. The electors in each State shall have the qualifications requisite for electors of the most numerous branch of the State legislatures.

---

[6] Ratified February 3, 1870.

[7] Ratified February 3, 1913.

[8] Ratified April 8, 1913.

When vacancies happen in the representation of any State in the Senate, the executive authority of such State shall issue writs of election to fill such vacancies: Provided, That the legislature of any State may empower the executive thereof to make temporary appointments until the people fill the vacancies by election as the legislature may direct.

This amendment shall not be so construed as to affect the election or term of any Senator chosen before it becomes valid as part of the Constitution.

Amendment XVIII[9]

[**Section 1.** After one year from the ratification of this article the manufacture, sale, or transportation of intoxicating liquors within, the importation thereof into, or the exportation thereof from the United States and all territory subject to the jurisdiction thereof for beverage purposes is hereby prohibited.

Section 2. The Congress and the several States shall have concurrent power to enforce this article by appropriate legislation.

Section 3. This article shall be inoperative unless it shall have been ratified as an amendment to the Constitution by the legislatures of the several States, as provided in the Constitution, within seven years from the date of the submission hereof to the States by the Congress.] (*Repealed by Amendment XXI.*)

Amendment XIX[10]

The right of citizens of the United States to vote shall not be denied or abridged by the United States or by any State on account of sex.

Congress shall have power to enforce this article by appropriate legislation.

Amendment XX[11]

Section 1. The terms of the President and Vice President shall end at noon on the 20th day of January, and the terms of Senators and Representatives at noon on the 3d day of January, of the years in which such terms would have ended if this article had not been ratified; and the terms of their successors shall then begin.

Section 2. The Congress shall assemble at least once in every year, and such meeting shall begin at noon on the 3d day of January, unless they shall by law appoint a different day.

Section 3. If, at the time fixed for the beginning of the term of the President, the President elect shall have died, the Vice President elect shall become President. If a President shall not have been chosen before the time fixed for the beginning of his term, or if the President elect shall have failed to qualify, then the Vice President elect shall act as President until a President shall have qualified; and the Congress may by law provide for the case wherein neither a President elect nor a Vice President elect shall have qualified, declaring who shall then act as President, or the manner in which one who is to act shall be selected, and such person shall act accordingly until a President or Vice President shall have qualified.

Section 4. The Congress may by law provide for the case of the death of any of the persons from whom the House of Representatives may choose a President whenever the right of choice shall have devolved upon them, and for the case of the death of any of the persons from whom the Senate may choose a Vice

---

[9] Ratified January 16, 1919.

[10] Ratified August 18, 1920.

[11] Ratified January 23, 1933.

President whenever the right of choice shall have devolved upon them.

Section 5. Sections 1 and 2 shall take effect on the 15th day of October following the ratification of this article.

Section 6. This article shall be inoperative unless it shall have been ratified as an amendment to the Constitution by the legislatures of three-fourths of the several States within seven years from the date of its submission.

Amendment XXI[12]

Section 1. The eighteenth article of amendment to the Constitution of the United States is hereby repealed.

Section 2. The transportation or importation into any State, Territory, or possession of the United States for delivery or use therein of intoxicating liquors, in violation of the laws thereof, is hereby prohibited.

Section 3. This article shall be inoperative unless it shall have been ratified as an amendment to the Constitution by conventions in the several States, as provided in the Constitution, within seven years from the date of the submission hereof to the States by the Congress.

Amendment XXII[13]

Section 1. No person shall be elected to the office of the President more than twice, and no person who has held the office of President, or acted as President, for more than two years of a term to which some other person was elected President shall be elected to the office of the President more than once. But this Article shall not apply to any person holding the office of President when this Article was proposed by the Congress, and shall not prevent any person who may be holding the office of President, or acting as President, during the term within which this Article becomes operative from holding the office of President or acting as President during the remainder of such term.

Section 2. This article shall be inoperative unless it shall have been ratified as an amendment to the Constitution by the legislatures of three-fourths of the several States within seven years from the date of its submission to the States by the Congress.

Amendment XXIII[14]

Section 1. The District constituting the seat of Government of the United States shall appoint in such manner as the Congress may direct:

A number of electors of President and Vice President equal to the whole number of Senators and Representatives in Congress to which the District would be entitled if it were a State, but in no event more than the least populous State; they shall be in addition to those appointed by the States, but they shall be considered, for the purposes of the election of President and Vice President, to be electors appointed by a State; and they shall meet in the District and perform such duties as provided by the twelfth article of amendment.

Section 2. The Congress shall have power to enforce this article by appropriate legislation.

Amendment XXIV[15]

Section 1. The right of citizens of the United States to vote in any primary or other election for President or Vice

---

[12] Ratified December 5, 1933.
[13] Ratified February 27, 1951.

[14] Ratified March 29, 1961.
[15] Ratified January 23, 1964.

President, for electors for President or Vice President, or for Senator or Representative in Congress, shall not be denied or abridged by the United States or any State by reason of failure to pay any poll tax or other tax.

Section 2. The Congress shall have power to enforce this article by appropriate legislation.

Amendment XXV[16]

Section 1. In case of the removal of the President from office or of his death or resignation, the Vice President shall become President.

Section 2. Whenever there is a vacancy in the office of the Vice President, the President shall nominate a Vice President who shall take office upon confirmation by a majority vote of both Houses of Congress.

Section 3. Whenever the President transmits to the President pro tempore of the Senate and the Speaker of the House of Representatives his written declaration that he is unable to discharge the powers and duties of his office, and until he transmits to them a written declaration to the contrary, such powers and duties shall be discharged by the Vice President as Acting President.

Section 4. Whenever the Vice President and a majority of either the principal officers of the executive departments or of such other body as Congress may by law provide, transmit to the President pro tempore of the Senate and the Speaker of the House of Representatives their written declaration that the President is unable to discharge the powers and duties of his office, the Vice President shall immedi-

ately assume the powers and duties of the office as Acting President.

Thereafter, when the President transmits to the President pro tempore of the Senate and the Speaker of the House of Representatives his written declaration that no inability exists, he shall resume the powers and duties of his office unless the Vice President and a majority of either the principal officers of the executive department or of such other body as Congress may by law provide, transmit within four days to the President pro tempore of the Senate and the Speaker of the House of Representatives their written declaration that the President is unable to discharge the powers and duties of his office. Thereupon Congress shall decide the issue, assembling within forty-eight hours for that purpose if not in session. If the Congress, within twenty-one days after receipt of the latter written declaration, or, if Congress is not in session, within twenty-one days after Congress is required to assemble, determines by two-thirds vote of both Houses that the President is unable to discharge the powers and duties of his office, the Vice President shall continue to discharge the same as Acting President; otherwise, the President shall resume the powers and duties of his office.

Amendment XXVI[17]

Section 1. The right of citizens of the United States, who are eighteen years of age or older, to vote shall not be denied or abridged by the United States or by any State on account of age.

Section 2. The Congress shall have power to enforce this article by appropriate legislation.

---

[16] Ratified February 10, 1967.

[17] Ratified July 1, 1971.

Amendment XXVII[18]

No law, varying the compensation for the services of the Senators and Representatives, shall take effect, until an election of Representatives shall have intervened.

Recent Proposed Amendments that Failed Ratification

Proposed 1972, expired unratified 1982

Section 1. Equality of rights under the law shall not be denied or abridged by the United States or by any State on account of sex.

Section 2. The Congress shall have the power to enforce, by appropriate legislation, the provisions of this article.

Section 3. This amendment shall take effect two years after the date of ratification.

---

[18]Ratified May 7, 1992.

Proposed 1978, expired unratified 1985

Section 1. For purposes of representation in the Congress, election of the President and Vice President, and article V of this Constitution, the District constituting the seat of government of the United States shall be treated as though it were a State.

Section 2. The exercise of the rights and powers conferred under this article shall be by the people of the District constituting the seat of government, and as shall be provided by the Congress.

Section 3. The twenty-third article of amendment to the Constitution of the United States is hereby repealed.

Section 4. This article shall be inoperative, unless it shall have been ratified as an amendment to the Constitution by the legislatures of three-fourths of the several States within seven years from the date of its submission.

APPENDIX B

JUSTICES OF THE SUPREME COURT OF THE UNITED STATES

	ADMINISTRATION	CHIEF JUSTICE	2	3	4
1789	Washington Federalist	John Jay (1789–1795)	John Rutledge (1789–1791)	William Cushing (1789–1810)	James Wilson (1789–1798)
1790					
1791			Thomas Johnson (1791–1793)		
1792					
1793			William Paterson (1793–1806)		
1794					
1795		John Rutledge (1795)			
1796		Oliver Ellsworth (1796–1800)			
1797	J. Adams Federalist				
1798					Bushrod Washington (1798–1829)
1799					
1800					
1801	Jefferson Dem-Rep[1]	John Marshall (Adams) (1801–1835)			
1802					
1803					
1804					
1805					
1806			H. Brockholst Livingston (1806–1823)		
1807					
1808					
1809	Madison Dem-Rep				
1810					
1811				Joseph Story (1811–1845)	
1812					
1813					
1814					
1815					
1816					
1817	Monroe Dem-Rep				
1818					
1819					
1820					

[1]Democratic-Republican.

5	6	7	8	9	10
John Blair (1789–1796)	James Iredell (1790–1799)				
Samuel Chase (1796–1811)	Alfred Moore (1799–1804)				
	William Johnson (1804–1834)				
		Thomas Todd (1807–1826)			
Gabriel Duvall (1811–1835)					

ADMINISTRATION	CHIEF JUSTICE	2	3	4
1821				
1822				
1823		Smith Thompson (1823–1843)		
1824				
1825 J. Q. Adams Dem-Rep				
1826				
1827				
1828				
1829 Jackson Democrat				
1830				Henry Baldwin (1830–1844)
1831				
1832				
1833				
1834				
1835				
1836	Roger B. Taney (1836–1864)			
1837 Van Buren Democrat				
1838				
1839				
1840				
1841 W. Harrison Whig				
1842 Tyler Democrat				
1843				
1844				
1845 Polk Democrat		Samuel Nelson (Tyler) (1845–1872)	Levi Woodbury (1845–1851)	
1846				Robert C. Grier (1846–1870)
1847				
1848				
1849				
1850 Taylor Whig/ Fillmore Whig				
1851			Benjamin R. Curtis (1851–1857)	
1852				
1853 Pierce Democrat				

5	6	7	8	9	10
		Robert Trimble (1826–1828)			
		John McLean (1830–1861)			
	James M. Wayne (1835–1867)				
Philip P. Barbour (1836–1841)					
			John Catron (1837–1865)		
				John McKinley (1838–1852)	
Peter V. Daniel (Van Buren) (1842–1860)					
				John A. Campbell (1853–1861)	

	Administration	Chief Justice	2	3	4
1854					
1855					
1856					
1857	Buchanan Democrat				
1858				Nathan Clifford (1858–1881)	
1859					
1860					
1861	Lincoln Republican				
1862					
1863					
1864		Salmon P. Chase (1864–1873)			
1865	A. Johnson Democrat				
1866[3]					
1867					
1868					
1869	Grant Republican				
1870					William Strong (1870–1880)
1871					
1872					
1873			Ward Hunt (1873–1882)		
1874		Morrison R. Waite (1874–1888)			
1875					
1876					
1877	Hayes Republican				
1878					
1879					
1880					
1881	Garfield Republican/ Arthur Republican				William B. Woods (1881–1887)

[2]In 1863 Congress established a tenth seat, to which Stephen J. Field was appointed.

[3]In 1866 Congress reduced the size of the Court to six justices. Consequently, the seats of Justices Catron and Wayne remained unfilled after their deaths in 1865 and 1867. Congress restored the Court to nine seats in 1869.

5	6	7	8	9	10
Samuel F. Miller (1862–1890)		Noah H. Swayne (1862–1881)		David Davis (1862–1877)	
					Stephen J. Field[2] (1863–1897)
	Joseph P. Bradley (1870–1892)				
				John M. Harlan (1877–1911)	
		Stanley Matthews (Garfield) (1881–1889)			

ADMINISTRATION	CHIEF JUSTICE	2	3	4
1882		Samuel Blatchford (1882–1893)	Horace Gray (Arthur) (1882–1902)	
1883				
1884				
1885	Cleveland Democrat			
1886				
1887				
1888		Melville W. Fuller (1888–1910)		Lucius Q. C. Lamar (1888–1893)
1889	B. Harrison Republican			
1890				
1891				
1892				
1893	Cleveland Democrat			Howell E. Jackson (Harrison) (1893–1895)
1894		Edward D. White (1894–1910)		
1895				
1896	McKinley Republican			Rufus W. Peckham (1896–1909)
1897				
1898				
1899				
1900				
1901	T. Roosevelt Republican			
1902			Oliver W. Holmes Jr. (1902–1932)	
1903				
1904				
1905				
1906				
1907				
1908				
1909	Taft Republican			

5	6	7	8	9	10
		David J. Brewer (1889–1910)			
Henry B. Brown (1890–1906)					
	George Shiras (1892–1903)				
			Joseph McKenna (1898–1925)		
	William R. Day (1903–1922)				
William H. Moody (1906–1910)					

Administration	Chief Justice	2	3	4
1910	Edward D. White (1910–1921)			Horace H. Lurton (1910–1914)
1911		Willis Van Devanter (1911–1937)		
1912				
1913	Wilson Democrat			
1914				James C. McReynolds (1914–1941)
1915				
1916				
1917				
1918				
1919				
1920				
1921	Harding Republican	William H. Taft (1921–1930)		
1922				
1923	Coolidge Republican			
1924				
1925				
1926				
1927				
1928				
1929	Hoover Republican			
1930		Charles E. Hughes (1930–1941)		
1931				
1932			Benjamin N. Cardozo (1932–1938)	
1933	F. D. Roosevelt Democrat			
1934				
1935				
1936				
1937		Hugo L. Black (1937–1971)		

5	6	7	8	9	10
		Charles E. Hughes (1910–1916)			
Joseph R. Lamar (1911–1916)				Mahlon Pitney (1912–1922)	
Louis D. Brandeis (1916–1939)		John H. Clarke (1916–1922)			
		George Sutherland (1922–1938)			
	Pierce Butler (Harding) (1923–1939)			Edward T. Sanford (Harding) (1923–1930)	
			Harlan F. Stone (1925–1941)		
				Owen J. Roberts (1930–1945)	

	ADMINISTRATION	CHIEF JUSTICE	2	3	4
1938					
1939				Felix Frankfurter (1939–1962)	
1940					
1941		Harlan F. Stone (1941–1946)			James F. Byrnes (1941–1942)
1942					
1943					Wiley B. Rutledge (1943–1949)
1944					
1945	Truman Democrat				
1946		Fred M. Vinson (1946–1953)			
1947					
1948					
1949					Sherman Minton (1949–1956)
1950					
1951					
1952					
1953	Eisenhower Republican	Earl Warren (1953–1969)			
1954					
1955					
1956					William J. Brennan (1956–1990)
1957					
1958					
1959					
1960					
1961	Kennedy Democrat				
1962				Arthur J. Goldberg (1962–1965)	
1963	L. B. Johnson Democrat				
1964					
1965				Abe Fortas (1965–1969)	
1966					

5	6	7	8	9	10
William O. Douglas (1939–1975)	Frank Murphy (1940–1949)	Stanley F. Reed (1938–1957)	Robert H. Jackson (1941–1954)	Harold H. Burton (1945–1958)	
	Tom C. Clark (1949–1967)		John M. Harlan II (1955–1971)		
		Charles E. Whittaker (1957–1962)		Potter Stewart (1958–1981)	
		Byron R. White (1962–1993)			

	ADMINISTRATION	CHIEF JUSTICE	2	3	4
1967					
1968					
1969	Nixon Republican	Warren E. Burger (1969–1986)			
1970				Harry A. Blackmun (1970–1994)	
1971					
1972			Lewis F. Powell (1972–1987)		
1973					
1974	Ford Republican				
1975					
1976					
1977	Carter Democrat				
1978					
1979					
1980					
1981	Reagan Republican				
1982					
1983					
1984					
1985					
1986		William H. Rehnquist (1986–)			
1987					
1988			Anthony M. Kennedy (1988–)		
1989	Bush Republican				
1990					David H. Souter (1990–)
1991					
1992					
1993	Clinton Democrat				
1994				Stephen G. Breyer (1994–)	

Sources: *The Supreme Court of the United States: Its Beginnings & Its Justices 1790–1991* (Washington, D.C.: Commission on the Bicentennial of the United States Constitution, 1992); Henry J. Abraham, *The Judicial Process*, 6th ed. (New York, NY: Oxford University Press, 1993).

5	6	7	8	9	10
	Thurgood Marshall (1967–1991)				
			William H. Rehnquist (1972–1986)		
John Paul Stevens (1975–)					
				Sandra Day O'Connor (1981–)	
			Antonin Scalia (1986–)		
	Clarence Thomas (1991–)				
		Ruth Bader Ginsburg (1993–)			

GLOSSARY OF LEGAL TERMS

a fortiori   Latin. With stronger reason, much more by relation to another.

abatement   A reduction, decrease, or diminution. As used in reference to actions at law, an action that is utterly dead and cannot be revived except by commencing a new action.

abrogation   The destruction or annulment of a former law by an act of the legislative power, by constitutional authority, or by usage.

ad hoc   Latin. For this; for this special purpose.

adjudicate   To pass on judicially; to decide, settle, decree, sentence, or condemn.

adverse   Opposed or having opposing interests. In resistance or opposition to a claim, application, or proceeding.

affiant   A person who makes and subscribes an affidavit.

affidavit   A written or printed declaration or statement of facts, made voluntarily, and confirmed by the oath or affirmation of the party making it, made before an officer having authority to administer a legal oath.

amicus curiae   Latin. "Friend of the court." A person who has no right to participate in a suit but is allowed to introduce argument on behalf of a party.

annul   To reduce to nothing, to make void or of no effect.

appeal   Resort to an upper court or tribunal for review of a lower court's action.

appellant   The party who takes an appeal from a lower court to a higher court.

appellee   The party in a cause against whom an appeal is taken, the party who has an interest adverse to setting aside or reversing the judgement of a lower court.

arguendo   Latin. For the sake of argument.

bailee   In contract law, an agent to whom movable property is committed in trust for another.

bill   In equity practice, a formal written complaint addressed by a suitor to a court, showing the names of the parties, stating the facts that make up the case and allegations of wrong, averring that the acts disclosed are contrary to equity, and praying for specific relief.

bill of attainder   A legislative act directed against a designated person pronouncing him guilty of an alleged crime without trial or conviction according to recognized legal process.

Black Codes   Body of laws regulating the institution of slavery prior to 1865, and subsequently applied to Freedmen.

Primary reference: *Black's Law Dictionary*, 5th rev. ed. (St. Paul, MN: West, 1979).

bona fide Latin. "In good faith." Without fraud or deceit.

capitation tax A tax or imposition on a person, such as a poll tax.

casus foederis Latin. "A situation anticipated." In contract law, a case or event contemplated by the parties to a contract or coming within the terms of the contract. In international law, a particular act or situation contemplated by a treaty or stipulated for in a treaty.

certificate of division A statement that judges of an appellate court disagree among themselves and that there is not a majority in favor of any one view.

certification A process by which judges of one court state uncertainty about the rule of law to apply in a case and request instructions from a higher court.

certiorari Latin. "To be informed of, to be made certain in regard to." The name of a writ requesting appellate review. An appellate procedure for reexamining the action of an inferior tribunal, commanding judges of the inferior court to certify or return records of the proceeding for judicial review of their actions.

class action An action brought on behalf of one's self and others similarly situated. As a general rule, the named plaintiff controls the litigation and may discontinue or settle at will.

cloture Closure of a legislative debate.

commission A warrant or authority issuing from the government, or one of its departments, empowering a person or persons named to do certain acts or to exercise jurisdiction, or to perform the duties and exercise the authority of an office.

common law As distinguished from Roman, modern civil, canon, or other systems of law, the body of law and juristic theory originated, developed, formulated, and administered in England, which has obtained among most of the states and people influenced by Anglo-Saxon heritage, including the United States.

community property Property owned in common by a husband and wife as a kind of marital partnership.

complaint The first or initiatory pleading on the part of the plaintiff in a civil action, designed to give the defendant information of all the material facts on which the plaintiff relies to support his demand. In criminal law, the charge made before a proper officer that an offense has been committed by a person named or described.

concurrent jurisdiction The power of more than one tribunal to take cognizance of the subject matter of a case.

consideration In contract law, the motive, price or impelling influence that induces a contracting party to enter into a contract.

consignee In merchant law, the person to whom goods are shipped for sale; the one to whom merchandise has been delivered.

constructive Inferred, implied, or made out of legal interpretation.

constructive bailment A contract arising where the person having possession of goods holds it under such circumstances that the law imposes a duty to deliver it to another.

contempt Willful disregard or disobedience of a public authority. In court, committed by a person who does any act in willful contravention of the court's authority or dignity, or tending to impede the administration of justice. Each house of Congress, state legislatures, and some administrative agencies also have power to hold persons in contempt.

contract A promissory agreement between two or more persons that creates, modifies, or destroys a legal relation. An agreement, upon sufficient consideration, to do or not to do a particular act.

conveyance In the law of real property, the transfer of legal title to land.

corum non judice Latin. A suit brought in a court that has no jurisdiction.

counterclaim A claim presented by a defendant in opposition to a claim of the plaintiff, intended to defeat or diminish the plaintiff's demands.

cross-complaint In civil cases, a complaint filed by the defendant in an action seeking affirmative relief against any party that gave rise to the litigation.

declaratory judgment A ruling that declares the rights of parties or expresses the opinion of the court on a question of law, without ordering anything to be done.

decree The judgment of a court of equity or admiralty, answering for most purposes to the judgment of a court of common law. A declaration of the legal consequences of the facts found.

deed In property law, a writing signed by a person with legal title to real estate, transferring that title to another.

de facto Latin. "In fact."

defamation The taking of one's reputation. The offense of injuring a person's character, fame or reputation by false or malicious statements. Includes both libel and slander.

defendant The person against whom relief or recovery is sought in an action

or suit; the person defending or denying.

de jure Latin. "Of right." Legitimate, lawful, by right and just title.

delegata potestas non potest delegari Latin. A delegated power cannot be delegated.

de minimis Latin. "Of nothing." So minor as to lack legal significance.

demurrer An allegation by a defendant that even if the facts alleged were true, their legal consequences are not such as to require an answer or further proceedings in the cause.

derogation The partial repeal or abolition of a law, as by a subsequent act that limits its scope or impairs its utility and force.

devise Testamentary disposition of land or realty; a gift of real property by the last will and testament of the donor.

distress warrant Writ authorizing an officer to seize personal property, usually for nonpayment of rent.

double jeopardy Common law and constitutional prohibition against a second prosecution after a first trial for the same crime, transaction, or omission.

eleemosynary Charitable.

eminent domain The power to take private property for public use.

en banc French. "In the bench." A meeting of all the judges of a court, as opposed to a panel of the judges of the court.

enjoin To require a person, by writ of injunction from a court of equity, to perform or to abstain or desist from performing some act.

enjoined Required, commanded, directed.

eo nomine Latin. "By that name."

equity The spirit and habit of fairness or justness. A system of remedial justice administered by certain tribunals, distinct from common law courts, empowered to decree remedies beyond the stringent lines of positive law in a given situation. Equitable remedies are governed by rules, principles, and precedents developed by courts.

error A mistaken judgment or incorrect belief. In appellate law, the name of a writ of review issued from a court of appellate jurisdiction to the court of record requiring it to send to the appellate court the record of the action named in the writ for an examination of errors alleged to have been committed, so that the appellate court can determine whether to reverse, correct, or affirm the decision of the court of record.

escheat Reversion of property to the state in consequence of the lack of any competent individual to inherit.

estop To bar, impede, stop, prevent, or preclude.

eviction Pursuant to the judgment of a court, the process of depriving a person of the possession of lands that he has held.

exclusionary rule Refusal to allow the prosecution's case in chief against a defendant to use evidence acquired by the government illegally.

ex directo Latin. "Directly." Immediately.

ex parte Latin. "One side only." Done for, in behalf of, or on the application of one party only.

ex post facto Latin. "After the fact."

ex post facto **law** One passed after the occurrence of a fact or commission of an act that retrospectively changes the legal consequences of such a fact or action.

express Clear, definite, explicit, unmistakable.

expressio unius est exclusio alterius Latin. "The expression of one thing means the exclusion of another."

ex proprio vigore Latin. "By its own force."

expunge Destroy or obliterate.

ex vi termini Latin. "From or by the force of the term." From the very meaning of the expression used.

fee simple absolute An estate in property in which the owner is entitled to the entire property, with unconditional power of disposition during the owner's lifetime, descending to the owner's heirs and legal representatives if the owner dies without a will.

felony A crime of a serious nature, for which the maximum penalty can be death or imprisonment, regardless of the fact that a lesser penalty may in fact be imposed.

foreclosure Termination of all the rights of a mortgagor in the property covered by the mortgage.

functus officio Latin. A task performed.

grantee One to whom a grant or bestowal is made.

grantor The person by whom a grant or bestowal is made.

guardian ad litem Latin. A person appointed by a court to prosecute or defend for an infant in any suit to which the infant may be a party.

habeas corpus Latin. "You have the body." Words used in writs commanding one who detains another to bring him or her, or have him or her brought, before the court issuing the writ. Typically issued to a jailor accused of detaining a prisoner contrary to law.

immunity Freedom from duty or penalty. Exemption from performing duties the law generally requires other citizens to perform.

implied Not manifest by explicit or direct words but rather by implication or necessary deduction from circumstances, general language, or the conduct of parties.

in camera Latin. "In chambers"; in private. A hearing conducted with no spectators present.

incorporation The act or process of forming or creating a corporation; the formation of a legal or political body, with the quality of perpetual existence and succession, unless limited by the act of incorporation.

indemnify To hold harmless; to secure against loss or damage; to give security for the reimbursement of a person in case of an unanticipated loss.

indictment A written accusation presented by a grand jury to a court, charging that a person has done some act or omission that by law is a punishable offense.

in forma pauperis Latin. "In the manner of a pauper." Permission given by a court to a poor person to sue without liability for costs.

information An accusation against a person for a criminal offense without indictment. Presented by a competent public officer on his oath of office rather than by a grand jury.

injunction A prohibitive writ issued by a court of equity to a defendant following a suit of a complaining party, forbidding the defendant to do some act that he is threatening or attempting to commit, or restraining him from the continuance thereof. The act must be injurious to the plaintiff and not such as can ade-

quately be redressed by an action at law.

in re Latin. "In the matter of." The usual matter of entitling a judicial proceeding in which there are no adversary parties, but some *res*, or thing, about which judicial action is to be taken. Sometimes used in a proceeding where the party makes a direct application.

inter alia Latin. "Among other things."

interlocutory order An order that does not decide an action itself but settles some intervening matter relating to the action.

interrogation The process of examining by formal questioning.

intervene To interpose an action or other proceeding with leave of the court.

intestate Without a will.

in transitu Latin. "In transit." On the way or passage; while passing from one place to another.

ipse dixit Latin. "He himself said." The base assertion of an individual alone.

ipso facto Latin. "By the fact itself." By the mere fact.

judicial notice The act by which a court, in conducting a trial or framing its decision, will, of its own motion, and without the production of evidence, recognize the existence and truth of certain facts, which, from their nature, are not properly the subject of testimony, or which are universally regarded as established by common knowledge.

jure belli Latin. "By the right or law of war."

juris privati Latin. "Of private right." Subjects of private property.

jus belli Latin. The law of war.

jus commune Latin. In English law, the common and natural rule of right.

laches Unreasonable delay; neglect to do something in time.

libel In admiralty law, to proceed against by filing an action in a court of equity. In tort law, a method of defamation, expressed by print, writing, pictures, or signs; generally, any publication injurious to the reputation of another.

libel *per se* A publication of such a character that an action may be brought without the necessity of showing any special damage, the imputation being that the law will presume that any one so described must have suffered damage.

lien A charge, security, or incumbrance on property.

mala in se Latin. "Wrongs in themselves." Acts morally wrong.

mala prohibita Latin. Acts made offenses by law.

malfeasance The doing of an act that is wrong or unlawful.

mandamus Latin. "We command." A writ issuing from a court of superior jurisdiction to an inferior court or governmental officer commanding the performance of an official act.

ministerial duty A definite duty, leaving nothing to discretion, imposed by law and arising under conditions admitted or proved to exist.

misdemeanor A crime or offense less serious than a felony.

misfeasance A misdeed or trespass. The improper performance of some act that a person may lawfully do.

mortgage A conveyance of property on a condition that becomes void upon payment or performance according to stipulated terms. Also, the instrument by which a mortgage conveyance is made.

nugatory Futile; ineffectual; invalid.

nuisance That which annoys and disturbs one in possession of his property, rendering its ordinary use or occupation physically uncomfortable. Anything that is injurious to health, or is indecent or offensive to the senses, or an obstruction to the free use of property. Commonly classed as private, public, and mixed.

obiter dictum Latin. Judge's opinion with no legal bearing on the case at hand.

omnis ratihabitio retrotrahitur et mandato prioriti æquiparatur Latin. "Every ratification relates back and is equivalent to a prior authority."

oyer and terminer Higher criminal court authorized to "hear and determine" certain cases.

parens patriae Latin. "Father (parent) of his country." The sovereign power of guardianship over persons under a disability, including minors, the insane, and the incompetent.

per curiam Latin. "By the court." In law reports, distinguishes an opinion of the whole court from an opinion written by one judge.

per se Latin. "By itself."

plaintiff A person who brings a legal action; the party who complains or sues in a personal action and is so named on the record.

plea in abatement A plea objecting to the place, mode, or time of asserting a claim without commenting on its merits.

pleadings The parties' formal allegations of their respective claims and defenses.

plenary Full, entire, complete.

police powers Inherent power of government to regulate in order to preserve public order, and to promote health, safety, and morality.

prima facie   Latin. "At first sight." A fact presumed to be true unless disproved by some evidence to the contrary.

pro forma   Latin. "As a matter of form."

prohibition   The name of a writ of review issued by a superior court commanding the judge and parties to an action in an inferior court to cease carrying on the litigation because the court lacks jurisdiction to hear the case.

propio vigore   Latin. "By its own force." By its intrinsic meaning.

quash   To overthrow, abate, annul, or vacate.

recuse   Purposely absent; remove.

redemption   A repurchase or buying back. The process of annulling and revoking a conditional sale of property, by performance of the conditions on which it was stipulated to be revocable.

remand   To send back.

removal jurisdiction   The power to transfer a cause from one court to another. Also, the transfer of a cause, before trial or final hearing, from a state court to the U.S. district courts pursuant to acts of Congress.

remove   To transfer an action from one court to another.

seize   To put in possession of or to invest with fee simple possession.

seriatim   Latin. "Severally." Separately, individually or one by one.

sic utere tuo ut alienum non laedas   Latin. "Use your own property in such a manner as not to injure that of another."

sovereign   A person, body, or state in which independent and supreme

authority is vested; a chief ruler with supreme power.

special verdict   A jury's special finding of the facts in a case, leaving to the court application of the law.

specific performance   A remedy in equity compelling a party to a contract to perform what was agreed to, because damages would provide inadequate compensation for breach of the contract.

stare decisis   Latin. "Let the decision stand."

statute of limitations   A statute prescribing the time period within which an action must be brought.

stay   A stopping. A court order stopping a judicial proceeding.

stipulated   Arranged by agreement, settled.

subpoena   Latin. "Under penalty." A process to cause a witness to appear and give testimony, commanding appearance before a court or magistrate at the time specified to testify for the party specified.

subpoena duces tecum   Latin. A subpoena commanding a witness who possesses or controls some document or paper that is pertinent to the issues of a pending controversy to produce it at trial.

sui juris   Latin. Possessing full social and civil rights.

supersede   Obliterate, set aside, annul.

suppress   To prohibit, prevent, subdue, or end.

tort   Latin. "To twist." A private or civil wrong or injury.

trespass   Doing an unlawful act, or a lawful act in an unlawful manner, that injures another's person or property.

uniform commercial code   A compilation of the statutory law of commerce adopted by most states during the 1950s and 1960s in an effort to replace commercial code diversity among them.

vacate   To annul, cancel, set aside, rescind, or render void.

voir dire   Latin. "To speak the truth." Preliminary examination of jurors by a court.

vested   Fixed, accrued, settled, absolute, not contingent.

vested right   A right that has so completely and definitely accrued or settled in a person that it is not subject to be defeated by the act of another private person, and that should be recognized and protected by the government. A right of such a nature that it cannot be divested without the consent of the person to whom it belongs and of which a person cannot be deprived arbitrarily without justice.

warrant   A writ or precept from a competent authority in pursuance of law, directing the doing of an act by a person competent to do it, and offering that person protection from damage if the act is done.

writ   A written order issuing from a court and requiring the performance of a specified act or giving authority to have the act done.

TABLE OF CASES

*Bold face type indicates excerpted cases.